PEACE AND CONFLICT SERIES
RON MILAM, GENERAL EDITOR

Also in the series:

Admirals Under Fire: The US Navy and the Vietnam War
by Edward J. Marolda

Crooked Bamboo: A Memoir from Inside the Diem Regime
by Nguyen Thai, edited by Justin Simundson

Girls Don't: A Woman's War in Vietnam
by Inette Miller

Rain in Our Hearts: Alpha Company in the Vietnam War
by James Allen Logue and Gary D. Ford

THE
AIR WAR IN
VIETNAM

MICHAEL E. WEAVER

TEXAS TECH UNIVERSITY PRESS

Copyright © 2022 by Texas Tech University Press

All rights reserved. No portion of this book may be reproduced in any form or by any means, including electronic storage and retrieval systems, except by explicit prior written permission of the publisher. Brief passages excerpted for review and critical purposes are excepted.

The views expressed in this book are those of the author and do not reflect the policy of the United States government, the Department of Defense, or Air University.

This book is typeset in EB Garamond. The paper used in this book meets the minimum requirements of ANSI/NISO Z39.48-1992 (R1997). ♾
Designed by Hannah Gaskamp
Cover design by Hannah Gaskamp
Cover photo courtesy of the Naval History and Heritage Command

Library of Congress Cataloging-in-Publication Data
Names: Weaver, Michael E., 1962– author. Title: The Air War in Vietnam / Michael E. Weaver.
Description: Lubbock: Texas Tech University Press, [2022] | Series: Peace and Conflict | Includes bibliographical references and index. | Summary: "An examination of the effectiveness of American air power—air superiority, aerial refueling, airlift, close air support, reconnaissance, and coercion & interdiction—during the Vietnam War"—Provided by publisher.
Identifiers: LCCN 2020053161 (print) | LCCN 2020053162 (ebook) |
ISBN 978-1-68283-085-7 (cloth) | ISBN 978-1-68283-264-6 (paper)
ISBN 978-1-68283-086-4 (ebook)
Subjects: LCSH: Vietnam War, 1961–1975—Aerial operations, American. | Air power—United States—History—20th century. Classification: LCC DS558.8. W43 2021 (print) | LCC DS558.8 (ebook) | DDC 959.704/3480973—dc23
LC record available at https://lccn.loc.gov/2020053161
LC ebook record available at https://lccn.loc.gov/2020053162

First paperback edition 2024

Texas Tech University Press
Box 41037
Lubbock, Texas 79409-1037 USA
800.832.4042
ttup@ttu.edu
www.ttupress.org

Dedicated to all who fought for freedom in Southeast Asia.

Contents

ILLUSTRATIONS / IX
MAPS / X
ACKNOWLEDGMENTS / XI

Introduction / 3

PART I
AIR SUPERIORITY AND NATIONAL POLICY DURING THE VIETNAM WAR / 9

1. Aerial Refueling: The Air War's Operational Foundation / 11
2. Achieving Air Superiority by Destroying Enemy Aircraft on the Ground / 21
3. Pursuing Air Superiority in the Presence of Antiaircraft Artillery and Surface-to-Air Missiles / 39
4. Air Superiority by Shooting Down MiGs / 61
5. Punch and Counterpunch / 72
6. The Imagined Weapon: Immature Technology / 84
7. Air Superiority Refinements, 1968–1972 / 94
8. Air Superiority Efforts during Linebacker / 100
9. Technology, Organization, and Management of the Air Superiority Mission / 109
10. Air Superiority during Linebacker II / 120

PART 2

AIR SUPPORT AND AIR POWER EFFECTIVENESS / 125

11. Photo Reconnaissance: Significance for Strategy and Policy / 127
12. Airlift Effectiveness / 158
13. The Effectiveness of Air Strikes against Ground Forces / 184

PART 3

COERCION AND INTERDICTION / 253

14. Air Coercion and Air Interdiction Effectiveness Over Southeast Asia / 255
15. Laos and the Ho Chi Minh Trail Become the Focus of the Air Campaign / 313
16. Restrictions and Rules of Engagement during the Air Campaign / 344
17. The Easter Offensive and the Revolution in Bombing Accuracy / 360
18. Toward Another Confrontation / 386

Conclusions / 407

NOTES / 415
BIBLIOGRAPHY / 573
INDEX / 589

Illustrations

13	KC-135 refueling B-52
52	F-105Gs refueling from KC-135
63	F-100D Super Sabres
65	F-104C Starfighter
67	Four F-4C Phantoms
69	F-4B Phantom
73	Vietnamese MiG-17 and pilots
75	Vietnamese MiG-21 at US Air Force Museum
81	EC-121 with two F-104As
82	E-2 Hawkeye
85	AIM-7 Sparrow missile
86	AIM-9B Sidewinder on F-8 Crusader launch rail
89	AIM-4 Falcon missile
130	RF-101C Voodoo
137	F-8 Crusader with drone
142	RF-4C Phantom
144	RA-5C Vigilante
160	C-123 Provider
166	C-7 Caribou
167	C-130 Hercules
203	A-4E Skyhawk with Marine pilots
204	A-7 Corsairs
215	Bomb craters from B-52 strike
268	F-105Ds refueling from KC-135
292	EB-66 leading F-105s on Sky Spot bombing mission
331	USS *Constellation*, 1969
334	A-4F Skyhawks over USS *Hancock*
370	F-4D with two laser-guided bombs
383	Aircrew in front of F-111A
392	B-52D taking off

Maps

14	Southeast Asia
23	Air bases in Southeast Asia
45	North Vietnam
64	Air bases in North Vietnam
186	Air bases in South Vietnam
270	Route Packages

Acknowledgments

Researching and writing this book would not have been successful without the assistance of several archivists. John Darrell Sherwood, Laura Wayers, and Dale J. Gordon of the Naval History and Heritage Command ensured the project would include substantial US Navy sources. Annette Amerman and Christopher Ellis guided me to documents at the Marine Corps History Division I never would have found otherwise. At the Air Force Historical Research Agency, Tammy T. Horton scanned numerous Air Force photographs, Sylvester Jackson pulled at least a hundred cartons, and Archie DiFante declassified several thousand excerpts of never-before-used documents. More than anyone, Mr. DiFante made possible the writing of a history based on newly accessed sources. His support has been indispensable for the completion of this project. Dr. Earl Tilford provided inestimable critiques that improved the book's readability. They are due more credit than these words convey. James Campbell, Allen Peck, and Stephen Randolph read and critiqued earlier versions. Richard Immerman and Gregory Urwin continue to give encouragement two decades after my years at Temple University. Dr. Immerman introduced me to the issue of force and diplomacy, a theme of this book. My wife and several deans and department chairs have supported this project unreservedly. Colonel Robert Smith helped jump-start this project with a research sabbatical in 2012. Over the years, Drs. Budd Jones, Ron Dains, John Terino, Michael Pavelec, and James W. Forsyth made possible researching, writing, and completing this project. Colleagues, coworkers, and our officer-students have offered constant encouragement. At Texas Tech University Press, Travis Snyder, Joanna Conrad, Christie Perlmutter, Hannah Gaskamp, John Brock, and Ron Milam shepherded the book to completion.

THE
AIR WAR IN
VIETNAM

Introduction

Any history of the Vietnam War is a serious undertaking for a number of reasons.[1] Policy makers and military professionals want to avoid repeating the mistakes made during that war. Many readers seek explanations as to why a country as powerful as the United States lost a war to such a seemingly inconsequential political actor. Historians strive for clearer understanding, a challenge when it comes to Vietnam. Researchers and writers face tensions between their preferences and the findings their research produces. One therefore has to get the story right and then analyze it with all the care one can muster. I embarked on this project with several goals: write an up-to-date history of the air war using heretofore unused sources, produce a history that was distinct from other examinations, and solidify my own understanding of this extremely complex war so that I could speak about it more intelligently. Analyzing the effective use of the air weapon during Vietnam has left me with several convictions I hope to convince others to adopt. As important as tactical and operational proficiency are in the employment of air power, they can be all for naught if nothing but dogma and faulty assumptions inform the strategy. Tactical actions and military operations have to advance policy goals in order to be considered truly effective. Air warfare is effective when it advances the war toward the goals the policy makers have set, even if executed without the utmost skill or proficiency. Geopolitics can hamstring military strategy. This research has convinced me that the troubles this air war experienced ultimately lay within the realms of geopolitical contexts, cognition, underlying assumptions, and analytical approaches. Indeed, pursuing a full understanding of air power in Vietnam takes one into a world beyond aircraft, air power, and even combat to the ways in which leaders conceive of war and conflict.

Air power was of supreme importance to the defense of the United States during the middle of the twentieth century. Long-range bombers carrying nuclear weapons helped form the bedrock of its nuclear deterrent force and the Navy continued to make the aircraft carrier the centerpiece of its fleet. Intercontinental jet airliners opened the North American continent and then the world to fast air travel, and the United States led the way with its revolutionary Boeing 707 and Douglas DC-8. Aerial refueling tankers enabled small jet fighters to cross oceans and deploy American air power to hotspots in Europe and Asia. Expectations for the capabilities and effectiveness of air power were high, and revolutionary technological change was the order of the day in the thirty years following World War II. Beliefs about effective military air power had become unquestioned assumptions, and then came the Vietnam War.

Aircraft flew millions of missions trying to collapse communist fighting capability and will. The effectiveness of air warfare is a fair question; the inquiry is necessary for understanding the course of the war and the opportunities for the proper use of the air weapon that did and did not exist. Examining air power's effectiveness is difficult because Vietnam was a complex and bewildering war. It simultaneously displayed the traits of an insurgency, a conventional war, a revolution, a civil war, a proxy war, and later a mechanized invasion of one country by another. Vietnam was a hybrid that confounds to this day.

INTRODUCTION

The 1969 edition of the *Military Assistance Command, Vietnam* (MACV) annual history wrote that it could not carry out the war without air power. Aircraft enabled the Army and Marines to shift men and supplies wherever they were needed quickly, photograph and surveil the whole of the region, and provide massive firepower quickly. Indeed, "airpower performed a decisive service."[2] But the war was lost.

What did air actions accomplish during the Vietnam War? By that I do not mean sortie rates, bomb tonnage, and body count, although those are starting points. The ultimate measure of military effectiveness is the event's contribution to the state's policy goals. Air actions mattered a great deal, and it is important to develop a more refined understanding of how air power affected the war. This book examines the air war from several perspectives in pursuit of understanding these interrelationships more clearly. It examines tactical capabilities and activities because they decide what a president's orders can and cannot actually achieve through combat. Weapons capabilities and their uses contribute to the analysis of air power's strategic significance for the same reason. Tactical actions take place in order to produce successful operations, but not for their own sake. Militaries conduct operations, fight battles, and wage campaigns in order to execute a strategy that achieves the country's policy goals. So when I examine, for example, bombing accuracy during close air support missions, tactical airlift during sieges, and missile reliability, my intention is to derive conclusions as to why this mattered to the higher levels of war.

The effectiveness of air power forms this book's unifying theme. Both a narrative and an analysis, it examines air power effectiveness from the tactical level of war to the level of national security policy. Most importantly, to what extent did successes or failures in the air war contribute to the president's goals? Both approaches—examining war from the bottom up and the top down—drive one toward the other. In other words, I seek to integrate the anthill perspective with that of the satellite. My interest in the air war began at the tactical level with an interest in how aircraft and munitions were employed in combat, but further study reinforced my belief that political consequences are what is most important.

One of the assumptions prominent in the war's memory is that if we had waged the air campaign in a certain way—unrestricted—victory was assured and inevitable. One might claim that defeat was a result of not following Air Force doctrine. Is following doctrine correctly the source of victory? Not if it is incomplete. Furthermore, a president's agenda may ignore important factors to the point that a well-fought war cannot overcome the flaws in his strategy. Neither is victory an automatic consequence of practicing the craft of war correctly, although that certainly helps. Victory results when force is applied in a way that convinces the enemy that submission is better than fighting. This is profoundly more difficult to accomplish than is at first apparent, especially when one sees the disparity in political commitment between two adversaries, such as existed between the warring parties in Southeast Asia. Actually, the communists had an advantage in terms of commitment, will, and ruthlessness. Can firepower negate and overcome those advantages?

Accomplishing this task requires a broad approach to the history of the air war. Therefore, sections of this book examine, for instance, missile and aircraft capabilities and tactics, subsequent portions trace a narrative of the air war, other parts walk through presidential debates inside the Johnson and Nixon administrations, and yet more paragraphs analyze the effectiveness of the air war. Explaining connections is another goal: for example, how did aftershocks from the Korean War affect the way the United States fought the air war? Substantiating one claim regarding air power's effectiveness might require a sampling of air combat engagements while explaining another requires a sampling of White House meetings.

I chose effectiveness as the unifying theme because of the influence of books like *Military Effectiveness: Volume 2, The Interwar Period* that Allan Millett and Williamson Murray edited in the late 1980s. Its title alone was enough to provide the foundational question. Michael Doubler's *Closing with the Enemy: How GIs Fought the War in Europe, 1944–1945*, encouraged me to take another look at what to many are settled issues and definitive conclusions. *Strategic Air Power in Desert Storm* by John Andreas Olsen refined my understanding of the relationships between military operations and the achievement of policy goals, and Richard Overy's *The Battle of Britain: Myth and Reality* provided an example of writing a history first and foremost from the most primary of sources. Those are but a few of the works that informed this study. The extent to which aircraft and air power are effective in war has also been a basic question with which my colleagues, adult learners, and I at the Air Command and Staff College wrestle constantly.

Six air power missions—air superiority, aerial refueling, tactical airlift, photo reconnaissance, close air support, and coercion and air interdiction—further refine this narrative and analysis. Questions about effectiveness take the book beyond simply relating what took place over Indochina. How effective were close air support bombing missions in terms of responsiveness and bombing accuracy, for example? What difference did they make to the furtherance of American and South Vietnamese military strategy? To what extent did bombing operations against North Vietnamese supply lines ultimately contribute to the goals of the South Vietnamese and American presidents? How did American air coercion efforts affect policy decisions in Hanoi? Did airlift operations generate any unintended consequences along with their many benefits? How were photographic reconnaissance missions flown, in what ways did those missions contribute to the war, and were there insurmountable technological barriers between capabilities and wants? How does an air force pursue dominating the airspace over enemy territory? Were aerial tankers really indispensable?

In addition to an analysis of the war, this work reports my findings that come out of an intensive sifting of sources not available during the first generation of Vietnam air war histories. The Air Force Historical Research Agency contains millions of pages of documentary evidence, much of which are seeing the light of day here for the first time because they simply were not accessible until the late 1990s and 2000s. I found plenty that had been declassified only in 1997, a small portion that had been declassified in 2001, and a remainder that I was able to get declassified locally with but rare exceptions. In the intervening years since beginning the project in 2012 I mined the Naval History and Heritage Center in 2014, and in 2016 the Marine Corps archives and a collection at the Air Force History Studies Division at Bolling Air Force Base for archival sources regarding the participation of the Navy and the Marines in the air war, as well as new materials on the Air Force's 1972 campaign. Using sources from these three services helped make this less of an Air Force history and instead more of an air power history. From time to time the book also functions as a compendium of new information.

The State Department's *Foreign Relations of the United States* series for the Johnson and Nixon administrations form the second major group of primary sources. They make it possible to examine links between air operations and national strategy and policy. Their availability is also comparatively recent; the 1968–1969 Johnson administration volume was only published in 2003 and the October 1972–January 1973 volume from the Nixon administration came out in 2010. They contain more information on military operations than one might expect.

The process of studying the air war over Indochina spawned two additional themes. It is helpful to view the air war as a siege because of the resemblance between siege warfare and the air campaign against North Vietnam and Laos. Second, the study of the air war and the war in its entirety reveals that the concept of limited war is misleading. Limited war was a device that leaders in Western Europe agreed upon in the aftermath of the Thirty Years' War of 1618–1648 in order to retain war as an instrument of statecraft without destroying their societies in the process. For the century and a half that followed the Peace of Westphalia, sovereigns used war in limited ways with limited means for limited ends. That changed with Napoleon's rise and continued for another century and a half until Hitler's fall. During the 1950s the great powers were faced with a geopolitical situation in which major war was no longer a rational option for policy makers because it could lead to catastrophic thermonuclear war. Theorists such as Robert Osgood suggested limited war as a viable option for political leaders in spite of and because of the nuclear standoff. The limited war concept suggested war could be throttled, managed, and steered toward the achievement of vital interests with a stingy use of military force to a degree it could not. National goals and geopolitics led to imbalances that made limited war a much more challenging tool than the discourse surrounding it would lead one to believe.

Additional decisions limited the scope of this work. The book does not examine helicopter airlift nor helicopter gunships. Doing so would have required years of additional research, and I wanted a finished book, not a never-ending project. The issue of effectiveness in and of itself is sufficiently clear to provide the roadmap. Because of this choice, veterans' accounts form only a small portion of the source material. As much as possible I have stricken the term "strategic bombing" because those words confuse more than they illuminate. The term is often conflated with bombing by large, long-range multi-engine bombers against economic or population targets, and the use of nuclear weapons is often implicit. Instead, in a literal sense strategic bombing is any kind of bombing that furthers one's own military strategy and undercuts that of the enemy, but instead of trying to force readers to submit to a redefinition of this label, I have opted for two terms that better describe the strategy behind the bombing of targets in North Vietnam and Laos: interdiction and coercion. The latter I define as simply using force to persuade a political actor to accede to one's demands. The former means destroying war materiel and disrupting the enemy's supply lines.

There is something in this book for several audiences. The heavy use of the *Foreign Relations of the United States* series should please diplomatic historians. Air power advocates and critics will find plenty of grist for their mills. Military historians will see a foundation of archival sources; historians of technology and aviation will discover new facts about the air war—particularly the war between aircraft. In these ways the book is holistic in its approach.

My overall argument is the American, and to a lesser extent South Vietnamese, air forces flew missions and carried out operations skillfully. They achieved air superiority, built a catalog of reconnaissance photographs for making strategy and assessing the consequences of military operations, and airlift successfully supported the ground war. Aerial refueling was an eminently successful operation and was foundational to the air war. Close air support enabled ground forces to wage war with fewer casualties and decided many an engagement in favor of the Americans and South Vietnamese. Ultimately, close air support was not melded with ground warfare sufficiently. The air campaign against targets in North Vietnam and Laos did not achieve what American policy makers wanted. Bombardments neither persuaded the enemy to give up his goal of taking over South Vietnam nor reduced the sum total of supplies and soldiers flowing down the Ho Chi Minh Trail to amounts small enough to ruin the communists' strategy and operations. The broader lack of success was due more to the refusal to employ ground and air warfare against the centers of gravity in North Vietnam, a decision arising from geopolitical realities and constraints. The nature of the American policy goals and strategy dragged the air war into a broader failure of war.

The character of the wider conflict predetermined many of the strategic options for the use of air power. Ultimately what resulted was not a failure of air power but a failure of war. The ways and means the United States was willing to employ were a mismatch with the ends of the North Vietnamese leaders. America's commitment to the war was insufficient for persuading the political actors who held the decisive reins of power in the Communist world to cease and desist to the point a permanent peace for South Vietnam had any chance of being anything more than an interregnum. American power was a misalignment not because of the weight of military force but because of the nature of the political goals each side pursued. The Johnson administration's refusal to address that mismatch was a failure of war in the broadest sense. No amount of unrestricted firepower, deft strategy, or tactical skill could grapple with that limitation unless American leaders first owed up to the reality of what they wanted to accomplish and, more importantly, what the leaders of the Lao Dong Party, North Vietnam's Communist Party, sought to achieve.

This book begins with an examination of aerial refueling because that capability enabled the Air Force to participate in the air campaign against North Vietnam. The character of the war would have been far different if the only bombers that could reach targets in North Vietnam were those flying off aircraft carriers. Fuel and range are critical to effective air power. Flying tankers is not a glamorous mission, but students of the Vietnam War and historians of air power need to understand its importance.

The book is arranged in three sections that examine the air missions in the order that makes the most sense for understanding the air war's relationship to national policy. Following an introduction to aerial refueling, an analysis of the quest for control of the skies over North Vietnam forms the first section since that mission was also foundational to the execution of the air war. This examination of air superiority tackles the assertion that North Vietnamese airfields were always sanctuaries for that air force and that Air Force and Navy pilots were never allowed to attack North Vietnamese airfields. It then looks at the ongoing battle with North Vietnamese surface-to-air missiles (SAMs), as well as the methods the North Vietnamese used to defend their airspace. It concludes with a study of the on-and-off battles between North Vietnamese and American fighter aircraft through the end of 1972.

Air support is the theme of the second section. Its study of aerial reconnaissance is a new contribution to the history of the air war. For instance, the United States made extensive use of reconnaissance drones for gaining photo intelligence of targets in North Vietnam, and their photographs were of great importance to leaders in Washington, DC. The second section traces the use of airlift aircraft in the support of combat troops. I found that in some ways the great success these pilots achieved actually worked against South Vietnam's policy goal of controlling the Vietnamese hinterland. The use of aerial bombing against enemy troops comprises the bulk of this section. Here, for example, I share my findings about the effectiveness of B-52 strikes against communist forces.

The final section examines the bombing campaign against targets in North Vietnam and Laos. Among other contributions to our understanding of the war, it analyzes the air campaign against the Ho Chi Minh Trail in depth, and later argues that the revolution in precision-guided munitions such as laser-guided bombs took place in 1972, not during the 1991 Persian Gulf War. As far as it went this air war was reasonably well managed. The bombing campaign was by its nature, however, a limited war campaign attempting to persuade the North Vietnamese to abandon a political goal of total victory that was not up for negotiation.

INTRODUCTION

A war as confounding as Vietnam requires a regular reexamination by citizens, historians, veterans, statesmen, and military officers. What follows is both a narrative of the war and an analysis; think of the storyline as the interstate and the analytical sections as exits for historical markers.

PART 1

AIR SUPERIORITY AND NATIONAL POLICY DURING THE VIETNAM WAR

Chapter 1

Aerial Refueling: The Air War's Operational Foundation

Brief Background

America's involvement in the Indochina war took place within several contexts and it escalated into a major war because of a series of decisions. To begin with, the United States was competing against the aggression of the Soviet Union and China. The United States' strategy for dealing with their agendas was to contain, not roll back, the efforts of those two countries to expand their power and influence. The United States took that approach because it recognized its own power was limited, and because those communist states' nuclear arsenals were powerful enough to persuade American leaders to tread carefully. The Munich Crisis of 1938, during which the leaders of France and the United Kingdom tried to appease Hitler by acceding to his demand that they agree to his annexation of a portion of Czechoslovakia, cast another shadow over American security strategy. The Munich analogy postulated that it was better to stand up against aggression sooner rather than later, and the United States attempted to follow that approach when the Cold War broke out after World War II. Communists spoke of spreading their revolution around the world, communist revolutions occurred in places as far apart as China and Cuba, and concerns grew that if one country fell to such a revolution, another of its neighbors would do likewise, then another, like dominoes, and then the United States and its friends would be faced with fighting not a limited war on the other side of the world, but a major war closer to home that simply had to be won. Only ten years prior to President John F. Kennedy's assassination, China and the United States had fought a war against each other from 1950 to 1953—the Korean War (an incomplete moniker for that bloody struggle)—and the Americans badly wanted to avoid another war with the Chinese. The US Air Force had engaged in air battles with Soviet pilots over Korea, an occurrence that American leaders also did not want to repeat because of the risks of escalation. Although Korea, and later Vietnam, were in East Asia, America's most vital overseas interests lay in Europe, so it had to divide its attention between the two carefully. The US was also engaged in the space race with the USSR, which stoked the competition between the two. Theorists of limited war wrote of that form of war as an adjunct to nuclear deterrence—thus, particularly with the advent of Kennedy's flexible response strategy, policy makers considered the range of options that lay before them. Perpetuating the Truman Doctrine, President Kennedy promised aid to countries under assault from communist insurgencies. Even cartography influenced the context of the coming war. The Mercator Projection makes Southeast Asia appear much smaller than it actually is; how could war with a tiny country like North Vietnam be anything but a quick victory?[1]

The United States military entered the 1960s organized, trained, and equipped for nuclear deterrence and for fighting "general war," one in which all resources, including nuclear weapons, are used to fight for national survival. The Air Force's official concept of limited war was vague: "Armed conflict short of general war, exclusive of incidents, involving the overt engagement of the military forces of two or more nations." That branch of the armed forces conceded that many factors limited war: geography, political goals, resources, geographical factors, and safe havens.[2] In order to deal with those challenges, President Kennedy had given specific orders for the military to develop limited war and counterinsurgency capabilities, but overall the services were not interested in adding those cognitive approaches to their quiver, and thus it was neither intellectually nor doctrinally oriented in a way to carefully analyze the problems conflict in Indochina presented.[3] Nevertheless, the United States' support of South Vietnam and its war against the communist insurgency grew during the first four years of the 1960s. By the time President Kennedy was assassinated, more than 16,000 American advisors were trying to provide leadership and training to South Vietnam's military forces. His successor, Lyndon B. Johnson, looked for options, and one of those was an escalated air war.

Tankers: The Great Enablers of Air Operations

Air power offered political leaders a form of firepower that did not portend the kind of commitment that came with sending in ground combat soldiers. Furthermore, a new technology added flexibility to the air weapon in the early 1960s: the air-to-air refueling tanker. With their ability to replenish aircraft in flight, tankers, especially KC-135 Stratotankers, extended the flying distance of any aircraft able to receive fuel from them. Tankers not only increased the endurance of large multi-engine bombers, they also turned short-range fighter aircraft into medium-range bombers, opening up many new possibilities for the conduct of war.

Mid-air refueling was foundational to the air war in Southeast Asia. The ability to fly large strike missions beyond South Vietnam depended directly on the presence of dozens of tankers; tanker availability determined how many missions Air Force aircraft could fly to North Vietnam. Tanker activities, however, typically receive no more than passing mention in histories of the air war. Operations Rolling Thunder and Linebacker I and II and the overall strategy they supported were possible because of aerial refueling that extended the ranges of the aircraft best suited for missions in the dangerous airspace around Hanoi and Haiphong.[4] The distances from their bases to targets in North Vietnam made en route refueling a necessity for F-105s, F-4s, and their escorts; they simply could not reach their targets otherwise. An F-4C carrying bombs had a maximum combat radius of about 360 miles. If not for KC-135s, only the Navy's tactical aircraft would have been able to reach targets in the Red River Valley; without mid-air refuelings, Air Force assets would have been restricted to targets in Laos, Cambodia, and South Vietnam.[5] Pacific Air Forces (PACAF) considered aerial refueling "absolutely indispensable."[6] Military Assistance Command, Vietnam (MACV), the lead organization for the American war in Southeast Asia, recognized that tankers made it possible to use fighter-bombers—fighter aircraft used as bombers—with the most "efficiency and effectiveness."[7] Air strategy would have been fundamentally different without the plentiful supply of air-to-air refueling aircraft.

This use of tankers to extend the range of tactical fighters during operational missions was a new task for tankers. In the late 1950s and early 1960s, the Air Force used them to enable fighters to deploy overseas without the need to stop and take on fuel at land bases, but mostly reserved them for extending the range of B-52 nuclear bombers. The Air Force had originally developed aerial refueling aircraft—the KC-97 and then the KC-135—to increase the range of its B-47 and B-52 bombers on missions against the Soviet Union, but

KC-135 refueling B-52 (Air Force Historical Research Agency)

the shooting war they fought was the Vietnam War. On average, a KC-135 could fill the tanks of one B-52 or up to six F-4s.[8]

The tankers suffered from just one major limitation: hot weather prevented them from taking off with a full load of fuel. It was so hot at the air bases in Thailand that the KC-135s could not take off with their maximum of 200,000 pounds of fuel; 150,000 pounds was their limit. Tankers that staged out of Kadena Air Base, Okinawa, would show up with only 30,000 pounds of fuel to offload; hot weather could reduce this by as much as 10,000 pounds.[9]

The bulk of the tanker sorties—one flight by one aircraft—went to supporting fighter-bombers on their way to and from North Vietnam and Laos. Typically, the aircraft comprising the strike force would top off prior to their run into North Vietnam, and then take on fuel again during the return home.[10] Navy F-4s, for example, might receive up to 3,000 pounds prior to commencing a combat air patrol (CAP) mission. Taking on fuel during the return approach to the aircraft carrier meant that, during this one cruise of the USS *Midway*, at least, no F-4 found itself dangerously low on fuel while in the landing pattern.[11] Tankers also orbited just outside of the range of MiG fighters so as to provide fuel to fighters that had burned most of their JP-4 fighting enemy interceptors.[12] Refueling made it possible for MiGCAP fighters to persist in their combats because the F-4 crews knew that a tanker was just minutes away once they disengaged from their adversaries. Tankers also enabled photo reconnaissance jets to keep making passes until they had completed their mission.[13]

Flying tankers was not a duty pilots eagerly pursued; top graduates of Air Force pilot training classes preferred fighters.[14] But tanker crews on assignment in Southeast Asia were not "sitting alert" at their nuclear bomber bases; they were supporting actual combat operations and quickly grasped the seriousness of their tasks. They knew the fighters' missions depended on their ability to manage and fly their tankers well. The whole modus

operandi was rather invigorating, particularly the fact that they had to think for themselves and improvise when events did not go as planned. Major Fred W. Sternenberg Jr. observed that tanker aircrews often had to make irreversible decisions that determined whether or not a mission was going to be successful or if a distressed aircraft was going to make it back to base. He added, "Most crews thrive in this environment. We finally have a chance to go out and do what we have been practicing for years and we do it well."[15]

In one sense, there just was not much to it and it was not that complicated. A tanker arrived at its orbit when it was supposed to, offloaded fuel to the aircraft that needed it, and then returned to base. Enabling the missions against North Vietnam was rewarding enough. Executing these missions required disciplined fuel allocation; an aircrew receiving fuel had to consider the needs of aircraft besides those assigned to them. Strategic Air Command (SAC), who owned the KC-135s, did not allocate enough fuel for each jet flying to top off with the maximum amount of fuel it could hold. Pilots who took all the fuel they could take would short shrift the last jet to take fuel from that tanker.[16]

Actual practice was more interesting, and tanker crews did all they could to help individual flights. Often, they came to the aid of a fuel-starved aircraft in time to prevent it from crashing due to bone-dry tanks. Known as a "save," accomplishing this kind of improvised mission also made it less necessary for aircrews to bail out of an damaged aircraft, no small thing given the opportunities that bailouts presented for injuries during the ejection or landing, and even capture or death. These situations demonstrated the need to fly missions the right way the first time—not to stay out of trouble but to avoid contributing to an aircraft loss. Time was of the essence and one incident taught everyone that too many agencies trying to help just clogged the radio frequencies, led to confusion, and could lead to a fighter-bomber with empty fuel tanks. On August 11, 1966, an F-4C had taken fire, was losing fuel, and called for a tanker. Three different stations tried to help at the same time, jamming the frequency, preventing the tanker crew from getting an azimuth of the F-4's radio transmission. Worse, one of the ground-controlled intercept (GCI) stations gave the tanker the wrong vector. They eventually found each other, but during the second approach to the KC-135 refueling boom, the fighter's engines quit. The pilots bailed out and a Navy helicopter crew retrieved them in good form.[17]

Fighter pilots valued tankers because their fuel enabled them to return to base instead of abandoning a fuel-starved aircraft. For example, after leaving his target over North Vietnam on November 22, 1965, "Oak 4," an F-105 Thunderchief, began losing fuel because enemy fire had damaged the jet. The pilot had to get more fuel—midair—if he wished to get back to his base. If he could not find a tanker aircraft in time, he would have to bail out and likely become a prisoner of war. An air traffic controller provided directions to Oak 4 and a KC-135A Stratotanker Captain Ross C. Evers piloted. They rendezvoused over North Vietnam in the nick of time. The damaged fighter had only 200 pounds of fuel left when it started receiving fuel and took on enough to stay aloft and managed to get back to its base with this help.[18] The story of Major Albert Hamblet Jr. and First Lieutenant T. H. Amos was the same: fuel from a KC-135 enabled them to fly back to base. Cannon shells had struck their F-4C Phantom northeast of Kep Airfield damaging one of their engines, so they headed for the Gulf of Tonkin where a US Navy ship could rescue them in case they had to bail out. Two North Vietnamese MiG-17s jumped them en route, so they dove for cover between some mountains while their flight leader drove away the MiGs. After that they managed to refuel from a KC-135 with one engine out and then landed at Da Nang Air Base in South Vietnam. When an F-105G pilot realized one of the fuel tanks was not going to be able to transfer fuel to his engine during a mission in October 1972, he looked for a tanker. He only had 1,000 pounds of fuel remaining when he joined up with one he found in a holding pattern nearby in case it was needed. He returned.[19]

Pilots appreciated the difference their tanker cohorts made. By July 1966 Brigadier General M. S. Tyler, commander of the 4252 Strategic Wing (SW), concluded that emergency tanker refuelings had saved at least fourteen distressed fighters. He suspected that more had taken place, but that fighter pilots had not documented them because, having deviated from procedures, they were at least partially responsible for their low fuel state.[20] In May 1967, Captain Howard L. Bodenhamer, an F-105 pilot of the 354th Tactical Fighter Wing (TFW), recommended Captain Richard E. Hughes's KC-135 crew for the Distinguished Flying Cross. Bodenhamer and three other Thunderchiefs had to fight MiGs during their April 19, 1967, mission and consequently left for home very low on fuel. Bodenhamer received a heading to Hughes's tanker and asked him to ascend to his flight level of 30,000 feet, which Hughes did. Bodenhamer then asked Hughes to slow down and begin a descent, because by that time he may have had only 100 pounds of fuel left, and he was around three to four miles astern. Entering some bad weather, Bodenhamer began suffering from spatial disorientation as he flew toward the refueling boom. Airman First Class Douglas D. Lueskow, the boom operator, plugged the boom into the F-105 despite Bodenhamer's "erratic" approach. Bodenhamer added, "I estimate that at the time I got on the boom I had less than thirty seconds of fuel remaining. It is my contention, as well as that of my fellow flight members, that this crew ... performed expertly, fearlessly, and perfectly. If at any point they had performed in any manner other than which they did, I would have bailed out over hostile territory." The accompanying tanker, commanded by Major Winfred T. Newsome, received a similar nomination because its crew had saved the two other F-105s.[21]

Another KC-135 aircrew (Major Alvin L. Lewis, Captains Kenneth H. Kelly and Manuel Micias, and Technical Sergeant Walter T. Baker) carried out a rescue of two fuel-starved F-105s, Wabash 1 and 2, in June 1967. Providing cover for a rescue operation used most of their fuel, then they had trouble finding a tanker because bad weather and an unusual number of in-flight emergencies had cascaded into a chaotic situation, delaying their chances of finding a tanker. Lewis was nearby, found them by listening to what was happening, and flew toward Wabash flight. When Wabash 2 declared "zero fuel," Lewis radioed that they were less than fifteen miles away. Wabash saw the tanker and turned to rendezvous. Lewis then entered into a dive because the F-105 could barely maintain its airspeed. The boom operator connected with his first attempt, and then Wabash 2's engine quit just as the jet fuel started flowing, so the tanker entered a thirty-degree dive so the F-105 could refuel while gliding. The F-105 pilot managed to relight his engine and get enough fuel to allow his leader, Wabash 1, to gas up. After topping off, both made it to their home base, and the fighter pilots credited the tanker crew with saving their jets.[22] On February 3, 1967, an F-4C, Rainbow 02, was down to 800 pounds of fuel due to damage taken during the mission. The refueling control agency sent two tankers to a successful rendezvous that enabled the damaged F-4 to take on enough fuel so as to land.[23] Yet another tanker towed a distressed fighter that was burning fuel faster than it could receive it from the tanker back to base, whereupon the fighter detached itself just before reaching the runway. Occasionally tankers even flew into prohibited airspace over Laos or North Vietnam to get fuel to distressed receivers. Rendezvous foul-ups were rare. Altogether, tankers saved eighty-one jets during Operation Rolling Thunder.[24]

Stratotankers helped Navy aircraft as well. On February 4, 1967, Anchor 02 Papa assisted an F-8 Crusader from the USS *Ticonderoga* that was about to run out of fuel. The F-8 made it back to its carrier after taking on more than 5,000 pounds of JP-4.[25] Three months later a tanker Major John H. Casteel commanded was refueling a pair of F-104Cs when it received direction to go help a couple of KA-3 Skywarriors, themselves carrier-borne tankers. As soon as they rendezvoused, the Skywarrior with three minutes of fuel remaining hooked up, followed by the second shortly thereafter. While the second Skywarrior was still taking on fuel, a pair of F-8 Crusaders arrived in desperate straits. Forlorn, one Crusader did not wait for the KA-3 to unhook but plugged into its basket while the "Whale," a nickname for a KA-3, took on fuel from the KC-135. At the same time, the other KA-3 offloaded fuel to the other F-8. No sooner were they done helping these Whales and Crusaders than two Navy F-4s showed up. After passing 3,000 pounds to them so they could return to the USS *Constellation*, Casteel topped off his escorting F-104Cs and made for Da Nang, because he was now relatively short of fuel himself. Casteel's aircrew received the McKay Trophy "for the most meritorious flight of the year."[26]

Aerial refueling served different purposes for carrier aviation than it did for land-based tactical aviation. The Navy used its tankers primarily to refuel carrier-based aircraft that were leaking fuel due to battle damage, less so to extend their range into North Vietnam. Aircraft carriers steamed sixty to one hundred miles off the coast, so their aircraft had enough fuel to reach their targets. Comparisons between these jets and the KC-135 are not that helpful because they had two different primary missions. Aircraft range extension was the primary purpose for the KC-135; the saving of distressed aircraft was the priority for Navy refuelers, with range extension running a close second. There was no comparison in the amount of fuel each could offload. On average, a KC-135 could transfer 116,000 pounds, while a KA-3 could offload 13,500, and an A-4 Skyhawk with a refueling "buddy pack" had only 4,000 pounds of fuel.[27] Navy strike aircraft also took on fuel in order to not carry as many external fuel tanks so as to carry more bombs. A-4C aircraft, for instance, could carry another 500-pound bomb and fly ten more minutes when topped off by a Navy tanker. Because of tankers, Skyhawks deposited an additional 422 tons of bombs on enemy targets.[28]

Navy KA-3s orbited as close to air strike locations as they safely could so as to refuel jets post-strike. During one particular event, the tanker squadron from the USS *Constellation* saved nine A-4s, six F-8s, and two F-4s, making it possible for six more jets to avoid having to do a barrier landing. The planes then refueled fifty-three jets that were in a holding pattern waiting for sailors to clear a flight deck fouled by debris or that had had trouble catching a cable. They also saved ten jets from other carriers. When the tailhook on Lieutenant Bob Stricker's F-8 broke when he tried to land, he did not have enough fuel to get to an airfield. A KA-3 scrambled from a standing start and rendezvoused in three minutes. A couple of years later an A-7E from the USS *Ranger* found itself down to 700 pounds of fuel forty miles from the carrier. A refueling from a KA-3B enabled it to make it back to the ship.[29]

A-6 Intruders—carrier-based bombers—were also used as tankers. While steaming in the Tonkin Gulf in December 1970, the USS *Kitty Hawk*'s A-6 squadron flew several of these bombers with refueling packs because the carrier had to take care of all refueling contingencies; there were no other carriers around with tankers to bail out the *Kitty Hawk*'s air wing in case something unusual happened. They saved, for instance, two F-4s that had to wait for a crashed jet to be cleared from the flight deck before landing themselves. As one commander wrote, "Best advice is for all A-6 squadrons to do a lot of thinking about tanking—it's a real requirement and can make or break you with the ship, regardless of what else you're doing."[30]

Marine KC-130 tankers provided a similar function: prolonging on-station time for Marine fighters.[31] Lieutenant General Victor H. Krulak considered them key elements of Marine air power.[32] They increased the effectiveness of A-4Es flying off of the short airstrip at the Chu Lai Forward Base; the jets had to take off with partially loaded tanks because of the short length of the runway, and the tankers topped them off. Because it was a straight-wing turboprop aircraft, the KC-130 was not what the Marines really needed. Its low speed and inability to fly at higher altitudes made it less compatible with tactical fighters. A KC-130 might, for instance, have to go into a shallow dive in order to have enough speed for an F-4 to remain attached to its refueling basket.[33]

There never seemed to be enough tankers. Following an August 1967 request, U-Tapao Air Base maintained thirty-two KC-135As, Takhli Air Base eight, and Kadena Air Base twenty-five. By early 1968 fifteen more tankers operated out of Ching Chuan Kang, Taiwan. PACAF appealed for more so as to increase daily sorties from fifty-three to sixty-six. Because North Vietnamese air defenses had improved, strike packages—groups of fighter-bombers and their escorts—needed more escort fighters, creating a need for more tankers. A loosening of the rules of engagement for striking in Hanoi meant that strike aircraft could fly more indirect approach routes that required more refuelings. There was also a greater need for bombing in Laos because of stepped-up guerrilla activity, and the F-100s flying there needed tanker support.[34]

Officers from tanker and fighter units met with air traffic controllers and discussed ways of improving procedures. These meetings made it possible for them to explain to one another what each needed to complete their missions. Timing, for instance, was very important for both tankers and receivers. Both had to be where they were supposed to be so the fighter-bombers would get their fuel on time and reduce the opportunities for mid-air collisions. Refueling tracks also needed to be located so that tankers parted with their receivers with all the fighter-bombers together because they had neither the time nor the fuel to find one another and form up before entering hostile airspace.[35]

Tanker crews and air traffic controllers displayed noteworthy flexibility when bad weather forced them to deviate from their standard orbits. Bad weather was particularly disruptive to missions over North Vietnam. During one Linebacker mission, tankers had to offload so much fuel prior to the fighter-bombers heading toward their targets that they did not have enough fuel left for post-attack refuelings. Tanker crews might find a gap in the clouds in which they could refuel only to see it close before a receiver could complete a rendezvous.[36]

Fighter pilots recognized the operational importance of tankers. The 355th Tactical Fighter Wing (F-105s) included the tanker crews in the wing's mission briefings to reinforce the essential nature of the tankers to the wing's operational success. Fighter pilots had the greatest respect and appreciation for the KC-135 crews because they took initiative and risks to reach them, flying into North Vietnamese airspace in order to effect a rendezvous. Recognizing their importance, the 388th Tactical Fighter Wing threw a party for the men of the 4258th Strategic Wing in May 1968 to show their appreciation and thankfulness.[37]

Basing tankers in Thailand improved the effectiveness of the entire operation. Since they were closer to their refueling orbits, they had more fuel available to offload. Flying KC-135s out of Thailand also highlighted the relationship between diplomacy and aircraft basing privileges. They initially flew out of Don Muang Air Base, which doubled as Bangkok International Airport. The Thai government valued its image as a commercial airport and did not want it overrun with foreign military aircraft, so Takhli became a base for ten to fifteen tankers in December 1965. Another base and the advent of the 4258th SW commenced in June 1966 at U-Tapao. The opening of that base simplified the logistical support of this fueling operation because it was next to a deepwater port, easing the transferral of fuel from ships to the air base; tankers began flying out of U-Tapao Air Base in August. Thailand bases had the added benefit of being less controversial for the Thai government domestically than Kadena Air Base on Okinawa was for the Japanese government. Ching Chuan Kang Air Base on Taiwan was also a more sensitive issue given the concerns of the government in Peking, so initially the Air Force did not use its tankers over Indochina. Having tankers based at both U-Tapao and Takhli also ensured at least one runway would be open in case a crash brought flight operations to a temporary halt at the other.[38]

Tankers proved especially enabling for the interdiction campaign against the Ho Chi Minh Trail in Laos, therefore Seventh Air Force (AF) did not want to give up any tankers in 1969, even though there had been a reduction of fighter-bomber sorties down to 14,000 per month. The end of the rainy season meant the communists were going to be repairing their roads more, and thus there was a greater need for interdiction sorties, hence KC-135s. Fewer tankers, Admiral John S. McCain Jr., the Commander-in-Chief, Pacific warned, would reduce the air interdiction effort over Laos.[39]

Air Force and Navy aerial refueling interoperability left much to be desired. KC-135s had been designed primarily to support Strategic Air Command bombers, so they employed the "boom" method of fuel transfer, while Navy tankers trailed a "drogue," a basket receptacle for refueling probes. In order to refuel F-100s, F-104Cs, and Navy aircraft, ground crews had to reconfigure a KC-135's boom with a drogue. As a result of two different fuel transfer methods—boom on the one hand and probe and drogue on the other—KC-135s could be nearby receivers that needed them and be unable to transfer fuel.[40] The probe and basket method the Navy and Marines used made refueling a bit trickier for their aircraft. In turbulent air the basket could move around enough to make completing a hookup a challenge, "like trying to spear a fish."[41]

The Air Force avoided a mistake in 1965 by retaining the Stratotankers under SAC's control, rather than siphoning off the tankers to PACAF. If PACAF had gotten its own tanker fleet, it would have required half again as many tankers to support the same number of missions as the previous arrangement. Another bone of contention concerned efficiency versus effectiveness. SAC measured refueling in terms of sorties, not aircraft refueled, so its management of tankers was more efficient.[42] So that its planes could offload the most fuel, it wanted to sequence tanker use so 40 percent flew in the mornings, 40 percent in the afternoon, and 20 percent at night. Seventh Air Force, however, wanted tankers to fly at the times they were needed. Similar negotiations lowered tanker orbits to altitudes more suitable for bomb-laden jets: 15,000 feet for F-105s and 16,000 to 18,000 feet for F-100s.[43]

The reaction to the North Vietnamese invasion in 1972 well illustrated the long-touted flexibility of air power. Tankers made it possible to transfer fighter aircraft from bases in the United States to Southeast Asia in a couple of days.[44] During Operations Constant Guard and Bullet Shot, F-4, F-105, and B-52 units deployed to Thai air bases accompanied by KC-135 tankers in April and May of 1972. The Marines sent a pair of A-4E Skyhawk squadrons and five of F-4s, and the Navy added four aircraft carriers to the two already operating near Vietnam.[45] Tankers were needed as urgently as any of those aircraft, and thirty-two more were brought into the theater. One hundred fourteen covered the ramps of Korat, Takhli, and Don Muang by the end of June, and there were fifty additional KC-135s at Clark Air Base (AB) in the Philippines and Kadena AB in Japan to refuel B-52 sorties.[46]

Not surprisingly, aerial refueling was indispensable to the success of Operation Linebacker, the air campaign against North Vietnam in 1972.[47] At first there were not enough tankers to support other missions besides those over North Vietnam. The strike packages swelled to more than 100 aircraft, making refueling difficult to manage.[48] Nevertheless, pre- and post-strike rendezvous typically proceeded smoothly, and "Tanker support was considered outstanding" was a pretty common assessment during the campaign, but not universally.[49] On August 2, General John W. Vogt, the Seventh AF commander, complained about the management of the previous day's post-strike tanker rendezvous.[50] There were some significant setbacks at times and they got worse that month. Often, tankers were "not where they should be, and in some cases do not provide the fighters with rendezvous assistance." For this reason, Seventh AF once again asked for the installation of air-to-air tactical air navigation (TACAN) black boxes in its F-4s. With that capability a tanker could broadcast its location in bearing and range and a receiver could locate and fly toward the tanker. Frequently the problems resulted from last-minute changes in operational plans. Furthermore, well-meaning tanker crews trying to assist receivers by deviating from the script would often disrupt the mid-mission air refueling sequence.[51]

Complaints during Operation Linebacker II, the eleven-day bombing campaign in December 1972, were the exception, and mainly concerned receiving the flying schedule at the last minute, which created problems meeting up with receivers at the scheduled place and time. While tankers had to be on time, the fighter-bombers were warned to not be late as well, because loitering for late arrivals would put other receivers behind schedule.[52] A couple of simple adjustments, providing more tankers for post-strike refueling, and tanker pilots transmitting their locations every couple of minutes after the jets left their targets, helped rectify the problem. Twenty-five more tankers made it possible to support 105 sorties each day at fifteen separate orbits. So many things had to function correctly, or aircraft could go down. On one mission an F-4 with numerous malfunctions was not able to contact the emergency tanker because of confusion over radio frequencies.[53] More common was the positive experience of fighters with emergency refueling support. Without the KC-135s, B-52s from Andersen AFB in Guam would not have been able to reach North Vietnam.[54]

Strategic Air Command measured the effectiveness of their tankers in terms of task completion: Did they all reach their orbits, how much fuel did they offload, did they take off as scheduled, how many sorties did they fly?[55] From June 1964 through August 1973, tankers "flew 194,687 sorties . . . providing 813,878 aerial refuelings, transferring a total of 8,963,700,000 pounds of fuel, equating to 1.4 billion gallons."[56] The Air Force recognized the importance of this mission to the execution of the air war in Southeast Asia, but it would have heightened the understanding of air power had it more frequently explained the relationship between air refueling and achieving national policy goals.[57]

This large-scale availability of aerial refueling may have unwittingly functioned as an enabler of a dysfunctional military strategy, the idea that bombing targets in North Vietnam and Laos could influence policy makers in Hanoi as thoroughly as could an Army-Marine conquest and occupation. An absence of KC-135 tanker support would have resulted in three more-restricted theaters of operation: the portion of the Red River Valley in range of Navy aircraft, the sectors of Cambodia and Laos in range of land-based aircraft, and all of South Vietnam. The close air support and some of the interdiction efforts were doable without refueling, but the coercion campaign against the North Vietnamese heartland would have been a Navy-only task. How many carriers would that have required to remain on station continually? Seven? Eight? The need for that number of carriers and the number of tankers actually used also suggests that Vietnam was not a so-called small war.

The Air Force recognized that tankers were indispensable. During June 1972, Air Force Lieutenant General George J. Eade wanted to field the optimum mix of air bombardment capabilities and wrote, "I hope we will give John Vogt all the tanker sorties he needs to make the most of this unique opportunity to prove the effectiveness of airpower."[58] In the end, the availability of a large fleet of tankers "provided a new range of operational possibilities for commanders," which in turn enabled them to provide national leaders more flexible options.[59] Given the United States' global commitments, air-to-air refueling was indispensable. The tankers made it possible to execute national policy. Without the KC-135 the president would have had to pursue different, more restricted national defense goals. Aerial refueling shaped, modified, and enabled national military strategy during the Vietnam War.

Chapter 2

Achieving Air Superiority by Destroying Enemy Aircraft on the Ground

Introduction: Why Fighter Combat Matters

Tales of fighter pilots, fighter planes, and air combat have dominated the literature surrounding airspace control over the past century, but in fact the ability to carry out military operations in hostile airspace has been a substantive priority for presidents and prime ministers since World War I. For an air force to accomplish its wartime missions over enemy territory, its aircraft have to be able to complete their operations without prohibitive losses. If that becomes impossible, then an air force has three options: continue to fly through enemy defenses until all that is left of its own aircraft is a negligible remnant; halt all air operations; or, figure out a way to defeat the defending air force. When fighting for airspace control during these kinds of situations, air superiority, a condition where one can complete missions without undue interference from enemy defenses, is generally the goal. Ideally, one attains air supremacy where one's aircraft can range over enemy territory with little risk of damage. If an air force cannot attain air superiority, then a state's political leaders cannot accomplish their goals as far as air warfare is concerned.

From the perspective of presidents, prime ministers, and chiefs of staff, day-to-day air superiority takes place in the background at the operational and tactical levels of war, somewhat like information technology and its technicians within a company's IT infrastructure. When those operations go well, an executive normally will not notice; air superiority simply enables other missions. When airspace control is in question, however, the apex of the government becomes intensely interested in what its fighter squadrons are doing. Prime Minister Winston Churchill, for example, personally visited a Royal Air Force air operations center on September 15, 1940, when the outcome of the Battle of Britain was unresolved.[1] On the eve of the Soviet counteroffensive at Stalingrad two years later, Stalin commented, "The experience of war ... indicates that we can achieve a victory over the Germans only if we gain air supremacy."[2] After the Israeli Air Force was unable to intercept a Soviet reconnaissance jet in 1971, the cabinet in Tel Aviv made the matter its first order of business.[3] In June and July 1972, the chief of staff of the US Air Force became very directive toward his subordinate commander in South Vietnam when air-to-air kill ratios approached a ratio that favored the North Vietnamese; the American National Security Advisor, Henry Kissinger, needed the air war to be going in America's favor while he negotiated with his North Vietnamese counterpart.[4]

Achieving control of airspace has been a national priority for warring states since the First World War. The first great campaign for air superiority took place in 1916 between the French and German air forces when the French realized air superiority was necessary for them to outlast the Germans during the Battle of Verdun.[5] World War II saw several battles for air superiority. The French Air Force never gained control of the air over the battlefield in May and June 1940, and that contributed to the defeat of France. The German Luftwaffe lost its attempt to control the skies over southeast England in 1940 when it slammed into Great Britain's integrated air defense system, which employed centralized management of interceptors through radar, telephones, and radio to inflict unsustainable losses on German bombers and fighters.[6] The Soviet Union fought for and gained air superiority in 1943 after the Luftwaffe had crushed its air force in 1941.[7]

At the same time, the United States chose to suspend its effort to bomb targets in Germany from October 1943 to February 1944 because it did not have air superiority and the Luftwaffe's interceptors were progressively destroying the American bomber force. The Army Air Forces won air superiority over Germany in the spring of 1944 by having bombers attack targets the Germans had to defend. When they attempted to do so, hordes of P-47s and P-51s shot the Luftwaffe out of the sky.[8] A year later, the XX Bomber Command with its B-29s possessed de facto air superiority over Japan because the bombers were so fast that Japanese fighters could not systematically intercept and shoot them down.[9] During the Korean War, Chinese Army generals railed against the absence of air cover as American aircraft pounded their soldiers. Two years later an Air Force operation to press their airspace control over North Korea to the Chinese border and beyond helped persuade their adversaries to negotiate a truce in 1953.[10] The Israeli Air Force carried out swift operations to gain control of the air over the Golan Heights and the Sinai as a necessary precursor to national survival in 1967. They did not rack up great tallies of air-to-air kills; fighter-bombers destroyed the Arab air forces on the ground.[11] Six years later in 1973, Israeli air forces fought for air superiority by defeating surface-to-air missiles (SAMs) and antiaircraft artillery (AAA) as well as Egyptian and Syrian MiGs.[12]

When the North Vietnamese could not dominate the airspace over their capital in 1972 they had to make significant concessions to the United States and South Vietnam during cease-fire negotiations.[13] In 1982 the air battles over the Bekaa Valley demonstrated that superior technology was no luxury. Israeli F-15As and F-16As achieved an 85:0 kill ratio against Syrian aircraft, helping decide that war.[14] As a consequence, the Israelis were able to extend their offensive into the Bekaa Valley, and Syria and Palestinian Liberation Organization ground units lay open to air attack.[15] When the United Nations coalition attacked Iraqi air defenses in 1991, it gained control of the skies over Iraq in a matter of hours.[16] The twentieth century closed with an air campaign complicated by Serbian SAMs, a demand that no enemy noncombatants be killed, fears of escalation, an enormously complex alliance, and United Nations politics. NATO air leaders were confident that achieving air superiority over Kosovo was a certainty, and that would provide the springboard for a quick successful air campaign.[17] National leaders monitored these air campaigns with the greatest of interest.

Political leaders and governments supported these air campaigns because from 1916 it was clear that dominance of the skies was necessary if one wished to wage successful military operations without taking severe losses. Air superiority simultaneously worsened the enemy's situation and losses and enabled one's own air and ground forces to accomplish their tasks more easily and with fewer losses; air superiority, therefore, was more than just tactical operation akin to artillery fire support.

Air superiority is important because it furthers one's military strategy, degrades the enemy's military strategy, and because an air force cannot sustain operations with

Air Bases in Southeast Asia

ongoing heavy losses; it will see most of its aircraft destroyed after a relatively small number of missions; an air arm of 100 aircraft that suffers a 10 percent loss rate, for example, would number about thirty-five aircraft after ten missions. High loss rates not only attrit an air force but also provide prisoners to the enemy, present graphic imagery of defeat and victory, and can encourage harsh scrutiny of the war within domestic political circles. Air superiority has therefore been a vital interest to policy makers for the past century.

This section of the book examines several issues surrounding air superiority effectiveness during the Vietnam War. It first assesses the extent to which the Johnson and Nixon administrations denied the Air Force and the Navy permission to achieve air superiority through cratering runways and destroying North Vietnamese interceptors on the ground. Leaders from the president and his cabinet down to individual aircraft commanders changed the way they executed the war because of the surface-to-air guided missiles the North Vietnamese fired at American aircraft. The North Vietnamese Air Force regularly evaluated its air defense methods and carried out improvements to try to defeat the Americans, but ultimately failed. This war witnessed a watershed in the technology of air weapons: SAMs and air-to-air missiles. As an immature technology, air-to-air missiles were a disappointment. When the North Vietnamese put up a stiff fight over their home territory, the results prodded the Americans into making changes in the ways they carried out and trained for the air superiority mission, and the course of the air siege reminded air leaders on both sides of the importance of the success of tactical missions to negotiations between states.[18] After the Americans made adjustments to their tactics in December 1972, North Vietnamese surface-to-air missiles were unable to stem the bombing missions sent against them, and the United States achieved its policy goals within a month.

Understanding the quest for air superiority over North Vietnam requires studying the execution of that mission from the bottom up, the top down, and the connections between the two. While the crux of the air war rested at the level of national policy, tactical and operational capabilities determined what policy makers could achieve, so a thorough investigation warrants a study not only of the ministers of war but also the operations, the aircraft, and the munitions they used. Since achieving command of the air can determine who wins or loses a war, it is imperative that historians, policy makers, and informed citizens scrutinize case studies like the Vietnam War.

In March 1965, the United States started flying sustained bombing missions over North Vietnam, first as reprisals for attacks by Viet Cong (VC) insurgents, and then as an ongoing air interdiction campaign against military targets. In its attempt to help render South Vietnam free of the communist insurgency and stave off eventual conquest from the North Vietnamese Peoples' Army of Vietnam (PAVN), the United States pursued a strategy of shoring up the South Vietnamese government, defeating the National Liberation Front/Viet Cong insurgency, and waging a bombing campaign against North Vietnam to help persuade Hanoi to stop sending supplies and troops into South Vietnam and to give up their effort to conquer South Vietnam.

The United States could not carry out its coercive air strategy against North Vietnam successfully unless it had the ability to fly and bomb without undue disruption from the North Vietnamese Air Force. While it is true pushing air strikes through skies the enemy dominates may still result in strike aircraft reaching and destroying important targets, the attacker will suffer substantial losses that will soon become prohibitive. That was not a risk in 1965, but as the North Vietnamese air defense system expanded, maintaining air superiority required more and more effort and resources from the US Air Force and the US Navy.

There were a number of means available for achieving air superiority. Aircraft could destroy surface-to-air missile sites before they were completed, as well as the SAMs themselves when found in warehouses, assembly areas, or at launch sites. Another option was destroying interceptors only in the air and attacking SAM sites after their completion when they were positively identified and operating. Antiaircraft artillery for its part does not have the range or reach to dominate the skies over a country, although it can inflict serious attrition on attacking forces near targets. One has to destroy those sites piecemeal, but the costs of that may outweigh the benefits. The most effective way to command the sky was to destroy enemy interceptors at their air bases and crater their runways to render them unusable.[19] One aviator later wrote that MiGs would not have shot down as many American aircraft if only he and his compatriots could have bombed the PAVN air force's primary bases sooner.

Why didn't the United States destroy the North Vietnamese air force on the ground like the Israelis had done to their adversaries during the 1967 Six-Day War?[20] The military repeatedly sought permission to establish air superiority over North Vietnam by destroying the enemy air force on the ground, but policy makers refused to allow a no-holds-barred campaign because they believed such an effort would result in an escalation of the war, which clashed with the basic policy goal of avoiding a military confrontation with China. Besides, American policy makers added, attacking airfields was not vital for achieving air superiority. This explanation brimmed with geopolitical logic, but to the aircrews getting shot at the reasoning defied common sense.

Frustration was the theme of the air superiority campaign for both sides. It was more than two years before airmen could employ the most effective kind of operation for achieving air superiority: bombing aircraft at their bases and cratering their runways. Furthermore, new technologies demonstrated chronic deficiencies. Aircraft that ought to have been more capable were not. Despite their preponderance of assets, American strike packages often did not know where MiG interceptors were flying or when they were about to attack. North Vietnamese SAMs did not function well and were terribly inefficient weapons. Achieving decisive effects against them was so difficult for American crews that they opted for "suppressing" the SAM threat, inadvertently developing a more mature understanding of air superiority. North Vietnamese sanctuary bases in China were off limits to American attack for reasons having nothing to do with American air power capabilities or effectiveness, and everything to do with not bringing China into the war. Aircrews entered battle without sufficient training in aerial combat and then suffered most of their losses to the random chance of antiaircraft artillery that was too ubiquitous and too well hidden to destroy. The US Air Force and US Navy always had air superiority over Vietnam, but all that seemed to accomplish long term was to enable the interminable air siege of North Vietnam to continue—which is what Presidents Lyndon B. Johnson and Richard M. Nixon needed from the fighter community. Air superiority was a necessary enabler that could help decide the course of the war, but achieving the president's policy goals on its own lay outside of its nature.

Destroying North Vietnamese interceptors on the ground became a consideration for the United States when U-2 photos first revealed MiG-17s on the tarmac at Phuc Yen Air Base just outside of Hanoi on August 7, 1964. Their presence was a troubling development for American reconnaissance pilots.[21] Geopolitical concerns made the Johnson administration very nervous about bombing airfields, especially those near Hanoi. A comprehensive airfield attack campaign might draw the Chinese directly into the war, something Johnson strongly wished to avoid.[22] For the first two years of the war civilian leaders removed most MiG bases from the target lists the Joint Chiefs of Staff (JCS) presented, despite the military's insistence that airfield attack was a necessity.[23] When concerns about Chinese reactions lessened during 1967 the White House permitted more and more air strikes against MiG air bases.

The need to gain air superiority was an outgrowth of the reprisal air strikes that commenced on February 20, 1965. Political leaders rejected airfield attack even though this would have been the easiest way for the Americans to gain air superiority over North Vietnam. PAVN jets were not protected in concrete aircraft shelters, and runways were easy to find. Likewise, the US could have solved the threat of an attack by the few IL-28 "Beagles" the North Vietnamese possessed against air bases in South Vietnam by blasting them to pieces on the ground as soon as they arrived in North Vietnam in May. Secretary of Defense Robert McNamara, however, would not allow that, and General William C. Westmoreland and U. Alexis Johnson, the Deputy Ambassador to South Vietnam, did not think that Hanoi would actually use the Beagles anyway.[24]

Among political leaders, bombing airfields was not an automatic choice. Former President Dwight D. Eisenhower advised against bombing the MiG bases near the capital after Viet Cong insurgents attacked American facilities on February 7, 1965; the Americans and South Vietnamese should instead limit air attacks to targets in the North Vietnamese panhandle.[25] McNamara initially concluded in February that American raids would lead to a battle with MiG-17s and that the United States would have to bomb the aircraft at their airfields. The rest of the National Security Council largely agreed, although Ambassador-at-Large Llewellyn Thompson Jr. was concerned about a Soviet reaction to attacking MiG bases.[26] With that apprehension in mind, the White House normally prohibited airfield attacks altogether when high-level Soviet bloc officials were in North Vietnam. The President's advisors, for example, warned against air strikes while Soviet Premier Alexei N. Kosygin was in Hanoi. Even if the administration waited until Kosygin left North Vietnam, one should still expect the air strikes to result in more Soviet military aid to North Vietnam.[27]

Concerned the PAVN air force might carry out attacks as retaliation for the initial reprisal air strikes—Operation Flaming Dart in February 1965—the Commander of the 2nd Air Division, Major General Joseph H. Moore Jr., suggested a major strike against their air bases even before the beginning of the operation.[28] Logically, destroying the MiGs on the ground would have resulted in fewer downed American aircraft.[29] Airfield attack, however, did not offer a permanent solution to the MiG threat, because the Soviet Union would provide replacement aircraft, the Chinese would allow the North Vietnamese to use their air bases as sanctuaries, and the North Vietnamese themselves repaired runways whenever the Americans bombed them.[30] Aside from these operational and material concerns, uncertainty about the Chinese reaction functioned as the great deterrent against targeting those jets.[31]

MiGs became a threat early on, attacking American aircraft for the first time on April 3, 1965. Three MiG-17s attacked a Navy strike force that was targeting the Dong Phuong Thuong Bridge. One of the MiGs scored some hits on an F-8E Crusader, and the MiGs escaped. The following day antiaircraft artillery downed an F-105D bombing the Thanh Hoa Bridge, and MiG-17s shot down two F-105s—the first American aircraft lost to MiGs during the war. Admiral Ulysses S. Grant Sharp, the commander-in-chief of Pacific Command (PACOM), recommended that air strikes against Phuc Yen Air Base follow any attacks by MiGs.[32] The primary consequence of MiG attacks was one out of every four fighter-bombers jettisoned its bombs in order to evade and survive these attacks. Measured another way, however, the loss rate was low. Of the 7,751 Air Force strike aircraft that entered Route Package VI, the most hotly contested airspace from April 1966 through March 1967, the loss rate was one aircraft out of a thousand.[33]

One American pilot believed he might have shot down a MiG, an action that President Johnson found "unduly inflammatory." Thereupon the president "informed the service chiefs he did not want any more MiGs shot down," a perspective astonishing to the aircrews under attack.[34] The JCS nevertheless listed air bases first on each target list it submitted in 1965.[35] In May Pacific Air Forces wished to crater Phuc Yen and destroy its MiGs with a strike force making a low-altitude attack at daybreak. It also recommended using tactical fighters instead of B-52s, as fighters had a better chance of achieving surprise and were less escalatory politically. The Joint Chiefs repeatedly asked permission to bomb it but were denied until October 24, 1967.[36]

Some outlying North Vietnamese air bases were in fact bombed in 1965. Although naval aircraft struck the airfield at Vinh in June, a base located in the middle of the panhandle, MiGs were not stationed there.[37] Navy and Air Force jets cratered runways at Dong Hoi and Dien Bien Phu airfields twice in July.[38] When strike aircraft cratered the outlying airfields at Na San, Dien Bien Phu, Dong Hoi, and Vinh, the North Vietnamese repaired them, and American aircraft returned to knock them out of commission month after month.[39] Although fighter-bombers repeatedly struck these staging bases, the major bases near Hanoi and Haiphong remained off limits. When a new airfield for MiG-17s came online at Kep in fall 1965, PACAF was unable to gain permission to strike it.[40] As an alternative to the prohibition against bombing airfields, the Air Force and Navy developed a plan in 1965 to bomb certain targets in order to draw the MiGs into the air and destroy them. Secretary McNamara received the plan on April 22 and sat on it.[41]

President Johnson worried an American fighter might actually shoot down a Chinese or Soviet MiG fighting on behalf of North Vietnam, and in fact, the president was not inventing a concern. Pilots claimed they had seen MiGs wearing Soviet and Chinese national insignia, but the national insignia of China and North Vietnam are quite similar. China's is a red star with red bars, and North Vietnam's is a yellow star on a red circle with red bars. Navy A-4E Skyhawk pilots reported on November 26, 1965, however, that they saw MiGs wearing Soviet markings. On April 18, 1966, Air Force F-4C Phantoms engaged a pair of MiG-21s wearing Chinese markings and shot down one of them.[42] Five days after that F-4Cs encountered another Chinese MiG-21 attacking an RB-66 reconnaissance aircraft but were unable to shoot it down.[43] Then on May 12 it appeared F-4Cs escorting an RB-66 had shot down a Chinese MiG-17, but the jet's identity was uncertain: "Jupiter 2 observed red star on top of both wings of one MiG. No bars were observed on either side of stars"—the markings for a Soviet aircraft. In any event, Jupiter 3 shot down a MiG-17 with a Sidewinder missile.[44] These encounters were rife with geopolitical risks and continued; Chinese MiG-19s fired missiles at an F-4B over North Vietnam on August 13, 1967, but failed to shoot down the Navy jet.[45] Publicized Chinese kills of American fighters, or vice versa, would have exacerbated tensions between the two countries, something President Johnson wished to avoid, and reports like these likely made him more nervous about the possibility of such an incident escalating.

President Johnson's goals regarding the war further explain why he prohibited the cleaning out of MiGs and SAMs. As early as April 1965 he publicly proposed "unconditional discussions" with Hanoi in order to bring the war to an end.[46] Perhaps he thought there was no reason to escalate if it might be possible to bring the war to some sort of a resolution before the end of the year. Indeed, the administration believed the inducement of a bombing pause and the threat of renewed bombing could persuade Hanoi to negotiate.[47] Bombing airfields would have been inconsistent with that initiative. He did grant permission, as mentioned earlier, to bomb the airfield at Vinh, possibly because of its distance from Hanoi and Haiphong, which thus made it less escalatory. Fighter-bombers from the USS *Midway* cratered Vinh's runway on May 8, 1965, and jets from the USS *Coral Sea* and USS *Oriskany* returned to do the same on June 30.[48]

Permission to bomb airfields was nevertheless rare during the first two years of Rolling Thunder. Even though fighter-bombers struck some, the five main bases of Bac Mai, Gia Lam, Kep, Kien An, and Phuc Yen remained off limits.[49] Instead, a pattern formed in which the Joint Chiefs of Staff pointed to the tactical and operational threats MiGs and SAMs posed, requested permission to destroy them proactively, and were denied by their civilian leaders who worried about the geopolitical consequences. This happened, for example, when they noted the presence of more than sixty MiG-17s at Phuc Yen as well as SAMs within the Hanoi and Haiphong restricted areas in August 1965. The Secretary of Defense refused permission again in September. He remained concerned about escalation, and he had been advised that there was little chance the North Vietnamese would use their aircraft to bomb the air base closest to North Vietnam located at Da Nang, South Vietnam.[50] McNamara subsequently denied eleven requests from November 1965 to March 1966 for permission to bomb targets like Phuc Yen.[51] Admiral Sharp insisted SAM sites and air bases be wiped out as soon as the bombing halt ended, but when Rolling Thunder recommenced in January 1966, the JCS ordered that strike aircraft were "*not authorized to attack DRV* [Democratic Republic of Vietnam] *air bases, from which attacking aircraft may be operating* [italics in original]."[52] McNamara was convinced they would be fighting "Chinese aircraft" within the year.[53] Interestingly, Secretary McNamara was not the sole source of these kinds of prohibitions. Not all military brass believed carrying out airfield strikes was of critical urgency. During a February 1966 briefing, Pacific Command explained to McNamara that "it was not necessary to strike the north's air bases until the MiGs began to interfere seriously with US air operations. Then, striking them would not draw the Chinese into the war." American fighter jets were sufficient for handling the MiGs.[54] The JCS asked again in March 1966 for permission to bomb the primary bases ahead of striking high-value targets in northeast Vietnam, but "political risks" were too great for McNamara to accede.[55] This restriction continued into the summer.[56] Operationally, MiG attacks forced the Americans to set aside more and more of their aircraft for aerial combat and the escort of fighter-bombers, which meant fewer aircraft were used for actual bombing missions. An aircraft carrier air wing, for example, "diverted as much as 28 percent of its strike force to MiG patrols," but this requirement did not render the air strikes ineffective, only less so.[57]

Had the American air forces been permitted to take out MiGs and SAMs on the ground, the consequences would have been significant only at the tactical and operational levels: air strikes would have suffered fewer losses, strike packages would have required fewer escorts, more aircraft could carry out bombing missions rather than escort missions, and not as many aircrew would have had to rot in the Hanoi Hilton. These were not trivial matters, but frustration over the effectiveness of the Rolling Thunder air strikes would have remained, because important as it was, an efficient, aggressive, and thorough campaign to achieve air supremacy (complete dominance of the air) would not have generated a strategically conclusive outcome for the war; the ability of American warplanes to fly over North Vietnam at will would not have been enough to convince the North Vietnamese that they were defeated. Air superiority was a necessary enabler for the bombing missions, but North Vietnamese political leaders and military personnel were determined, persistent, and ingenious. They found ways to circumvent the damage resulting from the bombing and simply refused to admit defeat. In spite of the two-year delay in permission to bomb airfields, the US achieved and maintained air superiority over North Vietnam and did so again whenever it wished throughout the war. The North Vietnamese air defense system never persuaded the Americans to stop sending missions north, although they raised the costs for them. The repeated requests to bomb the airfields were more about following doctrine and common sense than about following strategy or achieving strategic effectiveness.

The MiG arsenal grew in the spring of 1966, numbering sixty-three MiG-17s and fifteen new MiG-21 "Fishbeds" at Phuc Yen. Reconnaissance photos revealed fifty-three crates of fuselages and wings out in the open on the ramp at Phuc Yen, and because of the targeting prohibitions they were completely safe from air strikes.[58] While the prohibitions continued, the Air Force prepared a proposal that spring for a mission to destroy the North Vietnamese Air Force on the ground and crater its air bases' runways. If carried out, thirty B-52s would pound Phuc Yen at night at a very low altitude in two streams from two different directions. Planners expected a loss rate of 11 percent; because the B-52s were going to fly singly, one minute apart, AAA gunners would have had a chance to zero in on each jet. Fighter-bombers would follow up with strikes the next morning against Phuc Yen and all the other jet bases. If successful, this operation would have virtually eliminated the MiG threat, which was worsening—but only until the USSR provided replacement aircraft. It would also eliminate the IL-28 threat, which was not a serious problem. The proposal acknowledged the risk of escalation: "B-52 employment against Phuc Yen would represent a significant change in the overall conduct of the war in SEA. The change could be viewed as an unnecessary or undesirable escalation of the conflict and an intensification of the threat to CHICOM security [all caps in original]."[59] Eleven percent was a very high loss rate for assets like B-52s, especially since the Soviets could replace the MiGs and the North Vietnamese could repair the airfield. This operation remained a proposal and nothing more.

There were exceptions to the rule, as on June 23, 1966, when carrier air strikes hit the ground-controlled intercept station at Kep. That site was unable to provide guidance to MiGs for some time. A dozen F-105s left Bai Thuong airfield pockmarked on November 6, 1966. The norm returned that month, when Rolling Thunder 52 ordered that aircrews were to make every effort to avoid any kind of attack on Kep or Phuc Yen.[60]

While air-base attack was the best way to achieve air superiority, that method was risky and challenging. A study at the end of 1966 of what it would take to really disable the North Vietnamese air bases revealed a requirement for more than 1,000 sorties, including returning on three subsequent days to disrupt repair work. A planned September 1966 strike using B-52s at low level exploiting nighttime as cover would have sent twenty-nine against Phuc Yen and eleven against Kep. The Air Force completed tests of cluster bombs against revetted aircraft and seemed confident the bomblets could destroy parked aircraft. But there were 250 revetments in North Vietnam, and total destruction might eventually require fighter-bombers to carry out follow-on attacks with rockets and gunfire and suffer losses from the AAA that defended the bases. There were additional challenges: Spies might alert the enemy of the coming attack, some of the MiGs might be away on training missions, and some were always up in China. Ideally, massive numbers of aircraft would attack the bases at the same time, but the Americans could not launch all their aircraft quickly enough to arrive over the bases simultaneously. This battle would have instead been rather long and drawn out. Bad weather could also erode its effectiveness, and the North Vietnamese would be able to use the few MiGs on strip alert to attack the strike packages. Cratering the runways sufficiently would have required "about 600 bombs" in order to put "20 craters on each of the 7 runways" and the proposal assumed a loss rate as high as 5 percent.[61]

This plan also argued that F-4 Phantoms could not defeat MiG-21s in a force-on-force air battle; it projected that over time MiG-21s would shoot down three F-4s for every MiG that the F-4s killed. For that reason the air bases had to be knocked out. The secretary of the Air Force, however, exposed errors in this argument. Harold Brown noted that in actual experience the Phantoms had a 7:0 kill ratio against MiG-21s (that was just for the month of January 1967; the total was actually 14:1 through the end of January 1967), and that less-capable MiG-17s comprised the majority of the air threat. This briefing to the USAF Headquarters was designed to justify a decisive and comprehensive attack against air bases, but a key aspect of its own data undercut this argument. While it is true that eliminating MiGs would have resulted in more fighter-bombers reaching their targets without having to jettison their bombs in order to evade and survive an attack, the MiGs were not inflicting prohibitive losses, especially against escorting fighters. By the end of January 1967, in fact, F-4Cs had a 14:3 kill ratio against MiG-17s in addition to their 14:1 ratio against MiG-21s. F-105s were at least breaking even at 4:4 when pitted against MiG-17s. The Navy had a 12:6 kill ratio by this time. With these kinds of numbers the American air forces were not losing the air battle; there was no urgent need to take out the bases. Even with a successful operation, some MiGs would probably survive and escape to China from where they could still fly and provide some coverage to the northern quarter of North Vietnam.[62]

The proposal also argued that a comprehensive attack against runways and aircraft parked on the ground should be carried out only if it could completely remove the MiG threat, because even a remnant MiG capability would still require the flying of escorting fighters. Further complicating this proposed mission, not all the MiGs were sitting out in the open like the ones at Kep (revetments were available for twenty-two, and there were ninety parking spaces on the ramp); the off-limits base of Phuc Yen had revetments for 121 jets, making Phuc Yen a more difficult target.[63] Another look at the issue two years later did not reveal a reduction in the challenges. In October 1969, Chief of Staff of the Air Force General John D. Ryan informed President Nixon that complete destruction of North Vietnamese runways, air base infrastructure, and the like would require "three weeks" of air strikes.[64]

Although MiGs were not preventing strike aircraft from completing their missions, they were shooting down American aircraft while flying from sanctuary bases within North Vietnam itself, and that was absolutely galling to American aircrews. Those MiGs turned their buddies into corpses or prisoners of war. The worst point of frustration was flying over those bases, seeing MiGs parked out in the open, and not being allowed to bomb them. American aircrews found this indefensible. Americans were being shot down, captured, and killed so as to avoid an escalation that might not happen.[65] "I've flown over Phuc Yen and looked down and saw all kinds of MiGs and you can't do a thing. Flown over Gia Lam, which is right in the heart of Hanoi, you can't hit them. Why? If we're going to worry about the MiGs coming out of these bases, why not blast them and kill them on the ground, why take the chance of getting hit in the air?"[66] When Senator Stuart Symington spoke with pilots in Thailand who flew over the Red River Valley, he recalled that "the pilots almost got to their knees asking that Phuc Yen be knocked out."[67] He added that, "It seems we are running a rather extraordinary war when we don't even explain why a military target that is taking out our people is not hit, when the pilots plead that it be hit and when it is strictly a military target."[68] But from February through March 1967, MiGs achieved no kills against American aircraft.[69] Chairman of the Joint Chiefs of Staff General Earle G. Wheeler, US Army, nevertheless considered striking MiG bases in the heartland of North Vietnam "absolutely essential."[70] General John P. McConnell, the Air Force chief of staff at the time, conveyed to President Johnson's cabinet the aircrews' frustrations at flying over MiG bases, seeing the enemy fighters parked on them, being refused permission to destroy them on the ground, and then getting shot at by those same jets a few minutes later. These complaints were later brought up in Senate hearings in January 1967.[71]

Although the favorable kill ratio against the MiGs continued through the first six months of 1967, the trends were not positive, because while the communists lost fifty-one MiGs, they shot down nine American jets during 171 hostile encounters. This latter statistic was the best measure that the skies were becoming more dangerous for the Americans.[72] MiGs shot down an F-105F and an A-1E on April 19 and although President Johnson continued to fret about actions that might draw China into the war, on April 22, 1967, he permitted "limited attacks on Kep . . . and Hoa Lac" airfields. Colonel Robin Olds's 8th Tactical Fighter Wing received the mission, and on April 24 he was the lead pilot of a group of eight F-4s that went after Hoa Lac, attacking about twelve MiGs on the ground with cluster bombs, hitting seven. A contemporary analysis admitted that no one could be certain how many jets had been damaged; moreover, MiGs could be repaired unless cluster bombs destroyed them outright.[73] Air Force and Navy sources claimed at the time that the April 24 mission was the first American attack on a North Vietnamese airfield, which suggests that the prohibition against airfield attack had taken on some of the characteristics of a myth.[74] The president may have permitted the missions because of increased MiG activity, or it may have resulted from pressure by Senator John Stennis, who listened to the generals' complaints. Rolling Thunder 55 stated that these strikes had to be modest, seemingly random attacks avoiding the appearance of a major escalation, but that went against Admiral Sharp's operational goal of driving the MiGs into China, whereupon American fighters would intercept them as they emerged from the southern border of the buffer zone, meaning that American interceptors would be between the MiGs and the bombers.[75]

Navy jets from the USS *Kitty Hawk* bombed Kep the next day. They dropped a string of bombs from one end of the runway, but a second string missed the runway, hitting protected parking spaces. Jets from the USS *Bonhomme Richard* left at least three MiG-17s in flames on May 1.[76] Hoa Lac was bombed not only on April 24, but also on April 28, May 1, 3, and 7. Fighter-bombers returned to Hoa Lac three more times: May 8, 19, and 24, 1967. Navy jets bombed Kep airfield on May 17 and 21, and Haiphong's Kien Airfield was bombed on May 10, 1967. The May 21 bombing of Kep caught nineteen MiGs on the ground resulting in six being either damaged or destroyed. All told, missions against Kep and Hoa Lac Airfields destroyed an estimated sixteen aircraft on the ground. Twelve craters from an April 30, 1967, strike rendered the Bai Thuong runway unusable.[77]

Striking airfields also provided opportunities for destroying aircraft in the air. MiG-17s attacked the May 1 Navy strike group and were soon tracking an A-4E, which evaded long enough to give an F-8E time to get behind the MiG to fire a Sidewinder missile, which flew up the MiG's tailpipe and blew it to pieces.[78] Both services got stung as a result of kicking this hornet's nest. The Navy lost an F-4B on May 24 and an A-4C the next day, and MiGs shot down four Air Force F-105s from April 28 to 30 and downed two F-4Cs in May.[79] The May 10 strike by aircraft from the USS *Hancock* encountered bad luck. There were no MiGs in Kep's revetments, and a SAM downed one of their strike aircraft.[80]

Initially these were small attacks by about eight bomb-carrying jets, which fell within the guidelines stipulating random, small, harassing attacks. Because strike forces of this size were not sufficiently damaging, this restriction was done away with.[81] The JCS then fretted "that the airfield attacks had been too vigorous," but soon thereafter, President Johnson allowed the military to attack the air base of Kien An as well.[82]

There was no consensus regarding the wisdom of these operations among American political leaders. Senator Mike Mansfield warned that serious escalation would just drive the North Vietnamese Air Force into China, creating the temptation for American fighter pilots to chase MiGs into China in order to shoot them down, thus increasing the risk of war with China and encouraging a rapprochement between Moscow and Peking.[83]

One measure of the effectiveness of bombing airfields was whether or not the North Vietnamese continued to repair and fly from the bases thus bombed, something the Seventh AF recognized.[84] The greater number of aerial engagements may have been a sign that the missions hurt PAVN air force operations and they may have sent more interceptors aloft to defend their bases. Bombing the bases consequently provided more opportunities for air-to-air kills.[85] The commander of the Pacific Fleet, Admiral Roy L. Johnson, believed these airfield attacks prompted the North Vietnamese to more aggressively use their MiGs, in turn contributing to the greatest number of aircraft losses (ninety-eight to all causes) the US suffered thus far from April through June. PAVN forces fired 431 SAMs, causing nine American losses. American operations destroyed forty MiGs through air strikes and aerial combat during this time.[86] The Defense Intelligence Agency concluded that attacking targets the North Vietnamese valued around Hanoi was what persuaded them to sortie their MiGs.[87] As a consequence of the air strikes on MiG bases and air-to-air battles in the spring of 1967, MiGs became an uncommon sight, except to the F-4C they shot down in June; the planes hunkered down at Phuc Yen, Gia Lam, and on Chinese air bases.[88]

At the height of the summer of 1967, McNamara believed that MiGs were "of no threat to us at this point."[89] Why risk losing strike aircraft in airfield attacks when interceptors were not downing American jets, McNamara asked, as there were no losses to MiGs thus far in July 1967.[90] Secretary of State David "Dean" Rusk defended these choices before the Senate during the Stennis Hearings, and in July 1967, the US had lost just one aircraft to MiGs, so the secretary of defense was correct in the short term.[91] When MiGs became more aggressive in August 1967, Seventh AF asked permission to bomb all the airfields in North Vietnam. Navy A-6A Intruders and A-4C Skyhawks returned to Kep in August, damaged a couple of buildings, spread Mk-36 mines, and produced a lot of smoke, but there were no aircraft of any type on the airfield.[92]

Johnson's reluctance to renew the airfield bombing effort received support from a surprising source: Robin Olds. He preferred to leave the air bases intact because he would then know where the MiGs would come from. Olds's point of view left General John P. McConnell nonplussed. The president revealed some understanding of force and diplomacy when he later gave the go-ahead for an airfield bombing mission after the North Vietnamese had stiff-armed a "peace initiative" Henry Kissinger had attempted.[93] Kissinger was somewhat of a freelance diplomat at this time. Assistant Secretary of State William P. Bundy asked him to float the idea of American–North Vietnamese negotiations at an East–West conference in 1966. During the summer of 1967 he initiated the "Pennsylvania Initiative" after developing a series of useful relationships with prominent individuals in the Eastern bloc. He appeared to have gained an opening for serious negotiations with the North Vietnamese, but that was a mirage; the latter had no intention of moving toward a settlement.[94] The North Vietnamese were not interested and reacted to the offer of a bombing halt in return for productive negotiations with a demand for an "unconditional and permanent cessation of bombing raids."[95]

Concerns over escalation, aircraft losses, and civilian casualties clashed with a doctrinal conviction that bombing interceptors on the ground and their runways was simply what was done—period.[96] Bombing Phuc Yen would raise the morale of the American pilots and reduce the MiGs' effectiveness by forcing them to operate out of bases farther away from the targets they were trying to defend. That would result in fewer attack runs against American strike aircraft and thus fewer situations where F-105s had to jettison their bombs in order to evade attacking MiGs. Phuc Yen was the primary interceptor base for the North Vietnamese, so bomb it. There were concerns, however, that Communist bloc advisors were present on that base, and killing them would not support American goals. Whatever the concerns, MiGs shot down four aircraft in August 1967: MiG-21s downed two F-4Ds on August 23, and two A-6As were shot down on August 21, possibly by Chinese MiG-19s.[97]

On August 24, President Johnson spent almost an hour discussing with Rusk, McNamara, Army Chief of Staff General Harold K. Johnson, General McConnell, and Deputy Secretary of Defense Paul Nitze whether Phuc Yen should be bombed, and the meeting made clear that the choice was not an obvious one. Again, flying over an air base that essentially functioned as a sanctuary for MiG-21s and not hitting it vexed the aircrews who got shot down by those aircraft. In their minds, it made no sense to not bomb when cratering the runway and destroying the jets parked on the ramp was something the Americans had the capability to do any day the weather was halfway decent. When General McConnell informed the meeting that there were presently eleven MiGs at Phuc Yen, President Johnson asked a question that was more insightful than it first appeared: "Why is it so important to get eleven airplanes?" He understood that they were not strategically significant. The Soviets could replace them ad infinitum, they could stage out of China, and the North Vietnamese would repair the runway every time the Americans bombed it to the point that re-attacks would be necessary twice a week. The president was still concerned that a persistent effort could lead to a confrontation with the USSR and the PRC, and the secretary of state pointed out that if the North Vietnamese adjusted by flying their interceptors out of China, that "would be considered Chinese intervention." Phuc Yen's location increased the likelihood of civilian casualties (propaganda for Hanoi), and bombing it could result in F-105s getting shot down during the mission's execution. The fact of the matter was that the MiG attacks were not stopping the air strikes, and F-4s and F-8s could effectively deal with the MiGs in the air.[98]

The operational ability to destroy the MiGs parked at Vietnamese airfields could not solve the strategic fact of their resupply and sanctuary. In that sense, the US military could not keep the North Vietnamese Air Force destroyed. Even with restrictions on American targeting, North Vietnamese air defenses were operationally ineffective. It inflicted losses and forced some individual bombers to jettison their bombs before reaching their targets, but most of the bombers got through. The North Vietnamese Air Force could not stop the American air strikes, and it could not inflict strategically significant losses on the Americans. Neither could the Americans achieve a permanent solution to the MiG problem, and the reason was not President Johnson's "restrictions" or timidity. The sanctuary of China and the willingness of the Soviet Union to replace the interceptors meant that there was no one-time permanent solution to the MiG problem. It was as if the Americans could besiege a four-sided castle on only three sides. It seemed both the US and the North Vietnamese would continue to fly and die in this stalemate.

President Johnson approved the bombing of Phuc Yen on September 26, 1967, following several MiG attacks, but he canceled it hours later because of the impending arrival there of the Romanian prime minister.[99] Continuing this pattern, Seventh AF got authorization to bomb it three days later only to see the JCS revoke it. Admiral Sharp begged his superiors for permission, pointing out that his aircrews pressed "home their attack[s] while getting shot down by jets that took off from a sanctuary airfield [Phuc Yen had been off the target list]." He then appealed to their managerial sense, noting the wastage the MiGs caused in forcing fighter-bombers to dump their bombs prematurely, and closed with common sense: "The most effective method of denying an air capability to an enemy is the destruction of his aircraft on the ground and the neutralization of his airfields. Recommend strike restriction against Phuc Yen airfield be lifted at earliest possible date."[100] The same arguments for and against returned: airfields do not remain knocked out; work crews repair them and return attacks after this initial one would be necessary. Furthermore, such an operation might see more American planes shot down than enemy planes destroyed. Besides, General Wheeler expected Phuc Yen's destruction to require about 200 aircraft. Nevertheless, on October 23, Rusk and McNamara endorsed the bombing of Phuc Yen. Throwing up his hands, the president was despondent over issues larger than an enemy runway. He was becoming convinced that the US and South Vietnam could not "win the war militarily.... We can't win diplomatically, either." He wished to convey to the public the extent to which the US had negotiated with Hanoi before escalating: "We must show the American people we have tried and failed after going the very last mile" with diplomatic efforts.[101]

From April 24 to September 10, the Navy flew fourteen airfield strikes and the Air Force seventeen, but none against the primary base. The MiGs flew less as a result of the attacks, and a number evacuated to China. Estimates as to the number destroyed on the ground varied from five to twenty.[102] Finally, on October 23, President Johnson removed the bombing restrictions around Hanoi, so Navy and Air Force jets finally received orders to bomb Phuc Yen for the first time on October 24 and 25, and destroyed or damaged "five MiG-21s and seven MiG-17s" out of a total of eighteen present. An F-4 managed to shoot down a MiG that got off the ground. A week later there were only ten functioning MiGs in North Vietnam. Most of their inventory, between sixty and eighty, had escaped to China.[103] A Walleye guided bomb destroyed the control tower for good measure.[104] Navy strikers also bombed Bac Mai and Kien An Airfields that month, the latter while it was under repair from previous attacks. The Navy returned again in November.[105] Air Force and Navy jets struck every major airfield in North Vietnam except the commercial airport Gia Lam by November 1967, and barely twenty MiGs were left in North Vietnam at year's end.[106]

Unleashing air attacks against the bases placed the North Vietnamese Air Force on the horns of a dilemma. They had best not just sit on the ground awaiting attack, but flying to defend the bases subjected them to airborne attrition from American fighters. They could wait and be bombed or fly and get shot down. They fought back and consequently, Air Force fighters shot down forty-eight and the Navy got twelve. Bombings destroyed as many as sixteen on the ground, and "For all practical purposes" the North Vietnamese "Air Force was destroyed." This analysis made no mention of the number of MiGs that escaped to Chinese sanctuary bases. Nevertheless, because of the aggressive action against the MiGs, fighter-bombers had to abandon their bombs much less frequently in order to defend themselves, and the pilots could devote more of their attention to bombing accurately.[107] In the end, however, this air battle did nothing to prevent the next offensive the enemy had been preparing for months: the Tet Offensive in January 1968.

The MiG problem did not go away, and the air threat expanded in 1968 when the North Vietnamese installed a GCI facility near Vinh in the panhandle. Intelligence obtained evidence that the North Vietnamese were practicing air-to-ground bombing tactics in February 1968, which led General Wheeler to express concern for Da Nang Air Base. When IL-28s returned to Phuc Yen in February 1968, Wheeler once again pointed out to the president that they could reach and bomb the air base at Da Nang.[108] McNamara noted that such an attack would not be that consequential militarily, but the appearances would be terrible, and it would shock and embarrass the Americans' air defense capabilities. The president's reaction was an order to "Go in and get those MiGs at Phuc Yen."[109] Not waiting for good weather, Lieutenant General William W. Momyer, the Seventh AF commander, tasked the 8th Tactical Fighter Wing (Wolfpack) with the job. They flew it with four F-4Ds flying a reconnaissance mission profile at 250 feet above the ground in order to deceive the PAVN Air Force. Two of them flew up to a higher altitude and turned on their transponders to attract the enemy's attention, while the other two streaked across the ramp dumping cluster bombs that damaged and perhaps destroyed both IL-28s, not much bang for their efforts. Alerted flak crews damaged the engine of the F-4 Captains Tracy K. Dorsett and John A. Corder flew to such an extent that they had to abandon their Phantom on the return trip over Laos. A helicopter picked them up after they avoided enemy troops. The Wolfpack hit the base two days later in a completely different manner. Sixteen cluster bomb–laden F-4s zoomed up suddenly five miles from the target and released their bombs, which arced toward the base in a mist of bad weather. A third strike by four F-4s on February 14 found no IL-28s, or MiG-21s for that matter, on the ramp. As a consequence, only two IL-28s were kept at Phuc Yen; whenever American jets approached, these two would take off and orbit north of the airfield, waiting out of range for the Americans to leave. The North Vietnamese parked most of them on Chinese airfields along with the majority of their interceptors.[110] The effect of the strikes was not the destruction of a large portion of the enemy's air forces; the strikes encouraged the North Vietnamese to base their MiGs out of range of their targets, the American strike packages, thus nullifying the MiGs' intercept capabilities—a good outcome. This "Valentine's Day Raid" also witnessed two more MiG kills. Escorting F-4Ds shot down two MiG-17s: one with a Sparrow missile and the other with twenty-millimeter (20mm) gunfire.[111]

While the White House remained nervous about striking air bases in the heart of North Vietnam, it continued to be more permissive regarding outlying bases. As of March 1968, the air bases at Vinh, Dong Hoi, and additional airfields in the A Shau Valley were bombed regularly to prevent the North Vietnamese from using them as forward bases.[112] A-6A Intruders visited and cratered Cat Bi three times in February 1968.[113] The Vietnamese in turn deceived American bomb damage assessment efforts, painting fake "bomb craters on runways after" repairing them, or emitting smoke from impact sites after the Americans had missed their targets.[114] Vinh's runway was pulverized but, as always, rebuilt.[115]

Diplomatic efforts also interacted with airfield attacks. In May 1968, the Paris negotiations made the Johnson administration reluctant to bomb Bai Thuong Airfield out of concern that such an operation might jeopardize the talks. Therefore B-52s and aircraft flying over Laos had to endure greater risk; according to General Wheeler, the communists were staging MiGs there to take potshots at B-52s and other aircraft flying missions in the Laotian panhandle.[116]

A 1968 study concluded that plastering airfields generated only temporary consequences because the North Vietnamese were able to fill the craters in about one to three days. The primary consequence of runway bombing was the Vietnamese decision to move their MiGs to the sanctuary bases in China.[117] Leaders of the Seventh Air Force reached this conclusion again in 1972 when airfield attack became a regular occurrence. Cratering runways brought flight operations to an end at the targeted airfield for little more than a full day because the North Vietnamese were able to rebuild them, but the Americans kept their plans updated in case attacking an airfield was deemed felicitous.[118] The bombing halt shelved the possibility of further airfield attack for four years.

North Vietnamese airfields were no longer sanctuaries in 1972, even before the North Vietnamese invasion. During the last week of January 1972, General Creighton W. Abrams, the MACV commander, received permission to not only use anti-radar missiles against the radar targeting systems the North Vietnamese used to guide their interceptors, but also to execute reactive strikes against airfields on the panhandle.[119] Abrams warned that the North Vietnamese had been stationing MiGs at bases in the panhandle and would be close enough to attack targets in South Vietnam and southern Laos.[120] Henry Kissinger, President Nixon's national security advisor, was concerned, however, about the reaction of the press to bombing those airfields.[121] Many would consider them escalatory, but media considerations would not prevent airfield attacks once North Vietnam's invasion began that spring.

After the North Vietnamese Army invaded South Vietnam, US Air Force and Navy aircraft bombed airfields on a regular basis through October 1972 and once again during Linebacker II in December. On April 13, 1972, during Operation Freedom Train, eighteen B-52s, along with a supporting strike force, bombed the Bai Thuong Airfield at night, a base noted for its remoteness and lack of strategic importance. They left behind twelve craters in the runway, nine in the taxiway, and a destroyed MiG-17.[122] Wisely blended with diplomatic efforts, the intent of these strikes was to bolster Henry Kissinger's negotiating position for his April 20–24 trip to Moscow.[123] The majority of airfield attacks that month targeted locations in the panhandle, which kept the North Vietnamese from stationing their interceptors that far south. This was not an overly aggressive approach, because their fighters flew primarily out of four bases up north: MiG-21s were based at Phuc Yen, MiG-19s at Yen Bai, Kep housed MiG-17s, and there was also Gia Lam Airport at Hanoi. The North Vietnamese now protected a considerable number of their interceptors "in caves or bomb shelters," a defensive measure that made a direct hit by a large bomb necessary to destroy an aircraft thus protected.[124] A pair of laser-guided bombs did just that on June 15, gliding into the caves that held MiG-21s at Bai Thuong. Navy strikes cratered the runways at Vinh and Quan Lang Airfields but failed to render Dong Hoi's runway inoperable.[125] Fighter units urged the bombing of these primary airfields so as to drive the MiGs into China. North Vietnamese MiGs flying from China would begin to run low on fuel just as they intercepted American strike packages, resulting in a reduced threat for the American jets.[126]

When Operation Linebacker commenced on May 10, 1972, the entire air defense system outside of the Hanoi–Haiphong safe zones was fair game, including airfields. The extent of airfield attack has not been emphasized in reports of the 1972 air campaign. One popular account, for instance, only mentions a single airfield attack mission, and that on October 1, 1972. The American air forces did not knock out the air defenses first and then commence bombing in sequential order; they carried out those operations in parallel. Fighter-bombers hit Cat Bi and Kien An Airfields on May 10, and eight F-4s bombed Bac Mai Airfield the next day, though after bombing the runway was still open for operations. Laser-guided bombs added four craters to the Khe Phat runway on May 24.[127]

Air strikes went after airfields regularly during the summer of 1972, but not as an all-out effort because other targets were more important and MiGs were not stopping the strike packages from reaching their targets. In mid-summer, airfields were still not a priority target, suggesting that North Vietnamese interceptors were not a major threat. Instead, the JCS stipulated that airfields, SAM sites, and such were to be "attacked as necessary to provide maximum freedom of action [and] safety for friendly strike and reconnaissance forces."[128] The history of the Seventh AF explained the rationale this way:

> We have deliberately chosen to strike those targets which will cause the most damage to the enemy's capability to sustain his offensive. Airfields and SAM sites do not fall in this category. We have occasionally conducted strikes on airfields for harassment purposes and have destroyed the underground central command and control facility at Bac Mai. Also, "wild weasel" aircraft supporting Linebacker missions are targeted against SAM radars and EW [Early Warning]/GCI installations.... In summation, the game plan has been to use a minimum force to bomb high value targets. We have struck air defense targets when necessary but not at the expense of our primary mission.[129]

Even though missions against airfields were not the top priority, they were not an intermittent effort, either. Fighter-bombers hit Yen Bai on June 2, 1972, Khe Phat on June 13 and 14, Bai Thuong on June 15 and 25, Quan Lang on June 15 and 24, Vihn on June 17 and 21, Dong Hoi on June 18, Bac Mai on June 27, and the Navy hit Kep on June 29. There were six major strikes against airfields in July.[130] One mission against Dong Hoi proved devastating: each bomb hit the runway, and each was evenly spaced from the other. These were, one should note, dangerous missions. The F-4s (both bomb carriers and laser-guidance pod carriers) had to fly between 12,000 and 22,000 feet—right in the heart of a SAM's envelope, the altitude where the missile functioned most effectively. The lasing F-4 had to fly a steady turn in order to keep the laser on the target until the bombs hit, heightening its vulnerability.[131]

Seventh Air Force leadership did not compromise its priorities, deciding that the sorties and effort needed to keep the primary airfields closed "would require a continuing level of resources all out of proportion to the priority of the airfields." Air strikes removed the fields south of the 20th parallel from action in June, and the North Vietnamese had not sent any MiGs to them by the first week of July. They instead dispersed and camouflaged their MiGs at the main bases, rendering them somewhat secure from aerial attack. Caves and tunnels at Yen Bai offered good protection for MiG-19s, for instance.[132] US Air Force jets hit Yen Bai on June 2, and Kep on July 1. Altogether the US Navy sent eight missions against four airfields in July: Kep, Quan Lang, Vinh, and Phuc Yen. Not until August 17, 1972, did Seventh AF and PACAF decide to keep the southern airfields out of action, although a night attack struck Vinh on August 14. Regular air attacks continued, such as the September 2 attack against Phuc Yen. F-4s still managed to leave craters in its runway and parking ramp even though they dropped their laser-guided bombs (LGBs) without the benefit of laser guidance since cloud cover interfered with the laser illuminator. Then in September, targeteers could schedule airfields as alternate targets. US Air Force and Navy aircraft carried out a series of strikes against eleven airfields spanning the last five days of September, and repeated attacks continued through October. Swing-wing F-111A "Aardvarks" joined the action on October 14 and 17.[133]

Airfield attacks continued during Linebacker's final four weeks. Yen Bai was targeted on September 26 in an effort to destroy MiG-19s the US believed had been flown in from China. Fighter-bombers saw a secondary explosion (explosions that occurred after the bomb detonated; enemy ammunition and fuel created them) when they bombed the base again on September 29, which suggested they had struck something significant. Strike aircraft pummeled Yen Bai (every single bomb hit the target) on October 10.[134] When fighter-bombers hit it again on October 15, they destroyed at least one jet. The airfield was twice an alternate target, again suggesting the Air Force did not consider MiGs a serious threat. Phantoms cratered the runway on October 19 as an alternate target because clouds obscured the primary objective.[135] Aircraft from the USS *Midway* left Quan Lang Airfield cratered on December 6 because of a warning of a possible MiG attack. Four LGB F-4s bombed Bai Thuong ten days later.[136] Clearly the US Air Force and Navy were not having to pursue air superiority with one hand tied behind their backs. There was even an operation known as Taxi Road planned "against the entire North Vietnamese tactical order of battle," with the intent of using pretty much every available Air Force F-4 in Southeast Asia, plus three carrier air wings, thirty-six B-52s, and F-111As, but it was never executed for reasons left unstated, probably because of progress in the peace talks between Kissinger and Le Duc Tho, special adviser to the North Vietnamese delegation.[137]

When Operation Linebacker II kicked off on December 18, 1972, most of the bombing missions against runways relied on radar-aimed methods by jets flying at medium altitudes, and "In no case did the airfield damage level exceed 10 percent"—a far cry from predictions as high as 85 percent.[138] Seven three-jet B-52 "cells" went after three North Vietnamese airfields on December 18: Phuc Yen, Kep, and Hoa Lac, and fighter-bombers struck Yen Bai the next day.[139] B-52s bombed Quang Te and Bac Mai before dawn on December 21, and the rules of engagement permitted "Iron Hand" strikes (missions against SAM sites) to drop unexpended cluster bombs on Yen Bai, Kep, and Phuc Yen Air Bases if the pilots wished on their return routes.[140] Led by pathfinder F-4s using LORAN (long-range air navigation equipment used when clouds covered the target area), A-7D Corsairs bombed Yen Bai on December 22 and again the next day, followed by a strike against Hoa Lac.[141] North Vietnamese airfields received 10 percent of the strike sorties, and only the F-111 mission against Yen Bai inflicted severe damage. B-52s cratered runways and squelched MiG activity, but an A-7D/F-4 strike against Yen Bai did not inflict serious damage. The study that is the source of this information did not draw definitive conclusions about airfield attack. The most damaging strikes kept airfields out of action only temporarily, but the missions may have been more effective than was understood; cratering runways may have been the reason MiG sorties were relatively few during the campaign.[142]

The White House permitted extensive airfield attacks during the Vietnam War, and US Air Force and Navy aircraft flew effective airfield attack missions during Vietnam when ordered to do so. These missions did not—nor did their absence—decide the air war. Once military leaders received a free hand to attack airfields in 1972, they did not reflexively attack them, but valued their destruction below other objectives, indicating airfield destruction was not their highest priority. The experience of the Vietnam War suggests airfield complexes, parked aircraft, and especially runways were harder to knock out than might be expected. Work crews repaired and filled the craters, and spare interceptors flew in from China. Effective airfield attack required not only aggressive bombing, but also follow-up missions that had to return on a regular basis if they wished to keep bases inoperable. Since the North Vietnamese had a sanctuary in China and the Soviet Union functioned as a supplier, the PAVN could replenish its losses as soon as runways were operable, and the labor crews they marshaled were going to repair the runways no matter how many times they had to. There was no single-point panacea solution to the MiG problem during Rolling Thunder and Linebacker. Maintaining air superiority during Vietnam required an ongoing combination of airfield attack, air-to-air combat, and operations against surface-to-air missiles.

Chapter 3

Pursuing Air Superiority in the Presence of Antiaircraft Artillery and Surface-to-Air Missiles

The North Vietnamese emphasized antiaircraft artillery as their most widespread air defense weapon because it was plentiful, easy to use, and effective. They shot down more American aircraft with antiaircraft artillery than with any other means. As of June 24, 1965, they had already shot down twenty-six Navy, twenty-four US Air Force, and seven South Vietnamese Air Force (VNAF) aircraft; MiGs were responsible for only two of these losses. Antiaircraft artillery also damaged an additional 161.[1] Antiaircraft artillery was the most intractable weapon against American aircraft the North Vietnamese possessed and there were too many artillery pieces for the Americans to find and destroy all of them. Pilots' options were to evade known antiaircraft positions and persist with their missions. Early on, aircrews learned of the lethality of flak when during a 1965 mission against the Ban Ken Bridge in Laos, F-105s destroyed the bridge on the first pass, but some of the F-105 as well as F-100 pilots unwisely stayed to make repeated attacks. Triple-A (AAA, antiaircraft artillery) shot down an F-105 during one of these follow-on passes when it was firing an AGM-12 Bullpup air-to-ground missile. The main thing these pilots could have done differently to protect themselves was to leave after they had completed their first pass. This loss was unnecessary because flak downed the F-105 after the bridge had been destroyed.[2]

As weapons of attrition, AAA inflicted steady losses on American aircraft, disrupted their bombing runs, and harmed aircrews' bombing accuracy, lessening their effectiveness.[3] In North Vietnam the PAVN employed hundreds of large caliber weapons. Of the 978 guns the PAVN were believed to possess at the beginning of 1965, about two-thirds were 57mm or 85mm cannons. Nearly 60,000 troops manned AAA units, 21,000 of which were Chinese. A year into the war the Air Force estimated North Vietnam possessed 672 large machine guns, 1,452 37mm and 57mm guns, and 555 85mm cannons, dispersed among nearly 14,000 sites, about 4,000 of which were occupied at any one time. Through the first half of 1966, AAA inflicted most of the losses the American aircraft suffered, and the loss rate per 1,000 sorties increased to .0037 for the Air Force and to .0035 for the Navy.[4] The cumulative loss rates for Air Force aircraft over North Vietnam and Laos was .0027 and .0023 for the Navy in July 1966, and of the fifty-one aircraft shot down that month over Indochina, ground fire accounted for forty. One report noted in July 1966 that all the F-105s stationed in Thailand would be gone in another eight months if attrition rates continued.[5] The grand total of American aircraft lost to flak over North Vietnam and Laos was 384 by the end of 1966.[6] By the end of the war, ground fire claimed 1,161 USAF aircraft over all of Indochina. By contrast, surface-to-air missiles downed 106 and MiGs sixty-six Air Force aircraft.[7] Flak and small arms downed 293 Navy aircraft, SAMs destroyed eighty-one, and

39

MiGs took twelve more. Most Marine losses came at the hands of ground fire (105) while missiles brought down four and a lone MiG destroyed a single Marine aircraft.[8]

According to PACAF, antiaircraft guns were the most effective weapons the North Vietnamese possessed.[9] Antiaircraft artillery, however, needed the enemy aircraft to fly within range of their guns; if the attacking aircraft stayed out of range, they were safe from AAA fire. That was AAA's greatest shortcoming, unlike a MiG that could seek out and fly toward enemy aircraft. Flak was ubiquitous, but it could not make airspace dangerous enough to persuade the Americans to cease their attacks. Pilots were warned not to fly too low as VC would raise all their weapons and spray bullets at the attacking aircraft, which the US considered an effective use of small arms. During the Plei Me operation, for example, VC ground fire shot down six aircraft.[10] Triple-A units sometimes set up enticing targets to lure fighter-bombers to within the range of 37mm and 57mm guns. American pilots soon learned to avoid flying below 4,500 feet above ground.[11]

The US Air Force and Navy took antiaircraft artillery seriously and attributed its effectiveness to several factors. First, there were so many AAA locations where American aircraft often flew that they could almost saturate the air with exploding shells. The North Vietnamese (NVN) had such a surplus of these weapons that they could place them along roads and railroads as well as around high value targets. Triple-A batteries coordinated well with one another, and SAMs made flak more effective by driving jets down to the altitude where cannon shells could reach them. Seventh Air Force also suspected early warning radars were passing target data to AAA sites. The guns themselves had good optical sights and range finders, and some had fire control radars, but the small ratio of radars to guns was a weakness. In addition, the ones the North Vietnamese had were designed for use against high altitude bombers and could not keep up with low altitude fast targets. Moreover they could track only one target at a time. The larger 85mm and 100mm cannons had relatively low rates of fire, but these could still inflict lethal damage to aircraft, and they worried the aircrews.[12]

The Americans fought back. A lead aircraft on a bombing run, for example, would fire rockets to disrupt the cannon and automatic weapons, giving the trailing bomber a better chance of not getting hit. The downside to this tactic was that fewer jets actually bombed the target.[13] Moreover, these artillery pieces were difficult to destroy even when seen. The use of cluster bombs against AAA sites began in 1967 and paid off with fewer American losses, but those munitions were not the answer.[14] Neither was gunfire; 20mm cannon shells were accurate but not destructive enough against the hardened steel that comprised the artillery pieces. Given time, measures improved, and experience showed that a direct hit from a big bomb—2,000 or 3,000 pounds—smashed the cannons to pieces, and laser-guided bombs worked best to bring the blast effect close enough to dismantle the piece. Such bombs, for instance, were responsible for 58 percent of the AAA damaged or destroyed in Laos during the Commando Hunt VII operation in 1971–1972.[15]

The AAA threat worsened and moved farther south during the last couple of years of the war. During Operation Lam Son 719 in February 1971, fighter-bombers managed to destroy seventy AAA guns and damage five more in ninety-nine sorties. Then on July 11, 1971, a pair of F-4Ds used laser-guided bombs to destroy four pieces that had fired at aircraft over Laos.[16] Shortly thereafter, Seventh AF leadership admitted that antiaircraft artillery, automatic weapons, and small arms had also become a serious danger in Laos and Cambodia.[17] The communists had, for instance, studied the patterns AC-130 gunships followed, and achieved a direct hit on one in November 1971. A 57mm cannon shot down another AC-130 four months later, a day after an SA-2 surface-to-air missile destroyed one over the Ho Chi

Minh Trail.[18] Subsequently aircrews flying during Linebacker found ground fire to be exceptionally accurate, and that their jamming pods did not seem to work well. Triple-A at times got intense enough to drive away approaching American fighters.[19] During the final campaign year, flak shot down twenty-six American aircraft, about one aircraft for every 3,000 sorties.[20] Pilots also had to contend with the ZSU-23 starting in July–August 1972 when it arrived in theater. This was a radar-aimed, rapid-fire tracked vehicle that employed four 23mm cannons. The Americans were lucky it arrived so late in Southeast Asia because it was a buzzsaw of a weapon.[21]

While it took a couple of years before the Air Force and Navy regularly carried out airfield attacks, they went after a new kind of threat, the surface-to-air missile, with greater urgency and persistence soon after its appearance. The North Vietnamese tried to defend their airspace primarily with V-75 missiles, a surface-to-air missile known in the West as the SA-2 Guideline. Flak could only attrit fighter-bombers as they flew close to them, and MiGs were a secondary weapon the PAVN preferred to use only when the MiGs had an advantage.[22] Analysts in the US Air Force had trouble grasping this reliance on surface-to-air missiles over aircraft, referring in 1968 to the air bases with runways long enough for MiGs as "the most important" of the "33 targets" in their air defense network, and then citing the MiG threat as a distant second to AAA, followed by SAMs.[23]

The advent of surface-to-air missiles in the 1950s created a threat for aircraft that remains unsolved to this day.[24] Dealing with the SA-2 missiles complicated the Americans' efforts to dominate the airspace over North Vietnam, creating several problems for aircraft: the targeted aircraft had very little response time under the best of conditions; additionally, the missile's warheads were much more lethal than artillery shells or aircraft cannon fire, making evading the missile imperative. Finally, the evasive measures that aircraft take to survive SAM environments worsen bombing accuracy. Pilots needed an electronic warning that the missile was tracking it, and the aircrew needed to see it in order to outmaneuver the missile if electronic jamming proved inadequate. Guided missiles like the SA-2 were a challenge throughout the war because aircrews found it difficult to get timely warnings after SAMs had been launched, and the weapon's speed compressed the time available for the aircrew to figure out whether the SAM was zeroing in on their jet or someone else's. That left crews but seconds to find the missile with their eyes and then jettison their bombs and employ violent evasive maneuvers to make sure the missile did not get close enough to explode within lethal range. American forces never solved the problem that the firing of SAMs could force fighter-bombers to jettison their bombs to evade the missiles and survive, nullifying the effectiveness of the whole mission. Ten Navy F-4Js, for example, jettisoned their bombs during a single mission in April 1972 because of SAM firings. Missiles thus did not have to shoot down all the attacking aircraft to be effective, even those that missed a strike package. The SAMs' presence also eroded the overall effectiveness of US air strikes because planners and aircrews had to account for them and set aside more and more aircraft to locate the SAM sites, catalog their radio frequencies, figure out how often and where they were moved, and destroy them. Those aircraft tasked with destroying SAM sites could not carry out the actual air interdiction missions.[25]

The North Vietnamese air defense system was sophisticated and troublesome for American aircrews, and ground radars played a large role in the overall system. Their network consisted of one ground radar that guided MiGs (as ground-controlled intercept), seventeen that focused on fire control, and forty-one that concentrated on search.[26] The North Vietnamese faced challenges in creating effective defenses, building a system almost from the ground up. In fewer than eight months, however, they fielded a workable missile, antiaircraft artillery, MiG interceptor, and command and control system. The North Vietnamese early warning system was impressive. By 1966, they had a line of radars between themselves and the US air bases in Thailand that gave them coverage out to 160 miles and as low as 500 feet above the ground as aircraft approached the radar antennae. At first, they could not wield their MiGs aggressively, lest they put their most experienced aircrews at risk before building up a sustainably large cadre of interceptor pilots. This was the reason, Seventh AF leadership suspected in 1966, that only 25 percent of the MiGs that got in firing position actually opened fire; the PAVN air force was using the American bomber formations as training aids. In that way they would produce an air defense system that could continue to be effective while sustaining losses. Adding to the complexity, the extensive range of shooter options—missiles, flak, and MiGs—meant that the MiGs and SAMs had to be under tight control. Had the air defenders all been freewheeling, the MiGs would have been subjected to undue fratricide from SA-2s and ground fire. By early 1966, however, reports showed that North Vietnamese batteries "began to exercise a high degree of discipline . . . and these three systems were fully integrated under an apparently excellent command and control net."[27] It had taken time for the North Vietnamese Air Force to develop, but by 1966, one Navy pilot at least took them seriously, referring to his adversaries as "well-trained and disciplined pilots."[28]

Antiaircraft artillery was a somewhat predictable problem that the American air forces could not eliminate; each piece was useful on its own and did not have to be networked in order to be utilized. The rest of the air defense system—radars, SAMs, and MiGs— were fewer in number and therefore more valuable to Hanoi. Because the early warning radars formed the foundation of the North Vietnamese air defense network, the office of the Commander-in-Chief of the US Pacific Fleet (CINCPAC) wished to destroy the ones south of the 20th parallel from the beginning in order to increase the effectiveness of the bombing campaign. Their eradication would add to the survivability and surprise of American air strikes and would also constitute the destruction of valuable and difficult-to-replace assets and people. Destroying the radar network was never pursued because that risked killing Soviet or Chinese technicians working at the sites, and AAA was too omnipresent and hidden to neutralize.[29] So for eight years these radars provided early warning for surface-to-air missiles and MiG fighters, as well as intercept guidance for the MiGs. Combining the radar network with antiaircraft artillery, the North Vietnamese were able to make much of their airspace anywhere from hazardous to lethal. In sum, their strategy used SAMs to drive American aircraft down into the range of their flak guns and assigned MiGs airspace beyond the range of SAMs. They did not have the ability to use all three weapons together within the same space at the same time, but they learned to coordinate and deconflict MiGs and SAMs.[30]

North Vietnamese antiaircraft missiles spawned a new mission for US Air Force and Navy tactical aircraft: suppression of enemy air defenses, or SEAD (pronounced "seed"). Fighter-bombers needed specialized equipment in order to destroy AA missiles before they were launched, and as SEAD became a necessary mission, it pulled pilots, planes, and sorties away from the effort to coerce North Vietnamese leaders. Measures to destroy SAMs on the ground before they are fired kill people, and that complicated what seemed to be a clear-cut operational decision: attack missile sites. Air strikes against SAM sites involved geopolitical risks and drew the attention of the president himself.

An RF-101C Voodoo reconnaissance aircraft photographed construction crews carving out a SAM site in April 1965, and the first one became operational on May 1. An immediate consequence was the Air Force prohibiting its U-2 reconnaissance jets from flying closer than thirty miles to SA-2 batteries that had been identified.³¹ The Joint Chiefs asked for permission to bomb the first missile site on May 27, but Secretary of Defense McNamara was too concerned over aircrew losses and the "international reaction to comply."³² The State Department also vetoed striking the new SAM site the Soviets erected in April as far too escalatory and dangerous. It rejected the Central Intelligence Agency's (CIA) judgment that attacking North Vietnamese air defenses would not lead to the North Vietnamese conducting an all-out invasion of South Vietnam, nor to a Chinese army intervention, worrying instead that the Chinese might respond with some sort of air strike of their own in retaliation. McNamara then ordered that American aircraft were not to attack any air bases or SAM sites.³³ The Chinese foreign minister, however, passed a note to the US via the British on May 31 stating that China would only enter the war "if the war was expanded to Chinese territory." President Johnson received this message on June 4, 1965.³⁴

When the president put forth the possibility of destroying the missile sites, McNamara painted that action as extremely escalatory by arguing that B-52s, a weapon that personified escalation even when utilizing conventional weapons, had to first destroy the MiG bases before SAM sites were taken out. His assumption was peculiar, and he did not explain his reasoning. The risk of escalation evaporated President Johnson's interest in taking aggressive action.³⁵ Assistant Secretary of Defense for International Security Affairs John T. McNaughton did not believe the North Vietnamese would actually use their new SA-2 missiles against American aircraft, either; he believed the Soviet Union had installed them with the purpose of raising North Vietnamese morale—another odd conclusion. Admiral Sharp wanted to begin attacking SAM sites as they were being built, and the JCS urged the destruction of the growing number of SAM sites before the North Vietnamese completed a network of sites; better to destroy them piecemeal while under construction than after they were all up and running.³⁶ McNamara said no on July 11 because the Rolling Thunder strikes were still getting through without prohibitive losses, and again because he did not want to risk killing any "Chinese or Soviet technicians working at the sites."³⁷ Additional administration officials, such as Ambassador to the United Kingdom David K. E. Bruce and General Lyman L. Lemnitzer (Supreme Allied Commander, Europe) did not think such attacks would lead to Soviet military reprisals in Europe, but the fact that the consideration even came up demonstrates the administration's nervousness about the military escalation against North Vietnam inherent in SEAD operations.³⁸

Six weeks after these discussions, one of these missiles achieved its first kill on July 24, 1965, against an Air Force F-4C. The pilot, Captain Richard P. Keirn, survived and began an eight-year ordeal as a prisoner of war, while the radar intercept officer, Captain Roscoe H. Fobair, was killed upon impact with the ground. Admiral Sharp insisted the Pentagon clear him to retaliate, as the SA-2s had been fired from a site outside of the Hanoi safe area. Ambassador to South Vietnam Maxwell Taylor concurred, and in the aftermath of this shoot-down, Secretary Rusk thought that destroying the installations would function to warn against a repeat.³⁹ During that same meeting Secretary McNamara realized that destroying a SAM site was a possibility: fighter-bombers attacking SAM sites at very low altitudes would be below the SA-2's effective minimum altitude, lessening the likelihood that American aircraft would be shot down as a consequence of that kind of strike.⁴⁰

SAMs clearly affected American policy makers; both their capabilities and the fact that Soviets were involved in their use brought cabinet-level officials down into the working level of military operations and even individual missions because of the geopolitical risks. The White House involved itself in tactical operations like these because President Johnson feared bombing SA-2 sites could send shockwaves throughout the region, and a reprisal strike might result in the killing of Soviet technicians, which would affect relations between the US and USSR. Clark Clifford, one of Johnson's more trusted advisors, believed destroying a pair of SAM sites would signal American fortitude. Finally, President Johnson ordered their destruction, justifying it as defense of American strike aircraft.[41]

The Air Force carried out the mission on July 27, 1965, but it did not go well. The pre-strike reconnaissance missions alerted the North Vietnamese the Americans were coming after their missiles, so they moved them and set up an antiaircraft artillery ambush. Fifty-four F-105s attacked and ran into a barrage of flak, often used to protect SAM sites, which shot down four American aircraft. Two more planes crashed after colliding with each other on the way back to base. This was the first "Iron Hand" mission, as they came to be called by the Americans.[42]

This mission illustrated some of the practical difficulties SAMs caused, in addition to their political ones. Flying straight and level at low altitude in order to improve navigation to the target and avoid the missile engagement zone subjected wild weasel aircraft (generally speaking, aircraft performing an Iron Hand mission) to ground fire; SA-2s and flak mutually supported each other. PACAF analysts quickly concluded that a better way was to use small groups of fighter-bombers attacking from several different headings. Interestingly, the missiles' control van and radar were the primary targets, not the missiles themselves, because SA-2s cannot function without their ground radar system. This priority required an aircraft to fly near enough to the site to persuade its operators to track it, so as to give away the site's position. Given that the sites around Hanoi had overlapping coverage, all of them should have been struck at the same time in order to overwhelm them—if permission for such an aggressive mission could be obtained.[43]

Planners addressing the missile threat initially made some odd assertions. The arguments that MiGs had to be expunged before SAM sites were attacked, and that B-52s had to be the airframes to attack unprotected MiGs on the ground, were overly cautious. Fighter-bombers (in greater numbers) could carry adequate weapons loads and were more survivable against the North Vietnamese defenses. In fact, a group of just one A-6A and four A-4Es from the USS *Independence* got the first kill of a SAM site on October 17, 1965. This success had not come easy. Antiaircraft artillery shot down five aircraft during two days of Navy Iron Hand missions in August.[44]

By fall 1965, PACAF concluded that "SAMs probably cannot be eliminated from NVN but must be lived with," and that strike aircraft needed electronic countermeasure devices for self-protection. For the time being, the sites were to be attacked only when weasels possessed a clear advantage, and how to do so was to be left up to local commanders on the scene. Ideally, an aircraft with the men and the capability to synthesize targeting intelligence would be available to guide wild weasel aircrews. Pacific Air Forces also wanted the 2nd Air Division to coordinate with their naval counterparts in developing defenses.[45]

As expected, the number of SAM sites increased—from ninety-nine to 115 through the first six months of 1966—but their effectiveness declined. Despite firing fifty-five missiles, the enemy destroyed no American aircraft with them in May and June. American anti-missile efforts were gaining momentum, and most important, the SAMs failed to prevent American strikers from completing their missions. Iron Hand missions, jamming aircraft, warnings that a missile was in the air from an orbiting EC-121 early warning radar aircraft, and the violent maneuvers pilots executed when they saw the missiles coming after them were the reasons they were less effective. Although the SAMs' kill probability (Pk) decreased, their existence and use forced fighter-bombers down to lower altitudes where the more prevalent, if inaccurate, AAA could reach them, thus persuading the American air forces to devote

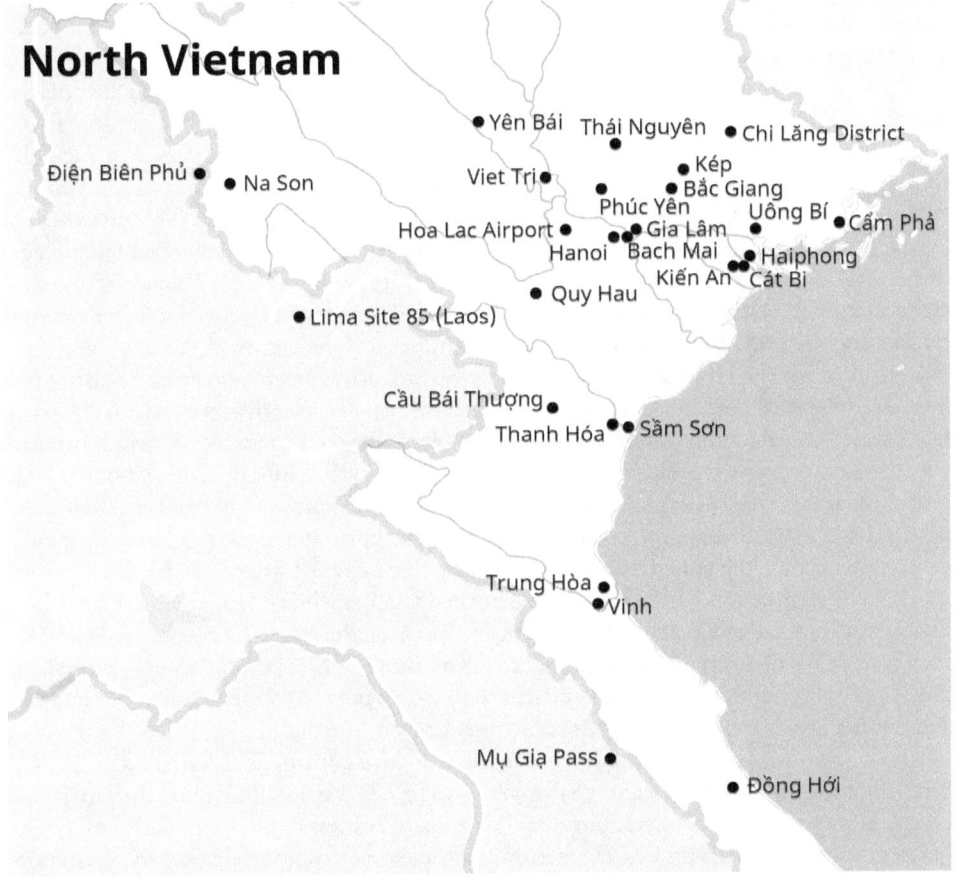

more and more aircraft to defeating the SAMs as opposed to carrying out bombing missions against North Vietnam. Those were their greatest effects. For the American air forces, their biggest challenge in defeating the SAM threat was finding the sites with missiles and guidance equipment with enough accuracy and timeliness to avoid or attack them.[46]

McNamara began to loosen the restrictions on attacking SAM sites in April 1966. The services could attack for the protection of their pilots and aircraft, but attacks against sites in Route Packages 6A and 6B required photographic confirmation of their existence beforehand.[47] His past refusals had begun to intimidate the generals, who were becoming somewhat culpable in the "restrictions controversy"—the assertion that various restrictions and rules of engagement decided upon in Washington, DC, prevented the United States from winning the air war, or at least waging it in the most sensible manner. In any event, in early May 1966 a reconnaissance drone photographed crates containing 132 SA-2 missiles along with the support equipment that went with the missiles at a barracks in Hanoi. These were as many SAMs as the North Vietnamese had launched since December 1965 and were an enticing target. The sensible next step was to destroy them before they were dispersed among the SAM batteries. Admiral Sharp asked for permission to do so, but General Wheeler replied that the JCS now wanted to bomb petroleum facilities near Hanoi and Haiphong, and were worried that asking to bomb a SAM site in such a sensitive area might alert the PAVN air force "to exercise greater vigilance in the vicinity" of similar targets.[48] That was an absolutely bizarre line of reasoning because the North Vietnamese were already vigilant since the

Americans had been bombing targets in North Vietnam for more than a year. Why not take away their main air defense weapon so that vigilance is their only option?

Their presence and use generated inefficiencies within the American air campaign. Warning receivers had to be retrofitted to fighter-bombers along with jamming pods, which occupied pylon space instead of bombs, weakening the striking power of each airframe. Jamming also advertises an aircraft's location to the enemy. One countermeasure, flying at extremely low altitudes, shortened an aircraft's range exponentially, and utilizing low-observable technology so as to fly at higher altitudes was beyond American technology in the 1960s. The US first attempted this last measure with the A-12 Mach 3 reconnaissance jet in 1967. Although the first mission in May went undetected, the North Vietnamese tracked and fired SAMs at the planes twice in October and then again in January 1968.[49]

Even though the United States possessed air superiority, defenses exacted a substantial levy. In addition to the toll flak took on aircraft, these missile sites distracted the Americans from their strategic efforts. The Air Force and Navy assigned these locations importance equal to that of other principal targets in North Vietnam.[50] Again, finding and destroying enemy radars and the missiles themselves drew additional aircraft away from the main purpose of using bombardment to coerce and interdict. Suppression required electronic intelligence to determine the radar frequencies, meaning those aircraft were also drawn away from the main mission. Pilots had to search for launched missiles while trying to find their target. Frequently they had to eject their bombs prior to reaching the target in order to evade SAMs, thus nullifying the Americans' mission as far as those fighter-bombers were concerned. Masses of fighter-bombers were less efficient than B-52s, but the former could often out-jam and out-maneuver the missiles; B-52s could only jam.

In the end, SAMs were not effective enough to seize control of the airspace, but they certainly added to the Americans' challenges. The SEAD mission illustrated the growth of complexity in aerial strike operations during Vietnam. Success required more and more different types of aircraft: wild weasel, electronic jammers, electronic intelligence detection aircraft, and later F-4s for dropping radar-confusing strips of aluminum chaff over the enemy instead of bombs (these F-4s were called "chaff bombers"). When twenty-three F-105s flew a mission as bombers on December 15, 1965, sixty-seven additional aircraft—electronic countermeasures (ECM), fighter escort, reconnaissance, aerial refueling—flew to support a single squadron of fighter-bombers. Only thirty-two bombers out of 120 aircraft comprised the actual pointy end of the spear for a May 1972 USAF mission.[51] A mission on September 5, 1972, required a supporting cast of thirty-two jets to ensure twelve fighter-bombers got through to their target. Another mission that month required more than sixty supporting jets for a dozen fighter-bombers.[52] In December 1972, for example, the USS *Midway*'s air wing split the difference half-and-half, flying 494 strike sorties and 468 in support of those.[53]

The Navy and the Air Force developed some sound tactics on surviving and defeating antiaircraft missiles and artillery. By 1967, the commander of Carrier Air Wing 14, Commander Ernest E. Tissot Jr., had his doubts about approaching at very low altitudes because the bombers had to pull up into a climb, which cost airspeed, look for and find the target, then aim and drop the bombs while the enemy shot at them. Generally, 12,000 to 18,000 feet was the best flight altitude; it placed one above the reach of AAA, and the air was still dense enough to provide good maneuverability for evading missiles. Missiles became more effective above 18,000 feet, so strike aircraft tended to stay below that altitude. In addition to a mid-altitude ingress route, pilots needed to make sure that every jammer on every aircraft was functioning properly before entering one of these hot zones. They needed to look for and see launched SAMs: "The ones that are not seen," Tissot warned, "are the most dangerous ones." High-speed approaches meant that aircraft could carry out high-G maneuvers, and the "Chances of being hit while executing high 'G' maneuvers are remote."[54] Evasive maneuvers to defeat SAMs, however, could be dangerous themselves, and result in a splendid euphemism: "inadvertent ground impact." The leadership of Carrier Air Wing 14 recognized this, warning aircrews to "Remember, the ground is the biggest threat, then comes AAA/small arms, then SAMs and finally MiGs [emphasis in original]."[55] For their part, the Marines refined their flak suppression tactics when their A-6s and F-4s began to be used for that mission in 1968. Close coordination with the bombing aircraft was essential, because the Marines found it best to carry out their flak suppression attacks no later than thirty seconds before the strike aircraft arrived.[56]

This attritional war against SA-2s actually takes one back to the issue of how the air war at the tactical and operational levels was related to the achievement of policy goals. American analysts were frequently looking for indicators that they were winning the war, but a military organization normally knows when it is winning or losing; if the evidence that it is winning is not incontrovertible, it is in a stalemate. One assessment further tried to speculate its way into the enemy's head: "the effects of our intensified operations in his heartland must be causing him to reconsider whether or not he can hold out until the United States' presidential election of 1968, when he hopes to see a change in our policy of contributing to the defense of South Vietnam."[57] Actually, the communists were formulating plans for an offensive that would lead to a battlefield victory that would force a change in American policy. The Tet Offensive would ideally decide the American election in favor of those politicians who wanted to leave the war. This was not a passive enemy who was merely acted upon and only reacted. The North Vietnamese shaped and dictated the course of the war to the extent that they could.[58]

The Americans tried to take the initiative and did not want the new weapon to inflict unsustainable losses on their aircraft. Without counters to the SAMs, aircraft losses would climb to the point of impinging on the president's use of force. In terms of devising countermeasures, the US responded to the SAM problem with urgency and success after some initial missteps. In October 1965, a study by the Joint Staff concluded that the air forces' greatest inadequacy was the inability of aircraft to radio warnings that SAMs had been launched quickly enough to give the aircrews a chance to spot and evade the missiles.[59] In the months that followed the services combined electronic intelligence, specialized weapons and aircraft, electronic countermeasures, daring tactics, and persistence to reduce the effectiveness of the North Vietnamese SAMs. The air forces did not eradicate the SAM sites and AAA batteries; they instead "suppressed" them, which reflected a more erudite and less literal understanding of what is involved in completing air combat missions successfully. Suppression of enemy air defenses is a part of the air superiority mission because it seeks the same effect as bombing aircraft and runways or shooting them out of the sky: the removal of threats to friendly aircraft so that they can complete their missions without getting shot down themselves—at least not in excessive numbers.

The Air Force, Navy, and Marines became quite good at SEAD, but at a cost in terms of risks, which led to aircraft and aircrew losses, and in terms of operational complexity, because SEAD missions involved the coordination of numerous kinds of aircraft. The first challenge was finding *active* SAM sites, because not every parking area the enemy had constructed had a missile battery located there. The Air Force used reconnaissance jets and drones for this task.[60] An additional method was applying electronic means to detect emissions indicating when a radar was tracking a jet and then when the site had launched a missile against it. In the first instance, a wild weasel could detect the emitters, and from April 1966, fire an "anti-radiation missile" (ARM) at the emitting radar. If the ARM destroyed the radar antenna, the SA-2s were useless until a replacement radar could be brought into action.

Weapons and munitions were important to the president and his cabinet because they determined the extent to which military activities could be effective and efficient. The Navy was better prepared for the SEAD mission in terms of equipment and training. It had produced the first ARM, the AGM-45 "Shrike," having begun work on that missile in 1958.[61] The Navy brought the Shrike into action in April 1965 and the Air Force began using it twelve months later on modified F-100Fs.[62] The Navy used A-4E Skyhawks against SAMs, and the aircraft carried two important black boxes: the APR-25 provided radar warning, the APR-27 SAM guidance warning, and its main weapon was the Shrike.[63] An A-4E pilot from the USS *Oriskany*, for example, planned and led a mission with four Air Force F-105s on October 31, 1965, because his equipment was better. Lieutenant Commander Richard Powers' A-4E had the capability to detect the radar, determine its direction, and fly toward it. Its black boxes told him where to look for the missiles, so he not only saw them when they were fired, he also saw where their site was located. He and the F-105s destroyed two sites and evaded several missiles during their mission.[64] For those missions the standard weapons load was four Shrikes or a pair of Shrikes and either two pods with "Zuni" rockets or Mark-82 500-pound bombs. Not surprisingly, one squadron wrote that for Iron Hand missions, no training environment existed that came close to simulating getting shot at by SAMs: "proficiency is acquired through combat experience only." This writer wished the Navy used two-seat TA-4Fs as wild weasel aircraft because the two crewmen could divide responsibilities. The one in back could focus on reading radar homing and warning (RHAW) instruments and evaluating the threat, leaving the pilot to fly the jet and look for SAMs.[65]

In November 1965, four Air Force F-100F Super Sabres, modified with avionics for determining where a radar signal was coming from, when a SAM radar was tracking it, and when a missile had been launched at it, touched down at Korat Air Base, Thailand. Since this two-seat version of the F-100F carried an electronic warfare officer, he and the pilot could segregate mission tasks. On Iron Hand missions, an F-100F "hunter" would lead three F-105D or F-4C "killers," and use its avionic suite to detect SAM sites, leaving most of the bombing to the killers.[66] Over the next few weeks, the Air Force began to develop effective SAM suppression methods with this jet. Ironically, on December 20, 1965, ground fire—not a missile—shot down an F-100F on just its second Iron Hand mission over North Vietnam.[67]

Two days later, PACAF concluded a strike force had "destroyed a SAM installation located in a small village well camouflaged in trees and under thatched structures." The aircrews observed that it was very difficult to see the target, even after an F-100 had placed smoke rockets on it. No one shot back, so the jets got to use all their ordnance against it. They attributed the mission's success to "terrain masking and tactical surprise," but that kind of run to the target, while increasing survivability, made it harder to verify the target's existence.[68] During the first months of Iron Hand missions, three-fourths of the time an aircrew would fly right over where a SAM site was supposed to be according to their instruments, but they were not able to see the site in order to bomb it.[69] Other tactics included terrain masking, then zooming up to an altitude above antiaircraft artillery range for weapons release in a dive bombing profile.[70] The possibility that the target hit on December 22 may not have been a SAM site since there was no AAA fire against the jets demonstrates that electronic identification of these sites was a necessary requirement, not just a preference. Secondary explosions of missile fuel or warheads could offer better confirmation that an Iron Hand mission had been effective. Navy strikes in November 1966, for example, against a missile warehouse in Haiphong generated fires and secondary explosions.[71]

The North Vietnamese could defeat the first-generation ARM, the AGM-45, by seeing the missile's radar echo on their radar screen, then turning off their radar, leaving the Shrike to "go ballistic" and hit the ground somewhere away from the radar. The trick for the North Vietnamese was detecting a missile with a small radar cross-section and a flight time of less than a minute before impact. Turning off their radar protected them from destruction because the Shrike needed a radar signal to home on, but it also meant that they could not guide any SA-2s. Thus, Americans got what they wanted: airspace free of SAMs—hence SAM suppression, as opposed to destruction. Shrikes encouraged the North Vietnamese to shut down their radars when they suspected wild weasels were near, which also functioned as a win for the Americans.[72] Navy A-4Es sometimes fired Zuni unguided rockets as simulated Shrikes and that tricked SAM crews to shut down their radar.[73]

The F-100Fs were an interim solution; the Air Force looked forward to using F-105Fs or F-4Cs as weasels.[74] Super Sabres were not adequate for the wild weasel role because an F-100's cruising speed was too slow to keep up with the F-105Ds they led during Iron Hand strikes. They also used the probe and drogue refueling system instead of the boom system of the F-105s, which meant that each needed its own tanker. Finally, the F-105F had more growth potential for the mission than the F-100F.[75] Eleven "wild weasel II" F-105Fs arrived in theater in May and July 1966 to replace the F-100Fs, after which the four modified F-100Fs returned to the US.[76] Pacific Air Forces also began modifying all its F-105s to carry Shrikes in April 1966.[77]

The greatest challenge for this mission did not lie in aircraft or missile capabilities; simply finding the sites was most difficult. Therefore, it was best to divert as many aircraft against a found site as possible, lest the North Vietnamese move the missiles and radars somewhere else. Survival was the next greatest challenge for these men. In fewer than eight weeks in the summer of 1966, five weasels were shot down.[78] Again, the SAMs indirectly degraded the effectiveness of the American air war because more and more aircraft were focusing on mission support, leaving fewer to carry out actual bombing missions.

Electronic jamming aircraft were a second component of the suppression effort and went hand in hand with the Iron Hand missions. Jamming SAM radars along with the use of cluster bombs against Triple-A led indirectly to increased bombing accuracy, not just fewer losses of aircraft, because SEAD and ECM aircraft interfered with enemy actions well enough that fighter-bombers could focus more on their bombing runs. The Air Force used EB-66Cs for electronic intelligence and EB-66Es for jamming; both were important for defending against SAMs.[79] The latter carried a suite of ALT-28 jammers tuned to the known frequencies of enemy radars. Flying in widely separated orbits about twenty-five miles from Hanoi, their crews detected and jammed radars for both missiles and AAA. In 1965 they had the ability to defeat radars that supported AAA as well as the Fan Song radars that guided the SAMs.[80] Sometimes their jamming caused SA-2 missiles to veer away from the jamming aircraft or fly "completely out of control."[81] They also detected missile firings and alerted aircrews over the radio.[82]

Jamming aircraft needed to be as close as possible to the radars in order to overwhelm them with their powerful signals, but that increased their vulnerability to SA-2s and MiGs. That meant putting scarce ECM aircraft at risk. EB-66 aircrews also insisted on receiving warnings of MiG attacks soon enough to turn and fly in the opposite direction. They were not skittish; in May 1966 a quartet of MiG-17s tried to shoot down an EB-66 but its escorts chased them away, downing one in the process.[83] An attempt to employ them against the radars more aggressively in November 1967 by sending them north of Thud Ridge, a mountain ridge northwest of Hanoi, nearly got some shot down, and on January 14, 1968, dangers worsened. Two MiG-21s flew southeast from Phuc Yen as if to protect the Thanh Hoa Bridge, but then turned to the west and struck an unescorted EB-66. In the end the EB-66s were not able to shut down the radar system with its jammers; they could only degrade it, and as Rolling Thunder wound down Seventh AF analysts concluded that it was too slow to fly over much of North Vietnam anymore.[84]

Marine aviation had had a great interest in tactical electronic jamming aircraft since learning of their importance during the Korean War, and the Corps contributed what they could with the obsolescent EF-10 Skyknight jamming aircraft they flew in the first years of Vietnam. A development of the F3D night fighter of Korean War vintage, the EF-10 lacked sufficient engine power to go fast enough to spin the turbines that powered its electronic jammers. An EF-10 pilot had to take his aircraft up high and then fly in a shallow dive in order to gain enough speed for the turbines.[85] The Skyknight squadron VMCJ-1 arrived in February 1965 and began participating in Iron Hand missions in March 1966. Their EF-10Bs completed most of the jamming and electronic detection missions flown at that time in support of Marine or Air Force fighter-bombers. Half of the squadron of ten jets were shot down and ten men died.[86] EF-10B ECM aircraft left Vietnam in October 1969 when brand-new EA-6As arrived.[87]

The Navy had twelve more capable EA-6As built, but the technical advisor to Secretary of Defense Melvin R. Laird, Dr. Gene Fubini, convinced him the new jets would be ineffective. Laird cancelled further purchases and cast off the jets to the Marine Corps. Lieutenant General Thomas H. Miller Jr., the chief of staff in the III Marine Amphibious Force, was adamant that the war effort needed more of them, pressed hard, and got fifteen more produced.[88] Actually, EA-6As were the only aircraft that could jam the new T8209 radar for the SA-2 when it came online.[89] The Marines may have considered the EA-6A their most valuable aircraft because when the issue of building revetments for their jets came up, it was given "first priority."[90]

During Linebacker, EB-66Es jammed SAM sites when B-52s were flying; otherwise they targeted GCI systems. By 1972 so much additional equipment had been installed that their weight increased until they could fly no higher than 24,000 feet—about 10,000 feet below where B-52s flew. This altitude difference degraded their jamming effectiveness and necessitated the use of more of these jamming aircraft. The most tangible support these jammers provided was to degrade the radars that initially detected and tracked American aircraft and supply data on the antiaircraft sites. Consequently, it took the enemy more time to detect and track strike aircraft, and even a few seconds were difference makers. The Navy's new cutting-edge EA-6Bs were better, generating a degree of confusion and frustration among SA-2 operators that American analysts could not measure with precision, but they saw SA-2s miss and fail more often.[91] In spite of their limitations, the EB-66 and EA-6B garnered considerable praise for their ability to increase the survivability of strike missions. Twenty-one of the former were still in Southeast Asia by fall 1972, and the much more advanced EA-6B arrived in May on the USS *America*.[92]

Over time the services developed different approaches to ECM. The Air Force fighter-bombers flew in formations whereby their jamming signals overlapped to create one large electronic blob on an enemy radar screen, noise jamming that degraded the enemy's ability to track an aircraft with any sort of precision. Navy fighters used on-board pulse deception jammers that created false targets. By the end of the war, electronic countermeasures reduced missile kill probability by half.[93]

It was difficult to tell how effective the effort to suppress enemy air defenses was. Were there fewer SA-2 firings because wild weasels were destroying sites, or were active SAM sites lying low by keeping their radars off, or were the weasels bombing decoys? Shrikes were not as effective as one would have liked and determining the actual effects of a Shrike launch was difficult. Pilots were often uncertain as to what their missiles accomplished. The silence of the Fan Song radars a few seconds after the launching of an AGM-45 could mean a direct hit, or it could mean that the radar operator detected the Shrike and momentarily stopped transmitting.[94] In any event, Air Force wild weasels fired 107 Shrikes from April 18 to July 15, 1966, "with only one hit confirmed as against 38 'probables.'"[95] Another way of assessing SEAD effectiveness was by the number of launch sites destroyed; Seventh AF leaders believed aircraft destroyed twenty-two in June and July 1966.[96] By 1968, the practice was to bomb sites even if no transmissions were coming from them. Indicative of these difficulties, analysts claimed that while there were few confirmed kills of missile batteries, "the daily harassment of suspected SAM areas seems to be valuable."[97] For the whole war the Air Force claimed to have destroyed 120 SAM sites.[98]

The air forces never completely solved the SAM problem; they just lessened its impact and found some better ways to exact a physical toll on the sites. Wild weasels could suppress SA-2 launches by trolling for them; any SAM operator who started tracking American aircraft was at the same time emitting signals the weasels could detect and target.[99] On December 24, 1972, for instance, an F-105G fired a Shrike at a signal from a radar and observed it stop transmitting. "Was that a hit or had an alert technician turned off the transmitter?" was always the question. The Shrike's warhead was not that effective against radars protected by embankments, but a subsequent mark included white phosphorus that created a flame bright enough on impact to provide a target for visual bombing.[100] A 1967 study concluded that only about 8 percent of Shrikes destroyed or seriously damaged the antiaircraft radar (eleven SAM installations), about 34 percent inflicted minimal damage to the site, and more than half of 232 assessed launches were effective. Firing them closer to the radar, of course, was better, but pointing the weasel at the site clued in the launch technicians that it was time to stop emitting. North Vietnamese operators turning off radars "accounted for approximately 30 percent of the ineffective missiles"; Shrikes seemed to function well whenever the target radar kept emitting.[101]

A 1968 study noticed that SAM sites fired much more often when weasels did not launch Shrikes at them, nearly half the time aircraft flew within fifteen miles of a site, but when weasels fired Shrikes, SAM sites did not fire back.[102] Thus its main effect was to persuade the enemy to not fire SAMs, which meant that aircraft flew by without getting shot at, which meant that the Iron Hand missions were effective at persuading the SAM sites to make themselves irrelevant. An A-4E Iron Hand mission demonstrated an ideal SEAD mission on December 24, 1968. Its pilot saw a missile lift off and fired two AGM-45s at once. One hit the site, stopping the guidance commands to the SA-2, which then "nosed over and dived into the ground."[103]

A Navy assessment in 1969 was skeptical of the actual effectiveness of SEAD. On the one hand, the North Vietnamese seemed to restrict their radar use due to the threat of ARMs. On the other hand, they fired SA-2s plenty of times at strike packages even though Iron Hand flights shot right back. The commander of Air Wing 14 believed that electronic jamming was a better weapon: "Iron Hand support, by itself, does not appear to provide the degree of defense against missile attack that some quarters would like to think it does." He looked forward to the greater prevalence of the jamming version of the A-6 Intruder because EKA-3 Skywarriors too often had to be used as tankers rather than jammers.[104]

The more advanced AGM-78 "Standard" ARM offered more potential as a destroyer of SAM radars because it had the ability to remember where it was aimed in case the radar

F-105Gs refueling from KC-135 (Air Force Historical Research Agency)

stopped emitting. It also had a larger warhead for ensuring the destruction of the site. It therefore still had a good chance of destroying the radar even if the operator turned it off, although it would probably not achieve a direct hit.[105] After in-theater tests, the Air Force found it suitable for employment from its F-105Gs in January 1968 and Navy A-6B Intruders began using them in March.[106] When a Fan Song radar threatened an A-6B on September 26, the crew fired an AGM-78 right after receiving warnings that the radar was tracking them. The Intruder's black boxes then indicated a missile was fast approaching, the pilot saw it, and evaded with a violent barrel roll. Afterward, electronic intelligence analysts concluded that in all likelihood the AGM-78 destroyed the radar.[107] Carrier Air Wing 6 credited the A-6B with keeping its losses to SAMs in 1968 to one aircraft. That same year the Air Force fielded a modified F-105F, the F-105G, and then the "Wild Weasel IV," thirty-six modified F-4Cs, which reached Southeast Asia in October 1969. They did not enter combat until after a subsequent deployment in December 1972.[108]

For all these efforts, the best way to defeat a SAM in flight was to receive an electronic launch warning, see the missile, and then employ the proper maneuver at the right time to evade it, most often rolling one's airplane upside down and pulling on the control column to fly a "split-S" toward the ground.[109] Naval aviators concluded: "The capability to counter the SAM threat is a combination of pods, pod formation, chaff, and evasive tactics. However, the most effective counter measure to date is visual acquisition and aircrew reaction." One also needed to stay about 8,000 feet above a cloud deck in order to have time to see and react to a launch.[110] A pair of F-8 Crusaders pilots found that one did not have to dive toward the ground if one saw the missile in time; they survived by making a series of hard turn reversals.[111] Seeing the missile in time and then outmaneuvering it remained the best countertactic through the end of the war.[112]

North Vietnamese launch crews adapted by emitting for only a minimum amount of time, which reduced the amount of time pilots had to look for airborne missiles.[113] By the spring of 1966, launch technicians were employing their weapons more skillfully, launching them only when targets were within the weapon's parameters and keeping their radars off as much as possible. Launch technicians were also shrewd and creative. One method was to gain target data from a GCI radar farther away, using its own tracking radar for the shortest amount of time possible, thus giving the victim less warning. Another tactic was to fire and explode a missile above an aircraft to induce the pilot to fly an evasive maneuver; he would then fly into two more missiles that were waiting for him, shot in anticipation.[114] The North Vietnamese adapted further by placing their search radar at a location remote from the missile launch site and the guidance radar. They also set up flak guns that evading aircraft would have to fly near while trying to outmaneuver a SAM by diving toward the ground. They used the placement of their surface-to-air missiles to support their propaganda war by locating them "on or near dikes, hospitals, and schools" with the hope that missiles and bombs would inflict propaganda-rich damage, an explicit violation of the laws of war.[115]

Rendering missile guidance signals irrelevant was a top priority for Air Force engineers. In the fall of 1966 the Air Force was confident the new QRC-160 ECM pod would defeat the SA-2 once there were enough for every aircraft, and at the same time General Wheeler worried as summer transitioned into fall that North Vietnamese efforts might reach a tipping point against American aircraft. A study in September–October 1966, however, found the pods to be completely effective against SAMs and AAA.[116] It assessed the experiences of nineteen flights of F-105s, each of which carried two pods, against air defenses. Bottom line: "There were no indications of radar-controlled AAA fire or of SAM launches being directed at an aircraft with operative QRC-160A-1 pods."[117] The penultimate test flight took F-105s with two pods apiece through the middle of a coven of SAM sites; not a single battery fired upon or even tracked the pod-equipped F-105s.[118]

From September 1966, their new ECM pods were effective enough against the missiles that by March 1967, the loss rate for F-4Cs using them was only .003 percent; from September through December, it rose to .026 percent—six F-4Cs lost out of 226 sorties. The F-105 loss rate to SAMs was .009 percent from January through March 1967, .020 percent July through September, and .006 percent through the end of the year; all the while the North Vietnamese fired SAMs at basically the same rate. While SA-2s downed five American strike aircraft on December 2, 1966, none used these jammer pods.[119] The commander of the 388th Tactical Fighter Wing, Colonel William S. Chairsell, commented that, "Seldom has a technological advance of this nature so degraded the enemy's defensive posture."[120] There were only two drawbacks to ECM pods. They occupied pylons that could have carried bombs, and they interfered with the onboard equipment that warned a pilot that a radar was tracking it. A more down-to-earth statistic was achieved in 1967: a kill rate of six aircraft per 1,000 SA-2s fired.[121]

The pods' effectiveness set off another round of move and countermove. In response the SAM operators adopted a three-point guidance method of pursuit tracking, which was easier to employ against a jamming aircraft, but it was easier for a targeted aircraft to outmaneuver a SAM thus guided.[122] The pod also effectively jammed AAA radars, forcing these sites to rely on barrage firing. Because of the pods' effectiveness, strike packages flew at medium altitudes, above AAA but more vulnerable to MiGs, which led in 1967 to the greater insistence for a MiG airfield bombing campaign.[123]

In the summer of 1967, airmen of the Seventh AF watched the North Vietnamese fire SAMs at an ever-increasing rate and concluded that the pods had induced the enemy to fire off missiles in desperation even without lock-ons.[124] The ECM pods remained effective as long as the jets flew in the proper formation. Too close together and they gave the enemy a more distinct target, too far apart and they lost the mutual support of one another's pods. The Americans believed by fall 1967 that the North Vietnamese SAM operators had resorted to tracking their aircraft optically because electronic jamming was ineffective against that method. In another adaptation, in December 1967, the pods were tuned to jam the signal from the missile back to the operator, who required it for guiding the missile.[125] Jamming this signal was more effective than most any other countermeasure. In turn, the North Vietnamese rotated about twenty-five SAM battalions, each with six missile launchers, among 150 different locations. What is more, the Vietnamese set up flak traps around dummy SAM sites so that the Americans would attack those locations and get shot to pieces for nothing.[126] Intelligence on site locations became obsolete quickly because the North Vietnamese moved missile batteries from place to place quickly.[127]

Surface-to-air missiles were not efficient weapons. The CIA observed it had taken the firing of more than 1,500 to shoot down forty-four American aircraft—not an impressive ratio. The ratio of missiles fired to aircraft shot down went from eighteen missiles in 1965 to thirty-two in 1966 to fifty-four in 1967. In 1967, the North Vietnamese fired 3,528 missiles and downed only sixty-one American aircraft.[128] By then the missiles usually missed their targets by a mile or greater. During the four years of Rolling Thunder, the PAVN air force fired 194 SAMs in 1965, 908 in 1966, 3,528 in 1967, and 667 in 1968. In each respective year they shot down eleven, thirty-four, sixty-one, and twelve American aircraft.[129] Later during the 1972 campaign, the North Vietnamese shot off 4,695 SAMs, but downed only sixty-five aircraft; they destroyed only 1.4 American aircraft for every 100 SAM firings.[130] SAMs were ultimately indecisive but nevertheless caused the Americans considerable difficulties and complications that they were able to overcome.

Some days the SAMs won, but those became rare as Rolling Thunder entered its final year. In a 1968 assessment, analysts believed the downturn in missile firings that year was due to intense and persistent Iron Hand strikes, of which there were more than 325 from April 1 to June 27. The QRC-160 pods were decisive. From the middle of December 1967 through the last day of March 1968 the North Vietnamese fired 495 SA-2s at American jets and shot down only one that was jamming. Furthermore, frequent action against sites south of the 19th parallel almost eliminated the threat.[131]

SAMs were able to dissuade low-speed aircraft from flying within range of their batteries. When the North Vietnamese moved SA-2s to sites just north of the DMZ (demilitarized zone, the boundary between North and South Vietnam) in 1972, AC-130s could no longer safely fly against Mu Gia Pass nor over the southern North Vietnamese panhandle. Knocking them out required sustained air strikes with more than just Shrike and Standard missiles. General Creighton Abrams, the commander of Military Assistance Command, Vietnam 1968–1972, informed Admiral John S. McCain Jr. that a thorough anti-missile effort also required clear weather so that aircrews could see and bomb the sites.[132] Abrams had also asked for permission to conduct a SEAD campaign in the southern panhandle, but the administration denied it because of the possible harm it could bring to critical diplomacy with the Soviets and Chinese.[133] In that sense the missiles forced the Americans to risk aircrews for the sake of diplomatic efforts.

With the end of Rolling Thunder, not much took place between North Vietnamese ground-based air defenses and their American adversaries until 1972. Beginning in 1969 the North Vietnamese began moving a few batteries down the panhandle to threaten aircraft flying over southern Laos and southern portions of North Vietnam. Following some firings at American aircraft, three Iron Hand missions struck back at the sites in February 1971. Harassment firings continued, but not to a degree that persuaded the Secretary of Defense to permit more air strikes against them.[134]

The greatest consequence of the battle between American aircraft and North Vietnamese surface-to-air missiles during the 1972 Linebacker campaign was that the Americans persisted with their attacks until the North Vietnamese made significant concessions during negotiations for American withdrawal. Continued air operations meant that the North Vietnamese did not gain a useful card to play in their negotiations with their counterparts. When Strategic Air Command mandated flawed B-52 tactics during Linebacker II in December, enough leaders at the headquarters in Omaha, Nebraska, recognized the problem in time to practice better methods before losses became too great. This back-and-forth battle took place just below the field of view of senior leaders in the White House, and when North Vietnamese SAMs finally began to impose significant losses, the president's attitude was that bombers get shot down during war, so keep fighting.[135]

The US did not make an all-out effort against SAM sites in 1972 because the Defense Intelligence Agency concluded that it was not possible to knock out all the sites. Continued suppression efforts would still form a part of every mission, but interdiction missions against supply lines were a higher priority. The Navy, for example, hit but five sites in August and eleven in September 1972.[136] Interestingly, an American strategic decision about the air war exerted a great influence on SAM suppression once the North Vietnamese invasion commenced. While they moved missile batteries down into Quang Tri Province during the beginning of the Easter Offensive because the Americans decided to wage a major air campaign against targets in North Vietnam, the North Vietnamese redeployed those southernmost SA-2s back to their heartland, thus leaving the airspace above the counteroffensives in Military Region 1 less dangerous than it could have been.[137] Overall the North Vietnamese air defense effectiveness declined in 1972. It suffered losses in MiGs and pilots, and its AAA shot down fewer aircraft.

Laser-guided bombs inadvertently functioned as the best counter to AAA not by destroying the pieces, but by enabling the jets to fly above ground fire's effective range. Air Force jets flew more missions in 1972 with LGBs, which kept them above flak. The Navy, by contrast, flew dive bombing profiles for most of its missions, and AAA accounted for half the Navy's losses. The Air Force also made a greater use of chaff, strips of aluminum foil that saturated radar pictures, and now carried more ECM pods. Surface-to-air missiles remained a threat; the enemy fired 777 in April and 429 in May 1972, with eleven and six kills in those respective months, but the Air Force estimated little more than 3 percent of those launched actually shot down an American aircraft.[138] From June through September the North Vietnamese launched fifty-six missiles on average per aircraft they shot down.[139] Because of the greater effectiveness of American jamming, the SAM operators once again incorporated greater use of "optical guidance" as a countermeasure, which lessened their kill probability.[140] During September 2 strikes against a pair of railroad targets and Phuc Yen Airfield, for example, the North Vietnamese fired an estimated twenty-four missiles at their attackers in under thirteen minutes, and relied on "visual tracking" quite frequently. At the same time, one Iron Hand officer commented that he had never experienced such dogged determination from the SAM operators. They kept their radars on throughout the wild weasel attacks so they could shoot back.[141] Achieving kills against radar sites was certainly desirable, and the dwindling kill rate Iron Hand missions achieved was disappointing, but the North Vietnamese were not winning, either. In order for their sites to survive they had to degrade their own radar search effectiveness by emitting for only short periods of time.[142]

There was not a great difference between the SAM suppression effort in 1972 compared with 1968: aircrews fired ARMs, dropped bombs, and asserted they had destroyed more sites than they probably had. A-6A aircrews, however, experienced something unexpected in August: an SA-2 radar tracking them when they flew as low as 200 feet.[143] Missile batteries continued to fire a missile at a jet in order to get it to take evasive maneuvers and dive toward the ground. They would then fire a second missile low where they anticipated the target to be.[144] This happened to an F-105G on September 17. When an SA-2 exploded between Condor 01 and 02, both turned toward the first missile when a second exploded about 200 feet behind the flight leader, damaging Condor 01 to such a degree that the men ejected over water, but "were dead when the swimmers reached them."[145] The North Vietnamese became more proficient at waiting until the last minute to turn on their guidance radars, thus defeating most ARM attacks, and they also waited to fire until the target was closer, improving their chances. Separate sites coordinated their radars by alternately turning them on and off, which complicated the decision making of weasel aircrews trying to decide where to fire. In addition, they would wait until the SAM's booster had dropped away before illuminating the target aircraft, which translated into a few seconds less warning time for the American jet.[146]

Because of the desire to destroy both the radar antenna and the stockpile of missiles at each site, Iron Hand strikes became comprised of two F-105G hunters with ARMs and two F-4E killers with cluster bombs for destroying the missiles themselves. Phantoms were used as killers since they could carry a wider variety of munitions than the F-105Gs, which needed to reserve their weapons stations for Shrike and Standard missiles. If the hunter-killer team saw a missile hit a site, the F-4E would bomb it.[147] The F-105G/F-4E hunter-killer team resulted in greater effectiveness because F-105Gs were more widely distributed, and the F-4Es were able to destroy more sites because they carried more ordnance. The 17th Wild Weasel Squadron found this pairing tremendously successful, but of course the North Vietnamese adjusted by switching to optical tracking again. When the SAM crews used that method, the aircrews did not receive any electronic warning as to the direction from which the missile was coming.[148]

Wild weasel aircrews and missile launch teams thrust and parried all year. One American adjustment came in April 1972, when A-6As bombed SAM sites near Haiphong, Vinh, and Thanh Hoa moments before B-52s reached the target. That caused enough disruption to allow the "BUFs" (big ugly fellows) to complete their missions without a loss. The enemy fired as many as thirty missiles at the B-52s bombing petroleum storage targets in Haiphong on April 13, but the SA-2s came no closer than a hundred yards to the bombers. The North Vietnamese found the Navy's tactics impressive; the carrier-based aircraft attacked so quickly the missile launch officers had no time to react.[149] During the first two months of Linebacker, the Navy and Air Force fired 486 Shrikes and Standards, ninety-nine functioning as "preemptive firings" intended to be detected so the enemy would shut down their radar. Based on aircrews actually seeing missile impacts against radars, only twenty-five out of 286 ARMs left the site damaged or destroyed. Aircrews witnessed the shut-down of the radars eighty-five times, so weasels were able to suppress SAM sites 110 times, an effectiveness rate of 38.5 percent.[150] Some in the Navy suspected that the North Vietnamese might be intercepting the radio call "shot gun" that went out when an aircraft fired a Shrike. That would be their cue to turn their radars off for a few minutes. To discourage SAM operators from turning on their radars in the first place, weasels started firing Shrikes at sites they knew of that were not emitting in order to deter missile launches. There was no way to know at the time how effective that was. Altogether the Air Force fired 678 AGM-45s and 230 AGM-78s through October, while Navy and Marine fighter-bombers fired even more, 1,257 and 165, respectively.[151]

Weasels made greater use of the AGM-78 Standard ARM in 1972, but its continued problems with bugs and their low numbers kept the AGM-45 as the predominate ARM. The aircrews of one Iron Hand mission found Standard missiles disappointing. Of the three AGM-78s fired, each scored a "no kill." During September weasels temporarily suspended using the new missile because of problems with its guidance controls and rocket motor, which had a failure rate as high as 25 percent.[152] When a weasel fired one on September 9, it suddenly flew up vertically and then reversed direction back toward the jets, passing between them and exploding about a mile away. There was even suspicion that the North Vietnamese had jammed one.[153]

The hunter-killer teams achieved reasonable success during Linebacker's latter stages. On September 16, 1972, AGM-78s probably destroyed one radar. An Iron Hand mission on October 6 saw kills of three sites confirmed, one by an AGM-78.[154] Determining the extent of the damage a strike had inflicted proved difficult because the North Vietnamese could move the batteries elsewhere, leaving an abandoned site for the post-attack reconnaissance aircraft. During Linebacker II, weasels attacked thirteen SAM sites, but by the time they reached two of them, the missiles and their attendant equipment were gone. Vietnamese missille crews could take down and redeploy a site in four hours.[155]

Weasels retaliated when fired upon. During a September 16 mission, Eagle 03 and 04 dropped cluster bombs on 85mm cannons that were firing at them from Yen Bai Airfield. Crown 03 discovered a previously unidentified site, peppered it with cluster bombs, and watched as SAMs went off like Roman candles. The 388th TFW concluded that the main effect of Iron Hand missions was to persuade the launch officers to not fire, lest they give away their position. The wing also found that their actions were persuading the enemy to fire their SA-2s at them more often than at the strike aircraft, which was one of the weasels' goals.[156] At this stage of the war these operations supported what was partially a siege and partially coercion, both of which had the purpose of supporting Kissinger's efforts to reach a negotiated settlement.

Surface-to-air missiles were terribly inefficient weapons during Linebacker II. On the first mission the North Vietnamese shot more than sixty at a wave of thirty B-52s striking but one: Rose 01. Another influx of fifty-one BUFs endured an onslaught of nearly 155 missiles but lost only a single bomber. Efficiency aside, SA-2s killed three B-52s on that first night. The North Vietnamese fired more than 180 at the next night's B-52 run but achieved no kills.[157] They were effective enough to persuade military leaders to give precedence to protecting the B-52s over thoroughly complying with the president's wishes for the bombing campaign. President Richard Nixon and his national security advisor, Henry Kissinger, had to remind them that the political priorities of maintaining coercive pressure took precedence over protecting the B-52 fleet.[158]

During the Christmas bombings, weasels unleashed Shrikes and Standards preventively against sites launching missiles, and against Fan Song radar emissions. On the December 22 mission weasels fired ten missiles, half of them against emitting sites, probably destroying but one.[159] Weasels flew in support of the nighttime missions B-52s were flying, but if they wished to see and bomb missile sites with cluster bombs, they needed clear weather and some moonlight. In their absence the bulk of the missions fired ARMs to dissuade SA-2 firings.[160] Altogether the Iron Hand missions were "ineffective" when flown in bad weather at night.[161] This inability to see their targets forced many to return without even expending their ordnance.[162] December 23 was unusual. The weasels encountered few indications of

SAM activity and fired only four AGM-45s—two against emitting radars and two preemptively.[163] As had been the case from the beginning the aircrews could seldom determine the results of their efforts. The next night may have seen one Shrike hit a radar, and December 26 seemed to produce better results. They believed they struck as many as seven radars with Shrikes and probably hit another with a Standard missile.[164]

Iron Hand missions continued to pursue suppression as their main goal. In order to do so they wanted the B-52s to inform them when they were three minutes from their target, so as to match the firing of the missiles with the time the sites preferred to turn on their radars. Interestingly, the message traffic of the Linebacker conferences—regular meetings on tactics that were held starting in July 1972—almost never mentions the heavy losses of the B-52s, but on December 28, representatives from the fighter wings unanimously asked to carry out a large-scale mission to destroy SA-2 sites as soon as the weather permitted so as to better protect the B-52s. F-111A Aardvarks, with their superior navigational aids, were sent on night missions against the sites.[165] The Navy did the same with their A-6As, sending the aircraft against either SAM sites or "lucrative targets in downtown Haiphong" in order to support the F-111 and B-52 missions. Flown at night at very low altitude into intense defensive fire, Intruder missions hit their targets to great effect more often than not.[166] The F-111As arrived over the missile sites just before B-52s reached the area, offering added protection by either destroying the missiles or disrupting their launch. General John C. Meyer, the commanding general SAC, wanted as many of these missions as possible. Accordingly, on December 26, Navy aircraft attacked SAM storage and assembly areas, and on the campaign's last day, December 29, weasels unloaded on signals from fourteen radars and saturated three sites with cluster bombs.[167]

The Air Force was uncertain about the effectiveness of its defense suppression effort during Linebacker II because some sites were not photographed after they were hit. Eight were not even damaged, and at times, regular high explosive bombs were used instead of cluster bombs, the best bomb for this target.[168] Considering the number of SA-2s fired, the SEAD effort was not as successful as it could have been. Furthermore, the stand-down prior to the operation was too extreme, and because of the momentary reduction in sorties, American forces failed to get the very latest intelligence on launch site locations. The decision to fly the B-52s in three waves each night meant that there were no weasels available for the third wave. Surprisingly, "Few strikes were sent against any Hanoi SA-2 sites until last three days." It was also unfortunate that F-111s were not certified to drop cluster bombs from low altitude. They would have been more effective against the sites than their conventional bombs.[169] Worst of all, the Air Force had identified the North Vietnamese ability to assemble, fuel, and transport SA-2s from their warehouses to the launch sites as the Achilles heel of their air defense network in 1968, but did not send bombing missions against those targets in earnest until the next to last day of Linebacker II on December 28.[170] Anti-radiation missiles destroyed few SAM radar sites during the last year of the war. Of 3,308 fired, 643 were preemptive firings, and 707 times the signal from the radar quit after the missile was fired; only 130 hit their target for sure.[171] Again, site destruction was not the necessary task; persuading the missile sites to not fire was the critical accomplishment.

There were rumors that more advanced SA-4s or SA-6s had been deployed in 1972, and that a third kind of missile was in the North Vietnamese inventory; it was actually a Chinese-manufactured SA-2. Of the newer medium-sized Soviet SAMs, only the SA-3 reached the theater, and it did not become operational until January 1973.[172] One aircrewman insisted that he had seen not one SA-4, but six of them. Not only did it look like the photographs he had seen, it also trailed black smoke—unlike an SA-2. "Having seen at least

100 SA-2s fired over the last ten months," he added, "it was quite evident that these missiles were different. They were slow, taking about 10 seconds to reach us from when first observed at about 5,000 feet." Its erratic flight path was odd, clear evidence of command guidance from the ground, and "The missiles were also painted black."[173] Navy pilots saw this missile as well, and noticed that it flew after them more intently, reacting quickly to each turn.[174] The commander-in-chief, Pacific later wrote, "Although the evidence was tenuous, the apparent characteristics of the missiles fired pointed to the ramjet powered SA-4 and SA-6."[175] At first, Chairman of the Joint Chiefs of Staff Admiral Thomas H. Moorer mentioned taking countermeasures against SA-4s in North Vietnam, but the JCS were cool on using and exposing America's best assets and knowledge against these missiles during Linebacker because they wanted to reserve what capability existed against these more modern weapons for the NATO theater. Later in August 1972, analysts decided that the new guided missile was not an SA-4, but was something else.[176] Had SA-3s or SA-4s been used, the distinct radar signals associated with them would have been detected; but in actuality, "There has been absolutely no SA-4 [electronic intelligence, photo intelligence, or human intelligence] obtained from any area of SEA."[177] More worrisome than these follow-ons to the already troublesome SA-2 was the SA-7, which Admiral Noel Gayler described as "the most significant development in Southeast Asia combat operations."[178]

Fired from a tube resting on one's shoulder, SA-7s were first observed when one sped by an F-4 on April 29, 1972. The capabilities of this small, rear-aspect infrared-guided missile caused a great amount of consternation when it appeared. An individual soldier could carry it anywhere, making airspace below 10,000 feet too dangerous for helicopters and slow-moving planes like C-123s and AC-130s. The new SA-7 was effective, shooting down thirty US aircraft at a rate of one kill for every thirteen firings.[179] On May 12, one struck and damaged an AC-130 near An Loc. Their presence drove helicopters to higher altitudes and led to the end of low-altitude napalm runs by A-37s. Because one shot down an O-2 forward air control (FAC) aircraft two days later, FACs who aggressively flew below 9,000 feet in order to support ground forces were now at greater risk.[180]

Not as well known are the kills the US Navy achieved with its shipboard SAMs. From 1967, the USS *Long Beach* and the USS *Chicago* fired eighteen RIM-8 "Talos" missiles between them against twelve flights of MiG-21s, destroying three. When the US caught wind of the possibility of MiG activity over South Vietnam in February 1968—near Khe Sanh in particular—General Wheeler reassured the president that the Navy was inserting RIM-2 "Terrier" and Talos-equipped ships into the Gulf of Tonkin as a countermeasure.[181] While functioning as a command-and-control ship on May 23, 1968, the USS *Long Beach* determined that a MiG-17 and a MiG-21 were closing on a group of American aircraft. It confirmed their identity by interrogating the MiGs' transponders so that they would self-identify as hostile. The *Long Beach* warned friendly aircraft to get out of the way, received permission to fire, and launched two Talos missiles at the MiGs. When the radar contact got bigger and stopped moving (the contact was now a debris cloud), it was clear the missiles had knocked the MiGs out of the sky.[182] Four months later on September 22, the *Long Beach* detected a hostile contact flying south past nineteen degrees north latitude, ordered friendly aircraft away from where the cruiser was going to fire its SAM, got permission to fire, and downed one of the MiGs with a Talos. Navy destroyers fired seventeen RIM-2 Terriers against MiGs from 1968 to 1972 and shot down three.[183] On April 19, 1972, for instance, the USS *Sterett* used a Terrier to destroy a MiG that was attacking the USS *Higbee*.[184] The USS *Biddle* achieved two more kills with Terriers in July 1972. Efficiency statistics for the ARM version of the Talos are even less well known. Cruisers fired ten missiles against North Vietnamese GCI sites in

1972 with at least two of them destroying a radar.[185] Admiral Moorer resented what he considered the underuse of Navy SAMs. He believed that ships using Talos missiles could have dominated the airspace over Haiphong and beyond: "They could have picked them [MiGs] off like flies, and they couldn't have flown over Hanoi for a hundred miles from that ship [the USS *Long Beach*]."[186]

Navy guided missile cruisers and destroyers carried out their most important mission on May 9, 1972, when three of them comprised the primary defense for Navy jets that dropped mines in Haiphong harbor—an operation of great importance to the Nixon administration's efforts to defeat North Vietnam's invasion of South Vietnam. The Navy recognized that using ships in this manner was unprecedented. F-4J Phantoms lurked to the east of this SAM belt, and at the same time Navy destroyers suppressed SAM sites and flak batteries near the harbor with gunfire. The mine-carrying jets—three A-6As and six A-7Es flying at 200 feet—encountered negligible antiaircraft fire, and three hostile SAMs exploded over a mile above them. When MiGs approached, a pair of Talos missiles from the USS *Chicago* almost certainly shot down one of them; the rest turned back to their base. The lightness of the North Vietnamese reaction to this mission may have been because Hanoi decided to not fight what was obviously on the way since President Nixon had announced the deadline for ships to get out of the harbor. Because this was no ordinary air strike—it reflected an escalation of the war—not only was the success of the airborne mining important to the achievement of American war aims, the success of the Talos/F-4 Phantom air escort mission was critical to the achievement of this politically risky mission. None of the mine-laying aircraft were shot down during this operation. The reliance on shipborne SAMs also fell in line with Kissinger's requirement to set aside the minimum number of aircraft for support missions.[187]

North Vietnamese surface-to-air missiles complicated the Americans' air war. US decision-makers had to worry about killing Soviet technicians and noncombatants if they decided to bomb the sites. The deadliness of the missiles—especially when aircrews did not see them coming—made confronting the problem a necessity. Addressing the SA-2 issue soaked up American assets and efforts. The damage they caused led to great efforts to rescue pilots they shot down, producing more variables for operations against North Vietnam. Indeed, so flummoxing were these new weapons that the logical next step was producing aircraft that were so hard to detect that they did not have to concern themselves so much with missile threats, low-observable aircraft like the F-117, F-22, and F-35, and fielding dozens of jamming aircraft such as the EA-6B. Because of surface-to-air missiles, air arms like the US Air Force and US Navy had to concern themselves more and more with surviving in the air instead of using aircraft as policy makers' weapons and tools.

Chapter 4

Air Superiority by Shooting Down MiGs

The prohibitions against an all-out effort to target surface-to-air missile sites and airfields meant the US Air Force and US Navy were going to have to shoot North Vietnamese MiGs out of the sky to achieve air superiority mission by mission. From the perspective of political leaders during the Johnson administration, this approach carried fewer geopolitical risks, but it required a greater level of danger for American aircrews. That defied common sense in the eyes of the military, but in the end, it was a mission the Air Force and Navy executed successfully, but not with the apparent ease of the air superiority fight during the Korean War.

The Americans and South Vietnamese possessed de facto air supremacy over South Vietnam, Laos, and Cambodia because the communists did not possess the means to challenge their dominance. Air supremacy over those areas greatly eased the execution of the war because Allied forces on the ground never had to worry whether "that airplane" overhead was hostile because it never was. This was easy to achieve since the North Vietnamese did not send air strikes south, but the Air Force wanted no chances after MiGs shot down two F-105s in April 1965. The JCS worried about a possible strike against Da Nang by IL-28s and MiGs with the potential of destroying dozens of aircraft and inflicting hundreds of casualties.[1] It needed some protection from the remote chance of a PAVN air force attack. Building an air picture was the first step, so five EC-121 airborne radar surveillance aircraft made their way to Tan Son Nhut Air Base in South Vietnam. They started flying during the third week of April 1965 with the mission of detecting North Vietnamese aircraft. They actually flew their orbits off the coast of North Vietnam, one at a higher altitude, and another down on the water (in order to provide some low-altitude coverage; their pulse-only radar could not detect aircraft flying below the horizon). For this reason, F-104Cs deployed to Da Nang in order to escort the EC-121s. In addition to the defending interceptors, there was a Hawk SAM battery at Da Nang as well, which PACAF believed would shoot down whatever aircraft might attack.[2]

Thailand's Don Muang Air Base benefitted from four F-102 Delta Daggers from the 509th Fighter-Interceptor Squadron since 1962. During the first week of August 1964 six touched down at Tan Son Nhut and Da Nang in South Vietnam to defend against incursions. Phantoms replaced the F-102s as air defense jets at Don Muang from November 1965 through June 1966. Six F-102s arrived at Udorn, Thailand, in April 1966. A pair of Delta Daggers was always ready to launch against intruders day or night. In June 1966, an increased threat encouraged Seventh AF to place four on alert at Da Nang and Tan Son Nhut. The Dagger would have been an able interceptor against North Vietnamese IL-28s, as long as the Beagles did not fly at very low altitudes. Somewhat belatedly, however, Pacific Air Forces realized its F-102s needed air combat maneuvering training. Since the F-102s might encounter MiG-21s, their pilots needed training in confronting fighter aircraft, not just bombers.[3] Eventually a MiG-21 shot down an F-102 in February 1968. A squadron of Australian CA-27 Sabres also provided air defense out of Ubon Air Base from 1962 to 1968.[4] The South Vietnamese Lieutenant General Ngo Quang Truong commented in October 1969 that North Vietnam would stage an air attack only if Hanoi believed it could somehow lead to winning the war.[5] The North Vietnamese Air Force never struck targets in South Vietnam or Thailand, but the F-102s remained, as much for diplomatic reasons as any. The presence of dedicated air defense assets met an American goal of assuring the Thai government of US support.[6] Air defense of South Vietnam and Thailand was a wise move; the absence of drama in that story was not only the result of a paucity of offensive air capability on the part of the North Vietnamese, but also due to the deterrent effect of the air defense system.[7]

The North Vietnamese used their MiG interceptors as a defensive force over their heartland, so that was where the United States focused most of its attention. On March 16, 1965, President Lyndon B. Johnson directed General Earle G. Wheeler to manage Rolling Thunder missions so that they would avoid encountering MiGs near Hanoi, but MiG-17s disregarded Johnson's wish and made their first attack on April 2 against four Navy F-8E Crusaders engaged in a flak suppression mission with A-4 Skyhawks. The MiGs did not shoot down any American planes, but that story would eventually change. The previous week Rolling Thunder VIII had targeted radar sites with the intent of lowering the danger to missions over North Vietnam. MiG attacks were a North Vietnamese countermove to that action.[8]

The United States needed to dominate the skies over North Vietnam in order for its fighter-bombers to be able to reach and bomb their targets without suffering more than the occasional loss to enemy action. Success was imperative if the president wished to use offensive air power to coerce the North Vietnamese into negotiations and if he wished to use air strikes to cut into North Vietnamese supply routes. His strategy of coercion and interdiction would be stillborn without a successful air superiority campaign, so although these missions took on a routine appearance, they were critical to the achievement of the president's objectives.

For its part, the Air Force eased into the air-to-air campaign with its newest fighter, the F-4C Phantom II, waiting in the wings. F-100D Super Sabres, an obsolescent air superiority fighter also known as the "Hun" (short for one hundred), flew escort missions only through April 1965. On April 4, one probably shot down a MiG-17 with gunfire. Captain Don Kilgus watched one of his cannon shells strike the MiG, which was then seen in a dive trailing smoke. The gun camera on his jet did not work correctly so there was no film of the engagement. The experiences of these two quartets of F-100Ds exposed the deficiencies in acceleration, maneuverability, and speed of the Hun, however, and the more capable F-4C took over the escort mission a couple of weeks later.[9] Huns flew only 200 combat air patrol sorties before giving way to the Phantoms.[10]

The Navy achieved the first MiG kills of the war on June 17, 1965, when a pair of F-4Bs downed two MiG-17s; the Air Force followed suit on July 10 when a flight of four F-4Cs brought down two more MiG-17s.[11] That day aircrews learned a lesson that remained relevant throughout the war: stay fast, avoid turning fights with MiGs, take advantage of the greater power of the American aircraft to exploit the vertical plane, and dive and zoom into position behind the MiGs for a good kill position. Indeed, during the fight the lead F-4C pilot pushed his jet into a dive, went to maximum power, reached a speed of Mach 1.2 (1.2 times the speed of sound—faster than the MiG-17 could ever fly), and went into a steep climb with the enemy fighters behind him. The MiG lost airspeed, tumbled sluggishly, and

F-100D Super Sabres (Air Force Historical Research Agency)

was now a vulnerable target for the American fighter. "Mink 4 executed a wing-over and a 180 degree turn to put himself on the enemy's tail. He fired four AIM-9B Sidewinder missiles and destroyed the MiG."[12] These kinds of tactical capabilities against enemy aircraft, though assumed, were necessary underpinnings for the American air war. Air-to-air combat over North Vietnam was one of seeking and pursuing advantages in support of an aerial siege campaign.

The president's decision to forego an all-out campaign against airfields and SAM sites did not make the achievement of air superiority prohibitively difficult. American forces only needed air superiority over North Vietnam for minutes at a time within the airspace used for the duration of each mission. Picture a bubble of American-controlled airspace surrounding a group of fighter-bombers as they flew over North Vietnam, similar to the way escorts at sea protect a convoy from approaching submarines. The Americans only needed to achieve enough airspace dominance within the air they flew to bomb accurately or take pictures without suffering serious losses—generally less than 3 percent for each trip north. Because American aircraft were able to achieve this kind of airspace control at will—MiG attacks were never able to severely maul a strike package—the president was able to employ air strikes as a coercive tool against North Vietnam indefinitely. The strategic policy shortcomings of the bombing campaign were never due to MiG or SAM effectiveness or weaknesses in American fighter aircraft. Had the United States achieved total air supremacy, that would have only altered the costs of the air war and simplified air operations; it would not have produced a strategic victory.

One may ask why the Air Force did not make greater use of the one purpose-built air superiority fighter in its inventory—the F-104 Starfighter. It had one wing of F-104Cs, a multirole version of a jet originally intended as a day fighter that seemed to some observers the

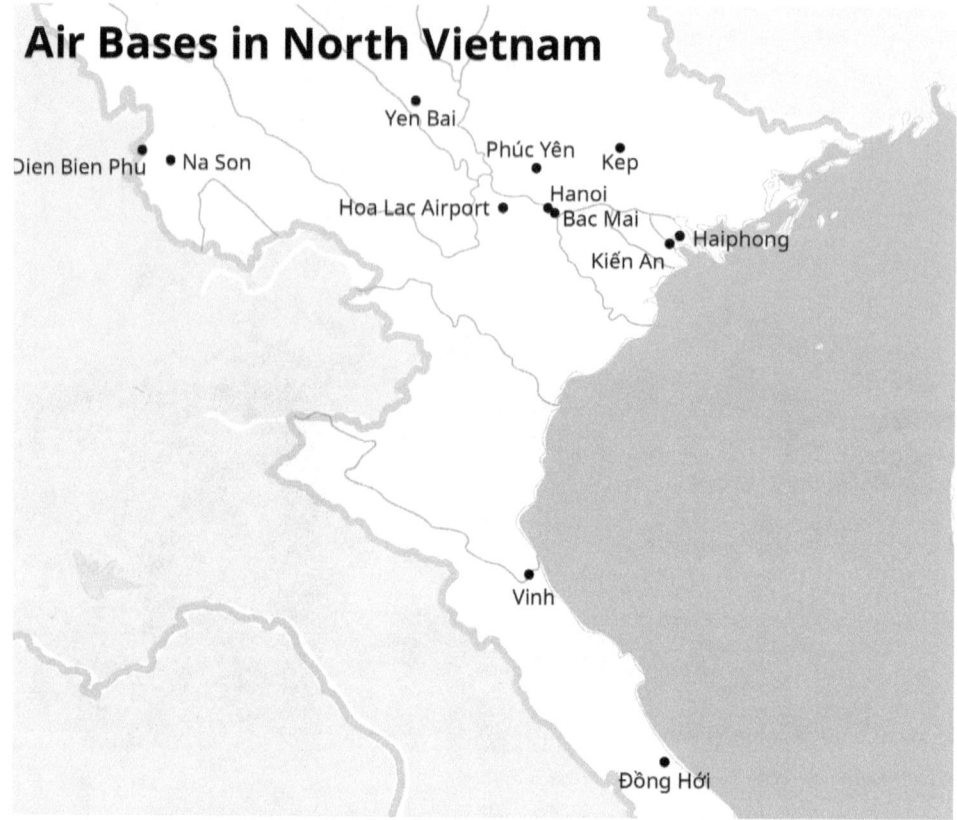

Air Bases in North Vietnam

Air Force's ideal answer for the MiGs. PACAF opposed the F-104C's use at first because that meant yet another aircraft type for the maintenance pipeline to support.[13] The Air Force nevertheless deployed the 479th Tactical Fighter Wing (TFW) a squadron at a time.[14] In April 1965 the first of those squadrons, the 476th Tactical Fighter Squadron (TFS), arrived in theater, forward deploying fourteen jets out of Da Nang with the remaining ten at Kung Kuan, Taiwan. These F-104Cs devoted half of their sorties to escorting EC-121s over the Gulf of Tonkin, with a quarter assigned to escort missions, 18 percent for close air support and 5 percent for weather reconnaissance. These escort missions could be particularly long, and there were discussions in February 1967 to restrict them to seven hours. When the 436th TFS took over in July, it allocated just 546 of 1,382 sorties to MiG combat air patrol (MiGCAP) and escort.[15] The third squadron, the 435th, flew 177 MiGCAP sorties out of 204.[16] Only two F-104 pilots ever saw a MiG. They left for the States in December.[17]

To partially compensate for the F-4C Phantom's lack of a gun, Seventh AF requested in May 1966 that F-104Cs return. The plan was to pair them "with the F-4s as air superiority teams."[18] It was believed that within this pairing the Starfighter could use its cannon in close quarters combat after the aircrews had identified the opponent as North Vietnamese, so F-104Cs returned to Southeast Asia in June.[19] They were based at Udorn, Thailand, because that base was closer to the northern quadrants of North Vietnam than Da Nang, and because the tankers that refueled the Starfighter flew out of Thailand.[20] When PACAF brought the 435th squadron back in June–July 1966, the MiGs were getting more rambunctious, but although they escorted F-105s on 100 sorties into fall 1966, most F-104C sorties (406) were ground attack missions over Laos and North Vietnam, even though the chief of

F-104C Starfighter (Air Force Historical Research Agency)

staff wanted them, as the only Air Force air superiority fighter with a gun until the F-4E entered service, preserved for use against MiGs, instead of exposed to the steady attrition inherent to close air support (CAS) and air interdiction missions.[21] Pacific Air Forces also warned the Air Staff that using them more aggressively over North Vietnam needed to wait until the F-104s received radar homing and warning (RHAW) black boxes, lest they be sitting ducks against SAMs. Seventh Air Force promised to return the Starfighters to the anti-MiG mission once the warning receivers were installed, but this was odd since F-4Cs did not have RHAW equipment themselves, and they flew through the skies of North Vietnam all the time.[22] It then hedged that the F-104 did not have the navigational capability to avoid the buffer zone along the Chinese border, understandable considering that the Chinese shot one down in 1965. When a team of specialists installed the display units of the RHAW in the Starfighter cockpit, the instrument cut off the pilot's forward view, which would not do.[23]

F-104C pilots managed to see a MiG-21 on August 7, 1966, and had their greatest chance for fighting MiGs when they participated in Operation Bolo on January 2, 1967, when they were used to protect F-4s returning from the operation with too little fuel remaining to defend themselves. Over the next six months of 1967, however, the squadron's primary mission was escorting electronic intelligence C-130s that flew over Laos and the Gulf of Tonkin. This was a tiring assignment because the pilots had to fly ten-hour missions every day; multiple aerial refuelings kept them airborne. An EC-121 monitored the airspace around them in order to vector the Starfighters against suspicious aircraft that might be coming after the C-130. The MiGs were either deterred or were not that interested in attacking this aircraft, so the F-104s never again had the opportunity to engage MiGs in combat.[24]

Those who flew the F-104C were confident in the combination of speed, small size, AIM-9B Sidewinder missiles, and its 20mm Gatling gun. A fighter possessing great acceleration and climbing abilities, the Starfighter was in fact not the best fighter for the air superiority mission. A series of practice combats between F-104Cs and F-4Cs (with a simulated gun, anticipating the introduction of the F-4E) in June 1966 demonstrated the Phantom's all-around superiority. Its beyond-visual-range missile, superior maneuverability, and a gun for close-in combat (in the form of a podded gun carried underneath its fuselage), meant that there were virtually no situations where an F-4 was at a disadvantage.[25] The Air Force had made the correct decision in going with the Phantom as its only air superiority fighter.

F-104s would have had a hard time against MiG-21s. It turned out the Fishbed was faster, more maneuverable, possessed greater acceleration, a better climb rate, and half the turn radius of the F-104.[26] The Starfighter's advantages were its gun and its size, which made it difficult to see. Against a MiG-17, an F-104C had a good chance of success if it executed a supersonic hit-and-run attack because the MiG would never see it coming; for it to get into a slow turning fight with a MiG-17 would have sacrificed all of the Starfighter's advantages.[27] Almost invisible a mile away when pointed straight at its adversary, an F-104 that got behind a MiG unseen would have a good chance to first take a lethal shot.[28] In the end, the underutilization of this aircraft contributed to the frustrating experience of the air siege of Vietnam because it defied what was to many common sense.

The leadership of Tactical Air Command (TAC) had been concerned about the ability of Air Force fighter pilots to handle the MiG threat even before large-scale participation in the war began. An absence of realistic training was the source of the problem, and discussions began in February 1965 on the need for substantive improvements. A Colonel Martin commented in Hawaii that, "I don't think we have any F-105 or F-100 pilots in Southeast Asia that could fight their way out of a paper bag if they were really contested by MIGs today. There has been no real training on air-to-air tactics for a good five [years]."[29] Indeed, while F-4 crews flew forty-four bomber intercept sorties a year, they practiced air combat maneuvering (ACM) only four times a year, and F-100 pilots were considered qualified on just twelve ACM sorties annually.[30] One veteran of combat over the Red River Valley observed that training had fallen off compared to what he had received prior to the Korean War. As a novice in the late 1940s he was trained day and night at all altitudes above 1,000 feet and was subject to attack at any time during a sortie. He stated, "The students learned to keep their heads on the swivel. We don't train that intensely now."[31] Colonel Abner M. Aust Jr. also observed, "our tactics/technics lessons learned during Korea and WWII were pretty much discarded."[32] The vice commandant of TAC, Major General Gordon Graham, called for training that better prepared pilots for the chaos of air combat: "Their training ... should go beyond gunnery school patterns, and airmen should relearn the technique of flying as a squadron."[33] The reason for this deficiency lay in assumptions the Air Force made after Korea: there would be no more medium-sized conventional wars due to the advent of nuclear weapons, thus there would be no more air-to-air fighter combat, and therefore the tactical fighter community concentrated on short-range nuclear bombing and neglected aerial combat. Consequently, one F-4C pilot, a Captain Ward, commented after a 1966 engagement with four MiGs that he had never received any training in close-in air combat maneuvering. His interviewer wrote, "This represented his first ACM practice ever and was his first and only combat encounter."[34]

The Navy's training suffered from similar shortcomings. Lieutenant Commander Spence Thomas, one of the F-8 Crusader pilots involved in the shooting fight with MiG-17s on April 2, 1965, "stressed the lack of training in air-to-air tactics" during an interview in

Four F-4C Phantoms (US Air Force)

1967.³⁵ A Commander Page, who was part of one of the first Navy F-4 units in the Gulf of Tonkin, recalled that his initial F-4 training centered around air defense intercepts. The squadron realized that in Southeast Asia, daytime air superiority was going to be their primary mission, so they set about to teach themselves tactics appropriate for that task. These aviators already realized that if they fired AIM-9B missiles against hard turning MiGs, the MiGs would employ sudden course changes to make the Sidewinder miss, and any MiG-17 they encountered would often be more maneuverable than an F-4B, therefore they emphasized using the radar-guided AIM-7D Sparrow in front aspect attacks. They also discerned they were going to have to visually confirm their target's identity, so the first jet would identify the MiG, the second would fire, and both would keep going, extending away from the MiG before turning back toward them.³⁶

The Air Force started to try to correct its share of these deficiencies at a conference in August 1965, where the participants exposed a host of problems. Air strikes were already following predictable patterns, so MiG pilots knew when and where to waylay the Americans if they so choose. Conferees agreed the Sidewinder was inadequate; fighters needed a short-range missile that could outturn and run down MiGs engaged in hard maneuvering. F-4C pilots thus far, however, considered the Sparrow to be "an extremely effective weapon despite some question as to reliability." A most serious constraint was the necessity to close with aircraft that were probably hostile in order to visually confirm their identity before shooting them. Given that nuclear weapons were not going to be used against North Vietnam, the conferees concluded, fighter pilots needed to spend less training time on nuclear tactics and more on air-to-air and conventional air-to-ground.³⁷

A year of war revealed that training remained seriously deficient in preparing aircrews for aerial combat, so in the spring of 1966, PACAF had its F-105 and F-4 pilots learn and practice offensive and defense air combat maneuvering tactics.³⁸ F-4 and F-105 pilots sought every opportunity to practice air combat. Because removing external fuel tanks was toilsome and inconvenient for maintenance personnel, PACAF allowed F-105 pilots to conduct air combat training with empty tanks still attached. F-4C crews used their time returning from North Vietnam strikes to practice, if they had enough fuel.³⁹ By February 1967, Seventh AF realized that its pilots were still not up to speed, endorsed this kind of post-mission training, and advised the Air Force that this too was not enough. One squadron tried to practice the air combat maneuvering tactics instructors at the Fighter Weapons School at Nellis Air Force Base, Nevada, had developed. The 391st TFS was fortunate to host two instructors from that school; the aircrews extracted as much knowledge from them as they could. Pilots needed more air combat practice during pilot training and at their follow-on replacement training units.[40] Years would pass before they received adequate preparation for war.

When the first American kills of North Vietnamese MiG fighters took place on June 17, 1965, the US Navy F-4B Phantoms responsible shot down two of them with AIM-7D radar-guided missiles.[41] With the F-4/AIM-7 combination, it appeared at first that American jets could simply sweep the skies of any MiGs that flew against strike packages. After all, the F-4s ought to be able to fire their missiles at the MiGs from "beyond visual range" (BVR) while the MiGs were unable to shoot back at that distance because they did not yet carry missiles. Indeed, the MiGs did not yet use radar homing and warning receivers (fuzz busters, essentially) to alert them that an enemy fighter was tracking them, so they might not even know that they were in danger until they exploded.[42] If the F-4s fired from behind, the MiG pilots would probably not see the missile coming—even though AIM-7s left a prominent white exhaust plume behind them—because of their poor rearward visibility from their cockpits and the AIM-7s' speed, which could top out at Mach 3.5.[43] Several factors, however, combined to complicate this scenario.

Fratricide was a major concern for the American air forces. First of all, how were pilots certain that the jet they targeted several miles away was an enemy aircraft? What if the MiGs were attacking American fighter-bombers; how could pilots make sure to not shoot down an F-105? For instance, on April 9, 1965, a Navy F-4B from the USS *Ranger* shot down a Chinese MiG-17 with a Sidewinder south of Hainan Island—and then may have blasted another Navy F-4B out of the sky by accident. There was never any firm evidence for this, except for Chinese accusations.[44] Navy vessels also wished to know which aircraft belonged to which side, so USAF aircraft had to contact the guided-missile cruiser that managed the airspace over the Gulf of Tonkin in order to avoid getting shot.[45] An F-4B shot down his wingman with an AIM-9 when they engaged in a confusing dogfight with two MiG-21s on August 17, 1968. Poor visibility and cloud cover made it difficult to tell who was who.[46] During Operation Linebacker, great concern lingered that an Air Force F-4 accidently shot down another Air Force F-4 (fortunately, it had not).[47]

The requirement for American aircraft to visually confirm their quarry before shooting sacrificed the option of long-range shots with AIM-7s. Ideally, F-4s would use their Sparrow missiles to shoot MiGs several miles away, but using that capability required certainty that the target was an enemy jet. This restriction cost some aircrews MiG kills, but it prevented a greater incidence of fratricide. The AIM-7 had a better chance of hitting a non-maneuvering unsuspecting target, but flying up to a suspected enemy sacrificed that advantage. Given the smokiness and size of American aircraft, the North Vietnamese pilots often saw their quarry first and started maneuvering to get into firing position themselves, which made it more difficult to get into the very limited firing parameters of the early Sparrow and Sidewinder missiles.[48]

Early efforts at electronic "identification: friend or foe" (IFF) were mixed. On December 23, 1965, the weapons director on an EC-121 believed a particular aircraft was making an attack run on it and gave Captain Arthur K. Ivins clearance to fire at it. The target was too far away from Ivins to see, and it just did not seem possible to him that the radar surveillance aircraft could positively identify an aircraft that far away. Ivins had also

F-4B Phantom (Naval History and Heritage Command)

just heard a Navy vessel ask everyone to make sure their transponder was on—and besides, he had previously been sent after several suspected hostile aircraft that turned out to be American, and this profile looked the same. He did not fire, closed on the target, and found himself looking at a US Navy A-3.[49]

One source of the issue was a turf war. The two services deconflicted rather than coordinated their air campaigns. For its part, the Navy worried its aircraft carriers could be subsumed into a "joint operation," quite possibly under Air Force control. Admiral Sharp, Rear Admiral James R. Reedy, and Major General Joseph H. Moore, commander of the Air Force's Second Air Division, divided North Vietnamese airspace into six sectors or "route packages" as a compromise solution.[50] Since the Navy and Air Force did not coordinate their air operations over the Gulf of Tonkin well that meant that the fighter pilots of both services had to exert care to avoid fratricide. A Navy memo written by a Navy squadron commander in 1966 noted that, "At present, each of the services operates aircraft over the Gulf without prior knowledge of, or coordination with, the other services. On several occasions a chance encounter between fighters has caused a potentially hazardous situation as both flights prepared for combat. Had visual identification been slow or erroneous, one or more aircraft might have been lost" to a fighter from its sister service. The skipper of VF-53, Commander Robair F. Mohrhardt, asked that some sort of provision be made for a radar site to manage airspace and deconflict the flight operations of the two services.[51]

A Navy warship became the facility that managed the airspace. A sophisticated guided-missile cruiser, the USS *Chicago*, as well as similar cruisers and destroyers, filled the bill, functioning as the first Positive Identification Radar Advisory Zone (PIRAZ) ship beginning in June 1966. It tracked everything flying west of 105 degrees longitude and above 18 degrees north latitude, issued MiG warnings, helped fuel-starved jets rendezvous with tankers, and coordinated air strikes. The sailors who functioned as weapons directors/GCI on these ships, known by their call sign Red Crown, greatly aided the air superiority mission for the rest of the war. When F-4s could function under control of a PIRAZ ship they could often fire their Sparrows BVR because the ships were able to identify aircraft as MiGs or friendlies using an identification friend or foe device and authorize them to fire without giving up the element of surprise by closing to confirm the aircraft's identity visually.[52] An experienced petty officer, the Red Crown controller sat in front of a radar scope, much like an air traffic controller, and exploited the expansive radar and IFF picture before him to provide threat warnings and attack vectors to aircrews, both Navy and Air Force. Their capabilities were highly regarded: "To the aircrews, the [USS] *Jouett* controller was almost like another aircrewman. . . . The *Jouett* proved to be an excellent CAP controller during several MiG engagements. Her controllers had a thorough knowledge of CAP capability and had a complete understanding of tactics to be employed." These weapons directors even met in person with members of aircraft carrier wings in order to develop and refine tactics and procedures: "This close working relationship decreased the reaction time and significantly increased the effectiveness of the Air Wing."[53] For example in 1968 a Navy wing wrote that it was feasible to make front-aspect AIM-7 shots because of the information, awareness, and guidance these ships provided.[54]

Discussions between Red Crown controllers and fighter pilots produced more effective air warfare that was safer for American pilots. During a December 1966 situation, Red Crown concluded that a pair of contacts were hostile because the Air Force confirmed it had no aircraft in that area. Two F-4Bs went after them and were authorized to fire. They detected the MiGs at thirty-three miles, locked on with their radar at ten, and fired one AIM-7E at six miles at one MiG that had turned tail for North Vietnam. Both F-4 crews saw it explode and crash. The second F-4B fired at his target from four miles back. The aviators never saw the MiGs prior to the fireball.[55] Events on June 27, 1972, demonstrated the importance of this Navy support to USAF aircraft for providing threat warning as well as intercept guidance. The PIRAZ cruiser had to leave the Gulf of Tonkin due to a typhoon, and "Before the day was over, four USAF F-4s had been shot down, three by MiGs."[56]

Some of the best examples of the effectiveness of these weapons director–aircrew teams occurred that year. The cruiser *Long Beach* showed more of what they could do on August 12, when its controller provided guidance, vectors, and information to an Air Force F-4 that shot down a MiG-21. The following month Red Crown on board the USS *England* vectored a Navy F-4J against a MiG-21 it destroyed. The next day, September 12, the controller on the USS *Biddle* received credit for three MiG-21 kills Air Force F-4s had made. In October the *Long Beach* once again provided GCI that led to the downing of a MiG.[57] After the war the commander of the 432nd Tactical Reconnaissance Wing (TRW) admitted that the Air Force was "dependent upon Navy ships for GCI information"—something that just would not do. The Air Force needed an airborne warning and control system, an "AWACS."[58]

Pilots were still responsible for their aircraft and had to remember that while the man in front of the radar scope on the ship possessed a bigger picture of the situation, his perspective was not complete. In the course of being dutiful and aggressive, he might vector a fighter toward MiGs that were trying to draw the American fighters into a SAM honey pot—a trap. The commander of Carrier Air Wing 14 warned that, "The over-zealous fighter pilot will soon be in deep trouble if he does not exercise good judgment in these cases."[59] Indeed, a flight of F-4s imperiled themselves in this way late in the war. They sped after two MiG-21s northwest of Hanoi on October 6, 1972, at Mach 1.2 drawing fuel from their wing drop tanks, closing and firing an AIM-7 from ten miles behind—too far for a Sparrow. When they dropped their tanks, the F-4s had 11,000 to 10,000 pounds of fuel remaining, and "All members of Buick flight remained in full afterburner for the duration of the engagement which lasted 1 minute and 59 seconds." When ground fire got too close and the flight lead reached the low fuel state that required them to return home, they turned toward their base. The MiG had probably tried to draw them over an AAA site on purpose. Buick 03 was unable to fly long enough to rendezvous with a tanker, and the aircrew ejected with just seventy miles to go when their engines quit running due to fuel starvation.[60]

There were still concerns in 1972 about fighters from one service accidentally firing on fighters from another, as in the case of Marine Corps F-4Js flying air patrols over North Vietnam. Air Force fighters kept making attack runs on these Marine aircraft and leadership warned that a friendly fire incident could still take place even though Air Force aircrews were briefed of Marine air activities and locations. For their part the Marines questioned the necessity of their mission, as they had been vectored toward possible enemy aircraft but twice during July and August of 1972; they never saw any MiGs. One source of confusion was that Air Force aircrews were not used to seeing uncamouflaged aircraft like the light gray and white Marine F-4s. A joint meeting solved the problem.[61] The need for a reliable electronic air-to-air IFF capability in fighter aircraft was clear. It would reduce the chances of fratricide and lessen the need to make visual passes before firing.[62] Red Crown prevented more fratricide during Linebacker's final month. An Air Force F-4 locked onto a target at seventeen miles for a Sparrow shot, when at a distance of eleven miles Red Crown informed the flight that the target was actually twenty-five miles away, "and there were friendlies in the area." Olds 01 had targeted an American aircraft, so he withheld fire, pressed on, saw a MiG-21, and maneuvered for the kill. The second Sparrow he fired dispatched the MiG.[63]

Chapter 5

Punch and Counterpunch

North Vietnamese MiGs were not a major threat during 1965; their mission was one of "harassment" and "disruption" rather than destroying American aircraft, and their efforts were not that effective.[1] A 2nd Air Division analyst argued, however, that both MiG-17 pilots who attacked F-100s on April 4, 1965, and the GCI that guided them performed with skill, probably due to the tutelage of the Chinese Air Force.[2] If the Soviet Air Force had had its way, their pilots would have flown some of the MiGs, but the North Vietnamese refused the Soviet request due to national pride.[3]

MiG-17s shot down too many aircraft to be called obsolescent; the aircraft was merely unsophisticated, though that did not keep it from remaining a problem throughout the war. With but half the speed of a MiG-21, it was still faster than bomb-laden jets, and its gun-only armament shot down twenty-four American aircraft. For its generation of fighter its only real weakness was the absence of powered control surfaces. At higher speeds such as Mach .9, the aerodynamic pressures on the ailerons and elevators were so great that it took all a pilot's strength to move the control stick enough to make a modest 2-G turn.[4] In fact, at those speeds the "anvil with wings," the F-4, was much more maneuverable than the much smaller MiG-17. At lower speeds, however, the same control inputs could generate a 7-G turn and no F-4 pilot wanted to get into a turning fight with the little bastard. Pilots were advised to remain fast, avoid turning fights, and climb steeply so as to exploit the Phantom's greater energy in order to defeat the MiGs.[5] F-4 pilot Max Cameron commented, "It was obvious that the MiG-17 could easily outturn the F-4, but the power and speed of the F-4 more than made up for this disadvantage."[6] Colonel Robin Olds found its low-speed turning capability astounding. Commander L. Wayne Smith of Carrier Air Wing Six avoided turning fights. Instead, attack and then keep flying straight through for at least a half minute and look for trailing MiGs.[7] Protracted dogfighting was not always the best choice for MiG-17s. On November 26, 1965, a group tangled with Navy A-4Es, a dangerous choice because A-4s were more maneuverable than the MiGs. In fact, on one mission, an A-4C fired a Zuni rocket with a proximity fuse that exploded close enough to a MiG-17 to cause it to dive into the ground.[8]

For its part, an F-105 coming off a bombing run could defend itself by outrunning MiGs. When some MiG-17s tried to close on some unladen F-105s during a December 1966 attack, they lost hope of overtaking them because the "Thuds," as the F-105s were called, accelerated to a blistering 900 miles per hour.[9] Even with external tanks an F-105 could exceed Mach 1.0 "in about five seconds."[10] Used as the primary fighter-bomber against North Vietnamese targets through 1968, the Air Force found that F-105s proved reasonably effective when defending each other. F-4Cs flying strikes carrying bombs also carried air-to-air missiles, switching from an air-to-ground to an air-to-air task within the same mission after bombing their targets. Sometimes after F-105s had dropped their bombs, they would fly MiGCAP while F-4s completed their bombing runs.[11]

North Vietnamese aircrews used their firing passes both to shoot and to learn. They often pulled back their MiG force after suffering a loss, and then developed and introduced

Vietnamese MiG-17 and pilots (US Air Force)

modified tactics before renewing attacks. During 1966 they were aggressive with their new MiG-21s during the last week of April and the first two weeks of May, when they targeted ancillary aircraft other than the F-105s and F-4s. Then after a month of practice, they began going after the jets weighed down with bomb loads, especially at low altitude. Another stand down followed and in August their attack methods became less predictable, with MiGs attacking anywhere from low altitude to four miles high.[12]

American sources reported that MiG-17s fired an AA-1 "Alkali" guided missile against F-4s twice during 1966. MiG-21s employed guns at least twice and relied on their missiles for eight firings. This study warned that these figures on MiG missile firings were not indisputable. Sometimes one could not be sure whether an AA-1 or R-13 (a Soviet copy of the American Sidewinder missile) had been fired, and the North Vietnamese could have taken shots that missed which American aircrews did not even see.[13] MiG-17s relied on guns, but used rockets at least twice during the first half of 1967, and there was at least one report of a MiG-17 firing R-13 infrared guided missiles at American aircraft. By the end of 1967, MiG-17 missile and rocket firings had failed to achieve a hit thirty out of thirty times.[14]

The MiG threat increased during the second year of the war due to better GCI, improved piloting, the addition of a few radar-equipped MiG-17s, and the introduction of top-of-the-line MiG-21Ds and Fs. Following many months of training and the installation of IFF transponders, not only the MiGs but also the entire air defense system improved. The transponders made it possible for the PAVN to fire SAMs and AAA at American aircraft while MiGs were engaged in the same general airspace, and they enabled SAM operators to differentiate MiGs from American aircraft and thus not shoot at their own.[15] MiG-17 pilots tried to entice the Americans into low-speed maneuvering fights (which played to their strengths), while MiG-21s hit and ran at high speed.[16] MiG-17s stayed close to their bases, below 9,000 feet, and flew in a pinwheel tactic while MiG-21s attacked jets as they left the target area. They were at their most aggressive during May 1967 and lost fifteen MiGs on the ground and eleven in the air, whereupon the PAVN air forces backed off for a couple of weeks. A renewal during June saw the loss of five MiGs, after which the bulk of their air force fled to the protection of Chinese air bases.[17] Halfway through 1967 the PAVN air force introduced more effective tactics. MiGs would attack American formations only when they had them outnumbered, could attack from an advantageous position, and when they achieved surprise. During November and December, they shot down nine aircraft with a loss of six of their own. As a further adjustment, MiG-21s attacked from high altitudes while MiG-17s attacked from below. December 1967 was their most aggressive month up to that time. Prior to the March 1968 bombing halt, they killed ten for the loss of nine. More telling was the fact that MiG attacks by 1968 accounted for a fifth of American losses. The MiGs would have had greater success, but their missiles suffered from the same problems as the Americans' weapons: they were designed to shoot down non-maneuvering bombers, not hard-turning fighters.[18] Robin Olds observed that shooting straight was the MiG pilots' greatest challenge, but he remarked, "All in all I feel they acquitted themselves reasonably well for a bunch of slobs."[19]

The MiG-21 posed a serious threat to American aircraft. While it did not have the range, on-board radar, or BVR missiles of the F-4, it did not have to fly as far or remain airborne as long as its counterparts in order to accomplish its task of local air defense. Ground radar stations could guide the aircraft to within visual range of American jets—often behind them— for hit-and-run attacks. The MiG-21 employed the R-13 "Atoll" as its primary weapon, and it was just as fast as any American fighter and more maneuverable than any except the F-8 Crusader, which it tended to avoid. A Navy squadron, VF-24, observed in 1968 that they were sent toward MiGs several times during their cruise, but the MiGs "always fled to their sanctuary before contact could be made."[20] Robert Sheffield, a pilot in the 4477th Test and Evaluation Squadron, the secret "Red Eagles" squadron that evaluated and flew MiG-17s, MiG-21s, and MiG-23s in the 1970s and 1980s, had flown F-4s before joining the squadron in 1979. In his opinion, "In the hands of a good pilot, versus the F-4, the MiG-21 wins every time."[21] Pilots in the 432nd TRW, disagreed: "The capability to fire ordnance from any aspect, coupled with the acceleration, zoom and sustained G advantage, makes the F-4 total weapons system superior to the MiG-21."[22] Tests of F-4Es against a MiG-21 in 1973 found "that the improved F-4E had a significant advantage over the MiG-21J, and that the F-4E with leading edge slats had a slight advantage over the MiG-21J at altitudes under 10,000 feet MSL."[23] The authors of the Red Baron III report took Fishbeds seriously: "If you know a MiG-21 in your area or you just lost sight of one and you want to find it again, ROLL OUT WINGS LEVEL 15 SECONDS THEN LOOK IN YOUR 6 O'CLOCK ABOUT 1.5 NM. IT WILL BE THERE [all caps in original]."[24]

The North Vietnamese's efforts were more than an inconvenience for America strike aircraft. From April 3, 1965, through December 31, 1966, there were 178 "incidents," when broken down include: fifty-four sightings of MiGs, fourteen situations where jets had to flee upon seeing a MiG, twenty-eight encounters, and eighty-two engagements—meaning one side or the other made a firing pass. MiGs shot down twelve American jets for the loss of twenty-five of their own.[25] The Seventh AF deputy chief of staff for operations argued, "In the mid and late summer of 1966 the enemy had achieved air superiority in the skies of his heartland. The SAMs were forcing us into the vulnerable 4500-foot area, the MiG attacks were being pressed with determination, causing us to jettison ordnance en route to the target and his Air Defense Control System was completely integrated and functioning with precision."[26] The situation was not as bad as the general opined. In actuality, Americans shot down twice as many of the enemy as they lost. More important, the fighter-bombers were reaching their targets, and the new QRC-160 ECM pod had entered service and rendered North Vietnamese SA-2s almost useless. Six months later, however, Admiral Sharp

Vietnamese MiG-21 at US Air Force Museum (US Air Force)

also overreacted, warning that North Vietnamese efforts could "make air operations in the Hanoi/Haiphong region too costly for the type of targets which could now be hit. Therefore, the US had the choice of abandoning the air war over the Red River Delta, which provided the enemy with a sanctuary needed to prolong the war, as well as to accept losses without commensurate return; or to expand the target list, and attack the enemy's air defense system, including MiG air bases and aircraft on the ground."[27] The admiral may have been painting a dire picture in order to gain permission to follow doctrine, first and foremost, and wipe out the North Vietnamese air force.

The primary effect of MiG attacks during 1966 was disruption: encouraging fighter-bomber crews to jettison their ordnance in order to become nimbler to escape attack. In July 1966 twelve aircraft dumped their bombs before reaching their target, nine did so in August, and seventy-nine in September. That continued a trend that had begun a year prior. PACAF anticipated that the North Vietnamese reaction to the QRC-160 pods would be to re-emphasize their MiGs, which is what happened after the pods proliferated in the fall.[28] Because of the effectiveness of the pods in degrading SA-2s and flak, MiGs had to take the fight to the Americans. The Navy also had good success with its ALQ-51 ECM suite, and found that aircraft that used it were shot down much less frequently than aircraft that did not have that defense against SA-2s, leaving no weak sibling for the North Vietnamese to focus on.[29] As MiGs became more active, aggressive, and successful in December 1966—a major change compared to previous months—MiG attacks forced more and more strikers to jettison their bombs before they reached their target. MiGs persuaded forty-four aircrews to dump their bomb load short of the target in order to survive and also shot down a pair of F-105s. For example, when four Thud pilots saw a pair of MiGs behind them and closing, they released their bombs to escape and the MiGs let them be.[30] By the end of the year 121 jets had jettisoned their bombs in order to survive. There was even a case where MiG-17s attacked some Marine F-4Bs on a night mission. American analysts worried that the PAVN pilots were improving and expected that attacks would increase in frequency and destructiveness.[31]

Frustrated, the Americans used guile and ingenuity to score a significant victory over the enemy interceptors. Colonel Robin Olds and General William W. Momyer came up with a plan over drinks at a conference in the Philippines that led to "Operation Bolo." Since the North Vietnamese had re-emphasized MiGs to compensate for the SA-2's shortcomings against jamming, the Americans needed to supplement electronic warfare with their fighter aircraft.[32] Bolo would take advantage of both. Its goal was to "destroy the airborne forces of the democratic republic of Vietnam."[33]

Intelligence analysts discovered patterns in the MiG's behavior of which they could take advantage: the aircraft flew whenever a strike package approached, and they normally set up about three orbits anywhere from ten to fifteen minutes before the F-105s and their escorts arrived. MiGs tried to avoid the F-4Cs when they attacked, pouncing on the bomb-carrying F-105s instead. American restrictions against bombing airfields and chasing down MiGs that fled for Chinese airfields helped shape the operation, resulting in four operational goals: entice the MiGs into the air, attack them aggressively enough that they had to fight and could not run away, have a CAP of Phantoms waiting for any that escaped and returned to their airfields low on fuel, and place another flight of F-4s between them and Ning Ming Airfield in China.[34]

The real trick would be to have the Phantoms fly the profile of a Thunderchief bombing mission and thus trick the North Vietnamese into attacking. Altitudes, airspeeds, radio frequencies, tanker orbits, flight routes, and such had to mimic those of a Thud strike. Another consideration was how long each kind of jet could stay in the air. Bolo's planners concluded the MiGs could remain airborne for fifty minutes, including five minutes of combat, therefore the F-4s covering their bases had to have enough surplus fuel to remain airborne for another fifty minutes. But an F-4 could only CAP that far away for five to twenty minutes, depending on whether it flew at maximum power, so they would have to shuttle F-4s to and from those CAPs. Consequently the operation ballooned into "16–18 flights of F-4 aircraft [and] 25 tankers to supply pre and post flight refueling." In order to not signal that anything unusual was up, the wing continued normal operations, and an order went out for "a normal strike force of [F-105s] to imply routine activities." To maintain secrecy, the 8th TFW sent hand-held orders to the 366th F-4C wing at Da Nang, and only the mission planners knew what was up until December 30.[35]

Major General Donovan Smith of Seventh AF came up with the idea of using the pods on F-4Cs to complete the deception. The factor that limited the number of F-4s that could participate was the availability of QRC-160 pods for self-protection against SAMs, and there were just fifty-seven in theater. The main reason for using the pods was to mimic the electronic footprint of F-105s; since F-105s used jamming pods, F-4s pretending to be F-105s had to as well. But there were no "adaptor kits" to connect them to an F-4's pylon, so a message was sent on December 23 asking for forty-eight. A C-141 transport arrived from the continental US five days later with the kits, plus an engineer. "This reaction time, without specific knowledge of the requirement, was remarkable."[36]

The mission went forward on January 2, 1967. An "east force" of seven flights of F-4s from the 8th TFW, and a "west force" of five flights from the 366th TFW comprised the Bolo F-4s. Additional aircraft included EB-66s for jamming, F-105s for Iron Hand, and F-104s to protect the Phantoms as they returned to base, by that time no doubt low on fuel and missiles and vulnerable to MiG attack, and of course the omnipresent KC-135 tankers.[37]

In order to gain the maximum number of kills, the F-4s had to be able to fire their AIM-7Es before the MiGs could see them, without having to identify who was who. That way they would get the first shot. The planners created a "missiles free" environment for the initial sweep by keeping American aircraft out of the airspace toward which they were flying and by orienting their Phantoms toward the empty airspace. For example, "Olds flight," the first in, could initially shoot at anything in front of it. It expected to kill MiGs above Phuc Yen, then proceed to a CAP above that base to shoot down anything that tried to take off or land there. The third flight in, "Rambler Flight," could shoot at anything in front of it when flying "headings between 140 degrees and 360 degrees." After these initial sweeps by Olds, Ford, and Rambler Flights, everyone would have to visually confirm the identity of any aircraft it was about to shoot, because the airspace would be a jumble of jets. In phase II, flights would cycle to and from the bases of Phuc Yen, Gia Lam, Kep, and Bac Mai at five-minute intervals, keeping fresh F-4Cs overhead to shoot down any MiGs they could. There were enough Phantoms to keep this up for at least fifty-five minutes and as long as an hour and ten minutes if the last F-4s only had to patrol and not fight.[38] That was long enough that any MiGs still in the air had to attempt to land, which meant fighting their way to their airfield, or running out of fuel and crashing.

The deception worked and the MiGs took the bait. This was an ingenious and successful concept, and only some unexpected weather conditions prevented it from becoming a catastrophe for the PAVN air force. There was an "8,000 foot undercast with unknown bottoms," conditions that signaled to the North Vietnamese that a strike may not occur that day. Nevertheless, they flew after the F-4s but did so "about 15 minutes later than expected." F-4s started to bunch up in the area that was to be the free fire zone, so Olds "cancelled the missile free options." The overcast made it more difficult for the CAPs to cover the airfields and provided cloud cover for the MiGs to escape into should they so choose. Because of the weather, more than half of the jets from the 366th TFW did not get to enter the battle area; ECM pod problems also contributed to that.[39]

Only three flights got to tangle with MiGs: Olds, Rambler, and Ford, fighting over Phuc Yen in an area thirty miles across for about thirteen minutes. Only MiG-21s came up after the supposed strike package, and F-4s shot down seven for zero losses of their own. Olds Flight fought four MiG-21s and expended four Sparrows and four Sidewinders, downing three. Ford Flight took on four more, killing one. Their missiles performed fairly well, and pilots fired three AIM-9s to try to persuade MiGs to react in a way that would nudge them into the Sidewinder's parameters. The one Sidewinder they fired with intent to kill worked. Of the two AIM-7s Ford Flight fired, one was a "no guide," and the other tumbled end over end. Rambler Flight faced uneven odds but shot down three of six MiGs with twelve Sparrow firings and four Sidewinders. After remaining in the area for another "15–20 minutes," the F-4s left for home.[40] Less than a year after sending their most advanced interceptor into combat, the North Vietnamese lost seven of their MiG-21s in a single day.[41]

Success in Operation Bolo was a consequence of creativity, deception, intelligence on MiG operational patterns, and detailed and thorough tactical and operational preparation on the part of the members of the fighter, tanker, and jammer units. Additionally, the engagements took place "between 9,000 and 15,000 feet," altitudes where the F-4C possessed greater maneuverability than it did at higher altitudes.[42] The wing achieved a similar result on January 6, when a pair deceitfully mimicked a high speed reconnaissance flight over the Red River Valley and shot down two MiG-21s.[43] The Air Force attempted this kind of ruse only once more—in January 1968—because Seventh AF considered MiG killing to be only a supplementary benefit; bombing was the primary mission.[44] The lack of a sustained follow-on campaign against MiGs was not that overly significant. Surface-to-air missiles were the more persistent problem, but as of March 1967, the new ECM pods seemed to have made fighter-bombers almost invulnerable to SA-2s. They shot down "only one pod equipped aircraft" during February, and that one had not been used correctly. That aircrew let themselves get shot down by drifting almost ten miles from the mutually supporting ECM their mates provided.[45] The weeks following Bolo saw a marked decrease in MiG aggressiveness, so operations against North Vietnam faced fewer challenges. That changed in April, and in response F-4s flew more escort missions to protect the F-105s.[46]

Operations like Bolo were helpful, but they could not generate strategically decisive effects given the war's political objectives. Therefore, the air superiority battle could not become strategically decisive. If the Air Force and Navy could execute this mission with great success air superiority would be one less issue to worry the president, and leaders could devote more energy into coercing North Vietnam and concern themselves less with just optimizing conditions for the air campaign. Eight months after Bolo, in August 1967, General Momyer testified to the Senate Preparedness Investigating Subcommittee of the Armed Services Committee that, "We have driven the MiGs out of the sky; for all practical purposes the MiGs are no longer a threat."[47] A few days later, on August 23, however, MiG-21s shot down two F-4s attacking the Yen Vien rail yard. Their success was the result of a modest tactical change that generated tactical surprise. Controllers vectored the MiGs toward the targets at low altitude inside clouds so that the F-4 pilots could not see them. The MiGs then maneuvered behind for a single-pass, hit-and-run attack with R-13 missiles. Colonel Robin Olds commanded the escort and was astonished shortly thereafter when he found out that Seventh Air Force Intelligence knew about the new tactic but failed to warn the aircrews.[48]

General Momyer's Senate testimony was not exactly correct. The North Vietnamese Air Force was down to thirty-four interceptors in August 1967—the ones that were located on North Vietnamese bases. Two-thirds staged out of sanctuary bases in southern China. One member of the intelligence community argued, "Our demonstrated capability of inflicting heavy damage will surely discourage the Sino-Soviet Bloc from significantly increasing North Vietnamese air resources." That proved to be wishful thinking.[49] Restocking their proxy's air force was too easy and paid too many dividends for the Soviets to do anything else. The war was an attritional siege sponsored by powerful state adversaries. Because external supplies were so important to the PAVN Air Force, cutting off those supply sources would have sharply diminished its effectiveness, but the United States did not have the geopolitical influence to persuade the Soviets to halt their support of Hanoi's air force.[50]

MiG attacks were not operationally or strategically effective. An April 1967 study by the Navy argued, "The effectiveness of enemy aircraft operations in preventing the execution of US air attack missions has been low. As of the end of 1966, thirty-six attack missions involving 112 sorties had been reported as aborted due to the presence or actions of enemy aircraft. However, protection of US attack aircraft from the MiG threat required approximately 0.30 support sorties per attack sorties in 1966."[51] They only inflicted attrition on the Americans: jets shot down, pilots captured, and most especially bombs jettisoned before reaching the target.

Halfway through 1967 MiGs became more aggressive, persuading forty-eight aircrews to jettison their bombs.[52] When a single MiG-21 fired an Atoll against a group of four F-4s they dumped their bombs, even though the missile exploded a half-mile behind—not a kill for the North Vietnamese, but a victory, nonetheless. An October 10, 1967, report to the Joint Chiefs of Staff outlining this trend may have been what finally persuaded the American national leadership to permit the bombing of the Phuc Yen MiG-21 Air Base. Forced jettisons, not losses to MiGs, had become the issue. If MiGs threatened fighter-bombers enough that they had to dump their bombs short of the target, that was a win for North Vietnamese air defense. Against one mission on December 19, 1967, the MiGs got no kills and lost two of their own, but twenty-four of forty fighter-bombers released their bombs early in order to dodge MiG attacks.⁵³ As 1967 waned, the enemy made further adjustments, firing barrages of SAMs and better integrating missiles, AAA, and interceptors into a coherent air defense system, which in spite of improved American ECM, "created a survivability situation that was only slightly better than it had been before the employment of the QRC-160 pod."⁵⁴ By year's end the number of MiGs in North Vietnam was down by about 80 percent, but cunning, aggressive, smart pilots flew what remained. Earlier in the year only about one percent of the Route Package Six sorties had jettisoned their bombs to evade a MiG attack, but as the end of 1967 approached MiGs became more effective and that rate increased to 10 percent before declining to 4 percent in January 1968.⁵⁵ President Johnson's March 31, 1968, bombing halt suspended this contest, but when the air campaign escalated in 1972, MiG attacks continued to force fighter-bombers to jettison their bombs through the end of the war.⁵⁶

A short-term answer was to get MiGs up in the air by attacking something Hanoi deemed worth protecting. That seemed to have been the case with raids against targets near Hanoi on December 17 and 19, 1967, when upward of twenty MiGs attacked on each of these days. During these battles MiG-21s employed hit-and-run attacks, while MiG-17 pilots tried to entice their opponents into close quarter fights at low altitudes. The Fishbeds got two kills for no losses, but four MiG-17s went down, having shot down one American jet.⁵⁷ MiGs attacking from multiple directions drew away fighter escorts and created opportunities for shooters.⁵⁸

General Momyer believed North Vietnamese pilots were more dear and harder to replace than airframes, and the way to get at them was through aerial battle. Therefore, he created another ruse similar to Bolo that took place on January 6, 1968. This time he used thirty-four F-105s loaded with AIM-9Bs only—no F-4s—which pretended to be on profiles that mimicked attacks on two railroad bridges and the airfields at Phuc Yen and Kep. Four MiG-21s attacked from behind, saw that the Thuds were carrying no bombs, figured out the subterfuge, blew through their formation, and informed their controllers that the Americans were attempting to entice them into another air battle and to not send up any more interceptors. Two of the F-105s fired AIM-9s at the MiGs but achieved no hits, and no one was shot down on either side.⁵⁹ This operation, and even Operation Bolo, illustrated a basic problem with the fighter sweep compared to bombing aircraft at their airfields: one cannot *make* the enemy commit aircraft to battle nor force him to remain in a fight once joined.

US Air Force and US Navy air leaders were frustrated at the beginning of 1968 because they thought it was necessary to sweep clean the skies of MiGs in order to be successful. Air Force F-4s had tried any number of tactical and operational methods: different timings for MiG sweeps, varied altitudes for escorts, close escort, free-ranging sweeps, and duplicity. The basic problem remained that the North Vietnamese held a better and more timely air picture than the American strike forces, which unless they were near the coast, closer to the radar of the PIRAZ ship, had to rely on information from Rivet Top: an EC-121M, a modified piston-engine Lockheed Constellation airliner that had long-range radars that could detect MiGs and radio their location and flight direction to American aircraft. Awareness, not airframes, was the basic problem; the Americans were "operating with less real time information while the enemy has this information available to him."⁶⁰ American aircraft normally did not know about incoming MiGs until they saw them, and neither airborne nor shipborne radar could detect low-flying aircraft.⁶¹ The situation proved worse the second half of 1967 regarding the warning of enemy aircraft. MiG-21 hit-and-run attacks accounted for every F-4 shot down, and "In every case, the detection of a missile in flight was the first indication of a MiG-21's presence."⁶²

An early Navy study previously concluded that the MiG warning system the US utilized was inadequate. It was not really a system. The Americans relied on four different sources of awareness of MiG activity: seeing them; detecting them with long-range search radar, either on a ship or an airborne early warning aircraft; electronic emissions, especially IFF; and the use of "special intelligence sources." Any of these could transmit a MiG warning over the radio, but only one every ten minutes, which was not frequent enough for jets under imminent attack. These warnings were very generalized, being most often a 30 x 30-mile map coordinate, and because they were so non-specific, they were almost useless tactically. During the first two years of the war, the on-board radars of American fighters almost never initially spotted enemy aircraft. In fact, out of nearly 180 encounters through the end of 1966, only six were initially detected by fighter aircraft radar, and all of those were F-4 detections. By the second half of 1967, MiG warnings were radioed in "bullseye" format: azimuth and range from Hanoi. An aircrew then had to figure out if those MiGs were near them.[63] All this presaged what eventually became known as "Teaball," a threat warning system the Americans cobbled together in 1972.

The fact that the earth's surface is curved and radar beams travel in straight lines means that low-level coverage is always a challenge for radars placed on the ground. Geography and technological limitations combined to give the North Vietnamese a couple of advantages in the fight for air superiority over their home territory. They got to place their GCI radars in the middle of the airspace they were defending, so they had some low-level coverage. As a result, their weapons directors were able to possess and exploit a picture of where their interceptors were as well as the locations of their adversaries. The closest the Americans were able to place their radars was in the Gulf of Tonkin. Consequently, they could only give threat warnings and intercept guidance to their aircraft if the MiGs chose to fly above 10,000 feet.[64]

The EC-121 had been designed as more of a search and early warning system to detect Soviet bombers at ranges beyond those of the radars along the North American coasts than as something managing fighter aircraft in offensive operations. Furthermore, its radars were pulse radars, not Doppler; therefore, they could only see aircraft above the horizon, a clutter of ground reflections hid the ones flying below the horizon. Until 1967, Seventh Air Force mainly used them to monitor the buffer zone along the North Vietnamese–Chinese border and yell at American aircraft that approached that no-fly zone to turn away from the border. Because it could not detect aircraft below the horizon, some were flown at a very low altitude—fifty feet over the Gulf of Tonkin wave tops—allowing the radar to be angled away from the ground and up into the sky. This gave them radar coverage over Hanoi down to 10,000 feet, but such sorties were hot, long, and bumpy for the aircrew due to atmospheric turbulence.[65] The radar return dots on the controller's screen represented pieces of the sky that were "30–40 miles" long, so radar data was useless for providing precise threat data to individual aircraft. It could not provide what the strike packages needed the most: warnings that MiGs were attacking, much less precise attack directions to escorting fighters.[66] A new black box, however, would help. During April–May 1967, "College Eye" EC-121Ds received QRC-248 transponders to interrogate North Vietnamese MiGs' transponders—triggering the MiG to tell the EC-121D who and where it was automatically, like civilian air traffic control managing airliners. Such information would not only help the weapons director differentiate hostile aircraft from friendly, the IFF return transmission would refine his radar picture and better enable him to vector fighters into an advantageous position, particularly after the introduction of the EC-121K later that summer. Now the National Security Agency (NSA) worried that if the Air Force used this capability to confirm the identity of every suspected MiG radar contact, the North Vietnamese would notice and the US would

EC-121 with two F-104As (US Air Force)

lose that source of information, but as August approached the JCS lifted this restriction.[67] Besides, Navy ships were already interrogating MiG transponders. The EC-121s could also share this aircraft identification data with Navy E-2 Hawkeye radar surveillance aircraft. Furthermore, Hawkeyes could "track NVN aircraft taking off from Phuc Yen and other NVN airfields"; if a jet takes off from a hostile airfield, it is hostile. As a result of these capabilities, the commander of the Seventh Fleet received permission to use this information to flag those aircraft as hostile.[68] Following a request from the 355 TFW, General Momyer in October 1967 allowed the aircrew on board the EC-121s to communicate with the fighters, and thus improve their chances of defeating the enemy.[69]

In August, modified EC-121K Rivet Tops arrived. The Rivet Top proved more capable because it had crew positions for communications intelligence personnel, the QRC-248 interrogator, and a panel displaying warning information on the SA-2's Fan Song radar. All this made a big difference against the MiGs; Air Force fighters shot down twenty by the end of 1967, and Rivet Top provided the key information used in thirteen of those kills.[70] Rivet Top EC-121s drew praise from the aircrews flying into hostile airspace. One from the 388th TFW commented that, "Rivet Top has provided outstanding real-time MiG information to our strike force." Other aircrews asked how the Rivet Top controllers obtained such good threat information, but an intelligence officer replied, "I don't know." Well, he did: they were listening to PAVN Air Force radio communications.[71]

The quality of this information varied, and pilots trusted each to differing degrees. One veteran, at least, Sammy White, did not consider the information from EC-121s to be that reliable: "Those warnings were very general, never of any particular or specific use to an individual flight. . . . No headings, no speeds, no altitudes, no particular tailoring of those warnings to any particular flight that I was ever aware of." He found the GCI from Red Crown to be considerably better: "They must have had a very good radar system, very good operators or controllers."[72] When the first Air Force ace of the war, Steve Richie, achieved his fifth kill, he and all the other F-4 crews on the mission considered guidance from EC-121s to

E-2 Hawkeye (Naval History and Heritage Command)

have been marvelous. Air Force leaders constantly praised Red Crown, particularly from the beginning to the end of 1972. The Navy recognized the breadth of contributions to the air war when it awarded Chief Radarman Larry B. Nowell the Distinguished Service Medal. A weapons director on the USS *Chicago*, Nowell provided radar guidance to interceptors in his role as Red Crown resulting in twelve MiG kills.[73]

These systems reduced American and increased North Vietnamese losses, so they contributed to the coercion strategy's staying power. Since they provided greater fidelity and awareness of what was happening over North Vietnam and near the Chinese border, the president could be less conservative in his use of aircraft there. An older system, the Navy's E-1B Tracer airborne radar surveillance aircraft, had some successful moments. On August 30, 1967, for instance, one tracked a strike group from the USS *Oriskany*, and using IFF was able to continuously follow American aircraft. The E-1B, Red Crown, and the mission commander flying in one of the strike aircraft communicated effectively with each other in terms of sending MiG warnings to the fighter-bombers, who confirmed that they had received that information. Better was the E-2 Hawkeye. The E-2 used a newer radar (an AN/APS-96) that could detect air and surface targets out to 200 miles and could also interrogate MiG transponders.[74] In 1968, an E-2 made the first radar contact on a MiG that a Navy F-4 subsequently shot down. It provided the directive guidance the F-4 needed, and the success of this team meant Naval aircraft were going to be used in this manner more often. The commander of the USS *America*'s air wing found that the E-2 offered enough capabilities to allow the air wing to carry out operations without the assistance of shipborne radar. After the 1968 bombing halt they functioned mostly as an air traffic control platform; the bombing restriction made MiG encounters unlikely. Hawkeyes monitored strikes, provided precise directions toward targets, lent navigation and rendezvous assistance, managed tankers, and guided search and rescue operations.[75]

As the bombing halt line moved to the south, the North Vietnamese pushed their air defenses farther into the panhandle. In January 1968, CINCPAC discovered evidence that the North Vietnamese were planning to station MiG-21s at Vinh Airfield in order to go after B-52s flying missions over Laos and South Vietnam. MiGCAPs were still necessary, and the Navy altered their tactics as a result, trying to overtake MiGs as they turned north for home. This protected strike packages (which was the point) but resulted in only twenty engagements (which are more interesting) and but six kills. When the enemy finally started going after the B-52s they would either send a MiG-21 below radar coverage for a sudden attack from behind or send three MiGs with the leader being a decoy to draw away the escorting fighters so that the trailers could attack unmolested. Nearly three years later, on the night of November 20, 1971, a Fishbed fired an R-13 against a B-52. The missile exploded underneath one of the bomber's wings but did not bring it down.[76]

Air combat declined after the March 31, 1968, bombing halt. Aviators maintained their CAPs, but air patrols in defense of the aircraft carriers, though necessary, actually eroded aircrews' readiness for combat; they simply burned holes in the sky except for the rare intercept. In another approach the Pentagon asked for permission to employ Talos SAMs from Navy cruisers against MiGs south of the 20th parallel so as to defend B-52s.[77] Then during the late spring of 1968, the Navy's 53rd Fighter Squadron noticed the enemy was falling into a predictable pattern. Its GCI controllers would send a pair of MiG-17s south from Bai Thuong to the 19th parallel at around 7,000 feet, looking for American aircraft to troll. Meanwhile a pair of MiG-21s would be sent to a low altitude orbit to the west, with the intent of pouncing upon American jets preoccupied with the MiG-17s.[78] Their operational area crept southward. MiGs took advantage of Bai Thuong as a forward operating base for attacking Navy aircraft, and in June a MiG-21 shot down an F-4J. Consequently, American aircraft, especially the slower ones, were more seriously threatened, so Seventh AF asked for a joint strike with carrier aircraft against this air base. A pair of F-4s engaged two MiG-21s on August 25 to no effect. General Wheeler interpreted North Vietnamese actions as a form of escalation, but it was just the ebb and flow of siege warfare. For the rest of 1968 there were but eighteen MiG encounters; MiGs lost six of these, while they downed two more F-4s.[79]

Chapter 6

The Imagined Weapon: Immature Technology

The air-to-air missiles the American fighters relied upon never justified the lofty assurances and press attention they had received.[1] Overpromised performance shaped expectations during the decade before the first MiG encounter of the Vietnam War as people read of near-magical weapons that avowed to destroy enemy targets in all kinds of weather conditions, at night, and with the reliability of mature technology. When missiles entered the inventory, defense officials of all stripes made extravagant assumptions regarding their reliability, lethality, and kill probability.[2] In reality, however, these highly sophisticated machines functioned only when fired within finicky parameters—if then. Picture a cone-shaped basket in front of a missile-firing jet that was fairly wide when both it and the target were flying straight and level. When both started turning, that basket quickly narrowed and would then disappear if both fighters were engaged in violent maneuvers. Like a defensive tackle chasing a rabbit, these early missiles could not keep up with a hard-turning target because they were not designed to shoot down fighters, only bombers. Neither were they intended to be manufactured to the standards necessary to handle the same abuse as a jeep or an artillery round, for example. The early Sparrow missiles—AIM-7Ds and Es—were in fact an immature technology, having been in existence for less than a decade at best.[3]

Prewar tests never mimicked combat situations. Engineers conducted missile trials "under controlled conditions, i.e., peaked aircraft and missile systems," and even then the AIM-7D had a kill probability of around 55 percent.[4] Wartime situations were neither controlled nor optimized, and aircraft and missiles were not "peaked." Air Force and Navy F-4s made only four kills with AIM-7Ds out of the twenty-eight times they fired the missile.[5] Tests of the AIM-4 Falcon pitted it against B-17s, trials the Air Force did not consider adequate.[6]

By May 1966, F-4 crews saw several firings of AIM-7s and AIM-9s in which the missiles did not fly toward the target or the rocket motor did not even ignite. An investigative team found no serious problems, just "some minor maintenance practices and instances where missiles were fired outside of their lethal envelope."[7] In actual service, however, several conditions produced adverse effects on each missile's internal components and electrical connections: the shaking and jarring the missiles endured on carts from the weapons bunker to the loading area, the rigors of repeated sorties before firing, maybe ten or more flights taking the missiles from 120 F to -60 F each time, through rain and vibration.[8] For example, something as bland as the "nozzle closure" on the AIM-7E missile was vital, so the Navy developed a new plastic nozzle that would maintain a seal despite the rigors of repeated flights. It would also seal off the rocket engine from rainwater, necessary because some of the motors' weather seals had ruptured.[9] Every single part and circuit of a missile had to function properly for it to work at all. As a consequence, within a quartet of AIM-7s on one F-4C, for example, only

AIM-7 Sparrow missile (USN)

two might even fire, and only one of those would actually guide toward the target. Then the fuse might malfunction, and the missile would not detonate. Sometimes Sparrows just broke. During its 1968 cruise, F-4B aircrews from the USS *Constellation* witnessed twenty Sparrows break during flying operations, and five were "lost on catapult launches."[10]

Six days after the first MiG attack, a flight of F-4Bs from the USS *Ranger* saw how oversold these immature technologies were. The aircrew had carefully inspected their missiles before takeoff on the morning of April 9, 1965, finding that the weather seals were good and that glass on the "seeker head and fuzing windows of the two Sidewinder missiles were clean." When one Phantom (Blue 2) fired an AIM-7D at a MiG, the aircrew only heard a "thud"; the missile had not fired, it just dropped off the jet into the ocean. The same thing happened when the crew fired a Sparrow at another MiG-17. On the third pass, one of the AIM-9Bs did not fire, and the other never appeared to track and follow its target. Another F-4B attempted to launch an AIM-9B, but it did not work. "Blue 1" fared no better, firing an AIM-7D "within range and steering limits. Lock-on was maintained but the missile did not guide and was observed to follow a ballistic flight path." They had done what they could: "All indications available to the crew were that the weapons system should have been functioning perfectly."[11]

An Air Force crew experienced a similar episode later that month. "Atlanta 4," one of four F-4Cs guarding an RB-66, suffered the frustrating reality of the missiles not functioning as advertised when they went after a MiG-21 on April 25, 1966. W. K. Darrow and L. R. J. Sonier attempted to achieve a radar lock-on but could not, so they fired three AIM-7s in "boresight" mode. "The first would not launch, the second launched but did not guide, the third would not launch. The fourth was fired with a radar lock on in a beam attack (.95 M 30,000') but missed."[12] That same day Detroit Flight (four F-4Cs) went after a MiG-21 that had attempted an attack against a U-2 flying at 70,000 feet. The MiG's target was too high, and soon it found itself the subject of the Phantoms' attention. Detroit 1 fired AIM-7s that refused to launch. It then fired two AIM-9s from too far behind; they blew up too far from the MiG to damage it. Detroit 2 fired a Sparrow head-on, which flew by the MiG. It then appeared that Detroit 2 was about to get lucky; the MiG turned toward him at fifteen miles after he had locked on for another Sparrow shot. Two AIM-7s flew straight ahead without guiding and the last one missed. Detroit 2 then fired a pair of Sidewinders from too far behind, which only blew up a piece of sky. When another MiG-21 attacked, and the F-4 crews saw how low their fuel state was, they dove into a cloud and wisely beat a fast retreat.[13] Problems like this continued and June 2, 1967, proved very frustrating for a group of F-4s from the 8th TFW. They engaged MiG-17s south of Kep and fired four Sparrows, three Sidewinders, and two Falcons; "no MiG kills resulted."[14]

Using and firing these missiles required aircrews to quickly complete complex tasks during life-and-death encounters. Aircrews also had to go through a series of switch functions and missile checks in flight. An F-4B crew from the USS *Midway* neglected to do so on June 4, 1965: "If pilot had 157 switch [in the] on position [instead of] standby, port missile

AIM-9B Sidewinder on F-8 Crusader launch rail (Naval History and Heritage Command)

should have tuned and been ready for firing.... In this case, pilot did not check for missile tuning until MiGs were encountered, thus did not know he had bad missile."[15] During another fight an F-4B from the USS *Constellation* was lucky to survive when it fired an AIM-7E at a MiG-17 because the missile exploded after traveling only a hundred feet. A Navy study found that as of December 1966 the guidance reliability of AIM-9s was 62 percent; that of AIM-7s was 42 percent.[16] It took more than reliable guidance systems for this missile to work.

This kind of poor performance should have been expected from these first-generation missiles. One of the problems seemed perceptual: just what is an air-to-air guided missile—a round of ammunition, something like a drone but with a host, or was it a sensitive, ultrahigh-tech machine? These were not rounds of ammunition, nor were they the equivalent of a complex appliance like a DVD player. They were more comparable to Formula 1 race cars or even robotics. Cubic inch for cubic inch, they were possibly the most complex machines in existence, but they had not been combat-tested. A further example of the fact that a guided missile was a machine distinct from its host (and not simply a round of ammunition) was that the missiles needed overhauls, thus PACAF asked for the establishment of an AIM-7 overhaul facility in the Pacific.[17]

The misses were not always the missile's fault, as when an F-4D aircrew fired an AIM-4D Falcon "head on" at a MiG completely outside of the missile's parameters. That missile simply had no capability to guide on a target flying toward it; the missile had to be able to view and home onto the target's jet exhaust. An aircrew might make a textbook intercept, as did Chevy Flight on September 9, 1972. It confronted MiG-21s head on, from 5,000 feet below so the radar would not have to deal with ground reflections, got a radar lock-on, fired AIM-7s at eight and six miles, only to see the F-4's radar break lock.[18]

Sometimes the missiles worked. The Air Force got its first AIM-7 kill on April 23, 1966, when Captain Robert E. Blake and First Lieutenant S. W. George downed a MiG-17. Their tactics were sound, as well; they carried out the intercept the way they had "planned and briefed" and, "None of the tactics utilized or required were of an extreme or unusual nature." This was doubly fortunate for they found their adversaries to be skilled and aggressive, but the MiG-17 could not outclimb or outrun the Phantom.[19] Blake later mentioned that they were able to stay out of reach of the MiGs by climbing, as did Neptune 3, an F-4 that dealt with an attacking MiG by accelerating to Mach 1.3 and climbing to get into a more advantageous position.[20] When a missile worked as advertised, the results were spectacular, as when Nitro 1 fired three Sidewinders at a MiG-21 whose pilot realized he was under attack and tried to escape at maximum power, giving the heat-seeking missile a perfect target. The third Sidewinder "went up the tailpipe [and] the MiG-21 disintegrated immediately."[21] A year later, on October 26, 1967, Red Crown vectored a pair of F-4Bs from the USS *Constellation* against a high-flying MiG-21. From about four miles back the aircrew fired an AIM-7E, which hit the MiG squarely in its left wing.[22]

Bureaucratic leaders within the Air Force were not slow to discover the seriousness of the missile deficiency problem. PACAF asked for replacements for its AIM-7D Sparrows, which suffered from a design flaw in its warhead. Its explosive would melt and run "between the steel rods" (which functioned as shrapnel) "during periods when the missile is subjected to abnormal heat," which was every single day in Southeast Asia. The warhead of the newer AIM-7E did not have this problem, was five pounds bigger, and its more powerful rocket motor gave the missile greater range.[23] Field units using the Sparrows did not have enough qualified technicians or manuals, and it took four months to get a guidance and control unit repaired.[24]

After the Air Force became concerned with the AIM-7 and AIM-9 failures, it sent an investigative team to Thailand to find out why so many were not guiding and some were not even firing. In May and June 1966, a team of specialists from the Air Force, Raytheon, Westinghouse, and McDonnell visited to try to determine the nature of the problems. They promptly saw how poorly the AIM-7D performed when in two-and-a-half weeks, twelve out of thirteen fired missiles missed their targets. Pilots fired four "outside designed parameters," three rocket motors failed, four did not guide, and no one had an explanation. Fifteen of twenty-one Sidewinders had been fired outside of the "design parameter."

In terms of effectiveness, the missiles had a kill probability (Pk) of 30 to 40 percent at best in real-world conditions. But these assessments demonstrated that for the weapon system to work, everything had to be done correctly: the aircrew had to fire the missile within the boundaries of the missile's capabilities, which they often failed to do; in order to launch the weapon they had to manipulate switches in the cockpit correctly, while in danger; and all of the various internal components of the missile had to work properly.[25] Actually, the guidance and control sections (again, these were not rounds of ammunition) of the AIM-7Ds and Es were failing at a rate of 15 percent. Furthermore, the missiles were not subjected to more intensive maintenance until after "250 operating hours."[26] By the end of 1966, Air Force Logistics Command ordered a "formalized reliability program on air-launched missiles," and set out to gather hard data on how well or poorly the missiles performed.[27] This kind of testing became a practice for PACAF in March 1967. One such program was Charging Sparrow, an initiative to assess the effects of the climate in Southeast Asia on the reliability of the F-4C-Sparrow missile combination. Combat Sage replaced Charging Sparrow in March 1967. The aims of Combat Sage included training aircrews on the use of air-to-air missiles, accumulating data on missile performance, and fine-tuning each aircraft's radar system prior to each mission.[28]

The Navy's experience mirrored that of the Air Force. During one particular month, a pair of F-4Bs fired three AIM-7Es and six AIM-9Ds to no effect against a couple of MiG-21s and once again, "most of these missiles were fired near or outside of recommended parameters."²⁹ AIM-7 problems plagued the Navy's squadrons. Navy depots tested each missile before sending them to an aircraft carrier, after which the missile would not be tested again unless it failed to tune or was flown thirty times. Then the missile would be sent to a maintenance facility on land to be tested and adjusted. More than 100 AIM-7Es were thus tested during the 1968 cruise and half failed. One particular air wing, Carrier Air Wing Six, tested each missile as soon as it arrived, whenever it failed to tune, and after it had been flown fifteen times, half of the original flight missions. Toward the end of the cruise each AIM-7E was tested after just ten flights. Ordnancemen also handled and moved the missiles far less frequently. These changes "proved to increase remarkably the reliability of the Sparrow."³⁰ Not everyone found the AIM-7E to be so unreliable. Carrier Air Wing 1 wrote in 1967 that, "They have proved to be highly reliable and very sensitive."³¹ But when the missile actually guided toward its target, the probability of kill was still only .375. After Operation Bolo, Colonel Robin Olds commented, "We were delighted with the effectiveness of our Sparrows," but he noted that his crews had "peaked" the missiles they used prior to the mission, which they were not always able to do.³²

Given the Air Force's experiences during Rolling Thunder, it could have arranged tests of the Sparrow from 1969 through the beginning of 1972, but it failed to do so. Nor did the Air Force improve its missile situation as quickly as it could have during Rolling Thunder. The Air Force wanted its own infrared guided missile, not the Navy's Sidewinder, so it attempted to replace the AIM-9B with an upgraded AIM-4 Falcon, a missile that originated in the late 1940s and was designed to hit Soviet bombers—large targets that could not maneuver quickly. The missile was the AIM-4D, which was supposedly "lighter, more maneuverable, self-tracking, and had a higher single shot probability of kill (.92 to .5)."³³ Engineers gave persuasive reasons to believe this Falcon would be an improvement over the Sidewinder: an AIM-4D was less likely to be distracted by the sun, flares, and reflective heat sources like clouds, and it was more sensitive to jet exhaust wavelengths. These would arm the new D-model F-4 in fall 1966.

Although F-4D pilots managed to shoot down five MiGs with Falcons, this missile was not an improvement. Within weeks PACAF identified a couple of extreme flaws. The seeker head had to be cooled from another component inside the missile, and this lasted for only two minutes; after that the missile could not be used. Therefore the pilot had better anticipate perfectly the time frame in which he would need and use his Falcons, or he would be flying around with unusable dead weight. Furthermore, the AIM-4D required a direct hit because it lacked a proximity fuse (a device in use since World War II), and it was not maneuverable enough to achieve a direct hit on a consistent basis. The sequence of switches and buttons the aircrew had to manipulate to fire the missile was cumbersome, an unacceptable trait for a dogfight missile.³⁴ One F-4D on October 26, 1967, for example, maneuvered to an ideal firing position behind a MiG-17, but the pilot had to flip the switch to select the missile, flip another to cool its seeker head, and wait for the tone indicating the missile was tracking the MiG's heat source. When the Falcon finally left the launch rail, the MiG had reversed course and was coming straight for the Phantom. Another aircrew managed to destroy a MiG with a Falcon missile during that same fight.³⁵ One has to wonder how the Air Force obtained that .92 probability of kill figure.

The Air Force tried to keep the AIM-4D in service with upgrades and better testing. Improved control surface actuators and new solid-state circuitry seemed to make for a more reliable missile. Further tests of the improved Falcons led PACAF to recommend their continued use in combat, and contractors modified missiles in Thailand.³⁶ The commander of

THE IMAGINED WEAPON: IMMATURE TECHNOLOGY

AIM-4 Falcon missile (US Air Force)

the 8th Tactical Fighter Wing at the time, however, Colonel Robin Olds, found the unreliability of the AIM-4D so frustrating that he refused to wait for the improvements and retrofitted AIM-9B launchers onto his F-4Ds. In the meantime, he prohibited his jets from flying over North Vietnam until remodified to carry AIM-9s again.[37] Pacific Air Forces followed suit when it did the same by taking Sidewinder launchers from F-4Cs and mounting them on Ds.

The Air Force introduced modified, improved AIM-4Ds to Indochina units in April 1968, but wanted PACAF's assessment of the missile's effectiveness first.[38] A modification allowed the seeker head to be cooled for three hours instead of two minutes, and later versions received a seventeen-pound warhead with a proximity fuse. The next month there was talk that its ineffectiveness against fighter targets should relegate it to air defense missions; they could hit targets like bombers that flew straight and level, that could not make the gyrations necessary to defeat a missile.[39] In October 1968, the 479th TFW completed a series of test firings of the yet-again modified Falcons, and the airmen were not impressed. While eleven of the twenty missiles fired achieved a direct hit, the tests were taking place "under extremely unrealistic conditions. Firings are being conducted using parameters that are ideal for the missile." Nine missed even though they were easy shots.⁴⁰ Seventh Air Force kept the dash-8 version of the AIM-4D until June 1972 only because its seeker could be slaved to the F-4 radar, a particularly useful capability at night.⁴¹

AIM-9 Sidewinders performed better, but still had their shortcomings. In a fight in which friendly and enemy aircraft were in front of a fighter that had a good lock-on tone for an AIM-9, the pilot could not determine whether his missile targeted friendly or enemy aircraft. A pilot would pass up a MiG kill to avoid killing one of his own, a choice a Navy pilot from the USS *Coral Sea* made during one mission.⁴²

The Air Force should have replaced its AIM-9Bs with the Navy's superior AIM-9D, which became available after 1965. Consequently, the Air Force's F-4s did not have a good dogfight missile until August 1972. From January to June 1967, the AIM-9D proved its reliability over the initial version of the Sidewinder. According to a Navy staff study, Air Force fighters achieved fifteen kills from seventy-eight missiles fired, while the Navy scored six killed from fifteen missiles—kill probabilities of 19 percent for the B and 40 percent for the D.⁴³ One F-4C pilot who spent a month on a couple of aircraft carriers praised the Navy's newer Sidewinder as a better missile: it could make tighter turns against a maneuvering target, it tracked the target better, and it performed better at shorter ranges. Major James A. Hargrove Jr. believed the Air Force was mistaken for not adopting AIM-9Ds.⁴⁴

The Air Force instead signed a contract for the development and production of the AIM-9E on March 23, 1967. The AIM-9E was a modified B with a better seeker head, greater range, a more forgiving firing envelope, the ability to hit targets in 5-G turns, and better performance at lower altitudes. Five thousand would be converted into E-models. Initial testing was okay: of the twenty-seven fired by June 1969, nineteen passed within lethal range of the target, and six of those achieved a direct hit. Just three miscarried.⁴⁵

The Navy and Air Force could not use their F-4s to their full potential because the AIM-7 had to be used at extended ranges. The Navy, on the other hand, could employ their F-8s in a manner that exploited their advantages of maneuverability to the full. The F-8 Crusader entered the war as the most glamorous of the fighters because it had been designed solely to defeat MiGs. Unlike the early F-4s, the Crusaders possessed four internal cannons designed to be handy in close-in fights. Celebrated as the "last of the gunfighters," missiles were actually the F-8's primary weapon; guns were "secondary."⁴⁶ The F-8's guns, in fact, usually jammed when in a turning fight—the time when they were most needed and appropriate.⁴⁷ The guns jammed or did not fire at all during three of the eight times they were fired in combat against MiGs through September 18, 1966. Furthermore, during early engagements, most pilots used their guns before maneuvering into a good firing position. Only one of these gun firings scored hits on a MiG-17.

AIM-9Ds were more promising. Of the three missiles that guided out of an early sample, one was fired too far behind the MiG, but the other two destroyed their targets. Six out of eleven that missed did so because the pilot fired them outside of the missile's parameters.⁴⁸ One squadron was nevertheless quite unsatisfied with the F-8's weapons. They reported that the 20mm cannons their F-8Cs used did not function well, and the gunsight also did not work correctly. An F-8C downed a MiG-17 with its cannon, but the pilot shot it at close range without the help of the lead-computing gunsight, and the MiG proved an easy target because it was not engaged in hard maneuvering. Commander J. D. Ellison blamed AIM-9D reliability problems on "the long periods of usage during which it undergoes months of successive flights, 'G' loading, and repeated arrested landings and catapult shots."⁴⁹ This squadron improved the guns' reliability with meticulous maintenance examinations but was unhappy with the way the cannon shells dispersed when fired. During its pre-deployment training its pilots achieved good success with Sidewinders but found that against enemy aircraft it was "extremely difficult to get in and stay in the missile envelope in a high 'G' turning fight."[50]

An F-8, Nickel 101, may have shot down a MiG-17 with its 20mm cannon on June 21, 1966. According to the contemporary account the pilot saw fuel stream from the MiG he had just struck with 20mm cannon shells. Another F-8's guns jammed during that fight.[51] In the same manner, after one F-8 damaged a MiG-21, the other Crusader finished him off with a Sidewinder. An F-8 with AIM-9Ds was lethal when it could attack a MiG unaware of its presence. On June 26, 1968, Batterup Flight received a series of vectors that brought them behind two MiG-21s who did not see them, one of which they shot down. The first F-8 kill of a MiG-21 was more spectacular. With intercept guidance from the USS *King*, an F-8E zoomed up behind it in maximum power. When the MiG pilot saw him, he began a split-S, which the Crusader pilot matched, shooting him with an AIM-9 before it went nose down.[52]

The F-8E also possessed an air intercept radar that could detect—after being pointed in the right direction by GCI—a MiG-sized aircraft as far out as thirty miles. Its maneuverability matched or exceeded that of the MiG-17, even when not flying at maximum throttle. A MiG-21 could not shake an F-8 if one got behind it; a pair of F-8Hs from the USS *Hancock* hounded two MiG-21s through seven complete turns during a September 17, 1968, engagement. When the leader fired four AIM-9Ds, however, none of them scored a lethal hit, and his wingman could not score with gunfire.[53] F-8s saw little air-to-air action during Linebacker, although they flew 413 patrol and escort missions during July, for example. Their last action occurred on May 22, 1972, when Nickel 101, an F-8J from the USS *Hancock*, attacked a MiG-17 that tried to outrun the faster jet. To save his own life the pilot bailed out and the abandoned aircraft crashed.[54] Nickel 101 did not get credit for a victory because the Navy argued that although the pilot cost the enemy a fighter jet, the pilot did not shoot down the MiG.[55]

The issue of which fighter could best perform the air superiority mission was a disputed matter. During the spring of 1965, the Navy completed a study of the capabilities of its F-4B Phantoms against F-104s, F-105s, and especially F-8 Crusaders. The Phantom aviators had little trouble with the Starfighter and Thunderchief, but they "heard the chuckles of the Crusader pilots in the office." To everyone's surprise, however, the Phantom was a better air superiority fighter than the Crusader—if employed correctly. Over the course of 125 missions, with about two-and- a-half engagements per and about fifteen missions each against Crusaders, F-4B aviators learned how to make best use of the Phantom's strengths. During the first three sorties, an F-4B crew would struggle somewhat against the Crusader, then hold its own on the next three, but "By the time they had had six missions in the F-4, they were calling the tune against the aggressive, experienced F-8 pilots." The combination of decent F-4 maneuverability and a power reserve greater than that of the F-8 highlighted the strengths of the F-4 over the F-8. The aviators learned to keep the F-4 fast and, most important, use all dimensions, especially the vertical plane, to defeat a first-rate adversary, in this case, the F-8 and its pilot.[56] F-4C aircrews soon applied similar methods for defeating MiG-17s: maneuver vertically until the MiG lost its airspeed, then shoot. Initial tactics against MiG-21s focused on driving the fight down to lower altitudes "where the aircraft are more equal in maneuvering ability."[57]

Aside from the problems of missile reliability, there was still a practical need for gun armament on fighters because the missiles of the day needed to travel hundreds of yards in order to arm the warhead, and that meant a pilot of an F-4 without a gun could not shoot at a plane at point-blank range. Less than a year into the war, Seventh AF recognized the deficiency. One pilot commented that if his Phantom had a cannon, he would be able to shoot MiGs that were so close that a missile did not have enough flight time to arm its warhead.[58] That minimum range was at the outer reaches of a 20mm cannon's effective envelope, so there would be times during close-in fights when a gun would be the ideal weapon. Furthermore, the gaggles of numerous aircraft in a tight airspace created situations where one could fire a missile at a MiG, and the missile would then go after a friendly aircraft. With a gun, one could shoot precisely at a MiG that was a few feet from a threatened American aircraft. A gun was the best option at very low altitudes, where heat and ground returns interfered with the guidance systems of the Sidewinder and Sparrow. While the Navy's F-8s made one or two gun or gun-assisted kills, the Air Force's F-105s made twenty-six with their 20mm cannon.[59] With the problems the air-to-air missiles demonstrated, the mounting of a gun in the F-4E got the attention and interest of Congress.[60]

Before the war a 20mm gun pod had been developed for Phantoms to use in ground attack missions. Colonel Frederick C. Blesse pursued this obvious solution to these variants' need for an air-to-air gun but did not get permission until the spring of 1967 to experiment with the external gun pod on the F-4s of the 366th TFW. F-4Cs achieved the first kills with the podded 20mm cannon on May 14, downing two MiG-17s. Proving its worth, the first MiG was shot well inside the minimum range of missiles, after failed AIM-7 shots. The second went down when Speedo 3 fired at a distance of 200 feet, something no missile could accomplish. Aircrews were extremely pleased with and confident in the cannon.[61] During Linebacker an F-4D managed to shoot down a MiG-21 from about 200 feet back with its gun pod after missing with a pair of AIM-9Es. A month later, Lark 01 switched to guns when Sidewinders twice failed to launch and scored enough hits to shoot down the MiG-21.[62]

From July to December 1967, guns accounted for half of American MiG kills, but that was as much an indicator of failure as of success. Five of these were by F-105 fighter-bombers. Attacking MiGs had gotten in among the bomb-carrying jets, which in self-defense sometimes had to jettison their bombs to avoid getting shot down. For instance, Crossbow 3 shot down a MiG-17 that was attacking another F-105 on August 23. The next month Wildcat 4 engaged a MiG-17 during a bomb run. The MiG got in front while trying to down another F-105 that had managed to drop bombs on the target. Thunderchiefs that fought MiG-17s on December 19 jettisoned their ordnance before attacking the MiGs, which was a victory for the enemy.[63]

These successes were significant to the aircrews involved, but the North Vietnamese made this period the most intense thus far. As the Americans hit more and more high-value targets, the PAVN air force put up a fight, downing forty-eight aircraft during the month following October 23. Analysts concluded the PAVN's great improvement in air combat during the second half of 1967 was due to the growth and maturation of their air defense system. The US had better carry out improvements of its own if it hoped to continue to possess air superiority, a necessity for the bombing campaign. Cratering air bases and cutting of air defense supplies from the USSR remained, in the Air Force's opinion, the best option for regaining the advantage. Air superiority efforts got the job done, but maintaining it was not an efficient operation for American air forces. As the March 31, 1968, partial bombing halt approached, the overall kill probability for Air Force–fired missiles, for instance, stood at 13 percent: 17 percent for Sidewinders, 14 percent for Falcons, and 10 percent for Sparrows. In raw numbers according to this review, 175 AIM-9s had been fired achieving twenty-eight kills and one probable, 224 AIM-7s fired for twenty kills, and forty-three AIM-4s fired for four kills and two probables.[64] Interestingly, this problem with reliability had been predicted eight years earlier by an author who noted that if each of the components of a 500-part missile demonstrated a 99.5 percent reliability rate, the "overall reliability" of the missile "is rather shocking only 8.13%."[65]

The best face one could place on the underwhelming results resided in the fact that all these were first-generation weapons, and it is rare for such a profoundly new and complex technology to not suffer considerable problems early on. Overeager expectations, however, led these air forces to handle missiles too roughly and to take their reliability for granted. Rhetoric surrounding missiles portrayed them as rounds of ammunition and they were treated as such, but they were complex aircraft in their own right. Altogether the combination of the harshness of the environment in which the missiles were carried, the requirement for jarring flight maneuvers to gain a good firing position, the complexity of their use, and the MiGs' defensive flying degraded the kill probability of the missiles greatly. The experiences proved infuriating for aircrews, but in the end, the problems were not strategically decisive.

Chapter 7
Air Superiority Refinements, 1968–1972

In 1968 the North Vietnamese MiG force was potent enough that the Air Force could barely maintain a 4:3 kill ratio; the Americans shot down sixteen MiGs but lost twelve of their own jets.[1] It "cost us an airplane almost every time we went up there," General John W. Vogt, the commander of Seventh Air Force, later commented.[2] This became somewhat of a moot point, however, when President Johnson moved the limit of bombing missions first to the 20th parallel in April 1968 and then to the 19th, just above the DMZ, in November.

The last MiG kills during Rolling Thunder took place on July 29, 1968, when an F-8E shot down a MiG-17, and on August 1 and September 16 when F-8s downed a MiG-21 on each day.[3] Altogether the air combat tally by the end of the campaign was in the United States' favor: its fighters shot down seventy-eight MiG-17s and thirty-three MiG-21s while losing twelve F-4Cs and Ds, four F-4Bs, three F-8s, twenty F-105s, two A-6As, two A-1s, and one RF-101, F-102, and A-4, each to MiG action.[4] As Rolling Thunder wound down and the three-and-a-half-year unilateral bombing halt commenced on November 1, 1968, the commander of Tactical Air Command, General Gabriel P. Disosway, told the United States Senate that American tactical air forces had the ability to complete their missions, which was correct.[5] Comparatively, however, American air forces struggled much more against North Vietnamese air forces than they had against those of North Korea, China, and the Soviet Union a decade and a half earlier. In spite of these struggles, one assessment warned against drawing too many lessons from this little war; after all, the enemy normally sent only half a dozen MiGs against American forces, and never more than twenty.[6]

The Air Force's response to the frustrations of air-to-air combat between the 1968 and 1972 bombing campaigns emphasized improving technology: better missiles and aircraft, rather than a smarter use of experienced aircrews and better air combat training. Ideally, the Air Force would have emphasized both approaches. For example, the organization wanted to make sure the service's primary tactical aircraft, the F-4E, received the technical upgrades necessary to keep it viable until F-15s entered squadron service in the mid-1970s. In fact, the Air Force was as concerned with overcoming a growing capabilities gap with the Soviets as it was with winning the next air campaign in Vietnam—and from the vantage point of 1969 another air campaign against North Vietnam was unlikely. The Air Force claimed that MiG-21s had a 4:1 kill ratio against American fighter aircraft, and the performance of the new MiG-25 Foxbat was frightening, so the need for a follow-on to the F-4E, what soon became the F-15 Eagle, was apparent.[7] In the meantime, the Air Force upgraded its F-4s and their missiles, but training lagged in its sophistication.

Some of the policies were astonishing given that the US military was fighting a major war. New F-4 pilots, for example, reached their units in 1968 without an adequate understanding of how to employ and fire their missiles. Although a missile shortage and the need to divert munitions to South Korea, due to the Pueblo Incident, led to a chief of staff decision that missile firing take place only in operational units and not training units, Air Force leadership was not convinced that proficiency with one's weapons was a priority for fighter pilots at this stage of the war.[8] Three years into the Vietnam War the chief of staff even wrote, "Training and individual aircraft verification are to be accomplished as secondary objectives.... Each aircrew will normally be provided a familiarization firing prior to serving in combat if resources are available." Some were even arguing that aircrews who were going to have to use missiles in combat could meet minimum qualifications without even firing real ones prior to going to war. According to General McConnell, the only thing that firing weapons was good for was "increas[ing] aircrew confidence," and weapons system evaluation program flights were sufficient for that. McConnell added that the rate of firing a single air-to-air missile each year and the firing of an air-to-ground missile every three years ought to be adequate during a war.[9] By 1971, the Air Force had "discontinued the allocation of missiles for training purposes only, and has directed that all firing be conducted with dual objectives: full weapon system evaluation, and aircrew training."[10] Consequently aircrews entered combat during Operation Linebacker in 1972 without enough training, particularly for fighting against MiGs; aircrews had to train in-theater before heading north.[11]

Right after the war the Air Force admitted its fighter pilots were not getting the aerial combat training they needed before entering combat. Air combat was not emphasized and, "The initial high loss ratio of F-4s to MiGs is an indication of this deficiency. By contrast, the Navy aircrews were prepared for air combat against other fighter aircraft. It is interesting to note," wrote the US Air Force author, "that after 21 June [1972] the MiGs engaged mostly USAF forces. In all probability this was because of their greater success against USAF crews."[12] That was understandable, because on average PAVN pilots had more air combat experience than F-4 pilots in 1972, the majority of whom had never fired a missile prior to deploying to Southeast Asia. Unforgivably, "Tactics and aircrew proficiency had to be developed after the Linebacker operations were initiated." F-4 aircrews still had to make the most of scraps of time for learning about and practicing aerial combat tactics after bad weather cancelled missions, sometimes after completing a mission—if they had enough fuel remaining.[13]

One squadron completed significant training before going to Southeast Asia—in 1969. The 469th TFS brought its F-4Es to Thailand having completed "four grueling months of ACM experimentation and training." They believed they were "the best trained squadron ever" since the war erupted, but Rolling Thunder was over; there was no way to put their dogfighting skills to use. The plan as of 1969 was to re-emphasize aerial combat training for Air Force fighters if the war escalated again but not before.[14]

Although the Air Force's training efforts between the air campaigns fell short, Tactical Air Command leaders made a major advance in its understanding of air superiority priorities with their realization that, "Air superiority cannot be achieved solely by destroying the enemy fighter force, rather the entire enemy air defense system must be systematically destroyed. To accomplish this task, approximately 25 percent of the fighter force must be optimized for destruction/suppression of the enemy ground radar defense system." The institution was maturing beyond the quest to produce another Red Baron.[15]

The Navy at this time admitted that it was also having problems achieving the effectiveness at aerial combat it desired. In June 1968, Navy F-4s fired twenty-five Sparrows against MiGs and scored not a single hit. F-4s and F-8s fired thirty-seven Sidewinders and achieved six kills—a 16 percent kill probability. There were hardware problems with the fire control system and the missiles themselves, but maintenance was also inadequate, and aircrews often mishandled their systems by continuing to fire missiles beyond their design limits or even by flying with cockpit switches in the wrong position. Consequently, the commander of Task Force 77 ordered an intensive training regimen for his aircrews. For instance, only half of the training targets for the missile firing program flew straight and level, the rest maneuvered, and half of the AIM-7 firings were against targets flying right at them from the front. The target was a BQM-34 drone, and the maneuver was a simple turn at a rate of twelve to fourteen degrees per second, simulating a MiG's turn rate.[16] Seventh Fleet believed this improved aircrew proficiency, skill, and confidence in their weapons stemmed from the crew's training, and decided in August 1969 that its aviators would continue live-fire training so as to sustain combat readiness. The USS *Kitty Hawk*'s F-4 squadrons benefitted from this new requirement, firing forty-seven Sparrows and three Sidewinders between them. Concerns about North Korea gave Seventh Fleet an additional impetus for keeping a sharp edge.[17]

When F-4Js, the Navy's newest fighter during Vietnam, entered the fleet it possessed the most advanced fighter radar in the world: the AWG-10 pulse-Doppler radar. It had the ability to search for and track aircraft that were flying close to the ground because its processors filtered out ground reflections. At sea, however, they had problems with the radar overheating while on the flight deck, and with short circuits due to moisture.[18] Problems with the core processor continued. "This unit is the heart of the AWG-10 system without which the radar will not operate in any mode. CVW-2 [Carrier Air Wing Two] F-4Js experienced 171 failures of this unit during the cruise."[19] To prevent malfunctions due to overheating and sudden jolts from catapult launches and arrested landings, aircrews turned the radar off before approach and waited until after takeoff to turn it on. Consequently, the radar worked 75 percent more often. Perhaps this was a reason Navy F-4s decided to rely on Sidewinders during Linebacker, but for the time being they emphasized speed and high aspect Sparrow shots. Commander L. Wayne Smith of Carrier Air Wing Six also recommended "carrying an attack straight through for at least 30 seconds searching for follow-on sections of MiGs. Always turn into the threat, never away."[20] This variant achieved the first nighttime kill of a MiG when an F-4J downed a MiG-21 on August 10, 1972.[21]

The Navy also emphasized a comprehensive training program in air-to-air combat that included firing at least ten missiles. Its pilots employed a two-jet side-by-side formation with enough lateral separation so as to enable each pilot to look over his shoulder and clear his wingman's blind spot well enough so that a MiG could not close to firing range without being spotted, something that had occurred far too often over the previous three years.[22] This formation, known as "loose deuce," made both fighters available as shooters who took turns as the leader, depending on which aircraft was in the more advantageous position. The Air Force's "fluid four" formation, in contrast, contained one shooter and three escorts for the flight leader. A pair of F-8s piloted by Lieutenant Anthony Nargi and Lieutenant J. G. Alexander C. Rucker illustrated loose deuce to great effect on September 19, 1968. The MiG-21 pilot appeared to see his enemies just as they attacked and started maneuvering violently, attempting a steep climb. Nargi maneuvered his F-8 well enough that the AIM-9 he fired not only tracked, it also flew "up the tailpipe and blew the whole tail end of the airplane off." Rucker, the wingman, saw a second MiG-21 first and took charge, per loose deuce tactical doctrine. He told Nargi to make a hard turn, which the latter completed, and very soon Nargi had flown into a firing position again. Nargi's missile missed, whereupon Rucker went after the MiG. The two decided to return to their carrier because they were running short on fuel and the MiG was outrunning them.[23]

In March 1969, the Navy began a more systematic program to teach and disseminate the knowledge and skills necessary for aerial combat when the "Top Gun" program was begun at Miramar Naval Air Station in San Diego, California. Top Gun had multiple founders, one of which was the F-8 "Crusader College" in Fighter Squadron 124 that had been teaching air-to-air combat for years. Another was a report Captain Frank Ault wrote in 1968 that called for the establishment of a more advanced school for fighter pilots. A third was the Navy's frustrating experiences against North Vietnamese MiGs during the war: a clear need existed for this kind of training.[24] The organization sought to produce instructors, not aces. As its first officer in charge Lieutenant Commander Dan Pedersen warned, "No egos, fellas. We're here to teach."[25] Three years later the first American ace of the war, Navy Lieutenant Randy Cunningham, stated, "I owe my victories to Top Gun."[26]

Beginning in 1970, Navy fighter squadrons based in the continental United States took advantage of an innovation the bomber interceptors of Air Defense Command initiated in 1966: dissimilar air combat tactics training (DACT), wherein pilots practiced combat against different kinds of aircraft from different services. Air Defense squadrons had been put on notice they might have to deploy overseas to conduct air defense operations against enemy MiGs, not Soviet bombers. Since Air Defense Command had not trained for combat against other fighter aircraft, it began to do so in 1966. Its program, Operation College Dart, became a standard part of the interceptor pilot's training program, and they welcomed participation by the Navy and Marines. Navy F-4 and F-8 squadrons flew to F-106 bases to engage in air combat training against airframes that did not fly like their own, and the F-106's flight characteristics even bore some resemblance to the MiG-21s that would form their main threat if the air war escalated in the future. Squadrons from Tactical Air Command did not participate until 1975.[27]

By 1970, the Air Force believed that there would not be any more air combat over North Vietnam because of the progressive drawdown and withdrawal from the war. After all, Nixon's policy was to turn the war over to the South Vietnamese and return American forces to the United States. This belief that the war was basically over may have encouraged the Air Force to not make short-term air superiority capabilities in terms of combat-ready aircrews a priority. Shortcomings in operational capabilities and an absence of good sense, however, made themselves known in December 1971 when a single F-4 flew a combat air patrol over Laos (doctrine called for flying in pairs) within range of North Vietnamese MiGs. That same month a pair of F-4s made their way past Hanoi without enough fuel to engage in a fight if the enemy chose to attack.[28] Another poor choice was the Air Force's assignment policy, which kept it from fully exploiting the experience its pilots gained in aerial combat. The system sent pilots to the theater for one year at the most and sent those who completed 100 missions over North Vietnam home. Unlike the Navy, the Air Force made no effort to return these experienced crews to the theater after a year in the States. The Navy, on the other hand, kept sending veterans back for repeated tours and although it sent a more experienced team into the war, it also wore out those pilots. As Wayne Thompson wrote, the Air Force's policy for personnel assignments kept sending inexperienced aircrews to Vietnam.[29]

As far as which formation to fly against MiGs, the four-ship fluid four or the two-ship loose deuce, the Air Force also did not resolve the dispute until after the war. During a 1967 mission that attempted to use loose deuce, the pilots found that the radio chatter clogged the radio frequency to such an extent that the mission commander could not manage the strike force.[30] Seventh Air Force began discussing serious doubts about the formation's desirability at the end of July 1972 when MiGs began attacking at very high speeds. Four-ship formations could not react quickly enough, but formations of two fighters could.[31] General Vogt added that although fluid four had been the Air Force way for years, "that is of minor importance if there is a better way to do it."[32] Preferences also depended on the mission:

those who flew MiGCAPs preferred finger-four while those escorting strike forces preferred loose deuce. The veterans of the 432nd Tactical Reconnaissance Wing (a wing composed mostly of fighter squadrons) concluded in August 1972 that the fluid four "has proven to be the most effective formation for maximum mutual support and lookout capability," up to three miles behind, for protecting the formation from surprise attacks and for a thorough radar search out ahead. Their wing tactics manual, however, had to devote more space and instruction to maintaining one's position in fluid four than in flights of two.[33] Major General Dewitt R. Searles commented that fighter wings agreed the element that was in the best position to attack ought to do so—at the expense of rigidly maintaining the formation. In the end, the trend favored the Navy's method, and the 432nd's wing commander, Colonel Scott G. Smith, found fluid four inadequate for meeting the threats over North Vietnam.[34] These wartime discussions led one to wonder how appropriate it was for two- and four-star generals to be involved in the details of fighter aircraft formations.

The North Vietnamese were anything but idle during the prolonged bombing halt. In the summer of 1969, they took delivery of forty-eight more interceptors, twenty-two of which were MiG-21s, although some analysts surmised that the aircraft may have been pulled from reserve storage. By fall 1969 the North Vietnamese possessed forty-seven MiG-17s, ten MiG-19s, and forty-eight MiG-21s. The PAVN forces then began to take more action against American aircraft. On January 28, 1970, a MiG-21 shot down a HH-3 helicopter near Mu Gia Pass when it tried to rescue a downed pilot. Two months later, a Navy F-4 chased away a MiG-21 that went after a reconnaissance aircraft. Subsequently the PAVN Air Force relocated all of the MiGs that had been at Vinh and Bai Thuong and all of the GCI radars that operated below nineteen degrees back north to the heart of North Vietnam as a temporary measure; they returned south the following year, and kept trying to shoot down O-2 and OV-10 FACs.[35] As PAVN forces extended their SAM deployments close to the DMZ and Mu Gia Pass in Laos, A-6As started flying orbits in order to take shots of opportunity at these sites. Their Rules of Engagement (ROEs) were liberal: A-6A aircrews were permitted to fire ARMs at sites as soon as they emitted. They did not have to wait for the site to track them, the final step before firing a missile.[36] When PAVN forces shot off three SAMs and a bunch of AAA fired at a reconnaissance aircraft on April 22, 1971, A-7 Corsairs retaliated and destroyed not only the antiaircraft artillery, but also a pair of MiG-21s on an airfield.[37]

As their 1972 invasion of South Vietnam approached, the North Vietnamese extended the reach of their air forces south once again. A MiG-21 fired at a B-52 over Laos on November 20, 1971, and another shot down an F-4 on December 18. A pair of MiG-21s arrived at Quan Lang Airfield in November, constituting a threat to B-52s bombing targets in Laos, and the year's end witnessed the downing of five F-4 Phantoms over Laos—three to MiG action. With this exception, however, the North Vietnamese did little more than harass flight operations over Laos. From December 1971 through January 1972, MiGs probed Laotian airspace fifty-seven times, but this resulted in only thirteen engagements, costing the North Vietnamese four MiGs while the Americans lost one F-4. During a reconnaissance mission over Dong Hoi Airfield in November 1971, flown to investigate the lone MiG-21 parked there, the aircraft's escorts returned fire against the flak batteries defending the airfield. The last such operation occurred while Congress was in recess, December 27–29, 1971. In response to the North Vietnamese challenge to airspace over southern Laos, Operation Proud Deep Alpha sent more than 200 Navy and Air Force aircraft against the North Vietnamese air defenses at the cost of three jets, but this operation did not bring the SAM threat in the panhandle to an end.[38]

Hanoi's aggressive actions raised concerns within the White House. The CJCS noted in January 1972 that the movement of MiGs and SAMs south improved the North Vietnamese abilities over Laos. Consequently, the Air Force halted the operations of low-speed aircraft there. Ambassador to Laos William H. Sullivan concluded that the North Vietnamese hoped to "cause some embarrassment to us in the air war," and the chairman of the JCS, Admiral Moorer, agreed: "The whole thing is designed to have a political effect."[39]

The North Vietnamese continued to exploit their superior radar and airspace picture over their heartland in early 1972, and General Abrams took the North Vietnamese air force seriously on the eve of the 1972 invasion. He sought to gain permission to send Iron Hand missions to destroy radars south of the 20th parallel because of the growing numbers of MiG-21s. He warned that PAVN GCI radar gave their MiG pilots *"vastly superior"* (italics in original) situational awareness for carrying out attacks on American aircraft. He also observed they had integrated their GCI radars with their SA-2 units. The former would give precise target data to the latter, enabling the missile site to launch and then turn on its guidance radar at the last second, almost eliminating electronic warnings to aircraft the guidance radar stalked.[40] Overall, the PAVN air force and the US Navy were well prepared for the upcoming campaign. The former had grown to eighty-four MiG-17s, thirty-three MiG-19s, and ninety-three MiG-21s. MiG-19s were the newest edition, having been added in 1969. Initially denigrated because it was an interim fighter between the MiG-17 and MiG-21, it actually had a thrust-to-weight ratio (.94:1) superior to the F-4's (.87:1) for greater acceleration, and lower wing loading—the weight each square foot of wing area an aircraft had to carry—of fifty-six pounds per square foot than the F-4 (eighty pounds), providing greater turning capabilities.[41] The US Air Force made some improvements in its equipment, but proved less prepared for battle because of its training deficiencies.

Chapter 8
Air Superiority Efforts during Linebacker

When the air campaign over the heart of North Vietnam reconvened in May 1972, the Air Force fielded better missiles and aircraft for the air superiority mission. The first AIM-7E-2 improved Sparrows had arrived in May 1968, too late for more than occasional use during the bombing halt years.[1] The F-4E arrived that same year. It had an internal gun, which was inherently more accurate than the gun pod F-4Ds had used. F-4s now employed the AIM-7E-2 "dogfight" Sparrow, and the AIM-9E Sidewinder, which possessed better guidance and turning capabilities than the AIM-9B. The dogfight Sparrow had modifications so that it could be launched at much shorter ranges: a half-mile from behind, one mile at medium aspect, and two miles against high aspect targets. It was also more maneuverable and performed better at high altitudes.[2] "Combat Tree" APX-80 air-to-air interrogators had been installed in three F-4Ds stationed at Udorn; they possessed the ability to interrogate MiG transponders, which meant they could confirm the hostile identity of aircraft too far away to be seen. Consequently, aviators could confidently use their AIM-7s at unfriendly targets without fear of hitting American planes by mistake. The Air Force could really emphasize the Sparrow as its primary air-to-air weapon. These specially equipped jets were in short supply until the third month of Linebacker when twenty flew in from the States. As one might expect, the North Vietnamese deduced Combat Tree's use and countered by turning off their transponders.[3] These changes were consistent with the Air Force's plan to emphasize technological improvements, but additional factors prevented their full exploitation.

Using BVR missiles requires verification of the target's identity and this remained an impediment to the full use of the F-4/AIM-7 combination, but a positive electronic identification of an aircraft as a MiG with Combat Tree was not enough of a confirmation to shoot at an aircraft; a second form of evidence confirming your radar had in fact locked on to a hostile aircraft was necessary. There were situations where visual identification was not always required. A controlling agency could designate an aircraft hostile and verify that there were no friendlies in an area. Controllers could also declare a track that took off from a North Vietnamese airfield as hostile, nullifying the need for a visual confirmation. Shipborne electronic IFF capabilities made it easier to sort out hostiles from friendlies. Better still, these aircraft and ships could pick up the IFF transmissions MiGs gave when their own ground control stations interrogated them. In this fashion, the Americans did not have to interrogate the MiGs' transponders but could track opposing aircraft positively without signaling that they were doing so. Exploiting the enemy's IFF in this way also made it possible to track MiGs flying at low altitudes that radar signals could not reach.[4]

The Americans made intelligent tradeoffs between preventing fratricide and giving the enemy more information on their fighters' whereabouts. American aircrews kept their own

IFF transponders turned on over North Vietnam so as to know where their own forces were, even though that made it easier for the enemy to track them. Fratricide nevertheless remained a threat through the end of Linebacker. On October 5, Lark 01 locked on to a MiG-21, fired, and the AIM-7 turned and started flying straight toward another F-4. Recognizing what was happening, the pilot turned off his radar so that the Sparrow would miss the American aircraft. The MiG-21 got away.[5]

When the North Vietnamese Army launched its mechanized invasion of South Vietnam on March 30, 1972, American and South Vietnamese air forces focused on defeating the invasion with close air support and air interdiction missions. Operation Freedom Train allowed strikes below the 20th parallel and several bombing missions above it during April. The South Vietnamese Army, its air force, and a large-scale effort by US Air Force and Navy air assets began slowing the invasion by May, and continued to fight the communists to a standstill, which required a few more weeks.[6] American forces relaxed their rules of engagement, and on April 16, 1972, the Navy received permission to use its Talos missiles against approaching enemy aircraft. The Navy and the Air Force were also cleared to attack North Vietnamese MiGs unless they were in the Chinese border buffer zone.[7] Hunting was good that day as fifteen MiGs took to the skies and F-4s shot down three, all of them with AIM-7s. Although upgraded, the missile was still not an automatic weapon. When the lead jet of Basco Flight locked on to a MiG-21 and shot off three Sparrows, the rocket motor of one did not even ignite. A second missed the MiG, but the third scored.[8]

Sparrows were still not highly reliable weapons. Imagine the frustration of the aircrew of Trigger 03 when on July 29 they "fired two AIM-7s in the boresight mode. The first missile did not guide and the second did not come off the aircraft." Pistol 01 had better luck when it spotted a MiG-21 in front of it less than a mile away. The Phantom crew "fired one AIM-7 with a full system lock on. The missile tracked smoothly and impacted the MiG, whose wing appeared to separate."[9] During July alone two remained attached to the aircraft after the pilot pulled the trigger, and the rocket motors of three did not fire after they launched.[10] The Navy was having problems with AIM-7s as well. Water was seeping through the "plugs and pins" resulting in short circuits—this on a missile that was used over the ocean and in clouds, where it is wet.

Not everything was the Sparrows' fault. Testing to see if missiles were properly tuned to its aircraft fire control system on the USS *America* found that "approximately 90 percent of all no-tunes were immediately traced to the aircraft," so the F-4s' fire control system received plenty of attention from the technicians on board; the system functioned better for the rest of the cruise. Navy Sidewinders also suffered from failures because ordnance men mishandled them.[11] The Air Force still struggled to figure out the problems with the AIM-7E-2 and asked a couple of weeks into Linebacker for the same kind of data it sought in 1966: details about the quality of the radar lock-on, and specifics "such as launch parameters, target speeds, ranges, angles off tail are required." Once again, a team of technicians at Udorn Air Base tried to figure out why the AIM-7 was unreliable.[12]

Seventh Air Force reacted to these recurring problems by establishing panels on the staff of each fighter wing with the task of investigating missile malfunctions. It brought in Air Force, Hughes, Raytheon, and Philco-Ford engineers to figure out the sources of the failures. One problem they found was that mechanical levers that armed Sparrow missiles as they were fired were worn out and failed. The immediate fixes included correcting "maintenance quality control deficiencies such as moisture intrusion sealing, tightening of boattails, cleaning and resealing aircraft fins, missile inspection between flights, missile flightline maintenance, checklist usage, changes in technical data, and missile handling."[13] One can again see that each missile was more akin to a compact aircraft requiring a level of meticulous maintenance and attention similar to a manned aircraft. They were, in fact, advanced machines and not because they were unnecessarily complex. These investigative panels found that the practice of carrying AIM-7s on F-4s used as bombers, just in case they needed them for self-defense, subjected more of the missiles to the stresses of repeated flights and thus lowered the overall reliability of the arsenal.[14] A writer from the 831st Air Division continued his own critique with an insightful treatise worth quoting in its entirety:

> Missiles are extremely more complex than our older air-to-air weapons (guns and cannon). Missile systems involve complex receipt and storage, missile assembly and operational aircraft fire control systems as well as aircrew knowledge and proficiency in the employment of air-to-air missiles. I believe the full spectrum of air-to-air missile operations must be exercised on a continuing basis to insure that we do have a fully reliable air-to-air weapons system. It is through use of the missile systems that we discover deficiencies and make modifications that improve equipment, procedures and techniques and in this manner contributes to an increased weapons capability. Initial SEA experience proved quite conclusively that the USAF was not prepared to employ the AIM-7 missile to its full capability because our personnel were not fully experienced in the receipt, assembly loading and firing the AIM-7.[15]

Perhaps the missiles should have been inspected and serviced before and after each and every flight, just like their host aircraft.

Sometimes the missiles just would not fire. During an October mission, Olds 01 saw its last AIM-7 hit the ground after firing it, and Olds 03 fired one at a MiG but the missile remained attached to the jet. One could still not count on Sparrows at the end of 1972, as when the pilot of "Togo 01" pulled the trigger four times, but the missiles remained locked in their recesses under the jet's fuselage.[16]

While engineers wrestled with these hardware problems, President Nixon decided that a new air campaign against North Vietnam was necessary to cripple its ability to overrun South Vietnam and to persuade it to negotiate a cease-fire, thus Operation Linebacker commenced on May 9.[17] The next day the North Vietnamese sent forty-one MiGs after American air forces and shot down two F-4s but lost eleven of their own interceptors. Kissinger's special actions group discussed this May 10 dogfight, commenting that it was probably the biggest "dogfight since World War II," but that honor goes to the Battle of April 12, 1951, during the Korean War. Either way, May was a deadly month; the Americans lost four F-4Ds, one F-4E, and an F-105G, but downed eleven MiG-17s, five MiG-19s, and eleven MiG-21s.[18] One Navy F-4J shot down three MiG-17s in one sortie but succumbed to a SAM while outrunning four other MiG-17s in pursuit.[19] Lieutenant Randy Cunningham and Lieutenant Junior Grade Willie Driscoll became aces as a result of this action. When asked if the Navy would bring Cunningham back to the States, Admiral Moorer replied, "No, we won't. We'll tell him to go out and get five more."[20]

Hanoi valued protecting the supply lines from China to the Ho Chi Minh Trail above all but found the return of the Americans formidable. Their jamming degraded the SA-2s, and the preventive firings of Shrikes and Standards persuaded more SAM sites to lie low. MiGs began to alter their tactics after their losses on May 10. At the beginning of the campaign they attacked in small, less disciplined flights but after suffering so many losses they returned to intercepts using a pair of MiG-21s with one trailing one to three miles behind. They also restricted MiGs to defending vital targets around Hanoi and Haiphong and used each kind of MiG at its optimum altitude. In spite of that, American jamming and the high numbers of fighters caused these adjustments to make no difference. Along with their return to hit-and-run attacks with pairs of MiGs, they reverted to firing masses of SA-2s to at least distract and disrupt the strike force cohesion, even though electronic countermeasures prevented many from guiding properly. American jamming, however, had no discernible effect on flak.[21]

In June, the North Vietnamese made more adjustments and began attacking the strike packages after they turned to fly back to bases in Thailand and on aircraft carriers. In this way they caught the American jets low on fuel and thus unable to engage in persistent air battles. MiGs concentrated against the more vulnerable jets—the chaff layers and the bomb carriers—because they had to fly straight and preferred to not maneuver until they had dispensed their load. On occasion MiG attacks forced fighter-bombers to either opt for a secondary target or jettison their bombs altogether. Consequently, the MiGs shot down seven F-4s while losing a MiG-19, two MiG-17s and two MiG-21s, but they did so after the strikers had dropped their bombs on their targets, making the MiG attacks tactically effective but operationally a failure. At times the North Vietnamese sent up to fifteen interceptors after the Americans and switched to high-speed attacks relying on R-13 missiles. As a result, the USAF devoted as many fighters to anti-MiG efforts as to actual bombing missions; altogether more than five support aircraft were aloft for every bomb carrier, such were the indirect effects of the PAVN air defense effort.[22]

The North Vietnamese demonstrated their capabilities to the full against a mission on July 6, 1972, when the Americans failed to jam their search radars and radio frequencies. They attacked the American jets almost all at once and coordinated their fighters and their missiles with precision, keeping the MiGs just beyond SAM engagement zones so missile operators could fire knowing that their own jets were at a safe distance. Ground control vectored the MiGs to approach from below, zoom up behind the Americans, fire, and escape at altitudes above the bombers. The Navy discovered MiGs liked to try to draw F-4s over a SAM site so as to fire missiles against them. A controller would send MiGs toward an American aircraft carrier, wait for the American GCI to dispatch F-4s after the encroaching aircraft, which then hightailed it back to Hanoi just above the wavetops with the intent of having a SAM site down a higher-flying American jet. Although the North Vietnamese tried this several times, Red Crown allowed patrolling F-4s to chase the MiGs only twice.[23] Here again this war resembled a siege, a series of efforts attempting to gain enough tactical successes that one might influence the war.

No North Vietnamese tactic was ideal. They gained an advantage, then lost it, and then found another way to achieve some success. Beginning in June, a highly polished bare-metal MiG-21 functioned as a decoy for a dull-gray camouflaged shooter trailing behind. After initially chasing after the shiny object and getting shot at by the second jet, the Americans figured out what was happening and learned to look for a second MiG when they saw a shiny one. Indeed, aircrews used their knowledge of enemy tactics to create advantages for themselves. When MiG-21s flew high speed (above Mach 1.2) stern attacks from 30,000 feet, American GCI shouted out warnings, and the escorting F-4s had time to turn and attack their adversary. When they switched to a low-altitude attack with a sudden climb at the end, Phantoms used their IFF to track the MiGs. By autumn, they orbited near Hanoi until their controller sent them after an American target. At maximum power, the MiGs would attack a vulnerable jet such as a chaff-laying F-4 and then climb away to a higher altitude. The F-4 chaff bombers, fully armed themselves, could turn on the attacking MiGs.[24]

Tacticians often sent MiG-21s in first and used smaller MiG-19s in trail as the shooters. When they figured out Phantom aircrews had gained the hardware to interrogate their transponders, they only squawked intermittently. Consequently, the F-4s could not fire their AIM-7s as aggressively, but enemy GCI had a harder time giving close control guidance to their own interceptors because of their decreased squawking. Typically, MiGs fled when F-4s turned toward them during the early stages of their intercept, but if MiGs were able to close on their quarry at high speed, the aircraft pressed home their attack. Ground controllers even tricked an American strike package on September 9 into thinking MiGs were airborne when they were not; the escorting fighters looked frantically for dangers that were not present.[25]

In September and October 1972, MiGs became less aggressive. On September 27, MiGs did not even take off to challenge one strike package. Their activity may have tapered off because of frustration, or because negotiations between the two countries were progressing and the North Vietnamese were husbanding their assets.[26] General Vogt believed Hanoi's reluctance to fly was because they had concluded that the US was taking advantage of "special intelligence." On October 6, however, two MiG-19s and four MiG-21s pestered a mission enough that only four out of twenty-six jets managed to drop their bombs.[27]

F-4 Phantom aircrews' understanding of the advantages and weaknesses of their own aircraft and those of the enemy matured by 1972. Consequently, they were able to exploit their aircraft's advantages and minimize those of the MiGs. During the first month of Linebacker air superiority units observed that like the polished aluminum MiGs, squawking MiG-21s often functioned as decoys for non-squawking MiG-19s and other MiG-21s following behind as shooters. MiG-21s also patrolled at lower altitudes and kept their transponders off while doing so to evade detection. They timed the launching of their fighters to have as much fuel remaining as possible for their attack run. Furthermore, "The enemy appears to know our on-station time, can detect our bingo fuel status, and is attacking our departing aircraft which are low on fuel." The 432nd TRW adapted by reminding its aircrews that once these attacks commenced, radar intercept officers were to function as visual lookouts: "We cannot over-emphasize how quickly some of these 'trailing' aircraft have closed to the six-o'clock position [dead astern]." Its pilots also exploited research that compared "energy maneuverability diagrams" of F-4s with MiGs. These charts revealed that the Phantom's best altitude for speed, maneuverability, and acceleration was 15,000 feet with at least 520 miles per hour of airspeed. Analysts warned pilots against devoting too much time in pursuit of a kill using their gun; doing so gave other MiGs the time to maneuver for their own kill shot from behind. Instead, maximize the Phantom's advantages, such as the Sparrow missile.[28]

The manner in which the leadership of the 432nd TRW described their adversaries demonstrates that US aviators took the MiGs seriously but were not intimidated by the enemy. Americans realized that their aircraft should always stay fast against all three kinds of MiGs, avoid turning fights in the horizontal plane, use their power in the vertical plane, and if flying a Combat Tree F-4, identify the enemy electronically and shoot him head-on with a Sparrow; from that aspect the MiGs could not shoot back. They cautioned that it was very easy to lose whatever advantage one had over a MiG-17 because of its maneuverability at lower speeds; the F-4 had speed and sustained turning advantages over the MiG-21 below 15,000 feet—the closer to the ground the better; and the fast and maneuverable MiG-19 was "a MOST formidable foe [all caps in original]."[29] Indeed, as far as the Americans could tell, a MiG-19 could outclimb and outturn the MiG-21.[30] Case in point, a MiG-19 got behind Eagle 03 and 04 on October 6, 1972, and stayed on their tail in spite of their best efforts. When they "performed a last ditch maneuver" they finished with a high speed dive with the MiG still latched onto them. The MiG pilot fired the whole time, lost track of the ground, and "crashed into the karst still firing his cannon."[31] Six days later intelligence sources conveyed that a MiG-21 met the same end trying to escape F-4s by diving into low-lying clouds. Late that summer, North Vietnam began flying the latest MiG-21 variant, the MiG-21MF, which carried four missiles instead of two, a pair of guns, and more fuel for more persistence in combat.[32] These sober understandings of capabilities and limitations contributed to greater effectiveness in this mission in 1972. MiGs remained dangerous into the fall, even though they attacked less frequently, as when a MiG-21 zoomed up from the deck and popped off a missile that shot down an F-4 just days before Linebacker ended.[33]

The PAVN further adjusted their SAM employment, better interpreting what they saw on their radar scopes even when the Americans exploited a full range of electronic countermeasures. Analysts realized the enemy had learned how to see an aircraft on their radar screen even in the midst of advance jamming if tracking an aircraft in close proximity from the side. They also seemed to have integrated their air defenses more completely, as when MiG-21s shot down an F-105G right after a SAM site fired six SA-2s right in front of it. That happened to Icebag 04: the missiles distracted the pilots and they never saw the attacking MiG. The opposing air force was a persistent and adaptive enemy, but too few trained pilots and skilled maintainers placed a ceiling on the number of interceptors the PAVN could send into battle.[34]

Some of the Americans' problems existed prior to Linebacker. The January 1972 Combat Sage report observed that aircrews were not fully readying their Sparrows for use, neglecting, for instance, electrical preflight tests. Aircrews who had been given written exams on these tests got "most" of their answers wrong.[35] Seventh Air Force concluded that Phantom aircrews were just not that skilled in placing their F-4s in the proper position relative to enemy aircraft in order to be in their missiles' launch window. They had not received enough training in operating an aircraft of the F-4's complexity within the chaos of aerial combat. The pilots were also too willing to fire when the target was at the edge of the missile's envelope, thus lowering the likelihood of a kill. In August 1972, for instance, Chevy Flight fired Sparrows at a MiG that had seen it and made a hard defensive turn, but the target was outside of the missiles' parameters and missed.[36] Aircrews often fired more than one missile to improve their kill chances in those situations that made the missiles' performance appear worse than its actual capabilities.[37] It became the practice in the 432nd TRW for an aircrew to fire all of its Sparrows at once because "most kills occurred from the third missile that was launched." Its aircrews employed Sidewinders the same way.[38]

Choices the Air Force made prior to Linebacker produced these deficiencies. F-4 aircrews possessed almost no practice in firing missiles or dissimilar air combat tactics. Tactical Air Command could have participated in Air Defense Command's dissimilar air combat tactics training program.[39] As Linebacker came to an end, tactics specialists concluded that aircrews had to know their weapons' firing parameters and understand the entire F-4 weapons system with complete thoroughness in order to be able to use them correctly during the stresses of combat. One possible solution involved a set rules of thumb. Aircrews, however, may have found remembering and using them in the heat of a MiG encounter, which were rare enough, one more challenge. The long-term solution was integrating a computer into the fire control system that would make those missile parameter computations instantaneously—but that technology would have to wait until the next generation of aircraft.[40]

In the meantime, analysts and F-4 aircrews in general grew in their understanding of the role of the radar operator in the F-4's back seat: the weapons system officer. In the past, aircraft commanders (the pilot in the front seat) had denigrated these officers as superfluous, but they were essential as lookouts for MiGs and for managing intercepts, and their ability to assess threats and issue warnings saved numerous lives.[41] Referred to variously as the "guy in back" or "GIB," the weapons system officer (WSO) was a true asset for the mission. Although pilots had a radar scope of their own in front of them, they were plenty busy flying the F-4 and looking out for other aircraft. The presence of a second pilot meant the WSO could devote his attention to scanning for enemy fighters with his radar, an analog system unadvanced enough to require the full attention of a second person who could make manual adjustments and tunings and interpret what was on the radar scope. Indeed, when an F-4 crew shot down a MiG with a radar-guided Sparrow, the WSO's bailiwick, the GIB might deserve more credit for the kill than the pilot. Until 1972, in fact, both aircrews only got credit for half a kill after destroying a MiG. General John D. Ryan changed this rule in 1972, retroactively, so that both the pilot and the weapons system officer received a full credit for each shoot-down.[42]

Infrared guided missiles had been improved but not perfected since Rolling Thunder. The Air Force developed an upgraded Sidewinder before Rolling Thunder came to an end. Introduced on November 30, 1968, the AIM-9E was an improvement over the AIM-9B in several respects. Its seeker could look for the target in a piece of sky wider than just right in front of the launch aircraft, it could focus on the target with more precision, follow it more easily, and at low altitude it could achieve 11-G turns when pursuing its target.[43] Infrared sources other than an aircraft's engine could still distract it, as happened when one "skipped off a rice paddy" instead of hitting a MiG-21 when fired at very low altitude in July 1972.[44] An F-4 got the first AIM-9E kill in May and the last in October.[45] It ought to have been a marked improvement over the AIM-9B, but again, missile effectiveness not only required the mechanical reliability of the missile itself, it also had to be fired within tracking and turn capabilities of the weapon, which pilots did not always do in the heat of battle. Ideally one would fire an AIM-9E before the target maneuvered, but the Echo version was supposed to be a weapon effective in a hard-turning fight. Navy efforts fared no better; Navy guidance also recommended firing its new AIM-9G before the target aircraft was aware of the danger. Neither the AIM-9G nor the AIM-9E proved "a satisfactory dogfight missile."[46] The AIM-9E achieved only six kills for seventy-one launch attempts.[47] In any event, the Air Force was not happy with the Echo version even though it was an improvement over the original Sidewinder and as of mid-May 1972, the chief of staff urged that every effort be made to bring AIM-9Js into combat before their projected in-service date of July 1972.[48]

With the AIM-9J the Air Force hoped to have a stern-aspect missile able to track and kill hard maneuvering fighters. Its seeker could track at sixteen degrees per second, compared to twelve degrees in the Echo. The biggest difference was in the amount of G-forces it could pull: twenty-two at sea level, and thirteen at 50,000 feet—twice as much as the Echo. The initial tests seemed promising, when in early 1969 twelve out of thirteen launched and guided when fired, and on average passed within fourteen feet of the target—close enough given its proximity fuse. Renewed tests in 1971 took a step backward; some missiles missed the target drone by more than a hundred feet, and the test missile did not give a "locked-on" audio tone any better than the earlier versions. The "Juliet" finally flew in combat on August 2, 1972, and achieved its first kill, a MiG-19, on September 9. The Juliet was no early version Sidewinder; Captains John A. Madden and Charles B. DeBellevue fired the missile at the rear quarter of the MiG about fifty degrees off centerline whilst in a 5-G turn.

The AIM-9J still did not function well at very low altitudes. Of the four missiles Chevy 1 fired at a MiG-21 on September 16, two flew into the ground.[49] The aircrew had, however, over-taxed the missiles, firing them from more than a mile behind at 750 miles per hour, which was right at the edge of the missile's range. With a follow-on shot the wingman achieved a kill. The last AIM-9J kill took place on October 15 against a MiG-21; only one of three fired hit home.[50] During the first Linebacker II mission Barracuda Flight thought one of the two AIM-9Js fired struck a MiG-21, but the missile did not detonate.[51] Its main shortcoming was that it was a stern-aspect missile; its seeker head was not designed to track on heat signatures other than those from an aircraft's hot exhaust, but that made it no more limited than all the other infrared guided missiles in existence at that time.[52] Aircrews were nevertheless pleased with the Juliet: "When fired within established missile parameters, the AIM-9J appeared to have a good Pk."[53]

The Navy achieved no breakthrough with its more advanced marks of the Sidewinder, the AIM-9G and H. By 1972, Navy F-4 squadrons relied mostly on the AIM-9G Sidewinder because the environmental conditions onboard their ships were even worse than those on land for the storage of the Sparrow. From April 1 through May 31, 1972, Navy F-4s fired only four AIM-7E-2s. After thirty-one AIM-9Gs had been fired in combat, it took about two missiles to achieve a kill, as compared to five for the earlier Sidewinder.[54] A pair of F-4Js, for example, pounced on two MiG-21s that were still climbing away from Kep Airfield on May 10. Silverkite 211 shot down one MiG with two AIM-9Gs. Both Silverkite 210 and 211 fired four between them at the second MiG, but all missed, although they exploded quite close to the MiG. They watched it fly away as a third MiG showed up, whereupon their low fuel state forced them to break off the engagement.[55] The Air Force recognized the superiority of the AIM-9G, but like the "D" from 1966–1967, that missile required a different launch rail and the ability to use a bottle of nitrogen the seeker head required for cooling. Air Force engineers investigated making the modifications necessary to use them, but efforts went no further. Both the AIM-9J and the Navy's brand-new AIM-9H were inherently more reliable machines because transistors had replaced all the vacuum tubes used in earlier models.[56]

These low figures, however, are misleading. Not infrequently, F-4 crews fired missiles head-on at attacking MiGs without being in the correct firing boundaries, deliberately, and with good reason. The escorts' purpose was to prevent strike aircraft from being shot down, and that did not necessarily require them to shoot down MiGs, only to disrupt their attacks or chase them away. Pilots fired missiles in front of attacking MiGs that had achieved a threatening firing position, often before they had time to gain a radar lock-on. In doing so, the escorts usually persuaded the MiG pilot to abandon his attack and focus on saving himself.[57] An aircrew might also fire a missile in order to nudge a MiG into a favorable turn into its missile tracking window, as Buick 01 did on August 28, firing off a pair of Sparrows: "The MiG turned after the first two missiles passed him, and Buick 01 fired his remaining two AIM-7s. The last missile impacted the MiG." That might have been an inefficient use of the missiles, but it was effective.[58] Fewer Sidewinder kills also resulted from a change in MiG-21 tactics that presented fewer opportunities for using the Sidewinder and the gun, but more occasions for the Sparrow. Because the MiGs flew high speed passes, they flew past the F-4s and beyond the Sidewinder's range, but not the Sparrow's. Because some F-4Ds could interrogate MiG transponders to get an accurate electronic identification, these MiGs were now more often subject to attack from long range with an AIM-7.[59]

Overall, when aircrews fired missiles within their designed parameters, and the missiles functioned, they were reasonably effective. That may explain why the Navy had an improved success rate with its AIM-9G. F-4Bs and F-4Js fired fifty of them from January through November 1972 and achieved kills 42 percent of the time. In addition, the fact that the Navy emphasized air combat maneuvering in its fighter training gave its pilots the ability to fly the F-4 into the Sidewinder's launch cone.[60]

Naval aviators found that the recent training upgrades from their Fighter Weapons School were worthwhile in combat. On May 18, aircrews from the USS *Midway* downed two MiG-19s. Lieutenant James M. Bell, the radar intercept officer, commented, "It was really amazing. It went just the way the fighter pilots and RIOs [radar intercept officers] are taught back at the Replacement Air Group Squadron 121 and also the Navy Fighter Weapon School. It was as though they read the book and knew the moves they were supposed to make, and they fell right into place just exactly as they are supposed to."[61]

Aircrews found better success with their missiles during Linebacker than during Rolling Thunder, but missile technology reliability remained below par. Leaders in Washington, DC, were aware of the comparative successes of these missiles.[62] General Vogt conceded that the AIM-7 concept was "still a pretty complex weapons system for the pilot to employ with a lot of built-in limitations."[63] During Linebacker the Navy fired seven of eighteen Sparrows outside of the missile's parameters. AIM-7s from Air Force F-4s destroyed thirty MiGs during all of 1972. They brought down six with the AIM-9E and four with the AIM-9J. Gunfire accounted for six. Four more MiGs smacked the ground trying to escape.[64] Through October 15, Air Force fighters had fired 299 Sparrows and Sidewinders, forty-five of which struck their targets, and downed thirty-five MiGs. Of the 224 missiles that were "noneffective," seventy-seven were because of missile malfunctions, sixty-three were because of aircrew mistakes, aircraft malfunctions caused forty more failures, and forty-four were non-effective for "unknown" reasons, although this latter category includes firings at altitudes very close to the ground where heat and radar reflections distracted both kinds of missiles.[65]

The AIM-7E-2 and the AIM-9J were better than earlier marks, but were still inefficient munitions. Juliets achieved a kill rate per missile fired of 13 percent, while the AIM-7E-2 and AIM-9E achieved rates of 5 and 8 percent, respectively.[66] Infuriating experiences with even the newest Sparrows continued through September: "As Finch 01 turned right the second MiG ended up in front of him at approximately 3,000 feet. He acquired a full-system radar lock-on on the MiG and attempted to fire two AIM-7s, both of which *did not launch*" [italics added]. Finch 03's AIM-7s fired but refused to guide. Three Sidewinders fared no better, so the pilot plastered the MiG-21's canopy and left wing with cannon fire, achieving a kill.[67] Altogether Air Force and Navy aircrews fired 235 Sparrows that shot down twenty-eight MiGs, about twelve MiGs shot down for each 100 times the pilot pulled the trigger. Aircrews fired 147 Sidewinders and downed thirty-two MiGs, a ratio of 22 shot down per 100 fired. Some Air Force squadrons were still flailing away with the AIM-4D Falcon; of nine fired, three either failed to launch or guide and none hit a MiG.[68] In sum, the fighter aircrews of the Air Force and Navy maintained air superiority over North Vietnam, so their missiles in the end functioned in an effective manner, but the inefficiency, unpredictable reliability, and wastage remained infuriating.

Chapter 9

Technology, Organization, and Management of the Air Superiority Mission

From the policy maker's perspective, the air superiority mission needs to proceed with enough success that he can focus on strategic and grand strategic issues: close presidential attention on air superiority operations means the effort is not up to par. For their part, general officers should execute that mission on the executive's behalf and solve shortcomings before they become strategically significant. With that in mind the PACAF commander, General Lucius D. Clay Jr., became very directive during the third week of May 1972 about how Seventh Air Force was going to improve its performance against MiGs. First, he instructed that the F-4E was going to be the primary air-to-air fighter, not the F-4D. Squadrons were going to specialize on a single mission. Two of the squadrons needed to focus on MiG killing, and specially selected aircrews, heavy on Fighter Weapons School graduates, were going to staff them. Flight discipline had broken down, he observed, and that was going to end. Lone jets had willingly been sent where MiGs were active and had attempted to engage them by themselves. Wingmen had become shooters instead of focusing on covering the flight leader, and flights had not been able to stay together during engagements. Tactics were going to change; flights were going to maneuver from the beginning for a gun kill because that would take them through the firing parameters for Sparrows and Sidewinders, the primary weapons. That sequence could then more seamlessly climax with a gun kill if the missiles failed. Careful missile maintenance and testing were to receive more attention. The air picture over North Vietnam must improve. For starters, the Navy's PIRAZ ship with its Red Crown weapons director would become the main control system for Air Force aircraft over North Vietnam. Clay concluded his directive, "In my opinion the building of a professional air-to-air team is going to have to be the result of an across-the-board effort to put properly trained crews into our most capable aircraft then guide them to the enemy in such a way that they can initiate combat from an advantageous position. Once this has been achieved the payoff will come from properly maintained missile and armament systems that perform as designed."[1]

One problem with Clay's order was that it sidelined an aircraft that held a unique capability: the F-4D's ability to electronically confirm the hostile identity of radar contact. General Vogt explained to Clay that neither the F-4E nor the F-4D were the preeminent Phantoms and both belonged in the air superiority mission. The F-4D had the Combat Tree system, while the F-4E had an internal gun. The D was better for high altitude fights, the E, lower altitude, where close-in gun fights were more likely.[2] General Vogt was slow to comply, and Clay became more assertive in June: "I note again that F-4Ds are predominately being utilized in the air-to-air role with MiG Cap escort, etc. The F-4E is the air-to-air combat airplane and prime effort should be placed on that aircraft in the air-to-air role. Let's get with it!"[3] Aircrews found that radio discipline was critical to mission success, and there was something to Clay's accusations that flight discipline was not where it needed to be. When an F-4 escorting some chaff bombers was shot down, so many aircrews had been talking on one frequency that "Gunsmoke 04" could not hear the warnings that MiGs were behind it and about to fire.[4]

Missile failure rates particularly bothered Air Force Chief of Staff General John D. Ryan. Although he tried to accelerate the delivery of AIM-9Js and AIM-7E-2s, conscientious maintenance of the missiles, the radar system, and proper mounting of the missiles onto F-4s was key to ensuring that the whole missile-radar-aircrew system worked. Clay sent a reminder of all this two weeks later and having listened to General Vogt made an exception to the earlier requirement: use Combat Tree and F-4Es as Vogt thought best. That was wise. Once Combat Tree equipment came into use, F-4 flight lead backseaters devoted much of their attention to finding and interrogating radar contacts and that proved worthwhile. Combat Tree F-4s functioned as flight leads as often as possible because they could confirm every radar contact.[5] As of September, the 432nd TRW reported that, "Approximately 17 of our last 20 MiG kills were made possible either directly or indirectly by the use of Combat Tree equipped aircraft."[6]

As June came to a close, General Ryan asked General Momyer, now the commander of TAC, if he had any recommendations on increasing the number of MiG kills.[7] Ryan pressed Clay and Vogt yet again for further improvements in air superiority effectiveness, noting the recent shoot down of five F-4Es in the past two days. The kill ratio was approaching the worst in American history, "which I find unacceptable," Ryan stated. The Air Force was losing an F-4 for every MiG shot down. Ryan told Clay to take a closer look at enemy and American tactics and reminded him that airfield attack was permissible.[8] Cratering their runways with LGBs after the MiGs were airborne could deny them a place to land given their low endurance and range; the MiGs might run out of fuel and crash. One might ask why the Americans chose not to target their GCI system. On July 4, 1972, American pilots did just that, placing a laser-guided bomb dead center into a control bunker at Bac Mai, but it did not seem to make any difference. Furthermore, targeting intelligence was not yet good enough to pinpoint any of the North Vietnamese control centers, so they did not receive a concerted amount of attention.[9]

Major General Carlos M. Talbott, the director of operations for the Air Staff, found Seventh AF "in utter chaos" when he investigated it in person in June.[10] The following month Brigadier General Frederick C. Blesse led an investigative team to the Seventh AF that forwarded a list of tactical and operational level recommendations for generating success in the air superiority mission. The suggestions seemed pretty simple: just change course headings and altitudes during the approach to the target, which should spoil the MiGs' intercept geometry, and use the most qualified crews in the specialized squadrons.[11]

Some flights forgot that their ultimate purpose was to protect strike forces, not rack up tallies of MiG kills. Consequently, the Air Force reemphasized training by bringing in weapons and tactics instructors from the Fighter Weapons School, and by modifying equipment with Operation Rivet Haste: F-4Es with leading edge slats for greater maneuverability, a video telescope, and the ability to fire the Maverick missile.[12] The Seventh Air Force director of operations also responded harshly to rumors that escort flights turned back to the target zone after the rest of the strike package headed home in order to bag more MiGs. He demanded an immediate end to that behavior.[13] Major General James D. Hughes, the deputy commander of 7/13 Air Force, all but accused MiGCAPs of putting the aircraft they were defending in peril in pursuit of MiG kills. He believed their overuse of the KC-135 that had been set aside for emergencies only was an indicator that they were pursuing kills at the expense of their mission of protecting strike aircraft. He also frowned upon the practice of F-4s trying to "decoy MiGs into a position from which they can be engaged." Worse: "Due to their losses to MiGs, the strike and chaff forces have not developed confidence in the ability of the MiGCAP and escort flights to provide proper protection against MiG attack. This has led to a 'do-it-yourself' attitude toward MiG defense on the part of strike/chaff aircrews. Flight leads have lately considered it necessary to jettison ordnance in order to perform defensive maneuvers." The Corona Harvest history reminded readers that fighters flew to protect other aircraft, not to rack up their personal scores.[14]

Methods for defeating MiGs evolved. Ideally F-4s would hit the MiGs shortly after the planes were airborne and before they had time to climb and position themselves for supersonic attacks. Chaff-carrying F-4s flew inbound profiles like MiGCAP F-4s, turned for home over the target, and then dispensed their chaff. This deception convinced the MiGs to delay taking off just long enough so they could not intercept the chaff layers in time. Finally, F-4s escorting chaff layers flew a weaving pattern behind them that made it easier to detect attacking MiGs. In this manner they kept their speed up without outrunning the jets they were escorting. Given some advanced warning, F-4s carrying chaff were not sitting ducks. A simple turn or two could frustrate the MiGs' intercept geometry, and trailing F-4s could provide cover for the leading chaff droppers. Using chaff was cumbersome but very effective at providing excess radar returns that disrupted the radar picture North Vietnamese GCI needed for managing their air defenses. The number of MiGs and SAMs the North Vietnamese sent after chaff-carrying F-4s was testament to their effectiveness. Chaff increased the enemy missile's miss distance, and only a single aircraft was lost to a SAM while in a chaff corridor.[15]

Ongoing evaluations comprised another solution. A successful air superiority campaign requires constant adjustments and Seventh AF began having meetings almost daily for self-evaluation in the summer of 1972. The "Linebacker Critiques/Linebacker Conferences" were General Ryan's idea. He wanted leaders from all the different flying units to meet in person and critique themselves and each other with the purpose of learning and improving operations.[16] General Vogt began holding these meetings in the latter half of July 1972.[17] The Linebacker conferences focused on the management of operations and the tactical effectiveness of counterair weapons and efforts; very little addressed the effectiveness of the bombing missions. The one for Linebacker Alpha V and Tango IV, for example, only mentioned that "Ubon strike package (Cedar and Elm) destroyed their primary targets."[18]

At the beginning of Linebacker, the MiGs shot down a substantial number of escorting F-4s because it was so hard to see one approaching at 1,000 miles per hour and because pilots received no warnings in time.[19] Perhaps the alteration that most improved effectiveness in the anti-MiG effort during the second half of Linebacker was not changes in missiles, tactics, equipment, or training but the development of the ability to build an understandable and usable picture of who was who—both friendly and hostile—where they were, what they were doing, which control agency they were talking to, and which control agency they were going to be under next.

The necessary breakthrough took place through the "Southeast Asia Tactical Data System Interface," a network of airspace control agencies linked by computer that evolved over time until it crossed a threshold of effectiveness in the summer of 1972. The formerly top secret (now declassified) 1972 history of Pacific Command was so cryptic about the network that the authors of the history wrote as if the reader was expected to already know about it, or if not, don't ask. Admiral Noel Gayler, CINCPAC, observed that "it had been an 'extremely effective' system for coordinating employment of Air Force and Navy assets, by permitting all participants to enhance warning and control through access to all source information from a variety of radar and signal intelligence sensors." Its main task was to warn aircraft about trolling MiGs, active SAM sites, and to steer wandering aircraft away from the Chinese border.[20] General Momyer chimed in from Tactical Air Command Headquarters and observed that the North Vietnamese possessed an excellent radar picture of their airspace while the Americans had "very limited radar coverage in most areas in route packs five and six and no coverage at all below 9000 ft, north and west of Hanoi," thus the MiGs could often attack unseen. An additional suggestion he made, along with bombing airfields, was greater use of "special intelligence resources." He realized the operational use of those resources could provide aircrews with useful information on what the enemy was doing in real time.[21] That adjustment would make the skies over North Vietnam safer for American aircraft. In the end, that sensitive intelligence was not that cosmic or surprising but was the equivalent of what is today called data mining.

General Vogt concluded the greatest danger American aircraft faced in enemy airspace was inadequate threat warning.[22] He received tips that both encouraged that conclusion and pointed him toward the solution. Analysts realized a variety of intelligence gathering methods during Rolling Thunder had acquired enough data day to day to construct a usable picture of what was taking place over North Vietnam: that data, however, was not collected and collated in a way that was usable in "real time." By the time they could have transmitted it to pilots in the combat zone, the threat information was so fleeting that it would have been too old to have been of any use. The solutions lay in technology and organization, and General Vogt pressed for improvements in these areas in July 1972.

The solution was to set up an operations center at Nakhon Phanom Air Base, Thailand, because the special intelligence operation was located there. This nexus collected data inputs and wrote them on a plotting board. A weapons controller then collated that information and coordinated with Red Crown and the controller on board the EC-121 College Eye aircraft, making particular use of enemy aircraft tracks they plotted using their ability to interrogate MiGs' IFF transponders. He then transmitted this information to fighter aircrews. The overall goal was to use "intelligence data in real time to reduce the MiG threat to Linebacker forces."[23] Vogt was trying to mimic the Navy's success of coalescing air intelligence from several sources in one place, and the resulting weapons control center at Nakhon Phanom began operations at the end of July. It was code named Teaball. Its major purpose "was preventing the shoot-down of F-4s."[24]

Teaball was a patched-together weapons control center that integrated every kind of available intelligence on the locations and intentions of all aircraft over North Vietnam and then used that information to assist American air operations. It blended data from three ground radar sites, an EC-121, a C-130 used to manage air-to-ground sorties, and actual data from over North Vietnam, ships, eavesdropping aircraft, and "special intelligence" or "SI." The information was specific and timely enough that the controller could advise a pilot when MiGs targeted him.[25] How could he do that? What was all this information and where did it come from?

The answer is that North Vietnamese radar sites sent their data to the air defense center in Hanoi via radio using unencrypted Morse code. A U-2 intercepted these radio telegraph communications and retransmitted them to linguists in Nakhon Phanom, who in turn translated the messages and wrote the data onto a chart. Teaball weapons controllers, therefore, got to use the same radar picture for North Vietnamese airspace as the North Vietnamese did by eavesdropping on their radar network. National Security Agency linguists also listened to and translated the intercepted communications between PAVN ground controllers and their pilots. In sum, Teaball exploited the enemy radar picture, the transmissions between enemy pilots and their controllers, and the commands their GCI center was giving to its interceptors to construct and plot a comprehensive picture of what was happening over North Vietnam. The Teaball controller would then use this information to vector F-4 Phantoms toward MiGs so the pilots would not be caught by surprise. As William L. Kirk, former commander of Teaball, said in 1996, "We were reading their mail, yes, and we were reading their mail in real time. In fact there were times when our plotting board was more current than the senior controller in Hanoi."[26] On September 19, 1972, for example, Teaball informed American forces when MiGs took off from Phuc Yen.[27]

Efforts like this went back thirty years. The Royal Air Force and the US Army Air Forces had some success in 1943–1944 intercepting Luftwaffe radio transmissions and using them to vector their own fighters toward the German interceptors. The United States had done almost the same thing during the Korean War when it set up a radio intercept site on the island of Paengnyong-do. Communications intelligence personnel listened to the orders sent to MiG-15 pilots and quickly relayed that information to American aircrews. More recently in 1970, the Israeli Defense Forces established a unit of Russian-speaking eavesdroppers to monitor Soviet MiG-21 pilots flying out of Egypt.[28]

Seventh Air Force had been working on a multi-source solution to building an accurate picture of what was taking place over North Vietnam since the start of Rolling Thunder. The National Security Agency initiated a program in 1965 called Project Hammock in which analysts eavesdropped on enemy GCI transmissions, translated them, and built an air picture by inserting these as radar tracks into a centralized radar presentation. Hammock information was passed on to other fighter controller agencies, but that required so much time that the process was just too slow to be tactically useful to airborne jets, who needed information in seconds. Annoyingly, Hammock would not forward tracks that were beyond the limits of American radars' ranges so that the North Vietnamese would not realize the extent of American monitoring.[29]

In 1966, Pacific Air Forces and the Pacific Fleet added procedures for the PIRAZ ship to exchange data with EC-121s and the Control and Reporting Center just outside of Da Nang on unidentified and hostile aircraft.[30] Seventh Air Force refined its efforts in 1967 with "Combat Lightning," combining data from ground radars, EC-121s, the Navy Tactical Data System, the Marine Tactical Data System, "Iron Horse" communications intelligence data, IFF data from North Vietnamese transponders, secure voice radio, and KC-135 radio relay aircraft. Preventing encroachment into Chinese airspace and enhancing combat operations was the purpose of all this. Furthermore, the supervising weapons director was able to monitor the air picture over North Vietnam, and a weapons director at Monkey Mountain South Vietnam could guide aircraft over North Vietnam. This control center received "data from other sources, (Annex A)," but the document does not elaborate the nature of those sources.[31] When the Air Force computerized this system in fall 1967, it became known as Seek Dawn. The coupling of Seek Dawn with radar data from Navy ships then resulted in the Southeast Asia Tactical Air Data System, a multi-source visual picture of what was taking place over North Vietnam.[32] Iron Horse was a National Security Agency computer that provided additional intelligence without revealing their sources or methods.[33]

This facility sounded quite a bit like Teaball in that it blended data from ground and airborne radars with communications eavesdropping into a comprehensive picture, but it was not yet. The system's first priority was threat warning for friendly aircraft flying over North Vietnam, but it was too slow to carry out that task well. Missions ran the gamut from guiding and controlling American aircraft in that airspace, committing fighters against airborne and surface-to-air enemy assets, to guiding search-and-rescue helicopters. One could also insert radar plots from sources not electronically linked into the computer. The control center was not co-located with the radar center because of the information the National Security Agency provided. Renamed once again as the North Vietnam Operations Control Center, it had the same mission, and there were hopes of using it in real time. What became Teaball may have been on the verge of implementation in the latter half of 1968, but the bombing halt resulted in the four-year delay in full implementation of this system.[34]

According to William Kirk, "Most of the elements of the system had been operating in Southeast Asia for some time prior to the development of the Teaball concept. It had not been possible, however, to transmit available operational intelligence, on a real-time or near-real-time basis, to those who needed it most—Linebacker aircrews facing the North Vietnamese MiG threat."[35] During the first week of July 1972, General Vogt complained that there just had to be a way to share this information with the aircrews under threat, so he pressed for the intelligence to be used and not just collected. Admiral Gayler gave Teaball permission to make use of this special intelligence in July.[36] Gayler's action tipped the scales.

July was a break-even month in terms of air-to-air kill ratios and explains why Gayler decided to risk the operational use of NSA SI: the North Vietnamese shot down five F-4Es and an F-4J while losing six MiG-21s. Since the beginning of June, the Air Force maintained a 2:3 loss ratio; for every two MiGs its fighters shot down, it lost three aircraft. Some argue that the introduction of Teaball in August turned the tables against the MiGs. As a consequence, F-4s achieved a 4:1 kill advantage by September.[37] Teaball improved the statistical kill ratio. From April to July, the number of American aircraft lost to MiGs per engagement each month was .33, .23, .28, and .33. The loss rate fell starting in August to .11, .08 in September, and .11 in October.[38] The utilization of Teaball improved the kill ratio to 3.8:1 in favor of the Americans.[39]

Gayler's and Vogt's implementation of Teaball was not the acting out of a technological fetish. Here was a case where air-to-air combat could directly influence strategy, diplomacy, and the achievement of policy goals. The South Vietnamese and the United States ground the North Vietnamese invasion to a halt and were trying to negotiate a settlement, but newspaper stories about the North Vietnamese Air Force defeating America's best fighter pilots—even achieving a marked advantage—would have placed Henry Kissinger in a weaker negotiating position. While the details of shooting down enemy air defense fighters is not usually a preoccupation of policy makers, shooting down MiGs was an intermediate step to the objective of persuading the Hanoi government to cease and desist its assault against South Vietnam. Air superiority missions became more significant in July and August 1972 because Henry Kissinger needed military success, not failure, to gain leverage during his negotiations with Le Duc Tho.

Teaball first supported a combat mission on July 29; the Teaball weapons director advised strike aircraft about possible and confirmed attacks, bearing and range to the threats, and additional helpful information.[40] Later that day SI confirmed that a MiG had been shot down that day, but it also underreported the number of MiGs aloft. Vogt believed because the Teaball controller was now committing the F-4s after the MiGs with such dispatch that it puzzled North Vietnamese GCI and injected a bit of hesitation into their management of their air defenses.[41]

According to Seventh AF, Teaball was an effective air battle management system. Once it came online, USAF fighters shot down nineteen MiGs while losing five. Previously, the AF had shot down twenty-four, losing eighteen of their own. General Vogt credited Teaball as the decisive game changer, but a definitive postwar analysis was more reserved in its conclusions.[42] The writers of Project Red Baron III hinted that while Teaball provided useful warnings to aircrews, a number of shortcomings that resulted from its patchwork nature made it less effective in supporting the offensive use of F-4s over North Vietnam. First, there were not enough people with the right training and clearances to fully man it for all missions, especially at night. Second, its reliance on radio relay aircraft provided more opportunities for system failure. Third, all the data was handled manually, which impeded its ability to provide real-time information. There were vulnerabilities to jamming, and Teaball was reliant on the NSA for its special intelligence. Moreover, the nature of the SI prevented the aircrews from understanding the trustworthiness and value of what the Teaball controller told them over the radio.[43]

Occasionally, Teaball's components failed individually or in concert.[44] The network relied on a KC-135 with a radio re-transmitter as a bridge from Teaball to the fighters over North Vietnam, but it did not always work.[45] Instructions were hard to understand, intermittent, and often confusing. For example, when the Teaball controller painted a picture of multiple hostile tracks, he was not always able to parse out specific, individual targets.[46] On September 23, one of the transmitters in the network sent out a noisy signal that was the functional equivalent of communications jamming and technicians were not sure what was happening.[47] Four days later, it transmitted, but it could not receive. The EC-121 airborne radar aircraft was not immune from trouble. Its own radios and interrogators malfunctioned. Then on October 29, all the components of Teaball worked fine—six days after Linebacker ended.[48]

Some of the fixes were easy: better antennae at Nakhon Phanom for transmitting to the relay aircraft, a triangular orbit for the radio relay that expanded the area where it could be heard, and the use of better headsets by the Teaball controllers themselves. Aircrews who had engaged MiGs rated Teaball third behind Disco and Red Crown in terms of usefulness, but the Corona Harvest history stated accurately that "it must be remembered that Teaball was primarily designed to prevent losses to MiGs, not to increase MiG kills."[49]

Teaball seemed to work as designed. MiGs did not always fly when strike packages showed up in September, which suggests that the North Vietnamese assumed they would have to take losses and decided against launching interceptors. In October, the Americans shot down seven MiGs for a loss of four of their own. During the October 15 mission F-4s downed at least three MiG-21s, maybe a fourth, and none of the aircraft in their strike package was shot down. Furthermore, the wings who participated in the missions praised the professionalism of the control agencies. Disco's radar and interrogator broke down, but Teaball provided pertinent and timely information, and Red Crown received its usual superlatives.[50] On the last day of September the Teaball/Red Crown/F-4 team functioned well. Prior to the mission, the Teaball liaison encouraged pilots to exploit their warnings. When the controller issued a radio call that MiGs were attacking, that was, he explained, "real time and means that the MiGs have decided to attack that particular element. The MiGs are anywhere from fifteen miles out to missile firing parameters." Afterward, the F-4 crews out of Udorn exclaimed that the guidance they received "was the best control ever from Red Crown and Teaball," despite enemy countermeasures. North Vietnamese controllers seemed to know that something was up because they jammed Teaball's radio frequency whenever Teaball issued a MiG warning.[51] In aggregate, from August 1 to October 6, MiGs threatened twenty-two out of forty-seven Linebacker missions, all the components of the Teaball network functioned on thirty-one missions, and MiGs shot down only one aircraft when Teaball functioned properly. Those statistics definitively show that Teaball was operationally effective. MiGs shot down four American jets flying missions when Teaball was down—usually due to communication problems. Consequently, only pairs and quartets of MiGs pursued strike packages in the latter months of Linebacker.[52]

At the same time, the North Vietnamese intercepted and exploited American radio transmissions. They sent their MiGs after jets having mechanical problems and targeted flights that were disorganized. Furthermore, they camouflaged their MiG-19s and equipped them with the same R-13 missiles their MiG-21s used. The North Vietnamese displayed proficient tactical control of their interceptors, using three separate pairs to hound a reconnaissance flight from behind, from in front, and from the side forcing him to flee.[53]

Teaball indirectly supported American diplomacy with the North Vietnamese by preventing a situation from arising in which MiGs were shooting down a prohibitive number of American planes. Such an occurrence would have given the opposition another card to play during the negotiations. Challenges with the system remained until the settlement was reached in 1973. Sometimes fighters saw MiGs of which Teaball was unaware. Another difficulty was distributing all the pertinent data to those who needed it most. For example, when MiGs attacked a strike force on July 29, enemy GCI vectored them against the chaff portion of the package so quickly that it appeared Red Crown had not received the SI-derived information quickly enough to react.[54]

A mid-summer evaluation offered a couple of forthright conclusions: (1) the best way to reduce losses to MiGs is an advanced warning of their attack profile; (2) all of the special intelligence the NSA obtains should be forwarded to aircrews as quickly as possible; (3) tactics should emphasize defeating MiG attacks before they reach firing range; (4) tactics should focus on shooting down MiGs soon after they take off because once they're going 1,300 miles per hour, they have a 500 miles per hour speed advantage and by the time pilots see them it is too late to react; and (5) at that speed defending fighters had no more than ten seconds to react before the MiGs were firing their missiles at vulnerable aircraft.[55]

Teaball's tactical utility was imperfect, like the rest of the command-and-control system. When eight F-4Es clashed with two MiG-21s on August 15, the aircrews never received any threat warnings, even though all the agencies knew about the MiGs.[56] Chaff and strike jets were glad to receive warnings from Teaball on a September 28 mission.[57] A flight of F-4s at one point received a thorough picture of what some MiGs were doing forty-two miles away—plenty of distance to set up an intercept. But then Red Crown lost contact with the MiGs, and the F-4s pressed on without any updates on where the enemy was or what they were doing. By the time Red Crown found the MiGs again, they were just eight miles from the F-4s, which had become targets themselves. No sooner had the leader seen the MiGs than his weapons system officer saw their wingman "explode." This incident further demonstrated the cobbled-together nature of what in reality was a semi-integrated system. At other times the warning and control system functioned like clockwork, as when Red Crown updated Pistol Flight throughout their attack run on a MiG-21 they shot down with a Sparrow missile.[58] Days later, however, Red Crown assured Teaball that his picture of events was comprehensive, so Teaball assumed Red Crown possessed the same threat information and kept silent when threat warnings should have been issued. When the strike force lost radio contact with Red Crown, Teaball did not know to step in and advise the flight of the dangers nearby. Fortunately, the MiGs only passed by and never attacked.[59]

"Finicky" was a polite word for the radio relay network. Teaball had to wait a second after all the other transmissions on its frequency ended before it transmitted, so the Teaball representative asked for "strict radio discipline," allowing the agency space to transmit.[60] Radio relay remained a weak link. During an August 28 engagement Disco vectored the

F-4s of Motion Flight, but because of the communication problems was not able to relay the MiGs' altitude information from Teaball. In fact, the F-4s merged with the MiGs on Disco's radar picture twice; they were at such different altitudes that Motion did not see the MiGs. The radio relay aircraft had to relocate away from the strike package because of bad weather, and after almost two hours of trying, Teaball could not establish the radio network connection.[61] Because of the radio relay problems there was a discussion of relegating Teaball to nothing but general threat warning and handing the fighter control responsibility back to Red Crown.[62] The Air Force finally started to bring some reliability to Teaball's communications network by flying the radio relay aircraft higher at 34,000 feet, establishing backup contingencies, and modifying antennae, which resulted in a great improvement in the transmissions' clarity.[63] On day ten of Linebacker II, however, the radio relay once again broke, sidelining Teaball for that mission. The Air Force lost a jet to a MiG on December 27, and General Vogt suspected that radio relay malfunctions may have played a role.[64]

When all the pieces functioned, Teaball provided strike packages some extraordinarily useful information on enemy MiG activity. On August 28, Buick Flight, three F-4Es and one F-4D, gained enough awareness from Disco, Red Crown, and Teaball that it detected MiGs on their radars sixty miles away. When Teaball gave Olds Flight a MiG warning on September 6, the crew was able to turn and find them with Combat Tree. Three more encounters on September 9 saw Teaball convey where to look for hostiles and the Combat Tree system on the F-4D confirmed it.[65] Teaball sent F-4s after MiGs that were just taking off from their base, robbing the MiGs of any chance to set up an intercept profile. The Teaball controller even provided individualized headings to Chevy Flight, vectoring it head-on against two MiG-21s; Chevy fired Sparrows, but before the missiles reached the target, the radar lock-on failed.[66]

The best information Teaball shared was the data it received from the NSA translators. During the September 11 mission, the Teaball controller told the strike force when it was under attack, and because the NSA was monitoring the transmissions from the MiG to its own GCI controller in real time, he informed the chaff flight *when the MiGs had visual contact on them*. Teaball controllers were also able to explain the latest MiG tactics to attendees of the Linebacker conferences; at this point in the campaign the MiGs preferred to target chaff F-4s.[67] When Captain Jeffrey Feinstein got his fifth kill on October 13, Vogt exclaimed that when Teaball, Red Crown, and the radio relay aircraft all functioned, "the system is unbeatable."[68]

During Linebacker's closing days the management of the air battles matured and gathered praise regarding the timeliness and relevance of Teaball's information.[69] On September 2 the EC-121 provided vectors toward attacking MiG-21s whereupon F-4s gained contact on the attackers at fifty miles using their onboard Combat Tree IFF. Although they were not able to shoot down the MiGs with the Sparrow shot, according to Teaball their attack run against the MiGs probably prevented the MiGs from reaching the chaff carriers.[70] On September 6, Teaball notified Olds Flight that MiGs were airborne, and the F-4s detected them at once using Combat Tree. They pursued the MiG-21s at their maximum speed but ran short of fuel before getting close enough for a shot. Because they charged the MiGs so soon, the F-4s' attack persuaded the MiGs to turn tail—attack defeated, strike package protected.[71] Teaball was not perfect, but even on days with intermittent communications fighters often received their threat warnings.[72]

On September 15, Teaball provided threat information and Red Crown used that to vector the fighters. The following day Disco relayed Teaball's information to Chevy Flight, and then took over control of the fighters when Red Crown could no longer detect the MiGs with its radar.[73] A September 17 Linebacker conference observed the radio network between Disco, Red Crown, and Teaball continued to not only function most of the time, but also sent prompt warnings.[74] The following month Teaball provided MiG warnings in time for Oriole Flight to turn, see, and attack the MiGs, who fled into a low cloud bank. The commander of the chaff bombers believed Teaball may have prevented one of his aircraft from being shot down.[75]

What this illustrated for effectiveness in the air superiority mission is that you *have to* be able to differentiate hostile from friendly aircraft; "probable" identities are too uncertain in a situation where jets shoot long-range missiles. There are too many risks to one's own aircraft to be without this kind of comprehensive picture, too many dangers from the enemy to not make full use of one's BVR missiles, and this kind of information is too useful to not exploit. These examples also teach that there was more to the air superiority mission than planes, pilots, and radars, and that masses of data that might appear to be "nice to know" are actually critical for successful military operations in the missile age. By fall 1972, Teaball's picture and the ability to interrogate MiGs' IFF with Combat Tree gave the escorting F-4s enough lead time to point themselves toward the enemy fighters and persuade many to simply turn away. The sum of the parts meant the F-4s could place themselves in such an advantageous position that they would defeat the MiGs' plan before they began their run against the American aircraft. Escorting fighters could persuade the enemy that an attack was pointless—don't even try.[76]

Teaball provided the first threat data for three more encounters in October, totaling just six times it had provided the initial threat data. Radar, especially from guided missile cruisers, was still crucial, providing the first warning on forty-one encounters. These cruisers did not see everything, however. In thirty-three other incidents, the first-time aircrews became aware of attacking MiGs was when they saw them. Wing commanders concluded by September 1972 that flights should not be left on their own to figure out attack profiles. They needed specific vectors from Red Crown or Teaball.[77]

This system, however, could not solve the shortcomings in aircrew preparation that persisted. General Vogt concluded the Air Force simply must confront its training inadequacies. "Our aircrews," he wrote in July 1972, "are inadequately trained for air combat." Out of six encounters examined, aircrews received solid MiG warnings, but the flight leaders failed to use them effectively. Furthermore, the general added, these aircrews required more training in air combat "so that they can fly the aircraft more instinctively and free them to concentrate on the tactical situation."[78] As an example, fighter aircrews received permission to practice aerial combat when Linebacker missions were scrubbed beginning in August—further indicating how little air combat maneuvering training they had received.[79]

In the rest of Vogt's twelve-page message, Brigadier General John J. Burns functioned as a squadron tactics officer—a captain's or major's billet—even though he was a staff officer at Air Force Headquarters. Burns' recommendations belonged in the "To Do" folders of flights and squadrons, and although they included issues at the operational level of war, most were tactical, such as his recommendation for utilizing voice tape recorders to a greater degree so that pilots could reconstruct what took place and draw and derive practical lessons. In fact, most of the message traffic from Seventh AF provides blow-by-blow tactical accounts (that are excruciating even for enthusiastic historians), ascends to the operational level of war occasionally, and rarely relates to strategic and policy level issues. Their level of detail is great for researchers reproducing the air war, but this tactical focus may point to the root of a challenge the Air Force faced for several decades after the war: the difficulty of focusing on strategic-level issues and the relationship between air power and national policy goals.

On the one hand, the chief of staff of the Air Force insisted in June that the kill ratio had to improve, so perhaps that order from a four-star general required the one-star to temporarily dive down to the tactical level of war in order to fix the problem.[80] On the other hand, General Ryan asked at the July 1972 meeting, "What are we doing about simplifying the call signs for Linebacker missions?"[81] Congress had not confirmed him as chief of staff of the Air Force to sort out aircraft call signs.

Where were the gun kills during Linebacker? The F-4E became the Air Force's predominant fighter and the Navy still used F-8s.[82] The decline in gun kills was due to a couple of factors. First, F-105s and F-8s achieved most of the gun kills through 1968: twenty-two and one, respectively. F-105s were far less prominent over North Vietnam in 1972, and F-8s had difficulties in persuading MiGs to fight.[83] An F-4E gained a gun kill on October 15 when Buick 03 shot a MiG-21.[84] The biggest change was that the services learned how to use their F-4s within an offensive counterair system and how to maneuver their F-4s into their missiles' firing parameters. Thus, the gun was a specialized secondary weapon for use when a fighter was too close to the enemy to use its missiles. If all went to plan, they would shoot down the MiGs before that happened. MiG-21s relied on supersonic firing passes to such an extent that they remained within gun range for only a second before entering the heart of the AIM-7's envelope.[85]

In addition to these technological factors surrounding the air superiority effort, an additional issue probably cost American lives and was certainly not managed as sensibly as it could have been: the overall theater-level management of the air superiority effort. There was none. The Air Force and Navy each carried out their missions separately, coordinating only the ECM effort and air superiority engagements. Vogt observed that during the summer 1972 air battles, for instance, the Air Force and Navy could have "saturated enemy MiG and SAM defense," but the route package system prevented that. "U.S. attacks were fragmented," one Seventh Air Force historian wrote, "and, consequently, more readily contended with by enemy defenses."[86]

During Linebacker's final three weeks, the North Vietnamese flew aggressively enough on October 6 to persuade three flights out of five to jettison their bombs. An F-4 downed a MiG-19, but another ran out of fuel over Laos. MiGs still tried to lure American aircraft over SAM sites.[87] Special intelligence verified the downing of two more MiGs on October 15, but the MiGs forced two flights to abort their missions against a fuel storage area in favor of an alternate target, and other MiGs forced a flight to dump its bombs in order to evade an attack. General Vogt exclaimed once again that Red Crown and Teaball had positioned escorting fighters in the right place quickly enough "to prevent damage to the strike force.... All our aircraft returned safely to base," but not all of the bombers completed their missions.[88]

Chapter 10

Air Superiority during Linebacker II

In December 1972, aircrews realized that a combination of measures was necessary to maintain sufficient control of the skies for the bombers to complete their missions. Defeating AAA was easy enough—fly over it—and darkness nullified most of the MiGs. Only the MiG-21s possessed an onboard radar that would have enabled them to zero in on a B-52 after receiving guidance from the GCI stations. If a MiG-17 or -19 closed to gun range on the tail of a BUF, the MiG would find itself within range of the B-52's radar-guided tail gun. Here the tail gunner would have the advantage over a MiG that was not violently maneuvering, thus presenting an easy target. Indeed, tail gunners claimed four MiG-21 kills, although only two were confirmed. A small number of MiG-21s flew against the B-52s each night but accomplished little.[1] There was speculation that the North Vietnamese used MiG-21s to determine the B-52s' altitude so SA-2 warhead fuses could be set for that same altitude. A couple of MiG-21s would level off at the bomber's altitude and then fly away whereupon the SAM sites fired accurate salvos of missiles. Ideally for the B-52s, the MiG would roll out behind one, right where F-4s trailing five miles behind could shoot it down with an AIM-7.[2]

There were few fighter-vs-fighter engagements during Linebacker II and altogether MiGs flew only twenty-seven intercepts in December.[3] F-4s still had not fully adapted to the MiG-21 high speed attacks. Close escort of bombers kept the escorts too slow to react, and B-52s' electronic countermeasures (ECM) jammed the F-4s' radars. B-52s were very difficult to see at night, so staying out of their way and maintaining radar contact with them proved taxing. A better method would have been a more free-ranging patrol at a higher speed in different altitude blocks.[4] As often as not, MiGs did not challenge daytime tactical fighter missions during the Christmas bombings, which seemed surprising given some of the opportunities, like when a LORAN F-4 led a group of A-7D Corsairs against a transformer in Hanoi, a Marine F-4 MiGCAP was airborne, but no MiGs came up after the relatively slow Corsairs.[5]

Teaball and Red Crown remained active during Linebacker II. When three MiG-21s went after a daytime strike package on December 22, information from Teaball and vectors from Red Crown positioned Buick Flight for an AIM-7 attack from below. A Sparrow reduced one of the MiGs to metal fragments, but the other two escaped. Teaball reassured the second wave of B-52s that night that no MiGs were airborne, and the third wave that only one MiG had taken off.[6] Two days later, a MiG-21 got close enough to Pontiac Flight to fire off two Atolls at the flight leader; fortunately their rocket motors gave out and exploded about a quarter mile behind them. Only one crewman, the backseater in Pontiac 02, even caught a "fleeting glimpse" of the MiG.[7] Relentless jamming signals that seemed to originate from Hainan Island, China, hampered Teaball on Day 4.[8] One evaluation wrote that

Teaball's only challenge during Linebacker II was manning shortages, but that was not the case. Radio relay remained unreliable, possibly due to EB-66 interference.[9]

Fighters functioned well enough, but still experienced difficulties. List Flight, a pair of Navy F-4Js, had just topped off from their tanker when Red Crown sent it after a MiG-21 on December 28. With full tanks they were able to close on the MiG. When it began a turn toward the fighters, the F-4s closed and downed it with multiple AIM-7s. Not surprisingly, B-52 crews openly expressed confidence in their fighter escorts after that.[10] Phantoms nevertheless continued to suffer problems with their fire control systems. For example, a quartet of F-4s, "Raccoon Flight," was sent after a MiG, given permission to shoot, achieved a good radar lock-on for its missiles, and just before it got into missile range the radar momentarily lost contact. The jet locked on again but could not maintain it, whereupon the MiG escaped by diving away.[11] Twelve upgraded Rivet Haste F-4Es were then flying out of Udorn, but they did not get the opportunity to use their air-to-air transponders against MiGs. No kills were in the offing, but one F-4E avoided shooting down another American aircraft on December 29 by using the electronic telescope mounted on the wing to verify its identity.[12]

Aircraft losses were not decisive for either side during the 1972 campaigns, although Hanoi lost nearly half of their MiGs: seventy-three out of 170. Those were numbers the Soviet Union could replace and given the communists' advantages on the ground and the reality of the American exit from the war, those losses were not going to wreck Hanoi's bargaining power with Kissinger. Their air defenses shot down a total of 116 American aircraft during 1972, about one for every 700 sorties. Surface-to-air missiles accounted for sixty-two of them, with MiGs and flak downing twenty-eight and twenty-six, respectively. The primary effect of their air defenses continued to be the draining off of bomb-carrying aircraft for defensive escort and support sorties: planners set aside 60 percent of all sorties to fly against air defenses, totaling more than 30,000.[13] In May 1972, for example, American air forces flew 5,678 sorties set aside for Linebacker objectives, and 2,899 of those were for dealing with the North Vietnamese missile and radar sites—not interdiction and strategic targets the destruction of which would more directly affect the course of the war. Combat air patrols and escorts formed the bulk of these sorties, with 2,229 set aside to deal with MiGs. Jamming aircraft flew seventy-four sorties, flak suppression required 211, reconnaissance flights got 201 fighter escorts, and FACs comprised 184 sorties. This does not include tanker sorties or reconnaissance flights. The kill ratio was favorable for the US in that American fighters shot down eight MiGs for every three American aircraft lost. Given the number of MiG sorties, approximately 54,000, there were not that many encounters; only 149 engagements took place during the 1972 campaigns.[14] The Center for Naval Analyses believed that these figures "probably underestimated . . . the effectiveness of the NVN air defense system."[15] The main impediment to achieving long-term air supremacy was the willingness of the Soviet Union to provide replacement aircraft to North Vietnam.

Conclusions

The United States always possessed air superiority over North Vietnam, although not with the ease American air leaders anticipated or thought appropriate given the power differentials between the two air forces. While worried about North Vietnamese air defenses, leaders understood the US possessed "relatively complete air superiority." The fact that the US could fly slower, more vulnerable aircraft such as helicopters, EC-121s, and tankers next to North Vietnamese airspace confirmed their assertion.[16] Since, barring weather aborts, their strike packages always got through to their targets, the Air Force and Navy maintained air superiority throughout the war. Significant numbers of attacking aircraft dumped their bombs when they came under attack, however, and escorting fighters were shot down, but the fighters largely succeeded in protecting the Thunderchiefs, Skyhawks, and Phantoms under their care.[17]

One consequence air superiority produced was that Americans could bomb as long as they wished, a strategically important result. The war was subsequently a test of wills between North Vietnamese endurance and American political will to continue the bombing. The North Vietnamese and the National Liberation Front had their ways of imposing their strategy on the United States and South Vietnam, as well: resisting in North Vietnam and fighting in South Vietnam, Laos, and Cambodia.

American airmen were slow to collate, analyze, and disseminate their experiences with air-to-air combat in ways that led to changes in tactics and training. When Tactical Air Command finally began to discuss changes in 1971, it was with an eye toward fighting Warsaw Pact air forces. TAC did not exploit the advent of air combat training between differing aircraft types that had begun in Air Defense Command during Rolling Thunder. The Navy did not make that same mistake and started flying against F-106s in 1971, in addition to initiating its Top Gun training program in 1969.[18] The Linebacker conferences were likewise years overdue. They were necessary and beneficial because they brought individuals together, each of whom was responsible for executing one portion of an operation, be it fighters, chaff bombers, or tankers. Tactics and operations at the very least would have improved had these kinds of conferences taken place from 1965. Perhaps their interrogative nature would have driven the discussions more toward making connections between operations and policy. Be that as it may, the air staff back in Washington, DC, evaluated the messages that came out of each conference and shared their findings with units in US Air Forces Europe (USAFE) and Tactical Air Command (TAC) as lessons learned.[19]

Looking at what the Air Force emphasized and what it ignored, one can see that by the early 1970s its military culture focused first on technological improvements; second on operational support, management, and coordination; and then on tactical skill. The tactical air forces were caught so unawares in 1965 by the requirements of and changes in air warfare the long air siege of North Vietnam exposed that their necessary responses rightly focused first on tactical and operational proficiency. Air Force decisions set the institution down a path that was good and bad at the same time.

The air forces learned how to sustain, coordinate, and fly big complex operations during Vietnam, and they improved weapons technology with their pursuit of the Combat Tree and Rivet Haste F-4s, the F-14, F-15, F-16, F-18, and A-10. The Air Force finally began to institutionalize tactics training in 1973, and to practice the execution of strike package missions with Operation Coronet Organ, the precursor to Operation Red Flag.[20] In the years following Vietnam the individual pilots, flights, and squadrons became very proficient. With those exercises and the advent of the Navy and Air Force Aggressor squadrons in 1969 and 1973, respectively, the American air forces developed superb tactical fighter expertise. Policy makers made the decisions on policy and strategy in the 1970s and 1980s; the air forces had enough on their plates trying to implement them. Emphasizing tactical and operational proficiency was necessary and appropriate for the standoff against the Warsaw Pact.

All these tactical-level issues adversely affected the relationship between the air war and the national policy goals in subtle ways. Although the North Vietnamese were not able to stop the bombing of their country, and although the Americans never lost air superiority, the losses the PAVN inflicted were substantial enough to drive the Americans into diverting more and more of their attention to the air superiority mission, which mostly resides at the operational and tactical levels of war. In turn, Americans paid less attention to the air interdiction campaign and its relationship to coercive and diplomatic efforts and the achievement of the strategic goals of the American and South Vietnamese presidents. With their persistence the North Vietnamese airmen lured American four-star generals away from dealing with strategic issues and toward solving tactical problems, such as the Air Force chief of staff asking the commander of TAC if he "had any ideas on what we might do to get more MiGs."[21] That was not a question on air strategy. Tactics for shooting down enemy air defense fighters is not usually a policy goal; shooting down MiGs was only an intermediate step to the objective of persuading the Hanoi government to terminate its war against South Vietnam.

The Air Force came to understand that the key to air superiority lay not merely in superior aircraft, missiles, or tactics, but more particularly in specified training in the air-to-air mission, maintenance of missiles and aircraft radars, an operations center that can integrate airspace information (probably inside an airplane), a multifaceted approach to gaining control of airspace, better radar warning equipment for fighters, and constant self-evaluation of how all this is playing out.[22] In the opinion of the commander of the 366th TFW, Colonel George W. Rutter, what air missions really needed was not a new fighter, it needed an advanced airborne radar warning, control, and radio communication system that could see aircraft at all altitudes. He believed that the "Availability of an AWACS-like aircraft could have reduced losses to MiGs by as much as 75 percent based on my observations of the results achieved by Teaball warnings."[23] Improvements after the war would need to focus on several variables, not on a single panacea solution. For the American tactical air forces, the next steps included not only new technology like the E-3 AWACS, new fighters and better missiles, but also better training, smarter tactics, and eventually a military intellectualism that ranged seamlessly from the tactical level of war to the policy and grand strategy issues presidents and alliances had to solve.

An examination of air superiority efforts during Vietnam drives one from aircraft comparisons and narratives of air combat engagements to questions about why the air war was waged in the manner it was. Geopolitical realities, concerns, and policy objectives placed limitations on the air superiority mission that may have been inevitable. The upwelling of frustration and rage that erupted during the war reveals that policy makers and military officers spoke past each other. The Johnson administration, in particular, never adequately explained the geopolitical sources of the restrictions on air power, and the airmen and aviators never adequately questioned their own doctrinal assumptions and dogma regarding the right way of conducting an air superiority campaign. Therefore, this study illustrates the necessity of communication between senior leaders executing grand strategy and the airmen fighting the war. Understanding the connections between air superiority operations and the war's policy goals must be made clear, not assumed or inferred. The United States may find itself again in a situation where it has to achieve air superiority in ways that run counter to commonsense doctrine because the geopolitical facts and objectives compel it. It will then be up to the air-minded officers of the United States military to bring operational plans to the president that will be successful in the constrained, complex world in which the president operates, whether or not those constraints conform to their personal preferences about how air superiority is to be achieved.

PART 2

AIR SUPPORT AND AIR POWER EFFECTIVENESS

Chapter 11

Photo Reconnaissance: Significance for Strategy and Policy

Visual reconnaissance was the first wartime mission airplanes undertook. During the 1911 war in Libya, Captain Carlo Piazza of the Italian Army used a Bleriot monoplane to ascertain the status of Turkish soldiers near the town of Azizia. A year later the French established an aerial reconnaissance squadron, a decision that produced a capability that affected the outcome of a war. On September 1, 1914, an observer and pilot found the German First Army moving in a direction that exposed it to a counterattack by the French Army along the Marne River. With that intelligence the French turned the invading army away from its capital. Gaining an awareness of enemy activity and providing targeting information became the primary operations for aircraft during the First World War; protecting these early reconnaissance planes was the reason the battle for air superiority took place.[1] Aerial reconnaissance gained a vital role in warfare before the war even ended. In spite of the airplane's revolutionary effects, aerial reconnaissance entered a period of stagnation after the Great War.[2]

Given the centrality of long-range bombing to the Allied effort during the Second World War, target photography rose again to importance. Even officers with access to decoded German radio messages considered photo reconnaissance to be the most important source of intelligence. Specialized aircraft did not fly these missions. Instead, the fastest fighter aircraft, such as P-38s and Spitfires, relied on speed for survival as they flew through the most dangerous airspace, although a B-29 Superfortress undertook what Major General Haywood Hansell considered the single most important aerial reconnaissance mission of the war—photographing Tokyo and Nagoya.[3]

The need for photo reconnaissance during the Korean War was crucial during its opening weeks since UN forces hardly knew what was taking place. Initially, converted WWII fighters and bombers flew missions alongside new RF-80 and RB-45 jets. Flights uncovered the Chinese troops massing for their invasion of North Korea, but senior commanders ignored that evidence. Afterward, reconnaissance aircraft carried out the usual missions of photographing potential targets and the aftermath of air strikes.[4] Tactical reconnaissance remained important enough that less than ten years after procuring 202 RF-101 Voodoos, the Air Force started fielding the first of 500 RF-4 Phantoms in 1962.[5]

The goal for missions like aerial reconnaissance is producing photographic intelligence the military and the president need for making sound national defense decisions. The United States' requirement for targeting intelligence on the Soviet Union, for example, led to the production and use of the U-2 aircraft in 1956. Improving missile and interceptor capabilities encouraged the pursuit of the more advanced SR-71 Blackbird and especially the Corona satellite reconnaissance programs. While technical issues can preoccupy the story surrounding this mission, those details do not really show up at the policy level of war unless they produce extraordinary opportunities or challenges, such as warnings of offensive threats like the ones from Cuba that President John F. Kennedy dealt with in October 1962.

Photo reconnaissance became integral to the Vietnam War, but was not necessarily part of the president's daily supervision of the war.[6] The air campaign could not have taken place without aerial reconnaissance because air strike planners needed photographs of enemy territory before they could assign targets. Reconnaissance missions found targets and thus enabled most kinds of bombing operations, the exceptions being those dependent on immediate targeting information, and taking advantage of fleeting opportunities. Those missions included armed attack aircraft seeking targets—armed reconnaissance—and flights against moving targets on the Ho Chi Minh Trail network in which aircrews had to attack trucks as soon as they found them. While photo reconnaissance could show whether or not bombs struck their targets and could confirm the extent of damage, this activity could not analyze how the North Vietnamese leadership reacted. That involved intelligence analyses collated with assumptions that the Johnson and Nixon administrations held on how bombing would influence Hanoi. US leaders thought the air campaign would persuade Hanoi to give up its goal of annexing South Vietnam, but the only way they could be certain of the air campaign's effects was when the government in Hanoi let the outside world know its internal conclusions about the extent of those effects—an uncommon occurrence. Along with electronic eavesdropping, aerial reconnaissance was the only form of intelligence the United States could extract from North Vietnam.[7]

The material that follows is a topical examination of photo reconnaissance over Indochina. This mission faced mostly technological challenges as opposed to geopolitical or strategic obstacles. Its demands pressed the technology of the 1960s to a limit that left combat troops depending on machinery that could not be responsive and timely enough for their immediate needs. Photo reconnaissance was effective as long as those who used it could wait for photographs to be developed, printed, analyzed, and distributed. At best that required hours for completion.

What Photo Reconnaissance Provided

Since geopolitical realities and national objectives required minimizing collateral damage and civilian casualties, mission planners needed precise photographs of their target zones. To take away aerial reconnaissance meant the air forces would be bombing blind. Military Assistance Command, Vietnam (MACV) recognized that it was necessary for prosecuting Operation Rolling Thunder, and so did the White House.[8] Photo reconnaissance not only documented what was happening, it also provided necessary targeting intelligence, as Secretary Robert McNamara explained to President Lyndon Johnson when increasing flights over Laos in 1964.[9] Another one of its elemental uses was photographing the results of bombing missions, known as bomb damage assessment, or "BDA."

Normally the national leadership interacted with reconnaissance only in an indirect manner—through targeting plans, assessments, and accuracy reports—but occasionally reconnaissance photographs became of immediate use to the president, as when photos made it possible for President Richard Nixon to reassure the Chinese that bombs had landed only on the North Vietnamese side of the border.[10]

The first priority for reconnaissance flights was obtaining strategic warning of aggression from China or North Vietnam, then conditions in the areas surrounding South

Vietnam came next, followed by photography of Viet Cong and PAVN activities. General William Westmoreland's command needed photographs that would aid the protection of American forces if the security situation in South Vietnam became unhinged, as in the case of civil unrest or actions against its leadership. It also needed progressively more reconnaissance flights as the war escalated in 1965. Since that required more aircraft, permission from Thailand to bring in more was necessary, which necessitated the assistance of the Department of State.[11] From the beginning Admiral Ulysses S. Grant Sharp assigned photo reconnaissance missions a top priority to support the planning and assessment of bombing missions.[12] Aerial reconnaissance was also necessary for assessing bombing effectiveness since on-site inspections were never a possibility in North Vietnam and were often quite difficult elsewhere in Indochina.

Reconnaissance flights commenced over Laos and South Vietnam well before the American bombing campaign against North Vietnam began. The first flights took place on October 21, 1961, in an effort to build a more accurate picture of the communist insurgency in Laos, and also to signal American concern about the state of affairs in that country.[13] The decision to coerce Hanoi made the comprehensive photography of North Vietnam a natural next step in March 1965. Haiphong and the area around Hanoi were initially excluded so as to not be overly provocative. U-2s carried out the preliminary reconnaissance and President Johnson tracked that information personally.[14] Every command level used reconnaissance flights, but many were examples of strategic reconnaissance since they informed policy makers' decisions. Targeting and post-strike reconnaissance remained a part of planning and executing the air war until the settlement of 1973. By then, Air Force reconnaissance flights alone numbered more than 650,000.[15]

Tactical reconnaissance jets commenced regular missions over Laos on May 19, 1964, but without, initially, the blessing of Souvanna Phouma, the premier of Laos, who wondered if they could be the first step in dragging Laos into a wider war.[16] After examining the resultant photographs and considering additional issues, he extended permission to the United States to begin combat operations against his communist enemies in Laos. Consequently, the United States initiated air strikes against enemy forces in northern Laos, Operation Barrel Roll, on December 14, 1964.[17]

Combined with the skills of a photo interpreter, photographs provided intelligence that visual observation could not. A pilot in a speeding jet could not always see and identify a target, but a photo interpreter studying a photograph often could. Aircrews could not see hidden truck parks, but analysts spotted them when given a chance to thoroughly examine photographs.[18] Thus in 1964 photo intelligence from high-altitude U-2s and low-altitude RF-101C Voodoos confirmed the North Vietnamese systematic infiltration of men and supplies through Laos into South Vietnam.[19]

Air Force and Navy aircraft began completing photo reconnaissance flights over North Vietnam in March 1965 in order to provide photos for refining the targeting plan and also to obtain post-strike photographs once the bombing began.[20] The JCS initially limited all the services to ten sorties per week. A huge number of missions took place during the succeeding years. Reconnaissance was necessary to verify what one suspected the enemy was doing; therefore MACV ordered a comprehensive pattern of photo reconnaissance flights over North Vietnam during the May 1965 bombing halt. When the Air Force and Navy completed 184 flights spanning a three-day period that month, that generated the unintended consequence of persuading the North Vietnamese to move their truck convoys at night, making them much harder to find and destroy.[21] Clearly the increase in targeting reconnaissance signaled an escalated bombing campaign, but reconnaissance was an irreplaceable component for bombing as a coercive instrument no matter the side effects.[22]

RF-101C Voodoo (Air Force Historical Research Agency)

Analyzing fixed targets and completing bomb damage assessments do not require very fast processing and interpretation times, in contrast to situations where troops are engaged in a shooting match with guerrillas. Thus, photo reconnaissance was more effective at supporting the air interdiction campaign than it was supporting firefights. Indeed, photographs were responsible for developing eighty-five out of 100 interdiction targets. As an example, a Navy photo interpreter saw a couple of long trains chugging toward the town of Ninh Binh in a September 14, 1966, photograph. Two days of air strikes from aircraft commenced, and subsequent photos from RA-5C Vigilante aircraft revealed the bombing smashed most of the railroad cars and two railroad bridges. Good photo intelligence made it possible for Washington to loosen targeting restrictions in 1966 when it permitted strikes against petroleum targets within the restricted areas around Hanoi and Haiphong. Military planners knew where civilians resided in relation to the targets so they could place aim points away from residences.[23]

Photographs provided the targets. On one mission in 1967 a single RF-101 Voodoo took enough good pictures to produce thirty-seven important targets next to the railroad it followed.[24] As a further example, pictures taken in 1968 revealed that the Thanh Hoa area had become once again a major storage and transshipment sector. Missions during 1969 exposed that, as expected, the North Vietnamese carried out extensive and sustained resupply efforts after the bombing above the 19th parallel stopped.[25]

Reconnaissance provided information decision makers needed. When proposing an increased use of air power against enemy troops, for example, Lieutenant General Victor Krulak wrote, "intensified shooting will certainly not be justified unless we are sure of what we are shooting at."[26] In March 1969, the JCS increased reconnaissance missions for three weeks to update target files in case the Nixon administration resumed Rolling Thunder.[27]

In 1972, Admiral Moorer reminded his subordinates of the critical necessity of systematic reconnaissance; the evidence extracted from the photographs was necessary for attacks against targets that had not been thoroughly destroyed. Ongoing reconnaissance by SR-71 planes and AQM-34L drones made it possible for President Nixon to initiate Linebacker II with little notice because those assets continued their surveys during the fall after Linebacker I ended. As was the case during Rolling Thunder, photographs of the results of Linebacker II missions were critical for decision makers. General Vogt recognized that he needed to know the precise impact point of each and every munition, not just for assessing the effectiveness of each bomb, but also to refute accusations that the military intentionally inflicted damage against targets that were out of bounds to military strikes.[28]

Photo reconnaissance was a necessary first step for effective air strikes anywhere in Indochina and was fundamental to the air interdiction campaign against North Vietnam. Photo reconnaissance could reveal, for example, that the Viet Cong were building trenches and fortifications, thus providing more targets for air strikes.[29] At first, aerial photography struggled to reveal the Ho Chi Minh Trail's presence. Thick, triple-jungle canopy hid what was underneath. This technological limitation led directly to policy-level issues: should the United States peel back the foliage hiding the trail with Agent Orange? Should aircrews release their bombs according to infrared cues instead of actually seeing the target? Would it be more effective to saturate a square mile with bombs from B-52s? Soon into the war, reconnaissance provided a plethora of targeting intelligence for the air interdiction campaign against the Ho Chi Minh Trail.[30] Strategists opted for bombing that depended on precise targeting intelligence. Later missions found trucks, antiaircraft artillery batteries, surface-to-air missile sites, gasoline and diesel fuel storage, and armored vehicles. Follow-on flights then confirmed the accomplishments of air strikes by taking before and after pictures.[31]

The air campaign needed photo reconnaissance to hit meaningful targets, and the air forces would have operated blindly without it. Reconnaissance verified active sections of the Ho Chi Minh Trail which led, for example, to two dozen B-52 sorties and 274 Marine sorties in September 1967 cratering the road and temporarily halting truck transportation through that section of the A Shau Valley.[32] Over the Mu Gia Pass in 1967, RF-101 photography discovered truck traffic and a follow-on sortie produced additional intelligence. These flights led to a successful air strike. Infrared imagery found targets for B-52 missions; clusters of campfires, for example, gave away the location of a Viet Cong base camp.[33] Photo reconnaissance robbed the North Vietnamese of surprise when flights discovered their movement toward a Marine fort in December 1967. During the siege of Khe Sanh less than a month later, reconnaissance missions made it possible to carry out air strikes that hit home around the clock. Photographs taken during reconnaissance flights uncovered eighteen specific targets that were very close to the encampment. Data from sensors and interrogations of prisoners helped refine decisions on where to take additional pictures.[34]

Photo reconnaissance also meant the US could partially map the Ho Chi Minh Trail, plot the locations of air defense equipment, capture the results of most bombing strikes, and occasionally find enemy infantry. It was not, however, able to detect the most elusive enemy forces. Due to the nature of insurgent warfare, for instance, photographs around Saigon in April 1968 were unable to identify the insurgents infiltrating rockets for an attack the next month.[35] On the other hand, reconnaissance was the reason the Air Force knew two years later that enemy forces were stockpiling supplies in Laos for transshipment into South Vietnam, and that antiaircraft artillery pieces had declined from 4,000 to 3,000 in southern portions of North Vietnam because the armaments had been moved into Laos. In another example, in 1969 photographs captured the North Vietnamese burying dozens of large fuel tanks in order to protect them from bombs.[36]

Reconnaissance was vital to the ground war. Soldiers needed photographs to locate enemy concentrations before they encountered them. During Operation Birmingham in April 1966, the 1st Infantry Division's commander praised reconnaissance technicians for the part their visual and infrared photos played. In another example, infrared photographs found the campfires of guerrillas at night near Ban Bang, and the division used that data to carry out an attack that destroyed a couple of trucks full of weapons and nearly 200 insurgents. Within South Vietnam, the Army provided its own reconnaissance for precise targeting in support of troops in combat while the Air Force aircraft photographed large swaths of ground and updated the overall database of targets. Twenty-Fourth Army Corps commented on the necessity of sufficient photographic coverage for sending air strikes against infiltrating enemy troops.[37] When reconnaissance was good the troops gained an understanding of the array of guerrillas and regulars they were about to fight, and consequently US forces employed smarter tactics and suffered fewer losses. General Creighton Abrams, MACV commander from June 1968 through June 1972, credited photo and visual reconnaissance—an aircrewman looking for enemy activity on the ground—with providing intelligence that enabled more effective air strikes against enemy troops. It was just as important in 1970 when photo reconnaissance afforded US and Army of the Republic of Vietnam (ARVN) forces with up-to-date information for their raid into Cambodia.[38]

Reconnaissance flights enabled Washington to push back against Hanoi's propaganda. When rhetoric erupted in 1966 that jets might bomb North Vietnamese dikes, American leaders not only denied any intention to do so, they also produced photographs showing how the North Vietnamese perfidiously embedded petroleum storage tanks in the dikes' banks, exploiting a humanitarian aspect of the laws of war to protect lawful targets in an unlawful manner.[39] Following more accusations, photographs showed that no bombs had struck buildings within a thousand-yard radius of the Romanian Embassy in Hanoi. Missions over the panhandle during bombing halts compiled useful portfolios verifying that the enemy was taking advantage of holiday truces, such as the one on December 23–25, 1966, and the New Year's stand-down a few days later.[40] The flights verified that the communists exploited the temporary suspension of hostilities by moving supplies in massive numbers of trucks and also repairing bridges. Photographs captured during reconnaissance missions revealed the same practice of rebuilding infrastructure and moving supplies forward during the 1967 Tet bombing halt and after the November 1, 1968, bombing halt.[41] Analysts estimated that in just five days of the latter occasion more than 4,000 trucks began their journey south, "enough to support four Viet Cong divisions with essential supplies for almost 4 years or the North Vietnamese Army divisions then in South Vietnam and Laos for more than a year."[42] Reconnaissance supported one American accusation definitively: the pictures proved the existence of persistent infiltration of North Vietnamese Army regulars and supplies into South Vietnam, countering the mantra that the war was only an internal civil war waged by guerrillas originating in South Vietnam.[43]

President Johnson worried that reconnaissance might be labeled an act of war; thus a bombing halt would inadvertently bring surveillance of North Vietnam to an end. His advisors reassured him and urged a continuance of reconnaissance flights if he suspended the bombing, which he did.[44] In fact, aerial reconnaissance "became the primary mission" over North Vietnam after LBJ ended Rolling Thunder. Furthermore, Seventh Air Force urged its reconnaissance personnel to increase their efforts because during the winter of 1968–1969 reconnaissance missions had not managed to take any photographs of trucks moving down the Ho Chi Minh Trail at night, nor had they photographed more than a handful of destroyed trucks along supply routes in Laos. Capturing the presence of truck traffic in Laos was a high priority, but too often reconnaissance flights over Laos were flown at too high an altitude to provide the maximum photographic fidelity and resolution.[45]

Photo reconnaissance interacted with diplomatic efforts. When the North Vietnamese fired at reconnaissance aircraft after the bombing halt, Acting Secretary of State Nicholas Katzenbach warned that continued firings put subsequent talks in jeopardy. On November 23, 1968, the North Vietnamese shot down a reconnaissance aircraft, whereupon American diplomats warned Ha Van Lau of the delegation to the Paris Peace Talks that the overflights were going to continue and that the United States would take all necessary measures to protect their aircraft. Lau replied that the flights violated their sovereign airspace and complained about numerous reconnaissance drone overflights. Then on November 25 the North Vietnamese downed a drone and an F-4D escorting another reconnaissance aircraft.[46] Although the North Vietnamese delegation considered these flights to be territorial encroachments, their American counterparts' reply was that when the bombing missions came to an end, everyone understood the tacit agreement that reconnaissance flights would continue. In 1970, Ambassador David K. E. Bruce reminded Xuan Thuy, a senior North Vietnamese negotiator, that the United States considered reconnaissance missions a requirement for the protection of American and South Vietnamese forces.[47] Bruce explained that these flights were "acts of force and not acts of war," which made sense since the administration used the photographs to confirm North Vietnamese actions and intentions but did not use them to support bombing operations.[48]

The missions continued and photographs documented North Vietnam's resuscitation after the November 1968 bombing halt. Haiphong was full of ships and barges, laborers repaired railroads, and supply troops drove truck convoys in broad daylight until they reached Laos. Because of the need to document this kind of behavior and persistence, the administration permitted reconnaissance flights over Hanoi.[49] After moving the bombing line south to the 19th parallel in 1968, Navy reconnaissance jets systematically recorded the communist rebuilding effort to the north of that line. The photographs revealed reconstruction not to get on with life, but to continue the war in South Vietnam, facts of geopolitical significance.[50] The findings did not, however, trigger adequate reconsiderations of the relationship between American war efforts and American war aims; that lay beyond the purpose of reconnaissance.

Photo reconnaissance documented activity on the Ho Chi Minh Road network and infiltration through Cambodia into South Vietnam. This knowledge quickly became dated, however, because the photos were snapshots in time; they were not persistent surveillance. Because the North Vietnamese altered their convoy schedules, good photos of their truck convoys produced an incomplete picture of what was happening. A Navy squadron commander noted that spotting a truck during daylight hours was a rarity because the enemy carried out most of their movements at night, and jungle canopy hid much of the rest.[51]

Reconnaissance provided hard evidence that the North Vietnamese were committed to continuing and even escalating their war effort in spite of the bombing campaign. Photographs alerted the Air Force to the state of enemy air defenses, finding, for example, the hardening of AAA in North Vietnam in 1967. Photographs also showed when the enemy began repairs on bombed targets. Logistical choke points, for example, were bombed again as soon as there were signs that traffic could once again flow through them. Photos of pontoon bridges and submerged fords across rivers made clear the North Vietnamese determination and capacity to rebuild, resupply, and persist; what reconnaissance could not discern was the breaking point of North Vietnamese political will. It was not possible, for example, to see in a photograph when a road repair crew on the Ho Chi Minh Trail might be so fed up that armed guards had to monitor them closely, nor could photographs of the Politburo building in Hanoi reveal the impact aerial bombing had on their policy decisions.[52]

Because planners must know whether or not air strikes destroyed their assigned targets, reconnaissance flights took pictures after bombing missions.[53] Was there evidence that all the bombs exploded? Did they hit the targets? How did post-strike pilot reports compare with what the photos showed? The prints revealed answers to those questions. For example, photos could show not only that a bridge was damaged but also which spans were sent into the water and which bombs missed.[54] A May 25, 1967, mission mapped the consequences of each bomb striking the Kinh No Storage Area, listing each crater, damaged structure, and destroyed building. Along with finding targets, bomb damage assessment via pre- and post-strike photography was a primary reconnaissance effort.[55]

The pilots carrying out the strikes also visually assessed their targets to determine the results, but pictures usually provided better imagery than pilot reports made while flying 650 miles per hour and evading antiaircraft fire. Moreover, evaluations based on what pilots thought they saw were often inaccurate. For example, "black smoke" was not necessarily an indicator that stored petroleum products had been hit; it could just be a burning truck or smudge pot.[56] Aerial reconnaissance by itself suggested that Operation Thor, a massive application of bombing and artillery in 1968 on an area from which the PAVN had been shelling South Vietnamese forces, did not accomplish what the mission planners hoped. Analysts concluded the missions knocked out the artillery pieces, but photography did not reveal destroyed pieces. Pilots in O-1 Bird Dog observation aircraft found through visual searches that American counterbattery fire actually destroyed sixteen cannons. Operations from July 10 to October 15 demonstrated to the Marine commanding general that intelligence assessments were difficult, and one had best combine as many sources as possible: agents, patrols, radar, aerial observers, and so on. Marines south of the DMZ noticed that they were not getting shelled as much, which was the most important measure of the effectiveness of the air strikes.[57]

Leadership in the 432 TRW realized a shortcoming of bomb damage photographs. Pictures of bombing results provided better information when they were taken right after the attack, ideally in the midst of secondary explosions, but oftentimes reconnaissance flights were either not scheduled or were sent to the wrong coordinates. Pilots had to know exactly where to photograph to not only assess bombing accuracy, but also photograph broader results like secondary explosions and fires. Photographing craters was not enough. Therefore, whenever RF-4Cs flew with strike aircraft, they took pictures right after the strikers were off target. Other reconnaissance pilots monitored the radio frequency on which strike aircraft asked for immediate bomb damage assessment photos from any available RF-4C with enough fuel to provide that service.[58]

There was always more to this mission than just flying over a coordinate with the camera running. On a June 1967 flight, photographs showed which MiGs at Kep Airfield had been struck by cluster bombs, but obtaining and determining the effects of airfield strikes was not, for instance, as easy as it first appeared. Aircraft that appeared intact could actually have been rendered unflyable, while the only way one could be certain that an aircraft was destroyed was if the damage was obvious. Sending an RF-4C over a targeted airfield before a strike package arrived in order to see how many MiGs were there before the bombing alerted the airfield that an attack was coming, giving the MiGs time to escape to China. Sending a jet over an airfield just after it was bombed resulted in too many getting shot down because the bombing alerted the antiaircraft gunners to attack the reconnaissance jet that followed. Sometimes the strike force pilot reports were all that was available to determine mission effectiveness. Nevertheless, nothing surpassed photographs for accurate assessments of bombing.[59]

Reconnaissance was vital to the 1972 air campaign by providing targeting photos and clarifying the results. This, however, was not a radical departure. American air forces flew reconnaissance missions regularly throughout the war. In the two years prior to the Easter Offensive, flights maintained a catalog of North Vietnamese SA-2 sites, among other things. During missions in April 1972, RF-4s photographed the results of attacks against antiaircraft artillery and SAM sites in the panhandle, and for the results of B-52 missions in the same area. SR-71 Blackbirds documented an increase in missile sites in Hanoi and Haiphong.[60] Flights also confirmed the accuracy and effectiveness of the April 16 B-52 mission against targets near Haiphong.[61] Reconnaissance photos guided air interdiction priorities; for instance, in the summer of 1972 photographs captured more than one hundred tanks and other vehicles strapped to railroad flatcars on their way to South Vietnam, providing all the more reason to bomb the railroad bridges between China and North Vietnam. Photos revealed nighttime truck convoys making their way south in July. They also showed that the North Vietnamese accumulated other supplies, providing targets vulnerable to air strikes, and soon thereafter Navy aircraft destroyed these valuable stocks and provisions.[62] Blackbird photographs made it possible to create new maps of portions of North Vietnam. RF-4 weather reconnaissance flights aided laser-guided bomb missions, and their possession of a shortwave radio enabled them to relay real-time weather reports. Flying an average of seventeen sorties a day during Linebacker, the 14th Tactical Reconnaissance Squadron (TRS) provided the photographs necessary to determine the consequences of the bombing missions. Seventh Air Force alone completed 2,307 RF-4C sorties during the last six months of 1972.[63]

Reconnaissance Platforms

Physical, technological, and geopolitical limitations combined to require a variety of photo reconnaissance platforms. Since the air campaign resembled an aerial siege of communist territory, the flights functioned as the equivalent of scouting probes, and their effectiveness depended on technical capabilities; therefore, much of this story concerns technological means. The variety of aircraft was also necessary because of the different kinds of data required and enemy air defenses. By 1967, U-2s were too vulnerable to SA-2 missiles to fly over North Vietnam, so in May A-12 Blackbirds displaced them. When cloud cover precluded photography, Blackbirds made scans using their high-resolution radar. U-2s subsequently added eavesdropping to their repertoire, collecting communications intelligence from North Vietnamese transmissions. U-2 flights also obtained high-resolution photographs of the Ho Chi Minh Trail throughout Laos and especially eastern Cambodia. They covered large areas, providing a good baseline for photo interpreters to notice changes indicating road work, the establishment of base areas, the location of noncombatant settlements, supply movements, and exits from the trail into South Vietnam. These photos supported B-52 missions and helped targeteers in their efforts to avoid hitting places where civilians lived.[64]

Reconnaissance satellites were invulnerable, making their use attractive, so the United States occasionally used its Corona satellites to photograph Indochina.[65] They suffered, however, from three significant and inevitable shortcomings. First, they could not take pictures through clouds, so aircraft were still needed for flying missions below cloud decks. Keyhole Mission 1041-1, for example, passed over North Vietnam in May 1967 and produced almost nothing but pictures of the clouds below it. Second, satellite orbits are so high—anywhere from 100 to 240 miles—that the resolution of their photographs is much lower than that of an aircraft flying at fourteen miles above ground, not to mention one at 4,000 feet.[66] Third, satellite orbits are almost inflexible; one basically has to wait until it flies over the target area before snapping pictures. This is because unlike a self-propelled aircraft, a satellite coasts; it essentially falls around the earth, therefore one cannot steer a satellite like an airplane.[67] So satellites were invulnerable and not provocative but were next to useless when one needed immediate photo intelligence. That was too bad because the resolution of their photographs had improved enough by 1967 to pick out individual vehicles.[68] In June 1967, the KH-4 mission 1042-1 produced photographs with good enough resolution to reveal that there was "no evidence or indication of offensive surface-to-surface missiles." Satellites also were able to show which of the dozens of SAM sites actually had missiles.[69]

The advent of the Lockheed A-12 Blackbird in 1962 provided national leaders with an aircraft that could provide timely reconnaissance and overfly almost any point on earth with impunity. With the ability to cruise at a speed of thirty miles per minute at an altitude of sixteen miles, knocking an A-12 out of the sky required either a perfect shot by a more advanced SAM like the SA-3 or a perfect intercept by the Mach 3 MiG-25—neither of which the North Vietnamese possessed—nor did anyone ever accomplish. Because it was an aircraft, A-12 flights generated airspace sovereignty violations, so they were sensitive and politically provocative missions. A-12s began photographing North Vietnam in May 1967, completing a series of flights over North Vietnam mapping both SA-2 sites and airfields.[70] Photographs from these and their replacement SR-71 Blackbirds were essential for policy makers' decision making in Washington, DC. Strategic Air Command managed their use, along with that of the U-2s and the reconnaissance drones, from its headquarters at Offutt AFB, Nebraska, but mission approval came from the JCS.[71]

The United States tasked A-12s, SR-71s, and Ryan Model 147 drones with the most dangerous missions over North Vietnam, and their data "constituted one of the greatest intelligence sources over high-threat areas."[72] Blackbirds replaced A-12s in 1968 as the main intelligence jet flown over North Vietnam, while low-altitude drones were used when higher resolution photographs were necessary, and when cloud cover masked that country from SR-71 photography.[73] Blackbird photographs achieved a resolution as small as one foot—seven times better than that of a satellite—and their high-resolution radar could point out when ships and trains had moved, the condition of bridges, and the stock levels of transshipment points.[74]

The SR-71 was not entirely flexible between the two collection modes. Optimizing a flight for the jet's high-resolution radar reduced its photographic capability, and vice versa. Not surprisingly, PACOM directed the Air Force to favor photo missions over those using high-resolution radar, scheduling the latter only when clouds obscured the target area. Since it took time to develop, print, and transport its photographs, SR-71s were not useful for time-sensitive reconnaissance. It took up to sixty hours to get its prints to Saigon when the development shop was still in Hawaii; moving it to Kadena AFB, Japan, cut the time to eleven hours. Blackbirds supported Linebacker II operations, but they could not provide immediately useful data. When an SR-71 flew on December 20 with a primary mission of checking on the status of mining operations, the weather over Hanoi and Haiphong prevented photography; it therefore relied on its high-resolution radar. The next night was the first time during the operation the weather allowed the SR-71 to take pictures of the area around the two main cities of Haiphong and Hanoi.[75]

Air defenses over Hanoi and Haiphong were too intense for most manned reconnaissance aircraft; loss rates would have been too high for jets flying below 80,000 feet. The

F-8 Crusader with drone (Naval History and Heritage Command)

United States therefore relied on pilotless aircraft—drones—that flew programmed missions for those two areas. Policy makers and military leaders found reconnaissance drones immensely useful from the beginning. They increased the Air Force's ability to obtain photo intelligence, their missions did not put aircrews at risk, and their photographs improved air strike effectiveness. The fact that drones received jamming support and were escorted by manned fighter jets further illustrates the importance attached to them.[76]

Strategic Air Command centrally managed the drones and treated them as platforms responsive to the needs of the JCS. They produced photographic intelligence of great importance; for instance, a drone brought back the first photographs of a SAM site under construction on April 5, 1965.[77] Just over a year later, on May 1, 1966, a drone photographed more than one hundred containers of SA-2 missiles at a Hanoi cantonment, leading Honolulu to request permission from Washington, DC, to bomb them. When Seventh AF got permission to bomb the primary MiG base in North Vietnam in 1967, it asked that a reconnaissance drone take the post-attack photos. Following the bombing reductions in the spring of 1968, drones flew low-altitude profiles below the cloud deck to provide coverage over the more contested areas.[78] Low-level drone flights were necessary during the December 1972 bombings because of the cloud cover that prevented SR-71s from using their cameras.[79]

The reconnaissance drone program originated in 1959 when Colonel Harold L. Wood of the US Air Force Director of Operations Reconnaissance Division proposed an unmanned reconnaissance aircraft as a solution to a problem that would arise sooner rather than later: what to do when the Soviets shot down a U-2? The Air Force procured some drones in 1963 and less than a year later they completed their first missions over North Vietnam in fall 1964.[80] These reconnaissance drones were BQM-34A "Firebee" target drones modified to carry cameras.⁸¹ A customized C-130 transport would launch one from underneath its wing, the drone would fly its route, and then a CH-3 helicopter would retrieve it midair as it hung from a parachute. The low-altitude version was the AQM-34L, which could fly at a speed of 550 miles per hour at 1,000 to 1,500 feet above the ground. Its camera could photograph 120 miles of ground below its flight path with a six-inch resolution. As long as the drone pilot, who resided on the DC-130 mothership, received good telemetry from the drone, he could send course corrections to low-altitude drones, which was important since they would drift as much as three miles off course per each one hundred miles they flew. Oftentimes, however, they lost the mothership connection and the drone had to rely on its on-board programming to complete its flight route. Altogether, however, low-altitude drone navigation was inadequate, and they often missed their targets. That was too bad, because according to one officer, the photographs from low-altitude drones were better than those from any other platform—provided they flew over the target. Because of the navigational drift and because they normally had to rely on their profile without any course corrections from the mothership, they only photographed what they were supposed to on about 40 percent of their missions. In sum, low-altitude drones were not that reliable in photographing their assigned targets because of shortcomings in their navigation and guidance systems.⁸²

The high-altitude versions, the Model-147H and 147T, could reach 70,000 feet, with a photographic resolution as tight as three feet. They were good for flights over high-threat areas, and they also flew low-altitude profiles. These versions were successful enough that the Air Force sought more drone sorties in 1968, enough to fly at a rate of ten high-altitude and thirty low-altitude sorties a month. When the Navy evaluated the SK-147 series drone for itself in November–December 1969, ten flights out of eleven succeeded, and its cameras produced excellent photographs.⁸³

During the first two months of Linebacker, all drones flew at low altitudes. Ten AQM-34s received long-range air navigation (LORAN) equipment to try to solve the navigation problem in July–August 1972, but two crashed, probably due to problems with their flight controls. Another pair of drones received television cameras so that the drone pilot on the mothership could correct for flightpath drift by seeing where the drone was going. These crashed, however, almost at once after their launch in June.⁸⁴

For most of the war drones were quite survivable. Their size imparted a low-radar cross section, but drones were not invulnerable to SAMs or MiGs. Missiles were a threat, but when five drone missions flew with an electronic countermeasure device which jammed the SA-2 in October 1966, the Air Force concluded that in all likelihood not a single missile had been fired at these drones—a credit to the new black box.⁸⁵ That advantage would not last. Drones overflew North Vietnam 291 times in 1970, for example, and enemy fire shot down nine. Missiles destroyed a drone flying at 63,000 feet over Dong Hoi on July 31, 1971, the first time the North Vietnamese downed a high-altitude drone so far south. That year SA-2s shot down five drones, MiGs three, and flak one. On September 19, 1972, F-4s chased away MiGs from a drone; it survived and was retrieved intact.⁸⁶

Sources vary regarding drone success rates during Linebacker II; one source stated that four out of forty-two failed to return, while another report stated forty-one launched and thirty-four were "effective." Four were either shot down or crashed. Nevertheless, drones covered 338 targets out of 1,007 scheduled. On December 21, for instance, there were four AQM-34L missions; three returned. An additional thirty drone sorties had flown earlier in the month before the bombing commenced. These drones not only took photographs, but they also distributed propaganda leaflets and recorded radar emissions for signals intelligence.⁸⁷

Drones suffered a significant attrition rate because of malfunctions and air defenses, but their losses did not carry the weight of the destruction of a manned aircraft. For instance, in 1969 the North Vietnamese recovered one of the drones; photography from another drone showed it sitting out in the opening at Phuc Yen. Three years later a significant percentage of drones were shot down during Linebacker. Of four drones launched on December 19, 1972, three were retrieved.[88] Neither the capture nor the loss rate felt catastrophic or alarming, highlighting one of the political values of drones: losing one was like seeing an expensive, replaceable appliance destroyed. A loss rate like that (of 25 percent) among manned aircraft would have sent shock waves through the White House. Using drones for reconnaissance meant the president could monitor what was happening in North Vietnam without risking aircrew lives, and without the risk of producing more prisoners of war because there were no aircrew in the aircraft to be captured in the first place.

Timing and deconfliction with manned aircraft were important because drones entered the same piece of airspace at the same time as manned aircraft, which would have to be on the lookout for the little jets.[89] The Navy Red Crown controller helped manage their flights and monitored efforts to shoot down drones. If it was a remotely piloted drone, Red Crown fed information to drone pilots so they could alter their drone's heading and altitude. Sometimes a drone pilot guided his charge into clouds to evade pursuing MiGs. These resulted in extraordinary pursuits: most of the time drones escaped, but in one instance nineteen MiGs tried "to shoot down a drone, and during another mission a North Vietnamese wingman shot down his lead MiG-21 while trying to bag a drone!"[90]

As drones successfully photographed high-risk, highly important targets, the Air Force chief of staff noted in April 1967 that drone reconnaissance had "been brought to the attention of the highest-ranking military and civilian officials in the Washington area."[91] After a November 1967 mission photographed thirty-four railroad cars and eighteen locomotives, Seventh AF complimented the quality and coverage of the pictures, adding that they would make important contributions to its target list. The Air Force chief of staff again noted in 1968 that drone photography was of supreme interest. When commending a subordinate on a recent run of seventeen successful drone missions in a row, he commented that the joint chiefs and the president examined the information those drones acquired. Indeed, the Nixon administration's Senior Review Group examined drone photographs of trucks on the Ho Chi Minh Trail while grappling with the effectiveness of the air campaign. During Linebacker II, in particular, General Vogt found drone photography so essential that he wished he had operational control of at least a few, but they were national assets: interests in Washington, DC, could send them after targets they wanted to see, irrespective of a theater commander's wishes. Vogt later commented that they were absolutely indispensable and were the only way he was able to gain the intelligence he needed during Linebacker II.[92]

Since drones used film cameras like the rest of the reconnaissance fleet, they were responsive enough only for strategic and operational reconnaissance. Several days would pass before a requesting agency had drone photographs on their desks. Nevertheless, by the end of the war they were flying 12 percent of all reconnaissance missions. Indeed, they obtained most of the bomb damage photographs during Linebacker II due to persistent cloud cover.[93]

Altogether the limitations of photographic aerial reconnaissance meant the attrition strategy could not be totally effective because to successfully search and adequately destroy insurgents, one had to detect and find them in real time. While these deficiencies existed because of technological limitations, the ultimate reason for the shortcoming had little to do with technology. In the end, this intelligence shortfall existed because political leaders decided not to send massive ground forces into Laos and North Vietnam. Their decision, reasonable given China's warnings and the limitations within American national interests, created a physical and temporal gap the military had to bridge by improving the capabilities of the reconnaissance platforms and their cameras.

Reconnaissance missions had to address several conflicting factors. While the highest-resolution pictures came from low-altitude flights, flying low required flying fast, which involved faster shutter speeds, decreasing picture quality. Flying low also resulted in a much smaller area photographed. Flying high for greater coverage resulted in diminished sharpness because of distance, haze, and smoke, and it could also get a reconnaissance aircraft shot down since every radar within a hundred miles could detect intruding aircraft. Consequently, missile batteries had time to coordinate their attacks. In addition, whatever the altitude, it was difficult for aircraft to navigate with precision.[94]

Manned tactical reconnaissance aircraft flew three basic profiles: high or low altitude in daylight, and night infrared. Several factors determined the profile: the capabilities of the cameras, the kinds of photos needed, the weather, and the antiaircraft threat. Weather could trump all; for instance, as the weather worsened in October 1972, determining the results of US air strikes became more difficult.[95]

When RF-101 flights commenced over Laos in July 1964 the JCS tightly controlled them to preclude losses to ground fire. Because of the technological limitations of their cameras, sharp, detailed photographs required flight at low level where AAA could shoot them down more easily. That factor conflicted with the American policy in 1964 of not getting more heavily involved in the war in Laos. Downed aircraft and dead pilots might lead to reprisal air strikes and escalation. Therefore, reconnaissance missions were kept above 5,000 feet and out of range of flak. Triple-A, therefore, indirectly reduced the quality of reconnaissance photographs.[96] Senator Mike Mansfield warned the president of this in June, writing, "if it is not in the national interest to become deeply involved in a military sense on the Laotian front, will avoid those actions which can impel us, *even against our inclination or expectation*, to become more deeply involved [italics in original]," but if the national interest compelled greater involvement, the senator added, "there is no issue."[97]

RF-101C Voodoos and then RF-4C Phantoms were the workhorses of the reconnaissance fleet. Voodoos flew the majority of their missions over South Vietnam to provide support for the Army, and also flew missions outside of South Vietnam during Rolling Thunder. On average, RF-101Cs from the 460th Tactical Reconnaissance Wing flew up to forty missions over South Vietnam each day.[98]

An aircraft of somewhat limited capabilities, the RF-101 initially did not have the navigational instruments necessary to fly night missions; its pilot had to see the flightpath and target in order to fly over it precisely. This inadequacy restricted RF-101s to mostly daytime missions. The Voodoo could take pictures at night utilizing flashbulbs dropped from a pod, but the light reflected from ponds and was insufficient to illuminate the foliage below. Improvements enabled RF-101s to take photographs at night of a village or outpost being attacked or of boats off the coast, but night photography remained a weakness. Another challenge was ensuring that the planes photographed the exact place, not an area a couple hundred yards away. That accuracy was difficult to achieve because there were not enough prominent geographic waypoints for determining one's position in Southeast Asia, and the further one flew after getting a precise fix, the more inaccurate one's location became.[99]

Reports differed on the quality of the RF-101's cameras, with one stating that the KS-72 failed at a high rate, but its replacement, the KS-72C1, was quite reliable and produced fine pictures. Another claimed the reliability of the newer camera was unpredictable.

Nevertheless, one had to use them either above 20,000 feet or below 8,000, so the Voodoo could not take first-rate photos from the airframe's ideal altitudes that lay between those two. The one advantage the RF-101 held over the newer RF-4C was its other camera, the KA-1, which had superior capabilities for low-altitude photography. Voodoos were able to take high-resolution photos that revealed the locations of artillery north of the DMZ. RF-4 photographs at that time lacked comparable resolution.[100]

RF-101s initially lacked the benefit of electronic countermeasures, so another jet with a jammer accompanied them. Voodoos tried carrying a QRC-160 jamming pod, but the pod caused instability at speeds approaching Mach 1.0, evasive maneuvering slowed the speed of the pod's ram air turbine that supplied it with electricity, and its drag reduced the jet's speed to such a degree that they had trouble outrunning MiGs. A better solution was relying on a jammer that was mounted inside the airframe: the ALQ-51, which was installed in 1967. Combined with an approach at a very low altitude, a sudden climb to the camera's best altitude, followed by an escape at high speed, the black box gave the pilot a better chance of achieving his mission and surviving.[101] When a MiG shot one down over North Vietnam in September 1967, however, Seventh AF decided to no longer send Voodoos that far north. Phantoms gradually supplanted them, with the last RF-101 leaving Vietnam in November 1970.[102]

The RF-4C sported several advantages over its older cousin. The second crewman enabled more precise navigation—as did its inertial navigation system—and its in-flight refueling capability extended its range. Recon Phantoms also possessed front and side quadrant mapping radars, and an infrared photographic capability. It could even develop negatives inside the aircraft so that they would be ready upon their return to base. In 1966 the RF-4 was the single reconnaissance platform that could fly night missions without any restrictions. Its terrain avoidance radar enabled it to fly at low altitudes over mountains, and it provided the majority of nighttime photographs taken over Southeast Asia. The infrared camera used at night, however, required flashbulbs—a dead giveaway to flak batteries. Phantoms flew almost 90 percent of the reconnaissance missions outside of South Vietnam because of their navigational capabilities, speed, and infrared camera.[103]

The reconnaissance version of the Phantom had a couple of shortcomings. Its KA-55 camera was out of place in Southeast Asia because it was designed for photography from 30,000 feet, but it was normally flown between 3,000 and 12,000 feet at speeds that challenged its abilities. The RF-4C's side-looking radar did not have the desired resolution, and the imagery it produced was of poor quality. Its daytime photographs were good, but because of the inevitable delays in developing the film and then studying the photos, photographs of trucks and such along the Ho Chi Minh Trail were not that tactically useful because by the time a bomber arrived the target had usually moved on. There was a direct relationship between the capabilities of the cameras and aircraft survivability; the cameras needed to focus and take pictures fast enough to keep up with the speed necessary to defeat antiaircraft weapons. The Phantom's KA-55 camera needed to be flown at 4,500 feet above ground, which kept within range of ground fire, and the limitations of its flashbulbs meant that it had to fly at 3,000 feet at night.[104] Worse, this camera broke during high-G maneuvers to evade SAMs. The RF-4's greatest shortcoming was debated. According to one assessment, its medium altitude cameras constituted "the greatest reconnaissance sensor system deficiency of the SE Asia war."[105] The absence of a real-time visual display was the RF-4C's most significant shortcoming, but that was a limitation of most reconnaissance airframes of the day.[106]

RF-4C Phantom (Air Force Historical Research Agency)

These limitations explain why sensors needed a wide variety of settings adaptable to different needs. For example, a requester might need KA-55 photographs that would match 1:4,000 scale maps, but that required the aircrew to fly at 350 miles per hour at 4,000 feet above the ground—making an RF-4C a ripe target for AAA, SAMs, and trolling MiGs if it was flying over North Vietnam. In order to use the KA-55 camera at medium altitudes of around 10,000 to 15,000 feet, the RF-4C had to fly at too slow a speed to survive hostile fire. Technicians in the 432nd TRW devised an interim modification in 1968 in which the KA-55 was relocated to the middle camera bay. It could then be flown up to 500 miles per hour and the pilot could carry out some mild evasive maneuvers while it was running. This modification, however, meant its stereo photography capability could not be used, which reduced the interpreters' abilities to pick out hard-to-find objects. Unfortunately, that which the RF-4C needed to survive hostile skies—speed and sudden maneuvers and heading changes—worked against optimal photography, which was its purpose.[107]

In 1969, the 432nd TRW also tried something new with the KA-1 camera. It experimented with a focal length of three feet and a negative of nine-by-nine inches, which permitted flying at an altitude above most antiaircraft artillery, an important capability because the RF-4C was not stout enough to keep flying after being struck by most ground fire.[108] A direct hit from a cannon shell usually destroyed a vital system or started a fire, requiring the crew to eject. Proposals to improve the jet's survivability with self-sealing fuel tanks, redundant fuel lines, a secondary flight control capacity, and armor protection of key components were turned down because they cost too much. Nothing really changed until July 1972 when a pair of RF-4Cs received new KA-90 high-resolution cameras. They performed adequately in combat conditions.[109]

The Deputy Chief of Staff for Intelligence, Seventh AF, Brigadier General George J. Keegan Jr., hated the RF-4C and found it completely inadequate. He preferred the OV-1 Mohawk because, "It provides me with the only real time index of where the traffic is flowing, where and what exactly—which is all I really need to know."[110] Keegan was, however, conflating two related but distinct capabilities: photo reconnaissance and real-time surveillance.

The KA-71 panoramic camera pods F-100s, F-4s, and F-105s carried to photograph their individual strike results produced first-rate photos measuring ten inches by seventy millimeters, and provided photographs of the target zone before, during, and immediately after bomb release. Photo interpreters found that they gave them information of conditions seconds after aircraft dropped their bombs. Photographs from these cameras proved ideal for determining exactly where the bombs and missiles struck.[111]

At first, some thought the capabilities of the RF-4C meant that the older RB-57E Canberra still in use was redundant. The two were equal in terms of photographic quality, but the Phantom possessed navigation capabilities for night and bad weather flying, a greater ability to acquire photo targets, and a side-looking radar for creating maps. It also had the ability to fly faster than pretty much anything else at low altitudes, and its night photo capabilities were superior. Soon thereafter, however, RB-57Es received better cameras. During the siege of Khe Sanh, RB-57Es could fly at 8,000 feet, where its KA-80 and KA-79 cameras captured images that provided resolution measured in inches instead of feet. The camera upgrade was a badly needed improvement, because a lack of photographic detail could result in a photo interpreter looking for objects that were not visible in the photo even though they were present on the ground.[112] RB-57Es were central to the task of uncovering camouflaged targets around Khe Sanh. They used a new Fairchild rotary lens camera that provided resolution four times better than other cameras. They also made use of a new film developed by Kodak specifically for detecting camouflage netting, which indicated the enemy's presence. Infrared film could differentiate camouflage from foliage, and interpreters could detect things, such as camouflaged huts, with color pictures, that one could not see with black and white.[113] RB-57Es were initially used for night infrared photography, but more and more they were tasked with daytime missions because of the aircraft's inability to pinpoint its location at night, and because analysts of B-52 strikes needed the superior resolution their large format cameras provided. RB-57Es were suitable, however, only for threat-free airspace, so as the enemy deployed SAMs farther south, Seventh AF restricted the RB-57Es to less dangerous missions over South Vietnam, Cambodia, and southern Laos.[114]

Navy aircraft also flew a major portion of the reconnaissance missions during the war, employing three different kinds of manned reconnaissance aircraft. Three-jet detachments of RF-8A Crusaders flew from *Essex*-class carriers, and larger carriers operated detachments of six RA-5C Vigilantes each. Three RA-3Bs flew out of Cubi Point, South Vietnam, providing a real-time infrared imaging capability. An RA-3B's aircrew could vector strike aircraft against targets at night and did so for the first time on August 8, 1966. The imagery this one jet produced was pretty important because it discovered the North Vietnamese were moving large amounts of materiel at night over roads the Navy thought it had rendered unusable. The intelligence also revealed the extent to which the enemy moved supplies in boats at night.[115]

When Vigilantes from the USS *Ranger* began flying missions between the 18th and 19th parallels in 1969, they received a higher priority than all other missions launched from the carrier. The number of aircraft that supported its missions bore witness to their importance: escorts, rescue flights, Iron Hand, jamming, tankers, and an E-2A Hawkeye to manage it all. Only the reconnaissance jet and its escorts penetrated North Vietnamese

RA-5C Vigilante (Naval History and Heritage Command)

airspace. For night missions Vigilantes teamed up with strike aircraft and were used effectively as long as the weather at night was clear.[116]

The RA-5C was a complex aircraft that to many promised much but did not deliver. Seventh Fleet's Vigilantes had problems with its side-looking radar, which functioned only about 40 percent of the time. Its failures were attributed to a number of causes that followed no pattern. Contractor support did not help.[117] A former skipper of the USS *Enterprise*, Kent L. Lee, considered the RA-5C "a disaster . . . in every way." He agreed that its cameras produced exceptional photographs, but his issue with the jet was the failure of its other systems to function. It contained a suite of sensors that were supposed to gather and collate electronic emissions and show where the missile batteries were, along with their radio frequencies. According to Lee, "The concept was marvelous, magic. It never worked. Never worked. Not once. . . . Not one time—for two tours with [Admiral James L.] Holloway and two tours for me."[118]

A source from the USS *Constellation*, however, wrote of the good enough success the Vigilante had with its side-looking radar sorties that their missions became staples over North Vietnam. Vigilantes also radar mapped Laos in order to provide the kinds of ground imagery A-6A Intruders required for flying night missions. The bombardier/navigator used the maps to steer his way to the target. The *Constellation*'s air wing used RA-5Cs to support the air superiority mission by detecting SAM sites and gathering emissions intelligence on SAM and GCI radars. Their efforts helped create a map of the locations of radar and missile sites.[119]

Upgrades slowly improved the Vigilante's capabilities. By March 1968, new infrared cameras had been installed for photographing enemy activity at night. The images were first rate, but the jet needed to fly no faster than 520 miles per hour to produce the best photographs, which made it vulnerable to SAMs and MiGs.[120] The RA-5C received a new thirty-six-inch focal length camera during the last year of the war that took especially good pictures when the jet flew an offset flight path—not flying directly over the target. The Vigilante flew at 10,000 to 15,000 feet and up to 700 miles per hour for these runs, which meant that it was more likely to avoid interception by MiGs and that speed gave it enough energy to outmaneuver SAMs.[121] As a testament to the danger of these missions, eighteen of these jets were shot down, primarily by AAA, and the Vigilante suffered "the highest loss rate of any Navy aircraft involved in the war."[122]

Aerial Reconnaissance Effectiveness

Effective photo reconnaissance occurred at the tactical level of war when aircraft photographed what they were assigned and supplied the resulting photograph to a photo analyst, a ground force combat unit, or a unit tasked with bombing enemy targets. Like the Air Force, the Navy measured reconnaissance effectiveness tactically and not strategically, assessing the RA-5C's success in terms of availability and sortie rates.[123] To be most effective, reconnaissance photographs needed to possess high resolution, be processed and distributed quickly, with precise details on exactly where the photograph had been taken, and analyzed in conjunction with other kinds of information.

Weather, not camera problems or enemy action, was the main impediment to successful reconnaissance missions, accounting for nearly three-fourths of the sorties over Laos and North Vietnam that could not produce useful photographs. Adding cloud cover and rain to the dense coverage of the region's tall trees made continuous, thorough photographic coverage impossible. Weather got so bad in December 1966 that jets stationed at Udorn either flew not at all or just carried out training missions.[124] Sometimes storms masked whole areas for months, forcing planners to work with progressively older information. Accordingly, the enemy took advantage of the concealment the cloud cover brought. As one example, when the weather cleared enough for missions in April 1969, imagery from an RA-5C revealed what was thought to be the largest collection of fuel storage tanks in North Vietnam. The ocean environment gave Navy missions additional difficulties; water and static electricity damaged camera film, and camera gears jammed. When A-7Cs were pressed into service to take bomb damage assessment photos with its KB18 camera system, hydraulic fluid and oil blurred the camera's window and did the same to the photographs—no surprise since the Corsair had never been designed as a reconnaissance aircraft in the first place.[125]

The nature of the Vietnam War amplified all the problems surrounding photo reconnaissance. Since the war was a siege, the reconnaissance apparatus could not investigate North Vietnam up close and certainly not from inside, only from above, and that limited the data one could obtain. As soon as a camera took a picture, the difference between the reality it captured at a moment in time and what reality would be when someone could finally use it began expanding. Since many of the targets moved, the photographs quickly became obsolete, sometimes before the aircraft even returned to its base. Aerial reconnaissance against the guerrilla war, especially in an environment that provided so much cover to insurgents, was maddening. Photographing a missile site or an entrenched infantry company was one thing, but how does one photograph an insurgency? Technological limitations of film cameras and the requirement to distribute most prints by courier created a barrier to timely photo reconnaissance that technology and procedures could not overcome. The reconnaissance community understood its limitations. For instance, its analysts realized that "finding the enemy" was the "basic problem of counterinsurgency"—a fact this contemporary analysis stated more than once.[126] Part of the reconnaissance story is of the efforts to use technology and efficiency to overcome these barriers.

Providing pictures and photo interpretation to users quickly enough to carry out effective air or ground strikes remained a challenge throughout the war. In 1973 the commander of the 432nd TRW commented, "The most significant organizational lesson learned was that there is no substitute for timely tactical reconnaissance properly exploited."[127] Technological limitations and bureaucratic realities were the reasons why aerial photos took so long to lead to actionable intelligence. One had to submit the request for a photo mission and then an aircrew had to fly over the areas to be photographed. It took time to develop the film and print the photographs, and then large numbers of interpreters had to study them for targeting intelligence. Each mission by a single aircraft produced 1,500 feet of film, requiring seventy-two technicians working up to twelve hours a day to process and interpret the transparencies and prints. One then had to get the intelligence to the user. In sum, there were five steps: asking for a mission, the time needed to fly the mission, film developing, analyzing the photographs, and distributing the results. It eventually became more than photo interpreters could analyze.[128]

The massive number of requests further slowed the effort to produce useful photographs and meaningful intelligence. The Army complained about the time it took to get their photos, but the Army requested the detailed photography of very large areas, developing transparencies and prints by the thousands took time, and the numbers were more than the 460th Reconnaissance Technical Squadron could produce given its personnel shortfalls. Aircrews completed so many missions that interpreters could analyze and use only about 20 percent of the photographs. For reconnaissance to be effective, timely, and responsive, requests had to be limited to truly important targets covering smaller areas, and in 1967, Seventh AF intelligence wanted the effort to give more consideration "to quality rather than quantity"—quickly. The Army wished the Air Force could provide actionable intelligence faster, but it seemed to want close-up photographs of every square inch of South Vietnam.[129]

Effective reconnaissance required sensible choices. In December 1965 the director of intelligence for the 2nd Air Division prioritized film consumption over intelligence production as a matter of policy. He ordered that "whenever the weather conditions were favorable, reconnaissance pilots would keep their cameras running while over enemy territory." Once they finished photographing the primary and alternate objectives, the pilots were to use all remaining film to photograph targets of opportunity or just whatever they happened to fly over. Miles of film rolled through the photo processing machines and across the photo interpreters' light tables, and the 2nd Air Division could boast about the tens of thousands of feet of film its jets had exposed. Repeated efforts by the intelligence staffs to reverse this trend failed, and analysts could exploit only a tiny percentage of the film to produce intelligence.[130]

Some considered massive amounts of photographs a measure of effectiveness. While the Army's OV-1 Mohawks produced about a hundred feet of film per day, Air Force reconnaissance aircraft produced "some 20,000 feet of imagery" each day.[131] Brigadier General Rockly Triantafellu, the director of intelligence in 1968, did not realize that the purpose of reconnaissance was intelligence production, not the manufacture of photographs. Furthermore, his obstinacy put aircrews' lives at risk for the production of meaningless statistics. General Robert N. Smith at US Air Force Headquarters in Washington, DC, noticed there were too many photos and too few interpreters: "We are processing 3–4 million ft. of film per month—most of which quality wise, is pure junk."[132] Major Arthur Andraitis of MACV explained that jets were sent on missions to inflate figures, not support intelligence gathering.[133] Brigadier General Jammie M. Philpott understood real operational and strategic effectiveness. He wrote in 1967 that, "For some reason we feel that our effectiveness is measured by hours of flying time, feet of film exposed or large numbers of sensor activations. On balance, we don't use recce this way in Route Packages V and VIa, and effectiveness is not questioned. One good picture of an important target is a success."[134] Six months later, jets flew numerous missions in support of Marines under siege at Khe Sanh and revealed the locations of artillery, troops, bases, and supply trails. That made it possible to bombard those targets with greater accuracy. Still, during three months, 1,398 missions produced 172 miles of photographic negatives, leaving one to wonder how a limited number of analysts could have scoured so many photos.[135]

Photo overload was another consequence of the character of this war. Since it was so difficult to determine where the enemy was and what was happening, take thousands of pictures to try and find out. Brigadier General Keegan understood how this impulse derived from the character of the guerrilla war: there were no fronts, and the enemy could be anywhere, so ground commanders naturally wanted thousands of square miles of ground photographed repeatedly. Even more, the scope of military operations spanned most of Indochina, so either way there were going to be thousands of photos to study. At the other end of the spectrum, Keegan found that when missions focused on one area intently, photo interpreters spent their efforts productively. When the siege of Khe Sanh escalated, presidential priorities forced him to focus on finding the most important targets. Spotting more than 600 targets, fighter-bombers hit all of them. Focused, in-depth photography and analysis of a small sector produced more actionable intelligence than widespread photography.[136] Nevertheless, mass instead of meaningful activity continued. During 1969 the 432nd TRW noted that it had exposed and developed more than three million feet of film in one quarter. It at least decided to print only the negatives that contained the specific objective the requester asked for.[137]

Technology limited the responsiveness of photo reconnaissance. Fighter-bomber units got target pictures from the reconnaissance squadrons anywhere from fifteen to thirty-five hours after they had been taken. A study of two sorties in 1967 found it took about an hour or two to unload the film, develop it, and send it on its way to the analysts. That of course did not include time for investigating each print or transparency. Fast enough for building an operational or strategic picture, this method, even at its most efficient, was too slow for quickly changing tactical situations. Another study found that a day and a half might have transpired before an aircraft was airborne following a request, processing and interpretation took sixteen hours, ten hours to fly the photos and the analysis to the Army, while getting the information out to the battalions took three to four days.[138] The quickest response time for producing usable photos was two hours, but that was a very special case: daytime photos near Saigon in which a courier was waiting for them as soon as they were developed.[139]

During the war's latter days drones were the most responsive, providing target photographs as quickly as ten hours if the weather was good. It initially took more than four days to provide SR-71 photography to MACV. By 1972, however, processing time had been reduced to only eighteen hours. A jet transport flew the photographs to Washington, DC, via Alaska.[140] Even as late as 1972 it took four days for Navy reconnaissance photographs to get from aircraft carriers to the fleet intelligence center, Pacific facility in Hawaii, something the Navy recognized as unsatisfactory for militarily effective action.[141]

Everyone from a battery commander to the president needed photographs faster than the technology of the day could deliver. The kind of photographs and intelligence the reconnaissance-intelligence community really wanted to provide was an electronic link that could deliver a printed photograph to a ground commander in sixty seconds. The need in

Washington, DC, for pictures spurred Project Compass Link, the electronic transmission of photographs. The Pentagon was obviously interested in pictures of what was taking place in North Vietnam, so squadrons selected fifteen to twenty of their most pertinent from each mission, some of which were sent by satellite link to the Pentagon.[142] When this capability came on line in July 1967, it cut the amount of time it took to get photos to Washington from days to minutes.[143] Users found, "The resolution of the transmitted photography was generally excellent, approaching an acuity of 30 lines per millimeter with up to 16 shades of gray under ideal conditions."[144]

Seventh Air Force was concerned the Army might find a way to carry out its own aerial reconnaissance, so it responded with a program that decentralized the mission, but photo interpretation and useful intelligence suffered as a result. The key element was setting up a photo processing and interpretation facility closer to the ground units. Brigadier General Keegan fought against this effort because he feared it would dilute the end product. Furthermore, he believed that the main mission of reconnaissance was supporting the air war over North Vietnam and Laos, not the counterinsurgency war in South Vietnam. Altogether the tactical reconnaissance intelligence system enhancement never received enough support in terms of facilities or personnel, and thus it was not able to provide an improved level of reconnaissance support for the Army.[145]

Several missions pulled the reconnaissance effort in competing directions: the need for photos of South Vietnam, missions that sought out targets over North Vietnam and Laos, and bomb damage assessment (BDA) photographs. Dissension resulted. Seventh Air Force's deputy chief of staff for operations in 1967, Brigadier General W. D. Dunham, argued that supporting Army operations was a waste of time because Air Force reconnaissance was more strategic than tactical in nature: "The Udorn squadrons [RF-4Cs] are really strategic reconnaissance units.... They do not support any army units in the field."[146]

A reconnaissance flight could provide accurate bomb damage assessment photographs. Because they focused only on a moment in time, enemy action could not immediately affect the perspicacity of post-attack photographs. A bombed site did not move but photo intelligence of a moving enemy for targeting purposes created a need for real-time intelligence that could follow him and keep up with the constant change of the battlefield. A mission might be lucky enough to photograph a moving target, but by the time the analysts turned it into intelligence, the target had moved. Efficient use of the day's technology could not act faster than the enemy's ability to react to a reconnaissance jet's overflight.[147]

Real-time reconnaissance was the ideal way to provide more timely intelligence, but except in rare forms, it did not exist. The Air Force recognized this limitation and the need for eliminating the time interval between photographing a target and getting the information to the user early in the war: "A real/near-real time reconnaissance capability is definitely required if the timeliness criteria is to be met."[148] Even if real-time visual data existed, it would not solve the need for a photo interpreter and his requirement for time to examine and study the imagery before him so that he could find the enemy. Moving targets needed an intelligence process that took no more than thirty minutes, but in 1966 extant technology could not meet that standard.[149] In daylight, a pilot could see the enemy on the ground and radio an Army contact what he saw, but he could not transmit what he saw in the form of a photograph or a television picture. When aircrews used flares at night to find the enemy, the flare signaled that they had been seen, so the enemy would scatter and hide. Therefore, the Air Force asked for a low-light television with a video link and either infrared or ultraviolet illumination for nights that were too dark. After all, most truck convoys moved at night. Pilots could compensate for this to an extent by seeing targets with their own eyes, but forwarding imagery at night without the enemy knowing he was been surveilled was impossible.[150]

The reconnaissance effort overcame darkness to an extent by using flashbulbs; flying at around 3,000 to 4,000 feet, aircraft ejected flashbulbs to provide light for their cameras. Because the aircraft sped up as soon as they started spitting out the flashbulbs, ground fire was usually not able to aim well enough to achieve hits. These aircraft also carried infrared cameras. Aircrews flew infrared missions at 500 to 1,000 feet, but that reduced their field of view so much that they had to make multiple passes over roads that twisted and turned. Night missions were prominent over Laos and resulted in finding trucks, encampments, and troops on the move. They too were used for bomb damage assessment. As with other aspects of the war, communist forces found ways to try to defeat these efforts. Dispersal and doing without cooking fires undermined infrared photography.[151] A laser illumination system for night photography arrived in 1969. The laser swept back and forth and was supposed to enable photography from 3,500 feet, but haze reduced the practical altitude to about 2,000 feet, and the photographic resolution was terrible.[152] In aggregate, night photography capabilities were seriously deficient for all parts of Southeast Asia. The same went for infrared photos over North Vietnam.[153]

The Air Force kept trying to provide something resembling real-time surveillance, fielding in 1966 an RB-57 that employed an infrared camera with a real-time display of what happened below in the dark. That same year the Air Force pursued Project Shed Light, which mated a camera with infrared sensors, a display within an aircraft, and a shortwave radio for transmitting the data. Furthermore, two projects, 665A and See Fast, demonstrated that real-time reconnaissance was feasible; they just needed funding and support. In the end the Air Force recommended pursuing Shed Light because of competition from the Army's Mohawk system. The OV-1 Mohawk had a side-looking radar capability that could detect moving targets, and an operator on board the Mohawk could view these readouts almost as they occurred. Shed Light was reasonably effective.[154]

The Atlanta/Bullwhip visual reconnaissance effort proved successful for finding new targets without relying on new technology. In October 1969, for example, the 432nd TRW kept at least one aircraft monitoring the Ho Chi Minh Trail continuously during daylight hours with just three sorties a day on average. Pilots looking for targets spotted more than one hundred in November and 172 in December. These missions were effective because the aircrews became so familiar with the terrain below them, they could tell when something had changed.[155] Quantifiable specifics about its effectiveness, however, were hard to come by because the only information catalogued was "sightings" and target types.[156]

In another compromise solution, forward air controllers provided a great deal of real-time spotting of enemy activity that the Air Force found trustworthy. Using hand-held cameras was another approach. Seventh Air Force bought more than 200 35mm cameras with telephoto lenses and it was well worth the money. They photographed much that would have otherwise been missed, from BDA to supply dumps. Handheld cameras still required time to get the pictures back to base, develop, and print them.[157]

The paucity of real-time photo intelligence had serious consequences. For example, a mission in the winter of 1969 photographed a platoon of enemy troops walking out in the open on a known road, but by the time interpreters could have fixed their location for an air strike, they were gone. One adjustment did not provide real-time photo intelligence, per se. During the third quarter of 1969, the 460th TRW began working with and flying with forward air controllers (FACs), with the FACs telling them where to take pictures. This did not improve the timeliness of the photographs, but it did improve their sagacity.[158]

Expectation management was important in gauging reconnaissance effectiveness and maintaining good relations with requesters. Seventh Air Force therefore educated personnel who asked for reconnaissance support as to the time and difficulty it took to fly the sortie, process the film, analyze the pictures, and then distribute the results. A requester was more likely to get what he wanted and not put an aircrew at undue risk when he explained his precise needs. Finally, if a requester was going to put someone's life at risk for some photo intelligence, use it.[159] Those facts of life did not satisfy the Army, which asked for fewer reconnaissance flights from the Air Force in 1968 and relied more on its OV-1 Mohawks for battlefield intelligence. At the same time, when Army commanders understood what aerial reconnaissance could and could not provide them, they submitted requests that were more focused on what the aircraft could provide. In 1968 the Army started asking the aircrews to use the best camera or sensor that would produce the best image in whatever scale that would produce images with greater resolution. Because of this change, the aircrews could more easily exploit the capabilities of their cameras.[160]

Photo request times for missions over South Vietnam ballooned, averaging ten days to complete. Three factors accounted for this: the Army relied more on its organic assets within South Vietnam, on real-time visual reconnaissance from FACs, and the Air Force gave other reconnaissance missions a higher priority. In May 1969, the management of the effort received a boost in the form of a computerized system for allocating photo reconnaissance assignments and priorities, and distribution lists for the photographs, but that could not meet the need for real-time imagery.[161]

A 1971 study covering 1965–1968 made the lack of jointness the first issue addressed in its critique of reconnaissance. Five different agencies conducted their own overflights: Seventh AF, the Army, the Navy, the Marines, and Strategic Air Command. In July 1966, Admiral Sharp had expressed support for a truly joint reconnaissance center. The Secretary of Defense had also called for the establishment of such an arrangement.[162] Westmoreland's command agreed, believing "that it is far easier for us to collect photography than it is for us to exploit it adequately."[163] Some in the Air Force were concerned such a clearinghouse might make some decisions that clashed with institutional interests. The JCS decided after further study a joint center would result in a redundancy in relation to the one that already existed in Hawaii, which should instead receive more personnel. This unresolved clash between centralization and decentralization existed at all levels; each reconnaissance squadron at Tan Son Nhut had its own lab, undercutting efficiency and effectiveness.[164] No one ever resolved this problem.

In addition to sensible priorities, effective reconnaissance needed adequate numbers of skilled photo interpreters, and a case in 1968 showed how vital they were. A site at Xom Trung Hoa was thought to have been an abandoned enemy barracks, but a photo interpreter figured out that it was a large fuel storage site. Consequently, an air strike from the USS *Enterprise* hit it, and "Credit for discovery of the target was given to a photo intelligenceman third class in *Ticonderoga*."[165] Similarly, developing and analyzing photographs generated opportunities like the one the USS *Hancock*'s air wing got on October 1, 1968. An RF-8 photographed an old SAM site to see if it was being used again. It was not, but the photo interpreter discovered a new site nearby, knowledge that generated an air strike by *Hancock*'s wing. Commander William F. Span, the mission commander, was ecstatic over the results: "I didn't see a single bomb outside the target area. There must have been a dozen fires burning with orange and black smoke up to two thousand feet. I saw two ignited missiles spinning around on the ground. I've never seen bombing like that. We must have caught them by surprise because there was only light flak and no missiles were fired. When you get a good reconnaissance photo of a place like that, it really helps." When the commander of the Seventh Fleet extended his congratulations, he praised the photo developers and interpreters first.[166]

Interpreters needed to be immersed into the significance of their mission, and one of the best ways was for them to fly over the areas where reconnaissance pilots were taking photographs.[167] In addition, Captain Larry L. Benson warned that a photo interpreter "must be allowed to spend as much time with a roll of film as necessary in order to provide the user with a meaningful product. The emphasis on speed and volume effectively destroy a man's capability to do this." Benson also argued that because of a shortage of photo interpreters, the Air Force was extracting under 25 percent of the intelligence it could have. Their shortage may have been the worst problem for the reconnaissance effort.[168]

Mission Danger

Major William J. Davies wrote in 1968, "Reconnaissance is a dangerous job, not only because the crews regularly get shot at but also because they can't shoot back!"[169] These jets carried no weapons for returning fire; they relied on speed, skill, and electronic countermeasures (ECM) for survival. Antiaircraft fire from the ground was a hazard from the very beginning. Subjected to small arms fire from the first day of their arrival, an RF-101C took a cannon shell in the front fuselage on August 14, 1962, while over Route 7 in Laos. The pilot and aircraft made a safe landing, but CINCPAC brought the flights to a halt for two weeks. Charles F. Klusmann, a Navy lieutenant, was not so lucky in June 1964 when gunfire shot down his RF-8 and he was captured. Ten months later machine gun fire downed a Voodoo.[170] The following year Captain Edward W. O'Neil Jr. confessed, "I have been so scared under fire that I once forgot to turn 'ON' my cameras (perhaps it was the fascination of seeing muzzle flashes for the first time)." Nevertheless, he and his squadron mates carried out their missions "because it was their profession."[171]

The dangers were extreme and fleeting. One RF-101 pilot on a mission saw a missile coming toward him, turned hard toward it, saw it pass within less than a hundred feet of his jet, and then felt his plane shudder from the explosion—fortunately out of range. When an RA-5C pilot on a 1968 mission spotted a SAM streaking after him, he flew toward it. A hard turn at just the right time outmaneuvered the missile so that when its warhead detonated, he would be beyond its lethal blast radius. That Vigilante suffered twenty-eight hits from shrapnel but managed to make "a fairly uneventful landing" on the USS *Ranger*.[172]

Others were not so lucky. When RA-5Cs arrived in theater in 1965, they did not yet have on-board jammers; they relied on speed and maneuvering to defeat SAMs. A Vigilante aircrew from the USS *Constellation* experienced the consequences of no ECM equipment firsthand on October 9, 1966. After radioing that a missile battery had fired at them, they were never heard from again.[173] The men in an escorting F-4 watched a Vigilante explode over Laos and crash on March 31, 1969, when a missile caught them unawares. In just two months of 1967, SA-2s targeted RF-101s at least thirty-five times. After a missile downed a Voodoo in August 1967, they all started carrying a pair of new ALQ-72 jamming pods in order to counter SAM radars. As a result of the pods' effectiveness, reconnaissance aircrews preferred to fly above flak and take their chances with the SAMs. MiGs were not as dangerous as flak, either. Voodoos, Phantoms, and especially Vigilantes simply used their speed to outrun MiG-17s.[174] The radar homing and warning receivers that equipped these jets could give aircrews some warning that a MiG was behind them. Additional help came in the form of jamming aircraft like Marine EA-6As that orbited off the coast of North Vietnam when reconnaissance aircraft were conducting their missions. During a 1969 mission an RF-4 zoomed up suddenly to arrive at the proper altitude for its cameras, but this time MiG-21s locked onto it with their radars. The Phantom survived when the pilot dropped its external fuel tanks in order to lessen drag and accelerated enough to avoid getting shot.[175]

Survival also necessitated flying unpredictable routes, random turns, fighter escort, and above all, vigilance.[176] An effective mission required careful planning. That and the danger highlighted the solitary nature of these flights. "When a Reece [reconnaissance] pilot plans a mission," Edward O'Neil Jr. wrote:

> [H]e alone is responsible for that plan, his life depends on the success of the plan, so *never, never volunteer* suggestions on how he should plan his flight [italics in original]. If he asks your opinion of his flight plan, tell him it is the best route you have ever seen. If you are asked for information, give it gladly, but do not be critical of anyone else's plan. Confidence in the mission is necessary, and the reasoning behind his plan is not known to you, so look and ask questions, but not volunteer information; one exception, something that happened to you in his proposed flight.[177]

Some missions were unusually dangerous, such as the one on June 18, 1968, in which an RF-4 crew flew an infrared photo mission in search of a North Vietnamese infantry division. They had to fly at 2,000 feet above the ground through mountains as high as 8,500 feet, utterly dependent on their terrain following radar, but it was worth it; they photographed five dozen enemy campfires, confirming the location of a PAVN division.[178] Flight operations outside of the heartland of North Vietnam were not as dangerous as those over Route Package VI, but dangers remained in 1969. The commanding officer of Reconnaissance Attack Squadron 6 warned that while none of them had seen any AAA thus far during their flights over Laos and the panhandle of North Vietnam they should not forget about the Vigilante that had exploded earlier than year. He warned his aviators against relaxing their guard, an attitude that threatened since as far as they knew none of them had been fired upon, and they had detected only a few brief lock-ons from Fan Song radars. He also reminded them to not make a second photography run over a target because it was too dangerous to fly over an alerted location.[179] During this time over Laos, the primary danger was colliding with other American aircraft at night or flying underneath a B-52 that had just unloaded its bombs. Navy–Air Force coordination and deconfliction of the effort remained inadequate.[180]

Verification of the agreements surrounding the November 1968 bombing halt meant that reconnaissance drones and manned jets were going to continue to fly over North Vietnam and get shot at. Indeed, five weeks into the halt the US had already lost four aircraft to enemy defenses. By January 6, 1969, ten drones had been shot down out of a total of seventy-seven missions; manned sorties totaled 453, nearly a quarter of which had been fired upon with four shot down.[181] These actions received the attention of President Nixon, who in 1970 considered reprisals for hostile action against reconnaissance aircraft. The shoot-down of one US aircraft on November 12, 1970, was the culmination of a number of attempts to down one of the jets. The incident came to the attention of Alexander Haig, who was surprised at the absence of any reprisals, though as it turned out, he would not have to wait long.[182] Hanoi's actions violated a tacit agreement that they would not fire on American reconnaissance jets, so Secretary of Defense Melvin Laird announced on November 21 that the US was going to carry out retaliatory air strikes against SAM and AAA sites south of the 19th parallel. Unimpressed, in 1970–1971 the North Vietnamese established sites farther and farther south in the panhandle, often firing against reconnaissance jets and their escorts, one of which they shot down on March 22, 1971.[183]

Aircrews and SA-2 operators thrust and parried throughout the war. The men who flew Vigilantes took risks to fly the optimum profiles for their cameras, flying toward North Vietnam at around 17,000 to 18,000 feet for the panoramic camera and 12,000 to 15,000 feet for the Tri Fan camera. Although too high for most guns, missiles could track and destroy them at those altitudes. An RF-4 crew might wait until a Fan Song radar illuminated them before activating their own jamming pods. Expending chaff at that moment, a rapid descent to low altitude, and turning off the pod would force the North Vietnamese weapons director to reduce and then increase the sensitivity of his radar presentation, by which time the RF-4 would be too low to track. His opponent might track an incoming jet with a ground-controlled intercept radar and predict when it would approach a SAM site, whereupon a missile crew would fire first and turn on their Fan Song at the last second. Reacting quickly enough to such subterfuge was no easy task.[184]

Each service rank ordered the danger in the same way: flak, missiles, then interceptors. RA-5C Vigilante doctrine recognized AAA as the greatest threat, so its pilots would not fly below 3,000 feet. Missiles found it difficult to hit jets below 4,000 feet, so they avoided flying higher than that. Fly fast; 650 miles per hour when escorted, and as fast as possible when alone. Do not fly straight and level, make frequent modest heading and altitude changes, not leveling out until the terminal phase of the photography run. When you hear the warning over the radio that a SAM site was tracking a jet, roll 130 degrees and make a 3.5G descending turn to 1,000 feet above the ground with a ninety-degree heading change. MiGs were almost never seen south of nineteen degrees, but over Route Package VI, an escort was certainly desirable. An attending F-4's centerline tank, however, limited it to 700 miles per hour, and it carried 7,000 fewer pounds of fuel than a Vigilante, so RA-5Cs might outrun their escorts—defeating their purpose. Finally, if attacked, accelerate as fast as you can, as low as you can, and try to hide in clouds.[185] Nevertheless, AAA downed nineteen RF-101s, SAMs destroyed one, and a MiG shot down another. Enemy action also achieved kills against nineteen RF-8s and seventy-six RF-4s.[186]

Nap-of-the-earth flying—or flying at very low altitude—offered protection from MiGs and SAMs up until the jet climbed to photographing altitude because search radars could rarely detect them when they flew that low. Flak, however, got bad enough over North Vietnam that aircrews began to discard the tactic of flying very low most of the way to the target because that profile kept them in range of machine gun and antiaircraft artillery for much of their route. RF-4Cs adapted by flying into hostile airspace at 800 to 1,000 miles per hour at 15,000 feet, and by employing their jamming pod and chaff to defeat the SAMs. The 11th TRS also found that two reconnaissance Phantoms provided some mutually supporting jamming energy, and two were easier to maneuver than was a formation of four. As the North Vietnamese became more skilled with SA-2s, they started tracking aircraft at very low altitudes. A Fan Song radar illuminated a Phantom flying at seventy-five feet for three minutes during one hairy mission. This countermeasure of flying very low meant that the aircrew had to time their climb precisely in order to photograph their target. They then minimized their exposure by remaining at, say, 3,000 feet for only five seconds, but that still left one in range of flak. MiGs may have been more disruptive to reconnaissance effectiveness than anything else because they could force an aircraft to evade to such a degree that it could not photograph its target.[187]

Fighter escort for reconnaissance aircraft varied. After ground fire shot down an RF-8A over Laos in June 1964, the JCS mandated escorts for reconnaissance aircraft. U-2 flights did not normally get them because Seventh AF assigned escorting fighter-bombers a greater priority and besides, MiG-21s would have had an impossible time reaching a U-2's altitude.

In June 1966, Seventh AF began sending RF-101s assigned to targets covered by the greatest amount of AAA and SAMs alone, without a wingman. The logic was that a lone jet might not attract as much attention and might be ignored, but of course the pilot was completely on his own if something happened to his jet. RF-4s did receive the protection of an escorting fighter-bomber that was there to retaliate against gun sites that fired against them. The first three years of war they got two escorts, but in April 1969 that went down to one because the enemy were not reacting to overflights as aggressively, and because one escort was easier to manage in bad weather than two.[188] When airspace became more dangerous during Linebacker, RF-4 Phantoms got four escorts, which would fly whichever altitude was best for protecting the photo jet from attack. Navy F-4s escorted RA-5Cs at night because the Phantom provided backup radar, navigation, radio, and identification friend or foe (IFF), and were there to see where the Vigilante crashed if it was shot down. A-7A attack aircraft that followed reconnaissance jets would shoot back so as to at least retaliate against the defenders.[189] On flights up north in April 1972, RF-4s had to fly without escorts, relying on their jamming pods, speed, and maneuvering to survive. One aircraft did not make it back.[190] During Linebacker II the RF-4s preferred to fly without escorts because when flying their maximum speed of Mach 1.3, escorting fighters could not keep up because of the aerodynamic drag of the missiles they carried.[191] The only other assistance they needed was a radio notification of when the last strike aircraft had departed the area they were to photograph. Besides, the MiGCAPs were sufficient for distracting MiGs, and higher priority missions received the F-4 sorties.[192]

For all their efforts, aircrews were not always informed of the extent to which their missions were militarily significant.[193] Lieutenant Colonel Clark H. Allison observed that sharing photographs he had taken with those airmen encouraged them that they were accomplishing something worthwhile, especially those who flew night missions. Aircrews—both strike and reconnaissance—often asked for post–bomb strike photographs, but reconnaissance technicians either could not sort out the relevant photos for them, or more often were too overworked to do so. Allison also firmly believed intelligence officers performed their duties better when they got to fly as passengers or aircrew on reconnaissance missions. Pilots could no longer pull one over on the photo interpreters, and at the same time they developed a greater rapport with one another. Debriefings improved, he stated: "When our airmen flew on combat aircraft, they felt that maybe they were really becoming involved in the operation.... Consequently, I felt that they were a lot more helpful to the crew members and the crew members respected them for what they did."[194]

Ongoing Efforts

Air Force measurements of reconnaissance effectiveness struggled between gauging what it could measure quantitatively and examining the operational and strategic consequences of the reconnaissance operations. One analyst wrote, "The effectiveness of reconnaissance operations is measured primarily by target coverage, timely delivery of data, and responsiveness to the tactical situation"—tactical effectiveness and mission completion.[195] If the mission was simply to take photographs of the assigned locations, reconnaissance could achieve a success rate of close to 100 percent.[196]

Reconnaissance activities during the siege of Khe Sanh demonstrated the difference between efficiency and effectiveness. Reconnaissance flights during that siege were not that efficient; each sortie produced on average only about one-and-a-half targets.[197] The aerial bombardment that the flights supported, however, ensured that the communists did not overrun the Marines, which was the critical goal according to the president, therefore aerial reconnaissance was effective in the most important way air power can be: supporting national policy goals.[198]

The best measure of operational effectiveness was the degree to which the photos uncovered targets, helped build an accurate picture of what was taking place, and provided clear photographs of targets after they had been bombed. One kind of report of bomb damage, for example, listed things destroyed, which is not the same as determining the ultimate consequences of the action, but it is a place to begin an assessment.[199] The point is, photographs can provide irreplaceable data on bombing accuracy and what the weapons destroyed, which is a part of effective reconnaissance, but determining the operational and strategic effects of those bombs was much more challenging. In fact, an accurately placed bomb may have nothing more than a tactical effect, or it may directly support policy goals.

A 1969 analysis concluded deficiencies in equipment, poor management in the allocation of limited resources, and too-few personnel combined to prevent reconnaissance from contributing as much as it could. For instance, there had not been enough photography of targets before and after strikes over North Vietnam. Because the system for deciding what got photographed was inadequate in terms of setting priorities, there were too many feet of film for the processing facilities to develop expeditiously, and too much for photo interpreters to study and analyze thoroughly. Too many chiefs were able to decide or deny photo coverage of an area, so there needed to be a re-evaluation of who could actually make decisions.[200]

The Air Force forwarded more than thirty-six recommendations in 1971 on how to improve. Among the most important, reconnaissance needed to be a joint operation managed by a single office, a request that dated from 1966 and had remained unmet. The Air Force needed to meet the Army's needs for timely reconnaissance lest the Army expand its own capability. Reconnaissance aircraft needed better ECM equipment, and jamming support needed to be a joint operation. Collectively, the reconnaissance effort required too many steps in terms of sending the request through the chain of command, processing film, analyzing photographs, and getting that information to the end user in time. One recommendation advocated for improved infrared reconnaissance capabilities, because daylight photographs provided far better intelligence than the infrared sensors RF-4Cs used.[201]

Sometimes one has to look at all the components in order to really determine the efficiency and effectiveness of a tactical procedure. Reconnaissance missions in support of laser-guided bomb targets seem excessive at first glance. They needed photos from 4,000 feet, 12,000 feet, and from the altitude necessary to scale the photograph to a 1:4,000 scale map. Given the accuracy, reliability, and destructiveness of just a single laser-guided bomb, however, multiple photo missions for one LGB-carrying aircraft actually constituted a very effective use of photo reconnaissance because the payoff was so great.[202]

As the withdrawal of American forces continued into 1971, there was not much in the way of Air Force reconnaissance flying in the second half of that year because Seventh AF was down to one RF-4C squadron, the 14th, while the South Vietnamese Air Force flew some missions with their RF-5s. The Phantom jets, however, received six KA-82 high-definition panoramic cameras from departing RB-57s that enabled the Phantoms to take sharper photographs. These cameras functioned very well in finding such things as SAM sites.[203] Indeed, they "yielded the best tactical photo reconnaissance yet seen in SEA."[204] The sharpness of their photographs enabled analysts to see enemy vehicles that had remained hidden. Unbelievably this improvement resulted in paperwork and harassment for Seventh AF because the modification had not been carried out through the proper channels. Bureaucrats in Hawaii tried to force the squadron to uninstall the cameras because the modification had not been authorized, but fortunately, common sense won that argument and the RF-4s got to keep their new cameras.²⁰⁵ Another innovation was the use of Polaroid photography. Polaroid film produced a print in seconds: take the picture, count to twenty, remove a protective covering, and you have a print. Visual reconnaissance flights took these pictures and then distributed them from Tan Son Nhut to other bases.²⁰⁶

In the three months before the Easter Offensive, the remaining reconnaissance squadron averaged but sixteen missions per day. A communist offensive was expected, so missions covered South Vietnam's borders. Flights detected the buildup of enemy vehicles, preventing the PAVN from achieving surprise. Strategic Air Command reconnaissance aircraft got busy after a December 30, 1971, request for pictures of the thirty-six most important enemy targets. By January 4, 1972, four drone missions had photographed twenty-four of these, and along with some reconnaissance assets from TAC, covered the rest by February 1.²⁰⁷

A variety of systems combined to provide targeting intelligence and BDA in 1972. The RF-4s had LORAN equipment that made them more useful for marking the location of targets. One kind in particular intimidated the South Vietnamese greatly: 130mm cannons. The use of stereo cameras produced pictures of such resolution that photo interpreters were now able to find the deadly weapons more quickly, and the combination of reconnaissance and laser-guided bombs helped solve what had been a chronic problem: finding and destroying these accurate, long-range pieces.²⁰⁸ Print processing was faster by 1972. A leader of a strike force could have a print of these cannons in hand within a day of the reconnaissance flight that took it.²⁰⁹

Exotic airframes carried out more of the reconnaissance missions during Linebacker; drones photographed the armored invasion of Quang Tri Province intensively. Low-altitude drones and SR-71s provided the post-attack photography that verified the effectiveness of air strikes, such as the B-52 raids of April 21 and 23 against targets around Thanh Hoa. Blackbird missions doubled and provided the confirmation of the results of a May 1972 bombing mission against a bridge in the buffer zone along China's border. In fact, drones and SR-71s flew the most reconnaissance missions in 1972, monitoring supply routes, air bases, Haiphong, the Hanoi Hilton, target sites, and the results of bombing missions.²¹⁰ When A-7D Corsairs began combat missions on October 16, 1972, the accuracy of its navigation system added to the flow of intelligence data. While on close air support missions, it could accurately "mark" places of interest a pilot saw, annotating the precise latitude/longitude location.²¹¹

In December 1972, six RC-135s, four SR-71s, two DC-130s for launching drones, and three U-2Rs were available to support Linebacker II. Tactics still mattered: the Air Force observed that Navy reconnaissance jets performed better because they accompanied the strike force instead of following later.²¹² The RF-4C squadron flew 604 sorties over North Vietnam from October through December, completing nine a day during Linebacker II. Thick clouds remained the primary adversary of useful photographs, with uncooperative weather preventing RF-4s from obtaining BDA prior to December 21 and then again on December 26.²¹³ The December 27 missions were uneventful; they photographed every target on their flight plan and the North Vietnamese Air Force did not even react—for a reason. Little did they know the North Vietnamese were running out of SAMs.²¹⁴ Manned reconnaissance aircraft completed their missions on December 29 because the weather was good enough for them to do so.²¹⁵ Because the weather at this time of the year over North Vietnam was wretched, low-flying drones became the primary means by which the US obtained photo reconnaissance and BDA. General Vogt characterized these drone missions as "extremely important," and a comparison with RF-4C missions sheds additional light on the transition from manned to unmanned reconnaissance that occurred. From December 18 to 29 a dozen RF-4C sorties covered forty-nine targets while seventy-seven drone flights photographed 632.[216] Demonstrating how the two platforms complemented each other, RF-4C missions supplemented those of reconnaissance drones when those aircraft could not provide adequate photographic coverage. Not until December 21 was the weather clear enough for an SR-71 to take pictures of Haiphong and Hanoi. Reconnaissance missions over North Vietnam came to a complete halt on January 15, 1973, because negotiations were progressing.[217]

By the end of the war, photo-reconnaissance aircraft could photograph fixed targets and analyze the effectiveness of bombing with photographs taken after an air strike, but the challenge of distributing photos to the fighter-bomber wings in time had not been resolved. Given the limits of film technology and the need for analysts to have time to scour photographs for indicators that the enemy was present, photo reconnaissance was simply unable to find enemy troops—particularly guerrillas—and immediately turn that into targeting intelligence for ground or air forces. Photographic reconnaissance was as effective as possible given the limitations of technology and the time needed for photo interpreters to do their job. This shortcoming once again demonstrates how improvement lay in joint efforts. In this case, infantry patrols and human intelligence were necessary to fill the gaps where high-resolution photographs run up against its inherent limitations.[218]

The Air Force and Navy fielded the best photo reconnaissance capabilities possible but did not manage them in the most efficient or effective manner. Technology for the kind of visual intelligence desired—reliable real-time remote video—did not yet exist. Neither did technology for providing real-time photographs to ground and air forces in the midst of battle or for providing targeting information on lurking hostile forces soon enough to strike them before they moved away. Photo reconnaissance was responsive enough to be consistently effective only at the operational and strategic levels of war.

Aerial reconnaissance over Indochina reflected how difficult it was to figure out what was happening on the ground in enemy territory. Its challenges were also byproducts of the massive sanctuaries in Southeast Asia—not only the ones that existed because of the decisions of policy makers not to widen the war, but also the ones that existed in South Vietnam where pacification had not been carried out fully. If friendly ground forces had been active over a greater portion of South Vietnam, the awareness they gained during the course of their operations would have produced more intelligence, and photo intelligence inside South Vietnam would have been less necessary and probably more focused. All this was an outgrowth of so-called limited war, of a war of ongoing attrition that was a natural consequence of this siege of North Vietnam. The kinds of side-looking radar imagery RA-5Cs took during Linebacker demonstrate how the siege drew everything toward finding and hitting targets for its own sake. This high-tech supersonic jet scanned for wooden boats in estuaries and for small targets of opportunity on trails in the jungle.[219]

Chapter 12

Airlift Effectiveness

Aerial transporting of soldiers and supplies opened new possibilities for waging war in the twentieth century. The ability to move vital items exponentially faster than ships, railroads, or trucks has been a self-evidently useful capability for armed forces since the 1920s when the Army Air Corps and US Marines began using transport aircraft for humanitarian relief and combat support.[1] Americans were not alone in recognizing the freight-carrying possibilities of aircraft during the biplane era. The British used this air capability in Iraq in 1920. During the 1930s the Air Corps exploited air transport to bring supplies to airfields quickly.[2] The United States Army Air Forces procured a large fleet of transports during World War II to deliver critical materials, from airplane parts to ammunition. American airlift into combat zones began in 1943 when C-47 Dakotas formed the only supply line sustaining Australia's Seventh Division in New Guinea. During the Berlin Airlift the United States and the United Kingdom used air transport to achieve a strategic purpose: defeating the Soviet Union's attempt to force the portions of Berlin it did not occupy to submit to its governance.[3]

A dearth of hard-surfaced airfields limited airlift within Korea, but Air Force transports dropped supplies to Army forces.[4] Korea's aftermath witnessed the production of a significant purpose-designed military transport, the C-123 Provider, which entered service in 1955 and later flew thousands of sorties in Vietnam.[5] By the time of the Vietnam War, the United States fielded a first-rate, long-range transport, the all-jet C-141 Starlifter, and the turboprop C-130 Hercules for tactical and intra-theater airlift—a design so ideal that it remains in production seven decades after it was conceived.[6] The US Air Force also had a network of bases and a management system for both intercontinental and intra-theater tactical airlift by the time the war escalated in 1965. By then, airlift had matured to the point that it provided the president with capabilities, options, and flexibility in military operations. Airlift made military operations easier to conduct, and in Vietnam took the possibility of another Dien Bien Phu off the table, thus eliminating one of President Lyndon Johnson's most persistent nightmares.[7]

Given America's worldwide security arrangements, transport aircraft had to be able to provide Army and Marine troops with supplies globally, for every kind of warfare, no matter the weather. Transport aircraft needed to do so while being shot at and while landing on gravel or dirt runways. Furthermore, tactical airlift needed the ability to transport cargo to users with as few in-between sorties as possible. This mission preceded the 1965 escalation in Vietnam by more than a decade.[8] In the opinion of one historian, airlift was, "In some respect . . . the glue that held the war effort together in South Vietnam."[9]

By tactical airlift I mean airlift "within a theater of operations, including within a combat zone, in direct support of tactical operations." The Air Force's main role for tactical airlift during Vietnam was to support the Army.[10] With escalation in 1965 the Air Force subdivided this role into five missions to include: flying forces to a strategically important hotspot, supplying forward deployed forces, flying them within theater, evacuating casualties, and supporting special operations.[11] This section highlights logistical supply, support, and air movement within South Vietnam.

The character of South Vietnam's transportation infrastructure created a need for airlift. Roads could turn into mud, which encouraged reliance on airlift. There were plenty of isolated detachments of troops too difficult to resupply by road, because of enemy activity, who needed urgent resupply when engaged with enemy forces.[12] Continued Viet Cong attacks on road transportation encouraged the use of airlift.[13] General William Momyer argued it was a necessary mission because in some places it just was not possible to move large amounts of supplies into a battle zone using trucks; the bogs, jungle, and terrible roads made aerial movement and supply necessary. Major General Gordon F. Blood of Seventh Air Force observed that tactical airlift was often the only way forward post could receive supplies, adding that the ability and willingness of transport aircrews to rush in ammunition and provisions "has provided the margin between survival and annihilation."[14] When aircraft supplied an outpost, there was no need to guard the road to that place, which meant that those troops could be used elsewhere. Completing this circle of support, aircraft also provided fuel to forces in areas where the VC controlled the roads.[15]

Although a support mission, tactical airlift in 1967, to cite one year, comprised a major portion of Air Force flying operations in South Vietnam, completing more than 32,000 sorties and landing at approximately 175 airports of all kinds.[16] Over the course of the war, transports moved enormous amounts of supplies within Vietnam. Fixed-wing American, South Vietnamese, and Australian transports carried more than 681,000 tons of supplies from 1965 to 1972, two-thirds by C-130s.[17]

One study observed that because airlift was not a glamorous undertaking it has received little limelight. The mundaneness of many of its daily activities carried over into the way the Air Force documented airlift accomplishments. The majority of the data revolves around tonnage, passengers, sorties, readiness rates, on-time rates, utilization rates, and so forth, but those are really just measurements of usage and efficiency, not indicators of operational or strategic effectiveness.[18] Most of the time the Air Force measured its airlift effectiveness not in the sometimes life-or-death consequences for people who received their assistance, but instead in terms of tons of freight delivered, sorties per day, average payload weight per sortie, and timeliness of deliveries in terms of meeting a schedule.[19] One reads assessments such as, "The average operationally ready rate from December 1967 to December 1968 for the C-130s was 74.8 percent. This figure was above the Air Force standard of 71 percent."[20]

Considering the consequences of airlift for the ground forces is necessary for comprehending its effectiveness. Colonel Theo C. Mataxis, a US Army advisor in Second Corps, claimed that several of his operations would not have been possible without tactical airlift. Transports, he wrote, made it possible to accumulate six battalions of infantry at Hau Bon over a day and a half in July 1965, utilizing an unimproved runway even though the weather made landing approaches a challenge. Airlifters enabled ground commanders to react more rapidly to opportunities and needs, flying for instance a group of Vietnamese Marines to take back their district headquarters at Dak To, and to reopen a highway the Viet Cong had seized in 1965. They also prepositioned the 173rd Brigade to Pleiku so it could stand by as the reserve during an operation in the Le Thanh District. As a customer, if you will, Mataxis expressed deep thanks for the airlift crews who had made these movements possible, flying into rough airfields while the enemy aimed mortars and small arms against them.[21]

Airlift was significant during the first year of heavy American involvement in the war and remained so throughout. Sampling its contributions, fifty-two C-130 sorties brought a Hawk missile battery to Da Nang in February, and the next month seventy-six sorties

C-123 Provider (National Archive)

deployed the 3rd Marine Combat Battalion Landing Team there. When F-105s deployed from Yokota, Japan, to Takhli, Thailand, C-130s brought in their support equipment. C-130s also dropped 1,125 Army of the Republic of Vietnam (ARVN) paratroopers against a VC-dominated sector in September 1965. Flying multiple missions each, just five shuttled the 1st Infantry Division (US) from Vung Tau to Bien Hoa in five days.[22]

Fairly soon into the war, analysts also considered the consequences of airlift: "The tactical airlift system is operating in an environment in which effectiveness cannot be measured solely in parameters such as ton-miles or tons per flying hour." A better measure was the speed and reliability of responses to requests. Efficiency and responsiveness were not synonymous, and responsiveness at times had to take priority over efficiency because the end-user might be fighting for his life. When possible, airlift managers strove for the efficient handling of cargo, but they also employed judgment to know when responsiveness took precedence over packing transports with as much and as many supplies as possible.[23] According to an experienced C-130 pilot, it was best to consider the strategic consequences of an airlift effort because quantitative measures painted an incomplete picture. David Mets wrote, "Ton-mile computations or even tonnage delivered per day are really inappropriate. In fact, they are not even demanded by Air Force doctrine, which explicitly states that responsiveness must always come first in tactical airlift. Thus, though the battle [of Khe Sanh] cost five airlift airplanes, one crew, and the lives of one full load of C-123 passengers, there can be no doubt that the garrison was sustained and that General Giap was denied his military and political goals partly because of the airlift."[24]

The Air Force's approach to effective airlift was based on the belief and experience that airlift was best managed in a more centralized manner whereby cargo could be delivered quickly to whomever needed it most. In contrast, the Army preferred to use its airlift—mostly helicopters—as an integral part of its units' moving supplies within the battle zone. The Army wanted to use airlift as an extension of the local commander, and Army commanders really wanted the Air Force's fixed-wing cargo aircraft to be theirs, sitting and waiting until they needed them. They wanted to own the supply chain, believing that ownership was the best way to make sure they got what they wanted whenever they wanted it, and individual Army commanders did not want to do without while a ground unit with more urgent needs received airlift support.[25]

The Air Force was convinced that placing airlift under the command of one person was the best way to deliver the most effective and efficient outcomes to the receivers of this service. One agency could sort needs within a larger operational and strategic context and focus its efforts on the greatest priority instead of diffusing efforts among a larger number of clients. A practice early in the war contradicted this approach: tying C-130s to individual sectors and keeping transports parked and ready for loading, but inactive. Cargo aircraft were better able to move more freight more responsively when centrally managed as one theater-wide entity.[26] The Air Force's system could access a larger reserve of aircraft, could bring transports in from outside of Southeast Asia, and could concentrate airframes that might be on standby in a less-busy corps to provide a surge of airlift to someone who needed more than his normal share.[27] General Westmoreland did not completely agree and argued that a permanently assigned C-130 wing in South Vietnam would result in easier command of the aircraft and continuity in the scheduling of flights, among other things. PACAF argued that his method would harm airlift efficiency throughout the rest of the Pacific theater.[28] These two different approaches were never completely resolved, but in 1966 the Army and Air Force chiefs of staff agreed at least that the Air Force would own fixed-wing transports, and the Army would own helicopter transport, with the Air Force retaining a few for special missions such as search and rescue. While Seventh AF got control of the 315th Tactical Airlift Wing, a C-123 unit, the C-130s remained with PACAF. Truly centralizing USAF airlift did not take place until after the war. In the meantime, Military Airlift Command handled strategic airlift, and Tactical Air Command managed tactical airlift, and in Indochina, Pacific Air Forces remained the central provider and manager.[29] Because transport aircraft were treated as theater-wide and not local assets, more were available to respond to sudden needs—a critical need could receive not just a proportional amount, but if the situation warranted, all the available transports. So ironically, the 315th Air Division argued that it could better serve General Westmoreland's goals by not stationing more C-130s in South Vietnam per se. That way his forces could have access to more of PACAF's resources even though they were a thousand miles away.[30]

While Army officers at all levels resented it when airlift was not on time, airlift was quite responsive to emergency taskings.[31] In one case during April and May 1966, sorties were "on time" for fifty-three of fifty-nine tactical emergencies and on "358 of 389 emergency supply" missions.[32] Nevertheless, there was too much duplication of effort, the Army did not follow the procedures the Air Force had developed, and the Air Force did not always get a chance to adequately explain its methods to Army commanders.[33] Effective airlift required modifying procedures, refining that took time. Dissatisfied with its responsiveness—it could take up to twelve hours to respond to an emergency request—the Air Force modified the method for submitting emergency requests that year. A brigade would send its application directly to the Direct Air Support Center, and the intervening levels of command would hear the request and could modify or deny it.[34] When the airlift system finally received adequate secure communications in 1968, management as well as security improved. Leadership's desire to manage the system via computer resulted in the Seek Data II program, which prepared orders for individual missions. Developments like these were more akin to garrison operations than mobile war operations and paint a picture not of a limited war or of a counterinsurgency, but of a siege.[35]

Several factors limited the effectiveness of helicopter airlift that often served as a bridge between the airfields where the transports landed and the troops in forward areas. Low speeds and cargo-carrying limitations were inherent to helicopters, and fixed-wing airlift possessed the capabilities helicopters lacked. Helicopter pilots often did not have enough practice in instrument flying, and there was no way for helicopters to fly in formation in low visibility, so they were not as useful when clouds, fog, and rain made visibility poor. Helicopters also could not lift much at higher altitudes. While they might lack enough landing zones, they certainly had more than did C-130s. In the end, fixed-wing and rotary-wing airlift complemented each other. Relying on the Air Force for heavy freight loads, Army and Marine helicopters moved troops into combat zones that had no airfields, evacuated casualties from within firefights, and flew individuals from command post to command post. Army and Marine commanders preferred to rely on USAF airlift for supporting air assaults because a C-130 could carry much more than a UH-1 or a CH-47. At the same time, helicopter airlift found a major role in Vietnam with air assaults into places fixed-wing airplanes could not reach, and there were a lot of places where fixed-wing transports could not land.[36]

Because of the characteristics of their operating environment and missions, C-7, C-123, and C-130 aircrews possessed a variety of skills. The weather was often cloudy and rainy, the remote airfields could be quagmires, ground fire was an almost constant threat, navigational aids were few, air drops demanded precise navigation, and assault landings were difficult and dangerous, so piloting transports on these missions required adroitness.[37] The very first airlift crews who deployed to Southeast Asia were rated as "well qualified" for the various tasks they had to fly, but those who followed had to build up their proficiency in theater. For example, C-123 pilots arriving in South Vietnam in 1965 were "not ready for combat operations upon arrival in Vietnam," and had not "practiced assault landings on short fields in heavily loaded aircraft." Navigators had not flown missions under fire while delivering paratroopers or freight and drop systems in use were new to loadmasters. Therefore, it took about six weeks to get them up to speed.[38] Eventually they were trained for the missions they had to fly.[39]

Nevertheless, there were not enough trained aircrews and many of the incoming pilots were older men who were returned to flying duties from staff jobs. In 1967, the typical airlift aircraft commander was on average more than forty years old. They needed a considerable amount of training specific to the Southeast Asia environment to become proficient enough for the missions they were about to fly; the remote airstrips were far more challenging than the practice ones stateside. Peacetime flying brought with it a repetitive kind of traffic pattern, but the threat of ground fire meant that every approach to an airfield needed to be unique to frustrate an enemy determined to shoot down transport aircraft. As a group and as individuals, these airlifters learned quickly and received consistent praise for their abilities and commitment.[40] Another personnel practice that improved airlift performance was keeping crews together; schedulers broke them up only for good reasons. Sometimes the aircrews could be quite a mix. Of the 127 new C-7 pilots as of April 1968, almost half were second lieutenants flying their first tours, more than fifty were lieutenant colonels, two had been aces during the Second World War, and six had doctoral degrees.[41]

The Air Force permanently stationed two C-130 wings in Southeast Asia in 1965, but the side effects devastated the availability of quality aircrews in subsequent years. After initially bringing in the very best aircrews, the Air Force's personnel center failed to identify who should go to Southeast Asia next in terms of abilities and experience, so the next group of airmen were a mixed bag. Combined with the refusal to give these men credit for a tour in a combat zone was the likelihood of an extended TDY (temporary duty) shortly after returning stateside after being away from home for a long time. Out of fifty-five pilots sent over in 1965, a year after they returned to the US fifteen switched to other commands to avoid another long stint away from home or had left the Air Force entirely. The airlifters were conflicted. They knew that their ethos required a willingness to deploy worldwide, but as one analysis observed, "Torn between the polarity of maintaining family integrity and the policies that were committing them to <u>unreasonable</u> demands, they opted in favor of their families [underline in original]" and left the airlift career field.[42]

One commander, Major Robert F. Ellington of the Airlift Control Element at Nha Trang, believed as of 1966 that the Air Force's policy for rotating its personnel in and out of Southeast Asia undercut airlift's flexibility. It rotated aircrews and airplanes from differing organizations into the theater, complicating everything.[43] Another officer observed that aircrews coming into the theater still lacked some necessary qualifications, and that PACAF did not get the most out of them because they normally remained for just one year instead of a normal three-year assignment. Captain Windsor noted the 315th Air Division performed "primarily a training function rather than its mission in transportation."[44] Furthermore, aircrews had to gain nine different kinds of ratings and qualifications to be able to fly into the different kinds of airfields that existed in Indochina. So airmen built up experience, knowledge, and practical abilities, and then aircrews without experience or proper training soon rotated in to replace them. As the need for transport pilots reached a critical shortfall, the Air Force sent in pilots who had no experience managing logistics or flying airlift missions. These included newly graduated pilots and crews from Strategic Air Command—men who had flown training jets or bombers and tankers. Brigadier General William G. Moore Jr., commander of the 834th Air Division, also observed that as soon as airlift personnel gained enough experience and knowledge, they did not need much in the way of supervision, but by then they were only weeks away from the end of their tour, a personnel management problem that continued. During the first couple of years of the war there was no other training option except on the job, and then as soon as the pilots and loadmasters knew what they were doing, their date for returning home neared. Their experience was then permanently lost, because they often took an assignment in a different Air Force specialty code. At times there was no handoff between leaders. Major Robert F. Ellington expected to receive some lessons learned from his predecessor, but that man left Vietnam three weeks before Ellington arrived.[45]

The pilots, loadmasters, and logisticians who conducted these operations were a mix of personnel on TDY and a small core of permanently assigned individuals, not a unified squadron or wing who trained together and then deployed together. Their skills varied, and one commander described them as "transient." Moreover, because the manning of these deployed groups was unstable, mid-level managers, supervisors, and commanders had a harder time identifying who was truly qualified and capable and best suited for missions of varying levels of danger and complexity. The nature of the Air Force's use of people also made it harder for commanders to develop unit-level esprit de corps. Further undercutting morale, the supervisors who wrote the performance reports could not witness the actions of their ratees because they resided in Okinawa or the Philippines. Brigadier General Moore argued that these factors combined to undercut the overall effectiveness of the mission.[46]

To be optimally effective, airlift squadrons needed a full complement of aircrews and maintainers. "Fully-manned" was uncommon and that produced serious consequences. In 1966 the 315th Air Commando Wing was so short of pilots that it could operate only a little more than 50 percent of its transports, and as a result it could fly about ten C-123s a day and deliver just 200 tons. Furthermore, this unit could not increase flying hours in an emergency because pushing aircrews beyond the twelve-hour-a-day limit risked wearing them out. Flight surgeons found the pace C-130 crews endured alarming and believed that fatigue would lead to carelessness and accidents. When Senator George Murphy of California investigated claims that aircrews were being exploited, PACAF assured him that crews were slated to fly ninety hours per month and were closely monitored if they flew up to 120 hours a month. Exceeding that limit required the consent of the Air Division commander, but no requests were made to him for that waiver.[47] The system of sending aircrews from main bases such as Naha and Clark to South Vietnam for fifteen-day TDYs helped mitigate long-term wear on the aircrews, but the time back at the primary base eroded their combat skills. The training sorties they flew were just not the same as working with the Army and the ARVN in combat conditions.[48]

Personnel managers found a new way of undercutting morale. The criteria airlifters had to meet to get credit for a combat tour were grossly unfair. Airlift crews had to stay in Vietnam for thirty days straight without so much as a single trip to a military base in the Philippines or Taiwan. If they did make such a trip, their clock returned to zero, even though they were getting shot at over Vietnam the next day. Loadmasters, pilots, and crew chiefs were resentful of this policy that treated their flying missions as equivalent to those crews who flew nowhere near a combat zone. Crews averaged forty-four combat sorties each month but were in South Vietnam on average nineteen days. This aggregate somehow did not count as combat flying. One commander, Colonel Arthur C. Rush, wrote, "They feel, and justifiably so, that they should receive credit for a tour due to the number of combat sorties and the combat hours they are flying. . . . Regardless of the manner in which this is justified, credit for, or towards, a tour must be provided."[49] Inequity in not receiving credit for combat flying overseas greatly harmed morale and the assignment process and stationing practices produced this inequity. C-130 crews were actually stationed outside of Vietnam at three bases: Naha Air Base, Okinawa; Clark Air Base, the Philippines; and Ching Cuan Kang, Taiwan. These crews flew a series of fifteen-day TDYs of intensive flying in Vietnam. During these stints they would quickly accumulate a considerable amount of time in high-threat airspace, but again, according to the rules, they did not and could not accumulate enough time to receive an overseas tour credit. Thus, a crewman could spend a year in the PACAF theater, rack up a host of combat missions, be transferred back to the US at the end of his tour, and then be immediately sent back to Vietnam.[50] Returning to a tour length of ninety days in June 1968 for TDYs solved this problem.

An additional issue was the question of what made for more proficient aircrews: shuttling them in and out of the country on those fifteen-day tours, or stationing them in South Vietnam as a permanent move? The shuttle system worked well, but keeping aircrews in-country for a year produced a set of very highly qualified pilots. In this quest for the most effective airlift force, however, one had to remember that even during a major war, PACAF had airlift obligations outside of Southeast Asia. Be that as it may, C-130 crews on shuttle TDYs carried out, for example, most of the air drops during the siege of Khe Sanh and operations in the A Shau Valley. Furthermore, an aircrew shortage developed, so those slated to return stateside were kept in the western Pacific for an extended stay. Finally, although the character of the war required a massive commitment from the United States, it was a limited war, and because it was a limited war, the Air Force would not involuntarily assign people to second tours in Southeast Asia.[51]

On the flip side, the autonomy and authority that aircraft commanders received to complete their missions pushed them to the limit of their flying abilities. They thrived on the challenge and high morale was a consequence: "For many it was the first opportunity they had to make decisions that matter, and its rewards were hard to equal. Every end of tour report stated unanimously that the tours in SEA were the most challenging and rewarding of their careers."[52]

Effective tactical airlift in a combat environment like Southeast Asia required a particular set of capabilities and infrastructure. South Vietnam alone, for example, had about 300 airstrips, most being rough, unpaved runways too short for all but the smallest cargo aircraft. With the war escalating, the Air Force did not have an airlift aircraft that could operate in and out of primitive airfields while carrying a load in the range of ten tons. As it was, only 38 percent of South Vietnam's airstrips could handle C-130s, the optimal aircraft in terms of freight tonnage and airfield capabilities. Navigation beacons and night/poor weather landing aids were sparse, so airlifters made their deliveries during daylight hours whenever possible, but that encouraged more enemy ground fire. Because ground fire was almost ubiquitous, pilots preferred to fly above it and make steep landing approaches.[53]

Aircraft completed the triad of infrastructure, aircrews, and airplanes. The C-123 Provider was an older design that could operate out of smaller airfields, the C-7 Caribou originally belonged to the Army and could take off and land from the most primitive strips, and the C-130 Hercules provided the ideal mix of rough field performance and freight capacity but needed a longer runway than the other two aircraft.

A Pentagon war raged between the Army and Air Force over the C-7 until the Army transferred its C-7 Caribous to the Air Force in January 1967 as part of an accord that settled the roles and missions of airplanes and helicopters in the two services.[54] When this took place, Army commanders were concerned about giving up aircraft that were answerable to the Army, but in the opinion of the Air Force, utilization rates and deliveries improved after the transfer.[55] The Air Force chief of staff had noticed that the Army was underutilizing the Caribous, but with the new arrangement these aircraft became his responsibility. After the handover, the Air Force made responding to the requirements of field commanders a top priority for C-7s in order to put Army concerns to rest. In 1968, however, the Caribous were still not 100 percent centrally controlled and managed. Four were dedicated to the III Marine Amphibious Force, and seven were dedicated to the Army's II Field Force Vietnam. The Air Force nevertheless soon found that through more efficient scheduling and management, it could accomplish with forty-eight transports what had required sixty under Army management. The commander of the 1st Infantry Division, however, bitterly disagreed, finding their arrivals tardy and poorly responsive to the local commander's needs, which in his opinion were what mattered the most.[56]

Interservice rivalry inserted itself into all this. In 1965, the Army built crude runways that were long enough (1,500 feet) for its C-7s, but not long enough for C-123s and C-130s. Pacific Air Forces realized it had better seize control of airfield construction and find a way to use its transports on very short runways if the Air Force wanted to retain the tactical airlift mission and not lose it to the Army.[57] Brigadier General Moore argued that Seventh AF ought to use C-7s to provide "unscheduled incidental airlift support" to the Army, not only because that mission met a legitimate Army need, but also because if the Air Force did not, the Army would.[58] Three months after the Air Force took over operations of C-7s, the commander of the 537th Troop Carrier Squadron crowed that his men were providing support that was just as effective and efficient as when the airframes were under Army control. The commander of the Army's 1st Cavalry Division (Airmobile), Major General John Horton, dubbed the squadron's efforts "outstanding."[59] There had been complaints among the Army about C-7 support, but the commander of the 834th Air Division, finding out about this via "bootlegged copies of messages," insisted that the division had provided the airlift the Army wanted.[60] The Air Force concluded by 1970 that a portion of transports should be set aside under the command of Army commanders, but that the joint command ought to decide who got what.[61]

C-7 Caribou (US Air Force)

The Caribou highlighted the tradeoffs between efficiency and effectiveness. It could reach places larger airplanes could not, so the ground forces involved received more logistical support and were less isolated—that was effectiveness. One disadvantage to the C-7, however, was one had to unload its cargo hold by hand, which was the least efficient method; but on the other hand, the C-7's responsiveness and capabilities were the reasons for its existence and use. Caribous provided airlift to forty runways that were too small for C-123s and C-130s.[62]

The next larger-sized aircraft, the C-123 Provider, surprised the Air Force with its effectiveness and capabilities given its fifteen-year age. A C-123 carried up to twelve tons of freight, cruised at a speed of 200 miles per hour, and could take off and land from dirt and gravel runways. It was both robust and dependable in no small measure due to the skilled efforts of its maintainers. It could land at 135 airfields, more than the C-130, because it did not need as long of a runway, so it was better for transporting materiel that needed to be extracted on the ground, not dropped by parachute. If one were going to paradrop supplies, it was better to do so in as large a package as possible, so the C-130 was the provider of choice for that task. Providers could usually bring supplies closer to troops in contact with the enemy, so it was effective in its own way even though it could not carry near the amount of freight of a C-130.[63] While the Provider's great assets were its reliability and ruggedness, early models were short on engine power. The simple modification of adding a small jet engine underneath each wing converted the C-123B to the C-123K, which doubled its rate of climb. The modified plane could reach altitudes above the range of small arms fire much more quickly. Entering service in May 1967, it could also take off with up to 100 percent more cargo than the version without the jet engines. The C-123s lacked, however, a radar for avoiding ground obstacles, and this led to some crashes. They would have been flown more frequently had there been enough aircrews for them.[64]

A C-130 Hercules could carry eighteen tons of cargo, cruise at more than 300 miles per hour, was powered by four turboprop engines of 4,000 horsepower each, and operated from

C-130 Hercules (Air Force Historical Research Agency)

fairly rough landing strips. The C-130 turned out to be not just an aircraft that aircrews adored because it was what they flew, it was a truly adaptable and capable aircraft. To begin with, while it had not been designed for aggressively landing on airstrips under fire, and struggled to perform the combat assault airlift missions under poor flying conditions, it soon proved to be a match for the challenges the war threw at it.[65] It not only proved its utility as an intra-theater airlifter between main bases, it also functioned as a dropper of flares to provide enough light for threatened outposts to see and fire at approaching troops and as a dispenser of psychological warfare leaflets. It was literally "the workhorse of tactical airlift in SEA."[66] Such were its capabilities that one did not require a large fleet of C-130s to satisfy the Army's requests. In 1967, Seventh AF found that forty-four were sufficient to meet MACV's requirements; thirteen C-130As, twenty-three C-130Bs, and eight C-130Es were permanently stationed in Naha, Clark, and Ching Cuan Kang, respectively. When in South Vietnam, they flew out of Cam Ranh Bay, Tan Son Nhut, and Nha Trang moving, on average, at least 1,600 tons each day. Even though they were practically brand new, there were concerns that the combination of frequent rough-field landings and maximum-weight takeoffs were wearing out the airframes and shortening their fatigue lives by as much as a factor of ten. Such are the consequences of wartime operations.[67]

The war's escalation exposed problems surrounding the infrastructure, management, and sustainment of effective airlift. Such things as air base facilities, spares, maintenance, forklifts, etc., were the key elements just as much as were airframes, and at an overall level airlift within Pacific Command (PACOM) none were sufficiently centralized. Effective airlift depended on more than just planes and pilots. Something as physically small as a radio that could encrypt transmissions would have made a big difference. During the siege of Khe Sanh, vital tactical information could not be passed in advance over radio because the transmissions were not scrambled, and the enemy might be listening. Portable scales for weighing cargo were also a mandatory piece of equipment because an overloaded transport could speed off the end of the runway, crash, destroy the plane and its cargo, and kill the people inside. Maintenance abilities, spare parts, and the availability of aircraft maintenance technicians had a direct bearing on how many airframes were actually operational.[68]

Another factor in airlift effectiveness was ramp space, which can be an operationally or even strategically decisive element of airlift. An outpost's runway was key to keeping it supplied—at least until North Vietnamese firepower made it too costly to use.[69] There was even a direct relationship between having spare tires and airlift effectiveness: rough, damaged, unimproved runways tore up tires at a fast rate. The 314th Troop Carrier Wing observed that Nhon Co's runway was "an absolute hazard. The surface is composed of large, sharp rocks that are tearing tires to pieces with every landing."[70] One also had to make sure that there were enough parachutes and parachute opening devices for paradrop missions as well as a capability for loading and securing pallets in cargo aircraft. The bottleneck might not be any of these, but instead the ability to unload cargo and send the plane on another mission could be the deciding constraint.[71]

Effective fixed-wing airlift required not only aircraft, but also runways, and Southeast Asia did not have enough good runways. As of January 1967, for example, there were only sixteen in South Vietnam that were at least 3,500 feet long and sixty feet wide. Runway length was not enough; the runway surface had to be strong enough to support an aircraft's weight. Reliance on short runways (under 2,900 feet long) resulted in cracked C-130 wings, landing gear, and engine mounts because landing on them required steep descent rates and hard landings. In fact, the sparsity of runways led the Air Force and CINCPAC to realize that they did not have an aircraft that could bring in ten tons of cargo onto runways that were substandard, bumpy, and short. MACV also concluded that the C-130, as good as it was, was not the ideal airlifter for counterinsurgency operations. If you wanted to use it, you had to build the runways.[72]

Cargo delivery to primitive airfields in the Vietnamese hinterland required combat controllers, air traffic controllers who often arrived via parachute to manage and control the airspace into which transports flew. It was not possible to overemphasize how important combat controllers were to remote airfield operations. Brigadier General Moore added that a pilot needed to lead these teams because transport pilots did not fully trust anyone else.[73] There was, however, already a pilot shortage in Vietnam.

Responding to urgent requests by ground forces resulted in racking and stacking priorities. Emergency airlift missions fell into three different priorities: "tactical emergency, emergency resupply, [and] combat essential," going from most urgent to least.[74] This functioned better than expected, because Tactical Air Liaison Officers (ALOs) found that they could often meet emergency requests by utilizing missions that had already been scheduled, which resulted in fewer disruptions that an emergency diversion of airborne supplies required. Consequently, deliveries were faster.[75]

Efficiency and effectiveness were often at odds, but the Air Force comprehended the difference between the two and understood when to emphasize one over the other. C-7s were not as efficient as C-130s, but there were outposts that needed their deliveries, so they were retained and used because they were effective at providing what those soldiers needed. Dirt strips could not support the weight of fully loaded C-130s, nor could a C-130 deliver a maximum tonnage load onto a 2,000-foot-long runway, though the need to do so persisted.[76] In order to get the most efficient and effective use out of its C-130s, PACAF eliminated the 1,000-foot buffer from the minimum runway length, but that increased risk. It also exploited a short runway on Ie Shima Island to train pilots on how to make these landings.[77]

Flying to these minimal runways meant that the transports could not be fully loaded, so that made those missions inefficient as far as tonnage was concerned, but of course if it was delivering critical supplies, that was an effective use of that sortie. In another example of common sense, the 315th Air Division soon realized that four C-130Es could deliver the fuel of six C-130Bs because of their greater fuel capacity, so they used C-130Es as the fuel carriers. Sometimes deliveries to outposts were quite fast. During an October 1965 operation, C-130s managed to take off with supplies needed at Plei Me as soon as an hour from the time the requests were received.[78]

To better manage tactical airlift in Southeast Asia, the Air Force activated the 834th Air Division on October 15, 1966, headquartered at Tan Son Nhut Air Base.[79] The issue of efficiency versus responsiveness gained additional scrutiny with the establishment of the emergency airlift request system (EARS) in fall 1966. With EARS, airlift got a separate communications network, and the dispatchers were collocated with the headquarters of II Field Force and the Third Direct Air Support Center. Airlift personnel were retained only at the division level and above, which increased the centralized management of airlift. A January 1967 analysis MACV conducted found that Seventh AF initiated 82 percent of the 176 emergency missions flown that month, suggesting that the Army was not dictating to the Air Force, but that airlift was trying to meet urgent needs. The nature of the requests for emergency airlift bore this out—of the freight delivered, 39 percent consisted of ammunition.[80]

Although the Army needed EARS, the communication network met the needs of both services. Not relying on emergency requests served the interests of both services, and the practice also better met the goals of efficiency, responsiveness, and effectiveness. An overreliance on reactive emergency requests would harm efficiency, and neglecting to pursue alternatives would put Army units in dangerous situations. The Seventh AF commander observed that airlift missions to build up reserves of ammunition and supplies near the enemy ahead of time had not been scheduled. Those were missions that should have been prioritized; emergency requests were unnecessary to stockpile ahead of time.[81] Everyone would win if regularly scheduled airlifts could keep receivers' stocks replenished, and if that was done, scheduled transports would not have to be suddenly diverted to meet the needs of imperiled units, thus resulting in a more efficient use of airlift. So when the Seventh AF commander sought to reduce emergency airlift sorties, the goal was not to neglect the needs of soldiers in the pursuit of efficiency for its own sake, it was to execute supply and airlift in such a way that those emergency needs would occur much less frequently, and so that when soldiers really needed emergency airlifts there would be no delays.

Airlift and the Tet Offensive

Airlift was particularly effective during the Tet Offensive, which began on January 29 and 30, 1968. "General Offensive-General Uprising," as the communists called it, was a sudden campaign in which anywhere from 84,000 to 124,000 Viet Cong and North Vietnamese regulars attacked more than a hundred cities and towns.[82] The communists assumed that the South Vietnamese people were just waiting for the right spark to set off a people's revolution and were spring-loaded to rise up and destroy the oppressive Saigon regime. A switch from guerrilla warfare to more conventional onslaughts provided the impetus for this uprising. Furthermore, the communists never sought any such thing as a mere psychological victory. They wanted a bloody conclusive military victory in the traditional sense, and badly wanted to seize and control a major city. Their optimal outcome would have been to persuade the

Americans to withdraw. The South Vietnamese and Americans, however, caught wind of their plans and were moving into place to carry out counterattacks when the Tet Offensive erupted on January 29. South Vietnamese armed forces, from the ARVN to the part-time territorials (Regional Forces and Popular Forces), fought with skill and anger and alongside the Americans and defeated the Tet Offensive.[83] They killed as many as 50,000 Viet Cong; in battle after battle, the South Vietnamese and Americans won.[84] The South Vietnamese people—ARVN, civilian irregulars, and regional forces— killed more than six in ten of the most stolid insurgents in South Vietnam, the most capable of Viet Cong.[85]

The chairman of the joint chiefs of staff recognized the operational and strategic significance of airlift during the Tet Offensive and explained to the president that operations in South Vietnam could use two more C-130 squadrons. General Wheeler knew that PAVN troops overrunning the Marine outpost of Khe San would have been catastrophic for the American war effort, so the ability to resupply it by air directly supported something critically important to the president. Westmoreland understood these relationships and declared airlift strategically important.[86] One could not meet the need for more airlift by just bringing in more aircraft. Too many would actually decrease efficiency and effectiveness, because there was only enough ramp space for fifty-four C-130s. Orbiting C-130s overhead while those on the ground were offloaded on a tiny parking area would have slowed the resupply effort.[87] The Tet Offensive exposed another problem with the management of airlift in SEA: the lack of headroom, or the inability to handle a surge in the need for airlift. The Air Force had to bring in transport aircraft from outside of Vietnam in order prevent the system from breaking down.[88] At the same time, the system was functioning as designed. These transports came from Tactical Air Command, which contained the strategic reserve of aircraft.[89] Saving aircraft from destruction by VC ground attacks by dispersing them to outlying airfields took the aircraft away from the cargo that they needed to deliver to imperiled units.

Enemy action cut off many roads, so the only way to get cargo and soldiers to quite a few places was tactical airlift. A runway and not a road might be the connective tissue between a unit and its destinations, as when Marine C-130s flew the 2nd Battalion of the 26th Marine Regiment from Da Nang to Dong Ha on March 8, 1967, and most especially during the Tet Offensive.[90] Sometimes necessary measures worked at cross purposes.

Air Force analysts concluded the responsiveness of the air logistical system was key, and aircrew persistence was another. During the Tet Offensive there was not a single case of transports encountering such resistance from enemy action that an operational plan had to be abandoned. Delivering cargo to Khe Sanh might require several attempts, but aircrews completed their missions. Two years prior, however, it took nearly four hours to load supplies on a transport responding to an emergency request. Consequently, aircraft got diverted to these higher priority missions. These perceptions, such as making responsiveness the highest priority and the necessity to fly planes that are less than fully and optimally loaded in order to be more responsive were not obvious to everyone, particularly those who measured airlift effectiveness by tonnage carried to the exclusion of all else.[91] Since responsiveness was the primary way of measuring airlift effectiveness, airlift during the Tet Offensive was a success. All the emergency requests were fulfilled, and the "combat essential and lower priority requests" were only delayed. The system was responsive enough to sustain Khe Sanh.[92] Up to the Tet Offensive, however, the airlift system demonstrated the least efficiency; but because the most urgently needed supplies got to the troops who needed them the most during the Tet Offensive, airlift was effective. Even with these successes, the Air Force realized it needed an even closer working relationship with and understanding of the Army's needs, lest it lose the tactical airlift mission to the Army.[93]

These were dangerous combat missions. Assault airlift—delivering troops and supplies to remote areas under fire—has yet to receive the attention of a Christopher Nolan movie, but those missions could be dangerous as hell.[94] During the first six months of 1966, for instance, ground fire struck airlift aircraft 463 times. C-130s carrying 40,000-pound loads of jet fuel to outlying airfields sometimes had to fly through flak and machine gun fire to complete their missions. Some did not make it to their destination. Viet Cong ground fire struck one C-130 thusly loaded on December 20, 1965, and it exploded, killing all five crewmen, representing the first North Vietnamese kill of a C-130. Altogether ground fire shot down nineteen C-130s, fourteen C-123s, and seven C-7s during the war.[95] Another C-130 crew was more fortunate when a parachute flare blew back into the cargo hold from outside and ignited another flare. One of the loadmasters saved the aircraft by grabbing and throwing the burning flare out of the airplane.[96] As dangerous as flying into Khe Sanh was, no crew ever refused to fly. Aircrews recognized the criticality of their task, and so they took the risks necessary to descend through the clouds and complete their air drops. As the ground fire worsened over succeeding days in the spring of 1968 at A Luoi, the aircrews opted for a nose-down, aggressive spiral descent. C-7 crews would pop out of cloud decks just a few feet above the ground, dispatch their cargo at the end of a parachute and then climb back into the soup.[97] Those aircrews providing supplies to forces in the A Shau Valley in April 1968 received special praise from their ground counterparts. Major General John J. Tolson, the commanding general of the 1st Cavalry Division, wrote, "I witnessed your C-130 crews in one of the most magnificent displays of courage and airmanship that I have ever seen. The low ceilings, mountainous terrain, lack of terminal navigation facilities and enemy anti-aircraft fires all combined to create an exceedingly hazardous environment for the planned resupply air drops."[98] He recognized that the missions were by nature inherently hazardous, what with the bad weather, primitive landing strips, and the necessity to fly the aircraft to the limits of their performance capabilities. Providers made approaches that left no margin: flying an assault approach was a "power-off stall plus ten knots . . . it is most certainly insufficient to allow recovery from an unexpected change in landing conditions."[99] Ray Bowers later wrote that flight operations into the A Shau Valley that spring were more demanding of the pilots' skills and fraught with more danger from antiaircraft artillery than existed at Khe Sanh.[100]

Camouflaged parked aircraft, helicopter rotors, undisciplined traffic patterns, rough landing surfaces, and even friendly artillery fire added to the opportunities for catastrophe on each transport aircraft sortie. The C-130 crews that completed thirty-two deliveries to Kontum on the nights of May 19 and 20, 1972, did so to an airfield that had been subjected to rocket attacks, one of which destroyed a South Vietnamese C-123. In the opinion of the operations analyst who examined the battle, C-130 resupply operations during May 1972 were among the Air Force's great achievements, and credit went to the men who flew them. Airlift crews landed at night no matter what, and on the night of May 22 loadmasters discharged seven planeloads of supplies.[101]

Deeming his C-130 Hercules "A big slow target made of aluminum," the commander of the 374th Tactical Airlift Wing, Colonel Andrew P. Iosue, considered low-altitude airdrops in support of An Loc four years after Khe Sanh so dangerous that he nominated every crew who completed one for the distinguished flying cross.[102] He was not exaggerating the danger: two of the 345th Tactical Airlift Squadron's crews were shot down and killed there.[103] An assessment late in the war wrote, "It is no wonder that many of their fellow pilots say that the C-130 crews have the most guts in South East Asia."[104]

The airlift mission required bureaucratic courage in addition to the physical bravery the flying environment made necessary. Aircraft commanders found themselves in situations where one imperative compelled them to take great risks to deliver cargo to people in need of their support, and the other imperative was to avoid destroying their aircraft and crew trying to complete the mission. Aircrews therefore needed their commanders' support in order to make tough decisions, like choosing not to fly into an airfield under mortar fire.[105]

Bad weather and limited navigational aids undercut tactical airlift. The closer one flew to the ground, the more accurate and responsive the information had to be concerning where the plane was in relation to the ground. When the weather was good, a pilot could simply see where he was and where he was going. When the weather was bad, he needed very accurate navigational aids and maps, items not always available in Southeast Asia. One solution for dealing with low cloud ceilings and poor visibility was to waive the rules so as to deliver supplies. In 1966 the 315th Air Commando Group lowered the minimums below cloud ceilings to 500 feet above the ground with three miles' visibility. Low ceilings made airlift operations more challenging and dangerous, but adverse weather was not a great impediment to airlift missions. In 1968 air and ground personnel developed methods for using a radar to guide C-130s to release paradrop points inside clouds that produced an average miss distance of about 133 feet.[106]

What if troops needed supplies and had no place to land near them? Airlifters developed three methods between 1963 and 1966 to meet this contingency. The first two were the "parachute low altitude delivery system" and the "low altitude parachute extraction system."[107] The former used a parachute to drop a bundle from an altitude of about 200 feet from a C-130 flying at 150 miles per hour, while the latter used a parachute to pull pallets out of the back end of a Hercules while it flew about twenty-four to sixty inches above the ground at the same speed. A third method was "ground proximity extraction system," in which a hook attached to the cargo pulled the load out of a C-130 or C-123 by hooking a cable on the ground. The aircraft would fly a touch-and-go approach, which required about 600 feet of open space, although the target area was only about seventy to 120 feet long.[108] Use of these methods began in May 1966 and were a hit with the Army. On average the pallets were dropped within forty-seven feet of where they were supposed to land. Right away most of the pallets reached their targets intact.[109]

When used at Khe Sanh for the first time, the pallet contained a delivery of fresh eggs, and the jolt of the landing broke only two. On May 13, men of the 25th Infantry Division received C-rations from a paradrop and a batch of rockets on a pallet ejected out of the back of a C-130 skimming over the ground; they planned on asking for the delivery of ammunition for their howitzers soon thereafter. These methods could provide significant numbers of artillery shells. Artillerists from the same division received ten tons of 105mm rounds (300 of them) and another pallet of 104 rounds of 155mm shells.[110] Airlift also delivered critically needed components, such as barrels for 175mm cannon, using these methods. Air deliveries in which the plane did not even land had been instrumental in supporting the Bu Dop Special Forces Camp in 1967. Two Viet Cong regiments were trying to overrun the camp, but air strikes beat back the enemy and air drops sustained it.[111] The 1st Cavalry Division was particularly impressed with the airdrops' accuracy in May 1968 during Operation Delaware, when twenty-seven drops arrived on average within seventy-three yards of the target—this under fire and in bad weather. The plan had been to take and repair the airstrip at A Luoi so that C-123s could land on it within six days. In reality, it was ten days before work could begin on the runway, and C-130 air drops had to make up the difference. During Khe Sanh, Hercules and Provider transports achieved average miss distances of ninety-five and seventy yards, respectively, under visual flying conditions; under instrument flying conditions, C-130s achieved an average 134-yard miss distance, although some drops were drastically inaccurate.[112]

There was also the ground radar aerial delivery system (GRADS) that was comprised of a radar plus wind information to locate and time an air drop. One would drop a pallet from about 15,000 feet that a drogue chute slowed to a speed of 130 feet per second. The main chutes would open in time to slow the pallet without subjecting it to too much drift.[113] What this meant was that if an airfield was under too much fire for a transport to land and offload supplies, or if there was no airfield at all but only an open field, transports could place pallets of vital supplies to within fifty feet of friendly forces, making it even more likely that surrounded forces would be able to fight on without being overrun. Consequently, this air drop capability lent flexibility to Army operations. The fact that Air Force transports and Army helicopters could be counted on to bring whatever troops needed, short of a main battle tank, supported ground force mobility.[114]

In other situations, a much more subtle approach was necessary, like resupplying covert special forces who wanted to avoid anything that might suggest their presence. The Fifth Special Forces Group got the Air Force to modify empty napalm canisters into parachute-retarded containers. In this way, an A-1 Skyraider could resupply them by flying what looked like a bombing run. An enemy observer might assume that it was going after communist troops, not supporting covert American Special Forces.[115]

This ability to resupply infantry constituted an operational revolution for infantry operating in remote areas: enemy possession of the ground around them could no longer cut off the troops from resupply. In fact, the commander of the air cavalry in the A Shau Valley did not consider his unit to be in an especially dangerous situation because he had good infantry, artillery, a dominant position, and a supply artery through the landing strip he controlled. He wrote, "With the airfield and approach facilities operational the weather is less of a consideration. Actually would like to see the enemy come after us for a change.... Am sure he realizes the high cost that would be to him."[116]

Supporting remote outposts was a vital airlift mission. The French attempted to use airlift to support their troops at Dien Bien Phu when Viet Minh troops surrounded it in 1954, but the freight-carrying capacity of their air force could not deliver the quantity of supplies necessary to sustain that outpost. The surrounded base at Dien Bien Phu required 200 tons of supplies per day, but the most their smaller transports were able to deliver was 120 tons. Consequently, the garrison surrendered in May 1954. A decade later, transports airlifted an average of 17,000 tons of supplies per month within South Vietnam, a daily average of more than 560 tons.[117]

As early as 1962 the South Vietnamese and US air forces had transports and air assault troops on alert day and night to provide relief to threatened outposts. During the defense of the outpost at Plei Me, resupply by air was essential to its survival. The aircrews completed their mission in airspace full of enemy ground fire, dropping bundles into a small drop zone, while tactical fighters provided close air support. Flares dropped from other transports provided light for five night airdrops.[118] General Hunter Harris of PACAF commented to his airlifters that, "It was only due to the day, night, and bad weather efforts of your airlift forces that the ground forces were able to get food, ammunition and supplies necessary to withstand the continuing Viet Cong assaults. Plei Me stands as a monument to what dedicated air and ground forces can accomplish by working in close harmony."[119] The following year C-123s air dropped supplies there with such accuracy that less than 2 percent were lost.[120]

Often, Special Forces camps were totally dependent on air supply. Special Forces commented in 1968 that C-7 deliveries were essential to their survival. Because of its short takeoff and landing capabilities Caribous could bring smaller but coveted loads to the most remote landing strips that were too short for C-123s and C-130s. They also were intended to be scheduled more flexibly, and the Air Force set aside eight Caribous for the support of the camps.[121] A soldier fighting the North Vietnamese in the A Shau Valley wrote that other than C-7s, "Nothing else could make it into the valley—no aircraft, no other forms of supplies. Helicopters weren't flying, there weren't any road supplies, the troops on the ground were very low on supplies, very low on ammunition, very low on water."[122] When the Viet Cong cratered the runway at Dak To during the Tet Offensive, leaving the usable portion too short for C-130s, C-7s still landed supplies. Aware of soldiers' dependence on them, some C-7 crews completed their missions with unusual determination, such as the one Major Clarence Beardsley commanded on May 12, 1967. A special forces camp at Con Thien badly needed 105mm artillery rounds, and Beardsley was going to make sure they received them. On the first pass for the airdrop, ground fire hit the Caribou and prevented the load from leaving the aircraft, so Beardsley made a second pass, took more hits, but delivered the ammunition.[123] Army helicopters in remote areas needed fuel, and C-7s were often the airframe that brought it to them. Tactical airlift thus made possible helicopter/infantry search-and-destroy missions out of the forward staging area of Cao Lanh in the summer of 1967. The 1970 siege of two Special Forces camps at Dak Pek and Dak Seang witnessed a most unstealthy means for getting supplies to friendly forces. After enemy fire shot down three C-7s, the airlifters switched to night operations and got help from a Fourteenth Special Operations Wing AC-119. As the Caribou made its approach, the gunship lay down suppressing fire and then aimed its spotlight at the drop zone. Over the course of seven weeks in April and May, not a single C-7 suffered so much as a bullet hole while conducting these night airdrops.[124]

Airlift repeatedly sustained Army and ARVN forces in battle. American and South Vietnamese forces won every engagement during a series of battles in July 1966 when airlift was the sole means of resupply. C-123s, for instance, delivered 6,100 artillery rounds to solitary batteries in the midst of Operation Paul Revere in August 1966. During Operation Attleboro, runways close to the action made it possible for the Americans to shuttle troops quickly to the operational area.[125] Units that needed reinforcements during Operation Greeley in June–August 1967 got them courtesy of C-130s that delivered an infantry brigade. When a road to Hue was cut in February 1968, Westmoreland had a battalion airlifted into that city.[126] That same month, supplies dropped on the garrison at Kontum were important to its ability to hold out. On the night of February 2, two C-123 crews paradropped their delivery into a drop zone not much larger than a football field.[127] Three hundred sorties meant that the 173rd Airborne Brigade fighting at Dak To was able to maintain three days of reserves. Consequently, the troops on the ground never faced the peril of running out of supplies. Provider and Caribou missions were essential for bringing troops and supplies to Ban Me Thuot because insurgents controlled all the roads to it. One Army officer noticed that the airlifters would do whatever was necessary to complete their missions.[128] Air-delivered supplies sustained a special forces outpost at Ben Het during a twenty-seven-day siege in June 1969. Later in the war, in 1970 and 1971, airlift using the ground radar delivery system made sure cut-off portions of the 101st Airborne Division were adequately supplied despite bad weather.[129] Airlift decided the fate of Bouam Long in northern Laos when it was besieged in 1970. Aircraft brought in fresh Laotian troops who subsequently drove away enemy forces. Transports supplied towns when insurgents made land or river transportation routes prohibitively dangerous. This took place not only in Vietnam and Laos but also in support of Cambodian troops, who for example received ammunition from air drops in the town of Kompong Thom in June 1970.[130]

The capabilities of airlift ensured American forces would not suffer a defeat like the French had at Dien Bien Phu in 1954, when Viet Minh surrounded them and compelled their surrender.[131] Westmoreland understood what General Raymond G. Davis later noted. When one's soldiers are isolated, whether in an outpost or because the enemy has surrounded them, "you can't walk to them. You can't supply them, you can't extract them, you can't get your casualties out. You're totally dependent on air for support to make your operation work, and the lives of your troops are in the hands of the aviators."[132] In April 1972, the besieged town of An Loc had been equated to the Alamo—a word associated with defeat as much as with heroic last stands—but Kissinger advised President Nixon that tactical airlift was instrumental for supplying An Loc, and three weeks later he commented that airlift was delivering supplies sufficient to sustain the town.[133]

Resupplying Civilian Irregular Defense Group outposts was another important task for airlifters.[134] Communist forces besieged Dak Seang on March 31, 1970, and the troops there needed helmets, gasoline, flak jackets, and, within a couple of days, water. In sustaining Dak Seang, airlifters modified their approach and paradrop tactics, and coordinated nighttime airdrops with the ground forces and AC-119 gunships. Most of the pallets landed in the drop zone; tactical fighters destroyed the few that landed outside the wire so that the VC would not retrieve them for their own use. The Caribou pilots brushed off hits from ground fire to complete their runs, and some died trying. One crashed a few miles away from its target—after delivering its cargo. The director of operations of the 483rd Tactical Airlift Wing observed that paradrops at night by one aircraft at a time were the best and simplest way of delivering cargo and that gunships were probably indispensable for their survival. Just by being in the vicinity of the landing zone, AC-119 gunships intimidated enemy troops into holding their fire. As a result of this support Dak Seang ultimately functioned as a death trap for attacking communists. Airlift alone, however, was not always sufficient to sustain surrounded outposts. Hercules's delivered sixty-three tons of supplies to the Duc Co Firebase in October 1972 but PAVN forces captured it in December.[135]

Saigon also tasked airlifters with evacuating untenable outposts. The short field capabilities of C-7 Caribous meant 3,130 refugees were able to flee Bung Lung and Ba Kev in northeastern Cambodia in June 1970, C-123s having been found too heavy for the soft runway. When communist troops got to within about a third of a mile of the runway, AC-119 gunships were brought in to fend them off until the last refugees could be flown out. In May 1968, MACV decided that the Kham Duc Special Forces Camp was no longer needed for the mission of assessing the movement of communist forces into the more populated areas along the coast of South Vietnam. Airlifters and close air support units received notice of just a few hours to begin the evacuation; nevertheless, Air Force, Army, and Marine forces completed the evacuation successfully. While fighter-bombers and B-52s suppressed enemy forces, transports evacuated a battalion-sized group of American and South Vietnamese soldiers, including some local civilian relatives on May 12. A battalion commander later wrote that airlifters were irreplaceable for its relief; infantry never could have done it alone.[136] Aircrews evacuated nearly 530 Vietnamese and American troops, but 150 died when the VC shot down a C-130 loaded with civilians that had just taken off.[137] Although successful airlift operations, evacuations were still defeats because the Viet Cong took ownership of the town after Americans and South Vietnamese fled.

Evacuating Kham Duc was not managed perfectly and unnecessarily directed aircrews into harm's way. One transport Lieutenant Colonel Jay Van Cleeff piloted was ordered to deposit a combat control team and ammunition there. Viet Cong lined both approaches to the runway and saturated the area with rifle fire. By the time they arrived over Kham Duc the camp was on fire, fighters were bombing the enemy all around it, and C-130s were already there landing and taking off, evacuating the camp. The combat control team was apparently supposed to direct the evacuation, and Van Cleeff managed to land successfully despite the crater in the runway and the debris on it. As he came to a stop he saw the remains of a burned-out C-130 on one side and a wrecked helicopter on the other. Although they could not see anyone left in the camp, the team departed the C-130, which then took off. In fact, the camp's evacuation had been completed and the team never should have stepped off their transport. C-123 pilot Lieutenant Colonel Joe M. Jackson landed there soon thereafter to retrieve the team. Jackson carried out an aggressive, high-descent approach, landed, waited for the three combat controllers to clamber aboard, and then took off through a hail of rifle and mortar fire. Guerrillas overran the camp after his plane departed. Jackson received the Medal of Honor for his courage.[138]

Airlift really stood out during the siege of Khe Sanh, an outpost that irregular forces and then Marines had held since 1962. Transports supported the Marines when they augmented the camp in spring 1967, and beginning that autumn the camp required aerial resupply to function.[139] During the stockpiling of the fort, enemy action progressively cut off Highway 9, the umbilical connecting Khe Sanh with the resources of Quang Tri: "It was almost impossible to get supplies into Khe Sanh by truck convoy, so the only way they could be resupplied was via aircraft." Caribous were often used because the runway was normally in such bad shape that the C-7s were the only aircraft that could land between the ruts and gouges on the landing surface.[140]

Khe Sanh's isolation worsened at the beginning of 1968. Enemy forces surrounded the Marine fort in January and PAVN artillery detonated a large portion of the Marines' ammunition and artillery shells on January 22. Now short of ammunition, the Marines at Khe Sahn were dependent on airlift for resupply and air strikes for a large portion of their firepower. General Wheeler reassured President Johnson that aircraft could keep the outpost supplied as long as the transports had the protection of B-52 and fighter-bomber strikes.[141] C-130s were central to the resupply effort, and their status and availability rates received the regular attention of the president. What with the Tet Offensive and the siege of Khe Sanh, Wheeler warned that airlift within Vietnam was the long pole in the tent.[142] Examples of the critical difference airlift missions made during 1968 fill volumes.[143]

The reason the PAVN besieged Khe Sanh has been debated at length. Some argue they intended to overrun and destroy Khe Sanh so as to deliver a mortal blow to American support for the war. PAVN offensives continued well after they had diverted the attention of their enemies, a sign that inflicting massive losses, not a diversion, was the purpose. In actuality, the North Vietnamese intended to use their operations against Khe Sanh as part of a larger strategy to draw American and South Vietnamese forces away from populated areas so that they would be too far away to respond to the Tet Offensive that would kick off at the end of January.[144] At the time, analysts were not certain of the ultimate purpose of the PAVN effort, but in any event American airlift capabilities, firepower, and South Vietnamese counterattacks denied the communists a battlefield victory. Both Westmoreland and Davis relied on air power to stave off defeat since the communists had Khe Sanh surrounded. Wheeler and Westmoreland discussed the use of nuclear weapons just in case the need arose for them, but President Johnson rejected out of hand any consideration of their use.[145]

AIRLIFT EFFECTIVENESS

Landing transports at Khe Sanh meant subjecting planes and crews to firepower of all calibers. One C-130 crew demonstrated a level of determination that defies credulity. A C-130 full of ammunition took fire upon landing on February 5, which ignited some of the ammo. The pilot guided the plane off the runway while the rest of the crew fought the fire. After the ammunition was offloaded, the plane took on a bulldozer. Then the mortars came. One struck within fifty feet of the transport, damaged an engine, and made it necessary to take off using just three engines. The Hercules, with bulldozer, made it to Da Nang. A week later, mortar and small arms fire seemed to have rendered a C-130 lost. Engines, tires, and hydraulics—all necessary for flight—were damaged. Instead of abandoning the aircraft, the crew and a mechanic repaired it and flew to Da Nang two days later.[146] It seems as though airlifters accepted hits from ground fire come what may, and that the only way the enemy could prevent the C-130s from landing where they wanted was to shoot one down. When the enemy gained control of lower altitudes, airlifters provided supplies via paradrop.

President Johnson told Chairman Wheeler, "I don't want any damn Dinbinphoo" at Khe Sanh.[147] The president monitored the siege during the Tet Offensive on a daily—and then an hourly—basis, and the ability of airlift to keep the fort supplied meant that he was not going to have to deal with the aftermath of 6,000 Marines having been slaughtered.[148] Nevertheless, Army Chief of Staff General Harold K. Johnson heightened the president's anxiety when he warned on February 9 that there was a possibility that the Viet Cong could capture Khe Sanh's airfield. If that happened, he placed the Marines' odds of holding out at "50–50."[149] When ground fire grew too intense, Seventh Air Force prohibited them from landing. For some time Providers and Caribous continued to offload on the ground, but their freight capacity was insufficient to fully supply the fort. After February 12 when mortar fire blew up a Marine C-130, the transports resupplied the outpost solely via airdrops. The first one occurred in instrument flying conditions at 400 feet with the C-130 flying at 150 miles per hour in order to increase drop accuracy. Given these challenges and the siege's importance to the White House, the Air Force allocated only the most experienced aircrews available for the airdrops to Khe Sanh. Their accuracy improved to an error of 115 yards, which meant that the besieged defenders could retrieve the supplies.[150]

Over the course of the seventy-eight-day siege, airlifters delivered 12,430 tons. The Marines judged it a success, and airlift was a key enabler to their survival. Over the course of the entire Tet Offensive, communist automatic weapons fire managed to shoot down only a single transport, and this C-130 was lost during its takeoff run at Song Be on February 28, not from Khe Sanh. All told, 10 percent of airlift capacity was lost to accidents and to enemy action while planes were on the ground. Communist firepower destroyed five Providers and eleven Hercules over the course of the battle.[151]

While the Air Force persistently measured airlift's effectiveness in tons, sorties, and timeliness, the Army saw it in terms of soldiers accomplishing their missions. During the 1970 raid into Cambodia, the commander of the 1st Cavalry Division exclaimed that, "Without this tremendous airlift capability, we could not have moved across the border to strike at the enemy's supplies and base areas nor could we have sustained our operations there."[152] Transports were critical for bringing ammunition close to the forward edge of the battle area, where helicopters then shuttled it into the hands of the soldiers.[153]

Transferring infantry from one place to another was another way the Army made good use of airlift, and transports carried out several large-scale troop movements. The responsiveness, flexibility, and freight hauling capabilities of the transports enabled them to reinforce garrisons and deliver supplies within hours of receiving requests—regardless of the situation along the roads that connected the myriad Allied units and South Vietnamese towns. The airplanes literally flew over obstacles. During the counterattacks against the communists in February 1968, airlift made possible the successful defensive strategy of the Americans and South Vietnamese. In one instance they moved a brigade of the 101st Airborne Division from Dao Loc to Song Be in January 1968, and eighteen C-130s moved a battalion in just five hours.[154] Air drops also empowered more conventional forms of warfare. In support of Operation Junction City, C-123s and C-130s moved pre-positioned supplies forward to the troops.[155] Airlift meant that resource-dependent formations like mechanized infantry could "roam the combat area at will, unencumbered by the requirements to maintain normal land lines of communications for necessary resupply."[156] During the run-up to the next enemy offensive of August 1968, General Abrams used airlift for operational level shifts of troops flying 1,300 sorties each day and adding up to a division's worth of troops and 3,000 tons of supplies. At the end of the year, Abrams moved the 1st Cavalry Division from I Corps to III Corps, distributing the troops as a screen along the Cambodian border.[157]

At the beginning of 1971, American airlift continued efforts to shore up South Vietnam's border with Cambodia. Transports moved South Vietnamese forces involved in a raid against communist forces in the Chup Plantation inside Cambodia, a raid designed to relieve pressure on both Cambodian forces and the ARVN Third Corps.[158] Because this took place during the American withdrawal, the magnitude of this action appeared to violate the spirit of American national policy and Secretary of State William P. Rogers became concerned about congressional reactions, but Admiral Moorer reassured him that Congress would be notified beforehand.[159] Nixon said, "If our goal is merely to withdraw that is one issue, but if our goal is to leave the South Vietnamese in such a way that they will have a chance for survival that is another." Secretary Rogers believed that because of American airlift capabilities, the Chup Operation was assured of success.[160] That this took place at all is surprising since Operation Lam Son 719 was more important and was just days away. When Chup ended in April nothing was fundamentally different.[161]

A month later, transports carried 36,000 passengers and 26,000 tons of cargo in 2,900 sorties in support of Lam Son 719/Dewey Canyon II—an operation that attempted to use ARVN troops and American and South Vietnamese air support to cut off the Ho Chi Minh Trail. Here airlift made possible the rapid movement of more than 9,000 soldiers in just seven days.[162] Transports moved supplies forward as far as Quang Tri, Phu Bai, and then Khe Sanh, where the airstrip had been refurbished. Hercules transports alone moved more than 13,000 people and 21,000 tons of freight. Helicopters then transported supplies from there to the troops waiting to cross into Laos. The jet fuel and ammunition the C-130s provided were particularly vital.[163] Pallets at Da Nang contained an excess of 350 tons of ammunition, fuel, and food for air drop resupply, but this fixed wing capability was set aside during Lam Son 719 in favor of helicopters. Instead, transports returned the beaten ARVN troops to their main bases in South Vietnam. There were plans for carving out a runway at Tchepone on which C-123s could land and thus sustain the raid, but the North Vietnamese were present in such great numbers and with such well-placed firepower that the runway was a forlorn hope.[164] The quick airlift of troops and supplies to the jumping-off areas was only a tactical success for the airlifters. Poor operational security and counterintelligence failures, and careful awareness on the part of the North Vietnamese, ensured that the enemy knew that something big was afoot to the east of Tchepone—a vital section of their supply line. They chose to defend that area and understood their opponent well enough for them to meet the South Vietnamese force of 10,000 with a counterattack of 23,000 that soon rose to 36,000.[165] It is rare indeed for any army to expect to defeat an enemy that outnumbers it three to one, especially when the side with the greater numbers also holds the high ground.

Airlift and the 1972 Offensive

By the time of the Easter Offensive in the spring of 1972, the airlift capacity had been drawn down to the level necessary to sustain the American forces still in Vietnam. The management of these aircrews, however, had not produced a bullpen of combat-ready pilots and navigators. The pilots brought in for the buildup proved capable of learning, adapting, and performing, but still were not fully ready for the kinds of operations they faced the moment they arrived; that took a few months of "on the job" experience.[166] Even by the war's last year, night airdrop training was virtually nonexistent because the host country for the 374th Tactical Airlift Wing, Taiwan, did not allow it. During the frantic missions of April 1972, for example, "'More than once,' just prior to takeoff for a night [container delivery system] mission, the navigator briefer 'was explaining basic Doppler techniques to the navigator and the pilot briefer was talking basic crew coordination problems.'"[167] One US Army captain, however, wondered why it took the US Air Force "26 days to get with the program to do a job that their pilots are supposed to be trained to do on a routine basis."[168]

Tactical airlift was essential to ARVN success in 1972. Airlifters provided them with great mobility during the 1972 Easter Offensive, flying troops into Hue to bolster its defense. A major component of North Vietnamese strategy was to cut off surrounded forces from their supply line, but airlift helped defeat that strategy. The White House recognized the importance of airlift and arranged to send a pair of C-130 squadrons to the theater in addition to the ones already there.[169] American and South Vietnamese reactions began as the invasion commenced by flying a battalion to Kontum from March 31 to April 1, 1972. Four days later, airlift shuttled 4,000 troops to Hue. Heavy airlift in the form of C-141 Starlifters were also brought in to release C-130s for airdrops. These flew four to eight sorties each day. Starlifters moved more than 15,000 troops from one part of South Vietnam to another by the end of May. Until the C-141s arrived, the Hercules was the sole American airlifter in the theater, because the Department of Defense had given the Caribous and Providers to the South Vietnamese. When the airstrip at An Loc fell to the invading forces a week into the invasions, air drops became critical to its survival. Supplies parachuted to the ground were once again vital to sustaining forces that had been cut off from ground resupply at Kontum and Minh Thanh. C-130s conducted all the air drops and most of those were devoted to Kontum and An Loc.[170]

A town north of Saigon, An Loc had to be sustained because President Nguyen Van Thieu attached his prestige to its protection.[171] Its aerial resupply began with helicopters from April 7 to 12. All of what they brought reached the ARVN defenders, but when ground fire shot down a CH-47 on April 12, helicopter resupply ended. From April 11 to 18, C-123s completed thirty-nine medium-altitude parachute deliveries, but those sorties came to an end when ground fire downed number forty.[172] South Vietnamese air drop accuracy was terrible. The transports approached at 5,000 feet giving wind currents plenty of time to push the bundles out of the drop zone into enemy hands. Consequently, ARVN troops recovered only about 30 percent of the ammunition and other supplies. The resupply task then fell to American C-130s, which delivered supplies using the low altitude container delivery system. This tactic required a C-130 to approach just above the treetops, climb to about 700 feet at the last minute, and then slow to 105 miles per hour whereupon the loadmaster ejected the pallets of supplies that a parachute slowed down. The transport then dove momentarily, accelerated, and escaped. Needless to say, the aircraft was an easy target at the apex of its profile, and this method also required a great deal of training. The first four made successful drops but each took a considerable amount of flak, which destroyed the fifth C-130.[173]

The C-130s had to switch from daytime operations to those at night after automatic weapons became prohibitively intense. Ground fire forced these aircrews to use the GRADS method of higher altitude precision air drops. Only two out of twenty-six tons of supplies reached the South Vietnamese on the first attempt. Worse, the force of impacting the ground damaged the paradropped 105mm shells.[174] Airlift had to sustain not only the allied forces that were cut off and under siege at An Loc but also the thousands of civilian refugees, whom the North Vietnamese allowed into the city to worsen the supply and food situation. More than 20,000 people were surrounded inside An Loc, half soldiers, the other half civilians. Logistical analysts originally believed the besieged would need 200 tons of supplies each day (mainly ammunition), but they survived on about sixty tons. South Vietnamese ground forces were going to stage a relief of An Loc, and airlift meant that relief troops did not have to walk or truck their way to the jumping-off point; transports airlifted a battalion of troops to their rally point five miles south of the town on May 16.[175]

Every C-130 supporting An Loc took hits. Because enemy forces filled the airspace over the drop zone with machine gun fire, pilots ejected their pallets from higher altitudes, which worsened accuracy.[176] It did not help that one of the main approach routes passed right over the command post for the 7th PAVN Division. An interim solution to the problem of dropping accurately at night was using a spotlight from an AC-119 or AC-130 to illuminate the drop zone at the last minute, but that meant the enemy shot at the gunship. Subsequent use of the high-altitude-low-opening parachute (HALO) method failed because the South Vietnamese parachute packers had not been trained well enough to pack them correctly so the triggering devices would function properly and open at the right altitude. All eight pallets either crashed or landed where enemy troops could retrieve the supplies. Low-level container drops recommenced on April 23, but when ground fire exploded another transport on April 26, the 374th Wing switched to nighttime container delivery system missions, but that tactic also failed. Friendly forces retrieved less than 30 percent of the pallets the Americans dropped, with a far lower rate for those the South Vietnamese dropped from their C-123s. According to MACV, the airdrops benefitted the enemy to a far greater degree thus far than they did the South Vietnamese. Misdirected pallets, for instance, introduced the VC to canned fruit cocktail.[177]

South Vietnamese troops occasionally retrieved a pallet, but the problem of inaccuracy and ground fire climaxed on May 3 when the enemy shot down another C-130. As a solution, the US Army flew in its own parachute packers, and the transports implemented a more accurate high drop speed system. They now combined a ground radar air delivery method to determine just when to drop the pallets with HALO parachutes that American experts had packed. Hercules transports flew one of these missions on the night of May 4 and South Vietnamese recovered twenty-three of twenty-four bundles. Less than a week after the air drop suspension of May 3, most bundles were landing close enough to friendly troops that they retrieved them. On May 4, after further adjustments to the system, fifteen of sixteen bundles reached the besieged. As a result of these adjustments, aircrews were able to accurately hit a drop zone of about 200 yards square. South Vietnamese recovered more than 90 percent of all the items dropped after May 4. Most of the cargo survived intact, except for cannon shells for 105mm guns and larger.[178] Rough landings burst open bags of rice, but not boxes of rice, and a parachute malfunction above a delivery of 105mm shells caused them to explode one at a time for hours. Providing at long last the correct drop zone coordinates, which had not been done, also helped.[179]

Another method initiated in May involved the use of adverse weather aerial delivery system (AWADS) equipped aircraft. AWADS were just as accurate as MSQ-77 Sky Spot radars, but using AWADS required a lot of training. All the PAVN could do after these adaptations was shell the drop zone after the pallets had landed. In response, the South Vietnamese developed the capability to retrieve all the supplies in just a minute and a half. South Vietnamese airlifters also learned how to carry out these high descent speed parachute drops from 9,500 feet themselves with great accuracy. The GRADS method, everyone concluded, was the most reliable means for guiding a transport to its release point.[180]

Because of these tactical changes, An Loc ultimately received enough supplies to hold on.[181] After another enemy attack commenced on May 11, airlift continued to sustain the defenders, while air strikes decimated the attackers. Within a week, enemy efforts to capture An Loc ended.[182] Once the paradrops hit their stride, the air bridge became reliable. From May 4 through June 25, 230 airlift sorties delivered "2,984 tons of supplies. The defenders received 2,735 tons; only 249 tons fell into enemy hands."[183] A recovery rate of 94 percent along with a successful helicopter medical evacuation turned around the confidence and morale of the defenders. Time eventually turned against the communists.[184]

Antiaircraft artillery caused plenty of trouble for the air delivery of supplies during the Easter Offensive, and it quickly worsened to the point that it made ordinary delivery methods too dangerous. Enemy 23mm guns were the worst because of their accuracy, density of fire, and the ease with which they were hidden. A combination of A-37 Dragonflies and AC-130 Spectres were good for destroying them, but the problem was never solved. When the North Vietnamese started using SA-7 antiaircraft missiles, that brought low-altitude air drops to an end. When these missiles were fired at some F-4 Phantoms, Seventh AF started canceling some C-130 missions.[185]

Military Assistance Command, Vietnam, temporarily denied airlift to the South Vietnamese in order to send them a message about the allied nature of air support. There was a problem with ARVN officers fleeing the onslaught instead of standing fast, so on May 2, General Abrams sent out this indictment: "Effective immediately no Vietnamese commander will be airlifted out of a unit defensive position by U.S. fixed wing aircraft or helicopter unless such evacuation is directed personally by the RVNAF corps commander. Inform your counterpart."[186] Not surprisingly, Abrams was worried that the South Vietnamese had "lost their will to fight . . . and that the whole thing may be lost."[187] They had not.

Although two North Vietnamese divisions lay siege to Kontum during April, it was not intense enough to prevent transports from reinforcing it. Over a span of three weeks beginning April 14, they brought in around 70,000 gallons of fuel each day.[188] The 50th Tactical Airlift Squadron conveyed supplies to Kontum night and day until the airspace got too crowded and the enemy started lobbing artillery shells at unloading C-130s. In response the squadron ended daytime missions but continued to land at night.[189] Disaster struck on May 17 when the PAVN subjected the airfield to 122mm rocket fire. "A US C-130 was offloading ammunition on the western end of Kontum airfield," John Paul Vann, the civilian advisor to II Corps, wrote, "when the airfield came under rocket fire." The pilot tried to take off at once, but the plane's loading ramp had not been raised and it scraped the ground, functioning as a brake. It never took off, careened into a building, tumbled, and exploded. Only two crewmembers survived. Then 3,000 105mm rounds at the ammunition dump started exploding. This closed the runway and led Vann to conclude that daytime deliveries were now at an end due to the rocket attacks.[190] Two days later twelve C-130s managed to land, unload their cargo and depart on the night of May 19, and thirteen C-130s were able to land and offload nearly 4,000 105mm rounds on the night of May 23.[191]

When enemy forces grabbed the eastern edge of the runway on May 25, the Americans countered with airdrops from C-130s, four of which carried out these missions on May 28, parachuting sixty-four tons of ammunition. They were accurate enough that the ARVN recovered all but a single ton. Kontum benefitted greatly from the lessons learned at An Loc and consequently efforts went more smoothly.[192] Pallets landing outside of the drop zone remained a challenge, but by June 5, all the air drops into Kontum were being recovered. Only two out of 176 parachutes failed, and only one of the twelve sorties failed to deliver. There the C-130s relied on the AWADS method and this proved very successful; no bundle missed the aim point by more than 330 yards, which kept them within the drop zone. Air drops sustained Kontum for two months while the enemy surrounded the town.[193]

Overall, however, the performance of the South Vietnamese airlifters demonstrated they were not yet ready or equipped to fight successfully on their own. The Vietnamization program to develop South Vietnamese military self-sufficiency, including an airlift capability, had come up short. Secretary of Defense Robert S. McNamara proposed it in fall 1967 and his replacement as secretary of defense, Clark Clifford, developed it in 1968 and forced it upon the Saigon government.[194] During Nixon's first year, the South Vietnamese handled 25 percent of their airlift requirements, which of course meant that they were dependent on the Americans for the rest.[195] While their airlift chipped in considerably during the Easter Offensive in 1972, the country had to have the help of the United States in order to complete an airlift effort that was operationally effective and strategically necessary for its national survival. By May 25, 1972, for example, South Vietnamese cargo aircraft had transported 77,191 passengers and 6,302 tons of supplies. Its primary transports were C-47s (forty-eight), C-119s (nineteen), and C-123s (forty-two), which were older and carried less freight than their American counterparts. By comparison, the USAF carried 128,586 passengers and 36,717 tons utilizing 3,657 C-130 and ninety-eight C-141 sorties.

Transports airlifted the equivalent of an infantry division, 15,892 troops to be exact, from one military region to another by May 28. The South Vietnamese had been able to accomplish about 85 percent of its airlift needs prior to the invasion, but the Easter Offensive showed that it was not up to fending off the North Vietnamese in yet another way: Saigon needed dozens more transports and with them, the pilots, maintainers, and infrastructure necessary to support their function—requirements far beyond South Vietnamese capabilities. For South Vietnamese forces to have flown as much freight and as many passengers as the American C-130s and C-141s had during the spring necessitated more than four times as many C-123s (229) as they had (forty-eight). The South Vietnamese struggled with tactical proficiency; too many of their missions had dropped supplies behind enemy lines. One solution John Paul Vann proposed was using C-130s as pathfinders for Providers because the American transport had better avionics that improved airdrop accuracy.[196]

An Loc and Kontum received most of the air drops during the first months of the Easter Offensive, 303 and 136 respectively, but twelve other threatened places also benefitted from 159 air drops. Aerial resupply not only sustained besieged cities but also provided relief to such places as the Dak Pek Ranger outpost. Airlifters had similar success at Duc Thanh, whose defenders nearly ran out of ammunition, but transports delivered pallets with enough accuracy that Duc Thanh was much more secure by June 3. Xuyen Moc was so small, however, that the parachute bundles really needed GPS-level accuracy. On June 16 a pallet of canned meat smashed the district headquarters to pieces, and a bundle of mortar rounds caught the village's small arms cache on fire. Nevertheless, its defenders held. Minh Thanh was so tiny that the whole place was a drop zone. South Vietnamese regulars were able to endure even though only a sixth of the drops landed where they could reach them.[197]

Hercules transports gave similar support to friendly forces in Cambodia, flying eighteen missions airdropping 213 tons to the harassed city of Kampong Thum. Air drops also sustained troops at Kompong Trabek and Svay Rieng. They continued these operations after the invasion ground to a halt because the South Vietnamese troops there still needed supplies.[198] Airlift around Angkor Wat was challenging and had to be kept to a minimum because the American operations nearby were politically sensitive.[199]

Soldiers and airmen at every level recognized the strategic significance of tactical airlift. General Vogt knew the aircrews had "materially assisted Allied ground forces in stopping the enemy offensive." An advisor at An Loc wrote that aerial resupply had an almost "undefinable impact in raising their morale, giving them hope and ... confidence. It was just totally, as far as I'm concerned, that single factor that has enabled them to sustain themselves, maintain hope, maintain desire, and maintain a limited offensive posture."[200] Airlift was effective because it made possible the execution of the American and South Vietnamese strategy and overturned the enemy's strategy.

This airlift capability may have come with a two-edged sword: it made military intervention easier and less risky for the United States. The eventual consequences of Vietnam serve as a warning against using capabilities as the starting point for military operations. Perhaps a downside of possessing a dominant tactical airlift capability is that as a result of that ability, a military force does not have to control all of the ground and all of the surface supply routes, which works against the ultimate policy goal of, and the essential strategic necessity for, winning a counterinsurgency war: governance—as governance takes place on the ground. The point in Vietnam was for the locals to control and govern their villages and hamlets and the surrounding countryside in tandem with their army and their central government in Saigon. That means that the non-communists of South Vietnam would have run things and would have been the sole possessors of violence to a degree that the police would have been able to identify and put down insurgent movements.[201] An absence of airlift means that an army has to completely dominate wherever it goes in order to advance farther, and that enables governance by the political actors who follow in its wake. In order to defeat an insurgency—which continued in 1972 in parallel with the invasion of North Vietnamese regulars—one still had to meet the same requirement whether or not air supremacy and loads of airlift capacity were yours. Airlift's remarkable capabilities can thus work against the ultimate policy goal of governance because the power in possession of that ability does not *have* to control *all* of the ground in order to wage successful military operations and support overextended or isolated outposts of troops, and thus an extensive airlift capability works against the ultimate political goal of a return to ordinary governance. This is not an argument to do away with or not use airlift; that would be senseless. The way to arrive at a better strategy is not to constrain military forces to the right options by taking away equipment. Instead, think through and create a strategy that will achieve the endgame. After all, the endgame in war is always political—who governs where and how—not military.

These tough choices illustrate one of the challenges of waging a supposedly limited war. Vietnam was a major war, and it required a level of commitment that was closer to a major war against a peer with great power than it was to a small war against insurgents like the Philippine War of 1899–1902. That should surprise no one since the Soviet Union and China were North Vietnam's sponsors. The infrastructural needs of tactical airlift—navigational aids, runways, ramps, maintenance, airspace control—further show that Vietnam was a major war. Indeed, airlift operations proceeded with the deliberateness of a siege, and airlift essentially needed the same kind of support infrastructure that existed in the United States transplanted to a location half a world away. Add close air support and reconnaissance aircraft (not to mention KC-135s, interdiction aircraft, and fighters) and it is clear that the US was fighting a major war.[202]

Chapter 13

The Effectiveness of Air Strikes against Ground Forces

C lose air support (CAS) comprised an enormous proportion of the missions flown in Southeast Asia. Daily experience revealed that when Viet Cong and PAVN forces gathered and friendly forces found them, aerial firepower devastated them. Close air support, however, suffered from the same challenge as ground forces: finding enemy forces. Air strikes were most effective when part of a joint operation because ground forces could impel the enemy to coalesce into targets vulnerable to bombing.

A Marine Corps definition of close air support has stood the test of time: "the attack by aircraft on hostile ground targets which are so close to friendly forces as to require detailed integration of each air mission with the fire and movement of forces."[1] A more down-to-earth report defined it as "fire support immediately available to the ground component *where* it is needed at the *time* it is needed [italics in original]."[2] Vietnam also saw thousands of "direct attack" missions, bombing strikes against enemy forces not in contact with friendly ground troops, mainly by B-52s.[3]

Aircraft have been used to bomb troops since Italian pilots bombed Turks in North Africa in 1911, and close air support became a basic mission of air forces in World War I. Britain's Royal Flying Corps, for instance, started using fighters to strafe and bomb German troops in May 1917 to support advancing soldiers. These air actions buttressed infantry operations.[4]

As mechanized warfare developed in the 1930s, even armies that envisioned air power supporting ground forces did not necessarily mean close air support because more lucrative targets existed farther behind the lines. Communication and coordination between ground and air forces was difficult, as was responding quickly to requests for support.[5] Nevertheless, Soviet and Nazi forces exploited the civil war in Spain to try out ground attack methods.[6] Germany already had its Ju-87 Stuka, and the Soviets designed a purpose-built close air support aircraft, the Ilyushin Il-2 Sturmovik, before the Second World War.[7] Airmen in the United States deemphasized direct support of troops in favor of bombing vulnerable industrial nodes. They did not consider targets within range of friendly artillery worth risking their aircraft. German successes against France in 1940, however, got the Americans' attention, and airframes and doctrine for the close air support mission followed.[8]

Close air support saw an uneven beginning in World War II, but by 1944 armies made constant use of fighter-bombers and purpose-built aircraft for that mission. It was a part of French doctrine, but their system (ground as well as air) was not responsive enough for the rapidly changing battlefield of May 1940.[9] While the Ju-87 Stuka dive bombers' reputation exceeded their effectiveness, they nevertheless spurred the evolution of aerial bombing close to friendly forces. The Soviets better integrated their Il-2s with ground armies, and it was superior to the Stuka.[10] Britain discounted close air support until the campaign in North Africa of 1941–1943, whereupon British and American air forces allocated large numbers of fighters to CAS while steadily improving command-and-control arrangements. Fighter aircraft like the British Hawker Hurricane increasingly flew close air support missions, beginning a practice that would continue through the rest of the century. In the summer of 1944, the Americans attached P-47s to tank formations via voice radio, and this aircraft designed as a high-altitude interceptor proved adept at destroying targets on the ground. Together with tanks, trucks, and infantry they raced across France and reached the German border in the first week of September.[11]

During the early weeks of the Korean War, massive amounts of close air support staved off defeat for the remnant holding out around the Port of Pusan. Once the front stabilized, CAS became a major source of firepower for UN forces. Because Chinese infantry resided in trenches for protection, the Air Force viewed CAS as a less effective use of air power. Nevertheless, approximately 45,000 close air support sorties were flown during the remainder of the war. Between the armistice and the escalation of the Vietnam War, however, this capability languished in the United States. The Air Force prioritized nuclear deterrence at the expense of conventional warfare capabilities, including air support for the Army. It only began to reinvigorate its capabilities just prior to the war's escalation in 1965.[12]

Close Air Support in Vietnam

Admiral Sharp and General Westmoreland agreed air support of ground troops engaged in firefights was the primary mission of American air power in Southeast Asia, with air strikes against Viet Cong base camps coming second. Reflecting this strategic priority, American forces flew more CAS missions than interdiction missions, completing more than a million sorties against targets in South Vietnam, while flying 172,138 interdiction sorties against North Vietnam.[13] The Air Force alone conducted more than 134,000 CAS sorties in 1968.[14] Close air support was essential. Helicopter operations, for example, often did not proceed without accompanying fighter-bombers.[15]

Bombing missions in support of troops began modestly in November 1961 when Air Force pilots flew missions with South Vietnamese copilots against insurgents. In addition, Air America pilots flew on behalf of the Royal Lao Government well before American involvement escalated.[16] As the Viet Cong achieved greater success in 1964, MACV began to look toward air power as an equalizer. When the Viet Cong destroyed two South Vietnamese battalions at Binh Gia at the end of 1964, an absence of effective close air support was one of the culprits. Westmoreland determined to change that.[17]

A month later he received clearance to use B-57s and F-100s on missions inside South Vietnam, with B-57s flying their first missions on February 19, 1965.[18] They proved effective against Viet Cong targets. Then in May pilots in A-1 Skyraiders killed sixty-four VC fighting ARVN forces in Binh Thuan Province.[19] Westmoreland also needed air support from the Navy, so carrier-based aircraft began flying CAS missions beginning April 15. Their targets were the same as for land-based aircraft.[20] The 2nd Air Division commander expressed doubts about their usefulness over South Vietnam, mainly due to their distance from the target area, but MACV needed their firepower through July 1966 because until that time there were too few air bases in South Vietnam.[21]

American leaders from the beginning realized firepower in the form of the overt involvement of American combat formations would result in the deaths of noncombatants in

Air Bases in South Vietnam

South Vietnam. That was a downside to aerial firepower supporting ground troops. The VC would take advantage of the consequent anger against American forces to further the goals of the National Liberation Front.[22] In 1965, the director of joint research and test activity, Brigadier General John K. Boles Jr., recognized this when he saw the results of an attack in An Xuyen Province. The bombs hit their aim point, but killed no VC, inflicting instead losses on local civilians. Bombing like that would only widen the rift between the Vietnamese people and the Saigon government.[23] Viet Cong treachery, such as placing mortars and recoilless rifles within a hamlet, presented American forces with the choice of pulverizing the enemy and risking civilians caught in the crossfire and lowering the risks to their own soldiers, or lessening the reliance on air support, a situation in which American forces would have suffered more losses.[24] The chairman of the Joint Chiefs of Staff believed bombing villages friendly to the communists ought to be permissible, but that would drive more peasants away from supporting the government of South Vietnam (GVN). Additionally, effective CAS required quick decisions because ground forces needed aircraft to deliver their ordnance within minutes. Preventing noncombatant deaths required time, careful study, and precise knowledge of who was who and where each individual was, time soldiers could not spare. Westmoreland's command also understood it was difficult for pilots from their vantage points several thousand feet above the ground to differentiate between enemy formations and noncombatants.[25]

The reliable availability of close air support was one reason the Army was willing to risk posting soldiers in isolated places. During an October 1965 operation, for instance, aerial cover defeated Viet Cong near the out-of-the-way Special Forces camp at Duc Co along the Cambodian border. When a PAVN regiment attacked the Plei Me Special Forces camp on October 19, aircraft inflicted extraordinary punishment.[26] For three days, air strikes kept the camp from being overrun until reinforcements arrived. Bombing wreaked such destruction near Hill 861 in February 1968 that grunts could finally move without anyone shooting at them.[27] An air liaison officer to the 5th ARVN Division believed CAS made successful small unit operations possible in the hinterland. Later in September 1968 the PAVN made a concerted effort to overrun the Special Forces outpost at Thuong Duc; Marine Corps A-6As were key to defeating their assaults.[28]

Bombing persuaded enemy forces to quit and friendly forces to persist. Fear of air strikes seemed to dissuade some of the Pathet Lao from waging offensives in 1964, and General Vang Pao of Laos commented that nothing had been more important to the successes against communist forces than the bombing from his own T-28 aircraft.[29] Classic examples of air power defending ground forces out in the hinterland took place throughout the summer and fall of 1968. On July 1, a Marine company fended off an assault, counterattacked, and then sent fighter-bombers after the retreating enemy. The bigger picture, however, was not as rosy; these Marines were covering the discarding and abandonment of the fortress at Khe Sanh. The following month, three VC regiments chased the defenders of Dong Xoai into a couple of buildings where they fought for their lives. These infantry survived because nearly 200 air support sorties killed 700 VC; Westmoreland credited air strikes with deciding the issue.[30] Laotian troops who suffered 60 percent casualties at Saravane, Laos, spanning three months in 1972 did not quit because they knew they had air cover. In November, intelligence revealed enemy forces were massing for an operation against Long Tieng, but F-111 and B-52 strikes compelled them to retreat. Enemy forces suffered the same fate from Corsairs, F-111s, and BUFs (B-52s) when Laotian troops held fast: the communists vacated the battle area.[31]

Close air support often prevented ground forces from being overrun, as in the case of the Bu Dop Special Forces Camp of 300 Vietnamese and six Americans on July 20, 1965. South Vietnamese A-1 Skyraiders and American F-100s pounded the VC while the infantry inside defended themselves. After the battle 122 VC lay dead, nearly half killed by air (KBA).[32] In an October 1965 battle, CAS inflicted around 500 KBA on the enemy. While fighting for Landing Zone Albany on November 17, Lieutenant Enrique Pujals claimed victory after Air Force planes napalmed PAVN about to finish him off.[33] Outnumbered in March 1966, the 2nd Battalion of the 28th Infantry turned to F-100 air strikes, which persuaded the VC to back away. After four A-1 Skyraiders and Army artillery worked over North Vietnamese forces attacking firebase Red Warrior, a helicopter observer submitted a body count of 400. During an enemy attack a forward air controller watched Viet Cong forces flee under the weight of Navy Skyhawk attacks.[34] Aircraft provided the same service for Loc Ninh in 1967, killing 852. One Army officer exclaimed, "If it hadn't been for air, we would have lost this place."[35] When a portion of the 5th Cavalry Regiment came under attack from a VC regiment on March 19, 1967, fighter-bombers made eighty-seven passes to help save it from destruction.[36] A 1970s study observed that nearly every soldier interviewed credited air strikes with either preventing the enemy from overrunning them, or for enabling them to overrun enemy forces themselves.[37]

Aircraft were essential to the defense of Special Forces forts along the border between South Vietnam and Laos in 1968. After Duc Lap came under attack in August, air strikes inflicted enough losses on enemy forces to prevent them from overrunning the camp. The

Army credited air support, but it still took an enormous amount of firepower to stave off defeat, including nine B-52 and thirty-four fighter-bomber sorties resulting in 715 enemy dead.[38] The following month air support for Thuong Duc led Lieutenant Colonel Daniel Connelly, the senior advisor to Special Forces in I Corps, to comment, "Air saved the camp. There is no doubt about it. Without that support from FACs and fighters, we would not be in Thuong Duc today.... I can't overemphasize the importance of air to this whole [special forces] operation."[39]

Marine A-4s showed aerial firepower could inflict tremendous harm against the enemy during a strike on June 9, 1966. Post-strike ground reconnaissance counted seventy-nine enemy dead. During Operations Union I and II, air support was the key to completing successful attacks against fortifications without suffering heavy losses of Marine infantry. When enemy forces attempted to overrun Fire Support Base Crook in June 1969, air support slaughtered 207 enemy soldiers; survivors were either captured or fled.[40] When a large enemy force threatened Long Tieng, Laos, in March 1970, air strikes hit the ammunition they had set aside for the assault, which stiffened the resolve of the defenders and gave them time to prepare—and ultimately to win. Civilians began returning to their homes at the end of the month, which may have been the best indicator of air power's effectiveness.[41] Back in South Vietnam, when enemy forces gathered in the A Shau Valley and threatened a fire support base, more than 4,000 sorties preempted their assault.[42] These actions saved friendly forces, but to what extent did the operations destroy the enemy sufficiently to undercut his strategy and advance the strategy of the Americans and South Vietnamese?

Success often required massive amounts of air support. Aircraft deposited nearly seventy tons of bombs and napalm over the course of a single day on a VC platoon that had seized the village of An Guong.[43] When a forward air controller saw soldiers and five tanks approaching Polei Kleng in May 1972, he thought they would probably overrun the camp, but a dozen aircraft, including an AC-130, repulsed the attack. During the defense of the area around Kontum in 1972, Lieutenant Colonel James W. Bricker recalled that they had killed close to half of the enemy, and air strikes were responsible for most of the carnage. When PAVN massed, air destroyed them.[44]

When infantry did not stand fast, air power was not enough to save ground forces from defeat. For example, B-52s were sent in against North Vietnamese troops in the Plain of Jars in Laos in February 1970.[45] The Plain of Jars fell three days later to the communists, which "showed what had been obvious to US air and ground commanders: air support alone could not sustain a ground battle when the support troops were unwilling to fight."[46] At the outset of the Easter Offensive, American and South Vietnamese forces learned at Loc Ninh there were some assaults air strikes could not stop. Two days of relentless infantry-tank attacks eradicated Loc Ninh, even though the defenders brought down gunship fire and cluster bombs on their own heads in a last-ditch effort to stave off the communist assaults.[47] Firepower plus infantry was not always enough, as when the 32nd ARVN Regiment advanced about a mile trying to sweep Highway 13 of enemy troops, but were unable to complete that task, even with the great number of fighter-bomber strikes and B-52 missions. On September 17, however, A-7 Corsairs from the USS *America* saved more than a hundred South Vietnamese and their American air liaison officers from an onslaught by three PAVN companies. The officers who recounted the events knew skill and bravery when they saw it; the aviators released their bombs as low as possible to avoid committing fratricide, and still placed ordnance within 300 feet of friendlies. It is clear this was an effective use of air power not because of casualties inflicted but because of what the enemy did: they stopped advancing and many retreated.[48]

Praise from the Army was frequent. In November 1965, for instance, Major General Jonathan O. Seaman of the 1st Infantry Division affirmed that teamwork between soldiers and airmen decided the issue at Bau Bang: "We simply could not have won such a complete victory without the timely, effective and continuous fighter support which was provided."[49] In 1970 Major General Lloyd B. Ramsey of the Americal Division found bombing from all the services excellent and accurate, as was the coordination between the FACs and the ground commanders. Numerous soldiers recounted instances of air support either enabling an assault or saving a unit from destruction.[50] Major General Arthur S. Collins Jr., commander of the 4th Infantry Division, cited a case from November 12 to 13, 1966, in which flare ships, gunships, and artillery a FAC had guided helped keep the enemy at bay through the night. In the morning, eighty-five flights from Navy and Air Force aircraft, flying under low ceilings, pounded the enemy. Another report from the 5th ARVN Division considered air support to be decisive for troops in contact because it inflicted high casualty rates on communist soldiers clustered together.[51]

During a battle in November 1967, elements of the 1st Cavalry Division found CAS very accurate, effective, and flexible. Just before commanders brought in some troops on helicopters, intelligence discovered a large group of VC close to the landing zone. The already inbound fighter-bombers adjusted their plan and bombed that target, and the second wave cleared out the area around the alternate landing zone. Helicopters encountered little resistance when they disgorged their soldiers. Marine air support was the difference maker in the A Shau Valley campaign in 1967, and they observed that their mobility via helicopters and the munitions from fighter-bombers were imperative for the success they achieved during Operation Harvest Moon.[52]

Not infrequently, soldiers testified to tactical fighters' bombing accuracy. Fending off the VC attacking Plei Me in October 1965, jets placed ordnance within forty feet of the camp.[53] Unable to move because of his wounds, Private First Class Jim Shadden watched PAVN murder wounded American soldiers where they lay when, "Before the North Vietnamese got to me, half a dozen of them, a pilot came over at treetop level, turned straight up, and dropped a canister of napalm dead center on them. I never cease to be amazed at the accuracy of that drop."[54] Colonel J. P. Lanigan of the 3rd Marine Regiment exclaimed in 1967, "The close air support was the most accurate and devastating that I have observed in three wars."[55] The ability of strike aircraft to drop bombs right next to friendlies ensured the district headquarters of Bo Duc did not fall to enemy forces in November 1967. While mopping up around Khe Sanh, Marine pilots brought their bombs to within twenty yards of their comrades on the ground. FACs heaped praise on several Marine aircrews during Linebacker for their marksmanship. Ordinarily B-52s aimed no closer than three kilometers from friendly forces since B-52s dropped unguided bombs from 30,000 feet. Their dispersal patterns from that height had to account for some significant margins for error so the bombs would not land on top of friendly troops.[56] South Vietnamese forces could be particularly trusting of American bombing accuracy. During Lam Son 719 in February 1971, the ARVN 1st Infantry Division would find enemy troops, request a B-52 strike of that location, bring the enemy into a firefight within the bomb zone, and then pull back just before the bombs arrived. A South Vietnamese battalion using this tactic netted twenty-nine killed by a February 27 B-52 mission.[57]

Briefly ascending into the relationship between military activities and policy, the heavy commitment to close air support constituted a political act. American leaders realized early on that one component of shoring up the Saigon government was ensuring the enemy never defeated South Vietnamese forces in a pitched battle, and close air support was a way of pursuing that outcome. Thus, it functioned as a political instrument. Westmoreland observed that air strikes against enemy forces made it possible for Saigon to maintain control in more and more sectors, thus air power generated political consequences. Reliance on firepower also inflicted powerful psychological effects on enemy troops and allowed American troops to avoid the greater casualties that normally arise from close infantry combat.[58] Both of these effects had political ramifications. Air power enabled the Johnson administration to take greater risks with the war because it might keep casualty figures relatively low. It made ground warfare less costly politically to President Johnson.

Close air support was one of the primary ways the United States assisted its allies. While South Vietnam received the majority of aerial fire support, the US allocated considerable forces to missions in Laos, and that help paid dividends. The American ambassador, Leonard S. Unger, forwarded this fact to Washington. When Rolling Thunder began, one F-105 squadron and two F-100 squadrons were on standby to aid the Laotians.[59] Commanders of the Lao infantry reiterated the following year that there was a direct relationship between air support and the success of their operations. They also considered "the psychological effect of air is of as great importance as the destruction of enemy positions."[60] Support from Lao T-28s in 1965 boosted the morale of the Royal Lao Armed Forces, which helped to keep the government in Vientiane afloat.[61] Thus all of it was ultimately political.

These relationships between air strikes, military effectiveness, and political support continued throughout the war. The threat of Laotian and American air strikes persuaded communist troops to attack only at night, and they persuaded some Pathet Lao soldiers to defect. After successful operations of Lao ground and air forces and American fighter-bombers in April 1966, the American ambassador maintained that American air strikes inflicted the majority of the losses on the enemy.[62] Then in 1967 the combination of steadfast fighting on the part of ground troops and air strikes resulted in government forces retaining two bases the communists had attacked. While defending Lima sites—outposts and radar stations in Laos that supported bombing missions over North Vietnam—Seventh AF noticed air support encouraged and stiffened the willingness of Laotian forces to fight. This combination, however, was not invincible. In 1969, the North Vietnamese had had enough and eliminated thirty-four of these locations.[63]

As a defense, enemy infantry tried to get near to American and South Vietnamese forces with the intention of being too close for the Americans to drop bombs and napalm down on their heads for fear of committing fratricide. This was a common tactic Viet Cong and PAVN used to try to nullify the Americans' firepower advantage and was known as "hugging." This may have taken place when Marine aviators found the enemy too close to friendlies to merit bombing without risking fratricide; a single errant bomb could kill dozens of friendly troops, such was the lethality of bombs against soldiers out in the open.[64]

Airmen took greater risks with air strikes against enemy forces that hugged; aircraft placed cannon fire and napalm dangerously close to friendly troops. After a portion of the 502nd Infantry Regiment found itself outgunned and outnumbered on September 18, 1965, the commander faced a grim situation. His artillery was too far away, his soldiers did not have heavy weapons with them, and antiaircraft fire was too severe for helicopters. Lieutenant Colonel Wilfrid Smith directed F-100 pilots to aim inside a hundred yards of his location, and the commander of the 1st Infantry Division asked for them to pour it on until they had no ordnance left. Weighing the options, Major General Jonathan O. Seaman understood the danger, and some of them were accidentally strafed and bombed as a consequence. Two infantrymen died, but the bombs prevented a catastrophe from overtaking the rest of the battalion. General Seaman took responsibility for the fratricide.[65] On February

28, 1967, Marine jets were able to work their napalm canisters and cannon fire close enough to where the enemy had concentrated. When two VC regiments threatened to overrun the Special Forces camp at Bo Duc in November 1967, the commander brought ordnance from fighter-bombers to within seventy-five yards of his troops' location, and the pilots released their munitions accurately enough to not kill them.[66] According to a 1970 Marine Corps history, "On occasion, Marine pilots conducted napalm and strafing runs as close as 15 meters from friendly troops but this was the case only under emergency conditions."[67] Not surprisingly, the AC-130 became the preferred weapon to defeat close contests because of its accuracy.[68]

Squadrons had some problems obtaining and training pilots to the level of skill necessary to drop bombs near but not on friendly forces. When the 366th TFW, for example, switched from F-4Ds to F-4Es in 1968, the pilots were not taken through the entire bombing course but received only a refresher. New pilots did not fly missions in support of troops engaged with enemy forces until they proved they could bomb with accuracy. Short rounds from artillery was a far more frequent problem, but those from aircraft were generally more lethal.[69] For example, a ground commander at Dak Seang said during an April 5, 1970, incident, "Do not bring the napalm closer," but the FAC heard "bring the napalm closer." It killed four South Vietnamese soldiers and wounded twenty-one.[70] Later in the war General Vogt complained some aircrews were failing to ensure they knew the locations of friendly forces or were hurrying their attack runs without making them along a heading that would put friendlies in less danger.[71]

Major General William E. DePuy warned against punishing the pilots for accidental fratricide or placing too many restrictions on aircrews and air liaison officers; he did not want concerns about friendly fire to make it harder for him to obtain support for his troops because bombing missions saved his men to a far greater degree than they accidentally killed them. There were even commanders who misled FACs as to their locations so pilots would drop bombs that much closer to friendly troops with the goal of destroying the enemy forces that were on top of them.[72]

Airmen-soldier operations involved more than aircraft dropping bombs on enemy troops; they required management and coordination. Planners had to anticipate sortie needs and then allocate aircraft missions so that the soldiers, Marines, and ARVN could count on some level of predictable air support. Since combat is not that predictable, this air management system had to set aside sorties to respond to unexpected threats to ground troops. It also needed the flexibility to divert aircraft flying to one location toward another in more urgent need of assistance. Since CAS is a joint operation, effectiveness demands liaison personnel to coordinate with the ground forces and forward air controllers, either on the ground or in the air, to give precise directions to the attacking aircrew. This kind of management was within the Americans' skill set because they had developed it in World War II and Korea. Ground-air teams could be very responsive, as when a Marine liaison officer observed a platoon of PAVN a mile away just as his strike aircraft arrived; on the spot he diverted them from the target they were slated to hit to this new one.[73]

The management of fire support aircraft was under the control of a single officer for only a few months in 1968, and that was only in response to the siege of the Marine fort at Khe Sanh. Marines normally integrated their air forces to the same degree as artillery and armor, for example, so they were reticent about turning over their jets to a single multiservice agency. They were also worried they would receive fewer sorties within a joint system. Missions Seventh AF scheduled for the Marines fell from 36 percent in April to 32 percent in May, and only 44 percent of scheduled targets were actually struck. Planned missions were ideal, but use of diverted aircraft instead of scheduled comprised 58 percent of the sorties flown in support of Marine operations. The III Marine Amphibious Force complained, and MACV accepted an Air Force proposal that allocated 70 percent of support to planned missions weekly and 30 percent daily. Even before this went into effect, joint air power relieved a Special Forces unit at Kham Duc on May 12 with 120 Air Force jets joining eighteen Marines to crush a PAVN attack. The Marine Corps history asserts this blending could have resulted in mid-air collisions, but the airborne forward air controllers from both services managed the airspace safely to ensure the ground below was perilous for the North Vietnamese.[74]

While pilots and their bomb-carrying jets conducted close air support operations, forward air controllers coordinated and deconflicted air strikes. Management by a skilled FAC was essential, and fixing the enemy in place by ground forces was necessary to maximize the bombers' usefulness. The FAC had to be able to find the troops of both sides and direct fighter-bombers against the enemy without killing friendly forces. During the siege of An Loc in 1972, ground commanders deemed FACs indispensable and marveled at their abilities.[75] Forward air controllers who flew over northern Laos—"Ravens"—supporting Vang Pao's forces against Pathet Lao guerrillas (sustained by the North Vietnamese) helped make Pao's men more effective. Raven FACs coordinated with Pao's artillery, which made it more accurate.[76] When the ARVN set their offensive in motion during Lam Son 719 in 1971, FACs and the aircraft they directed managed the airspace and the targeting of enemy forces well enough that the North Vietnamese could not achieve their goal of destroying their counterparts, although they drove them out of Laos. American FACs demonstrated great skill, were committed to the success of Army missions, and were easy to work with. South Vietnamese controllers, on the other hand, often avoided flying over enemy forces.[77]

A theme of these operations was the necessity and effectiveness of joint ground-air teams. Ground and air units reinforced each other. Steadfast infantry were essential to effective air support to compel enemy forces to concentrate, creating lucrative targets. In this way the two arms required each other in order to be most effective. One pilot concluded fighter-bomber support was most effective when ground forces fought the enemy within rifle range. He was not so sanguine about striking *alleged* Viet Cong locations.[78]

The availability of air support encouraged ground force commanders to move away from joint operations and instead rely on sequential operations. Air strikes would first bomb locations where the enemy was believed to be, based on a single intelligence source such as a long-range reconnaissance patrol or a forward air controller. Ground commanders preferred to use air strikes instead of their soldiers; they used direct attack by aircraft as a substitute for ground-only or joint operations.[79] Soldiers and Marines preferred to rely on artillery and air strikes over infantry assaults when confronting an enemy strongpoint. Indeed, they were the main killing force; infantry were supposed to find and then mop up after the firepower had done its work. Similarly, Victor Krulak pointed out to General Westmoreland that aerial firepower simplified and eased the Marines' tasks in combat.[80] When a Marine air liaison officer spotted a company of PAVN walking on a trail, he called in artillery and then aircraft to pulverize them. On March 3, 1967, a company of Marines trotted into position to flush the enemy the moment their commander had suspended the bombardment. These air-ground efforts scattered and then killed about 111 enemy troops.[81] In May 1968, another Marine ALO located his counterpart and sent strike aircraft instead of Marines against him. On January 9, 1970, Marines spotted an enemy platoon south of Da Nang. The air strikes they called in killed twenty-two. Later that month an A-6A killed all twenty enemy troops spotted south of the same area.[82] At times the Army used air strikes to fence off the battle zone and bomb exit routes the enemy sought to exploit and relied on close-in rifle fire to finish the enemy. General Davis realized the best time to use his infantry to attack an enemy ground force was right after B-52s bombed them. During a June 16, 1966, operation, American infantry followed up a series of fighter-bomber and B-52 strikes immediately with an attack into the bombed area, capturing or killing many who survived the bombs.[83]

South Vietnamese forces coordinated ground and air operations, especially later in the war. On January 21, 1967, they provided a textbook example when a force of about 125 riflemen, mostly civilian irregulars, formed a flushing force to herd a company of VC into the open, and drove a platoon-sized force toward a blocking force. A FAC watched this unfold and called in air strikes and artillery. When insurgents ambushed a smaller American force on June 8, 1966, at Ap Tau O, the 135 American and South Vietnamese troops along with twenty-five armored personnel carriers and seven tanks fought back. With artillery and nearly four dozen fighter-bomber sorties they decimated the attacking force of 1,200. At the outset of the 1972 Easter Offensive, Regional Forces and Popular Forces (part-time civilian soldiers) prevented enemy forces from moving and thus allowed South Vietnamese artillery and air strikes to destroy them.[84] In the opinion of the South Vietnamese Marine Division commander, Major General Bui The Lan, air support was essential for success. Facing five divisions and losing about a hundred soldiers per day, he informed the Seventh AF commander that his force would not be able to retake Quang Tri without a great deal more air support, which he received.[85]

American practice made it difficult to inflict the heaviest casualties on enemy forces and lessened the strategic effectiveness of both air and ground firepower. Although the Americans recognized the relationship between infantry combat and close air support, they did not always employ the two optimally. There was a preference for using them sequentially, softening up the enemy first before attacking or before American troops entered into a hostile area, but that was actually detrimental to the pursuit of MACV's attritional strategy. A better way would have been to let the enemy attack in large numbers so as to provide lucrative, concentrated, findable targets for aircraft because locating, identifying, and bringing enemy troops into close battle and keeping them fixed in place was the toughest tactical challenge the Americans faced when dealing with the enemy. During Operation Birmingham (April 24–May 17, 1966), for instance, the Americans witnessed how difficult it was to inflict decisive damage on them. While mopping up after the battle, ground teams found more than 9,000 ruined uniforms, but no one was wearing them. Army troops captured only twenty-one rifles and exchanged almost no fire with anyone in the area. MACV had believed 20,000 VC were in that area, but the operation produced only 115 enemy killed.[86] Seventh Air Force analysts concluded the enemy had chosen to not fight and defend this area because it was either not worth defending or because American forces were too powerful to defeat. Either way, the VC suffered losses they could replace. They were also aware of the offensive before it commenced because of the air strikes. One American analyst wrote that the VC "expected to lose the zone and took steps to minimize the impact of the loss."[87] The VC left behind a rear guard and evacuated.

Seventh Air Force argued that the enemy's intentions, whether they remained or fled, decided the extent to which air strikes were effective. The Air Force believed that instead of softening up places where someone thought the enemy might be, the Army should wait until it established meaningful contact that held them in place—then and only then bring in air strikes for the coup de grace. Ironically, while the 1st Infantry Division welcomed the liberal use of bombing prior to entering an area of enemy activity, Seventh Air Force was not keen about supplying firepower before American forces were fully engaged with the enemy because it knew that firepower used too soon would scatter the enemy instead of killing them. Aircraft should actually strike last, but the Army was wedded to preemptive bombardments.[88]

The relationship between troops massing and CAS effectiveness was known early on. The American ambassador to Laos in 1964, Robert Unger, realized using T-28 strikes against troops that were not tightly massed was ineffective.[89] The Army and the Air Force, however, had not comprehended the ineffectiveness of using ground forces to find the enemy and not fix them in place, but instead call in artillery and aircraft bombardment, then afterwards close in with foot soldiers after the bombing and shelling ceased. Instead, PACAF argued, "The threat of air power alone has prevented large scale attacks by massed troops and thus had contributed to the success of FAR [Royal Lao Forces] forces in operations against the Communists."[90] Maybe this concept applied in Laos, but in South Vietnam the enemy was so elusive that it was preferable for the enemy to concentrate so as to present a more "bombable" target for air strikes. Some in PACAF recognized this and chided the Army for wasting sorties, while an Army colonel explained as much to an ABC news reporter when asked in 1966 of the chances of another Dien Bien Phu. Roger R. Bankson replied that the VC would have to concentrate and mass in order to threaten a valuable place, turning themselves into a vulnerable target: "they would be decimated by the awesome firepower we have—particularly close air support."[91] The enemy was normally smart enough to not do that. Communist forces practiced dispersal, camouflage, and burrowing into the ground to gain some protection from bombs and to undercut the effects of air strikes. If, however, an objective was important enough they would mass in order to seize it. Troops who stood pat and fought would force the enemy to concentrate, easing the targeting challenges FACs and pilots faced.[92]

Westmoreland's approach lessened air power's effectiveness. He asserted that the enemy was most vulnerable when they were marshaling for an attack, so that was the time to bomb. Westmoreland was thrilled when American "spoiling actions" "disrupted enemy plans" in August 1966. He considered those operations to have "been highly successful [but] they had by no means eliminated the enemy's capability to mount attacks in the future."[93] Well, if they left the enemy in a condition where they could attack again, the operation had not been successful.

Westmoreland greatly favored B-52 strikes for this purpose and by 1967 wanted 800 sorties per month because they provided the Army with asymmetrical advantages, and because the bombing shattered the nerves of enemy forces who survived. Army commanders were convinced that without more sorties, greater numbers of ground troops would die because B-52 strikes were an essential prelude to successful infantry operations. Although Arc Light, as the B-52 missions against targets in South Vietnam were called, manifested a form of self-sabotage when used offensively, they were important for defense, as when General Creighton Abrams based his short-term strategy for defending the Quang Tri and Khe Sanh areas in the summer of 1968 on the capabilities of B-52s, and exploited those capabilities during the defense of South Vietnam in 1972.[94]

American leaders supported this firepower-first approach. The Army chief of staff advised the president, "the men got all the air cover they could use." Secretary of State Dean Rusk and President Lyndon Johnson recognized the importance of air support to infantry, and LBJ directed McNamara to apply as much air power against dug-in communist positions as American ground forces needed.[95] In line with that priority, PACAF became optimistic regarding the effectiveness of heavy conventional operations in the case of Operation Junction City in February–March 1967. At first the Viet Cong avoided contact with American troops, but over time, grunts engaged regiments of the 9th Light Infantry Division. Communist forces attacked only when they believed they were at an advantage, but air and artillery counterattacks made their efforts costly. Estimates by the end of March were that 1,871 VC had been killed, which was not a disaster for them. Most of the assessment of the damage to the enemy focused on materiel captured or destroyed.[96]

One of the common assertions about the Vietnam War in the United States remains, "we never lost a battle"—which unfortunately was not correct.[97] For instance Special Forces troops and an ARVN company had to evacuate Kontum Province's district headquarters in August 1965. Viet Cong overran it, even though air strikes hit the enemy day and night.[98] In March 1966, a couple of PAVN regiments lay siege to the A Shau Special Forces outpost. Two-hundred-thirty air strikes from American and South Vietnamese air forces spread bombs on the enemy, but "After two days, the camp, defended by 385 Americans, Chinese Nung mercenaries and Vietnamese irregulars, fell to the attackers."[99] By the time permission was granted to provide air support to the Laotian outpost at Ban Houei Sane in January 1968, approximately three PAVN battalions forced its evacuation. Even though the ARVN 3rd Airborne Brigade headquarters during Lam Son 719 received plenty of air support, PAVN overran and occupied it.[100] When Major David Brookbank exclaimed on April 30, 1972, "thank God for the U.S. Air Force," and "I can state without reservation that I have never witnessed such an impressive display of aerial cover and fire control as the Sandys provided," it was during the evacuation of Quang Tri.[101]

Assessing Effectiveness

Determining the exact impact that air strikes had on enemy forces was challenging and required data from several sources. According to historian John Schlight, analyzing effectiveness well "was extraordinarily difficult" and was "one of the larger disappointments of the war."[102] One method of finding out whether bombs had hit a military target was the observation of secondary explosions that occurred right after the bombs hit. The six bombs an A-6A Intruder, for example, dropped on a target in Laos on February 12, 1971, caused 152 such secondary detonations. These fireballs might be much larger than the bomb bursts of the munitions that caused them, and that helped observers differentiate between the bomb bursts and the materiel the bombs had ignited, which revealed the identity of the substance exploding.[103] When A-1s bombed a trench near Khe Sanh, explosions continued for another two-and-a-half hours, confirming the bomb had hit something really valuable: enemy ammunition. Observers counted the secondary explosions. During November 1968, the crews of the 4258th Wing (B-52s) counted a total of 408 secondaries. Intelligence analysts noted that 303 of these were the color of petroleum products, while the white and yellow ones marked the presence of munitions.[104] Aircrews recorded these statistics by looking down at the bombed area from high altitude, but that depended on air clear of clouds. As the weather worsened during April 1970, for instance, reported secondary explosions declined because the aircrews could not see them.[105] Counting secondaries was a necessary but insufficient form of bomb damage assessment. Ground reconnaissance teams also counted secondary explosions following an air strike.[106]

The region's foliage—tall trees and high grass—often forced aircrews to write "results not observed." Figuring out whether or not enemy personnel had been killed was not easy, either, because a dead soldier does not set off secondary explosions. Aerial or ground photography hours after a strike was not always optimal since it was not as timely as direct observations by aircrews; the attacking aircrews could often see the immediate consequences of their missions. When it took place, direct observation by troops walking the ground where the air strike had occurred was an accurate and often immediate source of bomb damage assessment. Testimonies of prisoners, information from spies, and enemy assessments of the effects were additional ways of figuring out what the bombs had really done. Taken together, analysts could build a decent picture of what CAS and direct attack accomplished.[107] Ground reconnaissance provided the most thorough assessment of air strikes. On November 3, 1967, for instance, some Marines completed a survey of bombed ground, but all they found were "fighting holes, cooked rice and assorted clothing and equipment. . . . No evidence of en[emy] casualties."[108] An examination on March 10, 1971, counted 745 dead as a result of B-52 bombings during Lam Son 719. An ARVN regiment credited air strikes for the several hundred bodies it found.[109]

Another metric used to measure close air support effectiveness was the number of sorties, which really only measured effort, not results. Others were "structures destroyed," "kill ratios," "bomb tonnage," freight "tonnage," and "body count"—useful but insufficient measures.[110] Pacific Command measured the rate of increase in secondary explosions B-52 crews observed in 1968, and it even counted how many sampans aircraft destroyed.[111] A January 1971 report noted that Marine squadrons dropped 2,979 tons of bombs, 718 napalm canisters, and fired approximately 11,000 rockets. Forty-nine percent of the 1,205 sorties were close air support, with interdiction and direct support accounting for the rest at 35 and 16 percent, respectively. The wing's aircrews killed thirty-one enemy over the previous two months. Sometimes body counts were large (325 in May 1968) and verified. Marine after action reports seldom mentioned the larger difference those sorties made for operations on the ground.[112] These were actually chronicles of flown sorties, expended munitions, and effort exerted, not really measures of effectiveness.

Accurate body counts were difficult because the enemy removed a large percentage of the dead. Air strikes and artillery saved Captain Raymond K. Bluhm's company on August 7, 1967, from being wiped out, although in their follow-up excursion on the ground his men found, "The North Vietnamese had vanished."[113] A FAC who examined the results of the Echo 78 B-52 strike of March 14 testified that it looked like survivors had removed the bodies of their dead comrades out of the bunkers.[114] In 1968 General Wheeler acknowledged this and claimed the American military counted "only the ones we find on the battlefield."[115] To compensate for the missing bodies, however, MACV employed statistical algorithms to estimate the percentage of casualties air strikes caused. These statistics suggested that 49 to 65 percent of the enemy troops engaged became casualties as a result of aerial bombardment. Survivors continued their body removal through the end of the war.[116]

The most important metric of effectiveness to soldiers and Marines was survival. A review of more than four years of Army after action reports and numerous personal interviews and questionnaire responses told the same story repeatedly. A friendly force came under fire; if the commander considered the situation beyond the capability of his own firepower or the enemy had burrowed into fortified positions, he requested immediate air support; after one or more air strikes the enemy either lay dead, put up little or no resistance to the assaults, or fled the scene.[117] By that metric close air support clearly demonstrated tactical and operational effectiveness.

A battalion commander rejected the idea that close air support was nothing more than a means of saving soldiers who were in a real tight spot. Air power was his asymmetric advantage, and he should exploit it. Air strikes were a necessary practice because the only alternative was huge casualties among one's own troops.[118] While each ground force commander used air support in a slightly different manner during their assaults, all of them relied on aerial bombardment when confronting a dug-in fortified enemy. Ground force commanders found that air strikes responded more quickly than gunships, were more accurate than artillery, and were far more destructive than artillery or helicopter gunships. Soldiers observed "artillery and gunships slowed the enemy down, but air strikes stopped him dead in his tracks."[119] When helicopters and artillery stopped firing, enemy troops crawled out of their trenches and opened fire—not so after bombs had landed on them. Another unit fired in excess of 200 90mm rounds from tanks into a bunker, assaulted it, and promptly suffered three casualties. A few well-placed bombs, however, terminated the bunker's existence.[120] The Marines found during the April–May 1967 battles around Khe Sanh that air strikes not only hurt dug-in PAVN, they also peeled back camouflage and made visible their fortifications and bunkers. Occasionally bombs could not root out enemy forces when they were well dug in and fortified. One brigade commander watched artillery and tactical air strikes pulverize an enemy position only to see them emerge from deep and well-built bunkers.[121]

Sometimes this use of aerial firepower was wise, but at other times it seemed terribly inefficient. On May 3, 1967, aircraft dropped 187 tons of ordnance at Khe Sanh, and analysts were only certain that they had killed three enemy. Two days later, 148 tons killed three more and persuaded one to join the South Vietnamese. Was it an efficient use of resources for F-4s to kill just ten enemy soldiers? Marines who did not have to close to within range of machine guns certainly thought so. But the question remains a legitimate one. A March 1969 history reported 5,017 ground attack sorties delivered more than 11,000 tons of bombs and 3,300 napalm canisters. Only 151 enemy were killed as a direct result of all that firepower.[122] On October 15, 1969, a pair of A-4 Skyhawks bombed a 12.7mm machine gun nest. They destroyed it, and observers counted ten secondary explosions, but two jet aircraft had been used against a machine gun. In July 1970 Marines flew more than 1,800 sorties dropping 7,665 tons of bombs, more than 2,100 napalm canisters, and fired 6,105 rockets, which killed nineteen of the enemy.[123] This ratio of firepower to results was problematic.

At other times air strikes were a necessity. They were necessary for blasting away the foliage covering bunkers and then more bombs were needed to destroy them. Their destruction required 1,000-pound Mark-83 bombs; smaller bombs and artillery shells only dented the log-dirt bunkers. Oftentimes PAVN entombed themselves when they rode out the bombing. An infantry–air operation on June 26, 1968, for example, credited F-4Bs responsible for fifty-three of the fifty-nine enemy dead. Marine ground teams frequently encountered enemy forces and then called in a FAC and fighter-bombers to destroy them. A reconnaissance team on January 9, 1969, spotted twenty-seven PAVN and informed a FAC who called in an air strike, resulting in twenty-two killed. In another example, on April 5, 1970, Marines found thirty communist soldiers and asked a FAC in a nearby OV-10 to bring in jets with bombs. Only seventeen survived.[124]

Communist forces made changes due to the air threat. In the latter part of 1969, they reduced their standard combat unit to the company because battalions and regiments were too vulnerable to air attacks. Air's constant threat also persuaded the enemy to compulsively build bunkers. Consequently, they had less time to attack their enemy and less energy for forcing neutral South Vietnamese to support their cause. The drudgery of constructing endless temporary bivouacs and field fortifications persuaded more than a few VC to defect or even to form bands of outlaws who survived by raiding villages in NLF-dominated areas. The air threat complicated their logistics terribly, but prisoners explained that while bombing inflicted hardship and death, they still received enough supplies to fight.[125]

Air strikes forced insurgents to practice good camouflage, hide themselves in plain sight among civilians, relocate at night, and attack when the weather was too bad for aircraft to fly.

But their measures attested only to the tactical and operational effectiveness of air strikes.¹²⁶ The enemy had to react and adjust; air strikes were a problem for them, but the difficulties close air support caused were not strategically decisive because the VC and PAVN never had to fundamentally change their strategy. As much operational trouble as air strikes wrought on the communists, the interaction revealed that the endurance and will of the enemy was the deciding factor. It also revealed their superior foot mobility. Of the American tactic of surrounding with soldiers and pounding with aircraft and artillery, "one Viet Cong officer said, 'Usually we could get away from that, even when they used helicopters to try and surround us, because we knew the countryside so well and could get out fast.'"¹²⁷ Not always. Once air strikes and artillery wounded the 93rd Battalion sufficiently on February 15, 1966, soldiers of the 7th Cavalry Regiment snapped bayonets onto their rifles, charged after two VC companies, and drove them into the arms of another platoon who killed more than fifty guerrillas.¹²⁸

The Implements of Close Air Support

Presidential policy for the air war depended on the capabilities of American aircraft and airmen. Each aircraft had its role, and the better each performed, the easier it was to achieve the war's goals. Capable aircraft and sound tactical effectiveness did not automatically translate into accomplishing the war's goals, however. That consequence further suggests the basic problems lay in strategy and policy. In any event, the more effective and efficient each aircraft and munition was, the less the policy makers had to concern themselves with basic warfighting issues.

The forward air controller's tasks are basic to close air support, and the aircraft the Air Force had on hand for its forward air controllers, the Cessna O-1 Bird Dog and the O-2 Skymaster, were inadequate airframes for the FAC mission unless the enemy could aim nothing more than rifles at them. An O-1 Bird Dog was a small, single-engine aircraft with a 200-horsepower engine capable of taking off from short, rough airfields, but it did not have the armor, radio capability, cockpit lighting, or engine power necessary to survive conditions over Indochina. It was too underpowered for flying missions in mountainous terrain, and the Bird Dog was too slow and underpowered to survive in areas with significant ground fire, but its presence was better than nothing at all.¹²⁹ The O-2 was a modified Cessna 337 Skymaster general aviation aircraft. It too lacked enough engine power, which meant it needed at least 2,000 feet of runway. It could not climb when it needed to evade AAA, and it could not slow down enough to confine itself to a small airspace while giving directives to attacking aircraft. It did not have any armor beyond a fiberglass plate to protect the pilot from ground fire. Because it was noisy, the enemy could hear it coming and hide. Perhaps worst of all, it was difficult for pilots and observers to see out of the aircraft toward the ground, which is where they had to look to direct bombing runs.¹³⁰ These shortcomings were so great that the Air Force sought out a new purpose-designed FAC aircraft.

The OV-10 Bronco resulted. It possessed the traits combat experience demonstrated were necessary: two powerful turboprop engines, plenty of windows in all the right places, short takeoff and landing ability, greater speed and range, room for two pilots, and the capacity for guns, rockets, and bombs. Its capabilities as an observation and FAC aircraft impressed Marines as soon as they started flying it over South Vietnam in 1968.¹³¹ Army commanders considered Broncos indispensable and praised them to no end. Arming it with rockets gave it the ability to provide some immediate firepower until more heavily armed aircraft responded.¹³² A modified OV-10 called "Pave Nail" entered service in March 1972 and sported new target acquisition laser designation equipment for supporting laser-guided bombs. While its optical system did not have enough magnification or low-light capability, Pave Nail OV-10s were effective enough to provide laser aiming for nearly a third of the LGBs used in Southeast Asia. During an August 1971 mission, for example, an F-4D released its bomb above a cloud deck. When the bomb broke out of the clouds it acquired the laser reflection from the OV-10 and struck the target dead center. Altogether the OV-10 was the ideal FAC aircraft for airspace its own forces controlled.[133]

For more dangerous airspace, FACs piloted faster F-100Fs beginning in June 1967. Pilots in this program, known as "Commando Sabre," flew them mainly over the lower half of the North Vietnamese panhandle and Laos. These F-100Fs were quite effective as a platform from which pilots could search for targets.[134] They helped fighter-bomber aircrews put bombs on targets and doubled the bombers' effectiveness. Because of the amount of time these aircrews spent looking for, finding, and marking targets, they set up a cross-training program to make pilots more proficient at armed reconnaissance. Their missions were more often in support of air interdiction than strikes against enemy troops. F-100Fs were good for this mission because of the cockpit visibility and the ability of the pilot in the back seat to use a camera with a telephoto lens. Given their familiarity with the mission, its aircrews became better at finding targets than other jet fighter pilots. The Hun—a nickname sprung from one hundred—could fly in its patrol area for almost an hour between refuelings, and although it was reasonably maneuverable and fast, the engine power was marginal enough to require the frequent use of its afterburner, lessening its endurance.[135]

Gunships—multi-engine transports modified to fire guns through portholes on the sides of the aircraft—proved particularly effective against enemy troops. Initially C-47s, a military version of the Douglas DC-3 airliner, were modified into the AC-47, but it proved deficient in firepower and flexibility. The way its guns were aimed was for the pilot to look through a gunsight to his left and make a left-hand turn in order to bring the weapons to bear, aiming the guns by banking the aircraft. Their firepower was too light against dug-in infantry in bunkers, and ground force commanders had to bring in tactical fighters to finish off attacking forces.[136] AC-47s remained effective in low-threat airspace and soldiered on in the Lao and South Vietnamese air forces.[137] Now one thing has to be addressed about the AC-47 because it always comes up. Aircrews nicknamed the AC-47 "Puff the Magic Dragon" after the Peter, Paul, and Mary children's song, and urban legends persist that the song was about a pot-smoking reptile that advocated marijuana use. The song's writer, Peter Yarrow, has repeatedly explained the song was a children's song, nothing more, nothing less, and had nothing to do with smoking pot, but the legend is so juicy it just won't go away.[138]

Next came the larger AC-119G Shadow, which proved successful in combat in 1969, but was really an interim platform. They were relatively responsive, often taking off in less than twenty minutes from the time they were scrambled. After its introduction, the AC-119's mission shifted from an emphasis on truck killing on the Ho Chi Minh Trail to lending support to troops under fire. Their best trait was the accuracy of their guns. Consequently, AC-119s circling overhead were able to either deter the enemy from attacking or defeat enemy forces trying to crush friendly positions. As an airframe, however, Lieutenant Colonel Edward A. Elbert of the 17th Special Operations Squadron found the AC-119G underpowered, and he was especially dissatisfied with the reliability of its engines, having dealt with one quitting right after takeoff.[139] Switching its machine gun ammunition from ball to armor-piercing incendiary greatly improved its effectiveness against vehicles, but the siege of An Loc revealed the ultimate shortcoming of the AC-119: the short range of its weapons meant it needed to fly at 3,500 feet above ground—well within the lethal range of the new SA-7 missile PAVN infantry brought with them in 1972 to fire against low-flying aircraft.[140]

AC-130 Spectres were the war's ultimate gunships and were formidable weapons. The first ones used four 7.62mm and four 20mm Gatling guns and had a computerized gunsight.[141] Beginning in the summer of 1970, they were modified to use two 40mm cannon along with a pair of 20mm and 7.62mm Gatling guns. "Pave Aegis" was the ultimate AC-130. It had a suite of sensors: a moving target indicator in its radar, a black box for detecting trucks and surface-to-air missiles, a television camera designed for nighttime use, a helmet-mounted sight, an inertial navigation system (INS), a laser for designating targets, long-range navigation equipment, and a fire control computer that compiled information from the suite of sensors.[142] Its 40mm cannon allowed it to fire against targets while flying at 8,500 feet at a slant range of three miles, but its best weapon was its 105mm cannon. An AC-130E was modified into the 16th Special Operations Squadron's first Pave Aegis gunship on February 18, 1972, and was immediately successful, demonstrating a one-shot, one-kill capability with its cannon. The cannon's range allowed the AC-130E to operate out of range of most ground fire, and it could fire at targets within a specific city block, such was its accuracy. An AC-130E's firepower was even used to herd enemy forces into an oncoming B-52's target box during one mission. Senior leaders in Washington recognized the AC-130's effectiveness and pressed for the conversion of more C-130s into gunships.[143]

AC-130s could persuade enemy forces to lay low simply by circling above friendly troops and dropping flares. They could not do so, however, in "high threat" areas, such as places defended by 85mm antiaircraft artillery pieces; gunships were too slow and low even at 10,000 feet. Moonlight also made it possible to see them, so they could not fly near concentrated flak when there was half a moon or greater.[144] They were vulnerable to SA-7 missiles, which became a serious concern in 1972 because of their ability to shoot slow moving aircraft as high as 8,000 feet above the ground. One hit and damaged an AC-130 over An Loc on May 12.[145]

Gunships were quite effective, as when a succession of gunships kept enemy infantry from overwhelming a South Vietnamese strongpoint on the night of February 25, 1971, during Lam Son 719. The director of Direct Air Support Center Victor was certain that PAVN would have overrun Hill 31 if gunships and fighter-bombers had not been present. During the 1972 campaign, PAVN frequently became inactive whenever one appeared overhead.[146] One that defended Tan Canh/Dak To wrecked at least seven tanks on April 23, 1972. John Paul Vann observed that AC-130s were particularly effective at Kontum. When a Pave Aegis AC-130E took out five tanks near Kontum, word spread to FACs across South Vietnam that there was an AC-130 that not only used a 105mm cannon—it was accurate.[147] An advisor at An Loc credited AC-130s with preempting several assaults. AC-130s proved devastatingly important to the outcome of the siege of the town, and a single mission received credit for killing 350, and for beating back a regimental attack.[148] One advisor, Major Ken Ingram, commented, "There is nothing the NVA could do when the Spectre was overhead except crawl into a hole and hope it didn't hit them."[149] In Laos near Saravane, Seventh AF recognized that friendly troops under siege in December 1972 had to have AC-130 fire support every night in order to prevent communist forces from overrunning them.[150]

Direct hits from its cannon obliterated the toughest targets: sandbag and log bunkers, tanks, and artillery pieces, and they had the ability to shoot within 100 yards of friendly forces; with the help of a ground radar beacon an AC-130 could fire without being able to see anything. An AC-130 locally updated the coordinates in its inertial navigation system during a June 1972 mission and fired at target coordinates the aircrew could not see. These beacons were critical for avoiding fratricide, and when ARVN troops did not have them at a fire base near Hue in 1972, Firebase Bastogne fell. Its firepower silenced the enemy near Dak Pek—without any rounds getting closer than 500 yards to ARVN troops.[151] This capability meant that given the air supremacy sustained over South Vietnam, American and ARVN forces could bring devastatingly accurate firepower onto the enemy's heads at almost any time, particularly at night from this aircraft. They were modern-day siege engines.

Close air support aircraft evolved in terms of the capabilities they brought policy makers and war fighters. The initial CAS aircraft in Southeast Asia was the T-28, which successfully supported Lao forces starting in 1961. The T-28 was a straight-wing, piston-engine training aircraft of post–World War II vintage that had proved effective against guerrillas who did not have much in the way of antiaircraft defenses. It used two 50-calibre machine guns and carried a ton of ordnance. With its training aircraft moniker, the T-28 was less provocative politically, and was capable enough against Pathet Lao guerrillas in northern Laos, although Americans flew most of the missions. These air operations were a vital interest to the Royal Lao government. Souvanna Phouma later exclaimed in February 1970 that if not for air support Laos would fall to the communists.[152]

An aircraft that should have been more at the forefront of policy makers' awareness was the A-1 Skyraider. It was a piston-engine aircraft developed after World War II that carried a heavy payload, could remain over the battle area for an extended period, and demonstrated great bombing accuracy. The Air Force found the Skyraider well suited for operations in South Vietnam and was more readily available to fly missions than any other aircraft. Early in the war they had left the ambassador to Laos impressed with their sturdiness against small arms fire when compared to jet fighter-bombers.[153] Ambassador Sullivan added that pilots preferred the Skyraider because of its endurance, ruggedness, and ability to maneuver in mountain valleys. It also had the ability to fly slow enough to escort rescue helicopters. FACs liked them because their low operating speed made them easier to manage when cloud ceilings were low.[154] Not everyone in the government was aware of the Skyraider's qualities. During a discussion of air support for the ARVN in January 1971, "The president commented that it would have been much better had we had some decent conventional close air support aircraft to give to the ARVN."[155] In the Skyraider the United States already did and already had.

The US provided A-1s to the South Vietnamese beginning in 1961. In addition to the combat qualities it demonstrated, it was ideal for them because its technology was conventional enough for them to maintain themselves. Greater capabilities and flexibility offered policy makers more options, but as the Americans provided more sophisticated airframes, their employment became more challenging to allies in Saigon because the maintenance of these aircraft was more difficult. Skyraiders, however, were viable only in areas where ground fire was light. Shoulder-fired SA-7 missiles the PAVN received in 1972 rendered the Skyraider less survivable because of its low speed, a vulnerability it shared with attack helicopters like the AH-1 Cobra.[156] On the other hand, A-1s flew missions despite the bad weather in I Corps when the Easter Offensive erupted. Many of their American peers considered South Vietnamese Skyraider pilots "world class," an assessment the White House was aware of.[157]

The F-100D Hun was the Air Force's primary CAS aircraft from 1965 to 1971, flying more than 360,000 sorties during those years. One-hundred ninety-eight were lost in combat over Southeast Asia. Its four 20mm cannon were lethal against personnel but lacked the punch necessary to destroy artillery.[158] Huns were most effective when flown in pairs, each carrying distinct kinds of ordnance so each could make only one attack run, thereby not giving an alerted enemy a second chance to fire against them. Originally designed as a mid-1950s vintage air superiority fighter, the Hun depended on piloting skill for bombing accuracy, as it did not carry precision-guided munitions like the Paveway laser-guided bomb, and it did not have any kind of radar or laser range finder for aiding in air-to-ground attacks. Another factor influencing its effectiveness was the munitions it used, and that depended on the target. The F-100 was most effective against enemy troops when utilizing cluster bombs or napalm, in that order. Against troop encampments, high-drag 500-pound bombs plus napalm worked the best, while 750-pound bombs were the weapon of choice against bunkers. There was some limited evidence the F-100 was a better truck killer than the F-4 when using unguided bombs, although the F-4 came into its own in that mission when it began using laser-guided bombs against trucks in 1968.[159]

Ground observers found the F-100 to be a very accurate bomber. The 1st Infantry Division's deputy commander, for instance, witnessed F-100s strikes attacking VC as close as seventy feet from his men, enabling them to drive the enemy away with a counterattack. It was also a rugged, reliable aircraft. One officer from the 3rd Tactical Fighter Wing observed that F-100s held up well despite the heavy payloads and high-G pullouts it flew. Their original design life was for 800 flying hours, but those in Vietnam averaged 2,700. F-100s needed, however, relatively high cloud ceilings in order to bomb with accuracy. When one particular pair carried out their attack run under clouds that were too low to give them adequate time to aim well, they not only struck VC, but their bombs also killed some of the South Vietnamese they were trying to defend.[160]

Pilots and soldiers praised the diminutive A-37B for its bombing accuracy. Lieutenant Gordo Weed used one during the siege of An Loc to destroy a North Vietnamese tank with a direct hit from a 250-pound bomb.[161] General Vogt considered it "indispensable," and called the 8th Special Operations Squadron's employment of Dragonflies "absolutely spectacular."[162] The Air Force noted the short amount of time necessary to refuel, rearm, and launch A-37s, and Brigadier General John R. McGiffert, deputy advisor in III Corps, concluded that it possessed the right combination of characteristics for a close air support aircraft in Vietnam. Another assessment noticed it could carry as much as an F-100, fly in gnarly weather as could the A-1, and was faster, more responsive, and survivable than the Skyraider.[163] A modified T-37 trainer with more powerful engines, A-37Bs were very small and fast. It was not a perfect airframe, however; when pilots tried to drop napalm canisters from them at high speed, "the sleek pods would often be forced up over the front of the wing before tumbling backward. It was an unnerving problem."[164]

The close air support mission has long faced a conundrum: aircraft speed and survivability versus bombing accuracy and endurance. Aircraft flying this mission needed to be fast to evade flak and missiles, and they also needed to be slow to find and bomb the target accurately; but it is not possible to fly at 600 mph and 150 mph at the same time. Skyraiders were accurate but vulnerable to guns and missiles, while F-100s and F-4s were more survivable but their speed harmed bombing accuracy.

The surprising success of the F-4—originally a Navy fleet air defense interceptor—at close air support had been recognized earlier in the war. In 1967, the Seventh AF deputy chief of staff for operations asserted that repeated data points proved its suitability for CAS. In his opinion, "The F-4C [h]as proven that a single aircraft type can successfully accomplish with superior results every mission in the tactical repertoire." Phantoms bombed accurately with a variety of munitions, routinely bringing ordnance to within a hundred yards of friendly troops without killing them.[165] A FAC from 1967 expressed a less-flattering opinion. He found F-4 pilots were unable to make aiming corrections any finer than seventy-five yards, and the napalm and high-drag bombs they dropped often missed the mark by a considerable

A-4E Skyhawk with Marine pilots (Jerome T. Bertrand Collection, Marine Corps History Division)

distance. He considered dropping more than one bomb to compensate for accuracy shortcomings to be a wasteful indicator of its inaccuracy and concluded the F-4C demonstrated only half the accuracy of an F-100D.[166] A forward air controller rejected the F-4 Phantom as a viable close air support aircraft because it was too much of a fuel guzzler to make more than one pass; it certainly could not wait around for the FAC to point out more targets. "The F-4 is just not a good close air support aircraft. . . . Any of our fast moving aircraft going below a 3,000 feet deck and trying to bomb a moving tank is trying to shoot a fish in a lake with a .22 off the bank."[167] One F-4C pilot found that just finding the target for the bombing run was the greatest challenge its pilots had to overcome. Nevertheless, by 1972 F-4s carried out the majority of CAS missions.[168]

Navy A-4 Skyhawks mainly flew against North Vietnamese targets, but when tasked they typically dropped their ordnance within seventy-five yards of friendly forces. It also had a good reputation and its simple design resulted in a high availability rate. Its pilots felt relatively safe inside because the jet was so small; it seemed like it would be hard for antiaircraft cannon shells to hit it. The F-8 Crusader, an air superiority fighter the Marines used for ground attack, had the speed necessary to survive, but lacked the F-4's stability and the A-4's maneuverability during bombing runs. As a result, the last Marine F-8 squadron left Da Nang for the United States in May 1968.[169]

The close air support mission lost a capability with the advent of jet propulsion: the ability to loiter over the battlefield waiting to be directed against targets. During Korea, for example, one could have four F4U-4s orbiting over some ground troops for a long period of time, but a decade later aircraft like the A-4E could not tarry waiting for a target. The A-7 Corsair II returned some of that ability to the air war, and was the best mix of speed, payload, endurance, and bombing accuracy. Developed as a carrier-based attack plane, the Navy had flown Corsairs since 1967 and pilots found its computer aiming system reliable enough and accurate enough that they preferred it over manual aiming, and on average one could

A-7 Corsairs (Naval History and Heritage Command)

drop a bomb within a hundred feet of the target—in test conditions. The main weakness of the initial variant, the A-7A, was engine power. The jet needed to carry only low-drag weapons because high-drag bomb racks for six bombs per pylon, for example, reduced its cruising speed so much that other jets in a strike package had to slow down so the Corsairs could keep up with them. Subsequent marks received more powerful engines starting in 1968.[170] The A-7E joined the fleet in 1970 and demonstrated an accuracy under "ideal conditions" of 180 feet, but in a "normal attack," that jumped to 320 feet. During a typical bombing run, the pilot used the radar to select the aim point and flew toward it. The computer took in all the available data, such as range, angle, and speed, and released the bomb at the proper time.

Corsair pilots also employed dive bombing and toss bombing techniques during their strikes. Corsairs were reliable, making it available for more missions, achieving a sortie rate of two sorties per day per aircraft by 1972.[171] Soldiers and aviators appreciated its flexibility.[172] During Lam Son 719 the A-7E flew its first missions defending troops and demonstrated its worth flying and bombing under low clouds with good accuracy. It could turn blind weather "runs into last minute visual attacks resulting in outstanding accuracies." Corsairs even flew in circumstances bad enough to ground slower-flying FAC aircraft. Its radar ranging and the M61 cannon were very precise and accurate. These traits made the Corsair the aircraft of choice for protecting helicopters rescuing a downed pilot.[173] On February 25, for example, A-7E aviators destroyed all three of the tanks a FAC had discovered just a hundred feet from friendly soldiers, then did the same to three more. Commander Jerry O. Tuttle put forth the most vociferous praise for the A-7E in comparison to the A-4 series, asserting it had the ability to place unguided bombs within fifteen yards of a target.[174]

By the end of June 1972, A-1 Skyraider attrition and losses had increased to the point that Seventh AF's ability to conduct search and rescue of shot down pilots was becoming compromised. In addition, all remaining Skyraiders were about to be transferred to the South Vietnamese Air Force, so General Vogt brought new Air Force A-7D Corsairs into Southeast Asia. The chief of staff brought up the issue a month later because with its greater endurance and accuracy the Corsair would be a better CAS aircraft than the F-4.[175] An A-7D wing, the 354th, received notice in July to prepare to deploy; the warning order came on September 21, and they left Myrtle Beach AFB, South Carolina, on October 10. Seventy-two Corsairs flew to Korat Air Base in Thailand, arrived on October 14 and flew their first combat missions two days later.[176]

The Corsair was a considerable improvement over the Super Sabre and the Skyraider. It had far greater endurance than the Hun and was almost as fast. Forward air controllers estimated that most of the bombs A-7Ds dropped struck within thirty feet of their aimpoint. Its radio could quickly home in on a downed airman's location, and once the pilot saw him his computer could "mark" his location. The Army had great confidence in the Corsair's ability to dispense weapons very close to friendly troops without harming them. It was the closest thing to an ideal ground support aircraft seen in the war.[177] When carrying two external fuel tanks it could range across much of Southeast Asia without any refuelings from KC-135s. By year's end they had flown approximately 14,300 sorties and only two had been shot down.[178]

Throughout the war the greatest weakness in the close air support effort was a shortfall in the capability to provide it during bad weather and low visibility. Clouds would drop so low as to preclude fixed-wing operations; aircrews flying missions in hilly terrain covered in clouds risked hitting the side of a mountain during a bombing run. The Air Force tried MSQ-77 radar-directed bombing as a stopgap measure, but it was neither accurate nor flexible enough. It was better than nothing, but the aim points were often no closer than 300 yards from friendly troops.[179]

One aircraft overcame the night and bad weather problem better than all the others: the Navy's A-6A Intruder, an aircraft possessing a suite of avionics conferring the ability to find and hit targets with relative accuracy at night and from inside clouds. Marines trusted them for close air support after dark. A single Marine Intruder supporting a combined action unit managed to kill a hundred enemy south of Khe Sanh on one mission in January 1968.[180] During Operation Dewey Canyon, January through March 1969, weather caused problems for Marine efforts more than half the time, but A-6As still managed to destroy 229 bunkers, thirty-two trucks, and seven 122mm cannon during 461 flights.[181] To provide target guidance to the aircrew, a ground FAC set up a beacon that would display its location on the bombardier-navigator's screen. The FAC then provided azimuth and range to the target, and the on-board computer then enabled the A-6A to hit targets its pilot could not see with almost as much accuracy as that of an A-4 Skyhawk in good visibility.[182]

Armed helicopters were used for close air support throughout the war, usually by escorting UH-1D Hueys transporting troops. Helicopter gunships sprayed the landing zone with rocket and machine gun fire before the UH-1Ds landed. A 1970 study found that Huey gunships and AH-1 Cobras provided fire support faster than artillery and fighter-bombers. Since helicopters used only machine guns and small rockets, they could fire closer to friendly troops with less chance for fratricide. Battalions did not have their own attack helicopters; these were "organic" only to the division level of command and not below, making them more like fixed-wing assets in terms of operational control. Indeed, according to a 1970 Air Force study, "from a battalion or lower echelon commander's standpoint, there is actually very little difference between the Army and Air Force systems providing fire support to his unit."[183]

Lam Son 719 cast doubt on the survivability of helicopter air assault against a determined enemy that camouflaged and concealed its antiaircraft weapons.[184] The 1971 battle revealed the endemic vulnerability of helicopters to concentrated automatic weapons—12.7mm and 14.5mm machine guns—not to mention larger caliber AAA. Machine guns and antiaircraft artillery also forced US Army helicopters to abandon flying just above the treetops in favor of altitudes of 4,000 to 6,000 feet, which placed them above the machine gun fire and below the optimal altitudes for guns like the 85mm cannon. Ground fire struck 695 helicopters during the operation, shooting down 122, with machine guns being the main culprit. Seventh Air Force managed to label this threat environment "as low, or at most a medium threat" by eliminating helicopter losses from the equation of all aircraft shot down and noting the absence of MiGs and near absence of SAMs.[185] Even though fighter-bombers and even B-52s pounded landing zones, helicopters suffered badly from ground fire. During the March 3 effort at one landing zone, ground fire hit forty-two helicopters, forced down twenty, and destroyed seven. Landing Zone Liz benefitted from fourteen B-52 strikes and sixty-one fighter-bomber sorties, but PAVN machine gunners destroyed two helicopters and forced down sixteen more. During subsequent missions to evacuate friendly forces, enemy forces lit into helicopter landing areas with a deluge of everything: AK-47, machine gun, mortar, rocket, and artillery fire, and inflicted great damage. In fact, helicopters needed a massive amount of support when used as the primary means of transportation. Ideally, C-130s dropping the 15,000-pound bombs that cleared landing zones for troop transport helicopters would follow close behind a B-52 mission. Massive preparatory bombardments were necessary for making landing zones safe enough for helicopters. The helicopters would then be able to land among enemy troops that were either dead or at least stunned and disorganized, but planners often spread out these three activities over a longer period of time than the Americans would have liked.[186] Regarding helicopter survivability, Marine Major General Marion E. Carl later commented, "They shoot you down as fast as you show up."[187]

The experience of Lam Son 719 suggested helicopters were ill-suited for combat zones unless they were armored against machine gun fire. This battle also suggested Vietnamization—even with large amounts of helicopters for airmobile operations and American fighter-bomber support—was not going to provide South Vietnam with as much offensive military capability as policy makers might have wished since helicopters needed so much fixed-wing fire support. This analysis also concluded ARVN forces needed enough firepower on the ground to thwart enemy attacks because bad weather limited close air support's availability.[188]

Targeting intelligence linked bombing with effectiveness: the greater its veracity, the more effective the aerial bombardment. An ideal example of ground troops providing targeting intelligence occurred in the summer of 1967. A ground controller diverted a Marine F-4B against some VC that a Special Forces group had just spotted. They knew where the enemy was and could provide accurate targeting guidance. When the Green Berets examined the results, they found nearly two dozen dead insurgents who likely "never knew what hit them."[189] The criticality of targeting intelligence cannot be overestimated.

General Momyer proposed a more deliberate use of aerial firepower against enemy troops. Concentrations of enemy forces created opportunities for American firepower. Assuming one could find the enemy, B-52s would soften up an area, tactical fighters would continue the bombardment, and ground forces would then go into the area to clean up. If the North Vietnamese were still full of fight, the ground troops could pull back, whereupon air strikes would repeat the process. Seventh AF Vice Commander Major General Robert F. Worley warned of the incessant need to ask province chiefs for permission to bomb first as an impediment to this use of B-52s. The opportunities, Worley believed, were too fleeting for that. This proposal, however, did not solve the more challenging problem of finding the enemy, which in a guerrilla-conventional war required ground forces and excellent human intelligence.[190]

Munitions used for close air support were effective as long as targeting intelligence was sound and pilot skill placed the weapon on the target. Since attrition was the war's predominant strategy, weapons makers produced a surfeit of munitions. The Vietnam War saw the advent of fuse extenders, which ensured bombs exploded above ground—very lethal against troops out in the open. Napalm was effective against troops and vehicles, and because the burning mixture spread out upon slamming into the ground, precision delivery was less important, provided friendlies were not close by. Similarly, cluster bombs were lethal against exposed troops. The Mark 20 Rockeye cluster bomb was used against armored vehicles and artillery. They were basically just as effective as CBU-24 cluster bombs, and experience revealed that both were three to ten times as effective as Mk-82s when it came to destroying trucks in Laos.[191] Some grunts rejected the use of cluster bombs near them because they were concerned about stepping on duds. Injuries also occurred from handling the bomblets: "One such incident ... involved a trooper who picked one up, looked at it, said, 'What's this,' showed it to his buddies, threw it over his shoulder, hit a tree and it exploded."[192]

The high-drag paddles that extended from 500-pound "snakeye" bombs slowed the bomb so the aircraft that dropped it would be outside of its blast radius when it hit the ground. A jet could therefore drop the bomb closer to the ground, which meant more accurate bombing. Aircrews fired unguided rockets, flares to provide light for night operations, and used gun pods. Ground forces favored gunfire and napalm because of their accuracy, while aircrews preferred tactics that enabled them to avoid ground fire and fly unpredictable attack patterns while putting weapons on target.[193] One squadron at least did not find the smaller 2.75-inch diameter rockets in use that effective because they dispersed, diminishing their hitting power. FACs also did not like them. The larger five-inch Zuni rocket, however, was a better munition. Its high speed improved its accuracy, and it could be fired individually.[194]

Some ideas for the use of munitions did not make sense, such as dropping cluster bombs from high-altitude B-52s over jungle areas. The bomblets scattered, got hung up in trees, and might then fall on friendly troops who followed up such a strike. A ground team, however, surveyed an enemy site pulverized by a mix of high explosive and cluster bombs and noticed the bomblets hit the areas between the bomb craters.[195] Enemy prisoners explained that they most feared bombs with delayed fuses because they were lethal against their bunkers. Cluster bombs were less effective because the enemy remained under cover most of the time. The same went for napalm, which also provided fodder for propagandists opposed to the war.[196]

This broad range of weapons makes sense since the Southeast Asia war was a siege that relied on attrition, but they also suggest the air forces were trying to make up for several problems the seriousness of which leadership never fully confronted: shortcomings in targeting intelligence, a reluctance to aggressively close with enemy ground forces, an incomplete understanding of the synergy between ground and air forces, the enemy's determination, and a geopolitical situation that really gave the United States no other choice.

Close Air Support Responsiveness and Bomb Damage Assessment

For soldiers under fire, response time—the interval between the receipt of the request for air support and the time the bombs dropped—could mean the difference between life and death.[197] The responsiveness of the system that sent close air support aircraft was a disputed issue. The Air Force asserted fixed-wing aircraft came to the aid of friendly troops quickly, but the system through which air support was requested, approved, and provided was cumbersome. A request had to gain approval through the US Army chain of command and often from a South Vietnamese representative. South Vietnamese approval made sense politically, but that slowed response time, which clashed with the needs of troops in contact. Speed was particularly important for troops fighting guerrillas because the ambushes and small battles were of such short duration.[198] American forces opened fire first "only 14 percent" of the time, and because communist forces initiated most battles, American and South Vietnamese forces were already behind once shooting began.[199]

Two studies completed in 1967 and 1968 claimed "USAF tactical air was not responsive to Army requests for close air support." Seventh Air Force, however, conducted its own study and issued a dissenting argument, asserting that computer-generated statistics failed to correctly portray how quickly flying units reacted to the most urgent requests. In fact, most of the time aircraft arrived before ground commanders had sorted out where they needed ordnance.[200] Westmoreland's headquarters expressed satisfaction with Air Force support, citing an operation the 101st Airborne Division undertook on June 2, 1966, in which immense air and artillery firepower greatly assisted the 1st Brigade's operation of hitting enemy forces from two different directions. The brigade had continual support day and night, and 531 soldiers of the 24th PAVN Regiment lay dead as a result.[201] Close air support was "effective only when it meets the fire support requirements of the Ground Commander," and that was certainly the case on that day.[202]

Some argued aircraft needed to be airborne right before ground forces encountered enemy formations, something difficult to anticipate. One Army officer observed that conditions changed too quickly for planned and scheduled air strikes. Another found that air strikes in support of troops in firefights had been especially good in terms of responsiveness, bombing accuracy, and destroying the target.[203] A Marine advisor observed in January 1967 that Seventh AF reacted quickly to their requests for support: "The reaction time varied from 10 minutes to 40 minutes but air responded as requested and was generally very effective."[204] Marines held their fighter-bombers at various levels of readiness: thirty, fifteen, five, or two minutes for armed aircraft manned with their engines started. During Operation Dewey Canyon, Marine jets required on average thirty-seven minutes to arrive overhead from the time a request was submitted. In general, it took about forty minutes before soldiers saw aircraft bombing their enemy. Troops often preferred the slower A-1 Skyraider over fast jets because of its ability to linger over the battlefield.[205]

Response times did not vary widely among different kinds of aircraft. During the Battle of Duc Lap in 1968 helicopter gunships arrived a half hour after the request went up the chain of command, and AC-47s showed up fifteen minutes later. During a series of operations in Binh Dinh Province, an ALO observed aircraft arriving anywhere from fifteen to twenty-four minutes after requested.[206] A December 1969 study found most armed OV-10 FACs were overhead in five minutes and other aircraft responded to nearly 60 percent of calls for "fleeting/perishable targets" in the same amount of time. More than half of tactical fighters flying from air bases such as Da Nang got to the target within forty minutes. Gunships were normally already airborne, and usually managed to arrive in under twenty-five minutes.[207] Over time, however, there just were not enough available airframes to respond to all the calls. In 1969 a system was set up by which F-4s on ground alert would take off after forty-five minutes and then wait for a call for air support, and once airborne they would reach their target in fifteen minutes.[208] How one measured time shaped the narrative: did the clock start when a soldier called for an air strike, or from the time the aircrew was told to man their jets and take off? The Air Force argued that diverts of airborne aircraft took place quickly; the aircraft would check in with the FAC about ten minutes after receiving the call. Yet another study in 1970 concluded that on average an hour would elapse from the time a ground unit first asked for assistance and the moment bombs fell on the enemy. Response time was important enough that it received the attention of the White House.[209]

Ground commanders normally reserved calls for heavy air support for times when they engaged larger enemy units. This involved fewer than 10 percent of infantry combat with enemy soldiers. More often they called on artillery or armed helicopters.[210] In actuality, most firefights were over before ground forces could ask for fire support; indeed, close air support was not always necessary. Only 4 percent of combat with the enemy, as of 1967, involved a formation larger than an infantry company.[211] An April 1969 examination of air support for the 25th Infantry Division found that more than half of the engagements its troops fought were against formations of no more than ten enemy, which did not warrant tactical fighter support because the division's own organic firepower was sufficient. Only 3 percent of the engagements were against more than forty hostile troops. Fifty-three percent lasted less than twenty minutes, so the fight would have been over by the time fighters arrived. Seventh AF also kept the division commander aware "that diverted or scrambled tactical air is available at all times to meet his needs, both by day and by night."[212]

Arc Light missions could not respond quickly to events on the ground; planners received their targets twenty-four hours before planes were scheduled to be overhead dropping bombs. Planning and briefing a mission could take thirteen hours, and then it took either two hours to fly from U-Tapao or six from Andersen. They were suitable only for scripted missions until methods for diverting them to new targets once over Indochina were developed. It took on average thirty-two hours to get a cell of B-52s over a target after the initiation of a request. The enemy troops likely would have moved out of the target box during the intervening time because targeting intelligence had a very short shelf life.[213]

Seventh Air Force and MACV pursued ways of reducing the response time of B-52s in the Arc Light program because of their devastating firepower. Handlers developed procedures to divert airborne cells to different targets, but in the opinion of the Eighth Air Force commander, few took advantage of that method. Quick reaction B-52s from Andersen AFB could show up in nine hours. Westmoreland wanted more B-52s based closer to the combat zone and got his wish when a wing was sent to U-Tapao, Thailand, in 1966. Thailand-based BUFs did not need a midair refueling and reached their targets hours sooner.[214] By May 1972, procedures had improved to such an extent that a B-52 cell could be diverted to a new target if it was notified just sixty minutes from its scheduled drop time. A later study estimated nine of every ten Arc Light missions were sent to a target different from originally assigned. This flexibility saved the lives of friendly soldiers and killed PAVN units. For example, at one point in May 1972, B-52s were diverted to aid the 81st Airborne Ranger Battalion. Their bombs landed within 600 yards of the friendlies and killed most of the communist regiment attacking the rangers.[215]

A few analysts realized that because many of the bombing missions struck targets on ground Allied forces did not subsequently capture, it was very difficult to figure out the results of these bombing raids. MACV believed, for example, 16,226 sorties from April to September 1967 were responsible for the deaths of 9,622 insurgents and enemy soldiers, but the latter number was not an absolute certainty.[216]

Analysts also understood early on that destroying thousands of "structures" in South Vietnam was not a decisive accomplishment. Bamboo and grass were the building materials, replacement costs were low, and the insurgents frequently abandoned them anyway.[217]

"Structures destroyed" nevertheless remained a metric. When raids commenced into Cambodia in the spring of 1970, the Air Force, Marines, and VNAF flew 6,844 CAS and interdiction sorties through May 31. Operations analysts tallied results in terms of something damaged or destroyed, and counted structures, bunkers, vehicles, secondary explosions, and enemy troops verified as killed as a result of air action. But what had they really accomplished?[218]

The most decisive effect air power can have is influencing enemy behavior—a compliant enemy is the best indicator of truly significant bomb damage. For example, the Air Force and the Marines carried out Operation Neutralize in fall 1967 to try to destroy PAVN artillery firing at friendly positions from north of the DMZ. Seventh Air Force provided 1,436 fighter-bomber and B-52 sorties, and the Marines 1,584. The Air Force considered the operation effective based on enemy behavioral change: dispersal of artillery and the firing of fewer rounds. Smashing enemy weapons dictated enemy actions. Marines noticed the next month that the artillery fire had stopped. Reconnaissance photos confirmed that additional air strikes had destroyed four guns. General Raymond G. Davis, commanding officer of the 3rd Marine Division, insightfully observed that a more strategic measure of effectiveness was what the enemy was and was not capable of accomplishing after being bombed.[219]

Many factors worked both against and for accurate appraisals of what bombing missions accomplished. Surviving enemy troops took actions to distort the accuracy of bomb damage assessment by removing or camouflaging destroyed equipment and dead bodies. South Vietnamese troops either were reluctant to leave their safe areas to determine the consequences of an air strike, or they would not make claims of the results unless they confirmed them with what they saw by scouting the ground where the bombs had fallen and counting each of the dead individually. Therefore, their KBA numbers were probably low. There were other cases where individuals made up BDA in order to please headquarters and aircrews, and to ensure they received substantial air support the next time they requested it. At the same time there were plenty of cases where ground teams did find numerous dead bodies, destroyed bunkers, and ruined supplies, but MACV had no way of confirming that those kinds of findings had made their way into the final statistical reports.[220] Analysts in CINCPAC admitted these problems halfway through the war. Among numerous charts and graphs of a 1968 report, the writer admitted that oftentimes it had not been possible to obtain bomb damage assessments, a problem that worsened as American troops left South Vietnam in the years that followed. There were simply too few people available for ground survey duty of bombed areas.[221]

B-52 Arc Light Missions

The close air support mission received a weapon in 1965 that only seemed new: B-52s carrying up to 108 conventional unguided bombs on each aircraft. Large multi-engine bombers had been used against ground forces before. In late July 1944, streams of B-17s and B-24s punched a hole in the German front around Normandy allowing Lieutenant General Joseph Collins to unleash his mechanized divisions toward Germany, and B-29s pummeled Chinese troops during the Korean War. In March 1965, the Joint Chiefs of Staff proposed using B-52s against the Viet Cong, in part to set a precedent for the bomber's use against North Vietnamese targets.[222] The Air Force began using compact formations of three to twelve B-52s for the "harassment, attrition [and] destruction of the VC and their facilities" in June 1965—direct attack. BUFs took on the ground support mission a few months later.[223] The effectiveness of these "Arc Light" missions, as they were called, was difficult to assess throughout most of the war, especially during the first three years. The available evidence suggests B-52 strikes were effective when used against concentrated enemy forces that were fighting American and ARVN ground forces. Their effectiveness against remote locales where VC and PAVN might or might not have been marshalling was questionable, spanning a range from very worthwhile to a complete waste of time.

As a use of B-52s, Arc Light missions were not a complete surprise. General Nathan Twining, chief of staff of the Air Force, wrote General Curtis LeMay in 1956 "that situations can and probably will arise in which military force must be brought to bear without the use of atomic weapons." Indeed, national policy required SAC as well as TAC to "maintain a conventional bombing capability."[224] Seven years later, SAC's commander, General Thomas Power, argued that the Secretary of Defense and the JCS ought to plan on making use of SAC forces "in contingency and limited war operations."[225]

The plane that executed them, initially B-52Fs but from 1966 on B-52Ds, had been designed as a nuclear bomber, and that remained its main mission. Strategic Air Command settled upon the D model because there were so many of them, and because they were slightly older than the newer more effective variants: better to pile flying hours on the airframes with more hours. Its huge bomb load, sufficient bombing accuracy, and all-weather abilities made it irresistible for direct attack against North Vietnamese and Viet Cong forces. A typical load might be forty-two 750-pound bombs and twenty-four 500-pound bombs, or eighty-four 500 pounders, and twenty-four 750-pound bombs for each aircraft. The optimal concentration was a "cell" of six B-52s within a square kilometer.[226] Often lauded as a most effective CAS platform, Westmoreland also appreciated that B-52s could pulverize spaces where the VC were hiding.[227] Since it was deemed possible, despite the jungle canopy, to determine the *area* in which a VC unit was operating, area bombing made sense. When the enemy was out in the open, the FAC/fighter-bomber team was more appropriate. General Westmoreland turned to B-52s after an operation relying on large numbers of fighter-bombers had failed to do much damage to an area from which the Viet Cong had been raiding. Fighter-bombers had used napalm, but the thunderstorms produced by the heat of the napalm doused the fires, and the guerrillas were too dispersed to make fighter-bombers anything but completely inefficient. The first Arc Light mission took place on June 18, 1965, against an area around Ben Cat, about forty miles northeast of Saigon.[228]

This first mission was a big operation: thirty B-52s and thirty-three KC-135s. Two B-52s crashed into each other on the way. Only fifty American and ARVN Special Forces examined the area after the bombs hit, and reports of their findings were not completely consistent on the details. One stated that the ground survey team found evidence of the enemy among the craters: bunkers, trenches, tunnels, and weapons, and that the bombs did not kill everyone, so the soldiers fought some VC, killing one and wounding two. "These were the only casualties observed by the three teams"; the ground was not littered with bodies like one might suspect, and in fact snipers harassed the reconnoitering soldiers. Major General Richard G. Stillwell answered reporters' questions about the mission forthrightly: "There was no damage seen by the teams from the bombs that were dropped by the B-52s. However, they saw about 5 percent of the known bomb craters that were in the area. They saw craters, no structures destroyed and no bodies . . . there was considerable evidence that there were people in there just a matter of hours before." Stillwell admitted to a reporter that enemy forces probably were not in the bomb zone when the bombs struck. He also conceded a much larger armed survey team could have more thoroughly assessed the results.[229]

This one mission illustrated some basics regarding effective use of bomber aircraft against troops: one must know where the enemy troops are, missions must hit them before they move away, and infantry must carefully examine the results. Not only did ground forces fail to comb the area with enough troops after the attack, it also appeared that their targeting intelligence was flawed or the enemy moved elsewhere before the bombers arrived. What is clear is Westmoreland and his SAC counterparts wanted the Arc Light concept to work, but they were so convinced of the inevitability of its effectiveness before the concept was tested, so wedded to its awesome display of firepower, that they ignored the powerful evidence from this first mission that effective saturation bombing of dispersed guerrillas may have been more difficult to execute than seemed plausible. Maxwell Taylor understood that Arc Light missions required reliable targeting intelligence to be effective, and that was something difficult to obtain in remote VC-controlled territory. There was also some understanding that these bombing missions needed to be combined with large ground operations to be effective. Taylor held hopes that MACV would send ground forces large enough to wipe out survivors of these attacks. There were, however, only enough soldiers available in 1965 to survey the results of just a few of the missions.[230] The armed forces were never able to reconcile 300 exploding bombs with the fact that enemy soldiers survived, ground survey teams never provided enough appraisals from troops poking around the wreckage, and no one ever insisted on targeting intelligence for each and every mission good enough to ensure that each one was as effective as it could have been.

The purpose of these missions varied with the needs of ground commanders and the abilities of airmen to find and attack the enemy. Military Assistance Command, Vietnam explained their purpose as assisting in "the defeat of the enemy through maximum destruction, disruption, and harassment of major control centers, supply storage facilities, logistic systems, enemy troops, and lines of communications in selected areas."[231] General Abrams similarly perceived the Arc Light sorties as a kind of fire brigade that he could shift to where most needed without the encumbrance of shuttling thousands of troops from one place to another. B-52s also provided a way of denying communist forces the freedom to choose when and where they would fight because the bombers brought the war to them.[232] Abrams saw cases where enemy forces besieged friendly forces, no soldiers were near enough to function as a relief force, and the only thing that prevented the destruction of friendly forces was a B-52 strike. Like Westmoreland, Abrams appreciated the ability of Arc Light missions to bomb enemy forces organizing themselves to attack. In addition, strikes to soften up the enemy had killed many and resulted in "negligible friendly casualties in follow-up ground operations." According to the commander-in-chief Pacific the consequence of all this was a reduction in the communists' will and ability to fight, but the enemy kept fighting.[233]

Arc Light missions were destructive, especially against massed enemy formations. "The psychological impact of the B-52 strikes on the enemy cannot be measured in quantitative terms. However, VC and NVA captives and returnees repeatedly state that they fear B-52 strikes more than anything else. This alone attests to far more effective results than are generally realized." Furthermore, the American strategy "has been to attack his forces during his preparatory phase and thereby keep him off balance."[234] That was a bad strategy because it worked against the decisiveness of the goal, which was killing off the enemy, not "keeping him off balance." Westmoreland also used B-52s "to disperse enemy concentrations in front of defensive positions," an approach that lessened casualties among American infantry, but "dispersal" was not the same as the killing off enemy forces and was not attritional.[235]

The bombers also gave him a way of striking forces that were beyond the reach of his own and for damaging their supply routes.[236] Destruction of substantial supplies, not "harassment," was the reason they were being used in Laos. Westmoreland believed, "The devastation and psychological effect achieved by B-52 bombing makes it the most effective and efficient weapons system available for striking area targets."[237] For instance, analysts discovered a location where the 325th PAVN Division was building a base camp, and on May 10, 1967, six B-52s softened it up before Marines attacked and routed them following the most concentrated bombardment of the war up to that time.[238] Routing the enemy, however, is insufficiently decisive when he will reconstitute and re-attack at a later date. Westmoreland should have allowed the enemy to become locked in battle with American forces, fixing them in place—the critical precursor to finishing them off—something American and ARVN forces had a terribly difficult time doing. Because this was a limited war for the United States, however, commanders were not going to subject their own forces to the losses endemic to utterly destroying an enemy infantry division.

General Abrams had no doubts as to B-52s' viability and usefulness. Air strikes, especially Arc Light, were central to his strategy of defeating enemy ground forces in 1968. He understood that every kind of intelligence needed to be studied and blended in order to provide aim points that would produce substantive results. The key to victory, Abrams added, was killing the enemy in decisive numbers before he reached major cities like Saigon and Da Nang, and B-52s were good at that. The way targets got assigned reflected either great care or micromanaging. Abrams decided where the bombs would go after three generals had examined intelligence reports, mission requests, and the situation on the ground—twice a day.[239]

It seems avoidance of American casualties was the ultimate purpose of these B-52 missions. Air Force Vice Chief of Staff General Bruce K. Holloway wondered in 1968 if a four-jet cell covering the same area could have the same basic psychological and material effects as six, but the Army did not like this proposal because it believed powerful Arc Light missions translated into fewer casualties among American ground forces. Admiral John S. McCain Jr. argued B-52 operations suppressed enemy activity and precluded greater losses among American and South Vietnamese troops.[240] For example in July 1968, Operation Thor comprised a four-day bombardment by 216 aircraft sorties and naval and ground firepower of an area that was too full of the enemy for American soldiers to enter. Major General Richard G. Stillwell concluded that Thor had hurt the enemy badly enough that soldiers could now enter the area without suffering too many casualties themselves: "An area denied to us for months is now open for hunting."[241] General Momyer wrote that MACV was going to rely on B-52s "as a principal means of achieving what his present troop strength will not permit him to do without risking unacceptable loss of lives, materiel, and territory. Use of the B-52 cannot be expressed in terms of BDA. Rather, it represents a major element in MACV's scheme of maneuver. B-52s were used as a spoiling force which assures an ability to meet major threats without putting at risk the defense of areas where ground forces were already heavily engaged."[242]

Was casualty avoidance an unreasonable goal during a war the winning of which was not necessary for national survival? Once again, the B-52s highlighted a conundrum: to really ensure that the enemy does not escape, infantry have to close with him and take casualties in the process. To what extent was that worth it to American soldiers during this limited war? Was it better to save lives for indeterminate results and bomb from afar, or was it better to close, finish off the enemy, and thus ensure that the higher losses among a commander's own troops accomplished something conclusive and lessened the need for more bloody combat in the future? That was another factor that made this limited war challenging and victory elusive. Over time, the draftee nature of the Army and the growing unpopularity of the war in the United States encouraged battle tactics that lessened the chance of conclusive action. As a consequence, the war lengthened, something that went against national policy. Air power offered a way out of having to explain high casualties among American infantry to an increasingly restless public.

Choosing to rely on firepower as opposed to men was not an either/or proposition. Just because an army was faced with an existential threat instead of a national security problem was not a reason to charge the guns; defeating the more serious threat may justify an even more liberal use of firepower. Since Vietnam was a limited war for the Americans, preserving men's lives was elevated to a national security and domestic political concern to a degree that moved the United States away from achieving the policy objectives it prioritized when deciding to embark on the war in the first place. Such was the manner in which so-called limited war generated more variables and more difficult challenges than a war that one truly had to fight. On the other hand, grunts encountered field fortifications so stout that no level of infantry maneuver, spirit, or dash could neutralize them, and heavy firepower was necessary.

The Americans' choice to rely on firepower instead of overly aggressive uses of infantry made waging a limited war more palatable—to a point. Firepower enabled the United States to avoid massive casualties among its own forces and wage an eight-year war, but firepower from the air generated mixed results. The clash between a dispersed hidden enemy armed with plenty of small arms and American forces that had access to the devastating firepower of aircraft created a conundrum. Again, in order to inflict a more decisive level of defeat on their enemy, American and South Vietnamese infantry had to close on them more aggressively in order to fix them in place. That resulted in greater losses of friendly soldiers. How could one justify those deaths when bombs from aircraft could kill some of the enemy and disperse them, without one having to rely on close-in infantry fighting to accomplish a decisive victory at the platoon or company level, a single firefight that by itself would not measurably move the war effort closer to conclusive victory? Perhaps, however, waging close quarters fighting at every opportunity in aggregate may have accomplished more to move the anti-communist forces toward their policy goals. In the end, firepower persuaded enemy insurgents and soldiers to avoid massed formations and to disperse. Political goals encouraged the free world forces to rely on firepower. Thus, it was harder for communist infantry to decimate American and South Vietnamese troops, but the enemy forces' dispersal made it more difficult for ARVN and US troops to inflict crushing losses and achieve their political agenda.

Ultimately the North Vietnamese possessed an asymmetric advantage over the Americans in terms of national interest and commitment. Choosing to rely on firepower made sense for the United States since Vietnam was a war of choice. It bears repeating that the nature of this war meant that the folks back home would never tolerate the magnitude of casualties necessary to close with enemy infantry to defeat them conclusively. It made no sense for the Americans to sacrifice the lives required to permanently destroy the National Liberation Front and the Lao Dong Party, even though their decimation was necessary to establish peace in Indochina. With their commitment to unlimited war aims the communists set the rules in their favor. They were willing to suffer enough to dissuade the Americans from paying their own high cost required to bring not only the war, but also the conflict, to a satisfactory and lasting conclusion.

Like all close air support missions, B-52 employment stressed placing bombs only where they were supposed to go. One method relied on the same MSQ-77 radar that transports used for paradrops to tell a bomber when to release his bombs. These devices covered almost all of South Vietnam and controlled thousands of sorties starting in 1966. They managed to achieve a bombing accuracy in December of that year of about 290 feet, not the "near pinpoint accuracy some claimed."[243] Accuracy was a closely scrutinized item, and if a B-52 cell was not precisely where it was supposed to be on a bombing run, the MSQ controller would terminate the bombing run. During September 1968, for example, 836 BUFs dropped

Bomb craters from B-52 strike (Air Force Historical Research Agency)

bombs on targets; three aircraft that were about to drop their payload did not because their MSQ controllers indicated the planes were not in the correct place. In addition, targeteers were required to select aim points at least a kilometer away from noncombatants as well as religious sites, monuments, or landmarks, the destruction of which would have political repercussions.[244]

Their bombs wielded substantial destructive power: an M-117 750-pound bomb had a kill radius of ninety feet while the Mk 82's was seventy-five feet, but looking at the bomb spread, Arc Light strikes might not have been as apocalyptic as they appeared. Vice Admiral Lloyd M. Mustin observed of the first mission in 1965 that the density of the bombs was surprisingly light, about one bomb for every two acres. The bombers were spaced to cover a kill zone a kilometer wide, and each B-52 dropped a string of 108 bombs about 5,000 feet long, resulting in an average distance between craters of forty-seven feet. A 1967 study concluded the bombs actually cratered only 2 percent of the target zone. While the lethal area around each impact point was greater than the crater's radius, for nearly all of the 1.3 square miles to remain uncratered after nine B-52s had struck suggests that this kind of area bombing covered like fishnet rather than a carpet. Therefore, the bomb spread was tightened. A preliminary test on March 10, 1967, found that this type of tactic, flown at night, appeared to close the roads bombed for four and five days in a row, and consequently, some North Vietnamese moved about during daylight hours.[245]

Most of the bombs the B-52s dropped were fused to explode at ground level to kill the VC; for that reason, the VC built bunkers and trenches forty feet deep and survived. Therefore, 25 percent of the bomb load needed to be penetrators with delayed fuses. Arc Light missions did not expend the firepower necessary, however, to collapse the deepest fortifications the enemy was able to dig. Colonel Joseph Pizzi compared one fortification at Kontum in 1972 to Monte Casino in World War II; a few of the caves were eighteen feet deep. B-52 bombs were not sufficient to destroy the enemy's deepest bunkers.[246]

Sometimes Army commanders found that the bomb spread left gaps wide enough that some of the enemy survived. General Collins of the 4th Infantry Division wrote that following an Arc Light mission against a target Alpha 96, his soldiers advanced into the bombed area and found themselves in a firefight with enemy survivors. The grunts backed away and brought in another Arc Light strike. When they surveyed the ground, they discovered most of the enemy had fled. Grunts found sixteen bodies and believed at least fifty more were dead inside a tunnel. On the locations where four other BUF strikes had laid down their bombs, "our forces were able to walk through the area without any opposition. While no enemy bodies were found in the area, there were many blood trails, and the area of strike Bravo 10 had the stench of death about it that one finds on a battlefield after many men have been killed." Similarly, Major General Raymond Davis saw thirty enemy combatants fleeing after B-52s bombed their location. Following another B-52 cell attack at that same area, Marines observed about twenty to thirty nearby "wandering about aimlessly." Artillery shells did them in.[247]

The B-52s nearly always put their bombs on the geographical target with accuracy, but that should have been only an initial goal. In light of Westmoreland's attrition strategy, the goal was to kill as many of the enemy as possible, and for all the effort put into the Arc Light missions, those B-52s dropping 324 bombs from each three-jet cell were not infrequently very efficient but not conclusively effective, especially in the early years of those missions. Whether or not the bombs actually killed a lot of Viet Cong and North Vietnamese Army troops was neither consistently measured nor tracked. Westmoreland realized that sound intelligence, responsiveness, and weight of ordnance went into effective B-52 missions.[248]

The Criticality of Targeting Intelligence

Putting the bombs on the target was not the challenge, finding the enemy was. Ideally, intelligence would guide planners where to focus their attention, whereupon B-52s and fighter-bombers would strike, and air and perhaps ground reconnaissance missions would follow.[249] Brigadier General John K. Boles Jr. concluded in 1965 that three-quarters of the bombing in South Vietnam was ineffective because the jets were sent on missions "based on little or no accurate intelligence." Boles maintained if just a fraction of the money spent on high-cost projects was shifted to improving intelligence capabilities, an exponential improvement in the bombing effectiveness would have been the result.[250] But accurate targeting intelligence was perishable, and quick responsiveness was seldom possible in order to exploit the B-52s' great firepower.[251] Bombers often hit locations based on the "suspicion" or "report" that enemy forces were there. For example, a mission took off on April 10, 1967, bound for a target in South Vietnam that was only suspected of being the location of a supply base and command post.[252] One-hundred-ninety-eight bombs pummeled that place, but the unit history lists no bomb damage assessment. Units might mark an area for bombing because they encountered enemy forces every time they tried to move into an area—conclusive evidence enemy forces were present. B-52s struck a target in the Quang Ngai Province on April 16 because human intelligence and evidence of the movement of supplies and soldiers placed headquarters of the Fifth North Vietnamese Army in that area.[253]

Targeting intelligence for Arc Light missions varied in detail and veracity. Triangulating radio transmissions was often a good way of finding enemy groupings. Bombers struck Viet Cong in Tay Ninh Province on July 20–21, and again on July 28–29, 1968, as a result of that kind of intelligence. Analysts suspected the first mission killed 33 percent of the enemy forces and claimed that the latter bombing killed more than a hundred and wounded about

150. Every kind of intelligence had to be integrated in order to know where and when to use the bombers.[254] The targeting intelligence for mission Hotel 8 relied on collecting a variety of data points. Ground reconnaissance teams observed a considerable number of enemy troops moving from place to place and that electrical generators were in constant operation. They also witnessed the enemy move supplies on boats, build earthworks, and enough activity occurred to produce a large pathway. Search lights that tried to illuminate the B-52s of mission Hotel 79 on the night of May 8 were further confirmations of the enemy's presence. Photo reconnaissance subsequently confirmed the enemy were concentrating in an area constructing encampments with defenses, suggesting the presence of company-sized units, not the 273rd Regiment suspected of operating in the area.[255] Roaming Special Forces might find and nominate a target like the one found on May 20, 1967. They found two base camps large enough for two battalions; subsequently, six B-52s bombed them. A captured soldier also might provide a target location. Nine B-52s struck the suspected location of two PAVN regiments on May 24 based on the interrogation of a prisoner.

Camouflage was a good indicator of enemy activity. Therefore, nine B-52s hit a group of camouflaged assemblages near Kin Giang the next day. Viet Cong wore visible footpaths into the earth where they walked in remote areas, and those drew Arc Light raids. Sometimes B-52s bombed targets that could only be military, such as enemy troops manning a system of trenches and bunkers that American observers had seen. A suspected PAVN headquarters always warranted a visit from B-52s. All agreed that Arc Light missions inflicted great harm when committed against enemy troops that were in contact with friendlies, and when the location of enemy forces was certain. Nonetheless, many missions targeted only suspected enemy locations.[256]

Arc Light missions were most effective when coordinated with ground operations. When ground forces found the enemy, artillery and aircraft then pounded him, but utter destruction of the enemy did not result unless the soldiers or Marines then attacked. Enemy forces consistently withdrew and reconstituted to fight again. Over time, however, B-52 operations were coordinated more effectively with ground forces. For example, when MACV gained intelligence of an impending offensive in August 1969, General Abrams gave B-52s a major role in attacking and disrupting North Vietnamese forces. He advised the commanding general of the 3rd Marine Division, Major General Raymond, that ground forces needed to search the ground the Arc Light mission just pummeled.[257] Deliberate coordination with ground force attacks became prominent in 1972 during Operation Linebacker.

Air Force Measurements of Effectiveness

The Air Force measured the effectiveness of Arc Light missions according to actions it controlled. If a cell of B-52s dropped all of its bombs where it was supposed to, that run was considered 100 percent effective. Efficiency was defined as the percentage of sorties that dropped their bombs where they were supposed to compared to the number scheduled to fly.[258] Superiors sent praise when ejector racks released 100 percent of their bombs: "The record shows all scheduled sorties flown, without an air abort, nor a bad bomb, for an effectiveness rate of 100 percent."[259] During its missions in the summer of 1966 the 91st Bombardment Wing reported whether all the bombs left their bomb racks and struck the plot of ground they were supposed to.[260] One report noted that reconnaissance photographs indicated at least 93 percent of the bombs landed within their target box. Another noted that a group of six B-52s were unable to release every bomb; they brought back a total of eight that were still attached to their carriages. The factors Strategic Air Command used to measure the effectiveness of Arc Light missions—no bombs remaining attached to bomb racks, percentage of bombs landing on the target, and percentage of bombs exploding—were relevant issues, but those metrics could not assess strategic effectiveness.[261]

Inconsistent certainty about the effects of Arc Light missions remained a theme for much of the war. A report on a June 1965 mission against a target in Binh Duong Province claimed more than 150 of the enemy killed or wounded, while other reports asserted up to 400 casualties resulted from a collapsed tunnel. The July 7 report expressed a common refrain: they did not *know* what the bombing had accomplished because no ground team surveyed the damage and photo reconnaissance could not pierce the dense tree canopy. Of twelve B-52 missions during the first two weeks of October 1965, a ground force operation complemented only six. Of five missions from late October to early November, ground reconnaissance followed up on only two, so what the other three actually accomplished remained unknown. On the morning of December 12, 1965, B-52s hit areas northwest of Cam Y, and a Marine battalion swept the area but found very little worth noting.[262] The fact that it was often difficult to accurately determine what took place as a result of a B-52 strike was documented at the highest levels. Westmoreland loved the BUFs, but his letter of October 16, 1967, is revealing. A month of bombings "disrupted" the enemy, he claimed, but they lacked precise data on the damage the bombing inflicted.[263]

The Air Force realized determining the effects of these attacks was very difficult because again, ground forces often did not follow up the bombing to assess the damage or finish off the survivors. During the first seven months of Arc Light missions, ground forces examined the bomb zone on only fifty-four of 150 Arc Light missions. That rate declined precipitously for 1966, when teams surveyed only twenty-three out of 219 strike zones.[264] Major General John D. Lavelle admitted that the Air Force had not confirmed the KIA claims regarding Arc Light missions because MACV would only accept confirmations from American forces about the effectiveness of air strikes, and ground teams surveyed less than half of the results of Arc Light missions up to that time.[265] A couple of years later the officer responsible for assigning targets to B-52s believed that direct observation, ground teams, photo reconnaissance, and special intelligence were adequate for determining the effectiveness of these but at the same time wrote, "Determining the actual effect of high altitude mass saturation bombing of non-strategic type targets was extremely difficult." His ultimate definition of effectiveness was so wide and broad that pretty much all the missions were effective: "There were very few strikes in which we did not feel we had accomplished the objective of either denying the area to the enemy, destroying the enemy and his supplies, or routing the enemy to assist ground operations."[266]

By 1971, one estimation concluded that, "Arc Light crews were unable to accurately determine if their bomb loads had struck paydirt."[267] During this time, however, when a ground team was able to examine the results of where bombs struck, the bombs usually destroyed something of value and significance. Following forty missions against the enemy in February 1971, ground survey teams concluded that they had killed at least 150 enemy troops (paltry numbers).[268] Eighth Air Force admitted in 1972 that, "Never more than 10 percent of the strikes have been evaluated and reported on by an intelligence source. This makes the quantification of the results of B-52 strikes a very elusive statistic indeed."[269] Strategic Air Command admitted that it was difficult to accurately assess the effectiveness of Arc Light missions without ground reconnaissance teams to confirm what had actually been destroyed.[270]

When infantry moved into an area just bombed by B-52s they confirmed the results and engaged with any survivors, as when the 9th ARVN and 1st US Infantry Divisions did following an April 22, 1967, Arc Light mission near Binh Duong.[271] During November–December 1967, ground or helicopter survey teams examined the bomb results anywhere from a few hours to a few days after the attack. Invariably they found damaged or destroyed structures, bunkers, and fortifications, perhaps a collapsed below-ground storehouse, but only mentioned the killing of a single enemy soldier. Regarding the effects of the November 24 mission, the ground reconnaissance team concluded that the enemy had been in the path of the bombs and "changed his plans for his defensive positions within that particular area."[272] That's it? Bombs from B-52s persuaded the enemy to "change his plans for his defensive positions"? The delay of several hours between the bombing and the survey probably allowed survivors to remove the dead and wounded, but there is no mention of body parts lying around, which one would expect after hundreds of bombs exploded among insurgents caught outside of bomb shelters. Maybe they had been gathered up, too. Other follow-ups to Arc Light sorties found, for example, hundreds of rifles, pistols, and mortar rounds. During one operation in the summer of 1968, Abrams sent in B-52s first and then followed up with significant numbers of troops both on foot and by helicopter.[273] This sort of joint warfare became much more common against the 1972 North Vietnamese invasion.

The most certain effect of Arc Light missions was to reassure and encourage American and South Vietnamese infantry. General Westmoreland asserted in September 1965 that they demoralized the VC and improved the combat capabilities of American and South Vietnamese forces. Two months later he forwarded his delight regarding the B-52 strikes in Pleiku Province on November 15, even though no one knew with any thoroughness exactly what they had accomplished.[274] Army and Marine generals lavished praise and thanks on the Air Force when B-52s pulverized enemy positions, whether suspected or certain. Lieutenant General Jonathan O. Seaman, the commanding general of II Field Force during Operation Cedar Falls, thanked the efforts of the 4133rd Bombardment Wing in February 1967 thus: "The accuracy and awesome firepower brought to bear upon the Viet Cong by your aircrews not only wreaked havoc with their fortifications but assisted materially in disrupting their morale thereby contributing materially to the success of the operation."[275] "Disrupting morale," however, was not a decisive use of firepower; nevertheless the MACV commander could not express more satisfaction with what the B-52s were doing, and no one was a greater advocate for their use than he.[276]

The Air Force struggled to assess the consequences of Arc Light missions. It recognized that B-52s had to actually hit the enemy in order to be worthwhile. It also realized that if ground forces did not follow up the strike and carry out on-the-spot BDA, one could not be certain of the results.[277] Too often there was a shortage of confirming, clear data on the missions. One study examined 110 B-52 missions during five weeks in September and October 1967. The analyst argued reasonably that if enemy forces were in a target area when the bombs arrived, they were "probably damaged either physically or psychologically; however, experience indicates that at times the enemy is willing to absorb this punishment." A target zone near Con Thien suffered five missions from September 19 to October 11, but enemy forces remained present, even though more than 1,000 tons of bombs fell in a 1.3 square mile rectangle.[278] Communist forces were willing to die in large numbers and were able to suffer the pummeling to a degree greater than expected.

After a year of B-52 missions over Southeast Asia, Seventh AF could not decide the extent to which they were effective and worthwhile. Momyer's intelligence director argued in June 1966 that the effectiveness and efficiency of B-52 strikes was not known.[279] He had surveyed bombed areas from the air and wrote that there had "been no killing of large bodies of enemy troops, no destruction of quantities of enemy materiel, and no denial of territory to the enemy."[280] Fourteen months after the first mission, Seventh AF concluded the Viet Cong did not mass their forces enough, nor did they possess vulnerable logistical tails that would have made them truly vulnerable to mass bombing. The heavy bombers were more effective as defensive weapons against condensed formations of infantry. Some message traffic illustrated this well: "The B-52 has made a significant contribution to the war, but a contribution which must be measured in terms of what it might have prevented, rather than in quantitative terms. This will continue to be the case unless the enemy commits the error of massing." Two B-52 squadrons were sufficient.[281]

The Air Force realized it was difficult to measure the consequences of these missions. The results of Operation Thor in the summer of 1969 were uncertain because no one inspected the area on foot and the observations from the B-52s were from as high as 30,000 feet or were from small aircraft avoiding friendly artillery while making their surveys. Many artillery and flak sites reported as destroyed did not have weapons on them, they were just cleared patches of ground. Bombs destroyed only two artillery pieces and eleven antiaircraft guns. Jungle cover made a thorough materiel assessment impossible, and the main indicator that the bombardment had been successful was the reduction in enemy artillery fire. Marine Lieutenant General Robert E. Cushman concluded that this was an effective operation and argued that a combination of air and ground-based firepower was the best way to defeat enemy artillery. A later assessment noted consequences that were of only local significance: the strikes silenced artillery that had been shelling Marine supply lines. Photographs B-52s took of their own bomb patterns, when the weather allowed it, only measured where the bombs landed, and how many bombs landed inside the intended target box. Ground teams provided the best assessments of the bombs' effects, but the boxes were often in terribly remote areas. Strategic Air Command held conferences to try to correct this problem but were befuddled.[282] Thing is, the Viet Cong were able to function in those secluded places, otherwise they would not have been there in the first place. Why was it that the Americans and the South Vietnamese found it too difficult to send ground reconnaissance teams into those same areas?

Photographs of the results of Arc Light strikes could provide only limited bomb damage assessment. When a group of bombs struck a previously hit piece of ground, photo-interpreters could not differentiate between the old and new craters well enough to assess the latest strike. In 1967, at least, "Items of military significance: none" was frequently the last sentence in a report that really only documented crater location and size, and damage to trees and terrain.[283] Other reports documented no damage at all to any of the specific targets in the bomb box—trenches, bunkers, road interdicted, and the like—while less frequently the photographs revealed that the bombs inflicted significant damage. An Arc Light mission on September 4, 1967, for example, destroyed but two bunkers, and caused 50 percent damage to foxholes. The reports noted whether or not a crater in a road could be bypassed; they usually could.[284] Of sixty-eight reports from March to October 1967, twenty-eight reported no damage. Of the occasional one that reported 100 percent damage, it would be to a road that the bombs had cratered, but that the enemy could bypass.[285] Another report considered a strike successful because the bombs blew away the jungle canopy; the enemy could thus no longer safely walk around out in the open in that newly exposed area.[286] "Unable to determine new impact areas due to previous strike in and around target area" was another common manner in which these reports were concluded.[287] One report from a pilot who flew over the bombed area and scanned it with his eyes noted that, "The strike caused extensive tree damage and uncovered one (1) foot trail."[288]

These were not a sample of a small group of reports: an inch-thick stack of paper makes up a single month's reports. Their content begs the question why no one insisted that without good human intelligence and large ground forces with which to fix the enemy in place Arc Light missions were not as effective as they could be. Without those measures, Arc Light needed the enemy to cooperate in the form of concentrating their forces, as with the siege of Khe Sanh in 1968 and the 1972 Easter Offensive. That the communists ever concentrated was surprising because they had conclusive experience that if intelligence sources found them, B-52s and fighter-bombers would destroy them if they packed themselves together in a small space. In fact, a part of MACV's strategy was to send an Arc Light mission against troop concentrations as soon as they were identified. Clearly firepower capabilities form but a portion of effective air power—targeting intelligence is key.[289]

Not infrequently Strategic Air Command wrote analyses on the ultimate effects of these missions that were not that flattering and revealed the mixed results of this kind of bombing. When ARVN forces spent three days searching the area macerated by twelve B-52s on January 9, 1967, they found "that surface bursts blew the tops from trees and had considerable effect on bamboo in the area." They also found that while the raid destroyed all of the bunkers, "there were no known enemy casualties as a result of this strike."[290] American forces might witness the same after a strike using high explosive and cluster bombs: "No bodies or signs of personnel casualties were observed in the areas covered by the recon team."[291] After one mission in February 1967, an analysis noted the bombing did not harm any of the twenty-five bunkers and tunnels made out of concrete and logs and that: "All installations discovered in the target areas during the ground follow-up operation were intact after these strikes took place." A captured VC explained that before the bombs fell, their commander had told them to leave the area in three separate groups and meet at the predesignated rendezvous location. The Army believed that headquarters elements were inside the target box, but the ground reconnaissance teams could not confirm whether that was true or not. The soldiers who combed the area could not tell whether the bombing killed anyone, but four Viet Cong surrendered and volunteered to fight for the South Vietnamese.[292]

That same month witnessed a much more effective mission, as stated by Major Tram Hung Tam, a captured VC officer. According to him, the dozens of bombs B-52s dropped on the Provincial Committee during mission Charlie 62 "killed 200 of 500 VC, destroyed 3,000 tons of rice and 30 tons of medical supplies ... the surviving members of the regiment scattered after the strike. Morale was low and many were willing to give themselves up to the government forces of SVN if afforded the opportunity."[293] One reason was "concussion sickness": the shock waves of the bomb explosions caused injuries that caused the afflicted to bleed "from the mouth, nose, ears, and internally."[294] A captured member of North Vietnam's 325th Division commented that they received no warning of the B-52s approaching on May 25, 1966; bombs just started exploding. He said once he gathered himself, he and the rest quickly left the bomb zone. While he only saw two dead, twenty soldiers were missing as a result, some of whom probably went over to the South Vietnamese. At times, B-52 strikes demoralized VC to the point that troops deserted and survived by banditry. To compensate, the VC elevated the intensity of their self-criticism talks and required constant supervision of everyone. The trauma of surviving a B-52 bomb spread was well known, so when possible, aircraft dropped psychological warfare leaflets a few hours after a mission to exploit this fact. Ambassador Sullivan added that B-52s were unique because they intimidated the enemy and projected a different kind of meaning than did fighter-bombers.[295]

B-52 attacks were not a wasted effort. Arc Light missions against Con Thien, a subject of fierce battle between Marines and PAVN, appeared to have not been that effective because enemy forces remained there and continued fighting. The area's value came under question, but Lieutenant General Victor Krulak, the commanding general of Fleet Marine Force, Pacific noted: "If it was not worth holding on to, why did the NVA want it so badly?"[296] They were more damaging to the enemy the more he was engaged with Allied forces. Their second most effective mission was against confirmed locations of supplies and troops. Communist troops became more concerned about being near bomb shelters than their main task at hand. The size differential between the bomb craters and their huts intimidated them and surviving under those bombs was frightful. Nothing scared VC and PAVN more than B-52s; they were one of the main reasons their troops deserted.[297] Arc Light missions persuaded the VC to place more emphasis on defensive measures—burrowing deep into the ground and staying on the move. A couple of insurgents captured from the 5th VC Division in 1969 attested to the results of American firepower, commenting that the combined weight from fighter-bombers, artillery, and B-52s had separated the smaller units from each other. Abrams's command noticed that the size of enemy battalions had shrunk on average from 330 to 250, it believed due to air strikes and artillery shelling. A prisoner in July 1972 claimed that a B-52 attack killed 110 out of the 180 in his unit.[298] Another testified that three bombings by B-52s had "severely reduced the battalion's capability to perform its mission."[299] Westmoreland argued they had dissuaded the VC from transitioning from guerrilla warfare to more conventional forms, deterred them from massing, undercut economic support for the insurgents, and "alienated noncombatants from the VC."[300]

After being on the ground near a strike Alexander Haig explained to President Nixon how the ground shook under the bombs.[301] A member of the MACV staff witnessed a B-52 strike during the siege of Khe Sanh from a distance of about a half mile and the concussions were so great that his trench fell in on him: "He felt as though he had been inside a large drum rolling down a steep, rocky hill."[302]

A 1966 assessment lauded Arc Light missions for the destruction they wrought on VC bases in remote areas. Other B-52 missions went after concentrations of troops close to where they were fighting American or South Vietnamese troops. The bombers were accurate with their bomb placement. Analysts tended to rely on photo interpretation to derive some conclusions regarding the consequences of Arc Light missions, such as counting the number of bomb craters inside the target box—a measure of bombing accuracy but not necessarily effectiveness. Photo interpreters, however, often discovered real evidence that the VC had been present, such as tunnels and fortifications. But the assessment confessed that, "This is about the best we can expect to see without detailed ground follow-up of each strike, because of the nature of the targets struck, the terrain and foliage restrictions, and the recognized VC policy to keep results of our actions hidden." This writer realized the shortcomings he was dealing with, adding that results such as killing important leaders, wrecking morale, and undercutting troop motivation and conviction were important consequences photographs and even ground surveys could not measure. He also understood that the ultimate effects of this kind of bombing may not manifest until combined with all the other actions against the enemy and produced consequences that could not be hidden.[303]

In the end, ground reconnaissance teams produced the most accurate assessments of B-52 effectiveness. They often found that B-52 strikes had done little conclusive damage or that they had struck nothing but jungle because targeting intelligence was inadequate. When a long-range reconnaissance patrol examined one site of an Arc Light attack, it considered the mission a success because either the B-52s' bombs damaged or destroyed six bunkers, or the patrol itself destroyed them. They found that the bombs had left a kitchen and the bunkers untouched. It mentioned no bodies. Another ground team found fifteen graves at a site, which meant that enough enemy survived nearby to bury them, or that insurgents from outside of the bomb zone had come in to bury them. At least the bombs from this mission smashed every bunker and foxhole.[304]

The Army was not carrying out enough post-strike searches on foot; doing so took a great amount of time and did not fit in with the larger operational tasks that the ground forces preferred. Strikes on March 19, 1967, were supposed to destroy enemy supplies, kill enemy troops, and render their fortifications useless. The battalion that examined the site found twenty destroyed bunkers, but mentioned no bodies, and a helicopter-borne search team saw no militarily significant items. The Golf 87 mission was deemed a great success because the bombing revealed the existence of what was either fuel or ammunition, destroyed some of both, and did the same to a cache of food supplies. The bombs destroyed seventy-five 100-pound bags of rice but missed two other large sets of bagged rice. Of the nineteen missions the 307th Strategic Bombardment Wing (SBW) flew in April 1970, ground reconnaissance teams put eyes on the results only five times and found at most six dead enemy soldiers. At the same time, airborne observers consistently observed incontrovertible evidence of enemy activity like trenches and bunkers and provided most of the BDA that month; one counted 130 bunkers destroyed.[305] A long-range patrol examining the results of a strike concluded that a battalion-sized formation reoccupied the area after the bombing, which suggests that the bombs missed the real target entirely.[306]

Sometimes post-attack ground reconnaissance teams came under enemy fire. The search of the area nine BUFs struck on January 20, 1967, found some undamaged huts that seemed to have been abandoned in the middle of a meal, but it found no indicators that anyone had been killed, probably because the VC removed all of their dead to frustrate body counting efforts, a common practice.[307] Another mission, on January 24, targeted what was probably the headquarters for the 9th VC Division, and nearly 600 bombs destroyed most of its base camp. In addition, "Numerous graves were found in the target area and 18 bodies were counted in one large grave. The ground follow-up force estimated that an additional 50 to 75 bodies were taken across the border to Cambodia."[308] Armed survey teams following a September 5, 1967, mission captured seventy-three enemy soldiers, including several outside of the target box who offered that the B-52 raid was the reason they had moved away from the blast zone. Concentrated bombing like that was supposed to leave no survivors; these strikes were not supposed to frighten the enemy or cause him to desert, but to kill him. The prisoners taken, however, demonstrated the significant consequences of B-52s working in conjunction with infantry; because friendly infantry was nearby, they were able to finish what the B-52s had started by capturing survivors of Arc Light missions.[309]

Sometimes Arc Light missions were sent against places where there was no actual enemy activity; targets were not always confirmed enemy locations. The three BUFs of mission Charlie 76 on January 30, 1967, struck what may have been a battalion headquarters and hurt what may have been a growing force of enemy infantry in Kontum Province.[310] In February 1967, a nine-jet mission hit its target, but, "There were no tunnels, installations or fortifications found in the area, nor was there any evidence of enemy units in the area during this strike."[311] Again, this time on February 7, twelve bombed their assigned target, possibly a long-term storage site. Follow-up did not find trenches, ammunition, bivouacs, or evidence of enemy dead.[312] The following week a mission "struck an unknown target area in Quang Ngai Province."[313] The wording of these reports was sometimes unclear, as with the ground reconnaissance of the area mission D-79 obliterated. The report states, "No items of military significance were observed by the follow-up operation."[314] Does that mean that they were annihilated, or nothing worth bombing was there in the first place? Similarly, the post-attack reconnaissance of Delta 88's mission repeated the same words.[315] More strikes in March, Echo 22 and Echo 36, which hit the same place seemed to be for nothing, as the BDA team found "no items of military significance" when surveying the site six days later.[316]

A broader assessment of March 1967 Arc Light missions commented that confirmed evidence of what the bombs had destroyed was not commonplace, apart from photographs that allowed one to count the number of craters. An agent claimed that B-52s on February 24 killed about 400 VC out of a total of 600 troops and 200 workers belonging to an unidentified VC unit. The PACAF analyst of this data was skeptical. Casualty figures that agents reported did not go into the totals that were tabulated, and he believed the data set was insufficient for drawing conclusions. He also warned against any quantification of letters, statements, and extolments.[317] These missions needed to destroy objects of value to the enemy, but in October, the 4258th flew 185 sorties against targets in the vicinity of the DMZ, but only 5 percent gave indications of destroying materiel of importance in the form of secondary explosions.[318]

At other times ground teams confirmed that Arc Light missions destroyed a lot of VC materiel and killed a significant number of soldiers. After a strike in October 1965, civilian irregular troops found that while the VC had moved on or been killed, they left behind 15,000 rounds of ammo, thousands of documents, and dozens of 60mm mortar rounds, among other things. A mission on June 20, 1966, killed fifteen enemy, wounded twenty more, and destroyed or damaged more than half of the 21st Regiment's equipment according to a captured PAVN sergeant. Nine B-52s bombed a tight concentration of bivouacs and field fortifications in support of an Australian operation on August 20, 1967. When troops examined the bombed-out area twelve hours later, they found the mission had destroyed a command post, a set of tunnels, and a trio of large encampments. They found footprints of more than a few insurgents and shot two they encountered. Missions on September 16 attacked an active VC base; the ground team found considerable quantities of food and military equipment and that all the bunkers, spider holes, and structures had been destroyed—but no bodies.[319] When nine B-52s struck a couple of VC companies on September 30, 1967, there were a reported thirty-eight killed and forty-seven wounded, along with a lot of damaged weapons. A day after a December 28, 1967, mission in support of MACV ground operations, the reconnaissance force wrote that they found evidence that enemy personnel had been killed or wounded but would not estimate numbers of killed. This target was no mistake. They found thirty destroyed bunkers, documents, and equipment. A few days later, the recon team found evidence of dead troops for the mission of January 10, but also would not attach a specific figure to the casualty count because it could not provide a verified number. The strike of February 1 hit something militarily significant, because 400-foot-tall flames raged for more than two hours after the bombs hit home.[320] Not until September 1968 is there any mention in the records of the 4258th SBW of missions killing substantial numbers of hostile troops. In this instance, a six-jet cell that flew on September 3 killed eighty-two. Missions on September 8–9 resulted in thirty-nine dead enemy according to FACs. Then on the September 16, six B-52s killed 300 of the 320th PAVN Division.[321]

At times the B-52s were used against completely unsophisticated targets, a fact one wing historian highlighted: "During December, something different was bombed. On 2 December 1968 Arc Light aircraft dropped 647 bombs on . . . 'bicycle repair bunkers with complete bikes and spare parts.'" Really? Six-hundred-forty-seven bombs from the bellies of the mightiest bomber in history to destroy bicycles?[322] Now it was true that these were not bikes for a merry ride on a Sunday afternoon; they were stout vehicles used for carrying cargo. A porter would load them down with 400 pounds of whatever, grab the handlebars, and push them along, walking them down the Ho Chi Minh Trail into South Vietnam.[323] But this strains only credulity, not targeting choices. This was an attritional war against a resolute enemy, and this was still a legitimate use of aerial bombardment against enemy logistics that required determination against determination. Nevertheless, sophisticated heavy bombers carry a certain meaning, and one intuitively expects them to be used in certain ways; bombing bicycles with a B-52 was no way to have your air campaign taken seriously. Such usage could too easily spin instances like these into an image of a sledgehammer smashing a gnat.

Military leaders considered Arc Light missions effective because ground commanders believed they were effective. For example, the Australian commander who led the survey of Foxtrot 70's bombing of a VC training area in Phuoc Tuy Province concluded the bombing had done great damage to the enemy since they encountered little resistance during the first phase of Operation Portsea.[324] Westmoreland believed the Army would not have attained its successes without the use of B-52s, which he described as a "major innovation of war." He wanted more and even mused about a single formation of one hundred B-52s for destroying entire regiments.[325] Likewise, General Wheeler lauded B-52s and fighter-bombers for what they were able to do to fielded forces, severely delaying PAVN plans for a spring offensive in I Corps, for example. The largest enemy attack on May 25, 1968, was only the size of a battalion, which American air forces placed under a relentless B-52 and tactical fighter bombardment. On June 5, the North Vietnamese force called off its assault, making the air strikes an effective bombing operation at the operational level of war, but to what extent did it undercut Hanoi's strategy and further that of the South Vietnamese and the Americans? General Momyer misapplied air power toward the destruction of enemy forces rather than the defeat of the enemy; the two are related, but are not synonymous. Massive bombing is fine when it works, but this group of generals was not learning during war. They overlooked the holistic necessity of joint and coalition operations—particularly against an enemy that was employing a sophisticated strategy of political action, terrorism, insurgency, and conventional warfare. A strategy beyond "more firepower" was necessary not to play nice with allies and other services, but to inflict the right kind of physical damage on the enemy so that they abandoned their war aims.[326]

At other times the bomb damage assessment teams on the ground killed more of the enemy than did the Arc Light missions. After the mission of March 5, 1967, the ground team spent three days examining the bombed area without finding any indication the enemy lived or patrolled there, nor signs that anyone had been killed. Near the target area, however, the team stumbled upon an insurgent platoon and shot thirty-five guerrillas. The battalion that verified the damage from a March 23 mission, however, combed the entire area and confirmed that the bombs destroyed a lot of foxholes and upward of forty bunkers. They only found one dead VC in a fresh grave, but they could tell by the smell that a number of bunkers still had bodies in them. This reconnaissance force killed twenty-three enemy troops during the survey. Eighty-five miles to the southeast a team also found the wreckage of a VC emplacement, and then encountered most of the 275th Viet Cong Regiment. According to the after-action reports, the mission was believed to have been decisive in preventing enemy forces from attacking nearby friendly troops.[327]

Bomb damage assessment teams seldom found the ground littered with bodies left from large infantry battalions or regiments. The indecisiveness of these firepower-based tactics at this stage of the war was in line with changes the Viet Cong were making in their own approach to the war. Robert W. Komer noticed in January 1967 that the VC were reverting from an attempt to escalate to conventional large unit operations back to guerrilla warfare due to the effectiveness of MACV's infantry/CAS firepower strategy. Guerrillas functioning as smaller covert units were by their nature much less vulnerable to blankets of firepower.³²⁸

The far more favorable Joint Staff assessment conceded that the green undercast of foliage limited aerial reconnaissance of B-52 strikes and the remoteness of their target boxes made ground reconnaissance follow-up difficult. When the JCS provided their judgment of Arc Light to Secretary McNamara in October 1966, they used bomb tonnage, response rate (100 percent), the fact that only 3 percent of the bombs failed to release from their carriages, and 98 percent of the aircraft reaching their bomb release points as determinants of effectiveness. Arc Light provided a unique capability that ground commanders had to have, and the bombings undermined VC morale, who realized the bombers could attack anywhere at any time.³²⁹

American political leaders cited evidence of the missions' effectiveness. Harry C. McPherson Jr., special counsel to the president, observed during a June 1967 fact-finding mission that B-52 strikes cratered the Ho Bo and Boi Loi forests, but enough VC survived that grunts had to close in to kill the survivors. He also warned against pursuing policy objectives by relying solely on military activities, because everything in Vietnam was interconnected: economic, military, racial, political, national identity, education—each affected the other. Ellsworth Bunker observed that artillery, tactical air strikes, and B-52s in particular, had contributed to beating back the enemy's most recent offensive. Defectors' reports reached the State Department, as in the case of a soldier who defected outside of Kontum in September 1968 who shared that air attacks killed 410 of 450 men in his battalion. Arc Light harmed the enemy up and down the length of South Vietnam.³³⁰

Air Strikes and the Defense of Khe Sanh

The Siege of Khe Sanh in 1968 was an example of the truly significant destruction air strikes could inflict on ground forces besieging a fixed target. Sometimes the PAVN operation against Khe Sanh is presented as something that surprised the Americans, but the Marines started anticipating the siege no later than October 1966. It did not begin until December 1967, when the North Vietnamese decided the base offered a good possibility for victory given its location closer to their supply lines. According to Lieutenant General Robert E. Cushman, the commander of the Marines in I Corps, the Marines at Khe Sanh had not adequately prepared for what was coming. They instead spent a lot of attention in 1967 initiating contact with PAVN infantry on the ground surrounding the fort. Furthermore, only one battalion manned Khe Sanh until December, and the bunkers were enough only for them; they were insufficient for the additional Marines who were brought in. Soon after the enemy escalated the siege of Khe Sanh, survival relied on the steadfastness of Marines and the weight of air strikes on enemy troops.³³¹

On January 22, 1968, Westmoreland directed everyone's attention to Khe Sanh: "I consider it imperative that we use the maximum air firepower available to meet the enemy threat in First Corps." He made General Momyer responsible for managing the proper use of Air Force, Navy, and Marine air strikes, with the caveat that the Marines would retain operational control over their aircraft. At the same time, the III Marine Amphibious Force was to hand over all its sorties that Marine units did not require as organic support to Seventh AF, but Marines at Khe Sanh would get the initial priority for those sorties anyway. Westmoreland made his intent clear: effective coordination was paramount: "I have directed my air deputy to insure [*sic*] in my name that these air resources are applied to this end."³³² General Momyer recognized the severity of the communists' intentions for Khe Sanh and ordered close air support for troops directly fighting the enemy to receive the greatest priority. Recognizing the expansiveness of the enemy onslaught, he did not become myopic on Khe Sanh but mandated aggressive air support of the men on the ground no matter where they were.[333] Air forces flew as many sorties as possible on the first day of the offensive against the outpost, "which was reported to be extremely effective."[334] General Cushman wanted as much air support as he could find, and he preferred CAS instead of artillery for two reasons. By relying on aircraft, he would not have to airlift artillery shells into the Khe Sanh area, and the weight the firepower aircraft could deposit was greater than what artillery pieces could send.[335]

Since President Johnson paid very close attention to the siege of Khe Sanh, the defense of this outpost remained a top priority for Westmoreland. Close air support, particularly by the B-52s, was instrumental. Not surprisingly its defense received first call on B-52 and fighter-bomber strikes, and it saw sixteen three-jet Arc Light missions each day. President Johnson warned General Wheeler that he wanted no repeat of the 1954 French defeat at Dien Bien Phu, and the air strikes were central to preventing the president's nightmare from becoming a reality. B-52 strikes around Khe Sanh not only killed a lot of enemy soldiers, but the air raids also persuaded the North Vietnamese to avoid coalescing into larger formations until within two miles of the Marines' perimeter.[336]

Mostly a Marine operation at first, tactical air strikes bombed targets that artillery could not reach or could not destroy. During the last eight days of January, artillery fired 13,457 shells, the Air Force contributed 2,092 fighter-bomber sorties, the Navy 811, and Marine air 1,087 of the same. Meanwhile the Marines in the compound waited for a major North Vietnamese assault that did not take place that month—perhaps because of the air strikes, they reasoned. Toward the end of January, approximately 500 tactical and forty B-52 sorties pounded the area daily, the consequences of which were readily apparent: plenty of secondary explosions and a marked erosion of enemy logistical efforts and moves to concentrate infantry for a serious assault. By February 10, it appeared that the air strikes had persuaded the communists to postpone whatever they had planned next for the outpost.[337]

The air strikes were a spectacle. During the siege an awestruck Marine noticed that an initial wave of B-52s did not kill all in their path; survivors ran hither and yon, and when a bomb from a second wave hit a group, they "utterly disappeared."[338] The Yankee 37 Arc Light mission later in February found a cache of munitions with its bombs, because secondary explosions continued to pop off for five hours. Individual strikes dropped bombs less than a mile from the fort. Marines cheered the BUFs from their trenches.[339]

The technological capabilities of B-52s and radar-directed fighter-bombers meant that the US could employ aerial firepower no matter Khe Sanh's weather. Furthermore, the CJCS reassured LBJ that if the enemy massed for an attack, that would exponentially increase their vulnerability to American air power and artillery. That relationship was a theme of warfare in Southeast Asia. When the communists concentrated their forces to attack an opponent, aircraft normally subjected them to great destruction.[340]

During the siege, MACV considered air power its guarantee that catastrophe would never happen. Westmoreland reminded General Momyer repeatedly that it was imperative for him to make Khe Sanh a priority above all other targets for tactical aircraft strikes. He supervised the provision for air support during the siege constantly, requiring them to reformat their reports to keep him better informed of what was happening. Westmoreland next delegated more authority to General Cushman by granting him the authority to employ the aircraft under his operational control. He reassured his Marine counterpart that he fully understood the dependent relationship Marine infantry had with their aircraft, and that he wanted Marine jets to support Marines as much as possible, but Cushman needed to be aware that a greater urgency for air support could arise somewhere else. He also asked Cushman to let him know if he was not getting enough air support. At the same time, Momyer was going to run the air war.[341] This was Westmoreland's way of telling Momyer that he was to support Cushman, and that he (Westmoreland) had the final say. He told them to work together, adding that there were to be no delays in providing air support to Khe Sanh. Further simplifying the issue, Westmoreland directed on March 8, 1968, that Seventh AF was going to manage all fixed-wing close air support missions, including those using Marine Corps aircraft.[342]

When Westmoreland found out the PAVN were digging tunnels and fortifications ever closer to Khe Sanh, he directed immediate action. Whenever there was any break in the weather, FACs and fighter-bombers had to be ready to exploit those opportunities against those fortifications at once. The need for aerial firepower peaked during February 29 to March 1 when the communists carried out their biggest attack thus far. The Marines perceived that another assault might be in the offing when the PAVN subjected them to bombardments on March 22 and 23, but Momyer reacted with more than a thousand tactical and 138 B-52 sorties. If an attack had been planned, it never happened, and enemy shelling declined. The Marines under siege did not forget the effectiveness of these missions.[343]

Quantifying the effectiveness of all this was elusive. Air strikes definitely pulverized the area: "the jungle literally looked like a desert. There was hardly a tree standing. It was just a landscape of splinters and craters."[344] Bombs triggered about 4,700 secondary explosions among the communists by the time Operation Niagara, Seventh Air Force's operation to defend Khe Sanh, was concluded on March 31, and B-52 aircrews counted another 1,300. Arc Light missions persuaded a lot of PAVN to desert, which prompted their leaders to assure them that a bomb had to hit within three yards to cause harm if the soldier was well entrenched. The Air Force believed that air power had inflicted losses much greater than what it measured but did not explain why. Given the amount of ordnance the Marines received (53,000 tons) and the damage it caused, the defeat of the siege was not a surprise.[345] Two facts were undeniable: the intensity of enemy attacks waned after March, and on April 12, 1968, the road connecting Khe Sanh to Ca Lu was reopened. By the last week of March, all the Marines' sources concluded that enemy troops were backing away from Khe Sanh.[346]

General Cushman gushed that the air support "has been greater than any other air support effort in the history of warfare." He credited not only air strikes but also the combined actions of ground forces for the infliction of losses on the enemy.[347] An Air Force study later reported, "In the words of a Senior Army Commander, the defense of Khe Sanh was 'probably the first major ground action won entirely or almost entirely by air power,'" although the document does not provide his name.[348] Cushman wrote that Arc Light missions were the most decisive of all, and Westmoreland credited B-52s as the saviors of Khe Sanh.[349] Admiral Sharp also credited air power with operational victories during the Tet Offensive. He gave particular credit to B-52 operations for helping prevent the VC from achieving their goals near Saigon, Dak To, and also Khe Sanh. One somewhat surprising lesson was that it was better to send six B-52s every three hours rather than three every ninety minutes. The larger cells pulverized the enemy to a greater extent and the longer time interval provided gave everyone more time to determine where the next set of bombers needed to hit before they arrived. The decision to bomb within 1,000 yards of the Marines proved decisive because that is where many of the enemy troops hid. The PAVN had been told that they were safe inside 1,000 yards because B-52s would not bomb closer than 3,000 yards of friendly positions.

According to prisoners, the Arc Light strikes by themselves inflicted 50–75 percent casualty rates; consequently, more and more defected to get away from the bombs. Most important, the bombing persuaded the PAVN to terminate their siege.[350]

Air power claimed an operational victory at Khe Sanh, but salvaging a strategic victory was challenging. General Cushman believed that defending Khe Sanh had been a strategically significant move because it prevented two PAVN divisions from participating in combat in more heavily populated and politically significant parts of South Vietnam. The shocking and surprising intensity of the enemy's escalated violence there and especially in conjunction with the Tet Offensive up and down the length of the country dismayed an American public that had been led to believe that the South Vietnamese and Americans were winning the war. Hanoi's goal had been to gain and maintain control of a major city, preferably Saigon, through conventional warfare across the country and, as Le Duan later wrote, inflict such a series of battlefield defeats as to persuade the United States to alter its strategy and leave the war.[351] The Americans and South Vietnamese, however, defeated them at every turn. The communists had pursued a military victory and had not achieved it.

When the Pentagon invented the "psychological victory" myth for the North Vietnamese and the Viet Cong—the assumption that the communists were trying to inflict only a psychological shock on the United States as opposed to a conventional military defeat—American doubts and confusion mangled what was a serious operational defeat for the Viet Cong into a strategically decisive psychological defeat for the Americans. The weeks before Tet, however, indicated a decisive lack of support for the Saigon government and a disturbing amount of acquiescence on the part of the South Vietnamese people: how did all those insurgents get into place and no citizen sound the alarm? If Saigon was winning, how was it the enemy was able to pull off a major countrywide offensive?[352] President Johnson stated during his January 17 State of the Union Address that "the enemy has been defeated in battle after battle," and then Tet erupted, wrecking his credibility.[353] Westmoreland at least recognized a connection between the war there and diplomatic posturing. He told his subordinates in the aftermath to "maintain maximum pressure on the enemy in the south" to prevent North Vietnamese diplomats from having the advantage of "some spectacular action or significant battlefield success."[354] His insight was too late. Regardless of what Hanoi's intentions may or may not have been, the Tet Offensive resulted in an irreversible consequence of doubt within the American public about the viability of the war.

An intelligence briefing in 1969 reiterated that assessing Arc Light effectiveness was still difficult.[355] The JCS commissioned a study of Arc Light effectiveness in September 1968, and its findings at the end of 1969 were inconclusive. B-52 strikes against troops had to have solid targeting intelligence and had to support the goals of the ground forces. A comment that "the ground force commander's subjective judgement" about the effectiveness of the strikes suggests again that reassurance was one of the main purposes of Arc Light. The report also admitted that secondary explosions were not the best means of evaluating what happened. Strategic Air Command continued to evaluate effectiveness by what it could measure, not on the mission's support for strategy or policy goals. Altogether, SAC still measured Arc Light effectiveness by how many bombs struck the geographical area on the ground as planned. There was almost no mention of the enemy or enemy reaction in this study.[356] The institution treated the missions as operations akin to engineering and timing projects. Lieutenant General Alvan C. Gillem, the commander of the 3rd Air Division who managed B-52s and KC-135s at Andersen Air Force Base, revealed during his end-of-tour interview that he did not have 100 percent confidence in Arc Light's effectiveness. B-52s were expensive in terms of airframes, support, and money, and it was difficult to assess the consequences of their operations because of the cover the jungle canopy provided; it made post-attack reconnaissance photographs problematic. Proper assessment required ground reconnaissance, but they occurred for only half of the missions. Reports from prisoners and FACs were very positive, but Gillem was not certain the effort and expense of B-52 missions were worth it. "Maybe post-war efforts will uncover it—and I'm sure there'll be efforts to do just that."[357]

Arc Light missions had their advantages. Another Air Force study in 1968 concluded they were preferable to artillery and tactical air strikes because they were more cost effective and put the ordnance on the target more quickly. To inflict the same kind of damage would have required 36,000 infantry, suffering on average 1,900 deaths of their own per year, or 180 155mm howitzers, or a mission by sixty fighter-bombers.[358] Another study in November 1968 lobbied aggressively that B-52 strikes were effective and should be continued. It ultimately based its case on individualistic and impressionistic evidence: "The most important expression of ARC LIGHT effectiveness is the subjective judgment of how well ARC LIGHT strikes fulfill the commander's objectives. All quantitative measurements are dwarfed by the importance the commander assigns to ARC LIGHT in its role of contributing to the success of the ground campaign." Furthermore, there was no way to specify within a narrow range how many B-52 sorties the Army needed. It needed a lot.[359]

Operations analysts were by 1968 sharing their suspicions. The fact that there were repeated studies to assess the effectiveness of the various kinds of bombing suggests aerial bombardment—strategic, interdiction, and close air support—was not strategically conclusive in its effects, not enough to permanently wreck the enemy's strategy and enable the Americans and South Vietnamese to establish lasting physical security for South Vietnam. Another 1968 analysis argued several debatable points on behalf of the efficacy of Arc Light missions. It asserted the methods for selecting targets were sound without explaining why, and it conceded that the evidence necessary to accurately tally the numbers of dead because of the missions was lacking but assured the reader that greater numbers of PAVN and VC had been killed without definitive supporting evidence. More convincing was its conclusion that the number of secondary explosions was evidence the bombings were destroying large numbers of vehicles and extensive amounts of ammunition. The study noted the shock and terror B-52 strikes inflicted on enemy troops, a piece of evidence that was repeatedly cited, but worn-down, shell-shocked troops were not necessarily defeated troops. As an example, the French Army spearheaded the decisive counteroffensive of 1918 on the Western Front a year after mutinying and after nearly four years of near-debilitating losses.[360]

In November 1968, the bombers modified the criteria for effectiveness, lowering standards greatly: only half the bombs dropped had to arm, and only 80 percent had to land where they were supposed to. The new criteria extended the target box "3,200 feet on each side." Consequently, an aircrew could release its bombs, see them hit 3,000 feet away from where they were supposed to land, "and still receive credit for an effective sortie."[361] The wing historian clearly found this change to be a graphic lowering of standards that allowed the missions to be portrayed as more accurate in terms of bombing effectiveness than was really the case, and he explicitly noted as much. Fortunately, such outcomes were rare. Out of 827 sorties, only two of them were not accurate, landing outside of the target box, but since they still hit within the larger target zone, higher headquarters considered them successful. The 4258th Strategic Wing did not.[362]

Analyses at CINCPAC in 1969 suggested B-52 missions were painful but not catastrophic for the enemy. Admiral McCain informed the joint chiefs that Arc Light missions harmed enemy logistics, destroyed a great deal of their war materiel, persuaded many North Vietnamese to desert, and imposed all kinds of difficulties on enemy preparations for their own offensives. He believed in the effectiveness of B-52s and opposed efforts to reduce their monthly sorties. President Nixon's assistant for national security affairs Henry Kissinger viewed B-52 missions as flexible forms of retaliation. He proposed their use if North Vietnamese forces waged an offensive against an important site in Laos later that year.[363] As the new decade began air leaders focused the use of B-52s against targets such as a mass of trucks parked for unloading and arranged for ground survey teams to gather BDA. As infantry examined strike areas more frequently, they found more and more evidence of their effectiveness.[364] At times enemy activity confirmed their presence and that B-52s had been given accurate targeting intelligence.[365]

Close Air Support and Direct Attack After the Tet Offensive

The Nixon administration valued B-52s and was concerned about the drawdown returning them to the United States. Admiral McCain agreed regarding their utility. Ambassador Ellsworth Bunker reminded Nixon of their psychological impact a couple of months prior to the 1972 Easter Offensive. Nixon suggested communicating the facts about the bombers to enemy forces in order to discourage them; let them know Arc Light missions had destroyed many regiments of the North Vietnamese Army.[366]

In broad terms, President Nixon used air power as a covering force for the withdrawal of American soldiers that began in 1969. Bombing sanctuaries in Cambodia preempted North Vietnamese operations, helicopter transport and close air support enabled the South Vietnamese to conduct a raid against the Ho Chi Minh Trail in 1971, and close air support in combination with the resolute fighting of the ARVN stymied the North Vietnamese invasion of South Vietnam in 1972. Air power was not a means to victory for Nixon because he was not pursuing victory, nor did he want the withdrawal to appear like cutting and running to Washington's allies. Perhaps American actions could strengthen South Vietnam and weaken North Vietnam in ways that would make it possible for Saigon to endure and resist for several years after American forces left the region.

General Abrams did not employ close air support in ways fundamentally different from General Westmoreland after he became the commander of MACV in June 1968. When intelligence indicated the communists were gearing up for an offensive, Abrams wrote, "I intend to accommodate the enemy in seeking battle and in fact to anticipate him wherever possible.... We cannot be forced into a position of merely reacting to the enemy. We must anticipate him, fix his major forces as far away from possible from our vital area, and defeat him decisively. His apparent offensive intent gives us a chance to strike him a crushing blow." He intended to divert firepower to units that found enemy forces, but finding them had always been the rub.[367] Abrams also reminded his generals that the war against Viet Cong political operatives and guerrillas, fundamental to defeating the insurgency, was a job still to be finished. Firepower nevertheless remained central. He sought to build on the attritional successes gained from the Tet Offensive by using aggressive combat actions to ruin the enemy's combat capability: "He must not be permitted to recover."[368] Abrams' approach of using large air strikes to soften up, preempt, disrupt, or prevent enemy forces from launching attacks on American and ARVN troops was not quite the same as the previous goal of utterly destroying PAVN and VC forces, and was more in line with Nixon's strategy of turning the war over to the South Vietnamese. Lessening American casualties had become a greater priority than achieving a victory over enemy forces. Ultimately, a successful withdrawal that was not precipitous was the primary measure of effectiveness.

Mission allocations reflected these policy and strategy changes. Once Vietnamization began, the weight of the total number of sorties set aside for CAS was reduced to 9 percent by the middle of 1970. Direct attack strikes against places where the enemy's presence was confirmed became a more common use of air power than close air support, per se, and 43 percent of sorties were used in that manner.[369] From July 1969 to March 1970, only 329 were scheduled, and aircraft that sat parked awaiting the call carried out just 722 more. Of improvised "immediate strike" sorties, 1,851 flew against targets where the enemy had been found and 778 hit "suspected enemy locations." Preplanned direct attacks against enemy forces received the bulk of the ground attack missions, with 3,470 going after confirmed enemy sites, and 3,996 against places where analysts believed they were operating.[370]

When North Vietnamese regulars used Cambodia as a sanctuary and a pathway to South Vietnam, they did not get themselves branded as aggressors, but instead created more complications for their enemies. Activities surrounding Cambodia illustrated a number of interrelationships between air power and national security. Air power could go forward instead of American or South Vietnamese infantry, but its expanded use would brand the United States as the state escalating the war, however justified that might have been by North Vietnamese actions. Bombing raids against PAVN forces inside Cambodia—forces the Cambodians wished were not there because they were violating their sovereignty—would run afoul of opponents to the war in Congress and enrage protesters within the United States. The Nixon administration walked a fine line between the two for more than a year, but its use of air power was not strategically decisive: it did not alter the scope of what was possible, nor did it persuade the communists to give up their policy goals.[371] It was, however, covering the American withdrawal.

The North Vietnamese had been using eastern Cambodia as a launch pad for their military activities in South Vietnam, as a route for the Ho Chi Minh Trail, and as a sanctuary for years. Air power in the form of B-52s flying covert missions provided President Nixon and General Abrams with a means of striking the sanctuaries without committing American or South Vietnamese ground forces. Abrams recommended the approval of just such an operation on February 9, 1969. The effectiveness of this kind of air strike depended on good targeting intelligence and as of February 18, 1969, Nixon's most senior advisors believed, "The intelligence on the target area [just west of the Cambodian-South Vietnamese border] appeared to be very accurate and the strike plans sound."[372] A deserter had just provided the location of the Central Office South Vietnam (COSVN), the elusive command post from which North Vietnam directed operations inside South Vietnam. Four days later, another offensive erupted across South Vietnam, violating a tacit agreement that in return for the bombing halt in 1968 the North Vietnamese and the Viet Cong would no longer carry out such operations.[373] The administration replied with B-52s.

Kissinger recognized the risks of secretly bombing PAVN forces in Cambodia. Ascribing the missions to pilots' navigational errors could harm the administration's credibility, lessen Americans' trust in the reliability and professionalism of Strategic Air Command, and subject both to the possibility Congress would investigate them with a mind to shackling further military operations. Bombing the sanctuaries in Cambodia in this manner reflected an imbalance between political goals, domestic politics, and military consequences. Was the bombing of a military command post and supply area in secret worth the backlash if it became public knowledge? Did not North Vietnam's treachery warrant a massive invasion of eastern Cambodia or a complaint to the UN? Melvin Laird worried that a preventive type of operation like this could undercut the entire war effort.[374]

Using B-52s in this way was strange because the United States and South Vietnam had legitimate reasons for carrying out reprisals for attacks on towns in South Vietnam. Instead of sending a strategic signal by bombing PAVN forces in the DMZ, for example, or hitting targets farther north, the administration opted for an operational target: COSVN, in the Cambodian sanctuaries. The secrecy was something Prince Sihanouk wanted; it kept the Cambodian leader from having to deal with the attention and communist hostility that would have come with full disclosure.[375] Bombing targets in yet another country certainly appeared to contradict Nixon's stated goal of deescalating the war, even if the target zone was awash in enemy troops.

Nixon directed the bombing of these sanctuaries on March 15, 1969, after a series of North Vietnamese attacks on urban areas in South Vietnam, and Abrams was confident that Arc Light strikes could destroy COSVN.[376] Nixon believed direct attack strikes against the sanctuaries in Cambodia was something the enemy would understand, and these bombings, code-named "Menu," first took place on March 17. This operation was carried out not only in response to communist military escalation but also to nudge the peace talks in Paris out of their somnolence. The extent of the secondary explosions from the first sorties told General Wheeler the bombs had hit a significant military target.[377] Ironically, the 1969 missions over Cambodia were gradualism continued. After all, Nixon was trying to communicate to the North Vietnamese that unless they "made significant concessions, tougher measures would follow."[378]

The methods the administration used to keep the Menu operations secret were pursued to achieve diplomatic and domestic political security. One order was sent through ordinary communication routes with an aim point just inside the South Vietnamese border. The real order went through channels with much more limited access and distribution. The only aircrew who knew where they were really flying and bombing were the pilot and the navigator. The ground-based MSQ-77 radar controller also knew and gave the order to each aircraft to release their bombs at the proper time. All were ordered to keep these measures top secret. Aircrews counted secondary explosions to determine the tactical effectiveness of their sorties and reported that BDA through special channels. The post-attack paperwork stated the bombs were dropped on targets in South Vietnam, not Cambodia.[379] Operation Menu was managed in such a way that the executive branch selected the kind of oversight Congress provided. Secretary of Defense Melvin Laird "briefed key members of the Armed Services Committee and Appropriations Committees of both houses. No one raised the issue that the full Congress should be consulted"; only select congressmen were consulted on secret operations, and this was standard practice. Senators John Stennis, Richard Russell, and Everett Dirksen and Representatives Mendel Rivers, Gerald Ford, and Leslie Arends were also informed.[380] Since these few congressmen did not raise probing questions, administration officials may have told themselves they had received a green light to add cooking the books to their operational methods.

The JCS and MACV later claimed these operations had been tactically successful and Ambassador Bunker and General Abrams informed Secretary Laird, "these raids have been 'one of the most telling operations in the entire war.'"[381] The ultimate consequence of the 1969 bombings of the Cambodian sanctuaries was, however, the encouragement of secrecy and aggressive leak plugging by Nixon's inner circle, which eventually led to the Watergate break-in.[382] Leaks such as Daniel Ellsberg's publishing of the "Pentagon Papers" so upset the president that he turned to J. Edgar Hoover, director of the Federal Bureau of Investigation, to solve the problem of leaks. Nixon gave Hoover permission to wiretap the telephones of unfriendly newspaper reporters and distrusted officials within the administration, including some members of the NSC staff Kissinger did not trust. Hoover even bugged the telephone of Melvin Laird's own assistant, Robert Pursley.³⁸³ Quite a train of events and consequences resulting from bombing legitimate targets in a sneaky manner.

The missions did not make it into the public discussion of the war as they took place; the handful of newspaper accounts that came out about Operation Menu never gained any traction, so in a sense these 1969 missions over Cambodia were effectively kept secret until congressional hearings brought them to light in 1973.³⁸⁴ A *New York Times* article only mentioned that Abrams had asked "permission" to order B-52 raids, and "high State Department officials" opposed such an operation.³⁸⁵ Thus far no one was blowing the whistle: not the Cambodians, not the North Vietnamese, nor the Soviets nor Chinese. The North Vietnamese were not going to flag the bombings because then the world would ask why they had 40,000 unwelcome troops in eastern Cambodia. Articles reported B-52 strikes against enemy forces on the Vietnamese side of the Cambodian border a month later in April, and *The New York Times* published a story on the missions on May 9, 1969, that mentioned the bombing on the Cambodian side of the border, but nothing came from that. The following week Prince Sihanouk spoke to the press and asserted that no Cambodians had been killed.³⁸⁶ Antiwar activists did not blow up over this, and it seems the leaks were actually less consequential than Nixon and Kissinger feared.

The American–South Vietnamese incursion into Cambodia that began in May 1970 developed in a context of a weakened and then chaotic Cambodian governance. Prime Minister Lon Nol raised the ante in the early spring by demanding that every Viet Cong and PAVN soldier leave Cambodia by March 15. That rankled Prince Sihanouk because he reserved foreign policy decisions for himself. On March 18, 1970, the Cambodian National Assembly voted to oust Sihanouk who then accused Lon Nol of treason. The next month Sihanouk sided with communist forces and in May announced a new government. The North Vietnamese exploited this chaos to expand their control of eastern Cambodia.³⁸⁷ Lon Nol asked the United States for assistance on April 14 after the North Vietnamese started fighting the Cambodian army. Because the North Vietnamese in the Cambodian sanctuaries were preparing to carry out operations against South Vietnam, the US decided to preempt with military operations of their own.³⁸⁸ Acting chairman of the JCS William Westmoreland believed a South Vietnamese–American operation into Cambodia would require only a small number of American soldiers, and North Vietnamese aggression provided an opportunity to push them out of their sanctuaries. Nixon then directed limited support for the Cambodians on April 22.³⁸⁹ If Cambodia fell to the North Vietnamese, PAVN forces would threaten the entirety of South Vietnam's border, a situation Nixon found unacceptable.³⁹⁰

The main purpose of this air-ground raid was to drive the enemy away from the South Vietnamese border and to destroy what enemy forces they could. The raid accomplished those objectives, for within a day PAVN were fleeing north. Furthermore, the main role for air strikes was close air support, not destroying pre-identified targets. Army commanders credited close air support and the air leadership of forward air controllers for minimal casualties among friendly forces. The operation was not a long-term expansion of the war because American and South Vientamese ground forces penetrated only thirty kilometers into Cambodia, and then returned to South Vietnam after a few weeks. South Vietnamese regulars moved against North Vietnamese base areas inside Cambodia on April 29.³⁹¹ Portions of the 1st US Cavalry Division crossed the border on May 1 and to their north troops from the 4th US Infantry Division helicoptered into a PAVN base area.³⁹²

Destroying enemy forces in Cambodia was going to be challenging because most intelligence data had not been updated in weeks. Nevertheless, the opening action of May 1 resulted in approximately 390 killed.[393] Nixon's goal of limiting American casualties encouraged MACV to repeat a mistake. The command believed the communists would resist with vigor, so MACV directed bombing places US and ARVN forces were going to enter with nearly 2,000 Vietnamese and American sorties during the second week of May alone, along with 633 B-52 sorties. The only way to defeat an enemy as determined as the PAVN, however, was to inflict casualties devastating enough that Hanoi could not recover. This use of air power backfired because the Allies had already established a pattern the enemy recognized: concentrated bombardments near American and South Vietnamese ground forces signaled a ground assault was coming and that it was time to withdraw. Related to this was the fact that a Seventh Air Force report got its measure of effectiveness for the Cambodian raid half-right; it reflected a mindset that measured success by how few of one's own troops were lost in an operation rather than the extent to which the operation had undermined the enemy's political goals and supported one's own:

> The retreat of the enemy allowed the friendly ground forces to sweep through the base areas with only 1,147 killed in action, compared to 11,562 enemy losses. These odds would likely have been much less favorable had tactical air not coerced the enemy out of his fortified defenses. Their experience with allied tactical air was undoubtedly a major factor in his decision to withdraw. Thus, the threat, as well as the employment, of air power contributed to the ground forces' ability to advance rapidly enough to uncover numerous caches and exploit them relatively unmolested.[394]

Air Force analysts concluded the operation inflicted damage on the enemy's logistical system with repercussions lasting for months.[395] American goals were to push away the North Vietnamese, not destroy them, to buy time for the American withdrawal. So in one sense the strategy was backward—more PAVN troops would survive for a later invasion of South Vietnam—but given the Americans' goals of protecting their own forces, and the fact that destroying the enemy was no longer the goal, it made some sense.

Ideally, the operation would have supported policy goals by devastating the PAVN, not casualty avoidance, but again the objective in May 1970 was not "winning"; the raid and bombardment drove the enemy away from South Vietnam as planned. Keeping American casualties low coincided with the withdrawal agenda. Many of those routed troops were probably fighting again during the 1972 invasion because only 926 had been confirmed dead along with an additional 1,358 more that air strikes probably killed. Nonetheless, the same report claimed more than 11,000 "enemy losses."[396] Forward air controllers managed 169 strikes from fighter-bombers that killed hundreds of the enemy with only a few wounded friendlies hurt by short rounds. Close air support from American and South Vietnamese aircraft also sustained Cambodian forces under siege in Kompong Thom.[397]

B-52 contributions commenced at four in the morning on May 1 with three dozen hitting inside the Fishhook, a portion of Cambodia that protrudes into South Vietnam. Abrams used them to pulverize enemy forces so they would not be able to counterattack.[398] Accordingly, American and ARVN forces encountered little enemy gunfire after thirty-five B-52s pounded the area during their mission of April 30–May 1. Right away a pair of stunned VC claimed the bombing killed at least thirty-five guerrillas. In the aftermath helicopter crews reported no ground fire, and soldiers credited the B-52s for that.[399] On May 21, Nixon approved B-52 strikes beyond thirty kilometers inside the border, targeting PAVN forces in northeast Cambodia, a sector where few Cambodians lived.[400]

The North Vietnamese made destroying COSVN difficult. Its troops kept moving, so radio direction finding of its position often found a location abandoned by the time bombers arrived. Adding to the confusion surrounding its identity, COSVN was not a single command post, but a set of encampments spread out over forty square miles of jungle. A total of forty-six B-52 sorties, for example, went after suspected locations on May 11 and 17. A communist mailman who came over to the South Vietnamese said casualties were considerable, but MACV concluded on May 18 that any chance of American and ARVN troops bagging large numbers of prisoners had passed.[401]

Another reason air strikes failed to destroy COSVN was the seven-hour warning the Soviets provided to the North Vietnamese. A Soviet trawler floating in international waters off Guam radioed when B-52s took off. There was nothing they could do about the trawler, so American operatives inserted false targets for the B-52s into the system managing air strikes and then radioed the actual target to the aircrews ninety minutes before their drop time. A prisoner explained that when the personnel at COSVN received the warning, two-thirds relocated while the rest stayed behind and died. The prisoner explained they placed their antennae about a mile or so from each command post, so radio direction finding could not locate manned command tents with precision.[402]

The bombings destroyed a lot of their supplies, but given time, the North Vietnamese could replace them. Air operations in Cambodia in June 1970 had to take place within twenty-one miles of the border and were inconsequential since nearly all the PAVN had departed. Nevertheless, North Vietnam still controlled the northeastern portion of Cambodia, including Angkor Wat. A detailed study of the operation lists what air power did, but not what it accomplished. Of note, air operations destroyed ninety-four vehicles, 135 boats, 1,431 structures, and but 206 enemy soldiers.[403] Nixon directed that air strikes against communist forces in Cambodia continue after American ground forces withdrew to keep pressure on the enemy, but of course air strikes alone did not constitute maximum pressure.[404] Fighter-bomber attacks continued through July 27.[405]

The best outcome for Washington relative to Hanoi was that the latter were unsure as to what the Americans might do: a meager success. These raids into Cambodia did not seem to directly affect American negotiations with the North Vietnamese, who blamed the United States for the coup in Phnom Penh. They denied the bombings were the reason for a temporary suspension of meetings between Brigadier General Vernon Walters and Le Duc Tho, and at the same time these military actions did not persuade the North Vietnamese to negotiate in good faith. They had no interest in a compromise negotiated settlement, only complete victory.[406]

Nixon's use of air power diverged from his desire to keep the war from further dividing the American people. He wished to use tactical aircraft and B-52s secretly—a difficult task, given the number of people involved and affected. Nixon informed no one else but Senator John Stennis, chairman of the Senate Armed Services Committee, and Senator Richard Russell. He assured the senators, "It's the best-kept secret of the war."[407] That was very risky considering the mood of the country. Nixon later wrote that he knew at the time the potential the operation had to create a "political catastrophe for me and my administration."[408] Abrams, on the other hand, was convinced that in a military sense the operation was an ideal choice.[409]

Whatever tactical and operational successes this operation produced were irrelevant because the bombings in Cambodia triggered a sustained political eruption in the United States. In addition to the four students shot at Kent State University, students protested or rioted at more than 450 campuses across the country and burned ROTC buildings, including two at the University of Wisconsin.[410] Individuals resigned from their National Security Council consultant jobs and from Kissinger's staff, while congressmen put forth resolutions to bring the war to an end. The lasting memory of the operation was not North Vietnam's violation of Cambodian sovereignty, but of the Ohio National Guard killing college students protesting at Kent State University.⁴¹¹ President Nixon subsequently had less political capital to spend, something Hanoi exploited.

Close Air Support and Lam Son 719

The White House intently monitored close air support during Lam Son 719, an operation against the Ho Chi Minh Trail, as soon as it began on January 30, 1971. South Vietnamese troops crossed the border with Laos on February 8, and the PAVN drove them out of the panhandle the following month.⁴¹² President Nixon tried to once again to frame American involvement as protection for American forces remaining in South Vietnam. The US provided air support but avoided calling it "close air support" because that term implied an integrated involvement with this ground operation that indicated the war was being expanded yet again. Nixon had promised to not provide that kind of assistance outside of South Vietnam, and Secretary of Defense Melvin Laird insisted that the US was not providing it because "close air support involved controllers on the ground and when this criteria was not met we did not have close air support." Semantics.⁴¹³ South Vietnamese regulars counted on heavy, well-placed aerial bombardment for success, and the Americans flew more than 9,000 sorties and dropped 20,000 tons of bombs over the course of the operation. Air strikes, however, did not support a South Vietnamese victory; they instead ameliorated a debacle.⁴¹⁴

Lam Son 719 was a disaster waiting to happen, not because the South Vietnamese were fighting without ground advisors nor because air support coordination was less than optimal. The North Vietnamese had been warned of the raid and were waiting for the attack with approximately 120 tanks and 35,000 soldiers. The ratio of offensive to defensive troops for this operation did not follow the rule of thumb of 3:1—far from it. The ARVN used 17,000 troops to carry out the raid, so they were outnumbered 2:1; expecting them to succeed was folly by any measure. The North Vietnamese Army had methodically surveyed the area and positioned their troops advantageously, and the possibility of achieving moral dominance and a strategic victory over President Thieu and his army instilled a willingness to suffer great losses. Saigon's planning and intelligence for Lam Son 719 was inadequate. More enemy soldiers were awaiting them than expected, and their antiaircraft fire was more lethal and denser than the Army anticipated.⁴¹⁵ Secretary of State Rogers warned beforehand, "The enemy had intelligence on our plans and we're now asking the South Vietnamese to conduct an operation that we refused to do in the past because we were not strong enough."⁴¹⁶

Lam Son 719 was an American initiative the South Vietnamese carried out. A successful operation would not only cut off the Ho Chi Minh Trail, Hanoi would also make concessions at the peace talks. Nixon and his advisors, however, realized the operation would be difficult and bloody, but went forward anyway. Not all ARVN forces participated; their armored forces held back. President Thieu killed their only chance for success—executing the operation with energy before the PAVN could react—by ordering a halt to its advance on February 12 when ARVN casualties passed the 3,000 mark. He then initiated a retreat on March 9 that was completed two weeks later.⁴¹⁷

Seventh Air Force's evaluation of air power effectiveness concentrated on tactical and operational lessons and did not address the larger campaign outcomes. In terms of attrition and body count, the operation exploited air power because it encouraged the enemy to mass, producing targets vulnerable to air strikes. It believed 13,642 enemy had been killed, 4,364 of those by air strikes.⁴¹⁸ South Vietnamese estimates were more conservative, counting 2,776 enemy KBA. Fighter-bombers destroyed seventy-four tanks, while armed helicopters were unable to knock out any. Laser-guided bombs left their mark: 173 Paveways destroyed seventy antiaircraft artillery sites.[419] The Air Force found that Mark 82 500-pound laser-guided bombs were very reliable and accurate against individual vehicles. On average, one required only 1.5 LGBs to destroy a truck, and when they missed, it normally was due to something other than a weapons malfunction.[420]

Inflicting a 37 percent casualty rate normally produces success, but not this time, because the South Vietnamese withdrew and then fled, battered and shaken. Indeed, the most important air strikes of the campaign occurred not during the advance but during the routing of ARVN forces out of Laos. For instance, when North Vietnamese T-54 tanks were chugging down Route 9 in an effort to cut off and trap South Vietnamese, F-100s wrecked the three tanks leading the charge, turning them into forty-ton roadblocks. One Navy squadron judged Lam Son 719 a success, pointing to the overall destruction and the likelihood the operation had put a considerable brake on the movement of enemy supplies. Lieutenant General James W. Sutherland, commander of XXIV Corps, credited American air power with preventing the destruction of South Vietnamese forces once they began their retreat into South Vietnam.[421] Three weeks into the operation, Henry Kissinger concluded Lam Son 719 was worthwhile: stopping infiltration on three roads, killing several thousand PAVN, and proving that the ARVN would fight. "Our air effort will be a deciding factor," he added.[422]

The US and South Vietnam continued to rely on B-52s during the operation. Kissinger kept Nixon informed, reporting B-52s had flown more than 500 missions and had inflicted massive damage. Even though ground teams examined only about one in ten bomb zones, "In virtually every case, the assessment showed the raids had been massively effective in destroying staging areas and achieving casualties."[423] The enemy had to concentrate to fight, and their mass infantry tactics made them terribly vulnerable to air strikes; B-52s killed 400 in just one bomb zone.[424]

Judging Lam Son 719 a success is an unreasonable conclusion because the North Vietnamese drove their adversary back into South Vietnam. Alexander Haig advised that US air strikes would be key for a successful withdrawal from Tchepone, which also meant the operation was a failure. Henry Kissinger believed the operation had accomplished its goals of harming communist supply movements and buying time for the South Vietnamese to improve their security situation, but Lam Son 719 was a disaster for the ARVN. The units involved were spent and ready to retreat just as Kissinger was making his positive claims. Admiral Moorer blamed the shortage of English-speaking officers among the ARVN for the less-than-optimal use of close air support. South Vietnamese dependence on American air support, however, pointed to the slow progress of Vietnamization, and Lam Son 719 suggested the South Vietnamese could not prevail in battle even with American assistance.[425]

Getting chopped up and driven from the battlefield dispirits an army. The imagery, even more than the fact, of panicked South Vietnamese troops unable to hold ground but instead fleeing bolstered the confidence of the North Vietnamese and confirmed in the minds of many Americans that the Saigon regime was beyond hope because it could never fend for itself. The operation also illustrated that a defending enemy with twice as many forces, good intelligence, the high ground, and the willingness to overcome severe losses is a serious challenge for aerial firepower to overcome. The best that could be said about it is the raid might have delayed a major PAVN offensive against I Corps by eight months. The worst consequences of the operation lay beyond the battlefield. The American people lost respect for South Vietnam's commitment to the war when they saw frightened ARVN troops clinging to helicopters flying back across the border.[426]

All of America's allies relied on air support. Right before the Easter Offensive, ARVN forces stabbed at the enemy with another raid into Cambodia; 310 sorties supported 2,100 soldiers, and sixty died for the attrition of 128.⁴²⁷ When Forces Armées Nationales Khmères (FANK) struck communist troops west of Phnom Pehn in November–December 1971, they relied on aerial firepower and suffered forty-three missing and 135 wounded while estimating that 1,238 enemy had been killed. Air strikes received credit for most of the enemy killed. FANK infantry did not attempt any major ground operations.⁴²⁸

During 1971, American air activity in Northern Laos was restricted to a handful of F-4s employing sophisticated ordnance beyond the capabilities of the Royal Lao Air Force (RLAF). They dropped cluster bombs on North Vietnamese supply routes, spread mines, and turned storage caves into stone caskets with laser-guided bombs. When supporting the campaign of Major General Vang Pao and his Hmong army in the Plain of Jars in June and July 1971, air forces were very effective because they functioned with ground forces. While American aircraft carried out interdiction strikes, half of the sorties—on average fifty-five a day—supported infantry, as did the RLAF with not quite as many sorties using their T-28s. It was a relatively small operation, facing about 20,000 enemy forces, but the troops functioned as beaters, flushing their enemy out for aircraft to bomb.⁴²⁹

The Hmong finished the 1971 campaign in a position stronger than they had begun, but with a dim future; the North Vietnamese brought in reinforcements. Would greater success in northern Laos have thrown a wrench into Hanoi's plans for March 30, 1972? North Vietnam may have been too strong, but the fact remains that Hanoi positioned up to three divisions along the eastern borders of the Plain of Jars, suggesting that those Laotian forces were not made of paper in the eyes of the North Vietnamese. In addition, what if those divisions had been available for operations in South Vietnam? By treating the region as a single theater, the air war helped pin down a PAVN army corps far from the war's decisive sector. As successful as this air effort was, it ultimately supported the policy of Laos, not the United States, which was withdrawing from Southeast Asia. The Americans recognized this disparity; Ambassador G. McMurtrie Godley wrote that Vang Pao was pursuing his own political agenda. The onset of the Easter Offensive in 1972 led to a drastically reduced number of sorties available to fight the North Vietnamese in all parts of Laos, from 9,295 in March to a low of 222 in July.⁴³⁰

As the troop withdrawals drove down the combat potential of American ground forces, Nixon and Kissinger reminded themselves that they would still possess a substantial instrument for defending South Vietnam: air power. Military Assistance Command, Vietnam had argued from the beginning of the withdrawal that reducing firepower in the form of artillery and close air support sorties would see more Americans killed in battle and produce serious political consequences, but that was a moot point, as withdrawal was Nixon's policy. The president sought to gain as much out of the air forces remaining as he could and maintaining high sortie rates was a priority for the Nixon administration at least until after November 1972.⁴³¹ While the North Vietnamese stockpiled supplies in Laos for their 1972 offensive, however, American sortie rates continued to decline. From an annual high of more than 370,000 in 1968, sorties decreased to roughly 106,000 through October 1971.⁴³² But given the demands, there were not enough available aircraft for operations in Laos and Cambodia, particularly after the Easter Offensive began. Air strikes were difference makers, but the ground forces under the command of the government in Vientiane were simply too few to withstand the growing numbers of North Vietnamese forces. Despite these weaknesses, Vang Pao's forces plus American air power helped keep North Vietnamese troops in place in northern Laos and prevent a collapse for the duration of 1972.⁴³³

Close Air Support and Direct Attack during the Easter Offensive

The United States and South Vietnam recognized the buildup for North Vietnam's next offensive during the late winter of 1972 and expected the North Vietnamese Army to carry out a conventional invasion using tanks but did not anticipate the size and scope of what was coming. The US was well aware of the armored buildup north of the DMZ, and the chairman of the Joint Chiefs of Staff recommended twice to Secretary Laird that the US attack it preemptively, but an effective military policy required the South Vietnamese and the Americans to attain victim status in order to possess more legitimacy for their military actions. Thus, Secretary Laird did not want to strike until the PAVN crossed the DMZ, otherwise the US would appear overly aggressive. As a stopgap the US commenced Operation Bullet Shot in February, the beginnings of a buildup of air forces throughout Southeast Asia that brought in ten KC-135s and twenty-nine B-52Ds.[434] After the invasion smashed into South Vietnam on March 30, Allied air forces devoted most of their efforts to stemming the tide of the PAVN onslaught, sending only 266 sorties into Cambodia in April.[435] In any event, the North Vietnamese attacked on three fronts: across the DMZ, from Cambodian sanctuaries toward An Loc, and a besieging of Kontum from sanctuaries inside Laos.

Named the Nguyen Hue Campaign by the North Vietnamese, the PAVN attacked from a position of strength. In addition to the 165,000 troops already in South Vietnam, another 36,000 moved in from Laos and Cambodia.[436] The invading North Vietnamese Army belied the image of the indigenous guerrilla warring against a technologically superior force. This was a conventional mechanized army bent on conquest and included antitank guided missiles and approximately 400 tanks.[437] The invasion's intent was to achieve military victories sufficient to ensure the United States had "to negotiate an end to the war from a position of defeat."[438] It erupted after the North Vietnamese had negotiated intransigently with Henry Kissinger for three years. Worried about the American effort to place a wedge between themselves and their patrons in Moscow and Peking, the leadership of the Lao Dong Party decided to act on behalf of their own interests. Once again battlefield events would be used to dictate what was possible diplomatically, and Le Duc Tho bargained even more fiercely as PAVN victories mounted, even denying the invasion was taking place.[439]

The initial American response to the Easter Offensive was tentative due to the unfavorable weather in Military Region 1 that limited air action. Weather remained bad enough during the first two weeks to greatly curtail flying close air support missions. Fortunately, MSQ-77 and LORAN, bombing navigation aids, made it possible to carry out some missions during bad weather.[440] This low sortie rate drew great criticism from the president, who asked why American fighter-bombers required a mile of clear airspace below clouds in order to bomb, but airliners could land when clouds were just 300 feet above the ground. Both Nixon and Kissinger should have realized that the military jets need the airspace for dive bombing, while the jet airliners were coming in to land at an airport.[441] In any event, Operation Freedom Train, the initial air response to the invasion, commenced on April 2, 1972. At first the JCS limited air operations no farther than twenty-five miles north of the DMZ, but this restriction moved northward throughout the rest of the month.[442]

Despite the shock of the invasion, the Americans and South Vietnamese shared the belief that air power was key to defending South Vietnam. President Thieu was certain the combination of American air power and ARVN ground forces could prevail.[443] Abrams and CJCS Moorer looked to B-52s as ready means of bringing intense firepower against the invaders. B-52s responded quickly, flying 1,806 sorties in April. Their targeting, however, was not as efficient as it could be; the ARVN would often base their targeting nominations on what their senior headquarters might approve, instead of what they recognized as a specific need for firepower.[444]

Nixon and Kissinger liked the symbolism of sending the bombers over the North Vietnamese panhandle: "this is music to my ears," said the president.[445] The US sought to stage more B-52s out of Thailand, but ramp space limited the number the Americans could base there.[446] Carrier air power escalated to its highest level of the war by the end of April, with six aircraft carriers conducting operations, one of which was off the coast of South Vietnam providing support to friendly troops. Marine squadrons began arriving in May 1972.[447] All would escalate into a decisive use of air power, particularly close air support and air interdiction.

For Nixon it was critical to win on the battlefield to support his diplomatic maneuvering with China and the Soviet Union.[448] He therefore informed the Washington Special Action Group on April 4, "there will be no consideration of restraints. We will do things that haven't been considered in several years.... Everything we do must be concentrated on breaking the enemy."[449] The next day he growled to aides, "the bastards have never been bombed like they're going to be bombed this time."[450] April's bombing missions flew against targets the nature of which made them more vulnerable to air power: a conventional army and its logistical tail—a key factor producing a war of a character different than the one of the previous seven years.

Air strikes continued to be most effective when carried out in conjunction with ground combat. South Vietnamese regulars, Marines, and Regional Forces coordinated with and followed up air strikes quickly and more intentionally than ever and conducted more post-attack surveys of B-52s strikes. They not only provided accurate BDA, but they also fought infantry they encountered during the course of those missions. For instance, soldiers examined the place near Kampong Trach that B-52s hit on April 4, found several destroyed bunkers, confirmed that the bombs had killed five, then fought survivors. A week later, ARVN confirmed a B-52 strike destroyed twenty-seven tanks. During a battle between Lai Khe and Loc Vinh on Highway 13, B-52s again decided the issue.[451] B-52s and regulars coordinated well on May 16, 1972, when a cavalry troop and a pair of battalions from the 7th Division stood ready to move into the B-52 target area between Dinh Tuong, Kien Tuon, and Kien Phong provinces the moment the last bomb detonated. Sometimes only the dead remained in the aftermath of an Arc Light mission, as the soldiers of two ARVN battalions found in Phong Dinh Province on June 11.[452] BUFs bombed the enemy in Dinh Tuong incessantly in August, and South Vietnamese forces moved into the strike area after most of these bombardments.[453]

On May 6, air cavalry surveyed the area B-52s pounded in Chuong Thien, received fire from enemy forces, called in tactical air strikes, and then helicopters flew a pair of Regional Forces battalions to attack the enemy on the ground while they were still gathering themselves after the bombardment. The use of B-52s at Chuong Thien elevated ARVN morale, and Major General Thomas M. Tarpley, commander of the Delta Regional Assistance Command, reported that the South Vietnamese soldiers were what made the Arc Light missions more effective.[454] South Vietnamese forces found that B-52 damage from the May 18, 1972, mission astride the border of Chuong Thien and Kien Giang was substantial, with bunkers either destroyed or pried open, but the two battalions that scoured the ground found only thirteen dead. B-52s and infantry coordinated once again that day when portions of the 9th Infantry Division along with Regional Forces combed the ground the bombs had struck right after the bombers departed.[455] One string of bombs persuaded enemy soldiers to flee toward the ARVN lines at An Loc, whereupon the South Vietnamese shot them.[456] When the South Vietnamese counteroffensive out of Kontum commenced on May 21, B-52s hit first, then infantry moved forward by design. After B-52s bombed what was thought to be the command post belonging to the 1st PAVN Division, a battalion from th 52nd PAVN Regiment, and a supply location on May 22, an ARVN cavalry troop and a ranger battalion surveyed the strike zone. John Paul Vann added that South Vietnamese still did not report KBA unless they saw the bodies with their own eyes, so he believed B-52 strikes had inflicted far more damage on the enemy than what was actually being reported.[457] Planners continued to position infantry battalions where they could follow up B-52s strikes immediately with their own attacks.[458]

Air strikes were key to draining the PAVN offensive of momentum during April and May 1972. Nixon's generals, in accordance with his priorities, used air strikes against targets over all of Vietnam.[459] General John W. Vogt, the Seventh Air Force commander at the time, informed Admiral Moorer, "Tac Air was the only thing that prevented the North Vietnamese from surging forward" after April.[460] Abrams agreed, crediting fighter-bombers and B-52s for the survival of Thieu's government. Tactical air strikes saved numerous posts from destruction, blew up enemy munitions, and in general protected friendly forces. When North Vietnamese tanks attacked at Dong Ha, South Vietnamese A-1 Skyraiders destroyed eleven on April 2. They destroyed five more at Firebase Pedro a week later, which helped to stall the North Vietnamese offensive at that location.[461]

Vogt compiled eight pages of ground commanders' effusive praise about the decisive difference air strikes made in fending off PAVN attacks. For example, as Major General James F. Hollingsworth observed:

> I estimate that the better part of the regiment operating southwest and west of Loc Ninh has been blown away by tac air strikes [April 7, 1972]. . . . The PW deserted his unit when ground troops fled from a Tac air strike. . . . The presence of US tac air in the delta has significantly bolstered the combat power as well as the morale of Vietnamese units [April 17, 1972]. . . . Other offensive contacts . . . were scattered and of relatively small size. This may indicate that the introduction of substantial US tac air into the delta, augmenting VNAF assets, has begun to limit the enemy's willingness to mass his forces during daylight hours [April 21, 1972]. . . . General Abe [Abrams] has repeated to many people in my presence that if it had not been for our air effort, South Vietnam would have crumbled and collapsed by this time.[462]

Abrams also praised the South Vietnamese Air Force for its close air support and argued that American air power may have played the deciding role during the campaign's first three weeks.[463]

All signs pointed toward An Loc, a provincial capital north of Saigon, as a key target of the North Vietnamese. A captured ARVN officer who escaped back to his own men confirmed the enemy intended to capture An Loc regardless of the losses and casualties. President Thieu decided that provincial capitals were going to be defended no matter the cost. Air support combined with army stamina to fend off repeated assaults, and later enabled a relief force to reach the town. Aerial firepower became doubly critical when shelling destroyed the defenders' artillery, leaving the soldiers nothing but mortar tubes as their remaining organic firepower. Carrier-based aircraft—Navy A-4Fs, for instance—ranged far inland from their ships to lend aid to An Loc, fend off enemy assaults, and encourage the defenders.[464] Major General Hollingsworth noted the Navy's contributions, and Navy strike aircraft flew sorties well into June in the attempt to lift the siege.[465]

The fanaticism of the PAVN—they either chained themselves to heavy weapons, such as tanks, or were chained to them—signaled this would be no ordinary campaign. The 15th Infantry Regiment similarly discovered communist troops with their legs bound so that they had to stay in their bunkers and fight.[466] When they imperiled An Loc, Nixon counted on American and South Vietnamese aircraft to tip the scales in the ARVN's favor. Holding onto An Loc was too critical to President Thieu for him to consider withdrawing, and therefore it was critical to Nixon's goals for Vietnam. An additional aim was killing enemy troops, and Nixon recognized after Haig explained to him air strikes could accomplish that as a result of the PAVN's decision to persist. B-52s pulverized a PAVN force lying in wait for the relief force coming from the south. Then the enemy concentrated to overrun the town on May 11, but just as their assault began, the first of sixty-six B-52s began their slaughter, making bombing runs hourly for the next day.[467] These Arc Light strikes inflicted an estimated 5,630 KBA. If PAVN forces were going to concentrate for an assault, BUFs would destroy them.[468] North Vietnamese analysts agreed air power played a key role in An Loc's defense. The South Vietnamese captured a report on April 18 stating that B-52s and poor combined arms teamwork on the part of PAVN forces were the two main reasons they failed to take An Loc on their first attempt. The town and its ARVN defenders stood, and they broke the siege by the end of May. Brigadier General John McGiffert credited air power, particularly from B-52s, with the successful outcome.[469]

Air operations included not only Air Force fighter-bomber aircrews, but also South Vietnamese, US Navy, and B-52s.[470] The South Vietnamese flew a third of all the fixed-wing sorties inside South Vietnam in May, totaling 5,586.[471] Their pilots received help from South Vietnamese soldiers, as when ARVN forces in Quang Tinh Province found and targeted North Vietnamese forces on May 4 and directed air strikes that killed more than 104, setting back the PAVN efforts to move supplies forward.[472] Army Cobra helicopters and Air Force Phantoms tailored the placement of their firepower to nudge the enemy into the target zone B-52s were about to bombard.[473]

B-52 firepower was central to Abrams's strategy for defeating the PAVN. Within the first month he commented that the combination of fighter-bomber strikes, B-52 missions, and ARVN fighting on the ground made it possible to resist the onslaught effectively and were the reason South Vietnam was still in existence.[474] Vice President Spiro Agnew had reported upon his return from Vietnam that B-52s were the main reason the ARVN's morale had not cracked and the Saigon government held together. Upon hearing that, the president told Strategic Air Command to transfer a hundred more of the bombers into Southeast Asia. Shortly thereafter up in Military Region 1, B-52 bombing patterns cleared pathways for troops defending Hue. According to prisoners' accounts, B-52 strikes kept breaking up their troop formations and inflicting serious losses.[475] When Abrams received intelligence of forces marshaling to finish off Hue, Kontum, and An Loc, he decided to use B-52s, fighter-bombers, and artillery to preempt their attacks. He concentrated his B-52s as a single hammer, allocating all of them to Military Regions 3, 2, and 1 on May 11, 12, and 13 respectively, for use against enemy troops and artillery near the three cities.[476]

The PAVN had decided to conduct a mass attack on the very day An Loc was scheduled to receive all the B-52 sorties. At least 1,000 PAVN lay dead in the aftermath. Aircrews placed the bombs within about 600 yards of friendly forces, decimating the enemy and wounding only a few South Vietnamese.[477] Following the thirty B-52 strikes during May 11, witnesses saw survivors running from the bombed area, whereupon aircraft and infantry took them under fire. Major General Hollingsworth's evaluation supported a more integrated form of warfare: by loosening requirements on the spacing of fighter-bomber and B-52 missions in the same airspace, planners increased continuous air support. Another six Arc Light missions on the night of May 12 seemed to have defeated the enemy's most recent push, although they had not given up. ARVN relief forces were moving north toward An Loc, but it took heavy air support to persuade them to continue toward the besieged town.[478]

As of May 19, Hollingsworth started to believe the enemy was withdrawing from An Loc because enemy activity declined, and the area became relatively quiet. Hollingsworth attributed the enemy's behavior to the death and destruction from aircraft.[479] According to two officers of the PAVN 7th Division, the bombing "was causing major breakdowns in [PAVN] morale and fighting spirit." Some soldiers were ignoring orders, all were malnourished, everyone feared the B-52s. On June 18, ARVN Lieutenant General Nguyen Van Minh announced the siege had been broken.[480] The North Vietnamese could not make good their losses under this onslaught, and the wrecking of three of the best PAVN divisions proved to be a strategic victory because the enemy no longer threatened Saigon.[481]

When the North Vietnamese lay siege to Hue, Nixon insisted B-52s be used against them. He valued the city because of its significance to the South Vietnamese: "You can lose Kontum, and you can lose a hell of a lot of other things, but you can't lose Hue."[482] President Thieu placed a greater value on An Loc, but Hue received air support as well. Laser-guided bombs destroyed bridges, and when thirty PT-76 amphibious infantry tanks forded streams anyway, fighter-bombers destroyed them. B-52s and fighter-bombers both had their roles. The BUFs pounded the PAVN, which then sought refuge within 3,000 yards of ARVN lines, normally too close for B-52s to drop, whereupon gunships and fast jets struck right up to the ARVN lines.[483] When a spread of bombs from BUFs damaged Colonel Pham Van Chung's bunker even though they landed the length of three football fields away, he was so impressed that he encouraged, "That was very good. . . . Do it again" to his American advisor.[484] When South Vietnamese began counterattacks to the west of Hue and southeast of Quang Tri, they coordinated with their air force counterparts. Consequently, South Vietnamese and American air strikes inflicted considerable losses and brought their attacks to a standstill. As soon as the PAVN launched human wave attacks on May 25, South Vietnamese Marines and air strikes mowed them down.[485]

Persistence and coordination prevented Kontum from being overrun. For instance, when troops completed a post-attack survey of a B-52 strike they counted hundreds of dead.[486] Outside of Kontum, ARVN infantry came upon a wounded soldier who revealed that his company numbered only twenty-five soldiers. Another prisoner relayed how his regiment, the 48th PAVN, was moving into place for an assault when bombs from B-52s killed many of his comrades. According to prisoners, air strikes inflicted most of the damage to their units.[487]

During the defense of Kontum, B-52 strikes preceded ground force assaults, and Vann believe missions like the Arc Light attacks of May 18–19 were what encouraged the 23rd ARVN Division to go on the offensive for the first time.[488] After these bomb strikes Major General Nguyen Van Toan, commander of II Corps, approved a plan to use ARVN to reopen Highway 14 into Kontum. When the PAVN launched their climactic attack on May 25, air strikes comprised the decisive element repelling the assault.[489] Most of the time whenever the enemy staged yet another attack, firepower destroyed it, although they managed to seize a command post and half of Kontum's airfield. Even though infantry and gunships repelled attack after attack, the corps commander asked for bombs aimed by Sky Spot and LORAN to be "brought to within 500 meters of friendlies and [he] will assume responsibility for the consequences." This was done.[490]

John Paul Vann declared on May 27, "the overall situation in Kontum City is critical but not at all hopeless." He believed heavy air strikes were necessary for its survival. Since the weather was worsening due to the seasonal monsoon, much of that had to consist of LORAN and Sky Spot missions.[491] When the enemy attacked again the next day, ARVN counterattacks were largely ineffectual. Firepower from American and South Vietnamese fighters and Army Cobra helicopters delivered most of the successes that day. An advisor also blamed PAVN incompetence at combined arms warfare for their failure to seize Kontum: they never coordinated infantry, armor, and artillery on a large scale.[492] Within a couple of days ARVN troops were mopping up the remaining enemy forces and processing surrendered infantry. Vann concluded air strikes had saved Kontum, which was not surprising given that an independent report in June placed North Vietnamese casualties at 33 percent.[493] In spite of accomplishments like these, word of air power's effectiveness was not getting out—quite the opposite.[494] Weather got so bad the first week of June that the only air strikes they received were from B-52s. Vann relied on B-52s as his killing force, particularly from mid-May onward, and his patrols found proof of their effectiveness in the form of mass graves. At the same time ARVN steadfastness was necessary for B-52 success. When they stood their ground, the enemy had to mass his infantry, serving themselves on a platter to the B-52s' bombs.[495]

These tactical and heavy bomber strikes assisted ground forces in an additional way: they allowed ground forces besieged in Kontum, for instance, to set aside artillery shells for critical moments when artillery was a necessity.[496] B-52s remained central to the continuing defense of Kontum, and also for breaking up any marshaling of forces the PAVN might attempt against another town. The B-52Gs brought into Guam were not that satisfactory because of their lighter bomb load, but Abrams wanted as many B-52 missions over South Vietnam as he could get. He found BUFs to be more efficient because it took about seventy-five fighter-bombers to bring the same firepower as three B-52Ds. Furthermore, B-52s could not bomb with the accuracy of fighter-bombers where precision was more important politically. Accordingly, send F-4s north with their laser-guided bombs and reserve B-52s for area targets in South Vietnam. Abrams realized bombing missions against North Vietnam meant nothing if the South Vietnamese collapsed, so provide Thieu's infantry with as much air support as possible. In other words, "it is not possible to lose the war in the North but it still is possible to lose the war in the South."[497]

Generals Abrams and Frederick C. Weyand, the new commander of MACV from June 30, were effusive in their praise for the B-52. Weyand wrote on July 18, "I could not ask for more nor better support than your command has given us. Next to the ARVN holding their positions, it has been the single decisive factor in our response to the enemy invasion."[498] According to Brigadier General Phan Van Phu, "If you want to kill people, you must use maximum air. What is maximum air . . . the B-52 of course."[499]

The South Vietnamese were winning after a month of fighting in and around Kontum, but its defense required persistent fighting well into the summer. June 18 was a blessedly quiet day until ARVN troops completed a raid against an enemy sector skillfully and with the support of their own fighter-bombers.[500] Vann exclaimed that theirs was the "best damn bombing I've seen in my 11 years over here. . . . In the defense of Kontum the VNAF has been magnificent, absolutely magnificent."[501] Vann credited them for a major portion of the success in the defense of the town. Other American observers also praised the South Vietnamese soldiers. They stood and fought hard, they did not run, they did not don civilian clothing and meld into the populace.[502]

By the third week of June 1972 daily summaries were consistently reporting low levels of enemy activity. Almost no one reported the presence of enemy troops near Kontum on June 29, the sole exception being Major General Tarpley's sector.[503] Although it is stated that air power inflicted most of the PAVN's estimated 16,000 casualties during the siege, the most significant measures of success was Kontum survived and the PAVN quit. The ground-air firepower team persuaded North Vietnam's army to give up its attempts to take the town.⁵⁰⁴ The Air Force's contemporary history of this battle highlighted every case of air power saving the day and being the decisive force. At the same time the USAF history added, "Airpower, in and of itself, cannot ensure victory; but in combination with a spirited ground defense it can prevent defeat."⁵⁰⁵

The fighting at An Loc and Kontum during spring 1972 once again demonstrated what took place when infantry stood fast and gave aircraft a chance to bomb suitable targets. Mutually supporting warfare of that kind, however, did not take place in April 1972 when the PAVN attacked Quang Tri just south of the DMZ: "The enemy was not pinned down so he could be hit by air strikes. Coordination was reportedly lacking among GVN ground, artillery, and air forces, and the commander of the 3rd ARVN Division could not effectively cope with the situation."⁵⁰⁶ North Vietnamese mechanized forces flushed ARVN troops out of Quang Tri who fled south despite the air support they received. These reports greatly worried the Pentagon, but Secretary Laird remained calm, noting that most of the South Vietnamese were fighting in place. Many ARVN troops who initially panicked actually rallied the following month, having found their backbones due to the leadership of Lieutenant General Ngo Quang Truong who replaced Lieutenant General Hoang Xuan Lam as the commander of I Corps on May 3. Truong made a good impression on his American counterparts, asking probing and detailed questions to determine what was happening before he acted, and appreciating the guidance of his American advisors.⁵⁰⁷

Air support was not a miracle worker. Enemy troops overran Loc Ninh on April 7 even though American advisors guided air strikes closer and then on top of the enemy forces inside their compound in a last-ditch effort to survive. More common were the actions at Pleiku on May 27 where a PAVN company attacked portions of the 3rd Cavalry. Eight F-4s arrived and bombed the enemy. Survivors fled as soon as the bombs stopped exploding.⁵⁰⁸ Because ARVN soldiers fought with more tenacity during the last week of May, they gave aerial firepower the time to work over the PAVN, who appeared spent by the first of June. Indeed, on June 7, the II Corps G-2 section drank toasts to the Air Force for the fire support it had provided.⁵⁰⁹

As North Vietnam's offensive leveled off, the Air Force found that most US Army officers credited air power as South Vietnam's salvation. Abrams wrote, "There is no question that the B-52s have been a major factor, and on occasion the deciding factor, in preventing the enemy's accomplishment of most of his major goals."⁵¹⁰ These successes in turn supported American diplomatic efforts.⁵¹¹ When General Vogt conveyed his assessment to Admiral Moorer over the phone, he gave more credit to air power, but discredited the MACV commanding general: "Abrams... has been out here too long. The whole ground war is screwed up. If it were not for the air and carriers offshore, the whole ground war would have gone down the drain a long time ago. That is 100 percent truth."⁵¹²

This kind of firepower reduced the losses for the side that used it. By the first week of June, American and South Vietnamese forces suffered 382 killed to at least 5,600 enemy killed. As vital as air support was to the ARVN, however, its availability and lethality generated an unhealthy dependency. The Air Force's senior representative for II Corps observed that the ARVN's favorite tactic was to unleash a B-52 attack on the spot the enemy probably was, and then call in fighter-bomber strikes.⁵¹³ In August, Lieutenant General Truong worried the bad weather he expected to begin the next month would hamper the availability of air support. General Vogt then commented somewhat dismissively that he was aware of Truong's dependence on it. Vogt promised bombing would continue during bad weather because of the availability of LORAN, adding, "As he always does, General Truong requested more B-52 support... he had no trouble producing lucrative targets for B-52 strikes."⁵¹⁴

The most accurate measure of effectiveness was the enemy's behavior. The North Vietnamese kept their stocks of supplies farther away from the battlefield because of the B-52s, and resupply columns had to endure well-directed air strikes. Because of American air supremacy over South Vietnam, the North Vietnamese were subjected to attack at the Americans' pleasure, which meant they had to win quickly, or they would have to work their way back to supply areas in the hinterland.[515] In June, a FAC reported the clearest evidence of how the battles had gone: "all the traffic we've seen since 10 June has been moving west." The North Vietnamese were returning to their sanctuaries in the interior.[516]

Aircraft wrought great destruction against T-34 and T-55 tanks during Linebacker. Nearly 40 percent of attacks by aircraft against armored fighting vehicles resulted in a destroyed or damaged tank, 8 percent a miss, with "results were not observed" on 53 percent of the attacks, resulting in at least 389 destroyed and 280 damaged.[517] For instance, during one encounter on May 5, 1972, FACs watched aircraft destroy eleven tanks and damage a dozen more. "They reported it had been a turkey shoot, with the tanks breaking wildly, some running into the sides of huts to hide under the roofs and others taking to the water to beat their way back."[518] According to a contemporary account, aircraft accounted for approximately 71 percent of all destroyed tanks.[519]

Precision-guided munitions came into their own in 1972, and the far greater effectiveness of laser-guided bombs was readily apparent before the end of May. Laser-guided bombs were ten times more effective against artillery pieces than unguided bombs. Achieving a direct hit on a tank with an unguided bomb required on average up to ten F-4 sorties, each carrying twelve 500-pound unguided bombs to destroy one tank—120 bombs. Each laser-guided bomb produced a kill up to 50 percent of the time, and each LGB sortie had an 80 percent chance of damaging or destroying a tank. Another source gives a lower kill rate for LGBs F-4s dropped of 37 percent, which was still exponentially more accurate and effective than unguided bombs.[520] While the LGB was the best and most accurate anti-tank weapon, the Rockeye anti-armor cluster bomb proved disappointing to some, but Marines found them useful. Among those attacking tanks with unguided bombs, the slower A-1s and A-37s tended to be the most effective, destroying on average 75 and 43 percent of tanks per sortie respectively, and South Vietnamese F-5As achieved a 54 percent kill rate. Army helicopter gunships struggled against tanks during Lam Son 719 but achieved good results with unguided rockets and guided missiles during the Easter Offensive. The new TOW (tube-launched, optically tracked, wire-guided) anti-tank missile ushered Army helicopters into the era of precision-guided munitions. Of the 127 fired from helicopters, ninety-six hit their target. Of these, forty were launched against tanks, twenty-seven of which did not survive. There were even cases of missiles aimed at, and hitting, the breach of an artillery piece. The main reason TOWs missed was because aircrews fired them out of range. With PGMs (precision-guided munitions), hitting a tank was no longer the most difficult challenge; confirming what happened was now more challenging than destroying a target. Over half the time pilots attacked tanks, they were not able to conclusively observe the result, understandable since they were evading ground fire, often at 500 miles per hour.[521]

Courage was a key component of these successes. Unfortunately, during the 1972 Easter Offensive, South Vietnamese FACs refused to fly into harm's way to such a degree that Americans had to take over all forward air controller duties. Some members of the ARVN would beg to differ on the origin and nature of this behavior. Regarding the reluctance of some South Vietnamese officers to send in ground teams to assess the effects of bombing missions, for example, Chief of the Joint General Staff General Vinh Loc replied, "If I send my people out, my losses are going to go up dramatically and I can't afford that. After all, we were taught the current tactics by US Army. You don't send your people out to get killed when you have airpower to do the job for you, so why would you expect me to do it?"[522] When the Americans expressed hopes their ally would wage some sort of a counteroffensive in fall 1972, General Vogt echoed the comments of General Loc. When General Weyand griped that Saigon's troops would not attack aggressively without massive air support, General Vogt observed, "Unfortunately, this is the way Westmoreland taught them to fight and you can't change that overnight."[523]

Close air support has to be carefully coordinated to be effective; one can receive too much of a good thing. During the siege of An Loc, for example, a ground commander needed accurate firepower very close to his troops' position, but "Tacair was trying to bomb, artillery was impacting in all quadrants, helicopters were flying through everyone's line of fire, Arc Light would come along and run off everyone within ten miles of the area, and the one weapons system that could really shoot in close, the gunship, was told to orbit, many times for three hours without firing a shot." A terribly wasteful practice was sending fighter-bombers on a mission with the hope the on-scene FAC would find something for them to do. They would wait past their minimum fuel state and then have to waste their bombs on a vacant field on their way home.[524] Deconfliction between B-52s and fighter-bombers was a necessity. On September 26, 1972, a bomb from a B-52 struck Lieutenant Commander John R. Paron's A-7 Corsair as it flew below. He and the jet survived and landed at Da Nang.[525]

American senior advisors functioned as a critical link between Vietnamese formations and American air power. More specifically, advisors' coordination with forward air controllers and the air strikes they controlled was essential for the successes the ARVN accomplished. A component of this was other airmen and soldiers understanding the capabilities and limitations of the aircraft, which was at times lacking. AC-130 crews in particular found that Army commanders were not familiar with how much destruction they could rain on the enemy, and they would end up wasting several days during which the ground force commander learned how to exploit them. Nor was efficient coordination automatic. During the opening weeks of the invasion, four out of ten fighter-bombers bombed without the guidance of a forward air controller.[526]

Perhaps the most important factor in the air forces' ability to hurt the North Vietnamese was the actions of the soldiers on both sides: ARVN dug in and fought, and PAVN massed together for their attacks against fortified fighting positions. Because the North Vietnamese undertook conventional attacks against ARVN strongpoints, they concentrated, which made them easier targets. The Americans and South Vietnamese thus knew where the enemy was, and so aircraft could bomb them to great effect. Air strikes were more effective when the enemy concentrated for an overland assault, and it was more difficult to mount effective missions when the enemy spread out and hunkered down.[527]

The North Vietnamese were on the horns of a dilemma because of their political goals; they had to mass their infantry to destroy their opponents, but that turned their own forces into the kinds of targets aircrews could find and destroy, which explains Major General Nguyen Vinh Nghi's concept of operations against PAVN forces. He used several infantry battalions to flush out enemy troops coming into South Vietnam from Cambodia, forced them to stand and fight and thus created targets aircraft could hit. Nixon's military advisors also understood this relationship.[528] During these battles between the 7th ARVN Division and those attacking from Cambodia, the battles were a complete success and air strikes were responsible for most of the 1,900 killed.[529] B-52s were excellent ground support weapons "in areas in which an established front exists."[530]

The PAVN, however, were not done. Their 130mm guns had been a primary concern of General Vogt because their shells, not PAVN infantry charges, were what caused ARVN infantry to run. In July air strikes focused on enemy artillery near Kontum because it was such a game changer—particularly the 130mm pieces. A North Vietnamese ground assault exploited their massive firepower, firing more than 10,000 rounds at three firebases, and their troops overran Bastogne on July 22.[531] South Vietnamese looked to air strikes as the solution to the problem of North Vietnamese 130mm cannon. Air strikes destroyed several every day, but 130mm rounds were shelling positions at an increasing rate. In fact, they were believed responsible for more than 80 percent of the casualties the Republic of Vietnam marines suffered, although General John D. Ryan later attributed the majority of the losses to mortars and recoilless rifle fire. The South Vietnamese Air Force provided only ten sorties each day near Quang Tri, and because none of these were at night, the PAVN poured on their attacks after dark.[532] The solution to the 130mm cannon was FACs looking for them, finding them, and calling in air strikes.[533] Laser-guided bombs were the best means for destroying them: Major General Alton D. Slay observed, "It would take 800 Mk-82s, under [instrument meteorological conditions], to get a 70 percent probability of kill against a 130mm gun; under [visual meteorological conditions] it would take one Paveway."[534]

BUFs proved instrumental to the retaking of Quang Tri, laying down a bombardment on June 28 in preparation for an ARVN assault.[535] As important as B-52s were to the retaking of the city, South Vietnamese marines decided the issue. They broke through the city walls on September 12 and three days later had control of it, killing considerable numbers of the enemy. When the North Vietnamese 312th Division began to mass near Quang Tri, B-52s were sent against the division to prevent it from making a successful attack. Their 700 sorties evened the playing field between it and weakened government forces nearby. South Vietnamese soldiers and marines expanded the ground they controlled around Quang Tri, and air strikes flew as much as possible, given the weather. Tactical and B-52 strikes remained worthwhile, the astounding number of secondary explosions serving as proof the bombs hit stores of enemy ammunition. Rainstorms, however, were so relentless during the last week of October that north of the city this effort came to a halt. Rain and flooding brought virtually all offensive action in this area to an end by the end of November.[536]

The difficulties in quantifying these effects encouraged American forces to adopt an indirect measurement of success that was at the same time less quantifiable and more substantively useful. Whether or not a friendly force under attack survived was the bottom line. Additional measures included the progressive disappearance of enemy positions and units and whether or not they continued to attack. If air forces pulverized known enemy forces that were attacking an ARVN position and the attacking stopped, analysts concluded the bombardment was the reason. "Situation quiet on departure," they wrote, was "a true measure of success." The encouragement air support gave friendly troops was another important if unquantifiable consequence. The responsiveness and accuracy of air strikes forced the enemy to make adjustments that weakened his effectiveness.[537] The writer of the Air Force report on close air support in 1972 offered some timeless analysis about the relationship of CAS to ground actions: "It must be remembered that airpower was not a panacea but was looked upon as one by many. No matter how effective airpower was, it could never capture and occupy terrain. The aforementioned statements give rise to questions about the willingness and capability of ground forces to purse their objective, as well as the need to capture and occupy terrain. These questions will not be answered; but instead, left to the reader to determine his position relative to these questions."[538]

By the middle of August, the ARVN-American team had staved off defeat, and then some. The Americans and the Vietnamese agreed, "The ARVN had already virtually recovered its equipment and manpower losses from the first phase of the 1972 offensive. But the enemy's main force capability had suffered severe losses in manpower and equipment, especially heavy weaponry, that he had little immediate prospect of recovering." General Weyand believed the US and ARVN inflicted 100,000 casualties on the PAVN thus far, and General Vogt believed less than 100 of the 750 tanks that were a part of the original PAVN order of battle still existed.[539] Then in September, joint use of ARVN probes that sought out enemy forces, and tactical air and B-52 strikes, wrecked a PAVN offensive in the Mekong Delta. Analysts also observed that enemy forces had transitioned to small unit activities.[540]

Ground combat and air strikes continued sporadically through the year's last four months. More than 1,200 B-52 sorties struck enemy targets through the end of 1972. The Air Force still sent BUFs after remote groupings of PAVN and their bases that were not fighting friendly troops.[541] Air still had opportunities to save the day as Linebacker wound down. On October 19, more than 250 Regional Forces soldiers along with a pair of American advisors found themselves under attack in the district of Phu Nhon at My Thach. A joint effort of Army AH-1 Cobras, jets from the USS *Saratoga*, and USAF A-7Ds that had been in country for only three days, saved the soldiers from certain destruction, something the A-7D pilots considered their greatest achievement during their portion of the war.[542]

Close Air Support Conclusions

The way one measures the results of air strikes and the conclusions one draws about their consequences in terms of supporting a strategy and especially a policy goal are related. The Air Force normally tried to determine results of its air strikes by first looking at bombing accuracy, then at the munitions' destructive effects, and often did not look beyond those two factors. There were times where analysts might ask how all this influenced the course of the war, but I get the impression that the prevalence of the purist attitude toward military professionalism, to borrow from Samuel P. Huntington, might have generated the inadvertent side effect of an officer corps that examined the effects of air power almost exclusively in terms of munitions' effectiveness and operational success. Officers examined tactical operational effectiveness, but seldom traced the impact of aerial bombardment through to the strategic and policy effects. That approach helps ensure the military stays out of politics and remains a compliant tool of civilian leaders, but it can also result in a military that struggles to conceive of tactics and operations that will clearly deliver what the president needs. One Air Force official history admitted that relating tactical effects to policy goals was terribly challenging.[543]

Still, tactical effectiveness is normally a prerequisite to strategic effectiveness, and in highlighting this capability, General Abrams may have been the most passionate advocate of fixed-wing close air support the war produced. Helicopters, the Army general told Congress, could not match the firepower and weight of effort of fighter-bombers and attack jets. He also contrasted the span, reach, and flexibility of helicopters to fixed-wing jets and favored the latter. In Vietnam he witnessed the shifting of much of the Air Force's close air support aircraft (mostly F-4s by the Easter Offensive) from Military Region-1 to Military Region-4 in an impressively short amount of time: "You switch that whole faucet, and you do it in about 45 minutes. The whole control system and base system that supports that, there is nothing in the Army like that. There is nothing anywhere in the world like it. . . . This can all happen in 2 hours." Abrams had observed that at times one Army division might not need any fighter-bomber support, while another in a different part of Southeast Asia might need all of it, so tying aircraft to individual divisions was not in the Army's interest.[544] In addition to Creighton Abrams, another Army general, Bruce Palmer Jr., heaped praise upon air support.[545] He also observed the downside of assigning aircraft to specific ground units during Operation Cherokee in May 1966, when fighter-bombers were bound to the 4th Marine Regiment, but were seldom needed—"only on two occasions." The rest of the time, except for their initial bombing runs, those jets were parked on a concrete pad being of use to no one.[546]

The crux of the problem for making the greatest use of aerial bombardment in support of one's own combat troops is knowing the location of enemy troops and keeping them in place until the bombs destroy them. Furthermore, the enemy troops somehow have to be forced to bunch close together above ground, not dispersed or inside fortifications, trenches, or bunkers—although if one can prevent them from leaving earthworks, close air support can turn those into sarcophaguses. Herding and fixing Viet Cong or North Vietnamese troops in place required two things difficult to obtain during this war: human intelligence—during an insurgency/guerrilla/conventional war no less—in order to know where the enemy is before they come in contact with friendly troops, and the proper use of ground forces in order to force the enemy to have to leave their hiding places, come out and fight, and remain in place, thus presenting hittable targets. Accomplishing that requires infantry willing to press the enemy enough that they take losses themselves. Now when ground forces compel the enemy to defend themselves openly, air forces really can finish them off, but this problem quickly drives us from the realm of tactics and joint doctrine to fundamental issues of war aims, national policy, and the extent of the threat to the country waging war against this kind of enemy. This was a limited war for the United States and the soldiers knew it; they were not going to fight with the same motivations that existed during the Battle of the Bulge, for example—Vietnam was not worth it to them. The geography of Vietnam made all this worse and success much more difficult to achieve; in desert, farmland, or steppe terrain, ground forces can close with and fix the enemy at a distance. In Vietnam, finishing off the enemy often required moving into point-blank range and subjecting one's infantry to heavy casualties from an enemy that still may be hidden by ten yards of intervening jungle.

When Nixon began his first term as president, everyone sensed the imbalance between American war aims on the one hand and the magnitude of force necessary to achieve American policy goals on the other. Secretary of the Navy John H. Chaffee confirmed this when he interacted with some aviators in May 1969. They believed the war was stalemated. Most telling were statements from the helicopter pilots who were on their second tour. They believed their day-to-day efforts were "futile" because they would "Take assault troops to LZ, dump them out, go back later to pick up dead and wounded. Then a few days later return to the scene, retract those who survive, then repeat the same cycle weeks or months later at the same place."[547]

In 1969, minimizing American casualties became a greater priority to policy makers than driving the communists into oblivion, and this encouraged a greater reliance on firepower during operations and resulted in military operations that inflicted less harm on the enemy.[548] For instance, when Marines observed enemy forces moving through the Plu Loc Valley on a regular basis in August 1969, the III Marine Amphibious Force decided to employ a new tactic it called the "air ambush." This tactic relied on sensors to find the enemy and artillery and air strikes to kill him. OV-10s guided two A-6As, four A-4s, and two F-4s against a platoon the Marines detected on the night of August 28. "The F-4 pilot salvoed his napalm right on target—six enemy were observed to get up and run. The second F-4 dropped his napalm in their midst." After four Skyhawks completed their bomb run the forward air controller did not see anyone moving on the ground. That changed after a few minutes and artillery opened up on the survivors. When Marines scoured the area on foot the next morning (close infantry action was the last step), they did not find a single body. Enough enemy had survived the hellish onslaught either within or near the target zone to remove those who were wounded or dead. Nevertheless, the Marines decided for the time being, "this technique will continue to be refined and future employment of the air ambush is planned."[549]

These tactical requirements to destroy the enemy and preserve oneself quickly led to some very important questions for voters and congressmen: are these human losses worth it to the commander, will the folks back home agree that Johnny did not die in vain? The nature of the Vietnam War and the outcome the United States wished to occur demanded the Americans fight with a level of aggression that put American troops at risk at a rate appropriate only for a war that was much more important to American national security than Vietnam could ever be. If the Americans wanted to win this limited war, doing so required killing off PAVN soldiers and communist operatives in demographically catastrophic numbers over a short period of time, generating a loss rate that even staunchly committed communists could not replace. The United States was not going to carry out a war with anywhere near that level of carnage not only because the optics would undercut the containment strategy, but also because of the costs to its own soldiers. It was this mismatch in terms of what was at stake for each country that made this kind of limited war more difficult to wage. In this way, the Vietnam War illustrates how misleading the discourse of the concept of limited war is. Limited war is commonly defined as war of limited means for limited ends, but for the Americans to have won the Vietnam War required them to employ means that were either more costly or riskier than the importance a victory was to American national security.[550] In this case the enemy, not the Americans, dictated the amount of force necessary for the Americans to achieve their objectives. The nature of the communists' goals—unification of Vietnam under one regime *no matter the costs*—gave them a great advantage.

A more direct strategy—conquest of North Vietnam and the cleaning out of the sanctuary areas of Laos and Cambodia—required the US to accept geopolitical risks and costs that were not worth it. Therefore, if the Vietnam War is conceptually restricted to South Vietnam, a stalemated war of mutual exhaustion with a Korea-like outcome was probably the best the US and South Vietnam could hope for; a successful "oil spot" strategy *may* have been successful with enough persistence. Accomplishing policy goals without winning a series of big battles, however, is almost culturally impossible for Americans to comprehend.[551]

Although the various ways in which the Allies tried to find enemy forces had their own challenges, the ultimate reason why close air support and direct attack did not achieve as great a measure of policy-level effectiveness as they could have was less the ambivalent commitment to joint warfare during Vietnam than it was the very nature of the war itself. While nothing can destroy ground forces like air strikes, nothing can fix them in place and force them to concentrate—and thus make them targets vulnerable to firepower—like ground troops. You do not want one without the other. General Taylor seemed to understand some of these limitations at the beginning of 1965. He agreed with President Johnson that the "guerrilla war cannot be won from the air . . . if we are thinking in terms of the physical destruction of the enemy."[552]

PART 3

COERCION AND INTERDICTION

Chapter 14

Air Coercion and Air Interdiction Effectiveness Over Southeast Asia

In early 1964, the consensus among the Johnson administration's civilian and military leadership was that the United States had to support South Vietnam to maintain the credibility of its containment policy.[1] Indeed, the United States was involved in an air war in Indochina before Operation Rolling Thunder, the air campaign against North Vietnam. The air war in Indochina began in Laos in 1964 when American-trained Laotian pilots began flying air strikes against communist insurgents using T-28 training aircraft that had been converted into light attack planes. This program evolved into the CIA's "Air America" covert war to get around prohibitions against American military involvement on behalf of Prime Minister Souvanna Phouma and his non-communist neutral government.[2]

In accordance with the 1962 Geneva Agreements Respecting Laos, signatories were supposed to respect "the neutrality, independence, and territorial integrity of Laos," but the North Vietnamese violated this agreement by functioning as a military belligerent in that country.[3] Their troops supported Pathet Lao Communist insurgents and protected their lines of supply through Laos to South Vietnam. Vientiane welcomed American assistance to defend Laos against Hanoi's aggression. Over time, the United States used air power in two related Laotian wars: first, to support the Royal Lao government against the Pathet Lao and North Vietnamese Army, and second, bombing North Vietnamese supply routes through the panhandle of Laos into South Vietnam and Cambodia. The former began in December 1964 as Operation Barrel Roll, and the latter, Operations Steel Tiger and Tiger Hound, commenced in April and December 1964.[4]

The Johnson administration discussed ordering an air strike in June 1964 to convince Ho Chi Minh that the United States was serious about containing North Vietnamese aggression, and President Johnson that same month approved a strike against antiaircraft artillery batteries in Laos as a reprisal for shooting down a US Navy RF-8A reconnaissance aircraft. Most of the administration saw air strikes as the best option from a set of not so promising alternatives, and Secretary of Defense Robert S. McNamara initiated planning for such operations.[5] Regarding the interdiction of the Ho Chi Minh Trail, Johnson, not ready in 1964 to employ American high-performance jets, approved Lao T-28s for that mission.[6] That interdiction effort diminished during summer 1964 when the North Vietnamese began transforming the Trail "from a network of jungle trails to a modern transportation system."[7]

Escalation took place following two years of discussion moving in that direction. President John F. Kennedy resisted recommendations for a large-scale military intervention in 1961. The next year, General Curtis LeMay opined that air power could decide the war in favor of Washington and Saigon, and also suggested enlarging Operation Jungle Jim, the

Air Force's special operations effort.[8] At the outset of 1964, the JCS called for a massive escalation of American involvement, including bombing North Vietnamese targets, mining the Haiphong Harbor, and perhaps invading North Vietnam. Days later, President Lyndon Johnson directed the development of plans to pressure and deter North Vietnam to support the policy of South Vietnam as non-communist and independent.[9] Of all the possibilities mentioned, the last one was "graduated overt military pressure by GVN and U.S. forces," which meant bombing factories, warehouses, and military sites.[10] In May and June the CIA, the State Department, and the president floated the possibility of bombing.[11] A June 1964 meeting in Honolulu that included Secretary of Defense Robert McNamara, Ambassador Henry Cabot Lodge Jr., Admiral Ulysses S. G. Sharp, and General William Westmoreland proposed "a series of graduated military pressures, culminating in limited air attacks against North Vietnam."[12] This, they believed, had some chance of influencing the Hanoi regime because losing what industrial facilities they had worried the North Vietnamese.[13]

The Johnson administration saw this region as a major national security interest, and Secretary of State Dean Rusk even asserted defending South Vietnam was just as important as protecting Berlin. A CIA assessment argued against the inevitability of the domino effect, the postulate that if South Vietnam fell, its neighbors would fall to communist insurgencies in quick succession, but the assessment warned if Laos and South Vietnam became communist the United States would suffer profound damage to its prestige and power in the Far East. Chairman of the Joint Chiefs of Staff General Earle G. Wheeler agreed when he argued that losing South Vietnam meant losing all of Southeast Asia to the communists.[14]

In the meantime, the South Vietnamese Navy had been raiding military targets on the coast of North Vietnam, and US Navy warships monitored the activities. Then on August 2, the North Vietnamese used torpedo boats to attack the USS *Maddox*. Two nights later the *Maddox*'s crew was convinced the torpedo boats had returned, but there was no attack. Inexperienced sonar operators thought they heard torpedoes launched against their ship. As reprisals for the supposed aggression, President Johnson ordered an air strike from the USS *Ticonderoga*.[15] Within three days Congress passed the Gulf of Tonkin Resolution, essentially giving the president a blank check for military action against North Vietnam. Days later National Security Advisor McGeorge Bundy proposed the first of January 1965 as a planning date for military escalation.[16]

August 1964 saw two doctrinal mismatches begin to affect the military options available to the president. The first was that the Air Force entered the war with doctrine rooted in the World War II bombing campaigns against vulnerable economic centers. The second held that if a certain target set was bombed aggressively enough over a short period of time the adversary would capitulate. Walt W. Rostow, chair of the State Department's policy planning council, urged bombing North Vietnam's domestic "sources of support," following antecedents from the bombing campaign against Germany. He somehow missed that North Vietnam's sources of support were the Soviet Union and China—neither of which could be bombed—and the economies of North Vietnam and Germany had nothing in common.[17] General Wheeler proposed a list of ninety-four vulnerable targets, arguing the administration needed to strike them immediately to maintain American credibility. Furthermore, he stated, bombing constituted a use of force most likely to destroy North Vietnam's ability to support its war in South Vietnam as well as its willingness to continue its aggression.[18] The JCS further believed "a sudden sharp blow" was the way to jolt Hanoi into ceasing its support of insurgencies beyond its borders.[19] A couple of weeks later the president found out, however, that his joint chiefs actually disagreed as to what should be done next. The chief of staff of the Air Force and the Marine Corps commandant believed a thorough campaign of air strikes was necessary, while the chief of staff of the Army, the chief of naval operations, and even the chairman of the JCS (despite what he said) believed such actions would work against American goals because an air campaign would overstress the Saigon government.[20]

Two months later, the Commander-in-Chief, Pacific, Admiral Sharp, recommended a mix of psychological operations and diplomacy with "gradually increased military pressures" in the form of aerial bombardments of the supply routes and other targets supporting the movement of insurgents and materiel into South Vietnam.[21] The admiral assumed successful destruction would generate strategically significant outcomes, including reduced support for the Viet Cong, although these effects would not be immediately evident.[22] All of these recommendations assumed Hanoi's policy goals were negotiable and that the Democratic Republic of Vietnam (DRV) was exceedingly vulnerable to military coercion. The ninety-four-target list initiated an argument that if only the United States' air forces got to destroy all those targets, Hanoi would inevitably comply with American demands.

Right before the 1964 United States elections, Viet Cong insurgents carried out a mortar attack on Bien Hoa Air Base on November 1, destroying five B-57 bombers and killing four Americans.[23] Ambassador to South Vietnam Maxwell D. Taylor recommended a large bombing operation against North Vietnam's main military airfield, Phuc Yen, in retaliation, and admitted such action would change the character of the American conflict with North Vietnam. Reprisal air strikes would have been justified, but President Johnson was not willing to take such action on the eve of Election Day.[24] His national security advisor inclined toward "a slow, controlled squeeze on North Vietnam in order to bring about negotiations, increasing gradually our present level of operations against the North."[25] McGeorge Bundy's option gained more attention during the remainder of the year.[26]

By the end of December, however, the president was skeptical about the merits of escalation: "Every time I get a military recommendation it seems to me that it calls for large-scale bombing. I have never felt that this war will be won from the air, and it seems to me that what is much more needed and would be more effective is a larger and stronger use of Rangers and Special Forces and Marines, or other appropriate military strength on the ground and on the scene."[27] A working group that included William Bundy, Vice President Hubert H. Humphrey, and Ambassador Taylor presented three options in December: stay the course and lose, implement a massive air interdiction campaign that included the ninety-four-target list, or attack the same target sets gradually over a longer period of time. Undersecretary of State George Ball warned if the United States used its asymmetric advantage—air power—the North Vietnamese would respond with their own asymmetric advantage: soldiers, which they had in huge numbers the Americans could not match. He also categorically rejected the assertion American credibility with her allies was on the line. The currents surrounding the various options and concerns were, however, moving the president toward open-ended military escalation, driven by an indeterminate strategy when Johnson had already approved an escalated air interdiction campaign against the Ho Chi Minh Trail in December.[28]

In January 1965, American policy makers were alarmed that communist military actions were becoming successful enough to defeat the counterinsurgency efforts of the Saigon government. The Johnson administration worried that political leaders in South Vietnam might reach an accommodation with the National Front for the Liberation of South Vietnam (NLF). In that case, Laos would become "untenable," Cambodia would appease the communists, and Thailand would lose confidence in the United States.[29] Administration officials believed if the US abandoned South Vietnam, a global "catastrophe" would soon follow.[30] Secretary of State Rusk believed a communist takeover of Southeast Asian countries would be a disaster for the United States and its friends; that made South Vietnam's preservation a vital interest—and a country goes to war over vital interests.[31]

For their part, McGeorge Bundy and Robert McNamara inclined toward using military means to force the communists to change their policy, but Rusk saw no good options.[32] Bundy proposed bombing MiG bases in North Vietnam to "stimulate Saigon to form a government that was viable," but he could not explain how bombing MiG bases in North Vietnam would persuade the South Vietnamese to strengthen their own government.[33] President Johnson was determined to go as far as necessary to defeat the communists' efforts in Vietnam. To that end the United States tried to influence Hanoi's behavior, using American support of Saigon's war as a first step. As these proved insufficient, President Johnson and his advisors looked to bombing targets in North Vietnam to try to alter Hanoi's actions.

The ensuing air campaign evolved as a coercive effort: persuade the North Vietnamese to end their support for the NLF by convincing the former that they could not achieve their goals in South Vietnam. In terms of target sets, it was mostly an interdiction effort that also bombed economically and politically valuable targets.[34] Operationally, Rolling Thunder was an air interdiction and armed reconnaissance campaign, but it also displayed some characteristics of a strategic bombing campaign because it was designed to decisively degrade Hanoi's war effort and persuade them to stop their efforts to conquer South Vietnam through destroying economic targets the Americans thought were irreplaceable to the North Vietnamese. The written goals of the Operation Rolling Thunder were, "restricting the flow of supplies into South Vietnam and Laos and coercing Hanoi to the conference table."[35]

A 1964 Navy study maintained that carrier air strikes could interdict North Vietnam's ground transportation system given there were so few infiltration routes. It also claimed only a couple of aircraft carriers would be sufficient. This analysis anticipated the North Vietnamese countering the effects of the bomb craters with human porters and repair parties and predicted they would repair bridges quickly. It also concluded interdicting supply movements between the Chinese border and Hanoi would be difficult, but that an effort to the south would be more promising. If the North Vietnamese were committed to using human transportation at night, the study conceded it would be difficult for air strikes to succeed, but supporting a war effort via porters and backpacks was not going to be able to sustain a large military operation.[36] These predictions were proven right. At the beginning of 1965 it appeared the limited bombing efforts had persuaded the North Vietnamese to switch from trucks to porters, but in reality "human portage" offered the greatest support not to the communists' logistical efforts, but to their propaganda campaign that theirs was but a determined, poor, peasant movement of dedicated agricultural revolutionaries. In reality, the North Vietnamese relied on road-bound trucks from the beginning. Naval aviators, for instance, counted a twenty-two vehicle/truck convoy near Tchepone, Laos, in April 1965.[37]

A consensus existed among the military leadership prior to Operation Rolling Thunder that a gradually escalating air campaign would achieve the president's policy goals. In January 1965, Maxwell Taylor saw air strikes as a way to compel Hanoi to alter its behavior. He assumed their leaders would find a series of gradually escalated strikes so unpalatable that they would negotiate with the South Vietnamese and Americans. Taylor also believed the United States could achieve its strategic goals by regulating "attacks not for the purpose of doing maximum physical destruction but for producing maximum stresses in" the "minds" of the leadership in Hanoi.[38] Taylor did not explain how aerial bombardment could generate unsurpassed stress within the minds of enemy leaders without great levels of destruction. Commander of the 2nd Air Division Major General Joseph H. Moore proposed a different approach: apply maximum force in small packages. Instead of the infrequent pattern of early air strike missions, Moore envisioned a continuous operation involving flights of no more than eight aircraft against fixed targets and supply lines. He believed this would convince the enemy there were no sanctuaries and no respites. Moore's assessment was overly optimistic, arguing the air campaign would generate massive and disruptive refugee flows, a great reduction in the amounts of supplies reaching communist forces, serious shortcomings in housing and transportation in the heart of North Vietnam, and that civilian protests in that country would demand a quick end to the war.[39]

Chief of Staff of the Air Force General John P. McConnell agreed with Ambassador Taylor's January assessment and the proposal Admiral Sharp made in November. On February 11, he wrote to the rest of the JCS: "I fully concurred in steadily increasing the military pressure on the DRV and pointed out that a Methodical increase will not only get the message across to the DRV but would accomplish it with the least chance of escalation and Chicom involvement." He added, "I strongly concur in the adoption of a graduated reprisal prgram [sic] as recommended by ambassador Taylor in Ref A [Saigon 2445 to State OF Feb 65]." In addition, serious reprisals would be in order if there was another communist attack. Convincing Hanoi their efforts could not gain the upper hand would save lives on both sides, and "Thereafter, we should resume the stance of continually and gradually increasing pressure."[40] General Westmoreland agreed: "A graduated reprisal program is obviously the most powerful persuader. RVN-US reprisal air strikes will be executed on basis on VC atrocities outrages and incidents against US and RVN [underlining in original]." As Westmoreland envisioned them, these air strikes would take place only below the 18th parallel in Vietnam and over northern Laos, not against the North Vietnamese heartland. Neither would jet fighters carry out the air strikes. He initially proposed using A-1 Skyraiders against more modest targets.[41]

Their conviction that only a little force would persuade Hanoi to yield was terribly flawed because it underestimated the amount of force required to persuade Hanoi to fundamentally and permanently change the policy goals for which it lived and died. Graduated limited destruction was completely insufficient; only severe devastation concentrated over a long period of time held the possibility of persuading North Vietnamese leadership into giving up vital national goals. Accomplishing such a feat was going to be difficult because of a major characteristic of Vietnamese identity: "resistance to foreign aggression."[42] Moreover, Hanoi was on the site of the Vietnamese capital of antiquity, Co-loa, which aided the Lao Dong Party in their assertions of greater legitimacy in contrast to the government in Saigon.[43]

Mobilizing their tradition of defiance was not innovative. Resisting invaders had been a component of Vietnamese history and identity long before this war. The Vietnamese defeated the Chinese during a war for independence in 938 and proclaimed coequal status with China in 966. Wars against Mongol and Chinese forces erupted again in the thirteenth, fifteenth, and eighteenth centuries. More recently they had been organizing and fighting for control of an independent Vietnam for decades. Vietnamese had fought the Japanese and defeated the French, but the Americans still did not take them as seriously as they should have.[44]

Taylor also assumed bombing missions carried out as reprisals for Viet Cong attacks would send signals that Hanoi would interpret correctly, boost South Vietnamese morale, and dissuade the Viet Cong from carrying out further attacks. Furthermore, reprisal strikes were meant to communicate to the leadership in Hanoi and Peking that similar military action would follow each Viet Cong attack.[45] Would those leaders perceive what American leaders thought were obvious and clear signals the way the Americans thought they would?

A couple of additional goals were naive: "air operations were designed to create acute management problems for the Civil Government and the military." Since when had an "acute management problem" persuaded a government to give up a vital national interest about which it held the deepest convictions? Degrading the morale and determination of the North Vietnamese was another goal.[46] How would morale only lowered, but not destroyed, persuade Hanoi to terminate its war? A more thorough memory of World War II would have warned American strategists of the ultimate irrelevance of low morale and defeatism within a population tightly controlled by an authoritarian regime.[47] To the contrary, the leadership in Hanoi was evincing a lot of confidence that South Vietnam would soon be theirs.[48]

Bombing Theory and Practice before Vietnam

The idea of using bombing aircraft against distant targets in urban areas dates from the first days of the age of flight. Futurists such as H. G. Wells foresaw flying machines terrorizing civilian populations. Bombing became a reality during the First World War when German multi-engine bombers and Zeppelin airships attempted to cow the populations of Paris and London into pressuring their governments to quit the war. They did not inflict much damage, cost the Kaiser points in the propaganda war, and provoked British retaliation.[49]

Theorists and practitioners exerted a great amount of effort to make the bombing of targets at long range a practical and strategically significant reality in the years that followed. Above all, everyone sought to avoid a repeat of the indecisive bloodletting of the Western Front, a field of such carnage that anything that held out the possibility of returning decisiveness to war while avoiding a repeat of the Great War was given a serious look. The Italian Giulio Douhet proposed preemptive airfield attacks to gain air dominance, followed by the bombing of urban targets to make the enemy capitulate.[50] American airmen proposed crippling attacks against key economic nodes to incapacitate an enemy's war-making capacity. The British intended to strike government and industrial centers as well, but with the intention of breaking civilian morale.[51]

The Germans were the first to put the idea to decisive use when they bombed Rotterdam and used the threat of further destruction to extract a Dutch surrender in May 1940. Their bombing of Warsaw the previous September was pointless because their ground army was taking over the whole country anyway. The German bombing of British cities failed. Not so the efforts by the Americans and British against the Nazi regime.[52] Great Britain's Bomber Command initially sought to score against key economic targets in Germany, but their bombers were too vulnerable to German air defenses, so they quickly switched to night bombing. Darkness provided some cover against German fighters but ruined British navigation and bombing accuracy. Targeting drifted toward bombing entire cities.[53] The US Army Air Forces persisted with high-altitude precision daylight bombing to achieve mixed results. Their raid of October 9, 1943, for instance, was destructive enough to bring all aircraft production at Marienberg to a halt for four months, but frequent undercast encouraged them to adapt radar-aimed bombing. In fall 1944, the bombing campaign wrecked German refineries and railroads, precipitating a collapse of their war economy. The greatest consequence of the bombing was political. It helped persuade the Soviet Union that the United States and the United Kingdom were sincere allies, and it helped leave no doubt that, unlike in 1918, Germany had lost the war. The bombing of Japanese cities generated similar effects.[54]

Labeled "strategic bombing," the World War II air campaigns produced some misleading aftereffects, rhetoric, and underlying assumptions. Douhet suggested using merciless air campaigns to win a war quickly before an enemy could bring his ground forces to bear. The potential of using air power alone to win wars is an idea that lingers as a tempting possibility.⁵⁵ The term "strategic bombing" and its practice were misleading and confusing. Bombing by long-range, multi-engine bombers was assumed to be strategic bombing, and after the advent of nuclear weapons the term became synonymous with nuclear warfare. It was simply bombing of economic and urban targets to weaken the enemy, in conjunction with a land war, perhaps to the point of capitulation.⁵⁶ To many in 1965 it only made sense that bombing North Vietnamese economic and logistical targets would be sufficient to coerce Ho Chi Minh into compliance.

Bombing North Vietnam

Not everyone saw the bombing of targets in North Vietnam as the optimal way to persuade Hanoi to stop its aggression. The way to win the war in South Vietnam was to win the war inside South Vietnam. United States intelligence analysts realized defeating the insurgency there faced immense challenges. Special National Intelligence Estimate 53-65 asserted in February 1965 that political and social revolution was roiling that country.⁵⁷ Such conditions were excellent either for the communists to advance their cause or for the United States to assist in a counterproductive manner; a country under such stress may be too overwhelmed to defeat an insurgency. When General Harold K. Johnson, the Army chief of staff, visited in March 1965, he found a country nearing disintegration.⁵⁸

The United States initiated Operation Rolling Thunder through a series of steps beginning with activities not widely advertised. Policy leaders first decided reprisal air strikes would be appropriate if the Viet Cong carried out another attack against an American base like the one on Bien Hoa in November.⁵⁹ Simultaneously, Ambassador Taylor, Alexis Johnson, General Westmoreland, and analysts from several governmental departments William Bundy chaired, met on February 6, 1965. They devised the notion of a series of measured actions that would persuade the DRV to end its activities in South Vietnam.⁶⁰

The steps the administration took during its decision to escalate reveal a deeply flawed cognitive approach to war. McGeorge Bundy proffered that conditions in South Vietnam were worsening by the day and an eventual loss of that country was a certainty within a year unless the United States took assertive action. America had invested a lot in South Vietnam, he argued, and now shared responsibility for that country's fate. With no way to negotiate a satisfactory outcome, and Saigon too weak to address the insurgency unaided, Bundy recommended "a policy of sustained reprisal" that was actually a strategy. He warned the war would be long and costly, but letting South Vietnam fall to the National Liberation Front was far worse. The geopolitical and security gains from paying the costs of intervention and attempting to turn the war around, even if Saigon fell, surpassed the consequences of cutting and running. Intervention would be worth it.⁶¹

The American strategy suffered from contradictions. While bombing North Vietnam, the United States would constantly announce it had no intention to take over or destroy that country. Bundy thought pressure should mount slowly to exert influence on the course of the war in South Vietnam. The intention was never "to win" the war but to keep South Vietnam free of insurgent warfare. Bundy believed that although the United States would be waging an offensive air war against North Vietnam, those air strikes "in no sense represent[ed] any intent to wage offensive war against the North. These distinctions should not be difficult to develop."⁶² A message from the 2nd Air Division in March regarding a Rolling Thunder mission, however, wrote of "punitive and crippling strikes"—not the language of a measured application of limited force.⁶³ The following month the president offered New Deal programs to both Vietnams—if Hanoi would relent.⁶⁴

The American strategy mismatched means and ends. For instance, the strategy advertised that American goals were limited, thus telling the North Vietnamese the level of pain they had to endure. The proposal for negotiations misread the North Vietnamese leadership badly by assuming their goals were negotiable. Bundy assumed limited air strikes against northern targets could have decisive effects on actions by Viet Cong guerrillas in South Vietnam. Somehow, rational political actors were to believe that an unremitting bombing campaign was not an offensive war. His plan of action was also contradictory and poorly reasoned. Altering Hanoi's willingness to supply the Viet Cong and give them political directions was something Bundy wished to pursue later, so he was unwilling to inflict decisive force against the enemy's center of gravity: the willingness of the politburo in Hanoi to continue the war. Instead, he believed a major air campaign would hurt communist morale and improve that of the South Vietnamese. Bundy even argued that other insurgent movements would examine this kind of continuous reprisal bombing campaign and be deterred from waging their own insurgencies—this as a result of an effort that "may fail." These recommendations did not even promise to accomplish American goals for Vietnam: "We cannot assert that a policy of sustained reprisal will succeed in changing the course of the contest in Vietnam.... What we can say is that even if it fails, the policy will be worth it."[65] Not exactly a firm foundation for an effective aerial bombardment campaign. Nevertheless, most of Johnson's advisors saw no alternative.[66]

One assumption may have been the most misguided: limited bombing could persuade Hanoi to end its support of the NLF and to negotiate a resolution; limited force could persuade them to give up a vital interest.[67] Admiral Sharp disagreed with an additional assumption: bombing would produce "only marginal effects." Instead, he believed, "Results will depend upon the nature of the campaign we wage." The admiral suggested that convincing Hanoi it could not win in the south would persuade the North Vietnamese leadership to negotiate dependably. A bombing campaign that made it more difficult for the North to support the insurgency was a preferable approach, he argued, to threatening North Vietnam with utter destruction. Such a threat, Sharp added, had little credibility given American policy and its geopolitical goals. Sharp believed the way to wage a persuasive air war was not only through destroying target sets, but also through an intense armed reconnaissance effort. These air strikes could be throttled up and pulled back in intensity. Additionally, the admiral realized operations in North and South Vietnam were interconnected in that combat in South Vietnam combined with air interdiction ought to suffocate the VC eventually. The administration intended to signal Hanoi that continued aggression would be costly for the North Vietnamese homeland.[68] Rolling Thunder could not succeed, however, if the North Vietnamese were willing and able to endure more punishment than the bombings could inflict. The policy goals and the assumptions that underlay it were more determinant of the effectiveness of air power than the skill, weight, or persistence of the air campaign itself.

Concerns that the war against the Viet Cong was going to be chronically indecisive encouraged the administration to "try something." Maxwell Taylor had thrown up his hands regarding the goal of decimating the insurgency because the Americans and South Vietnamese were never going to be able to put twenty soldiers in the field for every guerrilla, a widely accepted assumption for counterinsurgency. In fact, the South Vietnamese had killed thousands of insurgents, but the VC were still on the verge of conquering the country. This lack of success incentivized pursuing other avenues. Really, administration advisors did not know what to do to satisfy the myriad competing goals it had regarding Southeast Asia. The NSC staffer Chester Cooper recommended a bombing campaign against North Vietnam, but it needed to be restricted to targets below the 19th parallel, lest you use up all your targets and you no longer have air power as leverage against Hanoi. In addition, comprehensive bombing also risked encouraging greater Chinese and Soviet involvement.[69] That running out of targets would cause problems was an odd notion. Concerns that bombing all legitimate targets would probably lead to inconclusive results should have been a red flag regarding Rolling Thunder's potential for success.

In examining the air war in Vietnam, one can reach the vacuous conclusion that air power is indecisive, that it lacked the ability to produce "irreversible consequences." Such a criticism assumes one should expect individual forms of military power alone—land or sea or air—can and should be decisive by themselves without being coordinated with other forms of power, military or otherwise. One should instead ask that since an air campaign against North Vietnam could not be conclusive without the concurrent use of land and sea power—and vice versa—was not the decisive issue the refusal to invade North Vietnam? And from there, was not the decisive element the threat of Chinese intervention? Indeed, concerns over Chinese reactions, worries that had real merit, hung over decision after decision LBJ made. The Chinese had warned, for instance, that an American invasion of North Vietnam would trigger their own counterinvasion.[70] The Johnson administration could not know what level of violence would prompt Chinese intervention, and as George Ball warned in 1966, the administration would not know until it happened. Undersecretary Ball believed escalation was going to inexorably lead to war with China and perhaps even the Soviet Union. Better to give them a wide margin.[71]

Some administration officials preferred more nuanced uses of military force. Dean Rusk considered air strikes a way of communicating to North Vietnam that it could not expect to avoid the consequences of supporting the VC.[72] As Maxwell Taylor wrote from Saigon, the administration believed "a measured, controlled sequence of actions against the DRV . . . can be brought to bear on DRV to persuade it to stop its intervention in SVN."[73] Given Hanoi's requirements for just opening negotiations—the US leaving South Vietnam and the South Vietnamese acceding to the goals of the National Liberation Front, among others—it did not make sense to expect Hanoi to negotiate for settlement terms that conceded more than did its requirements to begin those negotiations. American leaders gravely overestimated Hanoi's openness to a negotiated settlement and planned a strategy that assumed Hanoi would at some point negotiate sincerely and respect South Vietnamese sovereignty—two assumptions that were chimeras.[74]

President Johnson accepted his advisors' counsel to rely on air strikes to achieve his ends, and in doing so, contradictions continued to characterize the policy goals and how the administration sought to achieve them. This campaign was not to be escalatory, but at the same time the United States held open the option of bombing for reasons other than retaliation for Viet Cong military attacks. State Department intelligence analysts cautioned that air strikes were in fact escalatory, citing Special National Intelligence Estimate 10-65 that warned China would in all likelihood employ its air force against American aircraft flying into North Vietnam.[75] Director for Central Intelligence (DCI) John A. McCone believed it unlikely the Chinese would counter with its armed forces, but the US should nevertheless be ready for Chinese countermoves.[76] The Chinese never responded with overt military action against the air campaign, but there were reports from time to time of MiG fighter aircraft bearing China's national insignia over North Vietnam, which meant a fatal clash between American and Chinese pilots was a possibility. In fact, Mao Tse Tung issued an order in April 1965 for his air force to deal aggressively with airspace incursions.[77] The Chinese proved their willingness to shoot down American aircraft that strayed over Hainan Island when two of their MiG-19s shot down an F-104C on September 20, 1965. Captain

Philip E. Smith flew into Chinese airspace after he received poor radar control directions and both of his compasses broke.[78]

Fear of Chinese intervention was the great geopolitical constraint facing the Johnson administration and it is difficult to overemphasize its influence. Because of this concern, Johnson concluded he could not unbridle his air forces against North Vietnamese targets, not to mention sending ground forces into North Vietnam. The president also feared bombing that was not closely monitored from Washington would accidentally lead to some kind of shooting war with China or the Soviet Union. Chinese threats of intervention worried the Johnson administration greatly; they had passed on subtle yet clear warnings about the consequences if air strikes became too aggressive and occurred too far above the 19th parallel.[79] A few months later the Chinese warned, "we are prepared to send our men to fight when Vietnam needs them," and China threatened to get involved on the scale it had during the Korean War if it appeared North Vietnam was about to go down in defeat.[80] China would not enter the war if the United States restricted its military actions against North Vietnam to air attacks, but if the United States "approached China," that was another matter. They sent warnings through third parties that if the US bombed China, China would defend itself.[81] Chinese warnings took any American amphibious operation against the North Vietnamese heartland off the table.[82]

War planners faced a dilemma. Avoiding escalation was necessary, but the belief of more than a few influential leaders, such as Dean Acheson (secretary of state for President Truman), that defeat in South Vietnam would so downgrade American credibility as to "lead to our ruin and *almost certainly to a catastrophic war* [italics in original]" pushed the country toward escalation at the very same time.[83]

Escalation resulting from aerial combat functioned under a different set of possibilities to constrain American actions. During 1965, 2nd Air Division discovered the Chinese air defense sectors north of Vietnam were upgrading their defenses, moving in a fighter regiment and an SA-2 battalion and constructing five additional air bases. Seventh Air Force remained aware of the buildup into 1966, including the movement of five air groups to sectors north of Vietnam. Undersecretary of State George Ball believed these were not defensive preparations but foreshadowed Chinese intervention. He also cited Chinese leaders speaking openly about war with the United States. His case was compelling. Secretary Rusk remained concerned that carelessness with a renewed bombing campaign in early 1966 could encourage China to enter the war. Avoiding that was his reason for maintaining a tight rein over air operations.[84]

Johnson raised his concerns over Chinese intervention once again in June 1966 by drawing a direct comparison between the 1950 Chinese intervention in Korea and the possibility of a recurrence in Vietnam. When General Wheeler suggested mining Haiphong Harbor and added that he did not believe it would lead to Chinese or Soviet countermeasures, the president asked, "Are you more sure than MacArthur was?" Wheeler pointed out a key difference: in 1950 American troops were approaching the Chinese border with Korea; in 1966 there would be no such similarity.[85] Nevertheless, Andrei Gromyko, the Soviet Union's foreign minister, bluffed in fall 1966 to an intermediary to get the word to LBJ that an American escalation would induce not only Chinese intervention, but also a "direct Soviet intervention with troops."[86] Why wouldn't LBJ remain concerned? There were three million Chinese soldiers on Vietnam's northern border, and the turmoil of the Cultural Revolution made China more unpredictable, not more distracted. In 1967, he even worried bombing targets in Haiphong could generate cascading effects like that of the *Maine* or the *Lusitania*. Consistent with this concern, when Johnson permitted the bombing of Cam Pha and Hong Gai in July, he would allow it only when there were no ships in the harbors.[87]

Such concerns formed one of the backdrops to the February 1965 discussions in the White House. While these meetings took place the Viet Cong mortared American forces on the airfield at Pleiku and did the same to some oil storage tanks close to Tuy Hoa on February 7, 1965, killing eight Americans and either damaging or destroying twenty aircraft. This generated a near consensus for reprisals. Accordingly, President Johnson authorized air strikes against four barracks in the North Vietnamese panhandle. Comprised of American and South Vietnamese aircraft, Operation Flaming Dart commenced the same day, but only one mission took off since bad weather had obscured three of the four targets. It did not inflict much in the way of material damage, but it was a step toward escalation.[88] The mission was believed to have accomplished McNamara's primary goal of communicating the administration's resolve, but their tactical effectiveness was poor, destroying or damaging only about 10 percent of the buildings targeted. Another VC attack three days later killed twenty-three Americans and seven South Vietnamese. A large air strike flew the next day.[89]

Johnson's advisors were divided between what to attempt next and what was possible. McNamara, Bundy, and Taylor believed great risks were worth taking if the US could achieve its goals, but George Ball was convinced that only "a crushing defeat" would persuade the North Vietnamese to fundamentally alter their pursuits—a course of action the administration could not consider because of China's threats.[90] The deputy assistant secretary of state for far eastern affairs, Marshall Green, doubted bombing would be persuasive; the more decisive locus was North Vietnam's sponsor China, a political actor who was untouchable.[91] Ambassador Taylor, for one, realized the most important target was the will of North Vietnam's leadership. The Joint Chiefs, who proposed an eight-week campaign, were skeptical it would persuade Hanoi to fundamentally change its ways. They also anticipated the communists using pauses in bombing as opportunities to build up their military capabilities.[92] Given the poor bombing accuracy of the first strikes, the JCS were concerned subsequent missions might struggle to be tactically effective.[93]

President Johnson's policy became one of supporting sociopolitical change in South Vietnam, halting infiltration, and making Hanoi stop its aggression. On February 13, he laid out three interrelated approaches: redoubling the effort to gain control of the countryside and its population, South Vietnamese Air Force bombing of targets in North Vietnam, and making the case in the United Nations that North Vietnam was the assailant as the aegis under which to pursue negotiations.[94] He was not, however, confident the limited methods he approved would achieve these goals: "bombers won't bring 'em to their knees—unless we do something we wouldn't do. We'll be called warmongers—elsewhere and here in the US."[95]

The president decided on February 19 to pursue the bombing campaign. The administration did not want to issue forth a public or a headline-making policy change; but bombing targets in North Vietnam was a public action, generally a loud one, so from the beginning yet another major contradiction existed in the administration's policy implementation: the desire to keep a major bombing campaign quiet.[96] The air strikes of February 27 were once again reprisals for VC attacks. Their objective was to make clear to Hanoi that similar air strikes would follow every Viet Cong attack against American bases. The first Rolling Thunder mission took off on March 2.[97] American policy objectives were not, however, definitively spelled out. John T. McNaughton, the assistant secretary of defense for international affairs, wrote a month later that the primary goal was predominantly avoiding the humiliation of defeat and the consequent blow to America's reputation as a steadfast security partner.[98]

Operation Rolling Thunder was an aerial siege in which the American aircraft destroyed the targets they could find, which the North Vietnamese rebuilt no matter how many re-attacks occurred. These air strikes were also coercive—the use of force to persuade the North Vietnamese to do what the Americans demanded. The bombing would stop, according to President Johnson, when the North Vietnamese stopped infiltrating supplies and soldiers into South Vietnam, brought an end to the military activities of the National Liberation Front, North Vietnamese soldiers returned to the Democratic Republic of Vietnam, members of the Viet Cong participated in South Vietnamese life and governance in a lawful manner, the organizations of the PAVN and VC in South Vietnam were disassembled, and international inspectors confirmed these actions had taken place. Additionally, President Johnson's desire to avoid accusations of being soft on communism tipped the scales in the decision to proceed.[99] Would these bombing raids be sufficient to persuade the communists to give up, for good, their most precious political goals?

While the administration seemingly believed a couple of dozen bombing missions would persuade Hanoi to do just that, the CIA warned against expecting productive negotiations. McGeorge Bundy concluded four days after the beginning of Rolling Thunder that those air strike missions had improved South Vietnamese morale, the extent to which was not known; but the CIA believed it to be substantial.[100] Maxwell Taylor concluded, however, the initial missions were ineffective in terms of the geopolitical purpose: "It appears to me evident that to date DRV leaders believe air strikes at present levels on their territory are meaningless and that we are more susceptible to international pressure for negotiations than are they."[101] The CIA disagreed, concluding the reactions from Hanoi and its allies exceeded their expectations after just a single air raid. Director of Central Intelligence McCone toned down his assessment a few days later, predicting the bombing campaign would not alter North Vietnamese actions until it threatened their industrial base, whereupon he thought they would make insincere offers to negotiate. He believed Rolling Thunder ought to be more aggressive, adding air bases, factories, power stations, and petroleum storage sites to the target list.[102] While scarce, these were not the most vital centers in North Vietnam. Industry comprised only 10 percent of their agricultural economy.[103] Admiral Sharp's command was already asserting that targeting North Vietnam alone was too narrow; the US also needed to escalate its air war in Laos to interdict the supply lines routed through that country.[104] Indeed, he believed that "with [the] proper use of air power we could bring the North Vietnamese to heel." The admiral also believed that there was no need to invade North Vietnam because the air campaign would be sufficient.[105]

Since the White House was the nexus of policy, diplomacy, and military force, the possibility existed for this air war to be managed in a way that would move the United States toward achieving its goals, but the manner in which the president handled military force undercut his own agenda. President Johnson wanted to avoid escalation, but only escalation offered the chance of forcing the North Vietnamese to back down. Johnson varied the strategy he thought would positively influence communist actions: the US would increase air strikes when the VC escalated, and lower sortie rates when the VC greatly reduced their operations over an extended period of time. He seriously undercut his goals by telling the communists that he was ready for discussions without any preconditions.[106] Hanoi responded by stipulating once again that before negotiations could even begin the US had to leave South Vietnam and stop attacking North Vietnam, and that South Vietnam's political affairs meet the requirements and demands of the National Liberation Front.[107]

The White House's offer and Bundy's air strategy signaled to the North Vietnamese that the United States was less than fully committed to winning. Methods such as throttling the bombing to the military activity of the VC meant that the enemy in a sense set the pace for the bombing campaign waged against itself. Another self-imposed restriction was keeping strike aircraft outside of the combat radius of MiG fighters to avoid escalation, but this placed a considerable percentage of North Vietnam off limits.[108] John McCone perceived the contradictions and argued the bombing had to be severe enough to persuade Hanoi it could not endure but had to negotiate. The current target set, however, conveyed that the US was more concerned that the war did not expand than it was with getting its way. McNamara, at least, had the JCS construct a three-month bombing plan, which was presented the last week of March 1965.[109]

Strategic worries and fears put a large brake on the scope of these missions. The United States took several threats off the table, such as terminating the current regime ruling North Vietnam, because LBJ wanted to avoid escalation. Consequently, air strikes were less likely to achieve policy goals because there was a level of damage the US was not going to inflict upon North Vietnam. They were going to be able to perceive this ceiling in the American use of force, which would guide their adaptations to the punishment. In Saigon, threatening South Vietnamese generals that the US would leave if they kept carrying out coups carried no weight. These generals knew such threats were diametrically opposed to demonstrating American determination to support friends against insurgencies.[110] The United States had made itself the hostage of its dysfunctional partner.

Operationally, air strikes were to be carried out predictably: twice a week with 100 aircraft missions against one target for American aircraft and another for South Vietnamese. The strikes were to creep up the panhandle toward the Red River Valley.[111] McNamara believed weekly missions "would make the air campaign sufficiently intense."[112] General Hunter Harris, the commander of Pacific Air Forces at the time, had mixed feelings about the management of the campaign from Washington. On the one hand, he understood that the president was dealing with geopolitical problems, but on the other hand he disliked the micromanaging: "it seemed to me that almost every military decision was based upon a political action," but that was the whole point. Harris noticed that communications technology enabled this kind of remote guidance as if the teletypes were connecting two separate spheres, but in fact political actions and military activities resided on the same spectrum, just at different places.[113]

Massive escalation was not feasible in 1965, so it should not have been presented as a possibility. One operational constraint was aircraft parking space; there was not enough in Southeast Asia because of the unanticipated number of support aircraft that vied for parking spaces with combat aircraft. Therefore, there was not enough room for the number of fighter-bombers necessary for an all-out air campaign against North Vietnam.[114] In order to send, for example, forty-eight F-105s north, those aircraft needed fighter escorts to protect them from MiGs, aircraft with jamming equipment to degrade the surface-to-air missile threat, reconnaissance aircraft for post-attack photography, and plenty of KC-135 tankers so that the F-105s could reach their targets from their bases in Thailand.

The Navy launched its first Rolling Thunder air strikes on March 15. Aircraft carrier aviation had its own space limitations, but it was more flexible in a couple of ways: it was more readily available, and in 1965 the carriers could reduce the distance their aircraft had to fly by moving closer to shore, and they were able to remain on station longer than initially expected. At the same time, longer term sustainment of carrier aviation placed greater demands on maintenance and personnel than the Navy anticipated. The Marines were able to deploy a single A-4 Skyhawk squadron to a temporary base at Chu Lai in September. The Air Force in contrast had to build seven additional bases in Thailand and South Vietnam.[115] Cam Ranh Bay Air Base was not finished until late 1965 and it was too far from North Vietnam to be useful without extensive aerial refueling. Phan Rang took another twelve

F-105Ds refueling from KC-135 (US Air Force)

months to complete. Da Nang opened its second runway in 1966.[116] Altogether a major air campaign against North Vietnam and the Ho Chi Minh Trail through Laos required a major materiel effort: airfields, maintenance, supplies; four wings of F-105s could not just show up in March 1965 and start flying missions.

Tracing the development of American strategy during the first six months of 1965 reveals that American leaders did not understand elementary concepts of coercion, nor of the relationship between military force and the goal of persuading the North Vietnamese to relinquish their policy goals. The president, for example, signaled his willingness to engage in talks without preconditions during an April 7 speech.[117] His proposal signaled weakness, so there was no reason for the North Vietnamese to negotiate. Maxwell Taylor turned force and diplomacy upside down. He actually thought the two main tools the US had for persuading the communists to submit to American demands were terminating Rolling Thunder and removing American troops from South Vietnam. Those were the very conditions Hanoi wanted. An end to the bombing campaign and a troop withdrawal could not function as coercive tools; Taylor was proposing ways the US could generate conditions North Vietnam needed to complete its takeover of South Vietnam. Dramatically escalating the bombing campaign and bringing in more American troops may have convinced the communists to give up their vital interests—maybe not, but relaxing pressure had no coercive value. Taylor at least recognized bombing could not be decisive unless the South Vietnamese started defeating the VC. Assessments like Taylor's demonstrate that a poor understanding of the basics of strategy and statecraft existed at the highest levels of the United States government. If individuals like the ambassador to South Vietnam had a deficient comprehension of the most elementary relationships between military action, vital interests, coercion, and such, then all that followed could only offer the United States time to recognize its mistakes and implement a new strategy that might work. The JCS chairman, General Wheeler, at least had the sense in April to admit that two months of bombing had not inflicted major damage on Hanoi's military capabilities, nor persuaded Hanoi to give up its goals.[118]

The administration, it must be noted, did not expect Rolling Thunder to be decisive immediately. On the contrary, it expected results would make themselves evident after six to twelve months, perhaps longer. Johnson and his advisors also expected worthwhile consequences even when not striking the most important targets: those in Hanoi and Haiphong. Taylor believed it wise to preserve those areas as "hostages," flawed logic because it disincentivized the Johnson administration from using full force, which again signaled a reluctance to act. It also assumed that the North Vietnamese recognized certain valuable targets were being held as hostages. At least some of Johnson's advisors recognized bombing needed to continue during negotiations. Others within the Air Force expected a long war early on because in May, it directed for aircraft to be painted in a camouflage scheme suitable for Southeast Asia.[119]

Bundy's recommendations remained flawed and trumped the strategic effectiveness air power could have exerted. He believed reducing the bombing would provide a more favorable environment for negotiations, when such an action actually signaled a lack of resolve and reduced incentives for the enemy to make concessions. His goal was "to get the war to the Conference table." He wished to persuade North Vietnam to give up vital interests by using a minimum of force and a maximum of nuance. He also believed, "By slowing down the bombing you are allowing them to talk without looking as if they are being bombed into submission." Bundy assumed that was possible, but in fact the North Vietnamese were not going to give up vital political goals unless they had been bombed past a point that they could stand. Given all that, there was no reason for Hanoi to give their enemies anything.[120]

The CIA, on the other hand, understood the nature of the problem and the director laid it out for the president: bombing had to hurt enough to convince the North Vietnamese to negotiate and make concessions to make the bombing stop. Bombing targets like bridges and barracks signaled that preventing escalation was a greater concern than achieving the administration's agenda.[121] Military power could not compensate for flawed inverted assumptions about the relationships between goals, force, and diplomacy. At the same time, insightful understanding of the geopolitical context, political goals, military operations, and diplomacy would not alleviate the necessity for force; it would have instead clarified the amount of force necessary.

The air campaign's goal was also to interdict the movement of supplies into South Vietnam to make it more difficult for Hanoi to support its war there, and for that reason the air strikes went after standard interdiction targets: bridges, railroad cars, transportation vehicles, warehouses, and fuel storage. Indeed, bridges were a major target of Navy strikes at the beginning of the escalation, and these missions were quite effective tactically. The JCS considered an attack effective when it caused enough damage to neutralize or render the object inoperable. Navy aircraft put spans of seven bridges into the water during April 1965 alone.[122] One could argue these kinds of missions would become strategically effective if Hanoi began to reconsider its overall agenda. As General Hunter Harris Jr. reiterated after a year and a half of indeterminate results: the "proper purpose of Rolling Thunder . . . is to punish enemy so that he will lose will to continue support of war in south."[123]

The services partitioned North Vietnamese airspace into seven sectors so that when one service was bombing in one segment, the other service was conducting flight operations in another. The "Route Package" system of dividing North Vietnamese airspace into zones for Navy operations and zones for Air Force operations had deconfliction rather than coordination or joint warfare as the goal. Preventing naval air operations from being subsumed into a joint operation was an additional reason Admiral Sharp, Rear Admiral James R. Reedy, and Major General Joseph H. Moore decided to make this partition. As the map shows, the

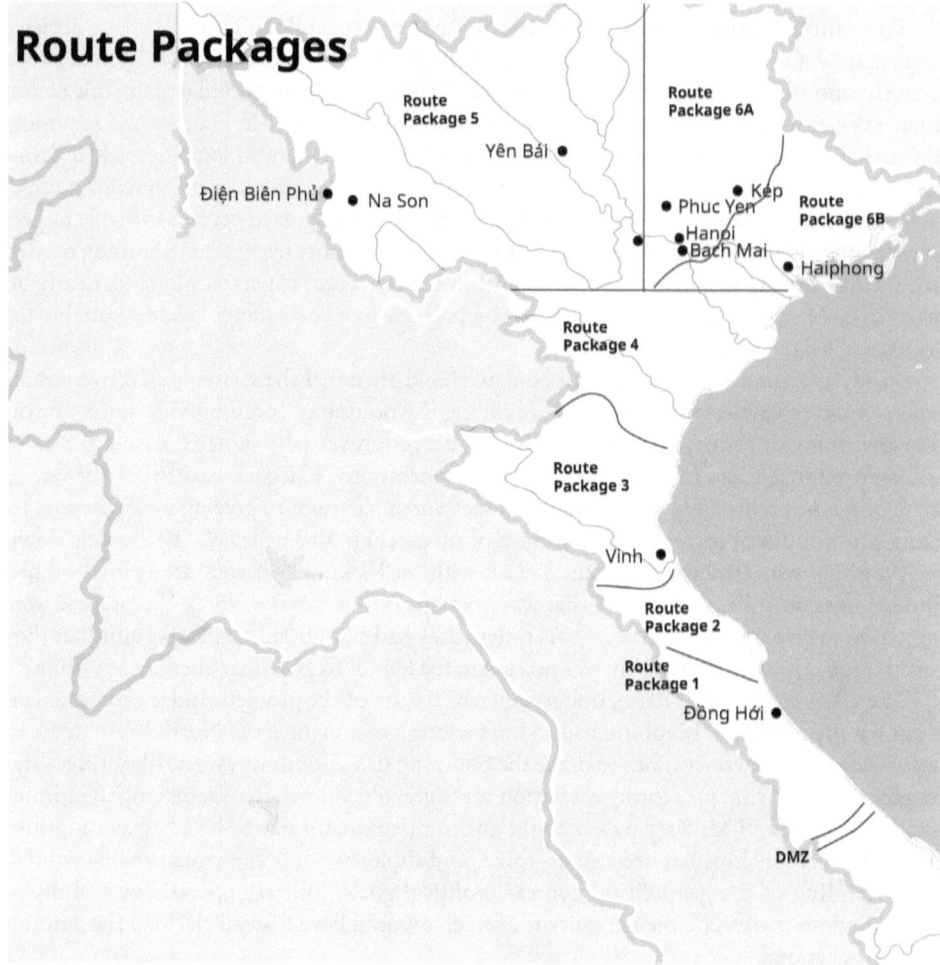

Navy set aside coastal targets closer to its aircraft carriers in Route Packages 1, 2, 3, 4, 6B, and received a larger area for its air strikes. Route Packages 5 and 6A went to the Air Force. Although these were closer to bases in Thailand, 6A in particular contained some of the most dangerous targets. Flying missions in another service's sector required coordination.[124]

These generals were not asking permission to bomb indiscriminately. They wanted to wage the war more efficiently because doing so would have at least nudged the air campaign toward greater effectiveness. Admiral Sharp was convinced restrictions on air power stood in the way of its most efficient use.[125] Sharp, in fact, hated the restrictions, blamed the restrictions for the defeat, was absolutely certain an unrestricted air campaign would have won the war, and categorically rejected the concept of restraint in warfare. Writing in 1978, he cited wartime documents that produced a persistent thesis. Indiscriminately killing civilians was out of bounds, but other than that, an air campaign had to be unrestrained to reach its maximum political effectiveness: "Once the decision is made to use military power to settle a political issue, that power should be used to its full effectiveness to get the war over with as quickly as possible. All other considerations should be secondary. *That* is the way to reduce *civilian and military* casualties [italics in original]."[126] His argument suggested political, military, and diplomatic actions occupy separate segments on a continuum of action when in actuality the three components mutually support and reinforce one another like the three cords in a rope. Sharp's perspective also assumed aerial bombardment could have been waged to a degree that even the political leaders in Hanoi could not have endured, and that other considerations were secondary.[127]

Pitting Sharp's insistence against the political goals of North Vietnam's leaders illustrates how misguiding the term "limited war" is for describing this war. The Americans employed limited means for limited ends, but Hanoi's goals were total: conquest of South Vietnam, or from their perspective, reestablishing proper governance for Vietnam. Moreover, the leaders of the Lao Dong Party were willing to pay a generational cost in terms of the damage to their infrastructure and deaths of their people. The United States was waging a war in a context of a threat of escalation that it badly wished to avoid. A total war in Indochina made no sense in terms of American policy goals nor in terms of the magnitude of military force necessary. So in one sense, the United States' choice was reasonable and rational. Where things went off the rails was miscalculating the difficulties present in limited wars in the presence of these constraints. Vietnam was not a limited war in the classic sense of eighteenth-century limited war in Europe. The label "small war" is even less helpful.[128] Words matter. Small war, limited war, war of containment—all these labels inadvertently deceived the Americans into perceiving of this war as easier and more manageable than it was ever going to be. Vietnam was a big, irregular, hybrid, major war fought by more than a million soldiers that involved a significant portion of Asia and concerned political actors from Tokyo to Canberra to Berlin, Moscow, Washington, and Peking.

While these issues remained in a state of flux, Sharp, Wheeler, Westmoreland, McNamara, McNaughton, and William Bundy held a meeting on April 20 and then told the president they agreed the pace of the air war was pretty much on target.[129] Opinions, however, would change. Two years later the JCS would argue, "From a military point of view, the most effective application of military force would have resulted from a sudden sharp blow followed by a full-scale air campaign against all of the targets."[130]

Pentagon planners initially rejected 138 of 140 targets that later were added after the first JCS target list because they were not going to support President Johnson's objectives.[131] Major General Moore understood, "air operations in SEA should support U.S. political objectives," but he protested interference in day-to-day operations by civilian politicians. He also misunderstood the relationship between combat action and the achievement of policy, assuming target destruction invariably supported national policy. His solution was to turn the war over to the military by removing civilians in the region from the "military chain of command" and "provide air commander in SEA broad military objectives and relative priorities instead of dictating specific targets, timing, force composition, and selection of weapons." Moore believed the "Air commander should have authority and information at his disposal to determine degree of destruction desired of each target using entire spectrum from harassment to total destruction, and be authorized to employ most effective weapons associated with nature and degree of destruction desired."[132] The former was something only a policy maker could decide because a policy maker could relate levels of destruction to policy goals better than a general concerned with day-to-day military operations. While military officers knew more about munitions than civilian leaders, the president's consultation was still merited because bomb types and levels of destruction affected the achievement of national objectives. Consultation, not demarcation, ought to have characterized this relationship. Because of the nature of war itself, there were legitimate reasons for political interference in military operations; it just needed to be competent interference.

Addressing these issues further had to wait because President Johnson ordered a bombing halt to begin May 13 in alignment with the birthday of Buddha. He wished to score points with world opinion and also to see how Hanoi reacted. Ho Chi Minh called it nothing more than a deceitful trick and refused to accept a letter from Dean Rusk.[133] Johnson was trying to demonstrate to those with dovish inclinations such as Abe Rosenthal and Ochs Sulzberger of *The New York Times* and Senator Mike Mansfield (D-Montana) that he was willing to try something different, but he complained six days into the pause that in response to this goodwill gesture, the Viet Cong had attacked and destroyed American aircraft at Bien Hoa Air Base. Their lack of appreciation for his magnanimity astonished the president, and McNamara commented that Hanoi's actions should have made its mendacity clear to Senator Mansfield.[134] The halt was short; Navy assets returned to bomb stored fuel at Phu Quy and the Phuc Loi Naval Base on May 19 and 20.[135]

American military leaders recognized the air campaign was not persuading Hanoi to alter its goals; the DRV was adjusting to the bombing. Admiral Sharp observed just before its suspension that Rolling Thunder had forced the North Vietnamese to change how they transported supplies to Laos. He did not, however, offer much concerning the larger effects of the air campaign, but noted that there were still plenty of targets left south of twenty degrees latitude. Sharp was comfortable with the number of aircraft he had for flying an unrelenting series of bombing missions and wished to continue to send a constant stream against military targets. General Wheeler added that the bombing forced the North Vietnamese to divert people and attention normally devoted to their civilian economy to instead defend their airspace and repair bomb damage. So the air campaign reduced North Vietnamese efficiency, but it had not diminished its military capability. Furthermore, their political leaders had not budged.[136]

A massive influx of soldiers and Marines was another available military option. Clark Clifford, Harry Truman's special counsel during his administration and someone Johnson relied on for advice, warned against sending a lot of ground troops to Southeast Asia, and cautioned it could evolve into a never-ending commitment "without a realistic hope of ultimate victory."[137] And there were limits to what military force could accomplish. The CIA believed events in South Vietnam would decide the war. Only a strong regime in Saigon and plenty of punishment of North Vietnam could produce a favorable outcome. The agency rejected escalation, forecasting a lot of dead Americans and a settlement too fragile for the South Vietnamese to sustain.[138] Ambassador Taylor held no confidence that bombing could force Hanoi to give up its goals. Rather, the Saigon government had to defeat the insurgency at the same time for bombing to generate decisive effects, something that appeared unlikely because the same day Taylor and Deputy Ambassador U. Alexis Johnson wrote their analysis, opponents of Phan Huy Quat, the South Vietnamese premier, attempted a coup against him. All this reminds us of something Gregory Daddis pointed out: military force by itself could not produce a functional political culture in South Vietnam.[139]

This Was Supposed to Have Been Quick and Easy

President Johnson's men thought bringing North Vietnam to heel would be easy and quick. They really did not believe Ho Chi Minh and Le Duan were as pertinacious regarding their national objectives as their public pronouncements claimed. Hanoi's intransigence surprised them, but overall, the Johnson administration believed the solution would ultimately be a simple one, whether it was bombing more comprehensively, or offering a better deal, or displaying sincerity of purpose, or negotiating more skillfully.

Beginning June 1, Dean Rusk initiated a discussion with Maxwell Taylor about the role of Rolling Thunder. Should it be emphasized as a war winner, or should it take second place to the war in South Vietnam? Taylor rejected the dichotomy, arguing the air campaign and the war against the Viet Cong were both necessary and mutually supporting. Bombing North Vietnam, even at a greatly escalated pace, would not persuade that regime to quit; the air campaign had to be coupled with progress in South Vietnam against the VC. Taylor warned against expecting to win quickly. He added that operationally, flying more missions comprised of fewer jets each seemed to result in a lower loss rate. He still recommended avoiding Hanoi and Haiphong out of fear of how the Chinese might respond.[140] It would seem the principals were not communicating well because McGeorge Bundy wrote a couple of weeks later that President Johnson rejected escalating the bombing because he did not believe that kind of coercion would produce negotiations. The administration was still trying to figure out what it wanted to accomplish, what lay in the realm of possibility, and what the risks were.

H. R. McMaster observed that the military chiefs emphasized interdicting materiel and decisively eroding the will of Hanoi to interfere in South Vietnam, while civilian leaders were more concerned about avoiding escalation, civilian casualties, and opprobrium at home and among other countries.[141] It is hard to envision air power being effective enough to undermine the enemy's strategy when it is pulled in opposite directions like that. Westmoreland was convinced the war was going to be long, while George Ball was convinced the war was unwinnable and believed widening the bombing effort would do nothing more than risk a more serious confrontation with the Soviet Union and China.[142] He believed aiding South Vietnam was the equivalent of giving radiation therapy to a cancer patient who was going to die anyway, but Johnson had already decided to move forward with escalation.[143]

Sharp understood that American and South Vietnamese forces had to defeat both the insurgents and the North Vietnamese regulars. A June 1965 message spoke in standard counterinsurgency doctrinal language: it discussed providing security for peasants, of defeating the VC where the people lived in the countryside, and of defeating soldiers that were coming from North Vietnam. To South Vietnamese commanders, however, the situation was so dire that issues of immediate survival took precedence over long-term strategy. Saigon needed American troops just to continue to exist. Westmoreland believed success in South Vietnam required not only an initial 175,000 American troops to keep it from collapse, but also much greater numbers, a prospect that rocked McNamara like no other.[144]

Meanwhile American air assets continued to hit army barracks, power stations, bridges, and such. Analysts at PACAF measured the immediate effects of these missions and provided long lists of the physical consequences. On a June 26, 1965, mission against the Qui Hau Ammo Depot West, for instance, Navy aircraft destroyed a building, severely damaged four more, inflicted moderate damage to five, barely touched seven, and left six unscathed. Assessing tactical effects was difficult; aircrews tended to overestimate the amount of destruction they witnessed.[145] This difficulty in comprehending what kinds of effects the bombing was having suggests that at best, damage bad enough to persuade Hanoi to accede was accumulating very slowly, or that the bombing campaign was simply inadequate by itself. The Navy's observation about the growing difficulty of finding significant targets illustrated a weakness of an attrition strategy: the better one is tactically, the sooner one runs out of targets, so capitulation must occur before that threshold. PACAF noticed the air strikes' effects were spread out in terms of time and geographic coverage, which allowed the destruction to remain at a level the enemy could tolerate.[146]

General Wheeler started to see cracks in assumptions about the air campaign by mid-summer. A study completed at his behest concluded the campaign could dramatically reduce North Vietnam's ability to support the insurgency, but a CIA estimate argued that although strikes against supply lines coming out of China hurt the enemy economy greatly, air interdiction was not going to push Hanoi to accede to American demands. Neither was it comprehensive enough to decisively harm the enemy's war in South Vietnam. Wheeler observed that the air strikes destroyed facilities it took the North Vietnamese years to build, but this destruction was not having much of an effect on North Vietnam's economy.[147] Days after Wheeler's note, McNamara recommended escalating from 2,500 sorties per month to 4,000. The administration also sought more armed reconnaissance missions to achieve some decisive effects and permitted air strikes against a highway bridge between China and North Vietnam.[148]

President Johnson's primary concern remained avoiding escalation instead of forcing the North Vietnamese to capitulate.[149] Consequently, the most valuable targets and the ones residing within Hanoi and Haiphong were hit the least; most of the bombing effort in 1965 went against less vital targets in outlying areas such as the panhandle. By July 22, ninety-one of 117 targets the JCS wanted to bomb south of twenty degrees latitude had been bombed, but only eighteen of the 132 targets north of twenty degrees had come under attack. By September 30 the trend continued with only twenty-five of 125 targets north of twenty degrees struck. As a result, the North Vietnamese found it easier to endure a campaign that produced fewer reasons to negotiate. North Vietnam also gained victim status, which proved to be a particularly powerful instrument in gaining international support. It was therefore not surprising that by July, Hanoi was settling in for a long war and gave no indication the bombing was close to forcing it to change its national objectives.[150] Visitors from African countries passed along their conclusion that Hanoi had "no intention of negotiating and is convinced that it is winning."[151] Given that level of determination, McNamara's goal of signaling a "credible threat of *future* destruction" was too nuanced to be compelling (italics in original).[152]

By August, air strikes had severely damaged most of the JCS list of 111 targets. CINCPAC found assessing the results of the air strikes challenging and criticized the limited nature of the program. Sharp added that, "all indications point to a major disruption of normal activity." His preference was to expand the strikes into the Hanoi and Haiphong areas, but if not, he was confident that more armed reconnaissance effort would bear fruit. He believed the bombing would make the war progressively more difficult for the North Vietnamese, and concluded, "We are on the threshold of realizing the full impact of a cumulative effect," but cautioned, "It is a campaign of pressure. Immediate and spectacular effects were not intended."[153]

When CINCPAC evaluated the progress of Rolling Thunder in August 1965, it did so in terms of comparing the effects it had generated with the goals of the campaign. The air campaign was designed to drive up the costs and the effort the North Vietnamese had to exert to support the war in South Vietnam. So, in a sense the North Vietnamese determined Rolling Thunder's effectiveness; the more they could take, the less effective the air campaign. Signaling that America's endurance was greater than Hanoi's was an additional purpose, along with casting doubt on their ability to continue to support the VC, make the possibility of defeat a point of discussion among the leadership, encourage defeatism among communist troops, worry their civilians, and ultimately create "an evergrowing management problem" that would draw attention away from combat operations in South Vietnam. Pacific Command's strategy for doing so was to bomb targets in the southern part of North Vietnam, drive air strikes toward the northwest part of the country, then shift operations to the northeastern section where Hanoi and Haiphong lay—somewhat akin to placing artillery closer and closer to a fort during a siege. At the same time, it remained an air interdiction campaign, particularly against routes from North Vietnam into Laos.[154] Analysts were pleased when bombs cut rail lines, stranding large numbers of rolling stock, and making them easy for follow-on bombings. Keeping railroad lines cut, however, was not as easy. Besides, North Vietnam's allies could replace these losses, rendering railroad cars an indecisive target set. If this air campaign was going to work, the president concluded, it would take quite some time.[155]

Assessments pointed to a North Vietnam hurt but not broken. Pacific Command concluded that by August 1965, the air campaign had inflicted considerable damage to most of North Vietnam's important military sites. They responded by dispersing materiel, generating many more targets to be found. Re-attacks against them were necessary to make sure they were not repaired. This interplay of move-countermove caused the campaign to evolve beyond set-piece bombing missions to a combination of surveillance and armed reconnaissance, which became a more frequent method for finding and destroying targets. In theory, these bombing missions would generate progressively greater effects, but this assessment hedged that generating really significant damage via armed reconnaissance was going to take time. Interdiction required cumulative destruction maintained over time, persistent enough to prevent reconstruction teams from overcoming the damage so that the bombing really would keep a road or railroad shut down. In terms of targets, it would be open season on all the usual kinds: roads, bridges, ferries, railroads, and military materiel along the way.[156]

Sharp's office recognized the difficulties: there was no single target whose destruction would generate cascading effects: "No one point of cratering or no one bridge destruction is likely to achieve any measurable degree of interdiction." Determining its effectiveness would be a challenge. Some actual effects and real changes in what the North Vietnamese were doing were there to be seen: truck traffic along targeted routes was way down and expected enemy offensives did not take place—probably because of the interdiction effort.[157] Armed reconnaissance was not that efficient, because one had to find a target before destroying it. A Navy study of these kinds of missions covering July 23–November 18, 1965, found them almost fruitless and repetitive: more than 2,500 nighttime sorties resulted in attacks on approximately 325 vehicles, while only 100 truck sightings occurred during 2,900 daytime sorties.[158]

A concurrent assessment observed that after about six months Operation Rolling Thunder had not significantly reduced North Vietnamese support for the Viet Cong, and security conditions in South Vietnam had not improved. In September data indicated isolated food shortages in North Vietnam and Laos, consequences that were not sufficiently dire to force an authoritarian regime to capitulate.[159] A CIA assessment agreed. The air strikes hurt North Vietnam's economy, transportation infrastructure, and food distribution, but Hanoi's posture remained unchanged. For instance, in addition to dispersing supplies, North Vietnam still sent troops south.[160] The Defense Intelligence Agency argued in October that the bombing was not reducing Hanoi's resolve.[161] Perhaps for that reason Pacific Command admitted that nothing decisive had been accomplished, but that: "We have created a base of destruction upon which we can capitalize during the next six months."[162]

Rolling Thunder was not an unlimited, massive air campaign. It was instead constrained and intermittent due to choices in Washington, DC, but also by monsoon weather. Consequently, the North Vietnamese had opportunities to rebuild and adjust that arrived with the predictability of the changing seasons. Weather was always a major determinant in the conduct of the air war and made the air campaigns less effective. Fighter-bomber dive bombing tactics required cloud bases no lower than 12,000 feet so pilots could find the target, attain a forty-five-degree dive angle, and have enough altitude to aim and then pull out of the dive before flying into flak. The jets had to release their bombs above 4,500 feet to avoid AAA, but that altitude hurt accuracy.[163]

Air leaders recognized bad weather as a major operational impediment from the very beginning. Half the time there were clouds down at 3,500 feet which obscured aim points. Worse, the weather usually did not improve until mid-afternoon, which meant the North Vietnamese knew when to be ready for American air strikes. Weather determined how many aircraft took off; missions diverted or got cancelled due to bad weather over the target.[164] Seventh Air Force scheduled more than 2,300 sorties against targets in Route Packages 5 and 6A from March through June 1966 but launched only 541. During one period, bad weather forced the cancellation of two-thirds of Navy air strikes.[165] Direct relationships between weather and sortie rates continued throughout the war, increasing over Laos, for example, as the weather improved from July to August 1972.[166]

Fortunately, in a seasonal sense weather was predictable. The weather was favorable over North Vietnam from May to October, and good over Laos from November to April, but airmen did not adequately convey this relationship to civilian leaders.[167] Late in the war President Nixon was beside himself over reports that the Air Force could not carry out a maximum effort against targets north of the DMZ at the beginning of April 1972. This problem was never solved, but weather affected the Air Force less than the Navy, because the Air Force could send missions against a wider range of targets geographically than could carrier aviation, so the Air Force had more opportunities to find a target that was not socked in.[168] Long stretches of bad weather meant that the campaign had to take place when weather permitted, which meant the bombing campaign could not be intensive. It would have done no good for President Johnson to permit an unrestricted bombing campaign only to see most of the missions cancelled due to bad weather for weeks on end.

Striking a wider variety of targets was an ongoing proposal for achieving greater strategic effects. General Hunter Harris was convinced air strikes could obliterate North Vietnamese gasoline, diesel, and jet fuel supplies with just 150 sorties, and those targets had been proposed on every target list up to October 1965. Furthermore, their locations were only at the edges of cities so noncombatants would not be placed under undue risk—a priority for air operations throughout Indochina. The target sets PACAF wanted to subject to comprehensive destruction—petroleum products, electricity, railroad equipment, airports, bridges and ferries, army buildings, radars and radios, navy facilities and boats, industry, and ports—were not inconsequential targets. Although an October 1965 PACAF assessment argued air strikes were very damaging because, for instance, the North Vietnamese had to make greater use of boat transportation, this example proved as much a sign of determination and adaptability as anything.[169] In fact, the center of gravity in this instance was the willingness of the North Vietnamese to endure sustained punishment, but breaking the will of the North Vietnamese people was not one of the goals of Rolling Thunder. A Polish journalist wrote that life went on almost as normal in Hanoi—an indicator that residents knew they were not targets. Hanoi's factories were working three shifts, shops were open in the evenings, and people were out and about—except when American air strikes took place. As a precaution, residents sought shelter between 11 a.m. and 3 p.m., emptying the streets.[170]

Analysts concluded the North Vietnamese were uncertain whether they could win militarily in South Vietnam, but they were confident that the political battle was theirs.[171] Here the analysis should have proceeded a step further. The whole point of war is "the political battle," so could the bombing decisively affect the political battle? The analyses of the war usually remained at the operational and tactical level and too infrequently did they examine their relationships to the achievement of political goals. That was a key omission in the application of air power in the Vietnam War: the absence of a systematic critical questioning as to whether the bombs destroying targets were or could decisively contribute to policy goals. There seemed to be an assumption that if only the airmen could bomb everything on the target list, North Vietnam's capitulation was inevitable.

An end-of-year summary noted only limited materiel damage on the country's infrastructure. The bombing had made the movement of military supplies more difficult, and hurt the economy, but analysts at Pacific Air Forces did not see with certainty any other favorable consequence of the bombing campaign.[172] Rolling Thunder also had not persuaded Hanoi to stop sending supplies down the Ho Chi Minh Trail; Ambassador Taylor reminded the president that no one had ever claimed air interdiction could prevent all supplies and PAVN soldiers from reaching South Vietnam.[173] Indonesia's military attaché to Hanoi, a Colonel Nurmanthias, concurred, stating that he did not see the slightest evidence that the North Vietnamese were anywhere close to giving in. Moreover, planning and stockpiling seemed to have preceded their ingenuity and rebuilding. He expected them "to fight to the end."[174]

Against this kind of intransigence, the United States considered Operation Rolling Thunder the centerpiece of a coercive strategy: "Air power has been the principle military tool used to dissuade the DRV from pursuing their political/military objectives." Pacific Air Forces analysts suspected the campaign had been unpersuasive because nearly half of North Vietnam's population and most of its urban dwellers resided in areas that were virtually free from US bombing.[175] They also warned that one could mistakenly conclude that because the United States had expended a great deal in terms of bombs dropped, aircraft shot down, and money spent, the targets destroyed were therefore of great value, but the analysis noticed that there was not a direct relationship between the effort put into destroying a target and its value, and that it was difficult to actually determine how the bombing had altered North Vietnamese strategic considerations. Indeed, by the end of 1965 North Vietnam was stronger than it had been a year prior because of the aid from the Soviet Union and China.[176]

The Johnson administration tried to blend force and diplomacy via bombing halts, but did so clumsily and based on flawed assumptions, believing the North Vietnamese would respond to suspensions of Rolling Thunder missions with gratitude and frank negotiations. McNamara promised the North Vietnamese would not exploit the bombing halt; how he arrived at that conclusion is unclear. During the December 23, 1965, to January 20, 1966, bombing pause, the North Vietnamese rebuilt bridges, patched roads, and moved supplies in large truck convoys in broad daylight.[177]

Much of the reasoning within the administration was incompetent. William Bundy believed a halt might exacerbate rifts between the North Vietnamese, Chinese, and the NLF. He also argued against threatening an expanded bombing campaign if Hanoi refused to negotiate; a softer touch, he believed, was more likely to encourage the Hanoi government to accede to American wishes. The May 1965 pause had been too short according to Bundy; a longer one, he argued, would have been more persuasive. He also argued that the administration ought to emphasize diplomacy in and of itself; he did not understand that separating force from diplomacy weakened the effectiveness of both. There was instead the belief that convincing skeptics and world opinion that the American desire for negotiating to be sincere and earnest was of more decisive importance than the opinions and actions of the North Vietnamese.[178] Perhaps the Soviet Union perceived this naivety. Its ambassador to the US, Anatoly Dobrynin, told the administration on December 18 that in return for a bombing halt, "the Soviets would attempt to persuade Hanoi to negotiate a settlement," an offer irresistible to LBJ. The ambassador never promised to compel them to reach a permanent resolution, which is what Johnson needed.[179] William Bundy failed to notice the contradiction between his hope that Hanoi would respond positively to the bombing pause and his expectation that they might condemn the bombing pause.[180]

What baffles many is that administration officials thought a country that refused to negotiate while being bombed would suddenly do so when the pain of bombing was removed. As a whole, the administration failed to understand that for Hanoi, South Vietnam's future was never negotiable. As far as the communists were concerned, South Vietnam was going to be merged into North Vietnam. Perhaps LBJ and his cabinet hesitated to admit that fact because of the implications of such a conclusion: if it were true, then President Johnson's limited methods could never work, so his administration would have been left with the options of defeat or an invasion of North Vietnam, neither of which he found palatable.[181] There was a shortage of understanding all around, one must add. Senator Sam Ervin, according to McNamara's December 9 memo, believed, "We ought to bomb North Vietnam out of existence because they are initiating the aggression. We can't afford to retreat further in the world."[182]

Admiral Sharp warned during the bombing halt that "extending the stand-down would weaken the U.S. negotiating position by removing the only pressure on Hanoi to come to terms."[183] The JCS also wondered whether the halt was helping or hurting diplomatic efforts.[184] McNamara examined the opposite of a bombing pause as 1965 waned: the JCS's desired escalation. The "sharp blow" operation it proposed would target airfields, transportation routes, energy supplies, and missile and flak sites. Even though armed reconnaissance would have continued to prevent rebuilding, this wave of attacks would last only a few days.[185] A renewed air campaign and more troops would follow. If it failed, however, then what? The United States would have made a visible use of military power, and unless the action persuaded the North Vietnamese to cave, the communists would have been given a huge victory of enduring the blows of a superpower. U. Alexis Johnson realized, "Bombing is our only bargaining counter," and the administration dare not fritter it away for something as inconclusive as negotiations that were only renewed. He realized that if an escalated campaign did not culminate in a North Vietnamese capitulation, the American war effort would be faced with a situation where it could either escalate further or capitulate itself.[186] General Victor Krulak advised McNamara that what the Americans and South Vietnamese needed most was perseverance; the North Vietnamese, he believed, were certain the United States did not have the resolve to see the war through. The United States had to support a policy of such indefatigability that it would convince Hanoi that their only hope of ridding themselves of the Americans was achieving either a complete and utter battlefield defeat of the US or vacating South Vietnam themselves.[187]

Sure enough, soon after the December 1965 bombing pause began, some in South Vietnam believed the halt signaled wavering American resolve. But 70 percent of the American people welcomed a bombing pause. President Johnson believed the pause showed the American people and the world he was willing to make every effort to provide negotiations the opportunity to produce peace.[188] He believed before he could ask the country to support a military escalation, he had to demonstrate his commitment to peace via making concessions. The president thought he needed to attempt a bombing pause to show he was willing to try such a stratagem, and if Rolling Thunder resumed the president could say, "We tried. The North Vietnamese would not talk. The resumption of bombing is a result of their intransigence, not impatience on our part."[189] The bombing pause began on December 23, 1965.[190]

The tone of the papers and discussions leading up to the decision to suspend bombing was one of doubt. Clark Clifford may have understood the reality with more clarity than anyone. The North Vietnamese believed they were winning, and they were not going to negotiate unless they believed that they were close to losing the war. As the administration mulled over its next course of action, it did so without a clear understanding of its opponent. U. Alexis Johnson admitted the United States understood neither the intentions nor the capabilities of their opponents—an abject failure in making war if there ever was one.[191]

While the Americans tended to separate the conduct of war and diplomatic efforts, the North Vietnamese realized that battlefield events determined what took place between diplomats. General Nguyen Van Vinh reminded NLF comrades that negotiations and fighting took place concurrently.[192] Later in January 1967, the Lao Dong Party Central Committee reaffirmed, "one could only win at the conference table what one had already won on the battlefield."[193] Westmoreland perceived this interrelationship but dimly. He believed a bombing halt was a bad idea because the air campaign was having trouble enough interdicting the communist supply chain. McNamara's assessments contradicted each other. On the one hand he insisted air strikes could destroy North Vietnamese bridges as they were repaired, so the North Vietnamese would not be able to exploit the bombing halt to move materiel into South Vietnam. In the very next breath he claimed that bombing had not reduced the number of soldiers reaching South Vietnam. Not surprisingly, McNamara began to doubt whether or not the war could be won.[194]

Initial Bombing Effectiveness against the Ho Chi Minh Trail

The aerial interdiction campaign included not only missions against targets in North Vietnam, but also thousands of missions against the Ho Chi Minh Trail through Laos. *Trail* is a terribly misleading label given the upgrades, bulldozing, and asphalt paving that took place to build and expand that network of supply roads. Trail conjured images of a narrow path through a jungle, not a road network that evolved into paved highways for trucks driving underneath a canopy of trees and camouflage netting. Early photographs of porters with backpacks trudging down what then resembled something no wider than a logging footpath burned this image into the memory of the war, and along with it, the meme of the dedicated impoverished revolutionary heartily and cheerfully using human muscle to overcome the machine warfare of the United States. By 1968 not only was the so-called trail a road network for trucks, but workers also used bulldozers and other forms of heavy machinery to maintain it. Thousands of miles of primary and secondary routes eventually comprised its length.[195]

Contemporary analysts described it accurately, as when a reconnaissance specialist referred to it as a "road network," the CIA wrote of it as a "road network" that "trucks" used because that is what it was, but their wording never replaced the evocative name of "trail."[196] Ambassador William Sullivan discovered its nature early on in 1965 when General Thao Ma took him to a section of the road network to prove the point: "Both Air Attaché and I," wrote the ambassador, "despite our several years' experience in this part of the world, were astounded by what we found. The 'trail,' even in this rainy season, was a thoroughly passable road. We drove two jeeps over it for more than a mile. It would have easily accommodated 4x4 trucks. Yet nowhere on this road, except for two very limited areas, was it open to the sky. Even flying over it slowly with a helicopter, [the] road was not discernible from above."[197] The occasional aerial photograph of bulldozers further betrayed the conventional nature of the road network. The myth that it remained "a dirt road" persists.[198]

Interdicting the Ho Chi Minh Trail was interminably difficult, and in April 1965 CINCPAC recognized opportunities and challenges would come with such an air campaign. Bad weather, cover provided by jungle canopy, enemy movement at night, roads one could easily repair, and the fact that the root sources of the supply line lay in two countries that could not be touched, combined to make effective air interdiction a serious challenge. The command concluded daylight strikes against concentrated fixed targets would be the most effective method, not only because that would destroy the most materiel, but also because bombing vehicles and porters on the move required finding them at night. Its night bombing effort was a difficult but necessary pursuit, because that was when the bulk of transportation movements took place. Because the North Vietnamese shifted so much of their logistical movements to the hours after sunset the capability to find and bomb targets at night became essential. Obtaining the appropriate airframe for night interdiction became a central consideration, and CINCPAC believed it had the aircraft, munitions, and know-how to wage an effective air interdiction campaign against supply routes. The imminent arrival of the Navy's A-6A Intruder (July 3, 1965) promised a resource to wage night interdiction more effectively. The A-6A was an aircraft carrier-based bomber whose systems enabled the aircrew to find and bomb individual targets darkness hid. The kinds of munitions proposed, however—fuses with delayed timers, steel tetrahedrons for puncturing truck tires, land mines, in addition to ordinary bombs—all pointed to the attritional and siege-like nature that would characterize this campaign for the next seven years.[199]

Siege warfare is a helpful concept and perspective for examining this air campaign. The target, like a castle or a city, did not move. Firepower, not infantry, pounded it. North Vietnam resembled a seaport enduring a landward siege; outside suppliers sustained it. Siege warfare and the air campaign against North Vietnam tested the endurance of both parties. The concept better conveys the strength of the Hanoi regime than words like "insurgency," "guerrilla," and "revolutionary." Enduring a siege was costly to noncombatants. Like a commander in medieval times, the North Vietnamese made victory so costly that the besiegers could not pay the price.[200] Just as armies carried out sieges to persuade the besieged to capitulate to demands, one purpose of the air campaign was, along with interdicting supply routes, to persuade the North Vietnamese to give up their war of conquest against South Vietnam.[201] True to form, the new commander of Seventh/Thirteenth Air Force in 1970, Major General J. Evans Jr., came from an ordnance assignment, and one of his goals was to continue to emphasize aerial firepower. He paid close attention to munitions, their use, and how well each weapon matched its target.[202]

The interminable secrecy of the air war over Laos arose from the United States' choice to protect the Royal Lao Government from having to really confront Hanoi's aggression, and the desire of both countries to not fully expose the North Vietnamese nature of the Ho Chi Minh Trail. All of this combined to undercut the narrative from Saigon and Washington that theirs was a defensive war against a threat from outside. Since the Johnson administration failed to fully convey the physical realities of the Ho Chi Minh Trail to the world, it prevented the public from comprehending the war's invasive character.

The extent of supplies the communist war in South Vietnam required was confusing. Before American involvement increased in early 1965 it was estimated that just a few days of truck convoys could provide sufficient ammunition, weapons, and the like to support a PAVN division for a year or a VC division for three-and-a-half years.[203] The Central Intelligence Agency, however, pointed out in December 1965 that the North Vietnamese had "been hard at work building additional truckable roads" and had "sent mechanical earth-moving equipment to the panhandle road program—a first in this remote part of Laos." As a result, the agency estimated that the North Vietnamese sought to move approximately 300 tons of supplies each day into South Vietnam.²⁰⁴ Over the next two years, North Vietnamese truck traffic increased by a factor of thirty. Apparently, someone inside South Vietnam had need for much more than the oft-cited fifteen tons a day the insurgency needed. One official historian found that the Viet Cong alone actually needed about 420 tons per month. In 1966, as an example, approximately eighty-two tons each day reached South Vietnam via the Trail.²⁰⁵ Along with 200 tons of supplies that went south daily through various means, about 4,500 soldiers each month made the journey. It was a road network by April 1966. Movement by foot became an alternative method when rain and mud brought truck movement to a halt. Since the Ho Chi Minh Trail already consisted of more than 2,700 miles of main and secondary routes, much of it hidden from view by overgrowth, expecting air strikes to be able to reduce its traffic to such a low throughput as to literally strangle the war in South Vietnam was expecting too much.²⁰⁶

The Hanoi regime did not merely endure the bombing; it adapted its transportation and repair methods. Aircrews conducting daytime surveillance saw evidence of logistical movement, such as tire tracks, but no trucks, and soon realized that the enemy was moving supplies exclusively at night. Night movement made it much more difficult for American forces to find and attack the supplies headed south. Technological limitations early in the war meant that aircraft had to use some sort of a light source to find and then illuminate the target, but that attracted return fire. The need for good weather also made night interdiction more difficult, and darkness made bomb damage assessment impossible for everything but immobile targets like truck parks.²⁰⁷

The extent to which the North Vietnamese kept this supply line open surprised the Americans. They repeatedly rebuilt bridges, used fords and ferries when they had to, and repaired everything tirelessly. Soon the Air Force anticipated that they would build more bypass roads and rely more on porters and boats to move supplies. According to a defector, shelters for trucks had been built along the trail, and each contained North Vietnamese soldiers who repaired the roads when damaged. These shelters even had tow trucks and repair shops.²⁰⁸ The communists constantly expanded alternative roads. As truck use increased, covert American road watch teams in 1966 observed the construction of bypass roads that shortened the route by many miles. Analysts soon warned that American tactics would have a short shelf life and would have to be revised on a regular basis given that the North Vietnamese constantly developed countertactics. The Air Force realized that it could not cut off the flow of supplies through Laos completely and settled for the more limited objective of disrupting the route to such an extent that enemy forces would see much of their fighting power wither.²⁰⁹

Initial assessments of air interdiction were not encouraging. From April 24 to May 24, 1965, air strikes attacked 179 trucks, damaging or destroying fifty-one of them. Thereafter, fewer trucks were seen, which could have been due to camouflage, their destruction, or a transition to night operations. Cratering a road was worthwhile where it narrowed, no bypass was possible, and where landslides were likely, or where there was a mountain on one side and a cliff on the other.²¹⁰ Cratering roads certainly caused problems for the enemy, but "Craters have been repaired rapidly when they could not be bypassed and *the enemy appears willing to make whatever effort is necessary to keep up the logistical flow* [italics in original]."²¹¹ Indeed, the communists employed about 11,000 workers on the trail, porters numbered around 6,000, and more than 100,000 repaired roads in the Vietnamese panhandle. Work crews doubled over the next two years, including more than 100,000 Chinese soldiers, according to John Prados and Xiaobing Li. Ambassador Sullivan doubted air strikes alone could sufficiently halt supply flows; ground forces equivalent to a pair of American infantry divisions would be necessary. That, however, would expand the war and enlarge the geographic scope of Indochina the United States sought to protect.[212]

Admiral Sharp explained the logic behind air interdiction: employ air strikes to destroy North Vietnam's military capability as far away from the front as possible; otherwise, friendly forces would have to fight an enemy who was better equipped and suffer more casualties unnecessarily.[213] In actuality, the air interdiction campaign as practiced was like cutting down a tree by starting at the outermost leaves and snipping one's way to the branches but leaving the trunk and roots intact. Aerial interdiction is more effective when it can cut choke points as close to the source as possible—the equivalent to cutting the base of a tree's trunk instead of its branches. The campaign, however, had to target the branches, not the roots that came through Haiphong and originated in China. Admiral Sharp realized interdiction was not going to be effective until missions could target the finite number of intermediate choke points, namely those around and through Hanoi and Haiphong. Until then, the air interdiction campaign would amount to nothing more than serious harassment. What is more, cutting off Haiphong as a choke point would have required regular and repeated bombing missions—a one-time strike would not have kept the port closed.[214]

During two weeks in 1965, for example, planners identified 108 interdiction targets, the majority of which were labeled bottlenecks. True bottlenecks number in the single digits; a number of choke points that large suggests that there were no vital logistical centers to destroy that would halt Hanoi's supply effort. Regarding these and additional factors, PACAF began to recognize challenges that would plague the air interdiction campaign for the rest of the war. The best choke points were bridges, fords, and ferries, since teamsters and porters could drive or muscle supplies around craters made by bombs. The alternate rainy and dry seasons brought some predictability as to when it would be easiest for the communists to transport supplies, and when it was easier or more difficult for air strikes to find and destroy them. Traffic jams photographed by reconnaissance sorties in 1966 proved the bombing campaign was at least impeding the North's logistical effort.[215]

The air campaign also involved targeting vulnerable parts of the trail with armed reconnaissance.[216] Admiral Sharp did not find the armed reconnaissance effort over Laos very effective, so he ordered missions to bomb stationary targets. The basic problem was finding trucks. Mobile ground teams along with aircraft functioned best for that mission, but the Laotian panhandle was remote, rugged country. Ideally, one would be able to find the concentrations of supplies at places where trucks were being parked or repaired, but it was hard to find and then strike them all at the same time, which was necessary in order to inflict enough damage that it would take a significant amount of time for North Vietnamese logistical troops to replace. Not only that, but air strikes also required large numbers of aircraft to inflict serious damage, along with a standby capability to bomb newly discovered targets. These efforts needed coordination between the US Air Force in Thailand, the American Embassy in Vientiane, the Royal Lao Air Force, intelligence sources, forward air controllers, and communications networks. One Navy wing found that armed reconnaissance during daylight resulted in very little destruction of trucks, and those missions further persuaded the enemy to move at night.[217]

An analyst lowered his expectations to such a degree that he advocated as successful a strategy "wherein by calculated moves, the enemy can be forced to react according to our plan," by which measure any American action could be labeled strategically successful. He also cited an assessment in which the operations were considered effective if they forced the enemy to arrange their convoys with greater spacing between each truck. Forcing enemy convoys to space their trucks 200 feet apart instead of ten feet is not a strategic victory. These pronouncements come across as arrogant: "we can force the enemy to increase the density of trucks on a route to coincide with scheduled air strike sorties along that route." Why would a thinking enemy conform to your agenda? Would not this enemy that had already adjusted devise a way to defeat this tactic as well? The proposal certainly overplayed the extent to which limited American military power could constrain the actions of a reactive, creative, camouflaged adversary. This analyst assumed that air strikes could ensnare and obliterate nearly all the trucks "within this geographic area."[218] Could not the North Vietnamese have simply moved their trucks to a different "geographic area," or taken a different route?

Efforts at increasing the pain of the war depended not only on what the US did, but also on how much the North Vietnamese could endure. An operational assessment which argued that the best outcome would be nothing more than additional strain on enemy efforts was not going to persuade the North Vietnamese they were being defeated conclusively.[219] Indeed, in the words of the commanders of Pacific Air Forces and Pacific Command, "we could not justify any strike program in NVN on basis of interdiction alone. Every study proves you can't stop infiltration with air interdiction. Only way to influence north Vietnamese support of war is by putting pressure on worthwhile targets. This can't be quantified because you cannot tell extent to which it is working until the enemy calls it quits."[220] Their judgment may help explain why General Westmoreland was not an enthusiastic supporter of bombing the trail because he thought those missions were not very effective; North Vietnamese forces still made it to South Vietnam.[221]

These findings can tempt one into restarting the polemic debate on the effectiveness or lack thereof of air power, but the decisive issues resided outside the realm of any one form of military force. The source problem was not supposed deficiencies in air power; that resembles blaming wrenches and robots instead of software for poorly constructing a car. The sources of the indecisiveness were cognitive and analytical, deeper problems involving policy. North Vietnam's agenda belonged in the realm of total war, but the ways and means the Americans pursued their goals were limited and did not line up with American policy. The Johnson administration did not realize that goals such as permanently halting the flow of supplies down the Ho Chi Minh Trail required the defeat of the Hanoi regime first—a defeat that had to occur inside North Vietnam. The nature of the American goals was such that North Vietnamese leaders would not consider discussing them, therefore the only way to bring lasting resolution to the conflict was completely subjugating the regime in Hanoi, which of course the United States was not going to attempt. The indecisiveness of the air interdiction campaign was a side effect pointing to a mismatch between ways and means, and end goals. More bombing was not the answer. Sound operational strategies are not rooted in magnitudes and quantities. Sound policy goals are the source of winning strategies.

Forgoing the option of expanding the ground war into North Vietnam placed an unrealistic set of expectations on air power. Just as ground warfare can only be decisive without suffering prohibitive losses when combined with air support, air interdiction really needs the complementary assistance of a high-intensity ground war to deny the enemy time to adjust and adapt in ways that can render indecisive an air interdiction campaign. The complementary effects of ground warfare with air power would have opened real possibilities to conclusively terminate the flow of supplies to the wars in South Vietnam, Laos, and Cambodia; but that option, a land interdiction effort combined with air interdiction, was not a possibility, not because of micromanagement from the White House, nor American-killing rules of engagement restrictions, nor because air power is not useful. The nemesis was what the Americans were trying to accomplish, what they wanted, the limited risks they were willing to take, the larger risks they were determined to avoid, and the limited costs they were willing to pay to try to win the war while minimizing its scope. The choice of an air-only campaign also tells the enemy that a state's commitment has limits and simplifies the actions the enemy must take to succeed.

Operation Rolling Thunder in 1966

During the December 1965 bombing pause the JCS recommended an immediate renewal of Rolling Thunder for several reasons. First, the pause weakened negotiations. Second, the North Vietnamese were increasing their military capabilities during this respite, and further delays would lead to more deaths of friendly troops. Finally, the bombing pause would gain momentum toward becoming the norm, making a renewed offensive more difficult. Admiral Sharp also wanted to renew the bombing because the pause had not persuaded Hanoi to negotiate. He concluded the North Vietnamese were willing to endure an enormous loss in lives if in the end that might win the war. They had indeed successfully implemented an information campaign that was persuading many they were the victims and the Americans the aggressors. The North Vietnamese commitment to their goal and their willingness to suffer unprecedented losses over a long period of time were what in Sharp's view made an escalation of Rolling Thunder necessary. General Wheeler believed Hanoi's intransigence required an intense, extensive air campaign. He argued there should be no limits on armed reconnaissance sorties, no restrictions on tactics or methods, and that only Hanoi, Haiphong, and the Chinese buffer zone be subject to restrictions.[222] Clark Clifford added another reason for renewing the air campaign: "We must fight the war where we are strongest and we are strongest in the air."[223] At the other end of the advisory spectrum, the State Department's legal advisor, Leonard Meeker, counseled a bombing suspension that allowed the members of the North Vietnamese politburo weeks, if not months, to sort out their own internal policy debates.[224]

Planning a renewed Rolling Thunder in January 1966, Seventh Air Force focused as much around the number of sorties as the targets or consequences of these air strikes, suggesting a preoccupation with means rather than political accomplishments. Both Rusk and McNamara favored resumption by January 27 as the best of a set of options they found unattractive. President Johnson decided to go forward the next day with the objectives of improving South Vietnamese morale, imposing serious military costs on the North Vietnamese, and greatly reducing their movement of supplies into South Vietnam. He saw it as his only option.[225]

Bombing resumed on January 31, 1966, but due to bad weather just fifty-six sorties reached their targets. At first, the only missions were armed reconnaissance sorties south of twenty degrees, thirty-one minutes latitude.[226] The North Vietnamese exploited the renewal for a propaganda victory by responding to the American negotiating position just hours after the first sorties, implying that the United States was unreasonably impatient.[227]

Rolling Thunder continued to pursue both coercion and interdiction in 1966. Broad goals were to worsen North Vietnam's condition and improve the situation in South Vietnam, killing, for example, as many VC and PAVN as possible as the communists infiltrated from North Vietnam, and attacking a greater portion in their staging areas and encampments.[228] Admiral Sharp's intent was clearly attritional: increase the costs and challenges the North Vietnamese faced in supporting combat operations in South Vietnam.[229] Sharp believed the most effective use of air power entailed destroying every piece of war materiel possible. For instance, the JCS observed cement and steel were needed to repair bombed roads and bridges and targeted both accordingly.[230] They also related air interdiction effectiveness to target vulnerability. Railroads, for instance, moved a third of North Vietnam's imports and were hit because "a train cannot drive around a crater or broken rail."[231] Ultimately, however, bombing could not keep the rail lines cut because work crews quickly rebuilt them.[232] Westmoreland agreed with Sharp: "Our operations must be oriented toward the destruction of these forces, and we must undertake an effective war of attrition against them."[233]

Destroying transportation routes and fuels remained tactical objectives, but the North Vietnamese had already begun transferring their gasoline and diesel from large storage tanks to smaller buried ones beginning in September 1965. The new national security advisor, Walt W. Rostow, saw comparisons between North Vietnam's reliance on such fuels and that of Germany during WWII, when there were in reality no comparisons. Consequently, he recommended targeting that could not be strategically decisive. Also seeking to expand the set of permissible targets, the JCS held that unless permitted to hit lucrative transportation targets in northeastern Vietnam, the air campaign could not inflict decisive costs because supplies from outside North Vietnam traversed that part of the country. These needed to be attacked before the supplies and armaments were dispersed.[234]

On February 26, 1966, Rolling Thunder 49 began with a monthly allocation of 3,000 sorties for missions against targets in Laos, and 5,100 for North Vietnam. Here, Westmoreland did not understand how to use aerial interdiction effectively as did Admiral Sharp. The general wanted more sorties assigned to the Ho Chi Minh Trail, but the admiral recognized that hitting targets as close to the seaport of Haiphong and the routes from China as possible provided for a more effective use of air power. The JCS split the difference.[235]

Military operations in 1966 failed to persuade Hanoi to seek terms. Sharp was not surprised, because he recognized by March that the materiel foundation for this war lay in the countries that supplied North Vietnam. The second-best option would have been to bomb the wharves in Haiphong and prevent ships from docking, but political worries sidelined that option. This let the enemy disperse their supplies before the Americans bombed them, violating basic principles of interdiction. It was as if the Americans were trying to strangle the enemy around the ankles instead of the neck. In any event, the CIA's deputy director for plans, Richard M. Helms, did not believe an increased bombing campaign could shut down the supply line.[236]

The Air Force concluded air interdiction had thus far not slowed the movement of materiel and soldiers, so the bombing campaign was not accomplishing its goals.[237] An intelligence appraisal was impressed with the degree to which the North Vietnamese adapted. The North Vietnamese resolutely pursued taking over South Vietnam. Against this goal the United States continued to implement a "carefully controlled means of gradual escalation to achieve strictly limited means."[238] While the United States used limited force, the American goal was almost as ambitious as Hanoi's, but the Johnson administration would not apply force sufficient to accomplish that goal. This was a major flaw in Johnson's strategy.[239]

In May 1966, the Air Force estimated enemy forces in SVN needed 380 tons of supplies per day to operate and only thirty-four tons had to be brought in from the north—mainly ammunition. Enemy forces engaged in combat only on an irregular timetable, the typical battalion fighting only one day out of thirty. At the same time, the Ho Chi Minh Trail's throughput approached a daily capacity of 600 tons. Both suggested the communists were about to escalate the tempo of their combat operations, or they needed more supplies than the Americans thought. This USAF study asserted an interdiction effort would be viable if the air campaign imposed costs the enemy either could not or would not pay to push troops and supplies south. Consequently, the lower the enemy's level of combat, the less effective interdiction would be, and vice versa. Once again, the JCS concluded the interdiction campaign had not significantly reduced the enemy's ability to support its combat operations. The communists were in fact planning to escalate in 1966 with the intention of destroying the ARVN, something that required more logistical support than guerrilla operations.[240]

It made no sense to President Johnson to only destroy the fuel the truck convoys needed to traverse the Ho Chi Minh Trail, so he extended the bombing to fuel storage sites in June 1966. The Air Force got to hit two prime targets, the one at Yen Bay on May 31 and a larger one near Hanoi on June 29.[241] One facility was within nine miles of downtown Haiphong; American political leaders warned their military commanders to take extra care to avoid civilian casualties. That kind of precaution was a component of effective air power; air forces had to destroy their targets without producing collateral damage that would harm the American cause and award the North Vietnamese the advantages of an aggrieved victim. They explain Admiral Sharp's strictures to bomb only with good visibility, execute bombing runs so that stray bombs would be less likely to harm noncombatants, make the maximum use of electronic countermeasures so SAMs were less likely to distract aircrews on their bombing runs, use the most accurate munitions, and rely on the most experienced aircrews available. These constraints served political rather than military ends.[242] The deputy commander of Seventh AF, General Gilbert Meyers, assessed the June 29 missions as more important and significant than any preceding them. Seventh Air Force concluded that the June 29, 30, and July 5 attacks destroyed anywhere from 35 to 45 percent of North Vietnam's fuel supplies.[243]

Rolling Thunder 51 opened more targets on July 6, including fuel storage and three bridges inside the Hanoi exclusion zone. Objectives included cutting fuel imports, destroying fuel storage sites, finding and bombing fuel the North Vietnamese were moving, and tracking results with aerial reconnaissance. Naval air strikes destroyed as much as 60 percent of the fuel depots in Haiphong, a target previously on the restricted list, leading Vice President Humphrey to praise the bombing accuracy.[244] The president exclaimed, "them sons-of-bitches are finished now."[245] The Air Force recognized, however, that bombing stored gasoline and diesel inflicted only short-term costs and encouraged long-term adaptations. Bombing fuel supplies compelled dispersal in fifty-five-gallon drums, even as petroleum supplies arrived on barges from Chinese ports. Soviet vessels simply offloaded the fuel they were providing at a Chinese port for railway transshipment.[246]

Navy aircraft destroyed more stored fuel, hundreds of trucks, barges, and railroad cars, and many bridges in August. Despite destroyed roadways and vehicles, the North Vietnamese still managed to move supplies. Carrier aircraft achieved the same kind of results the following month, flying more than 1,300 sorties from September 21 to 27. Hanoi's preconditions for negotiations remained unchanged, signaling that they were either mad or resolutely determined. As before, the Americans first had to stop the bombing, remove their troops from South Vietnam, and North and South Vietnam had to be reunified before negotiations could begin.[247]

Targets did not become easier to destroy with the loosening of restrictions. The Dao Quan facility with a capacity of 302 tons of fuel before a September 5, 1966, strike still had a post-strike capacity of 262 tons. After pilots delivered all their ordnance at La Danh, its capacity remained more than 1,200 tons. A September 11 attack on Trach Ban, however, wiped out the facility. Pacific Air Forces had held high hopes for the campaign against stored fuel but as of September its analysts realized it was not nearly enough to convince the leaders in Hanoi they could not win the war, which is not the same as a country conceding it had been defeated. PACAF then recommended a larger and broader set of targets, which assumed a decisive target set existed and current geopolitical realities would permit the United States to destroy it.[248]

Shortly thereafter, another CIA/DIA analysis repeated that the interdiction campaign was not decisively painful for the North Vietnamese, who still had enough fuel for their activities and remained able to move supplies effectively. Morale was only marginally down, with their economy still functioning. In fact, more men and supplies moved into South Vietnam than had a year earlier. Rolling Thunder operated under the flawed assumption that North Vietnam was a narrow bottleneck, but it simply was not. Furthermore, the enemy adjusted their means of transportation, shifting freight to trucks and boats.[249] Even the use of thirty B-52 sorties against the Mu Gia Pass in April only proved the ability of the North Vietnamese to repair damaged roads and get trucks moving again after a single day. Analysts saw it differently, arguing that the fact that the road was back in action so soon was an indication of the pass's strategic importance, not an indication of their ability to repair bomb damage to roadways.[250] The CIA argued North Vietnam was paying "a price it can afford and one it probably considers acceptable in light of the political objectives it hopes to achieve," but one consequence was encouraging.[251] By August, North Vietnamese shipping exports were down 40 percent from what they had been earlier in the year, even without a blockade. The war was having a material effect on that country, and the air campaign had worsened life for the North Vietnamese. More soldiers deserted, and morale was low. Seventh Air Force was convinced that the bombing had lowered their ability to wage war, but the goal of war is to win it, not reduce the enemy's ability to make it.[252]

Satisfied that bombing was the right instrument, Admiral Sharp believed the air campaign ought to be steadily intensified to force Hanoi to accede to American demands. Navy strikes month after month had pulverized roads, bridges, rolling stock, and trucks, and missions against these kinds of targets continued through the end of the year. A couple of months later naval air strikes wrecked oil storage facilities at Lim Hoanh and Kim Doi.[253] Hanoi, however, did not flinch. Bombing fuel storage did not significantly affect the course of the war, nor did it prevent an estimated 53,000 troops from reaching South Vietnam. McNamara expressed serious doubts about the effectiveness of the air campaign but suggested the United States continue it to buttress diplomatic efforts. The JCS continued to argue the only way to have an effective air campaign was to take away all of the constraints except the prohibition against the wanton killing of noncombatants, but such an unhindered campaign would have fed the Hanoi propaganda machine, an outcome diametrically opposed to the goals of policy makers in the White House. The JCS also assumed Hanoi would capitulate in the face of a maximum bombing campaign.[254]

An assessment by the JASON Summer Study Group argued in August 1966 that the attacks on fuel had barely dented North Vietnamese capabilities.[255] Stevedores continued to unload large amounts of war supplies from ships even though some bombing missions against Haiphong made the longshoremen's work more difficult. A later study estimated the air campaign would have needed 131,000 air strike sorties from September 1966 through December 1967 to prevent the North Vietnamese from building up a stockpile of supplies. Information gathered by the RAND Corporation later concluded the VC received just enough. In fact, even if the campaign prevented 80 percent of the supplies from reaching South Vietnam, enough arrived, nearly 5,000 tons each month, to support more than 80,000 soldiers.[256] Even though Rolling Thunder sorties rose from 4,000 to 12,000 a month by October, the damage had not been severe enough to reduce the flow of supplies to end the communist war effort. After McNamara finished reading the JASON group report in October, he recommended the president bring Rolling Thunder to an end.[257]

Westmoreland believed that the interdiction of the Ho Chi Minh road network was worth it because the bombing was hampering North Vietnam's effort to move supplies and people into South Vietnam. He concluded gradual escalation was not influencing Hanoi's leaders and that a change in operational strategy was in order: either a sudden, intense series of bombing missions against important targets, or a longer sustainable series of missions against those same targets. Either way, Rolling Thunder was a military means in which the US held the initiative. Admiral Sharp still believed bombing might persuade Hanoi to end its support for the Viet Cong. As it was, he recognized it was only preventing the enemy from bringing the full force of their military might against American and South Vietnamese ground forces.[258] Major General George S. Brown, assistant to the chairman of the JCS, briefed Secretary McNamara that whatever kind of interdiction strategy the US chose, the ability of the North Vietnamese to bounce back was the primary characteristic the US had to deal with.[259]

Given the targets not struck in 1966, one can understand why the argument that the air campaign had not been given a fair chance existed. Analysts at PACAF believed they had identified North Vietnam's key vulnerabilities and also the most fragile bomb aim points. Pacific Air Forces proposed a target system to affect large portions of the population, such as electricity generation. They assumed that bombing these, and others like the Thai Nguyen Army Supply Depot or the Thai Nguyen Steel Mill, would generate strategically decisive pressures that would persuade the leadership to negotiate. One can see, however, that PACAF's targeting occurred in reverse order. Targeting has to begin at the level of political and policy goals and work its way toward the tactical level of war. This assessment treated the campaign as an engineering problem in which the enemy reacted in predictable and favorable ways. An edition of "Effects of Air Operations in Southeast Asia" sheds light on their thought processes. Target destruction was the central focus, and interdiction created new targeting opportunities. Refined targeting aided aerial reconnaissance and bombing fixed targets near cities wore down the enemy psychologically.[260] Analysts hoped destroying certain targets would accomplish strategically important outcomes. Regarding the targeting of a railroad car repair facility, a shop for repairing motor vehicles, and a military supply depot, PACAF surmised that a large strike package attacking in an unpredictable sequence might produce some significant effects with only minimal losses. These were, after all, highly valuable facilities to the North Vietnamese as far as the American analysts were concerned.[261]

Since many targets remained unbombed and the North Vietnamese would not negotiate, military leaders sought to expand the air war. For instance, they sought to bomb the northeast railroad. Toward the end of the year, the JCS wished to expand the bombing into prohibited parts of Hanoi and Haiphong by reducing the size of the no-bombing zones to radii of ten and four miles, respectively. General Wheeler wished to bomb SAM sites, oil storage tanks, a steel and a cement plant, eight power stations, four locks, and the ports of Haiphong and Cam Pha. McNamara approved an escalation of the air campaign, but only against targets that were worth any losses incurred, and against ones that would result in few civilian deaths.[262]

Air strikes continued apace in December. Missions hit a motor pool and a railroad yard just outside of Hanoi, and their propaganda howled that the bombs had killed civilians. In spite of concerns about collateral damage, an A-6A strike destroyed most of a target that was very close to the center of Hanoi: the Van Dien Vehicle Depot. Jets from the USS *Kitty Hawk* completed strikes against SAM assembly warehouses in Haiphong. Strike packages exceeding 200 carrier and land-based aircraft hit targets near Hanoi on December 2; the two services coordinated the operation well and suffered minimal losses, but accumulated imports of Soviet fuel sustained the war effort through the autumn raids.[263] As far as Allied Forces could tell, truck traffic through Laos fell to almost nothing during the first three weeks of December 1966, then erupted, probably because the North Vietnamese expected fewer air interdiction missions during the Christmas holidays.[264]

The best indicators the bombing proved costly were the outcries of Hanoi's propaganda machine, but the JCS found the overall effectiveness disappointing.[265] While the CIA concluded that up to 20 percent of the North Vietnamese who trudged their way to South Vietnam died along the way, most died because of sickness, especially malaria. Only "10 percent were killed by air attacks and 5 percent were permanently lost through desertion." Air strikes encouraged soldiers to travel on foot as opposed to vehicle transportation, lengthening the journey and thus allowing more opportunities for sickness.[266]

Stalemate was not a word CINCPAC used when assessing 1966, but that is what its message traffic and analyses described. They called their own efforts a "successful spoiling operation" that persuaded communist forces to go on the defensive. Rolling Thunder had done next to nothing to cut off imports into North Vietnam, but CINCPAC argued the enemy held on because air forces had been allowed to strike only twenty of the 104 targets in the lucrative northeastern part of North Vietnam.[267] Sharp realized the collateral killing of civilians gave Hanoi a propaganda weapon but wondered why the US could not remind the world of what the PAVN were doing to South Vietnamese. His recommendation was to "get on with this war ... and when Hanoi screams in anguish, we should hit them again."[268] Sure enough, the screams following air strikes in December against targets close to Hanoi were those of Hanoi's friends in the international press who claimed the bombs killed a lot of noncombatants.[269] "In the final analysis," Sharp wrote, "it must be concluded that in 1966 our RT campaign did not apply adequate and steady pressure against the enemy." He was well impressed with the North Vietnamese counterefforts: "Despite our interdiction, the enemy has accommodated to our LOC attacks by ingeniously hiding and dispersing his logistic activity. His recuperative capability along these routes has been remarkable. However, it has been costly since he has been forced into a prodigious effort to continue to infiltrate men and material into south Vietnam."[270]

North Vietnamese determination to overcome the destruction of roads persisted throughout the war. On one day in July 1968, for example, Navy strikes pulverized a section of Route 71. While North Vietnamese defenses never stopped the air strikes, they always repaired the aftermath. A few days after these bombings, for example, Navy reconnaissance photographed "a footpath weaving through the heavily cratered area." A couple of days later they found a corduroy road made of logs, and a truck convoy ready to use it. A pair of A-4s cratered the road in front of them so they would have no place to go and called in more fighter-bombers to finish them off.[271] Then Skyhawks destroyed fifteen barges, and attacks with Bullpup missiles in September brought down the Tam Da Railroad Bridge for the remaining ten days of that month. Using Walleye guided bombs, A-4s returned to put this bridge in the water again on October 12. These tactical successes did not result in conclusive effectiveness operationally, because the North Vietnamese still managed to get supplies and troops to the front. An enemy can stalemate or defeat his adversary if he has the resources and willpower to keep repairing damage. Indeed, all of this demonstrated to General Krulak that a balance of force between the two sides characterized this war.[272] Vietnam was pure attrition, siege warfare.

As 1966 ended, North Vietnam had actually increased its ability to flow soldiers and supplies into South Vietnam. At best the bombing campaign had disrupted their efforts enough to prevent a conclusive campaign against South Vietnam. Preventing an ally from being overrun was not an inconsequential achievement, but the purpose of the Vietnam War was to produce security, safety, and independence for South Vietnam, not mere survival.[273]

Implements of Presidential Policy

Tactical capabilities of aircraft, munitions, and aircrews were directly related to the pursuit of policy goals because they determined what the president could actually ask Air Force, Navy, and Marine airmen to do. The physical capabilities of these weapons were the in-place executors of presidential intentions. Air strikes could destroy most targets in Indochina—provided the intelligence and reconnaissance community could find them. The need for bombing accuracy varied. Robust weapons like artillery pieces required a sharpshooter's exactitude, as did politically sensitive targets. Accurate bombing was necessary for hitting targets next to off-limit sites. Early in the war a target had to be finished off in just one day, which meant that a large force would bomb it. This caused a lot of smoke over the target for fighter-bombers arriving later in the mission, reducing their bombing accuracy.[274] Concerns about killing noncombatants and the issue of dead civilians, despite the doctrine of double effect, further connected bombing accuracy with the president's goals of shaping how everyone perceived the war.[275]

Visual dive bombing was the most used method during Rolling Thunder. A preliminary Navy study found this tactic resulted in an accuracy of about 250 feet for Mark 83, 1,000-pound and Mark 84, 2,000-pound bombs against heavily defended targets. Another case witnessed a seventy-five-foot miss distance against lightly defended targets. Each unguided bomb followed its own ballistic flightpath, and groups of bombs dropped from six-bomb carriages would disperse out to a distance of about a hundred feet from each other. The first couple of bombers had the best chance of hitting the target because they did not have to aim through the aftermath of exploding bombs; smoke from their bombs obscured the target for aircraft arriving last.[276] Air Force tactical units were ill-prepared for conventional warfare when Rolling Thunder began. A USAF study found that its fighter wings did not train in peacetime with the tactics—dive bombing angles, speeds, force package size—they would employ in wartime, nor were they practiced out of bases that possessed only the minimum of support equipment.[277]

The various types of aircraft used possessed differing capabilities, but there was not a wide variance in their bombing. F-105D Thunderchiefs functioned as the primary bomber over North Vietnam during Rolling Thunder, while F-4C and D Phantoms served as both bombers and fighters. The two F-105 wings did not agree on the best way to place their bombs on their targets, and pitted concerns over losses against bombing accuracy. The 355th TFW believed the best way was to approach at around 7,000 feet, climb up suddenly, find the target, and commence one's dive-bombing run. Its commander felt that this tactic resulted in greater bombing accuracy. The commander of the 388th TFW had his fighter-bombers approach at altitudes of around 16,000 feet in formations that provided effective overlapping coverage for their ECM pods before diving toward the target. He believed his unit's lower loss rates validated their tactics. Actually, the loss rate of the 355th TFW was not that much greater, and the losses could have been due to bad luck as much as anything. And besides, two different kinds of attack runs helped frustrate enemy defenses.[278] A study of F-105 bombing accuracy found that on average they dropped their bombs within about 405–540 feet of the target, and nearly 10 percent of sorties reported "a gross error of 1,600 feet or more." Their bombs hit within fifty feet of the target only 5 percent of the time. When they had to evade SAMs, the percentage of direct hits fell from 7 to 2 percent.[279]

Fighter-bombers from aircraft carriers provided a tremendous weight of effort against targets in North Vietnam and Laos, 50 percent through the war's first year. The Navy's primary strike aircraft during Rolling Thunder was the A-4E Skyhawk. It could carry half again as much ordnance as earlier variants, execute pop-up maneuvers at a greater speed, was safer, and possessed greater range. Violent maneuvers did not disrupt its bombing computer, and it could fire Shrike missiles against surface-to-air missile radars. Skyhawks approached at 10,000 feet, entered a forty-five-degree dive, released their bombs at 6,000 feet, and maintained more than 500 miles per hour as they pulled out of the dive. Although aviators from aircraft carriers flew multiple passes at targets if its destruction was particularly important, they soon learned to make, if possible, only one attack run to avoid excessive losses to antiaircraft artillery. An A-4C squadron, VA-153, forbade multiple attack passes in daylight, nor did it permit pilots to play chicken with flak sites. If one needed different kinds of ordnance to destroy the target, simply put it on two different aircraft so that no one has to make two passes.[280] After a few more months Air Force units also learned that the way to lose more jets was to make multiple bomb runs against the same target.[281] A more advanced Skyhawk arrived in 1967, the A-4F, which possessed a new computerized bombsight that was capable enough to persuade Luddites who had preferred to rely on their own skills to make use of it, especially during night bombing missions. It also improved bomb damage assessment.[282] Skyhawk pilots suffered high losses because they flew a third of the Navy's missions; 195 were shot down, the equivalent of sixteen squadrons.[283]

McDonnell F-4 Phantoms were also used as bombers. In June 1967, F-4Ds began using their radars for bomb aiming, but the best accuracy they could achieve was 300 feet. Fourteen percent of these kinds of bomb runs, however, resulted in miss distances of 4,000 feet.[284] None of these aircraft had the ability during the first three years of the war to bomb with pinpoint precision.

Early in the war the Air Force used dive bombing in good weather as its most accurate method of getting bombs on the target, but the coercive goals of Rolling Thunder needed a way of maintaining pressure on enemy forces when weather precluded visual bombing. Bombers relied on MSQ-77 Sky Spot radar guidance during bad weather. The two additional methods were "Buddy bombing," which comprised an EB-66 pathfinder leading fighter-bombers to a release point, and the F-105's toss bombing tactic utilizing its on-board computer and radar. Sky Spot achieved the greatest accuracy, but distance to the target was a limiting factor. When 200 miles from the radar, the error averaged 1,200 feet. At this distance, the jets had to be at least 30,000 feet above the ground to receive the radar signal, but F-105s could not reach that altitude with their full bomb load. None of these provided the accuracy needed for hitting something like a small building or a vehicle except by pure luck. The Air Force realized early on that accuracy would suffer when relying on these methods, but it wanted to deny the North Vietnamese the respite they would get if American strikes only took place when weather was good.[285] B-52s also made use of MSQ-77 along with radar mapping to determine their release points.[286]

To improve accuracy over North Vietnam, PACAF approached Ambassador Sullivan in November 1966 with a proposal to install an MSQ-77 in northern Laos. Several months later the United States placed one near the North Vietnamese border at Lima Site 85 in November 1967.[287] Since it was closer to the heartland of North Vietnam than transmitters in Thailand and South Vietnam, it provided greater bombing accuracy to aircraft dropping bombs through cloud decks. The North Vietnamese recognized the danger the site posed to them and overran it on March 10, 1968.[288]

General Momyer found this method of bombing too inaccurate for interdicting supply routes. Another problem with this kind of bombing was not only its inadequate accuracy for targets that required direct hits, but also the lack of BDA; the weather that made

EB-66 leading F-105s on Sky Spot bombing mission (US Air Force)

MSQ bombing necessary precluded obtaining post-attack photographs. Operations using MSQ-77 in interdiction operations forced the North Vietnamese to adapt, but they did not halt the movement of supplies and troops. While bombing supply routes nearly brought motorized infiltration through Laos to a halt toward the end of June 1966, their adjustment was to infiltrate through the DMZ. American air forces were able to flexibly strike infiltrating forces whenever they found them, but flexibility is not the purpose of interdiction; the goal is to stop the enemy.[289]

The Navy tried using A-3s and A-6As as pathfinders for other aircraft, but this too was not accurate enough. From late February to mid-March 1966, for example, the USS *Ranger* used A-3 Skywarriors as pathfinders for its bombers against targets along the Quan Deo Highway near Mui Ron. The only bomb that hit the target did so when the pilots could *see* the target. A-6As were coveted but scarce items; each carrier normally had just one twelve-plane A-6A squadron, and there were only 117 in the entire fleet as of 1966. The Navy did not want to use them as pathfinders but preferred to use them singly on night missions because with their moving target indicator capability they could hit vehicles at night; F-105s and A-4s could not.[290]

The Air Force tried to obtain a more accurate night-bombing capability by modifying RF-4Cs and F-105Ds and inserting various black boxes that exploited the day's best technology but were ultimately unsatisfactory. Thunderchiefs received LORAN, a radar for avoiding the ground, an inertial navigation system, and an ability to determine slant range with its radar. Altogether these modifications provided better target ranging, the ability to release bombs automatically when the device indicated the time was right, and most promising in theory, a continuously computed impact point. Collectively these were known as

"Thunderstick," but they provided a night and all-weather bombing accuracy of only 400 feet. All these systems were intended for releasing a free-falling, unguided bomb on the most accurate trajectory possible, but because of the changing wind currents between the release point and ground impact, even the best-aimed bombs drifted. Effective night bombing of the Ho Chi Minh Trail was difficult for several additional reasons. Aircrews seldom saw the trucks, precise navigation was difficult, damage assessment was a challenge, and bad weather caused the cancellation of half of night interdiction missions as of November 1966.[291]

Aircrews used weapons in ways designers had never considered. Pilots in F-105Fs modified for more accurate bombing at night used Sidewinder heat-seeking air-to-air missiles to destroy searchlights: the missile's heat seeker homed in on the searchlight's heat. A pair of F-8 pilots used Sidewinders to destroy two steam locomotives in North Vietnam in 1968.[292] Similarly, Seventh AF even used a high-tech bomber interceptor, the F-102, as a night ground attack aircraft. Its infrared search and tracking system was able to find vehicles by detecting their engine heat; they even found campfires. The pilot then fired heat-seeking guided missiles at the fires to kill the insurgents sitting around them. F-102 pilots used their radar to detect small boats darkness otherwise hid, and Navy S-2 Tracker antisubmarine aircraft fired AGM-12 Bullpup missiles to destroy wooden boats—probably not such a cost-effective measure.[293] While these were flexible uses of weapons in ways that were unconstrained by dogma, this was also an indicator that tactical challenges, such as fighter-bombers attacking search lights, had pulled the war effort away from strategic effectiveness toward solving tactical problems. Weapons use such as this also illustrated the attritional and siege warfare character of Vietnam.

Aircrews groped for solutions to the problem of accurate night bombing throughout the war. In 1965, for example, fighter-bombers successfully attacked roads and bridges by using flares to generate enough light so pilots could use daytime methods to find targets and aim their bombs. A C-123 transport with a night vision scope would look for trucks so that an accompanying A-26K could attack it. When the crewman found trucks, the transport would then eject a flare so that the bomber pilot could find the target. This method was slow, cumbersome, and crude. Oftentimes the truck drivers could hide their vehicles before the bomber started a bomb run. Their chances of finding trucks during a mission were only 15 percent and were almost zero if trucks turned off their headlights. Despite these challenges, individual bombers found and struck truck parks.[294] Serious tactical challenges like this one make it more understandable why the Americans pursued technological answers during the war. Additional solutions included using a laser as a light source for nighttime TV cameras, but it was not that effective in finding trucks hidden under trees. From 1971 there was "Green Weenie," a green laser that a gunship could use to show a laser-guided bomb-carrying aircraft where to lase, but enemy forces had an easier time seeing the laser spot than did the American aircrews. Nevertheless, better night attacks against trucks eventually persuaded them to drive their trucks during the day more often.[295]

The problem was not an obsession with technological solutions; these were needed. The fundamental problem was with the character of the overall strategy that forced the US to target the outer branches of the logistical system rather than the entryways into North Vietnam. Problems like these were symptoms of the consequences of geopolitical realities and policy-level choices, rather than endemic to American warfare preferences. Geopolitical concerns encouraged policy makers to attempt to use air interdiction in a manner that reduced its effectiveness. The Air Force and Navy had to carry out the air interdiction campaigns as a stand-alone effort without the benefit of a ground war campaign sufficient to compel the enemy to consume all of their supplies faster than they could be replenished.

For instance, had the American mechanized divisions slowly crept their way north across the DMZ, no more supplies or soldiers would have flowed down the Ho Chi Minh Trail; Hanoi would have diverted them against the more dangerous threat, but China's warnings consigned that option to MACV's hope chest.

All these tactical-level issues combined to create problems for the accomplishment of national policy. For all of this firepower, many targets were difficult to hit, harder to destroy completely, and very difficult to strike in bad weather. Consequently, the war became more and more attritional, operations generated cumulative but not conclusive effects, and the enemy gained time to adapt and gain strength and prestige. The enemy imprisoned shot-down pilots, filmed collateral damage that was not a violation of the laws of war, and developed alternatives to defeat American methods. These challenges produced a stalemate, to which military leaders believed they had the right answer.

Reluctantly Escalating the Air Campaign

As 1966 ended, CINCPAC set forth a trio of military objectives for 1967. The latter two were difficult but realistic: help the South Vietnamese in their efforts to defeat the communist military campaign and help the Saigon government expand its control of the country at the expense of the National Liberation Front's guerrilla war. The first objective, however, struck at the core policy goal of the communists and therefore would be more difficult to achieve: bring their support for and pursuit of the insurgencies in Laos and South Vietnam to an end.[296] General Harris argued that a gradually escalated campaign would not generate enough "psychological impact" on the people and leaders of North Vietnam to produce strategically important consequences. He believed the air campaign had to be stepped up in order to inflict enough of a shock on the politburo to convince them North Vietnam could not endure a long war. Air strikes needed to be intensified greatly and destroy heretofore off-limits, high-value targets, and he also advocated continuing the attrition strategy against supplies all along the communists' supply lines. He believed the targets in the core of the North were foundational to their ability to wage war, but one could argue that the will and endurance of the North Vietnamese Communist Party was the center of gravity. Harris realized an escalated air campaign would be challenging because of the number of bad weather days and the ability of the North Vietnamese to compensate for bomb damage. China's preoccupation with its own domestic issues (the Cultural Revolution) lessened the chance of intervention, he believed. Harris was optimistic, and believed that "Pressure on Hanoi, attrition of war materiel, and aggressive search and destroy operations in SVN, will bring about enemy exhaustion of men and materials."[297] There were a few reasons for believing that Hanoi might be near the breaking point. A CIA report in August 1967 asserted that Premier Pham Van Dong believed a negotiated settlement was imperative because Hanoi's war was not going well, and China threatened its own military intervention if Hanoi got weak-kneed, but the United States' paltry knowledge of the divisions within the enemy government was insufficient for contributing to strategic decisions.[298]

The new year brought no change in strategy even though military commanders had concluded their current approach was insufficient to change Hanoi's behavior. Admiral Sharp advocated destroying targets like power plants, and also cut off or at least reduce imports, destroy war resources, and inflict as many losses as possible against the supply routes through Laos. He did not necessarily seek "the total destruction of any given system but rather broad disruption, within defined limits, that will have important indirect economic and psychological as well as direct military effects." He warned, "We face a complex situation which will demand constant review of our tactics, adequacy of our forces and effectiveness of our operations against the enemy. In my opinion, the most important requirement for success is a demonstrated determination to stick to our guns," which made sense given the attritional character of American strategy. Sharp held out hope for a conclusion to the war that would be favorable to South Vietnam and the United States, but the air war against North Vietnam had to be escalated if such an outcome had any hope of occurring.[299]

Walt W. Rostow, President Johnson's special assistant, largely agreed. The air strategy, however, had not thus far persuaded Hanoi, otherwise Rostow would not have proposed another strategic reappraisal. Rostow's ideas were similar to those of Admiral Sharp: comprehensive interdiction of materiel entering North Vietnam, disrupting the entirety of Hanoi's economy, and focusing bombing in the panhandle, as if it was a narrowing funnel. Rostow even admitted in January 1967 that there had "been little systematic thought about a northern strategy as a whole"—a shocking confession. Rostow suggested that the administration consider a broader strategy, policy and strategy issues the administration should have resolved in 1965. He also believed time was of the essence as far as bombing or negotiating their way to a resolution, because the leaders in Hanoi were trying to outlast them through the completion of the next American election cycle in 1968.[300]

The chiefs of staff wanted to focus bombing against the more lucrative untouched targets that existed in the Hanoi–Haiphong complex.[301] President Johnson for his part started to change his mind about the focus of the war and "had begun to see the air campaign as a means to break the North's will to fight."[302] Rolling Thunder 53 constituted a renewal of the bombing campaign, but it did not reach the level of intensity the JCS sought. It at least decreased the no-bombing area to ten miles around Hanoi.[303]

The Johnson administration next undercut its agenda by offering to suspend the bombing campaign so negotiations could begin if North Vietnam would stop sending troops and supplies into South Vietnam. His missive made no mention of Hanoi removing its troops.[304] For his part, Secretary Rusk was fed up with the North Vietnamese government because the US had sent out probes and feelers and now a full offer to talk, but his counterparts were essentially nonresponsive.[305] When the US shut down bombing for four days during the 1967 Tet holidays, analysts estimated the North Vietnamese moved the same amount of supplies during that time that would have required nearly five weeks to move if attempted under the bombs. Rolling Thunder resumed on February 13, 1967, and Ho Chi Minh not only blamed the US for all that was happening in South Vietnam, but also reiterated his demand that the US remove its troops, stop its bombing, and recognize the NLF as a precondition to talks. The North Vietnamese anticipated attacks against vulnerable vital centers, such as large power stations, and began to disperse electricity production by switching to small portable generators.[306]

The renewal of Rolling Thunder continued the pattern of bombing for indeterminate strategic results. Once again, determining the effects of the missions was imprecise. The Navy bombed the Thai Nguyen Iron and Steel Plant, the Bac Giang Thermal Power Plant, and as always, they were heavily damaged.[307] General Wheeler argued the destruction of the latter would be a grave setback for North Vietnamese industry and their will to continue the war.[308] A Navy analysis asserted that destroying the pig iron processing plant hurt the country because they would now have to import iron.[309] But did North Vietnam have any plants for converting iron into finished products? The following month it was the turn for the Haiphong Cement Plant to be bombed, and the steel plant received another visit from A-6A Intruders. None of this was decisive, and CINCPAC assumed the bombings had degraded the tonnage of supplies sent into South Vietnam. The targeting of a concrete-producing facility has been criticized as mirror imaging, and maybe it was. On the other hand, Hanoi's propaganda movies had emphasized the building of it as a component of Vietnamese economic progress, and the North Vietnamese evidently really were quite proud of it. Navy A-4Es and A-6As bombed it on April 25, 1967.[310]

Destroying targets one at a time was insufficiently destructive, but President Johnson recognized this distinction only to a point. He exclaimed in February that North Vietnam was successfully waging a war against American morale and determination and was wearing down domestic support for the war.[311] If that was the case then the administration needed to base its use of force on the psychological effects of military actions on all of the relevant actors, and the extent to which those reactions would move the war toward or away from American policy goals.[312] Some in the Department of Defense (DoD) agreed, seeing Hanoi's strategy as endure losses, draw out the war so the Americans realized a stalemate existed, then the American public would withdraw its support for the war. According to the Vietnamese official history, their strategy was more aggressive, more centered around battle, and more focused on conventional forces than the Americans realized.[313] Whatever the communists' strategy was, American political and military leaders held interminable discussions on what to do next—actions confirming their strategy as insufficient, and the war stalemated.[314]

The president's advisors and generals disagreed on how to break the deadlock. Admiral Sharp believed escalating the bombing would advance American strategy and proposed hitting fifty-nine targets from April to October. Johnson permitted an escalation (although he denied it was taking place) in April when he approved the bombing of power stations within Haiphong's restricted area. In fact, targets were selected from each of PACOM's target sets.[315] Robert Komer, the president's acting national security advisor, did not believe bombing would ever persuade Hanoi to change its war aims. Senator Mike Mansfield, one of the most influential members of Congress, already believed the air interdiction/coercive bombings had failed.[316] The consul general in Hong Kong rejected the assertion that bombing would crack North Vietnamese will; they valued their political objectives more than they valued their limited industry.[317] During a meeting with Herbert Marcovich and Raymond Aubrac in July 1967, two functionaries for Henry Kissinger, North Vietnamese Prime Minister Pham Van Dong blustered, "We have been fighting for our independence for four thousand years. We have defeated the Mongols three times. The United States Army, strong as it is, is not as terrifying as Genghis Khan."[318]

McGeorge Bundy concluded Rolling Thunder was ineffective in persuading Hanoi to alter its fundamental goals, never would be able to do so, and never could have. He even wrote, "the president never claimed that it would," and that bombing as the way to squeeze fundamental concessions from Hanoi had "never been the official government position," but the White House certainly communicated through its actions that it believed the bombing campaign was a war winner.[319] Bundy by that time believed only air interdiction was warranted; bombing valuable economic targets in urban areas carried with it too many drawbacks for too little return, but contradictorily wanted that segment of the bombing campaign to continue.[320]

Hanoi's policy goals interacted with America's strategy: Ho and his government most certainly were determined to hold fast until after the November 1968 election, thus a dramatic American escalation could not achieve decisive results until 1969.[321] Adding to the challenge of successful coercion, the Americans were running out of major targets for bombing missions, excepting seaports. Secretary McNamara and Deputy Secretary of Defense Cyrus Vance believed little was to be gained by more bombing above the 20th parallel; sorties into that area would not make the North Vietnamese give in. Air missions should instead be devoted primarily to interdiction targets, they argued, along with the bombing of other targets that would force the North Vietnamese to devote a lot of effort to maintaining their air defenses. Their recommendation was flawed because the targets that would draw the most air defense attention were in the region they wanted to deemphasize or not bomb. Grasping at straws, McNamara hoped the Soviets would encourage the Vietnamese to talk. A marquee for incompetent statecraft, they wrote, "This proposed policy would not be done for the purpose of getting Hanoi to change its ways or negotiate." If not, then what was it good for?[322]

The administration was also trying to rewrite the history of its goals to match what limited military force could accomplish. Rostow insisted the administration had never said the bombing could cut off the movement of forces into South Vietnam. It would divert North Vietnamese efforts toward defense and might contribute in a meaningful way to the ending of the war. William Bundy proposed multiple options for continued bombing: interdiction, hitting bombed targets again, striking more targets above twenty degrees latitude, and escalating to targets like Haiphong Harbor, dams, and Phuc Yen Air Base. Maxwell Taylor adamantly defended air interdiction as effective and necessary; if it was not, the North Vietnamese would not have worked so hard to move supplies during the bombing halts. He was amazed anyone could propose reducing a military effort that destroyed men and materiel intended to kill Americans and South Vietnamese.[323]

Ultimately, the approved escalation had little of true worth to escalate against, besides Haiphong and other smaller seaports. The US already bombed most of the meaningful targets. Besides, McNamara warned, escalation would further damage the United States' image. Bombing thus far failed to make Hanoi give up its infiltration operations, and the enemy remained steadfast and determined. Better to bomb interdiction targets south of the Red River Valley. The only good the bombing accomplished that spring was to inflict a lot of damage on the few twentieth-century components of North Vietnam's economy; it was indecisive against North Vietnam's political will and its infiltration program.[324] The JCS nevertheless maintained their desire for escalation, and according to McNamara even suggested the use of nuclear weapons against supply routes from China into North Vietnam (the JCS memorandum makes no mention whatsoever of the use of nuclear weapons).[325] Chairman Wheeler added that the air interdiction effort had to stop not only flows through North Vietnam, but also imports, a point the military had been arguing for two years.[326]

When air attacks commenced against Hanoi's power generation facilities on May 19, 1967, the missions inflicted a great deal of damage, but since the government had distributed portable generators throughout the city, recovery did not take long. A quick recovery meant the mission had not inflicted decisive damage. On the other hand, French diplomats commented that morale in the Hanoi area was down, and the locals exhibited fear and weariness for the first time. Moreover, the bombing was not providing Hanoi with a propaganda coup. The diplomats noticed that nearly every bomb hit its target and that it was exceedingly rare for even one to hit a civilian residential area—right in line with the military's objective of not bombing people.[327] Nevertheless, the campaign seemed to be becoming a habit, a pursuit of narrow targeting results rather than something connected to a strategic-level coercion campaign, even though it may have begun to generate some strategic effects toward that end.

Stressing North Vietnam's war effort in the hope of producing a positive effect seemed to be the primary strategy. Admiral Sharp next wrote of cordoning off Hanoi and Haiphong by destroying internal transportation routes if his planes could not hit the piers and ships themselves.[328] Admiral Roy L. Johnson, however, was not so sure, having written in May that Navy bombing missions were only slowing rail traffic by destroying tracks and dropping bridges. Because the North Vietnamese determined how they responded to the air campaign, one had to talk of *keeping* something out of commission; they did not allow damage to remain permanent. Navy air strikes against the Dong Phong Thuong Railroad Bridge dropped one span on May 2; two days later it was back in use. It took another strike on May 7 to put it out of commission again.[329] Air strikes against the rail line from Hanoi northeast to China shut it down for nearly four weeks while those against the one from Thai Nguyen kept it inoperable for more than two weeks. One assessment argued that because sites lay unrepaired more than a month at a time the North Vietnamese did not have enough people available to rebuild. Sharp then asked permission to bomb a factory that produced fertilizer in order to force the North Vietnamese to require more imports of the materials necessary to continue production, chemicals that were similar to those for manufacturing explosives. Maybe that would push their ports and railroads to the breaking point.[330] Another assessment concluded effective interdiction required daily twenty-four-hour air strikes, a practice that, if fully executed, would have been enormously taxing on air assets.[331]

A majority of the president's advisors were starting to conclude that by itself the bombing campaign was unable to force Hanoi to capitulate. McNamara reiterated that escalation would not work and risked bringing the Chinese and Soviets into the war. Interdiction was less risky and most likely to achieve significant goals, endanger fewer airmen, and, he argued, supported the pursuit of a negotiated settlement. If the South Vietnamese could start to defeat the Viet Cong, the US could wage the air interdiction campaign in a way that would produce political gains. But the bombing continued as an attritional demonstration. All the while, more and more individuals in the US government denied that the war was "stalemated," which meant it was.[332]

The fact that the North Vietnamese kept demanding the bombing stop before they would negotiate suggested that Rolling Thunder was wearing them down. Had it really been decisive, the North Vietnamese would have offered major concessions to make it stop. The following month the State Department received feelers through Norwegian intermediaries that a bombing halt would result in talks. Days later, Alexei Kosygin privately pressed President Johnson to negotiate directly with Hanoi. In fact, the chairman received a communique from Hanoi during the lunch the two were enjoying during their summit in Glassboro, New Jersey: if the Americans would suspend the bombing, the North Vietnamese would negotiate. Kosygin ignored Johnson's concerns about the five PAVN divisions just across the DMZ he believed were poised to strike into South Vietnam. When President Johnson said that he was prepared to halt the bombing campaign and begin talks, Kosygin's reaction was tepid. These missives amounted to nothing.[333]

Materially, the 1967 bombings made the war more costly and difficult for the North Vietnamese and relatively less so for the South Vietnamese and Americans.[334] By the summer, Seventh AF saw the campaign generate several consequences: the North Vietnamese had to devote a lot of manpower and energy to rebuild rail lines and bridges and construct bypasses, move trains under the cover of darkness and bad weather, and rebuild roads. Troops had to march long distances because so many trucks had been destroyed. Additional effects were indirect: some people left the cities for safer ground, work teams dispersed fuel, as many as 500,000 laborers repaired the roads and railroad tracks and other bomb damage, while thousands manned air defense sites. None of this proved catastrophic for the North Vietnamese, although railroad damage was extensive enough to persuade China to switch to shipborne transportation to supply its surrogate.[335] Overall the bombing campaign was preventing throughput of materiel into South Vietnam from increasing; it was not cutting it off, but the bombing campaign was effective enough to keep the North Vietnamese from overrunning South Vietnam. Refusing to mine and bomb Haiphong really was a lost opportunity given that 75 percent of regime-sustaining imports flowed through that seaport.[336]

Pessimism took hold of the Johnson administration. During his July 1967 trip to Vietnam, Secretary McNamara and the military continued to disagree across the board. Changing his tune from the spring, McNamara rejected claims that interdiction was effective in August. Rostow commented that there was evidence the bombing might be reducing inflows of supplies by 50 percent, to which McNamara replied that he'd seen reports showing that the reduction was just one percent.[337] What alarmed President Johnson the most was the attitude of the American people, who seemed to think that the war had become unwinnable. He believed winning was possible, and that destroying the petroleum and electrical targets in North Vietnam would lead Hanoi to withdraw from the war. McNamara looked to South Vietnam as the most important factor, while the director of the CIA, Richard Helms, thought in terms of a withdrawal that would not impose too much geopolitical damage on the United States. Testifying before the Senate in August 1967, General McConnell believed the air campaign had been effective enough to prevent the PAVN from waging a greatly expanded war in South Vietnam.[338] The North Vietnamese would not have exerted such efforts as they were against an ineffectual air campaign.

Assessments pleaded that success was just around the corner. One analyst assumed the North Vietnamese truck fleet was of extreme value to them, so the losses on the Ho Chi Minh Trail were ruinous. Furthermore, consider the measures the enemy took during bombing halts to move supplies and repair routes; that meant constant bombing to nullify the Vietnamese countermeasures. Air interdiction had to continue because of its indirect effects on frontline soldiers; the more the PAVN hurt, the better for US grunts. Finally, the bombing destroyed a massive amount of materiel, something that should not be discounted. Tentative attacks against electricity production and the North Vietnamese air defense system passed up an opportunity to inflict greater shock and allowed the enemy to compensate for future losses by importing generators and improving defenses. In PACAF's judgment, the gradual and intermittent character of the bombardment effort weakened its shock value and gave the North Vietnamese time to adjust.[339]

Air Force and Navy evaluations saw the glass as half full. Seventh Air Force estimated air strikes destroyed more than 6,200 trucks and nearly 15,000 tons of supplies. Secondary explosions probably destroyed another 3,000 tons. According to this estimate, that 18,000-ton total would have supplied the PAVN for a year, assuming that they fought one day out of thirty or the VC for more than seven years. Communist forces, however, were waging a more intense war, meaning the losses were more costly.[340] The best a Navy analysis could say was the war was now a contest of resolve. It agreed that the efforts the North Vietnamese exerted against the air war proved Rolling Thunder was strategically effective. An assessment of the results of operations for July through September 1967 indicated they had isolated Hanoi and reduced the capacity of its primary roads and railroads to transport freight. Collectively it had only an erosive effect, reducing the transshipment of supplies the VC need. Since the enemy had not capitulated, the report recommended eliminating the no-bomb areas in North Vietnam, reducing the buffer zone along the Chinese border to fifteen miles, and bombings without restrictions against the roads and railroads from the Chinese border into North Vietnam.[341] The constancy and monotony of the Navy's monthly reports of bombing strategic targets further suggests the indecisiveness of this campaign.[342] In September, Seventh Air Force Intelligence was confident the air campaign had become effective enough that "the promise of an ever-increasing rate of destruction during the coming season cannot but help give North Vietnamese leaders cause to reflect and reconsider continued aggression."³⁴³ But what if after they paused and reconsidered they decided to press on? Another assessment noted that measurements of effectiveness were negative: cargo the trucks did not deliver, supplies enemy troops did not get, and battles the enemy did not wage due to shortages.³⁴⁴

After weeks of discussions on what to do next, President Johnson began providing clear guidance on August 16, 1967: "Our strategy, as I see it, is that we destroy all we can without involving China and Russia between now and September 1." He worried that if the US did not make a full effort against North Vietnam the war would lose the support of the American people. He permitted air strikes in Hanoi, Haiphong, and the buffer zone with China. The president wanted visible activity while the weather in Southeast Asia permitted bombing, and he wanted to hit most of the targets the military requested. Missions needed to bomb places that promised the most return for the least cost, but he set boundaries that contradicted the goal of making a full effort against North Vietnam: "We are not going to hit Haiphong Harbor because we are not going to hit any ships. We are not going to bomb Hanoi because we are not going to hit civilians. And we must be careful about the buffer zone because of the danger in going over the border. But we have got to put more pressure on."³⁴⁵ Johnson was never going to permit an "all-out" campaign.

Politics put the president in a quandary: he had to be aggressive to stave off hawks like Senator John C. Stennis (D-Mississippi), who might use either the need for escalation or its failure, to axe Johnson's Great Society social programs.³⁴⁶ Armed reconnaissance missions near the Hanoi exclusion zone could not appear too aggressive, and they could only hit Kep, Hoa Lac, and Kein An airfields—if American jets were chasing MiGs during an air strike against another target. After August 30, the Navy was not permitted to mine Haiphong, Hon Gai, or Cam Pha harbors; carrier aircraft waged air strikes against the roads and railroads radiating out from them in order to cut off those ports.³⁴⁷ The president who claimed he wanted an expanded effort could not bring himself to follow through.

When one considers the divided opinions within the administration, this auto-thrash of indecision is understandable. Secretary McNamara had lost hope, although he did not voice his doubts until fall 1967.³⁴⁸ Averell Harriman, the ambassador-at-large for President Johnson, noted that McNamara believed military victory was not possible, and that the US should press the Saigon government to enter negotiations with the National Liberation Front. Secretary Rusk believed the US could accomplish its goals, but Harriman believed Rusk "was asking for unconditional surrender of North Vietnam and the VC."³⁴⁹ The Secretary of the Air Force favored a marginally unchanged air campaign that would devote 20 percent of sorties to targets north of the 20th parallel, including routes from China and Vietnamese seaports. Rostow was steadfast that the bombing was more and more effective and supported additional missions.³⁵⁰ McNamara authorized many but not all of the targets that had been nominated, and Rusk wondered whether minor targets were worth American lives. Army Chief of Staff Johnson remained confident in the attrition strategy and the air campaign; one had to wait for the effects of the bombing to snowball. With an air campaign there was no way to know for sure which mission would reach the tipping point. He added that, "Every blow makes him stretch his resources and at some point his resources will not be able to be stretched anymore."³⁵¹

But there were no clear indicators and no consensus. While four-fifths of the air campaign was sent after the enemy's logistics and had caused a great amount of damage and diverted hundreds of thousands of people toward repair work, their damage control mollified many of the effects of the bombing.³⁵² According to McNamara, the chiefs were convinced that Rolling Thunder was advancing the president's goals but that he, "this poor, inexperienced civilian didn't know what the hell was going on and had a different view."³⁵³ On the other hand, several of America's east Asian allies—Australia, New Zealand, Thailand, South Korea, and South Vietnam—believed Rolling Thunder was essential. They also favored mining Haiphong Harbor and opposed bombing halts.³⁵⁴ In spite of that level of assurance from allies with much at stake in the war's outcome, fear of Chinese reactions intimidated some into opposing escalation.³⁵⁵

This was a failure of grand strategy and war, not of strategy nor of air power, because the Johnson administration was not coordinating the strong support it had from allies for a harder line with a willingness to justify escalation beforehand through the media and United Nations. Although Johnson had met with Premier Alexei Kosygin, he refused to aggressively press North Vietnam's sponsors to stop supporting Hanoi's aggression and violation of the sovereignty in Laos, Cambodia, and South Vietnam.

Leaders looked for some strategically significant effects after each mission. Admiral Sharp believed the dropping of two spans of the Paul Doumer Bridge in Hanoi on August 11 reduced the morale of the North Vietnamese, and that it was a testament to the capabilities, accuracy, and effectiveness of the bombing campaign. Soon thereafter, pontoon bridges and ferry boats carried supplies around the bombed-out Paul Doumer Bridge. As a consequence of bombing electrical power plants, the North Vietnamese suffered great inconveniences and morale fell—but life went on.³⁵⁶ What little industry the country had was now rubble, bridges were in rivers instead of over them, railroad lines were cut to pieces, but the director of the CIA noted again Hanoi found ways to transport war materiel to the battle zones in spite of difficulties and shortages.³⁵⁷

The administration's goals for these missions were contradictory: increase pressure while not signaling escalation. Therefore, the president had them spread out and not conducted continuously, possibly to support the Pennsylvania Initiative, an effort through a pair of Frenchmen and Henry Kissinger, the professor cum political operative, to pursue effective peace talks with North Vietnamese Prime Minister Pham Van Dong.³⁵⁸ Greater force would have made a settlement more attractive, so it is not surprising that these missions in August and September failed strategically even when they were operationally successful; the administration simply was not committed to them.³⁵⁹

"Bomb, bomb, bomb, that's all you know," President Johnson complained to the Army chief of staff in spring 1965.³⁶⁰ The president told General Johnson two-and-a-half years later to make the JCS develop new approaches for resolving the war. More troops or a switch to nuclear weapons were not options, LBJ warned. The president believed Congress would bring things to a head, either through escalation or withdrawal, when it reconvened in January 1968.³⁶¹

Weather cut Rolling Thunder sorties in September 1967 by a third, from 11,634 in August to 8,540 the following month. Strikes still managed to reduce transportation routes around Hanoi and Haiphong in accordance with the goal of cutting off those cities. The bombing that month was inconclusive because the North Vietnamese were able to repair the damage, and CINCPAC knew this from reconnaissance photographs. Worsening weather during the fall was going to mean more reliance on MSQ-77 missions and A-6A Intruder sorties, which would keep the pressure on, but the former lacked the accuracy to destroy targets and there were too few A-6As to wreck the North Vietnamese supply system.³⁶²

Air strikes hit a bridge and a warehouse two miles north of the center of Haiphong on September 11, but of course such an operation was not one of closing the harbor. The purpose of this attack seemed to be to demonstrate that American pilots could hit with enough accuracy so the North Vietnamese could not credibly accuse the US of recklessly putting civilians in danger. To try and have the same effect as closing Haiphong, CINCPAC had directed air strikes against bridges around that city, along with armed reconnaissance missions, since August 8. This operation was not carried out with the vigor the planners intended, and although the bridge-busting effort went well, the main consequence of this action seemed to be just another example of North Vietnamese persistence: moving supplies on barges. September bombings cut shipments from Haiphong to Hanoi by half, but 4,300 tons were still getting through each day.[363]

John Colvin, the United Kingdom's consul general in Hanoi, asserted that the American air campaign had North Vietnam on the ropes in September, and the bombing was coming close to persuading them to come to terms.[364] Perhaps LBJ's August restriction cost the air campaign an opportunity to effect negotiations in a conclusive manner, but CINCPAC concluded that North Vietnamese leaders believed eroding domestic support for the war in the United States would eventually result in an American withdrawal.[365]

Altogether, bombing and negotiating formed elements of gamesmanship of the highest order, and more often than not, Hanoi pursued its goals with more steadfastness and skill than did Washington. The world audience mattered greatly, because the US was trying to establish that it was making every effort to restrain its military campaign while at the same time trying to negotiate from a position of strength—contradictory efforts that rendered each ineffectual. North Vietnamese leaders knew this, and so did William Bundy, who observed that Hanoi practiced statecraft that was far more sophisticated than that of the Americans, and who had manipulated the United States into a position where if it pursued its own interests aggressively, the United States would get blamed for trying.[366] That they outmaneuvered their American counterparts is not surprising, considering that Johnson's national security advisor, Walt Rostow, exclaimed during a September Tuesday luncheon, "I do not see any connection between bombing and negotiations"—a statement that placed his understanding of basic statecraft in doubt.[367]

In September 1967, Seventh AF asked again for an escalation in the bombing campaign. The continuation of air interdiction against railroad and other transportation targets around Hanoi and Haiphong was not new, but Momyer also requested permission to strike ports and harbors. Bombing would not close Haiphong that fall, but the chairman of the JCS opened some targets within the ten-mile prohibited zone in Hanoi to limited attacks in October. These included a couple of storage areas and a railroad bridge, and follow-on strikes against a transformer, two storage depots, and two bridges. Furthermore, Phuc Yen Air Base, the main fighter-interceptor base for Hanoi, would finally be bombed again. Denied an all-out campaign, CINCPAC opted for sustained bombing against six groups of targets: electricity production, industry that supported the war effort, transportation, military bases, petroleum products, and ports—Haiphong in particular. The bombing halt six months later prevented their culmination.[368] Although the total set of available targets for bombing was huge at approximately 9,000, most were "worthless"; only about 400 were targets of substantial importance in the judgment of the JCS. Furthermore, of those the JCS considered important, political leaders granted permission to bomb only twenty-four of them.[369]

Instead of squeezing harder while he bombed more in order to compel the North Vietnamese to make concessions, President Johnson put forth his San Antonio Formula on September 29, offering to stop the bombing if North Vietnam promised to negotiate with the intention of reaching a compromise and not take advantage of a bombing halt, even though they always had in the past.[370] From the North Vietnamese perspective, negotiating before the bombing ended was too shameful, and they repeated their demanding terms the US and South Vietnam could not accept: a permanent bombing halt, and the "presence" of the NLF in negotiations.³⁷¹ After their response, President Johnson prophetically commented to his advisors, "History may make us look silly on this whole thing.... I think they are playing us for suckers. They have no more intention of talking than we have of surrendering ... all of this adds up. It is a question of which one can last the longest."³⁷² The war revealed that the North Vietnamese operated with a more sophisticated and holistic concept of what war was. For them, war involved not only military operations but also efforts to establish political control inside South Vietnam and gain diplomatic advantages in relation to their enemies.³⁷³

Three years prior, Walt W. Rostow warned that successful diplomacy required the president to confront his adversary with force, but LBJ was never committed enough to achieving his objectives in Vietnam.³⁷⁴ Johnson understood the interrelationships between domestic and foreign policy to an extent, but he never comprehended the degree to which diplomacy and military force were commingled. Furthermore, air power was now more than firepower. It had become a geopolitical tool, a meaning, an adjunct to diplomacy, and a factor in American domestic politics. Consider the reactions of the UN, student protesters, and the press. One had to assess an air campaign's effects in all those realms to assess its effectiveness.

President Johnson permitted more bombing following the rejection of his offer, approving half a dozen new targets in the Hanoi area, upon which American fighter-bombers pounced.³⁷⁵ Efforts in October continued to produce familiar results; 8,900 sorties managed to destroy or damage 1,500 vehicles. Weather was better than expected, allowing nineteen flying days, and the restriction on bombing inside the Hanoi ten-mile zone was suspended on October 23 so fighter-bombers could hit eight targets, including Hanoi's power station, a pair of bridges, and five brand new targets. The campaign produced considerable damage, all of it repairable. The North Vietnamese asked the USSR for more trucks, worked on building a new road from China, and repaired bomb damage.³⁷⁶ The hawkish Walt Rostow found himself agreeing with the CIA that although the air campaign had greatly increased the effort necessary to move supplies down into South Vietnam, and had drawn away hundreds of thousands of people from positive pursuits to work air defense and repair, "bombing cannot reduce their capacity to support the [insurgency in the] South to the extent that they would be forced to abandon the war in the South."³⁷⁷ The campaign may have, however, placed a cap on Hanoi's ability to cover manpower losses inside South Vietnam, which provided an opportunity for some success against the VC.³⁷⁸

Hanoi was closer to achieving its goals than was Washington. The CIA warned that although a bombing halt would probably result in "talks," North Vietnamese leaders differentiated "between *talks,* private, tentative, and exploratory, and *negotiations,* the formal settlement of outstanding issues [italics in original]." The North Vietnamese would perceive a unilateral bombing halt as a sign of weakness, and either way they would exploit a halt to repair damage and revamp its air defenses, and as always, send more troops into South Vietnam.³⁷⁹ The United States was on the horns of a dilemma. Terminating Rolling Thunder would weaken its negotiating position and strengthen North Vietnam's military campaign against South Vietnam. Continuing the bombing may not lead to decisive results, and that path risked portraying the US as stubborn and uninterested in solving the conflict, but it had to contribute to improved conditions in South Vietnam. McNamara, for one, favored a bombing pause because he believed that would increase domestic support for the war. His reasoning indicated how weak the American position was: the US had to base military operations on their relationships to its domestic audience rather than on their potential of persuading its enemy. No wonder LBJ asked, "How are we ever going to win?" McNamara replied, "I have no idea how we can win in the next 12 months."³⁸⁰

Their condition further illustrates this failure of war. The CIA concluded that bombing targets in Hanoi and Haiphong would not move the interdiction campaign closer to decisiveness, and the agency's leading analysts believed bombing would not cause Hanoi to throw up its hands within the next year or two. As had been the case, the North Vietnamese were not going to negotiate until the bombing stopped unconditionally.[381] Supreme Court Justice Abe Fortas understood the illogic of Johnson's desperation as well as anyone: why on earth would the North Vietnamese negotiate after the pressure of bombing was removed when they would not negotiate while suffering under the continued rain of bombs? Fortas stated, "This has always been incomprehensible to me."[382] Admirals Sharp and Charles Turner Joy argued for years that it was necessary to maintain the pressure of bombing *during* negotiations so as to not give up leverage over the enemy.[383] McNamara exclaimed the bombing campaign could not win the war on its own and, "The great danger is to lead our people to think we can win the war overnight with bombing." But that ship had sailed; the bombing campaign was treated as if it was a possible war winner but it could not even persuade Ho Chi Minh to talk.[384] Johnson at least had developed the sense to reject the suggestion that a unilateral bombing halt would result in honest negotiations from the North Vietnamese.[385]

Advisors still offered inverted logic to the president. How would a refusal to escalate the war and an eventual termination of bombing "increase pressure on Hanoi to reduce its military activities or to enter upon negotiations" when the escalation and bombing of the preceding two years revealed Hanoi's lack of interest in negotiating until the United States evacuated Southeast Asia, at which point negotiations would have been totally irrelevant?[386] Clark Clifford wrote on November 7, 1967, "I am at a loss to understand this logic." Further ridiculing the neurosis taking over the White House, he reminded the president that, "In World War I, World War II and the Korean War, the pressure was constantly increased until the enemy found it intolerable and capitulated."[387]

Policy makers were asking their military force to accomplish something that a military force cannot: persuade with limited force a group of totally committed political leaders to give up an unlimited political goal. The true logjam rested between two policies, not two military campaigns. The nature of Hanoi's political goals placed their immovable object against reluctant strength: the United States' desire to win the war on the cheap. In this Johnson was dishonest with himself. One moment he cited the relationship between bombing and a negotiated settlement, and the next he claimed Rolling Thunder had but three objectives, all of which the air campaign had already achieved and none of which were decisive: improve South Vietnam's morale, increase the cost of the war for North Vietnam, and elevate the cost of moving supplies down into South Vietnam.

When Senator Robert Byrd, however, got Secretary McNamara to admit that despite the campaign, the insurgents still had enough ammunition with which to fight, it was clear Johnson's military strategy had failed. Indeed, a few days later during another meeting, everyone present agreed with Secretary McNamara as he read a CIA analysis that bombing could not reduce the movement of soldiers and supplies down the Ho Chi Minh Trail to zero.[388] Dean Rusk was more measured. He did not believe escalating the bombing campaign could break Hanoi's will. He also rejected a complete cessation because bombing was one of the US's main forms of power and influence, the other being the war in South Vietnam.[389] The decision to neither escalate nor bail out put forth the façade of astute observation, but the discussions revealed that the strategy was to march in place and hope they got somewhere. For his part, Secretary McNamara was on his way out. An exhausted and beaten McNamara effectively left his post as secretary of defense on November 29, 1967. Johnson nominated him as president of the World Bank the following month.[390] As of that month McNamara was a broken man. According to Harry McPherson, special counsel to the president, during one meeting McNamara lost it, cussing about the Air Force's bombing campaign, and with tears, "McNamara went on for a full five minutes in 'rage and grief and almost disorientation.'"[391]

November witnessed the climax of Operation Rolling Thunder. Washington took more targets off its prohibited list, and the Air Force and Navy flew and bombed until the seasonal monsoon forced progressively more cancellations into 1968.[392] As 1967 ended, there was still no consensus on the effectiveness of the air interdiction campaign. The Defense Intelligence Agency was convinced bombing destroyed about 600 trucks in the panhandle of Laos. That was not a decisive kill rate given the reserves of trucks the North Vietnamese possessed, but this news excited the president and the CJCS, who cabled Westmoreland that he was certain that the effort was "reducing" their logistics, "and we are hurting him (I believe more than we realize)."[393] "Hurting" and "reducing" do not defeat committed enemies. Seventh Air Force argued Rolling Thunder was close to incapacitating the North Vietnamese economy, which would lead to its inability to function.[394]

The CIA examined the data and was more skeptical.[395] Secretary McNamara received another report from the JASON Division of the Institute for Defense Analyses, which argued the bombing campaign up to that time had been ineffective. In no way was the campaign having a significant effect on the war in South Vietnam, since communist forces grew in strength and the bombing had not truly harmed the supply side of the war because Eastern bloc countries, not North Vietnamese industry, supplied most of the materiel for the war. The campaign was not persuading Hanoi to alter its agenda. Nevertheless, Admiral Sharp still recited that the three-pronged strategy of offensive operations against enemy forces in South Vietnam, the bombing campaign against North Vietnam, and expanding Saigon's control over the countryside was working—victory was beyond the reach of the communists. The year ended predictably. The United States suspended bombing during the Christmas holidays and the North Vietnamese exploited the bombing halt to strengthen its military.[396]

A January 1968 assessment concluded bombing had either destroyed or rendered inoperable 100 percent of North Vietnam's chemical, cement, iron and steel, and explosives production, and 81 percent of its electrical production and stored fuel. Consequently, imports were up, especially food, which was 300 percent greater than in 1965.[397] In this sense the bombing campaign produced serious consequences that may have been debilitating if not for the imports the Soviet Union and China had provided. North Vietnam remained steadfast. The bombing created vulnerabilities—the transshipment pathways out of Haiphong and the road and railroad connections with China—but it had also exposed Hanoi's determination.

Admiral Sharp denied the air campaign was a failure because it had never promised to cut off the supply chain, only reduce it, which it did; however, the reduction had not concluded the war, which was what the president required.[398] The CIA posited that North Vietnamese leaders perceived their positions as strong as far as achieving long-term policy goals were concerned. If, as the Central Committee of the Lao Dong Party might expect, their opponents had no real hope of forming an anti-Communist government and army in South Vietnam that could stand on its own, even an American-led military victory was in the end a moot point. They also understood the relationship between diplomacy and military force, rebuffing American diplomatic efforts, appreciating that "nothing can be gained at the bargaining table unless it has already been won on the battlefield."[399] That was, in fact, a central tenet of their strategy, while the Americans demanded successful diplomacy in lieu of battlefield success.[400]

For doctrinal reasons the JCS persisted in calling for escalation and created another plan to escalate the air campaign against North Vietnam in 1968. The tone that comes through these three years of recommendations was, "you have never unleashed us. Of course, all we've ever recommended is 'bomb, bomb, bomb'—that is the nature of the one kind of offensive power we can use against North Vietnam"—and the generals had a point. Air strikes would exploit, in their opinion, the vulnerability of North Vietnam to interdiction, and this plan envisioned a much more aggressive and intense bombing effort. Bombing and mining would close ports, continuous bombing would make roads and railroads from China impassible, and supply line interdiction within North Vietnam would cut off Hanoi and Haiphong from each other. The safe areas in those cities would be reduced to radii of three and 1.5 nautical miles, respectively. The plan estimated the bombing could reduce imports as much as 90 percent for supplies arriving by sea, 80 percent by rail, and 70 percent via roads from China. Along with an escalated ground war in South Vietnam to attrit enemy supplies there, this campaign would harm Hanoi's war effort, perhaps conclusively. The generals believed it would force Hanoi to make serious concessions.[401]

The military wanted to carry out an unleashed effort to break the Lao Dong Party's commitment to victory, but by this time American civilian leaders had lost heart. McNamara opposed reducing the safe areas around Hanoi and Haiphong because he believed the US would pay a high price in aircraft and civilian casualties for little in terms of militarily worthwhile targets. He and the chiefs disagreed on every point except that American losses would climb. Wheeler noted that Vietnamese civilians received ample warning of air strikes and went into bomb shelters, which assisted the American goal of bombing war materiel and not civilian bystanders. Wheeler also argued that the kind of destruction Rolling Thunder caused for urban targets did not begin to approach what was done to German cities in WWII. Indeed, civilian casualties in North Vietnam caused him little discomfort when he considered the kind of slaughter and torture the Viet Cong and PAVN practiced in South Vietnam. Neither made any effort to minimize noncombatant casualties while US airmen went to great lengths to avoid killing enemy civilians. The North Vietnamese used populated areas as human shields for their AAA and SAMs. After this meeting Johnson terminated the safe zones and permitted fourteen authorized targets within the formerly restricted areas.[402]

During these debates the National Liberation Front unleashed its "General Offensive-General Uprising," more commonly known as the Tet Offensive. Hanoi had hoped to achieve a battlefield victory that would generate decisive political effects, but the relationship between events and American reactions did not occur in the way the North Vietnamese expected. The shocking sight of this countrywide explosion of violence after being told that the war was going well decisively undercut support for the war within the United States. The JCS argued that a far less restrained air campaign was now merited and appropriate, but the president would not unleash an expansion of Operation Rolling Thunder, a fatuous decision given the mendacity with which the communists had preceded the offensive with their calls for negotiations.[403]

During the Tet Offensive, the administration did not take advantage of the ARVN's stout defense against the VC, nor did it manifest greater pressure on the communists after American and South Vietnamese forces had killed thousands in a matter of days. Johnson instead met with UN Secretary General U Thant and reiterated his eagerness to stop Rolling Thunder if the North Vietnamese would just participate in sincere talks.[404] While the Tet Offensive produced a series of tactical slaughters and an operational defeat for the Viet Cong, President Johnson chose to respond as if nothing positive had taken place. He behaved like a weak, defeated leader begging for relief when the enemy had just gambled away their most committed veteran insurgents and Johnson's ally had demonstrated battle-winning tenacity. Lyndon Johnson needed to fight against his loss of will, but he was spent. Three years prior he had commented to Vice President Humphrey, "I'm not temperamentally equipped to be Commander-in-Chief.... I'm too sentimental to give the orders."[405] His reactions to the Tet Offensive confirmed his self-assessment in other people's blood.

While the Viet Cong attacked, the Joint Chiefs fought a rearguard action against the JASON Study's claims that Rolling Thunder had not been that effective. The US and South Vietnam gained nothing for their restraint and longanimity, the communists had replied with the Tet Offensive and a diplomatic pressure campaign. Ambassador Bunker wrote that a selective escalation of Rolling Thunder might be advantageous, especially as reprisals for the Tet Offensive. Given the administration's fear of possible Soviet and Chinese reactions to a major escalation of the war like an amphibious landing near Haiphong, a major change in military strategy was impossible.[406] The Air Force read the Tet Offensive as an indication that air interdiction was not effective enough. Movements of war materiel down the Ho Chi Minh Trail were higher than ever in December 1967, and even with the amounts air strikes destroyed, more than half got through to enemy troops. By now the Air Force had developed a better measure of air interdiction: how much war materiel enemy troops received. The Air Force therefore judged its 1967 interdiction campaign as anything but a success.[407]

The American response to Tet was not an escalated air campaign. Instead, General Westmoreland asked for 205,000 more troops to finish off the enemy after saying the VC had lost. That made no sense to Secretary of Defense Clark Clifford who wondered how the United States could assert the South Vietnamese and Americans had beaten the Viet Cong offensive and then ask for 200,000 more troops?[408] Clifford encountered more empty answers when he became secretary of defense: bombing alone would not win the war, and neither would the additional troops Westmoreland requested. Most distressing was the revelation that the military had "no plan in the traditional sense due to political restrictions imposed by Johnson," and all his briefers believed it would take several more years to achieve a military solution.[409]

By March the Johnson administration was moving not only toward a unilateral bombing halt, but also a major policy retreat. Senator J. William Fulbright, for one, tried to create political conditions in which the president could bring the United States out of the war without having won it. Johnson confessed that Fulbright understood sooner than he had that the war had poisoned everything. The United States was battering itself senseless over a war that it could not win; only the South Vietnamese could win it, if that was even possible. "I just think this war is a disaster," Fulbright said. "We just ought to get out of that country any way we can."[410]

Meanwhile, Senator Eugene McCarthy, a Democrat presidential candidate, won twenty of twenty-four delegates in the March 13 New Hampshire primary, putting him on a trajectory to defeat Johnson in the upcoming Wisconsin primary. Then Robert Kennedy entered the race. The USS *Pueblo* incident, the Tet Offensive, and economic problems all persuaded Johnson to carry out a most fundamental review of American goals for the war.[411]

Perhaps unilaterally implementing the San Antonio Formula and another bombing halt might provide some sort of a new start. Philip Habib, one of the "Wise Men" who met with Clark Clifford and Dean Rusk, said LBJ should end the bombing and talk with the North Vietnamese. Maybe they would negotiate, and perhaps diplomatic efforts could persuade the Soviets to pressure Hanoi to not take advantage of this bombing halt. The present time might be optimal for productive negotiations, the ambassador to the UN wrote, and they had never been as necessary.[412] Given these countries' past behavior, there was no reason to believe any of these hopes had any chance of producing positive results. General Wheeler advised that decisions on military strategy could wait; a short bombing halt would not matter that much militarily because the bad weather over North Vietnam through the middle of April forestalled most missions.[413] The argument that Hanoi would consider giving up on a vital policy goal after the United States removed an incentive for that choice—Operation Rolling Thunder—defies rational explanation. The administration held out hope based on the kind of reasoning it needed from the communists in order to achieve American objectives with the least strain on the United States instead of basing their strategy on the actual behavior coming out of Hanoi. But as March waned, more and more of the president's advisors concluded winning was impossible, and that continued war, especially the bombing of targets in North Vietnam, was wrecking America's standing in world opinion. Most argued it was time to terminate Rolling Thunder. Issues broader than the sound employment of force, diplomacy, and strategy overwhelmed the president. Fewer and fewer voters backed the war, domestic protests worsened, and a greater number of national leaders believed the war had become too challenging to win.[414] Secretary of Defense Clifford, who by March 30 believed the war was unwinnable, advised the president the US should withdraw. The president opted for de-escalation after receiving counsel from a wide-ranging set of advisors, particularly his secretary of state.[415]

Nevertheless, some military leaders still hoped for that comprehensive bombing campaign the Johnson administration had always denied them. Their recommendations did not advocate for an eruption of napalm rage, but instead emphasized coverage of every logistical supply route, leaving no sanctuary inside North Vietnam. Admiral Sharp believed an intense interdiction campaign as soon as the weather improved could deny logistical sanctuary and reinforce the message that the enemy simply could not wage unrestricted warfare in South Vietnam.[416] In his March 28 plan, General Momyer favored widening the bombing and terminating imports through Haiphong. He warned that targeting had to be comprehensive. For example, the bombing of Haiphong would not be that effective unless the railroads from China were also bombed, because supplies destined for the port could be rerouted through China. Targeting also needed to focus on choke points within North Vietnam, railroad yards and bridges in particular, places that took the most time to repair and where detours were difficult to construct. His proposal argued that air interdiction south of Vinh would be more difficult because the terrain allowed for more roads, many of which lay underneath trees. The North Vietnamese would find defeating the bombing in the panhandle easy: just drive the trucks around the craters, and the trucks that followed would soon compress the ground into a usable dirt roadway. Haiphong was an undeniably important target because it was the entry point for half of Hanoi's imports, but the North Vietnamese could also reroute those resources through China—thus the need for comprehensiveness. Without this renewed campaign North Vietnam's war would continue to bear fruit. This examination of the possible consequences of bombing halts was too narrow; by design it only considered military factors. Although it argued communist morale would improve as a result of a bombing halt, most of the assessments revolved around material effects: the ease and speed of the movement of supplies south, or the opportunity for MiGs to fly from sanctuaries inside North Vietnam.[417] Given events in the White House, Momyer's proposal was dead on arrival.

By March 29, President Johnson had decided to order another bombing halt, one that suspended bombing above twenty degrees latitude where the strategically significant targets lay. One reason was to gain more support within the US to continue the war and another was to defuse increasing protests across America. In addition, he sought to place the onus for the next step on Hanoi. Johnson still could not comprehend that the fate of South Vietnam was not open for discussion among the communists. He announced his decision on March 31, the bombing halt commenced on April 1, then expanded on November 1, when the administration moved the line two degrees south, about 138 miles. It also established a buffer zone around North Vietnam to preclude American aircraft from flying over that country by accident out of the concern that that could place the peace talks at risk.[418]

General Westmoreland favored this decision because it would free more aircraft for operations in South Vietnam. Since a greater air interdiction effort against the Ho Chi Minh Trail followed the halt, bringing Rolling Thunder to an end was not a complete cessation of the air campaign against the North Vietnamese war effort, and besides, the United States could shift the interdiction missions from Laos back to North Vietnam if necessary. The 1968 bombing halt was unpopular with the Air Force, and there were some within Southeast Asia who voiced disapproval with President Johnson's decision. The vice commander of Seventh AF, Major General Robert F. Worley, realized effective American military policy required military members to not openly criticize the president's decisions, and warned every airman to keep his opinions to himself, especially around the press.[419]

A cryptic response to Johnson's unilateral concession followed on April 3; the DRV was willing to determine "with the American side the unconditional cessation of the US bombing raids and all other acts of war against the Democratic Republic of Vietnam so that talks may start."[420] Next, as a component of their strategy to exhaust the Americans, the North Vietnamese wanted to have talks about having talks. Hanoi's fighting while talking strategy had lured the Johnson administration into a place where it actually had fewer options than it realized. The diplomatic aspect of this process, in this case deciding on where negotiations would take place, removed American military escalation as an option. Talks with the North Vietnamese were finally going to take place in Paris on May 10. Having made it so difficult to reach an agreement over a meeting place, Hanoi was betting Johnson would not be willing to sacrifice that progress with a resumption of Rolling Thunder, lest he be ridiculed for not giving diplomacy a chance. The communists provided Johnson with a pretense to resume bombing when they unleashed a smaller offensive in May, but by that time the Americans simply wanted out.[421] In this war, the variables of force and diplomacy interacted in unique ways. A gesture of goodwill actually set one up to be blamed for escalation when the offer was rejected, which meant that the US had fewer options since political realities precluded escalation.

Here again we see the difficulties of managing a limited war. Intense scrutiny and doubt were erasing the war's merits. In May a paper from the President's Science Advisory Committee concluded the bombing campaign was indecisive. Bombing had not persuaded Hanoi to change its ultimate agenda, nor had it inflicted decisive losses on the movement of supplies down the Ho Chi Minh Trail. The board offered nothing new except bombing executed more effectively with better technology. The JCS supported these recommendations.[422]

Into this push–pull of efforts and goals came the Soviets. Chairman Alexei Kosygin wrote President Johnson on June 5, "I and my colleagues believe—and we have grounds for this—that a full cessation by the United States of bombardments and other acts of war in relation to the DRV could promote a breakthrough in the situation that would open perspectives for peaceful settlement."[423] They were playing LBJ like a banjo. This was just what the administration wanted to hear: a "breakthrough" that could give them an opportunity to escape the war without making any more tough choices. Dean Rusk, however, recognized Kosygin was trying to persuade the US to stop the bombing without any reciprocity from Hanoi or Moscow.

Secretary of Defense Clifford, however, saw Kosygin's proposal as a prospect for moving forward; the Soviets could use their influence to bring the war to an end because they had leverage the United States did not. The North Vietnamese had the manpower capacity to continue the war for years and two allies supplied them. Seeking help from the Soviets was worth a try, and perhaps, Clifford reasoned, the Soviets would apply pressure if the US suspended Rolling Thunder. Give it two weeks and if nothing changed resume bombing. Maxwell Taylor warned that Kosygin's letter was a trap the administration should not trust.[424] Johnson's reply stated that he was prepared to terminate the bombing if he could have assurances that de-escalation would be the outcome. More likely, North Vietnamese leaders were insisting on a complete halt of the bombing because it was hurting them or because they thought the US was weak enough that it would give in to that demand. Communist forces were not de-escalating but were instead preparing for another offensive.[425] In the broadest sense, the United States had lost control of the bombing campaign as a military-diplomatic tool. Asking the Soviets to be peacemakers was a generous assessment of the potential magnanimity of a country that was in the middle of using tanks to squash a freedom movement in Czechoslovakia that summer.[426]

Talks regarding the possibility of ending the bombing south of the 20th parallel dragged on all summer. Walt Rostow wondered what the South Vietnamese must have thought: the United States restrained its bombing campaign against North Vietnam while gunfire and rockets pockmarked Saigon, Hue, and Da Nang.[427] No sooner had the US bombing halt taken effect than the North Vietnamese moved more weapons and supplies south. The rebuilding efforts within their own country focused on military, not civilian, projects. Stockpiles grew and waterborne transportation increased. North Vietnam provided a clear demonstration of what air power could do: look at what happened when bombing stopped, look at what it had prevented from taking place.[428]

Military leaders adjusted their operations, but not their suggestions, expectations, or plans in light of the 1968 peace talks. Over the summer they searched for actions to improve force effectiveness within the constraints imposed by civilian leaders, an exercise they found challenging. The JCS recommended in May, "an expanded air and naval campaign against NVN free of previous restraints," along with an expansion of Special Forces–type operations in Cambodia and Laos if the peace talks failed.[429] General Ralph Edward Haines Jr., the commander of US Army, Pacific, argued that the North Vietnamese were merely using the negotiations as a delaying tactic and the US should increase its military pressure on North Vietnam. He thought the fact that more enemy troops were surrendering and defecting indicated Hanoi might be more vulnerable to coercion than in the past. Haines also suggested that planning for an invasion of North Vietnam begin not only because of its coercive effects on Hanoi, but also because he believed the United States should settle the issue with an invasion of North Vietnam if the talks failed. He realized such an escalation risked running afoul of China and the American public, but communist intransigence, he believed, may make public opinion more receptive to American escalation. Refusing to at least prepare to escalate would surrender "the initiative to the enemy" and enable him to continue his protracted war on terms he could endure. General Joseph J. Nazzaro, commander-in-chief of Pacific Air Forces, believed that there were enough forces in the theater already to successfully carry out a more aggressive war if it could be conducted without restrictions from Washington. Admiral John J. Hyland, commander-in-chief of the Pacific Fleet, agreed but recognized proposing a military escalation would not be acceptable to American political leaders.[430]

Nazzaro also recognized the relationship between military action and diplomacy: "strong military actions must take place which would provide our negotiators with the advantage of bargaining from a position of visible strength. None of our current operations is having the effect of increasing enemy desires to negotiate," that is, the war was not hurting Hanoi enough to persuade them to make major concessions. He believed raids against militarily significant targets, not an all-out invasion, should take place. No targets in North Vietnam were worth an invasion, and such an endeavor, he realized, could escalate very quickly. Nazzaro was confident, however, that if the White House would permit the air forces to bomb every available target with a maximum level of force, the risks would not outweigh the consequences and results. Delay meant time for the North Vietnamese to disperse their valuable assets and strengthen their defenses to the point that an all-out air campaign would be less decisive.[431] Lieutenant General Henry W. Buse, commander of the Fleet Marine Force, Pacific, knew North Vietnam's negotiators needed battlefield victories during their talks to extract concessions from the Americans. Combat operations were the right hand of diplomacy, so he reminded Lieutenant General Cushman to deny the enemy battlefield successes so as to undercut communist bargaining.[432]

While their understanding of these connections was laudable, these generals were out of touch. The Office of the Chief of Staff of the Air Force offered that since the president had decided to not increase the size of military forces employed in Indochina, planners had to find ways to use force more effectively within that constraint, in light of the fact that the president was not about to escalate the war.[433] The generals should have realized that the chances of escalation during a presidential election in which the candidate from the president's own party was opposed to escalation and the challenger also sought a withdrawal were remote indeed.[434]

Even though the North Vietnamese were still sending about 31,000 troops each month into South Vietnam, more and more political actors ignored that fact and simply demanded that the bombing stop, so in July 1968 the president asked about the effects of a complete bombing halt. General Wheeler proffered a 30 percent increase in enemy soldiers and supplies reaching South Vietnam, while Secretary Rusk predicted a 50 percent increase. By this time in the war, however, international and domestic opinion, and ongoing and potential negotiations seemed to be more influential on the bombing campaign than military events and consequences on the ground.[435]

A fair question to ask is what this really demonstrated and accomplished? If the air interdiction campaign was achieving decisive effects, would not the North Vietnamese have stopped sending trucks south, knowing that they would simply be destroyed while in a traffic jam? On the other hand, the trends in the United States were toward a complete bombing halt and the beginnings of a withdrawal, so there were good reasons for the North Vietnamese to continue to press their advantage despite the serious losses that occurred from the summer into fall 1968. Certainly, their persistence demonstrated their determination to force as much war materiel south as possible, but their persistence may also have been an indicator that whatever large number of trucks the US destroyed, the damage was only enough to force the North Vietnamese to adapt, not to quit.

Stepping back for a moment, Vietnam reveals additional characteristics of the relationship between air power and the achievement of policy goals. Many variables make up this relationship, and some, like world opinion, may be beyond the control of the political actor using air power. A great power must think beyond the imposition of coercion and the reaction of his adversary. Furthermore, one has to consider more than just diplomacy and how international media coverage portrays the war. Statesmen also must anticipate how actions that are printed as efforts to end the war provide openings for other actors to attach additional meanings to this relationship between force, diplomacy, and policy goals. In addition, an action that counts on reciprocity from a hostile enemy actually changes the nature of the relationship by awarding leverage to the enemy. In this case, by curtailing the bombing the United States conceded much more than it thought, and North Vietnam gained more than was apparent. No longer were these two powers engaged in an air war; a superpower was now negotiating with a small power as if it were a peer. North Vietnam's tenacity and persistence continued until it cornered its adversary, pinning the United States into a space allowing little movement, a space the United States had created with its desperation to leave the war. President Johnson was willing to end the bombing for almost any reason if the enemy would just throw a few crumbs of "reciprocity" his way.[436] The suspension of bombing made it inevitable that if the communists did not de-escalate in kind and if the United States then reopened the bombing campaign, that renewal by the United States would cast it in the role of aggressor and North Vietnam in the role of victim, even though the communists had violated their part of the agreement. Consequently, North Vietnam gained an enormous amount of power when it lured the United States into the limited bombing halt of April 1, 1968, because of how aggressive a resumption of the bombing would appear, no matter how justified.

One can thus see that even in limited war, a great power has to exert an extreme amount of military force on its opponent in order to win, even when that opponent is far weaker. Achieving American and South Vietnamese objectives in this kind of limited war required the United States to crush North Vietnam; labeling this war "limited" may have been a war-deciding self-deception. At a bare minimum the administration should have realized that the possibility of the resumption of Rolling Thunder was not a threat sufficient to persuade Hanoi to give up its vital national interest.

Chapter 15

Laos and the Ho Chi Minh Trail Become the Focus of the Air Campaign

With the bombing restrictions of 1968, the campaign became primarily one of air interdiction limited to the panhandle and Laos. Although the bombing line was at twenty degrees north latitude, the US bombed targets in North Vietnam only as far north as the 19th parallel to avoid appearing too aggressive. This additional restriction forced the commander-in-chief, Pacific, to alter his air strategy to an even narrower form of attrition and interdiction: an aerial bombardment barrier running west to east.[1] Interestingly, the fall weather largely functioned as a bombing halt over the Vietnamese panhandle due to monsoonal factors. Weather was so bad during the fall that pilots could not see trucks, much less bomb them. Most of the time the only option was radar-aimed bombing against fixed targets like fords and ferries. Weather over Laos was more favorable to visual bombing during that time of year.[2]

The North Vietnamese responded by exploiting the restrictions to the full by accelerating their movement of troops into South Vietnam. This changing character of the war during 1968—more reliance on regular troops from North Vietnam—created logistical vulnerabilities. Because they needed more weapons, ammunition, and food, they needed more trucks to move the supplies. Since the North Vietnamese relied on truck traffic, that meant they needed roads through the mountains of Laos all the more. Ideally, creating blockages would lead to easily bombed traffic jams. American forces recognized this vulnerability and emphasized a technological solution to the challenge of finding trucks. The Igloo White system used sensors on or near routes where the enemy either drove trucks or moved on foot, along with the means to collate the data to generate targets for strike aircraft.[3] The primary targets were choke points along roads, sudden targets that were vulnerable to area bombing, and smaller fleeting targets of opportunity. Igloo White began in December 1967, and it was able to produce target intelligence for air strikes in real time by November the following year.[4]

Overall, the modified bombing effort proved inefficient and difficult. Seventh Air Force found aircrews spotted only a relatively small proportion of all the trucks observed during daylight hours, and the majority of the trucks destroyed by US aircrews were done so in daylight. Most trucks were seen at night, but those were bombed effectively at a lower rate. Assistance from FACs improved kill rates greatly.[5] The first major operation after the spring 1968 bombing halt, Operation Turnpike, targeted truck roads in Laos from April to June 1968. Air Force, Navy, and Marine aircraft flew nearly 13,000 sorties, almost half at night. For all that they estimated only 231 trucks were either damaged or destroyed, and their bombs put only 149 cuts in roads. One Navy wing perceived a slow but increasing rate of success. It sent its aircraft to the same place day after day and over time noticed the enemy needed more and more time to repair the bombed area well enough for trucks to operate. After cratering the road, choke point, or intersection, Navy jets dropped mines to frustrate repair efforts. Aircraft dropped mines by the thousands as part of the interdiction effort. One Navy assessment wrote that it was difficult to determine their effectiveness, and there was not a lot of confidence in their ability to decisively slow down truck and foot traffic.[6]

Alongside the air interdiction effort in Laos, the Air Force and Navy increased their interdiction efforts in Route Package 1 in July and August, which for the time being was still subject to attack. Finding and bombing choke points and bottlenecks among the system of roads and pathways was the focus of this bombing effort. Bombing would close crossroads and mines would help keep them closed. For instance, repeated bombings kept three choke points closed 23 percent, 60 percent, and 30 percent of the time, respectively, and the flow of communist supplies fell. The Navy identified seventy-seven choke points in the panhandle, twenty-one of which were particularly important. The North Vietnamese countered by shipping more stuff on boats along coastal waterways, but those were easier to find and destroy from the air. The campaign needed greater night bombing capability, because more than half of the vehicle movements took place after dark. There were not enough aircraft for these missions, although a number of aircrews were scheduled only for night missions in the same area, making them more familiar with the routes and more effective in their attacks.[7]

After a month, the campaign was clearly not inflicting enough damage to persuade the North Vietnamese to stop its aggression. Hanoi, however, put pressure on world opinion for the United States to bring its involvement to an end. Their emotional appeal, coupled with the American desire to withdraw, gave the North Vietnamese greater leverage than the bombing exerted on them. General Wheeler understood where that relationship was leading: a nullification of the effectiveness of American air power. He believed Hanoi would cut off preliminary talks while momentum compelled the United States to unilaterally terminate the air campaign for nothing in return. Diplomatic and media pressure would become too much for the United States to overcome, even if the current president or the next wished to renew bombing. Thus, Wheeler believed once the bombing campaign stopped, there was almost no chance of resumption.[8]

The course of the road interdiction campaign in September to October 1968 illustrated the dominance politics had over military operations. This air campaign actually achieved operational success and had it continued through November and December, it had a chance of forcing real concessions from Hanoi. But the die was cast, President Johnson's will was broken, and operational successes were insufficient to restore it.

The North Vietnamese continued nullifying the effects of bombing as best they could, innovating and improving their methods of camouflage, concealment, and repair. Whenever bombs destroyed a road or a railroad, work crews rebuilt it. After a Navy air strike pounded the railroad yard at Haiphong, reconnaissance photographs revealed four days later that the North Vietnamese had completed a rail line through the rubble.[9] A journalist from an East European country claimed repair teams worked all night and "often insist on continuing work even when a raid is in progress."[10] If bombs cratered a road, teamsters simply drove around the cratered area and shovel brigades filled them. As the air interdiction campaign continued along its course of pounding roads, bridges, and choke points, the North Vietnamese continued to repair or work around the damage no matter how many times bombs undid their work. The North Vietnamese compensated for the bomb damage through their own repair and rebuilding efforts, and their communist allies replaced hardware, including railroad cars the Americans destroyed.[11]

Their ingenuity matched their determination, as when they exploited rivers for floating drums of fuel downstream. They even built walls along riverbanks in order to increase the water's speed and depth so that river traffic could move more easily. Armed reconnaissance jets found and destroyed many of these. Maritime officials diverted tankers to Chinese ports for offloading, after which trucks, railroad cars, or boats shuttled the gasoline and diesel to North Vietnam. Sailors also transferred barrels from ships to smaller vessels at night to move the valuable commodity ashore. American analysts realized that made oil drum factories important targets, but bombing them was a move away from strategic targeting, because now one had to anticipate destroying oil drum factories to accomplish a tactical goal. Efforts against fuel for vehicles have been ridiculed as mirror-imaging, but the communists not only built pipelines along the Ho Chi Minh road network into South Vietnam, they also rebuilt them and installed bypass lines when American air strikes ruptured them.[12] Their actions surrounding the movement of gasoline and diesel fuel demonstrated the increasingly mechanized character of their war.

A standard innovation involved using ferries and pontoon bridges when a bridge was destroyed, as at the Ban Ton Phao Bridge in Laos in 1965. After A-4E Skyhawks scored direct hits on the Ha Thon railroad and highway bridges in August 1965 with Bullpup missiles, work crews installed a pontoon bridge by the next day.[13] Later in the war they placed "smoke pots on bridges to trick strike crews into thinking they had successfully hit those bridges."[14] When the interdiction campaign started to take a toll, the North Vietnamese compensated by obtaining more supplies from Cambodia, moving them on boats and adding infiltration routes across the DMZ.[15]

Analysts disagreed as to the effectiveness of bombing roads. The Office of Operations Analysis argued the road network, particularly in the Hanoi/Haiphong portions of North Vietnam, possessed too many alternate routes for the targeting of choke points to work. The primary mission type, in Route Package 1 at least, had been armed reconnaissance and accounted for the bulk of the truck kills in North Vietnam. The primary consequence was only the destruction of enemy war materiel and ammunition. Cratering roadways required hits within ten feet of each other, creating enough overlapping bomb craters so trucks could not drive over or around them. Marine tactical aircraft and B-52s, for example, formed two such obstacles in the A Shau Valley in September–December 1967. More than 1,300 Marine sorties pummeled the target, and this effort brought truck traffic to a halt and made foot travel difficult.[16] There was wide agreement that area denial weapons like delayed-fused mines could rarely close roads. One particular mission using bombs and mines closed a road for only an hour.[17]

These operations were object lessons in the difficulties of air interdiction against widely dispersed, well-hidden targets in which an entire country is available for alternate routes and bypasses. Finding and destroying the trucks in decisive numbers took an enormous amount of effort, first to find them and then to employ a wide variety of munitions. As summer turned into fall in 1968, however, the Air Force found that cratering roads was more effective than both armed reconnaissance and targeting stockpiles along the Ho Chi Minh Trail. Interdicting a few choice targets among the road network was effective but difficult to sustain. Targeteers needed to find more than one vulnerable spot along each roadway to bomb and allocate as many as thirty aircraft for each. Placing enough bombs to create a substantial cut in the road was even more difficult than subsequently keeping the road closed. Because work crews were often able to fill a crater in just a few hours, follow-on attacks were a necessity. One answer by November 1968 was to cut the road with AGM-12 Bullpup guided missiles and laser-guided bombs, then saturate the area with mines.[18]

Interdiction was less effective in the panhandle of North Vietnam because it was flatter and had more roads. After heavy rains had rendered many of the roads in the panhandle impassible in October 1968, reconnaissance jets photographed *more* trucks moving south.[19] That was quite a change from just one month prior, when General Abrams wrote, "It is our conviction that the air interdiction program in the North Vietnam Panhandle has been the primary agent which has reduced trucks detected from a level of 1000 a day in mid-July to between 150 and 200 a day at the present time."[20] The Navy believed its bombing and mining of road junctions in Route Packages 2 and 3 had produced a "36 percent drop in traffic," forcing the North Vietnamese to move supplies on roads through the mountains.[21] Abrams also believed the campaign was killing or wounding anywhere from five to ten thousand truck drivers and repair crews each month.[22]

Concerted, intense bombing of choke points greatly reduced the flow of supplies through Laos in fall 1968. The Navy had already found that bombing a road carved into a mountainside could send the roadway into the sea, and the Air Force applied this tactic to mountain roads in Laos. Direct hits left no room for bypassing the crater: it was mountain to one side and cliff on the other.[23] A three-week period of exhaustive choke-point bombing took place in July and August and appeared to reduce traffic by one-third. B-52s were instrumental in bombing supply dumps and groups of trucks parked underneath trees and camouflage. After this portion of the campaign, methods switched to armed reconnaissance and night attacks. "Key mountain passes were pulverized into basins of gravel," then the rains came in September and washed them out. By October 1968, "enemy traffic flow along infiltration routes was reduced by 97 percent." Intense attacks against work parties followed. When the North Vietnamese started building a bypass on an old railroad roadbed, planners sent more than 300 sorties against it. Xom Ve, another bottleneck, received 1,164 attacks that inflicted nearly 400 cuts and thirty-one landslides. It was closed almost 100 percent of the time after the first week of September. An intensive effort amounting to 2.3 million pounds of ordnance closed a bridge built just below the surface of the water at Ban Laboy for the month of October. Consequently, reports indicated, "The enemy's net tonnage through put into Laos was reduced from approximately 340 tons per day in early July to well below 35 tons per day in October. Much of the latter was carried on foot."[24]

This air interdiction campaign appeared operationally successful because movements were less than twenty-five trucks a day in October after numbering more than 1,100 in the third week of July. Seventh Air Force, now under the command of General George S. Brown, also estimated enemy killed at greater than 45,000. This evaluation argued that cratering choke points was far more efficient and effective than going after individual trucks. General Brown's command also concluded radar-guided bombing during the bad weather days of October had been effective at destroying choke points in Laos. Heavy rainfall contributed to the closings, so Brown tempered his glee with doubt as to how it could possibly do the same thing in Laos during the dry northwest monsoon during which time it was easier to carve bypasses and make repairs.[25] Persistence proved critical. The Navy became quite good at identifying successful repair efforts and then bombing them again and again. That was a tactical and operational success repeated ad nauseam, which in the short term produced a stalemate, but if continued over a longer period might have turned the screws on North Vietnam.[26]

With momentum driving the United States toward a complete bombing halt, the nature of the air campaign changed from a military operation to a diplomatic and informational chess match. Bombing's tactical, operational, or strategic effectiveness was no longer the central issue; its continuance or cessation in and of itself was the focus, as were the possible effects of its termination upon negotiations. National Security Advisor Rostow, for instance, wistfully thought on September 22 that, "I also have reason to believe the cessation of bombardment could lead to serious discussions which would move the war in Vietnam towards a settlement."[27] President Johnson assumed the North Vietnamese were reeling after their three offensives in February, May, and August had been blunted. He also believed that they might prefer to negotiate with the president they knew rather than Hubert Humphrey or Richard Nixon.[28] The United States was opposed to a scenario that ended Rolling Thunder only to be subjected to stonewalling, delays, and communist obfuscation. Those were practices the North Vietnamese knew how to exploit to their advantage. Any bombing halt would remove Washington's best form of leverage for coercing the North Vietnamese to not wrangle and Le Duc Tho, Hanoi's lead negotiator, may have recognized that very thing. Le Duc Tho insisted that an "unconditional cessation of bombing" was a precondition for discussing issues.[29] This momentum accelerated when the Democratic presidential nominee, Hubert Humphrey, promised to end the bombing "as an acceptable risk for peace." Humphrey added, "Now if the Government of North Vietnam were to show bad faith, I would reserve the right to resume the bombing."[30]

General Momyer shortsightedly informed President Johnson that a seasonal bombing halt did not really make much difference since the weather largely prevented the precise bombing needed for hitting truck convoys anyway. Momyer thought the bombing campaign was still just a military operation when it had become a pawn of perceptual warfare and a way for the North Vietnamese to influence and entice the Americans. Then the president deftly got his endorsement (and covered his own backside) by asking him the leading question of what would he do if he were president—go forward with the bombing halt? Of course, Momyer would stop the bombing if it had the best chance of producing peace.[31] Momyer mistakenly assumed restarting Rolling Thunder would be politically easy for the president when the weather improved or the North Vietnamese refused to budge.

As the day of the next bombing halt approached, air power could theoretically become a latent threat in case the North Vietnamese balked or recommenced attacking South Vietnamese cities.[32] Political realities in fall 1968, however, meant the possibility of renewing the bombing no longer existed, even if the capability did. Hope, not force, was now going to back the administration's efforts to negotiate. President Johnson counted on Soviet assistance toward this end: "Now that the bombing of North Vietnam is stopping, I hope and expect the full weight of the Soviet Union will be thrown into the balance to bring very quickly a firm, stable peace to Southeast Asia."[33] Why? The administration's use of force to encourage an end to the war was inconsistent, and sometimes lost touch with reality. Rusk actually urged President Thieu to "mount a major political and psychological effort in the days ahead to bring the VC over to your side," which revealed that Rusk had no comprehension of the depth of the National Liberation Front's commitment to its agenda. Removing Thieu from power was a major objective of the NLF: why on earth would they even consider siding with his government, a regime they had been trying to kill off for years?[34] Rusk also pressed Thieu, "we must maintain every bit of military pressure we can summon within South Vietnam and Laos. This is a time for more military pressure, not less."[35] Pursing a bombing halt completely contradicted this admonition.

Air Force and Navy efforts seemed to succeed in significantly reducing the flow of soldiers and equipment into South Vietnam, but then came the prohibition against bombing targets anywhere in North Vietnam on November 1, 1968, which according to General Momyer ended "one of the most successful interdiction campaigns in modern history." His long assessment concluded, "While the true magnitude of the logistic disaster inflicted upon the enemy may never be fully known, the data available thus far may help to explain Hanoi's growing urgency to bring about a cessation of the bombing."[36] The air wing commander from the USS *America* noticed, "For once it appeared that the North Vietnamese were having difficulty in keeping their roads open and the number of trucks sighted declined." Seasonal rains were going to force them to use boats and the Navy would be able to sink them, leaving the enemy no respite. Unlike a few weeks prior, he added, the air campaign seemed to actually be determining whether or not the communists in South Vietnam received supplies from the north.[37] If the United States had maintained this intense air interdiction campaign through the panhandles of North Vietnam and Laos into 1969, Hanoi may have agreed to negotiate, would have negotiated from a progressively weaker position, and may have made real concessions. The American air interdiction operation was showing success by November 1968, but the Johnson administration's will to persist was long gone, and once again, Hanoi's determination and willingness to suffer trumped American military successes.

After the enemy got what they wanted on November 1, 1968, a complete bombing halt of targets in North Vietnam, the United States now bargained as the weaker actor.[38] Instead of informing Hanoi it would stop the bombing once negotiations reached a satisfactory conclusion and a lasting settlement had been reached, the Americans stopped the bombing as soon the North Vietnamese promised to negotiate—without putting up any collateral. The United States thus awarded undeserved trust to a political actor who had never considered resolving the Vietnam conflict in any way short of South Vietnamese capitulation. President Johnson stopped the air attacks hoping for concessions, including the dream that Hanoi's negotiators would sit at the table with representatives from the Saigon government. Johnson promised to renew bombing immediately if the communists started shelling cities or the DMZ again, but that was unlikely during the presidential election or lame duck period.[39]

Rolling Thunder had only made it more difficult, not impossible, for North Vietnam to carry out its war.[40] According to one source, air strikes "destroyed 65 percent of the North's oil storage capacity, 59 percent of its power plants, 55 percent of its major bridges, 9,821 vehicles and 1,966 railroad cars."[41] Those were incomplete measures of effectiveness. Interrogations of captured PAVN soldiers at the end of 1968 revealed that they were still getting some supplies despite the bombing campaign.[42] Abrams understood that the best measure of effectiveness was what the enemy was able to do and what he attempted after sustained bombardments. Since the PAVN and VC could still carry the fight to their enemies, Rolling Thunder came up short.[43]

The reasons the bombing halt took place as it did remain hotly debated. According to Nixon's camp, Johnson's strenuous peace effort of 1968 was nothing more than an attempt to get Hubert Humphrey elected. According to the Johnson camp, Nixon persuaded President Thieu to refuse to participate in talks with the communists; Nixon was therefore responsible for a failed opportunity for peace. According to Ellsworth Bunker, however, Thieu would not join talks with the NLF for his own reasons; it had to function only as a component of the Hanoi delegation before Thieu would tolerate their presence. The bombing halt gave Humphrey a last-minute boost that was insufficient to overtake Nixon on Election Day. Humphrey could not openly complain about Nixon's chicanery, however, because he was informed about Nixon's dealings with Thieu from the eavesdropping the National Security Agency and the FBI had been conducting. The NSA and FBI recorded the correspondence between Americans and the South Vietnamese during the election campaign. Anatoly Dobrynin even offered money to Humphrey to help get him elected; Humphrey turned him down.[44]

If Thieu sat down with NLF representatives, that act would have conferred legitimacy to the insurgents and undercut his government's efforts to function as the sole voice for the South Vietnamese people.[45] Thieu had good reasons for being skeptical. Indeed, while he was meeting with Ambassador Bunker on the night of October 31, Saigon suffered rocket attacks three times in one night, leading Thieu to say, "You say they are ready for serious discussion. But look at what they are doing tonight."[46]

Thieu was prescient, for the North Vietnamese delayed serious discussions for weeks, haggling over things like the shape of the table and nameplates. Twenty-six days after the November 1 termination, the Americans were still waiting on their counterparts from Hanoi so talks could begin. Later, the United States decided against retaliatory air and naval gunfire strikes in March 1969 when communist forces struck Saigon with nearly a dozen 122mm rockets because public support in the US for the war was so fragile, and because retaliation would probably do little to deter subsequent attacks.[47]

Operation Commando Hunt

Terminating Rolling Thunder not only sacrificed a critical coercive tool, it also made execution of air interdiction much more difficult. Before the halt, supplies were subjected to destruction on their way to the Ho Chi Minh Trail and were easier to target because of the geography of North Vietnam and its transportation network. Once supplies reached Laos they vanished into the jungle. The air campaign had to then rely on an elaborate, complex, and inefficient system for finding, targeting, and destroying supplies dispersed on trucks. All of this complicated the effort to apply air power effectively and heightened the strategic importance of the bombing campaign in Laos.[48] Nixon had to reduce another instrument of leverage—US Army and Marine forces in Vietnam—when he began a phased withdrawal of American troops. Domestic political realities required him to do so, even though he could not extract a quid pro quo from the North Vietnamese.[49] The differing national goals of the US and South Vietnam, however, were going to undercut the strategic effectiveness of these actions. The United States wanted to exit the war, while the Saigon government wished to continue until it was secure. Achieving Saigon's goal was unlikely since there were still at least 250,000 communist troops in South Vietnam, around 130,000 of which were North Vietnamese regulars.[50]

These years of war after Tet settled into a monotonous campaign for land-based and carrier-based air power consisting primarily of air interdiction strikes over Laos and a progressively smaller quota of reconnaissance flights and close air support missions. Squadrons returned to the same area over and over so aircrews could become more familiar with what was happening on the ground. Their added familiarity improved the effectiveness of their armed reconnaissance missions and added to the intelligence picture of what was happening throughout their zones.[51]

Communist armies in South Vietnam needed support routed through Laos, so they were vulnerable to the effects of the campaign against the trail. Furthermore, the Army believed that combat in 1968 had wrecked the bulk of the PAVN forces that had been fighting in South Vietnam, and the PAVN forces needed replacements. Given that weakness, General George S. Brown, commander of Seventh Air Force after Momyer transferred to Tactical Air Command, saw air interdiction in Laos plus pacification as an opportunity to turn around the situation in South Vietnam. Furthermore, he measured success in terms of the degree to which air and ground operations supported these strategic and policy goals.[52]

After the late-summer, early-fall air interdiction campaign, Seventh AF initiated Operation Commando Hunt on November 15, 1968, an effort designed to decrease the amount of war materiel reaching South Vietnam by bombing trucks and supply dumps along the Ho Chi Minh Trail. Commando Hunt was consistent with the overall strategy to drive away and destroy communist forces in South Vietnam, and the administration believed continuing the air interdiction campaign in Laos would be productive. It also would force the enemy to set aside considerable manpower to maintain the road and the infiltration effort.[53]

Commando Hunt I was the first phase, and the program concluded on March 31, 1972, with Commando Hunt VII. With the focus of the air campaign switching to the Ho Chi Minh Trail, Operation Igloo White, the placement of sensors in Laos to detect traffic, became much more important, as was the case with Operation Prairie Fire, the emplacement of ground reconnaissance teams, and the somewhat odd effort of keeping it all a secret (with the blessing of the Laotian government). Together these provided targeting intelligence and political cover for the bombing missions.[54]

Commando Hunt was as large an operation as Rolling Thunder. During President Richard M. Nixon's first year approximately 400 fighter-bomber sorties bombed targets in Laos daily, along with from twenty to thirty B-52 sorties.[55] Commando Hunt I missions cut about forty-six roads each day and destroyed more than 4,000 trucks by the time it ended on April 15, 1969. Analysts believed "that only 18 percent of the enemy's logistical input into Laos reached South Vietnam," which if accurate made the campaign quite effective. In General Abrams's opinion, this five-month campaign was a success because it had left the enemy desperately short of supplies by the time the next wet season came around.[56] Initially, the Navy provided a quarter of the Commando Hunt sorties, sending more than 3,500 into Laos in December 1968 and January 1969. Their targets were basically the same as in North Vietnam: roads, storage sites, vehicles, and such.[57] Planners set aside the most "lucrative concentrations of vehicles in truck parks and storage areas" for Navy and Marine A-6As because of their ability to find and destroy smaller targets.[58] The Air Force sent more missions against the trail, upping its percentage of sorties outside of South Vietnam from 30 percent to 55 percent.[59]

Commando Hunt was going to have to suffice as an air interdiction campaign for the Nixon administration. While North Vietnamese perfidy in January 1969 warranted a resumption of the bombing of targets deep in North Vietnam, Nixon promised to de-escalate the war and no one in the administration wanted to renew Rolling Thunder. He recognized the domestic blowback would have been considerable had he canceled the bombing halt, no matter the merits and justification.[60]

The effort to inhibit the infiltration of North Vietnamese forces into South Vietnam by way of Laos was considered successful in 1969. The numbers were down to 104,000 soldiers in that year, a drop of 58 percent compared with the 246,000 estimated to have flowed south in 1968.[61] Soldiers felt like "hunted animals" there, and the bombing killed almost 15,000.[62] Still, more than 100,000 PAVN were reaching South Vietnam, so a 58 percent drop was insufficient. As Commando Hunt continued into 1970, CINCPAC believed the North Vietnamese had suffered losses numbering 22,000.[63]

In the context of previous North Vietnamese hints and promises, their continued pouring of 100,000 soldiers per annum into South Vietnam should have made it clear to Americans that Hanoi still had absolutely no interest in anything but total victory. Nevertheless, Henry Kissinger expressed aggravation over their intransigence to negotiating in person in August 1969 when he pointed out to Xuan Thuy and Mai Van Bo that the US had terminated its bombing of North Vietnam and had brought 25,000 soldiers home, without any reciprocation by Hanoi.[64] Why should they reciprocate? The point of war is achieving one's objectives, not reciprocity. Hanoi recognized Nixon's hands were tied by factors outside of military power: time and the will of the American people. In fact, Kissinger believed that *"The fundamental problem is time"*—the American people were running out of patience (italics in original).⁶⁵ They had decided winning would be too costly. The administration had few options, and if complete victory became one of them, it would lose the support of most voters. Thus, as far as coercing North Vietnam was concerned, the United States' big stick—military force—had been pruned because escalation was no longer an option. Kissinger nevertheless mused over the use of air strikes against North Vietnam in a sudden and harsh manner with the purpose of signaling dissatisfaction over the stalemate in the talks and a willingness to escalate further.⁶⁶

Military leaders continued to propose a renewed bombing campaign as a way to incentivize a negotiated settlement. In October 1969, the Joint Chiefs proposed an intensive operation, but Kissinger and Secretary of Defense Melvin Laird doubted its decisiveness, believed it would only make the United States look overly aggressive, and would result in adverse reactions from political opponents and friends alike. The target sets of Operation Pruning Knife were indeed quite extensive, envisioning destroying North Vietnam's air defense system, pulverizing interdiction targets in that country and in Laos, and mining Haiphong's harbor. Kissinger was concerned that if the administration carried out the JCS plan, which he believed was part of a quest for an extended bombing effort without restrictions, and it failed, the military would blame civilian leaders for not allowing the military to use all of its instruments of force in ways it knew best.⁶⁷

Chief of Naval Operations Admiral Thomas H. Moorer expressed the clearest insight of all: "When the US ceased bombing North Vietnam, we played our last trump card and lost all leverage which might be used to force concessions on their part . . . the NVN have the initiative and, as a result, are able to operate in the way calculated to best affect public opinion in the United States."⁶⁸ Now the domestic political climate had made escalation much less likely. Indeed, this changed relationship between military operations, world and domestic opinion, and Hanoi's steadfastness had created a situation where some senior members of Kissinger's staff opposed a renewed bombing campaign because it would damage the administration's relations with its friends and its own people more than it would harm North Vietnam. Moreover, according to a captured document, communist forces were still not going to agree to a cease-fire until such an agreement was a moot point: as always, the Americans had to evacuate South Vietnam and a coalition government in Saigon must include the NLF before negotiations began.⁶⁹

The war continued to intersect with the war between Pathet Lao insurgents, their North Vietnamese sponsors, and the Royal Lao Government in northern Laos. Prince Souvanna Phouma supported the bombing campaign over Laos because his army was too small to take on the North Vietnamese, and he believed American air strikes were the only substantial military defensive force at his disposal. He rejected assertions in 1969 that the Americans were violating the Geneva Agreements; the North Vietnamese had been violating them for years. Besides, he had invited the Americans to intervene because North Vietnam had violated Laotian neutrality first. Secretary of State William P. Rogers brought up an obvious issue when he visited Vietnam in May 1969: it made no sense that American troops could not venture into Laos—a friend and ally—when the North Vietnamese Army had parked itself there.⁷⁰

Interestingly, the sovereignty of the panhandle of Laos was not of great interest to Souvanna Phouma. The future of that air campaign, he commented, was "a matter for the Americans to decide." He was, however, convinced American air power was the reason the communists had not taken over Laos, which was important to American interests because the US wished for Laos to function as a buffer between North Vietnam and Thailand.[71] Souvanna Phouma did not mind the Americans there because the North Vietnamese had driven Laotians out of the area where the Ho Chi Minh Trail lay. "Come ahead and be my guest," he said to Admiral Thomas Moorer. "So long as you remain in that particular area of Laos, I couldn't care less."[72] This area was of "very little strategic interest to the Lao government itself," he added, asking only for the US to deny it was bombing targets in Laos, and to tailor its missions to not kill civilians who lived in the same general areas where the PAVN was active.[73] If the North Vietnamese wanted Souvanna Phouma to endorse a bombing halt, they would have to exit Laos.[74]

The effectiveness of this air campaign was among the very first issues the Nixon administration assessed. How much damage, really, did B-52 missions inflict? How effective was the bombing of supplies traversing Laos? How many tons were leaving North Vietnam for points south? How much essential materiel could get into North Vietnam from China if the United States sealed off harbors and sanctioned the use of ground forces to cut off supply routes through Laos?[75] Well, enough. Both the Office of the Secretary of Defense and the CIA concluded, as it had in years past, that the enemy's daily requirements of about ten to fifteen truckloads were so far below the enemy's logistical capacity "that the enemy can replace his losses easily by increasing his traffic flows to offset attrition and get through to SVN as much supplies as he wants to despite the bombing." These two agencies disagreed with the JCS and MACV about how much of a difference the termination of bombing in the North Vietnamese panhandle had made. The generals observed that supply movements grew quite a bit after the bombing ended but Pentagon analysts and the CIA credited improved weather for the uptick.[76]

Alongside this campaign, Nixon had Kissinger negotiate in secret because the president had no confidence in the ongoing four-party negotiations held in Paris. The president set out to achieve a suitable outcome because he believed a communist victory would stoke Chinese ambitions to an intolerable degree.[77]

Commando Hunt II commenced in April 1969 when the rainy season arrived. The bombing worsened the conditions of the roads and passes, slowing the movement of vehicles and porters. Aircraft made craters with laser-guided bombs, AGM-12 Bullpup air-to-ground missiles, and unguided bombs, then laced the area with mines. By the end of June all three passes through the Annam Mountains had been smashed, the Nape Pass was impassable, and there was a considerable decline in the number of trucks going through the passes at Ban Karai and Mu Gia.[78] With Commando Hunt III (November 1969–April 1970) daytime air strikes bombed the road network and the equipment used to maintain it during the day and went after the trucks at night. Laser-guided bombs proved especially effective for cutting roads, particularly at points where rebuilding was an engineering challenge. LORAN-equipped F-4s and A-6As were valued for destroying vehicles Igloo White sensors detected. Those missions were flown at dark or when the weather was bad, as opposed to the usual and more predictable times of during the day when the weather was favorable. It was important to strike with as little warning as possible so that the enemy could not react, and bombs from these aircraft, particularly the higher-altitude LORAN F-4s, arrived before the sound of the jets. As usual, repair teams got to work right after the explosions stopped. North Vietnam marshaled the manpower necessary to repair the roads, and drivers made sure there was plenty of space between their trucks so that a string of bombs would only take out one. The additional truck parks they built provided more places to hide, adding to the Americans' difficulties in finding all of them.[79] Precision-guided munitions did as much as anything to make sorties tactically effective.

The use of LGBs against trucks showed that just one of these munitions "achieved the same effect as about 80 unguided bombs."[80]

Assessing the effectiveness of strikes where sensor data determined the aim points and LORAN F-4s dropped the bombs was difficult. Aircrews witnessed a great number of fires and secondary explosions, but picking out and identifying trucks that had been damaged or destroyed was a great challenge. Photo reconnaissance was one method, but reconnaissance sorties did not follow every bombing mission. Because of smoke, clouds, jungle cover, and an enemy that was shooting back, it proved so difficult to obtain battle damage assessments from the air that aircrews reported they had not observed the results of bombing on 35 percent of the missions flown during Commando Hunt III. The Air Force tried to compensate by understating its assessments.[81]

A June 1969 study concluded Commando Hunt III had been successful enough at forestalling a buildup of enemy supplies that communist forces could not escalate their actions in South Vietnam: "The interdiction attacks by Air Force, Navy and Marine aircraft in Laos destroyed about 47 percent of the enemy's resupply input. Another 29 percent was consumed in maintaining and defending the LOC, and about six percent was stockpiled. The remaining 18 percent was delivered to South Vietnam." This amount, however, proved enough to replace the stocks and munitions the enemy used and the equipment the Americans and ARVN had captured and destroyed. Enemy forces consequently could not escalate their combat activities in South Vietnam, but neither was their ability reduced to zero.[82] True success would have inflicted starvation on VC and PAVN soldiers and forced them to fight without ammunition—a tall order—but Commando Hunt was not able to attrit them enough to do that. The stalemate continued.

Indeed, in summer 1969, Rear Admiral W. E. Lemos, director of Policy/Plans, OASD/ISA argued vociferously, "that the interdiction program in Laos is not effective," a conclusion others disputed, pointing out that seasonal rains washed out some of the roads the bombs had struck.[83] According to Colonel Lewis M. Jamison, deputy commander of operations of the 8th TFW, the combination of bombing and heavy rain rendered the Ho Chi Minh Trail impassable from July to October 1969. When the weather dried out, bombing roads became less effective because the North Vietnamese could more easily carve alternate routes.[84] During the summer of 1969, Seventh AF intelligence suspected the North Vietnamese were preparing to launch a major offensive during the second or third week of August against the very northern portion of South Vietnam, so it carried out an air interdiction campaign against the logistical buildup. It seemed to be effective since the throughput of supplies fell from about "340 tons per day in July to less than 35 tons per day in October."[85]

In spite of all these sorties against roads, the mileage of roadways ballooned from 465 miles in 1966 to more than 1,900 by the time Commando Hunt III ended in April 1970. Indeed, aircrews counted 143 road-building vehicles on the trail during the campaign. Convoys expanded, numbering as many as sixty trucks, and work battalions continued to employ thousands to build and repair the roads and disperse supplies awaiting transit.[86] The enemy also adjusted their supply lines to transit a sparsely populated section of Cambodia. They even bypassed the trail network entirely to send supplies by ship to the port of Sihanoukville, Cambodia, to supply forces in the Mekong Delta.

As the months passed, Seventh AF increasingly targeted vehicles instead of supply dumps, resulting in a 60 percent rise in destruction per sortie. But targeting individual vehicles was not as efficient as cratering choke points to make them impassable. Shutting down roads, according to Seventh AF, was better because altogether it took about $13,000 to destroy a ton of trucking, but closing a road cost only $1,000 per ton. The key remained selecting areas of the road network that could not be bypassed if cratered, and then sending enough sorties to keep the choke point closed.[87] This inefficient showing against trucks was a consequence of America's attritional strategy, which as far as the campaign against logistics in Laos was concerned, "was to attack them [trucks] whenever and wherever they could be found."[88] This violated a standard tenet of air interdiction—strike as close to the source of supply as possible (Haiphong and the railroads from China)—but that was no longer an option. The termination of Rolling Thunder forced the Commando Hunt campaign to function in an inherently inefficient manner and to wage interdiction in a way that violated the best potential of that form of air power.

For all this effort, analysts reached widely differing conclusions about the effectiveness of air operations as the decade wound down. Military Assistance Command, Vietnam argued Commando Hunt III was a success because it met the criteria Seventh AF set: inflict enough losses to make it impossible for the communists to stockpile enough supplies to carry out a big operation. Assertions that the air campaign ought to have reduced supply movements to zero constituted a completely unreasonable expectation. A 1969 PACAF study asserted that air, ground, and pacification operations had been destructive enough to render more than half of the PAVN units combat ineffective and weakened the VC even more. Abrams credited greater centralized management of air assets and the integration of different kinds of intelligence for the improvements. The JCS believed bombing forced the communists to lower the pace of combat operations in South Vietnam, but the CIA concluded that when roads were passable during the dry months the enemy continued their operations and stockpiled supplies. It also did not have any evidence the bombing had forced the PAVN to make major changes to whatever large combat operation it wished to undertake.[89] However, General Le Trong Tan of the People's Army of Vietnam later argued that had the Americans "cut a specific section of The Trail and taken over that area . . . we would have been stuck. We never would have been able to fight and win as we did."[90]

Because Hanoi's strategy was to outlast the United States, air strikes had to be far more destructive than they were to counter Hanoi's protracted war strategy.[91] George W. Anderson Jr., of the Foreign Intelligence Advisory Board, brought up the possibility of a renewed air campaign against North Vietnam during a meeting with President Nixon on July 18, 1970. Perhaps the cashing in of this last "blue chip that the US has left in trying to achieve a settlement" would persuade Hanoi to discuss a resolution to the war. President Nixon pointed out that domestic factors had taken away that option unless the North Vietnamese carried out a military operation so aggressive Nixon could not be heavily criticized for responding in turn.[92] This war illustrates that one must view coercive air power as something related to many more variables than just simple cause and effect. In this case, policy makers had to consider domestic reactions to a resumption of bombing, particularly after the protests against the bombings in Cambodia, the likelihood of such a campaign bringing about strategic breakthrough, the relationship of renewed bombing to ongoing diplomacy, and the fact that a failed campaign would move one further from, not closer to, a favorable resolution of the war.

The debilitating effects of air strikes on the enemy's health had long been significant. From the mid-1960s, enemy forces suffered from food shortages and a lack of medications, leading to a miserable existence. Weather was chilly during the rainy season and malaria endemic. The food shortages prodded the VC to operate among the South Vietnamese people even more, which supported the insurgents' agenda, even though their goal was to rule politically rather than extort food. One source claimed they took around 100,000 tons of rice from Cambodians, producing animosity, but not enough to turn peasants decisively against the insurgency.[93] The enemy, however, adjusted to food scarcity by waging combat operations less frequently and with less vigor. By 1970, the bombing was inflicting serious costs on the enemy. They were in such bad shape that they followed American soldiers and ate the garbage they left behind. Analysts concluded operations against the enemy in Cambodia had reduced the fighting power of the People's Army of Vietnam by an order of magnitude.[94]

After South Vietnamese and American troops pushed communist forces away from the Cambodian border in May 1970, Seventh AF commenced an air interdiction campaign in northeast Cambodia to make it more difficult for them to return. Executing it was difficult because of the lack of photographic targeting intelligence, and it was even more complicated because all agreed that Cambodians had to validate the targets. They also assumed the PAVN had created a network of roads that could be found and targeted. On May 21, 1970, reconnaissance flights commenced to support this new mission, dubbed Operation Freedom Deal. With the addition of air interdiction in northeast Cambodia, bombing hounded the North Vietnamese from their border through Laos and Cambodia thence into South Vietnam. A very aggressive series of missions closed out Commando Hunt IV, and Commando Hunt V commenced in September 1970 with an intense B-52 campaign.[95]

As during the previous two autumns, it appeared air interdiction and the northeast monsoon weather had brought truck traffic across these routes to a halt. Indeed, observers did not see any logistical traffic pass through that area during October, and the following month only a few trucks reached South Vietnam. November witnessed less than one truck per day reaching South Vietnam and two reaching Cambodia. In December, the throughput into South Vietnam crept up above one truck per day. Commando Hunt V came to an end on April 30, 1971, having been the major air operation in Southeast Asia, seeing 9,800 tactical sorties allocated monthly out of the total of 14,000 Washington scheduled each month. The operation also garnered nearly 1,000 B-52 sorties each month. All of this was estimated to have damaged or destroyed more than 20,000 trucks and forestalled the possibility of a major assault against South Vietnam in 1971, but ultimately it only perpetuated the stalemate.[96]

Nixon's advisors followed this campaign closely. In January 1971, Secretary of State Rogers observed the great increase in the number of trucks destroyed; where one hundred trucks had been destroyed each month, now the tally numbered 1,000. At the same time the enemy was still moving as much as 4,500 tons of supplies south each month. A skeptical Henry Kissinger pointed out that even if the Air Force achieved 8,000 truck kills a year as compared to half that number the year prior, the campaign was still destroying only a quarter of the total tonnage passing down the trail because the North Vietnamese sent so much into Laos.[97]

Commando Hunt dominated air operations in Southeast Asia. It received the lion's share of the 6,000 sorties per month aircraft carriers launched in 1969. By the second half of 1971, Seventh Air Force was sending most of its missions against the trail. Only 8 percent of its assets flew missions in South Vietnam during that time, while 9 percent went to Cambodia. As of October 1971, nearly all of Seventh AF's missions struck Ho Chi Minh Trail targets. General Winton W. Marshall, the Seventh AF's vice commander, believed this was an effective use of air power because fighter-bombers and gunships attacked trucks as soon as they were detected.[98] A mission in March 1971 against the supplies accumulated at Ban Ban, Laos, produced more than 4,000 secondary explosions, and an April 18 mission saw 1,000. Later, on April 30, "a flight of F-4s using laser-guided bombs produced another 4,000 secondary explosions from a storage area southwest of the PDJ [Plain of Jars]." Clearly these were tactically effective missions.[99]

Air power would, however, have fewer opportunities to affect the war in northern Laos, as planners allocated just thirty-two sorties each day starting July 1, 1971, a consequence of the continuing withdrawal from Southeast Asia. The withdrawal reflected contradictory policy goals: leave the war, sustain South Vietnam, and maintain Laos as a buffer between Thailand and North Vietnam, all of which required more firepower, not less. Although the individual capability and morale of the RLAF was very high and the pilots' bombing accuracy was impressive, it was comprised of just thirty-five T-28 light attack aircraft. Ambassador Godley understood that the war in northern Laos was not an integral part of the Southeast Asian War, but events there presaged a change.[100] The character of the war had made the enemy more vulnerable to air interdiction because "the war in Laos had long since ceased to be an unconventional war and had become instead a mobile conventional war employing regular forces."[101]

When Commando Hunt VI began in May 1971, analysts claimed it "came on the heels of the most successful dry season campaign to date."[102] As in previous wet season campaigns, bombing missions targeted points along the roads that were vulnerable to being washed out. The missions were as before: the bombing of sensor-indicated truck locations and the dispensing of thousands of mines along roadways. More than 20,000 sorties claimed to have destroyed or damaged an estimated 2,169 trucks—an inefficient campaign requiring on average ten sorties to destroy one truck.[103]

Meanwhile, during a July 1971 meeting with North Vietnamese negotiators, Henry Kissinger recognized his counterparts faced a conundrum: they did not see a way to achieve their agenda if they ended their combat operations, nor if they continued to fight, so there were reasons for the South Vietnamese to hold out hope.[104] Commando Hunt VI helped stalemate the enemy. In a peculiar twist, the Americans and South Vietnamese were in the same situation as their enemy. They lacked the capacity to win the war and a negotiated settlement would not bring about their national objectives.

Commando Hunt VII was the climactic air interdiction campaign against the Ho Chi Minh road network and was a major operation, with a monthly allocation of 10,000 Air Force fighter-bomber and 700 gunship sorties, with carrier-based aviation totaling another 10,000 sorties over the course of the operation. By its estimates the USAF damaged or destroyed 10,609 trucks. It took a lot of sorties, however, to yield this level of destruction. From November 23, 1971 to February 2, 1972, for example, 670 bombing runs against a set of roads in the area of Tchepone destroyed or damaged only eighty trucks and a single bulldozer.[105] The effectiveness of these intense, concentrated bombardments of choke points varied greatly. Bombing over a period of twenty-seven days kept "target 476" closed for twenty-six days, while the bombing of "point 475" from February 3 to March 31, 1972, closed it for just seven. The North Vietnamese overcame this campaign with their usual mix of persistence and resources, bypassing blocking points or using other roads, and kept the route through the area open nine out of ten days during February and March 1972: "They simply had more routes available than US air forces could adequately interdict with blocking points on a regular basis."[106] It was like trying to kill ants with a child's ballpeen hammer: the Ho Chi Minh Trail was now comprised of nearly 3,000 miles of paved and unpaved roads, detours, and tertiary routes. Air interdiction that focused on the roads' detours, bypasses, and exits rather than entryways and the sources of supply in North Vietnam—transportation pathways from China and Haiphong—was terribly inefficient, violated elementary doctrine, and in the end was a failure. Although they inflicted losses, they did not prevent the growing number of North Vietnamese regulars from reaching what would be jumping-off points for their invasion into South Vietnam.[107]

During the last week of 1971, the JCS sanctioned Operation Proud Deep Alpha, an interdiction operation against the buildup of war materiel in southern portions of North

Vietnam with the purpose of undercutting the looming invasion. The Navy flew 304 sorties and the Air Force 631. For all this, air strikes leveled thirty-nine buildings, put nineteen craters in runways, and destroyed or damaged 188 storage tanks of various sizes ruining 870,000 gallons of fuel, destroyed four trucks, and probably destroyed four SAM sites. Bad weather undercut the effectiveness of the operation.[108] Nixon relied on air strikes to weaken the buildup but was frustrated with the Air Force's tactical abilities. The North Vietnamese were building a road across the DMZ for their invasion and Nixon wondered aloud what was being done about it. Kissinger informed him the Air Force was bombing it, but derisively added, "it's one of the worst disgraces, that here the great US Air Force can't keep a road from being built."[109] Kissinger may have been willing to throw the Air Force under the bus, but General Vo Nguyen Giap, the North Vietnamese Minister of Defense, was more impressed than Kissinger with the consequences of American bombing. Giap believed the interdiction campaign might wreak enough destruction on PAVN stockpiling efforts at their jumping-off points to prevent the North Vietnamese from launching their invasion. Nevertheless, the North Vietnamese transported more than 4,000 tons of offensive war materiel into two provinces inside South Vietnam: Quang Tri and Thua Thien.[110] Although Nixon closed out 1971 by ordering five days of bombing during the Christmas holidays to demand the reinitiating of "serious negotiations," Le Duc Tho would not respond with any seriousness.[111] The North Vietnamese were three months away from their invasion of South Vietnam and were committed to seeing it through.

The effectiveness of Arc Light missions against the invasion force that marshaled during the first three months of 1972 remains uncertain because so little bomb damage assessment took place. The main targets were hostile base camps in Laos, Cambodia, and South Vietnam that were too remote for large ARVN formations to tackle. B-52 aircrews witnessed nearly 3,000 secondary explosions. Another way they assessed effectiveness was to first drop strings of sensors along the target area to detect the enemy's presence, and then use them to monitor what happened when the bombs arrived. These sensors could differentiate between cluster bomb explosions, for example, and secondary explosions. On the December 23, 1971, mission, "Acoustic sensors reflected secondaries [secondary explosions] for over one hour, as well as shouts, screams, horn signals, and other signs of human activity shortly after the strike." Eighth Air Force believed its series of B-52 strikes against base camps on February 11–14 delayed the invasion.[112] Not surprisingly, the allotment of B-52 sorties rose to 1,200 that month. Once the North Vietnamese launched their invasion of South Vietnam, air interdiction efforts over Laos were scaled back drastically. June 1972 saw only 394 American sorties there.[113]

The original goal of Commando Hunt was to reduce the logistical flow "to a point where it cannot support offensive military actions by the communists in South Vietnam."[114] Considering the materiel-heavy nature of the Easter Offensive, Commando Hunt was a failure. At best it weakened the PAVN enough to make it possible for the ARVN to fight them to a standstill in 1972—not an inconsequential outcome. The stockpiles the communists put in place for their invasion were enough for a single push of less than three months. The North Vietnamese did not have the logistical capacity to replenish their forces quickly enough to sustain their offensives.

Implements of the Aerial Siege

Since geopolitical constraints placed limits on military strategy, the importance of firepower and targeting intelligence was amplified. Those constraints calibrated the war around aircraft and munitions effectiveness, which resulted in a war of attrition that resembled a siege. The aircraft and weapons used brought a variety of strengths, weaknesses, and capabilities to this war. Their tactical capabilities provided capacities and placed limits on what policy makers could accomplish.

Attrition against truck traffic required pilots to find the targets and aim their weapons accurately. Flight-time endurance was therefore beneficial, which led to the conversion of transport aircraft into ships carrying the sensors and guns necessary to carry out that mission. Douglas C-47s were the first such aircraft converted, but they operated mostly over South Vietnam in support of troops fighting insurgents and regulars. The larger AC-119 carried heavier weapons, but initially AC-119s needed the assistance of a second aircraft, an OV-1 Mohawk, to find trucks. OV-1s used side-looking airborne radar and infrared sensors to detect vehicles for the gunship, and this team proved to be more than twice as effective over Laos as the gunship by itself. AC-119s found that the relaxed rules of engagement over northern Laos enabled them to fire at trucks more aggressively, but hitting a truck with gunfire was difficult because they could dart off the road and hide.[115] AC-130 Spectres were better because the airframe could carry more weapons and equipment, and with four engines it was more survivable. Spectres used 20mm Gatling guns, a 40 mm cannon, and from early 1972, a 105 mm cannon. They also carried a suite of sensors to find targets and aim their weapons with great precision. On average, Spectres destroyed twice as many trucks as its predecessor.[116]

The myriad of aircraft used against the Ho Chi Minh Trail demonstrated differing capabilities and levels of effectiveness. A variety were available, but none was ideal for the job. A 1968 study found that B-57s, A-26s, and T-28s were the most effective bombers over Laos at night, while A-1s, A-4s, F-4s, F-8s, and F-105s were unsuitable for night operations. Specialized aircraft like the B-57 achieved the same level of effectiveness at night as their day-only counterparts. F-4s were the best aircraft against roads during daytime strikes, and the B-57 was up to six times more effective than other aircraft used during the first three years of the air campaign.[117]

The most effective platform for truck destruction was the AC-130.[118] In spring 1970, for instance, AC-130s accounted for 49 percent of the trucks damaged or destroyed while flying just 6 percent of the missions. Their success rate continued during Commando Hunt III, when they accounted for 34 percent of the truck kills even though they flew less than 5 percent of the sorties, destroying on average seven trucks each time one flew.[119] Then during Commando Hunt IV, a group of seven AC-130s was responsible for nearly half of the trucks destroyed while flying under 2 percent of the missions Air Force aircraft completed. The terrible weather during Commando Hunt VI offered trucks great protection from gunships if they could travel through the mud. It took an average of ten gunship sorties to destroy a truck during Commando Hunt VI.[120] AC-130s continued their success through Commando Hunt VII, destroying or damaging five trucks per sortie. Right up to the end of Commando Hunt, they remained the best truck killer, destroying more than 7,000 from November 1971 to March 1972, nearly nine per flight. AC-119Ks followed with three trucks per sortie, and B-57Gs bagged two per sortie. Gunships had the loiter time and sensors necessary to find and destroy more targets, but they could only fly in areas where MiGs or SAMs were not present.[121]

Jet fighter-bombers flew 73 percent of the missions against trucks but accounted for only 35 percent of the kills. Their speed meant soldiers firing machine guns and cannon at them had a poor chance of scoring a hit, but that same speed made it more difficult for the pilot to find his target. In light of the introduction of newer aircraft, operations analysts examined and ranked the efficiency and effectiveness of aircraft a second time. AC-130s reigned supreme, and were followed by AC-119Ks, B-57Gs, A-6As, F-4s, A-7As, and A-4s.[122] Among fast jets, A-6As led with 70 percent of targets damaged or destroyed per sortie, while A-4 Skyhawks brought up the rear with a 20 percent rate. Sometimes A-7A Corsairs accompanied Intruders for extra firepower, and together they destroyed many a truck.[123]

The slow, but rugged, piston-engine A-1 Skyraider was favored by many for the war against trucks, and indeed, statistical analyses had found that aircraft like the Skyraider destroyed a truck every three sorties, while on average fast jets required four sorties to destroy one. These comparisons between the A-1 and jet fighter-bombers had been taken in airspace that was essentially unchallenged at night, was safe above 10,000 feet during daylight, and was relatively safe below that altitude. The Skyraider's low speed and long loiter time gave its pilot more opportunities to look for, find, and destroy trucks; but like gunships, it could only fly in airspace devoid of MiGs, missiles, and large caliber AAA. Much of Laos met that standard for most of the war.[124] Goals and capabilities clashed: destroying the target versus minimizing aircraft shot down; slowness improved bombing accuracy, but speed conferred survivability. Once targeteers demonstrated that a place was important enough to hold their attention, the North Vietnamese countered by placing more AAA at the site, eventually even in southern Laos.[125]

During Rolling Thunder's final months, Ambassador William H. Sullivan presented data that argued that piston-engine aircraft were twice as effective as jets in destroying trucks on the Ho Chi Minh Trail. Air Force leaders rejected those findings because propeller-driven Skyraiders, A-26s, and T-28s could only fly those kinds of missions during good weather, so the region's weather would ground them for half the year. Well, most of the jet aircraft needed good weather for seeing their targets as well. The deputy ambassador to Vietnam replied that if Skyraiders were capable, the Air Force should use them only when weather permitted.[126] In fact, another report argued that the slow aircraft were nine times more effective than fast jets, but General Wheeler doubted the accuracy of this claim, noting, for instance, that for the majority of the jet sorties no one was around to observe and determine what they had accomplished with their bombs. He also replied that the primary mission at the outset of 1968 remained bombing North Vietnamese targets, not those in Laos. He recommended against replacing a pair of F-4 squadrons with two of A-1s.[127]

Piston-engine aircraft had the advantage of maintainability, and Allied airmen found them easier to fly than jets. In 1966, Sullivan asked for AC-47s, and then PACAF accepted B-26K Invaders for use over Laos.[128] A leftover from the Korean War, the twin-engine Invader possessed great versatility and carried a maximum ordnance payload of six tons.[129] The lower speeds these aircraft flew meant that good pilots could bomb with considerable accuracy during daylight hours when the weather was clear enough for them to see their targets.[130] Over time, however, the skies became too dangerous for these slower aircraft and the Air Force phased them out in 1970.[131] The State Department wanted to transfer A-1s to the Royal Lao Air Force, but the DoD wanted to withdraw them. Kissinger commented, "We finally got a plane that can hit something," and the Defense Department wants to retire them.[132]

Munitions were important to policy makers because they needed accurate weapons to achieve their goals. The targets in Indochina were difficult to hit precisely: roads are long but very narrow, destroying trucks and artillery normally required a direct hit from a bomb, and without exacting precision one cannot bomb targets near populated areas lest civilians get hurt. Prior to precision-guided munitions the primary method was to aim dozens of bombs at a single point in hopes that one of them would strike true. For an unguided bomb to hit with precision—a direct hit on an artillery piece, for example—was an extreme rarity and not something to be relied on.

Hitting the target was the necessary first step toward achieving policy goals, and improvements in advanced technology increased the effectiveness of this air campaign. After laser-guided bombs reached the field on May 23, 1968, the teaming of AC-130s and F-4s proved very effective, averaging almost six destroyed trucks per sortie. F-4s carried the bombs and AC-130s found the target and marked them with a laser designator. Even though the laser-guided bomb was the most advanced conventional technology available, it reduced the cost of destroying small individual targets by 75 percent. Even with that level of efficiency, MACV estimated the Commando Hunt III campaign alone would need 10,000 LGBs. The enemy devised ways of undercutting the effectiveness of this team: more AAA, moving by day during cloudy weather, and even laying pipelines. Not all technological solutions were effective. An evaluation of TISEO (target identification system, electro-optical), a new system on the F-4E, found that it was not as effective for finding targets on the ground as looking with one's own eyes. It was useful for confirming the identity of other aircraft, which lessened the chances for fratricide.[133]

To improve bombing accuracy, engineers emplaced computational capabilities inside an aircraft, A-6A Intruder, that dropped unguided munitions with more accuracy than any other. Aircrews who flew A-6As relied on the jet's onboard guidance systems to carry out attacks without ever seeing the target. Intruders using their moving target indicator capability had success finding and bombing the enemy after dark.[134] The Intruder preceded the advent of precision-guided munitions, was the most accurate bomber in existence during the 1960s, and bombed quite accurately for one that did not use PGMs. One night in August 1966, for example, an A-6A flying a profile in which it relied on its precision guidance and radar capabilities sent a stick of bombs on their way with enough accuracy to drop a span of the Hai Duong Railroad and Highway Bridge into the water below. Even success like this, however, highlighted enemy persistence, because work parties constructed a railroad pontoon bridge next to the damaged one. Intruders probably knocked out the Uong Bi power station that same month, and bombs from A-6As went right where they were supposed to against the Hon Gai thermal power plant on March 2, 1967. They delivered a disproportionate amount of firepower compared to other jets that flew from aircraft carriers or Marine air wings in South Vietnam. In December 1966, the twelve assigned to the III Marine Amphibious Force—8 percent of the unit's aircraft—dropped 28 percent of the ordnance.[135]

Intruders completed missions when bad weather grounded workhorses like the A-4E and the F-105D, and for that reason were often the primary means by which the US attacked important targets.[136] They could be used individually or to guide less-sophisticated airframes, but the Navy preferred to reserve them for difficult targets that other aircraft could not hit.[137] The Intruder's ability to fly safely at very low altitudes at night and in bad weather provided a way to continue coercive bombing when poor weather kept other jets from flying. Because of that capability, the commander of Aircraft Carrier Task Force 77 recommended the Navy use A-6As primarily during those conditions, except when good weather was widespread and most any target would allow visual bombing. Marine A-6As followed suit, flying 94 percent of their May 1968 sorties at night.[138] During December 1966, the weather was too unfavorable over North Vietnam for most of the air wing of the USS *Enterprise* to fly missions, but not for its Intruders. Its Attack Squadron 35 flew its regular schedule of ten flights each day—not an overwhelming pace for the enemy, but enough to deny them respite. Attack Squadron 65 off the USS *Constellation* flew nearly a hundred strike sorties during that time in clouds that were so low that the aircrews were on instruments the whole time

USS *Constellation*, 1969 (Naval History and Heritage Command)

except for launch and recovery. In 1968, the jet gave the USS *Enterprise* the ability to fly eighteen attack sorties a day if the weather was too bad for other aircraft.[139]

An Intruder was dependent on the capabilities of its radar/computer bombing system. When the bombardier-navigator could not put the radar crosshairs on the target, the bombs were going to miss. About half of these misses were due to the nature of the target; if it did not present a sharp distinct image on the radar screen, the bombardier-navigator had a hard time determining the aim point. Thus, targeteers had to consider the clarity of the radar picture of a proposed target before assigning it to an A-6A. These missions were effective about 80 percent of the time.[140]

The A-6A's capabilities were widely coveted. The Marines liked using theirs for night close air support, and they also flew them against targets in Route Package 1. General Krulak told his commanders to only attempt difficult missions with fully capable jets. Those whose avionics were not fully functional could still fly less challenging support missions over I Corps. This aircraft's effectiveness became politicized, and the Marines had to manage its use with an eye not only on bombing missions, but also on the perceptions other federal agencies had of this airframe. Krulak warned that Congress and the Secretary of Defense as well as the Navy were closely monitoring its performance, so the Marines had to employ them only on missions that required their special capabilities or the Marines might lose them.[141] Carrier Air Wing Six found that the only way to use the A-6A was when its systems were fully functioning, so they performed the extra maintenance necessary to ensure every black box worked. Because of its capabilities, the chief of naval operations wished his air wings had more A-6As.[142] Admiral Sharp ordered the Marines in March 1967 to start employing their Intruders against targets deeper into North Vietnam. By ordering them to fly some missions there, he was protecting the Marines from seeing Seventh Air Force diverting the Marine

A-6As into their Rolling Thunder missions. Despite Sharp's protectiveness, Seventh AF got access to Marine Intruders, taking operational control in April 1967.[143]

The use of the A-6A as a night bomber over Laos was an exemplar of attrition warfare. Before they could be used, an extensive set of radarscope photography pictures of every potential target area had to be produced so that the aircrew would have aimpoints that stood out well enough for the radar to distinguish. Cutting a road with this jet using well-aimed but unguided bombs still required some good luck. Its accuracy increased the chances, and a larger bomb load of twenty 500-pound bombs did so as well, but in spite of the aircrews' best efforts, bombs often landed up to sixty feet from one another, which meant that it was possible for a string of bombs to bracket but not cut a road. For this reason, air leaders sent six A-6A sorties on a road-cut mission in hopes of achieving a 90 percent chance of producing one debilitating crater.[144] Bigger bombs were also used to accomplish this task. In 1971, the USS *Ranger*'s air wing complained it was a mistake for the Intruder to rely on Mk 82s because the craters were so small that the enemy could more easily drive around or fill them; they suggested using the 1,000-pound Mk 83 instead.[145]

Reliably accurate bombing was a capability policy makers needed in order to hit sensitive targets without too many bombs straying into civilian areas. The White House knew about the A-6A's capability and turned to it when President Johnson considered shrinking the prohibited zones around Hanoi and Haiphong in February 1968. When the thirty- and ten-mile restricted zones around Hanoi and Haiphong were lifted, Intruders carried out the bombing missions therein.[146]

Bomb tonnage is an inadequate measure by itself, but it is a testament to the utility of the A-6A that during 1969, those jets dropped 42 percent of all the bombs 1st Marine Aircraft Wing dropped while flying only 17 percent of the attack sorties. Nearly all were night missions. By 1970, a Navy study found that A-6As were more effective than every other platform—day or night.[147] After an A-6A, for example, found a truck convoy on Route 912 in Laos in December, it made a single bombing pass, and the aircrew counted eleven secondary explosions, six destroyed trucks, and a fire. Another study found that they suffered lower loss rates for each ton of ordnance on nighttime missions than those flown during the day.[148] A-6As also maximized their impact by bringing A-7As along with them; the Intruders found targets, and the Corsairs provided additional firepower.[149]

The A-6A functioned well when it worked, but malfunctions in the fire control systems plagued the aircraft, resulting in fewer missions and more sorties against targets that did not require the jet's precise capabilities. The complexity of the aircraft's fire control system resulted in poor reliability that was never solved during the war. Components often broke, and maintainers with the skills necessary to fix them were in short supply. It was a challenge to ensure as many as 40 percent of the airframes were fully functional.[150] In a June 1970 snapshot, for instance, of the Marines' twenty-five Intruders based at Da Nang, sixteen were operational, and on only ten were all the systems functioning. For one to take off with everything working was not routine, and rarer still did the jet land without some black box in need of repair.[151] Nevertheless, the accurate bombing of acutely important targets was so politically valuable that leaders coveted A-6A sorties and reviewed target lists for the targets most appropriate for Intruders first, such were its capabilities relative to other weapons systems. During the third quarter of 1967, for instance, they struck the Thai Nguyen thermal power plant, a railroad yard, and the Hoa Lac Airfield.[152]

Whatever its reliability problems, Seventh AF concluded that quality was irreplaceable for precision interdiction missions due to the bad weather endemic to Southeast Asia. It judged the Navy's A-6A Intruder the best aircraft for finding and destroying trucks due to its radar, navigation, and bombing systems. Its radar could pick out vehicles moving as slow as someone walking.[153] A later version, the A-6B, was able to defeat SAMs with a combination of chaff, violent turns, anti-radar missiles, and its electronic countermeasures suite. In 1972, the Joint Chiefs of Staff reminded air leaders to use A-6s exclusively at night and during bad weather.[154]

This aircraft and its aircrews cataloged some impressive feats. One of them completed their bomb run against the Thai Nguyen Steel Mill on March 26, 1967, with accuracy after making "a series of high 'G' ninety degree turns at very low altitudes and at night, with an airplane fully loaded with 13,000 pounds of bombs," avoiding five missiles along the way. It flew low enough to evade SAMs and MiGs, and it had three different jammers inside it to boot. The only part of the enemy air defense system that really concerned A-6 aircrew was a lucky shot from a random barrage of cannon fire.[155] The planes were not invisible to SAMs; a squadron found that even though they flew just 200 to 400 feet above the ground, escaping detection was nearly impossible. Tracking and shooting an A-6A at those altitudes with a SAM, however, was another matter.[156]

A closer look at all that was involved in executing these missions explains another rationale for high tech, expensive, highly capable aircraft like the A-6A and the later F-111. Not only were they more survivable because they flew below altitudes at which SAMs and jets could normally track them, but they also put far fewer support aircraft at risk in order to deliver their bombs. One of the consequences of North Vietnamese defenses was the expansion of the "strike package." In earlier wars strike packages consisted of just bombers and escorting fighters. Vietnam added jamming, wild weasel, and reconnaissance aircraft, tankers, chaff dispensing jets, airborne early warning, and rescue aircraft to the strike package's composition; a lot of aircraft had to fly for the bombing aircraft to reach their target. The advent of the A-6A Intruder and F-111A Aardvark revealed some ironic outcomes regarding the relationship between the cutting-edge nature of an aircraft, supporting aircraft, and loss rates. First, daylight fair weather bombers required more support during day missions than the A-6A did at night in bad weather. In aggregate, the low-tech fighter-bombers were more expensive because, "The aircraft supporting daylight strike missions suffered a greater combat loss rate per sortie than the strike aircraft being supported. In fact, the supporting aircraft suffered more total losses than the strike aircraft in these missions."

Intruders flying at night needed but a fraction of the defense suppression support daytime missions required. Furthermore, when one measured aircraft losses per sortie, the daytime missions using less sophisticated aircraft proved costlier than those A-6As flew. The Intruder's advantages increased when one factored in losses to accidents; the more aircraft in the air, the more likely one will suffer a debilitating failure of some sort. A-6A missions required fewer total aircraft. In addition, fewer were shot down per ton of bombs on target when compared to day missions. This study argued as well that a primary measure of effectiveness was the losses of all aircraft involved in a mission per sortie that dropped bombs on the target. By those measures, the Navy argued, the expensive, temperamental A-6A Intruder was more efficient and more effective than its counterparts.[157] To be fair, loss rates from all causes among naval aircraft on Rolling Thunder missions were not strikingly different. During the second half of 1967, A-4s flew 14,400 sorties for a loss rate of .26 percent, F-4s flew 5,460 for a .22 percent loss rate, F-8s flew 2,960 sorties for a .24 percent loss, A-1s completed 1,490 runs for a .07 percent loss, and A-6s flew 1,200 sorties for a .42 percent loss.[158]

The F-111A was another purpose-built bomber. They were needed to hit targets at night and in bad weather at ranges aircraft like the F-105D could not reach without repeated

A-4F Skyhawks over the USS *Hancock* (Naval History and Heritage Command)

in-flight refuelings.[159] The Air Force introduced the F-111A all-weather bomber in March 1968 in Operation Combat Lancer, but after three went down for reasons no one could determine, it grounded the rest until engineers could discover the causes of the crashes. Aardvarks did not fly any more combat missions that year but completed more than 500 training sorties by the time they left for the continental United States in November.[160] General Momyer suspected they crashed because of failures in their terrain-following radar, or because of pilot error. The F-111A would prove to be a much more successful and significant weapon when it reentered combat in 1972. F-111As did not, however, carry PGMs, and Vietnam revealed that for this era of air warfare, the best way for improving accuracy was changing the bombs, not the aircraft.

The Air Force and Navy held out hope that a new guided missile the Navy had developed, the AGM-12 Bullpup, would prove accurate enough.[161] The Bullpup came in two varieties: the AGM-12B with a 250-pound warhead, and the AGM-12C with one of 930 pounds. Its guidance system evolved over time. At first its control surfaces deflected fully with each command guidance input, making its flight path abrupt and degrading its precision. Modifying the guidance system to allow for gentler heading changes by allowing for all of the control surfaces to function concurrently improved its accuracy.[162] Early tests suggested that it might have a miss distance of seventy feet. The Navy had similar experiences in Vietnam with its accuracy, but occasionally it was spectacular, as when a pilot aimed two into a cave.[163] One air wing found Bullpups able to wreck several bridges unguided freefall bombs could not hit. Carrier Air Wing One liked using them against SAM sites.[164] A-7 Corsairs off the USS *Constellation* experienced an 80 percent reliability with their Bullpups, "with considerable success against well-defined point targets such as bridges, flak sites, and cave storage sites."[165]

During the 1969 interdiction campaign, the *Kitty Hawk*'s air wing found them accurate enough to cut roads. Carrier Air Wing Nine also found the AGM-12C to be a good weapon against AAA sites, and that it had decent accuracy—provided the launching pilot had recent and regular experience with practice firings.[166]

Fighter-bombers fired more than 9,000 Bullpups from 1965 through 1970; air forces did not use the AGM-12 in Southeast Asia after that. It was a reliable missile; only nine out of every 100 launches from Navy jets were misfires, while Air Force aircraft saw a 3 percent misfire rate. The warhead exploded about 99 percent of the time. Visibility problems and ground fire degraded its accuracy because they distracted the pilot, who had to continually guide the missile by watching its flight path, using a control stick to steer its flight direction while flying toward the target and the AAA that was often there. Overall, it worked right 73 percent of the time. Based on a fairly small set of Navy firings in which post-strike photographs verified the impact point, the accuracy for the AGM-12B was ninety feet, and that of the AGM-12C was 220 feet. One could not count on this missile destroying a heavy truss or girder-type bridge. Of thirty-five fired against truss bridges, all but one remained upright.[167]

Another new kind of guided weapon, an electro-optically guided bomb known as the AGM-62 Walleye, furthered the ability to attack vital targets with a much-reduced chance of inflicting casualties on noncombatants and a much greater likelihood of a single munition achieving a direct hit.[168] This weapon locked on to a high-contrast image with a television seeker and flew right toward the aim point. Its accuracy meant it was less risky for the president to designate targets in populated areas because the weapon was less likely to stray from its flightpath and kill civilians. Although accurate, Walleyes could not be used against all objectives because they required targets with visual features producing sharp contrasts.

Navy aircraft successfully employed the Walleye for the first time on March 11, 1967, against the Sam Son military barracks.[169] They used Walleyes again in May, wrecking the Bac Giang Thermal Power Plant, and by May 31, twenty-seven out of thirty-two hit their targets. At the time it garnered great attention; McNamara had looked forward to its use.[170] The Hanoi Thermal Power Plant was once again struck using Walleyes in June. Later that summer Walleyes destroyed or severely damaged three bridges and sank a barge.[171] The Air Force first used the AGM-62 on August 24 when a pair damaged a barge and a pier that were part of a ferry crossing. On August 30, two of the four F-4Ds that flew against the Long Khap Highway Bridge flew back to their base with their Walleyes intact because the first two jets dropped the bridge with their Walleyes. When Navy fighter-bombers sent two against the Hanoi Thermal Power Plant in August, both were true, blasting the southeast portion of the building that housed the boiler plant and one corner of the building housing the generator. Through August 1967, fifty-four of fifty-nine hit their targets.[172] In October, Walleye proved its worth against a power plant, an airfield hanger, and a control tower, and the next month a pair of A-4Es dropped the Hanoi/Haiphong Bridge with just one; the other missed. When the North Vietnamese countered with smoke generators, pilots defeated that countermeasure with a higher dive angle.[173]

The Walleye was far more accurate than unguided bombs.[174] Of the thirty-five dropped in theater during the first three months of 1969, nineteen scored a direct hit and one missed by only five feet. It met or exceeded expectations, which estimated an average miss distance of fifteen feet. AGM-62s also increased launch aircraft survivability because jets dropped them above the effective altitude of AAA, enabling pilots to take evasive measures against SAMs once the Walleye was dropped, since the Walleye was the first drop-and-forget guided bomb. A combination of SAMs, MiGs, and AAA, however, could disrupt attack runs. After

Otter Fight released their Walleyes as they were coming under attack on January 18, 1968, their Walleyes missed the Bac Giang Thermal Power Plant.[175]

In 1972, the Walleye II entered the inventory. It had a data link that allowed a controlling aircraft to monitor its progress and reacquire the target if need be. A Navy A-7E dropped the first one used, and it managed to seal up a cave at Xom Ram. One could even send it on its way and then lock on to the target after a few miles of flight in case one could not see it at first. President Johnson, however, had wanted something more accurate.[176]

American air forces needed a pinpoint bombing capability for a couple of reasons: not only did existing munitions risk too much collateral damage, the existing bombs simply could not hit pinpoint targets. Laser-guided bombs, with their ability to land within forty feet of the target, solved the accuracy problem.[177]

Laser-guided bombs were relatively simple devices. Mating a laser-seeker head, control mechanisms from a Shrike missile, and some guidance fins to a bomb were all that was necessary to make one. The other component was the laser, which functioned as a very narrow spotlight on the target the seeker saw and homed on.[178] The results from the prototype laser-guided bombs, named Paveway I, were spectacular. The first ones were dropped on May 23, 1968, and demonstrated profound accuracy at once. The 750-pound LGB achieved a 45-foot accuracy, the Mk-84, twenty feet. Examined another way, two sorties dropping two laser-guided Mk-84 bombs each had a 50 percent chance of hitting the target; otherwise it took 191 sorties—totaling several hundred bombs—to obtain the same effect with unguided Mk-84s.[179] Within months the bombs were often achieving direct hits: "The average miss distance was 17 feet; the CEP remained at zero."[180] In April 1969, 204 Mk-84 LGBs were dropped and 180 hit home. Nearly two-thirds of these first-generation laser-guided bombs scored direct hits, and the Paveway II recorded an accuracy of under seven feet.[181] Given that 25 percent of the JCS list of 240 targets at the time were bridges, which needed a direct hit to drop a span, that target type alone justified an accelerated production of these precision weapons. The main challenge these aircrews had was merely one of procedures and communication: making sure that the aircrew aiming the laser pointer and the crew in the jet with the bombs were going after the same target.[182]

The Walleye was not quite as accurate as the LGB, with the Air Force attaining a 52 percent direct hit rate out of 500 bombs, while the Navy achieved better results with a hit rate of around 65 percent. Numerical figures aside, photographs attest to its accuracy. Looking at the moment a Walleye impacted the Thinh Loc Railroad Bridge, it is hitting the bridge; the next photo shows the bridge as a tangled mess. All around are several dozen huge craters from previously dropped unguided bombs, some hundreds of feet from the target. These PGMs could enter buildings through openings and explode from within.[183]

Because LGBs could hit just about anything, just about anything could be the next target, and LGBs became the most high-tech weapon in existence against a vehicle of brute force. On August 30, 1971, for instance, an F-4 dropped one on a bulldozer. Even though an individual weapon was relatively expensive—a 2,000-pound LGB cost $12,000 in 1967—that expense was minuscule compared with the cost of the massive number of unguided bomb sorties needed to gain the on average kill probability of 85 percent of a laser-guided bomb. For instance, one would need thirty-seven F-4 or F-105 sorties dropping 220 M-117 bombs, which had only a 300-foot accuracy, to have a statistical chance of inflicting the same damage—and through random chance still not achieve a direct hit. Each LGB sortie cost on average just $26,000. Thus, the accuracy of LGBs generated an exponential improvement in accuracy for a much greater savings in money, risk, and flights.[184]

Measuring Air Interdiction's Effectiveness

During the ongoing stalemate, the United States pursued a variety of quantitative methods to determine whether or not the interdiction campaign was about to inflict decisive effects on the enemy's supply lines and capacity for waging war. Normally, analysts measured the effects of bombing in physical terms rather than on North Vietnam's behavior and policy. They particularly favored quantifiable metrics such as tons of supplies destroyed, sorties flown, and aircraft shot down. Right after quoting Secretary McNamara's goal of pressuring the North Vietnamese to bring their military campaign in South Vietnam to an end, a 1966 analysis listed mission costs, costs to the North Vietnamese, and the amount of supplies destroyed. The list did not include the achievement of the policy goal of McNamara just cited as a measure of success.[185]

The military measured damage and destruction: truck parks, locomotives, buildings, bridges, and so on. The Navy, like the Air Force, measured what it could quantify: sorties flown, tons of this or that kind of bomb exploded, number of rockets and cannon shells fired, number of buildings destroyed.[186] From September 18 to October 21, 1972, for instance, the USS *Midway*'s air wing destroyed a half-dozen pieces of rolling stock, more than fifty trucks and buildings, twenty-four bridges, and eleven piles of supplies. Its aircraft destroyed most of the depot at Thien Linh Dong, and a mission from the USS *Hancock* did the same to one at Phu Quy. A few days later *Coral Sea* aircraft wrecked oil tanks at the same place. Evaluations of air strikes also equated effort with effectiveness: one reads of sorties flown, stored fuel destroyed, trucks destroyed on the Ho Chi Minh Trail, bridges destroyed, and bombing missions flown. American air forces, for instance, flew 48,000 sorties against the trail in 1966. That same year armed reconnaissance missions tallied more than 9,000 trucks, 13,000 boats, almost 2,500 railroad cars, and thirty-one locomotives.[187]

Counting tonnage and trucks moving through Laos was one of the primary measures but doing so with accuracy remained an elusive challenge. "Road watch" teams of soldiers gathered accurate targeting intelligence and BDA. One road watch team on Route 6 forwarded reports on the movements of nearly 400 trucks spanning the course of three weeks, and another team on Route 7 tracked 325 trucks in May 1967.[188] The millions of trees that covered much of Indochina also made bomb damage assessment from aircraft exceedingly difficult. Smoke from one's own air strike made it common for pilots to not be able to report the results of their missions. Not only might a pilot see little damage from his bombs, he might also underestimate the effects. A strike by a pair of Thunderchiefs and a pair of Skyraiders against a truck park in Laos in 1967 seemed to do little from what the pilots saw, but the ground team that investigated the aftermath found sixty-five dead soldiers and 200 dead guerrillas. What is more, pilot reports of their mission results were often not tabulated until several weeks after the mission, thus losing any opportunity to exploit short-term advantages that may have been generated.[189]

Counting holes, cuts, and craters in roadways was a valid measure because they slowed or stopped the movement of supplies. Bombing missions during the fall of 1968 left more than 300 craters at one choke point in Laos, and later totaled about 3,600 over the course of Commando Hunt VI.[190] However much or accurate this was, these were measurements of destruction, and they were only a starting point for assessing effectiveness.

Initially, the US tried to interpolate the effectiveness of their effort by noting the increased presence of AAA where it was bombing, meaning that the bombing was effective. During Commando Hunt III the primary measurement of effectiveness was how many trucks were destroyed per sortie, and for all this an individual truck still had a .41 probability of reaching its destination. It was necessary to carry out a great number of strike missions in bad weather, which meant aircrews could not see, look at, or photograph the results of their missions, so the number of trucks listed as destroyed or damaged during those monsoons was probably low.[191]

As with close air support missions and air strikes against North Vietnamese targets, fires and secondary explosions were another method of assessing bombing effectiveness against the Ho Chi Minh Trail.[192] When bombers found and struck truck parks in Laos, secondary explosions verified that the ordnance had hit the target and not just a patch of ground. They were a primary measure for the B-52 strikes in Laos, but frequent cloud cover meant that counting them was often not feasible. During Commando Hunt IV cloud cover meant that for about half the sorties the aircrews could not assess what their ordnance had done, so they annotated, "results not observed."[193]

As had been the case with Rolling Thunder, it was apparent by the end of the first year of Commando Hunt that air interdiction's effectiveness in Laos was indeterminate. The 1965 PACAF history observed that the air campaign had persuaded the North Vietnamese to alter the way they transported freight down the Ho Chi Minh Trail. They reduced their reliance on immobile bases, moved more at night, improved their camouflage, relied on porters where air strikes had destroyed bridges, and employed more trucks. Thus, the air campaign made their effort more difficult, but did not end it. The history recognized already that reducing the movement of materiel to zero was unlikely because of the cover the terrain provided and the abundance of road workers and porters. Perhaps, as the command hoped, "the cost of maintaining his lines of communications was certainly made greater and perhaps raised to a level unacceptable to the enemy."[194]

The JCS measured effectiveness in terms of destroyed materiel and disruptions and delays in enemy operations. A 1966 report conceded their measurements of effectiveness were unable to read through the sparse and uncertain information coming out of Hanoi and argued that it might take "years" to accumulate definitive evidence about the consequences of the bombing campaign for North Vietnam. That was a reason, the generals argued, to continue the effort.[195] A 1967 study provided measurements from four perspectives. Strategic Air Command and the 3rd Air Division measured how many aircraft reached the target, the pattern the bombs created on the ground, and how many bombs struck compared with the number of bombs brought to the target area, and aircrews concerned themselves with bombing accuracy. American officials in Saigon measured dead enemy troops, destroyed equipment, harassment and disruption of enemy operations and plans, and how quickly air assets reacted to calls for assistance. The Department of Defense and the Headquarters Air Force measured costs, how destruction affected the enemy, weight of effort, and the effects of bombing on the will to fight.[196]

Another study found correlations between the amount of supplies making it through Laos to South Vietnam and the number of soldiers the enemy killed each month. Inflicting casualties on the enemy in South Vietnam was concurrently enormously expensive, requiring on average 28,000 pounds of munitions to kill an enemy combatant. The Army defended this, writing that it relied on firepower by design. Commanders moved their soldiers to find the enemy and to make the massive application of firepower more effective. For their part, VC and PAVN required about 600 to 700 pounds of supplies to kill one soldier, so even though their form of combat was far less expensive and more efficient, their combat actions were still relatively expensive and consumed a considerable amount of materiel to accomplish. Additional data asserted air interdiction cost much less than ground force firepower. Five-and-a-half sorties costing $56,000 destroyed a ton of supplies, while ground forces had to fire 162 tons of ordnance at a cost of $259,000 for the same outcome.[197] By this metric, air interdiction was a worthwhile effort.

One assessment was contradictory. On the one hand, Seventh AF concluded the scale and pace of the communist resupply effort through Laos during February 1967 was an indicator of just how bad the Rolling Thunder campaign hurt them. If Rolling Thunder was really that damaging, however, the PAVN would not have been able to build up supplies to the degree that it could: an estimated 9,600 tons. That was enough to support four Viet Cong divisions for almost four years, or four North Vietnamese Army divisions for more than one. If the enemy has potentially built up enough supplies for four years of war, you are not winning. This assessment at least had the momentary insight to realize that supply efforts like this indicated North Vietnam was going to continue to support the VC.[198] In any event, Westmoreland ordered more B-52 strikes against these supply lines in Laos and southern portions of North Vietnam in February 1967.[199] Because the United States did not use sizable numbers of troops in Laos (none were supposed to be there so as to avoid escalating the war), site surveys of the damage from these bombing raids was not done for Arc Light missions after the bombing halt.[200]

During a series of air strikes against the lower panhandle of North Vietnam in 1968, the information available to military analysts on its effectiveness was incomplete and contradictory. This operation produced "no dramatic breakthrough in interdiction tactics" but the results were assessed as "markedly successful."[201] While observers found nearly 6,000 trucks in Route Package 1 between mid-July and the end of October, "only 783 were estimated damaged or destroyed." How was such a low kill rate successful? The operation may have prevented the North Vietnamese from moving supplies into South Vietnam by truck, but they always found a way, as at Xom Ve where men carried supplies on their backs after bombs had rendered the road impassable to vehicles.[202]

Military Assistance Command, Vietnam realized determining the true effectiveness of the air campaign was enormously difficult and complex, and is worth quoting at length:

> Measurements, such as sortie rates, tons of ordnance dropped and troops airlifted, have given an indication of the magnitude of *effort* but then rarely reveal how effective that effort has been. It follows, therefore, that while statistics may be used to measure magnitude, the overall contribution must come in general terms related to support of other military operations, just as the military operations themselves must be related to the political and ideological objectives for which the war is being waged. On this plane, the contributions are too obvious to miss. Airpower has added astonishing firepower and mobility to battlefield and/or campaign situations. Indeed, in many instances, the operation would certainly have been ineffective if not impossible without it.[203]

Admiral Sharp warned against relying on sortie counts and sortie rates as a measure of effectiveness even more energetically. It would just lead to unproductive competition between the services: "Any statistical exercise which equates mission effectiveness to weights of ordnance serves no useful purpose."[204]

Another indicator that the American armed forces were having a difficult time measuring the substantive political effects of their campaign was their ongoing creation of new metrics. These relied on estimates, not hard facts. Analysts invented a "unit of destruction" and examined the number of units of destruction inflicted per aircraft lost, the units of destruction inflicted by Navy versus Air Force aircraft, the ratio of units of destruction to sorties, and how many tons of ordnance it took to destroy a target. By the end of 1965 the Air Force "inflicted 38 units of destruction for each aircraft lost," while "the Navy produced 29 units of destruction for each of its aircraft lost."[205] One proposal suggested a mathematical model for determining effectiveness: $E = (C_p \text{ or } C_a) \times K \times R$, or effectiveness as a result of multiplying the "probable or actual damage, destruction, harassment, or impedance of a specific target" by the certainty of the locations and type of target and multiplying that by the ordnance hitting it. An evaluator of this formula argued "mathematical discussion is useless and misleading." These were starting points for measuring tactical effectiveness, which is fine, but none of these considered the relationships between military actions and the achievement of the military strategy the United States was pursuing, nor the president's goals.[206] It was clear the bombing was not persuading the North Vietnamese to negotiate an end to the war. In fact, military action that produced decisive strategic effects would have been easy to read: a North Vietnamese plea to negotiate without preconditions and the granting of concessions on their part.

Analysts also attempted to measure the difference between the amount of supplies that entered Laos with those that exited and made it into South Vietnam. Throughput, the amount of supplies that actually reached communist forces in South Vietnam, became another measurement. Estimations instead of definitive data created the conclusions regarding Commando Hunt's effectiveness. Analysts had to estimate what supplies entered North Vietnam to approximate how much was destroyed by the time it reached the Ho Chi Minh Trail in Laos. Throughput for a 1968 estimate assumed 300 tons each month, the equivalent of a hundred trucks. After that, analysts estimated the damage air strikes inflicted, which they concluded amounted to 13,500 tons. That totaled just more than 20 percent of what entered the trail from North Vietnam, and it appeared that the communists used most of what they received in combat operations, stockpiling barely 400 tons, so at best air interdiction prevented them from stockpiling supplies.[207] It seems every assessment was an estimate, so that effectiveness was a summation of estimates. "Tons destroyed" was an estimate: "Its value was arrived at by making tonnage estimates of the goods destroyed or destroyed and damaged motor vehicles, water vehicles and railroad vehicles. In the same fashion, tonnage estimates were made for secondary explosions and fires. Combining these separate values gives the value of tons destroyed. Due to the uncertainty of the tonnage estimates, two estimates of tonnage were used [which] represent optimistic and pessimistic estimates."[208]

Throughput became a dominant measure during 1969 and continued through the rest of the war. Seventh Air Force used sensors, human intelligence, photo reconnaissance, and air observation to count the number of trucks that entered the Ho Chi Minh Trail, analyzed the ones destroyed along the way, and tried to count how many reached their destination—an inexact measure.[209] In fall 1969, the Air Force believed communist forces needed 9,000 tons of supplies, and the Directorate of Operations, HQ USAF, believed that 8,100 tons reached South Vietnam. Although some of this was from stockpiles—which were consequently being diluted—a 9 percent shortfall in throughput was unlikely to bring enemy forces to their knees. They also found destroyed trucks replaceable. Beginning in November 1969, air strikes destroyed more than 11,000, but they still had about 7,000 trucks on hand in March 1970. Statistical models also showed air interdiction against supply lines could not reduce throughput to zero; the campaign would eventually reach a point where additional missions did not make sense in terms of return on the effort. The bombing, however, was not irrelevant. It hurt enough and inflicted enough damage to persuade the North Vietnamese to demand the termination of the campaign before talks on Laos's future began, one of the more reliable indicators of its utility.[210]

A 1970 study also reached discouraging conclusions. Viet Cong and PAVN forces got about 70 percent of their provisions from within South Vietnam, another 10 percent from Cambodia, just 15 percent from the Ho Chi Minh Trail, and the small remainder crossed the DMZ. Only a third of the supplies that entered the trail reached South Vietnam. Some was consumed or used along the way, the communists stockpiled more, and air strikes destroyed the rest. The North Vietnamese ruthlessly compensated for attrition and losses. They assumed most would be destroyed before it reached soldiers in South Vietnam, so Hanoi imported more than twenty times the amount of war supplies that eventually reached their front in South Vietnam via the trail. "Even with the intensive bombing, the enemy still moves supplies adequate to continue, or substantially increase, his current operational level."[211] Interdiction improved that spring when analysts believed that of the 54,000 tons of supplies entering Laos, 19,000 tons made it to South Vietnam—a painful but not a decisive reduction. And these figures were provisional; Air Force Intelligence realized that measuring "input" was difficult and open to question.[212] Be that as it may, the administration already realized that bombing could not reduce throughput to zero. Analysts concluded at the end of 1971 that only 30 percent of the supplies that began their journey down the trail reached South Vietnam or Cambodia, which they deemed a success for the air interdiction campaign.[213] The materiel-heavy invasion the North Vietnamese mounted in March 1972 rendered that conclusion mistaken.

Ultimately, the availability of trucks for moving all this depended not just on US air power's ability to destroy them, but upon the will of the North Vietnamese to endure a tremendous amount of wastage to move minimal supplies forward, and the state of the relationship between North Vietnam and its suppliers: the Soviet Union and China.[214] That was one reason President Nixon sought better relations with the Soviets, to gain some leverage so they might reduce their support for Hanoi in order to gain better relations with Washington. The enemy still had enough capacity after the pounding they took to begin construction on a covert road network inside the northwestern part of South Vietnam. In response, the air forces devoted about thirty sorties each day against it. The enemy failed during this 1970 effort, but having to carry out air interdiction inside one's own country is not a sign the war is going well.

Extrapolation became another method of assessment. Seventh Air Force estimated from April to June 1970 that the communists lost 1,815 tons of supplies to air strikes and capture by ground forces. They derived this figure by multiplying each secondary explosion by 0.375 tons. A couple of pieces of indirect evidence were a bit more cut and dried. Enemy food shortages got severe enough that at times some of their soldiers starved to death. Another analyst noticed that they possessed almost no heavy weapons or high-tech systems in South Vietnam because they were unable to transport them there.[215]

With Commando Hunt VI, estimating throughput had become "the primary measurement of effectiveness" for the air interdiction campaign.[216] The methods by which this was done, sensor measurements of truck movements and through visual counting by road watch teams, also provided targeting coordinates. One must ask why those teams did not call in even more air strikes? The answer: because of the withdrawal policy, fewer and fewer aircraft were available. For fiscal year 1971, only 16,000 ground attack sorties were authorized. According to these measurements, approximately 1,400 tons of supplies reached South Vietnam during the rainy season of May through October 1971's logistical effort.[217]

Analysts used game theory to predict that random daytime attacks would be more fruitful than continuous ones. In other words, be unpredictable—a principle of war that preceded game theory. The study also wrote of inflicting a high enough kill percentage that the North Vietnamese would stop sending trucks down the trail because they had no hope of reaching South Vietnam, which also indicates that the campaign was not decisive, because if one could choose between destroy and deter, one would destroy all the trucks.[218]

The Nixon administration admitted air strikes carried out when targeting intelligence was poor were not that effective. Kissinger believed DoD and CIA assessments that the bombing could only make infiltration more difficult; it could not stop it.[219] By 1971, doubt expanded to include skepticism of the overall effectiveness of the sensor strings—so necessary for measuring throughput. A Seventh Air Force study noticed that many more trucks had been destroyed before the sensor network had been emplaced. How sensitive were the sensors, were fewer trucks operating than in previous years, had the bombing been effective enough to reduce truck traffic?[220] Altogether it was estimated that of 30,000 tons the North Vietnamese sent down the trail in 1971, only 5,000 tons of supplies reached South Vietnam.[221] Maybe the reason throughput got so low is because it was being stockpiled in Laos and Cambodia.

In 1971, an "econometric study" was conducted to demystify the ongoing question of how much reached South Vietnam. The analysts used advanced mathematical models and formulas to measure what had taken place, and more specifically to derive reliable throughput figures.[222] The analysts operated under significant constraints. The North Vietnamese were not advertising how many truckloads of ammunition, for example, they were sending down the trail, so these analysts had to estimate that. The next obvious measure was how much arrived in South Vietnam, but this too they had to estimate. They also examined the costs of the campaign. Because of these known unknowns, their conclusions could not have the conclusiveness and firmness they sought. The analysts concluded that sortie rates against these targets "was close to optimum." During the time they studied the campaign, costs increased by 20 percent, but effectiveness went up 150 percent, a conclusion that was based on a pyramid of interpolations and estimates.[223] The mere existence of this study proved that the war against trucks was indecisive—success would have been obvious.

While the air campaign destroyed supplies and bollixed the communists' resupply effort, a June 1971 assessment wondered about the extent to which it really impacted Hanoi's strategic goals. After all, their ultimate goal was to rule South Vietnam. The analysts could not agree as to whether the bombings had persuaded the enemy to change his strategy "from conventional back to guerrilla warfare."[224] On the other hand, the American objective had retreated from defeating Hanoi's political goals to one of inflicting enough damage on its military efforts that the Republic of South Vietnam could survive successive enemy onslaughts, albeit with the assistance of American air power and money. A July 1972 study confessed that analyses had still not produced definitive conclusions about the effectiveness of air interdiction. In fact, "the data are consistent with both interpretations, that: air power determined the output, or the enemy determined the output and we determined the price." This analyst favored the latter argument.[225]

A later analysis estimated that a total of 160,000 tons of supplies started down the Ho Chi Minh Trail from November 1968 through the beginning of 1972 and that 34,500 reached their destinations in South Vietnam. Seventy-nine percent destroyed and only 21 percent reaching South Vietnam would seem to spell victory, but it really needed to be complete enough to prevent the PAVN from launching its 1972 invasion. On the one hand, given the capacity the PAVN had to wage a mechanized campaign in 1972, Operation Commando Hunt was a failure. On the other hand, interdiction was essential to South Vietnam's survival in 1972: it inflicted enough losses to prevent the North Vietnamese Army from pre-positioning overwhelming forces against South Vietnam.[226] Whatever the effectiveness of the air interdiction campaign, the PAVN still managed to accumulate a mechanized army powerful enough to threaten South Vietnam with defeat at three different points of attack in spring 1972.

This campaign against North Vietnamese supply lines was in the end futile and tragic because it had to be waged in violation of the basic tenets of air interdiction: policy prevented the bombing from striking supply lines as close to their sources as possible. The war may have seen a different outcome had the air interdiction campaign been allowed to focus on the entryways from China and the port of Haiphong.

The most definitive metric for military effectiveness had always existed. General McConnell recognized that bombing's effects on the policy goals and behaviors of the North Vietnamese were the key measures of effectiveness.[227] An assessment the CIA and DIA wrote at the end of 1965 reached the same conclusion. The bombing campaign inflicted considerable damage, but the North Vietnamese were still able to move supplies and soldiers into South Vietnam, disperse war materiel and obtain more from other communist states. Altogether, what was taking place indicated "Hanoi's willingness to persevere indefinitely."[228] Westmoreland and Sharp likewise agreed. Changes in Hanoi's behavior were what Washington wanted, so those were the best measures of effectiveness.[229]

The ultimate problem was not with air power, technology, rules of engagement, or armed forces. In order to ruin North Vietnam's strategy, the air interdiction campaign had to be combined with a large ground invasion of southern Laos and probably the southern tip of North Vietnam because only a threat of that magnitude would have forced the North Vietnamese Army to use supplies at a rate greater than they could replenish. Adequate numbers of ground troops can cut off infiltration to virtually nothing. Much has been written on a proposed multi-division troop barrier running from the Gulf of Tonkin west to Thailand on a parallel just south of the DMZ. Advocates argue that it really could have cut off the supply pipeline from North Vietnam, while critics respond that the distance was longer than it appeared and that several corps of infantry would have been necessary. Besides, the North Vietnamese could have just extended the Ho Chi Minh Trail farther west through Thailand and Cambodia.[230] North Vietnamese Colonel Bui Tin argued twenty years after the war that the Americans could have won if they had cut off the Ho Chi Minh Trail with not only air forces but also ground forces, but geopolitics made that strategy a dead letter.[231] US Army operations north of the DMZ would have taken place on North Vietnamese soil, which would have been very escalatory, and sending a couple of American infantry divisions into Southern Laos would have put the friendly government in Vientiane at risk of an enemy counterstroke through Northern Laos. Even if a ground-air interdiction effort like that had proceeded in ways favorable to the South Vietnamese, Laotians, and Americans, an effective interdiction campaign would have meant little over the long haul without the development of a strong South Vietnamese state.

Chapter 16

Restrictions and Rules of Engagement during the Air Campaign

The White House and Pentagon required the Air Force and Navy to execute the air war with many restrictions on what they could do, how they could do it, what they could target, and the intensity of their bombing missions. Restrictions imposed by political leaders constitute one of the most contentious issues of the war. Military leaders believed the best way to achieve the administration's goals was for them to receive broad authority over targets, munitions, and methods, and for the politicians to get out of the way and let the military fight the war. Effective air power was unrestricted air power, and vice versa. They assumed that if they got to bomb whatever they wanted the way they wanted the achievement of policy goals was assured. A recurring argument has been, "if only the US could have bombed the hell out of whatever the JCS wanted to bomb in 1965 in the manner of the December 1972 Linebacker II campaign, the war would have been won in 1965. If only we had been allowed to wage the air war all out, without any restrictions, the US would have inflicted so much shock and destruction on North Vietnam that it would have let go of its goal of conquering South Vietnam in a matter of weeks."[1] The header for a 1997 article in *Vietnam* magazine asserted that, "Everyone in Vietnam knew that the restrictions imposed by the rules of engagement were insane."[2] More recently, in 2010 Harold Pease argued that, "it is because of them [the restrictions] that this 14-year-long war lasted so long and was lost."[3] Admiral Moorer commented, "Once you get into a war, the only thing to do is win it, in my view."[4] That assumes at the very least, according to one JCS report, "Restrictions on military operations in Southeast Asia have prevented the most effective application of allied military power."[5]

A related argument has been that the close management of the war from Washington by "unskilled amateurs" probably cost the United States the war.[6] Soon after the war, Ulysses S. Grant Sharp retired from his duties as a Navy admiral and wrote, "Civilian politico decision makers have no business ignoring or overriding the counsel of experience[d] military professional in presuming to direct the day-to-day conduct of military strategy and tactics from their desks in Washington, DC. . . . The aims or objectives of an internationally political strategy may quite reasonably legitimately be limited, as were ours in Vietnam, but the actual application of military force required to achieve those aims cannot and *must not* be tactically limited [italics in original]."[7]

General Joseph H. Moore Jr. worked under several seductive assumptions about the relationship between destroying targets and achieving policy goals. On the one hand, it would seem to make perfect sense that if policy makers gave the military a list of targets to destroy, got out of their way, and let them destroy them in ways guided by their professional expertise, that of course the enemy would capitulate. On the other hand, what if the enemy decided they could ride out whatever destruction American forces could mete out? What if the enemy's political goals were so fundamental and so nonnegotiable that such a bombardment operation would not come close to persuading them to change their minds? What if that level of destruction brought the enemy's patron states into the war? What if the bombing embarrassed American allies? Moore was correct, but only if the nature of war was the efficient destruction of military targets; war, however, resides ultimately in the province of political leaders. War is a form of communication and compulsion that strikes at values and agendas that peoples are willing to kill and die for in very large numbers. Who would understand better than political leaders (providing they were competent) the interrelationships between, for example, munitions used on a bombardment mission and the diplomatic and informational effects on key political actors? Political leaders should not interfere arbitrarily in military operations, but political interference in military operations is not interference at all since war is a political act.[8] The generals should have understood that, and the political leaders should have worked with them so that their manipulation of armed force was done in a manner that moved them toward the policy goals they had set rather than simply toward efficient destruction. Instead, Johnson placed his hand on the throttle of war in a way that worked against his own agenda. Unskilled political involvement in military affairs is as destructive of the national interest as is military force applied as if political interests were suspended during war. Collectively, American leaders failed to accurately assess the salient characteristics of the challenges the Vietnam War presented. Because of the shortcomings that characterized America's political and military leaders in 1965, what unfolded was neither a failure of diplomacy nor a failure of military force but instead it was a failure in the practice of war.

Unintelligent restrictions assisted the enemy. For example, by the middle of May 1965, the Commander-in-Chief, Pacific Fleet, Admiral Roy L. Johnson suspected the reason North Vietnamese air defenses were having successes against Rolling Thunder air strikes was due to repetitive, predictable operational patterns that made it easier for the North Vietnamese to anticipate American actions. Consequently, they could concentrate their antiaircraft guns near the targets the Americans would most likely attack. A good American countermove, in the opinion of Admiral Johnson, would have been to have more preapproved targets available for missions, which would have forced the enemy to disperse defenses. Expanding each Rolling Thunder from seven to fourteen days would also lessen the predictability of missions and would not intrude into the operation's effectiveness.[9] General Harris believed land- and carrier-based air power needed to be coordinated and jointly commanded on a larger scale.[10]

After the president sent a letter of sympathy to the parents of one airman shot down over North Vietnam, they returned it to the White House with the rejoinder, "We think you would be more sincere with your sympathy if you had taken the shackles off the fliers and let them hit more targets up north."[11] One veteran of a hundred combat missions agreed. Captain Leroy Thornal said, "I think we ought [to] just wipe out Haiphong, by hitting the dams up there." Since the United States was at war with North Vietnam it should pull no punches—the North Vietnamese certainly would not if they were waging war in the American homeland.[12]

One early constraint was bizarre. The Kennedy administration's State Department asserted American/South Vietnamese combat missions against communist insurgents constituted a "clear violation of the Geneva Accords."[13] The accords stated that "the introduction into Vietnam of any reinforcements in the form of all types of arms, munitions and other war material, such as combat aircraft, naval craft, pieces of ordnance, jet engines and jet weapons and armored vehicles, is prohibited."[14] A technical violation, perhaps, but states have the right to defend themselves, and have the right to call in assistance from other states.[15]

At first there were almost no rules of engagement; South Vietnamese pilots could bomb approved targets, they just could not cross international boundaries. The restrictions were initially more concerned with putting a South Vietnamese face on air operations and avoiding the appearance, at least, of overt American military activity. The commander of the T-28 squadron warned that restraints and care in the application of firepower were prudent because accidentally killing a noncombatant could nullify the successes of air-ground teams.[16] Some understood during the early days of the war that not only air power effectiveness but also military effectiveness in general were defined by their relationship to a host of critical factors: "political, psychological, sociological, and military."[17]

The main purpose of rules of engagement (ROE) in 1964 was keeping down the risks to aircrews, mainly those flying reconnaissance missions, and also the avoidance of giving the communists grist for their propaganda machine, thus, no napalm, no cluster bombs.[18] It was the Gulf of Tonkin incident that loosened the geopolitical restrictions on the use of air power: the US was able to openly deploy combat aircraft to South Vietnam, and the Thais allowed American aircraft to carry out combat missions from Thai bases. The ROE prohibited operations against North Vietnam in 1964. It was not until the president authorized Rolling Thunder—a policy decision—that operational restrictions began to be relaxed. Napalm was authorized against targets in North Vietnam on March 15, 1965, CINCPAC permitted armed reconnaissance missions, and Admiral Sharp received permission to use aircraft based in Thailand.[19]

Initially, there was a nuanced understanding of the relationship between restraint, restrictions, bombing accuracy, and careful targeting on the one hand, and the accomplishment of what were limited policy goals on the other. General Harris appealed to the professionalism of his airmen in his explanation for thoughtful restraint. Maximum destruction was not the purpose. Instead, bombing was intended to end Hanoi's aggression against South Vietnam. Only hitting authorized targets could further that agenda. "It is an essential part of our national policy," he added, "that rigid discipline continue to govern our actions." Restrictions were going to continue and, "They will not always be understandable at the operating level, but they must be observed nevertheless." Harris also realized "it is fundamental to the success of our national policy that the air crews continue to demonstrate extraordinarily high professional standards in this air war."[20]

The restrictions included not hitting targets within thirty miles of Hanoi and ten miles of Haiphong and staying at least thirty miles away from the Chinese border. Consequently, the North Vietnamese had two large internal sanctuaries, and these were where most of their industrial targets were located. For some time, MiG airfields could not be struck, but SAMs and AAA were the main threat, and they were targetable to varying degrees after July 1965. The buffer zone next to the Chinese border was understandable. These were not targets the destruction of which would have pushed Hanoi toward capitulation, but they fit a certain paradigm of what was a good target and what must be destroyed in any rational air campaign.[21] The chronic restrictions over Hanoi and Haiphong were probably the most bitterly disputed constraints. There were some permitted targets therein, but pilots had better positively identify them, and Washington had to receive "notification . . . of the plan to strike" and grant permission.[22] The president perpetuated the ten-mile Hanoi exclusion zone so that an errant bomb would not torpedo diplomatic efforts.[23]

Military leaders bristled against the tactical and operational restrictions on Rolling Thunder. Westmoreland opposed, but submitted to, the target approval process that routed everything through Washington.[24] Bruce Palmer Jr., an Army general who served in 1967 and 1968 as II Field Force commander, considered the myriad restrictions to be "simply unreasonable for men flying at 500 knots, trying to stay alive and yet close on their targets."[25] American military leaders soon pressed for the removal of most of the restrictions. They wanted permission to pursue Chinese aircraft into Chinese airspace if Chinese pilots attacked American aircraft, and they wanted to run down communist forces who fled into Cambodia during a battle. The State Department labeled napalm "a terror weapon," and opposed its use, riling the JCS who wished to use it against AAA sites. The president, however, gave his permission during Rolling Thunder's first month.[26] Some aircrews complained that the restrictions funneled them onto predictable flight routes that resulted in aircraft losses. Word that some referenced a portion of the ingress route into the Red River Valley as "slaughter alley" percolated up to the chief of staff of the Air Force. Second Air Division replied that no one had ever used that term. It did admit the combination of no-fly areas made flight routes more predictable, but that more than half of shoot-downs took place near the target, not en route.[27] General Momyer pointed out that the rules of engagement gave the enemy specific advantages—in particular, time to develop countermeasures and time to gain help from other countries. They also turned the northeastern portion of North Vietnam into a sanctuary. For instance, they parked trains in an off-limits railroad yard in August 1967.[28] A 1969 assessment encapsulated the continuing frustration well. Restrictions were excessive. Pilots could bomb "roads, railroads, and bridges outside of city limits, while within striking distance ships were unloading hundreds of thousands of tons of supplies," but the ships were off limits. The report indicated, "Trucks loaded with supplies were parked in courtyards, ball fields, and in towns that were restricted from strikes."[29]

All this baffled General John D. Ryan, who as commander of Pacific Air Forces thought it made no sense to steadily increase the size of forces in Southeast Asia without at the same time unleashing the full power of the Air Force and Navy. Westmoreland also supported a less-restricted target list that allowed for the bombing of strategically significant targets inside the Hanoi and Haiphong exclusion zones that contained, for instance, repair warehouses, facilities for assembling missiles, and a MiG base.[30]

Retired Major General Gilbert L. Meyers, recently the deputy commander of 2nd Air Division, argued the better alternative to "graduated pressure" was for the military to have "the latitude to fight the war the way the military people feel it is necessary to do so in order to win."[31] Momyer also believed the air campaign would have won the war if only the president had unleashed unrestrained force, adding, "don't get in a fight unless you are prepared to do whatever is necessary to win.... I suppose a military man will always be in the dilemma of supporting policy even though he knows it surely restricts the capacity of military forces to produce the desired effect."[32] The magazine *U.S. News and World Report* wrote in 1966 that General McConnell claimed "the Air Force could wind up the war in North Vietnam in two to three weeks if it were allowed to mount a powerful strategic air campaign."[33]

There are several assumptions implicit in these assertions: tactical effectiveness, liberal targeting, weight of effort, and unrestraint inevitably accomplish strategic goals; military activities during war are distinct from political and diplomatic concerns; war is distinct from politics; war is essentially a set of combat operations; and military leaders know best how to solve national security issues. Waging war successfully, however, requires leaders to deny sacred status to every preconceived idea and preference.

The operational management of missions became a bone of contention. From the very beginning, commanders believed the lack of flexibility in planning and flying strike missions resulted in more aircraft losses. They found the unpredictable changes authorities in

Washington issued after the completion of mission planning to be annoying at best, as were the differing rules of engagement for missions over North Vietnam and Laos.[34] Admiral Sharp wanted more flexibility in scheduling missions and primary and alternate targets to allow planners to exploit weather conditions to send aircraft against them at the most opportune times. General Harris wanted the authority for assigning targets and missions to reside at a level of command low enough to be able to react quickly to sudden opportunities, such as new information on where enemy forces were most active, something that made sense for an air interdiction campaign.[35] Harris also wanted to be able to re-attack when weather permitted. That way he could forestall the communists from completing repairs. Haiphong simply had to be bombed; supplies should be destroyed at their entry points into North Vietnam before being dispersed among the multitude of supply routes they had within their borders. Later in 1966, the chairman noticed air operations had become predictable and cited a study that argued predictability, whose roots lay in Washington's rules, contributed to greater loss rates.[36] General Harris longed for greater liberality for assigning targets, but he rejected target requests if they even came close to violating Washington's guidance.[37]

Admiral Sharp's command believed the air campaign would be more effective and sensible if they could "ease restrictions which might hamper the smooth, safe, and effective control of combat operations." He also wished to allocate decision making power to lower-level commanders to the greatest extent possible. In particular, he proposed: "rules of engagement should be recast in order to realize the full potential of U.S. military effectiveness." For example, allow reconnaissance squadron commanders to determine the best altitude for their jets to fly, and permit fighter squadrons to attack targets that avail themselves momentarily, adding, "If there are political considerations, the military commander should be kept continually appraised so as to reflect such ramifications in his actions."[38]

General Joseph Moore argued that giving commanders in the theater more flexibility would result in flying a greater number of missions using fewer aircraft each mission, increasing the likelihood of target destruction while putting fewer aircraft at risk. As things were, missions often had no alternate target in case the primary was socked in, so those aircraft flew over hostile territory for no reason. Flight limitations between missions made it more evident to spies when real missions were taking off. The JCS permitted only a single mission against each Rolling Thunder target. Each mission had to completely destroy the target, but that was not always possible. Thorough destruction was more difficult in a one-shot mission than was readily apparent with follow-up missions often needed but not permitted. It was as if there was an assumption that one mission equaled complete target destruction. Moore also observed that the respective services were waging separate deconflicted air campaigns rather than ones integrated in ways where each supported the other, an appropriate critique.[39]

General McConnell lay blame for the indeterminate progress on the bombing restrictions: "Our bombing is ineffective because of the restrictions place[d] upon the Air Force. We should lift these restrictions and we would then get results."[40] Major General John D. Lavelle pointed out in April 1966 that the US had not attacked the most important targets in North Vietnam, more than half of those the JCS recommended remained untouched. Commander-in-Chief, Pacific Fleet, Admiral Roy L. Johnson, argued that under the current set of restrictions, there were not any targets left worth bombing for aircraft losses. He counted sixteen prohibited targets valuable enough to risk losses if Washington would allow it, and cited eighty more whose destruction undercut Hanoi's support for the Viet Cong.[41]

Admiral Sharp believed the concern regarding civilian casualties was unfair, because while the US kept itself from destroying everything in North Vietnam relevant to the war, VC and PAVN soldiers terrorized and assassinated great numbers of South Vietnamese.

That was not an ROE problem, but instead was a failure of what is now referred to as information warfare, which highlighted the American and South Vietnamese failures in communicating those facts to the rest of the world in a convincing manner. A liberalization of rules and targets would not have solved that shortcoming. However, prohibiting bombing within ten miles of the center of Hanoi and four miles within the center of Haiphong certainly provided safe areas. Not mining Haiphong Harbor ensured North Vietnam could obtain the war resources it needed via the convenience of unrestricted shipping.[42]

Given all this, there is something to the argument that Johnson and McNamara should have contemplated more seriously a maximum effort that consisted of destroying all the targets, particularly Haiphong's harbor. But there is not an inevitable link between tactical efficiency, operational flexibility, and unrestrained violence on the one hand and the achievement of strategy and national policy objectives on the other. Achieving war aims is not the inevitable product of following favored methods, preferred doctrine, and weight of effort in a manner deemed efficient. Indeed, the American air forces could have bombed and destroyed all the targets only to see the Hanoi government defiantly call for the Americans to leave Southeast Asia as a precondition to talks. What would have followed next?

Not targeting civilians was a priority and the rules of engagement and restrictions toward that end served the war's goals. Large numbers of civilian casualties would have undercut the objective of winning the war and minimizing the deaths of noncombatants was necessary to avoid giving Hanoi ready-made propaganda, hence the limits on what fighter-bombers could strike.[43] An unrestrained bombing campaign would have placed aircrew safety and the destruction of assigned targets above the lives of noncombatants. That would have made the United States look like the aggressor and North Vietnam the victim. Such labeling can decide a war's outcome. For his part, Westmoreland did not seek to carry out unrestricted operations. He understood the relationship between restraint and the achievement of the war's goals and pursued both.[44]

Avoiding an unnecessary provocation of China lay at the heart of President Johnson's concerns, and his support for the political limitations on air operations over North Vietnam was a natural consequence. Since war is a political activity and not a realm separate from politics and diplomacy, those decisions lay within the president's prerogative. Nixon continued Johnson's practice of steering clear of confronting China. When the Chinese began lengthening a road in northern Laos in 1969, prohibitions expanded to prevent American aircraft from bombing "all known or suspected Chinese positions in Northern Laos."[45] Carrying out bombing missions with care enabled the US to inform the UN Security Council that it was waging war with restraint, but that body had not seen fit to hold the North Vietnamese and the National Liberation Front to the same standard.[46]

Some of the restrictions were odd. For instance, "only military targets would be attacked," but special care had to be taken when killing draft animals. The beasts must be used "in support of enemy operations" in order to be targeted, but aircrews could attack military targets of opportunity along their routes if they had leftover ordnance.[47] They could not attack lone vehicles because North Vietnamese propaganda claimed an isolated vehicle that got strafed was a school bus.[48] After the May 1965 bombing suspension, aircrews could not bomb stationary targets but targets that moved were permissible.[49] Rolling Thunder 53 stipulated, "No more than three repeat three of the nine (9) list D targets will be struck in any one week."[50] This stipulation, along with warnings to "Exercise extreme caution in conducting air strikes so as to avoid endangering foreign ships," was intended to avoid accusations the US was escalating the war.[51]

The administration believed its chosen level of force would be a sufficient persuader, but General Wheeler warned the Senate Armed Services Committee in 1967 that Hanoi would perceive of self-restrictions such as a reduction in the bombing campaign as weakness, a loss of confidence, doubt, and lack of fortitude. During Operation Commando Hunt III, attack aircraft were not allowed to bomb SAM sites until after the site had fired at them; it was a bit late at that point. Some self-imposed restrictions were just weird, like the JCS prohibition against weather reconnaissance aircraft taking photographs of what was happening on the ground below.[52]

Others made sense, like the requirement for fighters to visually identify aircraft they were about to shoot "only when possibility exists that the aircraft is either friendly or non-military." That possibility existed frequently, and American fighters did not have the ability to interrogate a MiG's transponder until 1972.[53] Another one that supported national policy was the prohibition against armed reconnaissance within twenty-five to thirty miles of the Chinese border. Not provoking the Chinese was a high priority for the Americans and flying over China, even by accident, would undercut that goal. If aircrews found "military targets in the vicinity of target areas [they] may be destroyed"—a quite liberal ROE because it granted the aircrew on the scene the power to determine if those objects were military targets. They could also return fire on their way to and from their bombing targets. The requirement that "collateral damage will be kept to a minimum consistent with desired damage objective" was also reasonable.[54] Aircrews in trolling fighter-bombers were to exercise the utmost care to not bomb places where noncombatants were close by. Accidentally bombing Lao villagers and soldiers, for instance, worked directly against the agenda of nurturing kinship between people in the hinterland of Laos and the central government. Rules of engagement, no matter how strict, could not eliminate accidental killings.[55]

Brigadier General George P. Simler, director of operations for the 2nd Air Division, understood the relationship between combat actions and geopolitics, and reminded his subordinates most forcefully in November 1965: "Air operations in Laos are extremely sensitive. It is absolutely imperative that your aircrews do not expend munitions outside of approved areas." He counted six ROE violations that month and if they continued, the US might lose the permission to attack North Vietnamese forces there preemptively.[56] Authorized JCS targets and only JCS authorized targets were to be bombed—also reasonable because the JCS were better positioned to coordinate military force with policy goals and diplomacy than were the commanders of Seventh AF or Pacific Command, not to mention wing commanders. Even before the generals issued this reminder, they had persuaded Washington to remove the requirement for a second approval of preplanned missions in December 1965.[57]

Restrictions slowly subsided, but always remained. At the end of 1965, there were no more time limitations or requirements for only one strike per target. By February 1966, the JCS lifted restrictions on how many aircraft could carry out combat missions on any particular day.[58] Which targets were to be authorized was the rub. Vice Admiral Kent L. Lee commented after the war that he never received directives on what tactics to employ, so the rules did not micromanage; instead they were simply told, "These are the targets you can hit."[59]

Reconciling the requirements for making Rolling Thunder strikes tactically and operationally as successful as possible with the requirements for making them compatible with international politics and propaganda vexed American generals. Wheeler tried to get Westmoreland to understand the reasons behind the restrictions and reassured him that he and McNamara were doing their "utmost to clear away the restrictions which hinder you in carrying out your mission."[60] The JCS also strongly opposed the practice of reserving a set of targets for later retaliation instead of bombing them now. The commander of PACAF tried to keep from annoying the JCS by vetoing requests from his commanders to bomb targets likely to be disapproved.[61] Wheeler tried to explain to his subordinates that the air strikes had to navigate a very difficult path in just attempting to achieve political goals, but over time, the limitations put on Rolling Thunder left the Air Force incensed. McConnell hinted the restrictions were a problem when he refused to answer a question regarding their impact on operational effectiveness. Military leaders saw no reason why worthwhile targets were off limits. They also argued the way air strikes were sequenced for them was arbitrary and made no sense militarily.[62]

Discussions like these illustrate two arguments on how to use air strikes most effectively: calibrated bombings, or the compressed, comprehensive destruction of targets of value to the enemy. The commander of PACAF also wrote, "should it become evident that lucrative fleeting targets must be struck in violation of above guidance, notify this HQ immediately following such attacks." He claimed that his purpose was not to violate the ROE, but to follow them carefully enough so that they could hit as much as they could. For example, he refused to permit the bombing of two oil storage sites "because they are border line with regard to the ground rules."[63]

Haiphong's harbor and waterfront, in particular, was one target set the generals believed essential to cutting off North Vietnam from their suppliers. Admiral Sharp lobbied for permission to bomb close to places that were off-limits. For example, air leaders believed dive bombing could be carried out with enough accuracy against Shipyard 4 in Haiphong to avoid hitting a nearby hospital wharf. Bomb, for instance, on the days when not a single foreign-flagged ship was docked nearby and avoid international incidents that way.[64] Two years into the war an incident occurred in which Air Force fighter-bombers accidentally struck a Soviet vessel, the *Turkestan*, with 20mm gunfire when they shot at a flak battery that had been placed right next to the ship.[65] When an aircraft dropped a Mk 36 mine too close for comfort to another Soviet ship in January 1968, Wheeler asked Sharp to ensure his aircrews bombed there only when the weather was good enough for them to place their bombs where they were supposed to go. This incident highlighted the challenge of deciding which political objective was more important: avoiding an incident with the United States' primary adversary, the USSR, or obtaining decisive results against a lesser threat during a shooting war. The admiral also complained that Washington always seemed to restrict him from finishing off a target, which gave Hanoi a chance to repair the damage and prepare for the next round just when bombing was inflicting serious damage.[66]

As the North Vietnamese adapted, they not only took advantage of the sanctuary status Hanoi and Haiphong had, they also exploited the buffer zone along the Chinese border to hold railroad cars until needed because the Americans would not bomb there.[67] For a few days in August 1967, however, the JCS lifted the restrictions against bombing targets inside what had been the Hanoi prohibited area: a ten-mile radius from the center of the city. Planners could also target rail lines with the zone along the Chinese border and authorized armed reconnaissance missions inside Haiphong's prohibited area, a four-mile radius from the center of the city.[68] The following year three A-6As were sent to bomb and mine Hanoi's river dock on February 24, 1968. Just days later, six targets were hit in metropolitan Hanoi, including Hanoi Radio, located eight miles to the south of the city.[69] Lifting these restrictions did not lead to decisive results.

Some rules were downright galling. Many found prohibitions against bombing military targets where ammunition and weapons were stored senseless and indefensible. For instance, fighter-bombers could not attack North Vietnamese air bases until 1967. Pilots hated it, and resented not being able to attack what was shooting at them or the ships unloading the supplies destined for enemy troops because doing so might expand the war, an argument many found unconvincing.[70] Many found fault with the restrictions as a whole and had written congressmen such as Senators Stuart Symington and Howard W. Cannon, one missive stating, "airpower was not being used to its best advantage."[71] One eloquent officer, an O-1 Bird Dog forward air controller named Captain Emery G. Cushing, expressed what became a common criticism of the war's air strategy in his end of tour report:

> Like many of my fellow officers, I have difficulty in accepting a policy of limited, protracted war with its very slow and sometimes, almost negligible progress.... In my opinion, if we are not supposed to win this war in the foreseeable future, then we should be straight forwardly advised. If air power alone is not sufficient to force Ho Chi Minh into a compromise, then why do we pursue the same path? I find it difficult to believe that we, one of the strongest, if not the strongest nation today, do not have the intestinal fortitude to face world opinion, as fickle as it is, and use the force necessary to remove this conflict from the realm of an endless nightmare.[72]

As discussed in chapter 2, President Johnson raised a worthwhile point during August 1967 discussions about removing the restriction against bombing the primary MiG base, Phuc Yen: why was destroying less than a dozen jets that the Soviets would replace so critical to the war?[73] How would destroying them produce long-term outcomes worth the risk and cost? Senator Symington, however, used the restriction against bombing that air base to point out an inconsistency in the White House's air war. Johnson and McNamara adamantly opposed hitting it because too many civilian deaths might result, but they had authorized targets closer to the center of Hanoi where even more noncombatants resided. Symington also prodded, and failed during the August 1967 Senate hearings, to get General Wheeler to publicly contradict the State Department and the secretary of defense regarding the skittishness over bombing North Vietnam's main air defense base.[74]

Many congressmen agreed with Senator John C. Stennis that military professionals were "best qualified to decide upon, plan, and carry out the purely military operations necessary to win the war."[75] They believed the restrictions were holding back the military from achieving a decisive victory. Senator Stennis was suspicious that the self-imposed restrictions and the withheld firepower were preventing the United States from achieving decisive effects, so he held hearings in August 1967.[76] "Gentlemen," he said, "it is well known that due to the restrictions placed on you, that you are not permitted to exert the full power and force you possess."[77]

General Wheeler believed a less-restricted air campaign against North Vietnam would by its nature reduce casualties in South Vietnam.[78] Wheeler denied the chiefs were proposing to bomb civilians and believed the assertion unrestricted bombing would topple the ruling party in Hanoi was "highly conjectural."[79] He observed that restricting bombing to below the 20th parallel would make military operations easier for the North Vietnamese.[80] Wheeler also asserted that destroying certain individual targets, like the Hanoi Thermal Power Plant, could bring that the war to an end sooner without explaining how.[81] One assertion from the hearings was that McNamara had arbitrarily prevented the JCS from authorizing missions against dozens of targets. Had certain targets been bombed earlier in the war, Wheeler believed, fewer pilots would have been shot down.[82] He made the same claims as McConnell regarding the ninety-four-target list during his August 16 testimony: "We supported a much sharper type of attack, Senator Thurmond, than the concept that was adopted."[83]

When Admiral Sharp testified, the thrust of the senators and his responses was that a plethora of important targets remained untouched that leaders in Washington would not permit the air forces to bomb, for no good reason. Their destruction, according to Senator Strom Thurmond, would bring the war an end and would do so more quickly. Sharp had asked for the removal of targeting restrictions in Hanoi, for instance, and was denied.[84]

Thurmond believed if only the air forces could bomb them continuously, without restrictions, capitulation would follow. Sharp agreed, adding that "indiscriminate bombing of civilian targets" was not necessary to achieve that result.[85]

McConnell testified that "the original concept of the Joint Chiefs of Staff was to go in there with a very severe application of airpower. In fact, our first target list was 94 targets which we intended to destroy in a total of 16 days. That process was disapproved."[86] NSC member Major General Robert N. Ginsburgh was convinced executing the ninety-four-target plan would have won the war had it been executed (he later suggested issuing evacuation warnings to the people of Hanoi and Haiphong and then turning those cites to rubble).[87] Moreover, McConnell agreed with Senator Margaret Chase Smith (R-Maine) that Rolling Thunder would "have been more effective and perhaps at an earlier date had it not been burdened with restrictions and prohibited targets. . . . Yes, ma'am, I am sure it would have been." When Senator Smith asked him about the political repercussions of these operations, he responded, "I don't know what the political implications might have been."[88] The senators and generals reemphasized "that the JCS had unanimously opposed Johnson's graduated pressure since March 1965."[89] The Air Force chief of staff had, in fact, vigorously endorsed a restricted air campaign in 1965 and had been confident that it would accomplish the president's goals.[90]

McConnell was in a precarious position where he needed to be aware of the relationships between military activities and international politics and had to avoid passing judgment on the policies of civilian leaders in the executive and legislative branches. That could poison relationships between the president, the secretary of defense, and himself. While doing so, he had to speak truthfully to Congress. During his testimony before the Senate Committee on Armed Services in 1967 he stated the JCS "were unanimous in our recommendations at that time as to what should have been done at that time," which was technically correct. The interchange between McConnell and Chief Counsel James T. Kendall, however, reads as if the JCS had recommended an all-out air campaign in 1965, but had been denied the chance to pursue that strategy, when in fact they had expressed firm confidence in the outcome of a gradually escalated bombing campaign.[91] McConnell made no claim that an unrestricted air campaign in 1967 would persuade the North Vietnamese to give in: "Now whether or not he will capitulate, I don't know what it takes to make him capitulate."[92] Shouldn't he have had a pretty good idea?

General Momyer argued that greater liberality in the freedom he had to select fleeting targets would make the air campaign more effective, but he rejected the claims that the restrictions had greatly weakened the effort against North Vietnam. American technology had improved effectiveness and lowered risks; the counter-air campaign was preventing MiGs from impeding bombing missions, the number of which had increased exponentially over the past fourteen months.[93] In fact, he added, the effects of the bombing were at last making themselves evident. Furthermore, "Morale is tremendous, and I have heard no dissatisfaction with the target system that the pilots are currently hitting."[94]

Saying the right things for that situation, Momyer wrote a proposal four years later that reinforced the demand that during wartime the civilian leadership should turn over the war to the military, which he believed knew what was best. In a letter to Major General George J. Keegan Jr., Momyer exclaimed, "I look back on the war with much regret that we were not permitted to take the action that would have won the war and saved many precious lives. What we the military could have done that we didn't do to break through the civilian decisions remains unanswered. I sometimes think the JCS should have resigned as a body to drive home the folly of the civilian strategy for fighting the war. I am sure this was considered but discarded because it wouldn't change the strategy." Blame the military for not resisting to a greater degree. Momyer was certain generals like George C. Marshall would never have permitted civilian leaders to impose a strategy the military had not created. Generals twenty years later should have been, he argued, equally assertive.[95] Momyer was repeating the binary nature of the options Americans perceived lay before them: either a war micromanaged by civilians or a war turned over to field commanders in which the civilians remained aloof until after the war. Success requires instead a cooperative melding of the two to ensure military force is used in a way that achieves the state's objectives.

When Secretary of Defense McNamara testified, he stated, "There can be no question that the bombing campaign has and is hurting North Vietnam's war-making capability" and that it harmed their ability to support their war in South Vietnam, but that the bombing was not persuading Hanoi to make fundamental changes to its political agenda.[96] Secretary McNamara stated that no amount of bombing could erode the flow of supplies into South Vietnam sufficiently to prevent the communists from continuing to engage in combat because the Ho Chi Minh Trail had too much headroom and capacity, and the communists could adjust their pace of operations to the ammunition and supplies at hand.[97] He did not believe an air campaign with fewer restrictions would accomplish anything more than the current "selective, carefully targeted bombing campaign, such as we are presently conducting."[98] Switching to a more indiscriminate campaign brought with it too many hazards and it probably would not produce decisive results. Moreover, bombing North Vietnamese targets left unaddressed the problem of the war against the Viet Cong in South Vietnam.[99] He rejected Sharp's assertion that, "The imposed restrictions have resulted in inefficient use of our airpower."[100] He also disputed arguments that the refusal to authorize fifty-seven targets the JCS had asked to bomb had substantively lengthened the war, and rejected a proposed objective of breaking the will of the North Vietnamese via a much less restricted bombing campaign.[101]

The thrust of the hearings was that unrestricted bombing would lead to victory. The senators ridiculed McNamara for his micromanagement of the war and the hearings produced two consequences: Johnson lost confidence in his defense secretary and he started including the chairman of the joint chiefs of staff in all the Tuesday lunchtime meetings.[102] The hearings showed that the appeal for a more violent and assertive air campaign not only ranged across the services, it also held considerable appeal among many civilian leaders. The Stennis Hearings also firmly rooted in American memory the argument that the restrictions on air operations lost the war for the United States.

So frustrated had the JCS become with the management of the war that, according to one source, Generals Wheeler, Johnson, and McConnell pondered resigning in protest on August 25. They slept on it, and then pulled back from the brink the following morning.[103] "We can't do it," Wheeler said to the other chiefs in an 8:30 meeting on the morning of August 26. "It's mutiny."[104] Whether or not this ever happened has been disputed.[105]

Although North Vietnamese propagandists howled that air strikes resulted in carnage, the chief of the North Vietnamese Mission in Paris confessed in 1968, "There was no particular fear of daylight bombing raids in NVN, the night raids and night alerts were bothersome as they kept people awake and nervous." The Canadian representative to the International Criminal Court revealed a nonkinetic effect of air power when he commented that he "could not understand why the US did not keep at least one aircraft over Hanoi constantly, since when air alerts sounded, all work stopped."[106] These and other accounts serve as evidence that the United States did not target civilians, suggesting that the restrictions were costly for American airmen, but shrewd politically. Indeed, the Hanoi ten-mile prohibited zone may have protected the United States from substantive accusations of trying to slaughter noncombatants in North Vietnamese urban areas. Clearly, American air forces aimed their bombs at military targets. Folk singer Joan Baez, for example, felt safe enough to record an album in Hanoi during the December 1972 bombings, which were among the war's least-restricted operations.[107]

The rules of engagement over Laos were sensible and were constructed to accomplish several goals: avoid killing noncombatants, avoid embarrassing the government in Vientiane, and destroy communist targets. Aircraft could not, for instance, fly within ten miles of the North Vietnamese–Laotian border so as to avoid incidents.[108] Pacific Command commented that while these controls reduced options for the use of air power, "The constraints imposed resulted from political-military considerations."[109] Once again that made perfect sense since war and politics reside next to each other on the same continuum. Restrictions existed in Laos because the Lao government wished to maintain the facade of neutrality. Ambassador Sullivan argued restraining American air power was worthwhile given the political goal of maintaining a relationship with Souvanna Phouma that did not embarrass his government, forcing him to undercut the whole enterprise. He added that Souvanna Phouma's confidence in the United States was unusually firm and maintaining that required five things: candor, an overlap of American actions with Laotian interests, not harming villagers, coordinating with the Lao military, and following the conditions he had set.[110] One of the policy goals was to "maintain this unique and essential political foundation for our operations. It means we must sometimes sacrifice maximum military opportunities in order to temper them to the political climate."[111] The constraints were designed to avoid unnecessary damage not only to the political-diplomatic effort, but also to the military effort as well. The rules did not result in the Americans having to fight with one hand tied behind their back, nor did these restrictions defeat Allied forces. The planning and attack cycle, however, was relatively slow, because every mission over northern Laos required approval in Washington. Delays like that had a negative impact because the lightly equipped Lao Air Force had greater success finding and destroying stationary targets using fewer aircraft flying more frequently under more liberal ROE.[112] An air force defending its own territory, however, is going to get away with more than an air force from another country even if its assistance is at the request of the local government.

Rules included the requirement for forward air controller and bombing aircraft to exploit "the most precise navigational aids available" to determine their location. Bombing when visibility was good could take place no closer than 500 yards of a prisoner of war camp; when visibility was poor, targets had to stay about two miles from a camp or from friendly troops. A wide variety of support aircraft were allowed, such as Iron Hand, reconnaissance, MiG combat air patrol, and such; only active jamming required specific authorization. The American Embassy had to validate each target. Other constraints included the presence of an observer from the RLAF on American aircraft for validating targets. Strike aircraft had to use the ordnance the embassy had approved, and they could jettison unused bombs in authorized areas. Wild weasels could shoot back at antiaircraft sites in much of Laos. Missions over northern Laos normally had to be monitored by an EC-121 College Eye aircraft and managed by a forward air controller. Targets in the buffer zone with North Vietnam could be bombed after validation and approval by the embassy, Honolulu, and the Pentagon. Armed reconnaissance aircraft could bomb targets of opportunity 200 yards each side of communist roads and paths if it was outside of the buffer zone. Aircraft could use napalm, but some targets required permission by the embassy for its use. The towns of Khang Khai and Phoung Savan could be bombed with the proper permissions. Fighter-bombers could hit targets as close as 500 yards of a village or a group of noncombatants if an airplane was receiving ground fire or providing close air support.[113] A January 1967 requirement stipulated American aircraft were to stay away from the populated parts of Laos to the best of their ability, and they were to stay ten miles away from five major towns, except for armed reconnaissance aircraft flying along Route 118 near Attopeu. From March 1967, every air strike in Laos had to be under the control of either MSQ-77 radar guidance or a forward air controller; most strikes had been FAC controlled anyway before the new rule. There were places where antiaircraft defenses were too dense to permit O-1s and O-2s to fly without undue risk, and requirements meant that armed aircraft diverted from North Vietnam sorties would not be able to expend their ordnance if they were not able to come under FAC control.[114] In sum, these parameters were pretty liberal and were designed to avoid making new enemies among the Laotian people and embarrassing the Laotian government.

It is not clear how a completely unrestricted bombing campaign in Laos would have shut down the Ho Chi Minh Trail when the most serious challenges there lay in finding trucks, truck parks, and bypass roads and not in getting permission to bomb. If the ultimate purpose of air interdiction was destroying as much of the enemy's ability to fight as possible without regard to other issues, liberal rules of engagement would not have overcome the challenge of finding targets. One must ask, how would looser ROEs that resulted in more noncombatant deaths, the accidental deaths of friendly forces, and casual border violations have helped the military find more targets? How would liberal targeting move the war effort closer to the achievement of the strategic and policy goals? The unconstrained use of aerial bombardment can only contribute to victory if other considerations, such as not making new enemies or losing allies or prestige, are not relevant to the war, or an existential threat has to be defeated no matter what, but they were in this case. South Vietnam faced an existential threat, but its sponsor, the United States, did not, which made sorting out the appropriate level of force all the more challenging. The multitude of variables, from respecting the lives of American aircrews to the usefulness of unrestrained American bombing to Soviet propaganda, all had to be taken into account—a difficult challenge.

An Air Force analyst from 1969 wrote, "It is fair to say that the rules are national policy translated to the battlefield. Each change, or threat of change, to the US political relationship with other nations, whether allies, enemies or potential enemies, was reflected in a corresponding alteration of the Rules of Engagement for the Vietnam conflict."[115] Defense Secretary Clifford argued in 1968 that geopolitical restrictions, not the rules of engagement or oversight from Washington, were the challenge. The US could not win by waging a war on the defense, and the sanctuaries of North Vietnam, Laos, and Cambodia posed an interminable problem. He is not to be confused with those in favor of escalation; Clifford badly wanted to get the United States out of the war.[116]

Rules of engagement for the 1970 raid into Cambodia were politically astute in one sense. The Americans did not want to make new enemies, so they coordinated with the Cambodian and South Vietnamese militaries toward that end, setting operational parameters to lessen the chance of harming noncombatants and avoid damaging cultural sites. Out of respect for Cambodia, the Cambodian Armed Forces (FANK) had to validate every target before bomb release. Additionally, if a Cambodian or South Vietnamese ground commander gave permission to hit a target, that was sufficient approval. The only exception was Cambodian national monuments. Reconnaissance aircraft located, mapped, and photographed shrines and culturally significant structures, photos were given to pilots, and under no circumstances whatsoever could they bomb those places. If enemy forces located elsewhere aimed ground fire at American aircraft, they could shoot back. They only needed

FANK permission if the fire was coming from a settled area.[117] Thus air forces could still bombard targets inside Cambodia, but in a way that demonstrated some respect for its sovereignty and concern for its cultural heritage.

The main factor affecting rules and restrictions over North Vietnam after Rolling Thunder was the November 1, 1968, bombing halt. Reconnaissance flights were a component of that decision, and those jets received escorts for their flights below the 19th parallel. The escorts could fire back at emplacements that shot at them. If MiGs attacked, the escorts could shoot them down. The overriding reason behind the prohibition against striking SAM sites before they fired was the belief that restraint aided the Paris Peace Talks.[118]

The JCS loosened some of the ROE in 1970. In particular, Iron Hand missions could hit batteries in North Vietnam below twenty degrees that either fired upon or illuminated American aircraft, and wild weasels could also place themselves between these threats and B-52s. Fighters could fight back against attacking MiGs. Fighter-bombers using Paveways (a type of laser-guided bomb) could overfly North Vietnam on their way to Laos. Arc Light and fighter-bomber missions could continue in Cambodia, specifically a series of interdiction and direct attack missions during the summer of 1970. Cambodia was opened to search and rescue, reconnaissance, and flare dropping aircraft, and FACs could operate in tandem with Cambodian forces.[119]

In 1971, the PAVN air force became more aggressive against aircraft flying over Laos and even tried to shoot down a B-52 on November 22. In response, Admiral Moorer forwarded an interpretation of ROE designating MiGs hostile when they were airborne south of nineteen degrees latitude when American aircraft were nearby, particularly B-52s. Moorer, General Abrams, and Admiral McCain permitted larger, more aggressive escort packages to fly. The rules assumed an interval of time between American aircraft receiving indications that missile sites were tracking them and the moment a battery fired, but a new PAVN tactic used search radars to provide targeting information to the site, which meant aircrews would receive no warning until the missiles were fired. They shot down two American aircraft in December.[120]

Considering that threat, Admiral McCain changed the rules of engagement in January 1972 to permit the firing of missiles against radars anywhere outside of Route Package 6 whenever MiGs were flying in a hostile manner.[121] A couple of weeks later Abrams permitted fighters to attack interceptors flying out of three panhandle airfields whenever they flew south of the 18th parallel.[122]

With the invasion of March 30, 1972, rules of engagement were found to be appropriate for every sector except for North Vietnamese airspace, where there was not, for example, enough flexibility in obtaining permission to bomb fleeting targets.[123] The Joint Chiefs directed planners and aircrews to take great care "to minimize civilian casualties and avoid known or suspected hospitals, religious shrines, POW camps, and third country shipping," a continuity with past rules. The secretary of defense had already granted the authority to engage hostile aircraft and missiles in March. Aircraft could attack sites that fired at American aircraft, and they could also bomb fire-control radars that only tracked them but did not fire, and shoot MiGs on sight below the 18th parallel.[124] While thoughtful restrictions were essential given the centrality of propaganda to the North Vietnamese war effort, a primary reason for relaxing them was the fact that the Soviets were more concerned over relations with the Americans than they were defending their client state, so there was less of a chance of upsetting them.[125]

The authorization of armed reconnaissance personified the liberalization of the rules because it delegated target identification authority to individual aircrews. Although the restrictions against bombing inside the buffer zone and the ten-mile radii from the centers of Hanoi and Haiphong remained, on occasion the JCS ordered strikes against specific targets inside those areas. Prohibitions—"prisoner-of-war compounds, foreign shipping, dikes and dams, fishing boats, hospitals, and shrines"—were sensible.[126] As for Laos, the JCS authorized the bombing of whatever the American Embassy wanted, excepting the portions of northern Laos where Chinese road builders were active.[127]

North Vietnamese willingness to sign an agreement by the end of October 1972 led to a bombing halt that month, so flights above the 20th parallel became prohibited in order to avoid disrupting negotiations.[128] When they broke down in December, President Nixon authorized a more unrestricted bombing campaign to persuade the governments in Hanoi and Saigon to reach a settlement. The claim of a postwar history, however, that the bombing operations "abolish[ed] nearly all restraints on the use of tactical air power over North Vietnam" is inaccurate because only "selected military targets" were authorized for targeting. Linebacker II was no Douhetian campaign to punish the North Vietnamese into compliance.[129]

The limitations inherent in the policy goals, not the rules of engagement, predestined military operations to a less than unrestricted use of air power. Although the rhetoric surrounding Linebacker was one of air power unleashed, restrictions remained, and Admiral Moorer still had to consult with Secretary Laird for permission to bomb targets in North Vietnam. An exchange between President Nixon and Admiral Moorer at the beginning of North Vietnam's offensive in April 1972 nevertheless illustrated the exasperating nature of the restrictions issue as well as any. The president was irritated that massive air strikes had not greeted the enemy troops streaming over the DMZ and accused the Air Force of refusing to take risks. Moorer explained that the North Vietnamese had moved SAMs into that area and kept moving them from site to site. For air strikes to take place without heavy losses, one had to first destroy those missile batteries, and that required finding them. Good visibility and weather were prerequisites, but those conditions were so intermittent in that area, he explained, local commanders had to have the predelegated authority to exploit fleeting breaks in the weather to launch missions. Four hours of good weather over the target might present itself without notice and only the theater commander could respond quickly enough to such an opportunity. His was the most reasoned explanation for delegating authority to theater commanders this author has seen. The chairman added that General Abrams and Admiral McCain had asked for permission to destroy those sites back in March, but Washington never granted clearance.[130]

Constraints increased in July after North Vietnam's mechanized offensive stalled and negotiations commenced. Moorer requested approval for twenty more targets, but Laird only approved a portion of them. When Moorer asked to bomb targets in Hanoi and Haiphong in August, Laird denied all of them except for a radio transmitter. Moorer also wanted to bomb more transportation targets inside the buffer zone, but when the Chinese asserted on July 5 that American bombs had struck China proper, Nixon, Laird, and Kissinger had a fit because of their concern of the missions' effects on diplomatic efforts.[131]

Wise, prescient limitations and guidelines on bombing, targeting, and weapons use were necessary for advancing the American and South Vietnamese war aims. Meshing rules of engagement with national policy, geopolitics, and tactical and operational needs of airmen required an effort at communication between civilian leaders and the generals that seldom took place. In the United States, the initiative for ensuring military operations, tactics, and weaponeering remain in lockstep with national policy goals ought to begin with the president and the secretary of defense. Given the proximity of their offices with those of the joint chiefs of staff, thoughtful coordination only required time and effort. In all wars, even in the scenario of an existential war between NATO and the Warsaw Pact, ROE and some avoidance of civilian casualties made military sense. In that situation, for example, every antitank missile that hit a noncombatant target did not hit a military target—the object that was trying to conquer American allies. Bombing places in Indochina because they had not been proven to be free of hostile troops would not have advanced the goal of defeating the North Vietnamese and the Viet Cong. When closely evaluated, the argument that unrestrained bombing would have won the war and that restrictions on bombing cost the war is not convincing. The controversy over rules of engagement and restrictions once again demonstrates that Vietnam was a failure of war.

Chapter 17

The Easter Offensive and the Revolution in Bombing Accuracy

When North Vietnam unleashed its mechanized invasion of South Vietnam in 1972, the capabilities and limitations of aircraft and their munitions would once again provide the president with opportunities and constraints as to what he could accomplish using war as an instrument of national policy. Changes in the relationships among the United States, China, and the Soviet Union made conventional military operations against the PAVN more effective. Nixon had recognized for years that convincing the Soviet Union to influence Hanoi—using the Soviets as a lever—was the way to persuade the North Vietnamese to alter their policy.[1] Détente and the desire of the Chinese and the Soviets to improve their relations with the United States at the expense of the other altered the geopolitical context to favor the United States and South Vietnam. American objectives shaped the tasks the air campaign sought to accomplish, which during this part of the war were quite different from those during Rolling Thunder. The United States left the ground war to the South Vietnamese and continued withdrawing even while the North Vietnamese invasion took place. Overturning the regime in Hanoi was not a goal; American military action did not threaten its existence. In fact, the United States wished to exit the war, which meant that its military and diplomatic forces had to achieve less: defeat the invasion and reach an interim settlement.

The United States became aware of the impending invasion in January 1972, although it was uncertain about the timing and particulars. Intelligence indicators convinced General Abrams that Hanoi intended a maximum effort, but the National Security Council staff believed they were going to wait until after the American presidential election to attack because they would gain more concessions after the election no matter who won.[2] The council's assessments were off the mark. North Vietnamese forces were about to wage a three-front offensive, and the air interdiction campaign against their supply routes had been insufficient to prevent the North Vietnamese from moving enough forces into position to launch the invasion.

America's effort over the Laotian panhandle was not extensive during the run-up to the invasion. Abrams pointed out that just as PAVN forces were forming, plenty of sorties were diverted away from a sector of Laos that was ripe with targets vulnerable to air strikes. They were sent to northern Laos and the area north of the DMZ. Abrams believed this looming invasion provided an opportunity: if the ARVN fought well and received massive support from American air forces, "the outcome will be a major defeat for the enemy, leaving him in a weakened condition and gaining decisive time for the consolidation of the Vietnamization effort."[3] He understood soldiers who stood their ground against a conventional invasion with the support of aircraft had a great chance of inflicting decisive losses on their opponent.

As of March 14, Melvin Laird believed air power was the reason the North Vietnamese had still not fully launched their offensive.[4] At the same time, Nixon and Kissinger realized air power was the country's one piece of hard power remaining in Southeast Asia. When informed of the imminence of the invasion Nixon commented, "We don't have any cards there, Henry, nothing but the damned Air Force, but we'll use it. We've got to use the Air Force."[5] Exasperated with them or not, Nixon looked to the air forces of the USAF and USN as his primary means to support South Vietnam—especially B-52s. "I would just double the number of '52s if necessary, whatever is necessary, so there's one hell of a show. We've got 400. I know a lot of them have to be refitted . . . but get them the hell over here right now. Let's have an awesome show of strength."[6] Consequently, Nixon ordered enough B-52s to the theater to sustain 1,500 sorties a month, sent three out of every four B-52 aircrews to Southeast Asia to fly missions, deployed more fighter squadrons, sent a fourth aircraft carrier, and removed sortie limits. Confident that air power could turn back the invasion, he also wanted air strikes to be as intense as possible against enemy troops. In fact, some air strikes were taking place already against enemy logistics while the enemy was still moving his forces into position. Behind this lay Nixon's belief that military success was necessary to convince the North Vietnamese to engage in worthwhile negotiations.[7]

One will notice that targets inside North Vietnam were not mentioned. America's military leadership wanted to take more serious preemptive action against the forces and logistical tails North Vietnam was marshaling, but that risked giving them victim status. Secretary Laird realized the US would get blamed for escalating the war if America and South Vietnam did not let Hanoi's army invade first. The policy goals of both countries would be better served by letting the North Vietnamese hit first so as to establish an iron-clad *casus belli* for Saigon and Washington. North Vietnamese actions ensured there was no doubt as to who the aggressor was. Their choice to invade when the Americans were on their way out puzzled everyone, but in the end, they carried it out to strengthen their bargaining position, discredit Vietnamization, and roll back the accomplishments of pacification.[8]

The invasion presented the Nixon administration and the Saigon government with an opportunity as well as a peril: the chance to practice the "Nixon Doctrine" in which the United States provided considerable support to friendly states threatened by aggressors, but would leave the American ally responsible for waging the ground war. Since it was also a test of Vietnamization, President Nixon commented, "if the ARVN pulls this off, let them have the credit. It's very important that they get the credit. . . . We'll get the blame if it fails, but we want them to get the credit."[9] That made sense because it would validate Nixon's agenda in which the South Vietnamese gained responsibility for fighting the ground war and defending themselves, something that furthered the interests of both countries.

When eight uniformed, conventionally armed PAVN divisions crossed into South Vietnam on March 30, the first thing they destroyed was the myth that the war in South Vietnam was strictly an internal grassroots guerrilla insurgency.[10] Their invading force of 125,000 sported more than 400 tanks and numerous artillery pieces.[11] The South Vietnamese waged the ground war against these regulars and contributed sorties to the air war. The conventional character of the offensive provided the allies an opportunity to exploit their superior firepower.

The American air response escalated quickly and briefly continued under the name Operation Rolling Thunder. Limited strikes into the heart of North Vietnam were underway less than three weeks into their invasion. On April 16, Navy A-6A Intruders struck SAM sites around Haiphong and seventeen B-52s bombarded the petroleum storage facilities near that city with the purpose of supporting the American negotiating posture. Air Force and Navy fighter-bombers followed, hitting additional targets. As a result, the communists lost more than a quarter of their fuel storage capacity at that location. This was Operation Freedom Porch Bravo, designed to signal to Hanoi the seriousness of the American commitment to resisting the invasion.[12] Le Duc Tho realized they were using military and diplomatic power to force concessions from his side. Carrier air power escalated to its highest level of the war by the end of April 1972 with six carriers, one of which was off the coast of South Vietnam providing infantry support. Their air strikes over North Vietnam focused on PAVN troops and their logistical tail in the southern panhandle.[13]

The North Vietnamese decided it was in their interest not to walk out of the negotiations, but to continue them for propaganda and to reach terms with the Americans.[14] As Henry Kissinger explained to Soviet Premier Leonid Brezhnev on April 21, 1972, the United States wanted only "an honorable withdrawal of all of our forces [and] to put a time interval between our withdrawal and the political process which would then start."[15] These aims were more achievable than those of 1965–1968. That air strikes into North Vietnam did not harm relations with the Soviets left the Nixon administration pleasantly surprised. The Soviets even relayed American messages and on April 12 invited Kissinger to Moscow.[16]

The Americans now had a free hand against North Vietnam because Zhou Enlai assured President Nixon that while China would maintain its support for Hanoi, it would not get involved militarily unless attacked.[17] Consequently, on April 22 and 24, targets around Thanh Hoa came under air attack by both B-52s and fighter-bombers without concern that such action might wreck improved Sino-American relations. April also saw the first Navy-tacair/B-52 joint operation against targets in Haiphong, Hanoi, Bai Thong, and Vinh. While all of this was taking place, the Soviets went forward with their talks with the United States and encouraged the North Vietnamese to reach a settlement with the Americans.[18]

Nixon's choice to intervene with Operations Freedom Train, Constant Guard, and then Linebacker surprised Hanoi.[19] They believed the American agenda vis-à-vis China and the USSR would trump concerns for Vietnam and the objectives of détente with China and the USSR during an election year would preclude a major military intervention. "This was a mistake," Le Duc Tho stated, "but not a catastrophic one." Tho was certain his people could endure, persist, and outlast the Americans. Wartime life was hard, but the country was structured for a long war. "What we hope to achieve," he added, "is President Thieu's departure. He, and he alone, stands in the way of the implementation of our plans, which have not changed since 1945."[20]

Hanoi underestimated the celerity with which American air forces could deploy additional aircraft to Southeast Asia. Constant Guard was the first time any country had flown several combat wings and their support equipment halfway around the world in a matter of days. With it, Nixon sent a message of determination along with combat capability.[21]

Given the clear military targets the invasion provided, Nixon was infuriated with the Air Force's inability to hit enemy forces due to bad weather in the panhandle. He had received inadequate information about the actual capabilities of American military aircraft to bomb with precision when weather obscured targets and reacted with contemptuous anger directed at the Air Force. Nixon commented to H. R. Haldeman, his chief of staff, "Our bombers . . . it's a colossal joke now. We can't hit anything unless the weather's perfect—ceiling unlimited."[22] Suggesting B-52s fly at "110,000 feet" betrayed woeful ignorance.[23]

Nixon also lost confidence in General Abrams: "He's had it. Look, he's fat, he's drinking too much, and he's not able to do the job." The president looked to an Air Force general to turn things around, Lieutenant General John W. Vogt, who had told Kissinger he was willing to go to Vietnam instead of NATO, even at the expense of a fourth star. Nixon made it so, and when the two met, told him his expectations with brutal clarity. The president was sick of weather excuses and prophesied this was going to be the Air Force's last chance to fight in a big war, "since this kind of war probably will never happen again, and that it would be a tragic thing if this great service would end its active battle participation in a disgraceful operation that this Vietnam offensive is turning out to be." Nixon's missive that Vogt was to circumvent Abrams in his communications with the administration left Vogt's eagerness to go to Vietnam unaffected. Vogt's suggestion to Nixon to make him deputy MACV did not go unheeded. Starting April 10, Vogt not only filled that role, but he also ascended to command Seventh Air Force, and he got his fourth star.[24]

Nixon looked forward to releasing unrestrained military might against North Vietnamese forces: "The bastards have never been bombed like they're going to be bombed this time."[25] According to Vogt, the president told him, "Now you, General, will have to get in there with air power and naval support and turn this whole thing around. I want you to crush the invasion and cause the North to get back to the negotiating table. Now you tell me what you need to do this."[26] Kissinger passed on to senior leaders such as Chairman Moorer, "I cannot stress enough the President's determination to do whatever is necessary. He will not be run out of Vietnam. He wants no excuses from subordinates or commanders that he has not done enough."[27]

Fighting that fervently required a sudden shift in mindset for the military. Stephen P. Randolph has pointed out that Nixon was suddenly demanding verve, initiative, and aggressiveness from his air forces after they had been tethered, muzzled, and micromanaged for years. General John D. Lavelle, the most recent commander of Seventh AF, had interpreted orders about his options for dealing with surface-to-air missiles above the DMZ liberally during the weeks before the invasion—and got fired. Lavelle authorized twenty-eight air strikes against radars and airfields from November 1971 through March 1972. He believed he had been relieved for his initiative, but General Ryan sacked him for falsifying after-action reports. Lavelle was accused of filing false reports that claimed reconnaissance aircraft had been fired upon as a pretense for what were actually planned air strikes. The Senate Armed Services Committee investigated, and Lavelle was forced into retirement at the rank of lieutenant general, a demotion. Later evidence revealed Lavelle falsified nothing. President Nixon, it turned out, authorized preventive air strikes against air defense assets that were targeting American aircraft on February 3, 1972.[28] The Air Force Board for the Correction of Military Records amended Lavelle's record on August 4, 2010, "and recommended his rank be restored. President Barak Obama endorsed this recommendation, but the Senate did not take action to restore him to the rank of general."[29]

Kissinger thought that if the United States wished to accomplish a negotiated settlement, it "had to create an impression of implacable determination to prevail."[30] Putting teeth to that understanding, Alexander Haig, deputy assistant to the president for National Security Affairs, suggested a more massive American military response to persuade the North Vietnamese to give up the ground they had taken thus far and to finally engage in serious negotiations that would lead to a settlement. Once forces were in place the Air Force and the Navy would conduct a massive aerial bombardment of North Vietnam. Any target could be bombed except those within the buffer zone along the border with China. The only real constraint would be bad weather. Targeting would take into account both psychological and military effects. Furthermore, "All possible diplomatic actions would be taken to pressure NVN to stop the aggression and negotiate."[31]

Operation Freedom Train formed the initial component of the air campaign in April. It was a close air support operation at first, while Linebacker would be an air interdiction effort. The hope was to undermine North Vietnamese military operations but also extract major policy concessions favorable to interests in Saigon.³² Disrupting supply lines was the first priority, fuel supplies were second, and the bombing of whatever else supported the war was third, although it ran concurrently with the first. Among the first targets hit on Freedom Train Bravo (April 9) was the railroad yard at Vinh, where the bombs cut rail lines in just four spots and destroyed only ten pieces of rolling stock.³³ B-52s made their presence felt when cells pounded enemy formations. The North Vietnamese Army, however, had brought SA-2 SAMs with them, firing at least fifty at B-52s and other aircraft during the first month of the invasion from sites northwest of the DMZ. All told they fired 742 times during April, and not one hit a B-52.³⁴ This gave the Americans confidence their ALT-28 jammers were completely disrupting the missiles' downlink signal. Marine EA-6A jamming aircraft contributed by supporting five missions. SAMs scored no hits against the aircraft the EA-6A planes defended.³⁵

Effective interdiction required action on multiple fronts. It was not enough to render the port of Haiphong inoperable because supply lines from China could handle almost twice the traffic of Haiphong. That meant rolling stock, trucks, and their fuel were especially important targets, and of course the railroad tracks had to be torn up. Nixon understood this and ordered B-52s to go after logistical targets like railroads during the second week of April. Vogt informed him that the bombers' accuracy was a disappointment, but they managed to cut three segments of rail lines in the Dong Hoi Railroad Yard.³⁶ When seventeen BUFs bombed a petroleum storage area near Haiphong on April 15, that was the farthest north they had ever struck. Their damage would not have an immediate effect, but North Vietnamese tanks and MiGs suffered fuel shortages in the coming weeks. The main purpose of these raids was to support diplomacy by signaling Nixon's seriousness and determination. They also left the leadership in Hanoi mortified over their air defense deficiencies against B-52s. Air raids were not going to coerce them by destroying economic targets because North Vietnam possessed too few to be decisively dependent on them. A contemporary Air Force analysis concluded that destroying North Vietnamese industrial facilities, what little there was to begin with, could not produce decisive results.³⁷

The way in which the Air Force and Navy assets were managed, a resuscitation of the route package system, meant the US could not fully concentrate its air power. For example, the Navy was assigned inland road targets in the panhandle, but their missions seldom reached far beyond the coast, accidentally creating a safe zone for the enemy. This decision lowered the air campaign's effectiveness because the Navy flew the majority of the strikes against North Vietnam: 7,917 sorties for two-thirds of the effort while the Air Force total was 4,169. By contrast, the Air Force flew 5,697 attack sorties over South Vietnam compared to the Navy and Marines who flew 3,909; the VNAF flew 4,152.³⁸ The Navy's smaller strike packages, on the other hand, were inherently more flexible and were thus able to find ways to hit their targets among thunderstorms and clouds to a degree greater than "the multi-wing 'mass gaggles' often employed by Seventh Air Force."³⁹ The Navy's targets were the same as the Air Force's: trucks, railroad lines, targets of opportunity. Over South Vietnam, the Air Force flew 47 percent of the American attack sorties, the Navy 34 percent, and the Marines 19 percent. Nearly half of this effort went against targets in the northern quarter of the country.⁴⁰ Aircraft from the USS *Midway*, for example, claimed ninety-six trucks, ninety-six bridges, and 113 structures destroyed from June 10 to July 7. All things being equal, the Navy was able to fly more sorties per day than the Air Force.⁴¹

The air forces were large enough to fulfill two roles at the same time: supporting the ground war and signaling enemy leaders. While the South Vietnamese Air Force focused on close air support, the American side of the air campaign went in multiple directions simultaneously, leaving General Abrams displeased. He wanted all air-to-ground sorties prioritized for use against the PAVN in South Vietnam. The country was in crisis and its defense needed every Air Force and Navy mission it could get. The president wanted to use bombing North Vietnam to coerce them to stop their invasion and to signal his determination to the Soviets. Kissinger believed all the Air Force wanted to do was bomb the enemy air force, and that Abrams only wanted to bomb the ground forces.[42] Abrams especially did not want to give up B-52s for operations up north and considered the proposal a serious mistake, but Nixon wanted an intensive bombing campaign, preferably concentrated in one place, because that would show a seriousness and steadfastness that Johnson's bombing halts made impossible. Abrams also believed it unnecessary since there were aircraft carriers and land-based fighter-bombers available for targets up north.[43] Although Abrams was pleased with the existence of Linebacker and the coercion-interdiction effort, he believed South Vietnam comprised the decisive theater.[44]

Nixon tried to convince Kissinger that he, in contrast to his predecessor, was completely determined: "Now Henry, we must not miss this chance. We're going to do it, and I'll destroy the g—n country, believe me. I mean destroy it, if necessary. And let me say, even the nuclear weapon if necessary. It isn't necessary, but you know what I mean. What I mean is that shows you the extent to which I'm willing to go. By—by a nuclear weapon, I mean that we will bomb the living bejeezus out of North Vietnam, and then if anybody interferes, we will threaten the nuclear weapon."[45] If North Vietnam wanted the bombing to stop, Nixon communicated, end its offensive against South Vietnam.[46] Nixon ordered an escalation of the air war on April 28: "If at all possible 1,000 sorties per day. This will have maximum psychological effect.... There are to be no excuses and there is no appeal."[47] Secretary Laird appealed; he disagreed with Nixon's sortie requirement, believing that there were already more than enough aircraft in South Vietnam to fight a defensive campaign.[48]

A month into the invasion, the American air campaign helped the ARVN fend off the PAVN, but it was not persuading Hanoi to quit. Hanoi would not even admit they had invaded South Vietnam, so Kissinger suspended his talks with Le Duc Tho because of Tho's recalcitrance. Bombing targets in Hanoi and Haiphong was necessary to try and hurt their war effort and coerce change, and it was going to have to begin in early May, right before the summit with the Soviets.[49]

A decision to carry out a major bombing campaign against North Vietnam—targets in Hanoi and Haiphong, especially—was much more than a military-operational issue. It could be tactically and operationally successful but wreck the upcoming summit with the Soviets—as Leonid Brezhnev had warned Henry Kissinger—and harm Nixon politically. As much as Nixon wanted the summit, a cancellation was something Nixon willingly accepted because saving South Vietnam was a higher priority than meeting with Brezhnev.[50]

Kissinger left for Moscow on April 20 to persuade the Soviets to pressure Hanoi. Nixon hoped Kissinger's trip would result in Hanoi feeling pressure to backtrack on some of its objectives, but he would be disappointed.[51] Kissinger concluded after the talks that "*we did not achieve a breakthrough on Vietnam*"; but he did communicate to the Soviets that the administration "*held Moscow to account* for the escalation ... and that we would prevent an allied defeat no matter what the risk to our other policies, including U.S.-Soviet relations and the summit [italics in original]."[52] Brezhnev told Kissinger during their April 21 meeting that the North Vietnamese hoped one of the consequences of their invasion would be a scuttling of the US–USSR negotiations, thus his meeting with Kissinger disappointed the politburo in Hanoi. Indeed, the summit went forward despite the bombings. Canceling it,

Anatoly Dobrynin later wrote, would have given Hanoi a "veto" of sorts over Soviet diplomacy, something the Soviets were not going to permit.[53]

As the administration deliberated whether or not to escalate further, Kissinger's advisors considered how the international community would respond, the appropriate level of violence, whether or not escalation would imperil the summit between Nixon and Brezhnev, adaptive North Vietnamese measures for obtaining supplies, South Vietnamese morale, and the effects on negotiations. The president recognized the importance of winning public support, and he wondered how this air interdiction campaign could improve over what Lyndon Johnson had attempted. Admiral Moorer explained that the mechanized nature of the enemy army and the character of the war created vulnerabilities favorable to air interdiction. Much greater rail traffic, more targets, and the logistical necessity to move during daylight hours presented American air forces with a plethora of targets. The North Vietnamese were now waging a conventional war rather than an insurgency, which played to the Americans' strengths. North Vietnamese fuel reserves, however, could last as long as "five months," according to Secretary Laird. Nixon ruled out an amphibious invasion of North Vietnam, but Hanoi did not need to know that, and the same went for nuclear weapons use.[54] But the American military itself was not going to win or lose the war; that was up to the South Vietnamese. Laird opined that, "If they don't have enough incentive, then all the equipment in the world won't save them."[55]

Nixon also gave first place to future American security goals: failing to adequately defend its ally could seriously undercut the credibility of its relationships with friendly and allied countries. Overall, he did not believe any of the options, from evacuating to an air and sea interdiction campaign, were ideal.[56] He believed, "The U.S. would cease to be a military and diplomatic power," and "Every non-communist nation in the world would live in terror [if he failed]. If the U.S. is strong enough and willing to use its strength, then the world will remain half-Communist rather than becoming entirely Communist." Treasury Secretary John Connally agreed, asking whether key Arab states might be the Soviets' next target.[57] He added that continuing to fight hard in Vietnam would serve American national interests by signaling that aggression had serious consequences, which the United States would deliver.[58]

Strategic signaling was the immediate purpose of the air campaign. Nixon intended to convince the Hanoi government that he was "absolutely determined to end the war and [would] take *whatever steps are necessary* to accomplish this goal [italics in original]."[59] An escalation would divide air power assets because some available for assisting the ARVN would be diverted to targets in North Vietnam. Kissinger believed escalation necessary because he saw a real risk of a South Vietnamese collapse—and a capture of most of the remaining 60,000 Americans in Vietnam—if the United States did not ramp up its air war. In addition, increased military action, such as a blockade, would give the US a bargaining chip for retrieving its prisoners. Nixon agreed.[60]

The administration believed North Vietnam received about 90 percent of its supplies through Haiphong, so cutting it off promised to pay good dividends. Therefore, on May 4, Nixon ordered Moorer to go forward with a major bombing campaign against military targets around Haiphong and to mine its harbor. The president timed this to support his concurrent diplomatic efforts.[61] The Soviet ambassador feared Moscow would overreact drastically but that never materialized. In fact, mining did not bring with it the threat of escalation at sea a blockade would.[62] Marine A-6As and Navy A-7Es from the USS *Coral Sea* carried out Operation Pocket Money on May 8, depositing mines in the harbor. Five ships evacuated before the mines activated, and North Vietnamese efforts to remove them failed. No ship entered or left the seaports through at least September 10, and the move basically terminated seaborne imports.[63] Navy aircraft laid additional mines during June, and occasional mining continued through December, eventually sowing more than 11,000 mines.[64] Not only was Pocket Money a tactical and operational success, but it also succeeded by what it did not do. The mines did not sink President Nixon's talks with Leonid Brezhnev, nor did they rupture recent breakthroughs in relations with China. During the summit the Soviets did not press the Americans on Vietnam, but merely brought up the issue enough to be able to tell Le Duc Tho they had done so.[65]

The mining of the ports did not result in immediate shortages in North Vietnam because it had stockpiled supplies. A month into Linebacker, American intelligence could not detect any major effects resulting from shutting down Haiphong Harbor and bombing supply lines; Hanoi had a history of solving those kinds of problems. But because of the closing of the harbor, problems multiplied, and they diverted shipping to Shanghai for overland transport. Altogether the Hanoi regime received but one-third of the imports it had in 1971. Ironically, the new American agreement to sell wheat to the Soviet Union made it easier for Moscow to feed its clients in Southeast Asia.[66]

Nixon expanded the air war to include a major interdiction effort against North Vietnam beginning the same day as the mining of Haiphong, but massive punishment raids by B-52s were never part of this campaign. It focused instead on the railroads from China and relied on fighter-bombers rather than B-52s.[67] Because the stakes were so high, Nixon decided conferring a greater latitude to the military would be more likely to produce strategically effective results. As he said to Admiral Moorer, "Do not go to secondary targets. We are going to get rail lines, POL, secondary planes [sic], power plants and airfields, but there is no damn excuse now. You have what the military claimed they never before got the authority to do."[68]

Operation Linebacker commenced on May 10. The top priorities were predictable for an interdiction campaign: "bridges, road and rail junctions, road and railroad repair equipment, railroad cars and locomotives, barges, and trucks," with the president assigning petroleum and transportation the highest initial priorities, including the "jolt" of striking a railroad yard next to Hanoi.[69] The purpose of destroying rail traffic was to force the North Vietnamese to drive trucks on highways and generate another vulnerability: reliance on more fuel and on roads. If bombing could drastically reduce overland transportation, that, combined with the closing of Haiphong Harbor, would force the North Vietnamese to use up their reserve supplies, eventually leading to a reduced combat capacity in the field. The Air Force recognized the North Vietnamese choice to carry out a mechanized conventional invasion meant that their forces were more dependent on logistics and therefore more vulnerable to air interdiction.[70]

The enemy did not have critically vulnerable targets that, if destroyed, made it impossible to wage war. Not until North Vietnam's assets were combined into a whole and struck was its logistical system in all its forms "strategic" in the sense that enough damage could be wrought to defeat Hanoi's strategy. Textbook interdiction was not exactly what the president had in mind for the initial phase of the air campaign; he wanted more. Nixon's intention was "to stop at nothing to bring the enemy to his knees," and he was "totally unsatisfied at this time at the plans the military have suggested as far as air activities are concerned."[71] As successes began to accumulate, however, Nixon did not follow up with further recriminations, but accepted the accomplishments in the forms they came.

Operation Linebacker had to achieve two goals: one coercive, the other physical. It was to shock and persuade the government in Hanoi to quickly accede to American demands, and it had to disable the supply system sustaining the war in South Vietnam. President Nixon wrote, "indiscriminate bombing of civilian areas is not what I have in mind. On the other hand, *if the target is important enough*, I will approve a plan that goes after it even if there is a risk of some civilian casualties [italics in original]."[72]

Air strikes thoroughly cut the rail lines into Hanoi during the first month, but they were not so effective against dispersed fuel supplies, estimated at enough for eight to twelve weeks of operations in South Vietnam. For this reason B-52s bombing fuel facilities at Haiphong was not as decisive as hoped.[73] By the time of the May 10 air strikes, fighter-bombers did not do as much damage because the North Vietnamese had drained the fuel tanks bombs had missed.[74] Laser-guided bombs appeared, however, to have wiped out "more than 5.5 million gallons of fuel" during a May 18 strike, a mission noteworthy because it took place well inside the old Hanoi exclusion zone.[75] Bridges such as the Haiphong Railroad Bridge were obvious targets and Navy A-7s wrecked it on May 18. Rail lines from China remained the number one air strike priority through the summer.[76]

Once again, the impressionistic meaning of the B-52 came up. The civilian leadership wanted to employ them against appropriate targets in North Vietnam, and so did Strategic Air Command. Kissinger asked Moorer whether the military was "willing to risk a B-52. [Moorer] said I do not have any problem with that and neither do the commanders. We do not want to go for nothing, we want a worthwhile target."[77] Then the president badgered him about why it was he had been given all these resources and leeway and "so far, nothing other than routine operations have occurred."[78] When Nixon brought up striking targets in Hanoi and Haiphong at the end of April, he wanted at least "100 B-52s" involved along with tactical aircraft over a span of three days. He wanted this because of the effects their presence would have on persuading the North Vietnamese to negotiate, the encouragement it would give to American public opinion that he was serious, and because the bombing would contribute to the goal of enabling South Vietnam to defend itself the next time North Vietnam attacked.[79] A couple of weeks later Nixon ordered twice as many B-52s: "Let them get a little frightened."[80] Nixon never followed up, however, and B-52s did not bomb targets in the Red River Valley until December.

The bombing added further stresses to life in Hanoi and Haiphong. According to Admiral Moorer, prices were rising, people were turning to the black market, and they were even protesting against the government. Overall, the attacks against the North Vietnamese transportation system made it more difficult for them to supply their invasion forces, but Admiral Moorer anticipated the North Vietnamese would find ways to work around the air campaign's damage. He was right. Within two weeks the Chinese permitted the Soviets to send supplies by rail through China.[81] Vietnamese efforts at filling the bomb craters had become more sophisticated, and they prefabricated bridge components as a counter to the bombing of one of the Americans' favorite targets.[82]

Kissinger was still concerned that the escalation of the air war might lead to the last-minute cancelation of the summit, and brought up his concern to Anatoly Dobrynin, who replied, "you have handled a difficult situation uncommonly well." All he asked, since the summit was still going to take place, was whether the Americans could scale back some of the air campaign while Nixon was in Moscow.[83] Nixon complied by establishing a no-bomb zone over Hanoi from May 21 through June 5.[84] Four days later on May 15, Brezhnev communicated to Nixon that he would press the North Vietnamese to confer with the United States "without preconditions" if he in turn would return the United States "to the plenary sessions in early June."[85] The summit began on May 22.

Nixon insisted the intense bombing continue during the summit, but the Air Force's inability to bomb in bad weather overrode his demands and left him nonplussed.[86] He said to Kissinger and Haig: "I want you to convey directly to the Air Force that I am thoroughly disgusted with their performance in North Vietnam. Their refusal to fly unless the ceiling is 4,000 feet or more is without doubt one of the most pusillanimous attitudes we have ever had in the whole fine history of the U.S. military." He blamed the commanders, not the pilots; their seniors wished to avoid losing, he believed, instead of playing to win. "Under the circumstances, I have decided to take the command of all strikes in North Vietnam in the Hanoi–Haiphong area out from under *any Air Force jurisdiction whatever*. The orders will be given directly from a Naval commander whom I will select [italics in original]."[87] What was missing here was an explanation to the president about the limitations of most aircraft when it came to bombing from inside clouds and what happened to aircraft that flew into flak traps below 4,000 feet. As discussed in chapter 14, a dive-bombing jet needed a ceiling of 8,000 to 12,000 feet in order to carry out a bombing run and to approach the target, see it, dive, drop its bombs, and then pull up and fly away without flying into the teeth of antiaircraft guns or smacking the ground outright. Moorer subsequently directed Admiral McCain to rely on A-6A Intruders against targets at night as a partial solution since they flew at very low altitudes and fulfilled the requirement for all-weather bombing.[88] Nixon's expectations may have been a consequence of advertisements by the services and aerospace contractors about "all weather" fighters over the past decade.[89] A more immediate cause was secondhand information from the vice president that the Air Force was unhappy with the target selection. Nixon's tantrum perplexed Kissinger because reports from the field were that the air forces were finally pounding the enemy with minimal constraints and morale was high.[90]

Other evidence revealed the fighter-bomber operations against targets in the Hanoi–Haiphong area rattled everyone who experienced them. Theo Ronco, a member of the French Communist Party visiting Hanoi, relayed in a letter:

> The bombings are appalling and murderous. The population, out of the habit, is beginning to suffer from shock, especially in Haiphong and Hanoi, where women are in the great majority. We (Hanoi) ask you to use all your influence to put an end to the bombings. In the end we will overcome the blockade, but the bombings must be stopped. . . . The explosives used at the present time are not only extremely murderous and devastating, but equally appalling because of the noise. How can Nixon be stopped? We have to find a way. It is indispensable. We believe that the best way is to obtain the resumption of the work of the Paris conference.[91]

The North Vietnamese had asked for talks in May, but the Americans rejected their requests because their counterparts had not given any indications about what the talks would cover.[92]

Admiral Moorer recognized the interrelationships between the bombing campaign, diplomacy, and the goal of wresting favorable concessions from the North Vietnamese. Good weather for bombing was going to last for three more months, and the campaign needed to center around the purpose of forcing Le Duan to negotiate. At the same time, the bombing had to destroy as much of their internal transportation network and their electrical generating capacity as possible.[93]

Because the political, diplomatic, and impressionistic effects of bombing helped determine whether national policy goals were achieved, it made sense for the chairman of the joint chiefs to become party to things like how close an unguided bomb or a PGM could be aimed against targets near sensitive facilities like ships in Haiphong Harbor that were not the property of the North Vietnamese. The accuracy of new weapons, namely laser-guided and electro-optical guided bombs, made the JCS more comfortable with bombing targets in the seaport and less concerned that a bomb would hit a ship. Moorer directed appropriate use of Walleyes against targets that needed a precise weapon.[94]

F-4D with two laser-guided bombs (US Air Force)

Improvements in munitions went far in enabling the president to use air power to achieve his goals, which were polar opposites from the mass bombing B-52s upon which the president mused. The air forces had a capability in 1972 that had not existed in 1965: an ability to achieve a *direct* hit with *one* bomb. It is surprising that the chairman did not point out the policy implications of these weapons to the president. One could reasonably target something in downtown Hanoi with a very good chance of hitting only that target, provided the weather was decent. The operational plans for the new air campaign emphasized their use. Interestingly, a strict reliance on what could achieve unprecedented tactical effectiveness and efficiency in terms of hitting targets precisely and nothing else did not jibe with one of Nixon's primary goals: to shock and coerce the North Vietnamese with massive numbers of bombs; reliance on precision-guided munitions required far fewer bombs for destroying targets.[95]

General Lucius D. Clay Jr., the PACAF commander, recognized the political advantages of using fighter-bombers with precision-guided munitions over B-52s, and toward the end of May he expressed doubts about the utility of ever using B-52s against targets in the far north if it came to that. Those bombers were useful against targets that covered large areas, but not many targets like that were left in North Vietnam. Using B-52s in those high threat areas also required the protection and support of a large variety of escort and support aircraft, which would be more productive on armed reconnaissance missions. Clay recommended against shifting them to targets in northeastern Vietnam. They were better for area-type targets in South Vietnam, many of which did not have the precise kinds of aim points precision munitions required but required lots of bombs. Fighter-bombers dropping LGBs were more effective tactically and politically: "we have been achieving outstanding results with tac air using laser guided munitions and have created a favorable impression on world opinion of pinpoint bombing against military targets with a minimum loss of civilian life." Up north, Clay advised, the Air Force and Navy could destroy their targets with far fewer sorties by relying on laser-guided bombs. Such missions required fewer support aircraft, fewer escorts, and fewer tankers, and thus fewer aircraft were exposed to the hazards of North Vietnamese airspace.[96] In addition, the media had given the weapons favorable coverage. News outlets such as *Aviation Week & Space Technology* and *The New York Times* reported the laser-guided bomb missions, making it possible for a wider range of policy makers to become aware of these capabilities.[97] General John D. Ryan Jr., now the Air Force chief of staff, disagreed, believing plenty of targets suitable to the bomb pattern from B-52s existed in the Red River Valley. Furthermore, B-52s could attack at night and through heavy cloud cover thus maintaining pressure on the regime. Ryan added that President Nixon had directed the use of B-52s up north so that was where they were going.[98]

The president wanted to use the B-52s to communicate and signal as much as to destroy, but again, Nixon did not follow up regarding where they were used, probably because of his preoccupation with the summit meeting with Brezhnev. In the end, the president let the airmen decide which aircraft and weapons were best suited and where. Most ironically, when the Air Force finally got the chance to bomb the hell out of North Vietnam with B-52s, it opted for pinpoint targeting using individual precision weapons from a handful of F-4D Phantoms dropping but a fraction of the tonnage of a B-52 raid. Fighter-bombers with PGMs, not B-52s, carried out the air war against targets in the North Vietnamese heartland during Linebacker. The Air Force's historical commitment to accurate, efficient, precise bombing from before World War II overcame a more recent and superficial impulse to pulverize. In a legalistic sense, the Air Force did not follow the letter of the president's directives. In the course of following its devotion to technology and efficiency, the Air Force serendipitously contributed more to the president's political goals than if they had sent a hundred B-52s north like he wanted.

Air power during Linebacker's first week focused on helping the ARVN resist assaults at An Loc and Kontum. At the same time, as the situation in South Vietnam improved, the JCS asked Secretary Laird for permission to ramp up the air war in the north. He approved twenty-eight of the forty-four targets they had requested on June 12. Moorer explained that the goal was to wear down their ability to carry out conventional warfare to such an extent that small unit guerrilla warfare would be their only choice after the air campaign was through. At the same time this bombing of warfighting capabilities was to persuade the leadership in Hanoi to negotiate the terms of their capitulations and break the will of the people to continue fighting. The kinds of targets were pretty much identical to those from the Rolling Thunder lists, but the bombs were different.[99]

The airmen emphasized precision-guided munitions to a degree that made Linebacker fundamentally different from Rolling Thunder.[100] When the first big strike of Linebacker flew against the Paul Doumer Bridge and the Yen Vien rail yard, twenty-nine precision-guided munitions (twenty-two LGBs and seven EOGBs, or electro-optical guided bombs) inflicted considerable destruction on the bridge, while 184 unguided Mk-82s left the railroad yard a mess.[101] The precision of laser-guided bombs allowed Moorer to tell the Air Force, for instance, to bomb the generators at the Lang Chi Dam with confidence the bombs would hit only the generators and not the dam itself, thus avoiding a flood. This fit in with the political goal of avoiding harm to noncombatants.[102] This tactical capability enabled the president to order more aggressive bombing with a greater assurance of target destruction and less chance of a collateral damage propaganda coup for Hanoi. And they inflicted real damage. By mid-summer the use of LGBs against railroad lines made the movement of freight a challenge despite the energy and persistence of work crews.[103]

Precision-guided bombs overcame some old countermeasures. The North Vietnamese parked valuable war items next to or in prohibited targets such as dikes or villages, using them as "shields," but PGMs made it possible to hit the targets and profoundly reduce collateral damage. Again, after four Paveways blew holes in the roof of the Lang Chi Power Plant, which was next to an off-limits dam, some more destroyed the turbines; the dam remained untouched—no banner headlines of flooded towns and drowned farmers.[104] These precision-guided munitions allowed a president to attack more aggressively with less risk.

The Air Force and Navy used quite a few laser-guided bombs. From April through August, they dropped twenty-eight 3,000-pound LGBs, 183 500-pound LGBs, and 2,715 2,000-pound laser-guided bombs. The LGBs comprised a small percentage of the total ordnance used; tactical aircraft dropped about 147,000 500-pound unguided bombs over North Vietnam during those same months and B-52s released more than 38,000 500-pounders alone.[105] They proved a watershed in aerial warfare not because they were used in preponderant numbers, but because each bomb could destroy its target, and their effectiveness ushered in new tactical possibilities for warfare, which in turn opened up new possibilities for achieving presidentially important goals.

Strike packages normally included only eight to twelve PGM-carrying F-4 Phantoms along with their escorts.[106] In fact, most of the bombing the Air Force carried out during Linebacker in Vietnam relied on "a small number of laser equipped aircraft."[107] Of the twenty-six major Air Force strikes listed for May 1972 over North Vietnam, twenty-five used laser-guided bombs. The other employed electro-optical guided bombs. June was a repeat; of the thirty major Air Force strikes against Route Package 6 targets, twenty-nine relied on Paveways.[108] Destroying two significant targets on June 21, a flight of four jets put one of the spans of the Lan Lau Railroad Bridge into the Song Cau River; that raid put out of action an alternate route into Hanoi. A pair of F-4s with LGBs precisely cut a section of the railroad line north of Hanoi.[109]

Carrier aircraft joined the laser-guided bomb club in June 1972, dropping ninety-two: at least forty-one hit their targets, twenty-five failed to guide, and seven did not explode. A Navy squadron used its three A-6Cs to test that airframe as a laser designator–carrying aircraft in August. They successfully dropped two bridges in November. Using one jet to designate targets for another was challenging. Everything on the A-6C had to function to near perfection, and both jets had to stay in the target area for an uncomfortably long time looking for the target—pretty much the same as the USAF experience.[110]

Smart bomb predominance continued in July, when the ratio was five missions using unguided bombs to thirty using precision. Missions in Route Package 1 wrecked the typical interdiction targets with newfound accuracy and greatly complicated North Vietnamese efforts to reinforce and resupply their forces. Of twenty-one major targets the USAF hit in North Vietnam in August, LGBs hit nineteen. Laser-guided bombs blew up twenty-two of the thirty-seven major targets in Route Package 6 in September, with only four of these missions failing to hit their target.[111] As Linebacker approached its final month in mid-September, Walnut Flight—three F-4s carrying two bombs each and one that used a new "Pave Knife" lasing pod—blew three bridges to pieces: three aircraft, three bridges.[112] October was different; only five out of twenty-three major missions employed LGBs because deteriorating weather covered too many targets with clouds and mist.[113]

In the middle of Linebacker, General Clay extolled the capabilities of laser-guided bombs: "With the laser we have achieved more meaningful BDA than was achieved in all of 1966 and 1967." He pointed out that just six of the bombs destroyed the Lang Bo Bridge, and eight downed the Lang Giai Bridge. It would have required an estimated 2,772 and 1,548 unguided Mk-82s, respectively, to accomplish the same thing against the two targets as those fourteen LGBs.[114] When a mission cut five bridges with just twenty-four Paveways, analysts noted that reaching the same result with unguided munitions would have required "2,400 bombs."[115] The Seventh AF director of operations called their performance "tremendous."[116] A reporter understood the change only in part when he wrote, "These aerial attacks have been far more destructive than ever before, primarily as a result of the new 'smart' bombs, which drop anything from five hundred to three thousand pounds of explosive with astonishing precision, through the use of either a laser beam or a small television camera."[117] A mid-summer study concluded that laser-guided bombs were ten times more effective in terms of sortie effectiveness than unguided bombs against antiaircraft artillery pieces, 3.5 times more effective against lines of communication, 2.8 against trucks, and 2.4 against tanks. On average, it only took about nine LGBs and five sorties to destroy a bridge. The Thanh Hoa Bridge was an outlier, but it still illustrated the capabilities of the weapons. Thousands of bombs during Rolling Thunder were unable to drop a span on that bridge; the second LGB mission against it did. This report concluded that Paveways not only provided a "two-fold" improvement in effectiveness, but fighter-bombers could "now attack targets not feasible before."[118]

Precision-guided munition accuracy was just remarkable. F-4s dropping them destroyed a specific transformer outside of Hanoi. Four F-4s put seven of their eight bombs on their target on May 24, the Thai Nguyen Thermal Power Plant. Eighty percent of the forty-one AGM-62 Walleye Is used in June scored hits, and all six of the new Walleye IIs hit their mark.[119] Compared to laser-guided bombs, the Air Force now considered bombing accuracy with free-fall bombs unsatisfactory. General Vogt, for example, found the results of a thirty-two-jet mission using unguided bombs against the Hanoi petroleum facility in May unimpressive because far fewer aircraft with a couple of Paveways each would have inflicted far greater damage.[120]

Although Walleyes had been in use since 1967 and Paveways since 1968, this expanded introduction of PGMs, especially the laser-guided bombs, heralded a revolutionary change in air warfare. With rare exceptions, each bomb precisely hit its target. Dropping the bombs from well above 10,000 feet, pilots did not have to fly their jets down into the range of antiaircraft fire, so the missions were less dangerous. Strike packages did not require as many aircraft, and overall, "the strike element size was determined by the number of targets, rather than by the difficulty of the individual target."[121] Single aircraft carrying two LGBs could destroy more than one target. Using smart bombs reduced the number of required sorties by as much as a factor of ten.[122]

Surprisingly, these were reliable weapons from the beginning. Immature technology often suffers through difficult teething problems, like those of air-to-air missiles; not the case for PGMs. The first generation of these weapons was tremendously successful under combat conditions. This capability did not fulfill a preference for accuracy; it was necessary for military reasons from the tactical level of war to the president's approval of an air campaign. Whereas before, concentrated spreads of bombs might hit a target and destroy it, a single laser-guided bomb would likely hit and destroy the target on the first attempt. This required far fewer aircraft and only one mission per target, and even allowed for two targets per sortie, as F-4s carried two LGBs. Of the 20,000-some-odd LGBs the Air Force dropped from 1968–1972, "84 percent successfully guided with approximately 60 percent direct hits," and the average miss distance was just "ten feet." The Navy did not have quite the success rate, obtaining 145 hits within thirty feet out of 330 bombs, but that was still an exponential improvement over unguided bombs.[123] Air Force planners had seen similar effectiveness against Ho Chi Minh Trail targets, months before the 1972 invasion. They appealed for more laser designators and more kits for turning a conventional bomb into a laser-guided one.[124]

Laser-guided bombs' limitations were not severe. For example, there were only six of the more effective Pave Knife laser illuminator pods in SEA at first, as well as "ten laser target designators (LTDs) that can be used in areas of lower threat." The North Vietnamese knew lasers could not penetrate smoke, so they used smoke generators to try to defeat this precision guidance system. Laser-guided bombs required fairly good weather—generally no worse than clouds covering three-eighths of the sky.[125] Oak Flight, however, managed to put six of their eight LGBs on target when clouds covered most of their target in September. Aircraft dropping them could complete missions on marginal weather days when a normal strike package would not go north. For example, General Vogt sent four F-4s after a railroad bridge on May 19 when skies were nearly overcast. After searching for a hole in the undercast near the bridge they found one, and their bombs hit the Vhu Xuyen Bridge. Four other F-4s with laser-guided bombs hit the Qui Hau Highway Bridge and a pontoon bridge at Giang Me Le—as stark a contrast in technology as one will find. Since the weather was so bad that day, the North Vietnamese assumed the Americans would not fly, so these jets did not have to suffer interference from flak, missiles, or MiGs.[126]

Because of the profound usefulness of laser-guided bombs, General Clay argued that the issue was "not one of increasing total sorties but one of increasing our laser-equipped force." He added, "More dumb bomb sorties will not help. They could, in fact, detract from our overall efforts when you consider the resultant civilian casualties that are inevitable in this type of operation [using unguided bombs]." Unfortunately, a new batch of Pave Spike pods would not arrive in theater until winter 1973. In the meantime, planners tried to modify tactics to mark more targets with the few laser designators they had. Nevertheless, the limited laser designator capability sufficed to destroy the highest priority targets without endangering people nearby.[127]

A late September Linebacker Conference (a regular meeting on tactics and effectiveness that commenced in July 1972) noted new tactics for the Pave Knife system. Four F-4s supported by one laser designator could release their Paveways as a group so that they would all hit the target within a couple of seconds of one another or the bombers could space themselves so that the laser operator could laze several different targets individually, one after another. An F-4 with an earlier laser-guidance pod would be sent after targets in less-dangerous airspace because the aircraft had to fly a steady turn without making sudden heading changes to defeat AAA. Either way, "A 24 ship strike force can roll-in and be off the target in one minute. The results on area targets have been extremely successful."[128]

While laser-guided bombs gained fame against tough-to-bring-down targets like the Thanh Hoa Bridge, only 8 percent of them were used against bridges. During Linebacker, more than a quarter cratered roads and railroads, and one in five were used against trucks. With two LGBs, an F-4 might destroy two tanks, in contrast to the free-fall bomb requirements to destroy a tank, which on average was at least seventy-two to 120 unguided bombs carried by six to ten aircraft.[129]

Seventh Air Force and PACAF leadership recognized the fundamental difference in reliability between good weather dive bombing, LORAN bombing, and missions using laser-guided bombs. One reads of inaccurate LORAN missions and aircrews' "guesstimates" of their dive bombing results, and it becomes understandable why a reader of a Linebacker summary wrote gleeful comments next to a report of the results from a laser-guided bomb flight that destroyed both the primary and secondary targets. A look at some of the post-bombing photography extant from the war makes the excitement even more understandable. Unguided bombs almost never hit their target directly. One photograph shows a nice line of craters so close together that they form a long shallow pond parallel to but never striking the railroad tracks right next to them which escaped unscathed. Another shows two bombs exploding directly on a pair of roads, but surrounding fields are covered with random craters for almost a mile.[130]

Headquarters PACAF asserted, "The success of the Linebacker operations is directly attributed to the application of the highly accurate laser guided bombs."[131] Vogt agreed, "The Laser Guided Bomb (LGB) has been the key to our successful interdiction campaign.... We have accomplished more in 3 months with the LB mission than we had accomplished in a single year under the RT operation."[132] Their ability to inflict so much meaningful damage may have outpaced the enemy's ability to repair or replace bridges over and over. A CINCPAC panel believed the frequency of laser-guided bomb strikes against bridges rendered rail lines unusable.[133]

Altogether the Air Force expended more than 10,500 laser-guided bombs from February 1972 to February 1973. More than 5,100 achieved direct hits, with 4,000 more missing by less than twenty-five feet.[134] In addition, from February through the end of December, Air Force jets dropped 329 Walleye TV-guided bombs, and within this narrower time frame the Air Force expended 9,094 LGBs. Interestingly, American air forces dropped more freefall PGMs during the 1972 air campaign—9,423—than were expended during the 1991 Gulf War, during which 9,342 were used.[135]

Their use of PGMs during 1972 constituted a revolution in military affairs, "a drastic change in military affairs resulting from a combination of technological change and operational and organizational innovation."[136] Thomas A. Keaney and Eliot A. Cohen argue that five technologies marked the revolution of the 1990s: low-observables, laser-guided bombs, portable encrypted telephones, aerial refueling, and anti-SAM radar missiles—AGM-88s.[137] Three of these were used during Linebacker: refueling, LGBs, and predecessors to the AGM-88. Indeed, "tank plinking"—using Paveways against tanks—was not invented during the Gulf War but originated over Vietnam in 1971.[138]

The options these munitions opened for the president and his aircrews are what marked Linebacker as the beginning of the late twentieth-century revolution in military affairs; the precision-guided munition breakthrough was in full swing in 1972, not 1991.[139] Not a completely new argument, Paul Gillespie wrote, "It would be difficult to overestimate the impact precision guided munitions had on U.S. military strategy in 1972.... 1972 marked a watershed in the application of modern air power."[140] This revolution in bombing accuracy greatly reduced the possibility of a string of bombs causing a mass casualty event among North Vietnamese civilians. Thus, the Americans were less likely to hurt their own cause and more likely to actually destroy targets and reduce enemy propaganda opportunities.

There is wide agreement that air power proved essential to beating back the Nguyen Hue Offensive. Bombing supply lines turned the course of the war against the North Vietnamese well enough that they could not achieve their goal of defeating South Vietnam. The air interdiction campaign inside I Corps of South Vietnam from May 31 inflicted enough damage that by the time the North Vietnamese commenced their June 20 secondary offensive, that effort proved so feeble that their opponents could not recognize its escalatory nature.[141] Air strikes continued to wear down their military capability as July approached, but the damage was not great enough to collapse the PAVN's offensive capabilities. Its army used less than 10 percent of its fuel in Laos and South Vietnam and the Allies had destroyed most of their tanks before July, so there was not as much of a need for gasoline in occupied South Vietnam. The rainy season and North Vietnam's inability to move tanks south to replace those destroyed hobbled mechanized operations. As predicted, air interdiction paid significant dividends—a couple of months after it began. A CIA assessment concluded air strikes would not be able to terminate the importation of fuel into North Vietnam, but they could inflict losses heavy enough to prevent the communist forces from sustaining high-tempo operations. The pipeline North Vietnam was building would be difficult to take out, but air power would have better results against fuel trucks. The grind of war was wearing down Hanoi's offensive capabilities, but not to the point that its formations could not wage defensive operations.[142]

While the PAVN's logistical situation was not good, their troops were in worse shape. A CIA analyst added that the killing and destruction in battle was a worse problem for the enemy than the conditions of their supplies and logistical train. One of Kissinger's advisors observed that bombing missions against supply lines had not directly altered the course of any battles, but it had reduced enemy morale and their government was feeling the strain of the losses.[143] Air interdiction was producing the effects it was designed to produce: interdiction does not directly or immediately affect battles; it takes place oftentimes hundreds of miles away from the battlefield. Effective interdiction disrupts and erodes an army's ability to wage and sustain combat operations and begin new ones.

Eleven weeks into the Nguyen Hue Offensive, Admiral Moorer reached several conclusions. South Vietnamese and American military action had stemmed the offensive and had greatly depleted North Vietnam's military power, which provided time for Saigon to reconstitute its defenses and prepare operations to retrieve lost territory.[144] But the interdiction campaign of harbor mining and air strikes had not completely cut off the enemy from their supply sources. The US did not have enough fighter-bombers to inflict sufficient damage, and the inability to achieve conclusive effects was not entirely surprising. Abrams commented that the air interdiction experience in Laos had "clearly demonstrated that even around-the-clock strike forces cannot completely stem the flow of truck traffic."[145]

Winning battles—which the ARVN/USAF/USN team had done in May and June—was only an intermediate step toward achieving strategic goals, which are only worthwhile if they achieve national policy goals. The United States had had a terrible time influencing the government in Hanoi. If an operation was persuading Le Duan and others to make changes, then that military operation was effective, and that happened in the summer of 1972. Linebacker missions against North Vietnam, close air support missions in South Vietnam, and the fighting power of Thieu's army combined to blunt the invasion and persuade the government in Hanoi to bend in accordance with the reality of what was taking place between Le Duan's army and Thieu's. Hanoi was going to have to ease up on some of the demands its diplomats were making. Military actions were strengthening the negotiating position of Washington and Saigon. Furthermore, American statecraft was good enough in combination with these activities that the USSR started pressing its client state to compromise.[146]

Military successes of the South Vietnamese and Americans began to stymie North Vietnamese objectives. In May, Le Duc Tho stated that Thieu was "our No. 1 enemy. His departure is imperative ... as soon as [Nixon] drops him, we will have won."[147] Four weeks later the CIA in Saigon received information from three different sources that communist leaders were no longer demanding the removal of President Thieu from office as a precondition to "substantive negotiations."[148] Military power was generating the most important kind of results: persuading the enemy to change their policy agenda. Not until the military effort had achieved that kind of movement did the Nixon administration suggest talks. On June 10, it proposed to their North Vietnamese counterparts in Paris that Henry Kissinger and Le Duc Tho meet on June 28.[149]

Given the president's goals—persuading the North Vietnamese to accede to a negotiated settlement—aircrew discipline in the broadest sense was vital. General Vogt recognized aircrews had to hit only the aim points they were given; collateral damage was impermissible. Having discussed the issue with Alexander Haig, he forwarded the president's goal to his commanders: "We are attempting to break the back of the NVA and get them to negotiate seriously in Paris. . . . We have definitely hurt them, and they are back to the negotiating tables now; we have to keep up the pressure now to make them negotiate seriously." Force and diplomacy were functioning in concert, but Vogt worried that a single stray bomb in a residential area could lead Washington to unilaterally stop the bombing campaign.[150]

The White House monitored the locations Seventh AF selected to bomb as well as the mission rates. Nixon and Kissinger were particularly desirous that missions against places around Haiphong and Hanoi continue on a regular basis to keep pressure on the enemy. Kissinger reminded General Vogt and the new MACV commander, General Frederick Weyand, of Nixon's priorities, and explained and clarified the slackening of pressure he noticed. Moorer told Haig that the weather had been bad enough to reduce the number of missions and reminded him that aircrews had to have good visibility to identify targets and then hit them with precision weapons. Those munitions were required because of the demands that dikes, hospitals, and other sensitive places not be inadvertently hit.[151] Senator Edward Kennedy accused the president of intentionally targeting dikes, which he had not. The annual late summer floods made it clear that heavy rains and not bombs were to blame for damage to dikes.[152]

Kissinger continued to insist on the melding of force and diplomacy, explaining to Moorer in August there was to be no decrease in air strikes during negotiations.[153] When the national security advisor met with Ambassador Bunker and Generals Weyand and Vogt in August, he explained, "it was necessary for Linebacker operations to be 'dovetailed' with his negotiations with the North Vietnamese." Kissinger wanted sortie rates to be consistent and requested that a strike against bridges in the buffer zone be delayed until the day before he met with the Chinese in order to strengthen his hand.[154] Vogt was convinced laser-guided bombs enabled him to safely hit targets inside the ten-mile buffer zone, but political goals took precedence. The diplomatic needs of improving relations with China hurt the operational effectiveness of the air interdiction effort because the administration could not allow further violations of the Chinese border while striking targets next to their border. Moorer had Admiral Noel A. M. Gayler, the new commander of Pacific Command, develop a planning cycle twelve days long in an effort to move the air campaign away from mere target selection toward greater coercive effects. Vogt also acted to make better use of LORAN missions to be able to maintain pressure through the monsoon season.[155]

General Vogt cautioned that shutting down truck traffic 100 percent was beyond the means of American air forces, but the bombing had made it more difficult for the enemy to supply and support their forces.[156] According to a PACAF assessment, the railroads between China and Hanoi were in such a state that trucks had replaced railcars for moving supplies. They were, of course, repairing the transportation routes, so air strikes had to return and bomb them again. Choke points were vulnerable, particularly in the buffer zone, but armed reconnaissance became preferable because the targets had dispersed as a result of bombing of railroads and highways. Air strikes claimed 450 trucks during July and downed more than forty bridges, slowing the North Vietnamese logistical effort.[157] The Defense Intelligence Agency also concluded the air campaign was wearing down the North Vietnamese. It had halted rail transportation from China. It had destroyed a thousand watercraft and shifted the movement of supplies to nighttime. Bombing caused serious damage to industrial targets, repair warehouses, electrical generation, and fuel. And yet in the midst of these bombardments, People's Army of Vietnam combat operations continued, even though ammunition shortages were making themselves felt. Interdiction bombing was finally producing the desired effect, sufficiently enough that the North Vietnamese invasion petered out by July.[158] That is how air power advocates had always argued air interdiction would affect ground warfare.[159]

Overall, General Vogt was pleased "that we have finally been able to mesh the military accomplishments to the diplomatic desires."[160] These military successes had also persuaded the Soviets to act. Nikolai Podgorny, chairman of the Presidium of the USSR Supreme Soviet, had flown to Hanoi in June "to persuade Hanoi to reach an agreement with the Americans."[161] Cumulative air strikes along with the efforts of the ARVN had depleted the North Vietnamese Army to the extent that Lieutenant General Ngo Quang Truong's ARVN offensive, Lam Son 72, which opened on June 28, was successful enough to bring the Easter Offensive to an end.[162]

Nothing was a done deal yet, and the military arm had to keep pressure on the leaders in Hanoi so that they would not protract negotiations. Admiral Moorer observed that missions against targets in the heartland of North Vietnam were insufficient for that purpose. Air strikes had not even reached 25 percent of the valid targets in Route Packages 5 and 6. He added hitting northern targets was a high priority and for McCain to increase the number, weight, and frequency of missions against targets there. Moorer also directed that the timing of missions—morning, noon, and afternoon, for example—was more important than providing more daylight hours for rescue missions of downed pilots by restricting missions to the morning hours. There one sees a side effect of how operations crowd out everything else in a limited war: the planners placed a higher priority on aircrew survival than strategic effectiveness because to the men organizing the missions losing aircrews was too high a cost for a campaign designed for exiting a war. Moorer also ordered McCain to schedule more nighttime A-6A missions over North Vietnam at the expense of those over South Vietnam so as to maintain as much round-the-clock pressure as possible, and shared his optimism that F-111As would be sent into Southeast Asia the next month. All this was about messaging and conveying resolution and determination, so there were to be more missions "against valid fixed targets" and fewer armed reconnaissance missions. Moorer wished for occasional B-52 missions into Route Packages 5 and 6 because their presence would also convey just how earnest the United States was about its goals, but these were not carried out.[163]

Optimal use was a theme. Admiral McCain informed his airmen on August 8 that to apply enough pressure to Hanoi he wanted to wage a more intense campaign against the core of North Vietnam. In line with Moorer's requirement, A-6A squadrons received the more difficult night bombing operations due to their greater capabilities.[164] The A-6A squadron VA-35 focused on, for example, a railroad line that ran through the northeastern part of Route Package 6 in September.[165] In addition, the Air Force improved the tactical and operational effectiveness of its instruments of coercion by having each wing execute one primary mission. The 8th TFW had the responsibility for guided bombs since they had all of the laser illuminators; the 432nd TRW had all of the F-4s equipped with Combat Tree IFF (identification friend or foe) interrogators, so MiG killing was its main job; naturally the 388th TFW provided the Iron Hand missions since it had the F-105Gs, EB-66s, and F-4s that dropped chaff.[166]

These aircraft were in theater to destroy targets, and one in particular, the Thanh Hoa Bridge, had been an irritant for years. In May 1965, General Hunter Harris Jr. complained about wasting dozens of bombs trying to obliterate its solid concrete piers instead of trying to drop a span into the river. Seven-hundred-fifty-pound bombs could not dent the forty-foot-thick concrete, and some bombs missed by as much as 700 feet. Better to put fewer jets at risk; just send four to eight against it from time to time until a munition with greater accuracy became available. Navy strikes in 1966 were not able to drop any spans, but they wrecked the tracks and decking on the bridge, which left it temporarily unusable but still repairable.[167] When Walleyes became available, Navy jets achieved three direct hits with them against a truss on the bridge, but it remained upright. General Clay observed in June 1972 that the Air Force and Navy had flown more than 1,000 sorties before they stopped trying to demolish the Thanh Hoa Bridge.[168]

A total of forty-three aircraft either crashed or got shot down trying to destroy it, but on May 13, 1972, fourteen F-4Ds with LGBs dropped the bridge into the Song Ma River with just fourteen bombs. Laser-guided bombs had already dropped another pesky target, the Paul Doumer Bridge, into the Red River, two days prior.[169] Workers repaired it over the summer, so Navy A-7Es used Walleye IIs to drop one of its spans into the river for a second time on August 10. That was not sufficient, as it always seemed to be with that structure, so the same squadron smashed the pontoons for the bypass bridge. Due to the inevitable repairs, A-4Fs from VA-164 had to hit again, this time with 1,000-pound LGBs, which managed to destroy about fifty feet of its decking. Aircrews were now able to achieve hits on the bridge consistently, but even that was insufficient for destroying it.[170]

Attack Squadron 164 was, incidentally, the only Navy squadron with aircraft equipped for using laser-guided bombs at that time; the squadron had eight from the first of the year. Weather had to be good for LGBs to work, but the greater annoyance for the Navy "was the total and absolute dependence on the U.S. Air Force for airborne laser designator services. Coordination and targeting was difficult and many sorties were aborted due to lack of designators." On August 8, a pair of TA-4Fs that were able to illuminate targets with a laser without the assistance of the Air Force landed on the USS *Hancock*. They started accompanying A-4Fs carrying 500- and 1,000-pound bombs on armed reconnaissance missions and regularly achieved great accuracy and effectiveness.[171] The *Kitty Hawk*'s F-4Js received hand-held laser designators and 500-pound LGBs over the summer. As with the Air Force, a jet with the laser had to fly a steady turn at about 10,000 feet so that the weapons system officer could aim the laser for the bomb-dropping F-4J. Targeteers assigned bridges and artillery sites along the coast to these F-4s.[172]

Navy A-7Cs finally wrecked the Thanh Hoa Bridge in October. Jets from the USS *America* dropped a span of the bridge on October 6. Laser-guided bombs hit two of the concrete piers, and then four 2,000-pound LGBs impacted the other half of the bridge. Photos from an RA-5C showed "the center pier down, the western section cut and the western end buckled, and one section in the river between the stumps of the severed highway and rail line." That day, "One of the attacking American pilots was reported to have said in disbelief as he pulled off the target: 'My God, I think we've dropped it.'"[173]

The Air Force turned to LORAN guidance once the northeast monsoon began so it could continue missions against North Vietnam; the thickness and expanse of the resultant cloud cover meant that there would be few chances to use Paveways and Walleyes.[174] Compared to PGMs, LORAN missions were demonstrations of intent. During one mission on September 21, the bombs created a string of impact points a mile and a half long. It provided accuracy no better than about 375 yards; the accuracy was simply terrible according to another evaluation.[175] Technological limitations made it unreliable because aircraft that maneuvered around thunderstorms often lost their connection with the transmitter.[176] During a September 17, 1972, mission, Corvette Flight suffered a break-lock within two miles of the drop point so it was unable to place its bombs on target. LORAN was also not the best system for use in high threat areas because the jets had to fly a single altitude and heading for the final twenty miles of the bombing run to release their bombs with maximum accuracy. A better use of LORAN missions was against targets not defended by weapons that required fighter-bombers to deviate from their flight paths.[177] Because of its accuracy shortcomings, any time a LORAN strike was planned near a populated area, planners screened the targets with extra care. Minimizing risks to civilians dictated the approach routes to the target.[178]

The bombing wreaked great destruction against power stations, enough to reduce electricity generation by three-quarters through the end of June, but PACAF concluded enough capacity remained to meet "essential requirements." Less than favorable weather and higher priority targets combined to lower the number of sorties against them over the rest of the summer into early fall. Four F-4s carrying LGBs, however, left the Viet Tri Power Station on fire on August 15, and these power plants generally needed months to repair once hit. Navy jets and Aardvarks made some of the last strikes against these targets in October.[179]

There was a lack of certainty about the effectiveness of Linebacker when one relied on statistical measures. The CIA did not expect bombardment and mining to alter fundamental policy objectives in Hanoi because at 3,000 tons a day imports were still above the 2,700-ton minimum. Furthermore, the CIA concluded the only real impact these interdiction missions had was limiting military equipment like tanks, SAMs, and artillery. Despite the effort, the North Vietnamese could still shift supplies from one place to another as necessary. A final recommendation pondered a wide use of force: "If air and mining alone won't turn Hanoi around, how can we combine it with ground operations in the South, psychological warfare, political steps, etc., to give us an overall impact that may cause Hanoi to change its policy?"[180] Those should have been the questions from the beginning because for air interdiction to damage an enemy supply chain well enough to decisively affect the operations of an enemy army, friendly ground forces must compel the enemy to engage in intense combat in conjunction with the air operations to force the enemy to use supplies to the point that they either run out altogether, or must focus their operations on avoiding the collapse that would take place if their supplies reached a critically low threshold. Although the tone of this memo was authoritative, the CIA also conceded that: "*We know very little about the situation in the North. Therefore, what we can say is limited and anything that is said is very tentative* [italics in original]."[181] While specific measurements were difficult to obtain, it appeared that the combination of ground and air power won nearly all the battles during 1972. Consequently, the PAVN offensive petered out during the summer, and they lacked the power to recommence their offensive following the pounding they had taken; South Vietnamese forces, at the same time, lacked the reserves in fighting power needed to drive the North Vietnamese out of their country. Another stalemate resulted.

Hanoi negotiated in fall 1972 more seriously because the American and South Vietnamese military operations had weakened them. The United Kingdom's consul in Hanoi, Joseph Wright, noticed some shortages during June.[182] Robert Thompson, the British counterinsurgency expert, investigated conditions in South Vietnam from June 17 to July 3 and concluded "that the North Vietnamese offensive has been militarily defeated and has caused little damage to the Vietnamization and Pacification programs."[183] The North Vietnamese agreed; its leadership admitted in June that their invasion "had failed to obtain its objectives." Air power and the ARVN frustrated the North Vietnamese enough that, "For the remainder of the war, then, VWP [Vietnamese Workers Party] leaders resigned themselves to struggle solely in the diplomatic arena."[184] At the same time, Vogt received reports that enemy troops were suffering severe shortages, reducing their offensive actions.[185]

Several variables interacted with each other to move conditions against North Vietnam. CIA director Helms shared a discouraging assessment with Kissinger on August 22: "The record of World War II, the Korean War, and Vietnam since 1965 strongly suggests that bombing alone is unlikely to transcend the realm of severe harassment and achieve true interdiction in the sense of stopping the movement of supplies a determined, resourceful enemy deems essential and is willing to pay almost any price to move."[186] Bombing by itself, however, never was the sole means during Linebacker, nor was it intended to be. The fighting the South Vietnamese Army engaged in during the seven months between the invasion and the October bombing halt was fundamental to persuading Hanoi to negotiate. The greater desire of the Soviets and Chinese to improve their relations with the United States also provided the Americans more coercive freedom against the North Vietnamese, and the bombing campaign must be evaluated in conjunction with the Americans' diplomacy with China and the Soviet Union, and with the agendas of those two countries. In a roundabout manner, these actions influenced Hanoi's patrons to press their client to compromise. China's premier Zhou Enlai told Le Duc Tho in July, "you have to negotiate." The North Vietnamese were pressed between the Chinese and the Americans, but the latter, Zhou reminded Tho, were exiting South Vietnam.[187]

Since North Vietnam shared a long and secure border with one of its main suppliers, it should have come as no surprise that the air campaign, successful as it was, in the end was unable to completely isolate North Vietnam from supplies originating in China and the Soviet Union.[188] Another consequence of Linebacker's continuance was a belief in South Vietnam that the war had finally turned in their favor and that the United States had shown itself to be a reliable friend.[189] Their self-assurance strengthened the United States' negotiating stance because Kissinger knew that President Thieu was not about to go wobbly and throw away the advantages gained as a result of fighting, and because the South Vietnamese had gained more confidence against their enemies.

Kissinger advised Nixon that military actions, the air and mine campaigns, specifically, had done enough damage so that the PAVN not only "suffered staggering losses," but was also depleting its reserves.[190] The mining of the harbors reduced shipping imports to almost nothing, and air interdiction slashed imports coming through China from 160,000 monthly to 30,000.[191] Vogt believed Linebacker was an irreplaceable factor in improving the environment for negotiations. The successes of military operations against North Vietnam encouraged Hanoi to look to other measures to influence American policy actions. Nixon and Alexander Haig became suspicious as early as late June that the North Vietnamese were making efforts to portray their looming concessions as magnanimous actions and were trying to portray them as a result of George McGovern's pressure on the Nixon administration, not because of American military successes.[192]

Indeed, the American presidential election factored greatly. Nixon believed his reelection hung in the balance, which focused his attention, but the timing of the North Vietnamese invasion actually favored Nixon's prospects. His and Kissinger's worst fear had been that the invasion would not commence until October, at which time a full-scale air war—justified though it would be—would wreck Nixon's reelection bid.[193] As of June, the North Vietnamese believed they could absorb the punishment the Americans could dish out until then, when a more amenable person, George McGovern, might get elected to replace Nixon.[194] Xuan Thuy, the head of the North Vietnamese delegation to the Paris Peace Talks, even "offered to help Senator McGovern's electoral chances in any way possible, including not doing anything during negotiations that might help Nixon."[195] These collusions between the McGovern campaign and the North Vietnamese had been going on for a year. In September 1971, Senator George McGovern met with North Vietnamese negotiators in Paris to persuade them to take actions—such as giving him a list of American prisoners of war held in North Vietnam—that would help him get elected president, an outcome that would be in the interests of the North Vietnamese.[196] The North Vietnamese also believed that if they waged diplomatic and military offensives during September and October they might be able to swing the American election to Senator McGovern. As Election Day approached, however, American domestic politics strengthened the negotiating hand of the US and South Vietnam. It was clear to Hanoi that Nixon was going to win reelection, so for the first time Le Duc Tho included the retention of President Thieu in a coalition government as a part of his new overture.[197]

The effectiveness of the air campaign and the ARVN's ground war enabled the Americans to wage their own talking-while-fighting strategy. Negotiations between Kissinger and Tho commenced on July 19 and as expected, Tho insisted the United States terminate its bombing campaign; he only partially understood the American goals. "Your bombardment," he proposed, "and your blockade of North Vietnamese seaports are aimed at forcing us to surrender [mistaken] and at winning a strong position in the negotiations for you [correct] ... the bombing will not succeed in subduing us and will not settle the fate of the war." When Kissinger offered a three-to-four-month cease-fire, Tho rejected the offer and the bombing continued.[198] Tho complained again about the bombing during an August 1 meeting with Kissinger, and once again turned down Kissinger's offer of a three-month cease-fire.[199]

Meanwhile, the Navy continued to fly 70 percent of Linebacker sorties in August. Most of the worthwhile targets had already been destroyed by then; the main function of bombing was to prevent repairs and rebuilding. The bombing forced the North Vietnamese to tap reserve materiel, but the Defense Intelligence Agency could not be certain as to how much was left. Vietnamese efforts centered on repair work and mitigating the effects of the bombing. They did so by moving supplies by truck, shuttling supplies in small boats from Chinese ships, and by continuing work on the pipeline that had been designed with easy repair in mind.[200]

Using air strikes to keep the pressure on Hanoi was a theme for the waning month of Linebacker. Kissinger needed to negotiate from a position of strength, so he and Nixon hounded Moorer about weather-canceled missions in August. Weather in September disrupted or cancelled more and more missions, but strike forces normally hit their targets weather permitting. On September 15, for example, fighter-bombers destroyed the bridge at Vu Chua, and all of the aircrews involved said that their bombs landed in the Bac Giang Railroad Yard. The next day, pilots testified that all of their ordnance landed within the Xoui Nien open air storage site and the Lang Chi Ammunition Plant, and laser-guided bombs wrecked two bridges on September 17.[201] In spite of the reduced bombing due to the monsoon, General Weyand believed enemy forces were "in deep trouble."[202]

In late September, A-6As received some help with the night bombing missions when two squadrons of F-111As arrived at Takhli Air Base, Thailand. This aircraft made it possible for the USAF to strike targets at night and in the bad weather endemic to that time of year with accuracy similar to that of the Intruder. Therefore, the US could better maintain pressure around the clock. Aardvarks carried enough fuel to not require tanker support, and they flew so close to the ground and so fast that the North Vietnamese could rarely detect them on radar and thus MiG-21s could not intercept them.[203] Their combination of speed, low altitude, heading changes, chaff, and jamming from their ECM pods made it very difficult

Aircrew in front of F-111A (US Air Force)

for missiles and guns to have any reasonable hope of bringing one down. Aircrews, to their surprise, discovered that SAM sites could momentarily track them down to 500 feet, and after three weeks of operations, the sites had tracked them more than seventy times, leading to sixteen missile firings. One exploded close enough to inflict damage.[204]

Bringing F-111As into the air war made sense for several reasons. The transferral of thirteen KC-135s back to the CONUS meant a greater need for a bomber that would not need mid-air refuelings. The bombers replaced an F-4D wing, and together with the A-7D wing brought in that fall, these longer-ranged aircraft made it possible to do without fifty-five tankers. Both were superior to F-4s for night missions.[205] General Ryan was ambivalent about the new mix of aircraft in Indochina. On the one hand, they sent home an F-4D wing that was having good success with daytime laser-guided bomb missions; replacing them with F-111As meant that a military capability was going to be lost. On the other hand, there were fewer and fewer opportunities to use LGBs because of the seasonal weather change. Political leaders needed the Aardvarks' ability to hit targets in North Vietnam at night to maintain constant pressure. Ryan also remained concerned about political aspects of bombing and coercion, reminding General Vogt that the air campaign was under scrutiny for its role in pressuring Hanoi. He had to make sure it passed the test. In sum, the US had aircraft that could strike most any target at almost any time and there was little the North Vietnamese could do about it as long as the jet functioned properly, and a few PGM-equipped F-4Ds remained for hitting targets requiring a level of precision F-111As could not provide. Another reason General Vogt wanted Aardvarks was because they did not need the support of jamming, chaff, fighter escort, and tankers like other aircraft did when they flew over the Red River Valley, and since they could fly against North Vietnamese targets, that freed more F-4s for missions in South Vietnam. Six of them flew their first combat mission against North Vietnam on September 28.[206] The fifteen that reached their targets on the night of October 13 hit home, but nine other jets aborted for a variety of reasons. The F-111s were especially valuable against railroads and railroad bridges during the fall months, and ground observers found F-111 accuracy to be exceptional.[207]

The F-111 required reliable terrain-following radar (TFR) to fly close to the ground in hostile airspace at night. The jets flew the first part of their mission in TFR mode to confirm the system was working and flew no lower than a hundred feet above the highest terrain feature five miles on either side of the approach to the target.[208] By the end of the year, however, six F-111s had failed to return from their missions. Pacific Air Forces suspected the losses were due to either some kind of "premature detonation" of one of their bombs or malfunctions in the terrain-following radar.[209] A couple of aircrews experienced jamming against their TFR, and the North Vietnamese may have developed a new countermeasure against the new threat: firing chaff up in front of approaching aircraft. The chaff could have tricked the autopilot to fly the jet up to a higher altitude where AAA could get them. Problems with the Aardvark's ability to fly very close to the ground, if unresolved, would nullify one of its primary advantages. The Air Staff only speculated that a combination of pilot error, TFR problems, and shrapnel from one of their own bombs were responsible for the lost jets.

Flak put F-111s in a quandary. When they flew missions against targets that required using Mk 84 bombs, their blast radius required the bomber to fly 1,000 feet above the ground to avoid the bomb blast, but that placed the jet where AAA could track them. Aardvarks could drop Mk 82 retarded bombs from lower altitudes, but they were not as effective against targets like bridges as was the Mk 84. In the end, using the high-drag Mk 82s for very low altitude drops won.[210]

Their missions continued for less than a month because bombing missions north of the 20th parallel came to a halt on October 23, 1972, as "a gesture of goodwill" toward the peace talks in Paris, a choice Secretary of Defense Laird disagreed with. The halt was not comprehensive, for SR-71 and drone reconnaissance flights continued, and strike aircraft destroyed North Vietnamese truck convoys funneling through a gap in the mountains about twenty-five miles north of Vinh on November 27. Similar missions continued in Route Package 2 and 3 right up to the commencement of Linebacker II, often by A-6As.[211]

Worsening weather left around ten good flying days in October, providing the enemy more time to bring damaged bridges back into service. Since LGBs needed good weather, Vogt made the northeast railroad bridges a priority on good weather days. The weather also meant fighter-bombers struck larger targets in line with the accuracy LORAN provided. Weather restricted which aircraft could fly, so the A-6A squadron was the USS *America*'s only aircraft to sortie against North Vietnam that month. Weather eroded mission effectiveness to a great degree. For example, from October 16 to 23, 1972, only 29 percent of 168 sorties allocated hit their targets in the area from Hanoi to Kep to Thai Nguyen. Fifty-four percent deviated to other targets, and 17 percent were cancelled outright.[212] The bad weather endemic over North Vietnam in December would make B-52s with their all-weather capabilities essential for Linebacker II, although Haig would remind the president that even an air campaign that relied on so-called all-weather aircraft like B-52s needed a modicum of decent weather.[213]

When the October bombing halt approached, Moorer assessed the results of Operation Linebacker as a partial success. For one, the mining of Haiphong had essentially shut down seaborne importation of materiel. The North Vietnamese had to transport supplies from China along a series of roads and railroads that aircraft repeatedly bombed. Since bombing destroyed many bridges and train repair warehouses, they had to offload and move supplies around ruptures in those transportation routes. There were plenty of untouched targets inside Hanoi and Haiphong, and Moorer intended to send missions against them whenever permitted by breaks in the weather. The Americans relied on A-6A missions for nighttime truck convoys, and on B-52s below the 19th parallel. The Intruders gained a new capability the first week of December when A-6As used Pave Knife laser pods with Paveways. Success was immediate.[214] The air campaign helped produce starvation among enemy troops and depleted their manpower reserves. Analysts wrote, "The caliber of NVA troops has declined markedly, with about 95 percent being recent recruits. Reinforcements sent into Quang Tri City who later became POWs stated they were sent forward without arms and were told they would have to find guns after they got to their fighting positions." The Americans concluded that this was due to their incessant air strikes on their supply lines.[215]

The war was once again a stalemate. Assessments from the DIA and CIA "concluded that North Vietnam could sustain the current level of fighting for the next two years, even with the heavy US bombing." While North Vietnam could continue to fight under the bombs, the combination of fighting and bombing had inflicted 100,000 casualties on communist forces (mostly PAVN), taken back the territory the North Vietnamese had seized the previous spring, and resulted in Saigon controlling territory where all but 400,000 out of nineteen million South Vietnamese lived.[216]

The North Vietnamese remained the stronger political actor. When Le Duc Tho presented Henry Kissinger with a new proposal on October 9, the American negotiator read an offer in which the major North Vietnamese concession was a willingness to permit Thieu to remain president of South Vietnam, but 100,000 North Vietnamese troops got to stay in South Vietnam. Kissinger did not consider conquest by fiat to be a deal breaker; he had posited in April the acceptance of a cease-fire even if nine of Hanoi's infantry divisions lingered in South Vietnam.[217] He believed the only way to remove the North Vietnamese troops was to expel them by force or kill them in place, but as things stood, the military power available to South Vietnam and the United States was insufficient to accomplish either. Thieu and the South Vietnamese were in an awful situation: an invader was occupying part of their country and they did not have the ability to remove him; there was no way the North Vietnamese were going to retreat when they had fought so hard and died in such numbers. Expelling the North Vietnamese Army was a fantasy, and in Kissinger's opinion, Thieu had better accept a compromise deal that conformed to the facts on the ground. Kissinger believed without justification that the PAVN would "go home once they realized that they could not move and could not reinforce."[218]

Chapter 18

Toward Another Confrontation

In anticipation of a renewed air campaign to break the logjam, General Clay proposed an operational change in October 1972 that should have been implemented in 1965: eliminating the Route Package system in favor of assigning targets to whichever weapon could best destroy them whether it be Navy or Air Force, because both services could get the job done interchangeably: "These targets require the same tactics and capabilities regardless of which force is assigned the task. The guidance factor should be the most economical and efficient use of the force."[1] Clay's observation was an advancement in operational warfare, but the bombing halt went into effect a week later.

Meanwhile, President Nixon failed to skillfully implement his "fighting while talking" strategy. Secretary of Defense Laird agreed to reduce bombing gradually from October 14, but he informed Kissinger he would intensify the bombing if there was no settlement. Vogt thought suspending the bombing before the North Vietnamese signed the final agreement was a serious mistake in coercive diplomacy.[2] Kissinger then violated Nixon's intent of maintaining pressure when he informed Le Duc Tho that the bombing of targets in Hanoi would subside.[3] Alexander Haig informed Kissinger that Nixon was convinced an agreement had to immediately follow a bombing halt, and Haig believed bombing had to form the backdrop of a settlement right up to the moment of signing, and that continued bombing incentivized serious negotiations on the part of the North Vietnamese. Neither happened.[4] In his memoirs, Nixon wrote that he told Kissinger that he would accept a 25 percent reduction in sorties, but that he was "absolutely opposed to [a bombing halt] before the election.... I would consider a bombing pause.... But there would be no bombing *halt* until the agreement was signed [italics in original]." Kissinger refused to comply with the president's wishes.[5] Nixon failed to enforce his requirement, perhaps because his election campaign was in its final stages. Kissinger informed Haig that bombing would be greatly curtailed to 150 missions each day, and targets in Hanoi were off limits; Laird had the Navy and Air Force comply with that directive. Kissinger gave General Weyand an additional task that did not match the military capabilities then in Southeast Asia: make clear to President Thieu the necessity of seizing as much territory before the cease-fire went into effect as possible—under a reduced allocation of combat aircraft sorties. Kissinger was unaware of sortie limitations Admiral Gayler had put forth from PACOM.[6] Kissinger then proposed a negotiating practice that had repeatedly failed during the Johnson years: "In order to show our good faith we will stop our bombing of the North and significantly reduce air activity in the South while this situation is being worked out."[7]

No one oversaw setting the specific goals and methods, the military actions taken, and that the concessions made did not support the United States' diplomatic aims. Nixon should have enforced compliance by his lieutenants, but Kissinger did whatever he wanted, and Kissinger's subordinate Alexander Haig had to rein in Kissinger for Nixon. In Haig's opinion, lessening military pressure during the negotiating endgame—in this instance by reducing air strikes in South Vietnam—"defies logic."[8] Bombing while negotiating would have lessened the need for the threat of escalation, but the president himself directed the maintenance of bombing only up to twenty degrees north latitude, which prohibited bombing the most politically useful targets.[9] Nixon also warned Andrei Gromyko, the Soviet ambassador to the United States, that he would escalate the bombing if the North Vietnamese did not accept Kissinger's offer.[10] Kissinger insisted that his requirement of a very short bombing halt—while he was flying back to Washington—was "not soft-headedness but to salvage what can be salvaged and give us the time we need."[11]

So the American national security team was divided. Kissinger and Nixon held opposing, conflicting convictions about the effects a continued application of force would have on their diplomatic efforts. Kissinger believed reducing bombing would encourage the Soviets to press the North Vietnamese, would reassure Thieu that the United States was serious, and would lessen any embarrassment for Hanoi. Nixon believed continued bombing would buttress diplomacy and public opinion. His lead negotiator believed continued bombardment would harm both. Regarding the secretary of state and the secretary of defense, Kissinger was also duplicitous: "With respect to Rogers and Laird, they should be told of developments but should be brutalized into total secrecy. As I have said, it is essential that we give the impression that major progress is being made."[12] In reality, Kissinger was brutalizing the South Vietnamese into signing "an agreement that was tantamount to surrender" as far as President Thieu was concerned, while the North Vietnamese skillfully orchestrated the various instruments of power at their disposal to advance their interests at the expense of their adversaries.[13] Kissinger admitted the management of these negotiations had come under threat after he digested Haig's messages: "I can only conclude that the breakdown in communications between us is so massive that I question how any discussion between us can be possible."[14]

Options, not communications, was the problem. The Americans had no good offers for the South Vietnamese, only proposals that were bad to varying degrees. Kissinger tried to explain on December 7 that the important thing was establishing some sort of documented obligation for the United States to be entitled to bomb North Vietnamese forces when they initiated their next offensive. He even worried that if he kept the president well informed, Nixon would accidentally disclose sensitive information and derail the talks. Meanwhile, Vogt complained that Admiral Gayler was a "disaster" and had prevented him from bombing productive targets in North Vietnam, and Kissinger's October 23 order to not bomb above twenty degrees latitude left Admiral Moorer puzzled because it followed neither rhyme nor reason.[15]

This was a failure of war. Force and diplomacy were no longer in sync, the chief negotiator was carrying out a strategy at variance with what the president ordered, Haig neglected to rat out Kissinger to the president, and Nixon neglected to enforce Kissinger's compliance. At the same time, Henry Kissinger refused to support an ally whose supposedly "unreasonable" demand was for occupying foreign troops to leave his country. He even perceived of "himself as the 'lone ranger' of American foreign policy," which assigned the president the role of the sidekick Tonto.[16] Altogether no one was on the same page and the United States was taking actions and pursuing objectives that ran counter to many of its own interests and those of its friend. If the secretary of defense, the chairman of the joint chiefs of staff, and the national security advisor will not meld force and diplomacy toward policy goals adequately, then the president has the obligation to force them to do so—accusations of running the war from the White House notwithstanding. Amazingly, Nixon and Kissinger did not meet with the JCS until November 30, the first time since the Easter Offensive began.[17]

Meanwhile, another indicator arose that the North Vietnamese were benefitting from the curtailed interdiction campaign. Intelligence discovered they still had enough supplies to move south for another offensive against the northern parts of South Vietnam. Moorer consequently directed a concentrated effort against those supply routes; B-52s flew 848 sorties through the rest of the month, not to mention fighter-bomber missions. Navy Attack Squadron 35 received high praise for the consequences of its bombing accuracy during these missions. Intruders from the USS *America*, *Saratoga*, and *Enterprise* destroyed forty-nine more trucks on November 30 and December 1.[18] But then after warning Hanoi that "a maximum effort" was to erupt on December 4, the president had bombing momentarily reduced as an act of "goodwill," a mistake akin to one of Johnson's bombing halts.[19]

Negotiations stagnated as December approached. Hanoi would not withdraw combat troops from South Vietnam, and Thieu would not accept an agreement that left enemy troops inside his country. Nixon and Kissinger tried to convey to Thieu the extent to which Congress was adamantly hostile to the war. They believed the only way to create hope Congress would support another American–South Vietnamese operation against North Vietnamese military action in 1973 or 1974 was for Thieu to show that he was trying to move forward by signing a settlement—no matter how disagreeable. Nixon decided the only way out of the impasse was to bomb the North Vietnamese in a manner that would get them to sign and would convince Thieu the Americans would unleash hell on the communists if they later renewed offensive action. Henry Kissinger voiced the basic policy objectives of what would become that hell—Operation Linebacker II—to President Nixon back in March 1971: achieve a cease-fire, the return of American prisoners, and the withdrawal of American forces, which ought to give Saigon a year to prepare for the next enemy offensive.[20] Author Jeffrey Kimball argued the Christmas bombings were aimed at persuading Thieu to get in line and as a way for Nixon to support a narrative that he had been strong and had persuaded Hanoi to accede to the Paris Peace Accords. The air raids were ultimately a coercive operation instead of one just centered around destroying a set of militarily significant targets that would alter options on the battlefield.[21]

Air Force Deputy Chief of Staff for Plans and Operations Lieutenant General George J. Eade had been thinking about the operational and strategic effects of respective weapons if the United States waged a more intense war against North Vietnam. He noticed the differing impressionistic effects of accurate precision-guided munitions compared to the psychological effects of B-52 night missions. General Vogt thus needed to rank order missions with those factors in mind. Eade believed the Air Force had made its case that B-52s were capable of striking targets up north if necessary.[22] This was true as long as it restricted B-52s to targets not requiring greater precision than they could deliver. With its advanced munitions, the United States now had the capability to destroy targets with little risk of collateral damage, while retaining the use of the B-52 as a weapon of intimidation.

As the administration saw that talks were probably going to break down, orders went out during the first week of December to prepare for air strikes against high value targets in the Hanoi–Haiphong region in case they were needed to squeeze concessions from Le Duc Tho. Haig directed these missions

> be so configured as to create the most massive shock effect in a psychological context. There is to be no dissipation of effort through scattered attacks against a number of varied targets, but rather a clear concentration of effort against essential national assets designed to achieve psychological as well as strategic results.... We cannot permit purely military considerations such as long-term interdiction, etc. to dominate the targeting philosophy. Attacks which are launched when the weather permits must be massive and brutal in character. No other criteria is acceptable and no other conceptual approach will be countenanced.[23]

The Air Force had been thinking about this, and the Joint Staff and Strategic Air Command had already written an operational plan that envisioned B-52s, fighter-bombers, naval gunfire, and minelaying hitting nearly sixty targets. President Nixon found it satisfactory when Admiral Moorer briefed him on December 7.[24] Nixon required their coercive effort to either extract concessions from the North Vietnamese or result in Le Duc Tho breaking off the talks and getting blamed for torpedoing the peace process. At the same time, Haig and Kissinger righted their ship and by December, Nixon and Kissinger were speaking from the same page, and the president approved of Kissinger's tactics for negotiating with Tho over the next couple of days. If Tho received guidelines for a settlement from Hanoi that were acceptable, Kissinger might be able to reach an agreement. If that was not the case, Kissinger would step away from the talks to consult with Washington and not return.[25]

When Admiral Moorer informed General Vogt of the deliberations about escalation, Vogt assured him that his forces were prepared to hit any target necessary even during the seasonal bad weather because planners had already tabulated each target's precise location. That was prescient because talks between Kissinger and Tho fell apart on December 13 when the North Vietnamese suddenly altered the text of the agreement seventeen different ways after agreeing to a version that had been finalized. Kissinger told the president it was time to bomb.[26]

Linebacker II: The Christmas Bombings

President Nixon decided on December 14 to alter the character, scope, and purpose of the bombing of North Vietnam.[27] Linebacker II, the new offensive, was a coercive campaign designed not to disable war-making capabilities, but to persuade the North Vietnamese government to do something they did not want to do: sign a cease-fire. Thus, on December 15 a set of thirty-one targets were sent out; thirty-nine more followed on December 19. They specified "railroad yards, storage facilities, airfields, surface-to-air missile sites, and bridges," and power stations.[28] Orders from the JCS directed the placement of bombs to be "close to the center of North Vietnam's government" and against "lucrative targets in the Hanoi and Haiphong areas."[29] The first ten targets included the Hanoi Radio Station, railroad yards and rolling stock repair warehouses, four airfields, a power station, and a logistical exchange facility. Railroad yards were more difficult to destroy than the other targets, so they received more than a third of the Air Force's effort, 484 sorties total.[30] North Vietnam's weather entailed reliance on B-52s and other aircraft possessing all-weather means, but fighter-bombers could still employ visual bombing when conditions permitted.[31]

Moorer transmitted the "execute message" on December 17 with a commencement time of 1200Z, on December 18. Restrictions were few. Laser-guided bombers were stipulated for certain targets to lessen the likelihood of collateral damage and strikes were to avoid damaging ships. The weather was so bad during Linebacker II, however, that USAF and Navy tactical aircraft used only twenty-eight laser-guided bombs. B-52s dropped more than 85,000 unguided bombs.[32]

Admiral Moorer ordered his commanders to take risks to comply with the president's orders: "We are counting on all hands to put forth a maximum, repeat maximum, effort in the conduct of this crucial operation."[33] Nixon's agents, however, struggled to understand what constituted a maximum B-52 effort. In Moorer's judgment, thirty jets per mission was the right amount and Laird agreed. That meant, however, that two-thirds to three-fourths of the available bombers were hitting targets outside of the Hanoi–Haiphong region, which explicitly violated the president's intent. Moorer promised Kissinger thirty B-52s every night over Hanoi and Haiphong. That, in his professional judgment, was what the political leaders wanted, but he was mistaken. Kissinger warned, "I will tell you you'll have massive problems with the president if there is any, under any guise whatever," any suggestion that the armed forces were executing anything but a maximum effort. "You know what the president wants." Kissinger added, "Now that we have crossed the bridge let's brutalize them."[34]

Problems with the president indeed. Nixon lit into the admiral on the phone when he said, "I don't want any more of this crap about the fact that we couldn't hit this target or that one. This is your chance to use military power effectively to win this war, and if you don't, I'll consider you responsible." Nixon added in his memoirs, "I stressed that we must hit and hit hard or there was no point in doing it at all. If the enemy detected any reticence in our actions, they would discount the whole exercise."[35] Nixon had informed Moorer on December 17 that this bombing operation was "the last chance for the Air Force and Navy to put forth a maximum effort against NVN," and that missions had better go forward. Moorer passed on to Admiral Gayler, his subordinate generals, and General John C. Meyer, the commander-in-chief of Strategic Air Command, that, "You will be watched on a real-time basis at the highest levels here in Washington."[36]

Moorer's bombing campaign was not as intense as it could have been and did not fully comply with the level of pressure Nixon wished to inflict on the North Vietnamese government. A crushing bombardment campaign was what the military had always demanded, but Admiral Moorer suggested a sortie rate of thirty B-52s each night after the third day. At least 129 B-52s were on hand for the first day; why not fly as many as possible around the political center each night? Using only 25 to 30 percent against a single objective violated the intent of the president's order.[37] Nixon had not followed up with his demands in May that B-52s be used, and the White House similarly did not follow up but sanctioned Moorer's choice to send "30 over Hanoi and scatter the rest over the rest of the country."[38]

Judging from its command history, it is not clear the extent to which Admiral Gayler understood this relationship between force and diplomacy the president was after, because after a few insightful sentences, the history then becomes preoccupied with SAM suppression. This portion of the military briefly recognized something beyond the tactical was taking place but did not seem to fully understand what or why. Operational goals focused on inflicting damage, first within the Hanoi–Haiphong region, then along supply routes between that region and China, including targets in the buffer zone. Ideally, the craters would function to quarantine Hanoi.[39]

The ultimate goal of this destruction was to persuade Hanoi to agree to a settlement, convince President Thieu to go along with that agreement and realize the United States was a steadfast ally, and force the North Vietnamese to return American prisoners of war. Nixon, however, refused to clearly explain his reasons or goals publicly, which only exacerbated the uproar from his critics.[40] *Newsweek*'s editor, Mel Elfin, wrote that Nixon had "ordered the most massive air raids in history without a word of explanation to anyone."[41] Nixon believed broadcasting clear reasons would undercut the negotiations. He later wrote that he needed to bomb heavily because only that would break Hanoi's intransigence, force a negotiated settlement Tho did not want, and convince Hanoi signing was a better choice for North Vietnam than the war's continuance.[42] The B-52 aircrews who were going to fly the missions were more concerned with hitting their targets and avoiding getting shot down than they were with geopolitics. Many were amazed they were finally flying into the teeth of the Red River Valley. Captain D. B. Kordenbrock commented that, "I thought they were pulling my leg when they said we were going to bomb Hanoi."[43]

Given that the operation's goals were to force the signing of an agreement by diplomats, one can better understand why the JCS took charge of selecting and confirming each target.[44] The closer one was to the nexus of power, the easier it was to perceive the interrelationships between military action, diplomacy, and the state's overall geopolitical goals. Kissinger, not surprisingly, monitored target selection. He promised Moorer permission to hit targets as close as five miles from the Chinese border, informed Laird that smart bombs were to be used on those missions, and issued a reminder on December 19 that the Hanoi–Haiphong area was to be the focus of bombing.[45] Officers at lower command levels had found this procedure insulting, but again, the goal was persuading the national leaders of other countries to conform to the American policy goals, which is not necessarily synonymous with carrying out the most militarily sound tactical operations.

To be effective, this coercive operation had to overcome the cloud cover rampant over North Vietnam in December. General Weyand was confident LORAN-guided USAF F-4s and A-7Ds could apply supplementary bombing pressure during daylight hours in places socked in by bad weather. General Vogt responded enthusiastically to his orders, appreciating the target approvals and flexibility he received.[46] After demonstrating their survivability during a rescue of two F-105 crewmen near Thanh Hoa, a high threat area that autumn, A-7Ds were sent against targets in Route Packages 5 and 6.[47] The A-7D crews were not rigidly bound to LORAN guidance; when they found breaks in the weather below them on their December 21 and 27 missions, they relied on their own eyes and on-board computer systems to hit their targets. Flying in groups of twenty to thirty-two aircraft, these missions struck Yen Bai and Hoa Lac Airfields, the Giap Nhi Railyard, the Viet Tri transshipment area, and storage sites and buildings in Hanoi and Trai Ca, among others.[48] They also achieved good bombing accuracy on December 22, combining LORAN guidance with their own radar mapping capabilities. Four days later they reported all these systems were functioning in the most trouble-free manner thus far. Surprisingly, the North Vietnamese did not send MiGs after them.[49] Their bombing accuracy was not the most important aspect of the daytime bombings. The mere fact of their presence made twenty-four-hour bombing a reality and exerted additional pressure on Hanoi to sign the peace accord.

Navy all-weather jets also threw their weight against these targets. A-6As from VA-35 joined VA-115 in mining Haiphong Harbor on December 18, and hit Haiphong's shipyard, nearby SAM sites, and the Kien An Air Base the next day. On the nights of December 19 and 20, three more groups returned to Haiphong, bombing the same targets and adding the Song Bi Thermal Power Plant to their list. During the rest of Linebacker II, this squadron bombed missile and logistical sites, dropped mines, and hit the Cat Bi Airfield.[50] These tactical fighter capabilities made it possible to apply pressure during the hours B-52s were not flying, and target places requiring a level of precision B-52s could not provide.

Given the Nixon administration's goals and the precision of laser-guided bombs, targets in Hanoi were now more acceptable, to include Hanoi's railroad station, Hanoi Radio, and the power station. F-4s aimed eight 2,000-pound Paveways against the railroad station on December 21, and all eight hit. A single flight of F-4s employing the weapons dropped a span of the Hanoi Railroad/Highway Bridge into the Canal des Rapides on December 28. Six bombs destroyed the generator plant, this during unfavorable weather and in the face of intense ground fire. Buildings around it were unscathed.[51] The LGB mission of December 24, however, never bothered to take off because of the extent of the cloud cover over their targets. In addition, the bombing strikes using unguided munitions destroyed the railroad yards, rolling stock, and nearby storage buildings. Aardvarks cratered the runways at Bac

B-52D taking off (Air Force Historical Research Agency)

Mai and Phuc Yen Airfields, but this was more the result of a large number of bombs; pinpoint accuracy was lacking.[52]

The bombing tactics Strategic Air Command assigned to its B-52s have been extremely controversial.[53] Initial runs flew in from the northwest in order to take advantage of the jet stream, which increased the bombers' ground speed toward their targets. Beginning on the night of December 18 and continuing during the next three, the B-52s approached in three groups timed to arrive over their targets at four-hour intervals. Planners believed that generated "the psychological impact of continuous bombing." The bombing, of course, was not continuous, and SAC soon admitted the four-hour gaps gave the defenders time to gather themselves and mount fresh missiles on their launchers.[54] Planners should have realized the extent to which these tactics were ill-suited for this operation. Their practice of predictable attack profiles proved catastrophic for several B-52s and threatened achieving the president's agenda. Eighth AF soon realized the first missions followed identical patterns to an extent that imperiled the accomplishment of their mission. The only changes it initially recommended was varying the times each group reached their target; hours still separated each wave of bombers.[55] Strategic Air Command routed the bomb runs this way because those tactics had worked well on Arc Light missions, because it had confidence in the B-52s' jammers, and because it wanted to lessen the risk of B-52s colliding with each other. But the skies of Laos, Cambodia, and South Vietnam, over which Arc Light missions had been flown, were threat-free zones compared to the airspace over Hanoi and Haiphong. Another choice—the post-attack turn "to escape the high threat area as soon as possible"—was not only unnecessary but also suicidal.[56] The turn was designed to avoid a nuclear blast, but of course there were not any nuclear blasts to avoid during these missions. The bombers should have just flown straight through and then turned when beyond the range of the SAMs. Seventh Air Force repeatedly scolded SAC for insisting on the post-attack turn because when the jets made their turns the B-52s' jamming antennae no longer pointed toward the tracking radars, enabling the SAM operators to track and shoot the bombers.[57]

Strategic Air Command's analysis of the capabilities of the B-52s' ECM was also flawed. Forty-one of ninety-eight B-52Gs still had the lower-powered 165-watt, ALT-6B jammers, while the rest of the B-52Ds had the 300-watt ALT-22. A test program found no significant difference between the two, but of course a nearly 50 percent increase in wattage is a major difference.[58] Worse, the Air Force had employed shrewder tactics on prior B-52 missions so there was little excuse for their thoughtless tactics. When eighteen struck targets in the Thanh Hoa area on April 21, they "approached the target on three separate headings and exited southeast." No SAMs hit them. A second group that approached on one heading nearly lost a bomber, which had to divert to Da Nang after a missile damaged it.[59]

On the third day, December 20, a SAM shot down the B-52G Quilt 03 in its post-attack turn. Not only was it performing the ill-advised but mandated turn that pointed its jamming signals away from the SAM batteries, two of its jammers had broken down. Another B-52G, Brass 02, was also hit during its turn. Three of its jammers were inoperative. It managed to crawl back to Thailand where the crew bailed out successfully. Orange 03, a B-52D, exploded after two SAMs hit it prior to bomb release. A missile exploded below Straw 02, another D model, while it was in its post-attack turn. The crew managed to keep it flying for another half hour but had to bail out over Laos. A SAM struck a B-52G that had not yet received the 300-watt jammers, Olive 01, while it was in its post-attack turn. Another unmodified G, Tan 03, veered steadily away from the other two B-52s in its formation when its radar failed until it was six miles from its wingmen—far too distant from the overlapping ECM their jammers provided. An SA-2 hit it before it released its bombs, and then after a couple of minutes another missile hit it. The crew ejected, and the one survivor, Staff Sergeant James L. Lollar, saw the plane explode. Altogether six B-52s were shot down that night, but it took greater than 220 SA-2 firings to do so—inefficient but effective. This strike and three previous against the Yen Vien rail yard inflicted meaningful damage on the yard—not surprising considering that more than 3,100 bombs had landed on it—but the issue that grabbed the most attention that night was the bombers' high loss rate.[60]

When the North Vietnamese shot down those six B-52s and an A-6A on December 20, the White House did not react with shock or despondency. The loss rate concerned the president, who "raised holy hell" over the predictable flight routes the B-52s were taking, but Nixon and Kissinger were more concerned about Thieu's insistence that the North Vietnamese withdraw their troops from his country as a condition for his signing the peace agreement, a concession the Americans knew they could not extract from the communists.[61] Haig believed Thieu was making the worst choice. The war was going to continue after the peace agreement signing, and he could either sign an agreement that would guarantee American military support, or insist on the expulsion of North Vietnamese troops, which was not going to happen, and see American support evaporate. Kissinger believed that because Thieu was rejecting the most reasonable option possible under the circumstances, Thieu had to be out of his mind.[62] The administration did not have the option of doing right by the South Vietnamese: continuing to apply greater and greater military force against the North Vietnamese to force them to withdraw from South Vietnam. Furthermore, American voters were tired of the war. War exhaustion had reached the point that a veto-proof number of congressmen promised to terminate American military involvement no matter the president's wishes and were prepared to cut off appropriations as soon as they convened after the Christmas recess. Senator Edward Kennedy harshly stated Congress must pass legislation terminating American participation in the war.[63] On the other hand, the Nixon administration was forcing its dependent to accept a stab in the face because capabilities, the politically possible, and the harshest of realities had combined to make Nixon's proposal the best offer Washington could give the Saigon government. Kissinger admitted that the United States was about to sell one of its friends down the river, and he channeled the ancient Greeks: "The strong do what they will, the weak suffer what they must." Kissinger even proposed forcibly removing Thieu from office, or opting for a two-way agreement with Hanoi, cutting out Saigon. He also believed South Vietnamese military forces had not exerted nearly as much effort as they could have to expel the PAVN.[64] General Vogt had found that all the ARVN "Corps Commanders think it is time for some kind of settlement and are all for it."[65]

The National Security Advisor had as much scorn for the Air Force's management of the B-52 strikes as he did for President Thieu. Each day, he observed, "they have flown these missions exactly at the same hour.... I told this to them yesterday. They said, 'Well, we got so much other stuff coming in.' But these North Vietnamese aren't stupid. They know at 7:10, the g__n B-52s are coming. That's what I think happened."[66] Admiral Moorer responded that it was not possible to achieve surprise since the North Vietnamese had comprehensive radar coverage of their airspace, but the problem was not the lack of surprise; Kissinger was referring to the lack of concentration of aircraft at a point in time that would overwhelm local air defenses. Just as bad, after three had been shot down on the first wave on December 20, General Vogt wanted to see the second wave canceled. Vogt's impulse to retreat went against the president's clear directive for a maximum effort. Then Moorer and Meyer redirected six B-52s from the second wave that were supposed hit targets in Hanoi to safer targets to protect them from SAMs. In the end, none were shot down during wave number two, but the final group of bombers saw three more shot down.[67]

From Nixon's perspective, bombers get shot down during war; that was just a problem to accept. He reminded his staff that the bombing would have to continue in order to force the return of American prisoners. Kissinger hinted that B-52 losses should decline because there were almost no targets left to bomb in the vicinity of Hanoi, and the missions might go elsewhere. Nixon replied that bombing targets in Hanoi had to continue, but it did not have to take place on the scale or intensity of the first three days. Despite all this, Kissinger believed they had a good chance of getting a favorable agreement with Hanoi because they were still talking, and because the reactions of the Soviets and Chinese had been moderate. Haig couriered a letter from Nixon to Thieu at the same time warning that when the communists returned to the peace talks, Thieu had better be ready to sign an agreement whether or not he found it satisfactory.[68]

Moorer reminded his generals he required them to fully exploit the good weather anticipated for December 21 and 22. He expected them to direct as many missions as possible above the 20th parallel on December 21 at the expense of bombing targets elsewhere. The Air Force and Navy also had to take advantage of this window to hit targets where good visibility was necessary for aiming with precision. These directives had the purpose of ensuring the North Vietnamese felt American air power in full measure.[69] Admiral Gayler therefore ordered Seventh AF to fly every last aircraft it could get in the air on both unguided and PGM missions even if that meant flying zero missions at night, thus lining up with Kissinger's intent.[70]

The story is not a sterile one of missiles versus machines. Escorting fighter crews watched these men die: "Rancor flight reported observing two B-52s on fire and subsequently exploding over the target area during numerous SAM firings."[71] At the worst phase of this mission, Scarlet 03 had fallen six miles behind the other two jets in its cell while carrying out a flight lead change. It exploded when a SAM hit. Scarlet 02 survived a MiG-21 attack unscathed, but then a SAM hit Blue 01, even though all the jammers in its cell were functioning. All its crewmembers ejected and survived but were captured.[72] The fighter pilots recognized bomber crews' bravery: Colonel Mele Vojvodich Jr. of the 388th Tactical Fighter Wing wrote, "From all the fighter jocks at Korat to all the bomber jocks at U-Tapao: congrats for a job well done. The courage displayed by your bomber crews over NVN is an inspiration to all. We'll do our best to give the 'Buff' drivers all the support we can. Also, thanks to the tankers for their vital support. Keep up the good work and good luck."[73]

On December 21, Kissinger conveyed an optimistic report on the day's missions and rejected a *Washington Post* assertion that these bombardments were just for "political" purposes: "What we are doing is all in the military category." George Wilson, the reporter, quoted officials from inside the Pentagon who insisted that "the bombing was part of the negotiating process rather than a military operation." Wilson should have realized that the two were synonymous; there is no more appropriate action for a military operation than to support political goals.[74] Nixon, however, was displeased when he read reports of only sixty B-52s total flying over North Vietnam, but Moorer reassured him the sortie rate was merely a consequence of day-by-day counting from halfway around the world. The sortie rate would return to a hundred the next day. Additionally, the 120 sorties of the first day was an aberration that occurred because the stand-down the day prior had given maintenance crews enough time to make all the jets ready to fly; maintenance requirements would not allow that to be repeated day after day.[75]

Following the unexpected and shocking B-52 losses, suggestions started flowing into SAC Headquarters from several commanders. The documentation of the Linebacker II conferences suggests air leaders did not discuss B-52 sequencing or tactics until December 29, but PACAF began making sound suggestions on December 22. General John C. Meyer of SAC offered that the best way CINCPAC could help the upcoming mission on December 22 would be to carry out SAM suppression and destruction missions to the greatest extent possible, particularly in the Hanoi and Haiphong areas. Ideally these missions would hit their targets just minutes prior to the B-52s' arrival.[76] Honolulu offered similar suggestions: exploit the capabilities of EA-6B electronic jamming aircraft, fly at several different altitudes within the chaff corridor, drop bombs from different altitudes, change their approach and departure routes daily, double the number of chaff aircraft, have B-52s use and dispense the chaff they themselves carried, and organize targets so only one chaff corridor is needed. Since defeating SAMs was easier in daylight, consider switching to daytime B-52 raids. Wild Weasel aircraft would be able to see and bomb missile launch sites if they could fly during the day. While it was true MiGs would be a greater threat, F-4 fighters were sufficient for defeating them.[77] Meyer expressed appreciation for the suggestions and stated SAC had already decided to make better use of EA-6Bs, and that "there will be occasions, particularly in heavily defended areas, where multiple simultaneous ingress routes would be preferred. This tactic denies the enemy the opportunity to consider shooting at all aircraft on one ingress route."[78] Cold comfort to the already dead airmen. Strategic Air Command altered their tactics, reducing the time between the cells to a minute and a half to two minutes. Eighth AF finally realized three ALT-28 jammers were necessary to jam an SA-2's radio link with its launch battery on the ground, which made it all the more urgent for B-52s to fly in groups of no fewer than three. Intelligence analysts also conveyed that even a single ALT-28 jammer was effective enough against the downlink transmission to afford a modicum of electronic self-defense. Jamming this signal was the critical ECM action.[79]

Overcast on December 22 forced a reliance on LORAN-guided, A-7D missions to hit targets during daylight hours. Regarding the nighttime bombings, Moorer believed "the

B-52s have just about hit every worthwhile target in the immediate vicinity of Hanoi and so we ought to begin to spread them out a bit away from the area not because so much of the defense," but because there were not that "many lucrative targets in there."[80] Admiral Moorer could not break out of the paradigm in which target destruction was the only thing bombing did, when in fact the purpose was not only destruction but also communication and coercion. This night's target was the Lang Dang Railroad Yard in Haiphong as well as a nearby oil storage facility, and the waves of bombers flew just two to four minutes apart, but they still made their post-attack turns. The B-52s approached at an altitude 1,000 feet above their bombing altitude, and the post-attack headings varied within an arc of twenty-five degrees. These modest changes were thought sufficient to disrupt SAM attacks.[81]

The sortie rate for December 22 enraged the president, and he was even more upset that only sixty B-52s were scheduled to fly on December 23. Moorer complied with Kissinger's guidance the next day and required the operations on December 26 (planning was two days in advance, and there would be no missions on December 25) be much larger and more intense in their scope. The CJCS got approval from the secretary of defense on Christmas Eve. Nixon's displeasure with Admiral Moorer was short-lived; Kissinger informed him on December 23 that Nixon had turned the day-to-day running of the operation over to the admiral.[82]

At first, Strategic Air Command insisted the loss rates were not so bad since they had not exceeded the 3 percent loss rate that its planners had projected, but they had set the predicted rates arbitrarily high in order to use statistics to mask the seriousness of the losses.[83] Meyer's command argued that a 97 percent success rate ought to greatly concern those responsible for Soviet air defense, which was a good point, but, "On the surface it may appear that our B-52 loss rates are high, [while] each and every loss is of concern, ou[r] B-52 loss rate is actually less than we calculated under the circumstances of repeated attacks against target areas highly defended by the most experienced defense forces in the world." The 307th wing's history was more forthright about the loss rate of December 20. It catalogued that the B-52Gs using the weaker ECM equipment suffered a 10 percent loss rate and that the jets that flew in pairs instead of three-aircraft cells experienced a 20 percent loss rate.[84]

On December 23, B-52 wings began moving toward implementing tactical changes that saved the campaign from defeat.[85] Headquarters SAC issued a further adjustment, agreeing that B-52s ought to approach from multiple axes, but for the time being planners only partially followed that advice. The bombers were still going to approach from essentially the same direction, the southeast, and leave the same way. They made a modest but insufficient modification to the post-attack turn: "two smaller post-target turns replaced the single large turn of 113 degrees–160 degrees that had been employed during the first five days." As a result, not all of the jets would be in the steep turn at the same time, nor would their ECM antennas be aimed away from the SAM radars for as long. SAM operators would still be able to detect them on radar in spite of their jammers. This phenomenon was "burn-through": the reflected signal from the enemy radar off of a target aircraft was greater than the signal the radar received from an aircraft's jammers, which made it possible for the radar return to appear on the radar scope.[86]

Brigadier General Glenn Ray Sullivan, commander of the 17th Air Division at U-Tapao, sent a message to General Gerald W. Johnson of 8th Air Force offering several suggestions. Since he was convinced the SAM sites were receiving accurate readings of the bombers' speeds and altitude, Sullivan recommended a change to the altitudes for the attacking B-52s. He also wanted B-52s to approach from different sectors of the sky and then leave the target area in different manners and headings to frustrate the SAMs. In particular, he suggested the bombers stop making their rote post-bomb-release turn. Finally, lay several different chaff corridors. Laying one single stream just told the North Vietnamese where to look for the bombers, who ought to be approaching from differing axes anyway.[87] At the same time, intelligence analyses caught up with operations. Analysts explained that the defenders were focusing their attention on firing against B-52s "during their post-target turns when the aircraft's jamming effectiveness was reduced due to high bank angles and their radar cross-sections were greatly increased."[88] Admiral Gayler then sent what was probably the best tactical advice offered thus far when he informed Admiral Moorer on December 23 that, "The North Vietnamese evidently waited to fire SAMs until B-52s had turned after dropping their bombs, when the planes made larger radar 'signatures' and the jamming chaff was less effective. Therefore, Gayler felt that they should fly straight on without turning."[89]

Despite the "maximum effort" order, B-52s flew but thirty-one missions over North Vietnam that night. The rest struck three SAM sites and the Lang Dang Railroad Yard, all of which hit their targets. Nixon's guidance, however, was inconsistent. He complained when only thirty B-52s flew north, and then accepted the reasons why the chairman had not complied with the spirit of his orders. Kissinger mentioned to Nixon on December 23 that thirty B-52s completed missions north of Hanoi just inside the buffer zone, and the president voiced no complaints that pressure on Hanoi had been diminished against his wishes.[90] Be that as it may, the bombing was enough to persuade the Soviets to prod the North Vietnamese into negotiating with the Americans again. Ilia S. Scherbakov, Moscow's ambassador to Hanoi, conveyed that desire on December 23.[91]

General Vogt tactfully offered some observations and suggestions on Christmas Eve. He blamed the weather for lack of Iron Hand success. He also noted they had doubled the amount of chaff F-4s but observed that the B-52s were not using their own chaff. Vogt also suggested using drones for dispensing chaff. The general reminded Gayler that Seventh AF was not responsible for the B-52 debacle, "Although we participate in a free exchange of information and ideas with SAC and HQ 8AF, the selection of routes, times, targets and tactics for the B-52 are made exclusively by them. They have altered altitudes during the last two missions but have not as yet elected to dispense the chaff carried on the B-52."[92]

Chaff corridor availability was one factor in determining the character of the attack runs, the presence of which degraded the ability of the missiles to guide accurately. Chaff-dispensing F-4s could lay six corridors over the course of a single night mission.[93] These jets were more at risk from midair collisions than from the enemy. Timing was important, as the F-4s would climb through the B-52s' altitude because at their weight they had to cruise at about 26,000 feet before briefly ascending to 36,000 to dispense their chaff. The F-4s also had to depend on their afterburners to get up to 36,000 feet for this kind of mission, which made fuel management and reaching their tankers critical.[94] Issues like this were just one of many reasons the operation needed an on-the-scene commander with enough authority and proximity to enforce the necessary tactical adjustments quickly because there were so many moving parts to the operation.

On December 24, a mere thirty B-52s went after North Vietnamese railroad yards. Tactics improved again with the decision for the bombers to fly a variety of headings when they vacated the target area, thence to the Gulf of Tonkin. They varied their altitudes by 1,000 to 2,000 feet, and they could also eject the chaff they carried for self-defense during their post-attack turn. General Meyer judged the December 24 B-52 missions successful. To minimize bombing on Christmas, Nixon permitted a one-day break in the action.[95]

Moorer assessed the campaign's first week as "remarkably successful to date," and promised a large air strike following the Christmas Day suspension.[96] Not every B-52 was going to be available for December 26 because thirty flew missions over South Vietnam on

Christmas. Nor could Moorer carry out both a continuous and a maximum effort at the same time because maintenance crews needed regular intervals to prep the bombers for their next missions, so the ones that flew on December 25 would not be available the next day. Eighteen B-52s flew missions over South Vietnam on December 28 and ten did likewise on December 29, but that still left plenty for targets up north.[97]

B-52 sortie rates north of the 20th parallel were to run about a hundred on December 26, sixty the following day, and thirty on each day after. These later sortie rates did not square with the "high priority requirement to maintain heavy pressure on Hanoi/Haiphong."[98] Intense bombing of targets close enough to the politburo so the members could hear the bombs characterized the missions on December 26, and that day did in fact see a larger effort that was more in line with Nixon's intent. Seventy-five B-52Ds flew against targets in and around Hanoi, and forty-five B-52Gs bombed targets near the less-heavily-defended Thai Nguyen, Haiphong, and Phuc Yen areas, sensible allocations given the weaker ECM capabilities of the B-52Gs. Day eight also witnessed a major improvement in tactics. All the B-52s arrived over their targets at basically the same time: only fifteen minutes passed from the time the first bomb exited a bomb bay to the last. They approached from many different directions, at different altitudes, and delayed their post-attack turns until well outside the range of the missile batteries, all with the intent of overloading the defenses.[99]

Most of the B-52s made modest, shallow-bank, post-attack turns; only the ones attacking the Thai Nguyen Railroad Yard made a 180-degree, high-bank turn but did so sufficiently far away from the SA-2s launch sites to evade the missiles (about twenty-one miles), and they broke it into two ninety-degree turns. In terms of jamming, two transmitters jammed the ground radars and a third jammed the missile downlink frequency. Another way the B-52s defended themselves was with a 1,000-foot altitude reduction two minutes before they opened their bomb bays along with sudden minor heading changes. A later evaluation argued that the new tactics, plus the addition of a chaff blanket, as opposed to chaff streams, were a marked improvement against the missiles.[100] While SA-2s did shoot down two B-52s that night, both were members of a two-jet cell, which of course had just two-thirds of the ECM wattage of a standard formation.[101] Flying in groups of less than three aircraft violated an earlier directive.

Tactically and operationally the December 26 missions were successful; at least the aircrews got to fly them with the most sensible tactics. One hundred thirteen B-52s hit "10 different targets at approximately the same time."[102] "This is the one that came from all directions at once and it worked out beautifully," Moorer wrote in his diary. Observantly, he and General Meyer believed the pace of American operations was persuading the North Vietnamese to use up their SAMs.[103] The magnitude of the supporting aircraft personified the force package: twenty-eight Iron Hand, twenty-four chaff, fifty-two escorts, and nine jammers. Ninety-five tankers fueled fighters and B-52s. In addition, strike aircraft from three aircraft carriers focused on SAM sites and SA-2 storage warehouses. Receiving their flight plans at the last minute complicated their efforts to fly where and when they were supposed to. The tactical changes for day eight were not magic. Bombers from the 307th Bombardment Wing did everything right. They attacked from multiple axes at the same time and flew straight through the missile engagement zone, but SAMs still shot down two of their bombers. One exploded in front of Ebony 02, and seconds later another struck the bomber's back end. Although a missile struck Ash 01, it made it back to U-Tapao, only to stall and crash while attempting to land.[104]

The North Vietnamese shot down thirteen B-52s and a pair of F-111s by this time, which amounted to a loss rate of 3.38 percent for the B-52s, and 2.25 percent for the F-111s. Hanoi asserted that machine gun fire downed one of the F-111s. The B-52 loss rate was worse than predicted, but the North Vietnamese could not stop Operation Linebacker II.[105]

The mission flown on December 26 helped produce the campaign's most important dividend to date. As the bombers returned to their bases, the North Vietnamese proposed that a resumption of negotiations take place on January 8, 1973, which Kissinger considered to be a great concession on their part. The American counteroffer was a promise to stop the bombing thirty-six hours after the North Vietnamese accepted the American terms.[106] In order to maintain pressure on Le Duc Tho, Kissinger decided the announcement would take place after they had stopped the bombing. It makes sense that the North Vietnamese complied on this day because they had hurt the Americans with their best effort, and then the Americans essentially escalated and carried out missions that were more damaging and more shrewdly flown. At the same time Moorer, Meyer, Gayler, and Vogt finally acceded to a sortie pace that would provide enough bombers over the targets to maintain pressure on Tho, saturate North Vietnamese SAMs, send a lot of bombers on each mission—ninety, on average—and provide some time for maintenance: send sixty one day and 120 the next.[107] Because the North Vietnamese were finally agreeing to discuss a cease-fire, the Air Force would not have the opportunity to fully implement this change.

On December 27, the B-52s once again flew smarter tactics, approaching from four different directions with most of the bombers arriving within a few minutes of each other. Most flew straight ahead after their bomb run; just one group made a big post-attack turn. Only sixty B-52s participated, but this was weightier than the thirty-jet missions. Supporting F-111s suppressed missile sites near Hanoi for the first time during the campaign, including the troublesome site VN 549. Chaff inconvenienced the SAM operators, forcing them to use less-effective firing and tracking methods. While they managed to shoot down one B-52, Cobalt 01, that would be their last. The one LGB flight that had good weather at its target placed seven out of eight bombs on target; a big cloud obscured the targets for the other one. The B-52 Ash 02 lost use of its electrical and hydraulic systems and all four engines under its left wing after a missile exploded nearby. It limped almost all the way to Nakhon Phanom, escorted by the other two B-52s, where its crew ejected successfully. Cobalt 01 was not so lucky. An SA-2 hit it squarely just before bomb release. Maybe if a large chaff cloud instead of corridors was created to the west of Hanoi, someone proposed, the winds aloft could take it to the target area.[108]

Sixty sorties hit five different targets on December 28, employing the same basic B-52 tactics as on days eight and nine, but three of the waves still made risky post-attack turns. A railroad yard, an SA-2 battery, and two SAM storage sites were their targets. Six B-52 cells arrived over the yard from different quadrants almost simultaneously.[109] Three flights of Paveway-toting F-4s went after Hanoi Radio; two of them achieved direct hits with their bombs, with the other scoring a "near miss."[110] Day ten's operation was quite successful and less dangerous. Against sixty bombers and seventy-five support jets, the North Vietnamese fired no more than twenty missiles.[111] That was because the North Vietnamese were running out of assembled and fueled SA-2s. The pace of operations had revealed the weakness in the North Vietnamese air defenses: the ability to assemble, fuel, and distribute SAMs quickly enough to have plenty available to fire. The US discovered this during the operation from intelligence sources; as Admiral Moorer recalled, "We were intercepting messages calling for more missiles."[112] North Vietnam was now almost defenseless, providing a textbook example of factors at the operational level of war exerting a direct and conclusive effect on national policy. The North Vietnamese could not defend their airspace anymore and they could not inflict losses on the B-52s, hence their concession and agreement to resume negotiations.

General Clay stated that there were almost no targets remaining worth risking another B-52. He believed that they should send B-52s against "targets of lesser military value in the lower threat areas of RP-5, 6A, and 6B." They would still be over North Vietnam, bombing; leave the remaining targets in high-threat areas to fighter-bombers. This would reduce the risk of continued B-52 attrition, but because of the inability of the North Vietnamese to assemble SA-2s for action quickly enough, the skies had already become much less threatening.[113] Clay's directive was contrary to the president's specific directions and the president's willingness to accept losses, and contrary to the spirit of using force to compel diplomatic concessions. It seemed to prioritize protecting airframes over completing the assigned mission.

Given the diplomatic agenda behind these missions, heavy bombing still needed to be conducted near Hanoi, even if meant rebombing empty craters. B-52s evince a different meaning than tactical fighter attacks, and its name intimidates. Only B-52s can signal and coerce in their unique way.[114] The ability to fire but a handful of SAMs at sixty B-52s bombing aim points around Hanoi and Haiphong that had already been hit would have only magnified the helplessness of Le Duan and the rest of the leadership of North Vietnam and heightened the coercive effects of their flights. So the latter days of Linebacker II presented an even greater opportunity to coerce concessions out of the North Vietnamese, and Clay and Meyer missed it. Meyer was still thinking tactically: it was all about destroying targets, efficiently, and with very low loss rates. Those were not even the issues; pressuring the North Vietnamese into diplomatic concessions was the crux of the matter.

The North Vietnamese formally accepted the terms on December 28, and the Americans suggested that a Linebacker III could take place if Hanoi failed to follow through with a settlement.[115] Moorer was nevertheless skeptical that force had been used in a way that would result in a signed agreement. He really wished they had bombed *"until they signed instead of bombing until they agreed to talk* [italics in original]."[116]

Strategic Air Command planners should have recognized the differences between nuclear and conventional tactics at the beginning of the planning process and directed the cells to fly from multiple directions from the beginning, had them continue to fly straight ahead past the SAMs' range, and allowed them to dump their own chaff to defend themselves. The principles of concentration and unpredictability were not abstract. While the B-52s should have been employing the appropriate tactics from day one, for an organization the size and mulishness of Strategic Air Command to recognize and implement effective changes in less than a week was actually pretty responsive.

Shortly after the war the author Alan Dawson cited reports from several Eastern bloc and North Vietnamese sources "that if the United States had kept up its bombardments and port blockades, it could have demanded the surrender of North Vietnam."[117] For his part, Haig believed the bombing should have been continued until Hanoi withdrew its troops from South Vietnam, but congressional and public pressure to stop the bombing once the communists had agreed to talk was too great for Haig's preference. B-52s continued bombing targets in Southeast Asia after Linebacker II, just not within the borders of North Vietnam.[118]

The Americans did not immediately relent. Two more missions flew on December 29 (day eleven), when F-4 pathfinders led A-7Ds on another LORAN strike and B-52s hit a missile storage site, a railroad yard, and Trai Ca just before midnight.[119] The sixty B-52s attacked from multiple directions at the same time. Missile batteries fired just twenty-three SAMs against the B-52s attacking targets near Hanoi, a greatly diminished response compared to what they had received in the past.[120] Hazel, Perch, and Yellow Flights waited until they had flown well past their target near Hanoi before turning ninety degrees to the south, and Plaid,

Sable, and Brass Flights flew straight ahead well past their target. Five of the six waves were over their targets for only eight minutes, then they were gone, and Linebacker II was over.[121]

Like General Clay at PACAF, Pacific Command measured the effectiveness of Linebacker II in tactical and operational terms: loss rates and target destruction. The bombing seemed pretty effective: "Preliminary analysis indicated that 15 of the 34 authorized B-52 targets were damaged to the extent that restrike was not immediately warranted.... Linebacker II appeared to have achieved its goals."[122] Materially, the bombing had inflicted serious damage to North Vietnam's transportation network and its ability to support its war-making efforts, but they would be able to recover and rebuild.[123] The conception of effectiveness PACAF and PACOM expressed was limited to the completion of tasks—all completely necessary—but there was no mention of supporting policy goals. Likewise, the character of the "Daily Wrap Up" messages from General Vogt and Seventh AF focused solely on tactical results. There were no discussions and no analyses—only exacting reports on the munition and bombing result of each individual sortie and detailed findings of post-attack photo reconnaissance. The report for operations on December 24, for example, stated, "The F-111s struck the Hanoi port and barge facility with photography confirming the destruction of eight buildings with heavy to moderate damage to an additional 23 buildings."[124] Oftentimes, the daytime strikes by fighter-bombers went well, as was the case on December 27, and the report for that day noted the photographic evidence of the damage A-7Ds had inflicted upon two radio transmitters. Typically, the B-52 strikes were labeled effective, meaning that they released their bombs when they were supposed to; out of 5,508 bombs dropped, 354 were noneffective.[125] Measurability remained the determining factor for assessing effectiveness: if a B-52 "released at least 50 percent of its internal or external weapons load in an armed configuration," it was considered effective. In the past "at least 80 percent of the released weapons" had to impact "within the target area" as well for the sortie to be "effective," but since the B-52s were only flying at night, that was a measure that could not be taken with precision.[126] Nine out of ten bombs dropped during Linebacker II were from B-52s and F-111s, both of which relied on radar for aiming. LORAN-guided jets dispensed 6.5 percent, and laser-guided bombs accounted for just 2 percent. The most effective platform against area targets was the B-52, and the most accurate munition was the LGB.[127]

A 1973 Air Force study similarly focused on measurements of destruction, a useful starting point for assessing the outcomes of these missions, but also delved into broader effects. It found that bombing accomplished the most destruction against railroad yards, not only from B-52s, but also from F-4s and A-7Ds using unguided bombs, and from F-4s with LGBs. It also expected that bombs dropping so close to Hanoi probably left the residents quite rattled. The study noticed that while Paveways were extremely accurate, adequate destruction, of railroad yards in this instance, required many more bombs than an LGB mission would deliver. Results from LORAN-aimed A-7Ds were generally less than what was desired, probably because the targets were so far away from the transmitter.[128] Indeed, "It appears, statistically, that LORAN bombing made no significant contribution to the overall damage level during Linebacker II... analysis of LORAN strikes during Linebacker II indicated that even area-type targets were missed by a considerable margin."[129]

Seventh Air Force and SAC both considered the F-111s' support to have been excellent. Bombing defensive sites just prior to the arrival of B-52s over their targets was their main task, although they also struck targets all over North Vietnam.[130] The F-111s' ability to arrive undetected unnerved bystanders, but its bombing system could not aim the unguided bombs it used with the precision of a laser-guided bomb. Just as the Air Force recognized the problems with its predictable B-52 attack profiles, Seventh Air Force also noticed Aardvarks needed to vary attack times, approach, and escape headings. It was not an infallible aircraft; an F-111 sortie against the Viet Tri Thermal Power plant did not seem to damage it much at all.[131]

On its final page of the Linebacker II survey the authors expressed great reluctance to measure anything beyond the physical and the immediate: "The psychological impact of LINEBACKER II operations is extremely difficult to measure." They noted that urban residents wanted to leave the cities, which was unprecedented. They assumed that morale went down among the people but observed at the same time that there were no indicators that the regime's hold on the people had lessened in any way. The study asserted that the most important outcome of the bombing was the damage to the enemy's rail system. Only the last sentence connected the operation to political goals: "However, it should be noted that the North Vietnamese did return to the peace conference table following LINEBACKER II."[132] At no point did this analysis suggest air power applied the way it was during Linebacker II could have won the war in years past.

Given that either some in the military did not understand the relationship between military operations and the achievement of policy goals, or the JCS had not adequately explained the purpose of Linebacker II, I expect that the campaign worked because the president and the JCS assigned the Air Force and Navy tasks that would support the president's goals, so a full understanding of that on the part of planners at the operational level of war was not indispensable to its success. How much more effective would Linebacker II have been had everyone from ground and aircrews to the planners, targeteers, and wing commanders fully understood the actual purpose of the bombing and the relationship between military actions, diplomacy, and policy objectives is something worth debating.

Losses were significant. North Vietnam shot down nine B-52Ds and six B-52Gs, along with twelve additional aircraft. Moorer predicted the B-52s would suffer a 2 percent loss rate. Some Air Force histories were coy regarding the downing of B-52s, briefly listing the shoot-downs and avoiding any explanation about why they occurred.[133] Two years after the Battle of Hanoi, Hoang Tung, a spokesman for the central committee of the Lao Dong Party, stated that, "If we had not been able to bring down the B-52s the situation might have been different. Their side would have made other steps forward to impose their conditions."[134]

Soon after the end of the operation, a study offered some initial conclusions about why B-52s suffered high loss rates. It posited that there might have been as many as six fewer shot down had the B-52Gs, with their less-powerful jammers, not been sent to the SAM-dense area around Hanoi. The B-52s with the weaker ALT-6B jammer were shot down three times as frequently as those with ALT-22s. Routes should have been varied and timed to overwhelm defenses. Analysts admitted the post-attack turn was a mistake. Although the B-52s received jamming support from specialized aircraft, that was not enough; their own on-board jammers were critical to survival.[135] The Air Force credited chaff as the B-52s' best protector. No B-52 flying in the middle of a chaff cloud was shot down.[136]

Strategic Air Command and Eighth Air Force backtracked, noting that they scheduled an intense sortie rate for the first three days because they did not expect a longer campaign. The SAC planners claimed that no one had ever flown "sustained operations over a heavily defended target area" before, which was an odd assertion considering that the generals and colonels in charge in 1972 had flown the bombing raids of World War II. They also conceded that the first missions were repetitive enough to allow the North Vietnamese to make adjustments sufficiently lethal that the bombers faced unsustainable loss rates.[137] That, frankly, was inexcusable. Anyone with an amateur's knowledge of past military operations would have known better than to fly the same approach heading, altitude, airspeed, separation, and post-attack turn night after night. Amateurs in operational art, Nixon and Kissinger, recognized at once that this predictability was an invitation to an enemy with a proven ability to learn and adapt to shoot down their bombers in significant numbers. The deeper cause was the lack of foresight within Strategic Air Command, which managed the operation from its base in Nebraska.[138]

The North Vietnamese had something to do with all of this, too. They kept their new T-8209 radar largely under wraps before the operation. It was able to provide range data to SAM batteries, and operators could blend that data with their own radar. Altogether the batteries could fire their missiles in such a way to leave the targeted aircraft less time to maneuver.[139] Months after the operation the commanding general of PACAF admitted the PAVN Air Force was able to learn quickly from their observations of American tactics, particularly the predictable and unimaginative way the B-52s flew their missions.[140]

Lieutenant General George J. Eade concluded in 1973 that Linebacker II's most significant outcome was the signing of a cease-fire and the extraction of the United States from the war. He concluded "the fact that a suitable climate was established for serious peace negotiations was in large part due to the constant pressure airpower was able to sustain."[141] The North Vietnamese also got what they wanted: the Americans out of the war. "According to the agreement, the United States was forced to recognize the independence, sovereignty, and territorial integrity of Vietnam."[142]

The annual history of CINCPAC argued the first priority for a successful air campaign is selecting targets the destruction of which would have the most impact on the enemy's ability to make war. The second was "the correct application of forces (in strength and frequency) to achieve the desired level of damage to the selected targets."[143] That line of reasoning assumed that if air power could destroy all the worthwhile targets in a relatively efficient manner, then victory was automatically achieved. Their thought process did not account for the ultimate political goals a president issued. It instead assumed a connection between the destruction of targets and the enemy's capability or will to continue the war. The thing is, an enemy subjected to such a focused and successful bombardment could still respond with a policy and attitude that they had not been defeated, they will not quit, and they will continue to wage war with the remaining capacity they still possessed. Furthermore, this 1973 analysis mentions North Vietnamese "war-making potential." The main war-making potential the North Vietnamese possessed was their people and their political will to continue the war; they did not have the large vulnerable industrial base of, say, Germany in 1943—not even close. Furthermore, China and the Soviet Union could sustain their physical means of waging war, particularly below the level of mechanized war that characterized the Easter Offensive, indefinitely. In addition, if a country's population embodies its war-making potential, a combatant state must try to kill off that enemy's population in order to force them to quit the war. Given America's policy goals in December 1972 of getting out of the war, not to mention its cultural traditions about war, including an ambivalence about targeting civilians, inflicting demographically devastating casualties on the North Vietnamese was not going to be considered. Almost as bothersome in this analysis is the absence of a thoughtful discussion regarding the president's policy goals. Nixon directed a coercive bombing campaign against the political will of a politburo, not a bombing campaign against economic targets.

The CINCPAC history mentions one train of thought that could have led the military toward a more explicit connection between targeting and policy goals: "As the LINEBACKER campaign continued, it became apparent that a more positive and rapid method of target selection and validation was required. Priorities were changing to include targets of high visibility and psychological impact," but the train of thought went back to a theme of the management of violence, not the use of violence to achieve policy goals.[144]

Some problems were recognized, and others were not perceived. The procedures for requesting permission to hit new targets were slow given the telecommunications technology of 1972. General Meyer's office noted that it recommended a SAM storage site for bombing on December 24 and did not get permission to hit it for two days. It took another two days for American bombers to be sent after that target. The greatest complaint, however, demonstrates a marked lack of understanding of the relationship between military force and policy goals. The commander-in-chief of the Pacific Fleet complained about having to select tactics that kept civilian casualties to a minimum, prevented bombs from landing on ships that did not belong to the North Vietnamese, and to not send flights through the buffer zone with China: "these policies restricted operational tactics and raised aircrew risk," and these "restrictions require aircrews to select approaches and tactics which may not permit optimum tactics or safe execution."[145] So apparently tactical considerations and the safety of airmen who were supposed to go in harm's way took precedence over not providing the North Vietnamese with a propaganda coup of dead civilians, not harming relations with neutral countries by bombing their ships, and not creating a diplomatic crisis with China by way of airspace violations—each of which was very important to the achievement of the president's agenda. These restrictions, however, were not the reason behind the shoot-downs of B-52s; credit for that goes to the tactical choices Strategic Air Command made on its own on how to employ B-52s and to the adaptations of the North Vietnamese Air Force.

Linebacker II was not a case of unrestrained bombing. It was actually a component of an exit strategy. Historian George Herring rejected comparisons between the Christmas bombings and operations like the bombing of Dresden and Tokyo: "American pilots went to extraordinary lengths to avoid civilian casualties, and large numbers of civilians had already been evacuated from the major cities."[146] Vietnamese leaders evacuated two-thirds of their people from Hanoi by the time the Christmas bombings began, which contributed to the low casualty rate that Hanoi reported of 1,318 killed and 1,261 wounded. The mayor of Hanoi, Tran Day Hung, asserted that the Americans bombed "our populated area," but that they killed so few because of the "evacuation plan." The North Vietnamese admitted that the Americans targeted the outskirts of Hanoi, not the city center, and asserted that they did so to kill more people, not fewer, because the people had been moved to the outskirts of the city. The *Washington Post* reporter who wrote this story added that the Americans "adamantly deny that their strategic objective was to kill masses of people in the Hanoi and Haiphong areas."[147] They were targeting the outlying areas because that was where the valuable targets were. The vice head of the hospital a stray bomb hit later noted that "none of our regular child patients was killed, for we had already evacuated," but forty members of the hospital staff died as a result of the bombing.[148] Indeed, the North Vietnamese asserted that they had achieved a victory of endurance against the American bombs.[149] In asserting that it was a victory for Hanoi, the mayor stated, "Without such a defeat [B-52 shoot downs] I don't think Nixon would ever have come to terms in Paris." They claimed kills of thirty-four B-52s, five F-111s, and forty-two additional aircraft.[150]

An irony was that Nixon and Kissinger provided civilian oversight and direction to the missions to a greater degree than President Johnson had. The civilian oversight in December 1972 helped maintain the high sortie rates and thus kept the pressure on the communists. The Nixon administration was also pursuing goals that were more achievable than President Johnson's, while the Johnson administration approached the use of force with reluctance.

In examining the effectiveness of Rolling Thunder and Linebacker, there is a consensus that Rolling Thunder did not achieve the Johnson administration's goals, but that Linebacker, and especially Linebacker II, were policy successes. Explanations diverge greatly. One school of thought argues Rolling Thunder failed because the bombing did not inflict enough pain and destruction in a sudden enough manner to shock the leadership in Hanoi into complying with American requirements. Because Rolling Thunder was a halting series of missions with a long list of sanctuaries and prohibited targets, the North Vietnamese had the chance to adapt and adjust. Restrictions were far fewer, and the intensity of the bombing was greater during Linebacker, particularly in December 1972. At first glance, the consequences of Linebacker II prove that unrestrained bombing will win a coercive campaign, and the manner in which it was waged served as an indictment of the gradual escalation policy of the Johnson years.[151] But the raids were neither indiscriminate nor unrestrained; ambassadors and their staffs, for instance, found Hanoi safe enough that they remained in the city. Admiral Moorer noted that intelligence eavesdropping revealed the government in Hanoi was confident the bombings were not taking place with the intent to destroy the city, so much so that they relocated supplies into Hanoi for safe keeping.[152] Target and weapon choices also undercut the carpet-bombing argument. Railroad yards cover the area of many football fields and were the B-52s' targets on December 24, for example; targets requiring more fidelity received the attention of fighter-bombers using either carefully aimed or laser-guided bombs. The places bombed were legal targets, and Bach Mai Hospital, accidentally hit by errant bombs (according to SAC), was next to a railroad line, a Radio Hanoi station, an airfield, and an army barracks.[153] The targets included Hanoi Railroad Repair Shops, Yen Vien Railroad Repair Yards, Ai Mo Warehouse, High No Vehicle Repair Shops, Kinh No Railroad Repair Shops, Kinh No Railroad Yards, Kinh No Railroad Spurs, Nguyen The Storage Area, Thai Nguyen Thermal Power Plant, Phuc Yen Airfield, Kep Airfield, Yen Bai Airfield, Hoa Lac Airfield, Bac Giang transshipment point—all of them lawful, legitimate targets.[154]

Rolling Thunder and Linebacker were waged under two profoundly different geopolitical contexts, against two very different kinds of invasions, for two differing reasons, pursuing different goals. These distinctions account for the relative success of Linebacker. In the late 1980s Earl H. Tilford and Mark Clodfelter first pointed out the flaws in the assertion that if only the United States had bombed in 1965 the way they had in December 1972 the war would have been won in a week.[155] During Rolling Thunder, the American goal was to persuade Hanoi to cut off its supplying, supporting, and infiltrating of troops and materiel into South Vietnam and evacuate it. President Johnson also wanted the communist government to give up its pursuit of taking over South Vietnam, a political goal of sacred importance to them, and leave it be. By December 1972, the United States' objective was to persuade the North Vietnamese to sign a cease-fire in which the United States largely left Southeast Asia behind, and in which the North Vietnamese army got to remain in South Vietnam—two things the North Vietnamese wanted most. In 1965, China promised to intervene in the war militarily if the US waged an overly aggressive bombing campaign against North Vietnam, and especially if American troops invaded the Red River Valley. Truly massive B-52 raids against North Vietnam were not even an option in 1965 because the Air Force did not begin modifying B-52Ds into "big belly" variants modified to carry 108 bombs until December; before that, they could only carry twenty-seven 500-pound bombs internally, in addition to the twenty-four carried under its wings. These modifications were not completed until 1967.[156] In 1972 the Chinese wished to nurture a friendship with the US as a counterbalance to the USSR, a goal more important to them than the absolute protection of North Vietnam against an enemy that was leaving the war. The infrastructure for land-based air power in Southeast Asia was sparse in 1965 compared to what was in place in 1972. In 1965 the United States was escalating its involvement; in 1972 it was leaving. In sum, the violence of Linebacker II, although more intense and concentrated than that of Rolling Thunder—especially as waged in 1965—was carried out in pursuit of more limited goals that were easier for the Americans to achieve and for the North Vietnamese and the Chinese to accept.

The cause-and-effect relationship between Linebacker II and the Paris Agreement has also been the subject of much debate. Gareth Porter concluded that Linebacker II did not coerce the North Vietnamese to negotiate, but instead left the Americans with no choice but to return to the talks in January. Ulysses S. Grant Sharp argued the bombing was persuasive enough, but the enemy also knew that political realities precluded a repeat of Linebacker II.[157] George Herring had no doubts the bombing persuaded the North Vietnamese to sign a peace accord, but that did not mean that the North Vietnamese capitulated to all American demands.[158] Robert Brigham relied on Mai Van Bo when claiming the communists returned to the talks "because Hanoi and the NLF had concluded that international public opinion and the U.S. Congress now demanded that the Nixon administration produce a final settlement," but the connection is not explained.[159] Timothy Lomperis believed the bombings were necessary to compel Hanoi to meet the United States halfway.[160] Robert Dallek and Dave Richard Palmer saw an obvious cause-and-effect relationship between the bombing and the settlement.[161] The operation did not lead China, one of North Vietnam's sponsors, to suggest that Hanoi stand fast against the perfidious Americans. On the contrary, Zhou Enlai encouraged Le Duc Tho to be flexible: "Let the Americans leave as quickly as possible. In a half year or one year the situation will change."[162] Sure enough, the third main actor, President Thieu, relented on January 22, 1973, and promised to endorse the ceasefire agreement. Bombing the North Vietnamese until they removed their army from South Vietnam was not going to happen because Nixon believed Congress would remove him from office if he embarked on that kind of operation. Air strikes continued to bomb the North Vietnamese Army south of the 20th parallel until the agreement was signed on January 27.[163]

The air war continued in Laos after the signing of the cease-fire between the Vietnams. American air forces flew a rush of missions against targets in that country before the cease-fire for Laos was enacted a few weeks later.[164] In the opinion of General Vang Pao, F-111s were instrumental prior to the February 22, 1973, bombing halt in forestalling another PAVN offensive. February 22 was a cease-fire in name only. Violations quickly mounted, as did American air sorties—nearly 6,000 that month—but they finally ended for good on April 17, 1973.[165] North Vietnamese forces initiated attacks against hundreds of villages in South Vietnam just before the armistice date. Subsequently, both sides fought pitched battles to seize control of as much territory as possible in South Vietnam. Irrespective of North Vietnamese violations, Congress forced an end to American military involvement, which terminated on August 15, 1973.[166]

Conclusions

Examining air power effectiveness during the Vietnam War drives one to examine deeper and larger issues. Air power has been put on trial for Rolling Thunder, but it is the wrong defendant. Air operations were only an accessory to an effort comprised of poorly thought-out strategies based on ill-thought assumptions. Assertions that air power failed to win the war in Vietnam flirt with the *post hoc ergo propter hoc* logical fallacy; Vietnam was not a failure of air power or ground power or a failure of counterinsurgency or conventional warfare, it was a failure of war. Senior leaders never executed the war in a manner the relational complexity of Southeast Asia required.

American air power was about as successful as it could have been given the character of the war. Even with the problems American air forces had with immature technology, atrophied tactical skills, and limitations in the air picture available to the pilots, air superiority was never really in doubt. It was no surprise they were eminently effective at airlift and air-to-air refueling because of their roots in American logistical practices. Tanker and airlift operations were exercises in logistics and scheduling, so they resided in the middle of America's managerial strengths. Likewise tactical airlift grew out of a country that always had to move freight and people over continental distances, on ships, railroads, and then through airliners. Photo reconnaissance required a series of processes of flying and photographing. Its shortcoming lay not in completing missions but in realizing at the strategic level how debilitating a problem it was to not be able to easily find the enemy underneath the cover of trees. Close air support was a tactical operation American forces conducted with considerable skill. In general, strike aircraft arrived quickly and bombed accurately. Bad rainstorms, nighttime, and low clouds could ground close air support aircraft, excepting the B-52 and the A-6A—thus the continuing need for artillery.

Operationally, the United States air forces were well organized to fly missions in ways that were reliable, reasonably efficient, and predictable to policy makers. The only serious glitch was the temporary bomb shortage of April–May 1966, an example of poor management. The practice of sending fighter-bombers on missions with just a couple of bombs to keep sortie counts up put men unjustifiably at risk, but it was not a truly significant event in terms of achieving strategic goals, since full bomb loads were not persuading the North Vietnamese anyway.[1] The strike package was a skillful adaptation to the threats the mix of SAMs, antiaircraft artillery, and MiGs produced. Large air operations were not new to the Air Force and Navy, given their experiences in World War II and Korea. Since they were management problems the Americans would conduct them efficiently. The main deficiency was the absence of a single manager for air operations. Even such an office existed, however, its efficiencies would not have been sufficient to win the war.

Close air support was most effective when combined with aggressive ground operations, particularly against conventional forces, a common practice by 1972. Close air support was operationally effective that year: air strikes combined with ARVN tenacity prevented the North Vietnamese from achieving their objective. Only the utter destruction of the PAVN would have been strategically conclusive given Hanoi's determination to conquer South Vietnam. Therefore, the strategic effectiveness of CAS was dependent not on tactical skill or operational execution, as important as those were, but on policy makers' intentions. To have concluded the war favorably, close air support would have to have been attached to a strategically decisive approach—in this situation, wiping out the PAVN. President Thieu's forces lacked the capacity to pursue that goal, starkly evident after the American withdrawal.

When it came to coercive bombing, air interdiction, and close air support, American aircrews could usually hit and destroy intended targets. Destruction became certain with the introduction of precision-guided munitions. Targeting intelligence was, as always, crucial. If one cannot find the enemy, whether through photographs or through human intelligence, then a military organization cannot fight him. Finding guerrillas and trucks was a particularly serious problem for this aerial siege.

Some of the lessons of Vietnam were self-evident from the beginning, others were not always learned or applied, and a few are faulty. Most aircrews discovered from the start that their training had not prepared them well for combat. Not until three years after the American withdrawal did the Air Force initiate the Red Flag exercises, turning American air forces into ready-to-use instruments of power. Missiles failed to work as advertised, but the services continued to treat them like rounds of ammunition and not as temperamental aircraft in their own right. Drones proved especially useful for photo reconnaissance. Managing close air support well enough to confer short response times is challenging. An air war needs a single person in charge. The more one coordinates air interdiction and close air support with ground war operations, the more effective each is at every level. Fighters can function well as bombers, tanker aircraft are indispensable, precision-guided munitions are revolutionary, and air strikes can and should be blended with diplomacy.

Nixon made a keen observation while the North Vietnamese flinched in 1972. He noticed the Soviets and Chinese gave their client material assistance but did not send their own infantry and fighter squadrons: "They've made the North do it themselves. . . . I think that one of the great lessons out of this war, looking to the future, is that Americans are basically paternalistic in our attitudes toward all countries we've helped, and we weaken them. We weaken them because we want to do it ourselves." Instead, the United States ought to require people under attack to fight the war themselves.[2] As a consequence, he developed the Nixon Doctrine. China already understood the wisdom of support that was narrow and focused. While more than 300,000 People's Liberation Army troops served in North Vietnam, they did not fight Hanoi's war.[3]

Other lessons are so rooted in anger they became part of the memory of the war, whether legitimate or not. Earl Tilford and Mark Clodfelter inflicted head shots to the "if only we'd bombed in 1965 like we did in 1972 we'd have won the war in a week" myth three decades ago, only to find that the assertion reanimates itself like a zombie. Similar is the argument that the bombing restrictions lost the war, an assertion seen as so obviously true that no one tests that thesis. It is as if the institutional memory conflates the failure of the war that included an air campaign with a failure of air power—the Vietnam War was not air power's to win or lose.

American air forces were able to inflict considerable costs on the communist war effort when targeting materiel and supply routes deep within North Vietnam. When the 1968 bombing halts shifted the air interdiction effort to a place replete with advantages for the enemy—Laos—it became impossible for bombing supply routes to generate conclusive effects. Policy decisions forced air power to be used against logistical routes in a manner that was worse than suboptimal, it was misleading. Bombing missions had enough trouble when they could hit targets inside North Vietnam. When they had to strike hundreds of miles away from the true choke points of Haiphong Harbor and the railroad lines from China, they had to find and destroy a dispersed, camouflaged enemy in Laos. For pilots and cameras to see all, through the jungle of Laos and Cambodia, and then destroy all with precision, was a physically impossible task that should never have been expected to produce decisive results in the first place. Doctrine on air interdiction was sound during Vietnam, but the air forces were prohibited from following doctrine sensibly until 1972. Fear of Chinese intervention, a factor outside of air power, ensured air interdiction could not be pursued in the most effective manner until policy makers addressed that concern.

American leaders assumed that a form of air warfare that was successful in one context would be equally successful in another. Why wouldn't bombing a weaker actor in the same manner that was successful against a stronger power work equally well? North Vietnam was weaker than Germany and Japan had been, but it was also far less vulnerable to coercive bombing and interdiction. So-called "strategic bombing"—actually the bombing of factories, refineries, and supply networks—was carried out under the assumption that if one destroys the factories that produce and fuel a mechanized armed force, that army can no longer wage war and will either capitulate or be destroyed. For bombing to hope to bring an enemy to its knees and to the negotiating table, that enemy must have vital centers it cannot live without. Those vital centers did not exist in North Vietnam. North Vietnam had no critical economic infrastructure or factories, and its economy had nothing in common with those of Germany and Japan in World War II. The vital targets lay in the Soviet Union and China. Rolling Thunder could not function as strategic bombing because there was no finite target set in North Vietnam that, if destroyed, wrecked Hanoi's strategy, or advanced Washington's to the point of concluding the war. Certainly the bombing halt of 1968 was an incompetent decision since it took away most of the incentives for the communists to ever negotiate in good faith, and it terminated an attrition campaign that was at least making it more difficult for the communists to wage their war, but broader issues exerted more influence on the effectiveness of military power.

Ultimately China's shadow meant the United States and South Vietnam would have to find a way to destroy the NLF and the PAVN without being able to attack either of the two centers of gravity: China's protection of its client and the Lao Dong Party membership themselves via an invasion and conquest of North Vietnam. Ensuring South Vietnam's sovereignty without slaying either of those foci was a tall and possibly hopeless order.

During the Vietnam War, air operations collided with problems that lay beyond the realm of air power, and an examination of air power in the Vietnam War drives us toward larger issues. Geopolitics disrupted the effectiveness of air power more than did the nature of air power or its machinery. The basic problem lay in the magnitude of the national security threats to the United States, the policy goals the United States set, and the commitment of the Vietnamese Communists to their agenda. One must remember that the Lao Dong Party weaved together extreme nationalism with fanatical communism. They were willing to endure massive death rates over a long period of time in order to unify Vietnam. They were willing to trade the destruction of their own country if in the end they could outlast the persistence of Saigon's sponsor. For them, the Southeast Asia War was more than a total war, it was existential and almost a religious pursuit. These facts provided them with a foundation of persistence the government in Saigon and especially the Americans likely could not match. In determining whether a war is limited or total, the other side has a vote, and a small regime may in fact be able to stuff the ballot box, if you will, in its favor if its commitment to its cause is exponentially greater than that of the great power it is fighting. In the end, the tie breaker goes to the side willing to suffer and endure more.

The Americans never understood the degree to which the Lao Dong Party devoted itself to absolute and complete victory. Because the members of that political movement were committed to victory at any and all costs, they had more leverage, and the only way South Vietnam and its sponsor could achieve their policy goals was to apply force in a manner and magnitude that permanently prevented the communists from reaching their ambition. Because the North Vietnamese considered the war their highest national priority, the Americans had to respond in kind to have a shot at winning the war and securing the peace thereafter. But of course the war was never the United States' greatest national security interest, so the value of the war to the communists gave Hanoi a strategic advantage. They were committed to an unlimited goal, which gave them more staying power and endurance, while the Americans did not really want to fight the war in the first place. They were engaged to preserve a friend of convenience and to protect their credibility with more important allies. The nature of the United States' purpose for involvement placed a cap on American commitment and endurance that was below that of their enemy.

The problems the air campaign had in stopping infiltration point to flaws in the policy and strategy choices presidents and their generals made. Since the United States refused to completely cut off the Ho Chi Minh Trail it had to use force that, to be decisive, required a concurrent ground war to bring the enemy to battle to such a degree that the combination of air and ground warfare forced the PAVN and VC to fight intensely until they ran out of supplies completely and collapsed. The US and South Vietnam would not fight that intensely, and the US was never going to use ground forces to cut off and shut down the Ho Chi Minh Trail. The US was never going to invade the Red River Valley either, because Hanoi's sponsors intimidated the United States into taking decisive operations off the table. Geopolitical concerns prevented interdiction from being fully implemented. Free from the most serious threats, North Vietnam could endure the siege secure in the knowledge that invasion did not threaten its territory. The geopolitical situation, not military factors, predetermined these choices.

Americans wanted tactical and operational excellence and weight of effort to overcome impossible geopolitical conditions. Two flawed assumptions surrounded the bomb-the-hell-out-of-them argument: the United States had the ability and the will to bomb North Vietnam sufficiently to persuade the Hanoi government to permanently withdraw its forces back into their own country, and the issue was up for negotiation in Hanoi. The argument replies that if only the Air Force and Navy could have been permitted to destroy every target the JCS could find, of course the North Vietnamese would have sought terms. But Vietnam was a clash of two wills, not target sets, and the Americans badly underestimated the willingness of their enemy to accept hundreds of thousands of bombs and thousands of dead kinsmen in order to outlast their attacker who wished only to win quickly, with the least possible losses, and leave. Not perceiving those relationships was a failure of war.

America's effort in Southeast Asia was, moreover, a failure of war in that its grand strategy did not adequately meld its elements of power into an application of force that maximized the effects of each. North Vietnam's aggression was a criminal violation of the UN charter, but President Johnson would not embark on a sufficiently assertive information campaign around the world, inside the UN and out, to label the Hanoi regime the aggressor and the South Vietnamese people the victims. Effective labeling of aggressor and victim would have given legitimacy to more aggressive actions on the part of the United States. Diplomacy and rhetoric had to precede American escalation, but that would have distracted political energy from Johnson's Great Society social programs. American policy was a failure of war because the Johnson administration refused to fully face up to and acknowledge all the difficult implications of the geopolitical situation and also of China's protection of North Vietnam; it instead tried to avoid them. Grand strategy had to undermine the communists' geopolitical situation if military coercion was going to resolve the conflict. No one seemed to realize South Vietnam's boundary with its enemy was an impossibly long geographical expanse to defend. That too was a failure of war. Its border with communist operating areas actually ran from the DMZ to the Gulf of Thailand.

The most fundamental failure of the war was not the misuse of air power but the lack of a competent understanding of statecraft on the part of the American executive branch. Leaders and advisors did not understand the relationship between diplomacy, national objectives, military force, communicating to the international public, and determination. Halting the bombing of targets in North Vietnam in the belief that that would encourage conclusive negotiations was asinine. Proof of the malpractice of statecraft came when the US attempted that failed tactic over and over after it had not only failed in May 1965, but after the North Vietnamese exploited each bombing pause to gain military advantages.

Since there was a mismatch between the respective forces in terms of policy goals, the United States was going to have to execute a war of limited aims with limited means with exquisite precision and skill, a rare occurrence. Given American traditions, the recent experiences of World War II and Korea, and the way in which the standoff with the Soviet Union in Europe had steered the American military toward mechanized warfare and away from being prepared for guerrilla warfare, not to mention the complex political-guerrilla-conventional warfare of Mao Tse-tung the Vietnamese Communists had adopted, selecting and executing the right strategy and tactics in Vietnam from the beginning and keeping it a war of limited commitment and means was beyond the cognitive capabilities of the United States' leaders.

It is commonly argued that great powers have the luxury and skill to wage small, limited wars successfully against hostile regimes with a minimum of commitment. Vietnam proved that to be a myth. The superpowers wanted to expand and defend their ways of life—communism and liberal democracy—and those were unlimited goals, but they dare not risk a direct clash with each other lest they find themselves hurtling toward a nuclear confrontation neither wanted. Supporting the wars of their client states was certainly a better choice for the superpowers than trying to settle the issue once and for all. But the pursuit of proxy wars, the theory of limited war, and the preponderance of military power the superpowers had relative to their smaller adversaries led the United States in particular to discount or even omit the ideological commitment and willpower of a small country such as North Vietnam and the National Liberation Front when assessing the relative power of each protagonist. Thus, we have the myth of limited war: that a great power can easily defeat a small, backward country with a minimum of commitment, materiel, violence, and time. The myth of limited war convinces great powers that they determine when victory or defeat takes place—but the other country has a vote, too. Indeed, in the case of the Vietnam War, the United States could not ultimately determine when victory occurred. It thought it could because of the preponderance of its material power, but in fact the communists were not defeated until and unless they had decided they were defeated.

These wars are neither small nor limited to the countries fighting them. The myth of limited war does not support arguments for a blunt force, unrestricted firepower kind of war in which the civilian leadership turns all aspects of war over to the military. That is not a path to victory, but instead is a lazy approach that finds the complexity of war, force, diplomacy, politics, and information warfare too challenging. The myth of limited war is also a chimera because it downplays or disregards the intangible strengths of the adversary. So-called small wars demand huge amounts of violence, killing, and destruction to convince the enemy that he has been defeated and that he will not be able to reconstitute himself after a time. Indeed, one must conceive all this in the simplest terms: victory takes place when force overcomes the enemy's will to resist and convinces the enemy that his defeated status is permanent, not temporary.[4]

Expecting an application of limited force to achieve complete success against an uncompromising policy does not add up. Victory for the United States would have required several choices too costly for the country to undertake. The "Wise Men" should have perceived this. The United States would have had to commit huge ground forces to a regional war because that is what the NLF and the PAVN were doing already. Were the American people willing to commit, say, an additional 750,000 draftees per year to such a war? Because of the commitment of the North Vietnamese to a unified Communist Vietnam, the United States would have had to invade and conquer North Vietnam. And it would have had to convince the world that the American action was neither neo-colonialism nor unduly cruel. The United States would also have had to convince the Chinese that an occupation of North Vietnam by a million mechanized American troops was no threat to their security. Defeating an enemy that was both rabidly nationalist and rabidly communist required persuading the adversary to give up core political and ideological values. Winning an ideological war like that is anything but limited. Achieving the desired outcome requires tools of persuasion that lie far beyond the components of air or ground warfare and requires the United States to blend battlefield events with the realm of governance, and further required the United States to see Vietnam as closer to a total war than a limited war.

An additional failure was the lost opportunity to learn during the war. The pounding North Vietnam was willing to take and the effort it was willing to expend should have made it clear that there was absolutely nothing limited whatsoever about the Hanoi government. Neither presidential administration, Johnson's especially, ever truly understood what it was dealing with: a regime willing to endure the destruction of its own country in pursuit of conquest. Furthermore, Vietnam was a hybrid of insurgency from within, conquest from without, terrorism, revolutionary activism, guerrilla warfare, and conventional warfare.

The United States understood military operations; it did not understand war as well as it thought it did. Neither administration understood how to measure success. Quants rarely measure policy success in war. If the enemy gives up its fundamental policy objective, you have succeeded in the most important way. Victory was not synonymous with successful operations or tactically effective applications of firepower, important as those are. The enemy's behavior is the ultimate metric. Victory would come when the United States and South Vietnam convinced their enemies that no matter what they did, they would be worse off tomorrow, and that there is no hope of anything better. The South Vietnamese would have achieved victory when the surviving communist revolutionaries voiced their complaints as a member of the loyal opposition, something beyond the nature of communism. Le Duc Tho observed: "You think military power can make our people submit. I think you are mistaken. Your defeat in Vietnam—where does it lie? Your defeat mainly lies in your wrong assessment of the political forces of our people in standing up against you."[5]

And what of the South Vietnamese; was it not their war to win? Not by themselves. They had to have a sponsor because their enemies had two who provided massive amounts of aid. South Vietnam was a weak state trying to develop beneficial connections between Saigon and outlying areas while overcoming its own authoritarian tendencies. It was a weak regime trying to construct a non-totalitarian state while subjected to a fierce guerrilla war by the National Liberation Front which had the full support of the North Vietnamese Army. North Vietnam was a strong, united authoritarian country. The stars would have had to align perfectly for the South Vietnamese to build a state and defeat an insurgency and later a conventional invasion at the same time.

Collectively, these failures poisoned the context within which air power expected to function and limited its possibilities for contributing to successfully concluding the war. It is doubtful Rolling Thunder could have ever coerced the North Vietnamese to evacuate their neighbors' territory, not because of the efficacy of bombing, but because of the monomania of the Communist Party in Hanoi. The overarching concern over escalation and Chinese intervention limited air power's ability to coerce. The limited commitment to the war led to casualty avoidance and undercut the effectiveness of close air support. Lyndon Johnson's feckless statecraft produced the bombing halts and prevented air interdiction from having any hope of decisive success. The chronic indeterminate results of air operations, counter-insurgency warfare, and operational strategies were symptoms of a lack of understanding of conflict, war, and peace.

A few authors have made compelling arguments that the Vietnam War was actually a strategic victory for the United States and its Asian friends in the Cold War. Although the United States lost the Vietnam War, it nonetheless achieved important geopolitical goals. John Colvin, the United Kingdom's consul general in Hanoi in 1966 and 1967, wrote in 1980 that American involvement gave other countries in the region time to establish growing free market economies and liberalizing polities. Moreover, "The existence in liberty of the Association of Southeast Asian Nations (Malaysia, Indonesia, Singapore, the Philippines, Thailand) and the prosperity and independence of Japan, South Korea, and Taiwan all spring from the United States' resistance to tyranny in Vietnam. They are living monuments to the American dead in Indochina and to all those men of the United States armed forces whose presence in Vietnam gave the rest of Asia the time to grow, un-harassed and at peace. The war was not in vain."[6] Bruce Palmer reached similar conclusions, and the war may have left North Vietnam too exhausted to knock over any more dominoes besides Laos and Cambodia.[7] Ironically, Warren Bell observed, the country that was defeated was and "remains more powerful than the one that won."[8] Michael Lind wrote an argument in 1999 I cannot counter that the Vietnam War, while a loss for the United States, was a strategic victory in the Cold War.[9] Most recently, Wen-Qing Ngoei assessed the Vietnam War as a successful containment of Chinese and Soviet expansionism that supported the agendas of regimes from Manila to Jakarta.[10] But what a costly victory.

Notes

Introduction

1. The views expressed in this work are those of the author and do not reflect the official policy of the United States government, the Department of Defense, or Air University.
2. United States Military Assistance Command, *Vietnam Command History 1969, Volume 1* (Saigon: Military History Branch, Office of the Secretary, Joint Staff Headquarters, 1969), p. v-192), found online at: https://www.scribd.com/document/81654495/Command-History-1969-Volume-I.

Chapter 1

1. For more background to the Vietnam War see John Lewis Gaddis, *The Cold War: A New History* (New York: Penguin, 2006). For a nice overview of the war, see Charles Neu, *America's Lost War: Vietnam, 1945–1975* (Hoboken, NJ: Wiley Blackwell, 2005). More extensive coverage is in John Prados, *Vietnam: The History of an Unwinnable War, 1945–1975* (Lawrence: University Press of Kansas, 2009).
2. The USAF Concept for Limited War, October 1, 1962, K417.01, July–December 1962, Vol. 3. Air Force Historical Research Agency, Maxwell Air Force Base, Alabama (hereafter referred to as AFHRA).
3. Andrew F. Krepinevich, *The Army and Vietnam* (Baltimore: The Johns Hopkins University Press, 1986), 29–33, 40.
4. Message from AFSSO 7AF to AFSSO CINCSAC, 140115Z, June 1972, Folder Gen. Vogt's Read File June 1972, Vogt Papers, Office of Air Force History, Air Force History Studies Division, Bolling Air Force Base (hereafter referred to as AFHSD). Charles K. Hopkins, SAC Tanker Operations in the Southeast Asia War (Offut, NE: Headquarters Strategic Air Command, 1979), 106. For a broader look at aerial refueling, see Vernon B. Byrd, *Passing Gas: The History of Inflight Refueling* (Chico, CA: Byrd Publishing, 1994).
5. Colonel Robert R. Scott, 355th TFW Combat Tactical Doctrine, December 28, 1967, M-U-41984-1, Air University Library, Maxwell Air Force Base, AL; History of 355th Tactical Fighter Wing 1 July 1965–31 December 1965, Document 23, K-WG-355-HI, July–December 1965; Message from CINCPACAF, KC-135 Tanker Support of PACAF, (no date time group), 11 September 1969, K712.312-3; Tanker Requirements, March 1968, K416.03-27, 1968–1969, AFHRA; Dennis R. Jenkins, *F-105 Thunderchief: Workhorse of the Vietnam War* (New York: McGraw-Hill, 2000), 75; TACOP Final Report, 45th TFS, 6 October 1965, K-WG-15-HI, Vol. 2. General Hunter Harris was the commander of PACAF from August 1, 1964, until February

1, 1967, when John D. Ryan replaced him. Joseph J. Nazzaro became its commander in August 1968 until retiring on August 1, 1971. Lucius D. Clay Jr. was the last PACAF commander during Vietnam. He held that post until October 1, 1973.

6. Major George R. Fessler Jr., Aerial Refueling in Southeast Asia, 1964–1970 (HQ PACAF: Directorate of Operations Analysis, CHECO/Corona Harvest Division, 1971), xi, K717.0414-21, AFHRA. Corona Harvest was an extensive series of contemporary studies written in an attempt to derive lessons from the war. Wayne Thompson, *To Hanoi and Back: The U.S. Air Force and North Vietnam, 1966–1973* (Washington, DC: Smithsonian Institution Press, 2000), 364. The CHECO Reports—contemporary historical examination of current operations—are an extremely useful, if at times uneven in quality, set of formerly classified histories written during the Vietnam War by Air Force staffers. While they have come under some criticism for being written in house, they are often quite helpful and provide historians with information that otherwise would be enormously difficult to find. Looking up the footnotes therein in order to verify their claims is difficult because they provide few suggestions as to where to find the message traffic and interviews on which they rely. See Major Daniel S. Hoadley, "What Just Happened? A Historical Evaluation of Project CHECO," thesis, School of Advanced Air and Space Studies, Maxwell Air Force Base, Alabama, 2013.

7. United States Military Assistance Command, Vietnam Command History 1966 (Saigon: Military History Branch, Office of the Secretary, Joint Staff Headquarters, 1966), 131, found online at: https://www.scribd.com/document/81654233/Command-History-1966.

8. Fessler, Aerial Refueling 1964–1970, 13; Thompson, *To Hanoi and Back,* 9; Robert Frank Futrell, *Ideas, Concepts, Doctrine: Basic Thinking in the United States Air Force, 1907–1960, Volume I* (Maxwell AFB, AL: Air University Press, 1989), 232–33; MACV Command History, 1972, B-31.

9. Fessler, Aerial Refueling, 1964–1970, 1; Message from 2nd Air Division to RUEAHQ/CSAF, 190710Z, March 1965, K526.1623, AFHRA.

10. Warren A. Trest, USAF SAC Operations in Support of SE Asia (HQ PACAF: Directorate of Operations Analysis, CHECO/Corona Harvest Division, 1969), 40–41, K717.0412-97; Fessler, Aerial Refueling, 1964–1970, 16–17.

11. Captain W. L. Harris, USS *Midway* to Commander Naval Air Force, US Pacific Fleet, 1971 Westpac Cruise Report, 11 November 1971, Ships History, Decommissioned, USS *Midway,* Box 527E, File CVA-41, Command History 1971, Naval History and Heritage Command, Washington, DC (hereafter referred to as NHHC).

12. F. A. Peck, Commander Attack Carrier Air Wing Nine to Commander Naval Air Force, US Pacific Fleet, Combat Tactical Supplement, 13 July 1968, Fleet Aviation Commands-Active, CVW-9, Box 18, File 1968, NHHC. Fleet Aviation Commands will be referred to as "Fleet."

13. Message to General Vogt from Major General Hughes, 161313Z, October 1972, K744.01, 1972, Vol. II, Appendix V; Major William J. Davies, History of the 12th Tactical Reconnaissance Squadron (hereafter referred to as 12th TRS), July–September 1968, K-WG-460-HI, Vol. 2, AFHRA; Commander L. Wayne Smith, Attack Carrier Air Wing Six Cruise Report of April 1968 to December 1968, 14 December 1968, Fleet Pre-1998, CVW-6, AR/229, Box 7, File F13, NHHC.

14. Steven A. Fino, *Tiger Check: Automating the US Air Force Fighter Pilot in Air-to-Air Combat, 1950–1980* (Baltimore: Johns Hopkins University Press, 2017), 159.

15. Staff Sergeant Stephen L. Y. Gammons, History of the 4258th Strategic Wing, January 1968, 28–30, K-WG-4258-HI, Vol. 1, AFHRA.

16. Interview of Captain Leroy W. Thornal by Major Harry Shallcross, September 13, 1967, location not provided, 2, K239.0512-012, AFHRA.

17. Hopkins, SAC Tanker Operations, 55; Trest, SAC Operations SE Asia, 45–46. Individuals called "weapons directors" functioned much like air traffic controllers, except they brought aircraft

NOTES FOR CHAPTER I

together, an activity collectively also referred to as "ground-controlled intercept" or "GCI" for short.
18. Hopkins, SAC Tanker Operations, 42–43.
19. Major Albert R. Hamblet Jr., Memo, 19 March 1966, K160.043-41, 26 April 1966; Message from 7th AF to RUEFHQA/CSAF/XOO, Linebacker Conference Charlie VIII and Uniform VII, 191300Z, October 1972, K740.3391, AFHRA.
20. The 4252nd was stationed at Kadena Air Base, Okinawa. Hopkins, SAC Tanker Operations, 54, 78.
21. Staff Sergeant Stephen L. Y. Gammons, History of the 4258th Strategic Wing, April–May 1967, 29–31, K-WG-4258-HI, Vol. 1; Colonel John W. Farrar, Citation for Award of the Distinguished Flying Cross, 19 May 1967, K-WG-4258-HI, Vol. 2, AFHRA.
22. History of the 4258th Strategic Wing, June–July 1967, 28–29, K-WG-4258-HI, Vol. 1, AFHRA.
23. The F-4C was from the 366th Tactical Fighter Wing. Message from 7th AF to RUMRDA/3 Air Div, F-4C Save, 3 February 1967, 090155Z, February 1967, K-WG-4258-HI, AFHRA.
24. Fessler, Aerial Refueling, 1964–1970, 17, 19; Trest, SAC Operations SE Asia, 46.
25. Report, Aircraft Save, Exhibit 20, K-WG-4258-HI, February 1967, AFHRA.
26. Holly Green Blue and Holly Green White were the two KA-3s. The KA-3 Skywarrior or "Whale" was a modified A-3 Skywarrior, a large nuclear bomber that flew from carriers. Its fuel system, however, was oddly designed. It could not transfer fuel from tanks that were used for refueling other aircraft to run its own engines. So one of these Navy tankers actually had 4,000 pounds of jet fuel on board when it had only three minutes of usable fuel left in its own tanks. Hopkins, SAC Tanker Operations, 68–69.
27. J. F. Brennan, Operations Evaluation Group of Center for Naval Analysis Study No. 172: Analysis of Tactical Aircraft Operations in Southeast Asia, 1965–1966, Vol. 1, 18 January 1968, 18, Coll/7 Publications of the Center for Naval Analysis, OEG, Box 63, Folder OEG, Vol. 1 #172, NHHC.
28. Heavy Attack Squadron Eight, A3 Utilization and Accomplishments, 17 November 1967; Fleet Pre-1998, AR/229, Box 107, File F13, NHHC.
29. Heavy Attack Squadron Eight, A3 Utilization and Accomplishments, 17 November 1967, Message from CTG 77.4 to RUMFAE/CTE 70.2.1.1, 040856Z, June 1967; Heavy Attack Squadron Eight, A3 Utilization and Accomplishments, 17 November 1967, Fleet Pre-1998, AR/229, Box 107, File F13; Commander J. E. McKnight, Commander Carrier Air Wing Two, Cruise Report of October 1970 to June 1971, 10 June 1971, Fleet Active, CVW-2, Box 13, File 7/70-6/71, NHHC. The barrier was a large nylon net stretched across the landing area of a carrier deck. It captured aircraft with malfunctioning landing gear, arresting hooks, or nearly out of fuel and brought them to a stop with minimal damage.
30. VA-52 First Line Period Report, 8–28 December 1970, Fleet Pre-1998, AR/229, VA-52, Box 130, File F10, NHHC; see also Carol Reardon, *Launch the Intruders: A Naval Attack Squadron in the Vietnam War, 1972* (Lawrence: University Press of Kansas, 2005).
31. Marine Fighter Attack Squadron 232 Command Chronology, December 1, 1972, found online at The Vietnam Center & Sam Johnson Vietnam Archive, Texas Tech University, http://vietnam.ttu.edu.
32. Message from CG FMFPAC to RUMSDN/CG First MAW, 180335Z, August 1967, found online at The Vietnam Center & Sam Johnson Vietnam Archive, Texas Tech University, http://vietnam.ttu.edu .
33. Lieutenant General Keith B. McCutcheon, Marine Aviation in Vietnam, 1962–1970, 68, Folder Aviation: Wars–Vietnam (2 of 3); Oral History Transcript, Lieutenant General Thomas H. Miller Jr., Interviewed by Benis M. Frank and Fred H. Allison, 18 August 1986, 217, History Division, Marine Corps University, Quantico, VA, 2006 (hereafter referred to HDMCU).

NOTES FOR CHAPTER I

34. History of Pacific Air Forces, 1 July–31 December 1965, Vol. 1, Part 2, 408–409, K717.01, Hopkins, SAC Tanker Operations, 72, 75; Message from CINCPACAF to RUHHHQA/CINCPAC, Tanker Requirements, 132149Z, February 1968, K717.1623, 1968, AFHRA.
35. Staff Sergeant Stephen L. Y. Gammons, History of the 4258th Strategic Wing, February–March 1968, 21–27, K-WG-4285-HI, 1967; Colonel Howard C. Johnson, Air Refueling, 15 May 1967, K-WG-4258-HI, Vol. 2, AFHRA.
36. M. F. Porter, Linebacker: Overview of the First 120 Days (HQ PACAF: Directorate of Operations, CHECO/Corona Harvest Division, 1973), 53, K717.0414-42, 1973; Message from 7th AF to RUHHABA/CINCPACAF, Linebacker Conference Juliet VI and Kilo VI, 261234Z, September 1972, K740.3391, AFHRA.
37. History of 355th Tactical Fighter Wing, 1 July 1965–31 December 1965, Document 22, K-WG-355-HI; Thornal interview, 23, K239.0512-012; Interview of Major James A. Hargrove Jr., by Lieutenant Colonel Robert Eckert and Major Harry Sallcross, September 19, 1967, 36–37, K239.0512-020; Sergeant David J. Hitchcock, History of the 4258th Strategic Wing, May 1968, 44, K-WG-4258-HI, Vol. 1, AFHRA.
38. Fessler, Aerial Refueling, 1964–1970, 31–32; Hopkins, SAC Tanker Operations, 46, 48, 50–51, 55, 67; Message from SAC to RUEFHQA/CSAF, Tanker Deployments, 191625Z, August 1967, K717.312, AFHRA.
39. Message from 7th AF to CINCPAC, SAC KC-135 Support for PACAF, 091245Z, October 1969, K740.03-58, 1969, AFHRA.
40. Hopkins, SAC Tanker Operations, 41–42.
41. Zalin Grant, *Over the Beach* (New York: W. W. Norton, 1986), 176.
42. Hopkins, SAC Tanker Operations, 43.
43. Ibid., 58–61; Staff Sergeant Arthur C. Warfel, History of 4258th Strategic Wing, November 1968, Vol. 1, 44, K-WG-4258-HI, 1968, AFHRA.
44. Hopkins, SAC Tanker Operations, 14.
45. History of the Pacific Air Forces, July 1971–June 1972, Vol. 1, 113–15, K717.01, AFHRA; History of the Pacific Air Forces, 1 July 1972–30 June 1973, 117, K717.01, AFHRA; Hopkins, SAC Tanker Operations, 84–87; Minutes of Washington Special Actions Group Meeting, May 24, 1972; Daniel J. Lawler, *Foreign Relations of the United States, 1969–1976, Volume XX, Southeast Asia 1969–1972* (Washington, DC: United States Government Printing Office, 2006), 361.
46. Message from 7AF to RHCOAAA/CINCSAC, 7AF Tanker Requirements, 030615Z, April 1972, K-WG-307-HI, Vol. 1; Message from CINCSAC to AIG 667/ Warning Order Young Tiger Surge, 041930Z, April 1972, K-WG-307-HI, Vol. 1; History of the Pacific Air Forces, July 1971–June 1972, Vol. 1, 122–23, K717.01, AFHRA.
47. Porter, Linebacker First 120 Days, 54, K717.0414-42, 1973, AFHRA.
48. Major Donald E. Cook, USAFTFWC Liaison Officer End of Tour Report, 14 August–15 November 1972, 1 December 1972, K417.0735, FY1973, Vol. 6, AFHRA.
49. See for example Message, Personal to General Vogt from Major General Hughes, Linebacker Conference Charlie VIII and Uniform VII, 191300Z, October 1972; Message, Personal to General Vogt from Colonel Olshefski, Linebacker Conference, 22 December 1972, Final Section of Six, 230645Z, December 1972, K744.01 1972, Vol. II, Appendix V, AFHRA.
50. Message from AFSSO 7AF TSN AFLD RVN to AFSSO Udorn, Linebacker Tactical Conference, 021150Z, August 1972, K143.044-90, Vol. 32, AFHRA.
51. Linebacker Conference Oscar IV and Papa IV, 230834Z, August 1972, K740.3391, AFHRA.
52. Message to General Vogt from Colonel Olshefski, Linebacker Critique 26 December 1972, 261355Z, December 1972; Message, Personal to General Vogt from Colonel Olshefski, Linebacker Conference, 24 December 1972, 241715Z, December 1972, K744.01 1972, Vol. II, Appendix

V; Message from 7th AF to RUEBHQA/CSAF/XOO, Linebacker II India Critique, 230108Z, December 1972, K740.3391, AFHRA.
53. Message, Personal to General Vogt from Colonel Olshefski, Linebacker II Critique 22 December 1972, Continued, 230645Z, December 1972, K744.01, 1972, Vol. II, Appendix V; History of the Pacific Air Forces, 1 July 1972–30 June 1973, 82, K717.01; A Strategic Air Command Study on the Effectiveness of Air Power in Southeast Asia, 16–17; Strategic Air Command Project Corona Harvest V, 1 July 1972–15 August 1973, K416.041-13, Vol. 1, Appendix A; Message from Colonel Olshefski to General Vogt, Linebacker II India Critique, 271115Z, December 1972, K168.06-230, AFHRA.
54. Message from General Vogt to Major General Hughes, Linebacker II Juliet Critique, 290945Z, December 1972, K168.06-230; Strategic Air Command Project Corona Harvest V, 1 July 1972–15 August 1973, 14, K416.041-13, Vol. 1, Appendix A, AFHRA (hereafter referred to as Corona Harvest V, 1972–1973, K416.041-13).
55. See for example Staff Sergeant Stephen L. Y. Gammons, History of 4258th Strategic Wing, September 1967, Vol. 1, 52, K-WG-4258-HI, 1967, AFHRA.
56. Hopkins, SAC Tanker Operations, 106, 108.
57. Fessler, Aerial Refueling, 1964–1970, 39.
58. Message from Lieutenant General G. J. Eade AF/XO, AFSSO USAF to SSO SAC, SEA Sorties, June 1972 [no date time group], K740.3391, AFHRA. Eade was deputy chief of staff for plans and operations.
59. KC-135s flew 4,593 sorties during Linebacker II. Hopkins, SAC Tanker Operations, 95, 108.

Chapter 2

1. Michael Korda, *With Wings Like Eagles: A History of the Battle of Britain* (New York: Harper Collins, 2009), 279; Winston Churchill, *The Second World War, Volume 2: Their Finest Hour* (Boston: Houghton Mifflin, 1976), 335–36.
2. Von Hardesty and Ilya Grinberg, *Red Phoenix Rising: The Soviet Air Force in World War II* (Lawrence: University Press of Kansas, 2012), 136.
3. Isabella Ginor and Gideon Remez, *The Soviet-Israeli War, 1967–1973: The USSR's Military Intervention in the Egyptian-Israeli Conflict* (Oxford: Oxford University Press, 2017), 250.
4. Message from AFSSO USAF to AFSSO PACAF, AFSSO 7AF, 271955Z, June 1972, Vogt Papers, Message Traffic June 1972, Office of Air Force History, AFHSD; 7th Air Force Commanders Conference, July 18–19, 1972, K168.06.228, 72/07/01–73/08/00, AFHRA.
5. John H. Morrow Jr., *The Great War in the Air: Military Aviation from 1909 to 1921* (Washington, DC: Smithsonian Institution Press, 1993), 149–51; Holger H. Herwig, *The First World War: Germany and Austria-Hungary, 1914–1918* (London: Arnold, 1997), 190–91.
6. Robin Higham, *Unflinching Zeal: The Air Battles over France and Britain, May–October 1940* (Annapolis, MD: Naval Institute Press, 2012), 167–209; Richard Overy, *The Battle of Britain: The Myth and the Reality* (New York: W.W. Norton, 2000).
7. Hardesty and Grinberg, *Red Phoenix Rising*, 228–57.
8. Stephen L. McFarland and Wesley Phillips Newton, *To Command the Sky: The Battle for Air Superiority over Germany, 1942–1944* (Washington, DC: Smithsonian Institution Press, 1991), 130–220.
9. Alvin D. Coox, "Strategic Bombing in the Pacific, 1942–1945," in R. Cargill Hall, ed., *Case Studies in Strategic Bombardment* (Washington, DC: Air Force History and Museums Program, 1998), 282, 285.
10. Xiaoming Zhang, *Red Wings over the Yalu: China, the Soviet Union, and the Air War in Korea*

(College Station: Texas A&M University Press, 2002), 69, 114, 117; Kenneth P. Werrell, *Sabres over MiG Alley: The F-86 and the Battle for Air Superiority in Korea* (Annapolis, MD: Naval Institute Press, 2005), 128–33; Conrad C. Crane, *American Airpower Strategy in Korea, 1950–1953* (Lawrence: University Press of Kansas, 2000), 164–67.

11. Alan Stephens, "Modeling Air Power: The Arab-Israeli Wars of the Twentieth Century," in John Andreas Olsen, ed., *Airpower Applied: U.S., NATO, and Israeli Combat Experience* (Annapolis, MD: Naval Institute Press, 2017), 244.

12. Ibid., 260; Kenneth M. Pollack, *Arabs at War: Military Effectiveness, 1948–1991* (Lincoln: University of Nebraska Press, 2002), 122.

13. Transcript of a Telephone Conversation between President Nixon and the President's Assistant for National Security Affairs (Kissinger), December 26, 1972, John M. Carland, ed., and Edward C. Keefer, gen. ed., *Foreign Relations of the United States, 1969–1976, Volume IX: Vietnam, October 1972–January 1973* (Washington, DC: United States Government Printing Office, 2010), 830 (hereafter referred to as *FRUS 1969–1976, IX*); Major Calvin R. Johnson, Linebacker Operations: September–December 1972 (HQ PACAF: Directorate Tactical Evaluation, CHECO Division, 1978), 63, K717.0413-102, AFHRA.

14. Benjamin S. Lambeth, "Moscow's Lessons from the 1982 Lebanon Air War," in R. A. Mason, ed., *War in the Third Dimension: Essays in Contemporary Air Power* (London: Brassey's, 1986), 132–33.

15. Richard A. Gabriel, *Operation Peace for Galilee: The Israeli-PLO War in Lebanon* (New York: Hill and Wang, 1984), 98; M. Thomas Davis, *40Km Into Lebanon: Israel's 1982 Invasion* (Washington, DC: National Defense University Press, 1987), 92; Yair Evron, *War and Intervention in Lebanon: The Israeli-Syrian Deterrence Dialogue* (Baltimore, MD: The Johns Hopkins University Press, 1987), 192–93.

16. Richard G. Davis, *On Target: Organizing and Executing the Strategic Air Campaign against Iraq* (Washington, DC: Air Force History and Museums Program, 2002), 257.

17. Robert H. Gregory Jr., *Clean Bombs and Dirty Wars: Air Power in Kosovo and Libya* (Lincoln, NE: Potomac Books, 2015), 30, 51, 57, 58; Dag Henriksen, *NATO's Gamble: Combining Diplomacy and Airpower in the Kosovo Crisis, 1998–1999* (Annapolis, MD: Naval Institute Press, 2007), 179.

18. Stephen Randolph's work may have prompted the train of thought of the war being like a siege. Stephen P. Randolph, *Powerful and Brutal Weapons: Nixon, Kissinger, and the Easter Offensive* (Cambridge, MA: Harvard University Press, 2007), 235.

19. Air forces had engaged in airfield attacks since World War I. The most influential air power theorist, Italy's Giulio Douhet, advocated that destroying aircraft on the ground where they were sitting ducks was the most sensible means for achieving air superiority, if not air supremacy. Giulio Douhet, *The Command of the Air*, trans. Dino Ferrari (New York: Coward-McCann, 1942), 34. Both the Germans and the British missed opportunities to at least attempt this during the Battle of Britain, but the Germans followed this doctrine well in June 1941 when they destroyed about 800 Soviet aircraft as they sat at their airfields. Hardesty and Grinberg, *Red Phoenix Rising*, 8. The Israelis fulfilled Douhet's vision most completely on June 5, 1967. Robert M. Citino, *Blitzkrieg to Desert Storm: The Evolution of Operational Warfare* (Lawrence: University Press of Kansas, 2004), 167.

20. John B. Nichols and Barrett Tillman, *On Yankee Station: The Naval Air War over Vietnam* (Annapolis, MD: Naval Institute Press, 1987), 70; J. Terry Emerson, "Making War without Will: Vietnam Rules of Engagement," in John Norton Moore, ed., *The Vietnam Debate: A Fresh Look at the Arguments* (Lanham, MD: University Press of America, 1990), 164.

21. William H. Greenhalgh, *The RF-101 Voodoo, 1961–1970* (Washington, DC: Office of Air Force History, 1979), 62. American sources often list these MiGs as "MiG-15/17s" because it was difficult to tell the difference from a distance, but the Vietnamese official history notes that in

1963 only MiG-17s comprised its fighter regiment. The Military History Institute of Vietnam, *Victory in Vietnam: The Official History of the People's Army of Vietnam, 1954–1975*, trans. Merle L. Pribbenow, foreword by William J. Duiker (Lawrence: University Press of Kansas, 2002), 96.

22. Editorial Note, John McCone, Memorandum for the Record, February 8, 1965, ed. David C. Humphrey, Ronald D. Landa, and Louis J. Smith, *Foreign Relations of the United States, 1964–1968, Volume II: Vietnam, January–June 1965* (Washington, DC: Government Printing Office, 1996), 694 (hereafter referred to as *FRUS 1964–1968, II*); Qiang Zhai, *China and the Vietnam Wars, 1950–1975* (Chapel Hill: University of North Carolina Press, 2000), 138–39; Robert D. Schulzinger, *A Time for War: The United States and Vietnam, 1941–1975* (New York, Oxford: Oxford University Press, 1997), 205; Robert S. McNamara with Brian VanDeMark, *In Retrospect: The Tragedy and Lessons of Vietnam* (New York: Times Books, Random House, 1995), 109, 213, 229.

23. Jacob Van Staaveren, *Gradual Failure: The Air War over North Vietnam, 1965–1966* (Washington, DC: Air Force History and Museums Program, 2002), 241; Memorandum for the Record by the President's Special Assistant for National Security Affairs (Bundy), September 20, 1964, ed. John P. Glennon, Edward C. Keefer, and Charles S. Sampson, *Foreign Relations of the United States, 1964–1968, Volume I: Vietnam 1964* (Washington, DC: United States Government Printing Office, 1992), 778 (hereafter referred to as *FRUS 1964–1968, I*).

24. Van Staaveren, *Gradual Failure*, 143–44. The Ilyuhin IL-28 Beagle was a subsonic light bomber that may have been able to evade detection by flying close to the ground and complete a nuisance raid on Da Nang. Yefim Gordon, Dmitriy Komissarov, and Sergey Komissarov, *OKB Ilyushin: A History of the Design Bureau and Its Aircraft* (Hinckley, England: Midland, 2004), 118, 137–40; Editorial Note, *FRUS 1964–1968, II*, 693–94; Graham A. Cosmas, *History of the Joint Chiefs of Staff: The Joint Chiefs of Staff and the War in Vietnam, 1960–1968, Part 2* (Washington, DC: Office of Joint History, 2012), 374.

25. Lieutenant General Andrew J. Goodpasture, Memorandum of a Meeting with President Johnson, February 17, 1965, *FRUS 1964–1968, II*, 301.

26. John McCone, Memorandum for the Record, February 8, 1965, *FRUS 1964–1968, II*, 193–94.

27. William R. Tyler, Memorandum from the Assistant Secretary of State for European Affairs (Tyler) to Acting Secretary of State Ball, February 8, 1965, *FRUS 1964–1968, II*, 198; William J. Duiker, *Sacred War: Nationalism and Revolution in a Divided Vietnam* (Boston: McGraw-Hill, 1995), 174.

28. Message from 2 Air Division to PACAF, 110748Z, February 1965, K526.1623, AFHRA; Van Staaveren, *Gradual Failure*, 77–78. The 2nd Air Division was the Air Force organization that managed its portion of the air war in Indochina until being upgraded to the Seventh Air Force on April 1, 1966. General William W. Momyer commanded Seventh Air Force from July 1, 1966, to August 1, 1968, when General George S. Brown succeeded him. Brown remained its commander until September 1970. John Schlight, *The United States Air Force in Southeast Asia: The War in South Vietnam, The Years of the Offensive, 1965–1968* (Washington, DC: Office of Air Force History, 1988), 129.

29. John Darrell Sherwood, *Afterburner: Naval Aviators and the Vietnam War* (New York: New York University Press, 2004), 10.

30. Message from CINCPACAF to RUMABA/13 AF, Phuc Yen Air Attack, SVN Air Defense, 092322Z, June 1965, K712.1623-2, AFHRA.

31. Memorandum from Secretary of Defense McNamara to the Chairman of the Joint Chiefs of Staff (Wheeler), September 15, 1965, ed. Edward C. Humphrey, Edward C. Keefer, and Louis J. Smith, *Foreign Relations of the United States, 1964–1968, Volume III, Vietnam, June–December 1965* (Washington, DC: United States Government Printing Office, 1996), 390 (hereafter referred to as *FRUS 1964–1968, III*).

32. Van Staaveren, *Gradual Failure*, 106–8; Message from CINCPAC, Optimum Military Air Strike Program for NVN, 040304Z, April 1965, K712-1623-2, AFHRA.
33. Department of the Air Force, Combat Alley Follow-On Study Report, K143.042-18, 19670922, AFHRA.
34. Van Staaveren, *Gradual Failure*, 106–8.
35. PACAF DI, Effects of Air Operations in Southeast Asia, 9 December 1965, 23–26, K717.6092, AFHRA; PACAF DI, Effects of Air Operations in Southeast Asia, 23 December 1965, figure 1, K717.6092, AFHRA.
36. Message from CINCPACAF to RUMSAL/2AIRDIV, Attack Plans, 310510Z, May 1965, K740.312-4, Vol. 3, AFHRA; Hearings before the Preparedness Investigating Subcommittee of the Committee on Armed Services, United States Senate, 90th Cong., 1st sess., August 22–23, 1967, 254.
37. Van Staaveren, *Gradual Failure*, 128; PACAF DI, Effects of Air Operations in Southeast Asia, 5 July 1965, 15, K717.6092, AFHRA; Effects of Air Operations in Southeast Asia, 22 July 1965, 18, K717.6092, AFHRA.
38. PACAF DI, Effects of Air Operations in Southeast Asia, 5 July 1965, 15, K717.6092, AFHRA. Each edition of this series contains detailed lists of bomb damage.
39. PACAF DI, Effects of Air Operations in Southeast Asia, 16 September 1965, 28, K717.6092, AFHRA; PACAF DI, Effects of Air Operations in Southeast Asia, 9 December 1965, 15, 17, K717.6092, AFHRA.
40. PACAF DI, Effects of Air Operations in Southeast Asia, 14 October 1965, 25, 27, K717.6092, AFHRA; PACAF DI, Effects of Air Operations in Southeast Asia, 11 November 1965, 24, K717.6092, AFHRA.
41. Van Staaveren, *Gradual Failure*, 118.
42. Message from 7AF to RUEKBA/National Military Command Center, 261340Z, 1966. The Americans shot down one of the MiG-21s. USAF Fighter Weapons School, Bulletin 4, K160.043-36, 23 April 1966; Colonel Herbert J. Rogers and Captain John H. Knops, A Study in Air Defense, North Vietnam: One Year (15 April 1965–15 April 1966), K470.40-22. See also Message from 7AF to RUCIRDF/FTD WPAFB, Air-to-Air Combat in SEA, 250740Z, May 1966, K717.312, AFHRA.
43. Rogers and Knops, Study in Air Defense, K470.40-22. For another "red star on fuselage" sighting, see Message from 366 TFW to RUEPJS/NMCC, 141410Z, May 1967, K717.312, AFHRA.
44. Message from PACAF to RUHLHQ/CINCPAC CC, 130138Z, May 1966, K160.043-46, 12 May 1966, Event 28. Given the challenges of seeing the details of other aircraft during close-in fights, my conclusion is that the MiGs wore North Vietnamese markings unless conclusive evidence demonstrates otherwise.
45. Lee Bonetti, et al., The War in Vietnam, July–December 1967 (HQ PACAF: Directorate Tactical Evaluation, CHECO Division, 1968), 107, K717.0414-17, AFHRA.
46. Speech by Lyndon B. Johnson, April 7, 1965, www.lbjlib.utexas.edu; Frank E. Vandiver, *Shadows of Vietnam: Lyndon Johnson's Wars* (College Station: Texas A&M University Press, 1997), 95–96.
47. Randall B. Woods, *LBJ: Architect of American Ambition* (New York: Free Press, 2006), 680–81; Van Staaveren, *Gradual Failure*, 191.
48. 7th Fleet Operational Summary, May 1965, Reference Files, Vietnam, A-Air Warfare (I), Aircraft Losses Folder, NHHC; 7th Fleet Operational Summary, June 1965, Reference Files, Vietnam, A-Air Warfare (I), Aircraft Losses Folder, NHHC.
49. Robert J. Hanyok, *Spartans in Darkness: American SIGINT and the Indochina War, 1945–1975* (Fort Meade, MD: Center for Cryptological History, National Security Agency, 2002), 252.
50. Van Staaveren, *Gradual Failure*, 188, 190; Memorandum from Secretary of Defense McNamara

to the Chairman of the Joint Chiefs of Staff (Wheeler), September 15, 1965, *FRUS 1964–1968, III*, 390–91.
51. Van Staaveren, *Gradual Failure*, 241.
52. Telegram from the Commander in Chief, Pacific (Sharp) to the Joint Chiefs of Staff, January 12, 1966, ed. David C. Humphrey, gen. ed. David S. Patterson, *Foreign Relations of the United States, 1964–1968, Volume IV, Vietnam 1966* (Washington, DC: United States Government Printing Office, 1998), 48 (hereafter referred to as *FRUS 1964–1968, IV*); History of the Pacific Air Forces, 1 January 1966–31 December 1966, 167, K717.01, Vol. 1, Part 2. See for example PACAF CC to 7AF CC, Rolling Thunder 51, 070828Z, June 1966, AFHRA.
53. Notes of Meeting, January 3, 1966, *FRUS 1964–1968, IV*, 9.
54. Van Staaveren, *Gradual Failure*, 233; Melyan and Bonetti, Rolling Thunder, July 1965–December 1966, 117, K717.0414-12, AFHRA.
55. Cosmas, *The Joint Chiefs of Staff, 1960–1968, Part 2*, 418.
56. Message from PACAF CC to 7th AF CC, Rolling Thunder 51, 070323Z, July 1966, K717.1623, AFHRA.
57. Navy History Division, History of U.S. Naval Operations in the Vietnam Conflict, Vol. III 1965–1967, Part 1 (February 1971), 118, Vietnam Command Files, COLL/372, Box 85, File CNO NHO, Vol. III, Part 1, NHHC.
58. Summary of Air Operations in Southeast Asia, 4–17 March 1966, 2–19, K717.3063, AFHRA; Captain Melvin F. Porter, Air Tactics against NVN Air/Ground Defenses (HQ PACAF: Directorate, Tactical Evaluation, CHECO Division, 1967), 25, K717.0414-16, AFHRA; Van Staaveren, *Gradual Failure*, 241.
59. HQ USAF, Directorate of Operations, DSC/P&O, Southeast Asia Counter Air Alternatives, 20 April 1966, K143.042-19, 1966. See also Lt. Col. L. V. Grosshuesch, Fact Sheet, Attack of NVN Airfields, 22 April 1966, K717.151-11, AFHRA; HQ PACAF, Assistant for Operations Analysis, R. E. Hiller, Southeast Asia Counter-Air Alternatives, 10 February 1967, K717.310-2, Vols. 1, 2, 10, February 1967, AFHRA; Van Staaveren, *Gradual Failure*, 272–73.
60. History Naval Operations, Vol. III, 1965–1967, Part 1, 109; USS *Constellation*, Highlights of 1966 Constellation/Attack Carrier Air Wing Fifteen Westpac Cruise (no date), Fleet Pre-1998, CVW-15, AR/229, Box 12, File F21, NHHC; DCS Intelligence, Headquarters PACAF, Effects of Air Operations Southeast Asia, November 1966, 28, K717.6092, November 1966; Message from JCS to RUHKA/CINCPAC, Rolling Thunder 52, 110425Z, November 1966, K717.1623, AFHRA.
61. Hiller, Southeast Asia Counter-Air Alternatives, K717.310-2, AFHRA.
62. Ibid.
63. Ibid.
64. Thomas H. Moorer, Memorandum for the Record, October 11, 1969, ed. Edward C. Keefer and Carolyn Yee, *Foreign Relations of the United States, 1969–1976, Volume VI, Vietnam, January 1969–July 1976* (Washington, DC: Government Printing Office, 2006), 459 (hereafter referred to as *FRUS 1969–1976, VI*).
65. Hearings before the Preparedness Investigating Subcommittee, August 22–23, 1967, 255. See also Nichols and Tillman, *On Yankee Station*, 16; David M. Barrett, *Uncertain Warriors: Lyndon Johnson and his Vietnam Advisors* (Lawrence: University Press of Kansas, 1993), 88; William W. Momyer, *Airpower in Three Wars: WWII, Korea, Vietnam* (Washington, DC: Superintendent of Documents, Government Printing Office, 1978), 140–41; U. S. Grant Sharp, *Strategy for Defeat: Vietnam in Retrospect* (San Rafael, CA: Presidio, 1978), 202; Ronald B. Frankum, *Like Rolling Thunder: The Air War in Vietnam, 1964–1975* (Lanham, MD: Rowman & Littlefield, 2005), 30; Michael O'Connor, *MiG Killers of Yankee Station* (Friendship, WI: New Past, 2003), 63.
66. Thornal interview, 18, K239.0512-012, 00/11/66–00/07/67, AFHRA.

NOTES FOR CHAPTER 2

67. Hearings before the Preparedness Investigating Subcommittee, August 16, 1967, 136.
68. Ibid., 137.
69. Summary of Air Operations in Southeast Asia, January–March 1967, Appendix 5A, K717.3063, AFHRA; Graham A. Cosmas, *History of the Joint Chiefs of Staff: The Joint Chiefs of Staff and the War in Vietnam, 1960–1968, Part 3* (Washington, DC: Office of Joint History, 2009), 18.
70. Memorandum from the Assistant Secretary of State for East Asian and Pacific Affairs (Bundy) to Secretary of State Rusk, May 19, 1967, ed. Kent Sieg, *Foreign Relations of the United States, 1964–1968, Volume V, Vietnam, 1967* (Washington, DC: Government Printing Office, 2002), 418 (hereafter referred to as *FRUS 1964–1968, V*).
71. Barrett, *Uncertain Warriors*, 88; Congress, Senate, Committee on Foreign Relations, *The World Situation: Hearing Before the Committee on Foreign Relations, 90th Cong., 1st sess., 16 January 1967*, 62–63.
72. Captain Arthur P. Geesey, Air-to-Air Engagements, 5, K717.601-9, AFHRA.
73. Thompson, *To Hanoi and Back*, 63–64; Major John C. Pratt, Air Tactics against NVN Air Ground Defenses: December 1966–1 November 1968 (HQ PACAF: Directorate, Tactical Evaluation, CHECO Division, 1969), 10–11, K717.0414-16, AFHRA.
74. TSgt. Kermit E. Andrews, History of the 8th Tactical Fighter Wing, January–June 1967, 12, K-WG-8-HI, Vol. 1, AFHRA; History Naval Operations, Vol. III, 1965–1967, Part 1, 134, NHHC.
75. Summary of Air Operations in Southeast Asia, April 1967, Appendix 5A, K717.3063, April 1967, AFHRA; Mark Clodfelter, *The Limits of Air Power: The American Bombing of North Vietnam* (New York: Free Press, 1989), 106; Cosmas, *Joint Chiefs of Staff 1960–1968, Part 3*, 21; Thornal interview, 19, K239.0512-012, 00/11/66–00/07/67, AFHRA.
76. History 555th Tactical Fighter Squadron January–June 1967, K-WG-8-HI, Vol.1, AFHRA; Editorial Note, *FRUS 1964–1968, V*, 333; Message from CTG 77.7 to AIG 7802, 011700Z, May 1967, History Naval Operations, Vol. III, 1965–1967, Part 1, 134, Reference Files, Vietnam, A-Air Warfare (I), File Vietnam Air Ops MiG Combat, NHHC.
77. DCS/Intelligence, 7th Air Force, An Assessment of Air Operations in Southeast Asia, 7 February 1965 thru 19 July 1967, 20, K740.04-20, 7 February 1965–19 July 1967; Geesey, Air-to-Air Engagements, 5; PACAF DI, Effects of Air Operations Southeast Asia, May 1967, 30, 46, 47, 73, K717.6092, AFHRA; HQ CINCPAC, Pacific Area Naval Operations Review May 1967, 15, Vietnam Command Files, Box 102, File May 1967, NHHC.
78. Message CTG 77.7 to AIG 7802, 011700Z, May 1967, NHHC.
79. Summary of Air Operations in Southeast Asia, April 1967, Appendix 5A, K717.3063, AFHRA; Summary of Air Operations in Southeast Asia, May 1967, Appendix 5A, K717.3063, Excerpt, AFHRA.
80. Commander P. T. Gillcrist, Fighter Squadron Fifty-Three to Chief of Naval Operations, 1967 Command History, March 9, 1968, Fleet Pre-1998, AR/229, VF-53, Box 257, File F4, NHHC.
81. Bonetti, The War in Vietnam: January–June, 102, K717.0414-17.
82. Thompson, *To Hanoi and Back*, 65.
83. Memorandum from Senator Mike Mansfield to President Johnson, April 29, 1967, *FRUS 1964–1968, V*, 355.
84. Message from 7AF to CINCPACAF, 150825Z, May 1967, K717.312-64, AFHRA.
85. Cosmas, *Joint Chiefs of Staff 1960–1968, Part 3*, 21.
86. Commander in Chief US Pacific Fleet to Commander in Chief, Pacific, Rolling Thunder Report and Analysis, 16 May 1967, Vietnam Command Files, COLL/372, Box 109, File CPF RT Rept 24 April–7 May 1967, NHHC; Pratt, Air Tactics against NVN Air Ground Defenses, 11, K717.0414-16, AFHRA.

87. Department of the Air Force, Combat Alley Follow-On Study Report, K143.042-18, 19670922, AFHRA.
88. Summary of Air Operations in Southeast Asia, June 1967, Appendix 5A, K717.3063, June 1967; Pratt, Air Tactics against NVN Air Ground Defenses, 11, K717.0414-16, AFHRA; Thompson, *To Hanoi and Back*, 74.
89. Tom Johnson's Notes of Meeting, July 18, 1967, *FRUS 1964–1968, V*, 623.
90. Summary of Air Operations in Southeast Asia, June–July 1967, Appendix 5A, K717.3063, AFHRA; Jim Jones, Assistant to the President, Notes of Meeting, August 18, 1967, *FRUS 1964–1968, V*, 709.
91. John S. Attinello, WSEG Report 116, Air-to-Air Encounters in Southeast Asia, Volume III: Events from 1 March 1967 to 1 August 1967 and Miscellaneous Events (Arlington, VA: Institute for Defense Analysis, February 1969), 20. This was an F-4C shot down on June 26. The CHECO Report Air-to-Air Encounters over North Vietnam 1 July 1967–31 December 1968 (HQ PACAF, 30 August 1969) does not list the loss. Stennis Hearings, 63.
92. Combined Campaign Plan 1967, TAB 1, Rolling Thunder/Barrel Roll Operations (July–September 1967), K740.317-3, 14 October 1967, AFHRA; Message from CTG 77.4 to NMCC, 241206Z, August 1967, Vietnam Air War Collection, Box 69, Folder 69/1, NHHC.
93. Thompson, *To Hanoi and Back*, 90; Chronology of Thirteenth Air Force, 1967, Pacific Area Naval Operations Review October 1967, 21, NHHC.
94. Niall Ferguson, *Kissinger, 1923–1968: The Idealist* (New York: Penguin, 2015), 734–58.
95. Woods, *LBJ: Architect of American Ambition*, 807.
96. William C. Sherman, *Air Warfare* (New York: Ronald Press, 1926), 32–33, 154, 190, 231; Douhet, *The Command of the Air*, 53; J. C. Slessor, *Air Power and Armies* (London: Oxford University Press, 1936), 37, 53–57; Momyer, *Air Power in Three Wars*, 5, 20, 22, 40, 111, 115; Robert Frank Futrell, *Ideas, Concepts, Doctrine: Basic Thinking in the United States Air Force, 1961–1984*, Vol. 2 (Maxwell AFB, AL: Air University Press, 1989), 468.
97. Memorandum from the President's Special Assistant (Rostow) to President Johnson, September 11, 1967, *FRUS 1964–1968, V*, 768; Van Staaveren, *Gradual Failure*, 59; Cosmas, *Joint Chiefs of Staff 1960–1968, Part 3*, 70; Summary of Air Operations in Southeast Asia, August 1967, Appendix 5A, K717.3063, AFHRA.
98. Tom Johnson, Notes of Meeting, August 24, 1967, *FRUS 1964–1968, V*, 723–25; Xiaobing Li, *Building Ho's Army: Chinese Military Assistance to North Vietnam* (Lexington: University Press of Kentucky, 2019), 174.
99. Notes of the President's Meeting with Secretary McNamara, Secretary Katzenbach, CIA Director Helms, Walt W. Rostow, George Christian. September 26, 1967, *FRUS 1964–1968, V*, 826; Thompson, *To Hanoi and Back*, 89; Cosmas, *Joint Chiefs of Staff 1960–1968, Part 3*, 81.
100. Message from CINCPAC to RUEKDA/JCS, 100325Z, October 1967, K717.312, AFHRA.
101. Notes of the President's Meeting with Secretary Rusk, Secretary McNamara, Walt Rostow, George Christian, General Wheeler, October 23, 1967, *FRUS 1964–1968, V*, 916–17.
102. Department of the Air Force, Combat Alley Follow-On Study Report, K143.042-18, 19670922, AFHRA.
103. Cosmas, *Joint Chiefs of Staff 1960–1968, Part 3*, 81–82; Message from CINCPAC to JCS, CINCPAC Monthly Rolling Thunder Summary, October 1967, 080330Z, November 1967, K717.1623-2, AFHRA; Chronology of Thirteenth Air Force, 1967, K750.01, Vol. 1, 1967, AFHRA; Pacific Area Naval Operations Review October 1967, 21, Commander in Chief U.S. Pacific Fleet, Analysis Staff Study 9-68, U.S. Air-to-Air Activity in Southeast Asia July–December 1967, Vietnam Command Files, COLL/372, Box 113, File CPF Staff Study 9-68, NHHC; Thompson, *To Hanoi and Back*, 90.

104. Bonetti, The War in Vietnam: January–June 1967, 11, K717.0414-17.
105. Pacific Area Naval Operations Review October 1967, 21, and Pacific Area Naval Operations Review November 1967, 14, Vietnam Command Files, Box 103, File November 1967, NHHC.
106. CINCPAC Message, Year-End Review of Vietnam, 1 January 1968, K712.1623-2, January 1968, AFHRA.
107. Brig. Gen. Jammie M. Philpott, DCS/Intelligence, to Maj. Gen. Jack E. Thomas, Assistant Chief of Staff, Intelligence, 13 September 1967, Atch 1: 7AF Air Effectiveness Trends during the Southwest Monsoon 1967, K740.04-18, AFHRA.
108. History of Pacific Air Forces, Vol. 1, Part 2, January–December 1968, 478, K717.01, Vol. 1, Part 2; Notes of the President's Meeting with the National Security Council, February 7, 1968, ed. Kent Sieg, *Foreign Relations of the United States, 1964–1968, Volume VI, Vietnam, January–August 1968* (Washington, DC: Government Printing Office, 2002), 142 (hereafter referred to as *FRUS 1964–1968, VI*); Thompson, *To Hanoi and Back*, 127.
109. Notes of the President's Meeting with the National Security Council, February 7, 1968, *FRUS 1964–1968, VI*, 142.
110. History of the 8th Tactical Fighter Wing, 1 January–31 March 1968, 26-29, K-WG-8-HI, AFHRA; Thompson, *To Hanoi and Back*, 127.
111. Thompson, *To Hanoi and Back*, 128; R. Frank Futrell, et al., *Aces and Aerial Victories: The United States Air Force in Southeast Asia, 1965–1973* (Washington, DC: Office of Air Force History, 1976), 78–79. The AIM-7E Sparrow (air intercept missile 7, "E" version) was a missile that homed in on the reflected radar returns its launch aircraft aimed at the target aircraft. Since the gun-armed F-4E was not yet available, F-4Ds often flew with a 20mm gun pod as a supplement to their missiles.
112. History of the Pacific Air Forces, 1 January–31 December 1968, 388, K717.01, Vol. 1, Part 2, 1968, AFHRA; HQ CINCPAC, Pacific Area Naval Operations Review January 1968, 14, Vietnam Command Files, Box 104, File January 1968, NHHC; HQ CINCPAC, Pacific Area Naval Operations Review February 1968, 10, Vietnam Command Files, Box 104, File February 1968, NHHC.
113. Pacific Area Naval Operations Review February 1968, 10, NHHC.
114. History of the Pacific Air Forces, 1968, 234–35, K717.01, Vol. 1, Part 2.
115. Pacific Area Naval Operations Review February 1969, 18, NHHC.
116. Notes of Meeting in the Cabinet Room, May 15, 1968, *FRUS 1964–1968, VI*, 669.
117. Lieutenant Colonel Donald M. Sorlie, An Analysis of the F-105 Weapons System in Out-Country Counter Air Operations, Maxwell AFB, April 1968, K239.042-3684, AFHRA.
118. Message from 7AF AFSSO to PACAF AFSSO, PACAF Team Visit 30 June–6 July 1972, 050720Z, August 1972, Folder General Vogt's Read File August 1972, AFHSD.
119. Memorandum from the President's Assistant for National Security Affairs (Kissinger) to President Nixon, January 29, 1972, ed. John M. Carland, *Foreign Relations of the United States, 1969–1976 Volume VIII: Vietnam, January–October 1972* (Washington, DC: United States Government Printing Office, 2010), 39–40 (hereafter referred to as *FRUS 1969–1976, VIII*).
120. Message from the Commander, Military Assistance Command, Vietnam (Abrams) to the Commander in Chief, Pacific (McCain), January 20, 1972, *FRUS 1969–1976, VIII*, 4.
121. Minutes of the Senior Review Group Meeting, January 24, 1972, *FRUS 1969–1976, VIII*, 26.
122. CINCPAC Command History 1972, Vol. 1, 153, K712.01, 1972, Vol. 1, AFHRA; Eighth Air Force Activity Input to Project Corona Harvest Phase V, 1 July 1971–30 June 1972 with Emphasis on Bullet Shot/Constant Guard, 15 October 1972, K520.041-2, AFHRA. Operation Freedom Train commenced on April 5.
123. Thompson, *To Hanoi and Back*, 225–27; Charles K. Hopkins, SAC Bomber Ops in SEA War, 734–35, K416.01-204, AFHRA; Henry Kissinger, *White House Years* (Boston: Little, Brown,

1979), 1154.
124. Thompson, *To Hanoi and Back,* 242; CINCPAC Command History 1972, Vol. 1, 153, K712.01, 1972, Vol. 1, AFHRA.
125. Message from AFSSO to AFSSO CSAF, Daily Wrap Up, 151115Z, June 1972, Vogt Papers, Message Traffic June 1972, AFHSD; History of the Pacific Air Forces, July 1971–June 1972, Vol. 1, 75–76, K717.01, AFHRA.
126. Message from 432 TACRECONWG/DO Udorn RTAFB to RUMMRSA/7AF/DO, MiG Tactics, 151140, May 1972, K717.03-221, July 1971–June 1972, Vol. 3, AFHRA.
127. John T. Smith, *The Linebacker Raids: The Bombing of North Vietnam, 1972* (London: Arms and Armour, 1998), 110. Michael O'Connor's narrative mentions the "campaign to cripple the North Vietnamese fighter fields." O'Connor, *MiG Killers of Yankee Station*, 230; CINCPAC Command History 1972, Vol. 1, 161, K712.01, 1972, Vol. 1; HQ PACAF, Directorate of Operations Analysis, Summary of Air Operations Southeast Asia, May 1972, pp. 4–B-2, 4–B-7, K717.3063, AFHRA; Message from AFSSO 7AF to AFSSO CSAF, Daily Wrap Up, 241100Z, May 1972, Vogt Papers, Message Traffic May 1972, AFHSD.
128. Air Operations in Southeast Asia, 1 July 1972–15 August 1973, Vol. 2, p. iv-14, K717.0423-23, AFHRA (hereafter referred to as Air Operations Southeast Asia 1972–1973, K717.0423-23).
129. Ibid., pp. iv-98 through iv-100.
130. Directorate of Operations Analysis, Summary Air Operations Southeast Asia July 1972, pp. 4-B-1 through 4-B-22, K717.3063, July 1972, AFHRA.
131. Message from 7AF to CINCPACAF, 060301Z, August 1972, K717.0423-21, AFHRA.
132. Air Operations in Southeast Asia, 1972–1973, Vol. 2, p. iv-100, K717.0423-23, AFHRA.
133. Ibid., p. iv-102; Message from 7AF to RUEFHQA/CSAF/XOOX, Vinh Airfield Strike, 140450Z, August 1972; Message from 7th AF to RUHHABA/CINCPACAF, Linebacker Conference Bravo V, 081218Z, September 1972, K740.3391; Air Operations in Southeast Asia, 1972–1973, Vol. 2, pp. iv-104 to iv-105, iv-121, K717.0423-23, Vol. 2, AFHRA.
134. Air Operations in Southeast Asia, 1972–1973, Vol. 2, p. iv-1233, K717.0423-23, 1; Message from 7th AF to RUHHABA/PACAF, Linebacker Conference Victor VI and Whiskey VI, 030216Z, October 1972; Message from 7th AF to RUEFHQA/CSAF, Linebacker Conference Quebec VII and Romeo VII, 141149Z, October 1972, K740.3391, AFHRA.
135. Linebacker Conference Charlie VIII and Uniform VII, 191300Z, October 1972, Message from 7th AF to RUEFHQA/CSAF/XOO, Personal for General Hargrove and General Blesse from General Talbot, 201052Z, October 1972, K740.3391, AFHRA; Message from AFSSO Udorn to AFSSO 7AF Personal to General Vogt from Major General Hughes, Linebacker Conference Delta VIII, 171210Z, October 1972, Vogt Papers, Message Traffic October 1972, AFHSD.
136. Colonel Scott G. Smith, End of Tour Report, 31 May 1973, K717.131, AFHRA. Smith was the commander of the 432 Tactical Reconnaissance Wing (hereafter referred to as the 432nd TRW).
137. Air Operations in Southeast Asia, 1972–1973, Vol. 2, p. iv-105, K717.0423-23, AFHRA.
138. Ibid., p. iv-265.
139. Message from CINCPACAF to AIG 7289, 090145Z, February 1973, NVN Air Defense Reactions against Linebacker II, K744.312, 1972–1973, Vol. 1; Message, Personal to General Vogt from Major General Hughes, Linebacker Conference 22 December 1972, 250645Z, December 1972, K744.01, 1972, Vol. II, Appendix V, AFHRA; Message, Personal to General Vogt from Colonel Olshefski, Linebacker II Critique 22 December 1972, Continued, 230645Z, December 1972, K744.01 1972, Vol. II, Appendix V, AFHRA.
140. Message, Personal to General Vogt from Colonel Olshefski, Linebacker Conference 24 December 1972, 241715Z, December 1972, K744.01, 1972, Vol. II, Appendix V, AFHRA; HQ 7th AF, History of Linebacker Operations, 10 May 1972–23 October 1972, 69, K740.04-24,

1972, AFHRA.
141. Message, Personal to General Vogt from Colonel Olshefski, Linebacker Conference 22 December 1972, Final Section of Six, 230645Z, December 1972; Message, Personal to General Vogt from Colonel Olshefski, Linebacker Conference 24 December 1972, 241715Z, December 1972, K744.01, 1972, Vol. II, Appendix V, AFHRA. LORAN triangulated three signals and compensated for wind in order to determine a bomb release point.
142. Colonel Herman L. Gilster and Captain Robert E. M. Frady, Directorate of Operations Analysis, Linebacker II USAF Bombing Survey, April 1973, 14–15, K143.054-1, Vol. 34, AFHRA.

Chapter 3

1. Van Staaveren, *Gradual Failure*, 141.
2. History of Pacific Air Forces, 1 July–31 December 1965, Vol. 1, Part 2, 107, K717.01, AFHRA.
3. PACAF DI, Effects of Air Operations in Southeast Asia, September 1966, 34, K717.6092, AFHRA.
4. Van Staaveren, *Gradual Failure*, 141, 267–68; Li, *Building Ho's Army*, 168–69.
5. Summary Air Operations Southeast Asia, July 1966, pp. 5-1 through 5-27, K717.3063, AFHRA.
6. History of the Pacific Air Forces 1966, 29, K717.01, Vol. 1, Part 1, AFHRA.
7. Michael McCrea, *US Navy, Marine Corps, and Air Force Fixed-Wing Aircraft Losses and Damage in Southeast Asia (1962–1973)*, Center for Naval Analyses Study, August 1976, 6–20. An earlier Air Force source lists higher numbers for losses to small arms and AAA at 1,443 and sixty-seven to MIGs. Directorate, Force Development and Analysis, DCS Plans, Tactical Air Command. Summary of USAF Aircraft Losses in SEA, 24, K417.042-16, AFHRA.
8. The Navy lost 136 more aircraft to unknown causes, and fratricide destroyed twelve Navy aircraft. McCrea, *US Navy, Marine Corps, and Air Force Fixed-Wing Aircraft*, 6-2, 6-11.
9. History of the Pacific Air Forces, 1966, 240, 242, 247.
10. PACAF DI, Effects of Air Operations in Southeast Asia, 28 October 1965, 16, K717.6092, AFHRA.
11. Van Staaveren, *Gradual Failure*, 186–87.
12. History of the Pacific Air Forces 1966, 248–53, K717.01, Vol. 1, Part 2, AFHRA; OPNAV 5750-1 Attack Squadron Fifty-Five Command History 1968, Fleet Pre-1998, AR/229, Box 132, File F13, NHHC.
13. Lieutenant Colonel Ralph F. Moody, et al., U.S. Marines in Vietnam, Part VII: Backing Up the Troops, 20: 20, 30 January 1970, Historical Division HQMC, Norman Anderson Collection, COLL/295, Box 2, Folder 13, HDMCU.
14. Thompson, *To Hanoi and Back*, 49.
15. Headquarters, Seventh Air Force, Commando Hunt VII, 1972, 138, K740.04-14, November 1971–March 1972, AFHRA; Brigadier General W. D. Dunham, End of Tour Report, 9 July 1967, K740.131, Dunham, Wm. D., August 1966–July 1967, AFHRA.
16. General L. D. Clay, HQ 7th AF, Lam Son 719 Operations: Lessons Learned, 18 May 1971, K740.04-15, February–March 1971, AFHRA; Southeast Asia Air Operations July 1971. K717.3063-1 July 1971, AFHRA.
17. History of 7th Air Force, 1 July 1971–30 June 1972, Attachment 4, K740.01-25, Vol. 4, Part 4, AFHRA.
18. Randolph, *Powerful and Brutal Weapons*, 53–54.
19. Message from 7th AF to RUHHABA/CINCPACAF, Linebacker Conference Yankee V and Zulu V, 211302Z, September 1972, AFHRA; Message from 7th AF to RUHHABA/CINCPACAF, Linebacker Conference Bravo IV and Charlie IV, 241202Z, September 1972, K740.3391, AFHRA.

20. OEG/OP-508W Summary of Air Operations in Southeast Asia, 1 January 1972–31 January 1973, Table 4-17, COLL/7 Publications of the Center for Naval Analyses OEG, Box 73, File OEG Memo 001448-73, NHHC.
21. Captain S. R. Foley Jr., USS *Midway* to Chief of Naval Operations, 1972 Command History, 14 March 1973, Ships History, Decommissioned, USS *Midway*, Box 527E, File CVA-41 Command History 1972, NHHC; Citino, *Blitzkrieg to Desert Storm*, 176; M. J. Armitage and R. A. Mason, *Air Power in the Nuclear Age* (Urbana: University of Illinois Press, 1983), 127, 129. ZSU-23s inflicted considerable losses on low-flying Israeli aircraft during the Yom Kippur War of 1973.
22. Van Staaveren, *Gradual Failure*, 201.
23. History of the Pacific Air Forces, 1968, 194, 458. K717.01, Vol. 1, Part 2, AFHRA.
24. Credit goes to then Major Ed Redman for making this point in a 2004 seminar at Air Command and Staff College (ACSC), Maxwell AFB, Alabama.
25. Message from COMSEVENTHFLT info CINCPACFLIT, from CTG 77.7 to CTU 78.1.1, 051252Z, April 1972, Vietnam Air War Collection, Box 69, Folder 69/5, NHHC; Melyan and Bonetti, Rolling Thunder, July 1965–December 1966, 5, 7, K717.0414-12, AFHRA; Rogers and Knops, Study in Air Defense. K470.40-22, AFHRA.
26. Van Staaveren, *Gradual Failure*, 141.
27. Rogers and Knops, Study in Air Defense, K470.40-22, AFHRA.
28. Message from CTG 77.8 to NMCC, CINCPAC, 131002Z, July 1966, Reference Files, Vietnam, A-Air Warfare (I), File Vietnam Air Ops MiG Combat, NHHC.
29. Message from CINCPAC to JCS, Radar Destruction in NVN South of 20 Degrees, 182219Z, March 1965, K712.1623-2, AFHRA; Notes of Meeting, July 26, 1965, 6:10–6:55 p.m., *FRUS 1964–1968, III*, 253–57; Li, *Building Ho's Army*, 169.
30. General Eggers, Deputy Director for Operations, J-3, Briefing: The Employment and Effectiveness of Missiles and Guided Weapons in SE Asia, circa 1973, K712.153-1, 72/03/00–72/10/00. This document does not give his first name, but he was probably Brigadier General George Dewey Eggers Jr., US Army. Project Red Baron III, Air-to-Air Encounters in Southeast Asia, Vol. 3, Part 1, 17, Roll 30, 153, Index 1109, K417.0735-7, AFHRA.
31. Greenhalgh, *The RF-101 Voodoo, 1961–1970*, 78; Pribbenow, *Victory in Vietnam*, 165; Van Staaveren, *Gradual Failure*, 114.
32. Editorial Note, *FRUS 1964–1968, II*, 693–94.
33. Van Staaveren, *Gradual Failure*, 128; Editorial Note, *FRUS 1964–1968, II*, 694.
34. Editorial Note, *FRUS 1964–1968, II*, 700.
35. Thompson, *To Hanoi and Back*, 35; Notes of a Meeting, May 16, 1965, *FRUS 1964–1968, II*, 667.
36. Van Staaveren, *Gradual Failure*, 114; Message from CINCPACAF to RUMABA/13 AF, Phuc Yen Air Attack—SVN Air Defense, 092322Z, June 1965, K712.1623-2, AFHRA.
37. Van Staaveren, *Gradual Failure*, 163; Cosmas, *The Joint Chiefs of Staff, 1960–1968, Part 2*, 371–72.
38. Memorandum from Secretary of Defense McNamara to President Johnson, June 2, 1965, *FRUS 1964–1968, II*, 707.
39. Melyan and Bonetti, Rolling Thunder, July 1965–December 1966, 2, K717.0414-12, AFHRA; Van Staaveren, *Gradual Failure*, 114, 163–64. Captain Fobair's remains were positively identified in 2001 by the Defense POW/MIA Accounting Agency (DPAA). See http://www.dpaa.mil/portals/85/Documents/VietnamAccounting/pmsea_acc_p_ca.pdf. Notes of Meeting, July 26, 1965, *FRUS 1964–1968, III*, 242.
40. Notes of Meeting, July 26, 1965, *FRUS 1964–1968, III*, 244.
41. Notes of Meeting, July 26, 1965, 6:10–6:55 p.m., *FRUS 1964–1968, III*, 253–57; Summary Notes of the 553d Meeting of the National Security Council, July 27, 1965, *FRUS 1964–1968, III*, 262.
42. History Naval Operations, Vol. III, 1965–1967, Part 1, 899, NHHC; *FRUS* states that the North

Vietnamese shot down six F-105s. *FRUS 1964–1968, III*, 257fn. Melyan and Bonetti, Rolling Thunder, July 1965–December 1966, 5, K717.0414-12; Thompson, *To Hanoi and Back*, 36.
43. Colonel Robert P. Parsons, Message from CINCPACAF to CINCPAC, SAM Site Problem, 30 July 1965, K717.01, July–December 1965, Vol. 2, Part 2. The term "wild weasel" generally refers to the aircraft performing an "Iron Hand" suppression of enemy air defenses mission. Lt. Col. Robert M. Burch, Tactical Electronic Warfare Operations in SEA, 1962–1968 (HQ PACAF: Directorate, Tactical Evaluation CHECO Division, 1969), 30, K717.0413-51, AFHRA; Cosmas, *The Joint Chiefs of Staff, 1960–1968, Part 2*, 372.
44. Intelligence Memorandum No. 2391/65, *FRUS 1964–1968, III*, 503; Van Staaveren, *Gradual Failure*, 143–44, 192; History Naval Operations, Vol. III, 1965–1967, Part 1, 89, NHHC; Cosmas, *The Joint Chiefs of Staff, 1960–1968, Part 2*, 373.
45. Message from PACAF to 2nd Air Division, 120208Z, October 1965, Telecon Number 184, K717.1623, AFHRA.
46. Message from CINCPAC to CINCPACFLT, 180054Z, September 1966, K712.1623-2; Van Staaveren, *Gradual Failure*, 267–69, 272.
47. Van Staaveren, *Gradual Failure*, 251.
48. Ibid., 256.
49. David Robarge, *Archangel: CIA's Supersonic A-12 Reconnaissance Aircraft*, 2nd ed. (Washington, DC: Central Intelligence Agency, Center for the Study of Intelligence, 2012), 35–37.
50. Cosmas, *The Joint Chiefs of Staff, 1960–1968, Part 2*, 515; History of Pacific Air Forces, January–December 1966, 29, K717.01, Vol. 1, Part 1, AFHRA.
51. Van Staaveren, *Gradual Failure*, 203; Randolph, *Powerful and Brutal Weapons*, 201.
52. Message from 7th AF to RUHHABA/CINCPACAF, Linebacker Conference South, 091131Z, September 1972 and Message from 7th AF to RUHHABA/CINCPACAF, Linebacker Conferences Charlie V/Delta V, 091132Z, September 1972, K740.3391, AFHRA.
53. Foley Jr., USS *Midway* 1972 Command History, 14 March 1973, NHHC.
54. Commander E. E. Tissot, Commander Attack Carrier Air Wing Fourteen to Commander Naval Force, U.S. Pacific Fleet, Addendum Report, 4 December 1967, Fleet Active, CVW-14, Box 20, File 1967, NHHC.
55. Tactics and Operating Procedures, CVW-14 Addendum Report, 4 December 1967, Fleet Active, CVW-14, Box 20, File 1967, NHHC. Another phrase is "the ground always wins."
56. Headquarters 1st Marine Aircraft Wing to Commandant of the Marine Corps, Lessons Learned from Combat Operations, March 29, 1968, Vietnam, Box 7, Folder 15, Archives Branch, HDMCU.
57. Assessment of Air Operations, 7 February 1965 thru 19 July 1967, 22, K740.04-20, AFHRA.
58. Lien-Hang T. Nguyen, *Hanoi's War: An International History of the War for Peace in Vietnam* (Chapel Hill: University of North Carolina Press, 2012), 80, 89, 90; Ang Cheng Guan, *The Vietnam War from the Other Side: The Vietnamese Communists' Perspective* (New York: Routledge Curzon, 2002), 120–35.
59. Van Staaveren, *Gradual Failure*, 195.
60. Ibid., 174–75.
61. Craig C. Hannah, *Striving for Air Superiority: The Tactical Air Command in Vietnam* (College Station: Texas A&M University Press, 2002), 8; R. T. Pretty and D. H. R. Archer, *Jane's Weapons Systems* (London: Jane's, 1969), 85.
62. Van Staaveren, *Gradual Failure*, 239, 270; Thompson, *To Hanoi and Back*, 103; History Naval Operations, Vol. III, 1965–1967, Part 1, 91, NHHC.
63. Tissot, Commander Attack Carrier Air Wing Fourteen, Addendum Report, 4 December 1967, NHHC.
64. These were the "panoramic SCA Receiver (IR-133), and a missile guidance warning receiver

(WR-300)." 355th Tactical Fighter Wing 1 July 1965–31 December 1965, Document 22, K-WG-355-HI.
65. Commander D. F. Mow, Attack Squadron One Hundred Sixty Four to Chief of Naval Operations, Command History 1 February 1967–1 March 1968, Fleet Pre-1998, AR/229, Box 175, File F8, NHHC. Zuni rockets were five inches in diameter and their high speed imparted better accuracy.
66. Directorate of Operations History, November 1965, K717.01, July–December 1965, Vol. 2, Part 2, AFHRA. The black boxes included the APR-26, the IR-133, and the WR-300. Peter E. Davies and David W. Menard, *North American F-100 Super Sabre* (Wiltshire, UK: Crowood, 2003), 107.
67. Porter, Air Attacks against NVN Air/Ground Defenses, 18-21, K717.0414-16, AFHRA; Van Staaveren, *Gradual Failure*, 197.
68. Directorate of Operations History, December 1965, K717.01, July–December 1965, Vol. 2, Part 2, AFHRA.
69. Vice Chief of Staff U.S. Air Force Conference, 25–26 April 1966, K717.151-11, AFHRA.
70. Colonel John W. Harrell Jr., Headquarters Pacific Air Forces, Historical Report for the Month of September 1965, 8 October 1965, K717.01, July–December 1965, Vol. 2, Part 2, AFHRA.
71. HQ CINCPAC, Pacific Area Naval Operations Review November 1966, 10, Vietnam Command Files, Box 102, File November 1966, NHHC.
72. Message from 7th AF to RUEFHQA/CSAF, Linebacker Conference 14 October 1972, 171222Z October 1972, K740.3391, AFHRA; Van Staaveren, *Gradual Failure*, 269.
73. Attack Squadron One Hundred Sixty-Four, 1 March 1968, NHHC.
74. Message from 2nd Air Division to CINCPACAF, Wild Weasel I Replacement Crews, 040224Z, January 1966, K240.03-37, 1965–1966, AFHRA.
75. Thompson, *To Hanoi and Back*, 36; Larry Davis, *Wild Weasel: The SAM Suppression Story* (Carrollton, TX: Squadron/Signal, 1986), 14; Davies and Menard, *F-100*, 109–11; Hannah, *Striving for Air Superiority*, 81.
76. Directorate of Operations History, May 1966, K717.01, Vol. 3, Part 1 and Directorate of Operations History, July 1966, K717.01, July–December 1966, Vol. 3, Part 3, AFHRA.
77. Colonel Mitchell A. Cobeaga, HQ PACAF, Weekly Activity Report, 18 April 1966, K717.01, January–June 1966, Vol. 3, Part 2, AFHRA.
78. Melyan and Bonetti, Rolling Thunder, July 1965–December 1966, 106–8, K717.0414-12, Porter, Air Tactics against NVN Air/Ground Defenses, 37–38, AFHRA.
79. Dunham, End of Tour Report, 9 July 1967, K740.131, CINCPACAF, Vice Chief of Staff U.S. Air Force Conference, 25–26 April 1966, K717.151-11; End of Tour Report, Lt. Col. John F. Hurst Jr., K717.131, John F. Hurst, August 1972–April 1973, AFHRA.
80. Van Staaveren, *Gradual Failure*, 196; Wolfgang W. E. Samuel, *Glory Days: The Untold Story of the Men Who Flew the B-66 Destroyer into the Face of Fear* (Atglen, PA: Schiffer Military History, 2008), 190; History of the Pacific Air Forces, 1 January 1967–31 December 1967, 69, 75, K717.01, Vol. 1, Part 1, AFHRA; DCS/Operations, History, Directorate of Reconnaissance, March 1967, K717.01, January–June 1967, Vol. 3, Part 1, AFHRA; History of 355th Tactical Fighter Wing 1 July 1965–31 December 1965, Document 22, K-WG-355-HI, AFHRA.
81. Porter, Air Tactics against NVN Air/Ground Defenses, 16, K717.0414-16, AFHRA.
82. Captain Mark E. Smith, USAF Reconnaissance in Southeast Asia, 1961–1966 (HQ PACAF: Directorate, Tactical Evaluation, CHECO Division, 1966), 40, K717.0414-14, AFHRA.
83. Pratt, Air Tactics against NVN Air Ground Defenses, 24, K717.0414-16; Message from 7th AF to RUHHABA/CINCPACAF, Personal for General Blesse and General Hargrove from General Talbot, 060815Z, September 1972, K740.3391, 21–29 September 1972; Summary Air Operations Southeast Asia, May 1966, 1–15, K717.3063, AFHRA.
84. Thompson, *To Hanoi and Back*, 98; Pratt, Air Tactics against NVN Air Ground Defenses, 22,

NOTES FOR CHAPTER 3

K717.0414-16, AFHRA.
85. Oral History Transcript, Lieutenant General Thomas H. Miller Jr., Interviewed by Benis M. Frank and Fred H. Allison, 18 August 1986, pp. 210–12, HDMCU.
86. Van Staaveren, *Gradual Failure*, 239; Lieutenant Colonel F. C. Opeka, Marine Composite Reconnaissance Squadron 1, 3 April 1966, found online at The Vietnam Center & Sam Johnson Vietnam Archive, Texas Tech University, http://vietnam.ttu.edu; Samuel, *Glory Days*, 190–91.
87. McCutcheon, Marine Aviation in Vietnam, 1962–1970, 65, HDMCU.
88. Miller Oral History Transcript, 210–12.
89. Fleet Marine Force, Pacific, Operations of U.S. Marine Forces in Southeast Asia, 1 July 1971 thru 31 March 1973, Vietnam, Box 14, Folder 3, Archives Branch, HDMCU; Fleet Marine Force, Pacific, Operations of U.S. Marine Forces, Vietnam, October 1969, found online at The Vietnam Center & Sam Johnson Vietnam Archive, Texas Tech University, http://vietnam.ttu.edu.
90. Message from Commandant of the Marine Corps to RUHHFMA/CG FMFPAC, RUMHAW/CG III MAF, RUMHAW/CG First MAW, Covered Revetments, 192154Z, February 1968, found online at The Vietnam Center & Sam Johnson Vietnam Archive, Texas Tech University, http://vietnam.ttu.edu.
91. End of Tour Report, Lt. Col. John F. Hurst Jr., K717.131, 1972–April 1973, AFHRA.
92. CINCPAC Command History 1972, Vol. 1, 169–71, K712.01, 1972, Vol. 1, AFHRA; Air Warfare Annex, Commander Seventh Fleet to Chief of Naval Operations, Command History 1972, 26 September 1973, Command File Post, 1 January 1946, Fleets, Box 714, File Seventh Fleet, CH, 1972, NHHC.
93. Hargrove interview, September 19, 1967, 123–24, K239.0512-020, 21/12/66 to 04/08/67; Eggers, Employment of Missiles, K712.153-1, AFHRA; Thompson, *To Hanoi and Back*, 51.
94. Message from CTG 77.5 to AIG 914, 210912Z, August 1967; Message from CTG 77.5 to AIG 914, 220438Z, August 1967, Vietnam Air War Collection, Box 69, NHHC.
95. Van Staaveren, *Gradual Failure*, 270–71.
96. Directorate of Operations History, July 1966, K717.01, July–December 1966, Vol. 3, Part 3, AFHRA.
97. Colonel Thomas J. Tiernan, HQ Seventh AF, Weekly Activity Report #14, 31 July 1968, K417.01, July 1968–June 1969, Vol. 12, AFHRA.
98. Thompson, *To Hanoi and Back*, 307.
99. Air Effectiveness Trends during the Southwest Monsoon 1967, K740.04-18, AFHRA.
100. Message from 7th AF to RUEFHQA/CSAF/XOO, Linebacker Critique 26 December 1972, 280410Z, December 1972, K740.3391, AFHRA; Thompson, *To Hanoi and Back*, 36.
101. Message from AFSCC San Antonio to RUEDNBA/TAC, 22121Z, August 1967, Shrike Effectiveness Evaluation, K417.01, July 1968–June 1969, Vol. 9, AFHRA.
102. Pratt, Air Tactics against NVN Air Ground Defenses, 31, K717.0414-16, AFHRA.
103. Southeast Asia Air Operations Briefing, 7 January 1969. Commander in Chief, U.S. Pacific Fleet, Rolling Thunder Operations Report and Analysis, January 1969. Vietnam Command Files, COLL/372, Box 111, File CPF RT Rept, 16–31 December 1968, NHHC.
104. Commander K. E. Enney, Commander Attack Carrier Air Wing Fourteen to Commander Naval Air Force, U.S. Pacific Fleet, CVW-14 Addendum Report, 11 February 1969, Fleet, Active, CVW-14, Box 20, File CVW-14 Cruise Report 1968–1969, NHHC.
105. Melvin F. Porter, Second Generation Weaponry in SEA (HQ PACAF: Directorate Tactical Evaluation, 1970) 62, K717.0413-80; Bernard Nalty, *Tactics and Techniques of Electronic Warfare in Vietnam* (Defense Lion Publications, 2013), 31; Pratt, Air Tactics against NVN Air Ground Defenses, 32, K717.0414-16, AFHRA.
106. Message from CSAF to RUEDFIA/AFLC/MCOO/MCSCA/MCMTA, 162112Z, January 1968,

Project Seed Hawk, K417.01, July 1968–June 1969, Vol. 9, AFHRA; Commander in Chief U.S. Pacific Fleet, Rolling Thunder Report and Analysis, 2, Vietnam Command Files, COLL/372, Box 110, File CPF RT Report, 16–29 February 1968, NHHC.
107. Pacific Area Naval Operations Review September 1968, 20, Message from AFSPCOMMCEN to AIG 8556, 052105Z, May 1972, Vietnam Air War Collection, Box 69, Folder 69/5, NHHC.
108. Smith, Carrier Air Wing Six Cruise Report April 1968 to December 1968, 14 December 1968, NHHC; Hannah, *Striving for Air Superiority*, 85–86; Air Operations in Southeast Asia, 1972–1973, Vol. 2, pp. iv-277, 278–79, K717.0423-23, AFHRA.
109. Van Staaveren, *Gradual Failure*, 271.
110. Message from AFSSO Udorn to AFSSO 7AF, Summary of the 20–21 October 1972 Linebacker Tactics Review Conference, 230427Z, October 1972, Vogt Papers, Message Traffic, October 1972, AFHSD.
111. Pacific Area Naval Operations Review, November 1966, 13, NHHC.
112. Message, Personal to General Vogt from Major General Hughes, Summary of the 20–21 October 1972 Linebacker Tactics Review Conference, 230427Z, October 1972, K744.01 1972, Vol. II, Appendix V, AFHRA.
113. History of the Pacific Air Forces 1966, 87–88, K717.01, Vol. 1, Part 2, AFHRA.
114. HQ PACAF, Assistant for Operations Analysis, Effectiveness of QRC-160-1 Pods, May 1967, K717.310-7; Summary Air Operations Southeast Asia, July 1966, 5–9, K717.3063, AFHRA.
115. Thompson, *To Hanoi and Back*, 37, 106; Guenter Lewy, *America in Vietnam* (New York: Oxford University Press, 1978), 404; International Committee of the Red Cross, Rule 23, Location of Military Objectives Outside Densely Populated Areas, found online at: https://ihl-databases.icrc.org/customary-ihl/eng/docs/v1_rul_rule23. See also International Committee of the Red Cross, Rule 35, Hospital and Safety Zones and Neutralized Zones, found online at: https://ihl-databases.icrc.org/customary-ihl/eng/docindex/v1_rul_rule35.
116. Message from CINCPACAF to RUHKB/CINCPAC, SA-2 Threat, 132045Z, October 1966, K717.03-38, AFHRA; Cosmas, *The Joint Chiefs of Staff, 1960–1968, Part 2*, 509.
117. Max J. Cleveland, Directorate, Tactical Air Analysis Center, HQ 7AF, On the Effectiveness of the QRC-160A-1 ECM Pods, 22 February 1967, K740.31067-4, AFHRA.
118. Porter, Air Tactics against NVN Air/Ground Defenses, 49, K717.0414-16, AFHRA.
119. Effectiveness of QRC-160-1 Pods, May 1967, K717.310-7, AFHRA; Thompson, *To Hanoi and Back*, 50–51.
120. Porter, Air Tactics against NVN Air/Ground Defenses, 53, K717.0414-16, AFHRA.
121. Pratt, Air Tactics against NVN Air Ground Defenses, 36, K717.0414-16, AFHRA; Air Effectiveness Trends during the Southwest Monsoon 1967, K740.04-18, AFHRA.
122. History of the Pacific Air Forces, 1966, 255–57, 263, K717.01, Vol. 1, Part 2, AFHRA; Directorate of Operations Plans History, October 1966, K717.01, July–December 1966, Vol. 3, Part 3, AFHRA.
123. Message from 7AF to RUEDHQA/CSAF, QRC-160-1 Pods for F-105, 220925Z, November 1966, K740.1623, AFHRA; Pratt, Air Tactics against NVN Air Ground Defenses, 17, K717.0414-16, AFHRA.
124. Assessment of Air Operations, 7 February 1965 thru 19 July 1967, 21, K740.04-20, AFHRA.
125. Thompson, *To Hanoi and Back*, 104–5; C. V. Sturdivant, Effect of Strike Force Size and Spacing on Vulnerability to SAMs and Suggested Delivery Tactics for Commando Club Missions, 15 February 1968, K717.310468-1, AFHRA; Nalty, Electronic Warfare, 39; Lieutenant Colonel Robert B. Weaver, Air-to-Air Encounters over North Vietnam, 1 July 1967–31 December 1968 (HQ PACAF: Directorate, Tactical Evaluation, CHECO Division, 1969), 26, K717.0413-22, AFHRA.
126. Thompson, *To Hanoi and Back*, 105, 40; Nalty, Electronic Warfare, 22.

127. Air Effectiveness Trends during the Southwest Monsoon 1967, K740.04-18, AFHRA.
128. Stennis Hearings, 165; Thompson, *To Hanoi and Back*, 50; Air Effectiveness Trends during the Southwest Monsoon 1967, K740.04-18, AFHRA; Bonetti, The War in Vietnam: January–June 1967, 102, K717.0414-17, AFHRA; Major James B. Overton, Rolling Thunder: January 1967–November 1968 (HQ PACAF: Directorate Tactical Evaluation/CHECO Division, 1969), Figure 6, K717.0414-12, AFHRA.
129. History of the Pacific Air Forces, 1968, 285, 466, K717.01, Vol. 1, Part 2, AFHRA; Air Effectiveness Trends during the Southwest Monsoon 1967, K740.04-18, AFHRA.
130. OEG/OP-508W Operations in Southeast Asia, 1 January 1972–31 January 1973, Table 4-14, NHHC.
131. Burch, Tactical Electronic Warfare Operations in SEA, 1962–1968, 41, K717.0413-51, AFHRA; History of the Pacific Air Forces, 1968, 468, 470–71, K717.01, Vol. 1, Part 2, AFHRA.
132. Message from the Commander, Military Assistance Command, Vietnam (Abrams) to the Chairman of the Joint Chiefs of Staff (Moorer) and the Commander in Chief, Pacific (McCain), March 8, 1972, *FRUS 1969–1976, VIII*, 122.
133. Randolph, *Powerful and Brutal Weapons*, 88–90.
134. Willard J. Webb and Walter S. Poole, *History of the Joint Chiefs of Staff: The Joint Chiefs of Staff and the War in Vietnam, 1971–1973* (Washington, DC: Office of Joint History, 2007), 109, 111, 113–14.
135. Conversation among Nixon, Kissinger, and Haig, December 20, 1972, ed. John M. Carland, gen. ed. Edward C. Keefer, *Foreign Relations of the United States, 1969–1976, Volume IX, Vietnam: October 1972–January 1973* (Washington, DC: United States Government Printing Office, 2010), 789 (hereafter referred to as *FRUS 1969–1976, IX*).
136. Air Operations in Southeast Asia, 1972–1973, Vol. 2, pp. iv-105 to iv-107, K717.0423-23, AFHRA.
137. Randolph, *Powerful and Brutal Weapons*, 257–58.
138. History of the Pacific Air Forces, July 1971–June 1972, Vol. 1, 84, K717.01, AFHRA; Summary Air Operations Southeast Asia July 1972, pp. 4-4 to 4-5, K717.3063, AFHRA; Thompson, *To Hanoi and Back*, 242–44.
139. MACV Command History 1972, B-12.
140. Randolph, *Powerful and Brutal Weapons*, 284; Eggers, Employment of Missiles, K712.153-1, AFHRA.
141. Linebacker Conference Bravo V, 081218Z, September 1972, K740.3391, AFHRA.
142. Message from CINCPAC to JCS, US Aircraft Losses to NVN Air Defense System, 202114Z, July 1972, Vietnam Air War Collection, Box, 67, File 67/1, NHHC.
143. OPNAV 5750-1, Attack Squadron Fifty-Five Command History, 1972, Fleet Pre-1998, AR/229, Box 132, File F11, NHHC; Attack Squadron Thirty-Five to Chief of Naval Operations, Command History, 22 February 1973, Fleet Pre-1998, AR/229, Box 122, File F7, NHHC.
144. Eggers, Employment of Missiles, K712.153-1, AFHRA.
145. Linebacker Conference Yankee V and Zulu V, 211302Z, September 1972, K740.3391, AFHRA.
146. Eggers, Employment of Missiles, K712.153-1, AFHRA; Air Operations in Southeast Asia, 1972–1973, Vol. 2, IV-170, K717.0423-23, AFHRA.
147. History of Linebacker Operations, 10 May 1972–23 October 1972, 47–48, K740.04-24, AFHRA; Deputy Commander, 7/13 Air Force, Linebacker Tactics Review Conference, 20–23 September 1972, 25, K744.01, 1972, Vol. 2, AFHRA; Message from 7th AF to RUHHABA/PACAF, Summary of Linebacker Tactics Review Conference, 011207Z, October 1972, K740.3391, AFHRA.
148. Cook, Liaison Officer End of Tour Report, 1 December 1972, K417.0735, FY1973, AFHRA; Message from 7th AF to RUHHABA/CINCPACAF, Summary of Linebacker Mission Foxtrot

NOTES FOR CHAPTER 3

IV, 051232Z, September 1972, K740.3391, AFHRA; Capt. Robert J. Pettit Jr. and Lt. Col. Edward T. Rock, History of the 17th Wild Weasel Squadron July—September 1972, K143.044-90, Vol. 55, AFHRA.
149. Attack Squadron Fifty-Two to Chief of Naval Operations, Command History, 26 February 1973, Fleet, Pre-1998, AR/229, VA-52, Box 130, File F9, NHHC; Strategic Air Command Corona Harvest, Summary of B-52 Arc Light Operations—NVN April 1972, K416.153-1, 25 May 1972, AFHRA; Randolph, *Powerful and Brutal Weapons*, 96.
150. OEG/OP-05W, Summary of Air Operations in Southeast Asia May 1972, Center for Naval Analyses, 4–13, COLL/7 Publications of the Center for Naval Analysis, OEG, Box 72, File OEG Memo 1368–72, NHHC.
151. Eggers, Employment of Missiles, K712.153-1, AFHRA; Commander J. A. McKenzie, Commander Attack Carrier Air Wing Eleven, Cruise Report of February to November 1972, 1 December 1972, Fleet, Active, CVW-11, Box 19, File 1971–1972, NHHC.
152. Message from 388 TFW to RUEKJCS/NMCC 040844Z, April 1972, Vietnam Air War Collection, Box 69, Folder 69/5, NHHC; Linebacker Tactics Review Conference, 20–23 September 1972, 25, K744.01, 1972, Vol. 2; Linebacker Conference Oscar IV and Papa IV, 230834Z, August 1972, K740.3391, AFHRA.
153. Message from AFSSO Udorn to AFSSO 7AF, Personal to General Vogt from Major General Hughes, Linebacker Conference Mike V and South II, 100620Z, September 1972, Vogt Papers, Message Traffic October 1972, AFHSD; Message from 7th AF to RUHHABA/CINCPACAF, 060815Z, September 1972, K740.3391, AFHRA.
154. Message from 7th AF to RUEFHQA/CSAF/XOO, Linebacker Conference Kilo VII and Juliet VII, 131333Z, October 1972 and Message from 7th AF to RUHHABA/CINCPACAF, Linebacker Conference Whiskey V and X-Ray V, 201236Z, September 1972, K740.3391, AFHRA.
155. Thompson, *To Hanoi and Back,* 243–44; CINCPACAF (DOAD) Lessons Learned Summary: Sam Sites, 9 April 1973, K168.06-239, 72/10/24–75/03/00, AFHRA.
156. Linebacker Conference Whiskey V and X-Ray V, 201236Z, September 1972, K740.3391, AFHRA; Air Operations in Southeast Asia, 1972–1973, Vol. 2, pp. iv-100, iv-203, K717.0423-23, AFHRA.
157. Corona Harvest V, 1972–1973, 62–64, 96, K416.041-13, AFHRA; Gillette, History 307th Strategic Wing, October–December 1972, Vol. 1, 60, K-WG-307-HI, AFHRA.
158. Transcript of a Telephone Conversation between the Chairman of the Joint Chiefs of Staff (Moorer) and the President's Assistant for National Security Affairs (Kissinger), December 19, 1972, *FRUS 1969–1976, IX*, 712; Transcript of a Telephone Conversation between Richard T. Kennedy of the National Security Council Staff and the Chairman of the Joint Chiefs of Staff (Moorer), December 21, 1972, *FRUS 1969–1976, IX*, 798; Corona Harvest V, 1972–1973, 77, 65, K416.041-13, AFHRA.
159. Message from 7th AF to RUEFHOA/CSAF/XOO, Linebacker II Arc Light Days 4 and 5, 291104Z, December 1972, K740.3391, AFHRA.
160. Message from AFSSO Udorn to AFSSO 7AF, AFSSO 13AF, Linebacker II Arclite Day Nine Critique, 290925Z, December 1972, Vogt Papers, General Vogt's Read File December 1972, AFHSD; Air Operations in Southeast Asia, 1972–1973, Vol. 2, pp. iv-277, iv-278, iv-279, K717.0423-23, AFHRA.
161. Message, Personal to General Vogt from Colonel Olshefski, Linebacker Conference 24 December 1972, 241715Z, December 1972, K744.01 1972, Vol. II, Appendix V, AFHRA; Message from AFSSO 7AF to AFSSO SAC. Ref your 210220Z, December 1972, 210540Z, December 1972, Vogt Papers, Message Traffic December 1972, AFHSD.
162. Air Operations in Southeast Asia, Lessons Learned Summary, K168.06-233, 73/01/31 –74/01/03, AFHRA.

163. Message to Gen Vogt from Col Olshefski, Linebacker Critique 26 December 1972, 261355Z, 1972, K744.01 1972, Vol. II, Appendix V, AFHRA.
164. Message to Gen Vogt from MG Hughes, Linebacker II Juliet Critique, 290945Z, December 1972, K744.01 1972, Vol. II, Appendix V, AFHRA; Message from 7/13AF/AFSSO to 7AF/AFSSO, Linebacker Conference 24 December 1972, 241715Z, December 1972 and Linebacker II Arclite Day Nine Critique, 290925Z, December 1972, Vogt Papers, General Vogt's Read File December 1972, AFHSD.
165. Message to General Vogt, info Lieutenant General Moore and Major General Talbott from Major General Hughes, Linebacker II Arclite Day 10 Critique, 300715Z, December 1972, AFHRA; Message to General Vogt from Major General Hughes, Linebacker II Arclite Day Nine Critique, 290925Z, December 1972, K744.01 1972, Vol. II, Appendix V, AFHRA.
166. USS *America* and Carrier Air Wing Eight 1972–1973 Westpac Deployment Cruise Report, 25, Ships History Decommissioned, *America* CV-66, Box 31B, File America (CV-66) III, NHHC.
167. Strategic Air Command Study on the Effectiveness of Air Power, 199, 206, K416.041-13, Vol. 1, Appendix A, AFHRA; Message to General Vogt from Major General Hughes, Linebacker II Kilo Critique, 300400Z, December 1972, K744.01 1972, Vol. II, Appendix V, AFHRA.
168. Gilster and Frady, Linebacker II USAF Bombing Survey, April 1973, 16, K143.054-1, Vol. 34, AFHRA.
169. Air Operations Learned Summary, K168.06-233, 73/01/31–74/01/03, AFHRA. The standard bomb for an F-111A was the 500-pound unguided Mark 82. An F-111 typically carried twenty-four.
170. Bonetti, The War in Vietnam: January–June 1967, 103, K717.0414-17; Marshall L. Michel, III, *The 11 Days of Christmas: America's Last Vietnam Battle* (San Francisco: Encounter Books, 2002), 212; Thompson, *To Hanoi and Back*, 269.
171. OEG/OP-508W Operations in Southeast Asia, 1 January 1972–31 January 1973, Table 4-22, NHHC.
172. Minutes of a Washington Special Actions Group Meeting, May 15, 1972, *FRUS 1969–1976, VIII*, 554; Summary Air Operations Southeast Asia July 1972, pp. 4-4 to 4-5, K717.3063; Rogers and Knops, Study in Air Defense, K470.40-22; Summary Air Operations Southeast Asia July 1972, p. 4-4, K717.3063. See also Office of PACAF History, History of Seventh Air Force, 1 July 1972–29 March 1973, 131, K740.10-25, Vol. 1 and Colonel James L. Passauer, End-of-Tour Report, K740.131, James L. Passauer, June 1972–July 1973, AFHRA; Randolph, *Powerful and Brutal Weapons*, 220; Thompson, *To Hanoi and Back*, 242–44.
173. Message from 8TFW to NMCC, 300800Z, July 1972, Vietnam Air War Collection, Box 67, File 67/1, NHHC.
174. Foley Jr., USS *Midway* 1972 Command History, 14 March 1973, NHHC.
175. CINCPAC Command History 1972, Vol. 1, 168, K712.01, 1972, Vol. 1, AFHRA.
176. Minutes of a Washington Special Actions Group Meeting, August 4, 1972, *FRUS 1969–1976, VIII*, 805; CINCPAC Command History 1972, Vol. 1, 168, K712.01 1972, Vol. 1, AFHRA.
177. Summary Air Operations Southeast Asia July 1972, 4-4, K717.3063 July 1972, AFHRA.
178. Minutes of a Washington Special Actions Group Meeting, August 4, 1972, *FRUS 1969–1976, VIII*, 805; CINCPAC Command History 1972, Vol. 1, 168, K712.01 1972, Vol. 1, AFHRA.
179. Message from AFSSO 7AF to AFSSO CSAF, Daily Wrap Up, 151100Z, May 1972, Vogt Papers, Message Traffic May 1972, AFHSD; Eggers, Employment of Missiles, K712.153-1, AFHRA; Randolph, *Powerful and Brutal Weapons*, 149, 150.
180. Major Paul T. Ringenbach and Captain Peter J. Melly, The Battle for An Loc, 5 April–26 June 1972 (HQ PACAF: Directorate of Operations Analysis, CHECO/Corona Harvest Division, 1973), 46, 47, K717.0413-196, AFHRA.

181. Eggers, Employment of Missiles, K712.153-1, AFHRA; Notes of the President's Meeting with the Joint Chiefs of Staff, February 9, 1968, *FRUS 1964–1968, VI,* 165.
182. Narrative Report USS *Long Beach* (CG (N) 9) Talos-MiG Engagement, 23 May 1968, Reference Files, Vietnam, A-Air Warfare (I), Vietnam Air Ops MiG Combat Folder. An ALQ-91 was an IFF interrogator that could interrogate MiG transponders, thus providing a reliable identification capability. The Long Beach used one to determine the identity of that contact. US Seventh Fleet Monthly Historical Summary, November 1967, 56, Vietnam Command Files, Box 117, NHHC.
183. Pacific Area Naval Operations Review September 1968, 18, NHHC; Pratt, Air Tactics against NVN Air Ground Defenses, 40, K717.0414-16, AFHRA; Eggers, Employment of Missiles, K712.153-1, AFHRA.
184. Commander Seventh Fleet to Chief of Naval Operations, Command History 1972, 26 September 1973, Command File Post 1 January 1946, Fleets, Box 714, File Seventh Fleet, CH, 1972, NHHC.
185. Message from USS *Biddle* to NMCC/RUEKJCS, 191630Z, July 1972, NHHC; Message from USS *Biddle* to NMCC, 192046Z, July 1972, Vietnam Air War Collection, Box 67, File 67/1, NHHC; Eggers, Employment of Missiles, K712.153-1, AFHRA.
186. Reminiscences of Admiral Thomas Moorer, USN (Ret.), Vol. III, 1254, Navy Department Library.
187. R. A. Ross, Memorandum: Air Defense during the Mining of Haiphong Harbor on 9 May 1972, CNA 00449-73, 16 November 1973, COLL/7 Publications of the Center for Naval Analyses OEG, Box 73, File OEG Memo 00449-73, NHHC; Randolph, *Powerful and Brutal Weapons,* 170, 175.

Chapter 4

1. Van Staaveren, *Gradual Failure,* 143.
2. These F-104s were in the 476th TFS. Ibid., 117–18; Hiller, Southeast Asia Counter-Air Alternatives, K717.310-2, AFHRA
3. History of the Pacific Air Force, 1 January 1967–31 December 1967, 46–49, K717.01, Vol. 1, Part 1, AFHRA; Message from 7th AF to AIG 7295, 25 June 1966, Increased Air Defense Posture, K717.01 January–December 1967, Vol. 2, Part 1, AFHRA; Directorate of Operations History, May 1966, K717.01 January–June 1966, Vol. 3, Part 1, AFHRA.
4. Chris Hobson, *Vietnam Air Losses: United States Air Force, Navy and Marine Corps Fixed-Wing Aircraft Losses in Southeast Asia 1961–1973* (Hinckley, England: Midland, 2001), 135; Alan Stephens, *The Royal Australian Air Force: A History* (South Melbourne: Oxford University Press, 2006), 254, 257.
5. Message from CG III MAF to COMUSMACV, Assessment of Enemy Situation in ICTZ, 030120Z, October 1969, found online at The Vietnam Center & Sam Johnson Vietnam Archive, Texas Tech University, http://vietnam.ttu.edu.
6. History of Pacific Air Forces, 1 July 1969–30 June 1970, 25–26, K717.01, FY 1970, Vol. 1, Part 1, AFHRA.
7. Lt. Col. Guyman Penix and Major Paul T. Ringenbach, Air Defense in Southeast Asia, 1945–1971 (HQ PACAF: Directorate of Operations Analysis, CHECO/Corona Harvest Division, 1973), K717.0414-36, AFHRA.
8. Message from CTG Seven Seven Pt Seven to JCS, 031451Z, April 1965, K160.043-16 April 1965–March 1967, AFHRA; John S. Attinello, Report R-123, Air-to-Air Encounters in Southeast Asia, Volume I: Account of F-4 and F-8 Events Prior to 1 March 1967 (Institute for Defense Analysis, Systems Evaluation Division, 1967), 33–34; Cosmas, *The Joint Chiefs of Staff, 1960–1968, Part 2,* 232, 234.
9. Colonel Robert R. Scott, PACAF Tactics and Techniques Bulletin, 45, 26 July 1966, K717.549-1, No. 45, 26 July 1966; Interview with Maj Keith B. Connolly, 8 November 1968, Interview with

Captain Donald Kilgus, no date, Captain Donald Kilgus, MiG Engagement of 4 April 1965, 19 February 1968, K740.04-25, 60/03/18–68/02/19, AFHRA; Institute for Defense Analysis, Air to Air Encounters in Southeast Asia, Vol. III, 1969, Event III-2, 37–38. Green 2 was the jet in Event III-2 that shot 20mm at the MiG. One source states that two MiG-17s were shot down on April 3 and 4, which suggests that Kilgus's shots on the MiG-17 downed it. Istvan Toperczer, *Air War over North Vietnam: The Vietnamese People's Air Force: 1949–1975* (Carrollton, TX: Squadron/Signal Publications, 1998), 12.

10. Summary of USAF Aircraft Losses in SEA, 42, K417.042-16, AFHRA.

11. Attinello, Report R-123, Air-to-Air Encounters in Southeast Asia, Volume I, 17; Colonel Robert R. Scott, PACAF Tactics and Techniques Bulletin, No. 25, 27 September 1965, K717.549-1, Nos. 22–31 (incomplete) 14 September–14 December 1965, AFHRA; Van Staaveren, *Gradual Failure*, 159.

12. The AIM-9B Sidewinder was a missile that guided on the heat signature of an enemy aircraft. A "rear aspect" missile, the ones used during the Vietnam War could only home in on the heat of the jet's exhaust, thus the launch aircraft had to be behind the target. Porter, Air Tactics against NVN Air/Ground Defenses, 5-6, K717.0414-16, AFHRA.

13. Message from Chief of Staff of the Air Force to RUHLKM/CINCPACAF, 092238Z, September 1966, F-104C Employment in SEA, K717.01 January–December 1967, Vol. 2, Part 1, AFHRA.

14. The first squadron was the 476th and was forward based at Da Nang until July 17, when the 436th TFS took over. Then on October 15, the 435th TFS replaced it for only a month, when an F-4C squadron, the 390th TFS, arrived from Holloman AFB. History, Twelfth Air Force, July–December 1965, K650.01-28, Vol. 1, AFHRA.

15. Lieutenant Colonel Howard H. Dale, TACOP Final Report, 5 August 1965, K-WG-479-HI January–June 1965, Vol. 1, AFHRA; Chronology of Thirteenth Air Force, 1967, K750.01, Vol. 1, 1967, AFHRA; Lieutenant Colonel Harlan E. Ball, TACOP Final Report, 8 August 1965, K-WG-479-HI, July–December 1965, Vol. 2, AFHRA.

16. Dale, TACOP Final Report, 18 January 1966, K-WG-479-HI, July–December 1965, Vol. 2, AFHRA.

17. John Attinello, Report R-123 Air-to-Air Encounters in Southeast Asia, Volume 1, October 1967, Institute for Defense Analysis, Systems Evaluation Division, WSEG Report 116, p. 17; Institute for Defense Analysis, Air-to-Air Encounters in Southeast Asia, Volume III, February 1969, 43, 115.

18. Directorate of Operations History, May 1966, K717.01, January–June 1966, Vol. 3, Part 1, AFHRA; Message from 7th AF to CINCPACAF, Early Deployment of F-104, 290634Z, May 1966, K717.312, 28–31 May 1966, AFHRA; Message from 8TFW to RUMBD FP/DEP Cmdr 7 13 AF, F-104/F4C Mission, 041351Z, June 1966, K717.312, AFHRA.

19. Message from 7AF to PACAF CC, MiG CAP, 290328Z, July 1966, K717.312, July 1966, AFHRA; History 479th Tactical Fighter Wing, 1 January–30 June 1966, K-WG-479-HI, January–June 1966, AFHRA. This was the 435th TFS.

20. F-104Cs used the probe and drogue method and could not be refueled via the boom method that was the primary means through which KC-135s refueled aircraft. Captain L. T. Harvey, Fact Sheet: F-104 Udorn, 21 April 1966, K717.151-11, 25–26 April 1966, AFHRA.

21. F-104C Employment, 092238Z, September 1966, K717.01, January–December 1967, Vol. 2, Part 1, AFHRA.

22. Message from PACAF CC to 7 AF, 110045Z, September 1966, F-104 Employment in SEA, K717.01, January–December 1967, Vol. 2, Part 1, AFHRA.

23. History of the Pacific Air Forces, 1967, 52–58, K717.01, Vol. 1, Part 1, AFHRA; Message from CSAF to RUHLKMCINPACAF, F-104 Utilization, 232206Z, December 1966, K717.312, AFHRA; HQ PACAF, Weekly Activity Report, 24 October 1966, K717.01, July–December 1966,

Vol. 3, pt. 3, AFHRA.

24. Attinello, Report R-123 Air-to-Air Encounters in Southeast Asia, Volume 1, October 1967, 18, AFHRA; Historical Record of the 435th Tactical Fighter Squadron, 1 January–30 June 1967, K-WG-8-HI, January–June 1967, Vol. 1, AFHRA; Robin Olds briefing to Corona Harvest Staff, September 29, 1969, 35, 40, K239.0512-222, 00/00/66–00/00/67, AFHRA; Van Staaveren, *Gradual Failure*, 182.

25. Gun pods arrived in 1967. History, Twelfth Air Force, July–December 1965, K650.01-28, July–December 1965, Vol. 1, AFHRA; Message from TAC to RUHLKM/PACAF, F-4/F-104C Systems Capability Evaluation, 241910Z, May 1966, AFHRA; Message from TAC to RUEDHQA/CSAF, 092005Z, June 1966, K717.312, 9–10 June 1966, AFHRA.

26. Abner M. Aust, Headquarters 6002nd Standardization/Evaluation Group (PACAF), PACAF Tactics and Techniques Program (Bulletin 5), May 17, 1965, K717.549-1, Nos. 1–13, 4 May–1 July 1965, AFHRA.

27. The Air Force used the F-86H as a stand-in for the MiG-17 to try to develop effective tactics against them. Lt. Col. Ralph S. Saunders, HQ 6002nd SEEG, PACAF Tactics/Techniques Bulletin #8, 2 June 1965, Attachment 1: ACT Evaluation of F-86H Versus Current TAC Fighters, K717.549-1, Nos. 1–13, 4 May–July 1965, AFHRA; Scott, PACAF Tactics and Techniques Bulletin, 45, 26 July 1966, K717.549-1, AFHRA.

28. History, Twelfth Air Force, July–December 1965, K650.01-28, July–December 1965, Vol. 1, AFHRA.

29. General Preston was the commander of Fifth Air Force. PACAF Commanders Conference Report, 23–25 February 1965, Headquarters PACAF, K717.151-13, AFHRA.

30. Captain Roger D. Tucker, "Should Aerial Combat Tactics Training be a Part of the Tactical Fighter Squadron Training Program?," thesis, Air Command and Staff College, Maxwell AFB, AL, 1965, 39–46.

31. Red Baron II, Volume 4, Event 87, K160.0311-20, Vol. 4, Part 2, January 1970, AFHRA. This interview was a part of the Red Baron project, which documented and analyzed air-to-air combat over Southeast Asia.

32. Colonel Abner M. Aust Jr., HQ 6002 SEG, PACAF Tactics/Techniques Program, 4 May 1965, K717.549-1, 4 May–1 July 1965, AFHRA.

33. Van Staaveren, *Gradual Failure*, 88.

34. Captain Ward, Dayton 2, Aircraft Commander, interviewed by Lt. Col. Agnew and Mr. Rubio, 13 December 1966, K168.043-42, 29 April 1966, AFHRA.

35. Thomas's comment about a lack of air-to-air combat training is surprising since F-8 Crusader squadrons were known for their emphasis on air combat training. Interview of LCDR Spence Thomas by Mr. Betty and Cdr Stewart, 3 March 1967, Patuxent River, MD, K160.043-16 April 1965–March 1967, AFHRA; Barrett Tillman, *MiG Master: The Story of the F-8 Crusader* (Annapolis, MD: Nautical and Aviation Publishing, 1980), 126–27.

36. Commander Page, interview by Commander Hughes and Lt. Col. Conley, debrief for Event 5, Project Red Baron, 1966, K160.043-20, June 65–December 1966, AFHRA.

37. Colonel Ross L. Blachly, Fighter Seminar Report, August 1965, K417.101-1, Film K4473, Index 1223; Major General Walter B. Putnam, Letter of Appreciation to 12th Air Force, 7 September 1965, K-WG-479-HI, July–December 1965, Vol. 1, AFHRA.

38. Scott, PACAF Tactics and Techniques Bulletin 43, 1 June 1966, K717.549-1, AFHRA.

39. History of Pacific Air Forces, January–December 1966, 296–97, K717.01, January–December 1966, Vol. 1, Part 1, AFHRA; Directorate of Operations History, June 1966, K717.01, January–June 1966, Vol. 3, Part 1, AFHRA.

40. Lt. Col. Walter L. Doerty Jr., End of Tour Report, 391st Tactical Fighter Squadron, K740.131,

NOTES FOR CHAPTER 4

1966, AFHRA; DCS/Operations, History, Directorate of Training, 1–28 February 1967, K717.01, Vol. 3, Part 1, AFHRA.

41. Jack Langguth, "Navy Jets Down 2 MiGs," *New York Times*, June 18, 1965, 2; Van Staaveren, *Gradual Failure*, 144.
42. Pratt, Air Tactics against NVN Air Ground Defenses, 39, K717.0414-16, AFHRA.
43. Thompson, *To Hanoi and Back*, 34; Marshall L. Michel, III, *Clashes: Air Combat over North Vietnam, 1965–1972* (Annapolis, MD: Naval Institute Press, 1997), 152–53.
44. Van Staaveren, *Gradual Failure*, 111; Memorandum for the Executive Assistant and Naval Aide to the Secretary of the Navy, F-4/MiG-17 Engagement of 9 April 1965, 26 April 1966; 9 April 1965 MiG Engagement, Source: Murphy Casualty Report, K160.043-17, 9 April 1965, AFHRA; Message from COMSEVENTHFLT to AIG183, 160824Z, April 1965, COMSEVENTHFLT Weekly Summary, 7–13 April 1965, Vietnam Command Files, COLL/372, Box 120, File Com 7th Flt Weekly Summary 1965; Commander in Chief U.S. Pacific Fleet, U.S. Air-to-Air Incidents in S.E. Asia 3 April 1965–31 December 1966, 13 April 1967, Vietnam Command Files, COLL/372, Box 112, File CPF Staff Study 3-67, NHHC.
45. Directorate of Operations History, November 1966, K171.01, July–December 1966, Vol. 3, Part 3, AFHRA.
46. Fleet Operations Review, August 1968, 20; Vietnam Command Files, Box 105, File CPF Flt Ops Rev August 1968; Commander in Chief U.S. Pacific Fleet, Analysis Staff Study 2–70, Command and Control of MiG Interceptions with SAM and CAP: May–September 1968, Vietnam Command Files, COLL/372, Box 113, File CPF Staff Study 2–70, NHHC.
47. Todd P. Harmer and C. R. Anderegg, *The Shootdown of Trigger 4: Report of the Project Trigger Study Team* (Washington, DC: Headquarters, US Air Force, 2001).
48. Commander in Chief U.S. Pacific Fleet, U.S. Air-to-Air Incidents in S.E. Asia 3 April 1965–31 December 1966, 13 April 1967, Vietnam Command Files, COLL/372, Box 112, File CPF Staff Study 3–67, NHHC; Extracts from "Heat Treat" Team SEA Trip Report, Colonel Robert R. Scott, PACAF Tactics and Techniques Bulletin 44, F-4C Fighter Screen and Escort, K717.549-1, No. 44, 14 July 1966, AFHRA.
49. Captain Arthur K. Ivins, interviewed by Agnew/Walden, 9 January 1967, K160.043-27, December 1965–January 1967, AFHRA; these EC-121s were known as "College Eye" from March 13, 1967, K750.01, Vol. 1, 1967, AFHRA.
50. History Naval Operations, Vol. III, 1965–1967, Part 1, 94, NHHC.
51. Navy fighter squadrons receive "VF" numbers: VF-53 is Fighter Squadron 53. Memorandum from Commander W. A. Gureck, Commanding Officer, Fighter Squadron Fifty-Three to Commander Attack Carrier Air Wing Five, 29 April 1966, Fleet, Pre-1998, AR/229, VF-24, Box 257, File F5, NHHC.
52. History Naval Operations, Vol. III, 1965–1967, Part 1, 107; Enney, Commander Attack Carrier Air Wing Fourteen, Addendum Report, 11 February 1969, NHHC.
53. Peck, Commander Attack Carrier Air Wing Nine Combat Tactical Supplement, 13 July 1968, NHHC; see also pp. 80–93 of Sherwood, *Afterburner: Naval Aviators and the Vietnam War*.
54. Peck, Commander Attack Carrier Air Wing Nine Combat Tactical Supplement, 13 July 1968, NHHC.
55. Message from CTG 77.5 to CINCPAC, NMCC, 200430Z, December 1966, Reference Files, Vietnam, A-Air Warfare (I), File Vietnam Air Ops MiG Combat, NHHC.
56. Frank M. Machovec, Southeast Asia Tactical Data Systems Interface (HQ PACAF: CHECO/Corona Harvest Division, Operations Analysis Office, 1975), 47–48, K717.0414-51, AFHRA.
57. Commander Seventh Fleet Command History 1972, 26 September 1973, NHHC.
58. Colonel Scott G. Smith, End of Tour Report, 31 May 1973, K717.131, AFHRA. The Air Force

initiated production of the E-3 Sentry in 1975, see *Air International* 9: 1 (July 1975), 3.
59. Tissot, Commander Attack Carrier Air Wing Fourteen, Addendum Report, 4 December 1967, NHHC.
60. Linebacker Conference Kilo VII and Juliet VII, 131333Z, October 1972, K740.3391, AFHRA.
61. Linebacker Conference Oscar IV and Papa IV, 230834Z, August 1972, K740.3391, AFHRA; Marine Fighter Attack Squadron 232 Command Chronology, September 4, 1972, found online at The Vietnam Center & Sam Johnson Vietnam Archive, Texas Tech University, http://vietnam.ttu.edu.
62. Commander E. W. Wingerter, Commander Attack Carrier Air Wing One to Chief of Naval Operations, Cruise Report, 2 May 1967, Fleet, Active, CVW-1, Box 11, File 1966–1967, NHHC.
63. Linebacker Conference 14 October 1972, 171222Z, October 1972, K740.3391, AFHRA.

Chapter 5

1. History of Pacific Air Forces, 1 July–31 December 1965, 146, K717.01, Vol. 1, Part 2, AFHRA; Commander in Chief U.S. Pacific Fleet, U.S. Air-to-Air Incidents in S.E. Asia 3 April 1965–31 December 1966, 13 April 1967, Vietnam Command Files, COLL/372, Box 112, File CPF Staff Study 11–66, NHHC.
2. Message from 2 Air Div to all Barrel Roll, Rolling Thunder, and Steel Tiger Addressees, Current Estimate of DRV/CHICOM Air Order of Battle, April 7, 1965, K526.1623, 7 April 1965, AFHRA.
3. Memorandum from the President's Special Assistant (Rostow) to President Johnson, September 10, 1968, in ed. David C. Humphrey and Charles S. Sampson, *Foreign Relations of the United States, 1964–1968, Volume XIV, Soviet Union* (Washington, DC: United States Government Printing Office, 2001), 699.
4. Steve Davies, *Red Eagles: America's Secret MiGs* (Oxford: Osprey Publishing, 2008), 121; Hobson, *Vietnam Air Losses*, 271.
5. Scott, PACAF Tactics and Techniques Bulletin, 45, 26 July 1966, K717.549-1, AFHRA.
6. Captain Max F. Cameron to Director Weapons System Evaluation Group, Project Red Baron, 31 January 1967, K160.043-37, 23 April 1966, AFHRA.
7. Interview of Colonel Robin Olds, July 12, 1967, interviewer unnamed, K717.051, Olds, AFHRA; Smith, Carrier Air Wing Six Cruise Report of April 1968 to December 1968, 14 December 1968, NHHC.
8. Rogers and Knops, Study in Air Defense, K470.40-22, AFHRA; Pacific Area Naval Operations Review August 1966, 11; Message CTG 77.7 to AIG 7802, 011700Z, May 1967, NHHC.
9. Message from 7AF to RUHKA/CINCPAC, 141850Z, December 1966, K717.312, AFHRA; U.S. Air-to-Air Incidents in S.E. Asia 3 April 1965–31 December 1966, 13 April 1967, NHHC.
10. Jeffrey D. Glasser, *The Secret Vietnam War: The United States Air Force in Thailand, 1961–1975* (Jefferson, NC: McFarland, 1995), 37.
11. History of the Pacific Air Forces, 1966, 782, K717.01, Vol. 1, Part 2, AFHRA; History of the Pacific Air Forces, 1967, 69, 75, K717.01, Vol. 1, Part 1, AFHRA; DCS/Operations, History, Directorate of Reconnaissance, March 1967, K717.01, January–June 1967, Vol. 3, Part 1, AFHRA.
12. History of the Pacific Air Forces, 1968, 198–99, K717.01, Vol. 1, Part 2, AFHRA; Melyan and Bonetti, Rolling Thunder, July 1965–December 1966, 118, K717.0414-12, AFHRA.
13. "The Alkali is an X-band beam-riding missile with a 2–4 mile range," found in Commander in Chief Pacific Fleet, Analysis Staff Study 6-68, U.S. Air-to-Air Incidents in S.E. Asia, January–June 1967, Vietnam Command Files, COLL/372, Box 113, File CPF Staff Study 6-68, NHHC. The MiG-21 that aimed cannon fire against American aircraft would have been an early MiG-21F,

which carried a 30mm cannon. The Soviets made the same mistake the Americans made—deleting guns from their fighters in favor of a missiles-only armament on the next couple of MiG-21 variants, which carried only R-13 missiles.

14. Staff Study 6–68, U.S. Air-to-Air Incidents in S.E. Asia, January–June 1967, NHHC; Analysis Staff Study 9–68, NHHC; Message from 366 TFW to RUEPJS/NMCC, 141410Z, May 1967, K717.312, AFHRA.
15. History of the Pacific Air Forces, 1966, 234–36, K717.01, Vol. 1, Part 2, AFHRA.
16. Commander Robert E. Weedon, Fighter Squadron Fifty-Three to Chief of Naval Operations, 1968 Command History, Enclosure No. 1: Employment of the F-8E, Fleet, Pre-1998, AR/229, VF-53, Box 257, File F3, NHHC.
17. Bonetti, The War in Vietnam: January–June 1967, 113, 114, K717.0414-17, AFHRA.
18. Geesey, Air-to-Air Engagements, 5–6; Melyan and Bonetti, Rolling Thunder, July 1965–December 1966, 119, K717.0414-12, AFHRA; Fleet Operations Review, August 1968, 21, NHHC.
19. Interview of Colonel Robin Olds, July 12, 1967, interviewer unnamed, K717.051, AFHRA.
20. Commander M. H. Isaacks, Fighter Squadron Twenty-Four to Chief of Naval Operations, Command Histories 1968, 20 February 1969, Fleet, Pre-1998, AR/229, VF-24, Box 249, File F30, NHHC; Peter Mersky, *F-8 Crusader Units of the Vietnam War* (London: Osprey Publishing, 1998), 88.
21. Davies, *Red Eagles*, 121.
22. Colonel Scott G. Smith, Tactical Fighter Weapons Employment, 10-10, K-WG-432-SU-MA, 1 August 1972, AFHRA.
23. History, USAF Tactical Fighter Weapons Center, 57th Fighter Weapons Wing, 30, K417.0735, 73/07/01 to 74/06/30.
24. Project Red Baron III, Air-to-Air Encounters in Southeast Asia, Vol. 3, Part 1, 17, Roll 30, 153, Index 1109, K417.0735-7, AFHRA.
25. U.S. Air-to-Air Incidents in S.E. Asia 3 April 1965–31 December 1966, 13 April 1967, NHHC; History of the Pacific Air Forces, 1966, 240, K717.01, Vol. 1, Part 2, AFHRA.
26. Dunham, End of Tour Report, 9 July 1967, K740.131, AFHRA.
27. Bonetti, The War in Vietnam: January–June 1967, 111, K717.0414-17, AFHRA. Note: this is the CHECO reports' paraphrase of the CINCPAC message to the JCS dated January 4, 1967. Geesey, Air-to-Air Engagements, 3.
28. History of the Pacific Air Forces, 1966, 234–36, K717.01, Vol. 1, Part 2, AFHRA; Message SA-2 Threat, 132045Z, October 1966, K717.03-38, October 1966, AFHRA.
29. HQ CINCPAC, Pacific Area Naval Operations Review January 1967, 133, Vietnam Command Files, Box 102, File January 1967. The ALQ-51 was a fire control radar jammer. Tissot, Commander Attack Carrier Air Wing Fourteen, Addendum Report, 4 December 1967, NHHC.
30. Thompson, *To Hanoi and Back*, 52–53; Cosmas, *The Joint Chiefs of Staff, 1960–1968, Part 2*, 524; Message from 7th AF to RUHKA/CINCPAC, 7AF/JOPREP/OPREP-3/Pinnacle 008, 031342Z, December 1966, K717.312, 3 December 1966, AFHRA.
31. Air-to-Air Incidents in S.E. Asia 3 April 1965–31 December 1966, NHHC; Rogers and Knops, Study in Air Defense, K470.40-22, AFHRA.
32. Thompson, *To Hanoi and Back*, 52–53; see also Interview of John B. Stone by Major Christopher H. Oliver, USMC, March 25, 2006, ACSC; Pacific Area Naval Operations Review January 1967, 133, NHHC.
33. Lt. Col. C. H. Asay, Maj. J. D. Covington, Capt. J. B. Stone, History of Operation Bolo, 8th Tactical Fighter Wing, January–June 1967, Vol. 2, K-WG-8-HI, January–June 1967, Vol. 2. Olds later credited Captain Stone with designing the operation. Olds briefing to Corona Harvest Staff, September 29, 1969, 63, K239.0512-222, AFHRA.

34. Asay, Covington, Stone, History of Operation Bolo, K-WG-8-HI, January–June 1967, Vol. 2, AFHRA.
35. Ibid.
36. Message from CSAF to AFLC, Pylon Adaptors for F-4/QRC-160, 232319Z, December 1966, K717.312, December 1966, AFHRA; Asay, Covington, Stone, History of Operation Bolo, K-WG-8-HI, January–June 1967, Vol. 2, AFHRA; Interview of Robin Olds by Major Christopher H. Oliver, USMC, February 21, 2006, ACSC.
37. Asay, Covington, Stone, History of Operation Bolo, K-WG-8-HI, January–June 1967, Vol. 2, AFHRA; Olds briefing to Corona Harvest Staff, September 29, 1969, 35, 40, K239.0512-222, AFHRA.
38. Because the Navy was not flying over North Vietnam that day, a missiles free ROE was permissible. Olds briefing to Corona Harvest Staff, September 29, 1969, 60, K239.0512-222, AFHRA.
39. Asay, Covington, Stone, History of Operation Bolo, K-WG-8-HI, January–June 1967, Vol. 2, AFHRA.
40. Bolo. See Joprep and Oprep-3 messages, 021708Z, January 1967, 02122Z, January 1967, 021230Z, January 1967, and 030128Z, January 1967, K717.312, January 1967, AFHRA.
41. Olds believed they shot down eight MiG-21s. Olds briefing to Corona Harvest Staff, September 29, 1969, 52, K239.0512-222, AFHRA.
42. Major Gordon Y. W. Ow, Directorate, Tactical Air Analysis Center, DCS/Operations Headquarters, 7th AF, Mission Bolo, 13 February 1967, K740.31067-3, February 1967, AFHRA.
43. History of the 555th Tactical Fighter Squadron, January–June 1967, K-WG-8-HI, January–June 1967, AFHRA.
44. Hanyok, *Spartans in Darkness*, 254.
45. DCS/Operations, Directorate of Operations Plans History, 6 March 1967, K717.01, January–June 1967, Vol. 3, Part 1, AFHRA.
46. Interview of Olds, July 12, 1967, K717.051, AFHRA.
47. Hearings before the Preparedness Investigating Subcommittee, August 16, 1967, 168.
48. Red Baron II, Volume 4, Event 63, K160.0311-20, Vol. 4, Part 2, January 1970; Interview of Robin Olds by Major Christopher H. Oliver, USMC, February 21, 2006, ACSC; Thompson, *To Hanoi and Back,* 86.
49. Air Effectiveness Trends during the Southwest Monsoon 1967, K740.04-18, AFHRA.
50. Ilya V. Gaiduk, *The Soviet Union and the Vietnam War* (Chicago: Ivan R. Dee, 1996), 118–19, 139; Major General G. B. Simler, AFXOPG, A Review of Air-to-Air Kills, March 6, 1968, K143.042-25, AFHRA.
51. U.S. Air-to-Air Incidents in S.E. Asia 3 April 1965–31 December 1966, 13 April 1967, NHHC.
52. Message from CINCPAC to JCS, CINCPAC Monthly Rolling Thunder Summary, August 1967, 072059Z, October 1967, K712.1623-2, September 1967, AFHRA.
53. Message from CINCPAC to NMCC, Telecon Item #111/67, Lieutenant General Myer to Major General Allison, 100205Z, October 1967, K712.1623-2, 10 October 1967, AFHRA. This message is full of additional cases where jets jettisoned their ordnance when MiGs attacked. Thompson, *To Hanoi and Back*, 112.
54. Pratt, Air Tactics against NVN Air Ground Defenses, 21, K717.0414-16, AFHRA.
55. Thompson, *To Hanoi and Back,* 96; History of the Pacific Air Forces, 1968, 460, K717.01, Vol. 1, Part 2, AFHRA.
56. Linebacker Conference Kilo VII and Juliet VII, 131333Z, October 1972, K740.3391, AFHRA.
57. Thompson, *To Hanoi and Back*, 110–11.
58. HQ USMACV Command History, 1967, 438.
59. Red Baron II, Volume 4, Event 87, K160.0311-20, Vol. 4, Part 2, January 1970, AFHRA.

NOTES FOR CHAPTER 5

60. Message from 7th AF to CINCPACAF, 08073Z, January 1968, K740.1623-8, 8 January 1968; Burch, Tactical Electronic Warfare Operations in SEA, 1962–1968, 43, K717.0413-51, AFHRA.
61. Commander in Chief U.S. Pacific Fleet, U.S. Air-to-Air Incidents in S.E. Asia 3 April 1965–18 September 1966, 20 December 1966, Vietnam Command Files, COLL/372, Box 112, File CPF Staff Study 11–66, NHHC.
62. Analysis Staff Study 9–68, NHHC.
63. U.S. Air-to-Air Incidents in S.E. Asia 3 April 1965–18 September 1966, 20 December 1966, 13 April 1967, Analysis Staff Study 9-68, NHHC.
64. Linebacker Conference Kilo VII and Juliet VII, 131333Z, October 1972, K740.3391, AFHRA.
65. Thompson, *To Hanoi and Back*, 98–99; Major James W. Warren, EC-121D Constellation Operations in Vietnam, Seminar Paper, April 2006, Maxwell AFB, AL, Air Command and Staff College, 7.
66. Colonel Robert R. Scott, PACAF Tactics and Techniques Bulletin #35, 8 February 1966, K717.549-1, No. 35, 8 February 1966, AFHRA.
67. Hanyok, *Spartans in Darkness*, 255.
68. Message from CINCPACFLT to RUMGUL/COMSEVENTHFLT, NVN MiG Threat, 112107, December 1966, K717.312, 10–12 December 1966; Directorate of Combat Intelligence, 1 July 1967 to 30 September 1967, K740.07, AFHRA.
69. Message from 355 Tactical Fighter Wing to 7AF, Red River Rats Informal CO Report, 201135Z, May 1967, K717.0414-16, December 1966–1 November 1968, Vol. 2, AFHRA; Pratt, Air Tactics against NVN Air Ground Defenses, 25, K717.0414-16, AFHRA.
70. Hanyok, *Spartans in Darkness*, 255; Michel, *Clashes*, 101, 144; Weaver, Air-to-Air Encounters, 1 July 1967–31 December 30, K717.0413-22, AFHRA.
71. Pratt, Air Tactics against NVN Air Ground Defenses, 25, K717.0414-16, AFHRA.
72. Interview of Sammy C. White by Major Harmer, 13 February 2001, location not given, K143.044-90, Vol. 25, AFHRA.
73. Linebacker Conference Oscar IV and Papa IV, 230834Z, August 1972, K740.3391, AFHRA; United States Military Assistance Command, Vietnam Command History 1972–1973, Volume 1 (Camp Smith, HI: Military History Branch, Office of the Secretary, Joint Staff, 1973), p. B-12, found online at: https://apps.dtic.mil/dtic/tr/fulltext/u2/a955103.pdf.
74. Message from CTG 77.8 to AIG 914, 301002Z, August 1967, Vietnam Air War Collection, Box 69, Folder 69/1; Carrier Air Wing Seventeen 1968–1969 Air Wing Capabilities, Fleet, Active, CVW-17, Box 21, File 1968; Attack Carrier Air Wing Eleven, Cruise Report February to November 1972, 1 December 1972, NHHC.
75. Smith, Carrier Air Wing Six Cruise Report April 1968 to December 1968, 14 December 1968, NHHC; Attack Carrier Air Wing Eleven, Cruise Report February to November 1972, 1 December 1972, NHHC.
76. CINCPAC Command History 1968, Vol. 3, 147–48, K712. 01, 1968, Vol. 3, AFHRA; History of the Pacific Air Forces, 1968, 224. K717.01, Vol. 1, Part 2, AFHRA; Geesey, Air-to-Air Engagements, 9–11, AFHRA; CINCPAC, Pacific Area Naval Operations Review December 1968, A-2, A-3, NHHC.
77. Seventh Fleet Monthly Historical Summary, September 1969, 8, Vietnam Command Files, Box 119, File September 1969, NHHC; McKnight, Carrier Air Wing Two, Cruise Report of October 1970 to June 1971, 10 June 1971, NHHC; Notes of Meeting, January 30, 1968, *FRUS 1964–1968, VI*, 80.
78. Weedon, Fighter Squadron Fifty-Three, Enclosure No. 1: Employment of the F-8E, NHHC. For additional specifics on North Vietnamese tactics, see Bonetti, *The War in Vietnam: January–June 1967*, 108–9, K717.0414-17, AFHRA.

NOTES FOR CHAPTER 6

79. History of the Pacific Air Forces, 1968, 258, K717.01, Vol. 1, Part 2, AFHRA; Editorial Note, *FRUS 1964–1968 VI*, 978; Geesey, Air-to-Air Engagements, 7.

Chapter 6

1. The title of this chapter is borrowed from Timothy H. Breen's book, *Imagining the Past: East Hampton Histories* (Reading, MA: Addison-Wesley, 1989).
2. "The Defence Debate: Aircraft and Missiles Discussed, Notable Speech by Supply Minister," *Flight* (March 9, 1956), 272; Frank Harvey, *Strike Command: America's Elite New Combat Team* (New York: Duell, Sloan, and Pearce, 1962), 159; Stanley M. Ulanoff, ed., *Fighter Pilot* (Garden City, NY: Doubleday, 1962), 422; Nels A. Parsons Jr., *Missiles and the Revolution in Warfare* (Cambridge, MA: Harvard University Press, 1962), 155; Stanley Ulanoff, *Illustrated Guide to U.S. Missiles and Rockets* (Garden City, NY: Doubleday, 1959), 79, 86.
3. The Sparrow was a Navy project and was first fielded as the "Sparrow I" in 1956. It was not a successful machine. The initial "Sparrow III" entered the inventory in 1958 and was later known as the AIM-7C. The AIM-7D followed in 1959 and the AIM-7E in 1963. They used vacuum tubes that suffered from reliability problems. Tubes inside air-to-air missiles were subjected to three of the four main degraders of tube reliability: high temperatures, shock, and vibration, along with extreme cold. Lieutenant Colonel Armand L. Monteverde, "Vacuum Tube Reliability" (Maxwell AFB: Air Command and Staff College, 1955), 3. Vacuum tube failure had been found responsible for 70 percent of failures in electronic equipment. Monteverde, "Vacuum Tube Reliability," 8. "Immature technology" is not my own term. See for example Sean M. Maloney, "Secrets of the BOMARC: Re-Examining Canada's Misunderstood Missile, Part 1," *The Royal Canadian Air Force Journal* 3, No. 3 (Summer 2014), 34.
4. Extracts from "Heat Treat" Team SEA Trip Report, K717.549-1, No. 44, 14 July 1966, AFHRA; Colonel Robert R. Scott, PACAF Tactics and Techniques Bulletin #44, F-4C Fighter Screen and Escort, K717.549-1, No. 44, 14 July 1966, AFHRA.
5. U.S. Air-to-Air Incidents in S.E. Asia 3 April 1965–31 December 1966, 13 April 1967, NHHC.
6. Message from COMDR AFOTC to COMDR ADC, 091610Z, August 1957, K410.01-8, July–December 1957, Vol. 3; Message from Commander ADC to Chief of Staff, USAF, USAF Current Status Report, 071600Z, May 1958, K410.01-9, January–December 1958, Vol. 3, AFHRA.
7. Directorate of Operations History, May 1966, K717.01, January–June 1966, Vol. 3, Part 1, AFHRA.
8. Karl J. Eschmann, *Linebacker: The Untold Story of the Air Raids over North Vietnam* (New York: Ivy Books, 1989), 128.
9. HQ PACAF, DMW Weekly Activity Report, 13 February 1967. PACAF accelerated the replacement of AIM-7Ds with Es in 1967. HQ PACAF, DMW Weekly Activity Report, 20 February 1967, K717.01, January–June 1967, Vol. 3, Part 2, AFHRA.
10. This happened to missiles in the forward two stations; they stopped breaking in this way by carrying them only in the two aft stations. Enney, Commander Attack Carrier Air Wing Fourteen, Addendum Report, 11 February 1969, NHHC.
11. MiG Encounters 9 April 1965, K160.043-17, 9 April 1965, AFHRA. This document is a very poor copy, and the header is unreadable. One can verify it by the numbers 003542 and 01134844 at the bottom of the first page.
12. USAF Fighter Weapons School, Bulletin-4, 25 April 1966, K160.043-39, 25 April 1966, AFHRA. In boresight mode the aircrew aim the radar directly in front of the aircraft and attempt to keep the radar beam on the target through manual flying inputs, like moving one's car to aim its headlights.
13. Message from 7th AF to RUEKDA/National Military Command Center, 250933Z, April 1966,

K160.043-38, 25 April 1965. Despite the date of the file, the message is from 1966, AFHRA.
14. From Pat Patterson to R. E. Klein, Raytheon, June 6, 1967, Raytheon, K160.043-250, 2 May 1967–5 July 1968, AFHRA.
15. Message from CTG Seven Seven Pt Six to AIG Nine One Three, Rolling Thunder 17C1 OP-5, 040446Z, June 1965, K160.043-19, 4 June 1965, AFHRA.
16. Tissot, Commander Attack Carrier Air Wing Fourteen, Addendum Report, 4 December 1967, NHHC; U.S. Air-to-Air Incidents in S.E. Asia 3 April 1965–31 December 1966, 13 April 1967, NHHC.
17. Colonel Frank L. Rose Jr., HQ PACAF, DMW Weekly Activity Report, 19 April 1968 and 8 May 1968, K717.01, January–December 1968, Vol. 3, Part 2, AFHRA; Robert K. Wilcox, *Scream of Eagles: The Creation of Top Gun and the U.S. Air Victory in Vietnam* (New York: John Wiley, 1990), 106.
18. Message from 8TFW to RUEPJ/NMCC, 051430Z, June 1967, Red Baron Event 17, K160.043-36, 23 April 1966; Message from 7th AF to RUHHABA/CINCPACAF, Linebacker Conference November V and Prime Choke Alpha South, 170800Z, September 1972, K740.3391, AFHRA.
19. Message from 7 AF to RUEKDA/National Military Command Center, 240024Z, April 1966, K160.043-37, 23 April 1966, AFHRA.
20. Captain Robert E. Blake, Submission to Paragraph 2 to Attachment Number 3 to WSEG Log No. 118564, K160.043-37, 23 April 1966; Message from 6252 TFW (DOI), Da Nang AB, RVN to 29 Air Division, Tan Son Nhut AFID, RVN, 18 March 1966, K160.043-32, March 1966–January 1967, AFHRA.
21. Message from 7th AF to RUMBDQ/634 Combat Support Group, 142254, July 1966, K717.312, AFHRA.
22. Tissot, Commander Attack Carrier Air Wing Fourteen, Addendum Report, 4 December 1967, NHHC.
23. Weekly Activity Report, 8–14 May 1965, 17 May 1965, K717.01, January–June 1965, Vol. 3, Part 1, AFHRA.
24. Message from 8 TFW to RUHLKM/CINCPACAF, AIM-7 Condition Status Report, 240600Z, May 1966, K717.312, May 1966, AFHRA.
25. Extracts from "Heat Treat" Team SEA Trip Report, AFHRA; Peck, Commander Attack Carrier Air Wing Nine, Combat Tactical Supplement, 13 July 1968, NHHC.
26. Colonel James W. Brown, Director of Munitions, HQ PACAF DMW, Weekly Activity Report, 24 October 1966, K717.01, July–December 1966, Vol. 3, Part 3, AFHRA.
27. Colonel Dale L. Samuelson, Deputy Director of Munitions, HQ PACAF, DMW, Weekly Activity Report, 3 January 1967, K717.01, July–December 1966, Vol. 3, Part 3, AFHRA.
28. DCS/Operations History, Directorate of Training, 1–31 March 1967, K717.01, January–June 1967, Vol. 3, Part 1; Colonel Robin Olds, End of Tour Report, December 1967, 34, K717.131, Chronology of Thirteenth Air Force, 1967, K750.01, Vol. 1, 1967, AFHRA.
29. Fleet Operations Review, August 1968, 20, NHHC.
30. Smith, Carrier Air Wing Six Cruise Report April 1968 to December 1968, 14 December 1968, NHHC.
31. Wingerter, Attack Carrier Air Wing One, Cruise Report, 2 May 1967, NHHC.
32. Colonel Robin Olds, End of Tour Report, December 1967, 8, K717.131; Robin Olds, October 1966–August 1967, Olds briefing to Corona Harvest Staff, September 29, 1969, 59, K239.0512-222, AFHRA.
33. History of the Pacific Air Forces, 1966, 88, K717.01, Vol. 1, Part 2, AFHRA.
34. Colonel Hanson W. Brown, Director of Munitions, PACAF Weekly Activity Report, 7 November 1966, K717.01, July–December 1966, Vol. 3, Part 3; DCS/Operations History, Directorate of

35. Requirements, January 1967, K717.01, January–June 1967, Vol. 3, Part 1, AFHRA; Thompson, *To Hanoi and Back,* 91; Michel, *Clashes,* 110. F-4D aircrews downed four MiG-17s and one MiG-21 with AIM-4Ds. R. Futrell, *Aces and Aerial Victories,* 69, 157.
35. Message from 8 TFW to AIG 913, 271141Z October 1967, K717.312, AFHRA.
36. Colonel Frank L. Rose Jr., HQ PACAF, DMW Weekly Activity Report, 20 November 1967 and Colonel Frank L. Rose Jr., HQ PACAF DMW Weekly Activity Report, 4 December 1967, K717.01, July–December 1967, Vol. 3, Part 5, AFHRA; Colonel Frank L. Rose Jr., HQ PACAF DMW Weekly Activity Report, 22 January 1968 and Colonel Frank L. Rose Jr., HQ PACAF DMW Weekly Activity Report, 12 February 1968, K717.01, Vol. 3, Part 2, AFHRA.
37. Interview of Robin Olds by Major Christopher H. Oliver, USMC, February 21, 2006; Robin Olds, with Christina Olds and Ed Rasimus, *Fighter Pilot: The Memoirs of Legendary Ace Robin Olds* (New York: St. Martin's, 2010), 315–16; Thompson, *To Hanoi and Back,* 91; Olds, End of Tour Report, December 1967, 13, K717.131, AFHRA.
38. HQ PACAF DMW Weekly Activity Report, 13 May 1968, K717.01, January–December 1968, Vol. 3, Part 2; Message from CSAF to RUHHABA/PACAF/DO/DM, 021721Z, April 1968, AIM-4D Missile, K417.01, July 1968–June 1969, Vol. 9, AFHRA.
39. History of the Directorate of Operations Requirements and Development Plans, DCS/R&D, 1 July 1968–31 July 1968, K140.01, AFHRA; Message from CINCPACAF to RUKLAAA/TAC/DORQ, 70519Z May 1968, AIM-4 Requirements, K417.01, July 1968–June 1969, Vol. 9, AFHRA.
40. Message from 831 Airdiv to RUWTPGA/12AF/DO, 312215 October 1968, AIM-4D Live Fire, K417.01, July 1968–June 3, 1969, Vol. 9, AFHRA.
41. Geesey, Air-to-Air Engagements, 57.
42. Message from CTG 77.7 to CINCPACFLT, 040117Z, April 1965 and Message from CTG 77.7 to CINCPACFLT, 040221Z, April 1965, Reference Files, Vietnam, A-Air Warfare (I), Vietnam Air Ops MiG Combat Folder, NHHC.
43. Message from CINCPACAF to RUEFHQA/CSAF/AFXOP, 262045Z, September 1968, RAM Phase B Test Program, K417.01, July 1968–June 1969, Vol. 9, AFHRA; Commander in Chief Pacific Fleet, Analysis Staff Study 6-68, U.S. Air-to-Air Incidents in S.E. Asia, January–June 1967, Vietnam Command Files, COLL/372, Box 113, File CPF Staff Study 6-68, NHHC.
44. Hargrove interview, September 19, 1967, 14, K239.0512-020, AFHRA.
45. History of the Directorate of Operational Requirements and Development Plans, 1 January–30 June 1967, K140.01, January–June 1967, Vol. 3, AFHRA; History of the Directorate of Operational Requirements and Development Plans, January–June 1969, K140.01, January–June 1967, AFHRA.
46. Commander in Chief U.S. Pacific Fleet, F-8 Weapons Performance against MiG-17 Aircraft, 24 December 1966, Vietnam Command Files, COLL/372, Box 112, File CPF Staff Study 13-66, NHHC.
47. Navy MiG Encounter, 14 July 1966, Reference Files, Vietnam, A-Air Warfare (I), Vietnam Air Ops MiG Combat Folder, NHHC.
48. F-8 Weapons Performance against MiG-17 Aircraft, 24 December 1966, NHHC.
49. Commander J. D. Ellison, Fighter Squadron Twenty-Four to Chief of Naval Operations, Command Histories 1967, 26 February 1968, Fleet, Pre-1998, AR/229, VF-24, Box 249, File F31, NHHC.
50. Isaacks, Fighter Squadron Twenty-Four, 20 February 1969, NHHC.
51. Message from CTG 77.3 to CINCPAC/NMCC, 212246Z, June 1966, Reference Files, Vietnam, A-Air Warfare (I), Vietnam Air Ops MiG Combat Folder, NHHC; Bruce F. Powers, OEG Representative to Commanding Officer, USS *Hancock,* Analysis of MiG Encounter by USS *Hancock* Aircraft, 21 June 1966, K160.043-51, 21 June 1966, AFHRA.

52. Fleet Operations Review, August 1968, 20, Message from CTG 77.8 to RUMFUK/CTG 77.0, 261555Z June 1968, Reference Files, Vietnam, A-Air Warfare (I), File Vietnam Air Ops MiG Combat; HQ CINCPAC, Pacific Area Naval Operations Review October 1966, 13, Vietnam Command Files, Box 102, File October 1966, NHHC. This happened October 9, 1966.
53. Message from CTG Seven Seven Five to RULLHQ/CINCPAC, DRV Air Activity, 9 January 1966, K740.04-25, 60/03/18–68/02/19, AFHRA; Institute for Defense Analysis, Air to Air Encounters in Southeast Asia, Vol. III, 1969, Event III-147, p. 159, Event III-194, p. 222 and Event III-345, p. 392; HQ CINCPAC, Pacific Area Naval Operations Review September 1968, 17, Vietnam Command Files, Box 105, File September 1968, NHHC.
54. Message from CTG 77.5 to CJCS, 230830, May 1972, Reference Files, Vietnam, A-Air Warfare (I), Vietnam Air Ops MiG Combat Folder; OEG/OP-05W, Summary of Air Operations in Southeast Asia May 1972, Center for Naval Analyses, C-6, COLL/7 Publications of the Center for Naval Analyses, OEG, Box 72, File OEG Memo 1368-72; Commander W. B. Brown, Fighter Squadron Two One One to Chief of Naval Operations, 1972 Command History, 11 March 1973, Fleet, Active, Box 160, File 1972, NHHC; Summary Air Operations Southeast Asia July 1972, p. 4-A-3, K717.3063, July 1972, AFHRA.
55. OEG/OP-508W Operations in Southeast Asia, 1 January 1972–31 January 1973, Table 4-4, NHHC, found online at: https://www.aerosociety.com/media/8037/an-examination-of-the-f-8-crusader-through-archival-sources.pdf.
56. Aust Jr., HQ 6002 SEG, PACAF Tactics/Techniques Program, 4 May 1965, Attachment 1: F-4 Fighter vs Fighter Tactics, K717.549-1, AFHRA.
57. K-WG-8-HI, January–June 1966, Vol. 1, Document 7, AFHRA.
58. Directorate of Operations, History, Assistant for Requirements and Systems Programs, November 1965, K717.01, July–December 1965, Vol. 3, Part 1; Thornal interview, 15, K239.0512-012, 00/11/66–00/07/67, AFHRA.
59. John S. Attinello, WSEG Report 116. Air-to-Air Encounters in Southeast Asia, Volume II: F-105 Events Prior to 1 March 1967 (Arlington, VA: Weapons Systems Evaluation Group, Institute for Defense Analysis, 1968), Events 15, 35, 56, 57, 84; *Aces and Aerial Victories*, 118–22.
60. US House of Representatives, DoD Subcommittee of the Committee on Appropriations, DoD Appropriations for 1969, 90th Cong., 2nd sess., 1968, Part 2, 667.
61. History of the Tactical Air Command, July 1962–December 1962, 238–39, K417.01, July–December 1962, Vol. 1, AFHRA; Thompson, *To Hanoi and Back*, 64; Message from 366th TFW to RUEPJS/NMCC, 141800Z, May 1967, K717.312, AFHRA; Hargrove interview, September 19, 1967, 22–23, K239.0512-020, 21/12/66–04/08/67, AFHRA.
62. Linebacker Conference November V and Prime Choke Alpha S, 170800Z, September 1972, K740.3391; Message from 7th AF to RUEFHQA/CSAF, Linebacker Conference November VII and Papa VII, 141146Z, October 1972, K740.3391, AFHRA.
63. Analysis Staff Study 9–68, NHHC; *Aces and Aerial Victories*, 129.
64. *Joint Chiefs of Staff 1960–1968, Part 3*, 83; Simler, AFXOPG, A Review of Air-to-Air Kills, March 6, 1968, K143.042-25, AFHRA.
65. "ABC's of Missile Guidance," *Air Progress* (Fall 1959), 74.

Chapter 7

1. Overton, Rolling Thunder: January 1967–November 1968, 42, K717.0414-12, AFHRA.
2. Porter, Linebacker First 120 Days, 46, K717.0414-42, 1973, AFHRA.
3. History of the Pacific Air Forces, 1968, X, 283, K717.01, Vol. 1, Part 2, AFHRA; *By Sea, Air, and Land: An Illustrated History of the U.S. Navy and the War in Southeast Asia*, Appendix E, NHHC,

found online at: http://www.ussbhr.org/navy%20mig%20kills.pdf.

4. Monthly Statistical Summary Southeast Asia Combat Air/Surface Operations October thru December 1968, SEACAG/OP-05W/OEG, Vietnam Command File, COLL/372, Box 92, File CNO SEA Combat Air/Sur Ops October–December 1968, NHHC.
5. History Tactical Air Command, January–June 1968, 221–23, K417.01, January–June 1968, Vol. 1, AFHRA.
6. Lt. Col. Ralph A. Rowley, The Air Force in South East Asia: Tactics and Techniques of Close Air Support Operations, 1961–1973, Office of Air Force History, 1976, 168.7041-144, AFHRA.
7. Generals Joseph J. Nazzaro, William W. Momyer, and Joseph R. Holzapple to HQ USAF, F-4 Configuration Problem, 3 December 1969, K417.01, July 1969–June 1970, Vol. 9, AFHRA; History Tactical Air Command, January–June 1968, 227–46, K417.01, January–June 1968, Vol. 1, AFHRA; TAC Views on Major Program Memorandum on Tactical Air Forces, 12 June 1969, K417.01, July 1968–June 1969, Vol. 2, AFHRA.
8. Colonel Rodney H. Newbold, HQ Seventh AF, TACLO Activity Report #7, 15 April 1968, K417.01, January–June 1968, Vol. 10, AFHRA; Message from CSAF to RUEBABA/TAC, 082207Z, April 1968, AIM-7 (Sparrow missile) Combat Qualification Firings, K417.01, July 1968–June 1969, Vol. 3, AFHRA. North Korea highjacked the USS *Pueblo* on January 23, 1968.
9. Message from CSAF to RUEBABA/TAC, 270929Z, April 1968, AIM/AGM Non-Combat Firing Requirements, K417.01, July 1968–June 1969, Vol. 3, AFHRA.
10. USAF 1971 Tactical Fighter Symposium, Nellis AFB, Nevada, 14–19 June 1971, K417.01 FY1971 Vol. 12, AFHRA.
11. Cook, Liaison Officer End of Tour Report, 1 December 1972, K417.0735, FY1973, AFHRA.
12. History of Linebacker Operations, 10 May 1972–23 October 1972, 69, K740.04-24, 1972, AFHRA.
13. Geesey, Air-to-Air Engagements, 45–46, 57.
14. Weaver, Air-to-Air Encounters, 1 July 1967–31 December 1968, 36–37, K717.0413-22, AFHRA.
15. TAC Views on Major Program, 12 June 1969, K417.01, July 1968–June 1969, Vol. 2, AFHRA.
16. Seventh Fleet Monthly Historical Summary, August 1969, 10–11, Vietnam Command Files, Box 119, File April 1969 [misfile]; Commander L. C. Page Jr., Commander Attack Carrier Wing Two, Cruise Report, 17 May 1969, Fleet, Active, CVW-2, Box 13, File 1/68–5/69, NHHC.
17. Seventh Fleet Monthly Historical Summary, August 1969, 10–11, Carrier Attack Wing Eleven End of Cruise Report, 30 December 1968–4 September 1969, Ships History Post 2001, *Kitty Hawk* (CV-63), Box 189, File 1969 Cruise Reports, NHHC.
18. Page, Commander Attack Carrier Wing Two, Cruise Report, 17 May 1969, NHHC.
19. McKnight, Carrier Air Wing Two, Cruise Report of October 1970 to June 1971, 10 June 1971, NHHC.
20. Smith, Carrier Air Wing Six Cruise Report of April 1968 to December 1968, 14 December 1968, NHHC.
21. Commander Seventh Fleet Command History 1972, 26 September 1973, NHHC.
22. Geesey, Air-to-Air Engagements, 42.
23. Message from USS *Intrepid* to RUYVSYC/CTF 70.2.1.1, 191038Z, September 1968, Reference Files, Vietnam, A-Air Warfare (I), File Vietnam Air Ops MiG Combat, NHHC.
24. Michael E. Weaver, "An Examination of the F-8 Crusader through Archival Sources," *Journal of Aeronautical History* (2018), 80; Captain Frank Ault, Air-to-Air Missile System Capability Review, July–November 1968 (Naval Air Systems Command, 1969), 37; Dan Pedersen, *Top Gun: An American Story* (New York: Hachette Books, 2019), 105. An initial examination of the records of VF-124 and VX-4 at the Naval History and Heritage Command turned up little on the first year of this organization.

25. Pederson, *Top Gun*, 135.
26. Wilcox, *Scream of Eagles*, 288.
27. Michael E. Weaver, "Missed Opportunities before Top Gun and Red Flag," *Air Power History* (Winter 2013): 21–27.
28. Message from General Ryan to General Clay, 211700Z, December 1971 and Message from General Ryan to General Clay, 041920Z, January 1972, K740.3391, 72/12/27–72/12/31, AFHRA. This took place again a year later. Message from Major General Hughes to Major General Talbott, 200750Z, December 1972, Night MiG Engagement, K744.312 1972–1973, Vol. 1, AFHRA.
29. Michel, *Clashes*, 119; John Darrell Sherwood, *Fast Movers: America's Jet Pilots and the Vietnam Experience* (New York: Free Press, 1999), 181; Thompson, *To Hanoi and Back*, 35.
30. First Lieutenant Bill Meagher, interviewed by Agnew/Walden, no date, circa 1966–67, K160.043-32, March 1966–January 1967, AFHRA. For a well-argued case against the four-jet formation see Sherwood, *Afterburner*, 241–42, and Fino, *Tiger Check*, 179–81.
31. Linebacker Tactical Conference, 311150Z, July 1972, K143.044-90, Vol. 33, AFHRA.
32. Message from AFSSO 7AF TSN AFLD RVN to AFSSO Udorn, Linebacker Tactical Conference, 021150Z, August 1972, K143.044-90, Vol. 32, AFHRA. John Darrell Sherwood locates the date of the Air Force's conversion to loose deuce to May 1972. The death of Major Robert Lodge to a MiG attack was traced partially to the inflexibility of finger-four. Sherwood, *Fast Movers*, 182–201.
33. Smith, Tactical Fighter Weapons Employment, 9-1, 9-3, K-WG-432-SU-MA, 1 August 1972, AFHRA.
34. Message Personal for General Vogt from Major General Searles, Linebacker Tactical Conferences, 060750Z, August 1972, K143.044-90, Vol. 32, AFHRA; Colonel Scott G. Smith, End of Tour Report, 31 May 1973, K717.131, AFHRA.
35. History of Pacific Air Forces, 1 July 1969–30 June 1970, 73–74, K717.01, FY 1970, Vol. 1, Part 1, AFHRA; Geesey, Air-to-Air Engagements, 13, 14–16, AFHRA.
36. Commander D. R. McCrimmon, Attack Squadron Fifty-Two, Line Period Report 31 May 1971, Fleet, Pre-1998, AR/229, Box 132, File F10, NHHC; Tissot, Commander Attack Carrier Air Wing Fourteen, Addendum Report, 4 December 1967, NHHC.
37. McCrimmon, Attack Squadron Fifty-Two, Line Period Report 31 May 1971, NHHC.
38. Seventh Air Force, Commando Hunt VII, 51, 141, K740.04-14, November 1971–March 1972, AFHRA; Mel Porter, Proud Deep Alpha (HQ PACAF: Directorate Operations Analysis, CHECO/Corona Harvest Division, 1972), 1, K717.0423-24, AFHRA; Thompson, *To Hanoi and Back*, 205–6; Webb and Poole, *Joint Chiefs of Staff, 1971–1973*, 115, 117.
39. Minutes of a Meeting of the Senior Review Group: Vietnam Assessment, January 17, 1972, *FRUS 1969–1976, VII*, 1033, 1034.
40. Message from Abrams to McCain, January 20, 1972, *FRUS 1969–1976, VIII*, 5.
41. Air Operations in Southeast Asia, 1972–1973, Vol. 2, p. iv–112, K717.0423-23, Tactical Analysis Bulletin, 72-2, 1 July 1972, K143.054-8, Vol. 13, AFHRA.

Chapter 8

1. HQ PACAF Weekly Activity Report, 20 May 1968, K717.01, January–December 1968, Vol. 3, Part 2, AFHRA.
2. Message from USAFTAWC to RUMMWKA/6400 Test Squadron, 231415Z, August 1968, Combat Waltz, AIM-7E-2 Test, K417.01, July 1968–June 1969, Vol. 9, AFHRA; Geesey, Air-to-Air Engagements, 57–58.
3. Smith, Tactical Fighter Weapons Employment, 9-1, 9-3, K-WG-432-SU-MA, 1 August 1972; Colonel Scott G. Smith, End of Tour Report, 31 May 1973, K717.131, HQ PACAF, Evaluation

NOTES FOR CHAPTER 8

Report for the NVN Offensive (April–August 1972), V-9, K717.04-9, 1972; Eggers, Employment of Missile, K712.153-1; Message from 7th AF to RUHHABA/CINCPACAF, Linebacker Conferences Oscar V/Papa V, 170835Z, September 1972, K740.3391, AFHRA; Thompson, *To Hanoi and Back*, 239.

4. Thompson, *To Hanoi and Back,* 239; Michel, *Clashes*, 194; Interview of General William L. Kirk, ret., by Colonel Darrel Whitcomb, 10 June 1996, Maxwell AFB, AL, K143.044-90, Vol. 17; Eggers, Employment of Missiles, K712.153-1, AFHRA; Analysis Staff Study 2–70, Command and Control of MiG Interceptions with SAM and CAP: May–September 1968, NHHC.
5. CINCPAC to JCS, US Aircraft Losses to NVN Air Defense System, 202114Z, July 1972, NHHC; Message from 7th AF to RUHHABA/PACAF, Linebacker Conference Prime Choke Bravo and India VII, 121233Z, October 1972, K740.3391, AFHRA.
6. Porter, Linebacker First 120 Days, 10, 13, K717.0414-42, 1973, AFHRA.
7. CINCPAC Command History 1972, Vol. 1, 154, K712.01, 1972, Vol. 1, AFHRA; Paul W. Elder and Peter J. Melly, Rules of Engagement, November 1969–September 1972 (HQ PACAF: Directorate of Operations Analysis, CHECO/Corona Harvest Division, 1973), 54, K717.0414-20, AFHRA.
8. Message from AFSSO 7 AF to AFSSO USAF, 161115Z, April 1972, K717.03-221, Vol. 1, 20 June 1973, AFHRA.
9. Message from AFSSO Udorn to AFSSO 7th AF, Linebacker Tactical Conference, 311150Z, July 1972, K143.044-90, Vol. 33, AFHRA. See also in K143.044-90, Vol. 32, AFHRA.
10. 1st Test Squadron, 405th Fighter Wing, Combat Sage, PACAF Weapons System Evaluation Program, Monthly MiG Engagement Report, 1–31 July 1972, K143.044-90, Vol. 39, AFHRA.
11. USS *America* and Carrier Air Wing Eight 1972–1973 Westpac Deployment Cruise Report, 53, NHHC.
12. Message from WRAMA Robins AFB, GA to RUMMRSA/7AF/LG Tan Son Nhut Afld RVN, Air Intercept Missile Performance, 132105Z, May 1972, K717.03-221, July 1971–June 1972, Vol. 3, AFHRA.
13. Message from AFSSO 7AF to AFSSO PACAF, Air-to-Air Missile Effectiveness, 030820Z, June 1972, Folder General Vogt's Read File May 1972, Vogt Papers, AFHSD; History of Seventh Air Force, 1 July 1971–30 June 1972, 332–34, K740.01-25, Vol. 1, AFHRA.
14. Message to 7/13 AF/TRD, Unguided Bombing, 280215Z, September 1972, K744.01, 1972, Vol. 3, AFHRA.
15. Message from 831 Airdiv to RUWTPGA/12AF/DO, 312215 October 1968, AIM-4D Live Fire, K417.01, July 1968–June 3, 1969, Vol. 9, AFHRA.
16. Message from 7th AF to RUHHABA/PACAF, Linebacker Conference Yankee VI and X-Ray VI, 050130Z, October 1972, K740.3391, AFHRA; Message, Personal to General Vogt from Colonel Olshefski, Linebacker Conference 22 December 1972, 230645Z, December 1972, K744.01 1972, Vol. II, Appendix V, AFHRA; Message from 7th AF to RUEFHQA/CSAF/XOO, Linebacker Conference 22 December 1972, 280405Z, December 1972, K740.3391, AFHRA.
17. Porter, Linebacker First 120 Days, 10–11, 13, K717.0414-42, 1973, AFHRA; Memorandum from President Nixon to the President's Assistant for National Security Affairs (Kissinger), May 9, 1972, *FRUS 1969–1976, VIII*, 520.
18. History of the Pacific Air Forces, July 1971–June 1972, Vol. 1, 83–84, K717.01, AFHRA; Minutes of a Washington Special Actions Group Meeting, May 10, 1972, *FRUS 1969–1976, VIII*, 530; Werrell, *Sabres over MiG Alley*, 80.
19. Message from CINCPACAF to AIG7269, MiG/SAM Engagement–Showtime 100 (10/1302– 13100 May 1972), 110033Z, May 1972, Reference Files, Vietnam, A-Air Warfare (I), Vietnam Air Ops MiG Combat Folder, NHHC.

20. Minutes of a Washington Special Actions Group Meeting, May 11, 1972, *FRUS 1969–1976, VIII*, 543.
21. Randolph, *Powerful and Brutal Weapons*, 205, 223; Message to 7/13 AF/TRD, Report 8-72, Air Combat Tactics, 060707Z, October 1972, K744.01, 1972, Vol. 3, AFHRA; Summary of Air Operations Southeast Asia, May 1972, 4–6 through 4–7, K717.3063, AFHRA.
22. OEG/OP-05W, Summary of Air Operations in Southeast Asia May 1972, Center for Naval Analyses, 4–13, COLL/7 Publications of the Center for Naval Analyses, OEG, Box 72, File OEG Memo 1368-72, NHHC; History of the Pacific Air Forces, July 1971–June 1972, Vol. 1, 88–89, K717.01; Tactical Analysis Bulletin, 72-2, 1 July 1972, K143.054-8, Vol. 13; History of Linebacker Operations, 10 May 1972–23 October 1972, 13–17, K740.04-24, 1972; Porter, Linebacker First 120 Days, 44–45, K717.0414-42, 1973, AFHRA.
23. Message from AFSPCOMMCEN to AFG 8556, 062135Z, July 1972, Vietnam Air War Collection, Box 67, Folder 67/1, NHHC; USS *America* and Carrier Air Wing Eight 1972–1973 Westpac Deployment Cruise, 24, NHHC.
24. Air Operations in Southeast Asia, 1972–1973, Vol. 2, p. iv–117, K717.0423-23; Report 8-72, Air Combat Tactics, 060707Z, October 1972, K744.01, 1972, Vol. 3, AFHRA. See for example Message from AFSSO Udorn to AFSSO 7AF, Linebacker Conference South, 070420Z, September 1972, Vogt Papers, Message Traffic September 1972; Message from AFSSO 7AF to AFSSO CSAF, Daily Wrap Up, 261020Z, May 1972, Vogt Papers, Message Traffic May 1972, AFHSD.
25. Report 8-72, Air Combat Tactics, 060707Z, October 1972, K744.01, 1972, Vol. 3; Message from 7th AF to RUHHABA/CINCPACAF, Linebacker Conference Mike V and South II, 170805Z, September 1972, K740.3391, AFHRA. Close control is where a weapons director issues every heading, airspeed, and altitude change to an interceptor.
26. Message from 7th AF to RUHHABA/CINCPACAF, Linebacker Conference Sierra VI and Romeo VI, 010642Z, October 1972, K740.3391; Messages from 7th AF to RUHHABA/CINCPACAF, September 1972, K740.3391; Message from AFSSO Udorn to AFSSO 7AF, Linebacker Conference Quebec V and Romeo V, 150715Z, September 1972, Vogt Papers, Message Traffic September 1972, AFHSD.
27. Linebacker Conference Kilo VII and Juliet VII, 131333Z, October 1972, K740.3391, AFHRA.
28. Message from 432 Udorn, MiG Tactics, 151140, May 1972, K717.03-221, Vol. 3, AFHRA; Message from CINCPACAF to AIG 7289, MiG Encounters for 10 May, 112356Z, May 1972, Reference Files, Vietnam, A-Air Warfare (I), Vietnam Air Ops MiG Combat Folder, NHHC.
29. Colonel Scott G. Smith, Tactical Fighter Weapons Employment, 10-5 through 10-10, K-WG-432-SU-MA, 1 August 1972, AFHRA.
30. Red Baron III, Vol. 3, Part 1, 17, Roll 30, 153, Index 1109, K417.0735-7, AFHRA.
31. Linebacker Conference Kilo VII and Juliet VII, 131333Z, October 1972, K740.3391, AFHRA.
32. Message from 7th AF to RUEFHQA/CSAF, Linebacker Conference 13 October 1972, 180952Z, October 1972, K740.3391, AFHRA; Foley Jr., USS *Midway* 1972 Command History, 14 March 1973, NHHC.
33. Linebacker Conference Prime Choke Bravo and India VII, 121233Z, October 1972, K740.3391, AFHRA.
34. Minutes of a Washington Special Actions Group Meeting, May 15, 1972, *FRUS 1969–1976, VIII*, 554; Eggers, Employment of Missiles, K712.153-1; Air Operations in Southeast Asia, 1972–1973, Vol. 2, p. iv-9, K717.0423-23; Message from CINCPACAF to IG 7289, SAM and MiG Tactics, 170035Z, May 1972, K717.03-221, Vol. 3, AFHRA.
35. History of Seventh Air Force, 1971–1972, 339, K740.01-25, Vol. 1, AFHRA.
36. Linebacker Conference Oscar IV and Papa IV, 230834Z, August 1972, K740.3391, AFHRA; CINCPACAF/XOA, The USAF in Southeast Asia, 1970–1973: Lessons Learned and

NOTES FOR CHAPTER 8

Recommendations: A Compendium, June 16, 1975, K717.0423-11, AFHRA.
37. History of Seventh Air Force, 1971–1972, 33, K740.01-25, Vol. 1, AFHRA; Message from CINCPACAF to SCAF/XOOW/LGMM, SEA Air Intercept Missile Performance, 250334Z, May 1972, K717.03-221, July 1971–June 1972, Vol. 3, AFHRA.
38. Colonel Scott G. Smith, End of Tour Report, 31 May 1973, K717.131, AFHRA.
39. Colonel Arthur W. Owen Jr., Message from ADC, Advanced Aerial Combat Tactics, College Dart, 16 April 1970, K410.01-21, FY 1970, Vol. 4, AFHRA; Maj Gen Joseph L. Dickman, Message from ADC to CNO, Dissimilar ACT Training, 27 March 1970, K410.01-21, FY 1970, Vol. 6, AFHRA; Colonel Lauren B. Hollenbeck, Message from ADC to 21 AirDiv, Navy/ADC Training at Miramar, 16 August 1971, K410.01-21, FY 1972, Vol. 5, AFHRA; Weaver, "Missed Opportunities," passim.
40. Report 8-72, Air Combat Tactics, 060707Z, October 1972, K744.01, 1972, Vol. 3, AFHRA; Page, Commander Attack Carrier Wing Two, Cruise Report, 17 May 1969, NHHC.
41. Report 8-72, Air Combat Tactics, 060707Z, October 1972, K744.01, 1972, Vol. 3, AFHRA. See also Colonel Scott G. Smith, End of Tour Report, 31 May 1973, K717.131, AFHRA; Michel, *Clashes*, 167; Sherwood, *Afterburner: Naval Aviators and the Vietnam War*, 76.
42. Hargrove interview, September 19, 1967, 29, K239.0512-020, 21/12/66 to 04/08/67, AFHRA; Thompson, *To Hanoi and Back*, 111–12.
43. Major John W. Siemann, Combat Snap: AIM-9J Southeast Asia Introduction (HQ PACAF: Directorate of Operations Analyis, CHECO/Corona Harvest Division, 1974), 10–11, 18, K717.0414-45; Penix and Ringenbach, Air Defense in Southeast Asia, 1945–1971, 40, K717.0414-36, AFHRA.
44. Message from 366TFW to AIG 913, JPCCO/JOPREP JIFFY 1059/366 TFW DOI, 241257Z, July 1972, Vietnam Air War Collection, Box 67, Folder 67/1, NHHC.
45. Geesey, Air-to-Air Engagements, 57a, 59.
46. SEA Air Intercept Missile Performance, 250334Z, May 1972, K717.03-221, Vol. 3, AFHRA.
47. Siemann, AIM-9J Southeast Asia Introduction, 12, K717.0414-45, AFHRA.
48. CSAF to RUHHABA/CINCPACAF, Air Intercept Missile Performance, 162218Z, May 1972, K717.03-221, July 1971–June 1972, Vol. 3, AFHRA.
49. Siemann, AIM-9J Southeast Asia Introduction, 16–18, 23–26, K717.0414-45. The Air Force converted 5,800 AIM-9Bs into Juliets. Lieutenant Colonel William G. Dolan Jr., Final Report, Phase I, ADC/ADWC Project 70-37 F-106 Externally Mounted Missiles, 27 October 1971, K410.012, October–December 1971, AFHRA.
50. Linebacker Conference Whiskey V and X-Ray V, 201236Z, September 1972, K740.3391, AFHRA; Siemann, AIM-9J Southeast Asia Introduction, 23–26, K717.0414-45, AFHRA.
51. Linebacker Conference 22 December 1972, 280405Z, December 1972, K740.3391, AFHRA.
52. Thompson, *To Hanoi and Back*, 241; Siemann, AIM-9J Southeast Asia Introduction, 29, K717.0414-45, AFHRA.
53. Cook, Liaison Officer End of Tour Report, 1 December 1972, K417.0735, FY1973, AFHRA.
54. Thompson, *To Hanoi and Back*, 241; OEG/OP-05W, Summary of Air Operations in Southeast Asia May 1972, Center for Naval Analyses, 4–1, 4–7, NHHC.
55. Message from CTG 77.4 to CJCS, 100530Z, May 1972, Reference Files, Vietnam, A-Air Warfare (I), Vietnam Air Ops MiG Combat Folder, NHHC.
56. Air Intercept Missile Performance, 132105Z, May 1972, K717.03-221, Vol. 3, AFHRA; Ron Westrum, *Sidewinder: Creative Missile Development at China Lake* (Annapolis, MD: Naval Institute Press, 1999), 187–88.
57. History of Linebacker Operations, 10 May 1972–23 October 1972, 47, K740.04-24, 1972; Eggers, Employment of Missiles, K712.153-1, AFHRA.

58. Message from AFSSO Udorn to AFSSO 7AF, Linebacker Conference Kilo IV, 300404Z, August 1972, Vogt Papers, Vogt Message Traffic August 1972, AFHSD.
59. Thompson, *To Hanoi and Back,* 241; Futrell, *Aces and Aerial Victories,* 122–25; Siemann, AIM-9J Southeast Asia Introduction, 11, 13, K717.0414-45, AFHRA.
60. Eggers, Employment of Missiles, K712.153-1, AFHRA.
61. USS *Midway,* Release No. 39-72, May 27, 1972, Fleet, Pre-1998, AR/229, Box 289, VF-161, File F2, NHHC.
62. Minutes of a Washington Special Actions Group Meeting, May 11, 1972, *FRUS 1969–1976, VIII,* 544.
63. History of Seventh Air Force, 1971–1972, 340, K740.01-25, Vol. 1, AFHRA.
64. Eggers, Employment of Missiles, K712.153-1, AFHRA; Thompson, *To Hanoi and Back,* 241; Futrell, *Aces and Aerial Victories,* 122–25; Siemann, AIM-9J Southeast Asia Introduction, 12, K717.0414-45, AFHRA.
65. USAF Air-to-Air Combat Summary, 1 January–15 October 1972, K143.252-2, 72/11/07–72/11/10, AFHRA.
66. Siemann, AIM-9J Southeast Asia Introduction, 29, K717.0414-45, AFHRA.
67. Linebacker Conferences Oscar V/Papa V, 170835Z, September 1972, K740.3391, AFHRA.
68. OEG/OP-508W Operations in Southeast Asia, 1 January 1972–31 January 1973, Table 4-6 through 4-13, NHHC.

Chapter 9

1. Message from PACAF AFSSO to AFSSO HQ 7AF, Air-to-Air War North Vietnam, 222240Z, May 1972, Vogt Papers, AFHSD.
2. Message from AFSSO 7AF to AFSSO PACAF, Utilization of F-4D/F-4E Assets for Counter Air Role, 190600Z, May 1972 and Message from AFSSO PACAF to AFSSO 7AF, 120345Z, May 1972, Folder General Vogt's Read File May 1972, Vogt Papers, AFHSD.
3. Message from AFSSO PACAF to AFSSO 7AF, Call from Momyer, 012130Z, June 1972, Vogt Papers, Vogt Message Traffic June 1972, AFHSD.
4. Geesey, Air-to-Air Engagements, 45; Discussion, Conclusions, and Recommendations Resulting from 7AF/13AF Deputy Commander's Conference on 26 July 1972, K744.312, 1972–1973, Vol. 1, AFHRA.
5. Message from AFSSO USAF to AFSSO PACAF info AFSSO 7AF, 012100Z, June 1972 and Message from AFSSO PACAF to AFSSO 7AF, Air-to-Air War NVN, 060250Z, June 1972, Vogt Papers, Message Traffic June 1972, AFHSD; Report 8-72, Air Combat Tactics, 060707Z, October 1972, K744.01, 1972, Vol. 3, AFHRA; Smith, End of Tour Report, 31 May 1973, K717.131, AFHRA.
6. Johnson, Linebacker Operations: September–December 1972, 52, K717.0413-102, AFHRA; Smith, End of Tour Report, 31 May 1973, K717.131, AFHRA.
7. Message from AFSSO TAC to AFSSO 7AF, Tactics for SEA, 010354Z, July 1972, Vogt Papers, Message Traffic July 1972, AFHSD.
8. Message from AFSSO USAF to AFSSO PACAF, AFSSO 7AF, 271955Z, June 1972, Vogt Papers, Message Traffic June 1972, AFHSD.
9. Air Operations in Southeast Asia, Vol. 2, p. iv-107 to iv-109, K717.0423-23, AFHRA.
10. Randolph, *Powerful and Brutal Weapons,* 317.
11. Message from AFSSO PACAF to AFSSO USAF/CSAF, Air-to-Air War NVN, 290317Z, June 1972 and Message from AFSSO PACAF to AFSSO 7AF, PACAF Team Visit, 30 June–6 July 1972, 192249Z, July 1972, Vogt Papers, Message Traffic June 1972, July 1972, AFHSD.

NOTES FOR CHAPTER 9

12. Evaluation Report for the NVN Offensive (April–August 1972), p. v-9, K717.04-9, 1972; History of Seventh Air Force, 1971–1972, 337, K740.01-25, Vol. 1; Air Operations in Southeast Asia, 1972–1973, Vol. 2, iv-163, K717.0423-23. Rivet Haste was not a factor in air-to-air effectiveness during Linebacker. K717.0423-23, 1 July 1972–15 August 1973, Vol. 2, 164; TAC Project 72A-068F, Rivet Haste (Phase I), K417.0735 FY 1973, Vol. 5, AFHRA.
13. Air Operations in Southeast Asia, 1972–1973, Vol. 2, p. iv-133, K717.0423-23, AFHRA.
14. Ibid., iv-144.
15. Eggers, Employment of Missiles, K712.153-1, AFHRA; Air Operations in Southeast Asia, 1972–1973, Vol. 2, p. iv-130, K717.0423-23, AFHRA; History of Linebacker Operations, 10 May 1972–23 October 1972, 39–42, K740.04-24, 1972, AFHRA.
16. Message from AFSSO 7AF to AFSSO PACAF, Visit of CSAF, 101345Z, July 1972, Folder General Vogt's Read File July 1972, Vogt Papers, AFHSD.
17. Deputy Chief of Staff, Plans and Operations, Memo for General Ryan, Linebacker Critiques, 26 July 1972, K740.3391, AFHRA.
18. Message from AFSSO Udorn to AFSSO 7AF, Linebacker Conference Alpha V and Tango IV, 030945Z, September 1972, Vogt Papers, Message Traffic September 1972, AFHSD.
19. History of Linebacker Operations, 10 May 1972–23 October 1972, 47, K740.04-24, 1972, AFHRA.
20. CINCPAC Command History 1972, Vol. 1, 171–73, K712.01, 1972, Vol. 1; CHECO Reports were similarly cryptic. Porter, Linebacker First 120 Days, 46–47, K717.0414-42; Johnson, Linebacker Operations: September–December 1972, 50, K717.0413-102, AFHRA.
21. Message from AFSSO TAC to AFSSO, Tactics for SEA, 7AF, 301930Z, June 1972, Vogt Papers, Message Traffic June 1972, AFHSD; History of Linebacker Operations, 10 May 1972–23 October 1972, 51, K740.04-24, 1972, AFHRA.
22. Message from AFSSO 7AF to AFSSO PACAF, Linebacker Victor III Mission, 301120Z, July 1972, Folder General Vogt's Read File July 1972, Vogt Papers, AFHSD; Thompson, *To Hanoi and Back*, 239.
23. Evaluation Report for the NVN Offensive (April–August 1972), pp. v-10 through v-11, K717.04-9, 1972, AFHRA; Linebacker Conference Oscar IV and Papa IV, 230834Z, August 1972, K740.3391, AFHRA.
24. Thompson, *To Hanoi and Back*, 239; Colonel Scott G. Smith, End of Tour Report, 31 May 1973, K717.131, AFHRA. For one of the first discussions of Teaball's existence see Doyle Larson, "Direct Intelligence Combat Support in Vietnam: Project Teaball," *American Intelligence Journal* 15, no.1 (Spring/Summer 1994): 56–58.
25. Machovec, Southeast Asia Tactical Data Systems Interface, 28, K717.0414-51; Message from 7/13AF to RUMMRSA/7AF, A-TACC-NS Concept of Operations, 061115Z, June 1972, K239.031-36, AFHRA; Message from AFSSO PACAF to AFSSO 7AF, MiG Warning Assistance Team, 020256Z, September 1972, Vogt Papers, Message Traffic September 1972, AFHSD.
26. Interview of General William L. Kirk, ret., K143.044-90, Vol. 17, AFHRA; Message from DIRNSA to NSA NCR NMCC SSO Da Nang SSO, 31, 2030Z, July 1972, K143.044-90, Vol. 40, 2001, AFHRA.
27. Linebacker Conference Bravo IV and Charlie IV, 241202Z, September 1972, K740.3391, AFHRA.
28. McFarland and Newton, *To Command the Sky*, 165, 228; Werrell, *Sabres over MiG Alley*, 106; Ginor and Remez, *The Soviet-Israeli War, 1967–1973*, 162.
29. Hanyok, *Spartans in Darkness*, 249–51.
30. CINCPAC, Pacific Area Naval Operations Review November 1966, 15, NHHC; Machovec, Southeast Asia Tactical Data Systems Interface, 28, K717.0414-51, AFHRA.
31. Lieutenant General Glen W. Martin, Combat Lightning in SEA Tactical Control Environment,

NOTES FOR CHAPTER 9

5 October 1967, K168.06-167, 1966–1970; Seventh Air Force Tactical Air Control Center (North Sector) Concept of Operations, Project Combat Lightning, K740.03-34, 22 October 1966, AFHRA.

32. Air Operations in Southeast Asia, 1972–1973, Vol. 1, p. ii-28, K717.0423-23, AFHRA.
33. Machovec, Southeast Asia Tactical Data Systems Interface, 7, K717.0414-51, AFHRA.
34. Colonel John W. Harrell, DOCOA, North Vietnam Operations Control Center, 8 September 1968, K740.03-38, 1967–1968, AFHRA; Communications Equipment in Southeast Asia (no date), K168.06-162, AFHRA; Machovec, Southeast Asia Tactical Data Systems Interface, 10, K717.0414-51, AFHRA.
35. Air Operations in Southeast Asia, 1972–1973, Vol. 2, p. iv-146, K717.0423-23, AFHRA.
36. Ibid., iv-147; Interview of General William L. Kirk, ret., K143.044-90, Vol. 17, AFHRA.
37. Summary Air Operations Southeast Asia July 1972, p. 4-2, K717.3063, July 1972, AFHRA; Machovec, Southeast Asia Tactical Data Systems Interface, 28, K717.0414-51, AFHRA; Porter, Linebacker First 120 Days, 46, K717.0414-42, 1973, AFHRA.
38. OEG/OP-508W Operations in Southeast Asia, 1 January 1972–31 January 1973, Table 4-9, NHHC.
39. Johnson, Linebacker Operations: September–December 1972, 52, K717.0413-102, AFHRA.
40. History of Linebacker Operations, 10 May 1972–23 October 1972, 51–53, K740.04-24, 1972, AFHRA.
41. Message, 291155Z, July 1972, K143.044-90, Vol. 32; History of Seventh Air Force, 1972–1973, 129, K740.10-25, Vol. 1, AFHRA.
42. History of Linebacker Operations, 10 May 1972–23 October 1972, 53, K740.04-24, 1972, AFHRA; Porter, Linebacker First 120 Days, 67–69, K717.0414-42, 1973, AFHRA.
43. Project Red Baron III, Air-to-Air Encounters in Southeast Asia, Volume 1: Executive Summary, 26, K417.0735-7, Vol. 1, 1974, AFHRA; Linebacker II Arclite Day 10 Critique, 300715Z, December 1972, K744.01, AFHRA; Message from 7th AF to RUHHABA/CINCPACAF, Linebacker Conference Prime Choke, 301136Z, August 1972, K740.3391, AFHRA.
44. Message from 7th AF to RUHHABA/PACAF, Linebacker Conference Alpha VII and Zulu VI, 051335Z, October 1972, K740.3391, AFHRA; Message from AFSSO Udorn to AFSSO 7AF, Linebacker Conference Prime Choke, 271020Z, August 1972, Vogt Papers, Read File August 1972, AFHSD; Message from AFSSO Udorn to 7AF, Linebacker Conference Delta VI and Foxtrot VI, 220859Z, September 1972, Vogt Papers, Message Traffic September 1972, AFHSD.
45. Interview of General William L. Kirk, ret., K143.044-90, Vol. 17, AFHRA; Linebacker Conference Bravo IV and Charlie IV, 241202Z, September 1972, K740.3391, AFHRA.
46. Message from AFSSO Udorn to AFSSO 7AF, Linebacker Conference Mike Four Blue, 190419Z, August 1972, Vogt Papers, Read File August 1972, AFHSD.
47. Message from 7th AF to RUHHABA/CINCPACAF, Linebacker Conference November VI and Lima VI, 280451Z, September 1972, K740.3391, 21–29 September 1972, AFHRA; Linebacker Conference Prime Choke, 301136Z, August 1972, K740.3391, AFHRA.
48. Linebacker Conference Sierra VI and Romeo VI, 010642Z, October 1972, K740.3391, AFHRA; Linebacker Conference Victor VI and Whiskey VI, 030216Z, October 1972, K740.3391, AFHRA.
49. Air Operations in Southeast Asia, 1972–1973, Vol. 2, pp. iv-154 through iv-56, K717.0423-23, AFHRA.
50. Linebacker Conference Juliet VI and Kilo VI, 261234Z, September 1972; Message from 7th AF to RUHHABA/CINCPAC, Linebacker Conference Oscar VI and Papa VI, 290545Z September 1972; Linebacker Conference Charlie VIII and Uniform VII, 191300Z, October 1972, K740.3391, AFHRA.
51. Message from 7th AF to RUHHABA/PACAF, Linebacker Conference Yankee VI and X-Ray VI,

NOTES FOR CHAPTER 9

050130Z, October 1972, K740.3391, AFHRA.
52. Air Operations in Southeast Asia, 1972–1973, Vol. 2, pp. iv-157, iv-158, iv-116, K717.0423-23, AFHRA.
53. Ibid.; Message from 7AF to RUHHABA/CINCPACAF, TACLO-7AF Activity Report NBR 17-72 (1–15 September 1972), 160200Z, September 1972, K744.01, 1972, Vol. 3, AFHRA.
54. Linebacker Conference Whiskey V and X-Ray V, 201236Z, September 1972, K740.3391; Linebacker Tactical Conference, 311150Z, July 1972, K143.044-90, Vol. 33, AFHRA.
55. Linebacker Tactical Conference, 311150Z, July 1972, K143.044-90, Vol. 33, AFHRA.
56. Red Baron 75, Incident #91, 15 August 1972, Vietnam Air War Collection, Box 67, File 67/3, NHHC.
57. Message from 7th AF to RUEFHQA/CSAF/XOO, Linebacker Conference Tango VI and Prime Choke Bravo, 010644Z, October 1972, K740.3391, AFHRA.
58. Message from AFSSO Udorn to AFSSO 7th AF, Linebacker Conference Oscar IV and Papa IV, 211040Z, August 1972, K744.312, Vol. 1, AFHRA; Linebacker Conference Foxtrot IV, 051232Z, September 1972, K740.3391, AFHRA.
59. Message from 7th AF to RUHHABA/CINCPACAF, Linebacker Conference Whiskey IV and X-ray IV, 021135Z, September 1972, AFHRA; Message from AFSSO Udorn to AFSSO 7AF, Linebacker Conference X-Ray IV and Whiskey IV, 291015Z, August 1972, Vogt Papers, Read File July 1972, AFHSD.
60. Message from 7AF to RUHHABA/CINCPACAF, Linebacker Conference Sierra V, 180708Z, September 1972, K740.3391, AFHRA.
61. Linebacker Conference Kilo IV, 300404Z, August 1972, Vogt Papers, Read File August 1972; Message from AFSSO Udorn to AFSSO 7AF, Linebacker Conference Bravo V, 040800Z, September 1972, Vogt Papers, Message Traffic September 1972, AFHSD.
62. Linebacker Conference Alpha V and Tango IV, 030945Z, September 1972, Vogt Papers, AFHSD.
63. Message from AFSSO PACAF to AFSSO 7AF, Teaball Communications, 050259Z, October 1972, Vogt Papers, Message Traffic September 1972; Message from AFSSO PACAF to AFSSO 7AF, Linebacker Conference Echo VIII, 181034Z, October 1972, Vogt Papers, Message Traffic October 1972, AFHSD.
64. Linebacker II Arclite Day Nine Critique, 290925Z, December 1972, Vogt Papers, AFHSD; Air Operations in Southeast Asia, 1972–1973, Vol. 2, pp. iv-124 through iv–125, K717.0423-23, AFHRA.
65. Red Baron 79, Incident 97, 28 August 1972, Red Baron 84, Incident 104 and Incident 105, and Red Baron 82 Incident 106, 9 September 1972, Vietnam Air War Collection, Box 67, File 67/3, NHHC; Message from AFSSO Udorn to AFSSO 7AF, Personal to General Vogt from Major General Hughes, Linebacker Conference India V, 080540Z, September 1972, Vogt Papers, Message Traffic October 1972, AFHSD.
66. Message from AFSSO Udorn to AFSSO 7AF, Linebacker Conference Bravo VI and Charlie VI, 210954Z, September 1972, Vogt Papers, Message Traffic October 1972, AFHSD; Linebacker Conference November V and Prime Choke Alpha S, 170800Z, September 1972, K740.3391, AFHRA.
67. Message from 7th AF to RUHHABA/CINCPACAF, Personal for General Hargrove and General Blesse from General Talbott, 170810Z, September 1972, Linebacker Conference Whiskey V and X-Ray V, 201236Z September 1972, K740.3391, AFHRA; Message from AFSSO Udorn to AFSSO 7AF, Linebacker Conference Golf V and Hotel V, 130409Z, September 1972, Vogt Papers, Message Traffic September 1972, AFHSD.
68. Air Operations in Southeast Asia, 1972–1973, Vol. 2, iv-125 through iv–126, K717.0423-23, AFHRA.

69. Message, Personal to General Vogt from Major General Hughes, Linebacker Conference Charlie VIII and Uniform VII, date-time-group unreadable, K744.01 1972, Vol. II, Appendix V, AFHRA.
70. Linebacker Conference Bravo V, 081218Z, September 1972, K740.3391, AFHRA. Another source states that a MiG-19 was shot down. Air Operations in Southeast Asia, 1972–1973, Vol. 2, iv-121, K717.0423-23, AFHRA.
71. Message from 7th AF to RUHHABA/CINCPACAF, Linebacker Conference South, 091131Z, September 1972, K740.3391, 21–29 September 1972; Message from 7th AF to RUHHABA/CINCPACAF, Linebacker Conference India V, 121005Z, September 1972, K740.3391, 21–29 September 1972, AFHRA.
72. Linebacker Conferences Oscar V/Papa V, 170835Z, September 1972, K740.3391, AFHRA.
73. Message from 7th AF to RUHHABA/CINCPACAF, Linebacker Conference Uniform V and Victor V, 190546Z, September 1972, 21–29 September 1972, AFHRA; Linebacker Conference Whiskey V and X-Ray V, 201236Z, September 1972, K740.3391, AFHRA.
74. November V and Prime Choke Alpha S, 170800Z, September 1972, K740.3391, AFHRA.
75. Tango VI and Prime Choke Bravo, 010644Z, October 1972, K740.3391, AFHRA.
76. Summary of Linebacker Tactics Review Conference, 011207Z, October 1972; Message from 7th AF to RUEFHQA/CSAF, Quebec VI and Uniform VI, 030207Z, October 1972, K740.3391, AFHRA.
77. Red Baron 106, Incident 142, 12 October, Red Baron 107, Incident 144, 13 October, and Red Baron 109, Incident 149, 15 October 1972, Red Baron Reports, Vietnam Air War Collection, Box 67, File 67/3, NHHC; Message for General Hargrove and General Blesse from General Talbott, 170810Z, September 1972, AFHRA.
78. Message from 7AF to CSAF/AFSSO 314 AD, 040600Z, July 1972, Vogt Papers, Read File July 1972, AFHSD.
79. Visit of CSAF, 101345Z, July 1972, Vogt Papers, AFHSD.
80. Message from 7AF AFSSO to PACAF AFSSO, PACAF Team Visit 30 June–6 July 1972, 050720Z, August 1972, AFHSD; Message from 7AF to CSAF/AFSSO 314 AD, 040600Z, July 1972, Vogt Papers, AFHSD.
81. Visit of CSAF, 101345Z, July 1972, Vogt Papers, AFHSD.
82. Eggers, Employment of Missiles, K712.153-1, AFHRA.
83. Robert F. Futrell, *Aces and Aerial Victories*, 157; Mersky, *F-8 Crusader Units*, 101.
84. Message, Personal to General Vogt from Major General Hughes, Linebacker Conference Charlie VIII and Uniform VII, date-time-group unreadable, K744.01 1972, Vol. II, Appendix V, AFHRA.
85. Thompson, *To Hanoi and Back*, 241.
86. History of Seventh Air Force, 1972–1973, 148, K740.10-25, Vol. 1, AFHRA.
87. Air Operations in Southeast Asia, 1972–1973, Vol. 2, pp. iv-125 through iv-126, K717.0423-23, AFHRA.
88. Ibid., p. iv-127.

Chapter 10

1. Message, Personal to Gen Vogt from Col Olshefski, Linebacker Conference 22 December 1972, Final Section, 230645Z, December 1972, K744.01 1972, Vol. II, Appendix V, AFHRA; Thompson, *To Hanoi and Back,* 270, 274.
2. Linebacker Conference 22 December 1972, Final Section of Six, 230645Z, December 1972, K744.01, 1972, Vol. II ,Appendix V, AFHRA; Message from 7th AF to RUEFHQA/CSAF/XOO, Linebacker Conference 22 December 1972, 280405Z, December 1972, K740.3391, AFHRA; Smith, End of Tour Report, 31 May 1973, K717.131, AFHRA; Thompson, *To Hanoi and*

Back, 270, 274.
3. Directorate of Operations Analysis, Summary Air Operations Southeast Asia December 1972, 2, K717.3063, December 1972, AFHRA.
4. Linebacker Conference 22 December 1972, 230645Z, December 1972, K744.01 1972, Vol. II, Appendix V, AFHRA; Air Operations in Southeast Asia, 1972–1973, Vol. 2, pp. iv-295 through iv-296, K717.0423-23, AFHRA; Linebacker Conference 22 December 1972, 280405Z, December 1972, K740.3391, AFHRA.
5. Message to General Vogt from Colonel Olshefski, Linebacker II India Critique, 271115Z, December 1972, K744.01 1972, Vol. II, Appendix V, AFHRA.
6. Message from 7th AF to RUHHABA/CINCPACAF, Linebacker II Foxtrot, 270756Z, December 1972, K740.3391; Linebacker Conference 22 December 1972, 280405Z, December 1972, K740.3391, AFHRA.
7. Linebacker Conference 24 December 1972, 241715Z, December 1972, Vogt Papers, AFHSD.
8. Johnson, Linebacker Operations: September–December 1972, 68, K717.0413-102, AFHRA.
9. Message, Personal to General Vogt from Colonel Olshefski, Linebacker II Foxtrot, 231530Z, December 1972, K744.01 1972, Vol. II, Appendix V, AFHRA; Air Operations in Southeast Asia, 1972–1973, Vol. 2, p. iv-312, K717.0423-23, AFHRA; Thompson, *To Hanoi and Back*, 240.
10. Message to General Vogt from Major General Hughes, Linebacker II Arclite Day Eleven Critique, 310310Z, December 1972, K744.01 1972, Vol. II, Appendix V, AFHRA; Message from CTG 77.5 to CJCS, 280659Z, December 1972, Reference Files, Vietnam, A-Air Warfare (I), File Vietnam Air Ops MiG Combat, NHHC.
11. Linebacker II Arclite Day 10 Critique, 300715Z, December 1972, K744.01, 1972 Vol. II, AFHRA.
12. Thompson, *To Hanoi and Back*, 274–75.
13. OEG/OP-508W Operations in Southeast Asia, 1 January 1972–31 January 1973, 1-2, 1-3, NHHC.
14. OEG/OP-05W, Summary of Air Operations in Southeast Asia May 1972, Center for Naval Analyses, 4–15, OEG/OP-508W Operations in Southeast Asia, 1 January 1972–31 January 1973, 4–5, NHHC.
15. Ibid., 4-1.
16. History of the Pacific Air Forces, 1968, 210, K717.01, Vol. 1, Part 2, AFHRA.
17. Thompson, *To Hanoi and Back*, 243.
18. USAF 1971 Tactical Fighter Symposium, Nellis AFB, Nevada, 14–19 June 1971, K417.01 FY1971, Vol. 12; Lieutenant Colonel Carl E. Bratfisch, Historical Record of the Interceptor Weapons School, for the period ending 30 June 1971, K410.012, April–June 1971, AFHRA.
19. Message from AFSSO CSAF to AFSSO 7AF, Linebacker Mission Critiques, 061230Z, September 1972, Vogt Papers, Message Traffic September 1972, AFHSD.
20. Michael E. Weaver, "Exercise Coronet Organ and the Real History behind Red Flag," *Journal of Cold War Studies*, forthcoming in 2022.
21. Message AFSSO TAC to AFSSO 7AF, Tactics for SEA, 010354Z, July 1972, Vogt Papers, AFHSD.
22. Evaluation Report for the NVN Offensive (April–August 1972), V-12, V-13, K717.04-9, 1972, AFHRA.
23. Geesey, Air-to-Air Engagements, 3.

Chapter 11

1. Basil Collier, *A History of Air Power* (London: Weidenfeld and Nicolson, 1974), 41; Morrow, *Great War in the Air*, 15, 69, 151; Robert A. Doughty, *Pyrrhic Victory: French Strategy and Operations in the Great War* (Cambridge, MA: Belknap Press of Harvard University Press, 2005), 86–87, 93, 256.
2. Terrence J. Finnegan, *Shooting the Front: Allied Aerial Reconnaissance and Photographic

Interpretation on the Western Front—World War I (Washington, DC: National Defense Intelligence College Press, 2006), 459, 462.
3. John F. Kreis, *Piercing the Fog: Intelligence and Army Air Forces Operations in World War II* (Washington, DC: Air Force History and Museums Program, 1996), 80–82.
4. Samuel T. Dickens, "USAF Reconnaissance during the Korean War," in ed. Jacob Neufeld and George M. Watson Jr., *Coalition Air Warfare in the Korean War, 1950–1953* (Washington, DC: Air Force History and Museums Program, 2005), 240–51.
5. Ray Wagner, *American Combat Planes* (Garden City, NY: Doubleday, 1968), 274; Anthony M. Thornborough, *USAF Phantoms* (London: Arms & Armour, 1988), 154.
6. Presidents Eisenhower and Kennedy followed certain kinds of reconnaissance missions very closely from time to time: U-2 flights over the Soviet Union and Cuba, and then Corona spy satellites from 1960. See for example Dino A. Brugioni, *Eyes in the Sky: Eisenhower, the CIA and Cold War Aerial Espionage* (Annapolis, MD: Naval Institute Press, 2010); Michael Dobbs, *One Minute to Midnight: Kennedy, Khrushchev, and Castro on the Brink of Nuclear War* (New York: Alfred A. Knopf, 2008); and Dwayne A. Day, John M. Logsdon, and Brian Latell, *Eye in the Sky: The Story of the Corona Spy Satellites* (Washington, DC: Smithsonian Institution Press, 1998).
7. Notes of Meeting, July 22, 1965, *FRUS 1964–1968, III*, 216. The study of reconnaissance operations quickly takes one into the realm of intelligence analysis, which is beyond the scope of this work. American intelligence during the Vietnam War warrants a separate book.
8. HQ USMACV Command History, 1966, 421.
9. Michael Forrestal, Summary Record of the 533rd Meeting of the National Security Council, June 6, 1964, ed. Edward C. Keefer, *Foreign Relations of the United States, 1964–1968, Laos, Volume XXVIII* (Washington, DC: United States Government Printing Office, 1998), 142 (hereafter referred to as *FRUS 1964–1968, XXVIII*).
10. Message from AFSSO 7AF to AFSSO CSAF, Daily Wrap Up, 221120Z, May 1972, AFHSD; Message from AFSSO 7AF to AFSSO CSAF, Daily Wrap Up, 261020Z, May 1972, Vogt Papers, Message Traffic May 1972, AFHSD.
11. Maj. Gen. Richard G. Stillwell, MACV Chief of Staff, to CINCPAC, Reconnaissance Support for MACV (working paper, no date), K717.03-40 July 1966–June 1967, AFHRA; HQ USMACV Command History, 1965, 49, 51, 151, Telegram from the Embassy in Thailand to the Department of State, March 23, 1965, ed. Edward Keefer, *Foreign Relations of the United States, 1964–1968, Volume XXVII, Mainland Southeast Asia; Regional Affairs* (Washington, DC: Government Printing Office, 2000), 617.
12. Command History, United States Military Assistance Command, Vietnam, 1965, 205.
13. Memorandum of Telephone Conversation between the Undersecretary of State for Political Affairs (Harriman) and the President's Special Assistant for National Security Affairs (Bundy), May 20, 1964, *FRUS 1964–1968, XXVIII*, 92; Summary Record of Meeting, June 2, 1964, *FRUS 1964–1968, XXVIII*, 125; Greenhalgh, *The RF-101 Voodoo, 1961–1970*, 27, 36; John J. Sbrega, "Southeast Asia," in *Case Studies in the Development of Close Air Support*, ed. Benjamin Franklin Cooling (Washington, DC: Office of Air Force History, United States Air Force, 1990), 426.
14. Telegram from the Department of State to the Embassy in Vietnam, March 30, 1965, *FRUS 1964–1968, II*, 493; Woods, *LBJ: Architect of American Ambition*, 513, 599.
15. Dunham, End of Tour Report, 9 July 1967, K740.131, AFHRA; Message from General Clay to General Vogt, 220305Z, April 1972, K717.03-221, Vol. 1, AFHRA; Hannah, *Striving for Air Superiority*, 10.
16. Timothy N. Castle, *At War in the Shadow of Vietnam: U.S. Military Aid to the Royal Lao Government, 1955–1975* (New York: Columbia University Press, 1993), 68–69; William E. Colby, Memorandum for Record, May 24, 1964, *FRUS 1964–1968, XXVIII*, 109.

17. Lt. Edward P. Brynn, Reconnaissance in SE Asia, July 1966–June 1969 (HQ PACAF: Directorate of Operations Analysis/CHECO Division, 1969), 6, K717.0414-14, 1969, AFHRA; Smith, USAF Reconnaissance in Southeast Asia, 1961–1966, 23, 24, K717.0414-14, AFHRA.
18. Smith, Carrier Air Wing Six Cruise Report April 1968 to December 1968, 14 December 1968, NHHC.
19. Castle, *U.S. Military Aid to the Royal Lao Government, 1955–1975*, 68–69; William E. Colby, Memorandum for Record, May 24, 1964, *FRUS 1964–1968, XXVIII*, 109.
20. Smith, USAF Reconnaissance in Southeast Asia, 1961–1966, 29, K717.0414-14; Message from COMUSMACV to RUMSAL/CMDR 7AF, Blue Tree Requirements for December, Daily Addition, 120605Z, December 1966, K717.312, AFHRA; Telegram from the Chairman of the Joint Chiefs of Staff (Wheeler) to the Commander in Chief, Pacific (Sharp), February 27, 1965, *FRUS 1964–1968, II*, 380; HQ CINCPAC, Pacific Area Naval Operations Review November 1968, 5, Vietnam Command Files, Box 105, File November 1968 History Naval Operations, Vol. III 1965–1967, Part 1, 76, NHHC; Van Staaveren, *Gradual Failure*, 85.
21. US Seventh Fleet Monthly Historical Summary, April 1968, 22, Vietnam Command Files, Box 117, NHHC; Greenhalgh, *The RF-101 Voodoo, 1961–1970*, 74, 77–78; Command History, United States Military Assistance Command, Vietnam, 1965, 202.
22. Holland Jr., Input on Tactical Air Reconnaissance, K417.367-2, November 1969, Vol. 1, AFHRA.
23. June Conference Book (PACAF), Section II, K717.151-12, 1966; Smith, USAF Reconnaissance in Southeast Asia, 1961–1966, 35, K717.0414-14, AFHRA; USS *Constellation*, Highlights of 1966 Attack Carrier Air Wing Fifteen Westpac Cruise, NHHC.
24. Lt. Col. Floyd Herbert, PACAF Tactics and Techniques Bulletin No. 67, RF-101 and RF-4C Reconnaissance, 11 August 1967, K717.549-1, AFHRA; PACAF DI, Effects of Air Operations Southeast Asia, August 1966, 64–65, K717.6092, AFHRA.
25. US Seventh Fleet Monthly Historical Summary, June 1968, 30, Vietnam Command Files, Box 117, NHHC; Overton, Rolling Thunder: January 1967–November 1968, 44, K717.0414-12, AFHRA.
26. Message from CG FMFPAC to RUHHMF/CG III MAF, 04003, August 1967, found online at The Vietnam Center & Sam Johnson Vietnam Archive, Texas Tech University, http://vietnam.ttu.edu.
27. Commander in Chief Pacific Command History, 1969, Vol. 3, 83, K712.01, Vol. 3, redacted, 1969, AFHRA; Corona Harvest V, 1972–1973, 39, K416.041-13, AFHRA.
28. Corona Harvest V, 1972–1973, 2, K416.041-13, AFHRA; Johnson, Linebacker Operations: September–December 1972, 69–70, K717.0413-102, AFHRA; Transcript of a Telephone Conversation between Moorer and Vogt, December 22, 1972, *FRUS 1969–1976, IX*, 807.
29. 2nd Air Div to RUEAHQ/CSAF, 190710Z, March 1965, K526.1623, AFHRA; Commanding officer 4th Marines, Colonel D. W. Sherman, to Commanding General, Third Marine Division, Combat Operation After Action Report, 24 May 1966, Vietnam, April–December 1966, Box 4, Folder 8, Archives Branch, HDMCU.
30. Greenhalgh, *The RF-101 Voodoo, 1961–1970*, 118; Memorandum from the Director of Intelligence and Research (Denney) to Secretary of State Rusk, January 27, 1965, *FRUS 1964–1968, XXVIII*, 323; Telegram from the Embassy in Laos to the Department of State, June 21, 1965, *FRUS 1964–1968, III*, 371, 372.
31. Capt. Charles E. Hogan, History of the 460th Tactical Reconnaissance Wing, 1 July 1968–30 September 1968, 17, 21 22, K-WG-460-HI, Vol. 1, AFHRA; Message from 7th AF to RUHHABA/CINCPACAF, Linebacker Conference Kilo V, 170820Z, September 1972, K740.3391, AFHRA; Message from 7th AF to AIG 919, Blue Springs Special Photo Interpretation Report MSN Q540, 252131Z, December 1966, K717.312, AFHRA.
32. Fleet Marine Force, Pacific, Operations of U.S. Marine Forces Vietnam, December 1967 and 1967

Summary, Vietnam, Box 13, Folder 4, Archives Branch, HDMCU.
33. History of the Deputy Commander for Intelligence, 1 January to 31 March 1967, K-WG-460-HI, AFHRA; History, 432nd TRW, January–June 1967, 9–10, K-WG-432-HI, January–June 1967, Vol. 2, AFHRA; Major William J. Davies, History of the 12th TRS, April–June 1968, 5–6, K-WG-460-HI, AFHRA; Smith, USAF Reconnaissance in Southeast Asia, 1961–1966, 45, K717.0414-14, AFHRA.
34. Mr. K. Sams, et al., The Air War in Vietnam: 1968–1969 (HQ PACAF: Directorate, Tactical Evaluation, CHECO Division, 1970), 25, K717.0413-143, AFHRA; Warren A. Trest, Khe Sanh (Operation Niagara) 22 January–31 March 1968 (HQ PACAF: Directorate, Tactical Evaluation, CHECO Division, 1968), 448, K717.0413-35, AFHRA; Message from CG III MAF to COMUSMACV, CG 7th AF, 290225Z, January 1968, found online at The Vietnam Center & Sam Johnson Vietnam Archive, Texas Tech University, http://vietnam.ttu.edu.
35. Greenhalgh, *The RF-101 Voodoo, 1961–1970*, 119.
36. History of Pacific Air Forces, 1 July 1969–30 June 1970, 69–73, K717.01, FY 1970, Vol. 1, Part 1, AFHRA; Major Dale L. Emerson, History of the 460th Tactical Reconnaissance Wing 1 January 1969–31 March 1969, K-WG-460-HI, Vol. 1, AFHRA (hereafter referred to as the 460th TRW).
37. Smith, USAF Reconnaissance in Southeast Asia, 1961–1966, 10, 45, K717.0414-14, AFHRA; Dunham, End of Tour Report, 9 July 1967, K740.131, AFHRA; Message from SSO XXIV Corps to CG III MAF, Air Photo Coverage of Laotian Border, 030116Z, December 1969, found online at The Vietnam Center & Sam Johnson Vietnam Archive, Texas Tech University, http://vietnam.ttu.edu.
38. Sams, et al., The Air War in Vietnam: 1968–1969, 6, K717.0413-143, AFHRA; John M. Shaw, *The Cambodian Campaign: The 1970 Offensive and America's Vietnam War* (Lawrence: University Press of Kansas, 2005), 61.
39. Greenhalgh, *The RF-101 Voodoo, 1961–1970*, 97–98.
40. Message from 7AF to RUMSMA/COMUSMACV, Special Operating Rules, Christmas 1966 Truce, 201159Z, December 1966 and Message from CINCPAC to RUCSAAA/CINCSAC, SEA Recon during Truce Period, 212225Z, December 1966, K717.312, AFHRA; Message from 7AF to RUHLKM/CINCPACAF, Christmas Ceasefire, 150630Z, December 1966, K740.1623-5, AFHRA; Message from 7AF to All ALFA Frag Addressees, Instructions for Christmas Ceasefire Period, 231150Z, December 1967, K740.1623, AFHRA; Message from CINCPAC to CINCPACFLT, Recon Effort during New Year's Stand-Down, 310242Z, December 1966, K712.312-25, AFHRA.
41. Greenhalgh, *The RF-101 Voodoo, 1961–1970*, 85, 99, 101; Recon Effort during New Years Stand-Down, 310242Z, December 1966, US Seventh Fleet Monthly Historical Summary, December 1967, 23, 26, Vietnam Command Files, Box 117, NHHC; HQ CINCPAC, Pacific Area Naval Operations Review November 1968, 15–18, 21–22, Vietnam Command Files, Box 105, File November 1968, NHHC.
42. Greenhalgh, *The RF-101 Voodoo, 1961–1970*, 101.
43. 1Lt. Harold D. Ryan, History of the 12th TRS, January–March 1969, 13, 15, K-WG-460-HI, AFHRA; Francis FitzGerald, *Fire in the Lake: The Vietnamese and the Americans in Vietnam* (Boston: Little, Brown, 1972), 67, 139–40, 160–61; Jonathan Neale, *A People's History of the Vietnam War: A New Press People's History* (New York: New Press, 2001), 41, 176.
44. Information Memorandum from the President's Special Assistant (Rostow) to President Johnson, July 1, 1968, *FRUS 1964–1968, VI*, 831; Notes of Meeting, October 14, 1968, *FRUS 1964–1968, VI*, 180–81; Memorandum for Record, October 23, 1968, ed. Kent Sieg, *Foreign Relations of the United States, 1964–1968, Volume VII, Vietnam September 1968–January 1969* (Washington, DC: United States Government Printing Office, 2003), 312 (hereafter referred to as *FRUS*

NOTES FOR CHAPTER II

1964–1968, VII).

45. Message from 7AF to RUMBDFK/TFA, Night Reconnaissance Operations in Laos, 100105Z, January 1969, K-WG-432-HI, Oct–Dec. 1968, Vol. 2, AFHRA; Message from 7AF to RUMBDFM/TASM Force Alpha, 101045Z, January 1969, K730.312-4 1968–1969, AFHRA; Reconnaissance Attack Squadron Nine, 8 January 1969, Newsletter, Supplement, Fleet Aviation Commands, Pre-1998, AR/229, Box 107, File F9, NHHC.

46. Memorandum of Conversation, November 13, 1968, *FRUS, 1964–1968, VII*, 633; Telegram from the Embassy in France to the Department of State, November 24, 1968, *FRUS, 1964–1968, VII*, 689, 690; Notes on the National Security Council Meeting, November 25, 1968, *FRUS, 1964–1968, VII*, 696, 698.

47. Memorandum from the President's Assistant for National Security Affairs (Kissinger) to President Nixon, November 23, 1970, *FRUS 1969–1976, VII*, 187. Bruce was the Ambassador to the Paris Peace Talks at this time. Notes of the President's Meeting, October 29, 1968, *FRUS, 1964–1968, VII*, 402; Nguyen, *Hanoi's War*, 118.

48. Notes of the President's Meeting, October 29, 1968, *FRUS, 1964–1968, VII*, 402; Memorandum from President Nixon to Secretary of State Rogers, Secretary of Defense Laird, and Director of Central Intelligence Helms, November 30, 1970, *FRUS, 1964–1968, VII*, 201.

49. HQ CINCPAC, Pacific Area Naval Operations Review February 1969, 16–26, Vietnam Command Files, Box 105, File January 1969, NHHC; Extract of message from CINCPACAF TO CSAF, ROE, 032143Z, January 1967, K717.312, January 1967, AFHRA.

50. Commander in Chief, U.S. Pacific Fleet, Rolling Thunder Operations Report and Analysis, 8 October 1968, Vietnam Command Files, COLL/372, Box 111, File CPF RT Rept, 16–30 September 1968, NHHC; Enclosure: Intelligence Analysis of North Vietnam 1–31 December 1968, Vietnam Command Files, COLL/372, Box 111, File CPF RT Rept, 16–31 December 1968, NHHC.

51. Davies, 12th TRS, April–June 1968, 10, K-WG-460-HI, AFHRA; Reconnaissance Attack Squadron Nine, Newsletter 6 February 1969, Fleet Aviation Commands, Pre-1993, AR/229, Box 107, File F8, NHHC.

52. Captain Jim Perokis, Input to Project Corona Harvest, 8 August 1970, K717.6001-6, 8 August 1970, AFHRA; Captain J. S. Christiansen, USS *Constellation* to Commander Naval Air Force, U.S. Pacific Fleet, 1968–1969 Cruise Report, 30 January 1969, Ships History Post 2001, *Constellation* CV-64, Box 70, File *Constellation* 1968, NHHC.

53. Message from COMUSMACV, from CINCPAC to CINCPACFLT, Arc Light Photography, 0180955Z, June 1965, K712.1623-2, AFHRA; Davies, 12th TRS, July–September 1968, 4, 12, K-WG-460-HI, AFHRA.

54. Message from 7th AF to PACAF, DOCO-66-TS-13602, July 1966, K740.1623-5, 25 July 1966, AFHRA; Message from 460 Recon Tech Squadron to AIG 7840, Significant Photo Interpretations, 182035Z, December 1967, K717.312, AFHRA.

55. Message from 13 RTS Tan Son Nhut AB RVN to AIG 919, 250122Z, May 1967, K717.312, AFHRA; Major S. R. Neiley Jr., AFXOPFR, Input Paper on Reconnaissance Forces in SEA, K143.5072-16, September 1965–November 1966, AFHRA.

56. Transcript of a Telephone Conversation between President Nixon and His Assistant for National Security Affairs (Kissinger), November 21, 1970, *FRUS 1969–1976, VII*, 184; DCS Intelligence, Headquarters PACAF, Effects of Air Operations Southeast Asia, October 1966, 41, K717.6092, AFHRA.

57. Message from CG III MAF to COMUSMACV, Evaluation of Thor, 212932Z, October 1968, found online at The Vietnam Center & Sam Johnson Vietnam Archive, Texas Tech University, http://vietnam.ttu.edu.

NOTES FOR CHAPTER II

58. 432nd TRW, Reconnaissance of BDA, 16 February 1969, K-WG-432-HI, January–March 1969, Vol. 2, AFHRA.
59. Message from 7AF to RUHLKSP/PACAF CC, 120256Z, June 1967, K717.312-64, AFHRA; Message from 7AF to CINCPACAF, 150825Z, May 1967, K717.312-64, AFHRA.
60. Robert F. Colwell, USAF Tactical Reconnaissance in Southeast Asia July 69–June 71 (HQ PACAF: Directorate of Operations Analysis, CHECO/Corona Harvest Division, 1971), 17, K717.0414-14, AFHRA; Captain William A. Gauntt, History of 14th TRS, April–June 1972, 8–9, K-WG-432-HI, Vol. 3, AFHRA; Message from AFSSO 7AF to AFSSO CSAF, Daily Wrap Up, 201130Z, May 1972, Vogt Papers, Message Traffic May 1972, AFHSD.
61. Message from 15 AF to AIG 712/IN/DOI/DOXI, Fifteenth Air Force Intelligence Summary 15-16-70, 182145Z, April 1972, K-WG-307-HI, April–June 1972, Vol. 1, AFHRA.
62. Air Operations in Southeast Asia, 1972–1973, Vol. 2, iv-73, K717.0423-23, AFHRA; Attack Carrier Air Wing Eleven, Cruise Report February to November 1972, 1 December 1972, NHHC.
63. Gauntt, 14th TRS, April–June 1972, 4, K-WG-432-HI, Vol. 3, AFHRA; SSgt. Donald L. Canney, History of 432nd TRW, 1 October–31 December 1972, 54, 55, K-WG-432-HI, Vol. 1, AFHRA; Margaret C. Mell, History of the Directorate of Operations, 1 July–31 December 1972, 290, K143.01 1 July–31 December 1972, AFHRA; Message from AFSSO 7AF to AFSSO CSAF, Daily Wrap Up, 261020Z, May 1972, Vogt Papers, Message Traffic May 1972, AFHSD.
64. Corona Harvest V, 1972–1973, 39–40, 176, K416.041-13, AFHRA; Message from SSO MACV to SSO SACRECONCEN, 130743Z, April 1967, K416.03-60, AFHRA; Major Arthur Andraitis, interview by Captain Benson, circa 1969, K717.0512, AFHRA.
65. Clarence E. Smith, "CIA's Analysis of Soviet Science and Technology," in Gerald K. Haines and Robert E. Leggett, *Watching the Bear: Essays on CIA's Analysis of the Soviet Union*, chapter iv, found online at: https://www.cia.gov/library/center-for-the-study-of-intelligence/csi-publications/books-and-monographs/watching-the-bear-essays-on-cias-analysis-of-the-soviet-union/article04.html.
66. Memorandum, Preliminary Assessment of Keyhole Mission 1041-1, 10–15 May 1967, found online at: http://www.nro.gov/foia/CAL-Records/Cabinet5/DrawerA/5%20A%200078.pdf; Day, Logsdon, and Latell, *Eye in the Sky: The Story of the Corona Spy*, 34, 76.
67. A satellite falls through space around the earth at around 16,000 to 17,000 miles per hour, so to turn its orbit ninety degrees would require enough of an engine burn to stop a 17,000 mile-per-hour forward vector and continue it in another direction at the same speed, and that would require an enormous amount of fuel for one orbit change for one target each time. Jerry Jon Sellers, with contributions by William J. Astore, Robert B. Giffen, and Wiley J. Larson, *Understanding Space: An Introduction to Astronautics*, 2nd ed. (New York: McGraw-Hill, 2000), 203–4, 207.
68. Day, Logsdon, and Latell, *Eye in the Sky: The Story of the Corona Spy*, 179.
69. National Photographic Interpretation Center, "KH-4 Mission 1042-1, 17–22 June 1967: South China and North Vietnam Edition," found online at: https://www.cia.gov/library/readingroom/docs/CIA-RDP99T01396R000100440001-4.pdf.
70. Peter W. Merlin, *From Archangel to Senior Crown: Design and Development of the Blackbird* (Reston, VA: American Institute of Aeronautics and Astronautics, 2008), 1, 3, 87; Colwell, Tactical Reconnaissance July 69–June 71, 24, K717.0414-14, AFHRA. The A-12 was produced for the CIA to fly "covert strategic reconnaissance," while the SR-71 was an Air Force platform that was an improvement over the A-12, and originally had the "mission of general war strike reconnaissance." C. W. Fischer, Memorandum for the President, "Advanced Reconnaissance Aircraft," December 26, 1966, found online at: http://nsarchive.gwu.edu/NSAEBB/NSA3BB74/. The A-12 had only a pilot, while the SR-71 had a systems officer sitting behind him. National Photographic Interpretation Center, Black Shield Mission X-001, 31 May 1967, found online at: http://nsarchive

gwu.edu/NSAEBB/NSAEBB74/.
71. Commander in Chief Pacific Command History, 1969, Vol. 3, 83, K712.01, Vol. 3, redacted, 1969, AFHRA; Corona Harvest V, 1972–1973, 39, K416.041-13; History of SAC Reconnaissance Operations, FY72, 1, 7, 12, K416.01-125, AFHRA. SR-71s flew out of Kadena Air Base, Okinawa, where a four-plane detachment was based.
72. Brynn, Reconnaissance in SE Asia, July 1966–June 1969, 29, K717.0414-14, 1969, AFHRA.
73. History of SAC Reconnaissance Operations, Historical Study No. 125, 18 April 1974, 1, 7, 12, K416.01-125, Vol. 1, 1 July 1971–30 June 1972, AFHRA; Corona Harvest V, 1972–1973, 39–40, 176, 178, K416.041-13, AFHRA.
74. Memorandum for Director, Office of Special Activities, Technical Evaluation of Mission BSX 001 of 31 May 1967, BYE-50249/67, 21 June 1967, found online at: https://archive.org/stream/HistoryOfTheOfficeOfSpecialActivitiesFromInceptionTo1969/CIAhistOSAincep-1969Final_djvu.txt; History of SAC Reconnaissance Operations, FY72, 14, K416.01-125, AFHRA.
75. Message from CINCPAC to SSO CINCPAC/J231, Coastal Reconnaissance, 112118Z, May 1972, Vogt Papers, Read File May 1972, AFHSD; History of SAC Reconnaissance Operations, FY72, 20–21, K416.01-125, AFHRA; Air Operations in Southeast Asia 1 July 1972–15 August 1973, Vol. 5, 131, 147, K717.0423-23, AFHRA.
76. Bonetti, The War in Vietnam: January–June 1967, 13, K717.0414-17, AFHRA; Message from 7AF to CINCPAC, Blue Springs, 060632Z, 1966, K740.1622, 7 July 1966, AFHRA; Colwell, Tactical Reconnaissance, July 69–June 71, 56–57, K717.0414-14, AFHRA.
77. Paul W. Elder, Buffalo Hunter: 1970–1972, (HQ PACAF: Directorate of Operations Analysis, CHECO/Corona Harvest Division, 1973), 2–12, K717.0414-39, AFHRA; Penix and Ringenbach, Air Defense in Southeast Asia, 1945–1971, 40, K717.0414-36, AFHRA.
78. Message from CINCPACAF to 7AF, 072252, May 1966, K717.1623, AFHRA; Message from 7AF to RUCSAAA/SAC, Bold Warrior Message, 240524Z, October 1967, K717.312-64, AFHRA; Davies, 12th TRS, April–June 1968, 9, K-WG-460-HI, AFHRA. The code name of the reconnaissance program changed several times, from Blue Springs to Bumble Bug, to Bumpy Action, then to Buffalo Hunter in 1970. Elder, Buffalo Hunter: 1970–1972, xi, 1, K717.0414-39, AFHRA.
79. Study on the Effectiveness of Air Power in Southeast Asia, 101, 178, K416.041-13, AFHRA; Air Operations, 1 July 1972–15 August 1973, Vol. 5, 101, 303, K717.0423-23, AFHRA.
80. William Wagner, *Lightning Bugs and Other Reconnaissance Drones* (Fallbrook, CA: Aero Publishers, 1982), 26; Zaccagnini, History of 4080th Strategic Wing, January–March 1966, 21, K-WG-4080-HI, AFHRA; Colwell, Tactical Reconnaissance, July 69–June 71, 52, K717.0414-14, AFHRA.
81. Zaccagnini, History of 4080th Strategic Wing, January–March 1966, 14–15, K-WG-4080-HI, AFHRA.
82. Elder, Buffalo Hunter: 1970–1972, 2–4, 6, 9, 31, K717.0414-39, AFHRA; Rolling Thunder-Linebacker: A Preliminary Comparative Analysis, June 1972, Tab 7, K143.042-11, AFHRA.
83. Elder, Buffalo Hunter: 1970–1972, 3, 4, K717.0414-39, AFHRA; Notes of Meeting, July 26, 1965, FRUS 1964–1968, III, 241; Message from SAC to RUHHHQA/CINCPAC, Low Bumpy Action Report, 192011Z, March 1968, K740.626-4, AFHRA; Colwell, Tactical Reconnaissance, July 69–June 71, 52, K717.0414-14, AFHRA; Naval Historical Division, United States Naval Operations Vietnam, December 1969 Highlights, 10–11, Vietnam Command File, COLL/372, Box 88, File CNO NHD: US Naval Ops VN Dec. 69, NHHC.
84. Rolling Thunder-Linebacker Comparative Analysis, June 1972, Tab 7, K143.042-11, AFHRA; Mell, History Directorate of Operations, 1 July–31 December 1972, 298, K143.01, AFHRA.

85. Message from 7AF to RUHLKSP/PACAF CC, 120256Z, June 1967, K717.312-64, 10–12 June 1967, AFHRA; Message from SAC to RUEDHQA/CSAF, Preliminary Wide Bush Activity Report, 172325Z, November 1966, K143.5072-14, 17 November 1966, AFHRA; Message from SAC to 7AF, Wide Bush/Lightning Bug, 071625Z, September 1966, K717.312, AFHRA. The jammer was known as Wide Bush/Rivet Annie.
86. Southeast Asia Air Operations July 1971, K717.3063-1, July 1971, AFHRA; Colwell, Tactical Reconnaissance, July 69–June 71, 56–57, K717.0414-14, AFHRA; Linebacker Conference Bravo VI and Charlie VI, 241202Z, September 1972, K740.3391, AFHRA.
87. Corona Harvest V, 1972–1973, 303, K416.041-13; Air Operations in Southeast Asia, 1972–1973, Vol. 5, 101, 130–31, 303, K717.0423-23; Mell, History Directorate of Operations, 1 July–31 December 1972, 296–97, K143.01, AFHRA.
88. Elder, Buffalo Hunter: 1970–1972, 2, K717.0414-39; Corona Harvest V, 1972–1973, 101, K416.041-13, AFHRA.
89. Coordination and File Copy, April 1967, K416.03-2, 12 April 1967–18 March 1968, AFHRA.
90. Machovec, Southeast Asia Tactical Data Systems Interface, 40, K717.0414-51, AFHRA. This source does not give a date for this incident, but it was brought to light during a December 24, 1972, interview found on page 58.
91. Message from CSAF, K416.03-2, 12 April 1967–18 March 1968, AFHRA.
92. Message from HQ 7AF to RUCSBB/SAC DOSR RIR DISC, 091410Z, November 1967, K740.367-1, AFHRA; Message from CSAF to [unreadable], 091650Z, February 1968, K416.03-2, AFHRA; Elder, Buffalo Hunter: 1970–1972, 36, 37, K717.0414-39, AFHRA; Minutes of a Meeting of the Senior Review Group, April 13, 1971, *FRUS 1969–1976, VII*, 546.
93. Thomas P. Ehrhard, *Air Force UAVs: The Secret History of Drones* (Washington, DC: Mitchell Institute, 2010), 24, 28, 29.
94. Herbert, Bulletin No 67, RF-101 and RF-4C Reconnaissance, 11 August 1967, K717.549-1, AFHRA; Smith, USAF Reconnaissance in Southeast Asia, 1961–1966, 16–17, K717.0414-14, AFHRA.
95. Message from PACAF to AFCP, Operation Neutralize, 011415Z, October 1967, K717.312, AFHRA; History of Pacific Air Forces, Vol. 1, Part 2, 1968, 497, K717.01, AFHRA; Air Operations in Southeast Asia, 1972–1973, Vol. 2, p. iv-94, K717.0423-23, AFHRA.
96. Message from CINCPAC to COMUSMACV and CINCPACFLT, Operational Policy—Yankee Team, 080009Z, July 1964, K712.312-40, 8 July 1964, AFHRA; Greenhalgh, *The RF-101 Voodoo, 1961–1970*, 62.
97. Memorandum from Senator Mike Mansfield to President Johnson, June 9, 1964, *FRUS 1964–1968, XXVIII*, 166.
98. Message from CINCPAC to CINCPACAF, Realignment of Able Mable Reconnaissance Posture, 221220Z, January 1965, K712.1623-2, AFHRA; History of Pacific Air Forces, Vol. 1, Part 2, 1968, 506, K717.01, Vol. 1, Part. 2, 1968, AFHRA; Lieutenant Colonel George Stalk, An Analysis of the Objectives of Out-Country Aerial Reconnaissance in Southeast Asia, 1965–1967, 51–52, Air War College Research Report 3686, K239.042-3686, 1968, AFHRA. RF-101s were based at Tan Son Nhut Air Base, South Vietnam, in 1965 and from 1966 to 1970, with an interlude at Udorn Royal Thai Air Base from November 1965 to August 1966.
99. Thorndale, Tactical Recon Photography Request/Distribution, 33, K717-0413-53, AFHRA; Greenhalgh, *RF-101 Voodoo, 1961–1970*, 51–52, 70; Herbert, Bulletin No 67, RF-101 and RF-4C Reconnaissance, 11 August 1967, K717.549-1, AFHRA.
100. Stalk, Out-Country Aerial Reconnaissance, 1965–1967, 51–52, K239.042-3686, 1968, AFHRA; Colonel Pat E. Goforth, HQ PACAF, Hypothesis on the Adequacy of Tactical Aerial Reconnaissance, 2 October 1969, K717.03-43, AFHRA; Greenhalgh, *RF-101 Voodoo, 1961–1970*,

NOTES FOR CHAPTER II

69, 71, 111.

101. Stalk, Out-Country Aerial Reconnaissance, 1965–1967, 51–52, K239.042-3686, 1968, AFHRA; Message from CSAF to RUHLKM/PACAF, Use of QRC-160 Pods on RF-101 Aircraft, 052053Z, December 1966 and Message from 7AF to PACAF, QRC-160-1 Pods, 110455Z, December 1966, K717.312, AFHRA; Greenhalgh, *RF-101 Voodoo, 1961–1970*, 84, 109.

102. Greenhalgh, *RF-101 Voodoo, 1961–1970*, 109; Colwell, Tactical Reconnaissance, July 69–June 71, 7, K717.0414-14, AFHRA.

103. Van Staaveren, *Gradual Failure,* 205; Vice Chief of Staff U.S. Air Force Conference, 25–26 April 1966, K717.151-11, AFHRA; Air War College Research Report 3686, K239.042-3686, 1968, AFHRA.

104. Stalk, Out-Country Aerial Reconnaissance, 1965–1967, 54–56, 64, K239.042-3686, 1968, AFHRA; Brynn, Reconnaissance in SE Asia, July 1966–June 1969, 5, 38, K717.0414-14, AFHRA.

105. Lieutenant General Alvan C. Gillem, II, to HQ USAF, Review of the Reconnaissance Report, 4 August 1971, K239.031-67, 65/01/01–68/03/31, AFHRA.

106. Stalk, Out-Country Aerial Reconnaissance, 1965–1967, 51–52, K239.042-3686, 1968, AFHRA.

107. Lt. Col. Vernon L. Allgood, History of the 12th TRS April–June 1968, K-WG-460-HI, AFHRA; Brynn, Reconnaissance in SE Asia, July 1966–June 1969, 39–40, K717.0414-14, Lieutenant Colonel Floyd Herbert, PACAF Tactics and Techniques Bulletin #53, RF-4C Operations in SEA, 30 December 1966, K717.549-1, No. 53, AFHRA.

108. Sgt. Steven Landry, History 432nd TRW, October–December 1969, 18, K-WG-432-HI, Vol. 1, AFHRA.

109. Message from HQ 7AF to RUEFHQA/CSAF/AFRDQ P/AFXOPWG, Combat ROC 7AF 5-70, Improved F/RF-4 Survivability, 090700Z, May 1970, K740.85170-5, AFHRA; Brigadier General Clifford W. Hargrove to HQ USAF, Review of the Reconnaissance Concept, 6 August 1971, K239.031-67, 65/01/01–68/03/31, AFHRA; Gillem, Review of the Reconnaissance Report, 4 August 1971, K239.031-67, AFHRA; Mell, History Directorate of Operations, 1 July–31 December 1972, 292, K143.01, AFHRA.

110. Brigadier General George J. Keegan Jr., to General Robert N. Smith, Asst. DCS/P&O, HQ USAF, 5 February 1968, K740.626-6, October 1967–February 1968, AFHRA.

111. Message from 2nd Air Division to RUEAHQ/CSAF, Report from USAF Analysis Team, 150020Z, March 1965, K526.1623, AFHRA; Captain O.P. Ditch, KA-71 Strike Photography, K717.03-39, July 1967–January 1970, AFHRA; Major General Gordon F. Blood, Bombing Accuracy Measurement, December 30, 1968, K-WG-432-HI, October–December 1968, Vol. 2, AFHRA.

112. Message from 7AF to RUHLKSP/CINCPACAF, Pat Lynn, 041220Z, July 1966 and Message from 2nd Air Division to 13th Air Force, 060924Z, June 1965, K526.1623, AFHRA; CHI Contact Report, Captain Larry L. Benson discussion with Major Nicholas Mavrotheris, HQ USAF, 20 January 1970, K717.03-39, AFHRA.

113. Message from 7AF, info CSAF, Compass Haste, Part II, 041644Z, March 1968, K740.920-1, AFHRA; Colwell, Tactical Reconnaissance, July 69–June 71, 24, K717.0414-14, AFHRA; Message from 7AF to RUHLKSF/CINCPAC DI, For General Traintafellu from General Keegan, Compass Haste, Part II, 260855Z, February 1968, K740.626-4, 1968, AFHRA; Landry, History of 432nd Reconnaissance Wing, January–March 1970, 14, K-WG-432-HI, AFHRA; Trest, Khe Sanh, 52, K717.0413-35, AFHRA.

114. Detachment 1, 460th TRW, RCS: AU-D5-Historical Data Record from 1 January 1966 to 30 June 1966, K-WG-460-HI, Det 1, AFHRA; Colwell, Tactical Reconnaissance, July 69–June 71, 24, K717.0414-14, AFHRA.

115. HQ CINCPAC, Pacific Area Naval Operations Review March 1967, 25, CINCPAC, Pacific

Area Naval Operations Review December 1966, A-1, Vietnam Command Files, Box 102, Files December 1966, March 1967, NHHC; Commander in Chief US Pacific Fleet to Commander in Chief, Pacific, Rolling Thunder Report and Analysis, 1 May 1967, Vietnam Command Files, COLL/372, Box 109, File CPF RT Rept 3-23 April 1967 HQ, NHHC. The system was called RECONOFAX VI.

116. Reconnaissance Attack Squadron Nine, 8 January 1969, Newsletter, Supplement, Seventh Fleet Monthly Historical Summary, June 1969, 8, Vietnam Command Files, Box 119, File June 1969, NHHC.
117. Seventh Fleet Monthly Historical Summary, August 1967, 23–24, Vietnam Command Files, Box 117, NHHC.
118. Kent L. Lee, *Reminiscences of Vice Admiral Kent L. Lee, U.S. Navy (Retired)*, Vol. II (Annapolis, MD: US Naval Institute, 1990), 687–88. Lee had commanded Carrier Air Wing 6.
119. USS *Constellation*, Highlights of 1966 Attack Carrier Air Wing Fifteen Westpac Cruise, Reconnaissance Attack Squadron Nine, Newsletter 6 February 1969, Reconnaissance Attack Squadron Nine, 8 January 1969, Newsletter, Supplement, and Reconnaissance Attack Squadron Six, Newsletter, 26 June 1969, Fleet Aviation Commands, Pre-1993, AR/229, Box 104, File RVAH-6, 1969, NHHC.
120. US Seventh Fleet Monthly Historical Summary, March 1968, 35, Vietnam Command Files, Box 117, US Seventh Fleet Monthly Historical Summary, April 1968, 22, NHHC. The cameras were new AAS-21s.
121. USS *America* and Carrier Air Wing Eight 1972–1973 Westpac Deployment Cruise Report, 27, NHHC.
122. Lawrence B. Brennan, "Wings of Gold: The Loss of LTJG Lee E. Nordahl, USNR and LCDR Guy D. Johnson, USN, RVAH Thirteen, on 20 December 1965 Over North Vietnam: The Conclusion," *Universal Ship Cancellation Society Log* (May 2006), 18.
123. Southeast Asia Air Operations Briefing, September 1971, K717.3063-1, September 1971, AFHRA; McKnight, Carrier Air Wing Two, Cruise Report of October 1970 to June 1971, 10 June 1971, NHHC.
124. Stalk, Out-Country Aerial Reconnaissance, 1965–1967, 54–56, 64, K239.042-3686, 1968, AFHRA; Smith, USAF Reconnaissance in Southeast Asia, 1961–1966, 16–17, K717.0414-14, AFHRA; Message from 7AF to RUHLKM/PACAF, Use of Recon Forces, 22 December 1966, 220159Z, K717.312, AFHRA.
125. Reconnaissance Attack Squadron Nine, Newsletter 7 May 1969, Fleet Aviation Commands, Pre-1993, AR/229, Box 107, File F8, NHHC; Commanding Officer, Reconnaissance Attack Squadron Six, Newsletter, 26 June 1969, NHHC; Reconnaissance Attack Squadron Nine, Newsletter 6 February 1969, USS *America* and Carrier Air Wing Eight 1972–1973 Westpac Deployment Cruise Report, 25, NHHC.
126. Smith, USAF Reconnaissance in Southeast Asia, 1961–1966, 54, K717.0414-14, AFHRA.
127. Colonel Scott G. Smith, End of Tour Report, 31 May 1973, K717.131, AFHRA.
128. C. William Thorndale, Tactical Recon Photography Request/Distribution (HQ PACAF: Directorate, Tactical Evaluation, CHECO Division, 1969), 4, 48, K717-0413-53, AFHRA; Interview of Captain John J. McGuire Jr., by Lieutenant Colonel I. R. Little, no date or location given, 20, K239.0512-320, 00/07/64–00/10/66, AFHRA.
129. Brigadier General Jammie M. Philpott, In-Country Reconnaissance, 3 October 1967, Message from 460 TRW to 7AF, UMD Authorization, 180200Z, November 1967, K740.626-6, AFHRA. Philpott was deputy chief of staff for 7th AF intelligence.
130. Greenhalgh, *The RF-101 Voodoo, 1961–1970*, 83–84.
131. Contribution of Army OV-1 to Recce Program in SEA, 100411Z, August 1966,

K143.5072-16, AFHRA.
132. Keegan Jr., to Smith, Asst. DCS/P&O, HQ USAF, 5 February 1968, K740.626-6, AFHRA.
133. Andraitis interview, K717.0512, 1969, AFHRA.
134. Philpott, In-Country Reconnaissance, 3 October 1967, Message from 460 TRW to 7AF, UMD Authorization, 180200Z, November 1967, K740.626-6, AFHRA.
135. Davies, History 12th TRS, April–June 1968, 5, K-WG-460-HI, AFHRA; MACV Command History 1968, Vol. 1, 426.
136. Keegan Jr., to Smith, Asst. DCS/P&O, HQ USAF, 5 February 1968, K740.626-6, AFHRA.
137. Landry, History of 432nd Reconnaissance Wing, January–March 1970, 14, K-WG-432-HI, AFHRA.
138. Holland Jr., Input on Tactical Air Reconnaissance, K417.367-2, November 1969, Vol. 1, AFHRA; Thorndale, Tactical Recon Photography Request/Distribution, 52, K717.0413-53, AFHRA; Smith, USAF Reconnaissance in Southeast Asia, 1961–1966, 45, K717.0414-14, AFHRA.
139. Question and Answer Paper on Reconnaissance Operations in RVN, January 1966, K143.5072-16, AFHRA; Colonel Lewis M. Jamison, End of Tour Report, 1 March 1970, K717.131, AFHRA; Jamison, Lewis M. 12 March 1969–28 February 1970, Davies, 12th TRS, July–September 1968, K-WG-460-HI, AFHRA.
140. Major Niles F. Smith, HQ 7AF, Working Paper 68/7 Photo Reconnaissance Support to Tactical Fighter Wings, 1 August 1968, K740.31068-7, AFHRA; History of SAC Reconnaissance Operations, FY72, 6, K416.01-125, AFHRA; Rolling Thunder-Linebacker Comparative Analysis, June 1972, Tab 7, K143.042-11, AFHRA; Corona Harvest V, 1972–1973, 139–40, 176, K416.041-13, AFHRA.
141. Seventh Fleet Operations in SEASIA (1 April 1972 to 27 January 1973) and Intelligence Lessons Learned, Vietnam Command Files, Box 121, File Com 7 Flt Project LLIVN: 7 Flt, NHHC.
142. Smith, USAF Reconnaissance in Southeast Asia, 1961–1966, 64, K717.0414-14, AFHRA; Seventh Fleet Monthly Historical Summary, November 1967, 24, Reconnaissance Attack Squadron Nine, Newsletter 6 February 1969, NHHC.
143. Colwell, Tactical Reconnaissance, July 69–June 71, 15, K717.0414-14, AFHRA.
144. Ibid., 16.
145. Brynn, Reconnaissance in SE Asia, July 1966–June 1969, 19–21, K717.0414-14, 1969, AFHRA; CHI Contact Report, Benson and Mavrotheris, HQ USAF, 20 January 1970, K717.03-39, AFHRA; Gillem, Review of the Reconnaissance Report, 4 August 1971, K239.031-67, AFHRA. The program was called TAC RISE for short.
146. Dunham, End of Tour Report, 9 July 1967, K740.131, AFHRA.
147. Stalk, Out-Country Aerial Reconnaissance, 1965–1967, 51–52, K239.042-3686, 1968, AFHRA; Jamison, End of Tour Report, 1 March 1970, K717.131, AFHRA.
148. HQ USAF Tactical Air Reconnaissance Center, Required Operational Capability (ROC) RF-4C Modernization, 24 June 1968, K417.0733-3, 24 June 1968.
149. Brynn, Reconnaissance in SE Asia, July 1966–June 1969, 2, K717.0414-14, 1969, AFHRA; Gillem, Review of the Reconnaissance Report, 4 August 1971, K239.031-67, AFHRA; Smith, USAF Reconnaissance in Southeast Asia, 1961–1966, 63–64, K717.0414-14, AFHRA.
150. DCS Research and Development, Operation Shed Light: An R&D Study of Night Air Attack Capabilities and Developments, Vol. 1 (Washington, DC: HQ USAF, April 1966), IA-5; HQ USAF Tactical Air Reconnaissance Center, Required Operational Capability (ROC) Low Light Level Sensor System, June 1967, K417.03-7, 2 June 1967; Colonel C. George Whitley, Real-Time Reconnaissance Capability—Southeast Asia, September 22, 1966, and Colonel Henry M. Henington, Real-Time Reconnaissance Capability—Southeast Asia, September 22, 1966, K143.5072-16, AFHRA.

NOTES FOR CHAPTER II

151. History, 432nd TRW, January–June 1967, 9–10, K-WG-432-HI, Vol. 2, AFHRA; Smith, USAF Reconnaissance in Southeast Asia, 1961–1966, 50, K717.0414-14, AFHRA.
152. Colonel Ralph F. Findlay, 432 TRW Oplan 25-69, Annex B, Concept of Operations, K-WG-432-HI, April–June 1969, Vol. 2; Colonel Thomas G. Monroe Jr., Request for R&D Requirements, 6 January 1970, K740-03-4; Sgt. Steven A. Landry, History of 432nd TRW, January–March 1970, 17, K-WG-432-HI, Vol. 1; Colwell, Tactical Reconnaissance, July 69–June 71, 32, K717.0414-14, AFHRA. The laser was an AN/AVD-2 Compass Count.
153. Goforth, Adequacy of Tactical Aerial Reconnaissance, K717.03-43, October 1967–October 1969, AFHRA.
154. Henington, Real-Time Reconnaissance Capability, 28 April 1966, K143.5072-16. The program was called Patricia Lynn. Message from CINCPACAF to CSAF, Contribution of Army OV-1 to Recce Program in SEA, 100411Z, August 1966, K143.5072-16, AFHRA; General Joseph P. McConnell, AFCCS to AFSC, Operation Shed Light, July 15, 1966, K243.03-58, AFHRA.
155. Landry, History 432nd Reconnaissance Wing, October–December 1969, 15, 19, K-WG-432-HI, AFHRA.
156. C. William Thorndale, Visual Reconnaissance in I Corps (HQ PACAF: Directorate, Tactical Evaluation, CHECO Division, 1968), 25, 26, K717.0413-36, AFHRA.
157. Contribution of Army OV-1 to Recce Program in SEA, 100411Z, August 1966, K143.5072-16, AFHRA; Message from 7AF to PACAF, FAC Hand Held Cameras, 042308Z, January 1967, K712.1623-1 1968, AFHRA; Brynn, Reconnaissance in SE Asia, July 1966–June 1969, 41, 44, K717.0414-14, 1969, AFHRA.
158. Hargrove, Review of the Reconnaissance Concept, 6 August 1971, K239.031-67, AFHRA; Captain Dabney L. Bowman, History of 16th TRS, January–March 1969, 14, History of the 460th TRW, July–September 1969, K-WG-460-HI, AFHRA; Folkman and Caine, The Cambodian Campaign, 21, K717.0413-84, AFHRA.
159. Message from CINCPACAF to RUEDHQA/CSAF, Daytime Photographic Scale Requirements, 160424Z, October 1966, K143.5072-16, September 1965–November 1966, AFHRA; Seventh AF DCS/1, Seventh Air Force Intelligence Reconnaissance Plan, February 1967, K740.626-3, AFHRA.
160. Andraitis Interview, K717.0512, AFHRA; History of Pacific Air Forces, Vol. 1, Part 2, 1968, 491, 494, K717.01, Vol. 1, Part. 2, 1968, AFHRA; Davies, 12th TRS, July–September 1968, 14, K-WG-460-HI, and Davies, History 12th TRS, April–June 1968, 5, K-WG-460-HI, AFHRA.
161. Thorndale, Tactical Recon Photography Request/Distribution, 1, 3, K717-0413-53, AFHRA; Brynn, Reconnaissance in SE Asia, July 1966–June 1969, 27–28, K717.0414-14, AFHRA; Colwell, Tactical, July 69–June 71, 9–10, K717.0414-14, AFHRA.
162. Gillem, Review of the Reconnaissance Report, 4 August 1971, K239.031-67, AFHRA; Message from CINCPAC info COMUSMACV, Southeast Asia JRC, 212120Z, July 1966, J717.312, AFHRA.
163. Stillwell, Reconnaissance Support for MACV, K717.03-40, July 1966–June 1967, AFHRA.
164. Brynn, Reconnaissance in SE Asia, July 1966–June 1969, 17, K717.0414-14, AFHRA; Stalk, Out-Country Aerial Reconnaissance, 1965–1967, 14, K239.042-3686, 1968, AFHRA; CHI Contact Report, Benson and Mavrotheris, HQ USAF, 20 January 1970, K717.03-39, AFHRA.
165. Message from Comseventhlft to AIG 183, Weekly Summary 8–14 May 1968, 181436Z, May 1968. A reader wrote on this message, "NOTE: Why every man is important!" Ships History Post 2001 Enterprise CV-65, Box 108, File Enterprise Vietnam Message File, NHHC.
166. Message from USS *Hancock* to CTE 70.2.1.1, 011325Z, October 1968, PAO Strike Presrel, NHHC; Message from COMSEVENTHFLT to CTG 77.5, SAM Site Strike, 021108Z, October 1968, Fleet Aviation Commands Pre-1998, AR/229, Box 175, File F7, NHHC.

167. Interview of Captain John J. McGuire Jr., 22, K239.0512-320, AFHRA.
168. CHI Contact Report, Benson and Mavrotheris, HQ USAF, 20 January 1970, K717.03-39, AFHRA.
169. Davies, 12th TRS, July–September 1968, 8, K-WG-460-HI, AFHRA.
170. Greenhalgh, *RF-101 Voodoo, 1961–1970*, 44, 87, Summary Record of the 533rd Meeting of the National Security Council, June 6, 1964, *FRUS 1964–1968, XXVIII*, 141; Castle, *U.S. Military Aid to the Royal Lao Government, 1955–1975*, 70. Klusmann was shot down on April 29, 1965, and escaped three months later.
171. Captain Edward W. O'Neil Jr., "Flying 'In the Barrel,' Summer 1966," K740.549-1, Summer 1966, AFHRA. The 20th TRS flew RF-101Cs.
172. Smith, USAF Reconnaissance in Southeast Asia, 1961–1966, 42, K717.0414-14, AFHRA; Message from 7th AF to UREKDA/NMCC, SA-2 Sighting, 191431Z, July 1966, K717.312, AFHRA; Reconnaissance Attack Squadron Nine, 8 January 1969, Newsletter, Supplement, NHHC.
173. Brennan, The Loss of LTJG Lee E. Nordahl, USNR and LCDR Guy D. Johnson, USN, 18, HQ CINCPAC, Pacific Area Naval Operations Review October 1966, 13, NHHC.
174. History, RVAH-6, 1969, 4, Fleet Aviation Commands, Pre-1993, AR/229, Box 104, File RVAH-6, 1969, NHHC; Message from 7 AF to RUEFHQA/CINCPACAF, Combat Employment of ALQ-51, 061050Z, August 1967, K717.312, AFHRA; History of Pacific Air Forces, 1 July –31 December 1965, Vol. 1, Part 2, 58, K717.01, AFHRA; Brynn, Reconnaissance in SE Asia, July 1966–June 1969, 37, K717.0414-14, AFHRA; Greenhalgh, *RF-101 Voodoo, 1961–1970*, 90.
175. Landry, History 432nd Reconnaissance Wing, October–December 1969, 15, K-WG-432-HI, AFHRA; Herbert, Bulletin No 67, RF-101 and RF-4C Reconnaissance, 11 August 1967, K717.549-1, AFHRA; Fleet Marine Force, Pacific, Operations of U.S. Marine Forces Vietnam, December 1969 and 1969 Summary, Vietnam, Box 14, Folder 1, Archives Branch, HDMCU.
176. Pratt, Air Tactics against NVN Air Ground Defenses, 27, 28, K717.0414-16, AFHRA.
177. O'Neil, "Flying 'In the Barrel,' Summer 1966," K740.549-1, Summer 1966, AFHRA.
178. Davies, History 12th TRS, April–June 1968, 5-6, K-WG-460-HI, AFHRA.
179. Reconnaissance Attack Squadron Six, Newsletter, 26 June 1969, NHHC.
180. Reconnaissance Attack Squadron Nine, 8 January 1969, Newsletter, Supplement, NHHC.
181. Memorandum from the President's Special Assistant (Rostow) to President Johnson, December 12, 1968, *FRUS 1964–1968, VII*, 748; Editorial Note, Notes of a Meeting between Secretary Clifford, the JCS and additional DoD individuals, January 6, 1969, *FRUS 1964–1968, VII*, 801.
182. Memorandum from the Senior Military Assistant (Haig) to the President's Assistant for National Security Affairs (Kissinger), April 1, 1970, *FRUS 1969–1970, VI*, 747; Memorandum from the President's Deputy Assistant for National Security Affairs (Haig) to the President's Assistant for National Security (Kissinger), November 13, 1970, *FRUS 1969–1976, VII*.
183. Message from Robert S. Leonard, CINCINFO MACV to Commander 7th AF, SSCDSF Statement of 21 November 1970, 210916Z, November 1970, found online at The Vietnam Center & Sam Johnson Vietnam Archive, Texas Tech University, http://vietnam.ttu.edu; Colwell, Tactical Reconnaissance, July 69–June 71, 22, K717.0414-14, AFHRA.
184. Smith, Carrier Air Wing Six Cruise Report April 1968 to December 1968, 14 December 1968, NHHC; Bonetti, The War in Vietnam: January–June 1967, 34, K717.0414-17, AFHRA.
185. Reconnaissance Attack Squadron Nine, RA5C Tactical Handbook: Recommendations and Comments, 28 April 1966, Fleet Aviation Commands-Pre-1998, AR/229, Box 107, File F11, NHHC. See also Reconnaissance Attack Squadron Seven, RA-5C Tactics and Operating Procedures in North Vietnam, 13 May 1967, Fleet Aviation Commands-Pre-1998, AR/229, Box 105, File F5, NHHC.
186. Greenhalgh, *RF-101 Voodoo, 1961–1970*, 166–68; Mersky, *F-8 Crusader Units of the Vietnam War*,

103; Thompson, *To Hanoi and Back,* 310.
187. History 432nd TRW, January–June 1967, 8–10, K-WG-432-HI, Vol. 2, AFHRA.
188. Greenhalgh, *RF-101 Voodoo, 1961–1970,* 58, 96; Message from 7AF to RUHLKM/CINCPACAF, Trojan Horse, 170425Z, August 1966, K717.312, AFHRA; Message from HQ 7AF to RUSOTA/432 TRW, Reconnaissance Escort, 121110Z, April 1969, K-WG-432-HI, Vol. 2, AFHRA; Col Ralph F. Findlay, Reconnaissance Escort Tactics, 16 March 1969, K-WG-432-HI, Vol. 2, AFHRA.
189. Smith, End of Tour Report, 31 May 1973, K717.131, AFHRA; Reconnaissance Attack Squadron Six, Newsletter, 26 June 1969, Reconnaissance Attack Squadron Nine, 8 January 1969, Newsletter, Supplement, NHHC.
190. Gauntt, 14th TRS, April–June 1972, 8–9, K-WG-432-HI, AFHRA.
191. Canney, 432nd TRW, 1 October–31 December 1972, 57, K-WG-432-HI, Vol. 1, AFHRA.
192. Message from AFSSO Udorn, Linebacker II Kilo Critique, 300400Z, December 1972, Vogt Papers, AFHSD; Smith, End of Tour Report, 31 May 1973, K717.131, AFHRA.
193. Allgood, History 12th TRS April–June 1968, K-WG-460-HI, AFHRA.
194. Interview of Lt. Col. Clark H. Allison by Lt. Col. I. R. Little, United States Air Force Oral History Program, date not shown, K239.0512-298, 00/12/65–00/10/66, AFHRA.
195. Stalk, Out-Country Aerial Reconnaissance, 1965–1967, 64, K239.042-3686, 1968, AFHRA; History of the 460th TRW, January–March 1969, 114, 120, 1Lt. Harold D. Ryan, History of 12th TRS, January–March 1969, 10, and Captain Dabney L. Bowman, History of 16th TRS, January–March 1969, 15, K-WG-460-HI, AFHRA.
196. Southeast Asia Air Operations Briefing August 1971, K717.3063-1, August 1971, AFHRA.
197. Trest, Khe Sanh, 51. K717.0413-35, AFHRA.
198. Notes of the President's Meeting with the Senior Foreign Affairs Advisory Council, February 10, 1968, *FRUS 1964–1968, VI,* 171; George C. Herring, *LBJ and Vietnam: A Different Kind of War* (Austin: University of Texas Press, 1994), 152; Phillip B. Davidson, *Vietnam at War: The History, 1946–1975* (New York: Oxford University Press, 1988), 565.
199. Captain Ralph O. Dorris, Cricket Historical Report, 10 March 1969 and Capt. Ralph O. Dorris, Cricket Historical Report, 4 April 1969, K-WG-432-HI, January–March 1969, Vol. 2, AFHRA.
200. Goforth, Adequacy of Tactical Aerial Reconnaissance, K717.03-43, October 1967–October 1969, AFHRA.
201. Hargrove, Review of the Reconnaissance Concept, 6 August 1971, K239.031-67, AFHRA; Gillem, Review of the Reconnaissance Report, 4 August 1971, K239.031-67, AFHRA; History of Seventh Air Force, 1971–1972, 266, K740.01-25, Vol. 1, AFHRA.
202. Captain L. W. Foley to 14 TRS PPIF Operations, Paveway II Photo Requirements, 23 January 1969, K-WG-432-HI, January–March 1969, Vol. 2.
203. History of Seventh Air Force, 1971–1972, 267, K740.01-25, Vol. 1, AFHRA.
204. Colwell, Tactical Reconnaissance, July 1969–June 1971, 39, K717.0414-14, AFHRA.
205. Ibid., 39, 40, 41.
206. TSgt John W. McCoy, History of 432nd TRW, January–March 1972, 36, K-WG-432-HI, Vol. 1, AFHRA; Thorndale, Visual Reconnaissance in I Corps, 30–31, K717.0413-36, AFHRA.
207. McCoy, 432nd TRW, January–March 1972, 30, 34, 36, K-WG-432-HI, AFHRA; History of SAC Reconnaissance Operations, FY72, 9, K416.01-125, AFHRA.
208. History of Seventh Air Force, 1971–1972, 266–67, 295, K740.01-25, Vol. 1, AFHRA; Interview of MG Norman J. Anderson, USMC, retired, March 17, 1981, by Benis M. Frank, Marine Corps Historical Center, Washington Navy Yard, Washington, DC, 244; Dale Andrade, *Trial by Fire: The Easter Offensive, America's Last Battle* (New York: Hippocrene Books, 1995), 131.
209. History of Seventh Air Force, 1971–1972, 299, K740.01-25, Vol. 1, AFHRA.

210. Message from AFSSO 7AF to AFSSO CSAF, Daily Wrap Up, 221120Z, May 1972, and Message from AFSSO 7AF to AFSSO CSAF, Daily Wrap Up, 261020Z, May 1972, Vogt Papers, Message Traffic May 1972, AFHSD; History of SAC Reconnaissance Operations, FY72, 2, 22, K416.01-125, AFHRA.
211. Corona Harvest USAF Air Operations in Southeast Asia, 1 July 1972–15 August 1973, Vol. 1, p. ii-44, K717.0423-23, AFHRA.
212. Corona Harvest V, 1972–1973, 20–23, K416.041-13, AFHRA; Message from General Clay to General Vogt, 220305Z, April 1972, K717.03-221, Vol. 1, AFHRA.
213. Gauntt, 14th TRS, April–June 1972, 4, and Canney, 432nd TRW, 1 October 31–December 1972, 57, K-WG-432-HI, AFHRA; Linebacker II India Critique, 271115, December 1972, Vogt Papers, AFHSD.
214. Message to General Vogt from Major General Hughes, Linebacker II Juliet Critique, 290945Z, December 1972, K744.01 1972, Vol. II, Appendix V, AFHRA; Diary Entry by the Chairman of the Joint Chiefs of Staff (Moorer), December 26, 1972, *FRUS IX, 1969–1976*, 826.
215. Vogt from Hughes, Linebacker II Kilo Critique, 300400Z, December 1972, K744.01, AFHRA.
216. Elder, Buffalo Hunter: 1970–1972, 29, 30, K717.0414-39, AFHRA.
217. Webb and Poole, *Joint Chiefs of Staff, 1971–1973*, 159; Air Operations in Southeast Asia, 1972–1973, Vol. 5, 147, K717.0423-23, Vol. 5, AFHRA.
218. Cook, Liaison Officer End of Tour Report, 1 December 1972, K417.0735, FY1973, AFHRA; TAC/PACAF/7AF SEAOR Working Group Final Report, K143.5072-22, September–October 1967, Vol. 1, AFHRA; History of Seventh Air Force, 1972–1973, 137, K740.10-25, Vol. 1, AFHRA.
219. USS *America* and Carrier Air Wing Eight 1972–1973, Westpac Deployment Cruise Report, 26, NHHC.

Chapter 12

1. Robert C. Owen, *Air Mobility: A Brief History of the American Experience* (Washington, DC: Potomac Books, 2013); ed. Neufeld and Watson, *Coalition Air Warfare in the Korean War, 1950–1953*, 8–9.
2. Charles J. Gross, *American Military Aviation: The Indispensable Arm* (College Station: Texas A&M University Press, 2002), 96; James S. Corum and Wray R. Johnson, *Airpower in Small Wars: Fighting Insurgents and Terrorists* (Lawrence: University Press of Kansas, 2003), 55.
3. Jeffery S. Underwood, "Presidential Statesmen and U.S. Airpower: Personalities and Perceptions," in Robin Higham and Mark Parillo, *The Influence of Airpower Upon History: Statesmanship, Diplomacy, and Foreign Policy since 1903* (Lexington: University Press of Kentucky, 2013), 189; Owen, *Air Mobility*, 54, 82.
4. Benjamin D. King, "Transportation in the Korean War," ed. Neufeld and Watson, *Coalition Air Warfare in the Korean War, 1950–1953*, 311–12; William W. Suit, "U.S. Air Force Korean Logistics," ed. Neufeld and Watson, *Coalition Air Warfare in the Korean War, 1950–1953*, 268.
5. Ray L. Bowers, *The United States Air Force in Southeast Asia: Tactical Airlift* (Washington, DC: Office of Air Force History, United States Air Force, 1983), 29.
6. Gross, *The Indispensable Arm*, 190; "C-130J Super Hercules," found online at: https://www.lockheedmartin.com/us/products/c130.html. Even the prototype YC-130 was recognized as "brilliant" from the beginning; see "Military Transports: Some Aspects of Current and Future Types," *Flight* (5 November 1954), 681.
7. Schulzinger, *A Time for War*, 260–61.
8. A Tactical Air Command Activity Input to Project Corona Harvest on Tactical Airlift in SEA,

NOTES FOR CHAPTER 12

1 January 1965–31 March 1968, i-23, K417.0734-1, Vol. 1; Lt. Col. B. A. Whitaker and L. E. Paterson, Assault Airlift Operations (HQ PACAF: Directorate, Tactical Evaluation, CHECO Division, 1967), 3, K717.0431-28, AFHRA.
9. Gross, *The Indispensable Arm,* 216.
10. Richard T. Drury, Dedication of Tactical Airlift to the Army, Professional Study No. 3903, Air War College, 9, 11, K239.042-3903, April 1970, AFHRA.
11. Corona Harvest Airlift in SEA, 1 January 1965–31 March 1968, p. i-23, K417.0734-1, Vol. 1, AFHRA.
12. HQ USMACV Command History, 1965, 60, 123; Bowers, *Tactical Airlift,* 174.
13. Tactical Airlift in SEA, 1 January 1965–31 March 1968, ii-77–ii-82, K417.0734-1, Vol. 2, AFHRA; Air University Designated Study #7, Tactical Airlift, 74, K239.0321-7, Vol. 6, 1968, AFHRA.
14. Tactical Airlift in SEA, Corona Harvest 1 April 1968–31 December 1969, Vol. 2, K417.0734-1, Vol. 2, AFHRA.
15. Bowers, *Tactical Airlift*, 219; Kenneth Sams and Lt. Col. Bert B. Aton, USAF Support of Special Forces in SEA (HQ PACAF: Directorate Tactical Evaluation, CHECO Division, 1969), 54, K717.0413-96, AFHRA; Whitaker and Paterson, Assault Airlift Operations, 51, K717.0431-28, AFHRA.
16. Brigadier General William G. Moore Jr., End of Tour Report, October 1966–November 1967, 37, K-DIV-834, 15 October 1966–30 June 1967, Vol. 2, AFHRA. Moore was the commander of the 834th Air Division.
17. Bowers, *Tactical Airlift*, 683.
18. Tactical Airlift in SEA, 1 January 1965–31 March 1968, ii-192, K417.0734-1, Vol. 2; Bonetti, The War in Vietnam: January–June 1967, 58, K717.0414-17, AFHRA.
19. See for example Historical Data Record, 384th Tactical Airlift Wing, K-WG-483-HI, October–December 1968, AFHRA; Whitaker and Paterson, Assault Airlift Operations, 70, 73–74, K717.0431-28, AFHRA.
20. Major David R. Mets, Tactical Airlift Operations, 30 June 1969 (HQ PACAF: Directorate, Tactical Evaluation, CHECO Division, 1969), 105, K717.0414-2.
21. Colonel Theodore C. Mataxis to Commander 2nd Air Division, Exceptional Performance of Duty by Officers and Men of the 315th Air Division, 19 August 1965, K-DIV-315-HI, July–December 1965, Vol. 3, AFHRA.
22. Colonel Charles W. Howe to All Wings, 315 Air Division Significant Airlift Accomplishments for 1965, no date, K-DIV-315-HI, July–December 1965, Vol. 3, AFHRA.
23. Jean Martin, History of 834th Air Division, 15 October 1966–30 June 1967, 124–25, K-DIV-834-HI, Vol. 1, AFHRA.
24. Mets, Tactical Airlift Operations, 30 June, 23, K717.0414-2, AFHRA.
25. Drury, Tactical Airlift to the Army, 15, 17, 43–44, 49, 15, K239.042-3903, April 1970, AFHRA.
26. Airlift in SEA, 1 January 1965–31 March 1968, I-25, I-26, K417.0734-1, Vol. 1, AFHRA.
27. Drury, Tactical Airlift to the Army, 52–54, K239.042-3903, April 1970, AFHRA.
28. Wesley R. C. Melyan and Lee Bonetti, The War in Vietnam 1966 (HQ PACAF: Directorate, Tactical Evaluation, CHECO Division, 1967), 150, K717.0414-75, AFHRA.
29. Drury, Tactical Airlift to the Army, 43–44, K239.042-3903, April 1970, AFHRA; Schlight, *The Years of the Offensive, 1965–1968,* 146, 297, 298.
30. Message from HQ 315th AD to CINCPACAF, Personal for General Martin from General Ellis, 120830Z, March 1965, K-DIV-315-HI, AFHRA.
31. Bowers, *Tactical Airlift*, 190.
32. Ibid., 189.
33. Captain Richard H. Prater, Evaluation of the Emergency Airlift Request System, November 1966,

K-DIV-834-HI, Vol. 3, AFHRA.

34. 7th Air Force Concept for Southeast Asia Airlift, 31 July 1966, K-DIV-834, Vol. 2, AFHRA; Brigadier General William G. Moore Jr., Emergency Airlift Request System, no date, K-DIV-834, Vol. 2, AFHRA; Lieutenant General William W. Momyer, Command and Control of In-Country Airlift in SVN, 10 July 1966, K-DIV-834, 15 October 1966–30 June 1967, Vol. 2, AFHRA. The Direct Air Support Center managed tactical air assets in South Vietnam. Captain Kenneth J. Alnwick, Direct Air Support Centers in I Corps, July 1965–June 1969 (HQ PACAF: Directorate, Tactical Evaluation, CHECO Division, 1969), x, K717.0413-58, AFHRA.

35. Mets, Tactical Airlift Operations, 30 June 1969, 47–49, K717.0414-2, AFHRA; Dan E. Feltham, *When Big Blue Went to War: A History of the IBM Corporation's Mission in Southeast Asia during the Vietnam War, 1965–1975* (Bloomington, IN: Abbott Press, 2012), 58–59.

36. Air University Designated Study #7, Tactical Airlift, 60, K239.0321-7, Vol. 6, 1968.

37. Martin, History of 834th Air Division, 15 October 1966–30 June 1967, 135, K-DIV-834-HI, AFHRA; Bowers, *Tactical Airlift*, 197.

38. Tactical Airlift in SEA, 1 January 1965–31 March 1968, ii-180–ii-182, K417.0734-1, Vol. 2, AFHRA.

39. Ibid., ii-178.

40. Air University Designated Study #7, Tactical Airlift, 67, K239.0321-7, Vol. 6, 1968, AFHRA; Tactical Airlift in SEA, 1 January 1965–31 March 1968, ii-176, K417.0734-1, January 1965–March 1968, Vol. 2, AFHRA.

41. Bowers, *Tactical Airlift*, 249, 369; David R. Mets, for instance, had a PhD from the University of Denver.

42. Quote on ii-199. Tactical Airlift in SEA, 1 January 1965–31 March 1968, ii-194–ii-199, K417.0734-1, Vol. 1, AFHRA.

43. Airlift in SEA, 1 January 1965–31 March 1968, i-25, i-26, K417.0734-1, Vol. 1, AFHRA.

44. Major Fred Gluck, Trip Report, no date, 315th Air Division Terminal, Tachikawa, Japan, K712.152-2, 8 October–11 November 1967, AFHRA.

45. Airlift in SEA, 1 January 1965–31 March 1968, i-25, i-26, i-75, i-76, i-77, K417.0734-1, Vol. 1, AFHRA; Moore, End of Tour Report, October 1966–November 1967, 13–14, K-DIV-834, AFHRA.

46. Moore, End of Tour Report, October 1966–November 1967, 27, K-DIV-834, AFHRA.

47. Tactical Airlift in SEA, 1 January 1965–31 March 1968, ii-167, ii-169, ii-184, K417.0734-1, Vol. 2, AFHRA; SSgt. James F. Smith Jr., and Jo H. Frazer, History of the 315th Air Division (Combat Cargo) PACAF 1 January–31 December 1966, 46–47, K-DIV-315-HI, Vol. 1, AFHRA.

48. Martin, History 834th Air Division, 15 October 1966–30 June 1967, 136–39, 147, K-DIV-834-HI, AFHRA.

49. Colonel Arthur C. Rush, Recognition of Service in SEA for Troop Carrier Personnel, 31 March 1966, K-WG-814-HI, Vol. 1, AFHRA.

50. "In order to receive credit for duty in SEA, crews had to spend 30 or more *consecutive* days in SEA [emphasis added]." This was rarely possible. Tactical Airlift in SEA, 1 January 1965–31 March 1968, ii-188–ii-189, K417.0734-1, Vol. 2, AFHRA.

51. Mets, Tactical Airlift Operations, 30 June 1969, 64, 69, K717.0414-2, AFHRA; Martin, History 834th Air Division, 15 October 1966–30 June 1967, 136–39, 147, K-DIV-834-HI, AFHRA; Bowers, *Tactical Airlift*, 351, 479.

52. Tactical Airlift in SEA, 1 January 1965–31 March 1968, ii-191, K417.0734-1, Vol. 2, AFHRA.

53. Ibid., ii-77–ii-82.

54. Mets, Tactical Airlift Operations, 30 June 1969, 3–4, K717.0414-2, AFHRA. The chief of staff of the Army, General Harold K. Johnson, signed off on this in order to gain leverage for the Army's

quest to keep the Air Force's hands off of Army helicopters. Lewis Sorley, *Honorable Warrior: General Harold K. Johnson and the Ethics of Command* (Lawrence: University Press of Kansas, 1998), 278–79.

55. Tactical Airlift in SEA, 1 January 1965–31 March 1968, ii-154, K417.0734-1, Vol. 2, AFHRA; The Air Force Concept for Southeast Asia Airlift, 31 July 1966, K-DIV-834, 15 October 1966–30 June 1967, Vol. 2, AFHRA.
56. Bowers, *Tactical Airlift*, 237; Drury, Tactical Airlift to the Army, 35–36, K239.042-3903, April 1970, AFHRA; BG Richard T. Knowles, Airlift Coordination and Operations, K-DIV-834, 15 October 1966–30 June 1967, Vol. 2, AFHRA.
57. Message from CINCPACAF to RUMSAL/2nd Air Div, Assault Airlift Airfields, 030212Z, December 1965, K-DIV-315-HI, Vol. 3, AFHRA; Message from 315 Air Commando Group to 315 Air Div, To Colonel Howe from Hannah, 290829Z, October 1965, K-DIV-315-HI, Vol. 3, AFHRA.
58. Brigadier General William G. Moore Jr., End of Tour Report, October 1966–November 1967, 20, K-DIV-834, Vol. 2, AFHRA.
59. Lieutenant Colonel Charles C. Smith, Memo, Is There Still Doubt?, no date, Major General Charles Horton to Commanding Officer, 537th Troop Carrier Squadron, 16 March 1967, Major General John Horton, to Commanding Officer, 537th Troop Carrier Squadron, Letter of Appreciation, 16 March 1967, K-WG-483-HI, AFHRA.
60. Moore to 7AF, Fixed Wing Cargo Airlift Support, 22 April 1967, K740.4501-2, AFHRA.
61. Drury, Tactical Airlift to the Army, 59–60, K239.042-3903, April 1970, AFHRA.
62. Mets, Tactical Airlift Operations, 30 June 1969, 52–55, 57, K717.0414-2, AFHRA.
63. K740.056-1, 1966–1967, Tab 20; Tactical Airlift in SEA, 1 January 1965–31 March 1968, pp. ii-156, ii-157, ii-159, K417.0734-1, Vol. 2; Smith and Frazer, History of the 315th Air Division, 1 January–31 December 1966, 40–41, K-DIV-315-HI, AFHRA; Schlight, *The Years of the Offensive, 1965–1968*, 143.
64. Bowers, *Tactical Airlift*, 197; Martin, History 834th Air Division, 15 October 1966–30 June 1967, 114, K-DIV-834-HI, AFHRA; Moore, End of Tour Report, October 1966–November 1967, 22–23, K-DIV-834, AFHRA.
65. K740.056-1, 1966–1967, Tab 22; Whitaker and Paterson, Assault Airlift Operations, 93, K717.0431-28, AFHRA.
66. Tactical Airlift in SEA, 1 January 1965–31 March 1968, ii-153, ii-157, K417.0734-1, Vol. 2, AFHRA; SSgt. James F. Smith Jr., and Margaret A. Myers, History of the 315th Air Division (Combat Cargo) PACAF, 1 July–31 December 1965, 27, K-DIV-315-HI, Vol. 1, AFHRA.
67. Martin, History 834th Air Division, 15 October 1966–30 June 1967, 113, 116, K-DIV-834-HI, AFHRA; Moore, End of Tour Report, October 1966–November 1967, 28, K-DIV-834, AFHRA.
68. Whitaker and Paterson, Assault Airlift Operations, 65–66, K717.0431-28, AFHRA; Airlift in SEA, 1 January 1965–31 March 1968, i-94, K417.0734-1, Vol. 1, AFHRA; Moore, End of Tour Report, October 1966–November 1967, 16, K-DIV-834, AFHRA; Air University Designated Study #7, Tactical Airlift, 63, K239.0321-7, Vol. 6, 1968, AFHRA.
69. James H. Willbanks, *The Tet Offensive: A Concise History* (New York: Columbia University Press, 2007), 61.
70. Smith and Frazer, 315th Air Division, 1 January–31 December 1966, 52–53, K-DIV-315-HI, AFHRA.
71. Martin, History 834th Air Division, 15 October 1966–30 June 1967, 55–56, K-DIV-834-HI, AFHRA; Major Ronald D. Merrell, Tactical Airlift in SEA, 15 February 1972 (HQ PACAF: Directorate of Operations Analysis, CHECO/Corona Harvest Division, 1972), 44, K717.0414-2, AFHRA.

NOTES FOR CHAPTER 12

72. Air University Designated Study #7, Tactical Airlift, 75–76, 96, 97, K239.0321-7, Vol. 6, 1968, AFHRA.
73. Moore, End of Tour Report, October 1966–November 1967, 14–15, K-DIV-834, AFHRA.
74. Airlift in SEA, 1 January 1965–31 March 1968, i-45, K417.0734-1, Vol. 1, AFHRA.
75. Ibid., i-49.
76. Mets, Tactical Airlift Operations, 30 June 1969, 124, K717.0414-2, AFHRA; Whitaker and Paterson, Assault Airlift Operations, 54–55, K717.0431-28, AFHRA.
77. Tactical Airlift in SEA, 1 January 1965–31 March 1968, ii-180, K417.0734-1. Vol. 2; Message from HQ 315 Air Div to 463 TCW, C-130 Minimum Runway Length Authorization, 020708Z, December 1965, K-DIV-315-HI, Vol. 3, AFHRA.
78. Smith and Myers, History of the 315th Air Division, 1 July–31 December 1965, 31, K-DIV-315-HI, AFHRA; Message from TACC C-130 to RUAUAL/315 Air Div, C-130 Tanker Operations, 221200Z, December 1965, Message from 315 Air Commando Group to 315 Air Div, C-130 Support, 240144Z, November 1965, K-DIV-315-HI, Vol. 3, AFHRA.
79. Moore, End of Tour Report, October 1966–November 1967, 2, K-DIV-834, AFHRA; Mets, Tactical Airlift Operations, 30 June 1969, 3, K717.0414-2, AFHRA.
80. Martin, History 834th Air Division, 15 October 1966–30 June 1967, 56, 62–64, K-DIV-834-HI, AFHRA.
81. Ibid.
82. Pribbenow, trans., *Victory in Vietnam*, 217; Editorial Note, *FRUS 1964–1968, VI*, 74. It was supposed to begin on the night of January 30, but due to miscommunication, a number of units began their part of the offensive on the night of January 29. Erik B. Villard, *The United States Army in Vietnam. Combat Operations: Staying the Course, October 1967 to September 1968* (Washington, DC: Center of Military History, United States Army, 2017), 281–82.
83. Duiker, *Sacred War*, 213; Marc Jason Gilbert, "The Cost of Losing the 'Other War' in Vietnam," in *Why the North Won the Vietnam War*, ed. Marc Jason Gilbert (New York: Palgrave, 2002), 180; Robert K. Brigham, *ARVN: Life and Death in the South Vietnamese Army* (Lawrence: University Press of Kansas, 2006), 97; Willbanks, *Tet Offensive*, 11.
84. Villard, *Staying the Course*, 436. Edwin Moise has recently argued that these figures have been overblown. See Edwin E. Moise, *The Myths of Tet: The Most Misunderstood Event of the Vietnam War* (Lawrence: University Press of Kansas, 2017), 163–64.
85. Circular Telegram from the Department of State to All Posts, February 14, 1968, *FRUS 1964–1968, VI*, 213; Duiker, *Sacred War*, 213–14; Villard, *Staying the Course*, 437; Brigham, *ARVN*, 97.
86. Memorandum from the Joint Chiefs of Staff (Wheeler) to President Johnson, February 3, 1968, *FRUS 1964–1968, VI*, 119; Telegram from the White House Situation Room to President Johnson, March 3, 1968, *FRUS 1964–1968, VI*, 310; Bowers, *Tactical Airlift*, 330; Lloyd Gardner, *Pay Any Price: Lyndon Johnson and the Wars for Vietnam* (Chicago: Ivan R. Dee, 1995), 417, 823; Woods, *LBJ*, 823.
87. Tactical Airlift in SEA, 1 January 1965–31 March 1968, pp. ii-299–ii-300, K417.0734-1, Vol. 1, AFHRA; Smith and Frazer, 315th Air Division, 1 January–31 December 1966, 45, K-DIV-315-HI, AFHRA; Bowers, *Tactical Airlift*, 175–76.
88. Tactical Airlift in SEA, 1 January 1965–31 March 1968, ii-298, K417.0734-1, Vol. 1, AFHRA.
89. Mets, Tactical Airlift Operations, 30 June 1969, 69, K717.0414-2, AFHRA. One should remember that the Pueblo Crisis, a serious confrontation with North Korea that mandated reinforcements from the United States, was also taking place at this time and further stretched airlift resources. Bowers, *Tactical Airlift*, 329.
90. Lt. Col. J. M. Cummings, Commanding Officer 2nd Battalion, 26th Marines to Commanding General 3rd Marine Division, Combat Operations After Action Report, March 25, 1967, Vietnam,

Box 6, Folder 2, Archives Branch, HDMCU.

91. Tactical Airlift in SEA, 1 January 1965–31 March 1968, pp. iii-302, ii-316, K417.0734-1, Vol. 1, AFHRA; Bowers, *Tactical Airlift*, 245.
92. Mets, Tactical Airlift Operations, 30 June 1969, 32, K717.0414-2, AFHRA.
93. Ibid., 33; Tactical Airlift in SEA, 1 April 1968–31 December 1969, Vol. 2, K417.0734-1, AFHRA.
94. Whitaker and Paterson, Assault Airlift Operations, 9, K717.0431-28, AFHRA.
95. Ibid., 118; Smith and Myers, History of the 315th Air Division, 1 July–31 December 1965, 30, K-DIV-315-HI, AFHRA; Bowers, *Tactical Airlift*, 689.
96. Message from 2 Air Div to RUAUAL/315 Air Div, C-130 Aircrew Rotation Da Nang, 271252Z, December 1965, K-DIV-315-HI, Vol. 3, AFHRA.
97. C. William Thorndale, Operation Delaware, 19 April–17 May 1968 (HQ PACAF: Directorate, Tactical Evaluation, CHECO Division, 1968), 36–37, K717.0413-33, AFHRA; Bowers, *Tactical Airlift*, 316, 335, 338.
98. Message from CG 1st Air Cav Div. to CG 7th AF, 282320Z, April 1968, found online at The Vietnam Center & Sam Johnson Vietnam Archive, Texas Tech University, http://vietnam.ttu.edu; Mets, Tactical Airlift Operations, 30 June 1969, 36, K717.0414-2, AFHRA; History of the 315th Air Division, 1 January–30 June 1968, K-DIV-315-HI, Vol. 1, AFHRA.
99. Whitaker and Paterson, Assault Airlift Operations, 60–61, K717.0431-28, AFHRA.
100. Bowers, *Tactical Airlift*, 339.
101. Mets, Tactical Airlift Operations, 30 June 1969, 70–71, K717.0414-2, AFHRA; Captain Peter A. W. Liebchen, Kontum: Battle for the Central Highlands (HQ PACAF: Directorate of Operations Analysis, CHECO/Corona Harvest Division, 1972), 49, 50, K717.0413-194, AFHRA.
102. Lt. Col. Allyn M. Devens, 50th Tactical Airlift Squadron Historical Report, 1 April 1972–30 June 1972, K-WG-374-HI, Vol. 3, AFHRA; Andrade, *Trial by Fire*, 455.
103. Captain Charles L. Lynch, History 345th Tactical Airlift Squadron, January–June 1972, K-WG-374-HI, Vol. 3, AFHRA.
104. Liebchen, Kontum: Battle for the Central Highlands, 78, K717.0413-194, AFHRA.
105. Tactical Airlift in SEA, Corona Harvest 1 April 1968–31 December 1969, Vol. 2, K417.0734-1, Vol. 2, AFHRA.
106. Air University Designated Study #7, Tactical Airlift, 71, K239.0321-7, Vol. 6, 1968, AFHRA; Mets, Tactical Airlift Operations, 30 June 1969, 21, K717.0414-2, AFHRA.
107. Smith and Frazer, 315th Air Division, 1 January–31 December 1966, 56–58, K-DIV-315-HI, AFHRA; Whitaker and Paterson, Assault Airlift Operations, 62, K717.0431-28, AFHRA.
108. Major Gordon Y. W. Ow, The Application of Aerial Delivery Systems to Cargo Airlift Operations in RVN, 12 January 1967, 2–5, K-DIV-834-HI, Vol. 1, also in K740.31067-1, 12 January 1967, AFHRA.
109. Smith and Frazer, 315th Air Division, 1 January–31 December 1966, 59, K-DIV-315-HI, AFHRA; Message from 8AERLPORTSQ to RUEDNBA/TAC, Peach Tree Activity Report, 250900Z, May 1966, K-DIV-315-HI, January–December 1966, Vol. 5, AFHRA. The message does not state where the camps were located.
110. Bowers, *Tactical Airlift*, 312; Message from 8AERLPORTSQ to RUEDNBA/9th AF, Peach Tree Activity Report, 190110Z, May 1966, and Message from 8AERLPORTSQ to RUEDNBA/TAC, Peach Tree Activity Report, 250900Z, May 1966, AFHRA.
111. HQ USMACV Command History, 1966, 283, Moore, End of Tour Report, October 1966–November 1967, 47, K-DIV-834, AFHRA; Villard, *Staying the Course*, 63.
112. Message from 315 Air Division to 314 Tactical Airlift Wing, 100041Z, May 1968, K-WG-316-HI, AFHRA; Mets, Tactical Airlift Operations, 30 June 1969, 34–36, 20, K717.0414-2, AFHRA; Bowers, *Tactical Airlift*, 312.

113. Colonel Richard J. Downs, End of Tour Report, 3 August 1972, K740.131, AFHRA. Downs was Seventh AF Director of Airlift. Major Ringenbach, Airlift to Besieged Areas, 7 April–31 August 1972 (HQ PACAF: Directorate of Operations Analysis, CHECO/Corona Harvest Division, 1973), 32, K717.0413-210, AFHRA.
114. Tactical Airlift in SEA, Corona Harvest 1 April 1968–31 December 1969, Vol. 2, K417.0734-1, Vol. 2, AFHRA.
115. Major D. E. Brock, 5th Special Forces Group (Airborne) 1st Special Forces, Lessons Learned, 20 April 1968, K740.5491-2, 20 April 1968, AFHRA.
116. Message from [unreadable] CG 1st Air Cav Div to COMUSMACV, [date time group unreadable, possibly 291415Z April 1968], found online at The Vietnam Center & Sam Johnson Vietnam Archive, Texas Tech University, http://vietnam.ttu.edu.
117. Corum and Johnson, *Airpower in Small Wars*, 148, 158, 159; Whitaker and Paterson, Assault Airlift Operations, 42, K717.0431-28, AFHRA.
118. Whitaker and Paterson, Assault Airlift Operations, 15-16, K717.0431-28, AFHRA; Message from 315 Air Commando Group, 240144Z, November 1965, K-DIV-315-HI, AFHRA.
119. Directorate of Operations, HQ USAF, Chronology on Effectiveness of Air Power in RVN, 13, K143.042-9, 12-27-1964–3-11-1968, AFHRA.
120. Bowers, *Tactical Airlift*, 212–13.
121. Whitaker and Paterson, Assault Airlift Operations, 27, K717.0431-28, AFHRA; Moore to 7AF, Fixed Wing Cargo Airlift Support, 22 April 1967, K740.4501-2, AFHRA; Sams and Aton, USAF Support of Special Forces in SEA, 56, K717.0413-96, AFHRA; Bowers, *Tactical Airlift*, 364, 372, 410, 412.
122. Thorndale, Operation Delaware, 19 April–17 May 1968, 36–37, K717.0413-33, AFHRA.
123. Bowers, *Tactical Airlift*, 323; Captain Joseph R. Brand, Narrative, no date, K-WG-483-HI, April–June 1967, AFHRA; 1Lt. Raymond Valentine, SSgt. Kenneth K. Karnes, and SSgt. Lewis D. Shedd comprised the rest of the aircrew.
124. Historical Data Record, 536th Tactical Airlift Squadron, 1 July 1967–30 September 1967, K-WG-483-HI, AFHRA; Major Grady W. Metcalf, History of the 14th Special Operations Wing, 1 April–30 June 1970, 16–17, K-WG-14-HI, AFHRA.
125. In addition, "C-130s and C-123s flew 6,650 sorties to move more than 30,000 troops and 19,000 tons of cargo." See Mets, Tactical Airlift Operations, 30 June 1969, 9–11, K717.0414-2, AFHRA; Lawrence J. Hickey, Operation Paul Revere/Sam Houston, 27 July 1967 (HQ PACAF: Directorate, Tactical Evaluation, CHECO Division, 1967), 1, K717.0413-16, AFHRA; Bowers, *Tactical Airlift*, 245.
126. Lt. Col. J. M. Cummings, Commanding Officer 2nd Battalion, 26th Marines to Commanding General 3rd Marine Division, Combat Operations After Action Report, March 25, 1967, Vietnam, Box 6, Folder 2, Archives Branch, HDMCU. See also George L. MacGarrigle, *United States Army in Vietnam, Combat Operations. Taking the Offensive: October 1966 to October 1967* (Washington, DC: Center of Military History, United States Army 1998), 299–304; Telegram from the Commander, Military Assistance Command, Vietnam (Westmoreland), to the Chairman of the Joint Chiefs of Staff (Wheeler) and the Commander in Chief, Pacific (Sharp), February 9, 1968, *FRUS 1964–1968, VI*, 155.
127. History of 315th Air Commando Wing, January–March 1968, 16, K-WG-315-HI, January–March 1968, AFHRA; Bowers, *Tactical Airlift*, 322.
128. C. William Thorndale, Battle for Dak To (HQ PACAF: Directorate, Tactical Evaluation, CHECO Division, 1968), 7, K717.0413-28, AFHRA; Bowers, *Tactical Airlift*, 321, 322.
129. Tactical Airlift in SEA, Corona Harvest 1 April 1968–31 December 1969, Vol. 2, K417.0734-1, April 1968–December 1969, Vol. 2; Major Ronald D. Merrell, Tactical Airlift in SEA, 15 February

1972 (HQ PACAF: Directorate of Operations Analysis, CHECO/Corona Harvest Division, 1972), 29, K717.0414-2, AFHRA.

130. Lieutenant Colonel Harry D. Blout, Air Operations in Northern Laos, 1 April–1 November 1970 (HQ PACAF: Directorate of Operations Analysis, CHECO/Corona Harvest Division), 11, K717.0413-65, AFHRA; Common Service Airlift Analysis, December 1969, K740.461-1, December 1969, AFHRA; J. D. Ryan, Air Operations in Cambodia, May–June 1970, 38, K740.04-16, AFHRA.
131. Davidson, *Vietnam at War*, 244, 252, 253, 259, 269.
132. General Raymond G. Davis, Oral History Transcript, Benis M. Frank, Interviewer, February 2–3, 1977, McDonough, GA, History and Museums Division, HQ USMC, 1978, p. 23, Archives Branch, HDMCU.
133. Minutes of a Washington Special Actions Group Meeting, April 12, 1972, *FRUS 1969–1976*, *VIII*, 240; Memorandum from the President's Assistant for National Security Affairs (Kissinger) to President Nixon, undated, *FRUS 1969–1976*, *VIII*, 311. This memo was written in late April. Memorandum from the President's Assistant for National Security Affairs (Kissinger) to President Nixon, May 19, 1972, *FRUS 1969–1976*, *VIII*, 611.
134. Sams and Aton, USAF Support of Special Forces in SEA, 11, K717.0413-96, AFHRA. Civilian Irregular Defense Groups, or CIDG, began as a CIA effort to train and equip villagers to defend themselves from Viet Cong insurgents. The number of encampments grew to several dozen and they were placed in areas too rugged for conventional forces. Graham A. Cosmas, *United States Army in Vietnam. MACV: The Joint Command in the Years of Escalation, 1962–1967* (Washington, DC: Center of Military History, United States Army, 2006), 78.
135. Colonel Roger P. Larivee, Mission Commander's Report of Dak Seang Aerial Resupply Operation, 1 through 12 April 1970, K-WG-483-SU-RE, AFHRA; SSgt. John R. Burton, 374th Tactical Airlift Wing History, 1 October–31 December 1972, K-WG-374-HI, Vol. 1, AFHRA.
136. Colonel William Pisaruck, Summary of 834th Air Div Support for Cambodian Operations, no date, K-DIV-834-HI, July 1968–June 1970, Vol. 2, AFHRA; Sams, et al., The Air War in Vietnam: 1968–1969, 33–34, K717.0413-143, AFHRA; History of the 315th Air Division, 1 January–30 June 1968, K-DIV-315-HI, Vol. 1, AFHRA.
137. 37th Tactical Airlift Squadron, After Action Report, 12 May 1968, K-WG-316-HI, AFHRA; Mets, Tactical Airlift Operations, 30 June 1969, 37–38, K717.0414-2, AFHRA; Bowers, *Tactical Airlift*, 343–47.
138. Jackson's copilot, Major Jesse W. Campbell, was awarded the Air Force Cross, with Silver Stars going to the remaining crewmen. Bowers, *Tactical Airlift*, 346.
139. Schlight, *The Years of the Offensive, 1965–1968*, 261; Bowers, *Tactical Airlift*, 290, 291.
140. 1Lt. Eric A. Garrison, History of 459th Tactical Airlift Squadron, July–September 1967, 12, K-WG-483-HI, AFHRA.
141. Trest, Khe Sanh, 22, 73, K717.0413-35, AFHRA. Notes of the President's Meeting with the Joint Chiefs of Staff, February 9, 1968, *FRUS 1964–1968*, *VI*, 165.
142. Notes of the President's Luncheon Meeting, February 13, 1968, *FRUS 1964–1968*, *VI*, 207; Memorandum from the Chairman of the Joint Chiefs of Staff (Wheeler) to President Johnson, February 27, 1968, *FRUS 1964–1968*, *VI*, 264; Woods, *LBJ*, 823.
143. The official history of Air Force airlift has summarized them well and conveys their significance, danger, and magnitude convincingly. Bowers, *Tactical Airlift*, 317–52.
144. Villard, *Staying the Course*, 260; Moise, *The Myths of Tet*, 134; Pribbenow, trans., *Victory in Vietnam*, 216, 230; Guan, *The Vietnam War from the Other Side*, 125; Gardner, *Pay Any Price*, 418; Bowers, *Tactical Airlift*, 292; Nguyen, *Hanoi's War*, 111; Peter Brush, "The Battle of Khe Sanh," ed. Marc Jason Gilbert and William Head, *The Tet Offensive* (Westport, CT: Praeger, 1996),

201; Woods, *LBJ*, 825; Davidson, *Vietnam at War*, 551–52; Bernard C. Nalty, *Air War over South Vietnam, 1968–1975* (Washington, DC: Air Force History and Museums Program, United States Air Force, 2000), 16.

145. Pribbenow, trans., *Victory in Vietnam*, 216; Moise, *The Myths of Tet*, 1, 110; Trest, Khe Sanh, 5, K717.0413-35, AFHRA; Davis Oral History Transcript, 23, HDMCU; Larry Berman, "The Tet Offensive," ed. Gilbert and Head, *The Tet Offensive*, 24; Memorandum of Conversation, April 3, 1968, *FRUS 1964–1968, VI*, 531.

146. Trest, Khe Sanh, 74, K717.0413-35, AFHRA; Tactical Airlift in SEA, 1 January 1965–31 March 1968, II-193, K417.0734-1, Vol. 1, AFHRA; History 315th Air Division, 1 January–30 June 1968, K-DIV-315-HI, AFHRA; Bowers, *Tactical Airlift*, 301.

147. Gardner, *Pay Any Price*, 417.

148. Woods, *LBJ*, 823; Gardner, *Pay Any Price*, 417.

149. Notes of the President's Meeting with the Joint Chiefs of Staff, February 9, 1968, *FRUS 1964–1968, VI*, 166; Gardner, *Pay Any Price*, 425.

150. History 315th Air Division, 1 January–30 June 1968, K-DIV-315-HI, AFHRA; Mets, Tactical Airlift Operations, 30 June 1969, 17, K717.0414-2, AFHRA; Bowers, *Tactical Airlift*, 302; Woods, *LBJ*, 823; Gardner, *Pay Any Price*, 417.

151. Mets, Tactical Airlift Operations, 30 June 1969, 20, K717.0414-2, AFHRA; Trest, Khe Sanh, 76, K717.0413-35, AFHRA; Bowers, *Tactical Airlift*, 295, 330, 351; MACV Command History 1968, Vol. 1, 426.

152. Pisaruck, Summary of 834th Air Div Support for Cambodian Operations, K-DIV-834-HI, July 1968–June 1970, Vol. 2, AFHRA; Shaw, *Cambodian Campaign*, 98.

153. Shaw, *Cambodian Campaign*, 99, 139.

154. Bowers, *Tactical Airlift*, 318–29; History 315th Air Division, 1 January–30 June 1968, K-DIV-315-HI, AFHRA; Charles K. Hopkins, History of the 315th Air Division, 1 July 1968–15 April 1969, 22, K-DIV-315-HI, AFHRA.

155. MacGarrigle, *Taking the Offensive*, 117.

156. Moore, End of Tour Report, October 1966–November 1967, 46, K-DIV-834, AFHRA. Junction City was "a massive conventional encirclement that required timely deployments and tightly controlled movements to isolate and reduce the enemy pocket." MacGarrigle, *Taking the Offensive*, 117.

157. Editorial Note on an August 12 Meeting between Clark Clifford and the Office of the Secretary of Defense Staff, *FRUS 1964–1968, VI*, 951; Lieutenant Colonel Bert B. Aton and E. S. Montagliani, The Fourth Offensive (HQ PACAF: Directorate, Tactical Evaluation, CHECO Division, 1969), 16, K717.413-107, AFHRA.

158. Memorandum for the President's File by the President's Deputy Assistant for National Security Affairs, January 18, 1971, *FRUS 1969–1976, VII*, 275. This operation was politically sensitive; it is nowhere to be found in Bowers' 1983 official history. James H. Willbanks, *A Raid Too Far: Operation Lam Son and Vietnamization in Laos* (College Station: Texas A&M University Press, 2014), 31. The Chup Operation was also called Toan-Thang, 1–71.

159. Memorandum for the President's File by the President's Deputy Assistant for National Security Affairs, January 27, 1971, *FRUS 1969–1976, VII*, 326.

160. Memorandum for the President's File, January 27, 1971, *FRUS 1969–1976, VII*, 328.

161. Willbanks, *A Raid Too Far*, 157.

162. SSgt. William A. Pierro, History of 834th Air Division, 1 January–30 June 1971, 41–44, K-DIV-834-HI, AFHRA. The second name, Dewey Canyon II, was supposed to confuse the enemy into thinking that the operation was a variation of Operation Dewey Canyon, but it only served to confuse the Americans. Merrell, Tactical Airlift in SEA, 47, K717.0414-2, AFHRA; Willbanks, *A Raid Too Far*, 73.

NOTES FOR CHAPTER 12

163. Bowers, *Tactical Airlift*, 514; Colonel J. F. Loye Jr., et al., Lam Son 719 30 January–24 March 1971: The South Vietnamese Incursion into Laos (HQ PACAF: Directorate of Operations Analysis, CHECO/Corona Harvest Division, 1971), 53, K717.0413-165, AFHRA; Merrell, Tactical Airlift in SEA, 52, 53, 58, K717.0414-2, AFHRA.
164. Pierro, History of 834th Air Division, 1 January–30 June 1971, 56, 58, K-DIV-834-HI, AFHRA; Merrell, Tactical Airlift in SEA, 61, K717.0414-2, AFHRA; Bowers, *Tactical Airlift*, 516.
165. Willbanks, *A Raid Too Far*, 57–69. The PAVN history states that upward of 60,000 North Vietnamese troops were involved in the counterattacks against the ARVN. Pribbenow, trans., *Victory in Vietnam*, 274.
166. Downs, End of Tour Report, 3 August 1972, K740.131, AFHRA.
167. Ringenbach, Airlift to Besieged Areas, 14, K717.0413-210, AFHRA.
168. Bowers, *Tactical Airlift*, 547.
169. Lynch, History 345th Tactical Airlift Squadron, January–June 1972, K-WG-374-HI, AFHRA; Ringenbach, Airlift to Besieged Areas, p. xviii, K717.0413-210, AFHRA; Minutes of a Washington Special Actions Group Meeting, May 11, 1972, *FRUS 1969–1976, VIII*, 544–45. This concept of defeating an enemy's strategy comes from the Chinese military philosopher Sunzi. Christopher C. Rand, *Military Thought in Early China* (Albany: State University of New York Press, 2017), 55.
170. Air Operations in Southeast Asia, 1972–1973, Vol. 1, p. iii-60, K717.0423-23, AFHRA; History of Seventh Air Force, 1971–1972, 288, 342, 343, K740.01-25, Vol. 1, AFHRA; Downs, End of Tour Report, 3 August 1972, K740.131, AFHRA; Bowers, *Tactical Airlift*, 540, 561, 565.
171. Ringenbach and Melly, Battle for An Loc, 16, K717.0413-196, AFHRA; Conversation between President Nixon and the President's Deputy Assistant for National Security Affairs, April 20, 1972, *FRUS 1969–1976, VIII*, 298.
172. Ringenbach and Melly, Battle for An Loc, 28, K717.0413-196, AFHRA; Andrade, *Trial by Fire*, 453.
173. Downs, End of Tour Report, 3 August 1972, K740.131, AFHRA; Ringenbach, Airlift to Besieged Areas, 2–3, K717.0413-210, AFHRA; Ringenbach and Melly, Battle for An Loc, 29–30, K717.0413-196, AFHRA; Bowers, *Tactical Airlift*, 259, 540–45.
174. Devens, 50th Tactical Airlift Squadron Historical Report, 1 April 1972–30 June 1972, K-WG-374-HI, AFHRA; Bowers, *Tactical Airlift*, 544–45; Message from JPV to Abrams, 310145Z, May 1972, Vogt Papers, Read File May 1972, AFHSD.
175. Ringenbach, Airlift to Besieged Areas, 1, 13, K717.0413-210, AFHRA; Bowers, *Tactical Airlift*, 540; Ringenbach and Melly, Battle for An Loc, 49, K717.0413-196, AFHRA.
176. Downs, End of Tour Report, 3 August 1972, K740.131, AFHRA.
177. Ringenbach, Airlift to Besieged Areas, 16, 18–19, 21, 28, K717.0413-210, AFHRA; Ringenbach and Melly, Battle for An Loc, 29–30, K717.0413-196, AFHRA; Bowers, *Tactical Airlift*, 545.
178. Ringenbach and Melly, Battle for An Loc, 34–36, K717.0413-196, AFHRA; Downs, End of Tour Report, 3 August 1972, K740.131, AFHRA; Ringenbach, Airlift to Besieged Areas, 32–33, K717.0413-210, AFHRA; Bowers, *Tactical Airlift*, 548.
179. Andrade, *Trial by Fire*, 459–61; Ringenbach and Melly, Battle for An Loc, 34–36, K717.0413-196, AFHRA; Ringenbach, Airlift to Besieged Areas, 12–13, K717.0413-210, AFHRA.
180. Downs, End of Tour Report, 3 August 1972, K740.131, AFHRA; Ringenbach, Airlift to Besieged Areas, 34, 36–37, K717.0413-210, AFHRA; Bowers, *Tactical Airlift*, 556, 554.
181. Ringenbach and Melly, Battle for An Loc, 34–36, K717.0413-196, AFHRA; Andrade, *Trial by Fire*, 459–61.
182. Ringenbach, Airlift to Besieged Areas, 33, K717.0413-210, AFHRA.
183. Andrade, *Trial by Fire*, 462.

184. Ringenbach and Melly, Battle for An Loc, 38–39, K717.0413-196, AFHRA; Air Operations in Southeast Asia, 1972–1973, Vol. 1, p. iii-60, K717.0423-23, AFHRA.
185. Directorate of Operations Analysis, Summary Air Operations Southeast Asia, April 1972, 2–5, K717.3063, April 1972, AFHRA; Ringenbach, Airlift to Besieged Areas, 16, 31–32, K717.0413-210, AFHRA; Message from Brigadier General Michael D. Healy to Abrams, DCE, 120244Z, June 1972, General Vogt's Read File June 72, AFHSD.
186. Message from General Abrams COMUSMACV to Major General Kroesen CG FRAC Da Nang, 020452Z, May 1972, Vogt Papers, General Vogt's Read File May 1972, AFHSD.
187. Richard Nixon, *RN: The Memoirs of Richard Nixon* (New York: Grosset & Dunlap, 1978), 594.
188. Ringenbach, Airlift to Besieged Areas, x, K717.0413-210, AFHRA.
189. Devens, 50th Tactical Airlift Squadron Historical Report, 1 April 1972–30 June 1972, K-WG-374-HI, AFHRA; Bowers, *Tactical Airlift*, 566–67.
190. Message from John P. Vann to Gen Abrams. Daily Commander's Evaluation, 180205Z, May 1972, Vogt Papers. General Vogt's Read File May 72, AFHSD.
191. Message from John P. Vann to General Abrams. Daily Commander's Evaluation, 190235Z, May 1972 and Message from Brigadier General John G. Hill to General Abrams, Commander's Evaluation, 2402024Z, May 1972, Vogt Papers, Read File May 1972, AFHSD; Bowers, *Tactical Airlift*, 568.
192. Liebchen, Kontum: Battle for the Central Highlands, 57, K717.0413-194, AFHRA; Ringenbach, Airlift to Besieged Areas, 42, K717.0413-210, AFHRA; Message from JPV to Abrams, DCE, 290220Z, May 1972, and Message from AFSSO 7AF to AFSSO CSAF, Daily Wrap Up, 291115Z, May 1972, Vogt Papers, Message Traffic May 1972, AFHRA.
193. Message from JPV to Abrams, DCE, 060215Z, June 1972, Vogt Papers, Read File June 72, AFHSD; Bowers, *Tactical Airlift*, 572; History of Seventh Air Force, 1971–1972, 288, K740.01-25, Vol. 1, AFHRA.
194. Prados, *Vietnam*, 261. Vietnamization is associated with the Nixon administration much more than with that of Lyndon B. Johnson. Jeffrey Kimball, *Nixon's Vietnam War* (Lawrence: University Press of Kansas, 1998), 72, 73.
195. Memorandum from the Chairman of the Joint Chiefs of Staff (Wheeler) to Secretary of Defense Laird, July 21, 1969, *FRUS 1969–1976*, VI, 310.
196. History of Seventh Air Force, 1971–1972, 303, 304, 341–45, K740.01-25, Vol. 1, AFHRA; Message from John P. Vann to General Abrams, Daily Commanders Evaluation, 110224Z, May 1972, Vogt Papers, Read File May 1972, AFHSD.
197. Bowers, *Tactical Airlift*, 574; Ringenbach, Airlift to Besieged Areas, 40–41, 44–48, K717.0413-210, AFHRA.
198. Burton, 374th Tactical Airlift Wing History, 1 October–31 December 1972, K-WG-374-HI, AFHRA; Ringenbach, Airlift to Besieged Areas, 48, K717.0413-210, AFHRA; Captain James A. Aston, History of 345th Tactical Airlift Squadron, June–September 1972, 10, K-WG-374-HI, July–September 1972, Vol. 2, AFHRA.
199. Message from Colonel Burnell to General Abrams, 220744Z, May 1972, Vogt Papers, Read File May 1972, AFHSD.
200. Ringenbach, Airlift to Besieged Areas, 48–49, K717.0413-210, AFHRA.
201. David Galula, *Counterinsurgency Warfare: Theory and Practice* (Westport, CT: Praeger Security International, 2006), 54.
202. This is an undercurrent throughout Schlight's *The Years of the Offensive, 1965–1968*, 113–84, passim.

Chapter 13

1. Marine Corps Direct Air Support Final Report, June 22, 1965, II-10, COLL/3746, Studies and Reports, Box 7, Folder Studies/Reports/Aviation 1 of 3, Archives Branch, HDMCU.
2. Lt. Col. H. W. Vincent, Advance Paper Panel V Allison Man/Mobility/Survivability Forum, 11–12 April 1967, Marine Close Air Support, p. i., COLL/3746, Studies and Reports, Box 258, Folder Allison Man/Mobility/Survivability Forum, Archives Branch, HDMCU.
3. See also David A. Deptula, Gary L. Crowder, and George L. Stamper Jr., "Direct Attack: Enhancing Counterland Doctrine and Joint Air Ground Operations," *Air & Space Power Journal* (Winter 2003), 6.
4. Collier, *History of Air Power*, 41; James Pugh, *The Royal Flying Corps, the Western Front and the Control of the Air, 1914–1918* (New York: Routlege, 2017), 72; Richard P. Hallion, *Strike from the Sky: The History of Battlefield Air Attack, 1911–1945* (Washington, DC: Smithsonian Institution Press, 1989), 20, 21.
5. Lee Kennett, "Developments to 1939," ed. Benjamin Franklin Cooling, *Case Studies in the Development of Close Air Support* (Washington, DC: Office of Air Force History, 1990), 28–29, 36–37.
6. Ibid., 39–41.
7. Hardesty and Grinberg, *Red Phoenix Rising*, 17.
8. Kennett, "Developments to 1939," 46–47, 52–53; David E. Johnson, *Fast Tanks and Heavy Bombers: Innovation in the U.S. Army, 1917–1945* (Ithaca, NY: Cornell University Press, 1998), 166.
9. Kennett, "Developments to 1939," 31.
10. Robert Allan Doughty, *The Breaking Point: Sedan and the Fall of France, 1940* (Hamden, CT: Archon Books, 1990), 324; Hallion, *Strike from the Sky*, 146; Hardesty and Grinberg, *Red Phoenix Rising*, 77, 86, 101.
11. Ian Gooderson, *Air Power at the Battlefront: Allied Close Air Support in Europe, 1943–1945* (Portland, OR: Frank Cass, 1998), 22; Robert V. Brulle, *Angels Zero: P-47 Close Air Support in Europe* (Washington, DC: Smithsonian Institution Press, 2000), 41–44; Hallion, *Strike from the Sky*, 152–62; Thomas A. Hughes, *Over Lord: General Pete Quesada and the Triumph of Tactical Air Power in World War II* (New York: Free Press, 1995), 183–84, 239.
12. Allan R. Millett, *The War for Korea, 1950–1951: They Came from the North* (Lawrence: University Press of Kansas, 2010), 188; John Schlight, *Help from Above: Air Force Close Air Support of the Army, 1946–1973* (Washington, DC: Air Force History and Museums Program, 2003), 134, 139, 139–40; Futrell, *Ideas, Concepts, Doctrine, 1907–1960*, 441.
13. Message from CINCPAC to COMUSMACV, Conduct and Control of Close Air Support, 242345Z, April 1965, K712.03-40, AFHRA; MACV Command History 1969, Vol. 1, p. v-192, The Single Management Issue, no date, 6, Vietnam, Box 21, Folder 3: Air Command and Control: Vietnam, Archives Branch, HDMCU; Thompson, *To Hanoi and Back*, 51.
14. Sbrega, "Southeast Asia," 465. Subsequently in 1969 the Air Force flew 96,543, 48,064 in 1970, 11,842 in 1971 and 40,322 in 1972.
15. Message from CG III MAF to CG FMFPAC, 031242Z, August 1967, found online at The Vietnam Center & Sam Johnson Vietnam Archive, Texas Tech University, http://vietnam.ttu.edu.
16. Sbrega, "Southeast Asia," 420, 423; Leonard Unger, Telegram from the Embassy in Laos to the Department of State, May 24, 1964, *FRUS 1964–1968, XXVIII*, 105; Victor B. Anthony and Richard R. Sexton, *The United States Air Force in Southeast Asia: The War in Northern Laos, 1954–1973* (Washington, DC: Center for Air Force History, United States Air Force, 1993), 106. Central Intelligence Agency pilots began flying transports in support of the war in Laos on a permanent basis in 1957. William M. Leary, "Supporting the 'Secret War': CIA Air Operations in

Laos, 1955–1974," *Studies in Intelligence* 42:2 (1999), 75.

17. Schlight, *The Years of the Offensive, 1965–1968*, 16; Sbrega, "Southeast Asia," 423.
18. Schlight, *The Years of the Offensive, 1965–1968*, 17; Dave Richard Palmer, *The Summons of the Trumpet: U.S-Vietnam in Perspective* (San Rafael, CA: Presido Press, 1978), 81; Sbrega, "Southeast Asia," 441.
19. Telegram from the Embassy in Vietnam to the Department of State, March 24, 1965, *FRUS 1964–1968, II*, 476; HQ USAF, Chronology on Effectiveness of Air Power in RVN, 3, K143.042-9, AFHRA.
20. 7th Fleet Operational Summary, April 1965, Reference Files, Vietnam, A-Air Warfare (I), Aircraft Losses Folder, History Naval Operations, Vol. III 1965–1967, Part 1, 185–92, NHHC.
21. Major General J. H. Moore, Study on Increased Air Effort in South Vietnam, 21 January 1965, K526.1623, AFHRA; Message from CINCPAC to COMUSMACV, Tactical Air Requirements, 070455Z, October 1965, K526.1623, AFHRA; History Naval Operations, Vol. III 1965–1967, Part 1, 181; Brennan, Analysis of Tactical Aircraft Operations, 1965–1966, Volume 1, 12, NHHC.
22. General Maxwell Taylor, Telegram from the Embassy in Vietnam to the Department of State, January 6, 1965, *FRUS 1964–1968, II*, 26.
23. Brig. Gen. John K. Boles, Bombing Mission from USS *Coral Sea*, 2 September 1965, K740.5492-2, 2 September 1965, AFHRA.
24. John M. Carland, *United States Army in Vietnam. Combat Operations. Stemming the Tide: May 1965 to October 1966* (Washington, DC: Center of Military History, United States Army, 2000), 84.
25. HQ USMACV Command History, 1965, 188, 758.
26. MACV Command History 1968 Vol. 1, 404, PACAF DI, Effects of Air Operations in Southeast Asia, 19 August 1965, 10, K717.6092, AFHRA; Warren Wilkins, *Grab Their Belts to Fight Them: The Viet Cong's Big-Unit War against the U.S., 1965–1966* (Annapolis, MD: Naval Institute Press, 2011), 92; Merle L. Pribbenow, "The Fog of War: The Vietnamese View of the Ia Drang Battle," *Military Review* (January–February 2001), 93.
27. Schlight, *The Years of the Offensive, 1965–1968*, 292; Prados, *Vietnam*, 135; Pribbenow, "The Fog of War," 96; Trest, Khe Sanh, 45, K717.0413-35, AFHRA.
28. Lt. Col. James E. Poore, 19th TASS/5th ARVN Div. ALO, 18 November 1966, Tactical Air Support Analysis Team, K740.4501-1, 27 October–8 November 1966, AFHRA; Fleet Marine Force, Pacific, Operations of U.S. Marine Forces Vietnam, October 1968, Box 13, Folder 8, Archives Branch, HDMCU.
29. Telegram from the Embassy in Laos to the Department of State, May 17, 1964, *FRUS 1964–1968, XXVIII*, 87.
30. Fleet Marine Force, Pacific, June 1968, Vietnam, Box 13, Folder 7, Archives Branch, HDMCU; Villard, *Staying the Course*, 602. The unit was 3rd Battalion, 4th Marine Regiment. HQ USAF, Chronology on Effectiveness of Air Power in RVN, 6, 8, K143.042-9, AFHRA.
31. William W. Lofgren Jr., The Air War in Laos, 1 January 1972–22 February 1973 (HQ PACAF: Directorate of Operations Analysis, CHECO/Corona Harvest Division, 1974), 242, K717.0413-65, AFHRA.
32. Effects of Air Operations in Southeast Asia, 22 July 1965, 10, K717.6092, AFHRA.
33. PACAF DI, Effects of Air Operations in Southeast Asia, 14 October 1965, 16, K717.6092, AFHRA; HQ USAF, Chronology on Effectiveness of Air Power in RVN, 10–13, K143.042-9, AFHRA. These were at Duc Co, Phu Cu and Phu Ly. Harold G. Moore and Joseph L. Galloway, *We Were Soldiers Once . . . and Young: Ia Drang, The Battle That Changed the War in Vietnam* (New York: Random House, 1992), 308.
34. Carland, *Stemming the Tide*, 177; MacGarrigle, *Taking the Offensive*, 74; History Naval Operations, Vol. III 1965–1967, Part 1, 185–92, NHHC.

35. Lee Bonetti, et al., The War in Vietnam, July–December 1967 (HQ PACAF: Directorate Tactical Evaluation, CHECO Division, 1968), 21, 23, K717.0414-17, July–December 1967, AFHRA.
36. Shelby Stanton, *The Rise and Fall of an American Army: U.S. Ground Forces in Vietnam, 1965–1973* (Novato, CA: Presidio Press, 1985), 151. Troop A of the 3rd Squadron, 5th Cavalry Regiment.
37. Maj. Leo J. Johnson, et al., Tactical Air in Support of Ground Forces in Vietnam (HQ PACAF: Directorate of Operations Analysis/CHECO Division, 1970), 22, K717.0414-71, 1970, AFHRA.
38. United States Military Assistance Command, Vietnam Command History 1968, Volume 1 (Saigon: Military History Branch, Office of the Secretary, Joint Staff, 1969), 403, 404, found online at: https://www.scribd.com/document/81653683/Command-History-1968-Volume-I; Sams, et al., The Air War in Vietnam: 1968–1969, 36, K717.0413-143, AFHRA; Sams and Aton, USAF Support of Special Forces in SEA, 29, K717.0413-96, AFHRA.
39. Sams and Aton, USAF Support of Special Forces in SEA, 21, K717.0413-96, AFHRA.
40. Fleet Marine Force Pacific, Operations of U.S. Marine Forces, Vietnam, June 1966, found online at The Vietnam Center & Sam Johnson Vietnam Archive, Texas Tech University, http://vietnam.ttu.edu; HQ USMACV Command History, 1966, 402, Marine Corps Forces in Vietnam March 1965–September 1967, Historical Summary, HDMCU; MACV Command History 1969, Vol. 1, v-195.
41. Kenneth Sams, John C. Pratt, and John Schlight, Air Operations in Northern Laos, 1 November 1969–1 April 1970 (HQ PACAF: Directorate of Operations Analysis, CHECO/Corona Harvest Division), 85, 90–92, 95, K717.0413-65, AFHRA.
42. MACV Command History 1970, Vol. 1, vi-50.
43. Wilkins, *Grab Their Belts to Fight Them*, 71; Otto J. Lehrack, *The First Battle: Operation Starlite and the Beginning of the Blood Debt in Vietnam* (Havertown, PA: Casemate, 2004), 100.
44. Liebchen, Kontum: Battle for the Central Highlands, 37, 42, K717.0413-194, AFHRA.
45. Memorandum from the President's Assistant for National Security Affairs (Kissinger) to President Nixon, February 27, 1970, *FRUS 1969–1970, VI*, 633.
46. Sams, et al., Air Operations Northern Laos, November 1969–April 1970, 21–22, K717.0413-65, AFHRA.
47. Commander Stanley R. Arthur, Commanding Officer, Attack Squadron One Six Four to Chief of Naval Operations, Command History 1972, 1 May 1973, Fleet Aviation Commands Pre-1998, AR/229, Box 175, File F3, NHHC; Nalty, *Air War over South Vietnam*, 385.
48. Message from MG Hollingsworth to Gen. Abrams. Daily Commander's Evaluation Report, 200230Z, May 1972, Vogt Papers, Read File May 1972, AFHSD; Captain Richard L. Poling and Captain Joseph A. Personett, USAF to Commanding Officer USS *America*, Letter of Commendation, no date, Refers to events of September 17, 1972, Fleet Aviation Commands Active, Box 132, File VA-82 Command History 1972, NHHC.
49. HQ USAF, Chronology on Effectiveness of Air Power in RVN, 18, 21, 23, K143.042-9, AFHRA.
50. Major David Folkman, Air Support in Quang Ngai Province (HQ PACAF: Directorate, Tactical Evaluation, CHECO Division, 1970), 44, K717.0413-142, AFHRA.
51. MG A. S. Collins, 4th Infantry Division, November 1966, LTC Robert H. Sigholtz, 173rd Abn Bde, 16 November 1966, Tactical Air Support Analysis Team, K740.4501-1, 27 October–8 November 1966, AFHRA.
52. 1st Air Cavalry Division, Combat Operations After Action Report, 19 December 1965, K712.03-43, AFHRA; Letter from CG III MAF to CMC, Quotes on Effectiveness of Marine Tactical Air, October 11, 1967, Folder Aviation: Wars-Vietnam (2 of 3), Marine Corps History Division, Fleet Marine Force Pacific, U.S. Marine Corps Forces in Vietnam March 1965–September 1967, Historical Summary, Volume 1, Vietnam, Box 13, Folder 1, Archives Branch, HDMCU.

NOTES FOR CHAPTER 13

53. Transcript of Report Lessons Learned, 25th Infantry Division, 1 November 1966–31 January 1967, K712.03-59, AFHRA; HQ USAF, Chronology on Effectiveness of Air Power in RVN, 12, K143.042-9, AFHRA; Major General John D. Lavelle, Analysis of Air Warfare in Southeast Asia, 6 April 1966, p. I-B-1. K143.505-13, AFHRA.
54. Moore and Galloway, *We Were Soldiers*, 307; Carland, *Stemming the Tide*, 142.
55. Lanigan, Combat Operations After Action Report, June 9, 1967, Vietnam, 1967, Box 5, Folder 12, HDMCU.
56. Bonetti, et al., The War in Vietnam, July–December 1967, 18–19, K717.0414-17, AFHRA; Fleet Marine Force, Pacific, Operations of U.S. Marine Forces Vietnam, May 1968, HDMCU; Marine Fighter/Attack Squadron 232 Command Chronology, August 9, 1972, found online at The Vietnam Center & Sam Johnson Vietnam Archive, Texas Tech University, http://vietnam.ttu.edu; MACV Command History 1968 Vol. 1, 418.
57. Loye Jr., et al., Lam Son 719 30 January–24 March 1971, 118, 55–56, K717.0413-165, AFHRA.
58. HQ USMACV Command History, 1965, 32; Cosmas, *MACV: The Joint Command in the Years of Escalation, 1962–1967*, 231; History of the Pacific Air Forces, 1966, 145, K717.01, Vol. 1, Part 2, AFHRA.
59. Telegram from the Embassy in Laos to the Department of State, August 20, 1964, *FRUS 1964–1968, XXVIII*, 260; Effects of Air Operations in Southeast Asia, 22 July 1965, 12, K717.6092, AFHRA; Message from 2nd Air Division to RUHLKM/CINCPACAF, Project Packrat, 190340Z, March 1965, K526.1623, 1965, AFHRA.
60. PACAF DI, Effects of Air Operations in Southeast Asia, 14 October 1965, 21, K717.6092, AFHRA.
61. Memorandum from the Deputy Director of the Office of Southeast Asian Affairs (Ewing) to the Director (Trueheart), December 16, 1965, *FRUS 1964–1968, III*, 427; Special National Intelligence Estimate 58–65, August 5, 1965, *FRUS 1964–1968, III*, 383.
62. PACAF DI, Effects of Air Operations in Southeast Asia, 19 August 1965, 12, PACAF DI, Effects of Air Operations in Southeast Asia, 16 September 1965, 19, K717.6092, AFHRA; HQ USAF, Chronology on Effectiveness of Air Power in RVN, 33, K143.042-9, AFHRA; Telegram from the Embassy in Laos to the Department of State, Effectiveness of USAF Operations in Northern Laos, August 3, 1966, *FRUS 1964–1968, XXVIII*, 483.
63. DCS Intelligence, Headquarters Pacific Air Forces, Effects of Air Operations Southeast Asia, Edition 37, 1967, 71, K717.6092, January 1967; Assessment of Air Operations, 7 February 1965 thru 19 July 1967, 34, K740.04-20, AFHRA; Prados, *Vietnam*, 355.
64. Wilkins, *Grab Their Belts to Fight Them*, 38–40, 108; Brush, "The Battle of Khe Sanh," in *The Tet Offensive*, 201; R. R. Dickey, III, 1st Battalion, 3rd Marines After Action Report, April 18, 1966, Vietnam, April–December 1966, Box 4, Folder 10, Archives Branch, HDMCU; Stanton, *Rise and Fall of an American Army*, 175.
65. History of the Pacific Air Forces, 1966, 125, K717.01, Vol. 1, Part 2, AFHRA; Carland, *Stemming the Tide*, 42.
66. Lieutenant Colonel E. R. Long, Commanding Officer 2nd Battalion, 3rd Marines to Commanding General, Third Marine Division (Rein), Combat Actions, After Action Report, March 5, 1967, Vietnam, Box 6, Folder 2, Archives Branch, HDMCU; Villard, *Staying the Course*, 63–64.
67. Moody, et al., U.S. Marines in Vietnam, Part VII: Backing Up the Troops, HDMCU.
68. Ringenbach and Melly, Battle for An Loc, 41–42, K717.0413-196, AFHRA.
69. Colonel Ernest D. Bryant, DOTACLO to TAC, TACLO (7AF) Activity Report #20, 1 November 1968, K417.01, July 1968–June 1969, Vol. 12, AFHRA; Project CHECO, Short Rounds and Related Incidents (HQ PACAF: Directorate of Operations Analysis, CHECO/Corona Harvest Division, 1971), 2–3, K717.0413-163, AFHRA.

70. Short Rounds, 17, K717.0413-163, AFHRA.
71. Major David R. Nelson, USAF Close Air Support in South Vietnam, 1 January 1972–31 January 1973 (HQ PACAF: Directorate of Operations Analysis/CHECO Division, 1974), 88, K717.601-8, 1 January 1972–31 January 1973, AFHRA.
72. Transcript of Message from Major General W. E. DePuy to COMUSMACV and Commander 7th AF, 270535Z, August 1966, K712.03-61, AFHRA; Johnson, Tactical Air in Support of Ground Forces in Vietnam, 23–24, K717.0414-71, 1970, AFHRA. The soldiers were from the Eighteenth Infantry Regiment.
73. Nelson, Close Air Support 1972, 19–25, K717.601-8, AFHRA; Message from CG III MAF to CG FMFPAC, 290334Z, June 1968, found online at The Vietnam Center & Sam Johnson Vietnam Archive, Texas Tech University, http://vietnam.ttu.edu; Lieutenant Colonel W. N. Vest, Commanding Officer 2nd Battalion, 3rd Marines to Commanding General, Third Marine Division (Rein), Combat Actions, After Action Report, March 5, 1967, Vietnam, Box 6, Folder 2. Archives Branch, HDMCU.
74. Fleet Marine Force, Pacific, Operations of U.S. Marine Forces Vietnam, May 1968, Vietnam, Box 13, Folder 6, Archives Branch, HDMCU.
75. Colonel Jones E. Bolt, 12th TFW, Tactical Air Support Analysis Team, K740.4501-1, 27 October–8 November 1966, AFHRA; James H. Willbanks, *The Battle of An Loc* (Bloomington: Indiana University Press, 2005), 157; Ringenbach and Melly, Battle for An Loc, 56, 57, K717.0413-196, AFHRA.
76. Blout, Air Operations in Northern Laos, 1 April–1 November 1970, 13, K717.0413-65, AFHRA.
77. Loye Jr., et al., Lam Son 719 30 January–24 March 1971, 104, K717.0413-165, AFHRA; Colonel John E. Lance, Senior Advisor IV Corps, 19 November 1966, Tactical Air Support Analysis Team, K740.4501-1, 27 October–8 November 1966, AFHRA; Randolph, *Powerful and Brutal Weapons,* 145.
78. Sams, et al., Air Operations Northern Laos, November 1969–April 1970, 91, 92, 95, K717.0413-65, AFHRA; Colonel George S. Weart, Tactical Air Support Analysis Team, K740.4501-1, 27 October–8 November 1966, AFHRA.
79. Johnson, Tactical Air in Support of Ground Forces in Vietnam, v. K717.0414-71, 1970, AFHRA.
80. Wilkins, *Grab Their Belts to Fight Them,* 35; Robert H. Scales Jr., *Firepower in Limited War* (Washington, DC: National Defense University Press, 1990), 77; History of the Pacific Air Forces, 1966, 134, K717.01, Vol. 1, Part 2, AFHRA; Lieutenant General Victor H. Krulak to General William C. Westmoreland, May 15, 1967, Krulak Papers, COLL/3064, Box 1, Folder 5, Archives Branch, HDMCU; Schlight, *The Years of the Offensive, 1965–1968*, 212.
81. Message from CG III MAF to CMC and FMFPAC, 01140Z, August 1967, found online at The Vietnam Center & Sam Johnson Vietnam Archive, Texas Tech University, http://vietnam.ttu.edu; Lt. Col. D. J. Fulham, Commanding Officer, 1st Battalion, 9th Marines to Commanding General 3rd Marine Division, Prairie II After Action Report, April 2, 1967, Vietnam, Box 6, Folder 2, Archives Branch, HDMCU.
82. Operations of U.S. Marine Forces Vietnam, May 1968, HDMCU; Operations of U.S. Marine Forces Vietnam, January 1970, found online at The Vietnam Center & Sam Johnson Vietnam Archive, Texas Tech University, http://vietnam.ttu.edu.
83. MacGarrigle, *Taking the Offensive,* 296; Interview with General Raymond G. Davis by Benis M. Frank, Transcript, 44–45, History and Museums Division, Headquarters U.S. Marine Corps, Washington, DC, 1978; Carland, *Stemming the Tide,* 287.
84. Message from CG XXX MAF to RUMSMA/COMUSMACV, Special Report: Thoung Duc CIDG/USASF, Camp Patrol Report, 241424Z, January 1967, found online at The Vietnam Center & Sam Johnson Vietnam Archive, Texas Tech University, http://vietnam.ttu.edu; Wilkins,

NOTES FOR CHAPTER 13

Grab Their Belts to Fight Them, 200–201; Message from Major General Cowles to General Vogt, Daily Commanders Evaluation Report, 301000H April thru 011000H May 72, 010250Z, May 1972, Vogt Papers, Read File April 1972, AFHSD.
85. Message from AFSSO 7AF to AFSSO PACAF, Sortie Requirements, 021120Z, August 1972, Vogt Papers, Read File August 1972, AFHSD; Andrade, *Trial by Fire*, 210.
86. History of the Pacific Air Forces, 1966, 145, K717.01, Vol. 1, Part 2, AFHRA.
87. Ibid., 146.
88. Ibid., 149; Notes of the President's Meeting with Foreign Policy Advisers, July 30, 1968, *FRUS 1964–1968, VI*, 921; Editorial Note on August 12 Meeting between Clark Clifford and the Office of the Secretary of Defense Staff, *FRUS 1964–1968, VI*, 952.
89. Telegram from the Embassy in Laos to the Department of State, March 3, 1964, *FRUS 1964–1968, XXVIII*, 29.
90. PACAF DI, Summary of Effects of Air Operations Southeast Asia, 1965, 10, K717.6092, AFHRA.
91. HQ USAF, Chronology on Effectiveness of Air Power in RVN, 38, K143.042-9, AFHRA.
92. Johnson, Tactical Air in Support of Ground Forces in Vietnam, vi–vii, K717.0414-71, 1970, AFHRA; Sams, et al., Air Operations Northern Laos, November 1969–April 1970, 65, K717.0413-65, AFHRA.
93. Message from CINCPACAF to CSAF, Westmoreland Meeting at CINCPAC 11 August, 120341Z, August 1966, K717.1623, March–December 1966, AFHRA.
94. Message from CINCPAC to RUEKDA/JCS, Arc Light Deployments, 160155Z, December 1966, K717.312 15–16 December 1966, AFHRA; HQ USMACV Command History, 1966, 400, Message from General Abrams to General Momyer, et al., 230757Z, June 1968, found online at The Vietnam Center & Sam Johnson Vietnam Archive, Texas Tech University, http://vietnam.ttu.edu.
95. Memorandum from the President's Assistant (Jones) to President Johnson, September 5, 1967, *FRUS 1964–1968, V*, 751–52.
96. DCS Intelligence, Headquarters Pacific Air Forces, Effects of Air Operations Southeast Asia, March 1967, 59, 60, K717.6092, AFHRA.
97. Barack Obama, Speech to 93rd Annual Conference of the American Legion, August 30, 2011, found online at: https://obamawhitehouse.archives.gov/the-press-office/2011/08/30/remarks-president-93rd-annual-conference-american-legion; Harry G. Summers, *On Strategy: A Critical Analysis of the Vietnam War* (Novato, CA: Presidio Press, 1982), 1.
98. PACAF DI, Effects of Air Operations in Southeast Asia, 19 August 1965, 10, K717.6092, AFHRA.
99. History of the Pacific Air Forces, 1966, 107, 110, K717.01, Vol. 1, Part 2, AFHRA. The document does not list the number of survivors. MacGarrigle, *Taking the Offensive*, 205.
100. Trest, Khe Sanh, 14–17, K717.0413-35, Loye Jr., et al., Lam Son 719 30 January–24 March 1971, 57, K717.0413-165, AFHRA.
101. MACV Command History 1972, L-18. Brookbank was an air liaison officer between the 3rd ARVN Division and the 20th Tactical Air Support Squadron. Andrade, *Trial by Fire*, 562.
102. Schlight, *The Years of the Offensive, 1965–1968*, 290.
103. Fleet Marine Force, Pacific, Operations of U.S. Marine Forces Vietnam, January and February 1971, found online at The Vietnam Center & Sam Johnson Vietnam Archive, Texas Tech University, http://vietnam.ttu.edu; Airman First Class Joseph Taylor, History of the 306th Bombardment Wing (Heavy), February 1967, Vol. 1, 49–50, K-WG-306-HI, Vol. 1, AFHRA; Staff Sergeant Stephen L. Y. Gammons, History of 4258th Strategic Wing, December 1967, Vol. 1, 33, Gammons, History of 4258th Strategic Wing, September 1967, Vol. 1, 48–49, K-WG-4258-HI, AFHRA.
104. Trest, Khe Sanh, 53, K717.0413-35, AFHRA; Gammons, History 4258th Strategic Wing, January

1968, Vol. 1, 35, K-WG-4258-HI, 1968; Warfel, History 4258th Strategic Wing, November 1968, 30, K-WG-4258-HI, AFHRA.
105. Sergeants Carl J. Trapolino and James D. Otis, III, History of the 307th Strategic Wing, April 1970, K-WG-307-HI, April 1970, AFHRA; Staff Sergeant Charles K. Wells Jr., and Sergeant Raymond A. Paoli, History of the 307th Strategic Wing, October–December 1970, Vol. 1, K-WG-307-HI, AFHRA.
106. Wells and Paoli, History 307th Strategic Wing, October–December 1970, K-WG-307-HI, AFHRA; R. R. Dickey, III, 1st Battalion, 3rd Marines After Action Report, April 18, 1966, HDMCU.
107. Nelson, Close Air Support, 1972, 75–77, 80–81, K717.601-8, AFHRA.
108. Message from Admino III MAF to CG FMGPAC, Combat Reporting, 29000Z, November 1967, found online at The Vietnam Center & Sam Johnson Vietnam Archive, Texas Tech University, http://vietnam.ttu.edu.
109. Loye Jr., et al., Lam Son 719 30 January–24 March 1971, 66, 70, K717.0413-165, AFHRA. For a more modest assessment, see Message from 8AF to 307 Strategic Wing, Arc Light/Lam Son 719 Operation, 220800Z, March 1971, K-WG-307-HI, January–March 1971, Vol. 1, AFHRA.
110. History of the Pacific Air Forces, 1966, 110–41, K717.01, Vol. 1, Part 2, AFHRA; Bonetti, et al., The War in Vietnam, July–December 1967, 18, 42, K717.0414-17, AFHRA; Fleet Marine Force, Pacific, Operations of U.S. Marine Forces Vietnam, May 1968, HDMCU; Fleet Marine Force, Pacific.
111. CINCPAC, Measurement of Progress in Southeast Asia, December 31, 1968, Vietnam, Box 7, Folder 7, Archives Branch, HDMCU.
112. Lieutenant Colonel D. J. Fulham, Commanding Officer 1st Battalion, 9th Marines to Commanding General 3rd Marine Division April 2, 1967, Vietnam, Box 6, Folder 2, Fleet Marine Force, Pacific, June 1968, and Fleet Marine Force, Pacific, Operations of U.S. Marine Forces Vietnam, December 1970 and 1970 Summary, Vietnam, Box 14, Folder 2, Archives Branch, HDMCU; Operations of U.S. Marine Forces, Vietnam, August 1966, Fleet Marine Force, Pacific, Operations of U.S. Marine Forces Vietnam, January and February 1971, found online at The Vietnam Center & Sam Johnson Vietnam Archive, Texas Tech University, http://vietnam.ttu.edu.
113. This was Company A, 2nd Battalion, 8th Cavalry Regiment. MacGarrigle, *Taking the Offensive*, 318, 319.
114. Taylor, History of the 306th Bombardment Wing, March 1967, Vol. 1, 43, K-WG-306-HI, AFHRA.
115. HQ USAF, Chronology on Effectiveness of Air Power in RVN, 5, 11, K143.042-9, AFHRA; Notes of Meeting, January 29, 1968, *FRUS 1964–1968, VI*, 71.
116. MACV Command History 1968, Vol. 1, 424; Message from John P. Vann to General Abrams, Daily Commander's Evaluation, 200225Z, May 1972, Vogt Papers, General Vogt's Read File May 1972, AFHSD.
117. Johnson, Tactical Air in Support of Ground Forces in Vietnam, 25, K717.0414-71, 1970, AFHRA.
118. Ibid., 24–28; Folkman, Air Support in Quang Ngai Province, 54, K717.0413-142, AFHRA.
119. Folkman, Air Support in Quang Ngai Province, 45, 46, K717.0413-142, AFHRA.
120. Johnson, Tactical Air in Support of Ground Forces in Vietnam, 24–28, K717.0414-71, 1970, AFHRA; Folkman, Air Support in Quang Ngai Province, 54, K717.0413-142, AFHRA.
121. Operations of U.S. Marine Forces Vietnam, December 1967 and 1967 Summary, HDMCU; Wilkins, *Grab Their Belts to Fight Them*, 81; David H. Hackworth, *Steel My Soldiers' Hearts: The Hopeless to the Hardcore Transformation of 4th Battalion, 39th Infantry, United States Army, Vietnam* (New York: Rugged Land, 2002), 157.
122. Colonel J. P. Lanigan, Commanding Officer 3rd Marines to Commanding General 3rd Marine Division, Combat Operations After Action Report, June 9, 1967, and P. C. Trammell, After Action

Report from 3rd Battalion, 9th Marines to Commanding General, 3rd Marine Division, May 14, 1966, Vietnam, April–December 1966, Box 4, Folder 12, Archives Branch, HDMCU; Fleet Marine Force, Pacific, Operations of U.S. Marine Forces, Vietnam, March 1969, found online at The Vietnam Center & Sam Johnson Vietnam Archive, Texas Tech University, http://vietnam.ttu.edu.

123. Fleet Marine Force, Pacific, Operations of U.S. Marine Forces, Vietnam, October 1969, and Fleet Marine Force, Pacific, Operations of U.S. Marine Forces, Vietnam, July 1970, found online at The Vietnam Center & Sam Johnson Vietnam Archive, Texas Tech University, http://vietnam.ttu.edu.

124. Lanigan, After Action Report, June 9, 1967, Vietnam, 1967, Box 5, Folder 12, Archives Branch, Fleet Marine Force Pacific, Operations of U.S. Marine Forces, Vietnam, June 1968, HDMCU; Fleet Marine Force, Pacific, Operations of U.S. Marine Forces, Vietnam, January 1969 and Fleet Marine Force, Pacific, Operations of U.S. Marine Forces, Vietnam, April 1970, found online at The Vietnam Center & Sam Johnson Vietnam Archive, Texas Tech University, http://vietnam.ttu.edu. These vignettes are a regular feature of these monthly reports, and their fundamental character does not vary from month to month.

125. Johnson, Tactical Air in Support of Ground Forces, 44, 45, 47–49, K717.0414-71, 1970, AFHRA.

126. History Naval Operations, Vol. III 1965–1967, Part 1, 192, NHHC.

127. David Chanoff and Doan Van Toai, *Portrait of the Enemy* (New York: Random House, 1986), 155; Wilkins, *Grab Their Belts to Fight Them*, 149.

128. Carland, *Stemming the Tide*, 209–10; Wilkins, *Grab Their Belts to Fight Them*, 154.

129. Schlight, *The Years of the Offensive, 1965–1968*, 48; Major Ralph A. Rowley, USAF FAC Operations in Southeast Asia, 1961–1965 (Washington, DC: Office of Air Force History, 1972), 48–49, 102, K168.01-43, 1961–1965, AFHRA; Major William C. Dale Jr., End of Tour Report, Tour dates: 23 May 1966–1 May 1967, Sector FAC, Nihn Thuan Province, K740.131, AFHRA; William C. Dale, 23 May 1966–1 May 1967, AFHRA; Message from CG 3rd Mardiv to CG III MAF, 1st Bn 4th Mar Contact of 11 April at LZ Torch, 120920Z, June 1968, found online at The Vietnam Center & Sam Johnson Vietnam Archive, Texas Tech University, http://vietnam.ttu.edu.

130. Message, 230948Z, April 1968, Improved Performance Characteristics and Crew Survivability for O-2A/B, K740.03-44, 7 November 1967, AFHRA; Thorndale, Visual Reconnaissance in I Corps, 29–30, K717.0413-36, AFHRA.

131. AFRDDE, Background Paper on OV-10A, 20 July 1966, K740.03-44, 7 November 1967, AFHRA; Message from CG III MAF to USMACTHAI, 140650Z, March 1969, found online at The Vietnam Center & Sam Johnson Vietnam Archive, Texas Tech University, http://vietnam.ttu.edu.

132. Nelson, Close Air Support, 1972, 73, K717.601-8; Captain Joseph V. Potter, OV-10 Operations in SE Asia (HQ PACAF: Directorate, Tactical Evaluation, CHECO Division, 1969, 7, K717.0413-60, AFHRA; MACV Command History 1969, Vol. 1, v-199 through v-200. Although the Bronco entered service in 1968, it did not fully replace the O-2 until 1972. Potter, OV-10 Operations, 7.

133. Seventh Air Force, Commando Hunt VII, 240, 243, K740.04-14, November 1971–March 1972, AFHRA; Southeast Asia Air Operations Briefing August 1971, K717.3063-1, August 1971, Potter, OV-10 Operations in SE Asia, 20, K717.0413-60, AFHRA.

134. Message from 7AF to CINCPACAF, Expanded F-100F FAC Program, 081151Z, September 1967, K717.312-1, AFHRA; Lt. Col. John Schlight, Jet Forward Air Controllers in SEASIA (HQ PACAF: Directorate, Tactical Evaluation, Checo Division, 1969), 2, 3, K717.0413-70; Air Effectiveness Trends during the Southwest Monsoon 1967, K740.04-18, AFHRA. Their call sign was "Misty."

135. Schlight, Jet Forward Air Controllers in SEASIA, 8–9, K717.0413-70; Operation Neutralize, 011415Z, October 1967, K717.312; AFXOPG, Report on Staff Visit to Southeast Asia, 9–19 November 1967, K143.152-1, 9–19 November 1967, Schlight, Jet Forward Air Controllers in SEASIA, 10, K717.0413-70, AFHRA.

136. Lieutenant Colonel Till, Major Thomas, Pave Aegis Weapon System (AC-130E Gunship) (HQ PACAF: Directorate, Tactical Evaluation, Checo Division, Project CHECO, 1973), 1, K717.0413-202, AFHRA; Sams and Aton, USAF Support of Special Forces in SEA, 18, K717.0413-96, AFHRA.
137. Captain James L. Cole Jr., Fixed Wing Gunships in SEA (Jul 69–Jul 71) (HQ PACAF: Directorate of Operations Analysis, Checo/Corona Harvest Division, 1971), 17, K717.0414-15, AFHRA.
138. Jordan Wouk, Letter to the Editor, "Magic Dragon's Not-So-Innocuous Puff," *The New York Times*, October 11, 1984, found online at: http://www.nytimes.com/1984/10/11/opinion/l-magic-dragon-s-not-so-innocuous-puff-002871.html; Belinda Goldsmith, "Just a Minute with: Peter Yarrow," Reuters, March 6, 2008, found online at: https://www.reuters.com/article/us-yarrow/just-a-minute-with-peter-yarrow-idUSSYD1071420080306; Kaili Bisson, "The Story Behind the Song 'Puff the Magic Dragon' by Peter, Paul, and Mary," Spindiddy, April 22, 2019, found online at: https://spinditty.com/genres/Puff-The-Magic-Dragon. Leonard Lipton co-wrote the song with Yarrow.
139. Nelson, Close Air Support, 1972, 59–60, K717.601-8, AFHRA; Lieutenant Colonel Edward A. Elbert Jr., End of Tour Report, circa July 1971, K740.131, AFHRA; Sams, Air Operations Northern Laos, November 1969–April 1970, 63, K717.0413-65, AFHRA.
140. Cole, Fixed Wing Gunships in SEA, 32, 33; Ringenbach and Melly, Battle for An Loc, 59, K717.0413-196, AFHRA. For a book-length examination of the AC-119, see William P. Head, *Shadow and Stinger: Developing the AC-119G/K Gunships in the Vietnam War* (College Station: Texas A&M University Press, 2007).
141. Lieutenant Colonel Till, Major Thomas, Pave Aegis Weapon System (AC-130E Gunship), (HQ PACAF: Directorate of Operations Analysis, Checo/Corona Harvest Division, 1973, 2, K717.0413-202, AFHRA. For more on the AC-130, see William P. Head, *Night Hunters: The AC-130s and Their Role in US Airpower* (College Station: Texas A&M University Press, 2014).
142. Till and Thomas, Pave Aegis Weapon System (AC-130E Gunship), 4, K717.0413-202, AFHRA; Monroe, Request for R&D Requirements, 6 January 1970, K740-03-4, AFHRA; Captain James L. Cole Jr., Fixed-Wing Gunships in SEA, July 1969–July 1971 (HQ PACAF: Directorate of Operations Analysis, CHECO/Corona Harvest Division, 1971), 47–48, AFHRA.
143. Till and Thomas, Pave Aegis Weapon System (AC-130E Gunship), 17–19, K717.0413-202, AFHRA; Nelson, Close Air Support, 1972, 68, 70, K717.601-8, AFHRA; Minutes of a Washington Special Actions Group Meeting, May 15, 1972, *FRUS 1969–1976, VIII*, 557.
144. End of Tour Report, Lieutenant Colonel John F. Hurst Jr., K717.131, 1972–April 1973, AFHRA.
145. Message from AFSSO 7AF to AFSSO CSAF, Daily Wrap Up, 151100Z, May 1972; Message from AFSSO 7AF to AFSSO CSAF, Daily Wrap Up, 131110Z, May 1972, Vogt Papers, Read File May 1972, AFHSD.
146. Loye Jr., et al., Lam Son 719 30 January–24 March 1971, 105, K717.0413-165, AFHRA; Evaluation Report for the NVN Offensive (April–August 1972), vi-1, K717.04-9, 1972, AFHRA.
147. Liebchen, Kontum: Battle for the Central Highlands, 21, K717.0413-194, AFHRA; Till and Thomas, Pave Aegis Weapon System, 21–22, K717.0413-202, AFHRA; Message from Mr. John P. Vann to Gen Abrams, Daily Commander's Evaluation, 060305Z, May 1972, Vogt Papers, Read File May 1972, AFHSD.
148. Ringenbach and Melly, Battle for An Loc, 60, K717.0413-196, AFHRA; Nelson, Close Air Support, 1972, 79, K717.601-8, AFHRA.
149. Willbanks, *Battle of An Loc*, 159.
150. The rest of the story is that the town fell to the PAVN on January 9, 1973, because it "did not have enough ground forces to survive." Air Operations in Southeast Asia, 1972–1973, v-102, v-104, K717.0423-23, 1 July 1972–15 August 1973, Vol. 3, AFHRA.

151. Summary Air Operations Southeast Asia, April 1972, 2–12, 2–13, K717.3063; Evaluation Report for the NVN Offensive (April–August 1972), vi-2, K717.04-9, 1972; Air Operations in Southeast Asia, 1972–1973, Vol. 1, iii-26, K717.0423-23, AFHRA; Liebchen, Kontum: Battle for the Central Highlands, 76, K717.0413-194, AFHRA.
152. Jacob Van Staaveren, *The United States Air Force in Southeast Asia: Interdiction in Southern Laos, 1960–1968* (Washington, DC: Center for Air Force History, 1993), 6, K740.056-1, 1966–1967, Tab 41; Sams, Air Operations Northern Laos, November 1969–April 1970, 20, K717.0413-65, AFHRA.
153. Message from 2 Air Div to PACAF, 170841Z, December 1965, K526.1623, AFHRA; Telegram from the Embassy in Laos to the Department of State, February 26, 1965, *FRUS 1964–1968, XXVIII*, 339.
154. Telegram from the Embassy in Laos to the Department of State, March 3, 1965, *FRUS 1964–1968, XXVIII*, 348; Warren A. Trest, *Air Commando One: Heinie Aderholt and America's Secret Air Wars* (Washington, DC: Smithsonian Institution Press, 2000), 178.
155. Memorandum for the President's File, January 27, 1971, *FRUS 1969–1976, VII*, 327.
156. Schlight, *The Years of the Offensive, 1965–1968*, 3. Dunham, End of Tour Report, 9 July 1967, K740.131, AFHRA; Message from Hollingsworth to Abrams, DCE, 210210Z, June 1972, Vogt Papers, Read File June 1972, AFHSD.
157. Randolph, *Powerful and Brutal Weapons*, 65, 134; Memorandum to Secretary of Defense Laird, July 21, 1969, *FRUS 1969–1976, VI*, 310.
158. History, Twelfth Air Force, July–December 1965, K650.01-28, July–December 1965, Vol. 1. History of Pacific Air Forces, 1 July 1972–30 June 1973, K717.01, AFHRA; Robert F. Dorr, "F-100 Super Sabre Flew Most Missions in Vietnam," *Defense Media Network* (September 12, 2013), found online at: https://www.defensemedianetwork.com/stories/f-100-super-sabre-flew-most-missions-in-vietnam/.
159. Maj. Edwin H. Snyder, HQ 7th AF, F-100 Strike Effectiveness in South Vietnam, 1 October 1968, K740.04-17, AFHRA; Bernard C. Nalty, *The War Against Trucks: Aerial Interdiction in Southern Laos, 1968–1972* (Washington, DC: Air Force History and Museums Program, United States Air Force, 2005), 66.
160. HQ USAF, Chronology on Effectiveness of Air Power in RVN, 8, 36, K143.042-9; Captain Donald R. Curtis, End-of-Tour Report, 7 January 1967, K740.131, AFHRA; Trest, *Air Commando One*, 176.
161. Nelson, Close Air Support, 1972, 64, K717.601-8, AFHRA; Ringenbach and Melly, Battle for An Loc, 43, K717.0413-196, AFHRA.
162. Message from AFSSO 7AF to AFSSO PACAF, 8 SOS, 020430Z, May 1972, Vogt Papers, Read File May 1972, AFHSD; Ringenbach and Melly, Battle for An Loc, 60, K717.0413-196, AFHRA.
163. Bonetti, et al., The War in Vietnam, July–December 1967, 18–19, K717.0414-17; Ringenbach and Melly, Battle for An Loc, 60, AFXOPG, Report on Staff Visit to Southeast Asia, 9–19 November 1967, K143.152-1, 9–19 November 1967, AFHRA.
164. Andrade, *Trial by Fire*, 403.
165. Dunham, End of Tour Report, 9 July 1967, K740.131, AFHRA.
166. 1st Lieutenant George R. Davis, End of Tour Report, 19th Tactical Air Support Squadron, no date, K740.131, 3 Feb 1967–11 Aug 1967, AFHRA.
167. Evaluation Report for the NVN Offensive, April–August 1972, v-6, K717.04-9, AFHRA.
168. Colonel Allan P. Rankin, 366th TFW, Tactical Air Support Analysis Team, K740.4501-1, 27 October–8 November 1966; Nelson, Close Air Support, 1972, 64, K717.601-8, AFHRA.
169. OPNAV 5750-1 Attack Squadron Fifty-Five Command History 1969, Fleet Aviation Commands Pre-1998, AR/229, Box 132, File F12, OPNAV 5750-1 Attack Squadron Fifty-Five Command

History 1968, NHHC; Peter Kilduff, *Douglas A-4 Skyhawk* (London: Osprey Publishing, 1983), 80–81; Moody, et al., U.S. Marines in Vietnam, Part VII: Backing Up the Troops, Operations of U.S. Marine Forces Vietnam, May 1968, HDMCU. The last squadron was VMF(AW)-235.

170. Davis Oral History Transcript, 30, HDMCU; W. Nunn, Operations Evaluation Group of the Center of Naval Analyses, Study No. 731, Combat Introduction of the A-7A Aircraft, 1969, COLL/7 Publications of the Center for Naval Analyses, OEG, Box 65, File OEG 731, NHHC; "A Corsair by Any Other Name," *Air International* 22:3 (March 1982), 146.

171. Lieutenant Commander Frederick J. West, Center for Naval Analyses Operations Evaluation Group Study 767, Evaluation of the A-7E Weapons System, December 1972, 6–7, 8, COLL/7 Publications of the Center for Naval Analyses OEG, Box 68, File OEG 767, Carrier Attack Wing Eleven End of Cruise Report, 30 December 1968–4 September 1969, Ships History Post 2001, *Kitty Hawk* (CV-63), Box 189, File 1969 Cruise Reports, NHHC.

172. Enney, Commander Attack Carrier Air Wing Fourteen, Addendum Report, 11 February 1969, Attack Carrier Air Wing Eleven, Cruise Report February to November 1972, 1 December 1972, NHHC.

173. McKnight, Carrier Air Wing Two, Cruise Report of October 1970 to June 1971, 10 June 1971, NHHC. Note: this is an outstandingly useful document on the capabilities of the A-7E.

174. Willbanks, *A Raid Too Far*, 105; Jerry O. Tuttle, Letters to the Editor, "A-4/A-7 Comparison," *Aviation Week and Space Technology* (July 10, 1972), 58.

175. Air Operations in Southeast Asia, 1972–1973, Vol. 1, pp. ii-41, ii-47, K717.0423-23, AFHRA; Message from AFSSO PACAF to AFSSO 7AF, Replacement of F-4s in SEA, 182253Z, July 1972, Vogt Papers, Read File July 1972, AFHSD.

176. Sidney G. Depner, History of the 354th Tactical Fighter Wing, 1 July 1972–30 September 1972, 2, K-WG-354-HI, Vol. 1, AFHRA; History of the Pacific Air Forces, 1 July 1972–30 June 1973, 129–32, K717.01, AFHRA; Message from 7/13 AF to RUKLAAA/TAC/DO, 090606Z, November 1972, Report 16-72, A-7 Operations, K717.01, AFHRA.

177. Message, Report 16-17, A-7 Operations, 090606Z, November 1972, K717.01; Personal from Colonel Knoles to General Momyer and General Rhodarmer, Report No. 2, 280148Z, October 1972, K-WG-354-HI, July–December 1972, Vol. 3; Nelson, Close Air Support, 1972, 65, 97, K717.601-8; Lieutenant General Carlos M. Talbott, Interview June 10–11, 1985, by Hugh N. Ahmann, 169, K239.2512-1652; Lieutenant Colonel William L. Ernst, The Rustic FACS To All of the Pilots of the 354th, no date, K-WG-354-HI, July–December 1972, Vol. 3, AFHRA.

178. Air Operations in Southeast Asia, 1972–1973, Vol. 1, p. iii-42, K717.0423-23; Sidney G. Depner, History of the 354th Tactical Fighter Wing, 1 October 1972–31 December 1972, 24, K-WG-354-HI, Vol. 1, AFHRA.

179. Fleet Marine Force, Pacific, Operations of U.S. Marine Forces, Vietnam, March 1966, found online at The Vietnam Center & Sam Johnson Vietnam Archive, Texas Tech University, http://vietnam.ttu.edu; Message from CSAF to RUEDNBA/TAC, Ground Directed Bomb System, 041818Z, August 1966, K717.312, AFHRA; Colonel J. P. Lanigan, Commanding Officer 3rd Marines to Commanding General 3rd Marine Division, Combat Operations After Action Report, April 3, 1967, and Lanigan, After Action Report, June 9, 1967, Letter from CG III MAF to CMC, October 11, 1967, U.S. Marine Corps Forces in Vietnam March 1965–September 1967, Historical Summary, Volume 1, Vietnam, Box 13, Folder 1, Archives Branch, HDMCU.

180. Fleet Marine Force, Pacific, Operations of U.S. Marine Forces, December 1966, found online at The Vietnam Center & Sam Johnson Vietnam Archive, Texas Tech University, http://vietnam.ttu.edu; Reardon, *Launch the Intruders*, 4; Fleet Marine Force, Pacific, Operations of U.S. Marine Forces, Vietnam, January 1968, HDMCU. January 21, 1968, to be precise.

181. Colonel E. J. Godfrey, Commanding Officer, 9th Marines to Commanding General 3rd Marine

Division, Combat Operation After Action Report, April 8, 1969, Vietnam, Box 9, Folder 14, Archives Branch, HDMCU. Dewey Canyon was an operation to take the A Shau Valley back from the communists. The valley was a major ground transportation route for the communists. Bowers, *Tactical Airlift*, 332.

182. McCutcheon, Marine Aviation in Vietnam, 1962–1970, 61, Marine Corps History Division. This system was known as "Diane." Sams, et al., The Air War in Vietnam: 1968–1969, 59–60, K717.0413-143, AFHRA.
183. Major John R. Bode, Command and Control of Air-Delivered Fire Support in Vietnam, K143.044-41, September 1970, AFHRA.
184. Major General Marion E. Carl, USMC oral history transcript, 43–44, Archives Branch, HDMCU; Message from CG III MAF to CG XXIV Corps, Enemy Caliber .50 Antiaircraft Fire, 230747Z, January 1970, found online at The Vietnam Center & Sam Johnson Vietnam Archive, Texas Tech University, http://vietnam.ttu.edu.
185. Clay, Lam Son 719 Operations: Lessons Learned, K740.04-15, AFHRA.
186. Ibid.; Message from USAFE to RUEDHQUA/CSAF, Close Air Support for the Army, 201709Z, July 1966, K717.312, July 1966, AFHRA; Shaw, *Cambodian Campaign*, 144.
187. Carl, USMC oral history transcript, 44, Archives Branch, HDMCU.
188. Clay, Lam Son 719 Operations: Lessons Learned, K740.04-15, AFHRA.
189. Moody, et al., U.S. Marines in Vietnam, Part VII: Backing Up the Troops, HDMCU.
190. Major General Robert F. Worley to Major General Royal N. Saker, MACV, Employment of In-Country Air, 3 April 1968, K740.31066-14, 3 April 1968, AFHRA.
191. Nelson, Close Air Support, 1972, 33–45, 50–55, K717.601-8; Sams, Air Operations Northern Laos, November 1969–April 1970, 40, K717.0413-65, AFHRA; Analysis Staff Study 3-70, Navy Combat Effectiveness of Rockeye, CBU-24, and Mk 82 GP Bombs against Trucks in Laos, November 1969–February 1970, Vietnam Command Files, COLL/372, Box 113, File CPF Staff Study 3-70, NHHC.
192. Major L. C. Edlund, End of Tour Report, K740.131, 28 April 1966–10 January 1967, AFHRA.
193. Blout, Air Operations in Northern Laos, 1 April–1 November 1970, 23, K717.0413-65; Nelson, Close Air Support, 1972, 33–45, 50-55, K717.601-8, AFHRA.
194. Excerpts from VA-153 Cruise Report, Fleet Aviation Commands Pre-1998, AR/229, Box 172 File F4, NHHC; 2nd Air Div to RUEAHQ/CSAF, 190710Z, March 1965, K526.1623, 19 March 1965, AFHRA.
195. Directorate of Operations History, December 1965, K717.01, July–December 1965, Vol. 2, Part 2; Message from 7 AF to CINCPACAF, Evaluation of CBU, 230420Z, July 1966, K717.312, July 1966, AFHRA.
196. Johnson, Tactical Air in Support of Ground Forces in Vietnam, 42–43, K717.0414-71, 1970, AFHRA; William H. Sullivan, Telegram from the Embassy in Laos to the Department of State, March 11, 1966, *FRUS 1964–1968, XXVIII*, 446; Dean Rusk, Telegram from the Department of State to the Embassy in Laos, March 23, 1966, *FRUS 1964–1968, XXVIII*, 451–52.
197. General Electric Company, Heavy Military Electronics Department, Marine Corps Direct Air Support Final Report, June 22, 1965, III-49, COLL/3746, Studies and Reports, Box 7, Folder Studies/Reports/Aviation 1 of 3, Archives Branch, HDMCU.
198. Michael H. Jones, Survey of Air Force Responsiveness to Immediate ASAP Requests for Air Support, December 1969, 1–2, K740.459-3, December 1969; Dunham, End of Tour Report, 9 July 1967, K740.131, AFHRA; Johnson, Tactical Air in Support of Ground Forces in Vietnam, 5–6, K717.0414-71, 1970; Major Frank Apel, Memorandum for Colonel Tighe, Close Air Support Responsiveness, 19 August 1969, DCS/Operations HQ 7th AF, Evaluation of the Adequacy and Timeliness of Immediate Close Air Support, June 1969, K740.459-2, AFHRA; Schlight, *The Years*

of the Offensive, 1965–1968, 293; Wilkins, *Grab Their Belts to Fight Them*, 149.
199. Gregory A. Daddis, *No Sure Victory: Measuring U.S. Army Effectiveness and Progress in the Vietnam War* (New York: Oxford University Press, 2011), 194; Wilkins, *Grab Their Belts to Fight Them*, 148.
200. Memorandum, Close Air Support Responsiveness, 19 August 1969, K740.459-2, AFHRA.
201. Message from CINCPACAF to CSAF, 221600Z, April 1965, K717-1623, AFHRA; HQ USMACV Command History, 1966, 377.
202. Lieutenant Colonel H. W. Vincent, Man/Mobility/Survivability Forum, 11–12 April 1967, HDMCU.
203. Lieutenant Colonel Henry L. Parker, I Corps DASC Deputy Director to HQ 7AF, 19 November 1966, Tactical Air Support Analysis Team, K740.4501-1, 27 October–8 November 1966; Lieutenant Colonel Robert W. Brownlee, 173rd Abn Bde, 15 November 1966, Tactical Air Support Analysis Team, K740.4501-1, 27 October–8 November 1966; Lance, Tactical Air Support Analysis Team, 19 November 1966, K740.4501-1, AFHRA.
204. Major Lawrence R. Gaboury to Commander U.S. Naval Forces, Vietnam, Combat Operations After Action Report, March 1, 1967, Vietnam, April–December 1966, Box 4, Folder 10, Archives Branch, HDMCU.
205. Colonel Gordon H. West, Tab E (Alert Status of Support Aircraft), April 1, 1966, Vietnam, April–December 1966, Box 4, Folder 1, and Godfrey, 9th Marines After Action Report, April 8, 1969, HDMCU; Colonel William Maddox, 21st Infantry Division Advisory Detachment, 22 November 1966, Tactical Air Support Analysis Team, K740.4501-1, 27 October–8 November 1966, AFHRA.
206. MACV Command History 1968, 403; Sams, et al., The Air War in Vietnam: 1968–1969, 36, K717.0413-143; Bonetti, The War in Vietnam: January–June 1967, 26–27, K717.0414-17, AFHRA.
207. Jones, Survey of Air Force Responsiveness to Requests for Air Support, 1–2, K740.459-3; Dunham, End of Tour Report, 9 July 1967, K740.131, AFHRA.
208. Captains David K. Mann and Edward P. Brynn, USAF Quick Reaction Forces (HQ PACAF: CHECO/Corona Harvest Division, Operations Analysis Office, 1974), 9, K717.0413-48, AFHRA.
209. Memorandum from the Central Intelligence Agency to President Johnson, July 31, 1967, *FRUS 1964–1968, XXVIII*, 608; Telegram from the Embassy in Laos to the Commander in Chief, Pacific (Sharp), May 30, 1968, *FRUS 1964–1968, XXVIII*, 725; ODASD(SA) Regional Programs, Southeast Asia Analysis Report, January 1970, Vietnam Command Files, COLL/372, Box 17, File DOD SEA Analysis Report, January 1970, NHHC; MACV Command History 1969, Vol. 1, v-201; MACV Command History 1970, p. vi-22.
210. MACV Command History, 1969, Vol. 1, v-201.
211. Schlight, *The Years of the Offensive, 1965–1968*, 293; Krepinevich, *The Army and Vietnam*, 192.
212. Memorandum, Close Air Support Responsiveness, 19 August 1969, K740.459-2, AFHRA; Sbrega, "Southeast Asia," 439.
213. Trest, SAC Operations SE Asia, 7–8, K717.0412-97; HQ USMACV Command History, 1966, 397, 2nd Lieutenant Robert L. Rhame, Sebron M. Haley, Arc Light Effectiveness Evaluation, 30 October 1967, K143.5072-22, Vol. 4, AFHRA.
214. Message from COMUSMACV, 120308Z, August 1966, K740.1623, 29 August 1966; HQ USMACV Command History, 1965, 197, Gillem, Corona Harvest on Arc Light, 130–31, K520.041-1, April 1968–December 1969; Warfel, History of 4258th Strategic Wing, December 1968, Vol. 1, 17–18, K-WG-4258-HI; Trest, SAC Operations SE Asia, 19, K717.0412-97, AFHRA.
215. Andrade, *Trial by Fire*, 477.
216. Air Effectiveness Trends during the Southwest Monsoon 1967, K740.04-18, AFHRA.
217. History of the Pacific Air Forces, 1966, 97, K717.01, Vol. 1, Part 2, AFHRA.
218. History of Pacific Air Forces, 1 July 1969–30 June 1970, 136, K717.01, FY 1970, Vol. 1, Part 1, AFHRA.

219. Schlight, *The Years of the Offensive, 1965–1968*, 271; The Single Management Issue, no date, 14, Operations of U.S. Marine Forces Vietnam, December 1967 and 1967 Summary, Davis Oral History Transcript, 34, HDMCU.
220. Nelson, Close Air Support, 1972, 81–83, K717.601-8; Liebchen, Kontum: Battle for the Central Highlands, 80, K717.0413-194, AFHRA.
221. CINCPAC, Measurement of Progress in Southeast Asia, December 31, 1968, HDMCU; Staff Sergeant Charles K. Wells Jr., and Sergeant Raymond A. Paoli, History of the 307th Strategic Wing, April–June 1971, Vol. 1, K-WG-307-HI, April–June 1971, Vol. 1, AFHRA.
222. Russell F. Weigley, *Eisenhower's Lieutenants: The Campaign of France and Germany, 1944–1945* (Bloomington: Indiana University Press, 1981), 136–37, 151–66; Millett, *The War for Korea*, 170, 445; Cosmas, *MACV: The Joint Command in the Years of Escalation, 1962–1967*, 231.
223. History of Pacific Air Forces, 1 July–31 December 1965, Vol. 1, Part 2, 83–84, K717.01; 1st Lieutenant Robert L. MacNaughton, First SAC B-52 Saturation Bombing in South Vietnam, 29 June 1965, K717.0414-53, AFHRA.
224. Message from Headquarters USAF to RJEDMH/CINCSAC, Personal for LeMay from Twining, 031815Z, November 1956, K416.03-19, 1965–1966, AFHRA.
225. General Thomas S. Power, SAC in the Limited War Role, 17 July 1964, K416.03-19, 1965–1966, AFHRA.
226. Trest, SAC Operations SE Asia, 19, 24–25, K717.0412-97; Gillem, Corona Harvest on Arc Light, 112, K520.041-1, April 1968–December 1969, AFHRA; HQ USMACV Command History, 1967, 404.
227. Willbanks, *The Battle of An Loc*, 82–83; Shaw, *Cambodian Campaign*, 141–42; Sbrega, "Southeast Asia," 446; History of Pacific Air Forces, 1 July–31 December 1965, Vol. 1, Part 2, 83, K717.01, AFHRA.
228. Message from AFFSO 2 AD to AFFSO PACAF, 210301Z, May 1965, K740.312-4, December 1964–January 1965, Vol. 3, AFHRA; Cosmas, *The Joint Chiefs of Staff, 1960–1968, Part 2*, 298; 1st Lieutenant Robert L. MacNaughton, First SAC B-52 Saturation Bombing in South Vietnam, 29 June 1965, K717.0414-53, 29 June 1965, AFHRA; Telegram from the Commander, Military Assistance Command, Vietnam (Westmoreland) to the Chairman of the Joint Chiefs of Staff (Wheeler), June 24, 1965, *FRUS 1964–1968, III*, 42.
229. MacNaughton, First SAC B-52 Saturation Bombing, 29 June 1965, K717.0414-53; History of Pacific Air Forces, 1 July–31 December 1965, Vol. 1, Part 2, 83–84, K717.01, AFHRA.
230. Telegram from the White House to the Embassy in the United Kingdom, June 16, 1965, *FRUS 1964–1968, III*, 11–12; Maxwell Taylor, Telegram from the Embassy in Vietnam to the Department of State, June 22, 1965, *FRUS 1964–1968, III*, 35; Cosmas, *The Joint Chiefs of Staff, 1960–1968, Part 2*, 346.
231. Trest, SAC Operations SE Asia, 3, K717.0412-97, AFHRA.
232. Ibid., 13.
233. Ibid., 15.
234. Message from COMUSMACV to RUHKA/CINCPAC, B-52 Strikes, 120308Z, August 1966, K740.1623, 29 August 1966, AFHRA.
235. Message from CINCPACAF, Westmoreland Meeting, 120341Z, August 1966, K717.1623, AFHRA.
236. Message from COMUSMACV, 120308Z, August 1966, K740.1623, 29 August 1966, AFHRA.
237. Telegram from the Commander, Military Assistance Command, Vietnam (Westmoreland) to the Commander in Chief, Pacific (Sharp), June 4, 1966, *FRUS 1964–1968, XXVIII*, 465–66; Telegram from the Commander, Military Assistance Command, Vietnam (Westmoreland) to the Commander in Chief, Pacific (Sharp), July 13, 1966, *FRUS 1964–1968, XXVIII*, 477.

238. History of 4258th Strategic Wing, April–May 1967, 44, 54, K-WG-4258-HI, Vol. 1; PACAF DI, Effects of Air Operations Southeast Asia, May 1967, 89, K717.6092, AFHRA.
239. Message from General Abrams to Lieutenant General Rosson CG III MAF, 2702300Z, July 1968, found online at The Vietnam Center & Sam Johnson Vietnam Archive, Texas Tech University, http://vietnam.ttu.edu; Trest, SAC Operations SE Asia, 14, K717.0412-97, AFHRA.
240. Message from SAC to CSAF/AFXDC/RUEFHQA, 181441Z, October 1968, K416.1623, 18 October 1968; Trest, SAC Operations SE Asia, 111–13, K717.0412-97; Pacific Command History, 1969, Vol. 3, 122, K712.01, Vol. 3, redacted, 1969, AFHRA. McCain replaced Admiral Sharp as the commander of Pacific Command in July 1968.
241. Sergeant David J. Hitchcock, History of 4258th Strategic Wing, July 1968, Vol. 1, 17–18, K-WG-4258-HI, AFHRA.
242. General William W. Momyer to General Bruce K. Holloway, 7 June 1968, K416.03-19, 1965–1966, AFHRA.
243. History of the Pacific Air Forces, 1966, 91, K717.01, Vol. 1, Part 2; Nelson, Close Air Support, 1972, 58, K717.601-8, AFHRA.
244. Gammons, History of 4258th Strategic Wing, September 1967, Vol. 1, 55, and Gammons, History of 4258th Strategic Wing, January 1968, Vol. 1, 27, K-WG-4258-HI, 1967; Warfel, History 4258th Strategic Wing, September 1968, 19–20, K-WG-4258-HI, Vol. 1; Trest, SAC Operations SE Asia, 25, K717.0412-97, AFHRA.
245. MacNaughton, First SAC B-52 Saturation Bombing, 29 June 1965, K717.0414-53; Message from COMUSMACV, 120308Z, August 1966, K740.1623, 29 August 1966; Trest, SAC Operations SE Asia, 26, K717.0412-97; Rhame and Haley, Arc Light Effectiveness Evaluation, 30 October 1967, K143.5072-22; Message from 7AF to RUHLKSP/PACAF CC, Report of 10 March B-52 strikes in Steel Tiger/ Laos, 111422Z, March 1967, K143.5072-70, AFHRA.
246. Staff Sergeant Stephen L. Y. Gammons, History of 4258th Strategic Wing, August 1967, Vol. 1, 35–36, K-WG-4258-HI, 1967; Liebchen, Kontum: Battle for the Central Highlands, 57, 61, K717.0413-194, AFHRA.
247. Trest, SAC Operations SE Asia, 31–32, K717.0412-97, AFHRA.
248. Message from COMUSMACV, 120308Z, August 1966, K740.1623, 29 August 1966, AFHRA.
249. Message from General Abrams to Lieutenant General Rosson, July 1968; Trest, SAC Operations SE Asia, 36, K717.0412-97, AFHRA; Telegram from Commander, Military Assistance Command, Vietnam (Westmoreland) to the Commander in Chief, Pacific (Sharp), September 16, 1966, 0518Z, *FRUS 1964–1968, XXVIII*, 493; Telegram from the Commander, Military Assistance Command, Vietnam (Westmoreland) to the Commander in Chief, Pacific (Sharp), September 16, 1966, 0519Z, *FRUS 1964–1968, XXVIII*, 497.
250. Brigadier General John K. Boles, Memorandum for Record, Bombing Mission from USS *Coral Sea*, 2 September 1965, K740.5492-2, 2 September 1965, AFHRA. Boles was the director of the Joint Research and Test Activity. He later commanded the 1st Armored Division. Jack S. Ballard, *Development and Employment of Fixed-Wing Gunships, 1962–1972* (Washington, DC: Office of Air Force History, United States Air Force, 1982), 221.
251. HQ USMACV Command History, 1966, 400.
252. History of 4258th Strategic Wing, April–May 1967, 42–43, 38–39, K-WG-4258-HI, Vol. 1, AFHRA.
253. Ibid., 40–41.
254. History 460th TRW, 1 July 1968–30 September 1968, K-WG-460-HI July–September 1968 Vol. 1, AFHRA; Graham A. Cosmas, *United States Army in Vietnam. MACV: The Joint Command in the Years of Withdrawal, 1968–1973* (Washington, DC: Center of Military History, United States Army, 2007), 188.

255. History of 4258th Strategic Wing, April–May 1967, 47–56, K-WG-4258-HI, Vol. 1, AFHRA.
256. Triantafellu from Keegan; Compass Haste, 260855Z, February 1968, K740.626-4; History of 4258th Strategic Wing, April–May 1967, 38–66, K-WG-4258-HI, Vol. 1, AFHRA; Summary of Interagency Responses to NSSM 1, March 22, 1969, *FRUS 1969–1976, VI*, 149, 151.
257. Wheeler, Memorandum for the President, 19 July 1968, K143.054-3 Vol. 7, 1969–1975, AFHRA; Message from CG III MAF to COMUSMACV, Visit of COMUSMACV to III MAF on 11 August 1969, 120025Z, August 1969, Message from LTG Zais CG XXIV Corps to LTG Nickerson CG III MAF, Visit of COMUSMACV to 3d Mar Div on 11 August 1969, 112343Z, August 1969, found online at The Vietnam Center & Sam Johnson Vietnam Archive, Texas Tech University, http://vietnam.ttu.edu.
258. Trest, SAC Operations SE Asia, 27, K717.0412-97, AFHRA.
259. Gammons, History of 4258th Strategic Wing, December 1967, 31–32, K-WG-4258-HI. See also Trapolino and Otis, History of the 307th Strategic Wing, April 1970, K-WG-307-HI, AFHRA.
260. Airman First Class Michael D. Clapsaddle, History of 91st Bombardment Wing (Heavy), July–September 1966, 22–48; quote from p. 26, K-WG-91-HI, July–September 1966, Vol. 1. See also Donald R. Burgin, History of 91st Bombardment Wing (Heavy) December 1966–January 1967, 13, K-WG-91-HI, December 1966–January 1967, Vol. 1, AFHRA.
261. Major Schulze, Effectiveness of B-52 Strikes, 22 April 1966, K717.151-11, 25–26 Apr 1966; Burgin, History 91st Bombardment Wing December 1966–January 1967, 26, K-WG-91-HI; Sergeant Joseph Taylor, History of the 306th Bombardment Wing (Heavy), March 1967, Vol. 1, 54, K-WG-306-HI, Vol. 1, AFHRA.
262. PACAF DI, Effects of Air Operations in Southeast Asia, 5 July 1965, 11, PACAF DI, Effects of Air Operations in Southeast Asia, 14 October 1965, 16–18, and Effects of Air Operations in Southeast Asia, 28 October 1965, 13–14, K717.6092, AFHRA; Operations of the III Marine Amphibious Force, Vietnam, December 1965, HDMCU.
263. Gammons, History of 4258th Strategic Wing, October–November 1967, Vol. 1, 61, K-WG-4258-HI, 1967, AFHRA.
264. 2nd Lieutenant Robert L. Rhame, Sebron M. Haley, Arc Light Effectiveness Evaluation, 30 October 1967, K143.5072-22, September–October 1967, Vol. 4; PACAF DI, Summary of Effects of Air Operations Southeast Asia, 1965, 8, K717.6092, AFHRA; HQ USMACV Command History, 1966, 395.
265. Lavelle, Analysis of Air Warfare in Southeast Asia, 6 April 1966, I-B-2, K143.505-13, AFHRA.
266. Colonel Dale A. Bozman, Corona Harvest Arc Light Questionnaire, 14 January 1971, K712.03-79, AFHRA.
267. Wells and Paoli, History of the 307th Strategic Wing, April–June 1971, K-WG-307-HI, AFHRA.
268. Staff Sergeant Joseph R. Quinn and Sergeant Tyrone K. Yoshida, History of 307th Strategic Wing, July–September 1971, Vol. 1. Wells and Paoli, History of 307th Strategic Wing, January–March 1971, K-WG-307-HI, AFHRA.
269. Eighth Air Force Activity Input to Corona Harvest Phase V, 1 July 1971–30 June 1972, K520.041-2, AFHRA.
270. Bonetti, et al., The War in Vietnam, July–December 1967, 43, K717.0414-17, AFHRA.
271. History of 4258th Strategic Wing, April–May 1967, 43, K-WG-4258-HI, Vol. 1, AFHRA.
272. Gammons, History of 4258th Strategic Wing, December 1967, 30–38, K-WG-4258-HI, AFHRA.
273. Message from COMUSMACV to RULKJSC/JCS, Commanders' Estimates of Arc Light Effectiveness, 190256Z, May 1970, K-WG-307-HI, May 1970, AFHRA; Editorial Note on an August 12 Meeting between Clark Clifford and the Office of the Secretary of Defense Staff, *FRUS 1964–1968, VI*, 951.
274. HQ USAF, Chronology on Effectiveness of Air Power in RVN, 11, 15, K143.042-9, AFHRA.
275. Major General W. J. Crumm, Message from 3rd Air Division to 2AF, 8AF, 15AF, Outstanding

Support of Operation Cedar Falls, 1 February 1967, K-WG-306-HI, January 1967, Vol. 1; HQ USAF, Chronology on Effectiveness of Air Power in RVN, 24, K143.042-9, AFHRA.
276. Notes of Meeting, November 21, 1967, *FRUS 1964–1968, V*, 1055; Colonel Edward Ratkovich, Asst. CoS, Intelligence, HQ USAF, The Selection of B-52 Targets in Southeast Asia, September 9, 1966, K143.5022-22, September–October 1967, Vol. 4, AFHRA.
277. Message from 2 AD to PACAF, 210301Z, May 1965, K740.312-4 December 1964–January 1965, Vol. 3, AFHRA.
278. Rhame and Haley, Arc Light Effectiveness Evaluation, 30 October 1967, K143.5072-22, AFHRA.
279. Melyan and Bonetti, The War in Vietnam, 140, K717.0414-75, AFHRA.
280. Van Staaveren, *Interdiction in Southern Laos*, 191.
281. Message from 7AF to RUHLKM/CINCPACAF, Ref JCS 9468, 291047Z, August 1966, K740.1623, 29 August 1966, AFHRA.
282. Melvin A. Porter, Operation Thor (HQ PACAF: Directorate of Operations Analysis, CHECO/Corona Harvest Division, 1969), 15, 19, 21, K717.0413-48; Overton, Rolling Thunder: January 1967–November 1968, 41, K717.0414-12; Trest, SAC Operations SE Asia, 30–31, K717.0412-97, AFHRA; Message from CG III MAF to COMUSMACV, Evaluation of Thor, 212932Z, October 1968, found online at The Vietnam Center & Sam Johnson Vietnam Archive, Texas Tech University, http://vietnam.ttu.edu.
283. Message from COMUSMACV to JCS, Bomb Damage Assessment, 240744Z, March 1967, and COMUSMACV to JCS, Bomb Damage Assessment, 250333Z, March 1967, K740.1622-3, 24 March–17 October 1967, AFHRA.
284. Message from COMUSMACV to JCS, Bomb Damage Assessment, 190214Z, September 1967; Message from COMUSMACV to JCS, Bomb Damage Assessment, 170951Z, September 1967; Message from COMUSMACV to JCS, Bomb Damage Assessment, 171030Z, September 1967; Message from COMUSMACV to JCS, Bomb Damage Assessment, 190206Z, September 1967; Message from COMUSMACV to JCS, Bomb Damage Assessment, 171215Z, October 1967, K740.1622-3, 24 March–17 October 1967, AFHRA.
285. Message from COMUSMACV to JCS, Bomb Damage Assessment, 022315Z, November 1967, K740.1622-3, 24 March–17 October 1967, AFHRA.
286. Message from COMUSMACV to JCS, Arc Light Strike Results 1086, 311108Z, March 1967, K740.1622-3, 24 March–17 October 1967, AFHRA.
287. Message from COMUSMACV to JCS, Bomb Damage Assessment, 052007Z, April 1967, K740.1622-3, 24 March–17 October 1967, AFHRA.
288. Message from COMUSMACV to JCS, Arc Light Strike Results 1123, 082035Z, April 1967, K740.1622-3, 24 March–17 October 1967, AFHRA.
289. MACV Command History 1968, Vol. 1, 423, Captain Robert C. Oliver, A Study: Military Intelligence Required for Initial Operation of Air Units, No date, written during or soon after 1938, File 248.501-25, AFHRA; J Kreis, *Piercing the Fog*, 1–2; Phillip S. Meilinger, *Airwar: Theory and Practice* (Portland, OR: Frank Cass, 2003), 4.
290. Airman First Class Joseph Taylor, History of the 306th Bombardment Wing (Heavy), January 1967, Vol. 1, 17-20, K-WG-306-HI, Vol. 1, AFHRA.
291. Message from 7 AF to CINCPACAF, Evaluation of CBU, 230420Z, July 1966, K717.312, AFHRA.
292. SAC Brasso Report on Arc Light Missions, prepared by SAC DITW, February 5, 1967, cited in History of the 306th Bombardment Wing (Heavy), January 1967, Vol. 1, 15, K-WG-306-HI, Vol. 1, AFHRA.
293. Taylor, History of the 306th Bombardment Wing, January 1967, Vol. 1, 17–20, K-WG-306-HI, AFHRA.

294. MACV Command History 1968, Vol. 1, 425.
295. Gammons, History of 4258th Strategic Wing, October–November 1967, Vol. 1, 57, K-WG-4258-HI; Folkman, Air Support in Quang Ngai Province, 37, K717.0413-142; Gillem, Corona Harvest on Arc Light, 103, K520.041-1, April 1968–December 1969, AFHRA; Memorandum from the Ambassador to Laos (Sullivan) to Assistant Secretary of State for East Asian and Pacific Affairs (Bundy), May 1, 1967, *FRUS 1964–1968, XXVIII*, 572.
296. *FRUS 1964–1968, XXVIII*, 572; Message from CMC to RUHHFMA/CG FMFPAC, 022005Z, November 1967, and Message from CG FMFPCA to RUCIHOA/CMC, 060312Z, November 1967, found online at The Vietnam Center & Sam Johnson Vietnam Archive, Texas Tech University, http://vietnam.ttu.edu.
297. HQ USMACV Command History, 1967, 406; Notes of Meeting, January 28, 1966, *FRUS, 1964–1968, IV*, 177; HQ USAF, Chronology on Effectiveness of Air Power in RVN, 19, 24–25, 41, K143.042-9; Wells and Paoli, History of the 307th Strategic Wing, October–December 1970, Vol. 1, K-WG-307-HI; HQ USMACV Command History, 1966, 400, SAC Brasso Report on Arc Light Missions, prepared by SAC DITW, February 5, 1967, AFHRA; Godfrey, 9th Marines After Action Report, April 8, 1969, HDMCU.
298. History of Pacific Air Forces, 1 July–31 December 1965, Vol. 1, Part 2, 31, K717.01, AFHRA; HQ USMACV Command History, 1966, 396, Message from General Abrams to Lieutenant General Cushman, 011510Z, March 1969, found online at The Vietnam Center & Sam Johnson Vietnam Archive, Texas Tech University, http://vietnam.ttu.edu; Transcript of a Telephone Conversation between President Nixon and the President's Assistant for National Security Affairs (Kissinger), August 11, 1972, *FRUS 1969–1976, VIII*, 824.
299. Message from Major General Tarpley to Gen Abrams, TAOR Assessment, 020200Z, June 1972, Vogt Papers, General Vogt's Read File June 1972, AFHSD.
300. Melyan and Bonetti, The War in Vietnam, 139, K717.0414-75, AFHRA.
301. Conversation between President Nixon and the President's Deputy Assistant for National Security Affairs (Haig), April 20, 1972, *FRUS 1969–1976, VIII*, 303.
302. Bozman, Corona Harvest Arc Light Questionnaire, 14 January 1971, K712.03-79, AFHRA.
303. Schulze, Effectiveness of B-52 Strikes, 22 April 1966, K717.151-11, 25–26 April 1966, AFHRA.
304. Message from COMUSMACV to JCS, Arc Light Results 1087, 31115Z, March 1967, K740.1622-3; Wells and Paoli, History of the 307th Strategic Wing, October–December 1970, K-WG-307-HI; Message from COMUSMACV to JCS, Arc Light Results 1120, 120520Z, April 1967, K740.1622-3, 31, AFHRA.
305. Bonetti, The War in Vietnam: January–June 1967, 41, K717.0414-17; Message from COMUSMACV to JCS, Arc Light Results 1078, 311111Z, March 1967, K740.1622-3; Message from COMUSMACV to JCS, Arc Light Strike Results 1098, 021027Z, April 1967, K740.1622-3; Message from COMUSMACV to JCS, Arc Light Results 1184, 030747Z, May 1967, K740.1622-3; Trapolino and Otis, History of the 307th Strategic Wing, April 1970, K-WG-307-HI, AFHRA.
306. Message from COMUSMACV to JCS, Arc Light Results 1115, 120728Z, April 1967, K740.1622-3, 31 March–16 October 1967, AFHRA.
307. Taylor, History of the 306th Bombardment Wing (Heavy), January 1967, 33, K-WG-306-HI, AFHRA; Wilkins, *Grab Their Belts to Fight Them*, 189, 200; Message from CG III MAF to CG FMFPAC, 010806Z, September 1969, found online at The Vietnam Center & Sam Johnson Vietnam Archive, Texas Tech University, http://vietnam.ttu.edu; Message from John P. Vann to General Abrams, Daily Commander's Evaluation, 200225Z, May 1972, Vogt Papers, Read File May 1972, AFHSD.
308. Taylor, History of the 306th Bombardment Wing (Heavy), January 1967, 37, K-WG-306-HI, AFHRA.

309. Gammons, History of 4258th Strategic Wing, October–November 1967, Vol. 1, 57, K-WG-4258-HI; Taylor, History of the 306th Bombardment Wing, January 1967, 42, K-WG-306-HI, AFHRA.
310. History of the 306th Bombardment Wing (Heavy), January 1967, Vol. 1, K-WG-306-HI, January 1967, Vol. 1 46, AFHRA.
311. Taylor, History of the 306th Bombardment Wing, February 1967, 12, K-WG-306-HI, AFHRA.
312. Ibid., 18.
313. Ibid., 19.
314. Ibid., 32.
315. Ibid., 33.
316. Taylor, History of the 306th Bombardment Wing, March 1967, Vol. 1, 33–34, K-WG-306-HI, AFHRA.
317. Effects of Air Operations Southeast Asia, March 1967, 61, 62, K717.6092, AFHRA.
318. Staff Sergeant Stephen L. Y. Gammons, History of 4258th Strategic Wing, October–November 1967, Vol. 1, 56, K-WG-4258-HI, AFHRA.
319. PACAF DI, Effects of Air Operations in Southeast Asia, 28 October 1965, 18, K717.6092; Gammons, History of 4258th Strategic Wing, September 1967, Vol. 1, 51, K-WG-4258-HI; Gammons, September 1967, 49-50, Operation Atherton, AFHRA.
320. Gammons, History of 4258th Strategic Wing, October–November 1967, Vol. 1, 60, and Gammons, History 4258th Strategic Wing, February–March 1968, Vol. 1, 60–61, 63, K-WG-4258-HI, 1967, AFHRA.
321. Staff Sergeant Arthur C. Warfel, History 4258th Strategic Wing, September 1968, 17–19, K-WG-4258-HI, Vol. 1, Warfel reported KBA; Gammons did not, AFHRA.
322. Warfel, History of 4258th Strategic Wing, December 1968, Vol. 1, 25, K-WG-4258-HI, AFHRA.
323. Assessment of Air Operations, 7 February 1965 thru 19 July 1967, 28, K740.04-20, AFHRA.
324. Ibid., 52, 53.
325. Message from CINCPACAF to CSAF, Westmoreland Meeting at CINCPAC, 11 August, 120342Z, August 1966, K717.1623, March–December 1966, AFHRA.
326. Earle G. Wheeler, CJCS, Memorandum for the President, Military Situation in South Vietnam, 19 July 1968, K143.054-3, Vol. 7, 1969–1975, AFHRA.
327. Taylor, History of the 306th Bombardment Wing, March 1967, Vol. 1, 32–33, and Taylor, History of the 306th Bombardment Wing, January 1967, Vol. 1, 54, K-WG-306-HI, AFHRA.
328. Memorandum from the President's Special Assistant (Komer) to President Johnson, January 23, 1967, *FRUS 1964–1968, V*, 56.
329. Cosmas, *The Joint Chiefs of Staff, 1960–1968, Part 2*, 470–71.
330. Memorandum from the President's Special Counsel (McPherson) to President Johnson, June 13, 1967, *FRUS 1964–1968, V*, 498, 499; Telegram from the Embassy in Vietnam to the Department of State, October 19, 1968, *FRUS, 1964–1968, VII*, 256.
331. Message from Lieutenant General Walt to Lieutenant General Krulak, October 7, 1966, Krulak Papers, COLL/3064, Box 1, Folder 4, Archives Branch, HDMCU; Fleet Marine Force, Pacific, Operations of the U.S. Marine Forces, Vietnam, January 1968, HDMCU; Message from CG III MAF to Commandant of the Marine Corps, 110914Z, March 1968, found online at The Vietnam Center & Sam Johnson Vietnam Archive, Texas Tech University, http://vietnam.ttu.edu.
332. Message from COMUSMACV to RUMSBJ/CDR 7AF Saigon, RUMMWAA/CG III MAF Da Nang, 220448Z, January 1968, found online at The Vietnam Center & Sam Johnson Vietnam Archive, Texas Tech University, http://vietnam.ttu.edu.
333. Trest, Khe Sanh, 23, K717.0413-35, AFHRA.
334. Telegram from the Commander of the Military Assistance Command, Vietnam (Westmoreland)

to the Commander in Chief, Pacific Forces (Sharp) and the Chairman of the Joint Chiefs of Staff (Wheeler), January 30, 1968, *FRUS 1964–1968, VI*, 77; Woods, *LBJ*, 823; Gardner, *Pay Any Price*, 417.
335. Trest, Khe Sanh, 10, K717.0413-35, AFHRA.
336. Memorandum from the Chairman of the Joint Chiefs of Staff (Wheeler) to Secretary of Defense McNamara, January 13, 1968, *FRUS 1964–1968, VI*, 31; Telegram from the White House Situation Room to President Johnson, March 3, 1968, *FRUS 1964–1968, VI*, 310; Trest, Khe Sanh, 66, 69, K717.0413-35; Bonetti, et al., The War in Vietnam, July–December 1967, 52, K717.0414-17, AFHRA; Gardner, *Pay Any Price*, 417.
337. Willbanks, *The Tet Offensive: A Concise History*, 62; Lanigan, After Action Report, June 9, 1967, Fleet Marine Force, Pacific, Operations of the U.S. Marine Forces, Vietnam, January 1968, HDMCU; Memorandum from the Joint Chiefs of Staff to President Johnson, January 29, 1968, *FRUS 1964–1968, V*, 70; Notes of the President's Meeting with the Senior Foreign Affairs Advisory Council, February 10, 1968, *FRUS 1964–1968, VI*, 169.
338. Trest, Khe Sanh, 71, K717.0413-35, AFHRA.
339. Gammons, History of 4258th Strategic Wing, February–March 1968, Vol. 1, 60–61, 63, K-WG-4258-HI, 1967, AFHRA.
340. Memorandum from Wheeler to President Johnson, February 3, 1968, *FRUS 1964–1968, VI*, 118; Loye Jr., et al., Lam Son 719, 30 January–24 March 1971, 7, K717.0413-165, AFHRA; MACV Command History 1972, K-14.
341. Message from COMUSMACV to RUMSAL/CDR 7th Air Force, Air Support of Khe Sanh, 131437Z, February 1968; Message from COMUSMACV to CDR 7AF, CG III MAF, Operation Niagara Reporting, 200200Z, February 1968 and Message from COMUSMACV to III MAF, info 7AF, 220420Z, February 1968, found online at The Vietnam Center & Sam Johnson Vietnam Archive, Texas Tech University, http://vietnam.ttu.edu.
342. Message from COMUSMACV to Zen/Depcomusmacv FWD, RUMSAK/CG III MAF Da Nang, RUMSAL/CDR 7AF Saigon, Air Strikes Khe Sanh Area, 290415Z, February 1968, found online at The Vietnam Center & Sam Johnson Vietnam Archive, Texas Tech University, http://vietnam.ttu.edu; Stanton, *Rise and Fall of an American Army*, 256.
343. Message from COMUSMACV, Air Strikes Khe Sanh Area, 290415Z, February 1968; Brush, "The Battle of Khe Sanh," in *The Tet Offensive*, 200; Trest, Khe Sanh, 89, K717.0413-35; Bozman, Corona Harvest Arc Light Questionnaire, 14 January 1971, K712.03-79, AFHRA; Fleet Marine Force, Pacific, Operations of U.S. Marine Forces Vietnam February 1968, 24, Vietnam, Box 13, Folder 5, Archives Branch, HDMCU.
344. History 8th Tactical Fighter Wing, 1 January–31 March 1968, 33, K-WG-8-HI, AFHRA.
345. Trest, Khe Sanh, 91–93, K717.0413-35, AFHRA; Message from CG III MAF to Two Six Marines Exclusive for Colonel Lownds from Lieutenant General Cushman, 111412Z, March 1968, found online at The Vietnam Center & Sam Johnson Vietnam Archive, Texas Tech University, http://vietnam.ttu.edu.
346. Trest, Khe Sanh, 98; Message from CG III MAF to CG Prov Corps V, 270934Z, March 1968, and Message from CG III MAF to CG Prov Corps, 261604Z, March 1968, found online at The Vietnam Center & Sam Johnson Vietnam Archive, Texas Tech University, http://vietnam.ttu.edu.
347. Message from CG III MAF to Two Six Marines.
348. Sams, et al., The Air War in Vietnam: 1968–1969, 29, K717.0413-143, AFHRA. See also Townsend Hoopes, *The Limits of Intervention: How Vietnam Policy Was Made and Reversed during the Johnson Administration* (New York: W. W. Norton, 1969), 214.
349. Message from CG III MAF to COMUSMACV, Air Support Khe Sanh, 080650Z, March 1968, found online at The Vietnam Center & Sam Johnson Vietnam Archive, Texas Tech University,

http://vietnam.ttu.edu; Willbanks, *The Tet Offensive*, 64.

350. Trest, SAC Operations SE Asia, 34–45, K717.0412-97; CINCPAC Command History 1968, Vol. 3, 293, K712. 01, 1968, Vol. 3; Bonetti, et al., The War in Vietnam, July–December 1967, 25–26, K717.0414-17, AFHRA.

351. Message from CG III MAF to CDR Seventh AF, 080752, April 1968 found online at The Vietnam Center & Sam Johnson Vietnam Archive, Texas Tech University, http://vietnam.ttu.edu; Woods, *LBJ*, 824–25; Guan, *The Vietnam War from the Other Side*, 126.

352. James S. Robbins, *This Time We Win: Revisiting the Tet Offensive* (New York: Encounter Books, 2010), 179–80. Lien-Hang T. Nguyen observes that "the majority of Vietnamese publications aver that the communist offensive achieved its primary aim of crippling the political will of the United States in a crucial election year." Nguyen, *Hanoi's War*, 112; Alexander Kendrick, *The Wound Within: America in the Vietnam Year, 1945–1974* (Boston and Toronto: Little, Brown, 1974), 248, 249; Prados, *Vietnam*, 240–43.

353. Herring, *LBJ and Vietnam*, 153.

354. Message from General Westmoreland and COMUSMACV to Lieutenant General Cushman CG III MAF et al., 041011Z, April 1968, found online at The Vietnam Center & Sam Johnson Vietnam Archive, Texas Tech University, http://vietnam.ttu.edu.

355. Lieutenant Colonel Charles Hope, HQ MACV J-2, Targets: October 1968–October 1969, K712.03-79, 5 March–1 September 1968, AFHRA; see also K712.03-76, AFHRA.

356. Gillem, Corona Harvest on Arc Light, 3–4, K520.041-1, April 1968–December 1969, AFHRA.

357. Ibid., 124–25.

358. J-3 Brief 205-68, HQ CINCPAC, of J3M 1540-68, 13 August 1968, Subj: USAF Arc Light Effectiveness Study, cited in CINCPAC Command History 1968, Vol. 3, 222–23, K712. 01, 1968, Vol. 3, AFHRA.

359. CAG-4, 18 Nov 68, cited in CINCPAC Command History 1968, Vol. 3, 223–24, K712. 01, 1968, Vol. 3, AFHRA.

360. Combat analysis group and strategic operation division, "Review and appraisal of arc light missions," CINCPAC Command History 1968, Vol. 3, 220–22, K712. 01, 1968, Vol. 3, AFHRA; Doughty, *Pyrrhic Victory*, 465–82.

361. Warfel, History of 4258th Strategic Wing, November 1968, Vol. 1, 22, K-WG-4258-HI, 1968, AFHRA.

362. Warfel, History 4258th Strategic Wing, September 1968, 35, K-WG-4258-HI, Vol.1, 1968, AFHRA.

363. Pacific Command History, 1969, Vol. 3, 120, 122, K712.01, Vol. 3, redacted, 1969, AFHRA; National Security Study Memorandum 74, September 17, 1969, *FRUS 1969–1976, VI*, 409.

364. Minutes of a Meeting of the Senior Review Group, Vietnam Military Assessment, May 24, 1971, *FRUS 1969–1976, VII*, 640; Staff Sergeant Charles K. Wells Jr., Sergeant James D. Otis, III, History of 307th Strategic Wing, June–September 1970, K-WG-307-HI, June–September 1970, Vol. 1, AFHRA.

365. See for example Arc Light Mission Summaries J-139T/112, 3 May 0208Z 1970; J-261T/254 12 May 0259Z 1970; J-352T/397 16 May 0301Z 1970; J-309T/381 18 May 0926Z 1970, Sergeants Carl J. Trapolino and James D. Otis, III, History of the 307th Strategic Wing, 1-31 May 1970, K-WG-307-HI, May 1970, AFHRA.

366. Memorandum from the President's Assistant for National Security Affairs (Kissinger) to President Nixon, April 16, 1970, *FRUS 1969–1970, VI*, 825–26; Editorial Note, *FRUS 1969–1970, VI*, 832; Conversation among President Nixon, the President's Assistant for National Security Affairs (Kissinger), and the Ambassador to South Vietnam (Bunker), February 3, 1972, *FRUS 1969–1976, VIII*, 71; Memorandum from President Nixon to the President's Assistant for National Security

Affairs (Kissinger), May 10, 1972, *FRUS 1969–1976, VIII*, 527.
367. Message from 7AF to Dep/Comdr 7/13 AF, Operational Guidance, 291155Z, July 1968, K-DIV-834-HI, Vol. 2, AFHRA.
368. Message from General Abrams to General Brown, et al., Special Guidance for General Officers Commanding, 010158Z, November 1968, found online at The Vietnam Center & Sam Johnson Vietnam Archive, Texas Tech University, http://vietnam.ttu.edu.
369. ODASD(SA) Regional Programs, Southeast Asia Analysis Report, June/July 1970, Vietnam Command Files, COLL/372, Box 17, File DOD SEA Analysis Report, June/July 70, NHHC.
370. Southeast Asia Analysis Report, June/July 1970, ODASD(SA) Regional Programs, Southeast Asia Analysis Report, June/July 1970, Vietnam Command Files, COLL/372, Box 17, File DOD SEA Analysis Report, June/July 70, NHHC.
371. Some comments by Steven Morillo at the 2018 Society for Military History Conference clarified some of the language I am using here, namely defining "strategically decisive" as altering the scope of what is possible.
372. Memorandum from the President's Assistant for National Security Affairs (Kissinger) to President Nixon, February 19, 1969, *FRUS 1969–1976, VI*, 68–69.
373. Henry Kissinger, *Ending the Vietnam War: A History of America's Involvement in and Extrication from the Vietnam War* (New York: Simon & Schuster, 2003), 57, 59.
374. Memorandum from Kissinger to President Nixon, February 19, 1969, *FRUS 1969–1976, VI*, 73; Melvin R. Laird, Message from Secretary of Defense Laird, February 25, 1969, *FRUS 1969–1976, VI*, 77–78.
375. Lewis Sorley, *A Better War: The Unexamined Victories and Final Tragedy of America's Last Years in Vietnam* (New York: Harcourt Brace, 1999), 101–2; Henry A. Kissinger, Memorandum for the President, Breakfast Plan, March 17, 1969, National Security Council, Vietnam Subject Files, Box 89, Nixon Library.
376. Kissinger, *Ending the Vietnam War*, 64; Henry Kissinger, Memorandum for the President, Breakfast Plan, March 16, 1969, National Security Council, Vietnam Subject Files, Box 89, Nixon Library; Kimball, *Nixon's Vietnam War*, 126.
377. Editorial Note, *FRUS 1969–1976, VI*, 124, 125; Memorandum from the President's Assistant for National Security Affairs (Kissinger) to President Nixon, *FRUS 1969–1976, VI*, 205; Shaw, *Cambodian Campaign*, 13; Kissinger, *Ending the Vietnam War*, 64; Nixon, *RN*, 381.
378. Charles E. Neu, *America's Lost War: Vietnam: 1945–1975* (Wheeling, IL: Harlan Davidson, 2005), 159.
379. Nalty, *Air War over South Vietnam*, 130–31. The 1973 DoD account referred to these procedures as "errors." Department of Defense Report on Selected Air and Ground Operations in Cambodia and Laos, September 10, 1973, 168.7122-16, 1974, AFHRA.
380. Kissinger, *Ending the Vietnam War*, 69.
381. Memorandum from the President's Assistant for National Security Affairs (Kissinger) to President Nixon, March 27, 1970, *FRUS 1969–1970, VI*, 741. H. R. Haldeman catalogued them as "a great success." H. R. Haldeman, introduction and afterword by Stephen E. Ambrose, *The Haldeman Diaries: Inside the Nixon White House* (New York: G. P. Putnam's Sons, 1994), 41.
382. Fred Emery, *Watergate: The Corruption of American Politics and the Fall of Richard Nixon* (New York: Times Books, 1994), 10.
383. Dale Van Atta, *With Honor: Melvin Laird in War, Peace, and Politics* (Madison: University of Wisconsin Press, 2008), 181.
384. Totaling 3,875 sorties, the Menu bombings continued through May 26, 1970. Webb, *History of the Joint Chiefs of Staff*, 137; Department of Defense Report on Selected Air and Ground Operations in Cambodia and Laos, September 10, 1973, 168.7122-16, 1974, AFHRA.

385. "U.S. Aides Oppose Raids in Cambodia," *New York Times,* March 26, 1969, 5.
386. Emery, *Watergate,* 9; Kissinger, *Ending the Vietnam War,* 66–68; "B-52 Raids Aim at Enemy Camps Near Cambodia," *New York Times,* April 10, 1969, 6; William Beecher, "Raids in Cambodia by U.S. Unprotested," *New York Times,* May 9, 1969, 1, 7; Schulzinger, *A Time for War,* 278.
387. Memorandum from the President's Assistant for National Security Affairs (Kissinger) to President Nixon, April 9, 1970, *FRUS 1969–1976, VI,* 802-03; Folkman and Caine, The Cambodian Campaign, 2–5, K717.0413-84, AFHRA.
388. Folkman and Caine, The Cambodian Campaign, 6, K717.0413-84, AFHRA; Telegram from the Staff Secretary of the National Security Council Staff Secretariat (Watts) to Winston Lord of the National Security Council Staff, April 20, 1970, *FRUS 1969–1970, VI,* 837.
389. Memorandum from the Acting Chairman of the Joint Chiefs of Staff (Westmoreland) to Secretary of Defense Laird, April 21, 1970, *FRUS 1969–1970, VI,* 845; Memorandum from President Nixon to his Assistant for National Security Affairs (Kissinger), April 22, 1970, *FRUS 1969–1970, VI,* 845; National Security Council Decision Memorandum 56, April 22, 1970, *FRUS 1969–1970, VI,* 851; Folkman and Caine, The Cambodian Campaign, 6, K717.0413-84, AFHRA.
390. Memorandum from the President's Assistant for National Security Affairs (Kissinger) to President Nixon, undated, *FRUS 1969–1976, VI,* 863; Folkman and Caine, The Cambodian Campaign 29 April–30 June 1970, 7, K717.0413-84, AFHRA; Nixon, *RN,* 451–52.
391. Folkman and Caine, The Cambodian Campaign, x, 18, 19, 23, K717.0413-84, AFHRA; Minutes of Washington Special Action Group Meeting, April 29, 1970, *FRUS 1969–1976, VI,* 912; Shaw, *Cambodian Campaign,* 76; Daddis, *No Sure Victory,* 210.
392. Folkman and Caine, The Cambodian Campaign, 9, K717.0413-84, AFHRA.
393. Ibid., 15, 17–18.
394. Directorate of Tactical Analysis, HQ Seventh AF, Air Interdiction in Southeast Asia, 15 April–15 June 1970 and August 1970, 108, 111, 113, K740.04-10, AFHRA.
395. Folkman and Caine, The Cambodian Campaign 29 April–30 June 1970, 33, K717.0413-84, AFHRA.
396. Seventh AF, Air Interdiction in Southeast Asia, April–June 1970, 115, 248, K740.04-10, AFHRA.
397. Shaw, *Cambodian Campaign,* 75; Ryan, Air Operations in Cambodia, May–June 1970, 39–40, K740.04-16, AFHRA.
398. Shaw, *Cambodian Campaign,* 25, 69, 142.
399. Message from 8AF to 307 Strategic Wing, For Commander from Gillem, 082323Z, June 1970, Trapolino and Otis, History of the 307th Strategic Wing, 1–31 May 1970, K-WG-307-HI, June 1970, AFHRA.
400. Footnote 5, *FRUS 1969–1976, VI,* 999; Memorandum from the President's Assistant for National Security Affairs (Kissinger) to President Nixon, May 25, 1970, *FRUS 1969–1976, VI,* 1004; Conversation with Lon Nol, Memorandum from the President's Assistant for National Security Affairs (Kissinger) to President Nixon, May 26, 1970, *FRUS 1969–1976, VI,* 1008.
401. Telegram from the Commander of the U.S. Military Assistance Command in Vietnam (Abrams) to the Chairman of the Joint Chiefs of Staff (Moorer), May 18, 1970, *FRUS 1969–1976, VI,* 984.
402. Memorandum of Conversation, May 31, 1970, *FRUS 1969–1976, VI,* 1018.
403. Memorandum from the President's Assistant for National Security Affairs (Kissinger) to President Nixon, May 19, 1970, *FRUS 1969–1976, VI,* 994; History of Pacific Air Forces, 1 July 1969–30 June 1970, 137–38, K717.01, FY 1970, Vol. 1, Part 1; Ryan, Air Operations in Cambodia, May–June 1970, 27, K740.04-16, AFHRA.
404. Memorandum from President Nixon to the Chairman of the Washington Special Actions Group (Kissinger), July 7, 1970, *FRUS 1969–1976, VI,* 1112.
405. Eds. David Goldman and Erin Mahan, gen. ed. Edward C. Keefer, *Foreign Relations of the United*

States, 1969–1976, Volume VII, Vietnam, July 1970–January 1972 (Washington, DC: United States Government Printing Office, 2010), 1 (hereafter referred to as *FRUS 1969–1976, VII*).

406. Memorandum from the President's Assistant for National Security Affairs (Kissinger) to President Nixon, May 19, 1970, *FRUS 1969–1976, VI*, 994; Memorandum from Richard Smyser of the Operations Staff of the National Security Council to the President's Assistant for National Security Affairs (Kissinger), June 8, 1970, *FRUS 1969–1976, VI*, 1040. Walters was the senior defense attaché to France. Kissinger, *Ending the Vietnam War*, 71.

407. Transcript of Telephone Conversation Between President Nixon, His Assistant for National Security Affairs (Kissinger), and the Chairman of the Senate Armed Services Committee (Stennis), April 24, 1970, *FRUS 1969–1976, VI*, 877.

408. Nixon, *RN*, 450.

409. Kimball, *Nixon's Vietnam War*, 205.

410. Howard Means, *67 Shots: Kent State and the End of American Innocence* (Philadelphia: DaCapo Press, 2016), 147–48.

411. Kendrick, *Wound Within*, 299–301.

412. Diary Entry by the Chairman of the Joint Chiefs of Staff (Moorer), February 12, 1971, *FRUS 1969–1976, VII*, 395; Prados, *Vietnam*, 412. See also Willbanks, *A Raid Too Far*. The source of the operation's name is contested. Lien-Hang Nguyen states that the term refers "to a famous Vietnamese battle in 1427 against the Chinese." Nguyen, *Hanoi's War*, 202. Phillip Davidson claims that the operation was "named after the village of Lam Son, the birthplace of Le Loi, a Vietnamese national hero of antiquity." Davidson, *Vietnam at War*, 637. The number came from the year 1971 and Highway 9. Willbanks, *A Raid Too Far*, 224.

413. Memorandum for the President's File, January 27, 1971, *FRUS 1969–1976, VII*, 321–22; Richard M. Nixon, *Public Papers of the Presidents of the United States, Richard Nixon: 1970: Containing the Public Messages, Speeches, and Statements of the President* (Ann Arbor: University of Michigan Library, 2005), 539.

414. Loye Jr., et al., Lam Son 719 30 January–24 March 1971, 13, 103, K717.0413-165, AFHRA; James H. Willbanks, *Abandoning Vietnam: How America Left and South Vietnam Lost Its War* (Lawrence: University Press of Kansas, 2004), 138.

415. Memorandum for the President's File, January 27, 1971, *FRUS 1969–1976, VII*, 327; Clay, Lam Son 719 Operations: Lessons Learned, K740.04-15; Loye Jr., et al., Lam Son 719 30 January–24 March 1971, 122, K717.0413-165, AFHRA.

416. Memorandum for the President's File by the President's Deputy Assistant for National Security Affairs (Haig), January 27, 1971, *FRUS 1969–1976, VII*, 329.

417. Prados, *Vietnam*, 406–7, 410, 416; Randolph, *Powerful and Brutal Weapons*, 14.

418. Clay, Lam Son 719 Operations: Lessons Learned, K740.04-15, AFHRA; Memorandum for the President's File, January 27, 1971, *FRUS 1969–1976, VII*, 327; Loye Jr., et al., Lam Son 719 30 January–24 March 1971, 27, K717.0413-165, AFHRA.

419. Wells and Paoli, History of 307th Strategic Wing, January–March 1971, K-WG-307-HI; Loye Jr., et al., Lam Son 719 30 January–24 March 1971, 9, 19, 43, 111, K717.0413-165, AFHRA.

420. William C. Momyer, Memorandum for David Packard, Deputy Secretary of Defense, Comments as Requested on the Close Air Support Summary Report to be Submitted to Congress, June 18, 1971, Section 9, p. 11/141, COLL/3746, Studies and Reports, Box 5, Folder 4. Archives Branch, HDMCU.

421. Loye Jr., et al., Lam Son 719 30 January–24 March 1971, 9, 75, 105, K717.0413-165, AFHRA; VA-52 Third Line Period Report, Fleet Aviation Commands Pre-1998, AR/229, VA-52, Box 130, File F10, NHHC; Willbanks, *A Raid Too Far*, 170; Transcript of a Telephone Conversation between President Nixon and the Chairman of the Joint Chiefs of Staff (Moorer), March 16, 1971,

FRUS 1969–1976, VII, 461.

422. Memorandum from the President's Assistant for National Security Affairs (Kissinger) to President Nixon, undated, *FRUS 1969–1976, VII*, 442. Probably March 2, 1971.
423. Conversation between President Nixon and his Assistant for National Security Affairs (Kissinger), February 18, 1971, *FRUS 1969–1976, VII*, 403; Memorandum from Kissinger to President Nixon, March 22, 1971, *FRUS 1969–1976, VII*, 489.
424. Minutes of a Meeting of the Washington Special Actions Group, March 23, 1971, *FRUS 1969–1976, VII*, 494; Memorandum from the President's Assistant for National Security Affairs (Kissinger) to President Nixon, Lam Son 719 Final Report, April 16, 1971, *FRUS 1969–1976, VII*, 552–53.
425. Backchannel Message from the President's Deputy Assistant for National Security Affairs (Haig) to the President's Assistant for National Security Affairs (Kissinger), March 19, 1971, *FRUS 1969–1976, VII*, 475–76; Memorandum from the President's Assistant for National Security Affairs (Kissinger) to President Nixon, March 22, 1971, *FRUS 1969–1976, VII*, 486; Moorer Reminiscences, III: 1228; Loye Jr., et al., Lam Son 719 30 January–24 March 1971, 84, K717.0413-165, AFHRA; Willbanks, *A Raid Too Far*, 171.
426. Loye Jr., et al., Lam Son 719 30 January–24 March 1971, 11, 82, 126; K717.0413-165, AFHRA; Randolph, *Powerful and Brutal Weapons*, 18–19; Prados, *Vietnam*, 415.
427. Seventh Air Force, Commando Hunt VII, 192, K740.04-14, November 1971–March 1972, AFHRA.
428. Ibid., 190.
429. Ibid., 58, 75.
430. Major William W. Lofgren, Air War in Northern Laos, 1 April–30 November 1971 (HQ PACAF: Directorate of Operations Analysis, CHECO/Corona Harvest Division, 1973), 65, 76, 88, K717.0413-65; Air Operations in Southeast Asia, 1972–1973, pp. V-21, V-22, K717.0423-23, Vol. 3, AFHRA.
431. Conversation among President Nixon, the President's Assistant for National Security Affairs (Kissinger), and the White House Chief of Staff (Haldeman), March 18, 1971, *FRUS 1969–1976, VII*, 475; Memorandum from the President's Assistant for National Security Affairs (Kissinger) to President Nixon, undated (circa March 1969), *FRUS 1969–1976, VI*, 155; Memorandum for the President's File by the President's Deputy Assistant for National Security Affairs (Haig), March 26, 1971, *FRUS 1969–1976, VII*, 510.
432. ODASD(SA) Regional Programs, Southeast Asia Analysis Report, August/October 1971, Vietnam Command Files, COLL/372, Box 18, File DOD SEA Analysis Report, August/October 71, NHHC.
433. Message from AFSSO, Sortie Requirements, 021120Z, August 1972, Vogt Papers, AFHSD; Air Operations in Southeast Asia, 1972–1973, pp. v-40, v-49, v-52, v-53, v-121, K717.0423-23, Vol. 3, AFHRA.
434. Evaluation Report for the NVN Offensive, April–August 1972, ii-3, K717.04-9; Porter, Linebacker First 120 Days, 12, K717.0414-42, 1973, AFHRA; Moorer Reminiscences, III: 1237; Cosmas, *The Joint Command in the Years of Withdrawal, 1968–1973*, 351; Nalty, *Air War over South Vietnam*, 329.
435. History of the Pacific Air Forces, July 1971–June 1972, Vol. 1, 83, K717.01; Seventh Air Force, Commando Hunt VII, 188–89, K740.04-14, November 1971–March 1972, AFHRA.
436. Willbanks, *Abandoning Vietnam*, 126; Ringenbach, Airlift to Besieged Areas, xiii, K717.0413-210, AFHRA; Ang Cheng Guan, *Ending the Vietnam War: The Vietnamese Communists' Perspective* (New York: Routledge Curzon, 2004), 93. Ringenbach recorded the campaign's name as Tri-Thien.

437. Liebchen, Kontum: Battle for the Central Highlands, 19–21, K717.0413-194, AFHRA.
438. Pribbenow, trans., *Victory in Vietnam*, 283; Guan, *Ending the Vietnam War*, 90.
439. Nguyen, *Hanoi's War*, 227; Larry Berman, *No Peace, No Honor: Nixon, Kissinger, and Betrayal in Vietnam* (New York: Free Press, 2001), 123–28.
440. Webb and Poole, *Joint Chiefs of Staff, 1971–1973*, 154; Nelson, Close Air Support, 12, K717.601-8, AFHRA; Lt. Col. Philip R. Harrison, Impact of Darkness and Weather on Air Operations in SEA (Headquarters PACAF: Directorate, Tactical Evaluation, CHECO Division, 1969), 10, K717.0413-97, AFHRA.
441. Telephone Conversation between President Nixon and the Chairman of the Joint Chiefs of Staff (Moorer), April 4, 1972, *FRUS 1969–1976, VIII*, 187, 188; Conversation between President Nixon and the President's Assistant for National Security Affairs (Kissinger), April 4, 1972, *FRUS 1969–1976, VIII*, 199, 200; Haldeman, *The Haldeman Diaries*, 435.
442. CINCPAC Command History 1972, Vol. 1, 149, K712.01, 1972, Vol. 1, AFHRA.
443. Backchannel Message from the Ambassador to Vietnam (Bunker) to the President's Assistant for National Security Affairs (Kissinger), April 5, 1971, *FRUS 1969–1976, VII*, 529; Andrade, *Trial by Fire*, 404.
444. Minutes of a Washington Special Actions Group Meeting, April 3, 1972, *FRUS 1969–1976, VIII*, 172. 182; Webb and Poole, *Joint Chiefs of Staff, 1971–1973*, 156; Summary Air Operations Southeast Asia, April 1972, 2–6, K717.3063, AFHRA; Randolph, *Powerful and Brutal Weapons*, 144–45.
445. Conversation between Nixon and Kissinger, April 4, 1972, *FRUS 1969–1976, VIII*, 210.
446. Minutes of Washington Special Actions Group Meeting, May 24, 1972, ed. Daniel J. Lawler, gen. ed. Edward C. Keefer, *Foreign Relations of the United States, 1969–1976, Volume XX, Southeast Asia, 1969–1972* (Washington, DC: United States Government Printing Office, 2006), 361.
447. Air Warfare Annex, Commander Seventh Fleet Command History 1972, 26 September 1973, NHHC. The carriers were the USS *Midway, Constellation, Kitty Hawk, Hancock, Saratoga*, and *Coral Sea*. Marines sent five fighter-bomber squadrons and an ECM squadron. Operations of U.S. Marine Forces in Southeast Asia, 1 July 1971 thru 31 March 1973, HDMCU.
448. Webb and Poole, *Joint Chiefs of Staff, 1971–1973*, 154; Kissinger, *Ending the Vietnam War*, 267.
449. Webb and Poole, *Joint Chiefs of Staff, 1971–1973*, 156. The WSAG was a committee the National Security Advisor, Henry Kissinger, chaired. It was comprised of "the second-ranking officers from the other national security agencies." Kimball, *Nixon's Vietnam War*, 144.
450. Seymour M. Hersh, *The Price of Power: Kissinger in the Nixon White House* (New York: Summit Books, 1983), 506; Kimball, *Nixon's Vietnam War*, 303.
451. Memorandum from the President's Assistant for National Security Affairs (Kissinger) to President Nixon, April 16, 1972, *FRUS 1969–1976, VIII*, 257; Message from Major General Tarpley to General Abrams, TAOR Assessment, 040230Z, April 1972, Vogt Papers, Read File April 1972, AFHSD; Message from 15 AF to AIG 712/IN/DOI/DOXI, Fifteenth Air Force Intelligence Summary 15-16-70, 112315Z, April 1972, K-WG-307-HI, Vol. 1, AFHRA.
452. Message from Major General Tarpley to General Abrams info General Vogt, TAOR Assessment, 160140Z, May 1972, Vogt Papers, General Vogt's Read File May 1972; Message from Major General Tarpley to General Abrams info General Vogt, 120305Z, June 1972, Vogt Papers, Message Traffic June 1972, AFHSD.
453. Major General Verne L. Bowers, Senior Officer Debriefing Report, Major General Thomas M. Tarpley, Commander, Delta Regional Assistance Command, 15 January 1972–13 January 1973, 13 April 1973, found online at: www.dtic.mil/dtic/tr/fulltext/u2/525122.pdf.
454. Message from Major General Tarpley to General Abrams, TAOR Assessment, 0703555Z, May 1972, and Message from Major General Tarpley to General Abrams, TAOR Assessment, 080315Z,

May 1972, Vogt Papers, Read File May 1972, AFHSD.
455. Message from Major General Tarpley to General Abrams, TAOR Assessment, 180325Z, May 1972, and Message from Major General Tarpley to General Abrams, TAOR Assessment, 190300Z, May 1972, Vogt Papers, General Vogt's Read File May 1972, AFHSD.
456. Minutes of a Washington Special Actions Group Meeting, May 11, 1972, *FRUS 1969–1976, VIII*, 543.
457. Message from Major General Kroesen to General Abrams. Commander's Daily Evaluation, 110255Z, May 1972; Message from John P. Vann to General Abrams, Daily Commanders Evaluation, 220213Z, May 1972; Message from Major General Tarpley to General Abrams, 220250Z, May 1972; Message from John P. Vann to General Abrams, Daily Commanders Evaluation, 210210Z, May 1972, Vogt Papers, Read File May 1972, AFHSD.
458. Message from Major General Tarpley to General Abrams, TAOR Assessment, 300240Z, May 1972, Vogt Papers, General Vogt's Read File May 1972, AFHSD.
459. Webb and Poole, *Joint Chiefs of Staff, 1971–1973*, 155.
460. History of the Pacific Air Forces, July 1971–June 1972, Vol. 1, 80, K717.01, AFHRA; Minutes of a Washington Special Actions Group Meeting, May 1, 1972, *FRUS 1969–1976, VIII*, 351.
461. Sorley, *A Better War*, 327–28; HQ PACAF, Evaluation Report for the NVN Offensive, April–August 1972, v-1, K717.04-9, AFHRA; Andrade, *Trial by Fire*, 87, 117.
462. Message from AFSSO 7AF to AFSSO USAF, 061045Z, May 1972, Vogt Papers, Read File May 1972, AFHSD.
463. Memorandum from the President's Assistant for National Security Affairs (Kissinger) to President Nixon, Abrams Assessment of Current Situation, no date, circa April 24–25, 1972, *FRUS 1969–1976, VIII*, 311; Message from Major General Tarpley to General Abrams, TAOR Assessment, 040230Z, April 1972, Vogt Papers, AFHSD; Summary Air Operations Southeast Asia, April 1972, 2–8, K717.3063, AFHRA.
464. Ringenbach and Melly, Battle for An Loc, 16, 21, 23, K717.0413-196, AFHRA; Attack Squadron One Six Four Command History 1972, 1 May 1973, NHHC.
465. Commander R. W. Peacher, Commanding Officer, Attack Squadron Two Hundred Twelve to Chief of Naval Operations, Command History 1972, 18 April 1973, Fleet Aviation Commands Pre-1998, AR/229, Box 183, File F25, Commanding Officer Attack Squadron Fifty-Six to Chief of Naval Operations, Command History, 1972, Fleet Aviation Commands Pre-1998, AR/229, VA-56, Box 133, File F14, OPNAV 5750-1; Attack Squadron Fifty-Five Command History, 1972, Fleet Aviation Commands Pre-1998, AR/229, VA-55, Box 132, File F11, NHHC.
466. Ringenbach and Melly, Battle for An Loc, 40–41, K717.0413-196, AFHRA; Message from Major General Hollingsworth to General Abrams, 260230Z, May 1972, Vogt Papers, Read File May 1972, AFHSD.
467. Conversation between President Nixon and the President's Deputy Assistant for National Security Affairs (Haig), April 20, 1972, *FRUS 1969–1976, VIII*, 296–99; Ringenbach and Melly, Battle for An Loc, 53, K717.0413-196; History of Seventh Air Force, 1971–1972, 264, 291, K740.01-25, Vol. 1; Eighth Air Force Activity Input, 1 July 1971–30 June 1972, K520.041-2, AFHRA.
468. Eighth Air Force Activity Input, 1 July 1971–30 June 1972, K520.041-2, AFHRA; Andrade, *Trial by Fire*, 373.
469. Randolph, *Powerful and Brutal Weapons*, 236; History of Seventh Air Force, 1971–1972, 264, 291, K740.01-25, Vol. 1; Eighth Air Force Activity Input, 1 July 1971–30 June 1972, K520.041-2, AFHRA; United States Military Assistance Command, Vietnam, *Command History January 1972–March 1973*, Volume II, J-13.
470. Message from AFSSO 7AF to AFSSO USAF, 061045Z, May 1972, Vogt Papers, AFHSD.
471. Summary Air Operations Southeast Asia, May 1972, 2–5, 2-A-5, K717.3063, May 1972, AFHRA.

472. Message from Major General Kroesen to General Abrams, Commander's Daily Evaluation, 050204Z, May 1972, Vogt Papers, General Vogt's Read File May 1972, AFHSD; Andrade, *Trial by Fire*, 127.
473. Liebchen, Kontum: Battle for the Central Highlands, 47–48, K717.0413-194, AFHRA.
474. Memorandum from the President's Assistant for National Security Affairs (Kissinger) to President Nixon, undated, *FRUS 1969-1976, VIII*, 308, 311; Message from the Commander, Military Assistance Command, Vietnam (Abrams) to the Commander in Chief, Pacific (McCain), May 18, 1972, *FRUS 1969-1976, VIII*, 580–81.
475. Webb and Poole, *Joint Chiefs of Staff, 1971–1973*, 167; Minutes of a Washington Special Actions Group Meeting, May 10, 1972, *FRUS 1969–1976, VIII*, 536; Minutes of a Washington Special Actions Group Meeting, May 19, 1972, *FRUS 1969–1976, VIII*, 593.
476. Message from General Abrams to Major General Kroesen, Instructions for Application of B-52 Effort, 100703Z, May 1972, Vogt Papers, Read File May 1972, AFHSD.
477. Message from AFSSO 7AF to AFSSO CSAF, 131110Z, May 1972, Vogt Papers, AFHSD. ARVN troops "confirmed over 200 hostile dead" that day. Ringenbach and Melly, Battle for An Loc, 45, K717.0413-196, AFHRA; MACV Command History, 1972, J-25.
478. Message from Major General Hollingsworth to General Abrams, Daily Commander's Evaluation Report, 120227Z, May 1972; Daily Commander's Evaluation Report, 130225Z, May 1972, Daily Commander's Evaluation Report, 160220Z, May 1972; Daily Commander's Evaluation Report, 180250Z, May 1972, Vogt Papers, Read File May 72, AFHSD; Andrade, *Trial by Fire*, 476.
479. Message from Major General Hollingsworth to General Abrams, Daily Commander's Evaluation Report, 170230Z, May 1972; Message from AFSSO 7AF to AFSSO CSAF, Daily Wrap Up, 191100Z, May 1972; Message from Major General Hollingsworth to General Abrams, Daily Commander's Evaluation Report, 190215Z, May 1972, Vogt Papers, Read File May 1972, AFHSD.
480. Ringenbach and Melly, Battle for An Loc, 52, 53, K717.0413-196, AFHRA.
481. Ibid., xi.
482. Editorial Note, Transcript of Conversation between President Nixon, Henry Kissinger, and Admiral Moorer, May 4, 1972, *FRUS 1969–1976, VIII*, 430; Nixon, *RN*, 1301.
483. History of Seventh Air Force, 1971–1972, 264, 282–83, K740.01-25, Vol. 1, AFHRA; Message from AFSSO 7AF to AFSSO CSAF, Daily Wrap Up, 231115Z, May 1972, Vogt Papers, Message Traffic May 1972, AFHSD.
484. Andrade, *Trial by Fire*, 168. Chung was the commander of the 5th Vietnamese Marine Battalion.
485. Summary Air Operations Southeast Asia, May 1972, 2–3, K717.3063, May 1972, AFHRA; Memorandum from the President's Assistant for National Security Affairs (Kissinger) to President Nixon, General Abrams Personal Assessment, April 26, 1972, *FRUS 1969–1976, VIII*, 330; Message from AFSSO 7AF to AFSSO CSAF, Daily Wrap Up, 251100Z, May 1972, Vogt Papers, Message Traffic May 1972, AFHSD.
486. Transcript of a Telephone Conversation between President Nixon and the President's Deputy Assistant for National Security Affairs, May 17, 1972, *FRUS 1969–1976, VIII*, 578; Lieutenant General Ngo Quang Truong, *The Easter Offensive of 1972* (Washington, DC: U.S. Army Center of Military History, 1977), 98.
487. Message from John P. Vann to General Abrams, Daily Commander's Evaluation, 160234Z, May 1972, Vogt Papers; Message from Vann to Gen Abrams, 180205Z, May 1972, Vogt Papers, Read File May 1972, AFHSD; Andrade, *Trial by Fire*, 249.
488. Message from John P. Vann to General Abrams, II Corps Operation to Open Highway 14 at the Kontum Pass, 180400Z, May 1972, Vogt Papers, General Vogt's Read File May 1972, AFHSD; Message from Vann to Abrams, Daily Commander's Evaluation, 200225Z, May 1972, Vogt Papers, AFHSD.
489. Message from Major General Cowles to General Vogt, II Corps Operation, 210217Z, May 1972,

NOTES FOR CHAPTER 13

Vogt Papers, Read File May 1972, AFHSD; Randolph, *Powerful and Brutal Weapons,* 269; Andrade, *Trial by Fire,* 399.

490. Message from AFSSO 7AF to AFSSO CSAF, Daily Wrap Up, 271100Z, May 1972, Vogt Papers; Message from AFSSO 7AF to AFSSO CSAF, Daily Wrap Up, 281100Z, May 1972, Vogt Papers, Message Traffic May 1972, AFHSD.
491. Message from John P. Vann to General Abrams. Daily Commander's Evaluation, 270300Z, May 1972, Vogt Papers, Read File May 1972, AFHSD.
492. Message from JPV to Abrams, DEC, 290220Z, May 1972, Vogt Papers, Read File May 1972, AFHSD; Liebchen, Kontum: Battle for the Central Highlands, 56, K717.0413-194, AFHRA.
493. Message from AFSSO 7AF to AFSSO CSAF, Daily Wrap Up, 3111207Z, May 1972, Vogt Papers, Message Traffic May 1972, AFHSD; Robert Shaplan, "Letter from Vietnam," *The New Yorker,* June 24, 1972, 70.
494. Message from AFSSO PACAF to AFSSO 7AF, Air Power Application and Effectiveness in Vietnam, 160150Z, May 1972; Message from AFSSO USAF to AFSSO PACAF, 7AF, CSAF XOO Msg, 131833Z, April 1972, 161300Z, May 1972, Vogt Papers, Read File May 1972, AFHSD.
495. Message from JPV to Abrams, DCV, 040135Z, June 1972, Vogt Papers, Read File June 1972, AFHSD; Andrade, *Trial by Fire,* 299–303.
496. Liebchen, Kontum: Battle for the Central Highlands, 72, K717.0413-194, AFHRA.
497. Message from the Commander, Military Assistance Command, Vietnam (Abrams) to the Commander in Chief, Pacific (McCain), June 6, 1972, *FRUS 1969–1976, VIII,* 649–50.
498. Eighth Air Force Activity Input, 1 July 1971–30 June 1972, K520.041-2, AFHRA.
499. Wells and Paoli, History of 307th Strategic Wing, January–March 1971, K-WG-307-HI, AFHRA.
500. Message from Brigadier General Michael to General Abrams. Daily Commander's Evaluation, 180144Z, June 1972, Vogt Papers, Message Traffic June 1972, AFHSD.
501. Liebchen, Kontum: Battle for the Central Highlands, 83, K717.0413-194, AFHRA.
502. Eighth Air Force Activity Input, 1 July 1971–30 June 1972, K520.041-2; Liebchen, Kontum: Battle for the Central Highlands, 86, K717.0413-194, AFHRA.
503. Message from Major General Tarpley to Abrams, TAOR Assessment, 190340Z, June 1972; Message from Major General Cooksey to Abrams, Commander's daily evaluation, 210231Z, June 1972; Msg from Hollingsworth to Abrams, DCE Report, 210210Z, June 1972; Message from Brigadier General Healy to General Abrams, Daily Commander's Evaluation, 290250Z, June 1972; Msg from Tarpley to Abrams, TAOR Assessment, 220200Z, June 1972, Vogt Papers, Read File June 1972, AFHSD.
504. History of Seventh Air Force, 1971–1972, 264, 289, K740.01-25, Vol. 1, AFHRA.
505. Liebchen, Kontum: Battle for the Central Highlands, 87, K717.0413-194, AFHRA.
506. Summary Air Operations Southeast Asia, April 1972, 2–3, K717.3063, AFHRA.
507. Nalty, *Air War over South Vietnam,* 365; Andrade, *Trial by Fire,* 142, 149; Van Atta, *With Honor,* 417; Summary Air Operations Southeast Asia, May 1972, 2–3, K717.3063, May 1972, AFHRA; Davidson, *Vietnam at War,* 637; Randolph, *Powerful and Brutal Weapons,* 253–54; Message from Major General Kroesen to General Abrams, Daily Commander's Evaluation, 040300Z, May 1972, Vogt Papers, General Vogt's Read File May 1972, AFHSD.
508. Ringenbach and Melly, Battle for An Loc, 5 April–26 June 1972, 10; Andrade, *Trial by Fire,* 411; Willbanks, *The Battle of An Loc,* 51; Message from John P. Vann to General Abrams, DCE, 280230Z, May 1972, Vogt Papers, Read File May 1972, AFHSD.
509. Liebchen, Kontum: Battle for the Central Highlands, 55–56, 63, 68, K717.0413-194, AFHRA.
510. Message from AFSSO PACAF to AFSSO USAF info AFSSO 7AF, Air Power Application and Effectiveness in Vietnam, 061750Z, June 1972 Vogt Papers, Message Traffic June 1972, AFHSD.
511. Berman, *No Peace, No Honor,* 135.

512. Webb and Poole, *Joint Chiefs of Staff, 1971–1973*, 188.
513. Liebchen, Kontum: Battle for the Central Highlands, 47, 67, 68, K717.0413-194, AFHRA; Andrew Wiest, *Vietnam's Forgotten Army: Heroism and Betrayal in the ARVN* (New York: New York University Press, 2008), 211, 212.
514. Air Operations in Southeast Asia, 1972–1973, Vol. 1, p. iii-19, K717.0423-23, AFHRA.
515. Andrade, *Trial by Fire*, 353.
516. Liebchen, Kontum: Battle for the Central Highlands, 89, K717.0413-194, AFHRA.
517. Majors Edward J. Dunne Jr. and Richard F. Quimby Jr., The U.S. Air War Against Tanks (HQ 7AF: Tactical Analysis Division, 1973), Figure 4, K740.041-2, 20 May 1973. Note: these statistics include all armored vehicles the PAVN used, including the lighter PT-76, which is not a main battle tank.
518. Message from AFSSO 7AF to AFSSO USAF, 061045Z, May 1972, Vogt Papers, AFHSD.
519. HQ PACAF, Evaluation Report for the NVN Offensive (April–August 1972), c-1, K717.04-9, 1972, AFHRA.
520. Summary Air Operations Southeast Asia, May 1972, 2-27, 2-32, 2-25, K717.3063, May 1972; Dunne, and Quimby, The U.S. Air War Against Tanks, 15, Figure 13, K740.041-2, 20 May 1973; HQ PACAF, Evaluation Report for the NVN Offensive (April–August 1972), c-1, 2, 3, 7, K717.04-9, 1972, AFHRA.
521. Marine Fighter Attack Squadron 232 Command Chronology, December 1, 1972, found online at The Vietnam Center & Sam Johnson Vietnam Archive, Texas Tech University, http://vietnam.ttu.edu; HQ PACAF, Evaluation Report for the NVN Offensive (April–August 1972), c-2, 3, 7, 9, K717.04-9, 1972; Eggers, Employment of Missiles, K712.153-1; Summary Air Operations Southeast Asia, May 1972, 2-27, 2-32, 2-25, K717.3063, May 1972, AFHRA.
522. Nelson, Close Air Support, 1972, 92–93, 96, K717.601-8, AFHRA.
523. Webb and Poole, *Joint Chiefs of Staff, 1971–1973*, 188.
524. Evaluation Report for the NVN Offensive, April–August 1972, iv-13. K717.04-9, AFHRA.
525. Commanding Officer, Attack Squadron One Five Five to Chief of Naval Operations, Command History 1972, 23 November 1973, NHHC.
526. Randolph, *Powerful and Brutal Weapons*, 75, 143; *Vietnam: A Staff Report Prepared for the Use of the Committee on Foreign Relations, United States Senate*, June 29, 1972 (Washington, DC: U.S. Government Printing Office, 1972), 11; Nelson, Close Air Support, 1972, 94, K717.601-8, AFHRA.
527. Summary Air Operations Southeast Asia, May 1972, 2–3, K717.3063, May 1972; Bozman, Corona Harvest Arc Light Questionnaire, 14 January 1971, K712.03-79, AFHRA.
528. History of Seventh Air Force, 1971–1972, 264, 294, K740.01-25, Vol. 1, AFHRA; Minutes of a Washington Special Actions Group Meeting, April 25, 1972, *FRUS 1969–1976, VIII*, 316.
529. Major General Verne L. Bowers, Senior Officer Debriefing Report, Major General Thomas M. Tarpley, Commander, Delta Regional Assistance Command, 15 January 1972–13 January 1973, 13 April 1973, found online at: www.dtic.mil/dtic/tr/fulltext/u2/525122.pdf.
530. HQ PACAF, Evaluation Report for the NVN Offensive (April–August 1972), VII-2-3, K717.04-9, 1972, AFHRA; History of Seventh Air Force, 1971–1972, 264, 290, K740.01-25, Vol. 1, AFHRA; Andrade, *Trial by Fire*, 212.
531. Message from AFSSO 7AF to AFSSO USAF, 061045Z May 1972, Vogt Papers, AFHSD; *FRUS 1969–1976, VIII*, 416; Air Operations in Southeast Asia, 1972–1973, Vol. 1, p. iii-26, K717.0423-23, AFHRA.
532. Air Operations in Southeast Asia, 1972–1973, Vol. 1, pp. iii-20, iii-21, K717.0423-23, AFHRA.
533. Message from AFSSO 7AF to AFSSO CSAF, Daily Wrap Up, 181100Z, June 1972, Vogt Papers, Message Traffic June 1972, AFHSD. Ryan was the Air Force chief of staff from 1969 to 1973.

534. Porter, Proud Deep Alpha, 52, K717.0423-24, AFHRA.
535. SSgt. Donald M. Tierney, History of 307th Strategic Wing, July–September 1972, K-WG-307-HI, July–September 1972, AFHRA; Truong, *The Easter Offensive of 1972*, 65.
536. Air Operations in Southeast Asia, 1972–1973, Vol. 1, pp. iii-18 through iii-24, K717.0423-23; Eighth Air Force Activity Input, 1 July 1971–30 June 1972, K520.041-2, AFHRA.
537. Nelson, Close Air Support, 83–84, K717.601-8, AFHRA.
538. Ibid., 85.
539. Memorandum from the President's Assistant for National Security Affairs (Kissinger) to President Nixon, August 19, 1972, *FRUS 1969–1976, VIII*, 906.
540. HQ PACAF, Summary Air Operations Southeast Asia, September 1972, 2–6, K717.3063, September 1972, AFHRA.
541. Directorate of Operations Analysis, Summary Air Operations Southeast Asia December 1972, 2–5, K717.3063, December 1972, AFHRA; Message from Major General Tarpley to General Abrams, TAOR Assessment, 170245Z, May 1972, Vogt Papers, General Vogt's Read File May 72, AFHSD.
542. Depner, 354th Tactical Fighter Wing, 1 October 1972–31 December 1972, 10, K-WG-354-HI, AFHRA.
543. Schlight, *The Years of the Offensive, 1965–1968*, 290–91.
544. Nelson, Close Air Support, 1972, 103, K717.601-8, AFHRA.
545. Bruce Palmer Jr., *The 25-Year War: America's Military Role in Vietnam* (Lexington: University Press of Kentucky, 1984), 160.
546. Air Support during Operation Cherokee, Annex 1 to 4th Marines After Action Report, May 24, 1966, Vietnam, April–December 1966, Box 4, Folder 1, Archives Branch, HDMCU.
547. Message from CG III MAF to CG FMFPAC, SECNAV's Visit to Westpac, 271346Z, May 1969, found online at The Vietnam Center & Sam Johnson Vietnam Archive, Texas Tech University, http://vietnam.ttu.edu.
548. Message from Admin FMFPAC to RHMMAFA/CG III MAF, Military Strategy in Southeast Asia (Memorandum by SECDEF 2 July 1969), 102005Z, July 1969, found online at The Vietnam Center & Sam Johnson Vietnam Archive, Texas Tech University, http://vietnam.ttu.edu.
549. Message from CG III MAF to CG FMFPAC, 010806Z, September 1969. See also Fleet Marine Force, Pacific, Operations of U.S. Marine Forces, Vietnam, August 1969, found online at The Vietnam Center & Sam Johnson Vietnam Archive, Texas Tech University, http://vietnam.ttu.edu.
550. Robert Endicott Osgood, *Limited War: The Challenge to American Security* (Chicago: University of Chicago Press, 1957), 238.
551. Antulio Echevarria, II, *Reconsidering the American Way of War: U.S. Military Practice from the Revolution to Afghanistan* (Washington, DC: Georgetown University Press, 2014), 4; Russell F. Weigley, *The American Way of War: A History of United States Military Strategy and Policy* (New York: Macmillan, 1973), 464–65. Gregory Daddis is more skeptical about the long-term prospects for this strategy. Daddis, *No Sure Victory*, 70.
552. General Maxwell Taylor, Telegram from the Embassy in Vietnam to the Department of State, January 6, 1965, 11 a.m., *FRUS 1964–1968, II*, 17.

Chapter 14

1. Robert S. McNamara, Memorandum from the Secretary of Defense to the President, January 7, 1964, *FRUS 1964–1968, I*, 13; John C. McCone, Memorandum from the Board of National Estimates to the Director of Central Intelligence, June 9, 1964, *FRUS 1964–1968, I*, 485–87. McNamara, *In Retrospect*, 106–7, 124–25.

NOTES FOR CHAPTER 14

2. Castle, *U.S. Military Aid to the Royal Lao Government, 1955–1975*, 65–76; Draft Paper Prepared for a White House Meeting, June 10, 1964, *FRUS 1964–1968, XXVIII*, 167.
3. Memorandum from the Joint Chiefs of Staff to Secretary of Defense McNamara, March 30, 1968, *FRUS 1964–1968, XXVIII*, 697; United Nations, "Declaration on the Neutrality of Laos, Signed at Geneva, on 23 July 1962," no. 6564, https://treaties.un.org/doc/Publication/UNTS/Volume%20456/volume-456-I-6564-English.pdf.
4. Nguyen, *Hanoi's War*, 163; Telegram from the Department of State to the Embassy in Laos, March 20, 1965, *FRUS 1964–1968, XXVIII*, 352–53; Castle, *U.S. Military Aid to the Royal Lao Government, 1955–1975*, 88.
5. Bromley Smith, Memorandum of Conference with President Johnson, June 8, 1964, *FRUS 1964–1968, XXVIII*, 153, 160; McNamara, *In Retrospect*, 114.
6. Editorial Note, *FRUS 1964–1968, XXVIII*, 279; Telegram from the Department of State to the Embassy in Laos, October 7, 1964, *FRUS 1964–1968, XXVIII*, 281.
7. Woods, *LBJ*, 513.
8. Gordon M. Goldstein, *Lessons in Disaster: McGeorge Bundy and the Path to War in Vietnam* (New York: Henry Holt, 2008), 54–61; Actions Resulting from the Chief of Staff's 12 February 1962 Staff Meeting, February 13, 1962, Papers of Curtis LeMay, Box B-153, Folder Chief of Staff Meetings, 1961–1962, Library of Congress. Thanks go to Dr. Trevor Albertson for sharing this document.
9. Editorial Note, January 22, 1964, *FRUS 1964–1968, I*, 35; Memorandum for the Record of a Meeting, White House, Washington, February 20, 1964, *FRUS 1964–1968, I*, 92–93.
10. Memorandum from McNamara to the President, March 16, 1964, *FRUS 1964–1968, I*, 159.
11. Memorandum by the Chief, Far Eastern Division, Directorate for Plans (Colby), and the Assistant Deputy Director for Policy Support, Directorate for Intelligence, Central Intelligence Agency (Cooper), May 21, 1964, *FRUS 1964–1968, XXVIII*, 95–98; Smith, Memorandum of Conference with President Johnson, June 8, 1964, *FRUS 1964–1968, XXVIII*, 158–59; Kai Bird, *The Color of Truth: McGeorge Bundy and William Bundy, Brothers in Arms: A Biography* (New York: Simon & Schuster, 1998), 278.
12. McNamara, *In Retrospect*, 121.
13. Bernard Fall, *Viet-Nam Witness: 1953–1966* (New York: Praeger, 1966), 114; Robert K. Brigham, *Guerrilla Diplomacy: The NLF's Foreign Relations and the Vietnam War* (Ithaca, NY: Cornell University Press, 1999), 41.
14. Memorandum of a Conversation, Department of State, Washington, July 1, 1964, *FRUS 1964–1968, I*, 535; John C. McCone, Memorandum from the Board of National Estimates to the Director of Central Intelligence, June 9, 1964, *FRUS 1964–1968, I*, 485; Memorandum of Meeting, White House, Washington, September 9, 1964, *FRUS 1964–1968, I*, 752–53.
15. The August 4 "attacks" were phantoms. Edwin Moise, *Tonkin Gulf and the Escalation of the Vietnam War* (Chapel Hill: University of North Carolina Press, 1996), 112–40, 242, 210.
16. Goldstein, *Lessons in Disaster,* 135; Memorandum from the President's Special Assistant for National Security Affairs (Bundy) to the President, August 13, 1964, *FRUS 1964–1968, I*, 678.
17. Tilford Jr., *Setup*, xvii, 79; Clodfelter, *Limits of Air Power,* 50; *The Pentagon Papers: The Defense Department History of United States Decisionmaking on Vietnam, Volume III, Senator Gravel Edition* (Boston: Beacon, 1975), 109, 200; David Milne, *America's Rasputin: Walt W. Rostow and the Vietnam War* (Hill & Wang, 2009), 134.
18. Memorandum from the Joint Chiefs of Staff to the Secretary of Defense, August 27, 1964, *FRUS 1964–1968, I*, 715; Charles Tustin Kamps, "The JCS 94-Target List: A Vietnam Myth that Still Distorts Military Thought," *Air and Space Power Journal* 68: 1 (Spring 2001), 77.
19. *The Joint Chiefs of Staff, 1960–1968, Part 2,* 48.

20. Memorandum of a Meeting, White House, September 9, 1964, *FRUS 1964–1968, I*, 749, 750.
21. Telegram from the Commander in Chief, Pacific (Sharp) to the Chairman of the Joint Chiefs of Staff (Wheeler), November 22, 1964, *FRUS 1964–1968, I*, 930.
22. Message, Optimum Military Air Strike Program for NVN, 040304Z, April 1965, K712-1623-2, AFHRA.
23. Schlight, *The Years of the Offensive, 1965–1968*, 16; Kendrick, *The Wound Within*, 184.
24. Telegram from the Embassy in Vietnam to the Department of State, November 1, 1964, *FRUS 1964–1968, I*, 873–75; Goldstein, *Lessons in Disaster*, 109; Vandiver, *Shadows of Vietnam*, 29.
25. Memorandum for the Record of a Meeting, White House, Washington, November 19, 1964, *FRUS 1964–1968, I*, 915; Bird, *Color of Truth*, 295–97.
26. Paper Prepared by the Ambassador in Vietnam (Taylor), undated [November 1964], *FRUS 1964–1968, I*, 955–57; Paper Prepared by the Executive Committee, December 2, 1964, *FRUS 1964–1968, I*, 973; Instructions from the President to the Ambassador to Vietnam (Taylor), December 3, 1964, *FRUS 1964–1968, I*, 977.
27. Telegram from the President to the Ambassador in Vietnam (Taylor), December 30, 1964, *FRUS 1964–1968, I*, 1058–59.
28. McNamara, *In Retrospect*, 160–62; Hearings before the Preparedness Investigating Subcommittee, August 16, 1967, 141; George W. Ball, *The Past Has Another Pattern: Memoirs* (New York: W. W. Norton, 1982), 381, 382; Editorial Note, *FRUS 1964–1968, XXVIII*, 303.
29. William P. Bundy, Memorandum from the Assistant Secretary of State for Far Eastern Affairs (Bundy) to Secretary of State Rusk, January 6, 1965, *FRUS 1964–1968, II*, 32; Bird, *Color of Truth*, 311. The NLF was established in 1960 and "was a northern response to genuine peasant uprisings at the village level in the southern countryside; it was a construct poised to reap the success of the spontaneous agitation and portray it as a 'concerted uprising' . . . orchestrated by communist cells under the direction of the" Vietnamese Workers Party. The NLF took "orders" from Hanoi. Nguyen, *Hanoi's War*, 53, 128.
30. Letter from the Ambassador to Vietnam (Lodge) to President Johnson, February 19, 1967, *FRUS 1964–1968, V*, 193. Anne Blair's biography of Lodge does little to illuminate Lodge's thinking about the war. Anne E. Blair, *Lodge in Vietnam: A Patriot Abroad* (New Haven, CT: Yale University Press, 1995). His own work from 1976 is similarly a blank page. Henry Cabot Lodge Jr., *As It Was: An Inside View of Politics and Power in the '50s and '60s* (New York: Norton, 1976).
31. Paper Prepared by Secretary of State Rusk, February 23, 1965, *FRUS 1964–1968, II*, 355.
32. McGeorge Bundy, Memorandum from the President's Special Assistant for National Security Affairs (Bundy) to President Johnson, January 27, 1965, *FRUS 1964–1968, II*, 96; Bird, *Color of Truth*, 303, 304.
33. McGeorge Bundy, Memorandum for Record, February 8, 1965, *FRUS 1964–1968, II*, 194.
34. Gardner, *Pay Any Price*, 167; PACAF DI, Summary of Effects of Air Operations Southeast Asia, 1965, 1, K717.6092, AFHRA; Barrett, *Uncertain Warriors*, 17; Clodfelter, *Limits of Air Power*, 134.
35. Assessment of Air Operations, 7 February 1965 thru 19 July 1967, 10, K740.04-20, AFHRA.
36. F. J. Olmer, Operations Evaluation Group Study No. 674 Interdiction of North Vietnam, 23 April 1964, pp. 3, 9–15, 17–19, COLL/7 Publications of the Center for Naval Analysis, OEG, Box 61, File OEG #674, NHHC.
37. Telegram from the Embassy in Vietnam to the Department of State, January 7, 1965, *FRUS 1964–1968, XXVIII*, 314; John Prados, *The Blood Road: The Ho Chi Minh Trail and the Vietnam War* (New York: John Wiley & Sons, 1999), 156; Van Staaveren, *Interdiction in Southern Laos, 1960–1968*, 69.
38. Taylor, Telegram from the Embassy in Vietnam to the Department of State, January 6, 1965, 11 a.m., *FRUS 1964–1968, II*, 17.

NOTES FOR CHAPTER 14

39. Major General J. H. Moore to COMUSMACV, 4 March 1965, Air Div to RUEAHQ/CSAF, 190710Z, March 1965, K526.1623, AFHRA.
40. Message from CSAF to JCS info PACAF, COMUSMACV, Graduated Reprisal Program against DRV, 110735Z, February 1965, K712.1623-2, 65/01/22 - 65/06/28, AFHRA.
41. Retransmission of a COMUSMACV Message to CINCPAC; Message from CINCPAC to CINCPACAF, Integration of Military Pressures on DRV, 190143Z, February 1965, K712.312-41, 19 February 1965, AFHRA; Westmoreland, *A Soldier Reports*, 117.
42. Patricia Pelley, "The History of Resistance and the Resistance to History in Post-Colonial Constructions of the Past," in Keith W. Taylor and John K. Whitmore, eds., *Essays into Vietnamese Pasts* (Ithaca, NY: Southeast Asia Program, Cornell University, 1995), 236; Staughton Lynd, *The Other Side* (New York: New American Library, 1966), 68.
43. Keith Weller Taylor, *The Birth of Vietnam* (Berkeley: University of California Press, 1983), 270.
44. Pelley, "History of Resistance," 235; Schulzinger, *A Time for War*, 4–5; Taylor, *Birth of Vietnam*, 280–81; William J. Duiker, "Victory by Other Means: The Foreign Policy of the Democratic Republic of Vietnam," in Gilbert, ed., *Why the North Won the Vietnam War*, 48–49.
45. General Maxwell Taylor, Telegram from the Embassy in Vietnam to the Department of State, February 6, 1965, 1 p.m., *FRUS 1964–1968, II*, 165; Message from CINCPAC to CINCPACFLT, Racing Motor, 170412Z, February 1965, K712.1623-2, AFHRA.
46. PACAF DI, Summary of Effects of Air Operations Southeast Asia, 1965, 1, K717.6092, AFHRA.
47. United States Strategic Bombing Survey, Summary Report (European War), September 30, 1945, 16; Gerhard L. Weinberg, *A World at Arms: A Global History of World War II* (Cambridge: Cambridge University Press, 1994), 479.
48. William Bundy, Memorandum to Secretary of State Rusk, January 6, 1965, *FRUS 1964–1968, II*, 31.
49. Collier, *History of Air Power*, 41; Morrow, *Great War in the Air*, 4, 154–56, 221, 244, 296; Tami Davis Biddle, *Rhetoric and Reality in Air Warfare: The Evolution of British and American Ideas about Strategic Bombing, 1914–1945* (Princeton, NJ: Princeton University Press, 2002), 22, 42–43, 61.
50. Douhet, *Command of the Air*, 28, 31, 53, 58.
51. Stephen L. McFarland, *America's Pursuit of Precision Bombing, 1910–1945* (Washington, DC: Smithsonian Institution Press, 1995), 90, 93; Michael E. Weaver, "International Cooperation and Bureaucratic In-Fighting: American and British Economic Intelligence Sharing and the Strategic Bombing of Germany, 1939–41," *Intelligence and National Security*, 23: 2 (April 2008), 156; Biddle, *Rhetoric and Reality*, 99, 178.
52. Eds. Klaus A. Maier, et al., *Germany and the Second World War, Volume II: Germany's Initial Conquests in Europe*, trans. Dean S. McMurry and Ewald Osers (Oxford: Clarendon Press, 1991), 121–22, 337; John Terraine, *A Time for Courage: The Royal Air Force in the European War, 1939–1945* (New York: Macmillan, 1985), 212.
53. Terraine, *Time for Courage*, 263, 283; Biddle, *Rhetoric and Reality*, 189, 197.
54. Conrad C. Crane, *American Airpower Strategy in World War II: Bombs, Cities, Civilians, and Oil* (Lawrence: University Press of Kansas, 2006), 35, 105; Weinberg, *World at Arms*, 419, 774–75; Alfred C. Mierzejewski, *Collapse of the German War Economy, 1944–1945: Allied Air Power and the German National Railway* (Chapel Hill: University of North Carolina Press, 1988), 183–84; Richard Overy, *The Bombers and the Bombed: Allied Air War over Europe, 1940–1945* (New York: Penguin Books, 2013), 101–2; Saburo Ienaga, *The Pacific War: World War II and the Japanese, 1931–1945* (New York: Pantheon Books, 1978), 229–31.
55. Douhet, *Command*, 58, 96; Olsen, *Strategic Air Power in Desert Storm*, 67; Meilinger, *Airwar*, 199; Clodfelter, *Limits of Air Power*, 10.

56. Craig F. Morris, *The Origins of American Strategic Bombing Theory* (Annapolis, MD: Naval Institute Press, 2017), 2, 8; Michael D. Gordin, *Five Days in August: How World War II Became a Nuclear War* (Princeton, NJ and Oxford: Princeton University Press, 2007), 19, 23.
57. Paper Prepared by Chester L. Cooper of the National Security Council Staff, January 6, 1965, *FRUS 1964–1968, II*, 34; Special National Intelligence Estimate 53-65, *FRUS 1964–1968, II*, 144.
58. Sorley, *Honorable Warrior*, 198.
59. *FRUS 1964–1968, II*, 17fn; Van Staaveren, *Gradual Failure*, 59.
60. Ambassador Maxwell Taylor, Telegram from the Embassy in Vietnam to the Department of State, February 7, 1965, *FRUS 1964–1968, II*, 31; Bird, *Color of Truth*, 293.
61. McGeorge Bundy, Memorandum from the President's Special Assistant for National Security Affairs (Bundy) to President Johnson, February 7, 1965, *FRUS 1964–1968, II*, 175, 181.
62. McGeorge Bundy, Memorandum to President Johnson, February 7, 1965, *FRUS 1964–1968, II*, 182–83.
63. Message from 2nd Air Division, Intell Annex to 2AD Frag Order, 110220Z, March 1965, K526.1623, 11 February 1965, AFHRA.
64. Bird, *Color of Truth*, 315; Milne, *America's Rasputin*, 151.
65. McGeorge Bundy, Memorandum to President Johnson, February 7, 1965, *FRUS 1964–1968, II*, 183–85.
66. Leslie H. Gelb with Richard K. Betts, *The Irony of Vietnam: The System Worked* (Washington, DC: Brookings Institute, 1979), 118.
67. Memorandum from Chester L. Cooper of the National Security Council Staff to the President's Special Assistant for National Security Affairs (Bundy), March 10, 1965, *FRUS 1964–1968, II*, 433; Dean Rusk, Telegram from the Department of State to the Embassy in Vietnam, March 16, 1965, *FRUS 1964–1968, II*, 450.
68. Message from CINCPAC to JCS, Rolling Thunder Eight Week Pressure Program, 271945Z, February 1965, K712.1623-2, AFHRA; Woods, *LBJ*, 602.
69. Memorandum from Cooper to Bundy, March 10, 1965, *FRUS 1964–1968, II*, 433–34. Some have argued—not conclusively—that the bargaining theories of Thomas Schelling "inspired" Rolling Thunder. Esther-Mirjam Sent, "Some Like It Cold: Thomas Schelling as a Cold Warrior," *Journal of Economic Methodology*, 14: 4 (December 2007), 16.
70. Executive Sessions of the Senate Foreign Relations Committee together with Joint Sessions with the Senate Armed Services Committee (Historical Series), Ninetieth Congress, First Session, 1967 (Washington, DC: U.S. Government Printing Office, 2006), 173; Zhai, *China and the Vietnam Wars, 1950–1975*, 138–39. I am borrowing definitions of "decisive" and "decisive battle" from Stephen Morillo. Decisive: irreversible consequences; decisive battle: a battle that causes a shift in the possibility space. His definitions strike me as more helpful than the definition of "decisive" that is often implied, which is actually confused with "conclusive"—a battle that concludes and terminates a war.
71. Memorandum from the Undersecretary of State (Ball) to President Johnson, January 25, 1966, *FRUS 1964–1968, IV*, 129–32.
72. Paper Prepared by Secretary of State Rusk, February 23, 1965, *FRUS 1964–1968, II*, 355.
73. Maxwell Taylor, Telegram from the Embassy in Vietnam to the Department of State, February 9, 1965, *FRUS 1964–1968, II*, 207.
74. Memorandum from the Office of Current Intelligence to Director of Central Intelligence McCone, February 23, 1965, *FRUS 1964–1968, II*, 360; Memorandum from the Assistant Secretary of State for Far Eastern Affairs (Bundy) to Secretary of State Rusk, March 5, 1965, *FRUS 1964–1968, II*, 398.
75. Summary Notes of the 547th Meeting of the National Security Council, February 8, 1965,

FRUS 1964–1968, II, 191; Thomas L. Hughes, Memorandum from the Director of the Bureau of Intelligence and Research (Hughes) to Acting Secretary of State Ball, February 8, 1965, *FRUS 1964–1968, II,* 200.

76. Memorandum for Record, Discussion with Secretary Rusk, March 18, 1965, *FRUS 1964–1968, II,* 457–58. McCone had been the Director of Central Intelligence since November 1961.
77. Message from 7 AF to RUEKBA/National Military Command Center, 261340Z, 1966, K160.043-36, 23 April 1966; Rogers and Knops, Study in Air Defense, K470.40-22; Message from 7AF Air-to-Air Combat in SEA, 250740Z, May 1966, K717.312, May 1966, AFHRA; Chen Jian, "China's Involvement in the Vietnam War, 1964–69," *The China Quarterly* No. 142 (June 1995), 377.
78. Peking Claims U.S. Plane," *New York Times,* October 6, 1965, 2, https://www.nsa.gov/news-features/declassified-documents/vietnam-powmia-documents/assets/files/DocC.pdf; Van Staaveren, *Gradual Failure,* 182.
79. Herring, *LBJ and Vietnam,* 43. See for example Memorandum from James C. Thomson Jr., to Chester Cooper, February 10, 1965, *FRUS 1964–1968, II,* 228–29. Additional documents in *FRUS 1964–1968, II,* 241, 248, 254–55; Gardner, *Pay Any Price,* 119, 122, 227.
80. PACAF DI, Effects of Air Operations in Southeast Asia, 5 July 1965, 2, K717.6092, AFHRA.
81. Zhai, *China and the Vietnam Wars, 1950–1975,* 138–39.
82. PACAF DI, Effects of Air Operations in Southeast Asia, 19 August 1965, 8, K717.6092, AFHRA; Prados, *Vietnam,* 190–91.
83. McNamara, *In Retrospect,* 195.
84. Rogers and Knops, Study in Air Defense, K470.40-22, AFHRA; Memorandum from the Undersecretary of State (Ball) to President Johnson, January 25, 1966, *FRUS 1964–1968, IV,* 134, 135; Notes of Meeting, January 27, 1966, *FRUS 1964–1968, IV,* 164.
85. Notes of President Johnson's Meeting with the National Security Council, June 22, 1966, *FRUS IV, 1966,* 450–51.
86. John Colvin, "Hanoi in My Time," *Washington Quarterly,* 138–54, (Spring 1981), 140.
87. Woods, *LBJ,* 758; Memorandum from the President's Assistant (Jones) to President Johnson, September 5, 1967, *FRUS 1964-1968, V,* 752.
88. Cosmas, *The Joint Chiefs of Staff, 1960–1968, Part 2,* 213–15; Woods, *LBJ,* 601; Bromley Smith, Summary Notes of the 545th Meeting of the National Security Council, February 6, 1965, *FRUS 1964–1968, II,* 156–57.
89. Cosmas, *The Joint Chiefs of Staff, 1960–1968, Part 2,* 216–17.
90. Memorandum from Acting Secretary of State Ball to President Johnson, February 13, 1965, *FRUS 1964–1968, II,* 258. Two months later Ball recommended withdrawal. Goldstein, *Lessons in Disaster,* 172.
91. Memorandum from the Deputy Assistant Secretary of State for Far Eastern Affairs (Green) to the Assistant Secretary of State for Far Eastern Affairs (Bundy), February 16, 1965, *FRUS 1964–1968, II,* 287.
92. Maxwell Taylor, Telegram from the Embassy in Vietnam to the Department of State, February 12, 1965, *FRUS 1964–1968, II,* 250–51; Memorandum from the Joint Chiefs of Staff to Secretary of Defense McNamara, February 11, 1965, *FRUS 1964–1968, II,* 240–49.
93. H. R. McMaster, *Dereliction of Duty: Lyndon Johnson, Robert McNamara, the Joint Chiefs of Staff, and the Lies that Led to Vietnam* (New York: Harper Perennial, 1997), 218–19, 220–21.
94. Bird, *Color of Truth,* 282; Vandiver, *Shadows of Vietnam,* 95, 130; Herring, *LBJ and Vietnam,* 109; McMaster, *Dereliction of Duty,* 229; George Ball, Telegram from the Department of State to the Embassy in Vietnam, February 13, 1965, *FRUS 1964–1968, II,* 263.
95. Robert S. McNamara, Personal Notes of a Meeting with President Johnson, February 16, 1965,

FRUS 1964–1968, II, 290.
96. McNamara, *In Retrospect*, 173; Memorandum from the President's Special Assistant for National Security Affairs (Bundy) to President Johnson, February 16, 1965, *FRUS 1964–1968, II*, 283.
97. Message from CINCPAC to RUHLKM/CINCPACAF, Rolling Thunder IV, 261924Z, February 1965, K712.1623-2 65/01/22 - 65/06/28, AFHRA; Telegram from the Chairman of the Joint Chiefs of Staff (Wheeler) to the Commander, Military Assistance Command, Vietnam (Westmoreland), March 4, 1965, *FRUS 1964–1968, II*, 396–97. Rolling Thunder was a set of discrete events. For example, Rolling Thunder 7 took place on March 19, 1965. Van Staaveren, *Gradual Failure*, 89, 94.
98. John T. McNaughton, Paper Prepared by the Assistant Secretary of Defense for International Security Affairs (McNaughton), March 10, 1965, *FRUS 1964–1968, II*, 427.
99. U. Alexis Johnson, Telegram from the Embassy in Vietnam to the Department of State, April 1, 1965, *FRUS 1964–1968, II*, 502; Paper Prepared by the Ambassador to Vietnam (Taylor), April 1, 1965, *FRUS 1964–1968, II*, 504; Bird, *Color of Truth*, 308.
100. John McCone, Summary Notes of the 550th Meeting of the National Security Council, March 26, 1965, *FRUS 1964–1968, II*, 482–83; Memorandum from the President's Special Assistant for National Security Affairs (Bundy) to President Johnson, March 6, 1965, *FRUS 1964–1968, II*, 402; Ray S. Cline, Memorandum Prepared by the Deputy Director for Intelligence, Central Intelligence Agency (Cline), March 8, 1965, *FRUS 1964–1968, II*, 422.
101. Maxwell Taylor, Memorandum from the Embassy in Vietnam to the Department of State, March 8, 1965, *FRUS 1964–1968, II*, 412.
102. Cline, Memorandum by the Deputy Director for Intelligence, March 8, 1965, *FRUS 1964–1968, II*, 421; Memorandum for Record, McCone Discussion with McNamara, March 18, 1965, *FRUS 1964–1968, II*, 459; John McCone, Memorandum for Record, April 21, 1965, *FRUS 1964–1968, II*, 580.
103. Schulzinger, *A Time for War*, 207; *The Pentagon Papers. The Defense Department History of the United States Decisionmaking on Vietnam Volume IV* (Boston: Beacon, 1975), 56.
104. Message from CINCPAC to RUMJFS Vientiane, U.S. Actions in Laos, 062141Z, March 1965; Message from Admino CINCPAC to CINCPACFLT, Barrel Roll/Steel Tiger, 242002Z, March 1965; Message from CINCPAC to CINCPACAF, Rolling Thunder IV, 261924Z, February 1965, K712.1623-2, AFHRA.
105. Sharp, *Strategy for Defeat*, 166–67.
106. National Security Action Memorandum No. 328, April 6, 1965, *FRUS 1964–1968, II*, 538–39; *Public Papers of the Presidents of the United States: Lyndon B. Johnson, Containing the Public Messages, Speeches, and Statements of the President, 1965*, Book 1–January 1 to May 31, 1965 (Washington, DC: United States Government Printing Office, 1966), 396.
107. U.S. Department of State, *American Foreign Policy: Current Documents, 1965* (Washington, DC: Department of State, U.S. Government Printing Office, 1968), 852.
108. McGeorge Bundy, Memorandum by the President's Special Assistant for National Security Affairs, April 1, 1965, *FRUS 1964–1968, II*, 510.
109. Letter from Director of Central Intelligence McCone to President Johnson, undated, *FRUS 1964–1968, II*, 521; Memorandum from Director of Central Intelligence McCone to Secretary of State Rusk, April 2, 1965, *FRUS 1964–1968, II*, 524; Cosmas, *The Joint Chiefs of Staff, 1960–1968, Part 2*, 233.
110. John T. McNaughton, Paper Prepared by the Assistant Secretary of Defense for International Security Affairs (McNaughton), March 10, 1965, *FRUS 1964–1968, II*, 428–31.
111. Ibid., 428.
112. McMaster, *Dereliction of Duty*, 225.

113. Project Corona Harvest, Oral History Interview #403, General Hunter Harris Jr., 22 April 1971, 46, Interviewed by Van Dunn, K239.0512-403, 00/00/64–00/00/67, Vol. 2, AFHRA.
114. Brennan, Analysis of Tactical Aircraft Operations, 1965–1966, Volume 1, xi–xii, NHHC.
115. History Naval Operations, Vol. III 1965–1967, Part 1, 76; Brennan, Analysis of Tactical Aircraft Operations, 1965–1966, Volume 1, xi–xii, NHHC.
116. Schlight, *The Years of the Offensive, 1965–1968*, 87, 155; Van Staaveren, *Gradual Failure*, 230.
117. Lyndon Johnson, Speech at Johns Hopkins University, April 7, 1965, www.Presidentialrhetoric.com; Sharp, *Strategy for Defeat*, 76.
118. Memorandum for Record, Meeting at CINCPAC Headquarters, April 4, 1965, *FRUS 1964–1968, II*, 534; Telegram from the Embassy in Vietnam to the Department of State, April 7, 1965, *FRUS 1964–1968, II*, 541; Memorandum from the Chairman of the Joint Chiefs of Staff (Wheeler) to Secretary of Defense McNamara, Overall Appraisal of Air Strikes against North Vietnam 7 February 1965 to 4 April 1965, April 6, 1965, *FRUS 1964–1968, II*, 537.
119. Memorandum from Secretary of Defense McNamara to President Johnson, April 21, 1965, *FRUS 1964–1968, II*, 574; Fact Sheet, Aircraft Camouflage, April 24, 1966, K717.151-11, 25–26 April 1966, AFHRA.
120. Memorandum from the President's Special Assistant for National Security Affairs (Bundy) to President Johnson, April 23, 1965, *FRUS 1964–1968, II*, 604–5.
121. Letter from Director of Central Intelligence McCone to President Johnson, April 28, 1965, *FRUS 1964–1968, II*, 614.
122. Cosmas, *The Joint Chiefs of Staff, 1960–1968, Part 2,* 363, 364; 7th Fleet Operational Summary, April 1965, NHHC; Melyan and Bonetti, Rolling Thunder, July 1965–December 1966, 15, K717.0414-12, AFHRA.
123. Message from CINCPACAF to CSAF, 080520Z, November 1966, K717.1623, AFHRA.
124. History Naval Operations, Vol. III 1965–1967, Part 1, 94, NHHC; Van Staaveren, *Gradual Failure*, 209–10, 240.
125. Message from CINCPAC to RUEKDA/JCS, Military Operations in Vietnam, 142140Z, January 1967, K717.01, 1 January–31 December 1967, Vol. 2, Part 2, AFHRA.
126. Sharp, *Strategy for Defeat*, 120, 128–29.
127. *The Pentagon Papers, Volume IV*, 57.
128. Eugenia C. Kiesling, "Total War, Total Nonsense, or The Military Historian Fetish," in Michael S. Neiberg, *Arms and the Man: Military History Essays in Honor of Dennis Showalter* (Leiden, The Netherlands: Brill, 2011), 215–42; David Chandler, *The Art of War in the Age of Marlborough* (New York: Sarpedon, 1995), 12–14; John Shy and Thomas W. Collier, "Revolutionary War," in *Makers of Modern Strategy*, edited by Peter Paret with the collaboration of Gordon A. Craig and Felix Gilbert (Princeton, NJ: Princeton University Press, 1986), 830.
129. Robert Buzzanco, *Masters of War: Military Dissent and Politics in the Vietnam Era* (New York: Cambridge University Press, 1996), 211–12; McMaster, *Dereliction of Duty*, 280.
130. Memo for the Secretary of Defense from the JCS, Rolling Thunder Targeting, September 15, 1967, attachment, K178.2-34, AFHRA.
131. Lavelle, Analysis of Air Warfare in Southeast Asia, 6 April 1966, I-B-9, I-B-11, K143.505-13, AFHRA.
132. Telecon Nbr 684, from 2nd Air Div to PACAF, 13 AF, 231050Z, March 1965, K526.1623 65/01/09–65/11/00, AFHRA.
133. Telegram from the Department of State to the Embassy in Vietnam, May 10, 1965, *FRUS 1964–1968, II*, 629; Telegram from the Department of State to the Embassy in Vietnam, May 11, 1965, *FRUS 1964–1968, II*, 636; Brigham, *Guerrilla Diplomacy*, 45.
134. Notes of a Meeting, May 16, 1965, *FRUS 1964–1968, II*, 665–67; Edwin Diamond, *Behind the*

Times: Inside the New New York Times (New York: Villard Books, 1994), 116, 122–24, 188–89.
135. 7th Fleet Operational Summary, May 1965, NHHC.
136. CINCPAC Communication Center, Rolling Thunder Program, 120314Z, May 1965, K712.1623-2, 65/01/22 - 65/06/28, AFHRA; Telegram from the Commander in Chief, Pacific (Sharp) to the Joint Chiefs of Staff, May 11, 1965, *FRUS 1964–1968, II*, 640–42; Memorandum from the Chairman of the Joint Chiefs of Staff (Wheeler) to Secretary of Defense McNamara, May 17, 1965, *FRUS 1964–1968, II*, 670–71.
137. Letter from Clark M. Clifford to President Johnson, May 17, 1965, *FRUS 1964–1968, II*, 672; John Acacia, *Clark Clifford: The Wise Man of Washington* (Lexington: University of Kentucky Press, 2009), 168, 171, 223, 236.
138. Memorandum Prepared in the Central Intelligence Agency, June 30, 1965, *FRUS 1964–1968, III*, 88, 89.
139. Paper Prepared by the Ambassador to Vietnam (Taylor) and the Deputy Ambassador to Vietnam (Johnson), May 20, 1965, *FRUS 1964–1968, II*, 675, 684; Gregory A. Daddis, *Westmoreland's War: Reassessing American Strategy in Vietnam* (New York: Oxford University Press, 2014), 169, 177–82.
140. Telegram from the Department of State to the Embassy in Vietnam, June 1, 1965, *FRUS 1964–1968, II*, 704–5; Telegram from the Embassy in Vietnam to the Department of State, June 3, 1965, *FRUS 1964–1968, II*, 710–13.
141. Telegram from the White House to the Embassy in the United Kingdom, June 16, 1965, *FRUS 1964–1968, III*, 12; Memorandum from the President's Special Assistant for National Security Affairs (Bundy) to President Johnson, June 21, 1965, *FRUS 1964–1968, III*, 27–33; McMaster, *Dereliction of Duty*, 286.
142. Telegram from Westmoreland to Wheeler, June 24, 1965, *FRUS 1964–1968, III*, 42; Paper by the Undersecretary of State (Ball), "Cutting our Losses in South Viet-Nam," no date (approximately June 28, 1965), *FRUS 1964–1968, III*, 62. Ball's June argument stands in contrast to his position after the VC mortared Pleiku in February during which he insisted on harsh reprisals. Woods, *LBJ*, 601.
143. Notes of Meeting, July 21, 1965, *FRUS 1964–1968, III*, 194; Goldstein, *Lessons in Disaster*, 208.
144. Telegram from the Commander Military Assistance Command, Vietnam (Westmoreland) to the Commander in Chief, Pacific (Sharp), June 13, 1965, *FRUS 1964–1968, III*, 2, 5; McNamara, *In Retrospect*, 188.
145. PACAF DI, Effects of Air Operations in Southeast Asia, 5 July 1965, 14, K717.6092, AFHRA; Sherwood, *Afterburner*, 59; Eduard Mark, *Aerial Interdiction: Air Power and the Land Battle in Three American Wars* (Washington, DC: Center for Air Force History, 1994), 359–60.
146. PACAF DI, Effects of Air Operations in Southeast Asia, 5 July 1965, 6, K717.6092, AFHRA.
147. Intensification of the Military Operations in Vietnam: Concept and Appraisal—Report of an Ad Hoc Study Group, July 14, 1965, *FRUS 1964–1968, III*, 187; SNIE 10-9-65, July 23, 1965, *FRUS 1964–1968, III*, 226, 228; Memorandum from the Chairman of the Joint Chiefs of Staff (Wheeler) to Secretary of Defense McNamara, Overall Appraisal of Air Strikes Against North Vietnam through 30 June 1965, July 14, 1965, *FRUS 1964–1968, III*, 143.
148. Memorandum from Secretary of Defense McNamara to President Johnson, Recommendations of Additional Deployments to Vietnam, July 20, 1965, *FRUS 1964-1968, III*, 176.
149. Cosmas, *The Joint Chiefs of Staff, 1960–1968, Part 2*, 368–69.
150. History of Pacific Air Forces, 1 July–31 December 1965, Vol. 1, Part 2, 44, 51, K717.01; Effects of Air Operations in Southeast Asia, 22 July 1965, 1–4, K717.6092, AFHRA.
151. PACAF DI, Effects of Air Operations in Southeast Asia, 19 August 1965, 1, K717-6092, AFHRA.
152. Clodfelter, *Limits of Air Power*, 71.

NOTES FOR CHAPTER 14

153. Message from CINCPAC to RUEKDA/JCS, Rolling Thunder Appraisal, 220043Z, August 1965, K717.01, July–December 1965, Vol. 2, Part 2, AFHRA.
154. Message from CINCPAC, Rolling Thunder Appraisal, 220043Z, August 1965, K717.01, AFHRA.
155. DCS Intelligence, Headquarters PACAF, Effects of Air Operations Southeast Asia, October 1966, 44, K717.6092; General J. P. McConnell, Chief of Staff, USAF, The Effectiveness of Air Interdiction Operations against Railroads in North Vietnam, 12 July 1966, K143.5072-66; Study of Effectiveness of the Air Campaign against NVN, K178.2-45 July 1967, AFHRA; Clodfelter, *Limits of Air Power*, 71.
156. Message from CINCPAC, Rolling Thunder Appraisal, 220043Z, August 1965, K717.01, AFHRA.
157. Ibid.
158. Commander in Chief U.S. Pacific Fleet, Preliminary Analysis of Data on U.S. Navy Rolling Thunder Armed Reconnaissance 23 July–18 November 1965, 13 June 1966, Vietnam Command Files, COLL/372, Box 112, File CPF Staff Study 7-66, NHHC.
159. Message from CINCPACFLT to RUHKA/CINCPAC, Effects of Rolling Thunder Program, 210228Z, August 1965, K717.01, July–December 1965, Vol. 2, Part 2; PACAF DI, Effects of Air Operations in Southeast Asia, 16 September 1965, 10, 19, K717.6092, AFHRA.
160. Intelligence Memorandum No. 2391/65, October 27, 1965, *FRUS 1964–1968, III*, 500–503.
161. Cosmas, *The Joint Chiefs of Staff, 1960–1968, Part 2*, 380.
162. Message from CINCPAC to RUEKDA/JCS, Rolling Thunder Appraisal, 210043Z, August 1965, K717.01, July–December 1965, Vol. 2, Part 2, AFHRA.
163. Message from CINCPAC, Rolling Thunder Air Campaign in NVN, April through September 1968, 1 March 1968, K712.1623-2; Air Operations in Southeast Asia, 1972–1973, Vol. 1, ii-39, K717.0423-23; History of the Pacific Air Forces, 1966, 88, K717.01, Vol. 1, Part 2, AFHRA.
164. Message from CINCPAC to JCS, Analysis of Aircraft Losses in Seasia, 040710Z, March 1965, K712.1623-2; Message from Admiral Sharp for General Westmoreland, Air Operations SEASIA, 190452Z, March 1966, K712.03-20, AFHRA.
165. McConnell, Effectiveness of Air Interdiction against Railroads, 12 July 1966, K143.5072-66, AFHRA; Message from CTG 77.4 to AIG918, 141548Z, August 1967, Vietnam Air War Collection, Box 69, Folder 69/1; Message from Comseventhflt to AIG 183, Weekly Summary 7–13 June, 170700Z, June 1967; Message from Comseventhflt to AIG 183, Weekly Summary 28 February–5 March, 110832Z, March 1968, Ships History Post 2001 *Enterprise* CV-65, Box 108, File Enterprise Vietnam Message File, NHHC.
166. Summary Air Operations Southeast Asia August 1972, pages 1-1, 4-1, K717.3063, AFHRA.
167. L. Standlee Steenrod and Lt. Col. George E. Yale Jr., The Bombing Campaign in North Vietnam and Laos: September 1966–April 1968, 28 June 1968, K143.5045-6, September 1966–April 1968, AFHRA.
168. Conversation among President Nixon, the President's Assistant for National Security Affairs (Kissinger), and the Chairman of the Joint Chiefs of Staff (Moorer), April 3, 1972, *FRUS 1969–1976, VIII*, 172; Brennan, Analysis of Tactical Aircraft Operations, 1965–1966, Volume 1, 14, NHHC.
169. PACAF DI, Effects of Air Operations in Southeast Asia, 14 October 1965, 25–30; PACAF DI, Effects of Air Operations in Southeast Asia, 28 October 1965, 1, K717.6092; General Harris interview, 22 April 1971, 78, K239.0512-403, Vol. 2, AFHRA.
170. PACAF DI, Effects of Air Operations in Southeast Asia, 28 October 1965, 1, K717.6092. 5-7, AFHRA.
171. PACAF DI, Summary of Effects of Air Operations Southeast Asia, 1965, 11, K717.6092, AFHRA.

172. History of Pacific Air Forces, 1 July–31 December 1965, Vol. 1, Part 2, 64, K717.01, AFHRA.
173. Melyan and Bonetti, Rolling Thunder, July 1965–December 1966, 20, K717.0414-12; Letter from the President's Consultant on Vietnam (Taylor) to President Johnson, December 27, 1965, *FRUS 1964–1968, III*, 712.
174. PACAF DI, Effects of Air Operations in Southeast Asia, 9 December 1965, 5, K717.6092, AFHRA.
175. PACAF DI, Summary of Effects of Air Operations Southeast Asia, 1965, 1, 3, K717.6092, AFHRA.
176. History of Pacific Air Forces, 1 July–31 December 1965, Vol. 1, Part 2, 67, 68, K717.01; PACAF DI, Summary of Effects of Air Operations Southeast Asia, 1965, 5–6, K717.6092; History of Pacific Air Forces, 1 July–31 December 1965, Vol. 1, Part 2, 30, K717.01, AFHRA.
177. Notes of Meeting, January 3, 1966, *FRUS 1964–1968, IV*; Summary Notes of the 556th Meeting of the National Security Council, January 29, 1966, *FRUS 1964–1968, IV*, 187; History of Pacific Air Forces, January–December 1966, 30–31, K717.01, January–December 1966, Vol. 1, Part 1, AFHRA.
178. "Elements of Second Pause Scenario," Draft Paper by the Assistant Secretary of State for Far Eastern Affairs (Bundy), October 22, 1965, *FRUS, 1964–1968, III*, 475–76.
179. Clodfelter, *Limits of Air Power*, 91.
180. Second Pause Scenario, Draft Paper by William Bundy, October 22, 1965, *FRUS, 1964–1968, III*, 478.
181. Duiker, *Sacred War*, 134, 173; Guan, *The Vietnam War from the Other Side*, 79.
182. Secretary of Defense McNamara, "Memorandum of Telephone Conversations with Members of Congress Relating to South Vietnam," December 9, 1965, *FRUS III, 1964–1968*, 634.
183. History Naval Operations, Vol. III 1965–1967, Part 1, 99, NHHC.
184. Melyan and Bonetti, Rolling Thunder, July 1965–December 1966, 31, K717.0414-12, AFHRA.
185. Draft Memorandum from Secretary of Defense McNamara to President Johnson, Courses of Action in Vietnam, November 3, 1965, *FRUS, 1964–1968, III*, 521, 528.
186. Memorandum for President Johnson, Courses of Action in Viet-Nam, November 9, 1965, *FRUS, 1964–1968, III*, 542. For a further examination of the concept of strategy as a process of seeking continuing advantage during a conflict or war, see Everett Carl Dolman, Lecture, Problems of Strategy, Air Command and Staff College, August 10, 2015, and Everett Carl Dolman, *Pure Strategy: Power and Principle in the Space and Information Age* (New York: Frank Cass, 2005).
187. Lieutenant General Victor H. Krulak to Robert H. McNamara, November 11, 1965, Victor H. Krulak Papers, COLL/3064, Box 1, Folder 3, Archives Branch, HDMCU.
188. Telegram from the Embassy in Vietnam to the Department of State, January 5, 1966, *FRUS 1964–1968, IV*, 15; Summary Notes of the 555th Meeting of the National Security Council, January 5, 1966, *FRUS 1964–1968, IV*, 21; Letter from the Permanent Representative to the United Nations (Goldberg) to the Ambassador to Vietnam (Lodge), January 6, 1966, *FRUS 1964–1968, IV*, 23.
189. Draft Papers, December 18, 1965, *FRUS 1964–1968, III*, 652–53.
190. *FRUS, 1964–1968, III*, 716.
191. Notes on Meeting, December 18, 1965, *FRUS 1964–1968, III*, 662, 665; Memorandum for President Johnson, November 9, 1965, *FRUS 1964–1968, III*, 538.
192. Elliot, *The Vietnamese War*, 1054–55.
193. Guan, *The Vietnam War from the Other Side*, 108, 114. The quotation is Guan's.
194. Telegram from the President's Special Assistant for National Security Affairs (Bundy) to President Johnson, in Texas, December 27, 1965, *FRUS, 1964–1968, III*, 703; Notes of Meeting, January 3, 1966, *FRUS 1964–1968, IV*, 9; McNamara, *In Retrospect*, 219–23; Joseph A. Fry, *Debating Vietnam: Fulbright, Stennis, and Their Senate Hearings* (Lanham, MD: Rowman & Littlefield,

2006), 119.
195. HQ 7th AF, Commando Hunt III, 123, K740.04-8, 69/11/00–70/04/00/, AFHRA; Prados, *The Blood Road*, 374.
196. Passauer, End-of-tour Report, K740.131, AFHRA; Intelligence Memorandum Prepared by the Directorate of Intelligence of the Central Intelligence Agency, May 18, 1968, *FRUS 1964–1968*, *XXVIII*, 713.
197. Telegram from the Embassy in Laos to Department of State, June 21, 1965, *FRUS 1964–1968*, *III*, 371.
198. PACAF DI, Effects of Air Operations Southeast Asia, May 1967, 102–3, K717.6092, AFHRA; Neale, *A People's History of the Vietnam War*, 141.
199. Message from CINCPAC to JCS, 211959Z, April 1965, K717.1623, April 1965, AFHRA; History Naval Operations, Vol. III 1965–1967, Part 1, 85, NHHC.
200. Philip Warner, *Sieges of the Middle Ages* (London: G. Bell and Sons, 1968), 59–60, 4. For helpful discussions of siege warfare, see Philippe Contamine, *War in the Middle Ages*, trans. Michael Jones (Oxford: Basil Blackwell, 1984), 102, 105, 115, 282; Paul Bentley Kern, *Ancient Siege Warfare* (Bloomington and Indianapolis: Indiana University Press, 1999), 286–98; Russell F. Weigley, *The Age of Battles: The Quest for Decisive Warfare from Breitenfeld to Waterloo* (Bloomington and Indianapolis: Indiana University Press, 1991), 55.
201. Action Memorandum from the Deputy Assistant Secretary of State for Far Eastern Affairs (Unger) to Secretary of State Rusk, Increased Military Pressures against North Viet-Nam, March 30, 1966, *FRUS 1964–1968, IV*, 310.
202. Blout, Air Operations in Northern Laos, 1 April–1 November 1970, 30–31, K717.0413-65, AFHRA.
203. Assessment of Air Operations, 7 February 1965 thru 19 July 1967, 31, K740.04-20, AFHRA.
204. Memorandum Prepared by the Central Intelligence Agency, 3097/65, December 9, 1965, *FRUS 1964–1968, III*, 423.
205. Assessment of Air Operations, 7 February 1965 thru 19 July 1967, 31, K740.04-20, AFHRA; Stanley Karnow, *Vietnam: A History* (New York: Viking, 1983), 455; Hearings before the Preparedness Investigating Subcommittee, August 25, 1967, 298; Van Staaveren, *Gradual Failure*, 153; Van Staaveren, *Interdiction in Southern Laos*, 301.
206. Memorandum from Secretary of Defense McNamara to President Johnson, January 24, 1966, *FRUS 1964–1968, IV*, 114; Lavelle, Analysis of Air Warfare in Southeast Asia, 6 April 1966, I-B-5, K143.505-13; Seventh Air Force, Commando Hunt VII, 1972, 133, K740.04-14, AFHRA; Prados, *The Blood Road*, 157.
207. History of Pacific Air Forces, 1 July–31 December 1965, Vol. 1, Part 2, 31, 119, K717.01; Message from 7AF to RUHLKM/CINCPACAF, Night Operations, 240655Z, November 1966, K740.511-1, AFHRA; Van Staaveren, *Interdiction in Southern Laos, 1960–1968*, 102.
208. Effects of Air Operations in Southeast Asia, 22 July 1965, 18, K717.6092; Effects of Air Operations Southeast Asia, Edition 37, 1967, 77, 79, K717.6092, AFHRA.
209. Major Gordon Y. W. Ow, Documentation and Analysis of Steel Tiger Interdiction Operations: November 1966–May 1967, 3, 11, 21, K740.31067-9; PACAF DI, Effects of Air Operations Southeast Asia, May 1967, 49, K717.6092, AFHRA.
210. History Naval Operations, Vol. III 1965–1967, Part 1, 208, NHHC; Message from CINCPAC to JCS, Steel Tiger, 180403Z August 1965. Message from CINCPAC to JCS, Infiltration Laos Panhandle, 0304119Z, November 1965, K712.1623-2 65/07/25–65/12/07; Southeast Asia Air Operations Briefing August 1971, K717.3063-1, August 1971, AFHRA.
211. History Naval Operations, Vol. III 1965–1967, Part 1, 208, NHHC.
212. Prados, *Blood Road*, 113, 193; Li, *Building Ho's Army*, 156; Telegram from the Embassy in Laos to

Department of State, August 9, 1965, *FRUS 1964–1968, III*, 387.
213. Telegram from the Commander in Chief, Pacific (Sharp) to the Joint Chiefs of Staff, October 26, 1966, *FRUS, 1964–1968, IV,* 780.
214. Message from CINCPAC to JCS, RVN Infiltration, 202213Z, November 1965, K712.1623-2, 65/07/25 - 65/12/07, AFHRA; Hearings before the Preparedness Investigating Subcommittee, August 16, 1967, 143.
215. PACAF DI, Effects of Air Operations in Southeast Asia, 19 August 1965, 3, K717.6092; General William W. Momyer, Letter to General Hunter Harris, Commander-in-Chief Pacific Air Forces, 15 July 1966, K143.5072-65, 15 July 1966, AFHRA.
216. Prados, *The Blood Road*, 158.
217. Enney, Commander Attack Carrier Air Wing Fourteen, Addendum Report, 11 February 1969, History Naval Operations, Vol. III 1965–1967, Part 1, 208, NHHC; Effects of Air Operations in Southeast Asia, 22 July 1965, 18, K717.6092, AFHRA.
218. Major Gordon Y. W. Ow, Some Thoughts on Road Interdiction Strategy, 1 February 1967, 1, K740.31067-2, 1 February 1967, AFHRA.
219. DCS Intelligence, Headquarters PACAF, Effects of Air Operations Southeast Asia, October 1966, 44, K717.6092, AFHRA.
220. Message from CINCPACAF to CSAF, 080520Z, November 1966, K717.1623, March–December 1966, AFHRA.
221. History Naval Operations, Vol. III 1965–1967, Part 1, 211, NHHC; MACV Command History 1965, 215–16.
222. Memorandum from the Joint Chiefs of Staff to Secretary of Defense McNamara, January 8, 1966, *FRUS 1964–1968, IV*, 35–36; Telegram from the Commander in Chief, Pacific (Sharp) to the Joint Chiefs of Staff, January 12, 1966, *FRUS 1964–1968, IV*, 47–51; Telegram from the Commander in Chief, Pacific (Sharp) to the Joint Chiefs of Staff, January 12, 1966, *FRUS 1964–1968, IV*, 49, 50; Memorandum from the Joint Chiefs of Staff to Secretary of Defense McNamara, January 18, 1966, *FRUS 1964–1968, IV*, 81; Telegram from Sharp to the Joint Chiefs of Staff, January 12, 1966, *FRUS 1964–1968, IV*, 82–83.
223. Notes of Meeting, January 28, 1966, *FRUS 1964–1968, IV*, 181.
224. Information Memorandum from the Legal Advisor of the Department of State to Secretary of State Rusk, January 20, 1966, Telegram from Sharp to the Joint Chiefs of Staff, January 12, 1966, *FRUS 1964–1968, IV*, 95–97.
225. History of the Pacific Air Forces, 1966, 166, K717.01, Vol. 1, Part 2, AFHRA; Notes of Meeting, January 27, 1966, *FRUS 1964–1968, IV*, 164–65; Notes of Meeting, January 28, 1966, *FRUS 1964–1968, IV*, 174–75, 181.
226. Cosmas, *The Joint Chiefs of Staff, 1960–1968, Part 2*, 408–9, 411; History of the Pacific Air Forces, 1966, 166, K717.01, Vol. 1, Part 2, AFHRA.
227. Gelb and Betts, *The Irony of Vietnam*, 141.
228. Paper Prepared by Secretary of Defense McNamara and Assistant Secretary of Defense for International Security Affairs (McNaughton), February 10, 1966, *FRUS 1964–1968, IV*, 217; Action Memorandum from the Deputy Assistant Secretary of State for Far Eastern Affairs (Unger) to Secretary of State Rusk, Increased Military Pressures against North Viet-Nam, March 30, 1966, *FRUS 1964–1968, IV*, 310.
229. History of the Pacific Air Forces, 1966, 153, K717.01, Vol. 1, Part 2, AFHRA.
230. Sharp, *Strategy for Defeat*, 109; Memorandum from the Joint Chiefs of Staff to Secretary of Defense McNamara, Air Operations against North Vietnam, March 26, 1966, *FRUS, 1964–1968, IV*, 300.
231. General William W. Momyer, Study of Bombing Alternatives, 28 March 1968, K740.04-21, 65/00/00–68/00/00, AFHRA.

232. Interview of General John W. Vogt by Claude G. Morita, 25 January 1973, K740.01-25 Vol. 1, p. 120, AFHRA.
233. HQ USMACV Command History, 1966, 346.
234. PACAF DI, Effects of Air Operations in Southeast Asia, 16 September 1965, 5, K717.6092, AFHRA; Cosmas, *The Joint Chiefs of Staff, 1960–1968, Part 2*, 408–9, 411; Clodfelter, *Limits of Air Power*, 96; Milne, *America's Rasputin*, 170–71; *The Pentagon Papers, Volume IV*, 5.
235. Cosmas, *The Joint Chiefs of Staff, 1960–1968, Part 2*, 413–16.
236. Message from Admiral Sharp, Air Operations SEASIA, 190452Z, March 1966, K712.03-20; Effects of Air Operations Southeast Asia, August 1966, 59, K717.6092, AFHRA; McNamara, *In Retrospect*, 228.
237. Lavelle, Analysis of Air Warfare in Southeast Asia, 6 April 1966, i-c-7, K143.505-13, AFHRA; Editorial Note, *FRUS 1964–1968, IV*, 192.
238. An Appraisal of the Effects of the First Year of Bombing in North Vietnam, June 1, 1966, *FRUS 1964–1968, IV*, 429–32.
239. Intelligence Memorandum Prepared in the Central Intelligence Agency, No. 1683/66, July 23, 1966, *FRUS 1964–1968, IV*, 517.
240. Operations Analysis Office, Vice Chief of Staff, HQ USAF, Analysis of Effectiveness of Interdiction in SEA, Second Progress Report, May 1966, K143.5072-13, May–July 1966, AFHRA; Wilkins, *Grab Their Belts to Fight Them*, 160; Guan, *The Vietnam War from the Other Side*, 105–6.
241. Telephone Conversation between President Johnson and Senator Mike Mansfield, June 10, 1966, *FRUS 1964–1968, IV*, 417–18; History of the Pacific Air Forces, 1966, 84, K717.01 Vol. 1, Part 2, AFHRA.
242. Cosmas, *The Joint Chiefs of Staff, 1960–1968, Part 2*, 424, 425; Notes of President Johnson's Meeting with the National Security Council, June 22, 1966, *FRUS 1964–1968, IV*, 450–52, Footnote 4, 452.
243. Clodfelter, *Limits of Air Power*, 98; History of the Pacific Air Forces, 1966, 84, K717.01, Vol. 1, Part 2, AFHRA.
244. Cosmas, *The Joint Chiefs of Staff, 1960–1968, Part 2*, 505, 506, OPNAV 5750-1 Attack Squadron Fifty-Five Command History 1966, Fleet Aviation Commands Pre-1998, AR/229, Box 132, File F15, NHHC.
245. Gardner, *Pay Any Price*, 307.
246. History of the Pacific Air Forces, 1966, 84, K717.01, Vol. 1, Part 2; Melyan and Bonetti, Rolling Thunder, July 1965–December 1966, 79, K717.0414-12, AFHRA; Telegram from the Embassy in Laos to the Department of State, January 5, 1966, *FRUS 1964–1968, XXVIII*, 435; History Naval Operations, Vol. III 1965–1967, Part 1, 110–11, NHHC.
247. Intelligence Report S-3690/AP-2F, August 1966, *FRUS 1964–1968, IV*, 615–16; HQ CINCPAC, Pacific Area Naval Operations Review August 1966, 8–9, Pacific Area Naval Operations Review September 1966, 7, Vietnam Command Files, Box 102, File August 1966, September 1966, NHHC; History of the Pacific Air Forces, 1966, 20–21, K717.01, Vol. 1, Part 1, AFHRA.
248. PACAF DI, Effects of Air Operations in Southeast Asia, September 1966, 35, 2, K717.6092, AFHRA.
249. Robert S. McNamara, Extracts from CIA/DIA Report, An Appraisal of the Bombing of North Vietnam Through 12 September 1966, *FRUS 1964–1968, IV*, 737; DCS Intelligence, Headquarters PACAF, Effects of Air Operations Southeast Asia, October 1966, 70, K717.6092, AFHRA.
250. Melyan and Bonetti, Rolling Thunder, July 1965–December 1966, 50, K717.0414-12, AFHRA.
251. Intelligence Memorandum Prepared in the Central Intelligence Agency, SC No. 09624/66, The Vietnamese Communists' Will to Persist," August 26, 1966, *FRUS 1964–1968, IV*, 601.
252. Assessment of Air Operations, 7 February 1965 thru 19 July 1967, 18–20, K740.04-20, AFHRA.

253. Melyan and Bonetti, Rolling Thunder, July 1965–December 1966, 88–89, K717.0414-12, AFHRA; HQ CINCPAC, Pacific Area Naval Operations Review August–October 1966, Pacific Area Naval Operations Review November 1966, Vietnam Command Files, Box 102, Files August–November 1966, NHHC.
254. Intelligence Memorandum, August 9, 1967, North Vietnamese Losses during Infiltration, *FRUS 1964–1968, V*, 679, 680; Robert S. McNamara, Extracts from CIA/DIA Report, An Appraisal of the Bombing of North Vietnam Through 12 September 1966, *FRUS 1964–1968, IV*, 740; Schulzinger, *A Time for War*, 209.
255. Clodfelter, *Limits of Air Power*, 99; *The Pentagon Papers, Volume IV*, 111–20.
256. Intelligence Note from the Director of Intelligence and Research (Hughes) to Secretary of State Rusk, September 14, 1966, *FRUS 1964–1968, IV*, 632; Major Edward J. Fisher, Flow of Goods to Meet Demands in NVN, AFGOA/RAND SEA Study Group, 23 July 1968, 20, 35, 39, K143.5045-10, 23 July 1968, AFHRA.
257. Memorandum from Secretary of Defense McNamara to President Johnson, October 14, 1966, *FRUS 1964–1968, IV*, 729–30; Herring, *LBJ and Vietnam*, 47.
258. Memorandum from the Commander, Military Assistance Command, Vietnam (Westmoreland) to the President's Special Assistant (Rostow), October 24, 1966, *FRUS 1964–1968, IV*, 778–79; Telegram from Sharp to the Joint Chiefs of Staff, October 26, 1966, *FRUS 1964–1968, IV*, 781, 782.
259. Transcript of Message from Gen Moore, CINCPACAF to Gen Momyer, 25 October 1966, Briefing Delivered by Major General Brown to SECDEF October 1966, K717.312-15, 25 October 1966, AFHRA.
260. PACAF DI, Effects of Air Operations in Southeast Asia, September 1966, 45, 65, 70, K717.6092, AFHRA.
261. DCS Intelligence, Headquarters PACAF, Effects of Air Operations Southeast Asia, October 1966, 49, K717.6092, AFHRA.
262. DCS Intelligence, Headquarters PACAF, Effects of Air Operations Southeast Asia, November 1966, 39, K717.6092, AFHRA; Memorandum from the Chairman, Joint Chiefs of Staff (Wheeler) to Secretary of Defense McNamara, November 8, 1966, CM-1906-66, *FRUS 1964–1968, IV*, 809–11; Memorandum from Secretary of Defense McNamara to President Johnson, November 9, 1966, *FRUS 1964–1968, IV*, 818.
263. Editorial Note, *FRUS 1964–1968, IV*, 897, 898; HQ CINCPAC, Pacific Area Naval Operations Review December 1966, 16–19, NHHC; Cosmas, *The Joint Chiefs of Staff, 1960–1968, Part 2*, 508.
264. Ow, Analysis of Steel Tiger Interdiction Operations, 5, K740.31067-9; Recon Effort during New Year's Stand-Down, 310242Z, December 1966, K717.312, December 1966, AFHRA.
265. HQ CINCPAC, Pacific Area Naval Operations Review December 1966, 10, NHHC; Message from CINCPAC 1967 Goals for Evaluation of Progress in Southeast Asia, 260403Z, November 1966, K712.1623-2, AFHRA; Document 70: Paper Prepared by Secretary of Defense McNamara and Assistant Secretary of Defense for International Security Affairs (McNaughton), February 10, 1966, *FRUS 1964–1968, IV*, Vietnam 1966, 216–18.
266. Intelligence Memorandum, August 9, 1967, North Vietnamese Losses during Infiltration, *FRUS 1964–1968, V*, 679, 680.
267. Message from CINCPAC, Military Operations in Vietnam, 142140Z, January 1967, K717.01, AFHRA.
268. Telegram from the Commander in Chief Pacific (Sharp) to the Chairman, Joint Chiefs of Staff (Wheeler), December 24, 1966, *FRUS, 1964–1968, IV*, 970.
269. Cosmas, *The Joint Chiefs of Staff, 1960–1968, Part 2*, 518.
270. Message from CINCPAC, Military Operations in Vietnam, 142140Z, January 1967,

K717.01, AFHRA.
271. Fleet Operations Review, August 1968, 11, NHHC.
272. HQ CINCPAC, Pacific Area Naval Operations Review September 1968, 12, 14, Pacific Area Naval Operations Review October 1968, 14, Vietnam Command Files, Box 105, Files September, October 1968, NHHC; Letter from the Commander of the Fleet Marine Force, Pacific (Krulak) to Secretary of Defense McNamara, January 4, 1967, *FRUS 1964–1968, V*, 16.
273. Intelligence Memorandum, November 1966, Effectiveness of the Rolling Thunder Program in North Vietnam, 1 January–30 December 1966, *FRUS 1964–1968, IV*, 803; Melyan and Bonetti, Rolling Thunder, July 1965–December 1966, 127, K717.0414-12, AFHRA.
274. Analysis of Aircraft Losses in Seasia, 040710Z, March 1965, K712.1623-2, AFHRA.
275. Within the doctrine of double effect, it is not immoral for noncombatant bystanders to be killed if an attacker makes a reasonable effort to place his bomb on a lawful target and does not seek wider damage via oversized bombs or lackadaisical accuracy. James Turner Johnson, *Morality and Contemporary Warfare* (New Haven, CT: Yale University Press, 1999), 130.
276. Commander in Chief U.S. Pacific Fleet, Navy Combat Accuracy Data, 10 March 1966, Vietnam Command Files, COLL/372, Box 112, File CPF Staff Study 4-66, Wingerter, Attack Carrier Air Wing One, Cruise Report, 2 May 1967, NHHC. To be exact, these figures measure "circular error probability" or "CEP," which was the radius in which half of the bombs dropped will hit. Another definition of circular error probability defines it as "the radius of the smallest circle with center at (x,y) which has a 50 percent probability of containing the true target coordinates." William Nelson, "Use of Circular Error Probability in Target Detection," Air Force Systems Command, 1988, 1.
277. Report from USAF Analysis Team, 150020Z, March 1965, K526.1623, AFHRA.
278. HQ PACAF, Assistant for Operations Analysis, Comparison of Dive Bomb Tactics between the 355th TFW and 388th TFW, K717.310467-5, May 1967, AFHRA.
279. Colonel Benton K. Partin, HQ 7th AF, Bombing Accuracy in a Combat Environment, Southeast Asia, August 1967–January 1968, K740.31068-4, 10 May 1968, AFHRA.
280. 7th Fleet Operational Summary, July 1965, Reference Files, Vietnam, A-Air Warfare (I), Aircraft Losses Folder, HQ CINCPAC, Pacific Area Naval Operations Review September 1966, 82, Vietnam Command Files, Box 102, File September 1966; Commanding Officer Attack Squadron One Hundred Sixty-Four, 1 March 1968, Memorandum from Commanding Officer, Attack Squadron One Five Three to Commander Attack Carrier Air Wing Fifteen, 13 November 1966, Fleet Aviation Commands Pre-1998, AR/229, Box 172 File F5, NHHC; History of Pacific Air Forces, 1 July–31 December 1965, Volume 1, Part 2, 107, K717.01, AFHRA.
281. Peter F. English and Bobby L. Marlow, Directorate of Operations Analysis, Reduction of Tactical Fighter Losses Over North Vietnam, 23 November 1966, K740.31066-13, 23 November 1966, AFHRA.
282. Page, Attack Carrier Wing Two, Cruise Report, 17 May 1969, NHHC. The black box was a CP-741.
283. Sherwood, *Afterburner*, 31.
284. Combined Campaign Plan Commando Nail Operations, K740.317-3, 14 October 1967, AFHRA.
285. Major Henry Triwush and Barthold W. Sorge Jr., USAF Tactical All-Weather Bombing Capability Over North Vietnam, 20 July 1966, K740.31066-8, 20 July 1966. The chief of staff of the Air Force was particularly interested in the accuracy of Sky Spot/Combat Proof. Message from CSAF to RUHLKM/CINCPACAF, Combat Proof, 232047Z, December 1966, K717.312, 23–24 December 1966; Vice Chief of Staff U.S. Air Force Conference, 25–26 April 1966, K717.151-11, AFHRA; T.O. 1F-105D-1 Flight Manual, (Fairchild Hiller, 1969), A4–8.
286. Trapolino and Otis, History of the 307th Strategic Wing, 1–31 May 1970, K-WG-307-HI, June 1970, AFHRA.

NOTES FOR CHAPTER 14

287. Telegram from the Commander in Chief, Pacific (Sharp) to the Chairman of the Joint Chiefs of Staff (Wheeler), February 25, 1967, *FRUS 1964–1968, XXVIII*, 559; Memorandum from the Director of Intelligence and Research (Hughes) to Secretary of State Rusk, February 28, 1968, *FRUS 1964–1968, XXVIII*, 658.
288. Telegram from the Embassy in Laos to the Department of State, March 11, 1968, *FRUS 1964–1968, XXVIII*, 665; Telegram from the Embassy in Laos to the Department of State, March 13, 1968, *FRUS 1964–1968, XXVIII*, 667. See also Timothy N. Castle, *One Day Too Long: Top Secret Site 85 and the Bombing of North Vietnam* (New York: Columbia University Press, 1999).
289. Message from 7AF, Night Operations, 240655Z, November 1966, K740.511-1; Effects of Air Operations Southeast Asia, August 1966, 112, K717.6092; History of the Pacific Air Forces, 1966, 93, K717.01, Vol. 1, Part 2; Message from CSAF to RUHLKM/CINCPACAF, Combat Proof, 232047Z, December 1966, K717-312, AFHRA.
290. History Naval Operations, Vol. III 1965–1967, Part 1, 101, NHHC; Colonel Kenneth L. Skeen, TAC Test 69-19 TACW Project 0010 Combat Thunder (RF-4C) Final Report, Vol. 1, June 1971, K417.01 FY1971 Vol. 13, AFHRA.
291. Skeen, TAC Test 69-19 Combat Thunder (RF-4C) Final Report, K417.01 FY1971 Vol. 13; Talking Paper on Night Operations in SEA, 15 November 1966, K143.5072-9, July 1965–November 1966, AFHRA.
292. Brig. Gen. Dale S. Sweat, HQ 7th AF to DXIH, Coordination of History, Tab 1, 3 September 1968, K740.07, July–December 1967, AFHRA; HQ CINCPAC, Pacific Area Naval Operations Review January 1968, 21, Vietnam Command Files, Box 104, File January 1968, Operation Focus-1, US Seventh Fleet Monthly Historical Summary, November 1967, 21–22, NHHC.
293. Colonel Robert R. Scott, PACAF Tactics & Techniques Bulletin, No. 20, 10 September 1965, K717.549-1, Nos. 19–21, 3–10 September 1965, AFHRA; HQ CINCPAC, Pacific Area Naval Operations Review January 1968, 24, Vietnam Command Files, Box 104, File January 1968, NHHC.
294. History of Pacific Air Forces, 1 July–31 December 1965, Vol. 1, part 2, 57, K717.01; Ow, Analysis of Steel Tiger Interdiction Operations, 7–8, K740.31067-9; Message from USAFE to RUEDHQA/CSAF, Comments on report of World-Wide Tactical Fighter Symposium, 190731Z, May 1966, AFHRA.
295. Seventh Air Force, Commando Hunt VII, 254–55, K740.04-14, November 1971–March 1972; Effects of Air Operations Southeast Asia, March 1967, 64, K717.6092, AFHRA.
296. Message from CINCPAC, 1967 Goals for Evaluation of Progress in Southeast Asia, 260403Z, November 1966, K717.01, 1 January–31 December 1967, Vol. 2, Part 2, AFHRA.
297. Message from CINCPACAF to RUHKA/CINCPAC, Rolling Thunder, 101946Z, January 1967, K712.1623-9, 10 January 1967, AFHRA.
298. Woods, *LBJ*, 754.
299. Message from CINCPAC, Military Operations in Vietnam, 142140Z, January 1967, K717.01, AFHRA.
300. Memorandum from the President's Special Assistant (Rostow) to President Johnson, January 19, 1967, *FRUS 1964–1968, V*, 49–50.
301. Gelb and Betts, *The Irony of Vietnam*, 168.
302. Clodfelter, *Limits of Air Power*, 106.
303. Memorandum from the President's Special Assistant (Rostow) to President Johnson, January 23, 1967, *FRUS 1964–1968, V*, 58; Cosmas, *The Joint Chiefs of Staff, 1960–1968, Part 2*, 520; HQ CINCPAC, Pacific Area Naval Operations Review January 1967, 12, Vietnam Command Files, Box 102, File January 1967, NHHC.
304. Johnson also wrote that the US would stop sending in more troops. Telegram from the Department

of State to the Embassy in the Soviet Union, February 7, 1967, *FRUS 1964–1968*, *V*, 92–93.

305. Summary Notes of the 568th Meeting of the National Security Council, February 8, 1967, *FRUS 1964–1968*, *V*, 98–99; Telegram from President Johnson to Prime Minister Wilson, February 12, 1967, *FRUS 1964–1968*, *V*, 143.

306. Hearings before the Preparedness Investigating Subcommittee, August 22, 1967, 203, Ho Chi Minh letter to President Johnson, February 15, 1967, *FRUS 1964–1968*, *V*, 173–74; Effects of Air Operations Southeast Asia, Edition 37, 1967, 50, K717.6092; Message from CINCPAC to JCS, CINCPAC Monthly Rolling Thunder Summary, September 1967, 072059Z, October 1967, K712.1623-2, September 1967, AFHRA.

307. HQ CINCPAC, Pacific Area Naval Operations Review February 1967, 15, Vietnam Command Files, Box 102, File February 1967; HQ CINCPAC, Pacific Area Naval Operations Review March 1967, 14, NHHC.

308. Notes of Meeting with President Johnson, February 17, 1967, *FRUS 1964–1968*, *V*, 183.

309. History Naval Operations, Vol. III 1965–1967, Part 1, 129, NHHC.

310. HQ CINCPAC, Pacific Area Naval Operations Review April 1967, 15, Vietnam Command Files, Box 102, File April 1967, NHHC; Tilford Jr., *Setup*, 78; PACAF DI, Effects of Air Operations in Southeast Asia, September 1966, 15, PACAF DI, Effects of Air Operations Southeast Asia, May 1967, 38, K717.6092, AFHRA.

311. W. W. Rostow, Notes of Meeting with President Johnson, February 17, 1967, *FRUS 1964–1968*, *V*, 185.

312. I have to admit that I am alluding to the concept of "the audience" in modern war. See Emile Simpson, *War from the Ground Up: Twenty-First Century Combat as Politics* (New York: Oxford University Press, 2013).

313. Editorial Note, *FRUS 1964–1968*, *V*, 366; Pribbenow, trans., *Victory in Vietnam*, 124–25.

314. Barrett, *Uncertain Warriors*, 62–92.

315. Memorandum for Record, March 21, 1967, *FRUS 1964–1968*, *V*, 278; Editorial Note, *FRUS 1964–1968*, *V*, 333; Cosmas, *Joint Chiefs of Staff 1960–1968, Part 3*, 20.

316. Robert W. Komer, Memorandum by the President's Special Assistant, April 24, 1967, *FRUS 1964–1968*, *V*, 344; Memorandum from Mansfield to President Johnson, April 29, 1967, *FRUS 1964–1968*, *V*, 355.

317. Edward Rice, Telegram from the Consulate in Hong Kong to the Department of State, May 1, 1967, *FRUS 1964–1968*, *V*, 360.

318. Gardner, *Pay Any Price*, 385.

319. McGeorge Bundy, Memorandum on Vietnam Policy, *FRUS 1964–1968*, *V*, 371.

320. Ibid., 372, 373.

321. Ibid., 375–76.

322. Memorandum from Secretary of Defense McNamara and the Deputy Secretary of Defense (Vance) to President Johnson, May 9, 1967, *FRUS 1964–1968*, *V*, 402, 403.

323. Memorandum from the President's Special Assistant (Rostow) to President Johnson, May 6, 1967, Bundy, Memorandum on Vietnam Policy, *FRUS 1964–1968*, *V*, 384; Memorandum by the Assistant Secretary of State for East Asian and Pacific Affairs (Bundy), May 9, 1967, *FRUS 1964–1968*, *V*, 404–5; Memorandum from the President's Special Consultant (Taylor) to President Johnson, *FRUS 1964–1968*, *V*, 410.

324. Draft Memorandum from Secretary of Defense McNamara to President Johnson, May 19, 1967, *FRUS 1964–1968*, *V*, 427, 430, 433; CIA, The Effectiveness of the Rolling Thunder Program and Enemy Countermeasures, 1 January 1966–30 April 1967, nsarchive2.gwu.edu/NSAEBB/NSAEBB348/jcsm.pdf.

325. McNamara, *In Retrospect*, 275; Memorandum for the Secretary of Defense, Operations against

North Vietnam, May 20, 1967, JCSM-286-67, Draft Memorandum from Secretary of Defense McNamara to President Johnson, June 12, 1967, *FRUS 1964–1968, V*, 474, https://www.cia.gov/library/readingroom/docs/CIA-RDP78S02149R000100310005-1.pdf.

326. General Earle G. Wheeler, Memorandum for the Secretary of Defense: Operations against North Vietnam, May 20, 1967, https://www.cia.gov/library/readingroom/docs/CIA-RDP78S02149R000100310005-1.pdf

327. PACAF DI, Effects of Air Operations Southeast Asia, May 1967, 8, 36, K717.6092, AFHRA; Berman, "The Tet Offensive," 28, Notes of Meeting, January 28, 1966, *FRUS 1964–1968, IV*, 177.

328. Message from CINCPAC to CINCPACFLT, CINCPACAF, Rolling Thunder, 140220Z, July 1967, K712.03-25, AFHRA.

329. Commander in Chief US Pacific Fleet, Rolling Thunder Report and Analysis, 16 May 1967, NHHC.

330. Overton, Rolling Thunder: January 1967–November 1968, 6, 7, K717.0414-12; Message from CINCPAC to RUEKDA/JCS, Rolling Thunder, 110237Z, June 1967, K717.312-64, AFHRA.

331. Howard A. Zwemer, Chief, Combat Analysis Division Operations Analysis, AFGOAC, Initial List of USAF Lessons Learned, 25 September 1967, K143.5072-22, Vol. 1, AFHRA.

332. Draft Memorandum from McNamara to President Johnson, June 12, 1967, *FRUS 1964–1968, V*, 481; Memorandum from the Deputy for Civil Affairs and Revolutionary Development Support (Komer) to the Commander, Military Assistance Command, Vietnam (Westmoreland), June 19, 1965, *FRUS 1964–1968, V*, 524; Bird, *Color of Truth*, 361.

333. Telegram from the Embassy in Norway to the Department of State, June 14, 1967, *FRUS 1964–1968, V*, 509–10; William D. Krimer, Memorandum of Conversation, June 23, 1967, *FRUS 1964–1968, V*, 547, 549, 551. The Glassboro Conference was a meeting between Kosygin and Johnson that took place in the small town of Glassboro, New Jersey, June 23–25, 1967. Gaiduk, *Soviet Union and the Vietnam War*, 132.

334. CINCPAC Command History 1968, Vol. 3, 118–20, K712. 01, 1968, Vol. 3, AFHRA.

335. Assessment of Air Operations, 7 February 1965 thru 19 July 1967, 10–11, 16–17, K740.04-20, AFHRA; HQ USMACV Command History, 1967, 24.

336. Study of Effectiveness of the Air Campaign against NVN, K178.2-45, July 1967, AFHRA.

337. Notes from Meeting of the President with Secretary McNamara to Review the Secretary's Findings during Vietnam Trip, July 12, 1967, *FRUS 1964–1968, V*, 604, 605; Barrett, *Uncertain Warriors*, 105.

338. Notes from Meeting of the President, July 12, 1967, *FRUS 1964–1968, V*, 609; Clodfelter, *Limits of Air Power*, 143; McNamara, *In Retrospect*, 283, 294; Hearings before the Preparedness Investigating Subcommittee, August 22, 1967, 201–2.

339. Assessment of Air Operations, 7 February 1965 thru 19 July 1967, 28, 30, K740.04-20; Message from CINCPACAF to CSAF, Effectiveness of Air Operations, 140335Z, July 1967, K717.01, Vol. 2, Part 2, AFHRA.

340. Assessment of Air Operations, 7 February 1965 thru 19 July 1967, 38, K740.04-20, AFHRA; MacGarrigle, *Taking the Offensive*, 257–60, 297–304; Prados, *Vietnam*, 180.

341. HQ CINCPAC, Pacific Area Naval Operations Review August 1967, 25, 29, Vietnam Command Files, Box 103, File August 1967, NHHC; Sweat, HQ 7th AF to DXIH, Coordination of History, Tab 1, 3 September 1968, K740.07, July–December 1967, AFHRA.

342. HQ CINCPAC, Pacific Area Naval Operations Review June 1967, 14–15, Vietnam Command Files, Box 103, File June 1967, NHHC.

343. Air Effectiveness Trends during the Southwest Monsoon 1967, K740.04-18, AFHRA.

344. Assessment of Air Operations, 7 February 1965 thru 19 July 1967, 23, K740.04-20, AFHRA.

345. Tom Johnson, Notes of Meeting, August 16, 1967, *FRUS 1964–1968, V*, 698.

346. Fry, *Debating Vietnam*, 86–87.
347. Message from 7AF to PACAF, 7AF 36 Hour Intent, 211040Z, July 1967, K717.312, 21–22 July 1967, AFHRA; History Naval Operations, Vol. III 1965–1967, Part 1, 150, NHHC.
348. McNamara, *In Retrospect*, 306–8.
349. W. Averell Harriman, Memorandum of Conversation between Ambassador at Large (Harriman) and Secretary of Defense McNamara, July 1, 1967, *FRUS 1964–1968, V*, 574–75.
350. Memorandum from the Secretary of the Air Force (Brown) to Secretary of Defense McNamara, July 3, 1967, *FRUS 1964–1968 V*, 580–81; Memorandum from the President's Special Assistant (Rostow) to President Johnson, July 22, 1967, *FRUS 1964–1968 V*, 631; Memorandum from the President's Special Assistant (Rostow) to President Johnson, July 31, 1967, *FRUS 1964–1968, V*, 652.
351. Memorandum from the President's Assistant (Jones) to President Johnson, September 5, 1967, *FRUS 1964–1968, V*, 751.
352. Earle G. Wheeler, Memorandum for Record, July 11, 1967, *FRUS 1964–1968, V*, 592.
353. Sorley, *Honorable Warrior*, 285.
354. Memorandum from the Deputy Assistant Secretary of State for East Asian and Pacific Affairs (Habib) to Secretary of State Rusk, August 5, 1967, *FRUS 1964–1968, V*, 668.
355. Lieutenant General Andrew J. Goodpasture, Memorandum for Record, Meeting with General Eisenhower, August 9, 1967, *FRUS 1964–1968, V*, 683–84; Memorandum from the Assistant Secretary of State for East Asian and Pacific Affairs (Bundy) to Secretary of State Rusk, August 14, 1967, *FRUS 1964–1968, V*, 688–89.
356. HQ USMACV Command History, 1967, 28, Overton, Rolling Thunder: January 1967–November 1968, 22, K717.0414-12, AFHRA.
357. Richard Helms, Memorandum from Director of Central Intelligence Helms to President Johnson, August 29, 1967, *FRUS 1964–1968, V*, 733–34.
358. Cosmas, *Joint Chiefs of Staff 1960–1968, Part 3*, 77; Prados, *Vietnam*, 207. The "Pennsylvania Initiative" failed. Cosmas, *Joint Chiefs of Staff 1960–1968, Part 3*, 81.
359. Dean Rusk, Telegram from the Department of State to the Embassy in France, September 12, 1967, *FRUS 1964–1968, V*, 785.
360. Fry, *Debating Vietnam*, 87; Tilford Jr., *Setup*, 147.
361. Memorandum from the President's Assistant (Jones) to President Johnson, September 12, 1967, *FRUS 1964–1968, V*, 779.
362. Message from CINCPAC to JCS, CINCPAC Monthly Rolling Thunder Summary, September 1967, 030001Z, September 1967, K712.1623-2, August 1967, AFHRA.
363. Dean Rusk, Telegram from the Department of State to the Embassy in France, September 13, 1967, *FRUS 1964–1968, V*, 796–97; Overton, Rolling Thunder: January 1967–November 1968, 10–11, K717.0414-12, AFHRA; Cosmas, *Joint Chiefs of Staff 1960–1968, Part 3*, 79.
364. Colvin, "Hanoi in My Time," 149–53; Jacksel M. Broughton, "Rolling Thunder from the Cockpit," in Moore, *The Vietnam Debate*, 149–50.
365. Message from CINCPAC to JCS, CINCPAC Monthly Rolling Thunder Summary, September 1967, 072059Z, October 1967, K712.1623-2, September 1967, AFHRA.
366. Memorandum by the Assistant Secretary of State for East Asia and Pacific Affairs (Bundy), September 28, 1967, *FRUS 1964–1968, V*, 835.
367. McNamara, *In Retrospect*, 301. These meetings over lunch on Tuesdays have become infamous. They began in February 1964, were not held on a regular basis once a week until 1967, and the participants discussed more than just the Vietnam War. The chairman of the JCS was not invited until October 1967. Some in the cabinet believed they were of great value, others noticed instead that it was difficult to translate the decisions into action. David C. Humphrey, "Tuesday Lunch

at the White House: A Preliminary Assessment," *Diplomatic History* 8: 1 (Winter 1984), 81–82, 90, 92–93.
368. Message from 7AF to CINCPACAF, Twelve Month Air Campaign against NVN, 181030Z, September 1967, and Message from CJCS to CINCPAC, Rolling Thunder, 232213Z, October 1967, K717.01, 1 January–31 December 1967, Vol. 2, Part 2; CINCPAC Command History 1968, Vol. 3, 115–16, K712. 01, 1968, Vol. 3, AFHRA.
369. Notes of the President's Meeting with Secretary McNamara, Secretary Rusk, Walt Rostow, George Christian, October 4, 1967, *FRUS 1964–1968*, *V*, 859.
370. Editorial Note, *FRUS 1964–1968*, *V*, 837. Johnson made the proposal at a speech in San Antonio.
371. Goldstein, *Lessons in Disaster*, 181; Woods, *LBJ*, 807.
372. Notes of the President's Meeting with Secretary McNamara, Secretary Katzenbach, CIA Director Helms, Walt W. Rostow, George Christian, September 26, 1967, *FRUS 1964–1968*, *V*, 825, 827; Woods, *LBJ*, 809.
373. Randolph, *Powerful and Brutal Weapons*, 23–24.
374. Memorandum from the Counselor and Chairman of the Policy Planning Staff (Rostow) to the Assistant Secretary of State for Far Eastern Affairs (Bundy), June 11, 1964, *FRUS 1964–1968*, *XXVIII*, 179.
375. Cosmas, *Joint Chiefs of Staff 1960–1968, Part 3*, 81.
376. Message from CINCPAC to JCS, CINCPAC Monthly Rolling Thunder Summary, October 1967, 080330Z, November 1967, K71.1623-2, AFHRA; Cosmas, *Joint Chiefs of Staff 1960–1968, Part 3*, 82.
377. Memorandum from the President's Special Assistant (Rostow) to President Johnson, October 4, 1967, *FRUS 1964–1968*, *V*, 855–56.
378. Memorandum from the Deputy for Civil Operations and Revolutionary Development, Military Assistance Command, Vietnam (Komer) to President Johnson, October 4, 1967, *FRUS 1964–1968*, *V*, 861–62.
379. The Consequences of a Halt in the Bombardment of North Vietnam, October 9, 1967, *FRUS 1964–1968*, *V*, 876–77.
380. Notes of the President's Meeting with Secretary Rusk, Secretary McNamara, Walt Rostow, CIA Director Helms and George Christian, October 16, 1967, *FRUS 1964–1968*, *V*, 880.
381. Memorandum from McGeorge Bundy to President Johnson, October 17, 1967, *FRUS 1964–1968*, *V*, 884; Notes of the President's Wednesday Night Meeting, October 18, 1967, *FRUS 1964–1968*, *V*, 894.
382. Notes of the President's Wednesday Night Meeting, October 18, 1967, 901.
383. Sharp, *Strategy for Defeat*, 155, 156.
384. See for example Draft Memorandum from Secretary of Defense McNamara to President Johnson, November 1, 1967, *FRUS 1964–1968*, *V*, 946. He also noted that many in the US believed that the bombing campaign kept "the war going," *FRUS 1964–1968*, *V*, 950.
385. Notes of Meeting, October 23, 1967, *FRUS 1964–1968*, *V*, 919.
386. Memorandum from the President's Special Consultant (Taylor) to President Johnson, November 3, 1967, *FRUS 1964–1968*, *V*, 978.
387. Memorandum by the Chairman of the President's Foreign Intelligence Advisory Board (Clifford), November 7, 1967, *FRUS 1964–1968*, *V*, 993, 994.
388. Notes of Meeting, October 23, 1967, *FRUS 1964–1968*, *V*, 923–24; Memorandum from the President's Special Assistant (Rostow) to President Johnson, November 2, 1967, *FRUS 1964–1968*, *V*, 952.
389. Memorandum from Secretary of State Rusk to President Johnson, November 20, 1967, *FRUS 1964–1968*, *V*, 1038, 1039; David Maraniss, *They Marched into Sunlight. War and Peace: Vietnam*

and America, October 1967 (New York: Simon & Schuster, 2003), 192. Rusk probably expressed this during the October 4, 1967, meeting.

390. Gardner, *Pay Any Price*, 404; Woods, *LBJ*, 809–10. McNamara formally left office on February 29, 1968.
391. Deborah Shapley, *Promise and Power: The Life and Times of Robert McNamara* (Boston: Little, Brown, 1993), 444.
392. Cosmas, *Joint Chiefs of Staff 1960–1968, Part 3*, 82–83.
393. Telegram from the Chairman of the Joint Chiefs of Staff (Wheeler) to the Commander, Military Assistance Command, Vietnam (Westmoreland), November 29, 1967, *FRUS 1964–1968, XXVIII*, 635.
394. Thorndale, Interdiction in Route Package One, 3, K717.0413-96, AFHRA.
395. Intelligence Memorandum Prepared by the Directorate of Intelligence of the Central Intelligence Agency, S-2543, December 1967, *FRUS 1964–1968, XXVIII*, 638.
396. Editorial Note, *FRUS 1964–1968, V*, 1116; CINCPAC Message, Year-End Review of Vietnam, 1 January 1968, K712.1623-2, January 1968, AFHRA; HQ CINCPAC, Pacific Area Naval Operations Review December 1967, 15, Vietnam Command Files, Box 103, File December 1967, NHHC.
397. AFXOP, Aerial Interdiction and Resupply Denial in NVN, 6 January 1968, 2, 5, K143.042-24, AFHRA.
398. History Naval Operations, Vol. III 1965–1967, Part 1, 166, NHHC.
399. Memorandum from the Board of National Estimates, Central Intelligence Agency, to Director of Central Intelligence Helms, January 18, 1968, *FRUS 1964–1968, VI*, 48.
400. Guan, *The Vietnam War from the Other Side*, 108, 114, 115; Guan, *Ending the Vietnam War*, 62, 74; Nguyen, *Hanoi's War*, 148, 228.
401. AFXOP, Aerial Interdiction and Resupply Denial, 6 January 1968, 8–16, K143.042-24, AFHRA.
402. Notes of the President's Tuesday Luncheon Meeting, February 6, 1968, *FRUS 1964–1968, VI*, 139, 140; Humphrey, "Tuesday Lunch at the White House," 91.
403. Robbins, *This Time We Win*, 91, 177–80, 238; Moise, *The Myths of Tet*, 95–96, 105, 114, 152; Cosmas, *Joint Chiefs of Staff 1960–1968, Part 3*, 150; *FRUS 1964–1968, VI*, 138–40.
404. Record of Meeting, February 21, 1968, *FRUS 1964–1968, VI*, 230–33.
405. Michael Beschloss, ed., *Reaching for Glory: Lyndon Johnson's Secret White House Tapes, 1964–1965* (New York: Simon & Schuster, 2001), 177. This took place on February 11, 1965, and is from the first lady's diary.
406. Cosmas, *Joint Chiefs of Staff 1960–1968, Part 3*, 150; Telegram from the Embassy in Vietnam to the Department of State, March 1, 1968, *FRUS 1964–1968, VI*, 299; Llewelyn Thompson, Telegram from the Embassy in the Soviet Union to the Department of State, March 1, 1968, *FRUS 1964–1968, VI*, 302–303.
407. Thorndale, Interdiction in Route Package One, 3, K717.0413-96, AFHRA.
408. Notes of the President's Meeting with the Joint Chiefs of Staff, February 9, 1968, *FRUS 1964–1968, VI*, 167; Daddis, *Westmoreland's War*, 143. Clifford replaced McNamara when he resigned on February 29, 1968.
409. Acacia, *Clark Clifford: The Wise Man of Washington*, 264–65.
410. Editorial Note, *FRUS 1964–1968, VI*, 341, 342; Randall Bennet Woods, *Fulbright: A Biography* (Cambridge: Cambridge University Press, 1995), 473.
411. Editorial Note, *FRUS 1964–1968, VI*, 373–74; Michael A. Cohen, *American Maelstrom: The 1968 Election and the Politics of Division* (New York: Oxford University Press, 2016) 109, 110–11; Acacia, *Clark Clifford*, 270; Lewis L. Gould, *1968: The Election that Changed America* (Chicago: Ivan R. Dee, 1993), 17–19, 47, 49–51.

412. Acacia, *Clark Clifford*, 277. The "Wise Men" were a group of experienced establishment advisors President Johnson turned to for advice. Telegram from the Mission to the United Nations to the Department of State, March 15, 1968, *FRUS 1964–1968, VI*, 391–93.
413. Memorandum from the Chairman of the Joint Chiefs of Staff (Wheeler) to Secretary of Defense Clifford, March 20, 1968, *FRUS 1964–1968, VI*, 422.
414. Notes of Meeting, March 26, 1968, *FRUS 1964–1968, VI*, 471–73; Cosmas, *Joint Chiefs of Staff 1960–1968, Part 3*, 169–70.
415. Acacia, *Clark Clifford*, 279; Townsend Hoopes, *The Limits of Intervention (An Inside Account of How the Johnson Policy of Escalation was Reversed* (New York: David McKay, 1969), 204; Barrett, *Uncertain Warriors*, 111. Barrett argues that the famous March 26 meeting with the Wise Men did not suddenly alter the president's policy direction, but instead confirmed what Johnson had already decided. If any one individual persuaded him to a final decision, it was Dean Rusk. Barrett, *Uncertain Warriors*, 148–53, 156.
416. Message from CINCPAC, Rolling Thunder Air Campaign in NVN, April through September 1968, 1 March 1968, K712.1623-2, September 1968, AFHRA.
417. Momyer, Study of Bombing Alternatives, 28 March 1968, K740.04-21, AFHRA.
418. Memorandum for Record, March 29, 1968, *FRUS 1964–1968, VI*, 488; Editorial Note, *FRUS 1964–1968, VI*, 494; Marc Jacobsen, "President Johnson and the Decision to Curtail Rolling Thunder," in Gilbert and Head, eds., *The Tet Offensive*, 227; Warfel, History of 4258th Strategic Wing November 1968, 11, 16, K-WG-4258-HI, 1968, AFHRA.
419. Jacobsen, Decision to Curtail Rolling Thunder, 226–27; Message from 7AF to AIG 7910, Exclusive for Commanders, 101320Z, April 1968, K740.1623 1-26 April 1968, AFHRA.
420. Editorial Note, *FRUS 1964–1968, VI*, 510.
421. Known as "mini Tet," an NLF offensive that was costly and indecisive and only weakened the communists. When they launched another "mini Tet" in August, it was so ineffectual that analysts had to examine the evidence carefully to determine that the communists had actually staged an offensive. Prados, *Vietnam*, 254, 262.
422. Editorial Note, *FRUS 1964–1968, VI*, 721.
423. Letter from Chairman Kosygin to President Johnson, Moscow, June 5, 1968, *FRUS 1964–1968, VI*, 754.
424. Notes of the President's Meeting with foreign Policy Advisers, June 9, 1968, *FRUS 1964–1968, VI*, 771; Memorandum from the President's Special Consultant (Taylor) to President Johnson, June 10, 1968, *FRUS 1964–1968, VI*, 779.
425. Letter from President Johnson to Chairman Kosygin, June 11, 1968, *FRUS 1964–1968, VI*, 783; Memorandum from Secretary of Defense Clifford to President Johnson, July 18, 1968, *FRUS 1964–1968, VI*, 875; Memorandum from the President's Special Consultant (Taylor) to President Johnson, August 2, 1968, *FRUS 1964–1968, VI*, 930; Acacia, *Clark Clifford*, 294–95.
426. Acacia, *Clark Clifford*, 308.
427. Memorandum from the President's Special Assistant (Rostow), July 7, 1968, *FRUS 1964–1968, VI*, 840; Telegram from the Commander, Military Assistance Command, Vietnam (Abrams) to the President's Special Assistant (Rostow), August 23, 1968, *FRUS 1964–1968, VI*, 971.
428. Deputy Chief of Staff for Intelligence, Headquarters, PACAF, The Effects of United States Air Operations in Southeast Asia, Volume 1, K717.6094, 1965–1968, Vol. 1, p. 7-1, AFHRA.
429. Background Paper on Possible Courses of Action and Alternatives in Vietnam, no date, K143,054-3, Vol. 33 1969–1975, AFHRA. See also JCS document to the Secdef, JCSM-343-68, May 29, 1968.
430. Message from CINCPACAF to CSAF, Possible Courses of Action and Alternatives in Vietnam, 090359Z, August 1968, K143.054-3, Vol. 33 1969–1975, AFHRA.

431. CINCPACAF to CSAF, 090359Z, August 1968.
432. Message from CG FMFPAC to CG III MAF, 222101Z, June 1968, The Vietnam Center & Sam Johnson Vietnam Archive, Texas Tech University, http://vietnam.ttu.edu. Cushman was the senior advisor to the ARVN in I Corps.
433. Draft Message from CSAF to CINCPACAF, Possible Courses of Action and Alternatives in Vietnam, circa 23 August 1968, not sent, K143.054-3, Vol. 33 1969–1975, AFHRA.
434. Gould, *1968*, 117–19, 164.
435. President's Meeting with Foreign Policy Advisers, July 30, 1968, *FRUS 1964–1968*, VI, 921, Footnote 2, 925.
436. Memorandum for Record, October 23, 1968, *FRUS, 1964–1968, VII*, 310.

Chapter 15

1. Notes on the Tuesday Luncheon, May 7, 1968, *FRUS 1964–1968, VI*, 648; Notes of Tuesday Luncheon, May 14, 1968, *FRUS 1964–1968, VI*, 665; CINCPAC, Pacific Area Naval Operations Review December 1968, A-1, NHHC.
2. Memorandum for Record, October 23, 1968, *FRUS, 1964–1968, VII*, 310–11.
3. Memorandum from the President's Special Consultant (Taylor) to President Johnson, May 13, 1968, *FRUS 1964–1968, VI*, 661; Thorndale, Interdiction in Route Package One, 4, K717.0413-96; Message from 7AF to RUEFHQA/CSAF, Impact of 7AF Summer Interdiction Campaign, 14 July through 31 October 1968, 140930Z, November 1968, K740.454-1; Colonel Jesse C. Gatlin, Igloo White, Initial Phase (HQ PACAF: Directorate, Tactical Evaluation, CHECO Division, 1968), 3, K717.0414-18, AFHRA; Guan, *The Vietnam War from the Other Side*, 133.
4. Pacific Command History, 1969, Vol. 3, 75, 178, K712.01, Vol. 3, redacted, 1969, AFHRA; Gatlin, Igloo White, Initial Phase, p. vi, K717.0414-18, AFHRA.
5. Thorndale, Interdiction in Route Package One, 38, K717.0413-96, AFHRA.
6. MACV Command History 1968 Vol. 1, 407–8; Smith, Carrier Air Wing Six Cruise Report April 1968 to December 1968, 14 December 1968, Peck, Commander Attack Carrier Air Wing Nine Combat Tactical Supplement, 13 July 1968, NHHC. These were Mk 36 DST destructor mines.
7. Commander in Chief, U.S. Pacific Fleet, Rolling Thunder Operations Report, 12 August 1968, Vietnam Command Files, COLL/372, Box 111, File CPF RT Rept, 1–31 July 1968, NHHC. Maj. Gen. Gordon F. Blood, 30 Day Interdiction Campaign in Route Package I and Tally Ho, 8 October 1968, K740.04-19, 5 September 1968, AFHRA.
8. Paper Prepared by the Chairman of the Joint Chiefs of Staff (Wheeler), September 11, 1968, *FRUS 1964–1968, VII*, 26, 27, 29.
9. Enclosure, Intelligence Analysis of North Vietnam, 1–15 March 1968, Commander in Chief U.S. Pacific Fleet, Rolling Thunder Analysis and Report, 23 March 1968, Vietnam Command File, COLL/372, Box 110, File CPF RT Rept 1–15 March 1968, NHHC.
10. PACAF DI, Effects of Air Operations in Southeast Asia, September 1966, 9, K717.6092, AFHRA.
11. Message from AFSSO 7AF to SSO 8AF, 150840Z, October 1970, K740.1623-5, 15 October 1970; Southeast Asia Air Operations Briefing, December 1971. K717.3063-1, December 1971. Pratt, Air Tactics against NVN Air Ground Defenses, 40–41, K717.0414-16; Bonetti, The War in Vietnam: January–June 1967, 109–10, K717.0414-17, AFHRA; Prados, *The Blood Road*, 191, 193, 315.
12. Assessment of Air Operations, 7 February 1965 thru 19 July 1967, 27, K740.04-20; HQ 7th AF, Commando Hunt III, 12, K740.04-8; Effects of Air Operations Southeast Asia, August 1966, 37, 41, 43, PACAF DI, Effects of Air Operations in Southeast Asia, September 1966, 81, K717.6092, AFHRA.
13. Effects of Air Operations in Southeast Asia, 22 July 1965, 35, and Effects of Air Operations

Southeast Asia, August 1966, 68, K717.6092; History of the Pacific Air Forces, 1966, 24, K717.01, Vol. 1, Part 1, AFHRA.
14. November V and Prime Choke Alpha S, 170800Z, September 1972, K740.3391, AFHRA.
15. Assessment of Air Operations, 7 February 1965 thru 19 July 1967, 28, K740.04-20; Message from CINCPAC, Military Operations in Vietnam, 142140Z, January 1967, K717.01, AFHRA.
16. Thorndale, Interdiction in Route Package One, 5-8, K717.0413-96; Air Effectiveness Trends during the Southwest Monsoon 1967, K740.04-18, AFHRA; Operations of U.S. Marine Forces Vietnam, December 1967 and 1967 Summary, HDMCU. B-52s in September committed 27 sorties to this operation; the remainder were Marine.
17. Thorndale, Interdiction in Route Package One, 3, K717.0413-96, AFHRA. The road was 1R-2748.
18. Walter F. Daniel End of Tour Report, K740.131, Daniel, 3 May 1968–2 May 1969, AFHRA. Daniel was Chief Fighter Division, Director Combat Operations for Operations outside of SVN, May 1968 to May 1969.
19. Rolling Thunder Operations Report and Analysis, 8 October 1968, NHHC.
20. Telegram from the Commander, Military Assistance Command, Vietnam (Abrams) to the President's Special Assistant (Rostow), August 23, 1968, *FRUS 1964–1968*, *VI*, 969.
21. Thorndale, Interdiction in Route Package One, 13–14, K717.0413-96, AFHRA.
22. Telegram from Abrams to Rostow, August 23, 1968, *FRUS 1964–1968*, *VI*, 971.
23. Message, Impact of Interdiction Campaign, 140930Z, November 1968, K740.454-1, AFHRA; HQ CINCPAC, Pacific Area Naval Operations Review September 1966, 8, Vietnam Command Files, Box 102, File September 1966, NHHC.
24. Message, Impact of Interdiction Campaign, 140930Z, November 1968, K740.454-1, AFHRA.
25. Ibid.
26. Rolling Thunder Operations Report and Analysis, 8 October 1968, NHHC.
27. Telegram from President Johnson's Special Assistant (Rostow) to President Johnson in Texas, September 22, 1968, Draft Contingency Presidential Statement, *FRUS 1964–1968*, *VII*, 76.
28. Herring, *LBJ and Vietnam*, 173.
29. Telegram from the Embassy in France to the Department of State, September 25, 1968, *FRUS 1964–1968*, *VII*, 81.
30. Transcript of Speech by Vice President on Foreign Policy, *New York times*, October 1, 1968, 33; Michael Nelson, *Resilient America: Electing Nixon in 1968, Channeling Dissent, and Dividing Government* (Lawrence: University Press of Kansas, 2014), 198.
31. Memorandum for Record, October 23, 1968, *FRUS, 1964–1968*, *VII*, 312.
32. Notes of the President's Meeting, October 29, 1968, *FRUS, 1964–1968*, *VII*, 411.
33. Letter from President Johnson to Chairman Kosygin, October 29, 1968, *FRUS, 1964–1968*, *VII*, 417.
34. Brigham, *Guerrilla Diplomacy*, 70, 98, 100.
35. Telegram from the Department of State to the Embassy in Vietnam, October 29, 1968, *FRUS, 1964–1968*, *VII*, 418–19.
36. Message, Impact of Interdiction Campaign, 140930Z, November 1968, K740.454-1, AFHRA.
37. Smith, Carrier Air Wing Six Cruise Report April 1968 to December 1968, 14 December 1968, NHHC.
38. Letter from President Johnson to Chairman Kosygin, October 31, 1968, *FRUS, 1964–1968*, *VII*, 472.
39. Transcript of Telephone Conversation Among President Johnson, Vice President Humphrey, Richard Nixon, and George Wallace, October 31, 1968, *FRUS, 1964–1968*, *VII*, 482.
40. MACV Command History, 1968, Volume 1, 3; Overton, Rolling Thunder: January 1967–November 1968, 43, K717.0414-12, AFHRA.

41. Clodfelter, *Limits of Air Power*, 134.
42. Message from CG III MAF to COMUSMACV, Aerial Interdiction in A Shau Valley, 220608Z, December 1968, The Vietnam Center & Sam Johnson Vietnam Archive, Texas Tech University, http://vietnam.ttu.edu.
43. Telegram from the Commander, Military Assistance Command, Vietnam (Abrams) to the President's Special Assistant (Rostow), August 23, 1968, *FRUS 1964–1968, VI*, 971.
44. Nelson, *Resilient America*, 218–19; Acacia, *Clark Clifford*, 318; Telegram from the Embassy in Vietnam to the Department of State, November 6, 1968, *FRUS, 1964–1968, VII*, 572; Cohen, *American Maelstrom*, 320; Anatoly Dobrynin, *In Confidence: Moscow's Ambassador to America's Six Cold War Presidents (1962–1986)* (New York: Times Books, 1995), 176; Jack Torry, "Don't Blame Nixon for Scuttled Peace Overture," http://www.realclearpolitics.com/articles/2015/08/09/dont_blame_nixon_for_scuttled_peace_overture_127667.html.
45. Cohen, *American Maelstrom*, 320; Brigham, *Guerrilla Diplomacy*, 82.
46. Telegram from the Embassy in Vietnam to the Department of State, November 6, 1968, *FRUS, 1964–1968, VII*, 577.
47. Editorial Note, November 26, 1968, *FRUS 1964–1968, VII*, 703. See for example Telegram from the Embassy in Vietnam to the Department of State, January 10, 1969, *FRUS 1964–1968, VII*, 813; Notes on Foreign Policy Meeting, November 26, 1968, *FRUS 1964–1968, XIV*, 765 and *FRUS 1969–1976, VI*, 88; Telegram from the Department of State to the Embassy in Vietnam, March 7, 1969, *FRUS 1969–1976, VI*, 88–89.
48. History of Seventh Air Force, 1971–1972, 264, K740.01-25, Vol. 1, AFHRA.
49. Ball, *Past Has Another Pattern*, 414.
50. Notes on Foreign Policy Meeting, November 7, 1968, *FRUS, 1964–1968, VII*, 585; Notes on President's Meeting with the Tuesday Luncheon Group, November 20, 1968, *FRUS, 1964–1968, VII*, 670; Message from General Abrams to General Brown Com 7AF, et al., Continuation of Bombing in Laos, 010415Z, November 1968, The Vietnam Center & Sam Johnson Vietnam Archive, Texas Tech University, http://vietnam.ttu.edu; Moise, *Myths of Tet*, 167, 208. The CIA believed that in counting the number of enemy forces—as opposed to combat troops—in South Vietnam, one should include political operatives and "irregulars." That put the strength of enemy forces at around 500,000. Moise, *Myths of Tet*, 167.
51. Naval Historical Division, United States Naval Operations Vietnam, January–December 1969 Highlights, Vietnam Command File, COLL/372, Box 88, Files CNO NHD: US Naval Ops VN January–December 1969; Commander A. R. Burt, Commander Attack Carrier Air Wing Nine, 1968 Command History, 25 February 1969, Fleet Aviation Commands Active, CVW-9, Box 18, File 1968, NHHC.
52. Message from 7AF to RUMBDFM/TASK Force Alpha, Personal for Commanders from General Brown, 101045Z, January 1969, K730.312-4, 1968-1969, AFHRA. Also catalogued at K740.1623 10 January 1969.
53. Pacific Command History, 1969, Vol. 3, 75, 178, K712.01, Vol. 3, redacted, 1969, AFHRA; Objectives and Courses of Action of the United States in South Viet-Nam, no date, Saigon, *FRUS 1964–1968, VII*, 720; Notes on the President's Meeting with the Tuesday Luncheon Group, November 20, 1968, *FRUS 1964–1968, VII*, 670.
54. History of Seventh Air Force, 1971–1972, 264, K740.01-25, Vol. 1, AFHRA; Notes on the President's Meeting, November 20, 1968, *FRUS, 1964–1968, VII*, 670.
55. Memorandum from Deputy Assistant Secretary of State for East Asian and Pacific Affairs (Sullivan) to the President's Assistant for National Security Affairs (Kissinger), June 10, 1969, *FRUS 1969–1976, VI*, 254.
56. HQ 7th AF, Commando Hunt III, 1, K740.04-8; Sams, et al., The Air War in Vietnam:

1968–1969, 39, 43, K717.0413-143, AFHRA.
57. Pacific Area Naval Operations Review November 1968, 6, 10; HQ CINCPAC, Pacific Area Naval Operations Review January 1969, 7, Vietnam Command Files, Box 105, File January 1969, NHHC.
58. HQ CINCPAC, Pacific Area Naval Operations Review February 1969, 9, Vietnam Command Files, Box 105, File February 1969, NHHC.
59. Sams, et al., The Air War in Vietnam: 1968–1969, 1, K717.0413-143, AFHRA.
60. Kissinger, *White House Years,* 239–40.
61. Pacific Command History, 1969, Vol. 3, 179, K712.01, Vol. 3, redacted, 1969, AFHRA.
62. Brigham, *Guerrilla Diplomacy*, 92–93.
63. Commander in Chief Pacific Command History, 1970, Vol. 2, 147, K712.01, Vol. 2, 1970, AFHRA.
64. Memorandum of Conversation, August 4, 1969, *FRUS 1969–1976, VI*, 332. Thuy was the head of the North Vietnamese delegation to the Paris peace talks; Bo was North Vietnam's delegate general in France.
65. Memorandum from the President's Assistant for National Security Affairs (Kissinger) to President Nixon, September 11, 1969, *FRUS 1969–1976, VI*, 383.
66. Minutes of National Security Meeting, September 12, 1969, *FRUS 1969–1976, VI*, 403; Memorandum from the President's Assistant for National Security Affairs (Kissinger) to President Nixon, October 2, 1969, *FRUS 1969–1976, VI*, 418–23.
67. Memorandum from the President's Assistant for National Security Affairs (Kissinger) to President Nixon, undated [October 1969], *FRUS 1969–1970, VI*, 447–49, 449; Cosmas, *The Joint Command in the Years of Withdrawal, 1968–1973*, 290.
68. Thomas H. Moorer, Memorandum for the Record, October 11, 1969, *FRUS 1969–1970, VI*, 457.
69. Memorandum from Roger Morris, Winston Lord, and Anthony Lake of the National Security Council Staff to the President's Assistant for National Security Affairs (Kissinger), April 22, 1970, *FRUS 1969–1970, VI*, 855–56; Memorandum from the President's Assistant for National Security Affairs (Kissinger) to President Nixon, December 27, 1969, *FRUS 1969–1970, VI*, 524–25.
70. Memorandum of Conversation, October 7, 1969, *FRUS 1969–1970, VI*, 438, 445; Message from CG III MAF to FMFPAC, Visit of the Secretary of State to ICTZ on 18 May 1969, 190606Z, May 1969, The Vietnam Center & Sam Johnson Vietnam Archive, Texas Tech University, http://vietnam.ttu.edu.
71. Blout, Air Operations in Northern Laos, 1 April–1 November 1970, 32–34, K717.0413-65; Major William W. Lofgren, Air War in Northern Laos, 1 April–30 November 1971, 29, K717.0413-65, AFHRA.
72. Moorer, Reminiscences, Volume 3, 1226, Navy Department Library.
73. Memorandum from Sullivan to Kissinger, June 10, 1969, *FRUS 1969–1976, VI*, 254.
74. Sams, Air Operations Northern Laos, November 1969–April 1970, 23, K717.0413-65, AFHRA.
75. National Security Study Memorandum 1, January 21, 1969, *FRUS 1969–1976, VI*, 10.
76. Summary of Interagency Responses to NSSM 1, March 22, 1969, *FRUS 1969–1976, VI*, 152.
77. Randolph, *Powerful and Brutal Weapons*, 9; Berman, *No Peace*, 49.
78. MACV Command History 1969, Vol. 1, v-217–v-218.
79. HQ 7th AF, Commando Hunt III, 6-11, 104, K740.04-8, AFHRA; OPNAV 5750-1 Attack Squadron Fifty-Five Command History 1968, NHHC.
80. History of Seventh Air Force, 1971–1972, 301, K740.01-25, Vol. 1, AFHRA.
81. Jamison, End of Tour Report, 1 March 1970, K717.131; HQ 7th AF, Commando Hunt III, 68, K740.04-8, AFHRA.
82. Pacific Command History, 1969, Vol. 3, 76, K712.01, Vol. 3, redacted, 1969, AFHRA.

NOTES FOR CHAPTER 15

83. Message from CINCPACAF to CSAF, Force Planning, 181933Z, June 1969, K143.054-3, Vol. 19, 1969–1975, AFHRA.
84. Wells and Paoli, History of the 307th Strategic Wing, April–June 1971, K-WG-307-HI; Jamison, End of Tour Report, 1 March 1970, K717.131; Elder and Melly, Rules of Engagement, 1969–1972, 8, K717.0414-20, AFHRA.
85. 1st Lieutenant Michael F. Revere, History of the 834th Air Division, 1 July 1968–30 June 1970, 17–18, K-DIV-834-HI, July 1968–June 1970, Vol. 1, AFHRA.
86. Lieutenant Colonel Herman L. Gilster, Maj. Richard D. Duckworth, Captain Gregory C. Hildebrandt, Master Sergeant Jack H. Besser, and Staff Sergeant Roy G. Crumrine, An Economic Analysis of the Steel Tiger Interdiction Campaign, 1 November 1969–30 June 1970, 17–19, K740.454-7, 70/06/30, AFHRA; Prados, *The Blood Road*, 191–93, 314; Nalty, *The War Against Trucks*, 5–6, 99; Air Interdiction in Southeast Asia, April–June 1970, 67, 75, 77, K740.04-10, AFHRA.
87. Sams, et al., The Air War in Vietnam: 1968–1969, 9, K717.0413-143; Thorndale, Interdiction in Route Package One, 4–5, K717.0413-96, AFHRA; Sorley, *A Better War*, 101.
88. HQ 7th AF, Commando Hunt III, 85, K740.04-8, AFHRA.
89. MACV Command History 1969, Vol. 1, v-225; Sams, et al., The Air War in Vietnam: 1968–1969, 2–4, K717.0413-143, AFHRA; Memorandum from Secretary of Defense Laird to President Nixon, September 4, 1969, *FRUS 1969–1976, VI*, 364.
90. Prados, *The Blood Road*, 325.
91. Memorandum from the President's Assistant for National Security Affairs (Kissinger) to President Nixon, September 10, 1969, *FRUS 1969–1976, VI*, 373.
92. Record of President's Meeting with the Foreign Intelligence Advisory Board, July 18, 1970, *FRUS 1969–1976, VI*, 1123.
93. Assessment of Air Operations, 7 February 1965 thru 19 July 1967, 34–35, K740.04-20, AFHRA.
94. Shaw, *Cambodian Campaign*, 157; Thorndale, Interdiction in Route Package One, 15, K717.0413-96; Seventh AF, Air Interdiction in Southeast Asia, April–June 1970, 55, K740.04-10, AFHRA.
95. Air Interdiction in Southeast Asia, 117–18; Folkman and Caine, The Cambodian Campaign 29 April–30 June 1970, 44–46, 59, K717.0413-84; Message from AFSSO 7AF to SSO SAC, Arc Light Targeting, 220450Z, September 1970, K740.1623 22 September 1970, AFHRA.
96. MACV Command History 1970 Vol. 1, pp. v-29, vi-31, vi-105, vi-108, vi-109, vi-111; Wells and Paoli, History of 307th Strategic Wing, January–March 1971, K-WG-307-HI, AFHRA.
97. Memorandum for the President's File, January 27, 1971, *FRUS 1969–1976, VII*, 328; Minutes of a Meeting of the Senior Washington Special Actions Group, February 2, 1971, *FRUS 1969–1976, VII*, 338; Minutes of a Meeting of the Senior Review Group, April 13, 1971, *FRUS 1969–1976, VII*, 545.
98. Naval Operations Vietnam, December 1969 Highlights, 8, Vietnam Command File, COLL/372, NHHC; History of Seventh Air Force, 1971–1972, 264, 270–71, K740.01-25, Vol. 1, AFHRA.
99. Lofgren, Air War in Northern Laos, 1 April–30 November 1971, 28, K717.0413-65, AFHRA.
100. Ibid., 33, 34, 48, 96.
101. Ibid., 30.
102. Captain Bruce P. Layton, Commando Hunt VI (HQ PACAF: Directorate of Operations Analysis, CHECO/Corona Harvest Division, 1972), 2, K717.0414-28, AFHRA.
103. Southeast Asia Air Operations Briefing, September 1971, K717.3063-1, September 1971, AFHRA.
104. Layton, Commando Hunt VI, 4, 31, K717.0414-28, AFHRA; Memorandum from the President's Assistant for National Security Affairs (Kissinger) to President Nixon, July 26, 1971, *FRUS 1969–1976, VII*, 838.

105. History of Seventh Air Force, 1971–1972, 307, 310, K740.01-25, Vol. 1; Seventh Air Force, Commando Hunt VII, 118–19, K740.04-14, November 1971–March 1972; Southeast Asia Air Operations Briefing, October 1971, K717.3063-1, AFHRA; Sherwood, *Afterburner*, 62.
106. Seventh Air Force, Commando Hunt VII, 132, K740.04-14, AFHRA.
107. Ibid., 133; Randolph, *Powerful and Brutal Weapons*, 48–49.
108. Seventh Air Force, Commando Hunt VII, 144–46, K740.04-14; Southeast Asia Air Operations Briefing, December 1971, K717.3063-1; Porter, Proud Deep Alpha, 51–52, K717.0423-24, AFHRA.
109. Conversation between President Nixon and the President's Assistant for National Security Affairs (Kissinger), January 20, 1972, *FRUS 1969–1976, VIII*, 9.
110. Message from AFSSO USAF to AFSO PACAF info AFSSO 7AF, Comments of Le Duc Tho, 242137Z, May 1972, Vogt Papers, AFHSD. This message relayed intelligence from earlier discussions between North Vietnamese leaders and leaders of the French Communist Party. Webb and Poole, *Joint Chiefs of Staff, 1971–1973*, 158.
111. Randolph, *Powerful and Brutal Weapons*, 51.
112. Eighth Air Force Activity Input, 1 July 1971–30 June 1972, K520.041-2, AFHRA; Nalty, *The War Against Trucks*, 197.
113. Memorandum from the President's Assistant for National Security Affairs (Kissinger) to President Nixon, February 8, 1972, *FRUS 1969–1976, VIII*, 85; Directorate of Operations Analysis, Summary Air Operations Southeast Asia June 1972, 1-1, K717.3063, June 1972, AFHRA.
114. Sams, et al., The Air War in Vietnam: 1968–1969, 39, K717.0413-143, AFHRA.
115. Blout, Air Operations in Northern Laos, 1 April–1 November 19, 20, K717.0413-65; Sams, Air Operations in Northern Laos, November 1969–April 1970, 63, K717.0413-65, AFHRA.
116. Till and Thomas, Pave Aegis Weapon System (AC-130E Gunship), 2, 4, 17–19, K717.0413-202; Monroe, Request for R&D Requirements, 6 January 1970, K740-03-4; Seventh Air Force, Commando Hunt VII, 1972, 81, K740.04-14, AFHRA. See also Memorandum from the Chairman of the Joint Chiefs of Staff (Moorer) to Secretary of Defense Laird, October 12, 1972, *FRUS 1969–1976, IX*, 117.
117. Steenrod and Yale, Bombing Campaign September 1966–April 1968, K143.5045-6, AFHRA.
118. Cole, Fixed Wing Gunships in SEA (July 1969–July 1971), 34, K717.0414-15, AFHRA.
119. Seventh AF, Air Interdiction in Southeast Asia, April–June 1970, 56, 58, K740.04-10; Till and Thomas, Pave Aegis Weapon System (AC-130E Gunship), 3, K717.0413-202; HQ 7th AF, Commando Hunt III, 86, K740.04-8, AFHRA.
120. End of Tour Report, Lt. Col. Ronald P. Hight, 7 December 1969–5 December 1970, K717.131; Layton, Commando Hunt VI, 31–33, K717.0414-28, AFHRA.
121. AC-119Ks destroyed 940 trucks, B-57Gs destroyed 461, and fighter-bombers destroyed 1,873. Headquarters Seventh Air Force, Commando Hunt VII, 83, 149–50, K740.04-14, AFHRA.
122. Seventh AF, Air Interdiction in Southeast Asia, April–June 1970, 56, 58, K740.04-10; Seventh Air Force, Commando Hunt VII, 83, K740.04-14, AFHRA.
123. HQ 7th AF, Commando Hunt III, 86, K740.04-8, AFHRA; HQ CINCPAC, Pacific Area Naval Operations Review September 1968, 12, 14, Vietnam Command Files, Box 105, File September 1968; Commander in Chief, U.S. Pacific Fleet, Rolling Thunder Report and Analysis, 9 September 1968, Vietnam Command Files, COLL/372, Box 111, File CPF RT Rept, 1–31 August 1968, NHHC.
124. Southeast Asia Analysis Report, June/July 1970, NHHC; Minutes of a Meeting of the Washington Special Actions Group: Laos, August 10, 1971, *FRUS 1969–1976, VII*, 857–58; Memorandum for the Record, June 8, 1971, *FRUS 1969–1976, VII*, 691. For more on the A-1 Skyraider, see Trest, *Air Commando One*, 178, 198.

125. Peter F. English and Bobby L. Marlow, Directorate of Operations Analysis, Reduction of Tactical Fighter Losses Over North Vietnam, 23 November 1966, K740.31066-13, 23 November 1966, AFHRA.
126. Memorandum by the Deputy Ambassador to Vietnam (Locke), September 12, 1967, *FRUS 1964–1968, XXVIII*, 621.
127. Memorandum from the Chairman of the Joint Chiefs of Staff (Wheeler) to Secretary of Defense McNamara, CM-2876-68, January 2, 1968, Use of Propeller and Jet Aircraft in Laos, *FRUS 1964–1968, XXVIII*, 645–47; Enclosure to Memorandum from Secretary of Defense McNamara to the Chairman of the Joint Chiefs of Staff (Wheeler), December 18, 1967, *FRUS 1964–1968, XXVIII*, 640–41.
128. Vice Chief of Staff U.S. Air Force Conference, 25–26 April 1966, K717.151-11, AFHRA. These were strengthened B-26s; earlier marks had been grounded in 1964 when their wings started breaking. Sbrega, "Southeast Asia," 441.
129. K740.056-1, 1966–1967, Tab 38, AFHRA.
130. Van Staaveren, *Interdiction in Southern Laos*, 160. The name of this aircraft was changed from B-26K to A-26K so that the Thais could claim that they had no bomber aircraft stationed on their soil. Melvin F. Porter, Interdiction in SEA, 1965–1966 (HQ PACAF: Directorate, Tactical Evaluation, CHECO Division, 1967), 58.
131. Nalty, *The War Against Trucks*, 29.
132. Minutes of a Meeting of the Washington Special Actions Group: Laos, August 10, 1971, *FRUS 1969–1976, VII*, 857; Transcript of a Telephone Conversation between Secretary of Defense Laird and the President's Assistant for National Security Affairs (Kissinger), August 12, 1971, *FRUS 1969–1976, VII*, 871.
133. Summary of Air Operations in Southeast Asia, June 1968, 1–7, K717.3063, June 1968; Pacific Command History, 1970, Vol. 2, 148–51, K712.01, Vol. 2, 1970; HQ 7th AF, Commando Hunt III, 15, K740.04-8; Seventh Air Force, Commando Hunt VII, 253; K740.04-14, AFHRA.
134. Enclosure 1, Commander A. H. Barie, Commanding Officer Attack Squadron Thirty-Five to Chief of Naval Operations, Command History 1966, 27 February 1967, Fleet Aviation Commands Pre-1998, AR/229, VF-35, Box 122, File F3; Enney, Addendum Report, 11 February 1969, 208, NHHC.
135. Effects of Air Operations Southeast Asia, August 1966, 52, K717.6092; Effects of Air Operations Southeast Asia, March 1967, 25, K717.6092, AFHRA; Marine Corps Forces in Vietnam March 1965–September 1967, Historical Summary, Volume 1, HDMCU.
136. HQ CINCPAC, Pacific Area Naval Operations Review October 1966, 9, Message from Comseventhflt to AIG 183, Weekly Summary 28 February–5 March 1968, 110832Z, March 1968, NHHC.
137. Directorate of Operations History, December 1965, K717.01, July–December 1965, Vol. 2, Part 2; Triwush and Sorge, USAF Tactical All-Weather Bombing Capability over North Vietnam, 20 July 1966, K740.31066-8, AFHRA.
138. Message from CINCPAC to CINCPACFLT, A-6 Operations, 030516Z, April 1967, K717.312, AFHRA; HQ CINCPAC, Pacific Area Naval Operations Review December 1966, 100, NHHC; Operations of U.S. Marine Forces Vietnam, May 1968, HDMCU.
139. Barie, Commanding Officer Attack Squadron Thirty-Five Command History 1966, USS *Constellation*, Highlights of 1966 Attack Carrier Air Wing Fifteen Westpac Cruise; Peck, Commander Attack Carrier Air Wing Nine Combat Tactical Supplement, 13 July 1968, NHHC.
140. Commander in Chief U.S. Pacific Fleet, Analysis 7-68: An Estimate of the Probability of a Gross Miss in A-6A Combat Systems Attacks, Vietnam Command Files, COLL/372, Box 113, File CPF Staff Study 7-68, NHHC. The sample size was 221 system run missions.

NOTES FOR CHAPTER 15

141. Message from CG FMFPAC to DDKE/CG III MAF, CG First MAW, Utilization of A-6 Aircraft, 252323Z, March 1967, and Message from CG FMFPAC to DDKE/CG III MAF, CG First MAW, 290355Z, March 1967, and Message from CG FMFPAC info DDKE/CG III MAF, DDKN/CG FMAW, Marine A-6A Employment, 140529Z, April 1967, The Vietnam Center & Sam Johnson Vietnam Archive, Texas Tech University, http://vietnam.ttu.edu.
142. Smith, Carrier Air Wing Six Cruise Report April 1968 to December 1968, 14 December 1968, NHHC; Hearings before the Preparedness Investigating Subcommittee, August 22–23, 1967, 263.
143. Message from CG FMFPAC Utilization of A-6 Aircraft, 252323Z, March 1967, and Message from CG FMFPAC to DDKE/CG III MAF, 290355Z, March 1967, The Vietnam Center & Sam Johnson Vietnam Archive, Texas Tech University, http://vietnam.ttu.edu; Message from 7AF to RUEFHQA/CSAF, A-6A Operations, 201200Z, December 1967, K717.312, December 1967, AFHRA.
144. Page, Attack Carrier Wing Two, Cruise Report, 17 May 1969, NHHC.
145. McKnight, Carrier Air Wing Two, Cruise Report of October 1970 to June 1971, 10 June 1971, NHHC.
146. Notes of President's Luncheon Meeting with Policy Advisors, February 20, 1968, *FRUS 1964–1968, VI*, 228. This document does not mention the A-6 Intruder; it uses the phrase "system run," a term used only with reference to A-6s. Moody, et al., U.S. Marines in Vietnam, Part VII: Backing Up the Troops, HDMCU.
147. Operations of U.S. Marine Forces Vietnam, December 1969 and 1969 Summary, HDMCU; Staff Study 3-70, Navy Combat Effectiveness of Rockeye, CBU-24, and Mk 82 GP Bombs, NHHC.
148. Operations of U.S. Marine Forces Vietnam, December 1970 and 1970 Summary, HDMCU. The A-6A was from VMA(AW)-225. H. Douglas Cluck and Robert L. Hubbard, Attrition Comparison: A-6A System Attacks vs. Visual Attacks, CINCPACFLT Analysis Staff Study 7-70, 26 March 1971, Vietnam Command Files, COLL/372, Box 114, File CPF Staff Study 7-70, NHHC.
149. Enney, Commander Attack Carrier Air Wing Fourteen, Addendum Report, 11 February 1969, NHHC.
150. Sweat, HQ 7th AF to DXIH, Coordination of History, Tab 1, 3 September 1968, K740.07, July–December 1967, AFHRA; Reardon, *Launch the Intruders*, 199.
151. Message from CG III MAF to CG FMFPAC, III MAF Daily Historical Summary Nr. 155 for PD 040001H to 042400H June 1970, 050333Z, June 1970, The Vietnam Center & Sam Johnson Vietnam Archive, Texas Tech University, http://vietnam.ttu.edu; Major General Marion Carl, Oral History Transcript, 61, Archives Branch, HDMCU.
152. Message from CINCPAC to RUMLKSF/CINCPAC, Rolling Thunder All-Weather Operations, 250004Z, February 1968, K717.01, 1 January–31 December 1968, Vol. 2; Combined Campaign Plan Commando Nail Operations, K740.317-3, 14 October 1967, AFHRA.
153. Colonel William B. Colgan, HQ Seventh Air Force, TACLO Activity Report #6, 31 March 1968, K417.01, January–June 1968, Vol. 10; Message from 7AF, A-6A Operations, 201200Z, December 1967, K717.312; Seventh Air Force, Commando Hunt VII, 1972, 81, K740.04-14, AFHRA.
154. Message from AFSPCOMMCEN to AIG 8556, 052105Z May 1972, NHHC; Air Operations in Southeast Asia, 1972–1973, Vol. 2, p. iv-15, K717.0423-23, AFHRA. The suite was an ALQ-100.
155. HQ CINCPAC, Pacific Area Naval Operations Review March 1967, 25, NHHC; Message from 7AF, A-6A Operations, 201200Z, December 1967, K717.312, AFHRA; Message from AFSSO 7AF to AFSSO TAC, Personal for General Momyer, 301105Z, September 1972, Read File September 1972, Vogt Papers, AFHSD.
156. Peck, Commander Attack Carrier Air Wing Nine Combat Tactical Supplement, 13 July 1968, NHHC.

NOTES FOR CHAPTER 15

157. Cluck and Hubbard, Attrition Comparison: A-6A System Attacks vs. Visual Attacks, NHHC.
158. Commander in Chief U.S. Pacific Fleet, Analysis Staff Study 4-68 Combat Attrition of Carrier-Based Aircraft during the Second Half of 1967, May 1, 1968, Vietnam, Box 7, Folder 22, Archives Branch, HDMCU.
159. Chronology of Thirteenth Air Force, 1967, K750.01, Vol. 1, 1967, AFHRA.
160. CINCPAC Command History 1968, Vol. 3, 175, K712. 01, 1968, Vol. 3, AFHRA.
161. Message from General William W. Momyer, 7AF, to AFSSO USAF, 250730Z, April 1968, K740.1623, 25 April 1968; Message from PACAF to RUMABA/13th AF, 140505Z, May 1965, K717.1623, 1965, AFHRA.
162. Robert L. Hubbard, Karen A. Free, Cynthia A. Rollins, Center for Naval Analysis, Operations Evaluation Group Study 734, Performance of Bullpup Missile in Combat, July 1971, COLL/7 Publications of the Center for Naval Analysis OEG, Box 65, File OEG 734, NHHC.
163. William Sanjour, Operations Evaluation Group Study No. 659, Predicted Combat Accuracy of Conventional Air to Surface Weapons, 7 November 1963, COLL/7, Publications of the Center for Naval Analysis OEG, Box 61, File OEG #659; Message from CTG 77.4 to AIG 914, 110832Z, August 1967, Vietnam Air War Collection, Box 69, File 69/1, HQ CINCPAC, Pacific Area Naval Operations Review December 1967, 9, NHHC.
164. Tissot, Commander Attack Carrier Air Wing Fourteen, Addendum Report, 4 December 1967, NHHC; Wingerter, Attack Carrier Air Wing One, Cruise Report, 2 May 1967, NHHC.
165. Enney, Commander Attack Carrier Air Wing Fourteen, Addendum Report, 11 February 1969, NHHC.
166. Carrier Attack Wing Eleven End of Cruise Report, 30 December 1968–4 September 1969, NHHC; Peck, Commander Attack Carrier Air Wing Nine Combat Tactical Supplement, 13 July 1968, NHHC.
167. Hubbard, Free, and Rollins, Study 734, Performance of Bullpup Missile, NHHC; Directorate of Operations History, November 1965, K717.01, July–December 1965, Vol. 3, Part 1, AFHRA.
168. Cosmas, *Joint Chiefs of Staff 1960–1968, Part 3*, 77.
169. Commanding Officer, Reconnaissance Attack Squadron Thirteen to Chief of Naval Operations, Command History 28 April 1968, Enclosure 3: Major Combat Reconnaissance Flights, Fleet Aviation Commands Pre-1998, AR/229, Box 110, File F3. Squadron VA-212 dropped the first Walleyes. The Walleye had a 450-pound warhead. History Naval Operations, Vol. III 1965–1967, Part 1, 132-33, NHHC.
170. PACAF DI, Effects of Air Operations Southeast Asia, Edition 41 May 1967, 68, K717.6092, AFHRA; History Naval Operations, Vol. III 1965–1967, Part 1, 136, NHHC; Memorandum from the President's Special Assistant (Rostow) to President Johnson, May 15, 1967, *FRUS 1964–1968, V*, 412.
171. HQ CINCPAC, Pacific Area Naval Operations Review June 1967, 14, Vietnam Command Files, Box 103, File June 1967, NHHC; Brig. Gen. Dale S. Sweat, HQ 7th AF to DXIH, Coordination of History, Tab 1, 3 September 1968, K740.07, July–December 1967, AFHRA.
172. Porter, Second Generation Weaponry in SEA, 4, 5, K717.0413-80; CINCPAC, Rolling Thunder Summary, August 1967, 030001Z, September 1967, K712.1623-2, AFHRA; Message from CTG 77.8 to CINCPACFLT, 221452, August 1967, Vietnam Air War Collection, Box 69, Folder 69/1, NHHC.
173. HQ CINCPAC, Pacific Area Naval Operations Review November 1967, 12–14, NHHC; Porter, Second Generation Weaponry in SEA, 8, 9, K717.0413-80; Message from CINCPAC to JCS, CINCPAC Monthly Rolling Thunder Summary, October 1967, 080330Z, November 1967, K71.1623-2, October 1967, AFHRA.
174. CINCPAC Command History 1968, Vol. 3, 146, K712. 01, 1968, Vol. 3, AFHRA.

NOTES FOR CHAPTER 15

175. Paveway Summary: E. O. Guided Bomb Drops, SEA, April 1969, K740.03-8, April–May 1968; Sanjour, Study No. 659, Predicted Combat Accuracy of Conventional Air to Surface Weapons, NHHC; Porter, Second Generation Weaponry in SEA, 13–16, K717.0413-80, AFHRA.
176. HQ PACAF, Summary Air Operations Southeast Asia, September 1972, 2-15 through 2-16, K717.3063, AFHRA; Harry McPherson, *A Political Education* (Boston: Little, Brown, 1972), 427.
177. Colonel Garth L. Reynolds, AFXOPGD, Lessons Learned in Air Force Operations, 11 October 1967, K143.5072-22, Vol. 1; Thorndale, Interdiction in Route Package One, 34, K717.0413-96, AFHRA. More specifically, this was a forty-foot circular error probable.
178. Porter, Second Generation Weaponry in SEA, 19, K717.0413-80, AFHRA. See Paul G. Gillespie, *Weapons of Choice: The Development of Precision Guided Munitions* (Tuscaloosa: University of Alabama Press, 2006), 66–122 for a discussion of the background and development of laser-guided bombs.
179. Porter, Second Generation Weaponry in SEA, 19, 21, K717.0413-80; Headquarters PACAF, Summary of Air Operations in Southeast Asia, June 1968, 1–7, K717.3063, AFHRA. These were M-117s and Mk 84s.
180. Porter, Second Generation Weaponry in SEA, 30, K717.0413-80, AFHRA.
181. Monroe, Request for R&D Requirements, 6 January 1970, K740-03-4; Paveway Summary: E. O. Guided Bomb Drops, SEA, April 1969, K740.03-8; Corona Harvest, USAF Air Operations in Southeast Asia, 1972–1973, Vol. 2, p. iv-205, K717.0423-23, AFHRA.
182. General B. K. Holloway, Vice Chief of Staff, AFCCS, Cost Effectiveness of Guided Bombs, 11 September 1967, K143.5072-22, September–October 1967, Vol. 1; Jamison, End of Tour Report, 1 March 1970, K717.131, AFHRA.
183. HQ CINCPAC, Pacific Area Naval Operations Review May 1967, 21, 22, NHHC; Eggers, Employment of Missiles, K712.153-1; Porter, Second Generation Weaponry in SEA, 4, K717.0413-80, AFHRA.
184. Southeast Asia Air Operations Briefing August 1971, K717.3063-1, August 1971; Holloway, Cost Effectiveness of Guided Bombs, 11 September 1967; K143.5072-22; Linebacker Conference Sierra V, 180708Z, September 1972, K740.3391, AFHRA.
185. Lavelle, Analysis of Air Warfare in Southeast Asia, 6 April 1966, I-B-12 to I-C-2, K143.505-13, AFHRA.
186. See for example Message from CTE 70.2.1.1 to Comseventhflt, 301030Z, April 1967, Ships History Post 2001 Enterprise CV-65, Box 108, File Vietnam Message Traffic 1965-1968; 7th Fleet Operational Summary, July 1965, Reference Files, Vietnam, A-Air Warfare (I), Aircraft Losses Folder; HQ CINCPAC, Pacific Area Naval Operations Review September 1966, 6–7, Vietnam Command Files, Box 102, File September 1966, NHHC; History of Pacific Air Forces, 1 July–31 December 1965, Vol. 1, Part 2, 41-47, K717.01, AFHRA.
187. Foley, USS *Midway* 1972 Command History, 14 March 1973, and 7th Fleet Operational Summary, May 1965, and 7th Fleet Operational Summary, June 1965, Reference Files, Vietnam, A-Air Warfare (I), Aircraft Losses Folder, NHHC; Effects of Air Operations Southeast Asia, Edition 32 August 1966, 14–37, K717.6092, AFHRA; Prados, *The Blood Road,* 163; Cosmas, *The Joint Chiefs of Staff, 1960–1968, Part 2,* 523.
188. PACAF DI, Effects of Air Operations Southeast Asia, Edition 41 May 1967, 102–3, K717.6092, AFHRA.
189. Assessment of Air Operations, 7 February 1965 thru 19 July 1967, 24, K740.04-20; Air Effectiveness Trends during the Southwest Monsoon 1967, K740.04-18, AFHRA; Message from CTG 77.4 to AIG 914, 071318Z, August 1967, Vietnam Air War Collection, Box 69, Folder 69/1, NHHC. This is a representative message of a common theme of these reports.
190. Message, Impact of Interdiction Campaign, 140930Z, November 1968, K740.454-1, AFHRA.

NOTES FOR CHAPTER 15

191. Assessment of Air Operations, 7 February 1965 thru 19 July 1967, 26, K740.04-20; HQ 7th AF, Commando Hunt III, 83, 93, K740.04-8; Seventh AF, Air Interdiction in Southeast Asia, April–June 1970, 55, K740.04-10, AFHRA.
192. Central Intelligence Agency to President Johnson, July 31, 1967, *FRUS 1964–1968, XXVIII,* 608; Assessment of Air Operations, 7 February 1965 thru 19 July 1967, 38, K740.04-20; Ow, Documentation and Analysis, 7–8, K740.31067-9; Lofgren, Air War in Northern Laos, 1 April–30 November 1971, 28, K717.0413-65; Southeast Asia Air Operations Briefing, September 1971, K717.3063-1, September 1971, AFHRA; Operations of U.S. Marine Forces Vietnam, December 1970 and 1970 Summary, HDMCU.
193. Ow, Analysis of Steel Tiger Interdiction Operations, 7–8, K740.31067-9; Air Interdiction in Southeast Asia, April–June 1970, 78–81, K740.04-10; Layton, Commando Hunt VI, 52, 54, K717.0414-28, AFHRA.
194. History of Pacific Air Forces, 1 July–31 December 1965, Vol. 1, Part 2, 120, K717.01, AFHRA.
195. Report Prepared by the Joint Staff, Joint Chiefs of Staff: An Evaluation of the Effects of the Air Campaign against North Vietnam and Laos, October 1966, *FRUS 1964–1968, IV,* 789–92.
196. A Survey of Analyses on B-52 Bombing Operations in Southeast Asia, K143.5022-22, September–October 1967, Vol. 4, AFHRA.
197. Comparative Analysis of Air Interdiction-Ground Force Operation in Southeast Asia (Second Look), 1 July 1970, K143.044-34, 1 July 1970, AFHRA.
198. Message from 7AF to RUHLKM/CINCPACAF, Enemy Movement of Supplies during Tet Truce Period, 110905Z, February 1967, K740.1623 11 February 1967, AFHRA.
199. Message from 7AF to RUEDHQA/CSAF, 151000Z, February 1967, K740.1623, AFHRA.
200. Trapolino and Otis, History of the 307th Strategic Wing, 1–31 May 1970, K-WG-307-HI, June 1970, AFHRA.
201. Thorndale, Interdiction in Route Package One, 46, 50, K717.0413-96, AFHRA.
202. Ibid., 51.
203. MACV Command History, 1968, Vol. 1, 402. Emphasis in original.
204. Message, Tactical Air Requirements, 070455Z, October 1965, K526.1623, AFHRA.
205. History of Pacific Air Forces, 1 July–31 December 1965, Vol. 1, Part 2, 68–70, K717.01, AFHRA.
206. Survey of Analyses on B-52 Bombing Operations, K143.5022-22, Vol. 4, AFHRA.
207. AFGOA 3859/68 Operations Analysis, Headquarters USAF, Measures of the 1968 Out-Country Bombing Campaign in Southeast Asia, K143.5045-11, January–October 1968, AFHRA.
208. Steenrod and Yale, Bombing Campaign September 1966–April 1968, K143.5045-6, AFHRA.
209. Seventh AF, Air Interdiction in Southeast Asia, April–June 1970, 86, K740.04-10, AFHRA.
210. Directorate of Operations, DCS/Plans and Operation, HQ USAF, Air Power in Southeast Asia, pp. iii-14 through iii-21, K143.042-28, 8 May 1969; HQ 7th AF, Commando Hunt III, 23, 90, K740.04-8; Gilster, et al., Economic Analysis of the Steel Tiger Interdiction, 39, 43–45, K740.454-7, AFHRA.
211. Southeast Asia Analysis Report, June/July 1970, NHHC.
212. HQ 7th AF, Commando Hunt III, 146, 148, 149, K740.04-8, AFHRA.
213. Memorandum from Winston Lord of the Planning Staff of the National Security Council to the President's Assistant for National Security Affairs (Kissinger), October 6, 1969, *FRUS 1969–1976, VI,* 429; Layton, Commando Hunt VI, 40, K717.0414-28, AFHRA.
214. HQ 7th AF, Commando Hunt III, 93, K740.04-8, AFHRA; Gaiduk, *Soviet Union and the Vietnam War,* 232; Memorandum from Winston Lord, October 6, 1969, *FRUS 1969–1976, VI,* 429.
215. Seventh AF, Air Interdiction in Southeast Asia, April–June 1970, 100, 106–7, K740.04-10, AFHRA.

216. Layton, Commando Hunt VI, 32, K717.0414-28, AFHRA.
217. National Security Decision Memorandum 77, August 12, 1970, *FRUS 1969–1976, VII*, 41; Layton, Commando Hunt VI, 67–69, 74, K717.0414-28, AFHRA.
218. Gilster, et al., Economic Analysis of the Steel Tiger Interdiction, 35–37, K740.454-7, AFHRA.
219. Memorandum from the President's Assistant for National Security Affairs (Kissinger) to President Nixon, August 7, 1970, *FRUS 1969–1976, VII*, 24.
220. History of Seventh Air Force, 1971–1972, 264, K740.01-25, Vol. 1, AFHRA.
221. Seventh Air Force, Commando Hunt VII, 61, K740.04-14, AFHRA.
222. Lt. Col. Herman L. Gilster, Maj. Richard D. Duckworth, and Capt. Gregory G. Hildebrandt, An Econometric Study of Aerial Interdiction in Southern Laos, 10 October 1970–30 June 1971, K740.04-12, AFHRA.
223. Gilster, Duckworth, and Hildebrandt, An Econometric Study, K740.04-12, AFHRA. This was not the first use of statistical analyses to try to determine bombing effectiveness. See for example the use of "a regression analysis" during Operation Commando Hunt III. HQ 7th AF, Commando Hunt III, 120, K740.04-8, AFHRA.
224. Webb and Poole, *Joint Chiefs of Staff, 1971–1973*, 107.
225. Charles J. Liddell Jr., Operations Analysis Office, Steel Tiger Output—Supply Limited or Demand Limited? 13 July 1972, K717.56-3, AFHRA.
226. Seventh Air Force, Commando Hunt VII, 4–7, 61, K740.04-14, AFHRA.
227. Cosmas, *The Joint Chiefs of Staff, 1960–1968, Part 2*, 403.
228. Special Intelligence Supplement, SIS 1221-65, An Appraisal of the Bombing of North Vietnam, December 21, 1965, *FRUS, 1964–1968, III*, 680–85.
229. HQ USMACV Command History, 1965, 11, 215; Telegram from the Commander-in-Chief, Pacific (Sharp) to the Joint Chiefs of Staff, January 12, 1966, *FRUS 1964–1968, IV*, 50.
230. Palmer, *The 25-Year War*, 187; Davidson, *Vietnam at War*, 352, 431.
231. Colonel Bui Tin, "How North Vietnam Won the War," *The Wall Street Journal*, August 3, 1995, A-8.

Chapter 16

1. Donald D. Frizzell, "Dissatisfaction with the Air War," in W. Scott Thompson and Donald D. Frizzell, eds., *The Lessons of Vietnam* (New York: Crane, Russak, 1977), 143; John F. Piowaty, "Reflections of a Thud Driver," *Air University Review* (January–February 1983), 52, 53; Broughton, "Rolling Thunder from the Cockpit," 149–50; John M. Gates, "If At First You Don't Succeed, Try to Rewrite History: Revisionism and the Vietnam War," in William Head and Lawrence E. Grinter, eds., *Looking Back on the Vietnam War: A 1990s Perspective on the Decisions, Combat, and Legacies* (Westport, CT: Greenwood Press, 1993), 177. This list is not exhaustive.
2. Joe Patrick, "Testing the Rules of Engagement," *Vietnam* (December 1997), 46.
3. Dr. Harold Pease, "Fighting with One Hand Tied Behind our Back in Vietnam and Afghanistan," August 25, 2010, http://libertyunderfire.org/2010/08/fighting-with-one-hand-tied-behind-our-back-in-vietnam-and-afghanistan/.
4. Moorer, Reminiscences, Volume III, 1228, Navy Department Library.
5. Analysis of COMUSMACV Force Requirements and Alternatives, March 1, 1968, *FRUS 1964–1968, VI*, 297; Melyan and Bonetti, Rolling Thunder, July 1965–December 1966, vi–vii, K717.0414-12; Captain William R. Burditt, Rules of Engagement October 1972–August 1973 (HQ PACAF: Office of History, Project CHECO, 1977), viii, K717.0413-227, AFHRA.
6. Emerson, "Making War without Will," 168.
7. Sharp, *Strategy for Defeat*, 270.

8. See Carl von Clausewitz, *On War*, eds. and trans. Michael Howard and Peter Paret (Princeton, NJ: Princeton University Press, 1976), 607–8.
9. Message from CINCPACFLT to CINCPAC, Rolling Thunder, 132111Z, May 1965, K712.1623-2, AFHRA.
10. General Harris interview, 22 April 1971, 74, K239.0512-403, Vol. 2, AFHRA.
11. Hearings before the Preparedness Investigating Subcommittee, August 16, 1967, 167.
12. Thornal interview, 20, K239.0512-012, 00/11/66–00/07/67, AFHRA.
13. L. E. Paterson, Evolution of the Rules of Engagement for Southeast Asia, 1960–1965 (PACAF: Directorate of Tactical Evaluation, CHECO Division, 1966), 5, K717.0414-20, AFHRA.
14. Ibid., 3.
15. Michael Walzer, *Just and Unjust Wars: A Moral Argument with Historical Illustrations* (New York: Basic Books, 1977), 54, 74, 90.
16. Paterson, Rules of Engagement for Southeast Asia, 1960–1965, 6, 7, 8, 14, K717.0414-20, AFHRA.
17. Ibid., 20.
18. Ibid., 29–33, 44–45.
19. Ibid., 37, 49–52, 58.
20. Message from CINCPACAF to RUAUE/5AF, 200100Z, April 1965, K717.1623, AFHRA.
21. PACAF DI, Effects of Air Operations in Southeast Asia, 11 November 1965, 24, K717-6092, AFHRA; History Naval Operations, Vol. III 1965–1967, Part 1, 97, NHHC.
22. Message from CJCS to RUHKA/CINCPAC, Rolling Thunder 53, 242039Z, January 1967, K717.01, 1 January–31 December 1967, Vol. 2, Part 2, AFHRA.
23. Cosmas, *Joint Chiefs of Staff, 1960–1968, Part 3,* 81.
24. Castle, *One Day Too Long,* 8–9; Jack Broughton, *Going Downtown: The War against Hanoi and Washington* (New York: Orion Books, 1988), xvi.
25. Palmer, *The 25-Year War,* 160.
26. Chester L. Cooper, Memorandum from Chester L. Cooper of the National Security Council Staff to the President's Special Assistant for National Security Affairs (Bundy), March 9, 1965, *FRUS 1964–1968, II,* 425, 426; Cosmas, *The Joint Chiefs of Staff, 1960–1968, Part 2,* 230.
27. Message from 2 Air Div to CSAF, 251246Z, March 1966, K526.1623, AFHRA.
28. History of the Pacific Air Forces, 1966, 74, K717.01, Vol. 1, Part 2; Message from CINCPAC to RUEKDA/JCS, Rolling Thunder, 270200Z, October 1967, K717.312-64, AFHRA.
29. TAC Views on Major Program, 12 June 1969, K417.01, July 1968–June 1969, Vol. 2, AFHRA.
30. Schlight, Rules of Engagement, 1 January 1966–1 November 1969 (HQ PACAF: Directorate, Tactical Evaluation/CHECO Division, 1969), 3, 13, Office of Air Force History. This document has no AFHRA number; it was only declassified in 2014. Melyan and Bonetti, Rolling Thunder, July 1965–December 1966, 92, K717.0414-12, AFHRA. Ryan was CINCPACAF from February 1967 until August 1968.
31. Hearings before the Preparedness Investigating Subcommittee, August 29, 1967, 495; Fry, *Debating Vietnam,* 129.
32. General William W. Momyer to General John P. McConnell, July 3, 1969, 168.7102-15, AFHRA.
33. "As the Air War Heats Up in Vietnam," *U.S. News and World Report,* May 9, 1966, 27.
34. Report from USAF Analysis Team, 150020Z, March 1965, K526.1623, AFHRA.
35. Message from CINCPAC to JCS, Rolling Thunder 7, 200445Z, March 1965, K712.1623-2, 65/01/22–65/06/28; Message from CINCPACAF to 7AF, Rolling Thunder, 151940Z, October 1966, K717.1623, AFHRA.
36. Melyan and Bonetti, Rolling Thunder, July 1965–December 1966, 129–30, K717.0414-12; Memorandum from Cooper to Bundy, March 9, 1965, *FRUS 1964–1968, II,* 426; Cosmas, *The Joint Chiefs of Staff, 1960–1968, Part 2,* 512.

37. Message from CINCPACAF to 7AF, Rolling Thunder Guidance, 040030Z, June 1966, K717.1623, AFHRA.
38. Message from CINCPAC to JCS, Shift to More Effective Footing for Prosecution of the War in South Vietnam, 211040Z, March 1965, K712.1623-2, AFHRA.
39. Message from 2 Air Div to RUEAHQ/CSAF, 160535Z, March 1965, K526.1623, 15 March 1965; Telecon Nbr 684, from 2nd Air Div to PACAF, 13 AF, 231050Z, March 1965, K526.1623, AFHRA; HQ USMACV Command History, 1966, 393, History Naval Operations, Vol. III 1965–1967, Part 1, 97, NHHC.
40. Summary Notes of the 556th Meeting of the National Security Council, January 29, 1966, *FRUS 1964–1968, IV*, 189.
41. Lavelle, Analysis of Air Warfare in Southeast Asia, 6 April 1966, pp. I-B-9, I-B-11, K143.505-13; Message from CINCPACAF to 7AF, Rolling Thunder, 151940Z, October 1966, K717.1623, AFHRA.
42. Message from CINCPAC, Rolling Thunder, 26 March 1968, K712.1623-2 March 1968, AFHRA. The document does not have a clearly delineated date time group. Sharp, *Strategy for Defeat*, 141–43, 183.
43. Telegram from the Embassy in Vietnam to the Department of State, January 6, 1965, *FRUS 1964–1968, II*, 26; Letter from Director of Central Intelligence Raborn to President Johnson, May 8, 1965, *FRUS 1964–1968, II*, 626; Memorandum from the President's Special Assistant for National Security Affairs (Bundy) to President Johnson, September 12, 1965, *FRUS 1964–1968, III*, 384; Van Staaveren, *Gradual Failure*, 130; An Appraisal of the Effects of the First Year of Bombing, June 1, 1966, *FRUS 1964–1968, IV*, 430. The US estimated that the bombing had killed about 3,000 North Vietnamese civilians, which it considered "a small number," because "over 350,000 persons died in 1965 from other causes and where the accidental deaths alone produced casualties some three to five times greater than those resulting from the Rolling Thunder Program." *FRUS 1964–1968, IV*, 431.
44. Daddis, *Westmoreland's War*, 75, 95, 96.
45. Elder and Melly, Rules of Engagement, 1969–1972, 16, K717.0414-20, AFHRA.
46. Schlight, Rules of Engagement, 1 January 1966–1 November 1969, 5, AFHRA.
47. History of the Pacific Air Forces 1966, 75, 77, K717.01, Vol. 1, Part 2, AFHRA.
48. Message from 41st ADIV to RUMSALA/2AD, 190908Z, May 1965, K717.1623, AFHRA.
49. Clodfelter, *Limits of Air Power*, 121.
50. Message from CJCS, Rolling Thunder 53, 242039Z, January 1967, K717.01, Vol. 2, Part 2, AFHRA.
51. Message from CJCS to RUHKA/CINCPAC, Rolling Thunder 57, 202044Z, July 1967, K717.01, 1 January–31 December 1967, Vol. 2, Part 2, AFHRA.
52. Hearings before the Preparedness Investigating Subcommittee, August 16, 1967, 150; HQ 7th AF, Commando Hunt III, 6, K740.04-8; History of Pacific Air Forces, 1 July–31 December 1965, Vol. 1, Part 2, 112, K717.01; Paterson, Evolution of the Rules of Engagement, 1960–1965, 62, K717.0414-20, AFHRA.
53. Thompson, *To Hanoi and Back*, 239.
54. Message from CJCS, Rolling Thunder 53, 242039Z, January 1967, K717.01, Vol. 2, Part 2, AFHRA.
55. Message from 7 AF to URHLKSP/PACAF CC, 130915Z, August 1966, K717.312-1; Letter from the Deputy Undersecretary of State for Political Affairs (Johnson) to the Deputy Secretary of Defense (Vance), March 8, 1966, *FRUS 1964–1968, XXVIII*, 445; Memorandum from the Director of the Joint Staff (Burchinal) to the Assistant Secretary of Defense for International Security Affairs (McNaughton), March 21, 1966, *FRUS 1964–1968, XXVIII*, 448.

56. Paterson, Evolution of the Rules of Engagement, 1960–1965, 68, K717.0414-20, AFHRA.
57. Message from 7AF to 355 TFW, 388 TFW, 8TFW, 35 TFW, Target Identification, 270200Z, 1966, K740.1623 26 July 1966; Paterson, Evolution of the Rules of Engagement, 1960–1965, 71, K717.0414-20, AFHRA.
58. Melyan and Bonetti, Rolling Thunder, July 1965–December 1966, 37, 48, K717.0414-12, AFHRA.
59. Reminiscences of Vice Admiral Kent. L. Lee, 678, NHHC.
60. Telegram from the Chairman of the Joint Chiefs of Staff (Wheeler) to the Commander, Military Assistance Command, Vietnam (Westmoreland) March 1, 1965, *FRUS 1964–1968, II*, 388–89.
61. Message from CINCPACAF, Rolling Thunder Guidance, 040030Z, June 1966, K717.1623, AFHRA.
62. An Appraisal of the Effects of the First Year of Bombing, June 1, 1966, *FRUS 1964–1968, IV*, 430; History of Pacific Air Forces, January–December 1966, 20, K717.01, Vol. 1, Part 1; Melyan and Bonetti, The War in Vietnam, 101, K717.0414-75, AFHRA; "Air Power—What It Is Doing in Vietnam War, Interview with the Air Force Chief of Staff," *U.S. News and World Report*, May 9, 1966, 28; Herring, *LBJ and Vietnam*, 46.
63. Message from CINCPACAF, Rolling Thunder Guidance, 040030, June 1966, K717.1623, AFHRA.
64. Message from ADMINO CINCPAC, Action Adm Sharp, 080346Z, December 1967, K712.1623-2; Schlight, Rules of Engagement, 1 January 1966–1 November 1969, 9, AFHRA.
65. Broughton, *Going Downtown*, 208–10. The incident happened on June 2, 1967.
66. Cosmas, *Joint Chiefs of Staff, 1960–1968, Part 3*, 84.
67. Effects of Air Operations Southeast Asia, October 1966, 98, K717.6092, AFHRA; Commander in Chief U.S. Pacific Fleet, Analysis Staff Study 11-68 A Case Study of A-6A Strikes against Hanoi Radcom, 21 March 1969, Vietnam Command Files, COLL/372, Box 113, File CPF Staff Study 11-68, NHHC.
68. The Hanoi and Haiphong areas were prohibited again on August 19. Bonetti, et al., The War in Vietnam, July–December 1967, 5–6, 8, K717.0414-17, AFHRA.
69. HQ CINCPAC, Pacific Area Naval Operations Review February 1968, 17, Vietnam Command Files, Box 104, File February 1968, NHHC; HQ CINCPAC, Pacific Area Naval Operations Review March 1968, 10–11, Vietnam Command Files, Box 104, File March 1968, NHHC.
70. Palmer, *Summons of the Trumpet*, 125; Message from CJCS, Rolling Thunder 53, 242039Z, January 1967, K717.01, Vol. 2, Part 2, AFHRA; Barrett, *Uncertain Warriors*, 123; McPherson, *A Political Education*, 426.
71. Hearings before the Preparedness Investigating Subcommittee, August 22, 1967, 227.
72. Captain Emery G. Cushing, End of Tour Report, 23rd Tactical Support Squadron, 8 June 1967, K740.131, Cushing, Emery G. 7 September 1966–15 June 1967, AFHRA.
73. Tom Johnson, Notes of Meeting, August 24, 1967, *FRUS 1964–1968, V*, 723.
74. Hearings before the Preparedness Investigating Subcommittee, August 16, 1967, 165, 167–68.
75. Fry, *Debating Vietnam*, 97.
76. Ibid., 98, 102; Cosmas, *Joint Chiefs of Staff, 1960–1968, Part 3*, 70.
77. Hearings before the Preparedness Investigating Subcommittee, August 9–10, 1967, 72.
78. Ibid., August 16, 1967, 131.
79. Ibid., 142.
80. Ibid., 133.
81. Ibid., 154.
82. Ibid., 154–59, 162–63, 177.
83. Ibid., 141.
84. Hearings before the Preparedness Investigating Subcommittee of the Committee on Armed

Services, United States Senate, 90th Cong., 1st sess., August 9–10, 1967, 38, 43, 45.
85. Ibid., 58.
86. Hearings before the Preparedness Investigating Subcommittee, August 22–23, 1967, 212.
87. Ginsburgh represented the CJCS on the National Security Council. Clodfelter, *Limits of Air Power*, 74, 144; Milne, *America's Rasputin*, 222.
88. Hearings before the Preparedness Investigating Subcommittee, August 22, 1967, 208.
89. Fry, *Debating Vietnam*, 108.
90. Message from CSAF, Graduated Reprisal Program against DRV, 110735Z, February 1965, K712.1623-2, AFHRA.
91. Hearings before the Preparedness Investigating Subcommittee, August 22, 1967, 230.
92. Ibid., August 22–23, 1967, 229.
93. Ibid., August 16, 1967, 168–69.
94. Ibid., 169.
95. General William W. Momyer to Major General George J. Keegan Jr., August 17, 1971, 168.7041-43, August 1971, AFHRA. Keegan was Deputy Chief of Staff, Plans and Operations, HQ Air Force Logistics Command. Momyer is mistaken about the assertiveness and wisdom of the World War II generals vis-à-vis the president. In summer 1942, for example, General George C. Marshall demanded the US Army invade northwest France that year, even though it was not ready, was too small, and would have been slaughtered. President Franklin D. Roosevelt recognized the premature invasion force Marshall proposed would have been destroyed and ordered the general to comply with his grand strategy of first keeping the Soviet Union in the war and more immediately to execute an invasion of North Africa. Marshall complied. Mark A. Stoler, *Allies and Adversaries: The Joint Chiefs of Staff, the Grand Alliance, and U.S. Strategy in World War II* (Chapel Hill: University of North Carolina Press, 2000), 89–90.
96. Hearings before the Preparedness Investigating Subcommittee, August 25, 1967, 277, 279.
97. Ibid., 279, 280; McNamara, *In Retrospect*, 287; Cosmas, *Joint Chiefs of Staff, 1960–1968, Part 3*, 72.
98. Hearings before the Preparedness Investigating Subcommittee, August 25, 1967, 281.
99. Ibid., 282.
100. Ibid., 357.
101. Ibid., 278, 279, 280.
102. McNamara, *In Retrospect*, 290; Cosmas, *Joint Chiefs of Staff, 1960–1968, Part 3*, 74–75.
103. Mark Perry, *Four Stars* (Boston: Houghton Mifflin, 1989), 163–65; Fry, *Debating Vietnam*, 137; Sorley, *Honorable Warrior*, 268, 286; Herring, *LBJ and Vietnam*, 56. Herring adds, "Perry's source for the story was an unnamed 'former JCS flag officer.' His account has been confirmed by a senior officer close to one of the deceased members of the JCS but denied by General Wallace Greene and Admiral Thomas Moorer." Herring, *LBJ and Vietnam*, 198.
104. Perry, *Four Stars*, 165.
105. Herring, *LBJ and Vietnam*, 198.
106. Message from CINCPAC to JCS, Rolling Thunder, 171925Z, March 1968, K712.1623-2, AFHRA. These quotations are from the message itself; they may be paraphrases or direct quotations of what the North Vietnamese and Canadian diplomats said.
107. Thompson, *To Hanoi and Back*, 262; Michel, *11 Days*, 184–85. The album was "Where Are You Now, My Son?" on A&M Records. The title cut has the sounds of jets and bombs in the background.
108. Pacific Command History, 1969, Vol. 3, 99, K712.01, Vol. 3, redacted, 1969, AFHRA.
109. Ibid., 84, 99.
110. Telegram from the Embassy in Laos to the Department of State, March 22, 1965, *FRUS 1964–1968, XXVIII*, 354.

111. Ibid., 355.
112. History of Pacific Air Forces, 1 July–31 December 1965, Vol. 1, Part 2, 109, K717.01, AFHRA.
113. Pacific Command History, 1969, Vol. 3, 102–5, K712.01, Vol. 3, redacted, 1969, AFHRA.
114. PACAF D.O. Read File, 14 January 1967, K712.1623-4, 1968; Message from 7AF to COMUSMACV, Use of FACs in Laos, 240910Z, April 1967, K717.312-1; Message from COMUSMACV to RUHKA/CINCPAC, Air Operations in Steel Tiger, 160340Z, May 1967, K717.312-64, AFHRA.
115. Schlight, Rules of Engagement, 1 January 1966–1 November 1969, xi.
116. Acacia, *Clark Clifford*, 298.
117. Commander in Chief Pacific Command History, 1970, Vol. 2, 179, K712.01, Vol. 2, 1970; Ryan, Air Operations in Cambodia, May–June 1970, 34, K740.04-16; Elder and Melly, Rules of Engagement, 1969–1972, 21, 22, 25, K717.0414-20; Folkman and Cain, Cambodian Campaign 29 April–30 June 1970, xvi, K717.0413-84, AFHRA.
118. Elder and Melly, Rules of Engagement, 1969–1972, 31, 37, K717.0414-20, AFHRA.
119. Commander in Chief Pacific Command History, 1970, Vol. 2, 143–44, K712-01, Vol. 2, redacted, 1970, AFHRA; Shaw, *Cambodian Campaign*, 144–45.
120. Elder and Melly, Rules of Engagement, 1969–1972, 40, 41, K717.0414-20, AFHRA.
121. Ibid., 44.
122. Ibid., 45.
123. Evaluation Report for the NVN Offensive, April–August 1972, iv-12, K717.04-9, AFHRA.
124. Porter, Linebacker First 120 Days, 10, K717.0414-42, 1973, AFHRA; Memorandum from Secretary of Defense Laird to President Nixon, March 8, 1972, *FRUS 1969–1976, VIII*, 117.
125. Jussi Hanhimaki, *The Flawed Architect: Henry Kissinger and American Foreign Policy* (Oxford and New York: Oxford University Press, 2004), 223–24.
126. Elder and Melly, Rules of Engagement, 1969–1972, 48, 49, K717.0414-20, AFHRA.
127. Burditt, Rules of Engagement October 1972–August 1973, 13, 15, K717.0413-227, AFHRA.
128. Ibid., 35–36.
129. Ibid., 38.
130. Conversation among Nixon, Kissinger, and Moorer, April 3, 1972, *FRUS 1969–1976, VIII*, 175.
131. Webb and Poole, *Joint Chiefs of Staff, 1971–1973*, 182. Moorer had been chairman of the JCS since July 1970.

Chapter 17

1. Nelson, *Resilient America*, 127.
2. Message from Abrams to McCain, January 20, 1972, *FRUS 1969–1976, VIII*, 1–2, 3; Memorandum from John D. Negroponte of the National Security Council Staff to the President's Assistant for National Security Affairs (Kissinger), February 15, 1972, *FRUS 1969–1976, VIII*, 102–3.
3. Message from Abrams to McCain, January 20, 1972, *FRUS 1969–1976, VIII*, 3, 6–7.
4. Memorandum from Secretary of Defense Laird to President Nixon, March 14, 1972, *FRUS 1969–1976, VIII*, 140. The two men did not see eye to eye. Nixon accused the secretary of watering down reports from Southeast Asia and delaying orders from the White House and erupted to the CJCS, "The Secretary of Defense is not Commander in Chief. The Secretary of Defense does not make decisions on those kinds of things. . . . He's a procurement officer." Conversation among Nixon, Kissinger, and Moorer, April 3, 1972, *FRUS 1969–1976, VIII*, 176.
5. Conversation between Nixon and Kissinger, January 20, 1972, *FRUS 1969–1976, VIII*, 10.
6. Conversation among Nixon, Kissinger, and Bunker, February 3, 1972, *FRUS 1969–1976, VIII*, 71.

By refitted Nixon meant that the ones configured for nuclear weapons had to be modified to carry conventional bombs—a time-consuming process.

7. Eighth Air Force Activity Input, 1 July 1971–30 June 1972, K520.041-2, AFHRA; Henry Kissinger, National Security Decision Memorandum 149, February 4, 1972, *FRUS 1969–1976, VIII*, 79; Memorandum from the President's Assistant for National Security Affairs (Kissinger) to President Nixon, February 16, 1972, *FRUS 1969–1976, VIII*, 109; Message from Abrams to Moorer and McCain, March 8, 1972, *FRUS 1969–1976, VIII*, 121. Kissinger, *White House Years*, 1101–2.
8. Memorandum from Laird to Nixon, March 14, 1972, *FRUS 1969–1976, VIII*, 139, 141; Randolph, *Powerful and Brutal Weapons*, 22, 26; Guan, *Ending the Vietnam War*, 82; Richard A. Hunt, *Pacification: The American Struggle for Vietnam's Hearts and Minds* (Boulder, CO: Westview Press, 1995), 252–55.
9. National Security Council Meeting, February 2, 1972, *FRUS 1969–1976, VIII*, 69; Memorandum from Philip A. Odeen of the National Security Council Staff to Richard T. Kennedy and John Negroponte of the National Security Council Staff, April 4, 1972, *FRUS 1969–1976, VIII*, 213.
10. MACV Command History 1972, B-5, FitzGerald, *Fire in the Lake*, 67, 139–40, 160–61; Neale, *A People's History of the Vietnam War*, 41, 176; Karnow, *Vietnam*, 401.
11. Dunne, and Quimby, The U.S. Air War Against Tanks, 3, K740.041-2, 20 May 1973, AFHRA; Davidson, *Vietnam at War*, 676, 678; Nalty, *Air War over South Vietnam*, 330. These totals include T-54s and PT-76s.
12. Commander Seventh Fleet Command History 1972, 26 September 1973, NHHC; Webb and Poole, *Joint Chiefs of Staff, 1971–1973*, 158; Summary of B-52 Arc Light Operations - NVN April 1972, K416.153-1; Porter, Linebacker First 120 Days, 13, K717.0414-42, 1973; CINCPAC Command History 1972, Vol. 1, 153, K712.01, Vol. 1; Eighth Air Force Activity Input, 1 July 1971–30 June 1972, K520.041-2, AFHRA.
13. Memorandum of Conversation, May 2, 1972, *FRUS 1969–1976, VIII*, 370; Air Warfare Annex, Commander Seventh Fleet Command History 1972, 26 September 1973, NHHC.
14. Guan, *Ending the Vietnam War*, 97.
15. Henry Kissinger, Memorandum of Conversation, April 21, 1972, in David C. Geyer, Nina D. Howland, and Kent Sieg, *Foreign Relations of the United States, 1969–1976. Soviet Union, October 1971–May 1972, Volume XIV* (Washington, DC: Government Printing Office, 2006), 486 (hereafter referred to as *FRUS 1969–1976, XIV*).
16. Randolph, *Powerful and Brutal Weapons*, 153–54; Gaiduk, *Soviet Union and the Vietnam War*, 234–35.
17. Memorandum of Conversation, February 22, 1972, Steven E. Phillips, ed., *Foreign Relations of the United States, 1969–1976, Volume XVII, China, 1969–1972* (Washington DC: US Government Printing Office, 2006), 717.
18. Hanhimaki, *The Flawed Architect*, 204; CINCPAC Command History 1972, Vol. 1, 154, K712.01, 1972, Vol. 1; Summary of B-52 Arc Light Operations—NVN Apr 1972, K416.153-1, AFHRA; Air Warfare Annex, Commander Seventh Fleet Command History 1972, 26 September 1973, NHHC; Guan, *Ending the Vietnam War*, 98.
19. Freedom Train was the name of the air offensive in April, Constant Guard was a set of trans-Pacific flights of combat aircraft from the US to Indochina, and Linebacker was the operation against North Vietnam that commenced on May 10. MACV Command History 1972, B-2, B-3.
20. Message from AFSSO USAF to AFSO PACAF info AFSSO 7AF, Comments of Le Duc Tho, 242137Z, May 1972, Vogt Papers, AFHSD.
21. Porter, Linebacker First 120 Days, 9, K717.0414-42, 1973, AFHRA; Randolph, *Powerful and Brutal Weapons*, 114.

22. Randolph, *Powerful and Brutal Weapons*, 85, 87.
23. Ibid., 95.
24. Conversation between Nixon and Kissinger, April 4, 1972, *FRUS 1969–1976, VIII*, 212; Diary Entry by the Assistant to the President (Haldeman), April 6, 1972, *FRUS 1969–1976, VIII*, 221–22. According to *History of the Joint Chiefs of Staff: The Joint Chiefs of staff and the War in Vietnam, 1971–1973*, Vogt replaced General John D. Lavelle at the suggestion of Admiral Moorer. Webb and Poole, *Joint Chiefs of Staff, 1971–1973*, 156.
25. Hersh, *The Price of Power*, 506. FRUS quotes it in a less colorful tone: "The bastards have never been bombed. [chuckles] They're going to be bombed this time." Conversation between Nixon and Kissinger, April 4, 1972, *FRUS 1969–1976, VIII*, 212.
26. General John W. Vogt, "A Commander's View, 185," Vogt Papers, AFHSD. Haldeman, April 6, 1972, 221–22.
27. Footnote 2, Summary of Conclusions of a Washington Special Actions Group Meeting, April 5, 1972, *FRUS 1969–1976, VIII*, 215.
28. Randolph, *Powerful and Brutal Weapons*, 91–92; Kissinger, *White House Years*, 1200; Kristina Ellis, 2016, "The Lavelle Affair: An Air Force Case Study in Ethics," Thesis, School of Advanced Air and Space Studies, Maxwell Air Force Base, AL, 48; Elder and Melly, Rules of Engagement, 1969–1972, 46, K717.0414-20, AFHRA; Lewy, *America in Vietnam*, 408; David Zucchino, "Fight to vindicate general dies in the Senate," *Los Angeles Times*, December 23, 2010, http://articles.latimes.com/print/2010/dec/23/nation/la-na-1223-lavelle-2010223.
29. Aloysius Casey and Patrick Casey, "Lavelle, Nixon, and the White House Tapes," *Air Force Magazine* (February 2007), 88; "Department of Defense Press Release, *Air Power History* (Fall 2010), 50–51; David Zucchino, "Fight to Vindicate General Dies in the Senate," *Los Angeles Times* December 23, 2010.
30. Kissinger, *White House Years*, 1116.
31. Memorandum from the President's Deputy Assistant for National Security Affairs (Haig) to the President's Assistant for National Security Affairs (Kissinger), April 6, 1972, *FRUS 1969–1976, VIII*, 224–25.
32. CINCPAC Command History 1972, Vol. 1, 164–65, K712.01, 1972, Vol. 1, AFHRA. The name Linebacker was used because that was the next code word "in the book." Moorer Reminiscences, Volume 3, 1242, Navy Department Library.
33. Seventh Fleet Operations (1 April 1972 to 27 January 1973) and Intelligence Lessons Learned, NHHC; Eighth Air Force Activity Input, 1 July 1971–30 June 1972, K520.041-2, AFHRA.
34. Minutes of a Washington Special Actions Group Meeting, April 3, 1972, *FRUS 1969–1976, VIII*, 180; Message from CINCLANT to AIG 84, 042030Z, April 1972, Message from 7th AF to AIG8306, 0213402Z, May 1972, Vietnam Air War Collection, Box 69, Folder 69/5, NHHC.
35. Message from AFSPCOMM to CSAF, 122358Z, April 1972, Vietnam Air War Collection, Box 69, Folder 69/5, NHHC; Operations of U.S. Marine Forces in Southeast Asia, 1 July 1971 thru 31 March 1973, Moody, et al., U.S. Marines in Vietnam, Part VII: Backing Up the Troops, HDMCU.
36. CINCPAC Command History 1972, Vol. 2, 539–40, K712.01, 1972, Vol. 2, AFHRA; Diary Entry by the Chairman of the Joint Chiefs of Staff (Moorer), April 12, 1972, *FRUS 1969–1976, VIII*, 237.
37. Thompson, *To Hanoi and Back*, 226; Minutes of a Washington Special Actions Group Meeting, April 17, 1972, *FRUS 1969–1976, VIII*, 271; Randolph, *Powerful and Brutal Weapons*, 126, 128; Air Operations in Southeast Asia, 1972–1973, Vol. 2, pp. iv-96 to iv-97, K717.0423-23, AFHRA.
38. Randolph, *Powerful and Brutal Weapons*, 197; Directorate of Operations Analysis, Summary Air Operations Southeast Asia June 1972, pp. 2–11, 4-1, K717.3063, June 1972, AFHRA.
39. Randolph, *Powerful and Brutal Weapons*, 257–58.
40. OEG/OP-508W Operations in Southeast Asia, 1 January 1972–31 January 1973, 2–9, Attack

Squadron Fifty-Two, Command History, 26 February 1973, Commanding Officer, Attack Squadron One Five Five to Chief of Naval Operations, Command History 1972, 23 November 1973, NHHC.

41. Foley, USS *Midway* 1972 Command History, 14 March 1973, Brennan, Analysis of Tactical Aircraft Operations, 1965–1966, Vol. 1, 13, NHHC. This data came from the comparison of the F-4 Phantom by both services by J. F. Brennan.
42. Diary Entry by Moorer, April 12, 1972, *FRUS 1969–1976*, VIII, 237–39; Memorandum from the President's Assistant for National Security Affairs (Kissinger) to President Nixon, General Abrams' Assessment of the Situation in Vietnam, May 1, 1972, *FRUS 1969–1976*, VIII, 346–48.
43. Message from the Commander, Military Assistance Command, Vietnam (Abrams) to the Chairman of the Joint Chiefs of Staff (Moorer) and the Commander in Chief, Pacific (McCain), May 4, 1972, *FRUS 1969–1976*, VIII, 413–14; Conversation between President Nixon and the President's Assistant for National Security Affairs (Kissinger), April 18, 1972, *FRUS 1969–1976*, VIII, 285–87; Message from Abrams to McCain, May 18, 1972, *FRUS 1969–1976*, VIII, 580–81.
44. Webb and Poole, *Joint Chiefs of Staff, 1971–1973*, 165.
45. Conversation between President Nixon and the President's Assistant for National Security Affairs (Kissinger), April 19, 1972, *FRUS 1969–1976*, VIII, 291.
46. Editorial Note, April 26, 1972, presidential address to the nation, *FRUS 1969–1976*, VIII, 331.
47. Memorandum from the President's Assistant for National Security Affairs (Kissinger) to Secretary of Defense Laird, April 28, 1972, *FRUS 1969–1976*, VIII, 332.
48. Van Atta, *With Honor*, 404.
49. Memorandum of Conversation, May 2, 1972, *FRUS 1969–1976*, VIII, 371; Memorandum from the President's Assistant for National Security Affairs (Kissinger) to President Nixon, May 2, 1972, *FRUS 1969–1976*, VIII, 387; Randolph, *Powerful and Brutal Weapons*, 156.
50. Kissinger, Memorandum of Conversation, April 21, 1972, *FRUS 1969–1976*, XIV, 501; Memorandum from Winston Lord of the National Security Council Staff to the President's Assistant for National Security Affairs (Kissinger), May 1, 1972, *FRUS 1969–1976*, VIII, 346; Robert Dallek, *Nixon and Kissinger: Partners in Power* (New York: Harper Collins Publishers, 2007), 377, 385.
51. Hanhimaki, *The Flawed Architect*, 207; Message from President Nixon to the President's Assistant for National Security Affairs (Kissinger) in Moscow, April 23, 1972, *FRUS 1969–1976*, VIII, 305.
52. Memorandum from the President's Assistant for National Security Affairs (Kissinger) to President Nixon, April 24, 1972, *FRUS 1969–1976*, VIII, 313.
53. Hanhimaki, *The Flawed Architect*, 208; Dobrynin, *In Confidence*, 248; Guan, *Ending the Vietnam War*, 99.
54. Memorandum for Record, Contingency Plan for Operations against North Vietnam, May 6, 1972, *FRUS 1969–1976*, VIII, 474–76; Memorandum from President Nixon to the Assistant to the President (Haldeman), May 7, 1972, *FRUS 1969–1976*, VIII, 481; Memorandum for the President's File, National Security Council Meeting, May 8, 1972, *FRUS 1969–1976*, VIII, 489–91.
55. Memorandum for the President's File, May 8, 1972, *FRUS 1969–1976*, VIII, 494.
56. Ibid., 485–86.
57. Ibid., 495, 496.
58. Editorial Note of a Conversation in the Oval Office, May 8, 1972, *FRUS 1969–1976*, VIII, 502, 503.
59. Memorandum from President Nixon to the President's Assistant for National Security Affairs (Kissinger), May 9, 1972, *FRUS 1969–1976*, VIII, 520.
60. National Security Council Meeting, May 8, 1972, *FRUS 1969–1976*, VIII, 485–86, 496; Editorial Note of a Conversation in the Oval Office, May 8, 1972, *FRUS 1969–1976*, VIII, 503,

NOTES FOR CHAPTER 17

504, 505–6.
61. Minutes of a Washington Special Actions Group Meeting, May 10, 1972, *FRUS 1969–1976, VIII*, 535; Conversation between Nixon, Kissinger, and Moorer, May 4, 1972, *FRUS 1969–1976, VIII*, 431–32; Cosmas, *The Joint Command in the Years of Withdrawal, 1968–1973*, 368.
62. Memorandum on Mining Haiphong, May 5, 1972, *FRUS 1969–1976, VIII*, 453; Memorandum of Conversation, May 8, 1972, *FRUS 1969–1976, VIII*, 511; Dallek, *Nixon and Kissinger*, 385.
63. Sherwood, *Afterburner*, 174; Porter, Linebacker First 120 Days, 16, K717.0414-42, 1973; History of the Pacific Air Forces, 1 July 1972–30 June 1973, 86, K717.01, 19720701–19730630, AFHRA; Editorial Note, *FRUS 1969–1976, VIII*, 507, Vietnam Command Files, Box 102, File 1967, Air Warfare Annex, Commander Seventh Fleet Command History 1972, 26 September 1973, NHHC; Webb and Poole, *Joint Chiefs of Staff, 1971–1973*, 184.
64. History of the Pacific Air Forces, 1 July 1972–30 June 1973, 86, 87, K717.01; Air Operations in Southeast Asia, 1972–1973, Vol. 2, pp. iv-3 to iv-5, K717.0423-23, 1, AFHRA; Editorial Note, *FRUS 1969–1976, VIII*, 507; Air Warfare Annex, Commander Seventh Fleet Command History 1972, 26 September 1973, NHHC; Sherwood, *Afterburner*, 213.
65. Memorandum of Conversation, May 12, 1972, *FRUS 1969–1976, XIV*, 825–26; Randolph, *Powerful and Brutal Weapons*, 217; Guan, *Ending the Vietnam War*, 99; Kissinger, *White House Years*, 1210.
66. Thompson, *To Hanoi and Back*, 228; Minutes of a Washington Special Actions Group Meeting, June 6, 1972, *FRUS 1969–1976, VIII*, 652–55; History of Seventh Air Force, 1972–1973, 138, K740.10-25, Vol. 1, AFHRA.
67. Webb and Poole, *Joint Chiefs of Staff, 1971–1973*, 161–62; Message from 15AF to AIG 712/IN/DOI/DOXI, 092105Z, May 1972, K-WG-307-HI, AFHRA.
68. Transcript of a Telephone Conversation between the Chairman of the Joint Chiefs of Staff (Moorer) and President Nixon, May 9, 1972, *FRUS 1969–1976, VIII*, 522; Webb and Poole, *Joint Chiefs of Staff, 1971–1973*, 162.
69. CINCPAC Command History 1972, Vol. 1, 160–61, K712.01, 1972, Vol. 1, AFHRA; Message from the Chairman of the Joint Chiefs of Staff (Moorer) to the Commander in Chief, Pacific (McCain), May 9, 1972, *FRUS 1969–1976, VIII*, 525; Memorandum from the Chairman of the Joint Chiefs of Staff (Moorer) to Secretary of Defense Laird, May 15, 1972, *FRUS 1969–1976, VIII*, 559; Transcript of a Telephone Conversation between the Chairman of the Joint Chiefs of Staff (Moorer) and the President's Assistant for National Security Affairs (Kissinger), May 8, 1972, *FRUS 1969–1976, VIII*, 503.
70. History of Seventh Air Force, 1972–1973, 121, 264, 295–96, K740.10-25, Vol. 1, AFHRA; Memorandum from Moorer to Laird, May 15, 1972, *FRUS 1969–1976, VIII*, 560.
71. Memorandum from President Nixon to the President's Assistant for National Security Affairs (Kissinger), May 9, 1972, *FRUS 1969–1976, VIII*, 520–21.
72. Ibid.
73. Summary Air Operations Southeast Asia, May 1972, pp. 4-4 through 4-5, K717.3063, May 1972, AFHRA; Moorer, Reminiscences, Volume III, 1243, Navy Department Library; Rolling Thunder-Linebacker Comparative Analysis, June 1972, Tab 7, K143.042-11, AFHRA.
74. Minutes of a Washington Special Actions Group Meeting, May 10, 1972, *FRUS 1969–1976, VIII*, 533.
75. Porter, Linebacker First 120 Days, 35, K717.0414-42, 1973, AFHRA.
76. Attack Squadron Fifty-Six Command History, 1972, NHHC; Air Operations in Southeast Asia, 1972–1973, Vol. 2, p. iv-13, K717.0423-23, AFHRA.
77. Diary Entry by the Chairman of the Joint Chiefs of Staff (Moorer), April 7, 1972, *FRUS 1969–1976, VIII*, 229.

78. Message from the Chairman of the Joint Chiefs of Staff (Moorer) to the Commander in Chief, Pacific (McCain) and Commander, Military Assistance Command, Vietnam (Abrams), April 8, 1972, *FRUS 1969–1976, VIII*, 231.
79. Memorandum from President Nixon to the President's Assistant for National Security Affairs, April 30, 1972, *FRUS 1969–1976, VIII*, 339.
80. Transcript of a Telephone Conversation between President Nixon and the President's Deputy Assistant for National Security Affairs, May 17, 1972, *FRUS 1969–1976, VIII*, 577.
81. Message from the Chairman of the Joint Chiefs of Staff (Moorer) to the Commander in Chief, Pacific (McCain), May 21, 1972, *FRUS 1969–1976, VIII*, 625; Memorandum from Moorer to Laird, May 15, 1972, *FRUS 1969–1976, VIII*, 561; Rolling Thunder-Linebacker: A Preliminary Comparative Analysis, June 1972, Tab 15, K143.042-11, AFHRA; "Soviet Is Reportedly Moving Aid for Hanoi across China by Rail," *New York Times*, May 19, 1972, 8.
82. Air Operations in Southeast Asia, 1972–1973, Vol. 2, iv-64, K717.0423-23, AFHRA.
83. Memorandum of Conversation, May 11, 1972, *FRUS 1969–1976, XIV*, 799.
84. Webb and Poole, *Joint Chiefs of Staff, 1971–1973*, 164.
85. Berman, *No Peace, No Honor*, 134–35; Hanhimaki, *The Flawed Architect*, 217.
86. Memorandum from President Nixon to the President's Deputy Assistant for National Security Affairs (Haig), May 18, 1972, *FRUS 1969–1976, VIII*, 584; Memorandum from President Nixon to the President's Deputy Assistant for National Security Affairs (Haig), May 20, 1972, *FRUS 1969–1976, VIII*, 623.
87. Memorandum from President Nixon to the President's Assistant for National Security Affairs (Kissinger) and the President's Deputy Assistant for National Security Affairs (Haig), May 19, 1972, *FRUS 1969–1976, VIII*, 618.
88. Message from the Chairman of the Joint Chiefs of Staff (Moorer) to the Commander in Chief, Pacific (McCain), May 21, 1972, *FRUS 1969–1976, VIII*, 627.
89. See for example Republic Aviation advertisement, "Getting Ready," *Flight International* (9 October 1959), 358; "Javelins of St. George: Profile of an All-Weather Fighter Squadron," *Flight International* (29 May 1959), 741; "Exercise Vigilant," *Flight International* (31 May 1957), 728; "Protecting the Heart of the Delta Dart," *Aviation Week and Space Technology* (January 25, 1960), 7.
90. Randolph, *Powerful and Brutal Weapons*, 230–32; Transcript of a Telephone Conversation between the Chairman of the Joint Chiefs of Staff (Moorer) and the President's Assistant for National Security Affairs (Kissinger), May 19, 1972, *FRUS 1969–1976, VIII*, 619–20.
91. Message from AFSSO USAF to AFSO PACAF info AFSSO 7AF, 242137Z, May 1972, Vogt Papers, AFHSD.
92. Editorial Note, June 22, 1972, *FRUS 1969–1976, VIII*, 659.
93. Diary Entry by the Chairman of the Joint Chiefs of Staff (Moorer), May 31, 1972, *FRUS 1969–1976, VIII*, 644.
94. Johnson, Linebacker Operations: September–December 1972, 40, K717.0413-102, AFHRA; Message from Moorer to McCain, May 9, 1972, *FRUS 1969–1976, VIII*, 526.
95. Randolph, *Powerful and Brutal Weapons*, 169, 191–92.
96. Message from AFSSO PACAF to AFSSO USAF info AFSSO 7AF, Concept for B-52 over North Vietnam, 260335Z, May 1972, Vogt Papers, Message Traffic May 1972, AFHSD.
97. Porter, Linebacker First 120 Days, 38, K717.0414-42, 1973, AFHRA; "U.S. Guided Bombs Alter Air War," *Aviation Week and Space Technology* (May 22, 1972), 16–17; David A. Brown, "U.S. Presses North Viet Air War," *Aviation Week and Space Technology* (July 3, 1972), 15; Charles Mohr, "Bombing of North Termed Highly Effective by U.S.: Accurate Laser-Guided Bombs Believed Freely Used—A Saigon Offensive East of Quangtri Is Reported," *The New York Times*, May 24,

NOTES FOR CHAPTER 17

1972, 1; Richard Witkin, "Accurate 'Smart Bombs' Guided to Objectives by TV or Laser," *The New York Times,* May 24, 1972, 20.
98. Message from AFSSO USAF to AFSSO PACAF info SAC, 7AF, Concept for B-52 over North Vietnam, 261831Z, May 1972, Vogt Papers, Message Traffic May 1972, AFHSD.
99. Webb and Poole, *Joint Chiefs of Staff, 1971–1973,* 173–74.
100. Attack Squadron Fifty-Six Command History, 1972, NHHC.
101. History of Linebacker Operations, 10 May 1972–23 October 1972, 10, K740.04-24, 1972, AFHRA.
102. Transcript of Telephone Conversation between the Chairman of the Joint Chiefs of Staff (Moorer) and Deputy Commander, Military Assistance Command, Vietnam (Vogt), June 8, 1972, *FRUS 1969–1976, VIII,* 656–57.
103. Air Operations in Southeast Asia, 1972–1973, Vol. 2, p. iv–9, K717.0423-23, AFHRA; Van Atta, *With Honor,* 409.
104. History of Seventh Air Force, 1971–1972, 264, 297, K740.01-25, Vol. 1, AFHRA; "North Viet Dikes Used for Guns, Storage," *Aviation Week and Space Technology* (August 28, 1972), 16–17.
105. Summary Air Operations Southeast Asia August 1972, p. 4-A-7, K717.3063, AFHRA.
106. Webb and Poole, *Joint Chiefs of Staff, 1971–1973,* 164.
107. Message from AFSSO to SSO DIA, Jerry W. Friedheim, Deputy Assistant Secretary of Defense, Public Affairs, Press Briefing, 021030Z, July 1972, Folder Gen. Vogt's Read File July 1972, Vogt Papers, AFHSD; Summary of Air Operations in Southeast Asia, K717.3063 April–October 1972, AFHRA.
108. Summary Air Operations Southeast Asia, May 1972, pp. 4-B-2 through 4-B-6, K717.3063, May 1972; Directorate of Operations Analysis, Summary Air Operations Southeast Asia June 1972, pp. 4-B-1 through 4-B-5, K717.3063 June 1972, AFHRA.
109. Message from AFSSO 7AF to AFSSO CSAF, Daily Wrap Up, 211145Z, June 1972, Vogt Papers, Message Traffic June 1972, AFHSD; Porter, Linebacker First 120 Days, 28, K717.0414-42, 1973, AFHRA.
110. Commander Seventh Fleet Command History 1972, 26 September 1973. See also the Air Warfare annex in this file. Attack Squadron Thirty-Five, Command History, 22 February 1973, NHHC.
111. Summary Air Operations Southeast Asia July 1972, pp. 4-B-16 through 4-B-22, K717.3063; History of Seventh Air Force, 1971–1972, 264, 298–99, K740.01-25, Vol. 1; Summary Air Operations Southeast Asia August 1972, pp. 4-B-19 through 4-B-21, K717.3063; Summary Air Operations Southeast Asia, September 1972, pp. 4-B-22 through 4-B-26, K717.3063; Summary Air Operations Southeast Asia October 1972, pp. 4-B-11 through 4-B-14, K717.3063 October 1972, AFHRA.
112. Message from AFSSO Udorn to AFSSO 7AF, Linebacker Conference Golf V and Hotel V, 13049Z, September 1972, Vogt Papers, Message Traffic September 1972, AFHSD.
113. Summary Air Operations Southeast Asia, September 1972, pp. 4-B-22 through 4-B-26, K717.3063, AFHRA; Directorate of Operations Analysis, Summary Air Operations Southeast Asia October 1972, pp. 4-B-11 through 4-B-14, K717.3063, October 1972, AFHRA; Thompson, *To Hanoi and Back,* 245.
114. Message from AFSSO PACAF to AFSSO 7AF, Linebacker, 272155Z, June 1972, Vogt Papers, Vogt—Message Traffic June 1972, AFHSD.
115. Porter, Linebacker First 120 Days, 25, K717.0414-42, 1973, AFHRA.
116. Talbott, Interview June 10–11, 1985, 231, K239.2512-1652, AFHRA.
117. Robert Shaplan, "Letter from Vietnam," *The New Yorker,* June 24, 1972, 73.
118. Walter F. Lynch, Operations Analysis Office, LGB Sortie Effectiveness, 21 July 1972, K717.56-2, 72/07/01, AFHRA.

119. Porter, Linebacker First 120 Days, 35, K717.0414-42, 1973, AFHRA; Message from AFSSO 7AF to AFSSO CSAF, 241100Z, May 1972, Vogt Papers, AFHSD; Commander Seventh Fleet Command History 1972, 26 September 1973, NHHC.
120. Evaluation Report for the NVN Offensive, pp. v-4, v-5, K717.04-9, 1972, AFHRA; Message from AFSSO 7AF to AFSSO CSAF, Daily Wrap Up, 171135Z, May 1972, Vogt Papers, Message Traffic May 1972, AFHSD.
121. History of Linebacker Operations, 10 May 1972–23 October 1972, 13, K740.04-24, 1972, AFHRA.
122. Porter, Second Generation Weaponry in SEA, 31, K717.0413-80; HQ PACAF, Evaluation Report for the NVN Offensive (April–August 1972), A-5, K717.04-9, 1972, AFHRA.
123. Eggers, Employment of Missiles, K712.153-1, AFHRA.
124. Message from CINCPACAF to RUEFHQA/CSAF XOOS, Laser Guided Bombs, F-4 Aircraft, 210321Z, July 1971, and Message from HQ 7AF to CINCPACAF/DOQ, Certification for High Speed Mk-82 LGB on F-4, 090203Z, August 1971, K740.01-25, 1 July 71–30 June 72, AFHRA.
125. History of Linebacker Operations, 10 May 1972–23 October 1972, 54, K740.04-24, 1972, AFHRA; Message from AFSSO PACAF, Linebacker, 272155Z, June 1972, Vogt Papers, AFHSD.
126. Message from AFSSO Udorn to AFSSO 7AF, Linebacker Conference Juliet VI and Kilo VI, 240509Z, September 1972, and Message Traffic September 1972, and Message from AFSSO 7AF, Daily Wrap Up, 291115Z, May 1972, Vogt Papers, AFHSD.
127. Message from AFSSO PACAF, Linebacker, 272155Z, June 1972, Vogt Papers, AFHSD.
128. Summary of Linebacker Tactics Review Conference, 011207Z, October 1972, K740.3391, AFHRA.
129. HQ PACAF, Evaluation Report for the NVN Offensive (April–August 1972), pp. v-4, v-5, b-4, b-50, K717.04-9, 1972, AFHRA.
130. Message from 7th AF to RUHHABA/CINCPACAF, Linebacker Conference November VI and Lima VI, K740.3391, 21–29 September 1972, K740.6271-1, Vol. 4; Photographs in K740.6271-1, Vol. 1, AFHRA.
131. HQ PACAF, Evaluation Report for the NVN Offensive (April–August 1972), pp. v-4, v-5. K717.04-9, 1972, AFHRA.
132. 7th AF Commanders' Conference, 18–19 July 1972, K168.06-228, 72/07/01–73/08/00, AFHRA.
133. Air Operations in Southeast Asia, 1972–1973, Vol. 2, p. iv-66, K717.0423-23, AFHRA.
134. Johnson, Linebacker Operations: September–December 1972, 38, K717.0413-102; Major Donald L. Ockerman, An Analysis of Laser Guided Bombs in SEA, June 28, 1973, 28, K740.041-4, 28 June 1973, AFHRA.
135. Colonel Breitling, Guided Bomb Operations in SEA: The Weather Dimension, 1 February–31 December 1972 (HQ PACAF: Directorate of Operations Analysis, CHECO/Corona Harvest Division, 1973), 22, 27, K717.0414-43, AFHRA; Thomas A. Keaney and Eliot A. Cohen, *Gulf War Air Power Survey Summary Report* (Washington, DC: Department of the Air Force, 1993), 226. To be fair, the US also fired 5,448 AGM-65 missiles during the 1991 Gulf War. Glenn C. Buchan, "Force Projection: One-and-a-Half Cheers for the RMA," in Thierry Gongora and Harald von Riekhoff, eds. *Toward a Revolution in Military Affairs? Defense and Security at the Dawn of the Twenty-First Century* (Westport, CT: Greenwood Press, 2000), 140.
136. Thomas A. Keaney and Eliot A. Cohen, *Revolution in Warfare? Air Power in the Persian Gulf* (Annapolis, MD: Naval Institute Press, 1995), 18, 132, 207.
137. Ibid., 189.
138. Loye, et al., Lam Son 719 30 January–24 March 1971, 19, 75, K717.0413-165, AFHRA; Nelson, Close Air Support, 1972, 33–45, 50–55, K717.601-8, AFHRA.
139. For contrasting views see Clifford J. Rogers, "'Military Revolutions' and 'Revolutions in Military

NOTES FOR CHAPTER 17

Affairs': A Historian's Perspective," in Gongora and von Riekhoff, eds., *Toward a Revolution in Military Affairs,* 21; Stephen Biddle, *Military Power: Explaining Victory and Defeat in Modern Battle* (Princeton, NJ: Princeton University Press, 2004), 20, 133; Keith L. Shimko, *The Iraq Wars and America's Military Revolution* (Cambridge: Cambridge University Press, 2010), 8–15.

140. Gillespie, *Weapons of Choice,* 118, 121.
141. Prados, *Vietnam,* 470; Robert Thompson, *Peace Is Not at Hand* (New York: David McCay, 1974), 109–10, 114; Summers, *On Strategy,* 103; George C. Herring, *America's Longest War: The United States and Vietnam, 1950–1975,* 3rd ed. (New York: McGraw-Hill, 1996), 274–75; Neu, *America's Lost War,* 194; Randolph, *Powerful and Brutal Weapons,* 274–79.
142. Memorandum from John H. Holdridge of the National Security Council Staff to the President's Assistant for National Security Affairs, June 27, 1972, June 22, 1972, *FRUS 1969–1976, VIII,* 677–80; Air Operations in Southeast Asia, 1972–1973, Vol. 2, pp. iv-78 to iv-79, K717.0423-23, AFHRA.
143. Minutes of a Washington Special Actions Group Meeting, June 28, 1972, June 22, 1972, *FRUS 1969–1976, VIII,* 687.
144. Message from the Chairman of the Joint Chiefs of Staff (Moorer) to the Commander in Chief, Pacific (McCain), June 22, 1972, *FRUS 1969–1976, VIII,* 667.
145. Air Operations in Southeast Asia, 1972–1973, Vol. 2, pp. iv-16, iv-81, K717.0423-23, AFHRA.
146. Gaiduk, *Soviet Union and the Vietnam War,* 241; Message from Moorer to McCain, June 22, 1972, *FRUS 1969–1976, VIII,* 668.
147. Message from AFSSO USAF to AFSO PACAF info AFSSO 7AF, Comments of Le Duc Tho, 242137Z, May 1972, Vogt Papers.
148. Memorandum from the Special Assistant to the Ambassador (Polgar) to the Ambassador to South Vietnam (Bunker), June 22, 1972, June 27, 1972, *FRUS 1969–1976, VIII,* 675.
149. Editorial Note, June 22, 1972, *FRUS 1969–1976, VIII,* 660.
150. 7th AF Commanders' Conference, 18–19 July 1972, K168.06-228, 72/07/01–73/08/00, AFHRA; Backchannel Message from the President's Deputy Assistant for National Security Affairs (Haig) to the President's Assistant for National Security Affairs (Kissinger), June 22, 1972, July 1, 1972, *FRUS 1969–1976, VIII,* 698fn.
151. Backchannel Message from the President's Assistant for National Security Affairs (Kissinger) to the Ambassador to South Vietnam (Bunker), July 30, 1972, *FRUS 1969–1976, VIII,* 778–79, 779fn.
152. Nixon, *RN,* 687; Van Atta, *With Honor,* 411.
153. Transcript of a Telephone Conversation between the Chairman of the Joint Chiefs of Staff (Moorer) and the President's Assistant for National Security Affairs, August 12, 1972, *FRUS 1969–1976, VIII,* 825.
154. History of Seventh Air Force, 1972–1973, 124–25, K740.10-25, Vol. 1; Air Operations in Southeast Asia, 1972–1973, Vol. 2, p. iv-70, K717.0423-23, AFHRA.
155. Message from 7AF to CINCPACAF, Linebacker Prime Choke Operation, 310830Z, August 1972, K168.060229; History of Linebacker Operations, 10 May 1972–23 October 1972, 27, K740.04-24, 1972, AFHRA; Randolph, *Powerful and Brutal Weapons,* 296, 322.
156. 7th AF Commanders' Conference, 18–19 July 1972, K168.06-228; Porter, Linebacker First 120 Days, 33, K717.0414-42, 1973, AFHRA.
157. Message from AFSSO PACAF to SSO CINCPAC, Linebacker Operations, 040136Z, July 1972, Vogt Papers, Gen Vogt's Read File July 1972, AFHSD; Air Operations in Southeast Asia, 1972–1973, Vol. 2, pp. iv-78 to iv-79, K717.0423-23, AFHRA.
158. Webb and Poole, *Joint Chiefs of Staff, 1971–1973,* 177–78.
159. Slessor, *Air Power and Armies,* 16, 91–93, 101, 111–18; Futrell, *Ideas, Concepts, Doctrine, 1907–1960,* 158; Meilinger, *Air War,* 41; Hughes, *Over Lord,* 129–31.

160. 7th AF Commanders' Conference, 18–19 July 1972, K168.06-228, AFHRA.
161. Guan, *Ending the Vietnam War*, 99.
162. Randolph, *Powerful and Brutal Weapons*, 279–80.
163. Message from the Chairman of the Joint Chiefs of Staff (Moorer) to the Commander in Chief, Pacific (McCain), August 6, 1972, *FRUS 1969–1976, VIII*, 815–16; Air Operations in Southeast Asia, 1972–1973, Vol. 2, pp. iv-15, iv-16, K717.0423-23, AFHRA.
164. Message from CINCPAC to COMUSMACV, CINCPACFLT, CINCPACAF, CINCSAC, Linebacker Operations, 090225Z, August 1972, K168.06-229; Message from CINCPAC Linebacker Operations, 090225Z, August 1972, K168.06-229, AFHRA; Foley, USS *Midway* 1972 Command History, 14 March 1973, NHHC.
165. Attack Squadron Thirty-Five, Command History, 22 February 1973, NHHC.
166. History of Linebacker Operations, 10 May 1972–23 October 1972, 21–22, K740.04-24, 1972, AFHRA.
167. Message from PACAF to RUMABA/13th AF, 140505Z, May 1965, K717.1623, 1965, AFHRA; USS *Constellation*, Highlights of 1966 Attack Carrier Air Wing Fifteen Westpac Cruise, NHHC.
168. History Naval Operations, Vol. III 1965–1967, Part 1, 133, NHHC; Message from AFSSO PACAF, Linebacker, 272155Z, June 1972, Vogt Papers, AFHSD.
169. History of Seventh Air Force, 1971–1972, 302, K740.01-25, Vol. 1, AFHRA; Thompson, *To Hanoi and Back*, 235; Drew Middleton, ed., *Air War: Vietnam* (New York: Arno Press, 1978), 85.
170. Attack Squadron Fifty-Six Command History, 1972, NHHC; Attack Squadron One Six Four Command History 1972, 1 May 1973, NHHC.
171. Attack Squadron One Six Four Command History 1972, 1 May 1973, NHHC.
172. Attack Carrier Air Wing Eleven, Cruise Report February to November 1972, 1 December 1972, NHHC.
173. Commanding Officer, Reconnaissance Attack Squadron Six Command History OPNAV Report 5750-1, 16 February 1973, Fleet Aviation Commands-Pre-1998, AR/229, Box 104, File F16; Message from [unreadable] to RUHGOAA/COMSEVENTHFLT, "PRESSL," 080630Z, October 1972, Fleet Aviation Commands Active, Box 132, File VA-82 Command History 1972, NHHC.
174. Porter, Linebacker First 120 Days, 51, K717.0414-42, 1973, AFHRA.
175. Message from 7th AF to RUHHABA/CINCPACAF, Linebacker Conference Hotel VI and India VI, 251149Z, September 1972, K740.339; History of Linebacker Operations, 10 May 1972–23 October 1972, 58, K740.04-24, 1972; Johnson, Linebacker Operations: September–December 1972, 43, K717.0413-102, AFHRA.
176. History of Linebacker Operations, 10 May 1972–23 October 1972, 71, K740.04-24, 1972, AFHRA.
177. Linebacker Conference Yankee V and Zulu V, 211302Z, September 1972, K740.3391; Linebacker Conference Bravo V, 081218Z, September 1972, K740.3391, AFHRA.
178. History of Linebacker Operations, 10 May 1972–23 October 1972, 29, K740.04-24, 1972, AFHRA.
179. Air Operations in Southeast Asia, 1972–1973, Vol. 2, pp. iv-95 to iv-96, K717.0423-23, AFHRA.
180. Memorandum from Philip A. Odeen of the National Security Council Staff to the President's Assistant for National Security Affairs (Kissinger), August 12, 1972, *FRUS 1969–1976, VIII*, 827–28.
181. Ibid., 826.
182. Randolph, *Powerful and Brutal Weapons*, 304.
183. Memorandum from the President's Assistant for National Security Affairs (Kissinger) to President Nixon, July 15, 1972, *FRUS 1969–1976, VIII*, 704. See also Thompson, *Peace Is Not at Hand*, 121–22.

184. Nguyen, *Hanoi's War*, 224–25.
185. Porter, Linebacker First 120 Days, 42, K717.0414-42, 1973, AFHRA.
186. *FRUS 1969–1976, VIII*, 945fn3.
187. Hanhimaki, *The Flawed Architect*, 233, 234.
188. Evaluation Report for the NVN Offensive (April–August 1972), p. v-3. K717.04-9, 1972, AFHRA.
189. Backchannel Message from the Ambassador to South Vietnam (Bunker) to the President's Assistant for National Security Affairs (Kissinger), July 26, 1972, *FRUS 1969–1976, VIII*, 767.
190. Memorandum from Kissinger to President Nixon, August 19, 1972, *FRUS 1969–1976, VIII*, 907.
191. Clodfelter, *Limits of Air Power*, 167.
192. Porter, Linebacker First 120 Days, 53, K717.0414-42, 1973, AFHRA; Note from the President's Deputy Assistant for National Security Affairs (Haig) to the President's Assistant for National Security Affairs (Kissinger), June 22, 1972, June 28, 1972, *FRUS 1969–1976, VIII*, 680–81.
193. Memorandum for the President's File, National Security Council Meeting, May 8, 1972, *FRUS 1969–1976, VIII*, 498; The White House Tapes, Conversation 697-2, March 30, 1972, *FRUS 1969–1976, VIII*, 154; Conversation between President Nixon and the President's Assistant for National Security Affairs (Kissinger), March 14, 1972, *FRUS 1969–1976, VIII*, 146; Dallek, *Nixon and Kissinger*, 381, 385; Van Atta, *With Honor*, 406.
194. Nguyen, *Hanoi's War*, 264, 268.
195. Berman, *No Peace, No Honor*, 95.
196. Ibid., 83, 89, 94.
197. Nguyen, *Hanoi's War*, 268; Duiker, *Sacred War*, 237; Nguyen, *Hanoi's War*, 251.
198. Memorandum of Conversation, July 19, 1972, *FRUS 1969–1976, VIII*, 723, 730, 736.
199. Memorandum from the President's Assistant for National Security Affairs (Kissinger) to President Nixon, August 3, 1972, *FRUS 1969–1976, VIII*, 797.
200. Summary Air Operations Southeast Asia August 1972, 3, K717.3063; Memorandum from Philip A. Odeen of the National Security Council Staff to the President's Assistant for National Security Affairs (Kissinger), September 8, 1972, *FRUS 1969–1976, VIII*, 943; Randolph, *Powerful and Brutal Weapons*, 286–89.
201. Transcript of a Telephone Conversation between the Chairman of the Joint Chiefs of Staff (Moorer) and the President's Assistant for National Security Affairs (Kissinger), August 24, 1972, *FRUS 1969–1976, VIII*, 914–15; Messages from 7th AF to RUHHABA/CINCPACAF, Linebacker Conferences, K740.3391, 19–29 September 1972, AFHRA.
202. Backchannel Message from the President's Deputy Assistant for National Security Affairs (Haig) to the President's Assistant for National Security Affairs (Kissinger), October 1, 1972, *FRUS 1969–1976, VIII*, 1024.
203. History of Linebacker Operations, 10 May 1972–23 October 1972, 32, 62, K740.04-24, 1972, AFHRA; Message from AFSSO PACAF to AFSSO 7AF, Replacement of F-4s in SEA, 192152Z, July 1972, Vogt Papers, Gen Vogt's Read File July 1972, AFHSD. The squadrons were the 429th and 430th TFS's from the 474th TFW, Nellis, AFB. HQ PACAF, The F-111 in Southeast Asia, 16, K717.0414-44, AFHRA.
204. Capt. Joseph F. Nerad Jr., Message to 7/13 AF/TRD, Report 14-72, F-111 Operations, 310905Z, October 1972, K744.01, 1972, Vol. 3; F-111 in Southeast Asia, 30, K717.0414-44, AFHRA.
205. Webb and Poole, *Joint Chiefs of Staff, 1971–1973*, 184; Message from AFSSO Replacement of F-4s in SEA, 192152Z, July 1972, Vogt Papers, AFHSD; Message from 7 AF to RUHHABA/CINCPACAF, 230838Z, August 1972, K740.3391, AFHRA.
206. Message from General Ryan for General Vogt, 112100Z, August 1972, K143.168-1, 71/12/21–72/08/11; Air Operations in Southeast Asia, 1972–1973, Vol. 1, pp. ii-51, ii-52, ii-54,

K717.0423-23, AFHRA.
207. Linebacker Conference 14 October 1972, 171222Z, October 1972, K740.3391; Air Operations in Southeast Asia, 1972–1973, Vol. 2, p. iv-77, K717.0423-23; Message from 7th AF to RUEFHQA/CSAF, Summary of F-111 Combat Operations through 8 October 1972, K740.3391, AFHRA; Message from AFSSO Udorn to AFSSO 7AF, F-111 BDA, 041205Z, December 1972, Vogt Papers, Message Traffic December 1972, AFHSD.
208. History of Linebacker Operations, 10 May 1972–23 October 1972, 63, K740.04-24, 1972, AFHRA.
209. History of the Pacific Air Forces, 1 July 1972–30 June 1973, 124–25, AFHRA; AFSSO 7AF to AFSSO PACAF, 170925Z, October 1972, Vogt Papers, Folder Gen. Vogt's Read File October 1972, AFHSD.
210. History of Seventh Air Force, 1972–1973, 141–42, K740.10-25, Vol. 1; Air Operations in Southeast Asia, 1972–1973, Vol. 1, p. ii-55, K717.0423-23, AFHRA.
211. History of the Pacific Air Forces, 1972–1973, 76, K717.01; CINCPAC Command History 1972, Vol. 1, 163, K712.01, 1972, Vol. 1, AFHRA; Attack Squadron Thirty-Five, Command History, 22 February 1973, NHHC; Van Atta, *With Honor*, 421.
212. History of Seventh Air Force, 1972–1973, 139–40, K740.10-25, Vol. 1; History of the Pacific Air Forces, 1 July 1972–30 June 1973, 77–78, K717.01, AFHRA; Attack Squadron Thirty-Five, Command History, 22 February 1973, NHHC.
213. Corona Harvest V, 1972–1973, 3–4, 8, K416.041-13, AFHRA; Conversation between President Nixon and the President's Deputy Assistant for National Security Affairs (Haig), December 12, 1972, *FRUS IX 1969–1976*, 601.
214. Memorandum from Moorer to Laird, October 12, 1972, *FRUS IX 1969–1976*, 115–17; Air Warfare Annex, Commander Seventh Fleet Command History 1972, 26 September 1973, NHHC.
215. Air Operations in Southeast Asia, Vol. 1, p. iii–22, K717.0423-23, AFHRA.
216. Webb and Poole, *Joint Chiefs of Staff, 1971–1973*, 187.
217. Berman, *No Peace, No Honor*, 156–57. *FRUS 1969–1976, VIII*, 319.
218. Ibid., 174.

Chapter 18

1. Message from AFSSO PACAF to AFSSO 7AF, Exclusive for General Vogt from General Clay, Linebacker Strategy, 070245Z, October 1972, Vogt Papers, Message Traffic October 1972, AFHSD.
2. Van Atta, *With Honor*, 421; Vogt, "A Commander's View," 188, Vogt Papers, AFHSD.
3. Memorandum of Conversation, October 11–12, 1972, *FRUS IX, 1969–1976*, 110–11.
4. Message from the President's Deputy Assistant for National Security Affairs (Haig) to the President's Assistant for National Security Affairs (Kissinger) in Paris, October 18, 1972, *FRUS IX, 1969–1976*, 177.
5. Nixon, *RN*, 694.
6. Message from the President's Assistant for National Security Affairs (Kissinger) to the President's Deputy Assistant for National Security Affairs (Haig), October 18, 1972, *FRUS IX, 1969–1976*, 178; Webb and Poole, *Joint Chiefs of Staff, 1971–1973*, 186; Randolph, *Powerful and Brutal Weapons*, 327.
7. Backchannel Message from the President's Assistant for National Security Affairs (Kissinger) to the President's Deputy Assistant for National Security Affairs (Haig), October 22, 1972, *FRUS IX, 1969–1976*, 246.
8. Backchannel Message from the President's Deputy Assistant for National Security Affairs (Haig)

NOTES FOR CHAPTER 18

to the President's Assistant for National Security Affairs (Kissinger) in Saigon, October 22, 1972, 1640Z, *FRUS IX, 1969–1976,* 268–69.
9. *FRUS IX, 1969–1976,* 265fn.
10. Nixon, *RN,* 689.
11. Backchannel Message from the President's Assistant for National Security Affairs (Kissinger) to the President's Deputy Assistant for National Security Affairs (Haig), October 22, 1972, 2050Z, *FRUS IX, 1969–1976,* 274.
12. Backchannel Message from the President's Assistant for National Security Affairs (Kissinger) to the President's Deputy Assistant for National Security Affairs (Haig), October 22, 1972, 1825Z, *FRUS IX, 1969–1976,* 265. Nixon and Kissinger had deliberately bypassed Rogers and Laird since May because the secretaries of state and defense did not support the president's goals or methods. Randolph, *Powerful and Brutal Weapons,* 164. As an example of Kissinger's opinion of the secretary of defense, he told Secretary Rogers that he thought Melvin Laird had leaked the Pentagon Papers. Dallek, *Nixon and Kissinger,* 310.
13. Berman, *No Peace, No Honor,* 163, 211.
14. Backchannel Message from the President's Assistant for National Security Affairs (Kissinger) to the President's Deputy Assistant for National Security Affairs (Haig), October 23, 1972, 0050Z, *FRUS IX, 1969–1976,* 275.
15. Hanhimaki, *The Flawed Architect,* 245; Kissinger, *White House Years,* 1351; Randolph, *Powerful and Brutal Weapons,* 329.
16. Hanhimaki, *The Flawed Architect,* 251.
17. Randolph, *Powerful and Brutal Weapons,* 331.
18. Air Operations in Southeast Asia, 1972–1973, Vol. 2, pp. iv-48, iv-54, K717.0423-23, AFHRA; Message from CTF 77 to CTU 77.6.1, 281416Z, November 1972; Message from COMSEVENTFLT to RUMFRBA/CTF 77/CTG 77.0, 030846Z, December 1972, Fleet Aviation Commands Pre-1998, AR/229, Box 122, File F7, NHHC.
19. Kissinger, *Ending the Vietnam War,* 397; Nixon, *RN,* 722.
20. Dallek, *Nixon and Kissinger,* 440–41; Berman, *No Peace, No Honor,* 185–97; Conversation among Nixon, Kissinger, and Haldeman, March 18, 1971, *FRUS 1969–1976, VII,* 474.
21. Kimball, *Nixon's Vietnam War,* 364; Neu, *America's Lost War,* 203.
22. Message from Eade AF/XO, SEA Sorties, June 1972 [date time group not written], K740.3391, AFHRA.
23. Message from the President's Deputy Assistant for National Security Affairs (Haig) to Richard T. Kennedy of the National Security Council Staff, December 6, 1972, *FRUS IX, 1969–1976,* 528.
24. Webb and Poole, *Joint Chiefs of Staff, 1971–1973,* 292; Message from Eade AF/XO, SEA Sorties, June 1972 [date time group not written], K740.3391, AFHRA.
25. Message from President Nixon to the President's Assistant for National Security Affairs (Kissinger) in Paris, December 7, 1972, *FRUS IX, 1969–1976,* 533; Message from the President's Deputy Assistant for National Security Affairs (Haig) to the President's Assistant for National Security Affairs (Kissinger) in Paris, December 12, 1972, *FRUS IX, 1969–1976,* 590.
26. Transcript of a Telephone Conversation between the Chairman of the Joint Chiefs of Staff (Moorer) and the Deputy Commander, Military Assistance Command, Vietnam (Vogt), December 14, 1972, *FRUS IX, 1969–1976,* 681; Clodfelter, *Limits of Air Power,* 181–82; Dallek, *Nixon and Kissinger,* 443; Hanhimaki, *The Flawed Architect,* 253. According to Larry Berman, Alexander Haig was the one who believed it was time to bomb. Berman, *No Peace, No Honor,* 214.
27. Message from the President's Assistant for National Security Affairs (Kissinger) to the Chief of the U.S. Delegation to the Paris Peace Talks (Porter), December 14, 1972, *FRUS IX, 1969–1976,* 683.
28. Air Operations in Southeast Asia, 1972–1973, Vol. 2, pp. iv-254, iv-2-55, K717.0423-23, AFHRA.

NOTES FOR CHAPTER 18

29. CINCPAC Command History 1972, Vol. 2, 542–43, K712.01, 1972, Vol. 2, AFHRA.
30. Corona Harvest V, 1972–1973, 4, K416.041-13; Gilster and Frady, Linebacker II USAF Bombing Survey, April 1973, 33, K143.054-1, Vol. 34, AFHRA.
31. Message from Richard T. Kennedy of the National Security Council Staff to the President's Deputy Assistant for National Security Affairs (Haig) in Paris, December 8, 1972, *FRUS IX, 1969–1976*, 540–41.
32. Message from the Chairman of the Joint Chiefs of Staff (Moorer) to the Commander in Chief, Pacific (Gayler) and the Commander in Chief, Strategic Air Command (Meyer), December 17, 1972, *FRUS IX, 1969–1976*, 712; Air Operations in Southeast Asia, 1972–1973, Volume II, p. iv-252, K717.0423-23; Directorate of Operations Analysis, Summary Air Operations Southeast Asia December 1972, p. 4-A-6, K717.3063, December 1972, AFHRA; Michel, *11 Days*, 210.
33. Air Operations in Southeast Asia, 1972–1973, Vol. 5, 43, K717.0423-23, AFHRA.
34. Telephone Conversation, Moorer and Kissinger, December 19, 1972, *FRUS IX, 1969–1976*, 759, 760.
35. Nixon, *RN*, 734.
36. Editorial Note, *FRUS IX, 1969–1976*, 725.
37. Corona Harvest V, 1972–1973, 77, 65, K416.041-13, AFHRA.
38. Conversation among President Nixon, the President's Assistant for National Security Affairs (Kissinger), and the Assistant to the President (Haldeman), December 20, 1972, *FRUS IX, 1969–1976*, 777.
39. CINCPAC Command History 1972, Vol. 1, 164–65, K712.01, 1972, Vol. 1, AFHRA.
40. Memorandum of Conversation, Saigon, December 19, 1972, *FRUS IX, 1969–1976*, 754; Berman, *No Peace, No Honor*, 215–18; Richard Reeves, *President Nixon: Alone in the White House* (New York: Simon & Schuster, 2001), 553; Stephen E. Ambrose, *Nixon: Volume Three. Ruin and Recovery, 1973–1990* (New York: Simon & Schuster, 1991), 39–41; Jonathan Aitken, *Nixon: A Life* (Washington, DC: Regnery, 1993), 455–56.
41. Reeves, *Alone in the White House*, 565. Raids during World War II were much bigger.
42. Nixon, *RN*, 733, 736.
43. Paul J. Gillette, History of 307th Strategic Wing, October–December 1972, Vol. 1, K-WG-307-HI, October–December 1972, AFHRA.
44. Gilster and Frady, Linebacker II USAF Bombing Survey, April 1973, 33, K143.054-1, Vol. 34, AFHRA.
45. Transcript of a Telephone Conversation between the Chairman of the Joint Chiefs of Staff (Moorer) and the President's Assistant for National Security Affairs (Kissinger), December 18, 1972, *FRUS IX, 1969–1976*, 734–35; Transcript of a Telephone Conversation between Secretary of Defense Laird and the President's Assistant for National Security Affairs (Kissinger), December 19, 1972, *FRUS IX, 1969–1976*, 757; Message from Richard T. Kennedy of the National Security Council Staff to the President's Deputy Assistant for National Security Affairs (Haig), December 19, 1972, *FRUS IX, 1969–1976*, 737.
46. Backchannel Message from the President's Deputy Assistant for National Security Affairs (Haig) to the President's Assistant for National Security Affairs (Kissinger), December 20, 1972, *FRUS IX, 1969–1976*, 765.
47. Captain Lonnie D. Ratley, III, History of 353rd Tactical Fighter Squadron, October–December 1972, 7, K-WG-354-HI, July–December 1972, Vol. 3, AFHRA.
48. Personal to General Momyer and General Rhodarmer from Colonel Knoles, A-7D Operations in SEA, Report No. 11, 291010Z, December 1972, K-WG-354-HI, July–December 1972, Vol. 3; Depner, 354th Tactical Fighter Wing, 1 October 1972–31 December 1972, 22, K-WG-354-HI, Vol. 1, AFHRA; Message from AFSSO Udorn to AFSSO 7AF, to Gen Vogt from MGen Hughes,

Linebacker II Kilo Critique, 300400Z, December 1972, Vogt Papers, AFHSD. For a detailed chronicle of the operations by Air Force tactical aircraft, see Karl Eschmann's *Linebacker*.
49. Linebacker II Foxtrot, 270756Z, December 1972, K740.3391; Message from 7th AF to RUEBHQA/CSAF/XOO, Linebacker II India Critique, 280108Z, December 1972, K740.3391, AFHRA; Linebacker II India Critique, 271115Z, December 1972, Vogt Papers, AFHSD.
50. Attack Squadron Thirty-Five, Command History, 22 February 1973, NHHC.
51. History of Seventh Air Force, 1972–1973, 143, K740.10-25, Vol. 1; Linebacker Mission Briefing, Slides 21, 23, K143.5072-102, 72/12/18–72/12/29; Air Operations in Southeast Asia, 1972–1973, Vol. 2, p. iv-241, K717.0423-23; Message, Personal to General Vogt from Colonel Olshefski, 230645Z, December 1972, K744.01 1972 Vol. II, Appendix V; Linebacker Mission Briefing, Slide 36, K143.5072-102, 72/12/18–72/12/29; Air Operations in Southeast Asia, 1972–1973, Vol. 2, p. iv-228, K717.0423-23, AFHRA.
52. Message from AFSSO Udorn to AFSSO 7AF AFSSO 13AF, 261355Z, December 1972, Vogt Papers, Read File Dec 1972, AFHSD; Air Operations in Southeast Asia, 1972–1973, Vol. 2, pp. iv-257, iv-258, K717.0423-23; Linebacker Mission Briefing, Slides 29, 30, K143.5072-102, 72/12/18–72/12/29, AFHRA.
53. Kendrick, *The Wound Within*, 383–85; Armitage and Mason, *Air Power in the Nuclear Age*, 109; Kimball, *Nixon's Vietnam War*, 365–66; Michel, *11 Days*, 139–63.
54. Corona Harvest V, 1972–1973, 11–12, K416.041-13, AFHRA.
55. Ibid., 27.
56. Ibid., 43.
57. Talbott Interview June 10–11, 1985, 229, K239.2512-1652, AFHRA.
58. Corona Harvest V, 1972–1973, 44, K416.041-13, AFHRA.
59. Summary of B-52 Arc Light Operations—NVN Apr 1972, K416.153-1, AFHRA.
60. Headquarters SAC, Corona Harvest USAF Air Operations in Southeast Asia, 1972–1973, Vol. 5, 109, 110, 118, 120, 121, 126, 128, K717.0423-23, AFHRA.
61. Memorandum from the President's Assistant for National Security Affairs (Kissinger) to President Nixon, December 20, 1972, *FRUS IX, 1969–1976*, 774–75; Nixon, *RN*, 737.
62. Memorandum of Conversation, December 19, 1972, *FRUS IX, 1969–1976*, 751; Conversation among President Nixon, the President's Assistant for National Security Affairs (Kissinger), and the Assistant to the President (Haldeman), December 20, 1972, *FRUS IX, 1969–1976*, 776.
63. Adam Clymer, *Edward M. Kennedy: A Biography* (New York: William Morrow, 1999), 195–96.
64. Conversation among President Nixon, the President's Assistant for National Security Affairs (Kissinger), and the Assistant to the President (Haldeman), December 20, 1972, *FRUS IX, 1969–1976*, 778, 779, 787–88.
65. Transcript of a Telephone Conversation between the Chairman of the Joint Chiefs of Staff (Moorer) and the Deputy Commander, Military Assistance Command, Vietnam (Vogt), December 22, 1972, *FRUS IX, 1969–1976*, 811.
66. Conversation among Nixon, Kissinger, and Haig, December 20, 1972, *FRUS IX, 1969–1976*, 777–78.
67. Webb and Poole, *Joint Chiefs of Staff, 1971–1973*, 154, 295.
68. Conversation among Nixon, Kissinger, and Haig, December 20, 1972, *FRUS IX, 1969–1976*, December 20, 1972, *FRUS IX, 1969–1976*, 780, 783, 787, 789; Zhai, *China and the Vietnam Wars, 1950–1975*, 206; Berman, *No Peace, No Honor*, 217–18.
69. Message from the Chairman of the Joint Chiefs of Staff (Moorer) to the Commander in Chief, Pacific (Gayler) and the Pacific Command Senior Commanders, December 20, 1972, *FRUS IX, 1969–1976*, 795.
70. Message from AFSSO 7AF to AFSSO SAC, Ref your 210220Z, December 1972, 210540Z,

December 1972, Vogt Papers, Message Traffic December 1972, AFHSD; Webb and Poole, *Joint Chiefs of Staff, 1971–1973*, 295.
71. Message, Linebacker II Arc Light Days 4 and 5, 291104Z, December 1972, K740.3391, AFHRA.
72. Air Operations in Southeast Asia, Vol. 5, 140–42, K717.0423-23, AFHRA.
73. Message from 388TFW to 307SW, 290309Z, December 1972, K-WG-307-HI, October–December 1972, Vol. 1, AFHRA. One officer refused to "obey an order to fly a combat mission in southeast Asia." He was investigated under Article 32 of the UCMJ. Message from CINCSAC to SECDEF, Media Query, Captain Michael J. Heck, 092255Z, January 1973, K-WG-307-HI, October–December 1972, Vol. 1, AFHRA.
74. Transcript of a Telephone Conversation between the President's Assistant for National Security Affairs (Kissinger) and the Chairman of the Joint Chiefs of Staff (Moorer), December 21, 1972, *FRUS IX, 1969–1976*, 797; George C. Wilson, "Officials Split on Bombing: Key Issue Is What U.S. Can Attain," *The Washington Post*, December 21, 1972, A11.
75. Transcript Richard T. Kennedy and Moorer, December 21, 1972, *FRUS IX, 1969–1976*, 798; Webb and Poole, *Joint Chiefs of Staff, 1971–1973*, 296.
76. Linebacker II Arclite Day 10 Critique, 300715Z, December 1972, K744.01, AFHRA; Message from SSO SAC to SSO CINCPAC, Linebacker II, 210200Z, December 1972, Vogt Papers, Message Traffic, AFHSD.
77. Message from AFSSO PACAF to AFSSO 7AF info AFSSO SAC, B-52 Operations, 221935Z, December 1972, Vogt Papers, Read File December 1972, AFHSD.
78. Message from SSO CINCSAC to CINCPACAF info 7AF, B-52 Operations, 232020Z, December 1972, Vogt Papers, Gen. Vogt's Read File December 1972, AFHSD.
79. Air Operations in Southeast Asia, 1972–1973, Vol. 5, 133, 135, 150–51, K717.0423-23, K416.0141-13 July 1972–August 1973, Vol. 1, Appendix A, AFHRA.
80. Transcript of a Telephone Conversation between Moorer and Vogt, December 22, 1972, *FRUS IX, 1969–1976*, 807, 808.
81. Headquarters SAC, Corona Harvest USAF Air Operations in Southeast Asia 1 July 1972–15 August 1973, Volume V, 149, 151, K416.0141-13 July 1972–August 1973, Vol. 1, Appendix A, AFHRA.
82. Memorandum for Record, Sequence of Events, 22–25 December 1972, Concerning Strikes on North Vietnam, December 27, 1972, *FRUS IX, 1969–1976*, 846–48.
83. Michel, *11 Days*, 11.
84. Message from CINCSAC to RUHJOFA/8AF, Linebacker II Update, 231739Z, December 1972, K-WG-307-HI, October–December 1972, Vol. 1, AFHRA.
85. Message from SSO CINCSAC to CINCPACAF info 7AF, B-52 Operation, 232020Z, December 1972, Vogt Papers, General Vogt's Read File December 1972, AFHSD; Air Operations in Southeast Asia, 1972–1973, Vol. 5, 166–68. K717.0423-23, AFHRA.
86. Message from SSO CINCSAC to CINCPACAF info 7AF, B-52 Operation, 232020Z, December 1972, Vogt Papers, Gen. Vogt's Read File Dec 1972, AFHSD; Air Operations in Southeast Asia, 1972–1973, Vol. 5, 166–68, K717.0423-23, AFHRA.
87. Lieutenant Colonel Charles E. Nicholson, Memorandum for Record, Arc Light Compression Tactics, December 22, 1972, 220806Z, December 1972, K-WG-307-HI, Vol. 1, AFHRA. The 17th Air Division vice commander, a Colonel Cody, took steps a week later to nominate General Sullivan for an award because he thought Sullivan "was instrumental in successfully altering B-52 tactics when striking within the Hanoi/Haiphong area." Message from Colonel Cody 17 AD to Colonel Morris 8AF, Rough, Repeat Rough Draft of Specifics to be Used Later as a Source for Formal Narrative Description of Proposed Award to 17AD CC, 311259Z, December 1972, K-WG-307-HI, October–December 1972, Vol. 1, AFHRA. According to Marshall Michel,

Sullivan had bypassed Eighth AF and sent the message straight to SAC to obtain a decision faster, but that violated the chain of command. Sullivan fell out of favor for violating the chain of command, and the Air Force sent a message when it did not promote him. He retired August 1, 1974. Michel, *11 Days,* 224.

88. Air Operations in Southeast Asia, 1972–1973, Vol. 5, 150, K416.0141-13 July 1972–August 1973, Vol. 1, Appendix A; Air Operations in Southeast Asia, 1972–1973, Vol. 2, p. iv-288, K717.0423-23, AFHRA.
89. Webb and Poole, *Joint Chiefs of Staff, 1971–1973,* 297.
90. Air Operations in Southeast Asia, 1972–1973, Vol. 5, 169–70, 173, K717.0423-23, AFHRA; Transcript of a Telephone Conversation between President Nixon and the President's Assistant for National Security Affairs (Kissinger), December 23, 1972, *FRUS IX, 1969–1976,* 819.
91. Hanhimaki, *The Flawed Architect,* 255; Gaiduk, *Soviet Union and the Vietnam War,* 244.
92. Message from AFSSO 7AF to AFSSO CINCPAC info AFSSO SAC, B-52 Operations, 240543Z, December 1972, Folder Gen. Vogt's Read File, December 1972, Vogt Papers, AFHSD.
93. Corona Harvest V, 1972–1973, 11, K416.041-13, AFHRA.
94. Linebacker II Arclite Day Nine Critique, 290925Z, December 1972, Vogt Papers, AFHSD.
95. Air Operations in Southeast Asia, 1972–1973, Vol. 5, 180, K717.0423-23, AFHRA; Message from CINCSAC to 7AF info CINCPACAF, CINCPACFLT, Linebacker II, 241800Z, December 1972, Vogt Papers, Read File December 1972, AFHSD.
96. Message from the Chairman of the Joint Chiefs of Staff (Moorer) to the Commander in Chief, Pacific (Gayler) and the Commander in Chief, Strategic Air Command (Meyer), December 23, 1972, *FRUS IX, 1969–1976,* 824.
97. Transcript of a Telephone Conversation between Nixon and Kissinger, December 23, 1972, *FRUS IX, 1969–1976,* 821; Study on the Effectiveness of Air Power in Southeast Asia, 183, 257, 282, K416.041-13, AFHRA.
98. Message from Moorer to Gayler and Meyer, December 23, 1972, *FRUS IX, 1969–1976,* 825.
99. Ibid., 824; Air Operations in Southeast Asia 1 July 1972–15 August 1973, Vol. V, 201, 207, K717.0423-23, Vol. 5, AFHRA.
100. Study on the Effectiveness of Air Power, 201, 203, 212, K416.041-13; Johnson, Linebacker Operations: September–December 1972, 62, K717.0413-102, AFHRA; Linebacker II Arclite Day Nine Critique, 290925Z, December 1972, Vogt Papers, AFHSD.
101. Air Operations in Southeast Asia, 1972–1973, Vol. 5, 223, K717.0423-23; Study on the Effectiveness of Air Power, 223, K416.041-13, AFHRA.
102. Air Operations in Southeast Asia, 1972–1973, Vol. 2, p. iv-284, K717.0423-23, AFHRA.
103. Diary Entry by Moorer, December 26, 1972, *FRUS IX, 1969–1976,* 826.
104. Air Operations in Southeast Asia, 1972–1973, Vol. 5, 193, 205, 206, 217, 220, 226. K717.0423-23; Study on the Effectiveness of Air Power, 206. K416.041-13; Linebacker Critique 26 December 1972, 280410Z, December 1972, K740.3391, AFHRA.
105. Lieutenant Colonel H. F. Hartsell, Linebacker II Operations, Briefing Slides, K143.042-12, 18–30 December 1972, Vol. 2; Pribbenow, trans., *Victory in Vietnam,* 324; Summary Air Operations Southeast Asia, May 1972, 4–12, K717.3063, May 1972, AFHRA.
106. Hanhimaki, *The Flawed Architect,* 255; Transcript of Telephone Conversation between Nixon and Kissinger, December 26, 1972, *FRUS IX, 1969–1976,* 830; Message from Richard T. Kennedy of the National Security Council Staff to the Air Attache at the Embassy in France (Guay), December 27, 1972, *FRUS IX, 1969–1976,* 845.
107. Transcript of Telephone Conversation between Nixon and Kissinger, December 26, 1972, *FRUS IX, 1969–1976,* 830; Webb and Poole, *Joint Chiefs of Staff, 1971–1973,* 298.
108. Air Operations in Southeast Asia, 1972–1973, Vol. 5, 231–36, 239–43, K717.0423-23, AFHRA;

Message from AFSSO Udorn to AFSSO 7AF, AFSSO 13AF, Linebacker II Juliet Critique, 290945Z, December 1972, Vogt Papers, Read File December 1972, AFHSD.
109. Air Operations in Southeast Asia, 1972–1973, Vol. 5, 253, 255. K717.0423-23; Linebacker II Operations, Briefing Slides. K143.042-12, 18–30 December 1972, Vol. 2, AFHRA.
110. Linebacker II Operations, Briefing Slides, K143.042-12, 18–30 December 1972, Vol. 2, AFHRA.
111. Linebacker II Arclite Day Eleven Critique, 310310Z, December 1972, K744.01 1972 Vol. II, Appendix V, AFHRA.
112. Moorer Reminiscences, Volume III, 1250, Navy Department Library; Johnson, Linebacker Operations: September–December 1972, 63, K717.0413-102, AFHRA.
113. Message from AFSSO PACAF to SSO SAC info AFSSO 7AF, B-52 Operations in NVN, 281913Z, December 1972, Vogt Papers, Read File December 1972, AFHSD; Study on the Effectiveness of Air Power, 251, K416.041-13, AFHRA; Message from AFSSO PACAF to AFSSO 7AF, B-52 Strikes, 300230Z, December 1972, Vogt Papers, Message Traffic December 1972, AFHSD.
114. Gillette, History 307th Strategic Wing, October–December 1972, Vol. 1, 44, K-WG-307-HI, AFHRA.
115. Message from the Air Attache at the Embassy in France (Guay) to the President's Deputy Assistant for National Security Affairs (Haig), December 28, 1972, *FRUS IX, 1969–1976*, 853; Clodfelter, *Limits of Air Power*, 196; Allan E. Goodman, *The Lost Peace: America's Search for a Negotiated Settlement of the Vietnam War* (Stanford, CA: Hoover Institution Press, Stanford University, 1978), 157.
116. Transcript of a Telephone Conversation between the Chairman of the Joint Chiefs of Staff (Moorer) and the Commander, Strategic Air Command (Meyer), December 29, 1972, *FRUS IX, 1969–1976*, 873; Moorer Reminiscences, Volume III, 1242, Navy Department Library. Robert Thompson, the British counterinsurgency expert, agreed. A. L. Gropman, "The Air War in Vietnam, 1961–1973," in Mason, ed., *War in the Third Dimension*, 57.
117. Alan Dawson, *55 Days: The Fall of South Vietnam* (Englewood Cliffs, NJ: Prentice-Hall, 1977), 123.
118. Dallek, *Nixon and Kissinger*, 447; Webb and Poole, *Joint Chiefs of Staff, 1971–1973*, 299; Diary Entry by the Chairman of the Joint Chiefs of Staff (Moorer), January 16, 1973, *FRUS IX, 1969–1976*, 1081.
119. Message for General Vogt from Major General Hughes, Linebacker II Lima Critique, 310320Z, December 1972, Linebacker II Arclite Day Eleven Critique, 310310Z, December 1972, Message to General Vogt from Major General Hughes, Linebacker II Day Twelve Critique, 310915Z, December 1972, K744.01 1972 Vol. II, Appendix V, AFHRA.
120. Air Operations in Southeast Asia, 1972–1973, Vol. 5, 277, 282, K717.0423-23, AFHRA; Message from AFSSO Udorn to AFSSO 7AF, 13AF, Linebacker II Arclite Day Twelve Critique, 310915Z, December 1972, Vogt Papers, Message Traffic December 1972, AFHSD. This message addressed the 11th mission, which occurred on December 29. Linebacker II Arclite Day Eleven Critique, 310310Z, December 1972, Vogt Papers, AFHSD.
121. Linebacker II Operations, Briefing Slides, K143.042-12, 18–30 December 1972, Vol. 2, AFHRA.
122. CINCPAC Command History 1972, Vol. 1, 165, K712.01, 1972, Vol. 1, AFHRA.
123. Air Operations in Southeast Asia, 1972–1973, Vol. 2, p. iv-314, K717.0423-23, AFHRA.
124. Message from AFSSO 7AF to AFSSO CSAF, AFSSO SAC, AFSSO PACAF, Daily Wrap Up, 260300Z, December 1972, Folder General Vogt's Msg File, Daily Wrap Up, 1 December 1972 thru 31 December 1972, Vogt Papers, AFHSD.
125. Message from AFSSO 7AF to AFSSO CSAF, AFSSO SAC, AFSSO PACAF, Daily Wrap Up, 281010Z, December 1972, Vogt's Msg File, Daily Wrap Up, December 1972, Vogt Papers, AFHSD; Message from 7th AF to RUEFHQA/CSAF/XOO, Linebacker II Juliet Critique, 311034Z, December 1972, K740.3391; Air Operations in Southeast Asia, 1972–1973, Vol. 5, 128,

K717.0423-23, AFHRA.
126. Study on the Effectiveness of Air Power, 288, K416.041-13, AFHRA.
127. Air Operations in Southeast Asia, 1972–1973, Vol. 2, pp. iv-300, iv-303, K717.0423-23, AFHRA.
128. Gilster and Frady, Linebacker II USAF Bombing Survey, April 1973, 6, 10, 22, K143.054-1, Vol. 34; Air Operations in Southeast Asia, 1972–1973, Vol. 2, p. iv-260, K717.0423-23, AFHRA.
129. Johnson, Linebacker Operations: September–December 1972, 44, K717.0413-102, AFHRA.
130. Air Operations in Southeast Asia, 1972–1973, Vol. 1, p. ii-59, K717.0423-23; Corona Harvest V, 1972–1973, 36, 82, K416.041-13, AFHRA.
131. Air Operations in Southeast Asia, 1972–1973, Vol. 2, p. iv-259, iv-265, iv-283, iv-284, K717.0423-23, AFHRA.
132. Gilster and Frady, Linebacker II USAF Bombing Survey, April 1973, 34, 37, K143.054-1, Vol. 34, AFHRA.
133. Air Operations in Southeast Asia, 1972–1973, Vol. 5, 290, K717.0423-23; Moorer Reminiscences, Volume III, 1272, Navy Department Library; Linebacker II Operations, K143.042-12, Vol. 1, 18–30 December 1972, AFHRA.
134. Gareth Porter, *A Peace Denied: The United States, Vietnam, and the Paris Agreement* (Bloomington: Indiana University Press, 1975), 165.
135. Air Operations Lessons Learned Summary, K168.06-233, 73/01/31–74/01/03; Linebacker II Arclite Day 10 Critique, 300715Z, December 1972, K744.01; Air Operations in Southeast Asia, 1972–1973, Vol. 2, p. iv-287, K717.0423-23, AFHRA.
136. Air Operations in Southeast Asia, 1972–1973, Vol. 2, p. iv-292, K717.0423-23, AFHRA.
137. Air Operations Lessons Learned Summary, K168.06-233, 73/01/31–74/01/03, AFHRA.
138. Conversation among Nixon, Kissinger, and Haig, December 20, 1972, *FRUS IX, 1969–1976*, 777–78; End of Tour Report, Lt. Col. John F. Hurst Jr., K717.131, 1972–April 1973; Air Operations in Southeast Asia, 1972–1973, Vol. 2, p. iv-288, K717.0423-23, AFHRA; Michel, *11 Days*, 122, 130, 223.
139. End of Tour Report, Lt. Col. John F. Hurst Jr., K717.131, 1972–April 1973, AFHRA.
140. Message from CINCPACAF to CINCPAC, Electronic Warfare Lessons Learned, 020401Z, October 1973, K168.06-239, 72/10/24–75/03/00, AFHRA. Marshall L. Michel does an excellent job conveying the North Vietnamese experience of Linebacker II from inside the SA-2 missile launch vans. Michel, *11 Days*, passim.
141. Air Operations in Southeast Asia, 1972–1973, Vol. 2, p. iv-316, iv-317, K717.0423-23, AFHRA.
142. Pribbenow, trans., *Victory in Vietnam*, 329.
143. CINCPAC Command History 1972, Vol. 2, 544, K712.01, 1972, Vol. 2, AFHRA.
144. Ibid., 546.
145. Air Operations in Southeast Asia, 1972–1973, Vol. 2, p. iv-269, iv-270, K717.0423-23, AFHRA.
146. Herring, *America's Longest War*, 280.
147. Murrey Marder, "North Vietnam: Taking Pride in Punishment," *Washington Post*, February 4, 1973, C4.
148. Kathleen Gough, *Ten Times More Beautiful: The Rebuilding of Vietnam* (New York: Monthly Review Press, 1978), 218.
149. Marder, "North Vietnam: Taking Pride in Punishment," C1.
150. Ibid., C4; Pribbenow, *Victory in Vietnam*, 327.
151. Palmer, *Summons of the Trumpet*, 259; Momyer, *Air Power in Three Wars*, 243; Sharp, *Strategy for Defeat*, 270; Douglas Pike, "The Other Side" in Peter Braestrup, ed., *Vietnam as History: Ten Years After the Paris Peace Accords* (Washington, DC: University Press of America, 1984), 72.
152. Moorer Reminiscences, Volume III, 1279, Navy Department Library.
153. Study on the Effectiveness of Air Power, 179, K416.041-13, AFHRA; Captain E. E. Tissot, Commanding Officer USS Enterprise, Deployment Report, 12 September 1972 to 12 June 1973, 3

July 1973, Marder, "North Vietnam: Taking Pride in Punishment," C4.
154. HQ SAC, USAF Air Operations in Southeast Asia, 1 July 1972–15 August 1973, Vol. 5, Addendum, 4, K717.0423-23, 1 July 1972–15 August 1973, Vol. 5, AFHRA.
155. Earl H. Tilford Jr., "Air Power in Vietnam: The Hubris of Power," in Lawrence E. Grinter and Peter M. Dunn, eds., *The American War in Vietnam: Lessons, Legacies, and Implications for Future Conflicts* (Westport, CT: Greenwood Press, 1987), 79–80; Clodfelter, *Limits of Air Power*, 206.
156. Gilbert, *Why the North Won the Vietnam War*, 24; William P. Head, "War from above the Clouds: B-52 Operations during the Second Indochina War and the Effects of the Air War on Theory and Doctrine," in David R. Mets and William P. Head, eds., *Plotting a True Course: Reflections on USAF Strategic Attack Theory and Doctrine: The Post-World War II Experience* (Westport, CT: Praeger, 2003), 58.
157. Porter, *A Peace Denied*, 165; Sharp, *Strategy for Defeat*, 255.
158. George C. Herring, "Fighting without Allies: The International Dimensions of America's Failure in Vietnam," in Gilbert, *Why the North Won the Vietnam War*, 92; Herring, *America's Longest War*, 280.
159. Brigham, *Guerrilla Diplomacy*, 111.
160. Timothy Lomperis, *The War Everyone Lost—And Won: America's Intervention in Viet Nam's Twin Struggles* (Baton Rouge: Louisiana State University Press, 1984), 94.
161. Dallek, *Nixon and Kissinger*, 446; Palmer, *Summons of the Trumpet*, 259.
162. Zhai, *China and the Vietnam Wars, 1950–1975*, 206.
163. Message from the President's Military Assistant (Scowcroft) to the President's Assistant for National Security Affairs (Kissinger), January 22, 1973, *FRUS IX, 1969–1976*, 1146; Dallek, *Nixon and Kissinger*, 447; Clodfelter, *Limits of Air Power*, 199.
164. Air Operations in Southeast Asia, 1 July 1972–15 August 1973, Vol. 3, p. v-30, K717-0423-23, AFHRA.
165. Air Operations in Southeast Asia, 1972–1973, Vol. 1, p. ii-61, K717.0423-23; Air Operations in Southeast Asia, 1972–1973, Vol. 3, p. v-31, K717-0423-23, AFHRA.
166. Willbanks, *Abandoning Vietnam*, 188, 190, 195.

Conclusions

1. History Naval Operations, Vol. III 1965–1967, Part 1, 103, Vietnam Command Files, COLL/372, Box 85, File CNO NHO, Vol. III, Part 1, NHHC; Van Staaveren, *Gradual Failure*, 263–65.
2. Conversation between President Nixon and Richard T. Kennedy of the National Security Council Staff, December 27, 1972, *FRUS IX, 1969–1976*, 840–41.
3. John Lewis Gaddis, *Strategies of Containment: A Critical Appraisal of Postwar American National Security* (New York: Oxford University Press, 1982), 298; Prados, *The Blood Road*, 363.
4. Carl von Clausewitz, *On War*, trans. and ed. Michael Howard and Peter Paret (Princeton, NJ: Princeton University Press, 1976), 80.
5. Memorandum of Conversation, April 4, 1970, *FRUS 1969–1970, VI*, 783.
6. Colvin, "Hanoi in My Time," 154.
7. Palmer, *The 25-Year War*, 173.
8. Warren Bell, et al., "Reporting the Darkness: The Role of the Press in the Vietnam War," ed. David L. Anderson, *Facing My Lai: Moving Beyond the Massacre* (Lawrence: University Press of Kansas, 1998), 72.
9. Michael Lind, *Vietnam, the Necessary War: A Reinterpretation of America's Most Disastrous Military Conflict* (New York: Free Press, 1999).
10. Wen-Qing Ngoei, *Arc of Containment: Britain, the United States, and Anticommunism in Southeast Asia* (Ithaca, NY: Cornell University Press, 2019), 149–50, 176.

Bibliography

Archival Sources

Air Force Historical Research Agency. Maxwell Air Force Base, Alabama.
Air Force History Studies Division. Bolling Air Force Base, Maryland.
Marine Corps History Division. Quantico, Virginia.
Naval History and Heritage Command. U.S. Navy Yard, Washington, DC.
Richard M. Nixon Library, National Security Council, Vietnam Subject Files.
The Vietnam Center & Sam Johnson Vietnam Archive, Texas Tech University, http://vietnam.ttu.edu.

Published Primary Sources

Carland, John M., ed. *Foreign Relations of the United States, 1969–1976, Volume VIII: Vietnam, January–October 1972*. Washington, DC: United States Government Printing Office, 2010.
Carland, John M., ed. and Edward C. Keefer, gen. ed. *Foreign Relations of the United States, 1969–1976, Volume IX: Vietnam, October 1972–January 1973*. Washington, DC: United States Government Printing Office, 2010.
Geyer, David C., Nina D. Howland, and Kent Sieg, eds. *Foreign Relations of the United States, 1969–1976, Volume XIV: Soviet Union, October 1971–May 1972*. Washington, DC: United States Government Printing Office, 2006.
Glennon, John P., Edward C. Keefer, and Charles S. Sampson, eds. *Foreign Relations of the United States, 1964–1968, Volume I: Vietnam 1964*. Washington, DC: United States Government Printing Office, 1992.
Goldman, David, and Erin Mahan, eds. Edward C. Keefer, gen. ed. *Foreign Relations of the United States, 1969–1976, Volume VII: Vietnam, July 1970–January 1972*. Washington, DC: United States Government Printing Office, 2010.
Humphrey, David C., Edward C. Keefer, and Louis J. Smith, eds. *Foreign Relations of the United States, 1964–1968, Volume III: Vietnam, June–December 1965*. Washington, DC: United States Government Printing Office, 1996.
Humphrey, David C., Ronald D. Landa, and Louis J. Smith, eds. *Foreign Relations of the United States, 1964–1968, Volume II: Vietnam, January–June 1965*. Washington, DC: United States Government Printing Office, 1996.

Humphrey, David C., ed. David S. Patterson, gen. ed. *Foreign Relations of the United States, 1964–1968, Volume IV: Vietnam 1966*. Washington, DC: United States Government Printing Office, 1998.

Humphrey, David C., and Charles S. Sampson, eds. *Foreign Relations of the United States, 1964–1968, Volume XIV: Soviet Union*. Washington, DC: United States Government Printing Office, 2001.

Keefer, Edward C., ed. *Foreign Relations of the United States, 1964–1968, Volume XXVII: Mainland Southeast Asia; Regional Affairs*. Washington, DC: United States Government Printing Office, 2000.

Keefer, Edward C., ed. *Foreign Relations of the United States, 1964–1968, Volume XXVIII: Laos*. Washington, DC: United States Government Printing Office, 1998.

Keefer, Edward C., and Carolyn Yee, eds. *Foreign Relations of the United States, 1969–1976, Volume VI: Vietnam, January 1969–July 1970*. Washington, DC: United States Government Printing Office, 2006.

Lawler, Daniel J., ed. *Foreign Relations of the United States, 1969–1976, Volume XX: Southeast Asia, 1969–1972*. Washington, DC: United States Government Printing Office, 2006.

Phillips, Steven E., ed. *Foreign Relations of the United States, 1969–1976, Volume XVII: China, 1969–1972*. Washington DC: United States Government Printing Office, 2006.

Sieg, Kent, ed. *Foreign Relations of the United States, 1964–1968, Volume V: Vietnam, 1967*. Washington, DC: United States Government Printing Office, 2002.

———, ed. *Foreign Relations of the United States, 1964–1968, Volume VI: Vietnam, January–August 1968*. Washington, DC: United States Government Printing Office, 2002.

———, ed. *Foreign Relations of the United States, 1964–1968, Volume VII: Vietnam, September 1968–January 1969*. Washington, DC: United States Government Printing Office, 2003.

U.S. Congress. Senate Committee on Armed Services. Hearings before the Preparedness Investigating Subcommittee of the Committee on Armed Services, United States Senate, 90th Cong., 1st sess. August 9–25, 1967.

Secondary Sources

"ABC's of Missile Guidance." *Air Progress* (Fall 1959): 74.

Acacia, John. *Clark Clifford: The Wise Man of Washington*. Lexington: University Press of Kentucky, 2009.

Aitken, Jonathan. *Nixon: A Life*. Washington, DC: Regnery, 1993.

Ambrose, Stephen E. *Nixon: Volume Three, Ruin and Recovery, 1973–1990*. New York: Simon & Schuster, 1991.

Anderson, David L., ed. *Facing My Lai: Moving Beyond the Massacre*. Lawrence: University Press of Kansas, 1998.

Andrade, Dale. *Trial by Fire: The Easter Offensive, America's Last Battle*. New York: Hippocrene Books, 1995.

Anthony, Victor B., and Richard R. Sexton. *The United States Air Force in Southeast Asia: The War in Northern Laos, 1954–1973*. Washington, DC: Center for Air Force History, United States Air Force, 1993.

Archer, Christon I., John R. Ferris, Holger H. Herwig, and Timothy H. E. Travers. *World History of Warfare*. Lincoln: University of Nebraska Press, 2002.

Armitage, M. J., and R. A. Mason. *Air Power in the Nuclear Age*. Urbana: University of Illinois Press, 1983.

Ball, George W. *The Past Has Another Pattern: Memoirs*. New York: W. W. Norton, 1982.

Ballard, Jack S. *Development and Employment of Fixed-Wing Gunships, 1962–1972*. Washington, DC: Office of Air Force History, United States Air Force, 1982.

Barrett, David M. *Uncertain Warriors: Lyndon Johnson and His Vietnam Advisors*. Lawrence: University Press of Kansas, 1993.

Beecher, William. "Raids in Cambodia by U.S. Unprotested." *New York Times*, May 9, 1969, 1, 7.

Berman, Larry. *No Peace, No Honor: Nixon, Kissinger, and Betrayal in Vietnam*. New York: Free Press, 2001.

Beschloss, Michael, ed. *Reaching for Glory: Lyndon Johnson's Secret White House Tapes, 1964–1965*. New York: Simon & Schuster, 2001.

Biddle, Stephen. *Military Power: Explaining Victory and Defeat in Modern Battle*. Princeton, NJ: Princeton University Press, 2004.

Biddle, Tami Davis. *Rhetoric and Reality in Air Warfare: The Evolution of British and American Ideas about Strategic Bombing, 1914–1945*. Princeton, NJ: Princeton University Press, 2002.

Bird, Kai. *The Color of Truth: McGeorge Bundy and William Bundy, Brothers in Arms: A Biography*. New York: Simon & Schuster, 1998.

Bisson, Kaili. "The Story Behind the Song 'Puff the Magic Dragon' by Peter, Paul, and Mary." Spindiddy, April 22, 2019. https://spinditty.com/genres/Puff-The-Magic-Dragon.

Blair, Anne E. *Lodge in Vietnam: A Patriot Abroad*. New Haven, CT: Yale University Press, 1995.

Bowers, Ray L. *The United States Air Force in Southeast Asia: Tactical Airlift*. Washington, DC: Office of Air Force History, United States Air Force, 1983.

Braestrup, Peter, ed. *Vietnam as History: Ten Years After the Paris Peace Accords*. Washington, DC: University Press of America, 1984.

Breen, Timothy H. *Imagining the Past: East Hampton Histories*. Reading, MA: Addison-Wesley, 1989.

Brennan, Lawrence B. "Wings of Gold: The Loss of LTJG Lee E. Nordahl, USNR and LCDR Guy D. Johnson, USN, RVAH Thirteen, on 20 December 1965 Over North Vietnam; The Conclusion." *Universal Ship Cancellation Society Log* 73: 5 (May 2006): 18–20.

Brigham, Robert K. *Guerrilla Diplomacy: The NLF's Foreign Relations and the Vietnam War*. Ithaca, NY: Cornell University Press, 1999.

———. *ARVN: Life and Death in the South Vietnamese Army*. Lawrence: University Press of Kansas, 2006.

Broughton, Jack. *Going Downtown: The War against Hanoi and Washington*. New York: Orion Books, 1988.

Broughton, Jacksel M. "Rolling Thunder from the Cockpit." In John Norton Moore, ed. *The Vietnam Debate: A Fresh Look at the Arguments*. Lanham: MD: University Press of America, 1990: 149–60.

Brown, David A. "U.S. Presses North Viet Air War." *Aviation Week and Space Technology*. July 3, 1972: 15.

Brugioni, Dino A. *Eyes in the Sky: Eisenhower, the CIA and Cold War Aerial Espionage*. Annapolis, MD: Naval Institute Press, 2010.

Brulle, Robert V. *Angels Zero: P-47 Close Air Support in Europe*. Washington, DC: Smithsonian Institution Press, 2000.

Bundy, McGeorge. *Danger and Survival: Choices about the Bomb in the First Fifty Years*. New York: Random House, 1988.

Buzzanco, Robert. *Masters of War: Military Dissent and Politics in the Vietnam Era*. New York: Cambridge University Press, 1996.

Byrd, Vernon B. *Passing Gas: The History of Inflight Refueling*. Chico, CA: Byrd Publishing, 1994.

"C-130J Super Hercules." https://www.lockheedmartin.com/us/products/c130.html.

Carland, John M. *United States Army in Vietnam. Combat Operations. Stemming the Tide: May 1965 to October 1966*. Washington, DC: Center of Military History, United States Army, 2000.

Casey, Aloysuis, and Patrick Casey. "Lavelle, Nixon, and the White House Tapes." *Air Force Magazine*, February 2007, 88.

Castle, Timothy N. *At War in the Shadow of Vietnam: U.S. Military Aid to the Royal Lao Government, 1955–1975*. New York: Columbia University Press, 1993.

———. *One Day Too Long: Top Secret Site 85 and the Bombing of North Vietnam*. New York: Columbia University Press, 1999.

Chandler, David. *The Art of War in the Age of Marlborough*. New York: Sarpedon, 1995.

Chanoff, David, and Doan Van Toai. *Portrait of the Enemy*. New York: Random House, 1986.

Churchill, Winston. *The Second World War, Volume 2: Their Finest Hour*. Boston: Houghton Mifflin, 1976.

Citino, Robert M. *Blitzkrieg to Desert Storm: The Evolution of Operational Warfare*. Lawrence: University Press of Kansas, 2004.

Clodfelter, Mark. *The Limits of Air Power: The American Bombing of North Vietnam*. New York: The Free Press, 1989.

Clymer, Adam. *Edward M. Kennedy: A Biography*. New York: William Morrow, 1999.

Cohen, Michael A. *American Maelstrom: The 1968 Election and the Politics of Division*. New York: Oxford University Press, 2016.

Collier, Basil. *A History of Air Power*. London: Weidenfeld and Nicolson, 1974.

Colvin, John. "Hanoi in My Time." *Washington Quarterly* (Spring 1981): 138–54.

Contamine, Philippe. *War in the Middle Ages*. Translated by Michael Jones. Oxford: Basil Blackwell, 1984.

Cooling, Benjamin Franklin, ed. *Case Studies in the Development of Close Air Support*. Washington, DC: Office of Air Force History, 1990.

Corum, James S., and Wray R. Johnson. *Airpower in Small Wars: Fighting Insurgents and Terrorists*. Lawrence: University Press of Kansas, 2003.

Cosmas, Graham A. *History of the Joint Chiefs of Staff: The Joint Chiefs of Staff and the War in Vietnam, 1960–1968, Part 2*. Washington, DC: Office of Joint History, 2012.

———. *History of the Joint Chiefs of Staff: The Joint Chiefs of Staff and the War in Vietnam, 1960–1968, Part 3*. Washington, DC: Office of Joint History, 2009.

———. *United States Army in Vietnam. MACV: The Joint Command in the Years of Escalation, 1962–1967*. Washington, DC: Center of Military History, United States Army, 2006.

———. *United States Army in Vietnam. MACV: The Joint Command in the Years of Withdrawal, 1968–1973*. Washington, DC: Center of Military History, United States Army, 2007.

Crane, Conrad C. *American Airpower Strategy in Korea, 1950–1953*. Lawrence: University Press of Kansas, 2000.

———. *American Airpower Strategy in World War II: Bombs, Cities, Civilians, and Oil*. Lawrence: University Press of Kansas, 2006.

Daddis, Gregory A. *No Sure Victory: Measuring U.S. Army Effectiveness and Progress in the Vietnam War*. New York: Oxford University Press, 2011.

———. *Westmoreland's War: Reassessing American Strategy in Vietnam*. New York: Oxford University Press, 2014.

Dallek, Robert. *Nixon and Kissinger: Partners in Power*. New York: Harper Collins, 2007.

Davidson, Phillip B. *Vietnam at War: The History, 1946–1975*. New York: Oxford University Press, 1988.

Davies, Peter E., and David W. Menard. *North American F-100 Super Sabre*. Wiltshire, UK: Crowood, 2003.

Davies, Steve. *Red Eagles: America's Secret MiGs*. Oxford: Osprey Publishing, 2008.

Davis, Larry. *Wild Weasel: The SAM Suppression Story*. Carrollton, TX: Squadron/Signal, 1986.

Davis, M. Thomas. *40Km Into Lebanon: Israel's 1982 Invasion*. Washington, DC: National Defense University Press, 1987.

Davis, Richard G. *On Target: Organizing and Executing the Strategic Air Campaign against Iraq*. Washington, DC: Air Force History and Museums Program, 2002.

Dawson, Alan. *55 Days: The Fall of South Vietnam*. Englewood Cliffs, NJ: Prentice-Hall, 1977.

Day, Dwayne A., John M. Logsdon, and Brian Latell. *Eye in the Sky: The Story of the Corona Spy Satellites*. Washington, DC: Smithsonian Institution Press, 1998.

Deptula, David A., Gary L. Crowder, and George L. Stamper Jr. "Direct Attack: Enhancing Counterland Doctrine and Joint Air Ground Operations." *Air & Space Power Journal* (Winter 2003): 5–12.

Diamond, Edwin. *Behind the Times: Inside the New New York Times*. New York: Villard Books, 1994.

Dobbs, Michael. *One Minute to Midnight: Kennedy, Khrushchev, and Castro on the Brink of Nuclear War*. New York: Alfred A. Knopf, 2008.

Dobrynin, Anatoly. *In Confidence: Moscow's Ambassador to America's Six Cold War Presidents (1962–1986)*. New York: Times Books, 1995.

Dolman, Everett Carl. *Pure Strategy: Power and Principle in the Space and Information Age*. New York: Frank Cass, 2005.

Doubler, Michael D. *Closing with the Enemy: How GIs Fought the War in Europe*. Lawrence: University Press of Kansas, 1994.

Doughty, Robert Allan. *The Breaking Point: Sedan and the Fall of France, 1940*. Hamden, CT: Archon Books, 1990.

———. *Pyrrhic Victory: French Strategy and Operations in the Great War*. Cambridge, MA: Belknap Press of Harvard University Press, 2005.

Douhet, Giulio. *The Command of the Air*. Translated by Dino Ferrari. New York: Coward-McCann, 1942.

Duiker, William J. *Sacred War: Nationalism and Revolution in a Divided Vietnam*. Boston: McGraw-Hill, 1995.

Echevarria, Antulio, II. *Reconsidering the American Way of War: U.S. Military Practice from the Revolution to Afghanistan*. Washington, DC: Georgetown University Press, 2014.

Ehrhard, Thomas P. *Air Force UAVs: The Secret History of Drones.* Washington, DC: Mitchell Institute, 2010.
Ellis, Kristina. "The Lavelle Affair: An Air Force Case Study in Ethics." Thesis, School of Advanced Air and Space Studies, Maxwell Air Force Base, Alabama, 2016.
Emery, Fred. *Watergate: The Corruption of American Politics and the Fall of Richard Nixon.* New York: Times Books, 1994.
Eschmann, Karl J. *Linebacker: The Untold Story of the Air Raids over North Vietnam.* New York: Ivy Books, 1989.
Evron, Yair. *War and Intervention in Lebanon: The Israeli-Syrian Deterrence Dialogue.* Baltimore, MD: The Johns Hopkins University Press, 1987.
Fall, Bernard. *Viet-Nam Witness: 1953–1966.* New York: Praeger, 1966.
Feltham, Dan E. *When Big Blue Went to War: A History of the IBM Corporation's Mission in Southeast Asia during the Vietnam War, 1965–1975.* Bloomington, IN: Abbott, 2012.
Ferguson, Naill. *Kissinger, 1923–1968: The Idealist.* New York: Penguin, 2015.
Finnegan, Terrence J. *Shooting the Front: Allied Aerial Reconnaissance and Photographic Interpretation on the Western Front—World War I.* Washington, DC: National Defense Intelligence College Press, 2006.
Fino, Steven A. *Tiger Check: Automating the U.S. Air Force Fighter Pilot in Air-to-Air Combat, 1950–1980.* Baltimore: The Johns Hopkins University Press, 2017.
FitzGerald, Francis. *Fire in the Lake: The Vietnamese and the Americans in Vietnam.* Boston: Little, Brown, 1972.
Frankum, Ronald B. *Like Rolling Thunder: The Air War in Vietnam, 1964–1975.* Lanham, MD: Rowman & Littlefield, 2005.
Frisbee, John L. "The Practice of Professionalism." *Air Force Magazine* (August 1986).
Fry, Joseph A. *Debating Vietnam: Fulbright, Stennis, and Their Senate Hearings.* Lanham, MD: Rowman & Littlefield, 2006.
Futrell, Robert Frank. *Ideas, Concepts, Doctrine: Basic Thinking in the United States Air Force, 1907–1960.* Volume I. Maxwell AFB, AL: Air University Press, 1989.
———. *Ideas, Concepts, Doctrine: Basic Thinking in the United States Air Force, 1961–1984.* Volume 2. Maxwell AFB, AL: Air University Press, 1989.
Futrell, Robert Frank, Gerald E. Hasselwander, William H. Greenhalgh, Robert F. Jakob, Carl Grubb, Charles A. Ravenstein, Walter Hanak, and Lawrence J. Paszek. *Aces and Aerial Victories: The United States Air Force in Southeast Asia, 1965–1973.* Washington, DC: Office of Air Force, History, 1976.
Gabriel, Richard A. *Operation Peace for Galilee: The Israeli-PLO War in Lebanon.* New York: Hill and Wang, 1984.
Gaddis, John Lewis. *The Cold War: A New History.* New York: Penguin, 2006.
———. *Strategies of Containment: A Critical Appraisal of Postwar American National Security.* New York: Oxford University Press, 1982.
Gaiduk, Ilya V. *The Soviet Union and the Vietnam War.* Chicago: Ivan R. Dee, 1996.
Galula, David. *Counterinsurgency Warfare: Theory and Practice.* Westport, CT: Praeger Security International, 2006.
Gardner, Lloyd. *Pay Any Price: Lyndon Johnson and the Wars for Vietnam.* Chicago: Ivan R. Dee, 1995.
Gelb, Leslie H., with Richard K. Betts. *The Irony of Vietnam: The System Worked.* Washington, DC: Brookings Institute, 1979.
Gilbert, Marc Jason, ed. *Why the North Won the Vietnam War.* New York: Palgrave, 2002.

Gilbert, Marc Jason, and William Head, eds. *The Tet Offensive*. Westport, CT: Praeger, 1996.

Gillespie, Paul G. *Weapons of Choice: The Development of Precision Guided Munitions*. Tuscaloosa: University of Alabama Press, 2006.

Ginor, Isabella, and Gideon Remez. *The Soviet-Israeli War, 1967–1973: The USSR's Military Intervention in the Egyptian-Israeli Conflict*. Oxford: Oxford University Press, 2017.

Glasser, Jeffrey D. *The Secret Vietnam War: The United States Air Force in Thailand, 1961–1975*. Jefferson, NC: McFarland, 1995.

Goldsmith, Belinda. "Just a Minute with: Peter Yarrow." Reuters, March 6, 2008.

Goldstein, Gordon M. *Lessons in Disaster: McGeorge Bundy and the Path to War in Vietnam*. New York: Henry Holt, 2008.

Gongora, Thierry, and Harald von Riekhoff, eds. *Toward a Revolution in Military Affairs? Defense and Security at the Dawn of the Twenty-First Century*. Westport, CT: Greenwood, 2000.

Gooderson, Ian. *Air Power at the Battlefront: Allied Close Air Support in Europe, 1943–1945*. Portland, OR: Frank Cass, 1998.

Goodman, Allan E. *The Lost Peace: America's Search for a Negotiated Settlement of the Vietnam War*. Stanford, CA: Hoover Institution Press, Stanford University, 1978.

Gordin, Michael D. *Five Days in August: How World War II Became a Nuclear War*. Princeton, NJ: Princeton University Press, 2007.

Gordon, Yefim, Dmitriy Komissarov, and Sergey Komissarov. *OKB Ilyushin: A History of the Design Bureau and Its Aircraft*. Hinckley, England: Midland, 2004.

Gough, Kathleen. *Ten Times More Beautiful: The Rebuilding of Vietnam*. New York: Monthly Review Press, 1978.

Gould, Lewis L. *1968: The Election That Changed America*. Chicago: Ivan R. Dee, 1993.

Grant, Zalin. *Over the Beach*. New York: W. W. Norton, 1986.

Greenhalgh, William H. *The RF-101 Voodoo, 1961–1970*. Washington, DC: Office of Air Force History, 1979.

Gregory, Robert H., Jr. *Clean Bombs and Dirty Wars: Air Power in Kosovo and Libya*. Lincoln, NE: Potomac Books, 2015.

Grinter, Lawrence E., and Peter M. Dunn, eds. *The American War in Vietnam: Lessons, Legacies, and Implications for Future Conflicts*. Westport, CT: Greenwood, 1987.

Gross, Charles J. *American Military Aviation: The Indispensable Arm*. College Station: Texas A&M University Press, 2002.

Guan, Ang Cheng. *Ending the Vietnam War: The Vietnamese Communists' Perspective*. New York: Routledge Curzon, 2004.

———. *The Vietnam War from the Other Side: The Vietnamese Communists' Perspective*. New York: Routledge Curzon, 2002.

Hackworth, David H. *Steel My Soldiers' Hearts: The Hopeless to the Hardcore Transformation of 4th Battalion, 39th Infantry, United States Army, Vietnam*. New York: Rugged Land, 2002.

Haines, Gerald K., and Robert E. Leggett. *Watching the Bear: Essays on CIA's Analysis of the Soviet Union*. https://www.cia.gov/library/center-for-the-study-of-intelligence/csi-publications/books-and-monographs/watching-the-bear-essays-on-cias-analysis-of-the-soviet-union/article04.html.

Haldeman, H. R. Introduction and afterword by Stephen E. Ambrose. *The Haldeman Diaries: Inside the Nixon White House*. New York: G. P. Putnam's Sons, 1994.

Hall, R. Cargill, ed. *Case Studies in Strategic Bombardment.* Washington, DC: Air Force History and Museums Program, 1998.

Hallion, Richard P. *Strike from the Sky: The History of Battlefield Air Attack, 1911–1945.* Washington, DC: Smithsonian Institution Press, 1989.

Hanhimaki, Jussi. *The Flawed Architect: Henry Kissinger and American Foreign Policy.* New York: Oxford University Press, 2004.

Hannah, Craig C. *Striving for Air Superiority: The Tactical Air Command in Vietnam.* College Station: Texas A&M University Press, 2002.

Hanyok, Robert J. *Spartans in Darkness: American SIGINT and the Indochina War, 1945–1975.* Fort Meade, MD: Center for Cryptological History, National Security Agency, 2002.

Hardesty, Von, and Ilya Grinberg. *Red Phoenix Rising: The Soviet Air Force in World War II.* Lawrence: University Press of Kansas, 2012.

Harmer, Todd P., and C. R. Anderegg. *The Shootdown of Trigger 4: Report of the Project Trigger Study Team.* Washington, DC: Headquarters, U.S. Air Force, 2001.

Harvey, Frank. *Strike Command: America's Elite New Combat Team.* New York: Duell, Sloan, and Pearce, 1962.

Head, William P. *Night Hunters: The AC-130s and Their Role in US Airpower.* College Station: Texas A&M University Press, 2014.

——. *Shadow and Stinger: Developing the AC-119G/K Gunships in the Vietnam War.* College Station: Texas A&M University Press, 2007.

Head, William, and Lawrence E. Grinter, eds. *Looking Back on the Vietnam War: A 1990s Perspective on the Decisions, Combat, and Legacies.* Westport, CT: Greenwood, 1993.

Henriksen, Dag. *NATO's Gamble: Combining Diplomacy and Airpower in the Kosovo Crisis, 1998–1999.* Annapolis, MD: Naval Institute Press, 2007.

Herring, George C. *America's Longest War: The United States and Vietnam, 1950–1975,* 3rd ed. New York: McGraw-Hill, 1996.

——. *LBJ and Vietnam: A Different Kind of War.* Austin: University of Texas Press, 1994.

Hersh, Seymour M. *The Price of Power: Kissinger in the Nixon White House.* New York: Summit Books, 1983.

Herwig, Holger H. *The First World War: Germany and Austria-Hungary, 1914–1918.* London: Arnold, 1997.

Higham, Robin. *Unflinching Zeal: The Air Battles over France and Britain, May–October 1940.* Annapolis, MD: Naval Institute Press, 2012.

Higham, Robin, and Mark Parillo, eds. *The Influence of Airpower Upon History: Statesmanship, Diplomacy, and Foreign Policy since 1903.* Lexington: University Press of Kentucky, 2013.

Hobson, Chris. *Vietnam Air Losses: United States Air Force, Navy and Marine Corps Fixed-Wing Aircraft Losses in Southeast Asia 1961–1973.* Hinckley, England: Midland, 2001.

Hoopes, Townsend. *The Limits of Intervention: An Inside Account of How the Johnson Policy of Escalation was Reversed.* New York: David McKay, 1969.

Hughes, Thomas A. *Over Lord: General Pete Quesada and the Triumph of Tactical Air Power in World War II.* New York: Free Press, 1995.

Humphrey, David C. "Tuesday Lunch at the White House: A Preliminary Assessment." *Diplomatic History* 8, no. 1 (Winter 1984): 81–101.

Hunt, Richard A. *Pacification: The American Struggle for Vietnam's Hearts and Minds.*

Boulder, CO: Westview Press, 1995.
Ienaga, Saburo. *The Pacific War: World War II and the Japanese, 1931–1945.* New York: Pantheon Books, 1978.
"Javelins of St. George: Profile of an All-Weather Fighter Squadron." *Flight International* (29 May 1959): 741.
Jenkins, Dennis R. *F-105 Thunderchief: Workhorse of the Vietnam War.* New York: McGraw-Hill, 2000.
Jian, Chen. "China's Involvement in the Vietnam War, 1964–69." *The China Quarterly*, no. 142 (June 1995): 356–87.
Johnson, David E. *Fast Tanks and Heavy Bombers: Innovation in the U.S. Army, 1917–1945.* Ithaca, NY: Cornell University Press, 1998.
Johnson, James Turner. *Morality & Contemporary Warfare.* New Haven, CT: Yale University Press, 1999.
Kamps, Charles Tustin. "The JCS 94-Target List: A Vietnam Myth that Still Distorts Military Thought." *Air and Space Power Journal* 68, no. 1 (Spring 2001): 67–80.
Karnow, Stanley. *Vietnam: A History.* New York: Viking, 1983.
Keaney, Thomas A., and Eliot A. Cohen. *Gulf War Air Power Survey Summary Report.* Washington, DC: Department of the Air Force, 1993.
———. *Revolution in Warfare? Air Power in the Persian Gulf.* Annapolis, MD: Naval Institute Press, 1995.
Kendrick, Alexander. *The Wound Within: America in the Vietnam Year, 1945–1974.* Boston: Little, Brown, 1974.
Kern, Paul Bentley. *Ancient Siege Warfare.* Bloomington: Indiana University Press, 1999.
Kilduff, Peter. *Douglas A-4 Skyhawk.* London: Osprey, 1983.
Kimball, Jeffrey. *Nixon's Vietnam War.* Lawrence: University Press of Kansas, 1998.
Kissinger, Henry. *Ending the Vietnam War: A History of America's Involvement in and Extrication from the Vietnam War.* New York: Simon & Schuster, 2003.
———. *White House Years.* Boston: Little, Brown, 1979.
Korda, Michael. *With Wings Like Eagles: A History of the Battle of Britain.* New York: HarperCollins, 2009.
Kreis, John F. *Piercing the Fog: Intelligence and Army Air Forces Operations in World War II.* Washington, DC: Air Force History and Museums Program, 1996.
Krepinevich, Andrew F. *The Army and Vietnam.* Baltimore, MD: The Johns Hopkins University Press, 1986.
Lambeth, Benjamin S. *The Transformation of American Air Power.* Ithaca, NY: Cornell University Press, 2000.
Langguth, Jack. "Navy Jets Down 2 MiGs." *New York Times*, June 18, 1965.
Larson, Doyle. "Direct Intelligence Combat Support in Vietnam: Project Teaball." *American Intelligence Journal* 15, no. 1 (Spring/Summer 1994): 56–58.
Leary, William M. "Supporting the 'Secret War': CIA Air Operations in Laos, 1955–1974." *Studies in Intelligence* 42, no. 2 (1999): 71–86.
Lehrack, Otto J. *The First Battle: Operation Starlite and the Beginning of the Blood Debt in Vietnam.* Havertown, PA: Casemate, 2004.
Lewy, Guenter. *America in Vietnam.* New York: Oxford University Press, 1978.
Li, Xiaobing. *Building Ho's Army: Chinese Military Assistance to North Vietnam.* Lexington: University Press of Kentucky, 2019.
Lind, Michael. *Vietnam, The Necessary War: A Reinterpretation of America's Most Disastrous Military Conflict.* New York: Free Press, 1999.

Lodge, Henry Cabot, Jr. *As It Was: An Inside View of Politics and Power in the '50s and '60s.* New York: Norton, 1976.

Lomperis, Timothy. *The War Everyone Lost—And Won: America's Intervention in Viet Nam's Twin Struggles.* Baton Rouge: Louisiana State University Press, 1984.

Lynd, Staughton. *The Other Side.* New York: New American Library, 1966.

MacGarrigle, George L. *United States Army in Vietnam, Combat Operations. Taking the Offensive: October 1966 to October 1967.* Washington, DC: Center of Military History, United States Army, 1998.

Maier, Klaus A., Horst Rohde, Bernd Stegemann, and Hans Umbreit. Translated by Dean S. McMurry and Ewald Osers. *Germany and the Second World War, Volume II: Germany's Initial Conquests in Europe.* Oxford: Clarendon, 1991.

Maloney, Sean M. "Secrets of the BOMARC: Re-Examining Canada's Misunderstood Missile, Part 1." *The Royal Canadian Air Force Journal* 3, no. 3 (Summer 2014): 33–43.

Maraniss, David. *They Marched into Sunlight. War and Peace: Vietnam and America, October 1967.* New York: Simon & Schuster, 2003.

Marder, Murrey. "North Vietnam: Taking Pride in Punishment." *Washington Post*, February 4, 1973.

Mark, Eduard. *Aerial Interdiction: Air Power and the Land Battle in Three American Wars.* Washington, DC: Center for Air Force History, 1994.

Mason, R. A., ed. *War in the Third Dimension: Essays in Contemporary Air Power.* London: Brassey's, 1986.

McCrea, Michael. *US Navy, Marine Corps, and Air Force Fixed-Wing Aircraft Losses and Damage in Southeast Asia (1962–1973).* Arlington, VA: Center for Naval Analyses, 1976.

McFarland, Stephen L. *America's Pursuit of Precision Bombing, 1910–1945.* Washington, DC: Smithsonian Institution Press, 1995.

McFarland, Stephen L., and Wesley Phillips Newton. *To Command the Sky: The Battle for Air Superiority over Germany, 1942–1944.* Washington, DC: Smithsonian Institution Press, 1991.

McMaster, H. R. *Dereliction of Duty: Lyndon Johnson, Robert McNamara, the Joint Chiefs of Staff, and the Lies that Led to Vietnam.* New York: Harper Perennial, 1997.

McNamara, Robert S., with Brian VanDeMark. *In Retrospect: The Tragedy and Lessons of Vietnam.* New York: Times Books, Random House, 1995.

McPherson, Harry. *A Political Education.* Boston: Little, Brown, 1972.

Means, Howard. *67 Shots: Kent State and the End of American Innocence.* Philadelphia: DaCapo, 2016.

Meilinger, Phillip S. *Airwar: Theory and Practice.* Portland, OR: Frank Cass, 2003.

Merlin, Peter W. *From Archangel to Senior Crown: Design and Development of the Blackbird.* Reston, VA: American Institute of Aeronautics and Astronautics, 2008.

Mersky, Peter. *F-8 Crusader Units of the Vietnam War.* London: Osprey, 1998.

Mets, David R., and William P. Head, eds. *Plotting a True Course: Reflections on USAF Strategic Attack Theory and Doctrine: The Post-World War II Experience.* Westport, CT: Praeger, 2003.

Michel, Marshall L., III. *Clashes: Air Combat over North Vietnam, 1965–1972.* Annapolis, MD: Naval Institute Press, 1997.

———. *The 11 Days of Christmas: America's Last Vietnam Battle.* San Francisco: Encounter Books, 2002.

Middleton, Drew, ed. *Air War: Vietnam.* New York: Arno, 1978.

Mierzejewski, Alfred C. *Collapse of the German War Economy, 1944–1945: Allied Air Power and the German National Railway*. Chapel Hill: University of North Carolina Press, 1988.

Military History Institute of Vietnam. *Victory in Vietnam: The Official History of the People's Army of Vietnam, 1954–1975*. Translated by Merle L. Pribbenow. Foreword by William J. Duiker. Lawrence: University Press of Kansas, 2002.

"Military Transports: Some Aspects of Current and Future Types." *Flight* (November 5, 1954): 681.

Millett, Allan R. *The War for Korea, 1950–1951: They Came from the North*. Lawrence: University Press of Kansas, 2010.

Millett, Allan R., and Williamson Murray. *Military Effectiveness. Volume 2: The Interwar Period*. Boston: Unwin Hyman, 1988.

Milne, David. *America's Rasputin: Walt W. Rostow and the Vietnam War*. New York: Hill & Wang, 2009.

Mohr, Charles. "Bombing of North Termed Highly Effective by U.S.: Accurate Laser-Guided Bombs Believed Freely Used—A Saigon Offensive East of Quangtri Is Reported." *New York Times*, May 24, 1972.

Moise, Edwin E. *The Myths of Tet: The Most Misunderstood Event of the Vietnam War*. Lawrence: University Press of Kansas, 2017.

———. *Tonkin Gulf and the Escalation of the Vietnam War*. Chapel Hill: University of North Carolina Press, 1996.

Momyer, William W. *Airpower in Three Wars: WWII, Korea, Vietnam*. Maxwell AFB, AL: Air University Press, 2003.

Moore, Harold G., and Joseph L. Galloway. *We Were Soldiers Once . . . and Young: Ia Drang, The Battle That Changed the War in Vietnam*. New York: Random House, 1992.

Moore, John Norton, ed. *The Vietnam Debate: A Fresh Look at the Arguments*. Lanham: MD: University Press of America, 1990.

Morris, Craig F. *The Origins of American Strategic Bombing Theory*. Annapolis, MD: Naval Institute Press, 2017.

Morrow, John H., Jr. *The Great War in the Air: Military Aviation from 1909 to 1921*. Washington, DC: Smithsonian Institution Press, 1993.

Nalty, Bernard C. *Air War over South Vietnam, 1968–1975*. Washington, DC: Air Force History and Museums Program, United States Air Force, 2000.

———. *The War Against Trucks: Aerial Interdiction in Southern Laos, 1968–1972*. Washington, DC: Air Force History and Museums Program, United States Air Force, 2005.

Neale, Jonathan. *A People's History of the Vietnam War: A New Press People's History*. New York: New Press, 2001.

Neiberg, Michael S. *Arms and the Man: Military History Essays in Honor of Dennis Showalter*. Leiden, Netherlands: Brill, 2011.

Nelson, Michael. *Resilient America: Electing Nixon in 1968, Channeling Dissent, and Dividing Government*. Lawrence: University Press of Kansas, 2014.

Neu, Charles E. *America's Lost War: Vietnam: 1945–1975*. Wheeling, IL: Harlan Davidson, 2005.

Neufeld, Jacob, and George M. Watson Jr., eds. *Coalition Air Warfare in the Korean War, 1950–1953*. Washington, DC: Air Force History and Museums Program, 2005.

Ngoei, Wen-Qing. *Arc of Containment: Britain, the United States, and Anticommunism in*

Southeast Asia. Ithaca, NY: Cornell University Press, 2019.
Nguyen, Lien-Hang T. *Hanoi's War: An International History of the War for Peace in Vietnam.* Chapel Hill: University of North Carolina Press, 2012.
Nichols, John B., and Barrett Tillman. *On Yankee Station: The Naval Air War over Vietnam.* Annapolis, MD: Naval Institute Press, 1987.
Nixon, Richard. *Public Papers of the Presidents of the United States, Richard Nixon: 1970: Containing the Public Messages, Speeches, and Statements of the President.* Ann Arbor: University of Michigan Library, 2005.
———. *RN: The Memoirs of Richard Nixon.* New York: Grosset & Dunlap, 1978.
"North Dikes Used for Guns, Storage." *Aviation Week and Space Technology* (August 28, 1972): 16–17.
O'Connor, Michael. *MiG Killers of Yankee Station.* Friendship, WI: New Past Press, 2003.
Olds, Robin, with Christina Olds and Ed Rasimus. *Fighter Pilot: The Memoirs of Legendary Ace Robin Olds.* New York: St. Martin's, 2010.
Olsen, John Andreas, ed. *Airpower Applied: U.S. NATO, and Israeli Combat Experience.* Annapolis, MD: Naval Institute Press, 2017.
———. *Strategic Air Power in Desert Storm.* Portland, OR: Frank Cass, 2003.
Osgood, Robert Endicott. *Limited War: The Challenge to American Security.* Chicago: University of Chicago Press, 1957.
Overy, Richard. *The Battle of Britain: The Myth and the Reality.* New York: W. W. Norton, 2000.
———. *The Bombers and the Bombed: Allied Air War over Europe, 1940–1945.* New York: Penguin Books, 2013.
———. *Why the Allies Won.* New York: W. W. Norton, 1995.
Owen, Robert C. *Air Mobility: A Brief History of the American Experience.* Washington, DC: Potomac Books, 2013.
Palmer, Bruce, Jr. *The 25-Year War: America's Military Role in Vietnam.* Lexington: University Press of Kentucky, 1984.
Palmer, Dave Richard. *The Summons of the Trumpet: U.S-Vietnam in Perspective.* San Rafael, CA: Presido Press, 1978.
Paret, Peter, ed., with the collaboration of Gordon A. Craig and Felix Gilbert. *Makers of Modern Strategy.* Princeton, NJ: Princeton University Press, 1986.
Parsons, Nels A., Jr. *Missiles and the Revolution in Warfare.* Cambridge, MA: Harvard University Press, 1962.
Patrick, Joe. "Testing the Rules of Engagement." *Vietnam* (December 1997): 46.
Pease, Harold. "Fighting with One Hand Tied Behind our Back in Vietnam and Afghanistan." August 25, 2010. http://libertyunderfire.org/2010/08/fighting-with-one-hand-tied-behind-our-back-in-vietnam-and-afghanistan/.
Pedersen, Dan. *Top Gun: An American Story.* New York: Hachette Books, 2019.
The Pentagon Papers: The Defense Department History of United States Decisionmaking on Vietnam, Volume III, Senator Gravel Edition. Boston: Beacon, 1975.
The Pentagon Papers. The Defense Department History of United States Decisionmaking on Vietnam, Volume IV. Boston: Beacon, 1975.
Perry, Mark. *Four Stars.* Boston: Houghton Mifflin, 1989.
Piowaty, John F. "Reflections of a Thud Driver." *Air University Review* (January–February 1983): 52–53.
Pollack, Kenneth M. *Arabs at War: Military Effectiveness, 1948–1991.* Lincoln: University of Nebraska Press, 2002.

Porter, Gareth. *A Peace Denied: The United States, Vietnam, and the Paris Agreement.* Bloomington: Indiana University Press, 1975.

Prados, John. *The Blood Road: The Ho Chi Minh Trail and the Vietnam War.* New York: John Wiley & Sons, 1999.

———. *Vietnam: The History of an Unwinnable War, 1945–1975.* Lawrence: University Press of Kansas, 2009.

Pretty, R. T., and D. H. R. Archer. *Jane's Weapons Systems.* London: Jane's, 1969.

Pribbenow, Merle L. "The Fog of War: The Vietnamese View of the Ia Drang Battle." *Military Review* (January–February 2001): 93–97.

"Protecting the Heart of the Delta." *Aviation Week and Space Technology* (January 25, 1960): 7.

Public Papers of the Presidents of the United States: Lyndon B. Johnson, Containing the Public Messages, Speeches, and Statements of the President, 1965. Book 1–January 1 to May 31, 1965. Washington, DC: United States Government Printing Office, 1966.

Pugh, James. *The Royal Flying Corps, the Western Front and the Control of the Air, 1914–1918.* New York: Routledge, 2017.

Rand, Christopher C. *Military Thought in Early China.* Albany: State University of New York Press, 2017.

Randolph, Stephen P. *Powerful and Brutal Weapons: Nixon, Kissinger, and the Easter Offensive.* Cambridge, MA: Harvard University Press, 2007.

Ray, John. *The Night Blitz, 1940–1941.* London: Arms and Armour, 1996.

Reardon, Carol. *Launch the Intruders: A Naval Attack Squadron in the Vietnam War, 1972.* Lawrence: University Press of Kansas, 2005.

Reeves, Richard. *President Nixon: Alone in the White House.* New York: Simon & Schuster, 2001.

Republic Aviation. "Getting Ready." *Flight International* (9 October 1959): 358.

Robarge, David. *Archangel: CIA's Supersonic A-12 Reconnaissance Aircraft*, 2nd ed. Washington, DC: Central Intelligence Agency, Center for the Study of Intelligence, 2012.

Robbins, James S. *This Time We Win: Revisiting the Tet Offensive.* New York: Encounter Books, 2010.

Samuel, Wolfgang W. E. *Glory Days: The Untold Story of the Men Who Flew the B-66 Destroyer into the Face of Fear.* Atglen, PA: Schiffer Military History, 2008.

———. *Warriors, Incredible Courage: The Declassified Stories of Cold War Reconnaissance Flights and the Men Who Flew Them.* Jackson: University Press of Mississippi, 2019.

Scales, Robert H., Jr. *Firepower in Limited War.* Washington, DC: National Defense University Press, 1990.

Schlight, John. *Help from Above: Air Force Close Air Support of the Army, 1946–1973.* Washington, DC: Office of Air Force History, 1988. Reprint, Washington, DC: Air Force History and Museums Program, 2003.

———. *The United States Air Force in Southeast Asia. The War in South Vietnam, The Years of the Offensive, 1965–1968.* Washington, DC: Office of Air Force History, 1988.

Schulzinger, Robert D. *A Time for War: The United States and Vietnam, 1941–1975.* New York: Oxford University Press, 1997.

Sellers, Jerry Jon, with contributions by William J. Astore, Robert B. Giffen, and Wiley J. Larson. *Understanding Space: An Introduction to Astronautics*, 2nd ed. New York: McGraw-Hill, 2000.

Sent, Esther-Mirjam. "Some Like It Cold: Thomas Schelling As a Cold Warrior." *Journal of*

Economic Methodology 14, no. 4 (December 2007): 455–71.
Shaplan, Robert. "Letter from Vietnam." *The New Yorker.* June 24, 1972, 70–90.
Shapley, Deborah. *Promise and Power: The Life and Times of Robert McNamara.* Boston: Little, Brown, 1993.
Sharp, U. S. Grant. *Strategy for Defeat: Vietnam in Retrospect.* San Rafael, CA: Presidio Press, 1978.
Shaw, John M. *The Cambodian Campaign: The 1970 Offensive and America's Vietnam War.* Lawrence: University Press of Kansas, 2005.
Sherman, William C. *Air Warfare.* New York: Ronald Press, 1926.
Sherwood, John Darrell. *Afterburner: Naval Aviators and the Vietnam War.* New York: New York University Press, 2004.
———. *Fast Movers: America's Jet Pilots and the Vietnam Experience.* New York: Free Press, 1999.
Shimko, Keith L. *The Iraq Wars and America's Military Revolution.* Cambridge: Cambridge University Press, 2010.
Simpson, Emile. *War from the Ground Up: Twenty-First Century Combat as Politics.* New York: Oxford University Press, 2013.
Slessor, J. C. *Air Power and Armies.* London: Oxford University Press, 1936.
Smith, John T. *The Linebacker Raids: The Bombing of North Vietnam, 1972.* London: Arms and Armour, 1998.
Sorley, Lewis. *A Better War: The Unexamined Victories and Final Tragedy of America's Last Years in Vietnam.* New York: Harcourt Brace, 1999.
———. *Honorable Warrior: General Harold K. Johnson and the Ethics of Command.* Lawrence: University Press of Kansas, 1998.
Stanton, Shelby. *The Rise and Fall of an American Army: U.S. Ground Forces in Vietnam, 1965–1973.* Novato, CA: Presidio, 1985.
Stephens, Alan. *The Royal Australian Air Force: A History.* South Melbourne: Oxford University Press, 2006.
Stoler, Mark A. *The Joint Chiefs of Staff, the Grand Alliance, and U.S. Strategy in World War II.* Chapel Hill: University of North Carolina Press, 2000.
Summers, Harry G. *On Strategy: A Critical Analysis of the Vietnam War.* Novato, CA: Presidio, 1982.
Taylor, Keith. *The Birth of Vietnam.* Berkeley: University of California Press, 1983.
Taylor, Keith W., and John K. Whitmore, eds. *Essays into Vietnamese Pasts.* Ithaca, NY: Southeast Asia Program, Cornell University, 1995.
Terraine, John. *A Time for Courage: The Royal Air Force in the European War, 1939–1945.* New York: Macmillan, 1985.
Thompson, Robert. *Peace Is Not at Hand.* New York: David McCay, 1974.
Thompson, W. Scott, and Donald D. Frizzell, eds. *The Lessons of Vietnam.* New York: Crane, Russak, 1977.
Thompson, Wayne. *To Hanoi and Back: The U.S. Air Force and North Vietnam, 1966–1973.* Washington, DC: Smithsonian Institution Press, 2000.
Thornborough, Anthony M. *USAF Phantoms.* London: Arms & Armour, 1988.
Tillman, Barrett. *MiG Master: The Story of the F-8 Crusader.* Annapolis, MD: Nautical and Aviation Publishing, 1980.
Tin, Bui. "How North Vietnam Won the War." *The Wall Street Journal,* August 3, 1995: A-8.
Toperczer, Istvan. *Air War over North Vietnam: The Vietnamese People's Air Force:*

1949–1975. Carrollton, TX: Squadron/Signal, 1998.
Trest, Warren A. *Air Commando One: Heinie Aderholt and America's Secret Air Wars*. Washington, DC: Smithsonian Institution Press, 2000.
Truong, Ngo Quang. *The Easter Offensive of 1972*. Washington, DC: U.S. Army Center of Military History, 1977.
Tuttle, Jerry O. Letters to the Editor. "A-4/A-7 Comparison." *Aviation Week and Space Technology*, July 10, 1972, 58.
Ulanoff, Stanley. *Fighter Pilot*. Garden City, NY: Doubleday, 1962.
———. *Illustrated Guide to U.S. Missiles and Rockets*. Garden City, NY: Doubleday, 1959.
"U.S. Guided Bombs Alter War." *Aviation Week and Space Technology* (May 22, 1972): 16–17.
Van Atta, Dale. *With Honor: Melvin Laird in War, Peace, and Politics*. Madison: University of Wisconsin Press, 2008.
Van Staaveren, Jacob. *Gradual Failure: The Air War over North Vietnam, 1965–1966*. Washington, DC: Air Force History and Museums Program, 2002.
———. *The United States Air Force in Southeast Asia: Interdiction in Southern Laos, 1960–1968*. Washington, DC: Center for Air Force History, 1993.
Vandiver, Frank E. *Shadows of Vietnam: Lyndon Johnson's Wars*. College Station: Texas A&M University Press, 1997.
Villard, Erik B. *The United States Army in Vietnam. Combat Operations: Staying the Course, October 1967 to September 1968*. Washington, DC: Center of Military, United States Army, 2017.
von Clausewitz, Carl. *On War*. Translated and edited by Michael Howard and Peter Paret. Princeton, NJ: Princeton University Press, 1976.
Wagner, Ray. *American Combat Planes*. Garden City, NY: Doubleday, 1968.
Wagner, William. *Lightning Bugs and Other Reconnaissance Drones*. Fallbrook, CA: Aero, 1982.
Walzer, Michael. *Just and Unjust Wars: A Moral Argument with Historical Illustrations*. New York: Basic Books, 1977.
Warner, Philip. *Sieges of the Middle Ages*. London: G. Bell, 1968.
Weaver, Michael E. "An Examination of the F-8 Crusader through Archival Sources," *Journal of Aeronautical History* (2018): 63–85.
———. "International Cooperation and Bureaucratic In-Fighting: American and British Economic Intelligence Sharing and the Strategic Bombing of Germany, 1939–41." *Intelligence and National Security* 23, no. 2 (April 2008): 153–75.
———. "Missed Opportunities before Top Gun and Red Flag." *Air Power History* (Winter 2013): 21–27.
Webb, Willard J. *History of the Joint Chiefs of Staff: The Joint Chiefs of Staff and the War in Vietnam, 1969–1970*. Washington, DC: Office of Joint History, 2002.
Webb, Willard J., and Walter S. Poole. *History of the Joint Chiefs of Staff. The Joint Chiefs of Staff and the War in Vietnam, 1971–1973*. Washington, DC: Office of Joint History, 2007.
Weigley, Russell F. *The Age of Battles: The Quest for Decisive Warfare from Breitenfeld to Waterloo*. Bloomington: Indiana University Press, 1991.
———. *The American Way of War: A History of United States Military Strategy and Policy*. New York: Macmillan, 1973.
———. *Eisenhower's Lieutenants: The Campaign of France and Germany, 1944–1945*. Bloomington: Indiana University Press, 1981.

Weinberg, Gerhard L. *A World at Arms: A Global History of World War II.* Cambridge: Cambridge University Press, 1994.
Werrell, Kenneth P. *Sabres over MiG Alley: The F-86 and the Battle for Air Superiority in Korea.* Annapolis, MD: Naval Institute Press, 2005.
Westrum, Ron. *Sidewinder: Creative Missile Development at China Lake.* Annapolis, MD: Naval Institute Press, 1999.
Wiest, Andrew. *Vietnam's Forgotten Army: Heroism and Betrayal in the ARVN.* New York: New York University Press, 2008.
Willbanks, James H. *Abandoning Vietnam: How America Left and South Vietnam Lost Its War.* Lawrence: University Press of Kansas, 2004.
———. *The Battle of An Loc.* Bloomington: Indiana University Press, 2005.
———. *A Raid Too Far: Operation Lam Son and Vietnamization in Laos.* College Station: Texas A&M University Press, 2014.
———. *The Tet Offensive: A Concise History.* New York: Columbia University Press, 2007.
Wilcox, Robert K. *Scream of Eagles: The Creation of Top Gun and the U.S. Air Victory in Vietnam.* New York: John Wiley, 1990.
Wilkins, Warren. *Grab Their Belts to Fight Them: The Viet Cong's Big-Unit War against the U.S., 1965–1966.* Annapolis, MD: Naval Institute Press, 2011.
Wilson, George C. "Officials Split on Bombing: Key Issue Is What U.S. Can Attain." *The Washington Post*, December 21, 1972.
Witkin, Richard. "Accurate 'Smart Bombs' Guided to Objectives by TV or Laser." *The New York Times*, May 24, 1972.
Woods, Randall B. *LBJ: Architect of American Ambition.* New York: Free Press, 2006.
Wouk, Jordan. Letter to the Editor. "Magic Dragon's Not-So-Innocuous Puff." *The New York Times*, October 11, 1984.
Zhai, Qiang. *China and the Vietnam Wars, 1950–1975.* Chapel Hill: University of North Carolina Press, 2000.
Zhang, Xiaoming. *Red Wings over the Yalu: China, the Soviet Union, and the Air War in Korea.* College Station: Texas A&M University Press, 2002.
Zucchino, David. "Fight to Vindicate General Dies in the Senate." *Los Angeles Times*, December 23, 2010.

Index

Note: Entry numbers referring to images are in italics.

1st Cavalry Division, 165, 172, 189
1st Infantry Division, 202
1st Marine Aircraft Wing, 332
2nd Air Division, 26, 44, 69, 72, 146, 185, 258, 261, 264, 347, 350
2nd Battalion of the 28th Infantry, 187
3rd Air Division, 229, 338
3rd Marine Combat Battalion Landing Team, 159–60
3rd Tactical Fighter Wing, 202
4th Marine Regiment, 251
5th ARVN Division, 187, 189
5th Cavalry Regiment, 187
5th Special Forces Group, 173
7th Cavalry Regiment, 198
8th Special Operations Squadron, 202
8th Tactical Fighter Wing, 30–31, 76–77, 378
9th Light Infantry Division, 195, 241
11th Tactical Reconnaissance Squadron, 153
14th Tactical Reconnaissance Squadron, 135
15th Infantry Regiment, 242
17th Air Division, 396
17th Wild Weasel Squadron, 56
24th Army Corps, 132
25th Infantry Division, 172, 209
26th Marine Regiment, 170
28th Infantry Regiment, 187
32nd ARVN Regiment, 188
50th Tactical Airlift Squadron, 181
53rd Fighter Squadron, 83
81st Airborne Ranger Battalion, 209
91st Bombardment Wing, 217
93rd Battalion, 198
101st Airborne Division, 174, 178, 208
173rd Airborne Brigade, 174
307th Strategic Bombardment Wing, 223, 398
314th Troop Carrier Wing, 168
315th Air Commando Wing, 163, 169, 172
315th Tactical Airlift Wing, 161, 163
345th Tactical Airlift Squadron, 171
355th Tactical Fighter Wing, 18, 290
366th Tactical Fighter Wing, 76–77, 92, 191
374th Tactical Airlift

INDEX

Wing, 179, 180
388th Tactical Fighter Wing, 18, 57, 290
391st Tactical Fighter Squadron, 68
432nd Tactical Reconnaissance Wing, 70, 74, 98, 104, 105, 110, 134, 142, 146, 147, 149, 378
435th Tactical Fighter Squadron, 64
436th Tactical Fighter Squadron, 64
460th Tactical Reconnaissance Wing, 149–50
469th Tactical Fighter Squadron, 95
476th Tactical Fighter Squadron, 64
479th Tactical Fighter Wing, 64, 89–90
483rd Tactical Airlift Wing, 175
502nd Infantry Regiment, 190
509th Fighter-Interceptor Squadron, 61
831st Air Division, 102
834th Air Division, 163, 165, 169
4133rd Bombardment Wing, 219
4258th Strategic Wing, 18, 195, 230
4477th Test and Evaluation Squadron ("Red Eagles"), 74

A-1 Skyraider, 173, 185, 195, 201, 205, 208, 247, 328, 329, 333
A-3 Skywarrior, 292
A-4 Skyhawk, 17, 188, 203, 328, 329, 333, *334*
   A-4C Skyhawk, 17, 31, 32, 72, 291
   A-4E Skyhawk, 17, 19, 27, 31, 44, 48, 49, 51, 84, 203, *203*, 291, 296, 315, 330, 335
   A-4F Skyhawk, 242, 290–91, 334, 379
A-6 Intruder, 17, 52
   A-6A Intruder, 32, 35, 44, 56, 58, 60, 94, 98, 141, 187, 192, 195, 205, 251, 280, 288, 292, 295, 301, 320, 322, 329, 330–33, 351, 361, 366, 368–69, 378, 382, 384–85, 391, 393, 407
   A-6B Intruder, 52, 333
   A-6C Intruder, 372
A-7 Corsair, 98, 145, 188, 203–4, *204*, 334–35
   A-7A Corsair, 154, 204, 329, 332
   A-7D Corsair, 37, 120, 156, 205, 250, 283, 391, 395–96, 401
   A-7E Corsair, 17, 60, 204, 336, 379
A-12 Blackbird, 46, 135, 136, 464
A-26, 293, 328, 329
A-37 Dragonfly, 181, 202, 247
AA-1 Alkali guided missile, 73
Abrams, Creighton W.
   airfield bombing, 35
   air interdiction, 315, 316, 376
   airlift, 178, 181
   Arc Light missions, 197, 212, 213, 217, 219, 233, 243
   Cambodia, bombing of sanctuaries, 232, 233, 234, 235
   close air support, 231, 250–51
   Easter Offensive, 240, 242, 243, 245, 246, 360, 365
   Nguyen Hue Offensive, 376
   Nixon loses confidence, 362–63
   North Vietnamese Air Force, 99
   Operation Commando Hunt, 324
   Operation Rolling Thunder, 54, 318
   photo reconnaissance, 132
   rules of engagement, 357
   suppression of enemy air defenses (SEAD), 54, 358
AC-47, 199, 208, 329
AC-119 Shadow, 175, 180, 328
   AC-119G Shadow, 199–200
   AC-119K Shadow, 328–29
AC-130 Spectre, 40, 54, 180, 181, 191, 200–201, 328, 329, 330
Acheson, Dean, 264
adverse weather aerial delivery system (AWADS), 180–81, 182
aerial reconnaissance. *See* photo reconnaissance
aerial refueling, *13, 52, 268*
   background to Vietnam War, 11–12
   as enabling air operations, 12–20
   importance, 7
AGM-12 Bullpup, 315,

590

322, 334–35
AGM-45 Shrike, 48, 49, 51, 56–57
AGM-62 Walleye, 335–36, 373
    AGM-62 II Walleye, 336
AGM-78 Standard ARM, 51–52, 57
AH-1 Cobras, 201, 205, 243, 245
AIM-4 Falcon, 84, *89*, 92–93
    AIM-4D Falcon, 86, 88–90, 108
AIM-7 Sparrow, 84–88, *85*, 90, 92, 101–2, 108
    AIM-7D Sparrow, 67, 68, 84–85, 87, 445
    AIM-7E-2 Sparrow, 100–101, 108, 110
    AIM-7E Sparrow, 70, 76, 84–86, 87–88
AIM-9 Sidewinder, 84, 92, 293
    AIM-9B Sidewinder, 63, 66, 67, 79, 85, 86, 88–89, 90, 100, 106, 438
    AIM-9D Sidewinder, 87, 90, 91
    AIM-9E Sidewinder, 90, 92, 100, 106, 108
    AIM-9G Sidewinder, 106, 107
    AIM-9H Sidewinder, 107
    AIM-9J Sidewinder, 106–7, 108, 110
air ambush, 251–52
"Air America" covert war, 185, 255
air combat maneuvering (ACM), 61, 66, 67–68, 107, 118
air combat training, 67–68, 95–97, 122. *See also* air-to-air combat
aircraft cannon, 15, 40, 62, 64, 90–92, 102, 104, 108, 190, 191, 200, 201, 204
aircraft carriers, 3, 13, 16, 19, 69, 83, 103, 241, 258, 267, 325, 361, 365, 398
Air Defense Command, 97, 105, 122
airfields
    Bac Mai Airfield, 27, 34, 36, 77, 110
    Bai Thuong Airfield, 29, 31, 35, 36, 37, 83, 98
    Ban Me Thuot, 174
    Bien Hoa Air Base, 160, 257, 261, 272
    bombing, 26–38, 302, 351–52
    Ching Chuan Kang Air Base, 17, 18, 164
    Chu Lai, 267
    Clark Air Base, 19, 164, 167
    Da Nang Air Base, 15, 16, 28, 34, 61, 64, 76, 159, 170, 177, 178, 203, 248, 268, 332
    Dong Hoi Airfield, 26, 27, 35, 36, 98, 138, 364
    Don Muang Air Base, 18, 19, 61
    Don Muang/Bangkok International Airport, 18, 19, 61
    Haiphong Kien Airfield, 31
    Hoa Lac Airfield, 30–31, 37, 300, 332, 391
    Kadena Air Base, 13, 17, 18, 19, 136
    Kep Airfield, 27, 29, 30, 31, 32, 36, 37, 77, 79, 85, 107, 134, 300, 384, 405
    Kien An Airfield, 27, 31, 34, 36, 391
    Korat Air Base, 19, 48, 205, 395
    Naha Air Base, 164, 167
    Nakhon Phanom Air Base, 112, 115, 399
    Nhon Co Airfield, 168
    North Vietnam, *64*
    Phuc Yen Air Base, 25, 26, 27, 28–29, 30, 32–34, 36, 37, 55, 77, 78, 79, 81, 113, 139, 257, 297, 302, 352, 392, 398, 405
    Pleiku, 159, 219, 246, 257, 265
    Southeast Asia, *24*
    South Vietnam, *186*
    Takhli Air Base, 17, 18, 19, 160, 382
    Tan Son Nhut Air Base, 61, 150, 156, 167, 169
    Thailand, 13, 18, 39, 42, 61, 62, 64, 95, 112, 129, 205, 209, 241, 257, 267, 270, 301, 322, 413
    Udorn Air Base, 61, 64, 100, 101, 115, 121, 145, 148
    U-Tapao Air Base, 17, 18, 209, 395, 396, 398
    Vinh Airfield, 26, 27, 35, 36, 37, 56, 83, 95, 98, 308, 362, 364, 384
    Yen Bai Airfield, 36, 37
Air Force, (South Vietnamese), 39, 155, 205, 210, 242, 245, 249, 265, 364
Air Force Historical Research Agency, 5
Air Force History Studies Division, 5
airlift, 158–69, 407
    assault airlift, 167, 171
    Easter Offensive (1972), 179–83

responsiveness, 160–61, 166, 169, 170, 177
Tet Offensive, 169–78
air power
  effective and unrestricted, 344
  effectiveness in Vietnam War, 3–5, 19, 20, 25, 62, 118, 123, 155, 176, 185, 188, 190, 194, 196, 210, 213, 221, 225, 227, 228, 229, 231, 232, 235, 236, 237, 238, 239, 240, 241, 242, 246, 250, 257, 260–61, 263, 269, 270, 273, 277, 283, 284, 286, 301, 303, 310, 311, 317, 319, 321, 324, 325, 342, 343, 344, 346, 352, 354, 359–60, 364, 371, 375, 378, 380, 402, 403, 407–13
  geopolitics, 409–11
  and ground warfare, 6–7
  importance to US defense, 3
  Nguyen Hue Offensive, 375
  policy goals, achievement of, 311–12
  restrictions, 270–71
air strikes against ground forces. *See* close air support
air superiority
  airfield bombing, 21–38
  antiaircraft artillery and surface-to-air missiles, 39–60
  fight for, 72–83
  MiGs, shooting down, 61–71
  Operation Linebacker I, 100–108
  Operation Linebacker II, 120–23
  refinements, 94–99
  technology, organization, and management of, mission, 109–19
  threat level management, 119
air-to-air combat, 62–63, 72, 94–95, 102. *See also* air combat training
air-to-air missile kill probability, 84, 87, 92–93, 95, 107
air-to-air missiles, 24, 72, 84, 87, 92, 95, 102, 293
  Charging Sparrow, 87
air transport. *See* airlift
Allison, Clark H., 154
ALQ-51 ECM suite, 75, 141
ALQ-72 jamming pod, 151
ALT-6B jammer, 393, 402
ALT-22 jammer, 393, 402
ALT-28 jammer, 49, 364, 395
Amos, T. H., 15
Anderson, George W., Jr., 324
Andraitis, Arthur, 146–47
An Loc, 171, 175, 179–80, 181, 182, 183, 192, 199, 200, 242–44, 246, 248, 371
antiaircraft artillery, 25, 26, 28, 37, 38, 39–40, 41, 42, 44, 46–47, 49, 53, 55, 71, 73, 79, 98, 131, 133, 140, 142, 145, 152, 165, 171, 181, 200, 206, 218, 238, 255, 276, 291, 306, 329, 330, 335, 337, 346, 373, 384, 407
  air superiority in presence of, 39–60
  Easter Offensive (1972), 181
  photo reconnaissance, 153
anti-radiation missile (ARM), 47–49, 51–52
Ap Tau O, 193
APX-80 air-to-air interrogator, 100
AQM-34L, 131, 138
Arc Light missions, 194, 209, 210–26, 228–31, 243, 327, 392
Arends, Leslie, 233
Army of the Republic of Vietnam (ARVN, South Vietnamese Army), 101, 132, 160, 164, 170, 174, 178, 179, 181, 182, 185, 187, 188, 189, 191, 192, 195, 196, 200–201, 206, 211, 213, 214, 219, 221, 231, 235, 236, 237–38, 239, 240, 241–46, 247, 248, 249, 250, 286, 306, 323, 327, 360, 361, 365, 366, 371, 376, 378, 380–82, 394, 408
A Shau Valley, 171, 173, 174, 188, 189, 195
Aubrac, Raymond, 296
Ault, Frank, 97
Aust, Abner M., Jr., 66
AWG-10 pulse-Doppler radar, 96

B-26K Invader, 329, 543
B-29s, 22
B-52
  aerial refueling, 12–13, *13*
  airfield bombing, 28–29
  Arc Light missions,

INDEX

210–26, 229–31
B-52D, 211, *392*, 393, 398
B-52F, 211
B-52G, 398
   Cambodia, bombing of sanctuaries, 235–36, 237
   capabilities, 388
   close air support, 188, 194, 209
   Easter Offensive, 240–42, 243, 244, 245, 248–49, 361, 368, 370–71
   Iron Hand missions, 58
   Khe Sanh, siege of, 227, 228
   missile sites, destruction, 43, 44
   Operation Commando Hunt, 327
   Operation Freedom Porch Bravo, 362
   Operation Linebacker II, 120–21, 389–90, 392–93, 394–401, 402, 404
   Operation Rolling Thunder, 291
   strengths and weaknesses, 370
   suppression of enemy air defenses, 46
   Tet Offensive, 231
B-57, 185, 328, 329
Bac Giang Thermal Power Plant, 295
Baez, Joan, 355
Bai Thuong Airfield, 29, 31, 35, 36, 37, 83, 98
Baker, Walter T., 16
Ball, George, 257, 263, 264, 265, 273
Ban Ken Bridge, 39
Bankson, Roger R., 194
Battle of Duc Lap (1968), 187, 208
Bau Bang, 189

Beardsley, Clarence, 174
Bekka Valley, 22
Bell, James M., 107
Bell, Warren, 413
Ben Cat, 211–12
Ben Het, 174
Benson, Larry L., 151
Bien Hoa Air Base, 160, 257, 261, 272
Bihn Duong Province, 218
Binh Dinh, 208
Binh Gia, 185
Binh Thuan Province, 185
black boxes, 19, 48, 52, 65, 80, 292, 331, 332, 431
Blake, Robert E., 86–87
Blesse, Frederick C., 92, 110
Blood, Gordon F., 159
Bluhm, Raymond K., 196
Bodenhamer, Howard L., 15–16
Bo Duc, 189, 191
body count, 4, 187, 196, 210, 211, 216, 219, 221, 222, 223, 224, 225, 237, 242
Boles, John K., Jr., 186, 216
bomb damage assessment (BDA), 35, 128, 134–35, 145, 148, 149, 155, 156, 195, 196, 210, 213, 216, 219, 220, 223–24, 225–26, 231, 233, 241, 281, 291, 327, 337–38, 372
bomb shortage, 407
bombing
   airfields, 26–38, 302, 351–52
   "Buddy bombing," 291

   cessation, 272, 277–79, 303, 307–10, 316–17, 318, 321, 357, 384, 386–88
   choke points and bottlenecks, 133, 282, 314, 316, 326, 377
   comprehensive, 262–63
   Easter Offensive, 360–85
   fuel storage sites, 286–87
   Ho Chi Minh Trail, 279–84, 287–88, 293
   inadequacy, 381
   jettisoning of bombs, forced, 29, 32, 33, 41, 74, 75, 78–79, 92, 103, 111, 119
   limited, 262
   night, 260, 280, 292, 293, 314, 382
   North Vietnam, 261–72
   Operation Linebacker II, 389–90
   pauses, 277, 278, 303
   railroad yards, 78, 308, 314, 364, 367, 371, 389, 397, 401, 405
   renewing, 317, 321
   strategic, 6, 258, 260–61, 409
   before Vietnam War, 260–61
   visual dive bombing, 290–91
bomb-the-hell-out-of-them argument, 257, 277, 344, 347, 353, 359, 371, 405, 408, 410
bottlenecks, 282, 314
BQM-34A "Firebee" target drones, 96, 137–38
Brezhnev, Leonid, 362, 365–66, 367, 368, 371
Bricker, James W., 188
Brigham, Robert, 406
Brookbank, David, 195

INDEX

Brown, George S., 288, 316, 319
Brown, Harold, 29
Bruce, David K. E., 43, 133
Bu Dop Special Forces Camp, 172, 187
Bui The Lan, 193
Bui Tin, 343
Bundy, McGeorge, 256, 257, 258, 261–62, 265, 266, 269, 273, 296
Bundy, William P., 32, 257, 261, 277, 278, 297, 302
Bunker, Ellsworth, 226, 231, 307, 318
bunkers, 215–16
Burns, John J., 118
Buse, Henry W., 311
Byrd, Robert, 304

C-7 Caribou, 162, 165–66, *166*, 168, 171, 174, 175, 176
C-47 Dakota, 158, 182, 199
C-123 Provider, 59, 158, 160, 161, 162, 163, 165, 166, 171, 172, 173, 174, 175, 176, 178, 179, 180, 182, 293
    C-123B Provider, 166
    C-123K Provider, 166
C-130 Hercules, 65, 112, 138, 158, 159, 160, 161, 162, 163, 164, 165, 166–67, 168, 169, 170, 171, 172–73, 174, 175, 176, 177, 178, 179–80, 181–82
    C-130A Hercules, 167
    C-130B Hercules, 169
    C-130E Hercules, 169

C-141 Starlifter, 76, 158, 179, 182
Cambodia
    geopolitical significance, 257
    incursions, 132, 175, 177, 178, 182, 210, 239, 252, 310, 347
    North Vietnamese activity in, 133, 143, 223, 232, 240, 248, 301, 315, 323, 340–42, 343
    Operation Commando Hunt, 324–25
    rules of engagement, 356–57
    sanctuaries, bombing, 231–36, 283, 325, 356, 357
Cameron, Max, 72
Carl, Marion E., 206
Carrier Air Wing 1, 71, 88, 334
Carrier Air Wing 2, 96, 145, 204, 291, 332
Carrier Air Wing 6, 56, 82, 96, 129, 153, 331
Carrier Air Wing 8, 58, 145, 157
Carrier Air Wing 9, 70, 330–31, 333, 335
Carrier Air Wing 11, 82, 204, 379
Carrier Air Wing 14, 46–47, 51, 70, 75, 85, 86, 87, 204, 282, 334
Carrier Air Wing 15, 330–31, 379
Carrier Air Wing 17, 82
Casteel, John H., 16
CBU-24 cluster bombs, 29, 30, 34, 37, 40, 49, 56, 57, 58, 134, 188, 202, 207, 239, 327, 346

Central Intelligence Agency (CIA), 269, 272, 280–81, 303, 380
Central Office South Vietnam (COSVN), 232, 233, 235–36
Cessna O-1 Bird Dog, 134, 198
Cessna O-2 Skymaster, 59, 98, 198, 356
CH-3, 138
Chaffee, John H., 251
Chairsell, William S., 53
China
    buffer zone, 31, 65, 80, 101, 156, 284, 299, 300, 346, 351
    confrontations with American aircraft, 27
    North Vietnam, support, 408, 409
    North Vietnamese policy, influencing, 360, 405
    Operation Rolling Thunder, impact, 305
    sanctuary for North Vietnamese aircraft, 33
    threat of entering the war, 263–64, 349, 350
Ching Chuan Kang Air Base, 17, 18, 164
choke points, 133, 282, 314, 316, 326, 377
Chuong Thien, 241
Chup Operation, 178
Churchill, Winston, 21
civilian casualties, 32, 33, 128, 175, 270, 273, 286, 288, 289, 290, 297, 300, 306, 322, 348–49, 354–55
Civilian Irregular Defense

Group outposts, 170, 175, 176, 193, 195, 224
Clark Air Base, 19, 164, 167
Clay, Lucius D., Jr., 109–10, 370, 372, 374, 379, 386, 400
Clifford, Clark, 44, 182, 272, 279, 284, 304, 307, 308, 310, 356
Clodfelter, Mark, 405, 408
close air support, 6, 184–95, 250–52, 407
   Arc Light missions, 210–26
   Easter Offensive, 240–50
   effectiveness, 6, 101, 195–98, 408
   implements, 198–207
   Khe Sanh, siege of, 226–31
   lessons, 408
   Operation Lam Son 719, 237–39
   responsiveness, 207–10, 249
   targeting intelligence, 216–17
   after Tet Offensive, 231–37
coercion, 5, 255–60
   bombing North Vietnam, 20, 57, 62, 257, 261–72, 278, 283, 284, 285, 296, 297, 302, 304, 310, 311–12, 314, 365, 368, 376–78, 380, 386, 388–90, 395, 400, 403, 405–6, 411
   bombing theory and practice before Vietnam War, 260–61
   defined, 6
   Ho Chi Minh Trail, bombing effectiveness, 279–84
   Operation Rolling Thunder, 284–89, 294–312
   presidential policy, implements, 290–94
   timing and complexity, 272–79
Cohen, Elliot A., 375
Collins, Arthur S., Jr., 189
Collins, Joseph, 210, 216
Colvin, John, 302, 413
Combat Lightning, 113
Combat Sage, 87
combat training. *See* air combat training
Combat Tree system, 100, 104, 109, 110, 117, 118, 122, 378
Commander-in-Chief of the US Pacific Fleet (CINCPAC), 42, 83, 210, 230–31, 274, 280, 289, 294, 302, 395, 403–4
Commando Sabre, 199
communications intelligence data, 112–14, 116–18
Connally, John, 366
Connelly, Daniel, 188
Con Thien, 174, 219, 221–22
Cooper, Chester, 262–63
Corder, John A., 34
Cunningham, Randy, 97, 102
Cushing, Emery G., 352
Cushman, Robert E., 220, 226, 227–28, 229, 311

Daddis, Gregory, 272
Dak Pek, 174, 201
Dak Seang, 174, 175, 191
Dallek, Robert, 406
Da Nang Air Base, 15, 16, 28, 34, 61, 64, 76, 159, 170, 177, 178, 203, 248, 268, 332
Darrow, W. K., 85
Davies, William J., 151
Davis, Raymond G., 175, 193, 210, 216
Dawson, Alan, 400
DC-130, 138, 156
DeBellevue, Charles B., 106
DePuy, William E., 191
Dien Bien Phu, 26, 27, 158, 173, 175, 177, 194, 227
diplomacy, 30, 303, 310–11, 377, 380–81, 382, 386–88, 390–91, 411. *See also* negotiations; statecraft
direct attack, 184, 192, 196, 210, 211, 232, 233, 252, 357
Dirksen, Everett, 233
Disosway, Gabriel P., 94
dissimilar air combat tactics training (DACT), 66, 95, 97
dive bombing, visual, 48, 55, 204, 240, 276, 290–91, 351, 369, 374
Dobrynin, Anatoly, 227–28, 318, 365–66, 368
dogfighting, 68, 88, 102. *See also* air combat training; air-to-air combat
Don Muang Air Base, 18, 19, 61

Dong Hoi Airfield, 26, 27, 35, 36, 98, 138, 364
Dong Phong Thuong Railroad Bridge, 298
Dong Xoai, 187
Dorsett, Tracy K., 34
Douhet, Giulio, 260, 420
Driscoll, Willie, 102
drogue (aerial refueling), 18, 49
drones, 96, 136–39, 147, 152, 156–57
Duc Co, 187
Duc Lap, 187–88
Duc Thanh, 182
Dunham, W. D., 148

E-1B Tracer, 82
E-2 Hawkeye, 81, 82, *82*, 143
EA-6A, 50, 152, 364
EA-6B, 50, 60, 395
Eade, George J., 20, 388, 403
EAK-3, 51
Easter Offensive (1972), 179–83, 188, 193, 240–50, 360–85
EB-66, 49–50, 76, 121, 291, 292, 378
EC-121, 44, 61, 64, 65, 68, 80–82, 112, 113, 115, 117, 121, 355
   EC-121D, 80–81
   EC-121K, 81
   EC-121M, 79
EF-10 Skynight, 50
"Effects of Air Operations in Southeast Asia," 288
Eighth Air Force, 209, 218, 327, 392, 396, 402
Eisenhower, Dwight D., 26

Elbert, Edward A., 199
electronic countermeasures (ECM), 46, 50, 53–54, 55, 74, 75, 77–79, 119, 120, 151, 155, 290, 382, 393, 395, 396, 398
   chaff, 46, 52, 55, 103, 110–11, 116, 117, 118, 122, 153, 333, 378, 382, 383, 384, 395, 397, 398, 399, 400, 402
electronic countermeasures aircraft, 46, 49–50, 53, 60, 102, 152, 364, 395
Elfin, Mel, 390
Ellington, Robert F., 163
Ellison, J. D., 90
Ellsberg, Daniel, 233
emergency airlift request system (EARS), 169
enemy aircraft, destruction on ground, 21–38
engagement, restrictions and rules, 344–59
Ervin, Sam, 278
Evans, J., Jr., 280
Evers, Ross C., 15

F-4 Phantom
   aerial combat training, 67–68
   aerial refueling, 13
   airfield bombing, 36, 37
   close air support, 202–3, 251–52
   F-4B Phantom, 27, 31, 62, 67, 68, 70, 75, 85–86, 87, 91, 94, 107, 197, 206
   F-4C Phantom, 12, 15, 16, 27, 29, 31, 32, 43, 48, 49, 52, 53, 62, 64, 65, 66, 67, 72, 76, 77, 84, 85, 87, 89, 90, 91, 92, 94, 203, 290
   F-4D Phantom, 32, 34, 35, 40, 86, 88, 89, 92, 100, 102, 107, 109, 117, 133, 191, 199, 291, 335, 370, 371, 379, 383
   F-4E Phantom, 56, 65, 66, 74, 92, 94, 95, 100, 102, 109–10, 114, 116, 117, 119, 121, 191, 330
   F-4J Phantom, 41, 60, 70–71, 83, 96, 102, 107, 114, 121, 379
   laser-guided bombs, 37, 40, 199, 202, 239, 245, 247, 325, 330, 370, 372, 373, 374, 379, 383, 391
   loss rate, 53, 96, 114, 115, 333
   versus MiGs, 29, 70–71, 72, 74, 107, 111
   Operation Bolo, 76–77
   Operation Linebacker I, 103–4, 105
   Operation Linebacker II, 121, 391, 397
   Operation Rolling Thunder, 291
   suppression of enemy air defenses, 46, 60
   Teaball, 116–18
F-8 Crusader, 16, 17, 26, 31, 33, 52, 62, 66, 74, 86, 90–91, 94, 95, 96–97, 119, 137, 203, 293, 328, 333
   F-8E Crusader, 26, 31, 62, 91, 94
F-15 Eagle, 22, 94, 122
F-100 Super Sabre, 39, 66, 72, 143, 185, 187, 190, 238
   F-100D Super Sabre, 62, *63*, 201–3
   F-100F Super Sabre, 48, 49, 199
F-102 Delta Dagger,

61–62, 293
F-104A Starfighter, *81*
F-104C Starfighter, 63–66, *65*, 91
F-105 Thunderchief, *292*
  aerial combat training, 67–68
  aerial refueling, 15, 16, 18
  versus antiaircraft artillery, 39, 46, 53, 72
  F-105D Thunderchief, 12, 15, 16, 18, 19, 26, 29, 31, 32, 33, 39, 44, 46, 48, 49, 52, 53, 61, 64, 66, 67, 72–76, 78, 79, 91, 92, 94, 119, 143, 160, 190, 267, *268*, 268, 290–91, 292, 328, 330, 336, 391
  F-105F Thunderchief, 30, 49, 52, 293
  F-105G Thunderchief, 15, 51, *52*, 52, 56, 102, 105, 378
  Ho Chi Minh Trail, aerial siege, 328
  Momyer ruse, 79
  Operation Bolo, 76
  Operation Rolling Thunder, 267, 268, 290
  "Thunderstick," 292–93
F-111A Aardvark, 58, 333–34, 382–84, 398–99, 401–2, 406
failure of war, 7, 304, 359, 387, 407, 410–11
Feinstein, Jeffrey, 117
fighter combat, significance, 21–38
Fighter Weapons School (Nellis Air Force Base), 68, 109, 110
First World War. *See* World War I
flares, 148–49, 171, 189,
293, 357
flashbulbs, 141, 149
Fobair, Roscoe, H., 43
food shortages, 275, 324–25, 341
Forces Armées Nationales Khmères (FANK), 239, 356
Ford, Gerald, 233
Foreign Relations of the United States series, 5, 6
formations, flight, 52, 54, 96, 97–98, 153
Fortas, Abe, 304
forward air controllers (FAC), 59, 98, 149–50, 188, 189, 191, 192, 193, 196, 197, 198, 199, 203, 204, 205, 209, 211, 247, 356
fratricide, 42, 68–71, 100–101, 188, 190–91, 200, 205, 330, 428
Fubini, Gene, 50
fuel, movement, 315
fuel storage sites, bombing, 286–87
Fulbright, J. William, 307
fuse extenders, 207

game theory, 341
Gayler, Noel, 59, 111–12, 114, 377, 386, 387, 390, 394, 397, 399
GCI radars, 53, 80, 98, 99, 144
General Offensive-General Uprising. *See* Tet Offensive
Geneva Accords, 345–46
geopolitics, 3, 6, 25, 27,
123, 266, 293, 409–11
George, S. W., 86–87
Gillem, Alvan C., 229–30
Gillespie, Paul, 375
Ginsburgh, Robert N., 353
Godley, G. McMurtrie, 239, 326
Graham, Gordon, 66
Green, Marshall, 265
Green Weenie laser, 293
Gromyko, Andrei, 264, 387
ground, destruction of enemy aircraft on, 21–38
ground-controlled intercept (GCI), 15, 29, 34, 36, 41, 50, 53, 59, 70, 72, 73, 80, 81, 91, 98, 99, 103, 110, 111, 113, 114, 116, 117, 120
ground radar, 41–42
ground radar aerial delivery system (GRADS), 173, 180
ground reconnaissance teams, 188, 195–96, 210–12, 216, 217, 218–19, 220–21, 222, 223, 226, 230, 231, 320
guerilla warfare, 225–26, 252
Gulf of Tonkin incident (1964), 346
Gulf of Tonkin Resolution, 256

Habib, Philip, 307
Haig, Alexander, 152, 222, 238, 243, 363, 368, 377, 381, 384, 386, 387, 388, 389, 393, 400

Haines, Ralph Edward, 310
Haiphong
    bombing prohibitions, 358
    imports, bombing and terminating, 308
    mining the port, 366–67
    Operation Linebacker II bombing, 391, 395, 396, 398, 400, 404
    SAM sites, bombing, 56
Haiphong Cement Plant, 295–96
Haiphong Harbor, 351, 366–67
Haiphong Kien Airfield, 31
Hamblet, Albert, Jr., 15
Hanoi
    Operation Linebacker II bombing, 391–92, 394, 395, 398, 400, 404, 405
    prohibited area, 36, 351, 354–55, 358
Hanoi Thermal Power Plant, 335, 352
Hansell, Haywood, 127
Hargrove, James A., Jr., 90
Harriman, Averell, 300
Harris, Hunter, Jr., 173, 267, 269, 276, 294, 345, 346, 348
Ha Van Lau, 133
helicopters
    airlift, 161–62, 173, 174, 177, 178, 179, 181, 189, 198, 231, 234, 241
    close air support, 185, 197, 205–6, 208, 209, 238, 243, 245, 247, 250, 251
    vulnerabilities, 190, 201, 206

Helms, Richard M., 285, 299, 381
Herring, George, 404, 406
HH-3, 98
high-altitude-low-opening (HALO) parachutes, 180
Hoa Lac Airfield, 30–31, 37, 300, 332, 391
Hoang Tung, 402
Hoang Xuan Lam, 246
Ho Chi Minh, 272, 295
Ho Chi Minh Trail
    aerial siege, implements, 327–36
    air interdiction, effectiveness, 299, 304, 307, 309, 322, 323, 326, 337–43, 354, 356
    bombing, 279–84, 287–88
    as focus of air campaign, 225, 232, 255, 257, 268, 279–81, 283, 285, 313–19
    night bombing, 293
    Operation Commando Hunt, 319–27
    Operation Lam Son 719, 237–39
    photo reconnaissance, 131, 132–33, 134, 135, 149
Hollingsworth, James F., 242, 243, 244
Holloway, Bruce K., 144, 213
Hoover, J. Edgar, 233–34
Horton, John, 165
Hotel 8, 217
Hotel 79, 217
Hue, 174, 179, 243, 244, 310
"hugging," 190–91

Hughes, James D., 110–11
Hughes, Richard E., 15
Humphrey, Hubert H., 257, 286, 317, 318
Hyland, John J., 310

"identification: friend or foe" ("IFF"), 68–71, 100–101, 118
Il-2, 184–85
Il-28, 25, 29, 34, 61, 421
immature technology, 84–93
information warfare, 349, 412
infrared guided missiles, 59, 73, 88, 106
Ingram, Ken, 200
interdiction, 255–60
    bombing North Vietnam, 261–72
    bombing theory and practice before Vietnam War, 260–61
    defined, 6
    doctrine, 409
    Ho Chi Minh Trail, bombing effectiveness, 279–84
    Laos and Ho Chi Minh Trail, air campaign focus, 313–19, 337–43
    Nguyen Hue Offensive, effectiveness, 376
    Operation Commando Hunt, 319–27
    Operation Rolling Thunder, 284–89, 294–312
    presidential policy, implements, 290–94
    Route Package 1, 314
Iosue, Andrew P., 171
Iron Hand missions,

37, 44, 48, 49, 50, 51, 54–55, 56–57, 76, 99, 143, 355, 357, 378
Iron Horse, 113
Israeli Air Force, 21, 22
Ivins, Arthur K., 68–69

Jackson, Joe M., 176
Jamison, Lewis M., 323
JASON Summer Study Group, 287
jettisoning of bombs, forced, 29, 32, 33, 41, 74, 75, 78–79, 92, 103, 111, 119
Johnson, Alexis, 261
Johnson, Gerald W., 396
Johnson, Harold K., 32, 177, 261
Johnson, Lyndon B.
  airfield bombing, 25, 26, 27, 30–31, 32–34
  bombing cessation, 272, 277, 278, 308–9, 312, 318
  bombing missions, limit, 94
  bombing North Vietnam, 264, 265, 266, 273, 274
  on Chinese intervention, 264
  close air support, 190, 195
  diplomacy and military force, understanding of, 303
  escalation, 12, 257
  failure of war, 7, 410–11, 413
  interdiction, 255, 256
  Khe Sanh, siege of, 177, 227
  missile sites, destruction, 43–44
  Operation Flaming Dart, 266
  Operation Rolling Thunder, 62, 258, 266, 269, 295, 296, 298, 299, 300, 301, 303, 405
  photo reconnaissance, 128, 129, 132
  "psychological victory" myth, 229
  rules of engagement, 349, 352
  San Antonio Formula, 302–3, 307
  on Soviet involvement and end of war, 317
  Tet Offensive, 306–7
Johnson, Roy L., 31, 297–98, 345, 348, 354
Johnson, U. Alexis, 25, 272, 278, 279
Joint Chiefs of Staff (JCS)
  airfield bombing, 36
  Arc Light missions, 210
  bombing cessation, 278
  bombing North Vietnam, 274
  Cambodia, bombing of sanctuaries, 233
  Easter Offensive, 240
  escalation, 256–57
  Laos and Ho Chi Minh Trail, air interdiction effectiveness, 338
  missile sites, destruction, 45
  Operation Commando Hunt, 324
  Operation Linebacker I, 371
  Operation Linebacker II, 389, 391
  Operation Rolling Thunder, 284–85, 286, 287, 289, 297, 306, 310
  photo reconnaissance, 129, 140
  rules of engagement, 348, 349–50, 353–54, 357, 358
Joy, Charles Turner, 304

JP-4, 13
Ju-87 Stuka, 184

KA-1 camera, 142
KA-3 Skywarrior, 16–17, 417
KA-55 camera, 141–42
KA-71 camera pod, 143
KA-79 camera, 143
KA-80 camera, 143
KA-82 camera, 155–56
KA-90 camera, 142
Kadena Air Base, 13, 17, 18, 19, 136
Katzenback, Nicholas, 133
KC-97, 12
KC-130 tanker, 17
KC-135 Stratotanker, 12–13, *13*, 14, 15–17, 18–19, 20, *52*, 76, 113, 115, 205, 211, 229, 240, 267, *268*, 383
Keaney, Thomas A., 375
Keegan, George J., 143, 147, 148
Keirn, Richard P., 43
Kelly, Kenneth H., 16
Kendall, James T., 353
Kennedy, Edward, 377, 393
Kennedy, John F., 11, 12, 255
Kennedy, Robert, 307
Kent State University, 236
Kep Airfield, 27, 29, 30, 31, 32, 36, 37, 77, 79, 85, 107, 134, 300, 384, 405
Keyhole Mission 1041-1, 135–36
Kham Duc Special Forces Camp, 175–76, 192

Khe Sanh, siege of (1968), 131, 143, 147, 154–55, 160, 164, 167–68, 172–73, 176–77, 189, 197, 226–31
Kien An Airfield, 27, 31, 34, 36, 391
Kilgus, Don, 62
kill ratios, 29–30, 54, 94, 95, 108, 110, 114, 121
Kimball, Jeffrey, 388
Kinh No Storage Area, 134
Kirk, William L., 113, 114
Kissinger, Henry
　airfield bombing, 35
　on Air Force's tactical abilities, 327
　Arc Light missions, 231
　bombing cessation, 387
　Cambodia, bombing of sanctuaries, 232
　close air support, 239
　Easter Offensive, 241, 361, 362, 363, 365–66, 377
　failure of war, 387
　Ho Chi Minh Trail, aerial siege, 329
　Laos and Ho Chi Minh Trail, air interdiction effectiveness, 342
　negotiations with North Vietnam, 21, 32, 37, 382, 385, 386, 388, 389, 399
　Operation Commando Hunt, 320–21, 322, 325, 326
　Operation Lam Son 719, 238
　Operation Linebacker I, 102, 381
　Operation Linebacker II, 57, 388, 389–90, 391, 394, 395, 397, 403
　suppression of enemy air defenses (SEAD), 60
　Teaball, 114
　on Thieu refusing to sign peace agreement, 393, 394
Klusmann, Charles F., 151
Komer, Robert W., 225–26, 296
Kontum, 171, 174, 179, 181–82, 188, 195, 200, 215, 226, 240, 242, 243, 244–46, 371
Kordenbrock, D. B., 390
Korean War (1950–1953), 11, 22, 112–13, 127, 158, 185
Kosygin, Alexei N., 26, 298, 309–10
Krulak, Victor H., 17, 130, 192, 222, 278, 289, 331
KS-72 camera, 140–41
　KS-72C1 camera, 140–41

Laird, Melvin R., 50, 152, 232, 233, 237, 240, 321, 358, 360–61, 365, 366, 371, 386
Lang Chi Dam, 371
Lang Chi Power Plant, 372
Lanigan, J. P., 189
Lao Dong Party, 7, 214, 240, 259, 271, 279, 305, 306, 402, 409–10
Laos
　air interdiction, effectiveness, 337–43
　air interdiction, implements, 327–36
　air interdiction, shift, 409
　air war, beginning, 255
　air war following ceasefire, 406
　airlift, 174–75
　close air support, 187, 188, 190, 201, 239
　as focus of air campaign, 313–19
　Ho Chi Minh Trail, bombing effectiveness, 280
　Operation Commando Hunt, 319–27
　photo reconnaissance, 129, 131, 140
　rules of engagement, 349–50, 355–56, 358
laser-guided bombs, 37, 40, 55–56, 110, 155, 238, 247, 249, 322, 323, 330, 336, 368, 370–75, 379, 380, 383, 384, 389, 391, 399, 401
Lavelle, John D., 218, 348, 363
Le Duan, 229, 272, 369, 376, 400
Le Duc Tho, 37, 114, 236, 240, 317, 327, 362, 365, 367, 376, 381, 382, 385, 386, 388, 389, 390, 399, 406, 412
Le Trong Tan, 324
Lee, Kent L., 144, 350
LeMay, Curtis, 211, 255–56
Lemnitzer, Lyman L., 43
Lemos, W. E., 323
Lewis, Alvin L., 16
limited war, 6, 7, 11–12, 157, 161, 164, 183, 211, 213, 214, 251, 252, 271, 309, 312, 378, 411
Lind, Michael, 413
Loc Ninh, 188

Loc Vinh, 247–48
Lollar, James L., 393
Lomperis, Timothy, 406
long-range air navigation (LORAN), 37, 120, 138, 156, 240, 244, 246, 292, 322, 323, 374, 377, 379–80, 384, 391, 395, 400, 428
Long Tieng, Laos, 188
Lon Nol, 234
loose deuce formation, 96, 97–98, 450
low altitude parachute extraction system, 172
Lueskow, Douglas D., 15
Luftwaffe, 22, 113

M-117, 202, 211, 215, 250, 336
Madden, John A., 106
Mansfield, Mike, 31, 140, 272, 296
Mao Tse Tung, 263, 411
Marcovich, Herbert, 296
Marines (South Vietnamese), 159, 191, 224, 249
Mark 20 Rockeye cluster bomb, 207, 247
Mark-82 500-pound bomb, 17, 48, 202, 207, 211, 215, 238, 247, 332, 336, 372, 379, 384, 405
Mark-83 1,000-pound bomb, 197, 290, 332
Mark-84 2,000-pound bomb, 40, 290, 336, 372, 379, 384, 391
Marshall, George C., 354, 552

Marshall, Winton W., 325
Martin, Colonel, 66
Mataxis, Theo C., 159
McCain, John S., Jr., 18, 54, 213, 230–31, 357, 368–69, 378
McCarthy, Eugene, 307
McCone, John A., 263, 266, 267
McConnell, John P., 30, 32–33, 95, 259, 299, 323, 351, 352, 353, 354
McGiffert, John R., 202, 243
McGovern, George, 381–82
McMaster, H. R., 273
McNamara, Robert S.
  airfield bombing, 25, 26, 27, 28, 33, 34
  airlift, 182
  bombing cessation, 277, 278, 279, 296
  bombing North Vietnam, 255, 256, 258, 265, 267, 271, 274
  close air support, 194, 195, 226
  coercion, 258
  escalation, 256, 273, 274, 288, 297, 298, 349
  interdiction, 255, 299
  Laos and Ho Chi Minh Trail, air interdiction effectiveness, 337
  leaves post as secretary of defense, 304–5
  on MiG threat, 32
  Operation Rolling Thunder, 272, 284, 287, 288, 296–97, 298, 300–301, 304, 306, 335, 337, 354
  reconnaissance, 128
  rules of engagement, 306, 349, 350, 352, 354

surface-to-air missile sites, destruction, 43, 45
  on winnability of war, 279, 287, 299, 300, 303, 304, 305, 306
McNaughton, John T., 43, 266
McPherson, Harry C., 226, 305
Meeker, Leonard, 284
Mets, David, 160
Meyer, John C., 58, 390, 395–400, 404
Meyers, Gilbert L., 286, 347, 400
Micias, Manuel, 16
MiGs, 25–37, 42, 49–50, 59–60
  anti-MiG operations, 80–82
  danger to American aircraft, 72–75
  F-4 head-on attacks, 107
  Hanoi raids, 79
  jettisons, forced, 78–79
  MiG-17, 15, 25–29, 31, 34, 35–36, 49, 59, 62, 67, 68, 72, 73, 75, 79, 83, 85, 86, 87, 88, 90–91, 92, 94, 98, 99, 102, 103, 104, 151, 421–22
  MiG-19, 27, 32, 36, 37, 98, 99, 102, 103, 104, 106, 107, 116, 119, 163
  MiG-21, 27, 28, 29, 32, 34, 36, 50, 59, 62, 65, 66, 68, 70, 71, 73, 74, 75, 77, 78, 79, 83, 85, 86, 87, 91, 92, 94, 96–99, 101, 102, 103–5, 106, 107, 108, 113–17, 119, 120–21, 139, 152, 153, 382, 394
  MiG-25, 94, 136

Operation Bolo, 65, 76–78
Operation Linebacker I, 102–5, 108, 119
Operation Rolling Thunder, 94
photo reconnaissance, 151–52
Seventh Air Force improvement against, 109–11
shooting down, 61–71
Teaball, 112–18
warning system, inadequacy, 80

Military Assistance Command, Vietnam (MACV)
aerial refueling, 12
airlift, 180
air power's importance to, 4, 54, 227, 231, 233
Arc Light missions, 209, 210, 212, 213, 217, 218, 219, 245
Cambodia, bombing of sanctuaries, 233, 235
close air support, 185, 192, 196, 239
conflict with ARVN commanders, 181
Laos and Ho Chi Minh Trail, air interdiction effectiveness, 339
Operation Commando Hunt, 324, 330
photo reconnaissance, 128, 129, 132

Miller, Thomas H., Jr., 50
missile malfunctions, 101–2
Model-147 drone, 138
Mohrhardt, Robair F., 69
Momyer, William W., 81, 206
air combat, 79, 81, 110
airfield bombing, 34
airlift, 159
Arc Light missions, 213, 219–20, 225
bombing accuracy, 291
bombing cessation, 317–18
on F-111A Aardvarks, 334
Khe Sanh, siege of, 226–27, 228
Operation Bolo, 76, 78
Operation Rolling Thunder, escalation, 302, 308
on radar coverage, 112
rules of engagement, 347, 353–54

Monkey Mountain South Vietnam, 113
Moore, Joseph H., Jr., 26, 69, 258–59, 344–45
Moore, William G., Jr., 163, 165, 168
Moorer, Thomas H.
on B-52s, 240, 395–96, 397–98
on bombing cessation, 321
on countermeasures against SA-4s, 59
Easter Offensive (Nguyen Hue Offensive), 242, 366, 368, 376, 377, 378
on Navy SAMs' underuse, 60
on North Vietnamese air power, 99
Operation Lam Son 719, 238
Operation Linebacker I, 102, 371, 376, 377, 378, 382, 384
Operation Linebacker II, 389–90, 394, 395–96, 397–98, 400, 405
photo reconnaissance, 131
on political interference in military operations, 271
rules of engagement, 348, 357, 358, 387
supply route attacks, 388
on winning war, 344, 399–400

mountain passes, 316
MSQ-77 radar-directed bombing (Sky Spot), 205, 214–16, 233, 240, 291–92, 301, 356
Mu Gia Pass, 54, 98, 131, 287
Munich Crisis (1938), 11
Murphy, George, 163–64
Mustin, Lloyd M., 215

Naha Air Base, 164, 167
Nakhon Phanom Air Base, 112, 115, 399
napalm, 59, 187, 188, 189, 190, 191, 196, 197, 202, 207, 211, 251, 346, 347, 355
Nargi, Anthony, 96
National Liberation Front (NLF), 24, 122, 186, 197, 214, 257, 258, 261, 262, 263, 266, 277, 279, 295, 300, 303, 317, 318–19, 321, 349, 406, 409, 411, 412, 413
Naval History and Heritage Center, 5
Nazzaro, Joseph J., 310–11
negotiations, 21, 30, 32, 37, 303–4, 318, 321, 322, 377, 380–81, 382–84, 385, 386–88, 389, 390–91, 399. *See also* diplomacy; statecraft
Newsome, Winfred T., 16
Ngoei, Wen-Qing, 413

Nguyen Hue Offensive, 375–76
Nguyen Van Minh, 244
Nguyen Van Thieu, 179, 237, 240, 242, 244, 317, 318–19, 362, 376, 382, 385, 388, 393, 394, 406
Nguyen Van Toan, 244
Nguyen Van Vinh, 279
Nguyen Vinh Nghi, 248
Nhon Co Airfield, 168
night bombing, 260, 280, 292, 293, 314, 382
night photography, 140, 148–49
Nitze, Paul, 32
Nixon, Richard M.
 air superiority, 25
 B-52s, psychological impact, 231, 241, 243
 bombing cessation, 318, 386–87
 Brezhnev, summit with, 368
 Cambodia, bombing of sanctuaries, 233–34
 Chup Operation, 178
 close air support, 239
 criticism of Air Force's tactical abilities, 327, 361, 362–63, 390
 Easter Offensive, 241, 242–43, 361, 362, 364, 365, 366, 368–69, 371, 377
 failure of war, 387
 Laos and Ho Chi Minh Trail, air interdiction effectiveness, 342
 negotiations, 388
 Operation Commando Hunt, 319, 320, 322, 324
 Operation Lam Son 719, 237
 Operation Linebacker I, 102, 367–68

Operation Linebacker II, 57, 388, 389, 390, 394, 395, 396, 397, 403, 404
photo reconnaissance, 128, 131, 152
public opinion on Vietnam War, 236–37
rules of engagement, 358
suppression of enemy air defenses, 60
Nixon Doctrine, 361, 408
North Vietnam
 aircraft interceptors, 98
 air defense system, 41–43
 airfields, 64
 antiaircraft artillery, 25, 26, 28, 37, 38, 39–40, 41, 42, 44, 46–47, 49, 53, 55, 71, 73, 79, 98, 131, 133, 140, 142, 145, 152, 165, 171, 181, 200, 206, 218, 238, 255, 276, 291, 306, 329, 330, 335, 337, 346, 373, 384, 407
 extends reach of air forces south, 98–99, 101
 ingenuity and determination, 314–15
 radar site data, 112–13
 Soviet and Chinese influence, 360
North Vietnamese Air Force (PAVN Air Force), 24–25, 31, 33, 42, 78, 94, 99
North Vietnamese Army (People's Army of Vietnam, PAVN), 187, 195, 197, 409
 1st Division, 242
 7th Division, 180, 244
 24th Regiment, 208
 320th Division, 224
 325th Division, 213
 artillery, 156, 181, 249

 in Cambodia, 234–35, 236
 combined arms ineptitude, 245
 fear of B-52 strikes, 222, 228
 Khe Sanh, 170, 176
 Lam Son 719, 237–38
 Nguyen Hue Campaign (Easter Offensive), 240, 242–50
Nowell, Larry B., 82
nuclear weapons, 11, 66, 67, 176, 185, 211, 261, 297, 301, 365, 366
Nurmanthias, Colonel, 277

Olds, Robin, 30–31, 32, 72, 74, 76, 78, 88, 89
O'Neil, Edward W., 151, 152
Operation Attleboro, 174
Operation Barrel Roll, 129, 255
Operation Birmingham, 132, 193
Operation Bolo, 65, 76–79
Operation Bullet Shot, 19, 240
Operation College Dart, 97
Operation Combat Lancer, 334
Operation Commando Hunt, 319–27, 337–38, 341, 342, 350
Operation Constant Guard, 19, 362
Operation Coronet Organ, 122
Operation Delaware, 172
Operation Dewey Canyon

603

INDEX

I, 205, 208
Operation Dewey Canyon II, 178
Operation Flaming Dart, 26, 266
Operation Freedom Deal, 325
Operation Freedom Porch Bravo, 361–62, 364
Operation Freedom Train, 35, 101, 240, 362, 363
Operation Greeley, 174
Operation Harvest Moon, 189
Operation Igloo White, 313, 320, 322, 327
Operation Junction City, 178
Operation Jungle Jim, 255–56
Operation Lam Son 72, 378
Operation Lam Son 719, 40, 178, 189, 192, 200, 204, 206, 237–39, 247
Operation Linebacker I
 aerial refueling, 12, 19
 airfield bombing, 36–37
 air strikes and negotiations with North Vietnam, 382–84
 air superiority efforts, 100–108, 111
 combat training, 95
 conferences, 111
 Easter Offensive, 362, 363
 effectiveness, 380–81
 F-8 action, 91
 final three weeks, 119
 first week, 371
 fratricide, 68
 goals and priorities, 367–68
 Kissinger's negotiations with North Vietnamese, 114, 358, 363, 365, 377, 382, 385
 laser-guided bombs, 370–73, 374–75, 379, 380, 383, 384
 photo reconnaissance, 154, 156
 precision-guided bombs, 371
 surface-to-air missiles (SAMs), 55, 57
 tank destruction, 247
 Teaball, 115, 116
Operation Linebacker II, 388–401
 aerial refueling, 12, 19–20
 airfield bombing, 37–38
 air superiority, 120–21
 contrast with Operation Rolling Thunder, 344, 404–6, 408, 410
 drone success, 138, 139
 effectiveness, 401–6
 laser-guided bombs, 391, 399, 401
 losses, 402
 photo reconnaissance, 131, 156–57
 rules of engagement, 358
 surface-to-air missiles (SAMs), 55, 57–58
 Teaball, 117–18
Operation Menu, 233, 234
Operation Neutralize, 210
Operation Niagara, 228
Operation Paul Revere, 174
Operation Pocket Money, 366–67
Operation Portsea, 225
Operation Prairie Fire, 320
Operation Proud Deep Alpha, 98, 326–27
Operation Pruning Knife, 321
Operation Rivet Haste, 110
Operation Rolling Thunder, 261–63, 265–66, 267–69, 272–78, 284–89
 aerial refueling, 12, 16
 air strikes, military effectiveness, and political support, relationship, 190
 aircraft, 290–93
 airfield bombing, 27–28
 bombing cessation, 272, 277–79, 303, 307–10, 317
 Easter Offensive, 361
 effectiveness, 299–300, 307, 309, 318, 339, 405–6, 413
 escalation, 294–312
 MiG attacks, 62, 94
 objectives, 304
 photo reconnaissance, 128
 progress evaluation, 274–76
 renewing, 317
 rules of engagement, 345, 346–47, 348, 349, 350–51, 353
 strategic bombing, 258, 409
 surface-to-air missiles (SAMs), 54
 termination, 319, 324
Operation Steel Tiger, 255
Operation Taxi Road, 37
Operation Thor, 134, 213, 220
Operation Tiger Hound, 255
Operation Turnpike, 313–14
Operation Union II, 188
Osgood, Robert, 6
OV-1 Mohawk, 143, 146, 149, 150, 328

OV-10 Bronco, 198–99, 208, 251

Pacific Air Forces (PACAF)
  aerial combat training, 67–68
  aerial refueling, 12, 17, 19
  air strikes, effectiveness, 273, 288, 324, 338, 370, 375, 380, 401
  airlift, 161
  bombing North Vietnam, 276, 282, 286
  close air support, 194
  immature technology, 88
  MiGs, shooting down, 64–65
  missile sites, destruction, 44
  missile testing, 87
  Operation Linebacker II, 395
  suppression of enemy air defenses (SEAD), 48

Palmer, Bruce, Jr., 251, 347, 413
Palmer, Dave Richard, 406
Pao, Vang, 187, 192
parachute low altitude delivery system, 172
Paris Peace Accords, 357, 388, 406
parking space, aircraft, 267
Paron, John R., 248
Paul Doumer Bridge, 301, 371, 379
Pave Aegis AC-130, 200
Pave Knife laser illuminator pods, 372, 374
Pave Nail OV-10, 198–99
Pease, Harold, 344
Pedersen, Dan, 97

"Pennsylvania Initiative," 32
Pham Van Dong, 294, 296
Phan Rang, 267–68
Phan Van Phu, 245
Philpott, Jammie M., 147
photo interpreters, 129, 130, 135, 142, 143, 146, 147, 148, 149, 150–51, 154, 155, 156, 157, 220, 222
photo reconnaissance, 127–28, 407
  effectiveness, 145–51
  information provided, 128–35
  mission danger, 151–54
  ongoing efforts, 154–57
  platforms, 135–45
Phouma, Souvanna, 129, 201, 255, 321–22, 355
Phuc Yen Air Base, 25, 26, 27, 28–29, 30, 32–34, 36, 37, 55, 77, 78, 79, 81, 113, 139, 257, 297, 302, 352, 392, 398, 405
Phuoc Tuy Province, 225
Piazza, Carlo, 127
Pizzi, Joseph, 215
Plain of Jars, 188, 239
Plei Me, 173, 187, 189
Podgorny, Nikolai, 378
Polaroid film, 156
Polei Kleng, 188
policy goals, achievement of, 311–12
political interference in military operations, 271, 344–45, 347, 352–55
Porter, Gareth, 406
Positive Identification

Radar Advisory Zone (PIRAZ) ship, 69–70
Power, Thomas, 211
Powers, Richards, 48
predictability, 67, 83, 191, 207, 267, 341, 345, 394
presidential election (1968), 47, 295, 296, 318
presidential election (1972), 360, 362, 381–82, 386
Project 665A, 149
Project Compass Link, 148
Project Hammock, 113
Project See Fast, 149
Project Shed Light, 149
"psychological victory" myth, 229
"Puff the Magic Dragon," 199
Pujals, Enrique, 187

QRC-160 ECM pod, 53–54, 74, 76, 141
Quang Tri, 246, 249
Qui Hau Ammo Depot West, 273

R-13 "Atoll," 73, 74, 78, 86, 90, 95, 103, 116, 120
RA-3B, 143
RA-5C Vigilante, 130, 143–45, *144*, 151, 153, 157
radar, 41–42, 80–82, 96, 110, 112–13, 118, 173, 180, 215, 383–84, 403
radar homing and warning (RHAW), 48, 65, 68
radio intercepts, 112–13
radio relay, 113, 115–17,

121

railroad yards, 78, 308, 314, 364, 367, 371, 389, 397, 401, 405

Ramsey, Lloyd B., 189

Randolph, Stephen P., 363

Raven forward air controllers, 192

RB-57 Canberra, 149, 155
  RB-57E Canberra, 143

reconnaissance. *See* photo reconnaissance; visual reconnaissance

Reconnaissance Attack Squadron 6, 152

Red Crown, 70, 71, 81–82, 115, 116, 117–18, 120, 121, 139

Red River Valley, 410

Reedy, James R., 69

refueling. *See* aerial refueling

refueling tankers, 12–20. *See also* aerial refueling

RF-4C Phantom, 134, 135, 140, 141–43, *142*, 153, 154, 155–57

RF-8A Crusader, 143

RF-101C Voodoo, 42, 129, *130*, 130, 131, 140–41, 151, 154

Richie, Steve, 81–82

RIM-2 "Terrier," 59–60

RIM-8 Talos, 59, 60, 83, 101

Rivers, Mendel, 233

roads, cratering, 281, 287, 289, 314, 315, 316

Rogers, William P., 178, 321, 325

Ronco, Theo, 369

Rostow, Walt W., 256, 285, 295, 297, 298, 300, 302, 303, 310, 317

Route Package 1, 26, 69, 79, 119, 152, 153, 269–70, 314, 315, 331, 339, 357, 364, 372, 378, 384, 386

Rucker, Alexander C., 96

rules of engagement, 344–59

runways, 25, 26, 29, 30, 35, 36, 37–38, 110, 165, 166, 168–69

Rush, Arthur C., 164

Rusk, David "Dean," 32, 256
  airfield bombing, 33
  bombing cessation, 272, 307, 309, 311
  bombing North Vietnam, 33, 263, 264
  close air support, 194–95
  on communist takeover of Southeast Asia, 256–58
  end of war, encourages, 317
  missile sites, destruction, 43
  Operation Rolling Thunder, 273, 284, 295, 300, 304
  Stennis Hearings, 32
  on winnability of war, 300

Russell, Richard, 233, 236

Rutter, George W., 123

Ryan, John D., Jr., 30, 106, 110, 111, 119, 249, 347, 363, 371, 383

SA-2 Guideline, 40–45, 47–51, 53–60, 74–77, 81, 99, 102, 120, 135–38, 151, 153, 264, 364, 395, 398–400

SA-3, 58, 59, 136

SA-4, 58–59

SA-6, 58, 59

SA-7, 59

San Antonio Formula, 302–3, 307

satellite reconnaissance, 127, 136, 464

Scherbakov, Ilia S., 397

Schlight, John, 195

Seaman, Jonathan O., 189, 190, 219

Searles, Dewitt R., 98

Second World War. *See* World War II

Seek Data II program, 161

Seek Dawn, 113

Senate Preparedness Investigating Subcommittee of the Armed Services Committee, 78

Seventh Air Force
  A-6A Intruder, 332
  aerial refueling, 18, 19
  AIM-4D Falcon, 90
  air combat training, 67–68, 96, 105
  airfield bombing, 33, 35, 36–37, 83
  airlift, 161, 165, 167
  air strike cancellations, 276
  antiaircraft artillery, 40
  Cambodia, bombing of sanctuaries, 235
  Chinese buildup, 264
  close air support, 193–94, 205, 208
  communications intelligence data, 113
  EC-121 airborne

radar surveillance aircraft, 80
emergency airlift request system (EARS), 169
F-102 Delta Dagger, 293
F-104C Starfighter, 65
helicopter air support, 206
Khe Sanh, siege of, 177
Laos, focus of air campaign, 313
Laos and Ho Chi Minh Trail, air interdiction effectiveness, 340, 341, 342
MiGs, improvement against, 109–11
missile malfunctions, 101–2
Operation Bolo, 76
Operation Commando Hunt, 319–20, 323, 325
Operation Freedom Deal, 325
Operation Lam Son 719, 237
Operation Linebacker I, 105
Operation Linebacker II, 392–93, 394, 397, 401–2
Operation Neutralize, 210
Operation Rolling Thunder, 284, 287, 298, 299, 302, 305
photo reconnaissance, 132–33, 137, 139, 146, 148, 149, 150, 154
RF-101C Voodoo, 141
self-evaluation, 111
suppression of enemy air defenses, 53–54
Teaball, 113, 114–15

Shadden, Jim, 189
Sharp, Ulysses S. Grant
airfield bombing, 26, 28, 33
on air interdiction, 282
air power restrictions, 270–71
American involvement, escalation, 256, 257, 259
on bombing and negotiations, 284, 288, 304
bombing cessation, 272, 278
bombing North Vietnam, 272, 274
bombing strictures, 286
close air support, 185, 228
Ho Chi Minh Trail, aerial siege, 331–32
Laos and Ho Chi Minh Trail, air interdiction effectiveness, 343
missile sites, destruction, 43, 45
Navy and Air Force turf war, 69
North Vietnamese air power, 74–75
Operation Linebacker II, 406
Operation Rolling Thunder, 262, 275, 284, 285, 287, 288, 289, 294–95, 296, 297, 305, 308
photo reconnaissance, 129, 150
rules of engagement, 344, 348, 351, 353
on winnability of war, 273, 305

Sheffield, Robert, 74
siege warfare, 5–6, 280, 289
Sihanouk, Prince, 233, 234
Simler, George P., 350
Six-Day War (1967), 22
Sky Spot, 244, 291, 292
Slay, Alton D., 249
Smith, Donovan, 76
Smith, L. Wayne, 72, 96
Smith, Margaret Chase, 353
Smith, Philip E., 263–64
Smith, Robert N., 146
Smith, Scott G., 98
Smith, Wilfred, 190
Sonier, L. R. J., 85
Southeast Asia Tactical Data System Interface, 111–12, 113
Soviet Union
aerial refueling, 11
airfield bombing, 33
bombing cessation, 227–28, 309–10, 317
bombing North Vietnam, 263, 264
North Vietnam, support, 26, 29, 33, 38, 43, 92, 121, 183, 256, 277, 303, 305, 341, 376, 381, 403
North Vietnamese policy, influencing, 360, 362, 365–66, 367, 378
Operation Rolling Thunder, impact, 305
relations with United States, 44, 127, 241, 260, 263–64, 273, 317, 351, 360, 362, 365, 367, 381, 411
Span, William F., 150–51
Special intelligence (SI), 92, 104, 114–16, 119, 218
Special National Intelligence Estimate 53–65, 261
SR-71, 121, 131, 135, 136, 137, 147, 156, 157, 384, 464
statecraft, 6, 297, 302, 376, 411, 413. *See also* diplomacy; negotiations
Stennis, John C., 31, 233,

236, 300, 352
Stennis Hearings, 32, 354
Sternenberg, Fred W., Jr., 14
Stillwell, Richard G., 211, 213
Strategic Air Command (SAC)
    aerial refueling, 14, 20
    Arc Light missions, 211, 218, 220, 221, 229–30, 232, 243, 338
    Operation Linebacker I, 338
    Operation Linebacker II, 55, 389, 390, 392–93, 395, 396, 400, 402–3
    photo reconnaissance, 136, 137, 150, 156
strategic bombing, 6, 258, 260–61, 409
Sullivan, Glenn Ray, 396–97
Sullivan, William H., 99, 201, 221, 279, 281–82, 329
suppression of enemy air defenses (SEAD), 42, 46, 47–58, 62, 95, 121, 333, 364, 390, 395, 430
surface-to-air missiles (SAMs), 22, 23–24, 25, 27, 28, 39–60, 151–53, 395, 396
Sutherland, James W., 238
Symington, Stuart, 30, 352

T-28, 194, 201, 328, 329
T-8209 radar, 403
TA-4F, 48, 379
Tactical Air Command (TAC), 66, 94, 95, 97, 105, 112, 122, 161, 170

tactical air navigation (TACAN) black boxes, 19
tail gunners, 120
Talbott, Carlos M., 110
Tam, Tram Hung, 221
Tam Da Railroad Bridge, 289
tankers, refueling, 12–20. *See also* aerial refueling
tank plinking, 375
tanks, 247
Tan Son Nhut Air Base, 61, 150, 156, 167, 169
targeting intelligence, 110, 127–28, 131, 146, 156, 157, 206, 207, 209, 212, 216–17, 221, 232, 408
Tarpley, Thomas M., 241
Task Force 77, 96
Taylor, Maxwell, 43, 262
    Arc Light missions, 212
    bombing cessation, 310
    bombing North Vietnam, 257, 258, 259, 261, 263, 265, 272
    coercion, 263, 268–69, 272–73, 310
    escalation, 258, 265, 266
    Ho Chi Minh Trail, aerial siege, 257
    interdiction, 277, 297
    Operation Rolling Thunder, 261, 262, 266, 269, 273
    on reprisal bombing missions, 259
    on winnability of war, 252, 257
Teaball, 80, 112–21, 123
technology, immature, 84–93
terrain-following radar

(TFR), 383–84
Tet Offensive, 34, 47, 228, 229
    airlift, 169–78
    close air support, 226–31
    Operation Rolling Thunder, 306
Thailand, 257, 291, 301, 322, 413
    air bases, 13, 18, 39, 42, 61, 62, 64, 95, 112, 129, 205, 209, 241, 257, 267, 270, 301, 322, 413
    Don Muang/Bangkok International Airport, 18, 19, 61
    Korat Air Base, 19, 48, 205, 395
    Nakhon Phanom Air Base, 112, 115, 399
    Takhli Air Base, 17, 18, 19, 160, 382
    Udorn Air Base, 61, 64, 100, 101, 115, 121, 145, 148
    U-Tapao Air Base, 18, 209, 395, 396, 398
Thai Nguyen Iron Steel Plant, 295, 298, 333
Thanh Hoa, 56, 130, 156, 362, 391, 393
Thanh Hoa Bridge, 26, 50, 373, 374, 378–79
Thao Ma, 279
Thinh Loc Railroad Bridge, 336
Thomas, Spence, 66–67
Thompson, Llewellyn, Jr., 26
Thompson, Robert, 380
Thompson, Wayne, 97
Thornal, Leroy, 345
threat warning, 112
III Marine Amphibious Force, 165, 192, 226, 251–52, 330

throughput, as measurement of air interdiction effectiveness, 281, 285, 298, 323, 325, 340–42
Thurmond, Strom, 352–53
Thuy, Xuan, 133
Tilford, Earl, 405, 408
TISEO (target identification system, electro-optical), 330
Tissot, Ernest E., Jr., 46–47
Tolson, John J., 171
Top Gun program, 96–97, 122
TOW (tube-launched, optically tracked, wire-guided) anti-tank missile, 247
Tran Day Hung, 404
Triantafellu, Rockly, 146
Truong, Ngo Quang, 62, 246–47
Tuttle, Jerry O., 204
Tuy Hoa, 265
Twining, Nathan, 210–11
Tyler, M. S., 15

U Thant, 306
U-2, 135, 136, 137, 153, 156
UH-1 Huey, 162, 205
Unger, Leonard S., 190
Unger, Robert, 194
United States Air Force. *See also* Eighth Air Force; Seventh Air Force
  479th Tactical Fighter Wing, 64, 89
  1965 fighter combat conference, 67
  AGM-62 Walleye, 34, 289, 335–36, 369, 373, 375, 379, 545
  airfield bombing, 32, 37, 53
  airlift, 158–59, 160, 161, 162–63, 165, 170–71
  air strikes, weather's impact on, 276
  air superiority, 21–24, 121–23, 127, 407
  air-to-air combat, response to frustrations, 94–95
  anti-MiG operations, 79, 80–81
  Arc Light missions, 210–11, 217–26, 230
  assignment policy, 97, 163, 164
  choke points, bombing, 282, 308, 313–16, 323–24, 326, 337, 409
  close air support, 185, 194, 201–2, 208–9, 250
  cratering roads, 232, 275, 281, 285, 308, 315, 316, 322, 323–24, 337, 374
  drone reconnaissance, 139
  Easter Offensive, 246, 361–62, 364–65, 368–69, 371, 378
  emergency airlift request system (EARS), 169
  F-4E, 109–10, 119
  fratricide, 68–70
  fuel storage sites, bombing, 131, 286, 287, 362, 367
  Ho Chi Minh Trail, bombing effectiveness, 281
  immature technology, 84–85, 87, 88–89, 90
  interdiction campaigns, 256, 293
  Laos and Ho Chi Minh Trail, air interdiction effectiveness, 339
  laser-guided bombs, 372, 373–74, 375
  limited war concept, 12
  loss ratio, 95, 114
  MiGs, shooting down, 61, 62, 66
  missile sites, destruction, 44, 46
  Operation Commando Hunt, 320, 323, 326
  Operation Lam Son 719, 237–38
  Operation Linebacker II, 392–93, 401–2
  Operation Neutralize, 210
  Operation Proud Deep Alpha, 98, 326–27
  Operation Rolling Thunder, 267–68, 285, 292–93, 299
  photo reconnaissance, 129, 136, 139, 146, 148–50, 154, 155, 156, 157
  refueling tankers, 12–20
  rules of engagement, 344
  suppression of air defenses, 42, 47–49, 51, 52, 55, 56–57, 58
  Teaball, 112–18
  Tet Offensive, 170–71, 307
  threat level management, inadequate, 119
  training inadequacies, 118–19
  victory and doctrine of, 4
United States Army
  airlift, 158–59, 160–61, 162, 165, 168, 174, 177–78, 180
  close air support, 187, 189, 192–93, 194
  emergency airlift request system (EARS), 169
  Laos and Ho Chi Minh Trail, air interdiction

effectiveness, 338
photo reconnaissance, 146, 148, 150
United States Marines, 220, 319, 364
  1st Marine Aircraft Wing, 332
  A-6A Intruder, 187, 205, 320, 331–32
  air ambush, 251–52
  air interdiction, 131, 313, 315, 323
  aircraft losses, 40
  airlift, 158, 162, 170, 175, 177
  close air support, 187–89, 190, 191–92, 196, 206, 208, 218
  F-4J air patrols, 71, 75, 120
  Fleet Marine Force, Pacific, 222, 311
  KC-130 tankers, 17
  Khe Sanh, siege of, 170, 176, 177, 226, 227–28
  Marine Tactical Data System, 113
  Operation Neutralize, 210
  Operation Rolling Thunder, 267
  photo reconnaissance, 150
  RVAH-6, 151, 154, 379
  RVAH-7, 153
  RVAH-9, 144, 151
  suppression of enemy air defenses, 47, 50, 57, 152, 364
  3rd Marine Division, 210, 217
  VMFA-232, 247
United States Navy
  aerial refueling, 16–17
  AGM-62 Walleye, 335
  air combat training, 95–97, 122
  airfield bombing, 31, 33–34, 35, 36, 37
  air strike cancellations, 276
  air superiority, 121–22

ALQ-51 ECM suite, 75
antiaircraft artillery, 40, 41, 46–47
anti-MiG operations, 79–80
Attack Squadron 35, 388
close air support, 185
cratering roads, 316
Easter Offensive, 361–62, 364
enemy aircraft operations study, 78
fratricide, 68–70
fuel storage sites, bombing, 286
Ho Chi Minh Trail, bombing effectiveness, 280
immature technology, 84–85, 87–88, 90
interdiction campaigns, 293
Laos and Ho Chi Minh Trail, air interdiction effectiveness, 337, 339
laser-guided bombs, 372, 373
MiGs, shooting down, 61, 62–63, 66–67
missile malfunctions, 101
missile sites, destruction, 46
missile study, 91
Operation Linebacker I, 103, 382
Operation Linebacker II, 391
Operation Pocket Money, 366–67
Operation Proud Deep Alpha, 327
Operation Rolling Thunder, 267, 269, 275, 287, 290–91, 292, 297–98, 299
Operation Turnpike, 313–14
photo reconnaissance, 129, 130, 145, 150, 157
Qui Hau Ammo Depot West,

mission against, 273
Route Package 1, 314
rules of engagement, 344
RVAH-6, 151, 154, 379
RVAH-7, 153
RVAH-9, 144, 151
suppression of air defenses, 42, 47, 48, 49, 50, 52, 55, 56–57, 58
surface-to-air missiles, shipboard, 59–60
Thanh Hoa Bridge bombing, 379
threat level management, inadequate, 119
training upgrades, 107
VA-35, 372, 378, 384, 391
VA-52, 17, 56
VA-55, 56, 203
VA-56, 242, 368
VA-115, 391
VA-146, 379
VA-153, 291
VA-155, 248, 364
VA-164, 48, 188, 291
VA-212, 242
VAH-8, 17
VF-24, 74, 90
VF-53, 69, 73, 83
VF-96, 107
VF-211, 91

USS *America*, 101, 379
USS *Biddle*, 59, 70
USS *Bonhomme Richard*, 31
USS *Chicago*, 69
USS *Constellation*, 17, 86, 144, 151, 330, *331*, 334–35
USS *England*, 70
USS *Enterprise*, 150, 330–31
USS *Hancock*, 150–51, 379
USS *Higbee*, 59
USS *Jouett*, 70
USS *Kitty Hawk*, 17, 31,

96, 335, 379
USS *Long Beach*, 59, 70
USS *Maddox*, 256
USS *Midway*, 85–86, 107, 337
USS *Ranger*, 143
USS *Sterett*, 59
USS *Ticonderoga*, 16, 256

Valentine's Day Raid, 35
Vance, Cyrus, 296–97
Vang Pao, 239, 406
Vann, John Paul, 181, 182, 200, 242, 244, 245
victory, 4, 410, 411, 412, 413
Viet Cong, 24, 26, 131, 132, 159, 169–70, 172, 174, 175–76, 177, 184, 185–86, 187, 190, 192, 194–95, 198, 211, 216–17, 219–20, 221, 225, 229, 231, 251, 257, 259, 261–62, 263, 265, 266, 272, 281, 288, 306–7, 339, 340, 348, 354, 359
Viet Tri Power Station, 380, 402
Vietnam War
　air power effectiveness, 3–5, 407
　American public opinion, 229, 236–37, 298
　bombing theory and practice before, 260–61
　failure, 7, 304, 359, 410–13
　Lao Dong Party's perspective, 409–10
　lessons, 408, 412
　as limited war, 252, 271, 312
　longevity and winnability, 270–71, 273, 347, 353–54, 359, 371, 410
　as major war, 11, 94, 164, 183, 271
　political battle, 276–77
　political interference in military operations, 271, 344–45, 347, 352–55
　political priorities, American, 251
　as siege warfare, 5–6, 24, 25, 57, 63, 66, 78, 83, 103, 122, 135, 145, 157, 161, 183, 201, 207, 265, 280, 289, 293, 328, 408, 410
　as stalemated, 251, 252, 298
　as strategic victory for American interests, 413
　success, measuring, 412
Vietnamization, 182, 206, 232, 238, 360, 361, 380
Vinh Airfield, 26, 27, 35, 36, 37, 56, 83, 95, 98, 308, 362, 364, 384
visual dive bombing, 48, 55, 204, 240, 276, 290–91, 351, 369, 374
visual reconnaissance, 127, 149, 199. *See also* photo reconnaissance
Vo Nguyen Giap, 160, 327
Vogt, John W., 19, 20, 104, 246, 363, 388
　on A-37B, 202
　on Admiral Gayler, 387
　on AIM-7, 108
　on Air Force kill ratio, 94
　on Air Force training inadequacies, 118
　airlift, 183
　bombing cessation, 386, 387
　close air support, 191, 205, 242
　drone reconnaissance, 139, 156
　Easter Offensive, 242, 246–47, 248, 249, 250, 362, 364, 377, 378
　on F-4D and F-4E, 109–10
　F-111A Aardvarks, 383
　on fluid four, 97
　on inadequate threat level management, 119
　laser-guided bombs, 373, 374, 375, 384
　Linebacker Critiques / Linebacker Conferences, 111
　Operation Linebacker I, 378, 381
　Operation Linebacker II, 131, 389, 391, 394, 397, 399, 401
　Teaball, 114–15, 117, 119
　on threat warning, 112
Vojvodich, Mele, Jr., 395

Walters, Vernon, 236
Ward, Captain, 66
warning receivers, 46
warning system, inadequacy, 116, 123
Watergate break-in, 233–34
weapons system officer (WSO), 105–6
weather, 13, 18, 29, 57, 77, 156–57, 172–73, 180–81, 182, 205, 246–47, 275–76, 313, 362–63, 368–69, 382, 384
Weed, Gordo, 202
Westmoreland, William C.

airfield bombing, 25
airlift, 161, 174, 175
American involvement, escalation, 256
Arc Light missions, 211, 212–13, 218, 219
bombing cessation, 279, 309
Cambodia, bombing of sanctuaries, 234
close air support, 185, 186, 190, 194
coercion, 259
Ho Chi Minh Trail bombing, 282, 287–88
Khe Sanh, siege of, 176, 226, 227–28
Laos and Ho Chi Minh Trail, air interdiction effectiveness, 343
longevity of Vietnam War, 273
Operation Rolling Thunder, 261, 285, 346–47
photo reconnaissance, 129, 150
rules of engagement, 349
supply line strikes, 339
Tet Offensive, 307

Weyand, Frederick C., 245, 248, 250, 377, 382, 386, 391

Wheeler, Earle G.
air combat, 83
airfield bombing, 33, 34, 35
airlift, 170, 176
Arc Light missions, 225, 227, 233
bombing cessation, 307–8, 311, 314
bombing MiG bases, 30
bombing North Vietnam, 256, 264, 268, 271, 272, 274, 295, 297, 306, 307–8
Chinese intervention, 264
close air support, 196, 329
considers resignation, 354
interdiction, 256, 297
loss of South Vietnam, 256
missile sites, destruction, 45, 288
Operation Rolling Thunder, 45, 62, 284, 288, 306
rules of engagement, 349–51, 352, 354
surface-to-air missiles, 53, 59
Tet Offensive, 170

White, Sammy, 81

Wilson, George, 395

Wood, Harold L., 137

World War I
aerial reconnaissance, 127
air superiority, 21–22
bombing, 260

World War II
air superiority, 22
bombing, 260
close air support, 184–85
photo reconnaissance, 127

Worley, Robert F., 206–7, 309

Wright, Joseph, 380

Xom Trung Hoa, 150
Xom Ve, 316
Xuan Thuy, 381–82
Xuyen Moc, 182

Yarrow, Peter, 199
Yen Bai Airfield, 36, 37
Yen Vien rail yard, 78, 371, 393

Zhou Enlai, 362, 381, 406
ZSU-23, 41
Zuni rocket, 207

www.ingramcontent.com/pod-product-compliance
Lightning Source LLC
Chambersburg PA
CBHW021413300426
44114CB00010B/473